Health Promotion in the Workplace
4th Edition

Michael P. O'Donnell, MBA, MPH, PhD, Editor

AMERICAN JOURNAL *of*

Health Promotion

Notice to the Reader

Publisher – American Journal of Health Promotion
Editor in Chief: Michael P. O'Donnell
Project Manager: Leslie Nye O'Donnell, Esq.
Production Coordinator: Allison Nye O'Donnell
Marketing Manager: Patti Weber

For information, use address American Journal of Health Promotion, P.O. Box 1254, Troy, MI or find us on the web at www.healthpromotionjournal.com
Copyright © 2014 by Michael P. O'Donnell
Second printing, 2015

ISBN-13: 978-1502509468
ISBN-10: 1502509466

CONTRIBUTORS

Wesley F. Alles, PhD
Director, Stanford Health Improvement Program
Stanford Prevention Research Center
Department of Medicine
Stanford University
Stanford, California

Judd Robert Allen, PhD
President
Human Resources Institute, LLC and
Wellness Culture Coaching, LLC
Burlington, Vermont

David R. Anderson, PhD
Senior Vice President & Chief Health Officer
StayWell Health Management
St. Paul, Minnesota

William B. Baun, MS
Program Management of Workplace Health
Promotion Programs
Wellness Officer
M.D. Anderson Cancer Center
Houston, Texas

Kamaldeep Bhui, BSc, MBBS, MSc, MD, Dipl. Clin. Psychotherapy
Wolfson Institute of Preventive Medicine
Queen Mary, University of London
Charterhouse Square, London, England

Richard Citrin, PhD, MBA
President
Citrin Consulting
Pittsburgh, Pennsyvlania

David M. DeJoy, PhD
Professor Emeritus
Director Emeritus, Workplace Health Group
Department of Health Promotion & Behavior
College of Public Health
University of Georgia
Athens, Georgia

Robert Eric Dinenberg, MD, MPH
Chief Medical Officer
Viridian Health Management
La Jolla, California

Sokratis Dinos, BSc, Cert, MSc, PhD
Psychology Programme Leader
School of Health
Department of Psychology
BPP University
London, England

Meridith Eastman, MSPH
Doctoral Student
The Gillings School of Global Public Health
Department of Health Behavior
University of North Carolina Chapel Hill
Chapel Hill, North Carolina

Edward M. Framer PhD
Director of Health and Behavioral Sciences
Health Fitness Corporation
Dallas, Texas

Jennifer L. Gay, PhD
Assistant Professor
Department of Health Promotion & Behavior
College of Public Health
University of Georgia
Athens, Georgia

Stefan B. Gingerich, MS
Senior Research Analyst
Staywell Health Management
St. Paul, Minnesota

Winifred A. Gebhardt, PhD
Associate Professor
Leiden University
Leiden, The Netherlands

Ron Z. Goetzel, PhD
Visiting Professor, the Johns Hopkins Bloomberg
School of Public Health
Director, Institute for Health and Productivity
Vice President, Truven Health Analytics
Bethesda, Maryland

Catherine A. Heaney, PhD, MPH
Associate Professor
Department of Psychology, Stanford Prevention Research Center
And Program in Human Biology
Stanford University
Palo Alto, California

Judith Hibbard, PhD
Senior Researcher, Health Policy Research Group
Professor Emerita, Department of Planning,
Public Policy & Management
University of Oregon
Eugene, Oregon

Andriana A. Hohlbauch, MPH, MA
Research Leader
Truven Health Analytics
Santa Barbara, California

Jayne K. Jeffries, MA MHS
Doctoral Student
The Gillings School of Global Public Health
Department of Health Behavior
University of North Carolina Chapel Hill
Chapel Hill, North Carolina

Gordon D. Kaplan, PhD
Senior Director, Health Intelligence
Alere Health
Fort Worth, Texas

Karen B. Kent, MPH
Research Program Manager
Bloomberg School of Public Health
Johns Hopkins University
Washington, DC

Brian A. King, PhD, MPH
Senior Scientific Advisor for Epidemiology
Centers for Disease Control and Prevention
Office on Smoking and Health
Atlanta, Georgia

Kristin Kirkpatrick, MS, RD
Manager
Wellness Nutrition Services
Cleveland Clinic Wellness Institute
Cleveland, Ohio

Laura Linnan, ScD
Professor
The Gillings School of Global Public Health,
Department of Health Behavior
University of North Carolina Chapel Hill
Chapel Hill, North Carolina

Seth Noar, PhD
Associate Professor
School of Journalism and Mass Communication
Member, Lineberger Comprehensive Cancer Center
University of North Carolina
Chapel Hill, North Carolina

Steven P. Noeldner, PhD
Partner at Mercer
4695 MacArthur Court
Suite 600
Newport Beach
California

Michael P. O'Donnell, PhD, MBA, MPH
Director & Clinical Professor
Health Management Research Center
School of Kinesiology
University of Michigan
Ann Arbor, Michigan
Editor in Chief and President
American Journal of Health Promotion
Troy, Michigan

Heather M. Padilla, MS
Research Director
Workplace Health Group
Department of Health Promotion & Behavior
College of Public Health
University of Georgia
Athens, Georgia

Michael Peterson, EdD
Professor and Chair
Department of Behavioral Health and Nutrition
University of Delaware
Newark, Delaware

James O. Prochska, PhD
Director of the Cancer Prevention Research Center
Founder of Pro-Change
University of Rhode Island
Kingston, Rhode Island

Janice M. Prochaska, PhD
President and CEO
Pro-Change Behavior Systems, Inc.
South Kingstown, Rhode Island

Judith J. Prochaska, PhD, MPH
Associate Professor of Medicine
Stanford Prevention Research Center
Department of Medicine
Stanford University
Stanford, California

Nico P. Pronk, PhD, MA
Vice President for Health Management and
Chief Science Officer, HealthPartners
Adjunct Professor of Social and Behavioral Science
Harvard School of Public Health
Bloomington, Minnesota
Boston, Massachusetts

James Pschock
CEO and Founder
Bravo Wellness
IncentiSoft Solutions
Cleveland, Ohio

Enid Chung Roemer, PhD
Visiting Associate Professor
Institute for Health and Productivity Studies
Department of Health, Behavior and Society
Johns Hopkins Bloomberg School of
Public Health
Washington, DC

Mari Ryan, MBA, MHP
Chief Executive Officer
AdvancingWellness, LLC
Watertown, Massachusetts

Erin L. D. Seaverson, MPH
Director, Research
Staywell Health Management
St. Paul, Minnesota

Alyssa Schultz, PhD
Assistant Research Scientist
Health Management Research Center
School of Kinesiology
University of Michigan
Ann Arbor, Michigan

Michelle Segar, PhD, MPH
Co-Director
Sport, Health and Activity Research and Policy Center
University of Michigan
Ann Arbor, Michigan

Colleen M. Seifert, PhD
Arthur F. Thurnau Professor
Department of Psychology
University of Michigan
Ann Arbor, Michigan

Anastasia Snelling, PhD, RD
Associate Professor, School of Education,
Teaching & Health
American University
Washington, DC

Kristyn J. Smith, BA
Medical Student
Rowan University School of
Osteopathic Medicine
Stratford, New Jersey

Maryam J. Tabrizi, PhD, MS
Research Leader
Truven Health Analytics
Bethesda, Maryland

Paul E. Terry, PhD
Chief Science Officer
Staywell Health Management
St. Paul, Minnesota

Jessica Fitts Willoughby, PhD
Assistant Professor
Edward R. Murrow College of Communication
Washington State University
Pullman, Washington

Mark G. Wilson, HSD
Associate Dean of Academic Affairs
College of Public Health
Professor, Department of Health
Promotion & Behavior
Director, Workplace Health Group
University of Georgia
Athens, Georgia

Kelly C. Young-Wolff, PhD MPH
Postdoctoral Fellow
Stanford Prevention Research Center
Department of Medicine
Stanford University
Stanford, California

Beverly Younger, LCSW, PhD
Clinical Associate Professor
Chair, Social Work & Business in a Global Society
University of Southern California School of Social Work
Los Angeles, California

CONTENTS

PREFACE

Michael P. O'Donnell, MBA, MPH, PhD, Editor

SECTION 1 THE HEALTH PROMOTION CONCEPT

Chapter 15.   Worksite Nutrition Programs   467
Anastasia Snelling, PhD, RN and Kristin Kirkpatrick, MS, RD

Chapter 16.   Stress Management in the Workplace   493
*Sokratis Dinos, CPsychol Richard Citrin, PhD and
Kamaldeep Bhui, BSc, MBBS, MSc, MD, Dipl. Clin.Psychotherapy*

Chapter 17.   Addressing Obesity at the Workplace   509
Ed Framer, PhD Gordon Kaplan, PhD and Nico Pronk, PhD

PREFACE

AUDIENCE FOR THE BOOK

This book is written with three audiences in mind. The first audience, and perhaps the most important, is students, most of whom are young people with open minds and passion, people who are still formulating career plans. Our hope is that this book opens their minds to a career path through which they can help individuals experience enhanced health and sense of wellbeing, transform workplaces into communities that care for their workers while they improve productivity and moderate medical cost increases, all of which will help them remain financially sustainable and commercially successful. The second, and probably the largest, audience is the rapidly growing network of professionals who have embraced health promotion as a career. Our hope for them is to provide the insights and tools they need to be as effective as possible in their work, and in turn improve the health and quality of life for millions of people every day. The third group is human resource professionals who have not chosen health promotion as a career, but have been tasked with implementing programs for their clients or in their own organizations. Our hope for them is to provide a tangible sense of how programs should work, so they know how to hire the best people to help them and how to monitor and oversee the successful rollout and evolution of a program.

WHAT'S NEW IN THIS EDITION?

The 4th edition of *Health Promotion in the Workplace* is significantly revised from the 3rd edition, which was published in 2002.[1] The overall book is organized around the Awareness, Motivation, Skills and Opportunity (AMSO) Framework, which I first articulated in 2005.[2] Of the 23 chapters, 9 are brand new. The AMSO Framework is described in chapter three and serves as the conceptual framework for the book. Another new chapter on marketing and communication supplements *three* other chapters on management issues. A new section of five chapters on core theories of behavior change has also been added, with separate chapters on goal setting and self-regulation, the Transtheoretical Model, intrinsic and extrinsic incentives, self-efficacy, and tailoring. The section on enhancing opportunities includes new chapters on social norms and social support. Finally, a new chapter on small business has been added. Of the remaining 14 chapters, 8 are authored or co-authored by authors new to the book, all of whom have added new perspectives. Six of the chapters are written by the same authors as the 3rd edition. All of these chapters have been updated to reflect new research and practices. For example, the chapter on how to design workplace health promotion programs has a new section on how to fund programs using methods beyond reducing medical costs. The weight control chapter reflects the global crisis that was not yet visible when the 3rd edition was written and the lack of effectiveness of most current approaches. The tobacco control chapter reflects the remarkable advances made in the science of smoking cessation that make eradication of this habit among working populations a reality.

HISTORICAL EVOLUTION OF THE FIELD

Earlier editions of this book included reviews of the historical evolution of the workplace health promotion field, and I will not repeat those reviews here. Instead, I will reflect on evolution of the field from three perspectives.

IT FINALLY FEELS REAL

From a personal perspective, workplace health promotion finally feels real. When I got involved in this field as a student in 1977, it was more an evangelical movement of a few thousand passionate health nuts, most of us in our 20's, than it was a field per se. It was wonderful. Every person I met was a soul mate; we were all committed to working out, eating right, helping others, and to making the world a better place. These were the kind of people you would meet for the first time and know within 30 minutes that you wanted to remain close for a lifetime. Indeed, many of my closest friends are people I met in those early years. But, jobs were hard to come by. A few lucky people, most of them with graduate degrees in exercise physiology, had jobs running corporate fitness centers within organizations. Others had jobs working for fitness equipment manufacturers, book publishers, colleges, or health risk assessment companies, but a lot of us were still trying to figure out how to work our way into the field. I had a degree from a top 20 college, an MBA from a top 10 business school, plus a masters in hospital management…and I could not find a real job in the field. My classmates from grad school were joining venture capital firms, new high tech startups, and management consulting firms, or working their way up the leadership ranks of hospitals. They were buying houses and starting to build investment portfolios. I was increasing the balance on my credit card and trying to earn enough from short term consulting contracts to cover the monthly interest payments on my credit card.

One great benefit of not having a regular job was having time to work on a book…the first edition of *Health Promotion in the Workplace*, which also happened to be the first textbook in the workplace health promotion field. The royalty advance from the publisher was enough to pay off my credit cards and support me for a few months. I started planning the book when I finished my MBA in the summer of 1979, finished it in 1982, and it was finally released in late 1983, with an official publication date of 1984.[3] By 1982, I had a great job, at director of Health Promotion Services at a hospital in the Silicon Valley. My job was to develop a health promotion program for the hospital employees and also build a business selling health promotion programs to employers in the Silicon Valley. I met with every single company in Santa Clara County that had more than 3000 employees, as well as many smaller fast growing high tech startups. I loved it. It gave me the chance to spread the word on workplace health promotion, and rub shoulders with business leaders who were creating great companies. I got to know some of them personally; one friend helped launch Osborne Computers. Another invented the original Amiga computer. I spoke with the CEO's of Hewlett Packard and Lockheed, and I even got to know Steve Jobs. Well, not really, at least not very well. In reality, I just waved at him from 10 feet away as he dashed out one door and in another. I don't know if he even noticed me. I was hoping to give him an autographed copy of the first edition of this textbook. Maybe he as least looked at the cover when his secretary gave it to him…if she gave it to him. He never called. Oh well. I still bought the Macintosh computer when it first came out, and indeed, wrote the business plan for *American Journal of Health Promotion* the first week I owned my Mac…but I digress (which seems to happen more and more as I get older). Anyway, despite my enthusiasm and a steady paycheck, launching a health promotion business was tough, even in the Silicon Valley, because the field was new and medical care costs were not a problem for employers. I had 150 companies on my "strong prospect" list, but in three years, I probably signed contracts with only 20 of them. By this time, my friends were in their early 30's, getting married and starting to have kids. Most of them quit the health promotion jobs they loved because they needed jobs that paid enough to support their families. At the same time, students who were reading my textbook were contacting me for advice on how to get a job in health promotion. My advice was typically to apply the principles from the book to their own lives and to get a job in another field that offered realistic opportunities for advancement.

Fast forward to the present. I know more than a dozen people in the health promotion field who are multimillionaires. Four of them sold their health promotion companies for more than 100 million dollars. These millionaires are still the very rare exceptions, and health promotion is not the right career choice for the person whose priority is to get rich. However, there are excellent satisfying career opportunities in health promotion that pay as well as careers in many other fields. In short, work place health promotion finally feels real. Cool. However, it is still a tiny field. My guess is that total annual revenues for the field are in the three billion dollar range, although I have heard estimates as high as six billion; but even at that six billion upper limit, the field is still smaller than a single hospital system, such as the Cleveland Clinic, or than the ten largest car dealerships in the city of Los Angeles.

Nevertheless, the field has grown and is poised for growth for several reasons.

WHAT WILL DRIVE FUTURE GROWTH?

Four factors are probably most important in helping the workplace health promotion field to continue growing.

First, programs work. Thousands of studies have demonstrated that workplace health promotion programs can improve health, and dozens have shown that they can reduce medical costs and absenteeism. The effects are discussed in detail in the first three chapters of the book. This is not to say that all programs work. In fact, I would estimate that 95% of programs are too superficial to have much impact at all.[4] However, when programs follow evidenced based approaches, and are implemented well, they improve health, reduce medical costs, and even enhance productivity, sometimes to a remarkable degree, especially given the low cost of comprehensive programs. These approaches are discussed throughout the book.

Second, medical care costs are continuing to increase. The impact of high medical costs on employers is discussed in detail in chapter two. These impacts are severe, but the biggest problem is not employer costs, it is costs to the federal government for older adults and low-income people. According to the non-partisan Congressional Budget Office, spending by the United States federal government on Medicare, Medicaid and Social Security are projected to grow from 1% of Gross Domestic Product (GDP) in 1970, to the current (2014) level of 6%, to 16% in 2085.[5,6] If this trend continues, federal spending on medical care will consume 100% of all federal income tax revenues by 2065, and will surpass that level in subsequent years. Spending on all other government programs, like defense, education, transportation, and others, would be funded by debt, or in reality, not funded at all. It is hard to imagine how the United States could survive as a nation if this transpires. Fortunately, it may be possible to avert this crisis by adapting the most effective workplace health promotion strategies and applying them to all aspects of people's lives.[7] If this is done well, it could improve health and reduce medical utilization of all Americans during their early and mid adulthoods, but equally important, it could compress the period of disability in the last years of life.[8] If this happens, the health promotion field could grow to ten or more times its current size.

Third, workplace health promotion has become a business. People with experience in running businesses have taken over. They know how to develop products, hire and train staff, implement quality control processes, penetrate new market segments, and secure funding for growth. In most cases, their focus has been on growth and growth they have produced. When they have built their businesses on a foundation of scientific evidence, best practice standards, and improving health, they also improved the quality and effectiveness of programs.

Finally, health promotion has begun to be integrated into national policy in the United States. The Affordable Care Act (ACA) passed in 2010 included several dozen provisions to advance the field.[9] Five of the most important are briefly described below. Only one of these five is directed at workplace health promotion, but the other four provide a fertile climate for health promotion within community and clinical settings.

- Wellness Incentives. Section 2705 of the ACA, and subsequent regulations, confirmed that employers can offer a health plan premium differential (or access to other health services) of up to 50% based on employees achieving health goals or participating in health promotion programs.[10] One of the primary impacts of these provisions is to provide a mechanism to engage more employees in workplace health promotion programs. A growing body of research is showing that incentive programs implemented well can push participation from the 20%-40% level to the 70%-90% level.[11,12] The other primary impact is to provide a mechanism through which employers can fund the entire cost of the health promotion program, including the incentive, through the health plan premium.

- Medicare Wellness visit. Section 4103 of the ACA authorizes reimbursement for an annual Wellness Visit with a physician as well as programs in tobacco cessation, weight control and other areas for all Medicare recipients. The important impact of these provisions will be to draw more physicians, nurses and other clinical health professionals into the health promotion field, which will help to enhance the prevalence of programs, and create opportunities for health promotion organizations that provide interventions in these areas.

- Medicaid study. Section 4108 provided $100 million in funding to test the impact of health promotion programs on health and medical costs with Medicaid recipients at the community level in ten test settings. The important impact of these provisions is to identify health promotion strategies appropriate for low income people, and identify approaches that can reduce Medicaid costs.

- Prevention Trust & Community Transformation Grants. Section 4002 authorized $10 billion over ten years to fund the development of health promotion programs, and Section 4201 articulated the idea of Community Transformation grants for innovative approaches that have the potential to produce transformative change.

- The potential impact of these provisions is to identify the community level strategies that have the greatest impact on health, and to implement these programs in hundreds of communities.

- National Prevention Strategy. Section 4001 directed the cabinet level secretaries of all the departments of the federal government to create a National Prevention Strategy. The primary impact of these provisions is to stimulate thinking about how policies in agriculture, transportation, education, commerce and all other areas of the federal government can improve health, and initiate implementation of some of these strategies.

WHAT COULD DERAIL GROWTH?

Workplace health promotion seems to be very well positioned for steady growth, but this growth could be derailed by several factors. Two of the most likely are briefly discussed below.

- Public and Private Exchanges. Section 201 of the ACA authorized creation of public and private health insurance market exchanges that allow individuals to purchase health insurance as individuals, without paying a premium if they have existing medical conditions. These market exchanges were created primarily to provide easy access to health insurance for individuals who did not have access through their employer. However, some employers, including large self-insured employers, are choosing to eliminate their internal health plans and instead provide a subsidy to help employees purchase insurance on the exchanges. The number of employers who choose to move to the exchanges is unknown. An early analysis by the Congressional Budget Office estimated that only 7% of people who had been covered by employer sponsored health insurance would move to the exchanges, but subsequent analyses by McKinsey & Company estimated that 50% to 60% of employers would consider

some major changes in their coverage plans, with some of them moving to public or private exchanges.[13] A more recent survey by Accenture estimated that 25% of employers would move employees to private exchanges.[14] One of the primary advantages to employers of shifting to the exchanges is to increase the predictability of the cost of health care by shifting from a defined "benefit" (in which full medical coverage is provided by the employer regardless of the cost) to a defined "contribution" (in which the employer pays a specific annual amount each year and employees are responsible for increase costs in the exchanges). If this shift to defined contribution occurs, employers will no longer be as motivated to control their medical costs because the risk of increases has been shifted to employees. The impact on workplace health promotion programs is unpredictable. Some employers may continue to provide health promotion programs with the goal of enhancing productivity, or of helping employees moderate their own costs. Other employers may continue programs as a strategy to attract and retain the most talented employees. Some may partner with exchanges that provide the health assessment and skill building elements of programs and focus their internal efforts on creating opportunities for healthy lifestyle, especially through policy and environmental approaches. It is entirely possible that the field of workplace health promotion will continue to grow within the context of the exchanges, just morphing to a new form. It is also possible that the field will contract.

- Losing its soul. In my opinion, the biggest risk to workplace health promotion programs is the possible loss of its soul. If the field becomes dominated by financial incentives that create winners among the healthy and losers among the unhealthy, or if the predominate programs are impersonal web based approaches, or if business people with a profit motive and no knowledge of the art and science of health behavior change become the driving force of the field, the workplace health promotion field has the potential to wither away. Changing health behaviors is hard. It requires reversing habits that have been formed over decades. It requires over coming the cultural norms of society, circumventing the food industry and normal modes of transportation, carving out time for health despite the demands of work and family, and it sometimes requires shifting to new sets of friends. In most cases, it requires soul searching and deep commitment to change. All of these changes require support from professionals who are passionate about health and are fulfilled when they help others. If we allow human connection or human touch to slip away, the field of health promotion could become irrelevant.

Michael P. O'Donnell

REFERENCES

1. O'Donnell MP, 2002. Health Promotion in the Workplace, 4th edition. Delmar Publishers, Albany New York.

2. O'Donnell MP, 2005. A Simple Framework to Describe What Works Best: Improving Awareness, Enhancing Motivation, Building Skills, and Providing Opportunity The Art of Health Promotion, American Journal of Health Promotion, 20,1.

3. O'Donnell MP, Ainsworth TH 1984, Health Promotion in the Workplace, John Wiley & Sons.

4. O'Donnell MP (2013) Does Workplace Health Promotion Work or Not? Are You Sure You Really Want to Know the Truth?. American Journal of Health Promotion: September/October 2013, Vol. 28, No. 1, pp. iv-vii.

5. O'Donnell MP. Can We Reduce Our Federal Deficit and Create Jobs by Making the Healthy Choice the Easiest Choice? November/December 2011, Vol. 26, No. 2, pp. viii –xii.

6. Congressional Budget Office. The 2013 Long-Term Budget Outlook, September 17, 2013 Available at http://www.cbo.gov/publication/44521. Accessed March 1, 2014.

7. O'Donnell MP, (2012) A Strategy to Create Jobs and Reduce the Deficit by Making the Healthy Choice the Easiest Choice. American Journal of Health Promotion: July/August 2012, Vol. 26, No. 6, pp. iv-xi.

8. Fries JF. Aging, natural death, and the compression of morbidity. N Engl J Med. 1980;303:130–135.

9. O'Donnell, MP. Integrating health promotion into national health policy. Am J Health Promot 2009 Jul-Aug;23(6):iv-vi.

10. O'Donnell, MP. Financial incentives for workplace health promotion: what is equitable, what is sustainable, and what drives healthy behaviors? Am J Health Promot. 2012 May-Jun;26(5):iv-vii. doi: 10.4278/ajhp.26.5.iv.

11. Taitel MS, Haufle V, Heck D, et al. Incentives and other factors associated with employee participation in health risk assessment. J Occup Environ Med. 2008;50:863–872.

12. Seaverson ELD, Grossmeier J, Miller TM, Anderson DA, The role of incentive design, incentive, value, communications strategy, and worksite culture on health risk assessment participation. Am J Health Promot. 2009; 23:343.

13. McKinsey and Company. How U.S. health care reform will affect employee benefits. Available at: http://www.mckinsey.com/insights/health_systems_and_services/how_us_health_care_reform_will_affect_employee_benefits. Accessed March 1, 2014.

14. Accenture. Are You Ready? Private Health Insurance Exchanges Are Looming. May 17, 2013. Available at: http://www.accenture.com/us-en/Pages/insight-private-health-insurance-exchanges-looming-summary.aspx Accessed March 1, 2014.

ABOUT THE EDITOR

Michael P. O'Donnell is the Director of the Health Management Research Center and Clinical Professor in the School of Kinesiology at the University of Michigan. Formed in 1978, the Center has helped more than 1000 worksites measure the health risks of their employees; calculate the link between health risks, medical costs and productivity; evaluate the impact of their health promotion programs; and in the process, establish the scientific foundation for this area of research.

Dr. O'Donnell is also the founder, president and editor-in-chief of the American Journal of Health Promotion, Inc. Launched in 1986, the *American Journal of Health Promotion* was the first scientific journal to address the health promotion field, focusing on the science of lifestyle change and the art of managing programs. It remains the most widely read scientific publication devoted exclusively to health promotion with subscribers in 42 countries. The *Journal* sponsors the annual Art and Science of Health Promotion Conference, which attracts more than 600 people each year.

As editor-in-chief, Dr. O'Donnell has completed composite editorial reviews of more than 1800 manuscripts. As President, he has organized 25 national conferences. Dr. O'Donnell is also founder and chairman emeritus of the Health Promotion Advocates, a non-profit policy group created to integrate health promotion concepts into national health policy. The group was successful in introducing several pieces of legislation in the United States Congress; several elements of these bills were incorporated into the Patient Protection and Affordable Care Act, including the formation of a cabinet level National Prevention Council responsible for creating an annual National Prevention Strategy.

Dr. O'Donnell has been responsible for launching and managing health promotion efforts that have served employees, patients, local employers and the community in three hospital systems including the Cleveland Clinic, William Beaumont Hospital and San Jose Hospital.

Dr. O'Donnell earned a PhD in Health Behavior and Health Education from the School of Public Health at the University of Michigan, an MBA in General Management and an MPH in Hospital Administration, both from the University of California, Berkeley. He completed his undergraduate work in Psychobiology at Oberlin College. During high school, he lived in Seoul, Korea with seven brothers and sisters while his father served in the Peace Corps.

Dr. O'Donnell's publications include more than 200 articles, book chapters and columns, books and workbooks. He has received 13 national awards including the Bill Whitmer Leadership Award from the Health Enhancement Research Organization (HERO), Elizabeth Fries Health Education Award from the James F. and Sarah T. Fries Foundation, Lifetime Achievement Award for Advancing Health and Wellbeing in the United States from WELCOA, Active Living

Person of the Year from the Active Living By Design Program of the Robert Wood Johnson Foundation, Alumnus of the Year from Seoul Foreign School, selection as a Senior Fulbright Scholar by the Council on International Exchange, Distinguished Leadership and Service Lifetime Achievement Award from the Association for Worksite Health Promotion, Young Professional Award from the Society for Public Health Education, Great Lakes Chapter, selection as a Fellow by the Association for Fitness in Business, and the Bausch Lomb Award in Science from the University of Rochester.

Dr. O'Donnell has presented more than 260 keynote, breakout, and workshop presentations on six continents, provided consulting services to almost 100 employers, health care organizations, government agencies and foundations and served on boards and committees for 48 non-profit and for profit organizations. He is an avid swimmer and hiker, and has been a vegetarian for 30 years. He strives to achieve the model of health promotion espoused by the *American Journal of Health Promotion*: a balance of physical, emotional, intellectual, social and spiritual health.

CHAPTER

1

Health Impact of Lifestyle and Health Promotion

Robert Eric Dinenberg

INTRODUCTION

Hippocrates spoke to the importance of healthy lifestyle and health promotion when he said some 2,500 years ago, "the function of protecting and developing health must rank even above that of restoring it when it is impaired." This chapter makes the current case for this ancient statement by describing the health impact of lifestyle and health promotion.

A common theme that runs throughout the sections of this chapter is the targeting and addressing of the three most important modifiable chronic disease risk factors: (1) tobacco use, (2) physical inactivity, and (3) unhealthy diet. The introduction provides the context for targeting and addressing these risk factors. The next section is a literature review on the health impact of lifestyle that examines how tobacco use, physical inactivity,

and unhealthy diet lead to disease and how healthy lifestyle change can positively impact health. The following section is a literature review on the health impact of health promotion programs that focuses on health promotion programs that address tobacco use, physical inactivity, unhealthy diet, and interventions that address multiple risk factors. The goal of this chapter is to convey the perspective that healthy lifestyle efforts and health promotion programs successfully address the root cause of disease and therefore are essential safeguards for good health. This chapter provides the kind of knowledge that leads to action; healthy lifestyle efforts and health promotion programs save lives and improve health, so these efforts and programs are needed now to help our communities, our nation, and our world.

The World Health Organization (WHO) estimates that if the major risk factors for chronic disease were eliminated, more than 40% of cancer cases would be prevented and at least 80% of all heart disease, stroke, and type 2 diabetes cases would be prevented. WHO notes the most important modifiable chronic disease risk factors to be tobacco use, physical inactivity, and unhealthy diet. These chronic disease "causes" are expressed through risk factors such as raised blood pressure, raised glucose levels, abnormal blood lipids (particularly low density lipoprotein [LDL] cholesterol), and overweight and obesity. The main chronic diseases include heart disease, stroke, cancer, chronic respiratory diseases, and diabetes. Importantly, WHO notes that socioeconomic, cultural, political, and environmental determinants are "causes of the causes" of chronic disease.[1] Figure 1-1 illustrates the flow of causation that progresses from underlying determinants of chronic disease to modifiable risk factors to intermediate risk factors to the main chronic diseases.

Figure 1-1 summarizes WHO research that demonstrates how underlying determinants of chronic disease, such as education, occupation, and income, can affect tobacco use, physical inactivity, and unhealthy diet, which are risk factors for chronic disease both directly and through intermediate risk factors such as raised blood pressure, raised glucose levels, abnormal blood lipids, and overweight and obesity. This multicausality means that various lifestyle and health promotion interventions can be used at various times in various settings for disease prevention.[2] A healthy lifestyle effort might address physical activity alone, while a health promotion program might address an underlying determinant of chronic disease such as work culture, a modifiable chronic disease factor such as physical activity, an intermediate risk factor such as raised glucose levels, and a disease such as diabetes.

It bears repeating that chronic diseases can be prevented through healthy lifestyle and health promotion. Modifiable behavioral factors, including diet, overweight and obesity, inactivity, and tobacco use, account for more than 80% of coronary heart disease,[16] more than 70% of stroke,[16] more than 70% of colon

Figure 1-1: Causes of chronic disease.

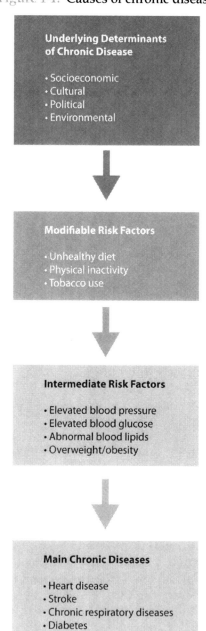

Adapted from:
World Health Organization. Preventing chronic diseases: a vital investment. Geneva: World Health Organization; 2005.

cancer,[17] and more than 90% of type 2 diabetes cases.[18] Eighty percent of lung cancer cases are caused by smoking/secondhand smoke. This means that 80% of coronary heart disease, 70% of stroke, 70% of colon cancer, 80% of lung cancer, and more than 90% of type 2 diabetes cases are potentially preventable by lifestyle modifications[19] (see Figure 1-2).

As much of chronic disease is caused by lifestyle factors, it follows that a focus on lifestyle is an essential part of any effort that seeks to address disease and promote health. Professionals who dedicate themselves to health promotion and disease prevention for populations and physicians who see individual patients share this common interest in

Figure 1-2: **Percentage of Major diseases caused by lifestyle factors.**

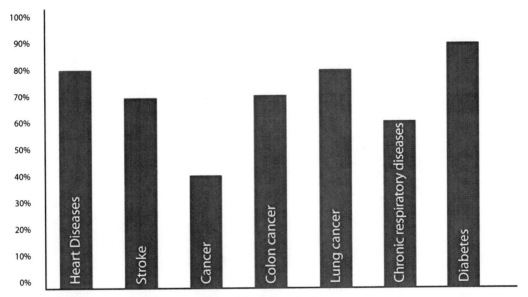

Heart disease: 80% of heart disease is caused by lifestyle factors
Stroke: 70% of stroke is caused by lifestyle factors
Cancer: 40% of all cancer is caused by lifestyle factors
       70% of colon cancer is caused by lifestyle factors
       80% of lung cancer is caused by smoking/secondhand smoke
Chronic respiratory diseases: 60% of chronic respiratory disease is caused by lifestyle factors
Diabetes: 90% of Type 2 diabetes is caused by lifestyle factors
Adapted from :
World Health Organization. Preventing chronic diseases: a vital investment. Geneva: World Health Organization; 2005. Available from:
http://www.who.int/chp/chronic_disease_report/full_report.pdf.

promoting a healthy lifestyle. Physicians who focus on promoting healthy lifestyle do so in a field called *lifestyle medicine*. Lifestyle medicine is defined as the evidence-based practice of assisting individuals and families to adopt and sustain behaviors that can improve health and quality of life. The American College of Preventive Medicine and American College of Lifestyle Medicine have endorsed a list of lifestyle medicine competencies that include checking lifestyle "vital signs" such as tobacco use, alcohol consumption, diet, physical activity, body mass index, stress level, sleep, and emotional well-being. A lifestyle medicine physician targets behaviors that include, but are not limited to, eliminating tobacco use, improving diet, increasing physical activity, and moderating alcohol consumption.[3] These behavior targets, which are targets that any professional who is in a position to promote healthy lifestyle can aim for, correspond with the list of top three actual causes of death in the Unites States seen in Figure 1-3.

The American College of Preventive Medicine notes that national guidelines emphasize lifestyle interventions for general health, as well as for most disease or high risk conditions. Commonalities from lifestyle recommendations put forward by national guidelines include the following:

1. If a smoker, quit smoking.
2. Engage in at least 150 minutes of moderate intensity aerobic activity per week. Also engage in muscle-strengthening activities that work all

Figure 1-3: Top 3 actual causes of death in the United States.

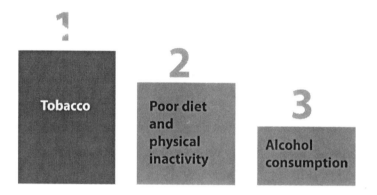

Adapted from:
Mokdad AH, Marks JS, Stroup DF, Gerberding JL. Actual causes of death in the United States, 2000. JAMA. 2004; 291:1238-1245.

major muscle groups on 2 or more days per week.
3. Use alcohol in moderation, if at all, and limit to two servings per day for men, one serving per day for women.
4. If overweight or obese, lose 5% to 10% of body weight.
5. Achieve weight loss by decreasing kilocalorie intake by 500 kcal/d and gradually increase physical activity to 60 min/d.
6. Consume a diet rich in vegetables and fruits, at least three vegetables, two fruits per day.
7. Eat whole-grain, high-fiber foods and make sure at least half of grains consumed are whole grains.
8. Eat fish, especially oily fish, at least twice a week.
9. Minimize intake of foods and beverages with added sugars.
10. Limit intake of saturated fat to less than 10% of energy, trans fat to less than 1% of energy, and limit cholesterol to less than 300 mg/d by choosing lean meats, choosing vegetable alternatives, choosing fat-free or low-fat dairy products,

and minimizing intake of partially hydrogenated fats.

Healthy lifestyle behaviors are included in national practice guidelines for chronic disease management and prevention.[4-9] The U.S. Preventive Services Task Force (USPSTF) recommends that clinicians screen all adult patients for tobacco use, obesity, and alcohol use. USPSTF recommends that clinicians offer tobacco cessation interventions for tobacco users, intensive multicomponent behavioral interventions to promote sustained weight loss for obese persons, counseling for reduced alcohol consumption in excessive alcohol users, and diet changes for all who have hyperlipidemia or other known risk factors for cardiovascular and diet-related chronic disease.[10]

The WHO defines health promotion as the process of enabling people to increase control over their health and its determinants, and thereby improve health.[11] A definition of health promotion published in the *American Journal of Health Promotion* is as follows:

Health Promotion is the art and science of helping people discover the synergies between their core passions and optimal health, enhancing their motivation to strive for optimal health, and supporting them in changing their lifestyle to move toward a state of optimal health. Optimal health is a dynamic balance of physical, emotional, social, spiritual, and intellectual health. Lifestyle change can be facilitated through a combination of learning experiences that enhance awareness, increase motivation, and build skills and, most important, through the creation of opportunities that open access to environments that make positive health practices the easiest choice.[12]

The urgent need to deliver health promotion programs to as many people as possible is best understood by considering how chronic diseases *that could be prevented*

are blocking the way to a vital and strong United States. Seventy-five percent of U.S. health care spending is on people with chronic conditions.[13] One of two American adults has at least one chronic illness[14] and about one-fourth of people with chronic conditions have one or more daily activity limitations.[13] Seven of 10 deaths among U.S. citizens each year are from chronic diseases.[15]

Efforts for healthy lifestyle and health promotion programs can save millions of lives. We can choose to do as Hippocrates, the father of modern medicine, urged us to do; instead of waiting for health to be impaired and then reacting, we can be proactive and set as our top priority "the function of protecting and developing health." This is an ancient call to action that needs to be answered today.

THE HEALTH IMPACT OF LIFESTYLE: LITERATURE REVIEW

The most important modifiable risk factors are tobacco use, physical inactivity, and unhealthy diet. Modifiable risk factors can lead to intermediate risk factors. Table 1-1 lists U.S. deaths from all causes in a single year attributable to both modifiable and intermediate risk factors. These risk factors are responsible for premature disability and premature deaths for millions of people in the United States and the world. This section examines the link between these risk factors and disease and points to how lifestyle impacts risk factors and health.

Most deaths attributable to these modifiable risks are from cardiovascular disease, while cancers, respiratory diseases, diabetes, and injuries account for more than 20% of all deaths caused by smoking, alcohol use, high blood glucose, physical inactivity, low intake of fruits and vegetables, and overweight-obesity. Tobacco use has the largest effect on cancer mortality, compared with any other risk factor, causing about 33% of all cancer deaths.[20] Tobacco use and the deaths attributed to poor diet and physical inactivity account for about one-third of all deaths in the United States.[21] The impact of tobacco use, physical inactivity, and unhealthy diet on health are discussed below.

Table 1-1: U.S. Deaths in a Single Year Attributable to Risk Factors.

1. Tobacco smoking (467,000 deaths)
2. High blood pressure (395,000 deaths)
3. Overweight-obesity (216,000 deaths)
4. Physical inactivity (191,000 deaths)
5. High blood glucose (190,000 deaths)

Adapted from Danaei G, Ding EL, Mozaffarian D, et al. The preventable causes of death in the United States: comparative risk assessment of dietary, lifestyle, and metabolic risk factors. *PLoS Med.* 2009;6(4):1–23.

Tobacco Use

Tobacco use is the leading cause of disease, disability, and death in the United States.[22] Tobacco use accounts for about one in five deaths in the United States.[20] The American Cancer Society Cancer Prevention Study Phase II (ACS CPS-II) demonstrates the link between tobacco use and heart disease,[23] stroke,[23] chronic obstructive pulmonary disease (COPD),[24] other respiratory diseases including asthma and lower respiratory tract infections,[24] and the following cancers: lung cancer; mouth, pharynx, and esophagus cancer; stomach cancer; liver cancer; pancreatic cancer; cervix uteri cancer; bladder cancer; leukemia; and kidney and other urinary cancers.[25] A meta-analysis of cohort, case-control, and cross-sectional studies demonstrates the link between tobacco use and tuberculosis.[26] A meta-analysis of 25 prospective cohort studies with 1.2 million participants concludes that active smoking is associated with an increased risk of type 2 diabetes.[27]

Evidence-based tobacco control programs have been shown to reduce smoking rates,

disease caused by smoking, and tobacco-related deaths.[28] Smoking cessation reduces the risk for lung and other types of cancer; reduces the risk for coronary heart disease, stroke, and peripheral vascular disease; reduces the risk of developing COPD; for women in their reproductive years reduces the risk for infertility, and for pregnant women reduces the risk of having a low-birth-weight baby. Eliminating secondhand smoke exposure reduces the risk of heart disease and lung cancer in nonsmoking adults and reduces the risk of sudden infant death syndrome, acute respiratory infections, and more frequent and severe asthma attacks in children. Smokeless tobacco cessation reduces the risk of developing oral cancer.[22,29] Table 1-2 describes tobacco use in the United States.

Table 1-2: Tobacco Use in the United States.

1. More than 43 million American adults (about one in five) still smoke.
2. Each year 443,000 people die from smoking or exposure to secondhand smoke.
3. Seventy percent of U.S. smokers want to quit, and around 40% try to quit each year, but most of these attempts are unaided and unsuccessful.

Adapted from CDC. *The Power of Prevention: Chronic Disease…the Public Health Challenge of the 21st Century.* Atlanta, Ga: Centers for Disease Control and Prevention; 2009.

Physical Inactivity

Physical inactivity is responsible for about 1 in 10 deaths in the United States.[20] Meta-analysis of the effects of physical inactivity on disease-specific mortality demonstrates the link between physical inactivity and heart disease mortality (meta-analysis of 20 prospective cohort studies), stroke mortality (meta-analysis of 8 prospective cohort studies), breast cancer mortality (meta-analysis of 12 prospective cohort and 31 case-control studies), colon cancer mortality (meta-analysis of 11 prospective cohort and 19 case-control studies), and diabetes mortality (meta-analysis of 13 prospective cohort and 9 case-control studies).[30] See Table 1-3 for estimates of the portion of diseases caused by inactivity.

Table 1-3: Worldwide Burden of Disease Due To Physical Inactivity.

Worldwide, physical inactivity is responsible for:

- 7% of the burden of disease of type 2 diabetes;
- 10% of the burden of disease of breast cancer;
- 10% of the burden of disease of colon cancer;
- 6% of the burden of disease of coronary heart disease.

Adapted from Bull F, Armstrong T, Dixon T, et al. Physical inactivity. In: Ezzati M, Lopez AD, Rodgers A, Murray CJL, eds. *Comparative Quantification of Health Risks: Global and Regional Burden of Disease Attributable to Selected Major Risk Factors.* Geneva, Switzerland: WHO; 2004:729–882.

Lack of physical fitness has been shown to be a predictor of cardiovascular events in healthy men and women.[32] For adults who are physically active there is strong evidence of reduced rates of coronary heart disease, stroke, metabolic syndrome, type 2 diabetes, breast cancer, colon cancer, depression, high blood pressure, and all-cause mortality.[33,34]

Sedentary lifestyle throughout the day is a risk factor even for people who do exercise on a regular basis. A prospective study on sedentary lifestyle examined mortality during a 12-year period for 7,278 men and 9,735 women from the Canadian Fitness Survey and reports that, even with physically active individuals, there is a strong association between sitting and mortality risk from all causes including cardiovascular disease. The highest mortality subpopulation group in the study is obese men and women who spend most of their waking time sitting. The study demonstrates that physical activity does not cancel out the ill effects of too much sitting during the day.[35] Research that points to sedentary behavior as an independent risk factor complements longitudinal research that looks specifically at the health impact of physical activity.

A longitudinal study followed two groups for more than 25 years–a physically active group (members of an "Age 50 Plus Runner's Club") vs. a matched comparison group drawn randomly from the same community. Over the years of the study, starting at study participant average age of 58 years through an average age of 80 years, differences in disability between the physically active group and comparison group grew steadily greater so that the postponement of minimal disability for the physically active group was 14 years over controls, and the postponement of a higher disability level for the physically active group was 16 years over the comparison group. For the first 8 years of the study, members of the physically active group had only 25% of the mortality rates of the control group. Postponement of mortality changed as subjects aged, so that at year 25 of the study, members of the physically active group had 60% of the mortality rate of members of the comparison group. At year 25, 48.9% of the comparison group had died compared with 30.5% of the physically active group.[36] Members of the physically active group used substantially fewer medical resources.[37]

Physical activity has also been studied as an intervention for healthy weight management. A meta-analysis of 43 randomized controlled trials that examined body weight change, using one or more physical activity interventions in adults with overweight or obesity, found that, compared with no physical activity intervention, physical activity resulted in small weight losses across studies and was associated with improved cardiovascular disease risk factors. The meta-analysis also concludes that exercise is associated with improved cardiovascular disease risk factors even if no weight is lost.[38] The health benefits of physical activity occur with 30 minutes of daily moderate activity.[39] Moderate intensity physical activity for 30 to 45 minutes per day on most days of the week can lower blood pressure in people with hypertension by an average of about 5 to 10 mm Hg over several months.[40] A meta-analysis of randomized controlled trials showed that in 30 hypertensive study groups, aerobic exercise training resulted in a net reduction in blood pressure of 7/5 mm Hg.[41]

Evidence from randomized controlled trials shows that exercise training in people with metabolic syndrome decreases blood pressure, increases insulin sensitivity, reduces triglycerides, and increases HDL.[42,43] Exercise alone (no changes in diet) accomplished with 30 minutes of brisk walking, three to seven times per week for 6 months, reversed insulin resistance in sedentary individuals with insulin resistance.[44] A review of 14 randomized controlled trials on the effects of exercise in type 2 diabetes found that the exercise interventions significantly improved glycemic control, decreasing hemoglobin A1c levels by .6%.[45] Physical activity reduces risks for metabolic syndrome, type 2 diabetes, some cancers, and cardiovascular disease. Physical activity also strengthens bones and muscles, improves mental health and mood, improves ability to do daily activities, and prevents falls among older adults.[46]

Unhealthy Diet

Healthy eating helps prevent high blood pressure and high cholesterol and is associated with reduced risk for obesity, heart disease, cancer, stroke, and diabetes.[47-53] A poor diet can increase the risk for lung, esophageal, stomach, colorectal, and prostate cancers.[54] Research on

specific eating plans shows the health impact of a healthy diet.

The Dietary Approaches to Stop Hypertension (DASH) eating plan consists of four to five servings of fruits; four to five servings of vegetables; two to three servings of low-fat dairy products; seven to eight servings of mostly whole grains; one serving of nuts, seeds, and legumes, limiting meats, poultry, and fish to two or fewer servings per day; and less than 2 mg of sodium per day. The DASH eating plan has been shown to be an effective first-line therapy for hypertension. The DASH multicenter trial showed that the DASH-based diet, with body weight, sodium intake, and physical activity held constant, could reduce blood pressure, by 11.4 mm Hg systolic and 5.5 mm Hg diastolic, in patients with hypertension.[55] The relevance of this change in systolic and diastolic blood pressure is understood through the perspective of research that shows that each 20 mm Hg increase in systolic blood pressure or 10 mm Hg increase in diastolic blood pressure above 115/75 mm Hg is associated with more than a two-fold increase in stroke mortality, and a two-fold increase in death from coronary heart disease. In the normal blood pressure reading of 115/75 mm Hg, the top number (115) is called systolic blood pressure and the bottom number (75) is called the diastolic blood pressure. An analysis of sodium restriction and the DASH diet showed that, compared to controls, hypertensive patients who followed the DASH eating plan and added sodium restriction to the plan achieved significantly more blood pressure control.[56]

A randomized controlled trial of the DASH diet on lipid levels showed that after 8 weeks patients with elevated cholesterol levels reduced total cholesterol relative to controls by 13.7 mg/dL and reduced LDL cholesterol by 10.7 mg/dL relative to controls.[57] A randomized controlled trial of the Third Report of the Expert Panel on Detection, Evaluation, and Treatment of High Blood Cholesterol in Adults (ATP III) recommended diet (low saturated fat with plant sterols and viscous fibers) showed that LDL cholesterol was reduced by 29% in the diet group, 31% in the drug therapy group, and 8% in the control group.[58] Replacing saturated fat intake with omega-3 fatty acids can lower LDL cholesterol.[59]

There is widespread support that a nutritious diet consists of a wide range of fruits, vegetables, beans, nuts, seeds, and whole grains. These conclusions have emerged from hundreds of studies on the relationship of diet, disease, and premature death. Several of the most important studies are summarized below. A review of 35 studies of the effects of the Mediterranean diet notes that adherence to the Mediterranean diet is associated with a reduction in both total and coronary mortality and, in the one study on Mediterranean diet and cancer incidence included in the review, a risk reduction of 60% in the Mediterranean diet group.

The Mediterranean diet consists of abundant plant foods including fruits, vegetables, beans, nuts, and seeds; minimally processed, seasonally fresh, locally grown foods; fresh fruits as the typical dessert; olive oil as the principal source of dietary lipids; cheese and yogurt consumed in low to moderate amounts; red meat consumed in low frequency and amounts; and wine consumed in low to moderate amounts with meals.[60] A typical Western dietary pattern that consists of meat, fried foods, and diet soda fails to provide the health benefits of a Mediterranean diet. In addition, research shows that the Western dietary pattern may be a health hazard. The Atherosclerosis Risk in Communities study found that long-term consumption of a Western dietary pattern (meat, fried foods, diet soda) increased the risk of developing metabolic syndrome.[61] Table 1-4 notes a trend toward unhealthy eating in the United States.

A Mediterranean diet study followed up study participants for 3 years and concludes that the adoption of a Mediterranean diet pattern reduced the likelihood of overweight people becoming obese. Among initially overweight subjects, 7.9% of women and 6.9% of men became obese in the 3 years of the study. High adherence to the Mediterranean diet was associated with a significantly lower likelihood of becoming obese among overweight subjects.[62] There is strong evidence to support that replacing refined grains with whole grains can lead to significant weight loss and helps reduce weight gain.[63] The Nurses' Health Study demonstrated that women in the highest quintile of fiber intake had a 49% lower risk of major weight gain than women in the lowest quintile. Participants in this study with the highest fruit and vegetable intake had a 24% lower risk of becoming obese than those with the lowest intake.[64]

Table 1-4: Unhealthy Diet in the United States.

1. Only 24% of adults consume five or more servings of fruits and vegetables per day.

2. Fewer than 22% of high-school students eat fruits and vegetables five or more times per day.

3. More than 60% of children and adolescents consume more than the *Dietary Guidelines for Americans* recommends for saturated fat.

Adapted from CDC. *The Power of Prevention: Chronic Disease…the Public Health Challenge of the 21st Century.* Atlanta, Ga: Centers for Disease Control and Prevention; 2009.

The Lyon Diet Heart Study compared a Mediterranean-type diet with a Western-type diet following an initial myocardial infarction. Compared to the Mediterranean-type diet, the Western-type diet includes more saturated fat, a higher percentage of total calories from fat, more omega-6 fatty acids, and less fiber. At 4-year follow-up, there was a 32% reduction in cardiac death and nonfatal myocardial infarction in the Mediterranean diet group compared to the Western diet group. The Mediterranean diet group had 95 hospital admissions and the Western diet group had 180 hospital admissions. The Mediterranean diet group had 14 nonfatal myocardial infarction events and the Western diet group had 44 nonfatal myocardial infarction events.[65,66] Evidence is clear that diet has an important impact on health.

Multiple Risk Factors or Positive Behaviors

Healthy and unhealthy behaviors rarely occur in isolation and have synergistic effects on health. For example, adherence to a Mediterranean diet and greater physical activity, for an age 70-to-90-years study group, was associated with lower mortality rates due to heart disease and cancer. Adherence to Mediterranean diet and greater physical activity was associated with 65% to 73% lower rates of all-cause mortality.[67]

The Nurses' Health Study followed 84,129 women and showed that with three of five healthy lifestyle factors, risk for coronary heart disease during a 14-year period was reduced by 57%. In this study, healthy lifestyle factors are defined as:

1. No current tobacco use;
2. Not overweight or obese;
3. Moderate alcohol use;
4. Engaged in 30 minutes per day of moderate to vigorous physical activity such as brisk walking;
5. Consumption of a diet high in fiber, high in omega-3 fatty acids, high in folate, with a high ratio of polyunsaturated to saturated fat, low in trans fat, low in glycemic load.

This study demonstrated that with four of five healthy lifestyle factors, risk for coronary

heart disease was reduced by 66%, and with all five healthy lifestyle factors, risk was reduced by 83%.[68]

These results were confirmed in a study that followed 42,847 men in the Health Professionals Follow-up Study. Healthy lifestyle factors for this study are the same as those used in the Nurses' Health Study (see Table 1-5). Men who adopted two or more healthy lifestyle factors had a 27% lower risk of coronary heart disease than men who achieved none of these factors. Men who achieved all five healthy lifestyle factors had an 87% lower risk of coronary heart disease.[69]

Table 1-5: Healthy Lifestyle Factors Used in the Nurses' Health Study and the Health Professionals Follow-Up Study.*

1. No current tobacco use
2. Not overweight or obese
3. Moderate alcohol use
4. Engaged in 30 minutes per day of moderate to vigorous physical activity such as brisk walking
5. Consumption of a diet high in fiber, high in omega-3 fatty acids, high in folate, with a high ratio of polyunsaturated to saturated fat, low in trans fat, low in glycemic load

*For those with all five healthy lifestyle factors, risk for coronary heart disease was reduced by more than 80%.

An analysis of data from the Health Professionals Follow-up Study and the Nurses' Health Study suggests that more than a third of all incident coronary heart disease in U.S. men and women may be attributed to excess weight. The study showed that the risk of coronary heart disease associated with obese men was more than twice that associated with men of optimal weight. The risk of coronary heart disease increased with excess weight both with and without comorbid conditions of hypertension, high cholesterol, and diabetes.[70]

A longitudinal study examining cardiorespiratory fitness and adiposity as mortality predictors shows that waist circumference becomes insignificant as a predictor of mortality when level of fitness is controlled for, except among the most obese. Cardiorespiratory fitness was shown to be a significant mortality predictor independent of overall or abdominal adiposity. These findings underline the importance of regular physical activity for both normal-weight and overweight individuals. Overweight individuals who improve their cardiorespiratory fitness can realize a health benefit whether or not this activity leads to weight loss.[71]

Research shows that, along with tobacco use, both overweight/obesity and lack of regular physical activity are risk factors that impact health. A longitudinal study followed 1,741 individuals who were categorized on the basis of three risk factors: current smoking, overweight or obesity, and physical inactivity. Individuals in the "low risk" category had none of the three risk factors, individuals in the "moderate risk" had one of the three risk factors, and individuals in the "high risk" had two or three of the risk factors. The most recent analysis of this study shows that high risk subjects are about twice as disabled as low risk subjects. Moderate disability was postponed by 10 years in low risk subjects compared with those at high risk. This research demonstrates that improvements in longevity do not necessarily lead to more people in poorer health, but, in fact, can lead to a postponement of functional declines so that morbidity is compressed into a shorter period later in life.[36] We all have to die of something, but if we die of that something in a short amount of time at the end of a long healthy life, then our health has been optimized.

Human health can be optimized through the prevention of chronic disease. The American Diabetes Association, the American Cancer Society, and the American Heart Association published a common agenda that notes that cardiovascular disease, cancer, and diabetes account for approximately two-thirds of all deaths in the United States and that the major risk factors for these diseases are tobacco use, physical inactivity, and unhealthy diet.[72] An important element of this common agenda is the call for greater awareness about healthy lifestyles. Evidence shows that lifestyle impacts health.

THE HEALTH IMPACT OF HEALTH PROMOTION PROGRAMS: LITERATURE REVIEW

Health promotion programs are important vehicles for public health because they can reach many people where they spend much of their time, because elements of health promotion programs can support individuals in changing health behaviors, and because health promotion programs can reach program participants and the family members of program participants as well. For example, a health promotion program that aims to reach people at work and that aims to support the population at work through group processes, policies, and environmental resources is a program that may improve the health of the population.[73] A comprehensive health promotion program offers programming that is integrated into the structure of the organization and can include tobacco cessation and prevention, regular physical activity, nutrition education and promotion, stress management, early detection/screening, weight management, disease management, and changes in the participant's environment to encourage healthy behaviors.[74] Health promotion programs can be provided in clinical, organizational, or community settings. A review of the literature on health promotion programs that address tobacco use, physical inactivity, unhealthy diet, and interventions that address multiple risk factors is below.

Tobacco Use

Direct exposure to cigarette smoke is associated with substantial morbidity and mortality, as is exposure to secondhand smoke. While smokers are two to three times more likely to die of cardiovascular disease,[75] nonsmokers who are exposed to secondhand smoke at home or at work have a 25% to 30% greater likelihood of developing heart disease.[76] Health promotion programs that target smoking prevention therefore protect smoker and nonsmokers alike.

A Cochrane review of 51 studies on workplace interventions for smoking cessation concludes that programs that offered group counseling and pharmacologic agents for smoking cessation yielded the highest participant quit rates and sustained smoking cessation rates for 6 to 12 months after the intervention. While this review did not include a meta-analysis, study outcomes from group-counseling and pharmacologic therapy interventions are as follows: A study on group counseling for smoking cessation demonstrated at 12 months that self-help participants achieved a sustained abstinence rate of 5.1%, and the group-counseling participants achieved a sustained abstinence rate of 31.2%. A study on pharmacologic therapy showed a 12-month continuous abstinence rate of 20.2% in the intervention group, compared with 8.7% among controls.[77] A review of 58 trials of telephone counseling for smoking cessation found telephone counseling to be an effective way to assist in smoking cessation and demonstrates that quit rates were higher for groups randomized to receive multiple sessions of proactive counseling. Evidence for a dose response was demonstrated; one or two brief calls are less likely to provide a measurable benefit, while three or more calls increase the odds of quitting, compared to a minimal intervention such as providing standard self-help materials.[78]

Statewide legislation prohibiting indoor smoking has decreased smoking prevalence.[79] A systematic review including 166 tobacco intervention studies examined studies on smoking bans and restrictions (bans or limits on tobacco smoking in workplaces and public areas) and concludes that such policies are effective in decreasing daily tobacco consumption among continuing users, increasing rates of tobacco cessation, and reducing workplace exposure to environmental tobacco smoke. Studies included in the review that measured components of environmental tobacco smoke (such as nicotine vapor) before and after implementation of a smoking ban or restriction demonstrate that environmental measurements of environmental tobacco smoke components decreased by a median relative percentage difference of −72% (range, −44% to −97%) in assessments conducted between 6 and 12 months after implementation of the ban or restriction.[80]

Research shows that a worksite health promotion program for tobacco cessation is more effective when occupational safety and health is integrated into the program. A randomized controlled study of 15 mid- to large-sized manufacturing worksites, ranging from 424 workers to 1585 workers, randomly assigned worksites to receive either worksite health promotion only or worksite health promotion integrated with occupational safety and health. In both cases the worksite health promotion program included a tobacco cessation program. Smoking quit rates among hourly workers in the health promotion plus occupational safety and health group more than doubled relative to those in the health promotion–only group.[81]

Physical Inactivity

Daily physical activity is recommended to promote and maintain health and to prevent the development of risk factors for chronic diseases.[82] Workplace health promotion strategies to promote activity at the worksite include educating employees about the benefits of activity, providing access to safe spaces for activity, and modifying the built environment so that employees can incorporate activity into their work days.[74]

A study on previously sedentary adults who used stairs instead of elevators at work during a 12-week promotional campaign for stair use demonstrated that the median daily number of ascended and descended one-story staircase units increased from a baseline of 4.5/d to 20.6/d. Measurements for stair-using participants at 12 weeks include significant declines in waist circumference (-1.7%), weight (-0.7%), fat mass (-1.5%) diastolic blood pressure (-1.8%), and LDL cholesterol (-3.0%). At 12 weeks, estimated maximal aerobic capacity for participants had increased by 9.2% At 6 months, the median daily number of ascended and descended stairs one story staircase unit had decreased to 7.2/d. Benefits of estimated maximal aerobic capacity (+5.9% from baseline) persisted.[83]

Maximal aerobic capacity is a measurement of fitness that is estimated through an exercise test and heart rate recording. The increase in estimated maximal aerobic capacity measured for participants in this study demonstrates an increase in fitness level for study participants.

A worksite health promotion program that aimed to help hypertensive employees achieve 10,000 steps daily demonstrated increases in physical activity, reductions in weight, and reductions in blood pressure among program participants. In this quasi-experimental design, hypertensive employees participating in an employer-based blood pressure screening program were divided as follows: employees at five sites, consisting of 6,319 employees, received the usual care of blood pressure screening plus education and served as the control group; while two sites, consisting of 9,534 employees, served as the experimental group. The experimental group received the usual care of blood pressure screening plus education and also received education designed to encourage physical activity.

At 1-year follow-up, the experimental group showed a decline in systolic blood pressure of 10.6 mm Hg while the control group showed a decline in systolic blood pressure of 6.1 mm Hg. The experimental group showed a decline in diastolic blood pressure of 7.4 mm Hg, while the control group showed a decline in diastolic blood pressure of 3.1 mm Hg. The reduction in blood pressure was significantly greater in the experimental group than the control group. Also significant, the weight of experimental group members decreased by, on average, 8.2 pounds, while the weight of control group members increased by, on average, 2.4 pounds. At baseline, 19.1% of the experimental group and 22.3% of the control group reported undertaking vigorous physical activity on 3 or more days per week. At the 1-year follow-up, 38.3% of the experimental group and 27.7% of the control group reported undertaking vigorous physical activity on 3 or more days per week. This represents a 23.8% increase in those undertaking vigorous physical activity in the control group and a 100% increase in those undertaking vigorous physical activity in the experimental group.[84]

A randomized controlled trial showed that worksite physical activity and nutrition counseling improve cardiorespiratory fitness among participants. In this trial, 168 employees in the control group received written educational materials on physical activity, nutrition, alcohol, smoking, and stress, while 131 employees in the intervention group received the same educational material and also received, during 9 months, seven 20-minute counseling sessions that took place during work time. The counseling was guided by the individual's stage of behavior change and aimed at the promotion of physical activity and healthy dietary habits. At 9-month follow-up, members of the intervention group demonstrated, on average, improved cardiorespiratory fitness levels, compared to controls.

Cardiorespiratory fitness in this study was measured by using a submaximal bicycle ergometer test. The average heart rate during the last 2 minutes of cycling was used as the submaximal heart rate measure. Members of the intervention group, on average, decreased their submaximal heart rate by 1.7 beats per minute, compared to baseline performance in the submaximal bicycle ergometer test, showing an improvement in fitness level; while members of the control group, on average, increased their submaximal heart rate by 1.6 beats per minute, compared to baseline performance, showing a deterioration of fitness level as measured by performance in the submaximal bicycle ergometer test.[85]

A systematic review of 47 studies of either physical activity or worksite nutrition or combined nutrition and physical activity interventions found strong evidence that worksite health promotion programs aimed at improving physical activity, nutrition, or both, are effective in reducing body weight. Employees showed a benefit of reducing weight by 2.8 pounds when compared to controls at the 12-month follow-up.[86]

Unhealthy Diet

Healthy food options in the cafeteria at work is an example of an environmental intervention, defined as an intervention that does not require individuals to self-select into defined educational programs but are implemented for all employees.[87] A review of randomized controlled trials that used environmental modifications in health promotion programs at worksites to increase consumption of fruit, vegetable, and fiber and to reduce fat intake demonstrated significant effects of environmental interventions on dietary intake. Of six studies that measured the effect of a worksite health promotion program on dietary fat intake, five studies demonstrated a significant decrease in dietary fat intake for program participants. Of six studies that measured the effect of a worksite health promotion program, including an environmental modification such as labeling on fruit and vegetable intake, all studies found significant positive changes, compared to controls.[88]

One study from the review, called the Working Well Trial, demonstrates that an intervention targeting healthy nutrition can lead to significant reductions in dietary fat intake and significant increases in fruit and vegetable intake. The Working Well Trial included a 2-year intervention that targeted both individuals and the worksite environment and used a randomized, matched-pair evaluation design with the worksite as the unit of assignment and analysis for 28,000 workers in 111 worksites. This study compared changes in intervention and control worksites and reports that the percentage of energy obtained from fat consumption decreased by 2.07 percentage points between baseline and follow-up for the intervention group, and that the percentage of energy from fat decreased 1.70 percentage points among employees in control sites. The intervention group achieved a net reduction in the percentage of energy obtained from fat consumption of .37 percentage points. The intervention group also achieved a net increase in fiber densities of .13 g/1000 kcal, but this was not a significant result. The largest net effect for nutrition was change in the consumption of fruits and vegetables; intake of fruits and vegetables increased by .20 servings per day between baseline and follow-up for the intervention group and only increased by .02 servings per day for the control group. The intervention group achieved an average increase in fruit and vegetable intake of .18 servings per day.[89]

A review on the effects of worksite health promotion programs evaluated different nutrition intervention strategies such as providing health education opportunities, changing the availability of healthy foods, and providing incentives for choosing healthy foods. The review reports that most strategies were associated with favorable outcomes, and benefits to employees included availability of nutritious foods, point-of-purchase information, incentives to encourage the purchase of nutritious foods, and training of health care providers to provide nutrition counseling. One worksite study from the review, called the Seattle 5 a Day, randomized 14 worksites to an intervention group and 14 worksites to a control group and then surveyed cross-sectional samples of 125 employees per worksite to compare worksite mean fruit and vegetable consumption at 2-year follow up with that at baseline. The Seattle 5 a Day intervention addressed both individual-level behavior change and changes in the work environment including point-of-purchase information, organizational support for healthy eating, and reducing access barriers to fruits and vegetables at work. Employees at intervention worksites increased their fruit and vegetable consumption by .3 more daily servings than employees at control worksites.[90]

A study examined whether a worksite nutrition program could significantly improve nutritional intake for employees. Employees who were overweight and/or had a pre-existing diagnosis of type 2 diabetes were recruited from two Government Employees Insurance Company (GEICO) corporate locations; one location with 65 employees was designated as the intervention site and one location with 44 employees was designated as the control site. The cafeteria at the intervention site included menu options that fit the program eating recommendations of low-fat foods rich in vegetables, fruit, grains, and legumes with no meat or dairy products included in the diet. Participants in the intervention group engaged in weekly lunchtime group sessions for instruction and support conducted by a physician, a registered dietitian, and/or a cooking instructor. The intervention group was asked to follow the nutrition intervention diet for the duration of the 22-week study. Results showed that in the intervention group, reported intake of total fat, trans fat, saturated fat, and cholesterol decreased significantly and fiber intake increased significantly, compared with the control group.[91]

A follow-up study examined whether the nutrition intervention program at GEICO reduced body weight and improved other cardiovascular risk factors in overweight employees. The study concludes that employees in the nutrition intervention group lost significantly more weight and had a significantly greater reduction in waist circumference than control-group participants. Weight loss of 5% of body weight was more frequently observed in the nutrition intervention group (48.5%) than the control group (11.1%).[92]

Multiple Risk Factor Interventions

A large National Institutes of Health–led multicenter clinical research study called the Diabetes Prevention Program (DPP) investigated whether modest weight loss through dietary changes and increased physical activity or treatment with the oral diabetes drug metformin (Glucophage) could prevent or delay the onset of type 2 diabetes in 3,234 study participants. At the beginning of the DPP, participants were all at risk for developing diabetes. Participants in the lifestyle intervention group that featured a 16-lesson training curriculum and motivational support on a healthy low-fat diet, physical activity for 150 minutes per week, and behavioral modification with a goal to lose 7% body weight reduced their risk of developing diabetes by 58%.[93] Table 1-6 describes DPP conclusions.

A multicenter randomized trial among 810 adults with above-optimal blood pressure evaluated the effects of implementing established lifestyle recommendations that reduce blood pressure such as weight loss, sodium restriction, increased physical activity, and limited alcohol intake. Participants were randomized to one of three groups: a behavioral intervention that implemented established recommendations, a behavioral intervention that implemented established recommendations and also implemented the DASH diet, or an advice-only comparison group.

Participant goals for the established intervention group and the established intervention plus DASH diet group were as follows: weight loss of at least 15 pounds at 6 months for overweight or obese participants, at least 180 minutes per week of moderate intensity physical activity, daily intake of 1 ounce or less of alcohol (two drinks) for men and ½ ounce of alcohol (one drink) for women, and daily intake of no more than 100 mEq of dietary sodium. Only the participants in the established plus DASH diet group received instruction and counseling on the DASH diet where the goals were 9 to 12 servings of fruits and vegetables, two to three servings per day of low-fat dairy products, and reduced intake of saturated fat and total fat. Only the participants in the established plus DASH diet group received instructions to substitute fruits and vegetables for high-fat, high-calorie foods. Compared with the baseline hypertension prevalence of 38%, at 6 months the hypertension prevalence in the advice-only group was 26%, the hypertension prevalence in the established intervention group was 17%, and the hypertension prevalence in the established intervention plus DASH diet group was 12%.[94]

Table 1-6: Diabetes Prevention Program (DPP) Conclusions.

1. DPP participants in the lifestyle intervention group reduced their risk of developing diabetes by 58% during the study.

2. DPP participants who took the oral diabetes medication metformin also reduced their risk of developing diabetes, but not as much as those in the lifestyle intervention group: participants taking metformin reduced their risk of developing diabetes by 31%.

3. People at risk for developing diabetes can prevent or delay the onset of diabetes by losing a modest amount of weight through diet and exercise.

Evidence from a review of 15 studies on comprehensive worksite health promotion programs indicates that multifactorial, comprehensive worksite health promotion programs focused on multiple risk factors are likely to reduce risks for chronic disease. All programs that focused on high risk employees or conditions in the review established a supportive worksite environment for all employees and then offered individualized risk reduction counseling to high risk employees. Multicomponent or comprehensive interventions rank higher in clinical effectiveness than single-factor disease management programs.[95]

A study that describes 7-year trends in the health habits of employees participating in a comprehensive workplace health promotion program initiated at Vanderbilt University demonstrates long-term changes in the health risks of participating employees. Participating university faculty and staff were asked to complete a health risk assessment, complete a self-directed lifestyle management tool for setting health improvement goals, and view an annual educational video. A financial incentive was provided to participants who engaged in all three steps of the program. Health coaching and targeted risk-reduction programs were provided for employees who needed additional support. Over the course of 7 years, reductions in the risk factors of tobacco use, physical inactivity, and poor nutrition were noted.[96]

A review of 36 studies examined worksite health promotion factors, including tobacco use, physical activity, and diet, and concluded that worksite health promotion programs showed short-term changes in awareness, behavior, and health.[97] A review of 47 peer-reviewed studies of multicomponent worksite health promotion programs found that workplace health promotion programs achieved long-term behavior change and risk reduction among workers, and that the most effective programs offered both targeted risk-reduction programs for employees at high risk and general health awareness initiatives for all employees.[98] A review of 33 studies evaluated the impact of worksite health promotion programs and concludes that 6 of 7 studies found significant reduction in tobacco use, 8 of 13 studies found improvements in physical activity, and 6 of 12 studies found improvements in diet.[99]

A review of more than 50 worksite health promotion studies released by the Centers for Disease Control and Prevention Community Guide Task Force concluded that evidence-based programs can achieve long-term health improvements in worksite populations. The task force notes the following benefits associated with workplace health promotion programs: reducing health risks, improving health-promoting behaviors, increasing appropriate referrals to health care professionals for high risk employees, increasing early detection of disease or risk of disease, and increasing employee awareness of health issues.[100]

A systematic review of selected interventions for worksite health promotion examined 37 studies that evaluated the effectiveness of an assessment of health risks with feedback, and 51 studies that evaluated the effectiveness of an assessment of health risks with feedback combined with additional interventions, to conclude that (1) health assessment and feedback alone is not likely to have a positive impact on health outcomes, and (2) there is strong or sufficient evidence for meaningful effects of assessment of health risks with feedback combined with additional interventions. Additional interventions had meaningful effects on the following outcomes: tobacco use, alcohol use, seatbelt nonuse, dietary fat intake, blood pressure, cholesterol, summary health risk estimates, worker absenteeism, and health care service use. Social support enhanced these impacts. An assessment of health risks with feedback is not likely to have a health impact by itself, but is useful as a gateway intervention to a broader worksite health promotion program that includes heath education lasting an hour or more or repeating multiple times during 1 year, and that may include skill-building opportunities and other health promotion activities.[101]

Research demonstrates that for some outcomes, including tobacco use, a comprehensive approach to worker health that integrates occupational safety and health with worksite health promotion is more effective than an approach that uses worksite health promotion alone.[102-104] A randomized controlled trial described earlier in this chapter examined two approaches to tobacco use: a worksite health promotion–alone approach and an approach that integrates occupational safety and health with worksite health promotion. This study demonstrates that smoking quit rates among hourly workers in the health promotion plus occupational safety and health group more than doubled relative to those in the health promotion–only group.[81]

Total Worker Health™ is a strategy developed by the National Institute for Occupational Safety and Health (NIOSH) "to integrate occupational safety and health protection with health promotion to prevent worker injury and illness and to advance health and well-being." Approaches that integrate occupational safety and health and health promotion programs in the workplace have been shown to improve health behaviors such as tobacco use,[82,102,103,105] physical activity,[105,106-110] and diet.[102,103,111-113]

Successful worksite health promotion programs reduce occupational injury rates; absence of chronic disease, good mental health, and good physical condition are associated with low occupational injury rates.[103,114-117] Workers with health risk factors, such as poorly controlled diabetes, smoking, drug and alcohol abuse, sleep deprivation, and obesity, are shown to be more likely to sustain injuries.[103,117,118] Evidence shows that when workers are aware of occupational safety and health changes made at the worksite, they are more likely to participate in healthy eating activities and smoking cessation programs.[102,103,119,120] Comprehensive approaches that address the physical and organizational work environment and promote personal health among employees and their families help sustain healthy workers and healthy communities.

UNANSWERED QUESTIONS

1. What factors contribute to differences in behavior change and health outcomes that may exist across different sectors, for different-size employers, and among different socioeconomic groups? Any undertaking that seeks to answer this question must reach small, midsize, and large employers in different sectors across the country, and do so in a way that includes all socioeconomic groups. The Centers for Disease Control and Prevention (CDC) launched the National Healthy Worksite Program (NHWP) to assist up to 104 small, midsize, and large employers in establishing comprehensive workplace health programs. The NHWP is designed to assist employers in implementing health protection and promotion strategies that will lead to specific, measurable health outcomes to reduce chronic disease rates. A useful tool that is integrated into this program is the CDC Health Scorecard that is designed to help employers assess the extent to which they have implemented evidence-based health promotion interventions or strategies. Another useful tool that is integrated into the program is a lifestyle risk algorithm that is designed so participating employees can answer questions regarding their health habits that inform a report on their risk for chronic disease. NHWP can help address unanswered questions about factors that contribute to differences in

behavior change and health outcomes for a diverse group of worksites.

2. How do we measure the effectiveness of combined health protection and health promotion programs, using a system that is standardized? The concept of integrating occupational safety and health with worksite health promotion is not new, although it points to how best to protect the safety and well-being of employees while providing them opportunities for health improvement. In 1984 NIOSH concluded that integrating occupational safety and health with worksite health promotion would "make possible a 'synergism of prevention' to improve the health of workers through comprehensive risk reduction"[124] and more recently, the American College of Occupational and Environmental Medicine Guidance Statement[103] titled "Workplace Health Protection and Health Promotion: A New Pathway for a Healthier-and-Safer Workforce" states, "Government and private sector organizations and agencies should expand research on the synergy between health protection and health promotion in the workplace." NIOSH has funded Centers of Excellence to research the health protection and health promotion integration concepts of Total Worker Health™, and these resources can help address unanswered questions about how to measure the effectiveness of combined health protection and health promotion programs, using a system that is standardized.

3. How can a worksite positively impact employee perception of worksite health culture and how do we measure culture within the worksite? Research shows that an

organizational change initiative is not likely to meet expectations if the initiative does not include a change in culture. A cross-sectional study on the worksite environment and employee perceptions of worksite culture examined 21 worksites with culture data from 2,467 employees to conclude that modifiable components of the worksite environment are strongly and positively related to employee perceptions of the worksite health culture.[125] This study used an instrument called Heart Check (HC) to measure the organizational support for employee health and an instrument called the Lifegain Health Culture Audit (LHCA) to measure health culture. HC scores were significantly and positively associated with LHCA total mean scores. Of HC factors, the most strongly correlated to LHCA total mean scores were (1) the tangible features of the workplace-built environment that impact health or health behavior and (2) the provision of information dissemination, and awareness building regarding the workplace health initiative. Further research that seeks to connect health-supporting features of the worksite with perceived health culture and health behavior can also use the CDC Worksite Health Scorecard, which helps employers evaluate the extent to which they have implemented evidence-based healthy worksite strategies, and The Human Resource Institute's Cultural Analysis Toolkit, which measures the influence of worksite culture on health behavior.

CONCLUSION

Evidence shows that, as Hippocrates said, the "function of protecting and developing health must rank even above that of restoring it when it is impaired." The most effective way to protect and nourish good health is to address the most important modifiable chronic disease risk factors, which are tobacco use, physical inactivity, and unhealthy diet. Tobacco use, physical inactivity, and unhealthy diet are risk factors for chronic disease both directly and through intermediate risk factors such as raised blood pressure, raised glucose levels, abnormal blood lipids, and overweight and obesity. If the major risk factors for chronic disease were eliminated, more than 40% of cancer cases would be prevented and at least 80% of all heart disease, stroke, and type 2 diabetes cases would be prevented.

Tobacco use and the deaths attributed to physical inactivity and poor diet account for about one-third of all deaths in the United States. Evidence shows that tobacco use, physical inactivity, and poor diet undermine good health, and evidence also shows that healthy lifestyle efforts and health promotion programs aimed at tobacco cessation, increased physical activity, and a healthy diet improve health. Yet, one in five Americans still smokes,[121] more than one in three American adults do not meet recommendations for physical activity,[122] and only 24% of U.S. adults eat five or more servings of fruits and vegetables per day.[123] Worksite health promotion programs are a proven strategy to prevent major risk factors for chronic disease.

In conclusion, we know tobacco use, physical inactivity, and unhealthy diet to be the three most important causes of chronic disease. We also know that efforts for healthy lifestyle change and comprehensive health promotion programs can positively impact tobacco use, physical inactivity, and unhealthy diet, and the underlying determinants of these causes such as, for example, whether a person works at a healthy worksite or an unhealthy worksite. Chronic disease risk factors that can stem from tobacco use, physical inactivity, or unhealthy diet, such as raised blood pressure, raised glucose levels, abnormal blood lipids, and overweight and obesity, are impacted by lifestyle choices. Efforts to promote healthy lifestyle and comprehensive health promotion programs help make the healthy choice the easiest choice and, in so doing, help people lead healthy lives.

SUMMARY

Healthy lifestyle efforts and health promotion programs successfully address the root cause of disease and therefore are essential safeguards for good health.

The World Health Organization (WHO) estimates that if the major risk factors for chronic disease were eliminated, more than 40% of cancer cases would be prevented and at least 80% of all heart disease, stroke, and type 2 diabetes cases would be prevented.

WHO notes the most important modifiable chronic disease risk factors to be unhealthy diet, physical inactivity, and tobacco use.

Tobacco use and the deaths attributed to poor diet and physical inactivity account for about one-third of all deaths in the United States.

Tobacco use is the leading cause of disease, disability, and death in the United States. Evidence-based tobacco control programs have been shown to reduce smoking rates, disease caused by smoking, and tobacco-related deaths.

Physical inactivity is responsible for about 1 in 10 deaths in the United States. Worldwide, physical activity is responsible for 7% of the burden of disease of type 2 diabetes, 10% of breast cancer, 10% of colon cancer, and 6% of coronary heart disease.

Healthy eating helps prevent high blood pressure and high cholesterol and is associated with reduced risk for obesity, heart disease, cancer, stroke, and diabetes. A poor diet can increase the risk for lung, esophageal, stomach, colorectal, and prostate cancers.

A large National Institutes of Health–led multicenter clinical research study called the Diabetes Prevention Program investigated whether modest weight loss through dietary changes and increased physical activity could prevent or delay the onset of type 2 diabetes in 3,234 study participants. Participants in the lifestyle intervention group (16-lesson training curriculum and motivational support on diet, physical activity for 150 minutes per week, and behavioral modification with a goal to lose 7% body weight) reduced their risk of developing diabetes by 58%.[71]

Evidence shows that lifestyle impacts health.

The American Diabetes Association, the American Cancer Society, and the American Heart Association published a common agenda that notes that cardiovascular disease, cancer, and diabetes account for approximately two-thirds of all deaths in the United States and that the major risk factors for these diseases are tobacco use, physical inactivity, and unhealthy diet. An important element of this common agenda is the call for greater awareness about healthy lifestyles.

The American College of Preventive Medicine and American College of Lifestyle Medicine have endorsed a list of lifestyle medicine competencies that include checking lifestyle "vital signs" such as tobacco use, physical activity, diet, alcohol consumption, body mass index, stress level, sleep, and emotional well-being.

Health promotion programs are important vehicles for public health because they can reach many people where they spend much of their time (at work, for example), because elements of health promotion programs (group processes, policies, environmental resources, for example) can support individuals in changing health behaviors, and because health promotion programs can reach program participants and the family members of program participants as well.

A review of more than 50 worksite health promotion studies released by the Centers for Disease Control and Prevention Community Guide Task Force concluded that evidence-based programs can achieve long-term health improvements in worksite populations. The task force notes the following benefits associated with workplace health promotion programs: reducing health risks, improving health-promoting behaviors, increasing appropriate referrals to health care professionals for high risk employees, increasing early detection of disease or risk of disease, and increasing employee awareness of health issues.

Comprehensive approaches to worker health that integrate occupational safety and health with worksite health promotion may be more effective than using either occupational safety and health or worksite health promotion alone. Approaches that integrate occupational safety and health and health promotion programs in the workplace have been shown to improve health behaviors such as tobacco use, physical activity, and diet.

Comprehensive approaches that address the physical and organizational work environment and promote personal health among employees and their families help sustain healthy workers and healthy communities.

The Centers for Disease Control and Prevention (CDC) responded to evidence that effective workplace programs, policies, and environments can significantly benefit employees, their families, and communities by launching the National Healthy Worksite Program (NHWP). NHWP is an initiative to establish and evaluate comprehensive worksite health promotion programs to improve the health of workers and their families.

NHWP assists up to 104 small, midsize, and large employers in establishing comprehensive worksite health promotion programs designed to reduce chronic disease rates. Useful tools and practices integrated into this effort include the CDC Health Scorecard (designed to help employers assess the extent to which they have implemented evidence-based health promotion interventions or strategies), a lifestyle risk algorithm (designed so the specific lifestyle practices of participating

employees inform a report on their risk for chronic disease), and the integration of occupational safety and health into worksite health promotion programs.

Comprehensive health promotion programs and other efforts to promote healthy lifestyle aim to make the healthy choice the easiest choice and, in so doing, help people lead healthy lives.

Glossary

Chronic disease, modifiable risk factors: Tobacco use, physical inactivity, and unhealthy diet are the most important modifiable risk factors that may lead to chronic disease directly or through intermediate chronic disease risk factors such as raised blood pressure, raised glucose levels, abnormal lipids, and overweight and obesity.

Diabetes Prevention Program (DPP): A large National Institutes of Health–led multicenter clinical research study investigated whether modest weight loss through dietary changes and increased physical activity could prevent or delay the onset of type 2 diabetes in 3,234 study participants at risk for developing diabetes and concluded that participants in the lifestyle intervention group reduced their risk of developing diabetes by 58% during the study.

Diet, Mediterranean: The Mediterranean diet consists of abundant plant foods including fruits, vegetables, beans, nuts, and seeds; minimally processed, seasonally fresh, locally grown foods; fresh fruits as the typical dessert; olive oil as the principal source of dietary lipids; cheese and yogurt consumed in low to moderate amounts; red meat consumed in low frequency and amounts; and wine consumed in low to moderate amounts with meals. A review of 35 studies of the effects of the Mediterranean diet notes that adherence to the Mediterranean diet is associated with a reduction in both total and coronary mortality.

Dietary Approaches to Stop Hypertension (DASH): The DASH eating plan consists of four to five servings of fruits; four to five servings of vegetables; two to three servings of low-fat dairy products; seven to eight servings of mostly whole grains; one serving of nuts, seeds, and legumes, limiting meats, poultry, and fish to two or fewer servings per day; and less than 2 mg of sodium per day. The DASH multicenter trial showed that the DASH-based diet, with body weight, sodium intake, and physical activity held constant, could reduce blood pressure, by 11.4 mm Hg systolic and 5.5 mm Hg diastolic, in patients with hypertension.

Health promotion, definition: Health promotion is the art and science of helping people discover the synergies between their core passions and optimal health, enhancing their motivation to strive for optimal health, and supporting them in changing their lifestyle to move toward a state of optimal health.

Health promotion program, comprehensive: A comprehensive health promotion program includes (1) health education programs, (2) a supportive social and physical environment, (3) integration of the program into organizational structure, (4) screening, including treatment and follow-up as needed, and (5) links to other assistance programs.

Lifestyle medicine: The evidence-based practice of assisting individuals and families to adopt and sustain behaviors that can improve health and quality of life.

Morbidity, compression of: A paradigm based on postponing functional declines into older ages with a goal of compressing morbidity into a shorter period later in life.

National Healthy Worksite Program, CDC: The Centers for Disease Control and Prevention (CDC) launched the National

Healthy Worksite Program (NHWP) to assist up to 104 small, midsize, and large employers in establishing comprehensive workplace health programs. The NHWP is designed to assist employers in implementing health protection and promotion strategies that will lead to specific, measurable health outcomes to reduce chronic disease rates.

Physical activity, recommendations: Adults need at least 150 minutes of moderate intensity aerobic activity per week. Adults also need to engage in muscle-strengthening activities that work all major muscle groups on 2 or more days per week.

Tobacco use, health impact: Tobacco use is the leading cause of disease, disability, and death in the United States. Smokers are two to three times more likely to die of cardiovascular disease, and nonsmokers who are exposed to secondhand smoke at home or at work have a 25% to 30% greater likelihood of developing heart disease. Eighty percent of lung cancer cases are caused by smoking/secondhand smoke.

Total Worker Health™, NIOSH: Total Worker Health™ is a strategy developed by the National Institute for Occupational Safety and Health (NIOSH) to integrate occupational safety and health protection with health promotion to prevent worker injury and illness and to advance health and well-being.

Worksite, healthy: A healthy worksite is one in which workers and managers collaborate to protect and promote the health, safety, and well-being of all workers and the sustainability of the workplace by considering (1) health and safety concerns in the physical work environment; (2) health, safety, and well-being concerns in the psychosocial work environment including organization of work and workplace culture; (3) structural features of the workplace including policies, the built environment, and health services; and

(4) ways of participating in the community to improve the health of workers, their families, and other members of the community.

Learning Objectives

1. Be aware of the World Health Organization's estimates for disease prevention that could occur with the elimination of the major risk factors for chronic disease.
2. Name the three most important modifiable chronic disease risk factors.
3. Know that tobacco use, physical inactivity, and unhealthy diet are referred to as chronic disease causes, and that these causes are expressed through four intermediate risk factors (raised blood pressure, raised blood glucose, abnormal blood lipids, and overweight/obesity).
4. Name three categories of underlying determinants ("causes of the causes") of chronic disease that can affect tobacco use, physical activity, and diet.
5. Be aware of the percentage of deaths in the United States that are attributable to tobacco use, physical inactivity, and unhealthy diet.
6. Be aware of the health impact of tobacco use and the health impact of tobacco control programs.
7. Be aware of the health impact of physical inactivity and the health impact of increasing physical activity.
8. Be aware of the health impact of an unhealthy diet and the health impact of a healthy diet.
9. Be aware of the Diabetes Prevention Program (DPP) and be able to describe DPP results.
10. Understand why health promotion programs are important vehicles for public health.
11. Be aware of the strategy to integrate occupational safety and health protection with health promotion and be able to describe the effectiveness of this strategy.
12. Be aware of the National Healthy Worksite Program, a program launched by the Centers for Disease Control and Prevention.

Discussion Questions

1. How do we go about eliminating the major risk factors for chronic disease?
2. Discuss the stepwise flow from (*step 1*) underlying determinants of chronic disease to (*step 2*) tobacco use, physical inactivity, and/or unhealthy diet to (*step 3*) development of additional risk factors to (*step 4*) development of chronic disease, giving specific examples for each step.
3. How does healthy lifestyle impact the postponement of disability? Compare the aim of prolonging the lifespan with the aim of postponing disability.
4. Consider different environments where heath promotion can take place and then discuss, in each environment, who is in the best position to help people make healthy choices about tobacco use, physical activity, and diet? Who does this person need to team with to help bring about healthy change? For each environment, discuss whether or not this role exists. Does a role need to be created?
5. Discuss the worksite as an environment in which to launch health promotion efforts. In the worksite environment, what strategies can be used to make sure that health promotion efforts engage as many people as possible? Discuss other environments in which to launch health promotion efforts that would engage as many people as possible.

REFERENCES

1. World Health Organization. Preventing chronic diseases: a vital investment. Geneva, Switzerland: World Health Organization; 2005. Available at: http://www.who.int/chp/chronic_disease_report/full_report.pdf. Accessed February 2, 2014.

2. Ezzati M, Hoorn SV, Rodgers A, et al. Estimates of global and regional potential health gains from reducing multiple major risk factors. *Lancet.* 2003;362:271–280.

3. Lianov L, Johnson M. Physician competencies for prescribing lifestyle medicine. *JAMA.* 2010;304(2):202–203.

4. Third Report of the National Cholesterol Education Program (NCEP) Expert Panel on Detection, Evaluation, and Treatment of High Blood Cholesterol in Adults (Adult Treatment Panel III): final report. *Circulation.* 2002;106:3143–3421. Available at: http://www.nhlibi.nih.gov/guidelines/cholesterol/atp3xsum.pdf. Accessed February 2, 2014.

5. Chobanian AV, Bakris GL, Black HR, et al. The Seventh Report on the Joint National Committee on Prevention, Detection, Evaluation, and Treatment of High Blood Pressure: the JNC 7 report. *JAMA.* 2003;289(19):2560–2572. http://www.nhlbi.nih.gov/guidelines/hypertension/express.pdf. Accessed February 2, 2014.

6. American Diabetes Association. Standards of medical care in diabetes–2009. *Diabetes Care.* 2009;32:S13–S61. Available at: http://care.diabetesjournals.org/cgi/content/full/32/Supplement_1/S13. Accessed February 2, 2014.

7. Lichtenstein AH, Appel LJ, Brands M, et al. Diet and lifestyle recommendations revision 2006, a scientific statement from the American Heart Association Nutrition Committee. *Circulation.* 2006;114:82–96.

8. Grundy SM, Cleeman JI, Daniels SR, et al. Diagnosis and management of the metabolic syndrome: an American Heart Association/National Heart, Lung, and Blood Institute scientific statement. *Circulation.* 2005;112:2735–2752.

9. National Institutes of Health, National Heart, Lung and Blood Institute, North American Association for the Study of Obesity. *The Practical Guide: Identification, Evaluation, and Treatment of Overweight and Obesity in Adults.* October 2000. NIH Publication No. 00-4084. Available at: http://wwww.nhlbi.nih.gov/guidelines/obesity/prctgd_c.pdf. Accessed February 2, 2014.

10. USPSTF. USPSTF A-Z topic guide. Available at: http://www.uspreventiveservicestaskforce.org/uspstopics.htm#AZ. Accessed February 2, 2014.

11. The Bangkok Charter for health promotion in a globalized world. Geneva, Switzerland: World Health Organization; August 11, 2005.

12. O'Donnell MP. Definition of health promotion 2.0: embracing passion, enhancing motivation, recognizing dynamic balance, and creating opportunities. *Am J Health Promot.* 2009;24(1):iv–iv.

13. Anderson G. *Chronic Conditions: Making the Case for Ongoing Care.* Baltimore, Md: John Hopkins University; 2004.

14. Wu SY, Green A. *Projection of Chronic Illness Prevalence and Cost Inflation.* Santa Monica, Calif: RAND Health; 2000.

15. Kung HC, Hoyert DL, Xu JQ, Murphy SL. Deaths: final data for 2005. *Natl Vital Stat Rep.* 2008;56(10):1–120. Available at: http://www.cdc.gov/nchs/data/nvsr/nvsr56/nvsr56_10.pdf. Accessed February 2, 2014.

16. Stampfer, MJ, Hu FB, Manson JE, et al. Primary prevention of coronary heart

disease in women through diet and lifestyle. *N Engl J Med.* 2000;343(1):16–22.

17. Platz EA, Willet WC, Colditz GA, et al. Proportion of colon cancer risk that might be preventable in a cohort of middle-aged men. *Cancer Causes Control.* 2000;11(7):579–588.

18. Hu FB, Manson JE, Stampfer MJ, et al. Diet, lifestyle, and the risk of type 2 diabetes mellitus in women. *N Engl J Med.* 2001;345(11):790–797.

19. Willet W. Balancing life-style and genomics research for disease prevention. *Science.* 2002;296:695–698.

20. Danaei G, Ding EL, Mozaffarian D, et al. The preventable causes of death in the United States: comparative risk assessment of dietary, lifestyle, and metabolic risk factors. *PLoS Med.* 2009;6(4):1–23.

21. Mokdad AH, Marks JS, Stroup DF, Gerberding JL. Actual causes of death in the United States, 2000. *JAMA.* 2004;291:1238–1245.

22. U.S. Department of Health and Human Services. How tobacco smoke causes disease: the biology and behavioral basis for smoking-attributable disease: a report of the Surgeon General. Atlanta, Ga: U.S. Department of Health and Human Services, Centers for Disease Control and Prevention, National Center for Chronic Disease Prevention and Health Promotion, Office on Smoking and Health; 2010. Available at: /tobacco/data_statistics/sgr/2010/index.htm. Accessed February 2, 2014.

23. Ezzati M, Henley SJ, Thun MJ, Lopez AD. Role of smoking in global and regional cardiovascular mortality. *Circulation.* 2005;112:489–497.

24. Thun MJ, Apicella LF, Henley SJ. Smoking vs other risk factors as the cause of smoking-attributable deaths: confounding in the courtroom. *JAMA.* 2000;284:706–712.

25. Ezzati, M, Henley SJ, Lopez AD, Thun MJ. Role of smoking in global and regional cancer epidemiology: current patterns and data needs. *Int J Cancer.* 2005;116:963–971.

26. Lin HH, Ezzati M, Murray M. Tobacco smoke, indoor air pollution and tuberculosis: a systematic review and meta-analysis. *PLoS Med.* 2007;4:e20.

27. Willi C, Bodenmann P, Ghali WA, et al. Active smoking and the risk of type 2 diabetes: a systematic review and meta-analysis. *JAMA.* 2007;298:2654–2664.

28. Centers for Disease Control and Prevention. Best practices for comprehensive tobacco control programs-2007. Atlanta, Ga: U.S. Department of Health and Human Services; 2007. Available at: http://www.cdc.gov/tobacco/tobacco_control_programs/stateandcommunity/best_practices/. Accessed February 2, 2014.

29. Bonnie RJ, Stratton K, Wallace RB, eds. *Ending the Tobacco Problem.* Washington, DC: Institute of Medicine, The National Academies Press; 2007.

30. Bull F, Armstrong T, Dixon T, et al. Physical inactivity. In: Ezzati M, Lopez AD, Rodgers A, Murray CJL, eds. *Comparative Quantification of Health Risks: Global and Regional Burden of Disease Attributable to Selected Major Risk Factors.* Geneva, Switzerland: WHO; 2004:729–882.

31. Lee I-M, Shiroma J, Lobelo F, et al. Effect of physical inactivity on major non-communicable diseases worldwide: an analysis of burden of disease and life expectancy. *Lancet.* 2012;380:219–229.

32. Kodama S, Saito K, Tanaka S, et al. Cardiorespiratory fitness as a quantitative predictor of all-cause mortality and cardiovascular events in healthy men and women: a meta-analysis. *JAMA.* 2009;301:2024–2035.

33. U.S. Department of Health and Human Services. 2008 Physical Activity

Guidelines Advisory Committee report. Available at: http://www.health.gov/paguidelines/. Accessed February 2,2014.

34. Warburton DE, Charlesworth S, Ivey A, et al. A systematic review of the evidence for Canada's Physical Activity Guidelines for Adults. *Int J Behav Nutr Phys Act*. 2010;7:39–39.

35. Katzmarzyk PT, Church TS, Craig CL, Bouchard C. Sitting time and mortality from all causes, cardiovascular disease, and cancer. *Med Sci Sports Exerc*. 2009;41(5):998–1005.

36. Fries J. The theory and practice of active aging. *Curr Gerontol Geriatr Res*. 2012;2012:420637.

37. Hubert HB, Fries JF. Predictors of physical disability after age 50: six-year longitudinal study in a runners club and a university population. *Ann Epidemiol*. 1994;4(4):285–294.

38. Shaw K, Gennat H, O'Rourke P, Del Mar C. Exercise for overweight or obesity. *Cochrane Database Syst Rev*. 2006;(4):CD003817.

39. Jakicic JM, Otto AD. Treatment and prevention of obesity: what is the role of exercise? *Nutr Rev*. 2006; 64(2, pt 2):S57–S61.

40. ACSM Position Stand. Physical activity, physical fitness, and hypertension. *Med Sci Sports Exerc*. 1993;25:i–x.

41. Fagard RH, Cornelissen VA. Effect of exercise on blood pressure control in hypertensive patients. *Eur J Cardiovasc Prev Rehabil*. 2007;14(1):12–17.

42. Carroll S, Dudfield M. What is the relationship between exercise and metabolic abnormalities: a review of the metabolic syndrome. *Sports Med*. 2004;34(6):371–418.

43. Hamdy O, Ledbury S, Mullooly C, et al. Lifestyle modification improves endothelial function in obese subjects with the insulin resistance syndrome. *Diabetes Care*. 2003;26(7):2119–2125.

44. Duncan GE, Perri MG, Threiaque DW, et al. Exercise training without weight loss, increases insulin sensitivity and postheparin plasma lipase activity in previously sedentary adults. *Diabetes Care*. 2003;26(3):557–562.

45. Thomas DE, Elliott EJ, Naughton GA. Exercise for type 2 diabetes mellitus. *Cochrane Database Syst Rev*. 2006;(3):CD002968.

46. Physical activity for everyone. Atlanta, Ga: Centers for Disease Control and Prevention; 2008. Available at: http://www.cdc.gov/physicalactivity/everyone/health/index.html. Accessed February 2, 2014.

47. Dietary Guidelines Advisory Committee. *Report of the Dietary Guidelines Advisory Committee on the Dietary Guidelines for Americans, 2010, to the Secretary of Agriculture and the Secretary of Health and Human Services*. Washington, DC: U.S. Department of Agriculture; 2010.

48. Appel LJ, Moore TJ, Obarzanek E, et al. A clinical trial of the effects of dietary patterns on blood pressure: DASH Collaborative Research Group. *N Engl J Med*. 1997;336(16):1117–1124.

49. Obarzanek E, Sacks FM, Vollmer WM, et al. Effects on blood lipids of a blood pressure-lowering diet: the Dietary Approaches to Stop Hypertension (DASH) Trial. *Am J Clin Nutr*. 2001;74(1):80–89.

50. Moore TJ, Conlin PR, Ard J, et al. DASH (Dietary Approaches to Stop Hypertension) diet is effective treatment for stage 1 isolated systolic hypertension. *Hypertension*. 2001;38:155–158.

51. Jenkins DJ, Kendall CW, Marchie A, et al. Effects of a dietary portfolio of cholesterol-lowering foods vs lovastatin on serum lipids and C-reactive protein. *JAMA*. 2003;290(4):502–510.

52. de Lorgeril M, Salen P, Martin JL, et al. Mediterranean diet, traditional risk

factors, and the rate of cardiovascular complications after myocardial infarction: final report of the Lyon Diet Heart Study. *Circulation.* 1999; 99(6):779–785.

53. Ornish D, Scherwitz LW, Billings JH, et al. Intensive lifestyle changes for reversal of coronary heart disease. *JAMA.* 1998;280(23):2001–2007.

54. Kushi LH, Byers T, Doyle C, et al. American Cancer Society guidelines on nutrition and physical activity for cancer prevention: reducing the risk of cancer with healthy food choices and physical activity. *CA Cancer J Clin.* 2006;56:254–281.

55. Harsha DW, Lin PH, Obarzanek E, et al. Dietary Approaches to Stop Hypertension: a summary of study results: DASH Collaborative Research Group. *J Am Diet Assoc.* 1999; 99(8 suppl):35–39.

56. Svetkey LP, Simons-Morton DG, Proschan MA, et al. Effect of the dietary approaches to stop hypertension diet and reduced sodium intake on blood pressure control. *J Clin Hypertens (Greenwich).* 2004; 6(7):373–381.

57. Obarsanek E, Sacks FM, Vollmer WM, et al. Effects on blood lipids of a blood pressure-lowering diet: the Dietary Approaches to Stop Hypertension (DASH) Trial. *Am J Clin Nutr.* 2001;74(1):80–89.

58. Jenkins DJ, Kendall CW, Marchie A, et al. Effects of a dietary portfolio of cholesterol-lowering foods vs lovastatin on serum lipids and C-reactive protein. *JAMA.* 2003;290(4):502–510.

59. U.S. Department of Agriculture, Agricultural Research Service, Dietary Guidelines Advisory Committee. *Report of the Dietary Guidelines Advisory Committee on the Dietary Guidelines for Americans*; 2005.

60. Serra-Majem L, Roman B, Estruch R. Scientific evidence of interventions using the Mediterranean diet: a systematic review. *Nutr Rev.* 2006;64:S27–S47.

61. Lutsey PL, Steffen LM, Stevens J. Dietary intake and the development of the metabolic syndrome: the Atherosclerosis Risk in Communities study. *Circulation.* 2008;117(6):754–761.

62. Mendez MA, Popkin BM, Jakszyn P, et al. Adherence to a Mediterranean diet is associated with reduced 3-year incidence of obesity. *J Nutr.* 2006;136(11): 2934–2938.

63. Williams PG, Grafenauer SJ, O'Shea JE. Cereal grains, legumes, and weight management: a comprehensive review of the scientific evidence. *Nutr Rev.* 2008;66(4):171–182.

64. He K, Hu FB, Colditz GA, et al. Changes in intake of fruits and vegetables in relation to risk of obesity and weight gain among middle-aged women. *Int J Obes Relat Metab Disord.* 2004;28(12): 1569–1574.

65. De Lorgeril M, Salen P, Martin JL, et al. Mediterranean diet, traditional risk factors, and the rate of cardiovascular complications after myocardial infarction: final report of the Lyon Diet Heart Study. *Circulation.* 1999; 99:779–785.

66. De Lorgeril M, Salen P. The Mediterranean style diet for the prevention of cardiovascular diseases. *Public Health Nutr.* 2006;9(1A):118–123.

67. Knoops KT, de Groot LC, Kromhout D, et al. Mediterranean diet, lifestyle factors, and 10-year mortality in elderly European men and women: the HALE project. *JAMA.* 2004;292:1433–1439.

68. Stampfer MJ, Hu FB, Manson JE, et al. Primary prevention of coronary heart disease in women through diet and lifestyle. *N Engl J Med.* 2000;343:16–22.

69. Chiuve SE, McCullough ML, Sacks, FM, Rimm EB. Healthy lifestyle factors in the primary prevention of coronary heart

disease among men: benefits among users and nonusers of lipid-lowering and antihypertensive medications. *Circulation.* 2006;114(2):160–167.

70. Flint AJ, Rexrode KM, Hu FB, et al. Body mass index, waist circumference, and risk of coronary heart disease: a prospective study among men and women. *Obes Res Clin Pract.* 2010;4(3):e171–e181.

71. Sui X, LaMonte MJ, Laditka JN, et al. Cardiorespiratory fitness and adiposity as mortality predictors in older adults. *JAMA.* 2007;298(21):2507–2516.

72. Eyre H, Kahn R, Robertson RM, et al. Preventing cancer, cardiovascular disease, and diabetes: a common agenda for the American Cancer Society, the American Diabetes Association, and the American Heart Association. *Circulation.* 2004;109:3244–3255.

73. Consensus Statement. Guidance for a reasonably designed, employer-sponsored wellness program using outcomes-based incentives. *J Occup Environ Med.* 2012;54(7):889–896.

74. AHA Policy Statement. Worksite wellness programs for cardiovascular disease prevention: a policy statement for the American Heart Association. *Circulation.* 2009;120:1725–1741.

75. Centers for Disease Control and Prevention, National Center for Chronic Disease Prevention and Health Promotion, Office on Smoking and Health. Fact sheet: health effects of cigarette smoking. Available at: http://www.cdc.gov/tobacco/data_statistics/fact_sheets/. Accessed February 2, 2014.

76. U.S. Department of Health and Human Services. *The Health Consequences of Involuntary Exposure to Tobacco Smoke: A Report of the Surgeon General.* Atlanta, Ga: U.S. Department of Health and Human Services, Centers for Disease Control and Prevention, Coordination Center for Health Promotion, National Center for Chronic Disease Prevention and Health Promotion, Office on Smoking and Health; 2006.

77. Cahill K, Moher M, Lancaster T. Workplace interventions for smoking cessation. *Cochrane Database Syst Rev.* 2008:CD003440.

78. Stead LF, Perera R, Lancaster T. Telephone counseling for smoking cessation. *Cochrane Database Syst Rev.* 2009:CD002850.

79. Shields M. Smoking bans: influence on smoking prevalence. *Health Rep.* 2007;18:9–24.

80. Hopkins DP, Briss PA, Ricard CJ, et al. Reviews of evidence regarding interventions to reduce tobacco use and exposure to environmental tobacco smoke. *Am J Prev Med.* 2001;20(2S):16–66.

81. Sorensen G, Stoddard A, LaMontagen A, et al. A comprehensive worksite cancer prevention intervention: behavior change results from a randomized controlled trial in manufacturing worksites (United States). *Cancer Causes Control.* 2002;13:493–502.

82. Haskell WL, Lee IM, Pate RR, et al. Physical activity and public health: updated recommendation for adults from the American College of Sports Medicine and the American Heart Association. *Circulation.* 2007;116(9):1081–1093.

83. Meyer P, Kayser B, Kossovsky MP, et al. Stairs instead of elevators at workplace: cardioprotective effects of a pragmatic intervention. *Eur J Cardiovasc Prev Rehabil.* 2010;17(5):569–575.

84. Gemson DH, Commisso R, Fuente J, et al. Promoting weight loss and blood pressure control at work: impact of an education and intervention program. *J Occup Environ Med.* 2008;50:272–281.

85. Proper KI, de Bruyne MC, Hildebrandt VH, et al. Costs, benefits and effectiveness of worksite physical activity counseling from the employer's perspective. *Scand J Work Environ Health.* 2004;30:36–46.

86. Anderson LM, Quinn TA, Glanz K, et al. The effectiveness of worksite nutrition and physical activity interventions for controlling employee overweight and obesity: a systematic review. *Am J Prev Med.* 2009; 37(4):340–357.

87. Story M, Kaphingst KM, Robinson-O'Brien R, Glanz K. Creating healthy food and eating environments: policy and environmental approaches. *Annu Rev Public Health.* 2008;29:253–272.

88. Engbers L, van Poppel MN, Chin A Paw M, van Mechelen W. Worksite health promotion programs with environmental changes: a systematic review. *Am J Prev Med.* 2005;29(1): 61–70.

89. Sorensen G, Thompson B, Glanz K, et al. Work site-based cancer prevention: primary results from the Working Well Trial. *Am J Public Health.* 1996; 86(7):939–947.

90. Matson-Koffman DM, Brownstein JN, Neinier JA, Greaney ML. A site-specific literature review of policy and environmental interventions that promote physical activity and nutrition for cardiovascular health: what works? *Am J Health Promot.* 2005;19:167–193.

91. Levin SM, Ferdowsian HR, Hoover VJ, et al. A worksite programme significantly alters nutrient intakes. *Public Health Nutr.* 2010;13(10):1629–1635.

92. Hope R, et al. A multicomponent intervention reduces body weight and cardiovascular risk at a GEICO corporate site. *Am J Health Promot.* 2010; 24(6):384–387.

93. Diabetes Prevention Program Group. Reduction in the incidence of type 2 diabetes with lifestyle intervention or metformin. *N Engl J Med.* 2002; 346(6):393–403.

94. PREMIER Research Group. Effects of comprehensive lifestyle modification on blood pressure control: main results of the PREMIER clinical trial. *JAMA.* 2003;289(16):2083–2093.

95. Pelletier KR. A review and analysis of the clinical and cost-effectiveness studies of comprehensive health promotion and disease management programs at the worksite: 1998-2000 update. *Am J Health Promot.* 2001;16:107–116.

96. Byrne D, Goetzel RZ, McGown PW, et al. Seven-year trends in employee health habits from a comprehensive workplace health promotion program at Vanderbilt University. *J Occup Environ Med.* 2011;53(12):1372–1381.

97. O'Donnell M. Health impact of workplace health promotion programs and methodological quality of the research literature. *Art Health Promot.* 1997;1(3):1–7.

98. Heaney CA, Goetzel RZ. A review of health-related outcomes of multi-component worksite health promotion programs. *Am J Health Promot.* 1997;11(4):290–307.

99. Osilla KC, Van Busum K, Schnyer C, et al. Systematic review of the impact of worksite wellness programs. *Am J Manage Care.* 2012;18(2):e68–e81.

100. Task Force Community Preventive Services. *Proceedings of the Task Force Meeting: Worksite Reviews.* Atlanta, Ga: Centers for Disease Control and Prevention; 2007.

101. Soler RE, Leeks KD, Razi S, et al. A systematic review of selected interventions for worksite health promotion: the assessment of health risks with feedback. *Am J Prev Med.* 2010;38(2S):S237–S262.

102. Sorensen G, Stoddard A, Hunt MR, et al. The effects of a health promotion-health protection intervention on behavior change: the WellWorks Study. *Am J Public Health.* 1998;88(11):1685–1690.

103. Hymel PA, Loeppke RR, Baase CM, et al. Workplace health protection

and promotion: a new pathway for a healthier-and-safer-workforce. *J Occup Environ Med.* 2011;53(6):695–702.

104. Sorensen G, Barbeau E. *Steps to a Healthier U.S. Workforce: Integrating Occupational Health and Safety and Worksite Health Promotion: State of the Science 2004.* Paper commissioned for the National Institute for Occupational Safety and Health; 2004.

105. Sorensen G, Landsbergis P, Hammer L, et al. Preventing chronic disease at the workplace: a workshop report and recommendations. *Am J Public Health.* 2011;101(suppl 1):S196–S207.

106. Sorensen G, Barbeau E, Stoddard AM, et al. Promoting behavior change among working-class, multiethnic workers: results of the healthy directions-small business study. *Am J Public Health.* 2005;95(8):1389–1395.

107. Lara A, Yancey AK, Tapia-Conye R, et al. Pausa para tu salud: reduction of weight and waistlines by integrating exercise breaks into workplace organizational routine. *Prev Chronic Dis.* 2008;5(1):A12.

108. Pronk NP. Physical activity promotion in business and industry: evidence, context, and recommendations for a national plan. *J Phys Act Health.* 2009;6(suppl 2):S220–S235.

109. Pronk NP, Kottke T. Physical activity promotion as a strategic corporate priority to improve worker health and business performance. *Prev Med.* 2009;49(4):316–321.

110. Yancy AK. The meta-volition model: organizational leadership is the key ingredient in getting society moving, literally! *Prev Med.* 2009;49(4):342–351.

111. French SA, Hannan PJ, Harnack LJ, et al. Pricing and availability intervention in vending machines at four bus garages. *J Occup Environ Med.* 2010; 52(suppl 1):S29–S33.

112. Lemon SC, Pratt CA. Worksite environmental interventions for obesity

control: an overview. *J Occup Environ Med.* 2010;52(suppl 1):S1–S3.

113. Lemon SC, Zapka J, Li W, et al. Step ahead a worksite obesity prevention trial among hospital employees. *Am J Prev Med.* 2010;38(1):27–38.

114. Maniscalco P, Lane R, Welke M, et al. Decreased rate of back injuries through a wellness program for offshore petroleum employees. *J Occup Environ Med.* 1999;41(9):813–820.

115. Musich S, Adams L, DeWolf G, Edington DW. A case study of 10-year health risk appraisal participation patterns in a comprehensive health promotion program. *Am J Health Promot.* 2001; 15(4):237–240, iii.

116. Musich S, Napier D, Edington DW. The association of health risks with workers' compensation costs. *J Occup Environ Med.* 2001;43(6):534–541.

117. Ostbye T, Dement JM, Krause KM. Obesity and workers' compensation: results from the Duke Health and Safety Surveillance System. *Arch Intern Med.* 2007; 1678(8):766–773.

118. Trogdon JG, Finkelstein EA, Hylands T, et al. Indirect costs of obesity: a review of the current literature. *Obes Rev.* 2008;9(5):489–500.

119. Sorensen G, Stoddard A, Ockene JK, et al. Worker participation in an integrated health promotion/health protection program: results from the WellWorks project. *Health Educ Q.* 1996; 23(2):191–203.

120. LaMontagne AD, Barbeau E, Youngstrom RA, et al. Assessing and intervening on OSH programmes: effectiveness evaluation of the Wellworks-2 intervention in 15 manufacturing worksites. *Occup Environ Med.* 2004;61(8):651–660.

121. National Center for Health Statistics. Health, United States, 2007: with chartbook on trends in health of

Americans. Hyattsville, Md: National Center for Health Statistics; 2007. Available at: http://www.cdc.gov/nchs/data/hus/hus07.pdf. Accessed February 2, 2014.

122. Centers for Disease Control and Prevention. Prevalence of self-reported physically active adults–United States, 2007. *MMWR*. 2008;57:1297–1300. Available at: http://www.cdc.gov/mmwr/preview/mmwrhtml/mm5748a1.htm. Accessed February 2, 2014.

123. BRFSS prevalence and trends data [online]. Atlanta, Ga: Centers for Disease Control and Prevention; 2008. Available at: http://apps.nccd.cdc.gov/brfss/gage.asp?cat=AC&yr=2007&state=US#AC. Accessed February 2, 2014.

124. National Institute for Occupational Safety and Health. *NIOSH Program Plan by Program Areas for Fiscal Years 1984-89*. Rockville, Md: U.S. Department of Health and Human Services, Public Health Service, Centers for Disease Control, National Institute for Occupational Safety and Health; 1984.

125. Hoebbel C, Golaszewski T, Swanson M, Dorn J. Associations between the worksite environment and perceived health culture. *Am J Health Promot*. 2012;26(5):301–304.

CHAPTER

2

The Employer's Business Case for Workplace Health Promotion

Michael P. O'Donnell and Alyssa Schultz

INTRODUCTION: WHY DO EMPLOYERS INVEST IN HEALTH PROMOTION PROGRAMS?

Approximately 94% of employers with 200 or more employees offer some form of **health promotion program**.[1] Furthermore, the percentage offering programs has been increasing[2,3] (See Tables 2-1 and 2-2). This begs the question: "Why do employers invest in health promotion programs?" That is the focus of this chapter.

Historically, employers invested in health promotion programs to reduce medical care costs, improve productivity and enhance image.[7,8] Since most published research focuses on those areas, discussions of those studies will be the focus of this chapter. Savings in these areas can justify a health promotion program, just as savings in electricity can justify the cost of using a new energy efficient light bulb. However, a health promotion program that contributes only cost savings will suffer the same fate as a light bulb. When it burns out, it will be discarded.

A subtle but important shift in the way we perceive and investigate the financial—or broader organizational—return of a health promotion program may help to prevent such a fate. To survive and be successful, a health promotion program must contribute to the mission, long-term goals, and short-term priorities of the organization it serves and to the special interests of those who approve its budgets.

This concept was crystallized by the results of a benchmark study conducted more than a decade ago on the best health promotion programs in the United States.[9] This study illustrated that the best programs really did take a different approach to the direction and evaluation of their programs. Most of them have well-structured studies on health improvement, medical care cost savings, and **absenteeism** savings, but they also had something else. They had qualitative impressions of how their program contributed to the organization's mission, long-term goals, short-term goals, and the personal priorities of those who approved their funding. Studies that show medical care cost savings or absenteeism improvements are important only to the extent that controlling costs in these areas is an important priority for the organization. They might also be important

Table 2-1: Percent of Employers Offering Health Promotion Programs at the Worksite according to Three Surveys.[1,2,4]

Employer Size	2012	2010	2008
3-24	58%	74%	48%
25-199	79%	72%	69%
200-999	93%	91%	85%
1000-4999	96%	96%	91%
5000+	99%	98%	98%
All Employers	63%	74%	54%

Source: Kaiser Family Foundation and Health Research and Educational Trust. *Employer Health Benefits: 2012 Annual Survey.* Menlo Park, CA. 2012.

Employer Size	2011	2008	2005
<500	27%	19%	16%
500+	73%	57%	46%
10000+	77%	67%	47%
All Employers	44%	33%	27%

Source: MetLife. 10th Annual Study of Employee Benefits Trends. New York, NY, 2012.

Employer Size	1999	1992	1985*
50-99	86%	75%	NA%
100-249	92%	86%	NA%
250-749	96%	90%	NA%
750+	98%	99%	NA%
All Employers	90%	80%	66%

Source: Association for Worksite Health Promotion, U.S. Department of Health and Human Services, William M. Mercer, Inc. 1999 National worksite health promotion survey. Northbrook, IL: Association for Worksite Health Promotion and William M. Mercer, Inc. 2000.
* The 1985 survey did not measure program prevalence by employer size.

Table 2-2: Percent of Employers Offering Specific Types of Health Promotion Programs at the Worksite.

Type of Program	2004[5]	1999[2]	1992[6]	1985[6]
Blood pressure screenings	36%	29%	32%	NA*
Cholesterol screenings	29%	22%	20%	NA*
Cancer screenings	22%	9%	12%	NA*
Health risk assessment	19%	18%	14%	NA*
Fitness programs	20%	25%	NA*	NA*
Nutrition or cholesterol education	23%	23%	NA*	NA*
Weight control classes or counseling	21%	14%	NA*	NA*
Quit smoking classes or counseling	19%	13%	NA*	NA*
Stress management classes or counseling	25%	26%	NA*	NA*
Alcohol or drug abuse programs	36%	28%	NA*	NA*
Back injury prevention	45%	53%	NA*	NA*
Maternal or prenatal programs	19%	12%	NA*	NA*
Balancing work/family education		18%	NA*	NA*
HIV/AIDS education	15%	25%	NA*	NA*
Workplace violence prevention programs		36%	NA*	NA*
Smoking policy	57%	79%	59%	27%

*Survey questions varied from year to year so not all categories are available for all years.

if external visibility or **external validation** of their programs is one of the short- or long-term goals of the organization, or the priorities of the person approving the program.

An early survey of senior managers[2] lends further support for this conclusion. Only 4% of senior managers listed employee health as their top priority, and only 35% listed it as near the top of their priority list (see Table 2-3). Health promotion programs must be tied to the items that are near the top of the priority list for the entire organization to be perceived as important to the organization. Much of our future research and evaluation efforts must address this new area of concentration... the

impact of health promotion programs on the organization mission, long-term goals, short-term goals, and the personal priorities of those who approve their funding. It is important to recognize that different types of companies will have different reasons for implementing health promotion programs. For example, all industries, but particularly those with a high ratio of labor costs to total costs (such as hospitals or educational institutions), are concerned about health care costs and **productivity**. However, technology companies may be more focused on attracting and retaining top candidates for employment. Manufacturing industries may place top priority on avoiding

Table 2-3: Where Does Employee Health and Well-Being Fall on Senior Management's Priority List? (Percentage of Companies).[2]

The number one priority	4%
Near the top of the priority list	35%
At the middle of the priority list	33%
Low on the priority list	16%
Not on the priority list	12%

employee injuries. Financial industries, whose employee demographics include a majority of younger females, may focus on work-life balance.

The purpose of this chapter is to help readers understand why employers invest in health promotion programs. The conceptual argument and the evidence to date linking health promotion programs to medical care cost containment, productivity enhancement, and image enhancement are described. This is followed by a brief review of the methodological quality of the evidence. Side bar discussions recognize that the decision to start, continue, or discontinue a health promotion program are not always rational. Even so, employers can use this **conceptual framework** to project the financial impact of their program and to help them determine if a program will be a prudent investment for their organization.

Workplace Health Promotion in the United States and around the World

This chapter primarily focuses on workplace health promotion in the United States where most large employers pay the health care costs of their employees. Under such a system, there is economic incentive for employers to become active in the area of employee health. In much of the rest of the world, employers do not pay those costs directly and so the reasons for investing in health promotion programs may be different than in the United States. A 1997 survey of European employers found the most important reasons for undertaking

such programs were because of government legislation encouraging workplace health promotion, problems with employee morale, and productivity problems.[10] These reasons were cited by more than 60% of companies surveyed. When respondents were asked to report the associated benefits for the company, it was notable that significant benefits were perceived in the areas of staff morale, health problems, reduced turnover, and reduced accident rates.[10]

A more recent study of European employers found a variety of **internal motivating factors** and **external motivating factors** for offering workplace health promotion.[11] Internal factors included evidence that programs had a significant impact on productivity, absenteeism, disability costs, job satisfaction, employee commitment, turnover, recruitment, and morale. Furthermore there was recognition that employee health and well-being are linked to accidents and injuries. Some of the external motivating factors reported by survey respondents were potential image enhancement for customers and future employees and support from local and government initiatives.[11]

Apart from the specific goal of health care cost containment, many reasons for investing in workplace health promotion are similar for companies across the world. Improved employee health has the potential for impacting the organization in myriad positive ways. In the United States, the Patient Protection and Affordable Care Act of 2010 created new governmental incentives that encourage employers to offer workplace health promotion programs. Therefore, external motivating factors may provide additional incentives for employers to invest in such programs.

RATIONAL REASONS FOR INVESTING IN HEALTH PROMOTION PROGRAMS

There are a number of rational reasons employees invest in health promotion programs. The most widely cited among these are **medical care cost containment, productivity improvement**, and **image enhancement**.

Medical Care Cost Containment

Medical care costs have risen substantially during the past four decades in many developed nations around the world. Increases have been most dramatic in the United States. As a percent of gross domestic product (GDP), medical care costs in the United States have been increasing for 50 years, growing from 5.1% in 1960 to 7.1% in 1970, 9.0% in 1980, 12.4% in 1990, 13.7% in 2000, to 17.6% in 2010.[12] In dollars, medical care costs in the United States increased from $27.4 billion in 1960 to $2.6 trillion in 2010.[13] In 2010, the United States spent two and a half times as much on health care as the average of the 33 developed nations participating in the Organization for Economic Cooperation and Development at that time. On a per-capita basis, the United States spent an average of $8,233 per capita in 2010, which was 57% more than the Netherlands, the nation spending the second most.

These cost increases have been of special concern to employers because employers have assumed a disproportionate share of the increases. In 1965, employers paid 17% of the total cost, and employees paid 61%.[14] By 1989, employers paid 30%, and employees paid 37%, with the federal government covering the rest. By 1994, employers were paying 35.3%. As this trend has continued, employers have become much more aggressive about managing their costs and passing more costs on to employees; by 1999, employers were paying only 29.2% of total costs.[15]

During the late 1980s and 1990s, employers implemented a wide range of medical care cost strategies, including sharing some costs with employees, training employees to be better consumers of medical care, forming coalitions of employers to negotiate bulk purchase discounts directly with medical care providers rather than insurers, and offering managed care as a preferred option—and sometimes the only option—to their employees. By 2000, an estimated 92,000,000 people were covered by **health maintenance organizations** (HMOs), compared to 54,000,000 in 1995 and 34,000,000 in 1990.[16] An estimated 92,000,000 additional people were members of preferred provider organizations (PPOs) by 1998.[17] Medical care providers also became very aggressive in their pricing. Development of health promotion programs was very compatible with these schemes and was often a part of cost-containment strategies. Although total medical care expenditures for the United States continued to increase in absolute dollars, as a percentage of GDP, medical care costs peaked in 1993 at 13.7%, dropped to 13.6% in 1994, increased to 13.7% in 1995, then dropped to 13.6% in 1996, and 13.4% in 1997.[18] Average medical care costs paid by employers seemed to be under control in the mid-1990s, dropping 1.1% in 1994, increasing only 0.2% in 1995, 1.4% in 1996, and dropping 2.9% in 1997.[19]

Unfortunately, the success in medical care cost containment of the 1990s appeared to be short-lived, and in the early 2000s the **consumer-directed health plan** (CDHP), also known as **high-deductible health plans** became popular with employers in another effort to moderate costs. The creation of CDHPs stemmed from the assumption that a major driver of increased health care costs was that the patient (the consumer of health care) was insulated from the cost of care.[20] These plans combine a high-deductible health plan structure with health savings accounts or health reimbursement arrangements to promote cost-aware patient decision making. As of 2010, an estimated 12.6% of employees with employer-provided health coverage were enrolled in CDHPs[21], a rapid rise from just 4% in 2006.[1]

The current spending on health care in the United States, 2.6 trillion dollars in 2010[13], is an incredible sum of money, and it is prudent business practice to take aggressive efforts to control it. A modest investment in health promotion that has a good chance of keeping employees healthy and out of the hospital is conceptually appealing, even without a lot of data to support the connection between health status and medical care costs, and most executives relied on their gut instincts to make decisions to invest in programs. However, in the past two decades, an impressive body of research has emerged to support this connection.

Health Risks are Associated with Medical Costs

The first significant study was conducted by Control Data Corporation.[22] After following 10,000 employees for four years, Control Data found that medical care claims were lowest for employees who exercised regularly, ate nutritious foods, fastened their seat belts, did not smoke cigarettes, and were not hypertensive. Similar results were found at Steelcase Corporation, an office furniture manufacturer.[23,24] Between 1985 and 1990, employees with zero risk factors had average annual medical care costs of only $250, while employees with six risk factors had costs of $1,600.

One of the early landmark studies[25] of the link between medical care costs and risk factors was produced through a collaboration of six employers (Chevron, Health Trust, Hoffman-La Roche, Marriott, State of Michigan, State of Tennessee) that was organized by the Health Enhancement Research Organization (HERO).

StayWell (a health promotion vendor) had health risk data and MEDSTAT (a medical care cost data management organization) had medical care cost data on these six employers. With the assistance of HERO and the permission of the employers, these two databases were merged to determine the relationship between ten **modifiable risk factors** and medical care costs. The strengths of this study include the large sample size, measurement of a wide range of risk factors, and the multivariate nature of the analysis. That study found eight risk factors (depression, stress, blood glucose, body weight, current or previous tobacco use, hypertension, and sedentary lifestyle) were associated with higher costs even after controlling for the other risk factors. That study was repeated again in 2012 with similar results. In that analysis, the health risks and costs of 92,486 people from seven companies were analyzed (see Table 2-4). Results again found that depression, blood glucose, blood pressure, body weight, tobacco use, physical inactivity, and stress were associated with higher costs after adjusting for all other risks.

Costs were higher for those with elevated cholesterol but not after adjusting for the other nine risk factors. The finding that higher levels of alcohol consumption are not related to higher costs is initially surprising but has been found in other studies; people who drink excessively often neglect their health and do not seek medical care when they need it. The finding related to nutrition was surprising but also has been seen in other studies. This study showed the medical costs for those with good nutrition habits were actually higher both before and after adjustment. Our suspicion is that the tool used to measure nutrition habits within the questionnaire was too short to capture the full scope of nutrition habits that would impact health and medical care utilization. It was remarkable that the two studies published more than a decade apart had such consistent findings which lends credibility to the relationships found.

Table 2-4: Medical Care Costs Associated with Risk Factors[26].

Risk Factor	Mean Cost With Risk Factor	Mean Cost Without Risk Factor	% Difference (unadjusted)	% Difference (adjusted)*
Depression	$6207	$3902	59.1%	48.0%
Stress	$5024	$4444	13.0%	8.6%
Blood glucose	$6532	$3842	70.0%	31.8%
Body weight	$4956	$3498	41.7%	27.4%
Tobacco use	$4192	$3784	10.8%	16.3%
Blood pressure	$5264	$4132	27.4%	31.6%
Exercise	$4477	$3537	26.6%	15.3%
Cholesterol	$4780	$4688	2.0%	-2.5%
Alcohol use	$3857	$4015	-3.9%	-9.5%
Nutrition	$3245	$4226	-23.2%	-5.2%

*The adjusted differences are the differences between those with and without each risk factor which persisted after adjusting for all of the other risk factors in a multivariate analysis. Costs are adjusted to 2009 dollars.

The 1998 HERO study also showed that employees who had a cluster of risk factors had strikingly higher costs. Employees with a cluster of seven heart disease risk factors had an average annual cost of $3,804, those with a cluster of risk factors for stroke had average annual cost of $2,349, and those with a cluster of psychological risk factors had average annual cost of $3,368. Employees with no risk factors had average costs of $1,166 (see Table 2-5). Others have found comparable results when examining different clusters of risk factors and points to the importance of addressing the whole person rather than just one risk factor at a time.[27,28,29]

A related study coordinated by HERO[30], used the data from the 1998 investigation to estimate the percent of total costs attributable to these risk factors. The first study identified the most expensive risk factors among those who had these risk factors. The second study identified the total cost of the risk factors,

Table 2-5: Medical Care Costs Associated with Clusters of Risk Factors, United States.[25]

Risk Factor Cluster	With Risk Factors	Without Risk Factors	% Difference
Heart disease risks	$3,804	$1,158	228%
Stroke risks	$2,349	$1,272	85%
Psychosocial risks	$3,368	$1,368	147%
No risk factors		$1,166	

factoring in the number of employees who had each of those risk factors. This changed the order of the most costly risk factors. For example, in the first study, depression was the most costly risk factor per person, but because less than 3% of employees in their sample suffered from depression, it did not have as significant an impact on total costs. Stress was the most costly risk factor because almost 20% of employees experienced high levels of stress. Almost 8% of total medical care costs were attributable to stress. Furthermore, this study showed that 24.9% of total costs were attributable to these 10 risk factors, all of which can be considered manageable through health promotion programs. This landmark study is very important because it indicates that 25% of annual medical care costs, or about $1,000 per employee, are attributable to risk factors that health promotion programs have been shown

capable of managing. This information will better help an employer make a decision to invest the $50, $100, or $200 needed to pay for a program or at least will give the employer the objective data required to justify an emotional or gut level decision to invest in a program (see Table 2-6).

A similar study was completed in South Korea and found analogous results.[31] Data on a randomly selected sample of over 180,000 employees were analyzed using a protocol similar to the HERO studies. This study found that employees with six heart disease risk factors had medical care costs 149% higher than those with none of these risk factors, and employees with three stroke risk factors had costs 52% higher than those with none of these risk factors (see Table 2-7). It is remarkable that similar trends persisted, even in a country where annual medical care costs are only

Table 2-6: Cost of Risk Factors as a Percent of Total Medical Care Costs.[30]

Risk Category	Cost/High Risk	#At High Risk	Total Cost Due to Risk	% of Total Costs	Cost/ Capita
Stress	$732	8,518	$6,236,880	7.9%	$136
Former tobacco smoker	$311	14,329	$4,455,029	5.6%	$97
Body weight	$352	9,197	$3,239,919	4.1%	$70
Exercise habits	$173	14,908	$2,574,760	3.3%	$56
Current tobacco user	$228	8,797	$2,004,045	2.5%	$44
Blood glucose	$587	2,271	$1,332,646	1.7%	$29
Depression	$1,187	997	$1,183,439	1.5%	$26
Blood pressure	$199	1,827	$363,317	0.5%	$8
Excess alcohol use	-$52	1,723	-$89,027	-1.1%	$2
High cholesterol	-$14	8,641	-$117,431	-1.5%	-$3
Nutrition habits	-$162	9,278	-$1,500,623	-1.9%	-$33
Total expenditures attributable to high risk per capita			$19,682,953	24.9%	$428
Total medical care expenditures			$78,959,286		

Table 2-7: Medical Care Costs Associated with Clusters of Risk Factors, South Korea.[31]

Risk Factor Cluster	With Risk Factors	Without Risk Factors	% Difference
Heart disease risks	190,568 won	99,457 won	149%
Stroke risks	157,922 won	98,707 won	52%
No risk factors		41,515 won	

one-eighth, or about $587 per year (1997 data), of those in the United States at that time.[32]

The work of the University of Michigan Health Management Research Center (UM-HMRC) provides additional support for the connection between health risks and medical costs. This Center has collected health care utilization and lifestyle behavior data during the past 30 years on more than 2,000,000 individuals working in more than 1,000 worksites. They have established long-term data management relationships with dozens of large employers. These data have allowed them to formulate and test a wide range of relationships between health risks and medical care costs, which are summarized in Table 2-8.[33] A number of these learnings are discussed in more detail.

After completing the UM-HMRCs **Health Risk Appraisal** (HRA), participants receive a personalized profile of their health risks as well as an overall score called a **wellness score**. The wellness score was found to be highly correlated with annual medical costs and is important because it allows a proxy measure of medical care costs that can be measured through a simple questionnaire.[34] These relationships are shown in Table 2-9.

The relationship between medical care costs and health risks is further illustrated in Table 2-10, which shows the relative cost of high-risk versus low-risk conditions for actual illness, perceived health problems, physiological measures, and lifestyle habits. Not surprisingly, the difference in medical care costs is greatest for people who actually have

a disease compared to those who do not have a disease, averaging 168% higher. Those who have risk factors measured by **biometric tests** have differences averaging 53% higher, which is very close to the differences for people who perceive problems related to health, satisfaction, and stress (48%). Costs for people with lifestyle risk factors are lowest among these four major categories but still average 16% higher than those without these risk factors.

Health Risks are Associated with other Cost Measures

In addition to medical costs, employee health risks have also been found to be associated with other health cost outcomes such as workers' compensation and pharmacy costs. In the 1980s and 1990s, pharmacy costs were a relatively minor component of employee health costs but they became the fastest rising contributor to total corporate health care costs[36] and represent the third-largest component of direct health care expenses after hospital care and physician services[37], comprising 15% of total health care spending in the United States.[38] As with medical claims, pharmacy claims have been found to be associated with employee health risks at corporations as diverse as a utility company[39] and a financial services organization.[40] The utility company found that approximately one-third of its pharmacy costs were attributed to excess health risks among the employees.[39] The financial services employer found that pharmacy costs increased in a stepwise manner as the number of employee health risks increased from zero to six or more.[40]

Table 2-8: Key Research Learning and Date Discovered, University of Michigan Health Management Research Center.[33]

Learnings	Year Discovered
1. High-risk persons are high cost (prospective data) a. individual risks b. cumulative risks	1991
2. Absenteeism and disability show the same relationship as medical costs	1993
3. Excess costs are related to excess risks	1993
4. Changes in costs (medical and pharmacy) follow changes in risks	1994
5. Risk combinations are the most dangerous predictors of cost	1995
6. Low-risk maintenance is an important program strategy	1996
7. Resource optimization: changes in risk drive changes in cost when targeted to specific risk combinations	1996
8. Wellness scores are highly correlated with medical costs	1997
9. Program participation is related to risk and cost moderation	1998
10. Wellness program opportunities are in preventive services, low- and high-risk interventions, and disease management	1998
11. Presenteeism is a measure of productivity and is associated with risks and disease	1999
12. Total value of health defined for the organization	2000
13. Natural flow of risks and costs; clusters of risks identified	2001
14. Focus on the person, not the risk or disease	2002
15. Time away from work responds to risks the same as medical costs	2002
16. Improved population health status as a result of employer-sponsored programs	2003
17. Benchmarks for bending population cost trend lines: 85%+ participation and 75%+ low-risks status	2004
18. Pre-retirement participation influences post-retirement participation	2005
19. Presenteeism changes follow risk changes	2005
20. "Don't get worse" philosophy, keep healthy people healthy	2006
21. Importance of culture of health	2007

Table 2-9: Relationship between Wellness Score and Medical Care Costs.[34]

Wellness Score	Annual Medical Costs
95	$1,415
90	$1,643
85	$1,800
80	$2,087
75	$2,369
70	$2,508
65	$2,817
60	$2,638
55	$2,818
50	$2,970

Changes in Risks are Associated with Changes in Costs

After consistently finding that health risks measured by self-report questionnaire are associated with health care costs, the next logical question for the field was whether or not changes in those risks were associated with commensurate changes in health care costs. The UM-HMRC has published those results from several different organizations.[41,42,43] In 2001, Edington summarized the UM-HMRC's research based on their health risk and cost database containing more than 2,000,000 covered lives and with multiple years of data.[44] They found that health care costs decreased an average (median) of $153 with every one decrease in number of risk factors and increased an average (median) of $350 with every one increase in number of risk factors.

A more recent study[45] found similar results after examining pre- and post-HRA questionnaires taken by employees of six large employers. Medical and pharmaceutical claims were collected as the **outcome measure** for the duration of the study from 2004 to 2009. After controlling for chronic conditions, health risk changes from pre- to post-test were associated with health care cost changes in the year following the post-test. Employees with chronic conditions had a $129 reduction in cost for each risk reduced and an increase of $210 for each risk added while the costs of employees with no chronic conditions increased $101 for each risk added and decreased $25 for each risk reduced.

The finding that reduced risk factors are associated with reduced costs provides further support for the risk reduction programs advocated throughout this book. The finding that increases in risk factors are associated with increases in costs was a breakthrough discovery that led to the notion that keeping employees healthy was a worthy goal of health promotion programs in addition to reducing health risks among those with high risk factors. This is a critical finding because health promotion programs in the early days of our field were often criticized for attracting the people who already practiced healthy lifestyles. Programs do need to learn how to better attract those with unhealthy lifestyle practices, but the studies cited above underscore the importance

Table 2-10: Medical Care Costs and Health Factors.[35]

Health Measure	Low Health Risk	High Health Risk	Difference
No Illness	$1773	$4168	140%
Disease			
Heart Disease	$1875	$8299	340%
Diabetes	$1975	$4669	140%
Cancer	$1981	$3456	70%
Other diseases	$1871	$4162	120%
raw average difference			168%
Biometric			
Blood pressure	$1810	$3732	110%
Relative body weight	$1881	$2633	40%
Cholesterol	$2033	$2276	10%
raw average difference			53%
Psychological Perceptions			
Physical health	$1751	$3756	110%
Life satisfaction	$2023	$2769	40%
Stress	$1857	$2572	30%
Job satisfaction	$2056	$2298	10%
raw average difference			48%
Lifestyle Habits			
Medication/drug usage	$1874	$3034	60%
Physical activity	$1865	$2462	30%
Smoking	$2023	$2290	10%
Seat belt usage	$2059	$2007	-3%
Alcohol usage	$2072	$1695	-18%
raw average difference			16%

of also helping those with healthy practices to continue those healthy practices.

Health Promotion Programs are Associated with Improvements in Risks and Costs

The link between medical costs and risk factors that can be modified by health promotion programs is fairly clear from the studies cited above. However, a separate question is whether health promotion programs can be successful in reducing employee health risks and ultimately in reducing health care costs. Dozens of studies have addressed this question, and a number of reviews have attempted to summarize the findings.[46,47,48,49,50,51,52,53] A large body of research has been compiled on the success of workplace health promotion programs in improving employee health risks, at least over the short-term. In terms of program impacts on costs, several literature reviews have attempted to summarize those findings. One such review was written by Aldana (1998)[54], who identified research on the impact of workplace health promotion programs on medical care costs. He then examined the methodology of each study, and determined which ones had **experimental**, **quasi-experimental** and **pre-experimental designs**. Aldana analyzed 24 studies: 21 (88%) of these studies showed that programs reduced medical care costs, and 3 (12%) showed no impact on medical care costs. Eight of the studies reported the cost of the program and the amount of savings achieved, thus allowing a calculation of the **cost/benefit ratio**. Savings ranged from $2.30 to $5.90 for every dollar invested and averaged $3.35. Also, the studies having experimental designs reported the highest levels of savings. Aldana repeated his analysis in 2001[55], with additional focus on assessing the quality of the research methodology. He reviewed 34 studies that examined the link between health risks (either single or multiple) and financial outcomes, 14 of which addressed health care costs, and 20 studies of absenteeism. The seven studies

which presented **returns on investment (ROIs)** for health care cost savings found an average savings of $3.48 for every dollar spent on the program while three studies of absenteeism had an average ROI of 5.82. The majority of those reviewed studies received a "B" rating for the methodological quality (see Table 2-11).

Chapman conducted a meta-analysis of ROI studies in 2003, 2005 and again in 2012 with somewhat more lenient inclusion criteria.[56,57,58] By 2012, his review included a total of 62 studies about the economic return of worksite health promotion programs. The methodological quality scores for those 62 studies ranged from 12 to 30 points, reflecting a wide variation in quality of research in our field although the more recent studies had larger sample sizes and higher quality methods and received more weighting in the meta-analysis. The final result of the meta-evaluation found an average cost/benefit ratio of 5.56 across 25 studies which reported a cost/benefit ratio including benefits from health costs, sickness absenteeism, workers' compensation and disease management costs.

In the same year, Baicker and colleagues completed a meta-analysis of the literature on health costs and savings associated with workplace health promotion programs.[59] **Meta-analysis** is a method of systematically combining data from similar studies and repeating the analysis with the combined larger data set. It often allows trends to be identified that were not apparent in the individual studies. Baicker's analysis included 22 studies, primarily conducted at large employers, and found that medical costs decreased $3.27 for every dollar spent on employee wellness programs. It is important to note that nearly all ROI analyses of workplace wellness programs have been limited to programs offered by large employers. Smaller employers may be less likely to have the **economies of scale** required to demonstrate a return on investment from health promotion programs but it does not mean that they would not receive benefits from such programs.

Table 2-11: Relationship between Health Risks and Health Care Costs and Absenteeism.[61]

Health Risk	Number of Studies	Positive Relationship	Negative Relationship	No Relationship	Literature Rating	Conclusion
		Relationship between Health Risks and Health Care Costs				
Obesity	6	5	-	1	Indicative	Likely
Cholesterol	6	1	2	3	Weak	Inconclusive
Hypertension	5	4	-	1	Weak	Inconclusive
Stress	5	5	-	-	Indicative	Likely
Diet	2	-	2	-	Weak	Inconclusive
Alcohol Abuse	4	2	2	-	Weak	Inconclusive
Seat belt usage	2	1	-	1	Weak	Inconclusive
Fitness/physical activity	6	3	-	3	Suggestive	Inconclusive
Multiple risk factors	5	5	-	-	Indicative	Likely
		Relationship between Health Risks and Absenteeism				
Obesity	5	5	1*	-	Indicative	Likely
Cholesterol	2	1	1	1†	Weak	Inconclusive
Stress	8	7	-	1	Indicative	Likely
Fitness/physical activity	7	2	-	5	Weak	Inconclusive
Hypertension	5	2	-	3	Weak	Inconclusive
Multiple risk factors	3	3	-	-	Indicative	Likely
Diet	0	-	-	-	No data	No data
Alcohol abuse	0	-	-	-	No data	No data
Seat belt use	0	-	-	-	No data	No data

* All five studies found that more obese women had higher absenteeism levels; four studies found that more obese men had higher absenteeism levels; one found that more obese men had lower absenteeism levels.
† One study found that employees with high cholesterol had higher rates of absenteeism; the other found that women with high cholesterol had lower rates of absenteeism, but there was no relationship for men.

How should we interpret the above findings? It is likely that studies that found negative or neutral results were not submitted for publication or were more likely to be rejected if they were submitted. Nevertheless, the trend of positive ROIs is very encouraging. We can conservatively conclude based on the research that some health promotion programs are clearly able to reduce medical care costs. We can also conclude that some programs are apparently able to produce medical care cost savings that far exceed their cost. We need to put these cost/benefit values in perspective. An employer never expects to make money on an employee benefit (like a health promotion program) and rarely, if ever, expects the program to pay for itself in directly measurable savings. Almost any employer would be more than satisfied with an employee benefit that produces a cost/benefit ratio of 1.00 which means $1.00 in savings for every $1.00 invested; returns of $3.00 for every dollar invested are clearly outstanding.

In conclusion, the relationship between medical care costs and risk factors that can be modified by health promotion programs is strong. Also, research on the impact of programs on medical care costs does support the claim that programs can reduce medical care costs. The quality of the research methodology is also adequate. This body of research should be sufficient to persuade an employer that health promotion programs can moderate medical costs. We could not make this statement in the early years of this field. Furthermore, we can probably increase the savings potential of health promotion programs if we design programs with the explicit goal of impacting medical care costs. To do this, we need to focus more attention on the health risks that are most costly, such as injury and musculoskeletal problems, instead of the health risks with the strongest links to death and chronic disease, such as cardiovascular disease and cancer. At the same time we need to address the needs of low-risk employees by providing them with encouragement and opportunities to remain healthy and stay low-risk. Many programs have already adopted the strategy of focusing on high-risk employees, but few have recognized the importance of keeping healthy employees healthy as a strategic focus.[60] We also need to incorporate programs on the wise use of medical services and encourage appropriate use of pharmaceuticals and medical care, particularly for those with chronic health conditions such as diabetes or asthma. A large percentage of services provided are medically unnecessary, and it is possible to educate employees to use care more appropriately.

Productivity Enhancement

We have long argued that health promotion programs enhance productivity, and as the research improves, we have more and more evidence to support this claim. Historically, research focused on employee absenteeism[24,61,62], then additional measures of workers' compensation absences[63], and short- and long-term disability outcomes were studied.[64,65] Finally, measures of on-the-job productivity losses, also known as **presenteeism**, were included in health promotion research. Productivity at work is difficult to measure, particularly in knowledge-based jobs. In general terms, employee productivity is defined as output per unit of labor. Among blue-collar workers, this might be measured in terms of automobiles, toys, tables, or any other product produced per hour. For white-collar workers, it might be designs created, insurance claims processed, or customer service calls handled per hour. For a sales person, it might be sales closed per month, and for a film producer, it might be films produced per year. In addition to the quantity of units produced, the quality of each unit produced is an important element of productivity; the automobiles, toys, and tables must meet all production standards. To be of value to the organization, designs, claims processed, and service calls taken must be free of errors. The sales closed must not be canceled, and the films made must be well made.

Within the health promotion community, most of the focus to date on productivity has been on absenteeism, primarily because absenteeism is easy to measure, but also because absenteeism is an important part of productivity. When a worker is absent, s/he may continue to get paid but produces no work. In some cases, s/he is replaced by someone else who must be paid. This raises the cost of producing the same level of output. In other cases, he or she is not replaced, and co-workers are required to disrupt their work to fill in for the absent employee. This reduces total output. In either case, output per unit of labor (i.e., productivity) drops. Health promotion programs are expected to reduce absenteeism by helping people stay healthy and thus reduce the need to be absent. This is reasonable as long as illness is the cause of the absence. Sometimes people take a "mental health" day when they need a break. Other times they call in sick when, in fact, they are staying home with a sick child. The impact of a health promotion

program on these cases is more complex and is better explained within a broader conceptual approach, which is illustrated in Figure 2-1.

The Concept

The basic concept, as illustrated in Figure 2-1, is that human performance is higher when people are physically and emotionally able to work and have the desire to work. Higher levels of human performance lead to higher levels of productivity, which in turn can lead to higher profit levels. Health promotion programs play a central role in this model because they can improve health by reducing health risks, helping to manage controllable diseases, and reducing use of mood-altering substances. These health improvements lead to improved physical and emotional ability to work. Health promotion programs also improve **organization climate**, which enhances people's desire to work and directly enhances human performance. This model also asserts that improved organization climate and higher profit levels directly reduce

Figure 2-1: Mechanisms linking health, productivity and profit.[91]

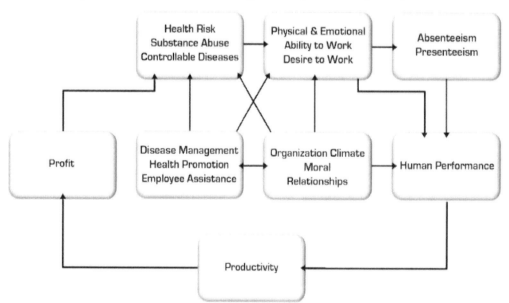

health risks. This is a preliminary model that must be tested and refined. Elements within the model may change and new mechanisms may be discovered.

Why is this Concept of Enhancing Productivity so Important?

The basic reason is that increased human productivity can lead to increased profits. In operational terms, higher productivity in a manufacturing setting means more product is produced with fewer labor hours of input. Increased productivity in research and development means more and better product enhancements emerge from research labs. Increased productivity in sales and marketing means more products are sold and sales revenues are higher. Increased productivity in management means people receive more effective guidance and coordination. Productivity enhancement has always been important for these reasons, but is even more important as businesses compete globally.

Corporations' desire to improve productivity is also important because American businesses have entered an increasingly competitive global business environment. American businesses lead the world in most measures of productivity[66]; however, labor costs in the United States are among the highest in the world, and U.S. markets have fewer limitations on imports than virtually any other major market in the world. If U.S. businesses want to continue to compete successfully, they must have higher quality products produced at lower cost through more productive processes. Finally, existing developments in computer technology and emerging developments in **measurement theory** are enabling businesses to measure productivity with greater accuracy and efficiency than ever before. Just as double digit medical care cost increases in the 1970s sparked a decades-long focus on medical care cost containment, this combination of events has sparked what we expect will be a decades-long focus on productivity enhancement.

How much more productive will employees be who are physically and emotionally able to work and motivated to work because they feel their employer is concerned about their well-being? This remains an open question; one that we expect will receive considerable attention in the next decade. The author has posed this question in formal discussions with hundreds of executives and dozens of scientists during the past few decades. The most common response from scientists is that employees will be 5% to 10% more productive. The most common response from executives is that employees will be 100% more productive! As we would expect and hope, scientists are more conservative in their estimates. However, executives think of themselves when they answer this question. They know how much more productive they are when they are full of energy, not distracted by emotional problems, and really want to work. They know they are far more likely to be effective in their creative thinking, negotiating, efforts to motivate people, strategic planning, and any other challenging activity when they feel good and are motivated. In reality, a factory worker or clerk who has little control over his or her work environment might be able to increase productivity by 5%, 10%, or even 30%. A knowledge worker, such as a lawyer, scientist, writer, salesperson, or senior manager, might be able to increase productivity by 50%, 100%, or even more.

To make this relevant to business, we need to quantify the value of productivity increases and losses. The data supporting a financial payoff from health promotion are probably strongest in the area of medical cost savings, but the greatest potential payoff for health promotion is probably in productivity enhancement. The reason for this is simple. The maximum benefit we can achieve in medical cost savings is to eliminate the cost, or more realistically, to eliminate the costs related to lifestyle risk factors. If we eliminate the total medical care cost, this will save approximately $6,000 per year per covered life (employee + dependents).

If we eliminate the 25% of costs that are related to lifestyle risk factors, we will save approximately $1,500 per year per employee. More realistically, if we eliminate one quarter of the 25% of costs that are related to lifestyle risk factors, we will save approximately $375 per year per employee. Savings at any of these levels would be significant and more than enough to pay for the health promotion program, but they are minor compared to the additional revenue and profit we could earn by increasing productivity.

If productivity increases by 1% in a company with a 10% profit margin and that increased productivity can be translated into increased revenues, this will increase profits by 10%. If the profit margin is 5%, profits will increase by 20%. If productivity increases by 10%, profits will increase by 100% with a 10% profit margin and by 200% with a 5% profit margin. A 1% increase in profits in the United States in 2012[67] would be worth $150 billion per year, a 10% increase worth $1.5 trillion, and a 20% increase worth $3.0 trillion. Potential returns of this magnitude will grab the attention of even the most skeptical executives and policy makers.

Measuring productivity is very difficult and measuring the on-the-job productivity losses associated with poor health (presenteeism) has been a topic of great interest in recent years. Dozens of **presenteeism questionnaires** have been created and tested in a variety of settings. Several reviews of these instruments and their use in employee populations have been published.[68,69,70,71] In general, these productivity loss instruments have been found to be **valid** and **reliable** in measuring the association between health conditions and health risks with on-the-job productivity in a variety of jobs and industries. In one study, an objective measure of productivity was used with telephone customer service operators in order to assess the relationship between health risks (measured by an HRA) and productivity at work.[72] As the number of health risks increased, employee productivity decreased; and disease states were associated with productivity reduction as well. Measuring productivity among telephone operators who are "plugged in" during their entire shift is not easily replicated in most other occupations. Hence, the presenteeism questionnaires attempt to quantify the loss of productivity in several different ways such as the physical demands of work, interpersonal communication, getting to work on time, working a full shift, and quality of work accomplished.

While it appears that we can reliably state that health risks and health conditions are associated with a certain degree of productivity loss on the job, there is much less agreement on whether or not we can monetize those results.[73,74] Presenteeism instruments have given wildly varying estimates of the cost of presenteeism associated with several health risks and conditions. But it is unknown exactly how those productivity estimates can be translated into dollars for the organization. If a worker is 10% less productive today because she is suffering from a migraine, does she work twice as hard tomorrow to catch up the work she couldn't get to the day before? Or, if a database programmer needs to take a stretch break every 20 minutes to alleviate back pain, is that time lost or is it recouped when the worker returns to his desk with renewed energy? How do you accurately measure the productivity of a knowledge based worker who may arrive at a solution to a design flaw while he or she is not even at work? In many situations, workers put in extra hours to make up for lost time on a previous day, or co-workers shoulder a heavier load while co-workers are not well. All of these factors create a very complex context in which to calculate the dollar losses associated with presenteeism.

Measuring the impact of health promotion programs on productivity is even more difficult. As we recognized above, most early efforts to measure the impact of health promotion on productivity have focused on absenteeism as an outcome measure. Aldana[54] reviewed the research on the impact of absenteeism on productivity. He found 16 studies on this topic; 14 (87%) of the studies reported reductions in absenteeism after the introduction of the health promotion programs, one study reported no change, and one study reported an increase in absenteeism as a result of the program. Five of the studies reported cost/benefit analysis values, with a range of $2.50 to $10.10 saved for every $1.00 invested and an average savings of $4.90. The studies with experimental designs had the highest level of savings values (see Table 2-11).

In 2004, a study of 500 employees found that a reduction of one health risk improved presenteeism by 9% after controlling for baseline risks and demographic factors.[75] A similar study[76] measured changes in presenteeism using a modified version of the Work Limitations Questionnaire and compared it with changes in health risks over a two-year period. Each risk factor increased or reduced from 2002 to 2004 was associated with a commensurate change of 1.9% productivity loss. Mills and colleagues[77] conducted a quasi-experimental study to evaluate the impact of a comprehensive health promotion program on employee health risks and work productivity measured by the Work Performance Questionnaire. They found that the intervention group of employees had a significant improvement in work performance compared to the control group after twelve months of follow-up.

One study combined the outcome measures of absenteeism, short-term disability, and workers' compensation into a sum of the cost of **time away from work (TAW)** and compared it with health risk status and individual health risks of 6,220 hourly workers at Steelcase Inc. from 1998 to 2000.[64] Higher TAW costs were associated with several individual health risks and Table 2-12 shows the association of overall health risk status with TAW which helps to illustrate the total value of employee health to the organization. The excess costs associated with excess health risks accounted for 36% of the costs totaled for medical, pharmacy, absence, disability and workers' compensation at the study corporation.[64] The importance of this concept is that much of what individuals and companies spend on health is excess relative to a baseline population of those with zero, one or two health risks (overall low-risk status).

Loeppke reviewed the research on the total value of health to individuals, corporations, populations and nations and concluded that there is good evidence that health promotion can lower health risks, reduce the burden of disease, improve productivity, and lower total health costs. He found the most important driving factors of successful programs to be the commitment to prevention and having the ultimate goal of creating a culture of health within organizations and communities.[78] It appears that business leaders agree. A recent survey of employers' health care strategies in 2012 by the Towers Watson/National Business Group on Health found that "developing a workplace culture where employees are accountable and supported for their health and well-being" was cited as a top focus area by 40% of respondents, the most frequently reported answer.[79]

The above results are very encouraging, and we should be comfortable in concluding that some health promotion programs can reduce absenteeism and presenteeism and that, in some cases, the savings in absenteeism may more than pay for the cost of the program. However, we are not yet comfortable in quantifying the monetary savings in improvements in on-the-job productivity.

Image Enhancement

We have very little data to support the impact of health promotion on company image, and most of it is out of date, but it remains a very important motivation for many employers who develop health promotion programs. In

Table 2-12: Total Value of Health: Excess Costs associated with Excess Risks.[64]

Outcome Measure	Low Risk	Medium Risk	High Risk	Excess Cost Percentage*
Short-term Disability	$120	$216	$333	41%
Workers' Compensation	$228	$244	$496	24%
Absence	$245	$341	$527	29%
Medical & Pharmacy	$1,158	$,1487	$,3696	38%
Total	$1,751	$2,288	$5,052	36%

*Excess cost column reflects the number of employees in each of the risk categories.

an early survey, attracting new employees was identified as an important reason for developing a health promotion program by 67% of employers and retaining existing employees was cited by 76% of employers.[2]

Some of the early health promotion programs were developed primarily for image-related reasons. For example, when the Silicon Valley was emerging in the 1970s, engineers were in great demand. Companies such as Apple, Advanced Micro Devices, and Hewlett-Packard were growing from zero to thousands of employees in just a few years. College graduates with bachelor's degrees were commanding salaries of $50,000, which is the equivalent of about $250,000 in 2012 dollars. Also, many of these companies were developing competitive products with great growth potential. Knowledge of how to develop these products had great market value, so retaining existing employees was even more important than attracting new ones.

Many of these companies realized they could not survive financially by competing for employees solely through salaries; it was much less expensive, and initially more distinctive and effective, to compete based on benefits. For example, an elaborate club-type fitness center could be built for an amortized cost of $500 per employee per year and serve as a beacon to new employees and a morale-boosting perk for existing employees. If that same $500 were added to an employee's salary, it would work out to an increase of about $0.24 an hour, even less after taxes. Most professional employees already earning a large salary would not even notice such an increase. The Silicon Valley is a unique environment, but we have seen similar growth of new health promotion programs in other geographic areas that have gone through rapid industrial growth.

Some companies add health promotion programs when it is consistent with their products. For example, during the late 1970s and early 1980s, over half of the hospitals in the United States started selling health promotion programs to corporations and individuals in their communities. Prospective employer clients naturally asked these hospitals how well the health promotion program for their own hospital employees was working. Most of these hospitals did not initially have programs in place but scrambled to launch them. Unfortunately, when hospitals realized it was very difficult to run a profitable hospital-based health promotion program, many discontinued their corporate and community programs, as well as their internal employee health promotion programs and most of these programs shut down. In recent years, there has been a growing interest in hospital health promotion, and the American Hospital Association is stepping up to provide guidance. This has manifested in their recently released report: A Call to Action, Creating a Culture of Health[80], which encourages hospitals to take a leadership role in developing health promotion in their communities, starting with developing excellent health promotion programs for their own employees.

Programs also seem to develop in industry clusters. For example, health promotion programs are common among employers in high technology, oil, insurance, consumer products, public utilities, government agencies, and, automotive companies. This industry **cluster effect** illustrates how benefits are typically added. A rational perspective would lead us to conclude that companies conduct organized prospective cost/benefit analyses to decide which benefits to add and retain. As discussed below, a rational analysis is not always the driving force in decisions about health promotion programs. How many companies have ever tried to measure the impact of their medical care coverage on productivity or even on the health of their employees? Very few. Instead, companies typically look at the benefits offered by their primary competitors and try to match those benefits. This does not mean that they spend their dollars frivolously. They are very aggressive in securing the best price/quality balance and in containing overall costs of their benefits... they just don't use the methods we might expect them to use to select benefits based on the returns they provide.

The auto industry in Detroit provides a good example of the clustering effect, the desire to have benefits comparable to competitors, and the nonscientific method by which programs are often added. In the Detroit area, large automobile companies set the standard of high pay and excellent benefits.

This started when the first large auto company was started by Henry Ford. Much like the high technology companies in California in the 1970s (and the present day), Henry Ford needed to hire a huge number of employees to keep up with the exploding demand for cars created when he was able to reduce the cost of each car with the development of the assembly line. He offered hourly wages that were more than double the normal wages for a factory worker. Until recently, the labor unions have been successful in keeping those wages and benefits above market levels. Major employers in the Detroit area set their salary and benefit packages to try to keep up with the automobile companies.

During the early 1980s, Ford, then Chrysler, started to add employee health promotion programs. These programs continued to grow in the late 1980s and 1990s despite the fact that in 1991 the United States auto industry had the worst financial performance in its history. Ford, Chrysler, and General Motors lost a combined $7.5 billion in 1991.[81] A few years later, General Motors began developing plans for its employee health promotion program, a program that was once the largest employee health promotion program in the United States and probably the world. General Motors did have good rational reasons to develop a program: they were the only major U.S. auto company that did not have a program, and they had a relatively old work force and very high medical care costs. Despite these rational motivators, the impetus came from two new members of their corporate board, one of whom was a previous Secretary of Health and Human Services. These board members figured out how to divert existing health-care-related funds; within a few months, efforts to develop a program were underway. Following the lead of the auto companies, employers in southeastern Michigan have continued to develop and maintain employee health promotion programs. By the early 2000s, health promotion had become part of the culture and business strategy for auto companies, which is probably the primary reason they maintained their programs even when several of them nearly went bankrupt in 2007.

This desire to match the benefits of major competitors is likely responsible for some of the spread of health promotion to workplaces internationally. As companies around the world compete globally, they need to establish an image at least as polished as their major American competitors. They also need to recruit employees from the same labor pools, and having comparable benefits will be part of the strategy to achieve this. This will be especially true in Asia, where establishing position and saving 'face' is such an important part of the culture.

Combined Motives

It is important to stress that most organizations will have multiple motives for establishing their health promotion programs; some of these motives may not be entirely rational (See side bar: A Counter Perspective: The Emotional Factor). Also, as suggested by Green and Cargo nearly two decades ago[82], health promotion programs are so common now that some employers will adopt programs because they realize health promotion makes good business sense. A process to help managers determine if a proposed health promotion program is likely to produce sufficient returns is described in the side bar titled "How Can an Employer Determine if a Health Promotion Program Will Be a Good Investment?"

A COUNTER PERSPECTIVE: THE EMOTIONAL FACTOR

Why, indeed, do employers invest in health promotion programs for their employees? In the past four decades we have spent untold hours examining this question. We have felt our efforts to answer this question were well spent, because the future of our programs depended on this data. We were right in that feeling, but we may have made a basic mistake in our assumptions.

We have assumed that a decision to invest in a health promotion program is made through a fully rational process, and we have scrambled to accumulate data that show the financial returns of programs.

Ironically, now that we have good data to support the financial returns that can be realized from health promotion programs, we need to recognize that this process of deciding to start or continue a program is not fully rational.

Basically, what we need to start or continue a health promotion program is the emotional buy-in of the person who has the authority to say "YES," the emotional buy-in of the individual who has the authority to approve spending of $100 to $250 per employee per year. That's how much health promotion programs cost. To most organizations that is not very much. On the lower end, it is the equivalent of taking all the employees out for a holiday dinner. At the upper end, it is about as much as landscaping or carpeting a new facility. Spending at this level is not frivolous. Spending at this level does require close supervision to make sure the money is well-spent. However, it does not require the level of sophisticated cost/benefit analysis we have conducted to defend health promotion investments. Major investments, such as the acquisition of another company or the launch of a new product, often have less data to support their returns than we have to support investments in health promotion.

If a health promotion program has the emotional buy-in of top management, it will be approved and continued.[33,83] If not, the program will never start or will be discontinued when budget problems occur. In a small- to medium-sized company, the president will have sufficient authority to approve investment in a health promotion program. In a large company, a senior vice president will have authority to make an investment of this order of magnitude.

The authors have come to this conclusion based primarily on experience in talking to the top managers who have approved, continued, and discontinued programs. However, there are a few studies that support this position. For example, a study by Wolfe, Slack, and Rose-Hearn[84] of a small group of Canadian companies showed that senior managers did not list financial savings as the primary management motivation for establishing and continuing programs, although program managers did. Senior managers wanted to enhance morale, and they were not looking for direct quantifiable financial returns. At a personal level, Gerry Greenwald, former Chairman and Chief Executive Officer of United Airlines and former Chairman of Chrysler Motors asked one of the authors if there was any evidence to show that programs work, especially if they save money. After hearing the findings from a dozen studies, he stopped the presentation, saying that was more than enough to convince him and that he usually had far less evidence to guide him in making investment decisions of hundreds of millions of dollars.

From another perspective, some employers have a philosophical opposition to interfering with employees' private lives, health habits and medical decision-making[85] and will be unlikely to ever invest in health promotion at the workplace.

Also, an early national survey of employers conducted by William M. Mercer, Inc., for the Department of Health and Human Services[19], "keeping employees healthy" was cited by 84% of employers as an important reason for establishing a program. Reducing medical care costs was listed by 75%, and improving productivity was listed by 64% (see Table 2-13). Cost containment was important but not the most important reason.

The Dupont and Pacific Bell health promotion programs may provide further support for this concept. Both of these programs received the C. Everett Koop Award from the Health Project in encouraging researchers to conduct higher quality studies. Both had published good quality studies illustrating cost savings[86,87], yet both programs were discontinued. The reasons these programs were discontinued were never publicized, so we cannot conclude that an "emotional" factor was the cause. However, we can conclude that something other than the medical care cost containment or absenteeism reduction outcomes, which these programs demonstrated, was more important to their respective organizations.

The authors have always been, and continue to be, strong advocates for excellent program evaluation and research on the health and financial benefit of health promotion programs, but think it is important that we be more aware of why and how organizations make decisions to develop and continue or discontinue programs. To be successful and survive, a health promotion program must contribute to the mission, long-term goals, and short-term priorities of the organization it serves, and to the special interests of those who approve its budgets. Sometimes these specific interests are unstated emotional factors. Our research and evaluation efforts should address all of these factors.

Table 2-13: Reasons Contributing to a Business Decision to Offer Health Promotion Program[19].

Keep workers healthy	84%
Improve morale	77%
Retain good employees	76%
Reduce medical care costs	75%
Attract good employees	67%
Improve productivity	64%

How Good is the Quality of the Evidence?

In 1984, we could only speculate about the financial impact of health promotion programs. Only a handful of studies had been published, and all of them had serious methodological flaws. By 1994, hundreds of studies had been published on the impact of workplace health promotion programs; a large number of them addressed financial outcomes. Our general conclusion at that time was that most of the studies did have some flaws in methodology that prevented us from making conclusive statements that programs do save money. We devoted a great deal of time examining the methodological flaws of the research and recognition of the outstanding quality of these programs. It is still important for practitioners to be aware of these problems, so we are including a list (see Table 2-14) on the most common potential threats to internal validity.[88] Despite these flaws, we made it very clear that the amount and quality of research

supporting the financial returns from health promotion programs was, even then, far superior to the research supporting business investments for decisions with costs similar to those of a health promotion program. After all, these programs cost from only $50 (or less) per employee for a basic program to $350 for the best comprehensive programs in the country. As mentioned earlier, this cost is about as much as a year-end party, carpeting, landscaping, etc. The quality of the evidence we had in 1994 was more than sufficient for an employer to make a decision to invest in a health promotion program. Indeed, by 1990, 81% of employers surveyed had decided to develop some form of health promotion program.[2] Since 1994, numerous additional studies had been published, and the quality of studies continued to improve. By 2002, the outcomes in our field of research expanded to include multiple measures of productivity, and the number of employers who scientifically evaluated the success of their programs grew. We had examples of successful programs in

Table 2-14: Potential Threats to Internal Validity.[88]

Validity Threat	Definition/Description
1. Selection	A threat when effect may be due to pre-existing differences between the kinds of people in the study groups.
2. Attrition	Refers to the dropping out of subjects over time such that the characteristics of remaining subjects at posttest are different from the characteristics of the full group at pretest. In multiple group studies, differential mortality occurs when the characteristics of subjects leaving the study are different between the experimental and comparison groups.
3. Maturation	Processes occurring within the respondents as a function of the passage of time; growing older, more experienced, more motivated. In multiple group studies, selection may interact with maturation such that respondents in one group "mature" faster than respondents in another group, regardless of the treatment.
4. History	Refers to the specific unintended events occurring between the pretest and posttest measurements in addition to the treatment variable. In multiple group studies, local history is a threat when events other than the treatment affect one group but not another.
5. Instrumentation	Operates due to improper precalibration of measuring instrument: changes in the calibration of the instrument between the pretest and posttest; or because scale intervals are not equal and change is easier to detect at some points on the measurement scale than on others.
6. Statistical Regression	Tendency for an unusually high or low score to regress or return to a more usual or mean level on subsequent measures.
7. Treatment Fidelity	Refers to the ability to infer that the treatment, or worksite health promotion program, exists in sufficient strength to cause the intended outcome.
8. Diffusion of Treatments	Occurs when experimental and comparison groups have contact, and the comparison group may receive the treatment or part of the treatment from the experimental group.
9. Testing	The effects of taking a test upon the scores of a future testing. Also referred to as **reactiveness of measures.**
10. Compensatory Rivalry among Respondents Receiving the Less Desirable/No Treatment	May operate in multiple group studies when rivalry is engendered among the subject receiving the less desirable treatment or no treatment. Also referred to as the **John Henry effect.**

Table 2-14: *continued*

Validity Threat	Definition/Description
11. Resentful Demoralization of Respondents Receiving the Less Desirable/No Treatment	May operate in multiple group studies when the comparison group gets discouraged because they were not given the favorable treatment and, as a result, their behavior is negatively affected.
12. Compensatory Equalization of Treatments by Administrators	May operate in multiple group studies when there is administrative reluctance to tolerate inequality of treatments among groups.
13. Ambiguity about the Direction of Causal Influence	Not clear if A caused B or B caused A.

many types of organizations with diverse workforces and from varying industries and geographic locations.

The Aldana reviews[54,55] and the Baicker et al. review[59] cited previously are probably the best reviews of the literature on the financial impact of workplace health promotion programs from the perspective of having a systematic search process, factoring in methodology quality and summarizing results of the literature as a whole. In addition to summarizing the impact of the studies, the Aldana review also critiqued the methodology of each study using the criteria in Table 2-15.

The most important methodological problems in the research on the financial impact of workplace health promotion programs have not changed much in the past decade; they include lack of sufficient randomized controlled designs, small sample sizes, short duration of the studies, inadequate measurement tools, and inappropriate analysis.[54] Despite these limitations, it is difficult to find many higher quality bodies of research in health care, business, or any of the social sciences for investments of a similar order of magnitude. From a practical perspective, the quality of evidence is certainly good enough for a business executive trying to determine if health promotion is a good investment.

Does this mean we rest on our laurels? Should we stop conducting research on the organizational or financial impact of workplace health promotion programs? Definitely not, but we should refocus our efforts in terms of methodology, the scope of our research outcomes, and where the research is conducted. The most important problems with health promotion research are: small number of randomized controlled designs; small sample sizes; short duration of the studies; lack of valid and reliable measurement tools; and inappropriate analyses.[54] Suggestions on how to address these problems are discussed below.

Individual employers should continue to conduct high quality evaluations of their programs, examining both the health and organizational outcomes of their programs. However, the primary focus of these evaluation efforts should shift to focus on how well the program supports the organization's mission, long-term goals, and current priorities. To the extent that these goals and priorities include containing medical care costs and enhancing productivity, those outcomes should be studied. Indeed, there was a burst of activity in

Table 2-15: Aldana and Pronk's Definitions of the Various Scoring Criteria.[61]

	Description
Study Rating	
A	Properly randomized, controlled study (experimental designs).
B	Well-designed controlled trials without randomization (quasi-experimental designs).
C	Well-designed cohort or case-control studies (pre-experimental designs).
D	Trend data, correlational and regression studies (correlational designs).
E	Expert opinions, descriptive studies, case reports, reports of expert committees.
Literature Rating	
Weak	Research evidence supporting relationship is fragmentary, nonexperimental, and/or poorly operationalized. A majority of experts in the field believe causal impact is plausible but no more so than alternative explanations.
Suggestive	Multiple studies consistent with relationship, but no randomized control groups. Most experts believe causal impact is consistent with knowledge in related areas but see support as limited and acknowledge plausible alternative explanations.
Indicative	Relationship supported by substantial number of well-designed studies, with few or no randomized control groups. Experts believe that relationship is likely causal, but evidence is still tentative.
Acceptable	Cause-effect relationship supported by well-designed studies with randomized control groups.
Conclusive	Cause-effect relationship between intervention and outcome; substantial number of well-designed, randomized, control studies.

the realm of measuring presenteeism in the past decade and we suspect it will continue to be an area of interest for researchers and practitioners. These individual program evaluation efforts should be upgraded to address two of the most common problems in research and evaluation: using valid and reliable measures, and using the appropriate analysis. For most employers, this will be difficult because, in a comprehensive program that includes organization level changes, the best unit of randomization will be at the organization level. Therefore, multiple organizations will be required to conduct this level of study.

The problems of small sample sizes and short duration of studies will be difficult to correct at the individual program evaluation level except with the largest employers. In examining medical care costs, study samples of at least 10,000 people are optimal to overcome analysis problems related to the volatility of the data. We also need cost data three years before and three years after the intervention. Ideally, we would like to have a situation in which the intervention is offered, withdrawn, and offered again. This type of research might be possible in a small number of very large organizations that have low turnover. These might include the United States Post Office, the military (focusing on career officers), or some of the twenty or so largest employers. However, this type of evaluation will be very difficult for most employers.

Even with the largest employers, it will be difficult to justify the high cost of high quality research. It is not unusual for a well-conducted study on the impact of a health promotion program on medical care utilization to cost $100,000 - $250,000 or more. Also, structuring a program to comply with research requirements might create significant delays in program implementation, causing resentment from the people not having access to the program. All of these extra problems and costs would serve no direct purpose to the employer as they already have sufficient data to show them the program can produce positive financial returns.

Another problem is the absence of a clear **temporal mechanism** to explain the link between health risks and medical care costs. For example, we would expect that people who have risk factors such as hypertension, excess stress, sedentary lifestyle, tobacco use, poor nutrition, and alcohol abuse to have higher medical care costs. However, it is reasonable to expect a lag of several years between the onset of these diseases and the increase in costs and between the elimination of the risk factor and a reduction in costs. If this lag time does exist, how should we interpret a reduction in medical care costs that occurs immediately after a health promotion program occurs? It would be reasonable to expect rapid cost reductions from programs in medical selfcare, seat belt use safety programs, and substance abuse treatment, but not in most of the other areas. For example, Musich et al. estimated that costs of former smokers returned to costs of non-smokers in five years for those with no chronic conditions and in 10 years for those with chronic conditions.[89] To fully understand the potential of health promotion programs to reduce costs, we need to conduct **longitudinal studies**.

To address the problems of study design, sample size, and duration of study, we need to create collaborative efforts among employers, private research foundations, and such government agencies as the National Institutes of Health, Centers for Disease Control and Prevention, Department of Commerce, or Department of Labor, to design, implement, and fund large scale research studies. The Health Enhancement Research Organization[90] and the American Journal of Health Promotion[91] made some progress in stimulating these efforts, but much work remains to be done. The results of these proposed studies would help set government policy, not necessarily to advise individual employers. This research might focus on producing standardized outcome measures and identifying a) which interventions are best in producing savings, b) characteristics of the most successful programs, c) how to improve the cost effectiveness of programs, and d) how to reach different gender, ethnic, and income groups.

HOW CAN AN EMPLOYER DETERMINE IF A HEALTH PROMOTION PROGRAM WILL BE A GOOD INVESTMENT?

A process is described below to help a manager determine if the program is likely to produce sufficient returns to justify its cost.

Cost/Benefit Analysis Projections

Like any other program in the organization, the health promotion program should not be a frill. It should pay for itself in terms of the benefits it brings to the organization. Some of these benefits will be tangible and measurable, such as reduced medical care costs or reduced absenteeism. Others will be more difficult to measure but equally valuable, such as improved image. Projecting the financial returns a program may generate is not simple, but it can be done and should be done as part of the **feasibility study** to determine if the program is a good investment for the organization. A **"macro-approach"** to cost/benefit analysis is described below.[4] The macro approach has seven basic steps that are also listed in Table 2-16.

Step 1: Identify and Quantify the Areas Affected by the Health Promotion Program

The first step in the prospective cost/benefit analysis is to determine the areas of the organization that are likely to be affected by the health promotion program, identify sources of information on each of these areas, and quantify these areas. Identifying areas that may be affected by the health promotion program will be relatively easy. A sample list of these is shown in Table 2-17. However, in most organizations, identifying good sources of this information and securing accurate values will be difficult. For example, many organizations track absenteeism at the department level but may not keep central records for the entire organization. Collecting data will often require a request from each department. This can be very cumbersome in an organization that has a large number of departments located in multiple geographic sites and can easily result in missing data from some departments. In some cases, absenteeism is tracked for hourly workers but not for salary workers. Other productivity related data, especially how much high quality work an employee completes per week, month, or year, is just not available in most organizations.

Collecting information on medical care spending is equally difficult. Surprisingly, even moderately large employers sometimes have trouble determining their annual medical care costs. In most cases they will know exactly how much they have paid a specific carrier, such as Blue Cross/Blue Shield, but their payments may not correspond to a specific calendar year. In other cases they may have additional commercial carriers, different carriers for active employees and retirees, and a number of HMOs, all using different calendar years for collecting premiums. This is not to say that the director of benefits could not come up with an accurate measure of current annual medical care costs if given such a directive by the president of the organization. However, it might be difficult to justify this much effort merely to provide information to facilitate a prospective cost/benefit analysis for a health promotion program. In most cases, the compilation of these figures will be left to the person conducting the study, and it is very easy to make mistakes in such compilations. This problem is compounded when collecting information on past years. This whole process is very time-consuming and subject to error due to missing or misinterpreted documents. Collecting information on productivity and image are, of course, far more difficult because most organizations do not keep information on these areas.

Step 2: Estimate the Cost Ranges of the Health Promotion Program

The next step is to determine the probable cost of the health promotion program. This may seem difficult to do before the program is fully defined, but in reality it is not difficult to project general ranges. For example, in the year 2010, the annual costs of an **awareness level** program would be between $20 and $70 per employee: a **behavior-change program** $60 to $150, including staffing; and a **comprehensive supportive-environment program** $150 to $350. During the design process, the principal designers often have a good general sense of the level of program and spending that is likely to be approved.

Step 3: Determine the Percentage Savings Required in the Areas to be affected in Order to pay for the Program

Determining the level of spending required for the program to pay for itself can be done by dividing the expenditures in the areas expected to be affected by the program by the cost of the program. For example, if annual medical care costs are $6,000 per covered life and the program is expected to cost $150 per life, the program must reduce medical care costs (or moderate future increases) by 2.50% to pay for itself ($150 ÷ $6000 = .025). Similarly, if the average employee is paid $25 per hour or $50,000 per year, the program would need to reduce paid staff time by 0.3% to pay for itself ($150 ÷ $50,000 = .003). (Paid staff time might be reduced by enhancing productivity or reducing absenteeism during hours worked. This is a very simple example used for illustrative purposes only.) Of course, if benefits are realized in both areas, the effect required in each would be reduced.

Step 4: Ask if it is Reasonable to Achieve the Level of Savings Required to Pay for the Program.

When determining whether the level of savings required to pay for the programs is reasonable if done right, the key is to ask the question not of the analyst or the health promotion expert but of the person(s) authorizing or paying for the program. This question should be asked twice. First, as part of a feasibility study senior managers should be asked to project in very rough terms how much they expect a health promotion program to affect the three major benefit areas: medical care costs, productivity, and image. Second, after the three steps above have been completed and a basic program plan has been developed, the senior executive should be shown his or her earlier estimate and the amount of savings required and asked if that level of savings seems reasonable at a gut level. The analyst can support this process by supplying research articles and answering any questions asked. The analyst should not be the one to answer the central question about whether the required savings are reasonable to achieve.

Step 5: Add Other Nonquantifiable Benefits

Some of the expected benefits will not be quantifiable, yet will be very important. For example, if the health promotion program provides an important publicity angle for the employer that is felt to be an important part of an overall image campaign, the program will provide a benefit that is very hard to quantify but is nevertheless important. Including such non-quantifiable benefits will be "frosting on the cake" if the quantifiable benefits show that the program makes sense; it may provide the necessary additional return if the quantifiable benefits are borderline.

Step 6: Compare Costs to Other Expenditures

Comparing the cost of the health promotion program to other expenditures helps the organization do a comparative **cost-effectiveness analysis** by considering how much benefit is received from current expenditures compared to those expected from the health promotion program. It is often useful to compare the program costs to each of the other employee benefits, such as paid vacation and holiday time; medical, disability, and life insurance; retirement benefits; and any subsidies for cafeterias, parking, club memberships, and other benefits. Comparing it to in-house training costs, tuition reimbursement, and out-of-town seminars helps to put these costs in perspective with other employee development costs. Comparing it to the cost of preventive maintenance and service for equipment and facilities allows developers to ask how much should be spent keeping employees in good working order as compared to equipment and facilities. Finally, it is often useful to identify all the annual expenditures of similar magnitude to the proposed health promotion program in order to allow direct comparison of the perceived benefits of these expenditures relative to the expected benefits of the health promotion program. In most cases such comparisons illustrate the relatively low cost of a health promotion program.

Step 7: Decide Whether the Program is a Good Investment

The final step, deciding whether the program is a good investment, is relatively easy if the first six steps are followed. This macro-approach provides a level of detail and sophistication that is acceptable to most business decision-makers. Although it is conceptually simple, it is a challenge to implement due to the difficulty of securing accurate information on the organization's financial expenditures.

Table 2-16: Steps in Determining Whether a Health Promotion Program Is a Good Investment.

Step 1:	Identify and quantify the areas affected by the health promotion program.
Step 2:	Estimate the cost ranges of the health promotion program.
Step 3:	Determine the percentage savings required in the areas to be affected in order to Pay for the program.
Step 4:	Ask if it is reasonable to achieve the level of savings required to pay for the program.
Step 5:	Add other nonquantifiable benefits.
Step 6:	Compare costs to other expenditures.
Step 7:	Decide whether the program is a good investment.

Table 2-17: Areas That May be Affected by a Health Promotion Program.

Impact Area	Source of Data
Productivity-related	
Absenteeism	Personnel records
Desire to work	Employee satisfaction surveys
Morale	Employee satisfaction surveys
Output per unit of time	Specialized studies
Physical and emotional disabilities	Personnel records
Recruiting success	Interviews with employment representatives
Turnover	Personnel records
Health-related	
Life insurance costs	Benefits records
Medical care costs	Personnel records
Other insurance costs	Benefits records
Type of medical claims	Medical utilization records
Worker's compensation claims	Personnel records
External Image-related	
Community	
• Current client's perceptions	Public relations department
• Potential client's perceptions	Public relations department
• Potential employee's perceptions	Public relations department

Table 2-17: *continued*

Impact Area	Source of Data
Product sales	
• Health promotion programs	Marketing department
• Other products	Marketing department

CONCLUSION

Keeping employees healthy is very important to most employers, and this is the reason most frequently cited by top managers for developing health promotion programs. Many top managers will fund a program because they want to keep employees healthy and because it is "the right thing to do." However, few programs will survive or thrive on a long-term basis unless they contribute to the mission, long-term goals, and short-term priorities of the organization, or to the special interests of those who approve program budgets AND top management sees data on a regular basis that shows the connection between the program and those organizational outcomes.

The most common justification for health promotion programs is medical care cost containment. A persuasive body of research has emerged that shows that people with unhealthy lifestyles do cost more and that health promotion programs can produce savings in excess of their costs. However, saving money through medical care cost containment will be important to employers only when medical care costs are perceived to be a serious problem.

Returns from productivity related outcomes including enhancing morale, reducing absenteeism, attracting and retaining good employees, and making sure that employees are physically and emotionally able to work are likely to be far greater than returns from medical care cost savings. These areas are also more likely to be closely related to the mission, longterm goals, and short-term priorities of the organization. Research

examining the relationship between health promotion programs and productivity does show that programs are associated with reduced absenteeism, and that the returns from absenteeism are greater than the returns from medical care cost containment when compared from a cost/benefit perspective. Predictions by the authors that this would be a rapidly growing area of research did not come true, probably because of the challenges in conducting this research.[92]

Research or program evaluation on the impact of health promotion programs on medical care costs or productivity is expensive to conduct for most employers. Therefore, most employers must rely on research conducted in other organizations and extrapolate those findings to their own employees. Furthermore, this research or program evaluation is very difficult to execute, and few if any studies have been able to eliminate all of the methodological problems.

Nevertheless, for the field in general, the data supporting the claim that health promotion programs can reduce medical care costs and reduce absenteeism is of higher quality than the data most businesses have to support other investments of similar cost and thus is adequate to justify an investment in a health promotion program. A protocol is described here which shows how employers can decide if a health promotion program is likely to produce a positive return for their organization without conducting expensive research or making precise assumptions about financial returns.

Program managers trying to justify their programs will probably be most successful if they determine the mission, long-term goals, short-term priorities of their organization, and the special interests of those who approve program budgets, THEN design their programs to enhance these organizational outcomes. Next, they should design their program evaluation plan to measure the impact of the program on these outcomes, and make sure top management sees those data on a regular basis.

Glossary

Mission: The central purpose or core objective of an organization.

Long term goals: The specific outcomes and organization strives to achieve over a period of years to achieve its mission.

Short term priorities: Specific issues an organization must address in the current month, quarter or year to capitalize on an opportunity or overcome a problem.

Cost Benefit Analysis: A wide range of analyses an organization can use to determine the benefit of an investment. Benefits can be quantitative or qualitative, include improved health, image in the community, recruiting and retaining talented staff, enhancing productivity, reducing medical costs, and other outcomes. Specific analyses might include payback (years to recover the investment), return on investment, internal rate of return, and other methods.

Return on Investment (ROI): Analysis to directly compare a financial investment with financial returns. The formula commonly used by Western businesses is Benefits/Costs. The formula commonly used by economists is (Benefits-Costs)/Costs.

Medical cost containment: Efforts by employers to control the rate of increase of their medical costs.

Productivity: The amount of work employees produce, commonly defined as output per unit volume of labor. Some definitions include measures of product quality.

Absenteeism: A tendency to be absent from work. Absences can be scheduled and have prior approval (jury duty, military service, vacations, etc) or unscheduled (personal illness, family illness, feigned illness, etc). Absenteeism rates are the (number of hours away from work)÷(total work hours possible).

Presenteeism: Being at work but not being productive because of illness, lack of motivation or other causes.

Employee Turnover: Employees leaving the organization for any reason. Turnover rate is the number of employees leaving in a year divided by the total number of employees.

Morale: The feelings of enthusiasm, commitment, or hopefulness employees hold for their work or organization.

Learning Objectives

After reading this chapter, readers will be able to do the following:

1. Describe the primary objective and subjective reasons employers invest in workplace health promotion programs.
2. Summarize the primary findings on the financial impact of health promotion programs.
3. Describe the quality of the evidence on the financial impact of health promotion programs.
4. Describe a process to predict if health promotion will be a good investment for employers.

Discussion Questions

1. How does the quality of evidence for health promotion programs compare to the quality of evidence for other business or health investments of the same order of magnitude?

2. Given the cost of health promotion programs, what is the most appropriate level of rigor for the evaluation effort? How much should be spent to evaluate a program?

3. In focusing on medical cost reduction and productivity enhancement, are employers focusing on the most important and appropriate outcomes? What other outcomes should employers consider?

4. What are the roles of the business leadership, internal program manager, external program suppliers and venders and out side consultants in planning and implementing the evaluation of the health promotion program?

REFERENCES

1. Kaiser Family Foundation and Health Research and Educational Trust. *Employer Health Benefits: 2012 Annual Survey.* Menlo Park, CA. 2012.

2. Association for Worksite Health Promotion, U.S. Department of Health and Human Services, William M. Mercer, Inc. *1999 National worksite health promotion survey.* Northbrook, IL: Association for Worksite Health Promotion and William M. Mercer, Inc. 2000.

3. U.S. Department of Health and Human Services. Healthy People 2020: Healthy people in healthy communities. ODPHP Publication Number B0132. Washington, D.C. 2010.

4. MetLife. 10th Annual Study of Employee Benefits Trends. New York, NY, 2012.

5. Linnan L, Bowling M, Childress J, Lindsay G, Blakey C, Pronk S, Wieker S, Royall P. Results of the 2004 national worksite health promotion survey. *Am J Pub Health.* 2008;98:1503-1509.

6. Department of Health and Human Services, Public Health Service. 1992 National survey of worksite health promotion activities: Summary. *Am J Health Promot.* 1993;7(6):452-464.

7. O'Donnell M, Harris J. Health Promotion in the Workplace (2nd ed.). Albany, NY: Delmar Publishers. 1994.

8. Goetzel R, Ozminkowski R. What's Holding You Back: Why Should (or Shouldn't) Employers Invest in Health Promotion Programs for Their Workers? *N Car Med J.* 2006;67:428-430.

9. O'Donnell M, Bishop C, Kaplan K. Benchmarking best practices in workplace health promotion. *Art Health Promot.* 1997;1:1.

10. European Foundation for the Improvement of Living and Working Conditions. *Workplace Health Promotion in Europe: Programme Summary.* Dublin, Ireland. 1997.

11. European Agency for Safety and Health at Work. *Motivation for employers to carry out workplace health promotion.* Publications Office of the European Union, Luxembourg. 2012.

12. Organization for Economic Cooperation and Development. OECD Health Data 2012 - Frequently Requested Data. Paris, France. 2012.

13. Centers for Medicaid and Medicare Services. *National Health Expenditure Data.* Baltimore, MD. 2011.

14. Levit K, Cowan C. The burden of health care costs: Business, household, government. *Health Care Fin Rev.* 1990;12(2):131.

15. Koretz G. Employers tame medical costs: But workers pick up a bigger share. *Bus Week,* January 17, 2000, p. 26.

16. Interstudy. The Interstudy Competitive Edge: HMO Industry Report, 9.1. Bloomington, MN: InterStudy Publications. 1999.

17. Hoechst Marion Roussell, *HMO/PPO/Medicare-Medicaid Digest.* Kansas City: MO; 1999.

18. Health Care Financing Administration. National Health Care Expenditures, 2000. Washington DC.

19. William M. Mercer, Inc. 14th Annual National Survey of Employer-Sponsored Health Plans. 2000. Northbrook, IL.

20. Finkelstein A. The aggregate effects of health insurance: evidence from the introduction of Medicare. *Q J of Econ.* 2007;122(1):1-37.

21. Haviland AM, Marquis MS, McDevitt R, Sood N. Growth of Consumer-Directed Health Plans to one-half of all employer-sponsored insurance could save $57 billion annually. *Health Aff.* 2012;31:1009-1015.

22. Brink S. *Health risks and behavior: The impact on medical costs.* Brookfield, WI: Millman and Robertson. 1987.

23. Yen L, Edington D, Witting P. Associations between health risk appraisal scores and employee medical claims costs. *Am J Health Promot.* 1991;6(1):46-54.

24. Yen L, Edington D, Witting P. Prediction of prospective medical claims and absenteeism costs for 1284 hourly workers from a manufacturing company. *J Occup Med.* 1992;34 (4):428-435.

25. Goetzel R. Relationship between modifiable health risks and health care expenditures. *J Occup Environ Med.* 1998;40:10.

26. Goetzel RZ, Pei X, Tabrizi MJ, Henke RM, Kowlessar N, Nelson CF, Metz RD. Ten modifiable health risk factors are linked to more than one-fifth of employer-employee health care spending. *Health Aff.* 2012;31:2474-2484.

27. Schultz AB, Edington DW. Metabolic syndrome in a workplace: prevalence, co-morbidities, and economic impact. *Met Syn Rel Disord.* 2009;7:459-468.

28. Braunstein A, Li Y, Hirschland D, McDonald T, Edington DW. Internal associations among health-risk factors and risk prevalence. *Am J Health Behav.* 2001;25:407-417.

29. Mayer JP, Taylor JR, Thrush JC. Exploratory cluster analysis of behavioral risks for chronic disease and injury: implications for tailoring health promotion services. *J Comm Health.* 1990;15:377-389.

30. Anderson DR, Whitmer RW, Goetzel RZ, Ozminkowski RJ, Dunn RL, Wasserman J, Serxner S. The relationship between modifiable health risks and group-level health care expenditures: Health Enhancement Research Organization (HERO) Research Committee. *Am J Health Promot.* 2001;15(1):45-52.

31. Jee S, O'Donnell M, Suh I, Kim I. The relationship between modifiable health risks and future medical care expenditures: the Korea Medical Insurance Corporation (KMIC) Study. *Am J Health Promot.* 2001;15(4):244-255.

32. Anderson G. Multinational comparisons of health care: Expenditures, coverage, and outcomes. New York, NY: The Commonwealth Fund; 1998.

33. Edington DW. *Zero Trends: Health as a serious economic strategy.* University of Michigan Health Management Research Center; Ann Arbor, MI. 2009.

34. Yen L, McDonald T, Hirschland D, Edington DW. Association between wellness score from a Health Risk Appraisal and prospective medical claims costs. *J Occup Environ Med.* 2003;45:1049-1057.

35. Edington D. *Worksite wellness; 20-year cost benefit analysis and report: 1979 to 1998.* Ann Arbor, MI: University of Michigan, Health Management Research Center. 1998.

36. Steinwachs DM. Pharmacy benefit plans and prescription drug spending. *JAMA.* 2002;288: 1773-1774.

37. Levit K, Cowan C, Lazenby H, Sensenig A, McDonnell P, Stiller J, Martin A,

Health Accounts Team. Health spending in 1998: signals of changes. *Health Aff.* 2000;19:124-132.

38. Milliman. 2012 Milliman Medical Index. Seattle, WA. 2012.

39. Yen L, Schultz AB, Schnueringer E, Edington DW. Financial costs due to excess health risks among active employees of a utility company. *J Occup Environ Med.* 2006;48:896-905.

40. Burton WN, Chen CY, Conti DJ, Schultz AB, Edington DW. Measuring the relationship between employees' health risk factors and corporate pharmaceutical expenditures. *J Occup Environ Med.* 2003;45:793-802.

41. Edington DW, Yen LT, Witting P. The financial impact of changes in personal health practices. *J Occup Environ Med.* 1997;39:1037-1046.

42. Edington DW, Musich S. Associating changes in health risk levels with changes in medical and short-term disability costs. *Health and Productivity Management.* 2004;3(1):12-15.

43. Schultz AB, Edington DW. The association between changes in metabolic syndrome and changes in cost in a workplace population. *J Occup Environ Med.* 2009;51:771-779.

44. Edington DW. Emerging research: a view from one research center. *Am J Health Promot.* 2001;15:341-349.

45. Nyce S, Grossmeier J, Anderson DR, Terry PE, Kelley B. Association between changes in health risk status and changes in future health care costs. *J Occup Environ Med.* 2012; 54:1364-1376.

46. Pelletier K. A review and analysis of the health and cost effectiveness outcome studies of comprehensive health promotion and disease prevention programs at the worksite. *Am J Health Promot.* 1991;5:311-315.

47. Pelletier K. A review and analysis of the health and cost effectiveness outcome studies of comprehensive health promotion and disease prevention programs at the worksite, 1991-1993 Update. *Am J Health Promot.* 1993;8:43-49.

48. Pelletier K. A review and analysis of the health and cost effectiveness outcome studies of comprehensive health promotion and disease prevention programs at the worksite, 1993--1995 Update. *Am J Health Promot.* 1996;10:380-388.

49. Pelletier K. A review and analysis of the health and cost effectiveness outcome studies of comprehensive health promotion and disease prevention programs at the worksite, 1995-1998 Update. *Am J Health Promot.* 1999;13(5),66-78.

50. Pelletier K. A review and analysis of the health and cost-effectiveness studies of comprehensive health promotion and disease management programs at the worksite: 1998-2000 Update. *Am J Health Promot.* 2001;16(2):107-116.

51. Pelletier K. A review and analysis of the clinical and cost-effectiveness studies of comprehensive health promotion and disease management programs at the worksite: update VI 2000-2004. *J Occup Environ Med.* 2005; 47:1051-1058.

52. Pelletier K. A review and analysis of the clinical and cost-effectiveness studies of comprehensive health promotion and disease management programs at the worksite: Update VII 2004-2008. *J Occup Environ Med.* 2009;51:822-837.

53. Loeppke R, Edington DW, Beg S. Impact of the Prevention Plan on employee health risk reduction. *Pop Health Mgmt.* 2010;13:275-284.

54. Aldana S. Financial impact of worksite health promotion and methodological quality of the evidence. *Art Health Promot.* 1998;2(1):1-8.

55. Aldana S. Financial impact of health promotion programs: a comprehensive review of the literature. *Am J Health Promot*. 2001;15(5):296-320.

56. Chapman LS. Meta-evaluation of worksite health promotion economic return studies. *Am J Health Promot*. 2003;17(3):1-10.

57. Chapman LS. Meta-evaluation of worksite health promotion economic return studies. *Am J Health Promot*. 2005;19(6):1-10.

58. Chapman LS. Meta-evaluation of worksite health promotion economic return studies: 2012 update. *Am J Health Promot* 2012;26(4):1-12.

59. Baicker KM, Cutler D, Song Z. Workplace wellness programs can generate savings. *Health Aff*. 2010;29:304-311.

60. Edington DW. Changes in costs related to changes in psychological and social support risk factors. Paper presented at Art and Science of Health Promotion Conference, Colorado Springs, Colorado. 2000.

61. Aldana S, Pronk NP. Health promotion programs, modifiable health risks, and employee absenteeism. *J Occup Environ Med*. 2001;43:36-46.

62. Serxner S, Gold DB, Bultman KK. The impact of behavioral health risks on worker absenteeism. *J Occup Environ Med*. 2001;43:347-354.

63. Musich S, Napier D, Edington DW. The association of health risks with workers' compensation costs. *J Occup Environ Med*. 2001;43:534-541.

64. Wright DW, Beard MJ, Edington DW. Association of health risks with the cost of time away from work. *J Occup Environ Med*. 2002;44:1126-1134.

65. Kuhnen AE, Burch SP, Shenolikar RA, Joy KA. Employee health and frequency of workers' compensation and disability claims. *J Occup Environ Med*. 2009;51:1041-1048.

66. International Labor Organization. *Key Indicators of the Labour Market*. Geneva, Switzerland. 2011.

67. U.S. Department of Commerce, Bureau of Economic Analysis. Gross Domestic Product. 2012. Available at http://www.bea.gov. Accessed March 2013.

68. Johns G. Presenteeism in the workplace: a review and research agenda. *J Org Behav*. 2009;31:519-542.

69. Mattke S, Balakrishnan A, Bergamo G, Newberry SJ. A review of methods to measure health-related productivity loss. *Am J Manag Care*. 2007;13:211-217.

70. Schultz AB, Edington DW. Employee health and presenteeism: a systematic review. *J Occup Rehab*. 2007;17:547-579.

71. Lofland JH, Pizzi L, Frick KD. A review of health-related workplace productivity loss instruments. *Pharmacoeconomics*. 2004;22:165-184.

72. Burton WN, Conti DJ, Chen CY, Schultz AB, Edington DW. The role of health risk factors and disease on worker productivity. *J Occup Environ Med*. 1999;41:863-877.

73. Brooks A, Hagen SE, Sathyanarayanan S, Schultz AB, Edington DW Presenteeism: critical issues. *J Occup Environ Med*. 2010;52:1055-1067.

74. Cyr A, Hagen S. Measurement and quantification of presenteeism: letters to the editor. *J Occup Environ Med*. 2007;50:163-171.

75. Pelletier B, Boles M, Lynch W. Change in health risks and work productivity over time. *J Occup Environ Med*. 2004;46:746-754.

76. Burton WN, Chen CY, Conti DJ, Schultz AB, Edington DW. The association between health risk change and presenteeism change. *J Occup Environ Med*. 2006;48:252-263.

77. Mills PR, Kessler RC, Cooper J, Sullivan S. Impact of a health promotion program on employee health risks and

work productivity. *Am J Health Promot.* 2007;22:45-53.

78. Loeppke R. The value of health and the power of prevention. *Int J Workplace Health Mgmt.* 2008;1:95-108.

79. Towers Watson/National Business Group on Health. Performance in an era of uncertainty: 17th annual employer survey on purchasing value in health care. New York, NY. 2012.

80. American Hospital Association. A Call to Action: Creating a Culture of Health. http://www.aha.org/aha/issues/Health-for-life/culture.html. Accessed April 5, 2013.

81. Kerwin K, Treece J. Detroit's big chance: Can it regain business and respect it lost in the past 20 years? *Bus Week*, June 29, 1992, p. 82.

82. Green L, Cargo M. The future of health promotion. In M. O'Donnell & J. Harris (Eds.) Health Promotion in the Workplace (2nd ed.,pp. 497-524). Albany, NY: Delmar Publishers. 1994.

83. Grossmeier J, Terry PE, Cipriotti A, Burtaine JE. Best practices in evaluating worksite health promotion programs. *Art Health Promot.* 2010. 12(1):1-9.

84. Wolf R, Slack T, Rose-Hearn T. Factors influencing the adoption and maintenance of Canadian facilities-based worksite health promotion programs. *Am J Health Promot.* 1993;7:189-198.

85. Goetzel R, Ozminkowski R. The health and cost benefits of worksite health promotion programs. *Ann Rev Pub Health.* 2008;29:303-323.

86. Bertera R. The effects of behavioral risks on absenteeism and health care costs in the workplace. *J Occup Med.* 1991;33,1119-1124.

87. Goetzel R, Juday T, Ozminkowski R. What's the ROI? A systematic review of return on investment studies of corporate health and productivity management initiatives. *Worksite Health.* 1999;6(3):12-21.

88. Conrad K, Conrad K, Walcott-McQuigg J. Threats to internal validity in worksite health promotion program research: Common problems and possible solutions. *Am J Health Promot.* 1991;6,112-222.

89. Musich S. Faruzzi SD, Lu C, McDonald T, Hirschland D, Edington DW Pattern of Medical Charges After Quitting Smoking Among Those With and Without Arthritis, Allergies, or Back Pain. *Am J Health Promot.* 2003; 18:133-142.

90. O'Donnell M, Whitmer W, Anderson D. Is it time for a national health promotion research agenda? *Am J Health Promot.* 1999;13:3.

91. O'Donnell M. Editor 's Notes: Building health promotion into the national agenda. *Am J Health Promot.* 2000;14:3.

92. O'Donnell MP. Health Promotion in the Workplace. 3rd ed. Albany, NY: Cenage, 2002.

CHAPTER

3

The Face of Wellness

A Conceptual Framework to Guide the Development of Effective Health Promotion Programs: The Awareness, Motivation, Skills and Opportunity (AMSO) Framework and the Face of Wellness Model

Michael P. O'Donnell

This chapter is organized around the Awareness, Motivation, Skills and Opportunity (AMSO) Framework (Framework), which is a component of the Face of Wellness Model (Model). It starts with a review of the process used to develop the Framework and the Model. Next, the three major components of the Model are briefly reviewed: Aspirational Vision of Health, Health Behavior Change Process, and the AMSO Framework. The description of the AMSO Framework includes discussions of the four basic components of the Framework: awareness, motivation, skills and opportunity, and the six components of opportunity: peers, organizations, the state, society, environment and equality.

PROCESS USED TO DEVELOP THE AMSO FRAMEWORK AND FACE OF WELLNESS MODEL

The AMSO Framework and Face of Wellness Model were developed based on a twenty-year quest to answer the question "What works best in workplace health promotion?" The systematic portion of the quest included a benchmarking study that involved collecting basic information on 76 *workplace health promotion programs* that had reported the health and financial impact of their programs in the peer-reviewed literature; additional detail collected through questionnaires on 26 of those programs and more complete information gathered through site visits to the six deemed best practice;[1] a systematic review of the literature on the health impact of workplace health promotion that synthesized the findings of 384 studies[2] and resulted in publication of more than 20 articles;[3,4] plus a systematic review of the literature on the financial impact of workplace health promotion programs that synthesized findings of 72 studies.[5] The non-systematic portion of the process included completing in-depth reviews of more than 2000 articles submitted to the American Journal of Health Promotion between 1986 and 2012, reviewing descriptions of more than 200 workplace health promotion programs submitted with applications for the C. Everett Koop Award[6] between 1994 and 2012, and being involved in the design and/or management of programs at more than 50 employers.

THE FACE OF WELLNESS MODEL

The image of a face (Figure 3-1) was chosen to provide a simple and memorable image to organize the principles gleaned from this quest. This image also reminds health promotion professionals that the core of what they do is not about theoretical concepts, analytic methods, budgets, incentives or equipment. It is about people. It is about understanding people's priorities and helping them change in ways that profoundly impact their lives. As the health promotion field becomes more complex, as it depends more on computer technology to deliver programs, as programs are pressured to show a positive *return on investment*, it is easy to forget that the core of health promotion is helping people in very personal ways.

The Face of Wellness model has three basic components: (1) an *Aspirational Vision of Health*, (2) a *Renewing Health Behavior Change Process*, and (3) a *Portfolio Balancing Approach to Planning Change Strategies*. The two eyes represent the Aspirational Vision of Health and the Renewing Health Behavior Change Process, while the nose represents the Portfolio Balancing Approach to Planning Change Strategies. These components are described in detail below.

Figure 3-1: The Face of Wellness: An Integrated Model for Planning Wellness Programs.

©2006, Michael P. O'Donnell MBA, MPH, PhD.

AN ASPIRATIONAL VISION OF HEALTH

Many health promotion professionals (including the author) are health nuts. We want to be physically fit. We eat a nutritious diet. We work at being effective in managing stress. We manage weight consistently. We would never consider using tobacco or putting any abusive substances in our bodies. We want to be healthy because we want to be healthy. We are a bit unusual in this regard, but often do not realize we are unusual. For us, health is the reward in and of itself. Not everyone feels that way.

Health nuts are like money nuts. Money nuts like to make money because they like to make money. Most other people work to make money so they can provide for their family, do fun things, help other people, or feel proud of themselves. Health nuts want to be healthy because they want to be healthy, while most other people who make a point of taking care of their health do so because it leads to other rewards. The more typical person might maintain good health to be a good role model for their kids, to allow them to work hard in a job, to make sure they are alive to see kids and grandkids reach important milestones, to be good at a sport, to look good, to excel at whatever is important to them in life. For example, I have a friend who works out two hours a day, six months a year and eats a nutritious diet because he spends the other six months living in remote parts of the world, hiking through pristine wilderness areas to study fish that have not been exposed to human influences. He is a fish nut. He maintains great health so he can study fish.

The mistake many health promotion professionals make is that they do not realize they themselves are health nuts. When they talk to people about health, they assume others care about health. Sometimes, maybe even most of the time, the people they speak to about health do not care about health – not as much as the health nut cares. When a teenage daughter talks to her dad about music groups, he tries to be polite, but he really doesn't care about the latest teen sensation. When a sports nut talks to a co-worker about basketball stars, the co-worker tries to be polite, but usually doesn't really care about the latest MVP. When a lawn nut talks to a neighbor about his lawn, the neighbor tries to be polite, but really doesn't care about the latest fertilizer mix. Get the idea? When people listen to health promotion professionals talk about health, much of the time they are just being polite; often they really don't care.

For this reason, health promotion professionals have more success in reaching people when they think and talk about health in very broad terms. This led me to defining optimal health as "a balance of physical, emotional, social, spiritual, and intellectual health"[7] when the *American Journal of Health Promotion* was launched in 1986. These five dimensions of optimal health are briefly described in Table 3-1. Most organizations have focused their programs on the physical and emotional dimension, but some have addressed all five areas. Note: See Appendix 3-A for brief comments on the historical roots of this aspirational vision.

This broad definition of optimal health is scientifically reasonable because there are compelling links between each of these dimensions and medically based measures of morbidity and mortality. Equally important, this broad definition is engaging to many lay people because it encompasses the elements of life that are typically important to them. This broad definition is inspirational or aspirational because it provides a vision of what might be. It stimulates thinking about personal growth. This is in contrast to compliance-oriented definitions that focus on limiting consumption of certain foods, maintaining a certain weight, exercising a certain number of minutes per week – in other words, directions for reducing "risk" factors.

Over time, it has become clear to professionals who use this definition that

Table 3-1: Dimensions of Optimal Health.

Physical Health is the condition of your body. Programs include fitness, nutrition, weight control, quitting smoking, alcohol and drug abuse prevention and medical self-care.

Emotional Health is the ability to cope with or avoid stress and other emotional challenges. Programs include employee assistance programs (EAP), stress management, and programs to enhance happiness.

Social Health is the ability to form and maintain nurturing and productive relationships with family, friends, co-workers, neighbors and others. Programs can include training in parenting, conflict resolution, assertiveness and other skill building areas, as well as opportunities for employees to get to know each other in fun social activities and to serve others through volunteer projects.

Intellectual Health encompasses achievements in academics, career, hobbies and cultural pursuits. Programs can include job-focused mentoring and skill enhancement programs, as well as more broadly focused tuition reimbursement policies, book clubs, and cultural outings.

Spiritual Health is having a sense of purpose, love, hope, peace and charity. For some people, this is drawn from being part of an organized religious group; for others, it is having a sense of values inspired by other influences. Programs can include workshops to help people clarify life priorities and set goals as well as allowing people to embrace their religious beliefs.

it is very difficult to know when one has achieved "balance" among the dimensions. It is also clear that different dimensions are more important to people at different times in their lives. People sometimes need to focus virtually all of their attention on their work (intellectual dimension) to complete an important project. Other times they need to focus time on family members (social) to help others through crucial periods. Other times they need to learn new strategies to help themselves through stressful circumstances (emotional). Even the most dedicated fitness nut and most conscious eater (physical), needs to be reminded to go to the doctor for preventive checkups. Most people need to step back periodically to reflect on what, indeed, is important in life, and get back on track (spiritual). Optimal health is not a static condition; it is a dynamic condition. It is not realistic to expect to reach that magic point of perfect balance and stay there. It is

more realistic to seek opportunities for growth and think in terms of a process of *striving* for balance under changing circumstances. Recognizing this, the *American Journal of Health Promotion* revised its definition of optimal health to reflect these circumstances. Table 3-2 shows the original and revised definitions of health promotion and optimal health.

People are more likely to strive for growth in each of the dimensions when they discover synergies between those dimensions and their personal passions. If a person's passion is to be a super athlete (physical), s/he can achieve that passion faster by embracing other dimensions of the model. S/he can engage a great coach to provide guidance and teammates for competition (social). S/he can learn how to harness failures and successes to push through challenges (emotional). S/he can learn more about physiology and the mechanics of motion (intellectual) to perfect technique.

Table 3-2: Evolving Definitions of Health Promotion and Optimal Health.

Original Definition
....

"Health promotion is the science and art of helping people change their lifestyle to move toward a state of optimal health. Optimal health is defined as a balance of physical, emotional, social, spiritual, and intellectual health. Lifestyle change can be facilitated through a combination of efforts to enhance awareness, change behavior and create environments that support good health practices." (O'Donnell, *American Journal of Health Promotion*, 1986, 1, 1, 1)

1989 Revision
....

"Health promotion is the science and art of helping people change their lifestyle to move toward a state of optimal health. Optimal health is defined as a balance of physical, emotional, social, spiritual, and intellectual health. Lifestyle change can be facilitated through a combination of efforts to enhance awareness, change behavior and create environments that support good health practices. Of the three, supportive environments will probably have the greatest impact in producing lasting change." (O'Donnell, *American Journal of Health Promotion,* 1989, 3, 3, 5)

2008 Revision
....

"Health promotion is the science and art of helping people change their lifestyle to move toward a state of optimal health. Optimal health is the process of striving for a dynamic balance of physical, emotional, social, spiritual, and intellectual health and discovering the synergies between core passions and each of those dimensions. Lifestyle change can be facilitated through a combination of efforts to enhance awareness, increase motivation, build skills and most importantly, to provide opportunities for positive health practices." (O'Donnell, *American Journal of Health Promotion*, 2008, 23, 2, iv-v)

2009 Revision
....

"Health Promotion is the art and science of helping people discover the synergies between their core passions and optimal health, enhancing their motivation to strive for optimal health, and supporting them in changing their lifestyle to move toward a state of optimal health. Optimal health is a dynamic balance of physical, emotional, social, spiritual, and intellectual health. Lifestyle change can be facilitated through a combination of learning experiences that enhance awareness, increase motivation, and build skills and, most important, through the creation of opportunities that open access to environments that make positive health practices the easiest choice." (O'Donnell MP American Journal of Health Promotion, 2009, 24, 1, iv-iv)

S/he can also work to understand how athletic aspirations can fit within broader life goals (spiritual). If a person's passion is to be a great parent (social), s/he needs to model nutritious eating habits and physical activity (physical) for children. S/he also needs to know how to keep his or her cool when children are misbehaving (emotional). S/he needs to know when and how to draw on other people for support (social), learn about effective parent skills (intellectual), and help children discover their own priorities in life (spiritual).

People are much more likely to be open to health messages when health promotion professionals help them discover their true passions and help them understand how the other dimensions of health can help them realize these passions. For this reason, one of the five dimensions of optimal health is placed at the center of the illustration (Figure 3-2). Placing physical health at the center is the default, because physical health is most closely aligned with medically inspired measures of health. This illustration will be most compatible with medically driven health promotion programs. However, the concept might be more engaging to each of the many individuals in an organization if each person is encouraged to put the dimension that best encompasses their passions in the center (Figure 3-3). Some organizations will choose to feature these five dimensions as central tenants of their programs and will offer specific opportunities to support each dimension. Other organizations will feel that this framework is not sufficiently scientific to feature it broadly, but will use it as an under girder to help them understand their population's needs.

These five dimensions allow a nice balance of parsimony and comprehensiveness and they align well with the types of programs that can be provided in a health promotion program. However, other aspirational definitions of health may work just as well or better for other groups. See definitions from the YMCA, World Health Organization and National Wellness Institute in Table 3-3. Additional dimensions that might be added include environmental sustainability and sexuality.

Figure 3-2: Aspirational Vision of Health with Focus on Physical Health.

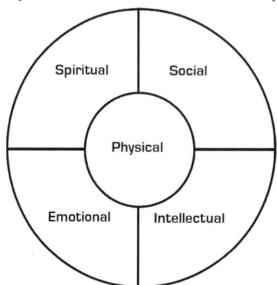

Figure 3-3: Aspirational Vision of Health with Focus on Each of the Core Dimensions.

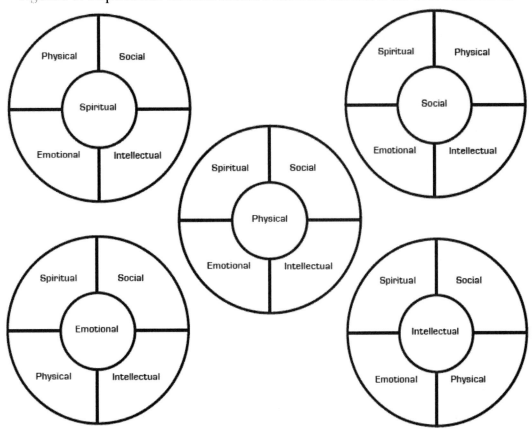

©2007, Michael P. O'Donnell MBA, MPH, PhD.

Regardless of the definition of health, the key is helping people discover their life passions and the synergies between those passions and each of the dimensions of optimal health.

RENEWING HEALTH BEHAVIOR CHANGE PROCESS

Health promotion programs typically engage people in lifestyle change by offering lifestyle questionnaires *(health risk assessments)* and *biomedical screenings* that identify health risk factors and help employees understand the link between lifestyle and health. The next step is to recruit employees into educational and activity programs to support these changes. The more systematic the program offerings, the more likely employees are to follow through. The six-step Renewing Health Behavior Change Process provides a structured approach to doing this. The usual approach is to encourage people to start at the first step and progress through each step sequentially, because this provides a logical approach to change. However, each person needs to be able to start where they are ready to start. Some people start in the middle or the end with no intention of following a set sequence, but eventually realize the wisdom of the sequential process. The goal in offering programs should be to help people eventually cover as many of the steps as

Table 3-3: Other Aspirational Definitions of Health.

World Health Organization

"Health is a state of complete physical, mental and social well-being and not merely the absence of disease or infirmity."
Source: Constitution of the World Health Organization, available at: http://www.who.int

National Wellness Institute

"Six Dimensions Model: Physical, social, intellectual, spiritual, emotional, occupational"
Source: National Wellness Website. Available at: http://www.nationalwellness.org

YMCA

"To put Christian principles into practice through programs that build healthy spirit, mind and body for all."
Source: YMCA website. Available at: http://www.ymca.net

---

possible. The six steps are listed and described below and illustrated (Figure 3-4). The process renews annually or when people are ready to adopt a new health habit. The steps in this process were inspired by a different but similar set of strategies developed by StayWell Health Management in the early 1980s.[8] These steps are similar to 12 step models used in addiction recovery programs.[9]

1. Get ready
2. Measure your health
3. Set goals
4. Build skills
5. Form habits
6. Help others

One of the keys to success in this process is to include activities in each step that stimulate the person to move to the next step.

Step 1. Get Ready

Getting ready is about opening your heart and mind to change. It is about imagining what might become of your life. It is about reflecting on what is most important to you in life and starting to think about health relative to other priorities. This is also a time to reflect on how better health can help you realize your passions. Asking people to open their minds in this way can reduce some of the resistance people often feel about making any type of change in life. This step can be part of the process that moves people from the precontemplation to the contemplation stage of *readiness to change*.[10] The critical element of this step is empowering people to dream about what might be and helping them believe they control their own destiny.

- A health promotion program can support the Get Ready step through multi-media promotional campaigns and interactive discussions.

Step 2. Measure your Health

People who open their hearts and minds to change will be eager to measure their health. In the context of a health promotion program, the best measures of health are a health risk appraisal (HRA) and a basic health

Figure 3-4: Renewing Health Behavior Change Process.

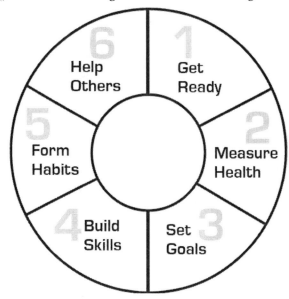

screening. Biometric measures included in screenings evolve over time, but the most common currently are blood pressure and resting heart rate; blood glucose, triglycerides and cholesterol (total, HDL, LDL and LDL/HDL ratio); and height, weight, waist and hip measurements. Collectively, these tests measure metabolic syndrome, which is the likelihood a person will contract diabetes, stroke or heart disease sometime in the future.[11] If a person has abnormal values in three of the five areas, they have metabolic syndrome.

Most HRAs focus on the physical dimensions of health and some examine the social or cultural dimensions. To measure the emotional, social and spiritual dimensions, free questionnaires offered by The Soul/Body Connection can be used. These questionnaires measure hope, humor, optimism, spirituality and well-being, forgiveness and gratitude (http://www.spiritualityhealth.com). Measures developed by the Authentic Happiness group assess core strengths, emotions, engagement, meaning and life satisfaction (http://www.authentichappiness.sas.upenn.edu/).

Another valuable supplement is the Physical Activity Readiness Questionnaire (PAR-Q) developed by the Expert Advisory Committee of the Canadian Society for Exercise Physiology and the British Columbia Ministry of Health (http://uwfitness.uwaterloo.ca/PDF/par-q.pdf). This is a good tool to identify physical conditions that require a physician's clearance before an exercise program.

- A health promotion program can support the Measure Your Health step by offering a health risk appraisal and health screening programs.

Step 3. Set Goals

Setting goals is important to success in any area of life. If you don't know what you want, how do you know the first step to take to get there? How do you know if you are making good progress? Setting goals is also one of the most important things you can do to improve your health. In fact, a review by Goetzel and Heaney[12] concluded that personal goal setting can double success rates in health promotion programs. Goal setting is part science and part art, but there is more science than most people think. Both are briefly summarized below.

Impact of Setting Goals

Setting goals, especially challenging goals, increases performance in many ways. Setting goals helps us focus our attention on activities that will lead to achieving these goals.[13] Setting goals also increases the physical effort we are willing to exert when we get fatigued, and helps us tolerate repetitive tasks that lead to our goal.[14] Setting goals also helps us prolong effort,[15] and stimulates us to draw on our knowledge to develop strategies to meet our goals.[16]

Types of Goals

There are three types of goals and different strategies are recommended for each type.[17] The goal types are aspirational, learning and performance. Aspirational goals are dreams about what the future may be. These might include career ambitions, romantic relationships, raising a family, athletic performance, a specific body image, a sense of confidence, living a life of integrity, or other dreams. Aspirational goals do not need to be realistic, specific or static. They should be about dreams, about what makes you feel fulfilled, about priorities in life. They often evolve as life evolves. Learning goals can be tied to gaining specific knowledge necessary to achieve an aspirational goal, but people tend to be more committed to learning and actually learn more, when they allow themselves some latitude to explore what interests them. This is especially true in areas that are complex or novel to them.[18] Once a person has acquired the knowledge and ability to perform specific tasks, setting specific goals leads to higher performance.[19] For example, the aspirational goal might be to get rid of all the junk food in your diet and replace it with nutritious food. The learning goal might be to learn how to identify, shop for and prepare delicious

nutritious foods. Once the knowledge and skills are acquired, the performance goal might be to eat nutritious foods at least 90% of the time.

Challenging Goals

Once skills and knowledge are acquired, setting specific performance goals increases performance by 42%-82%, while setting challenging goals tends to increase performance or effort by 52%-82%.[20] These results are likely to occur only when commitment to the performance goal is high, and the person possesses the necessary skills and the ability to achieve the goal. For example, it is realistic to set specific and ambitious goals related to performing specific amounts and types of exercises or activities, and eating specific amounts and types of food because these are behaviors that are under a person's control. It is not realistic to set a specific and ambitious weight loss goal, because losing weight is a condition, not a distinct behavior that is within a person's total control.

Setting your Own Goals

Setting your own goals rather than relying on an expert or advisor can increase performance by 11%[21], probably because people tend to better understand goals they set for themselves.[22] Nonetheless, skilled advisors can be very helpful in setting goals.

Commitment

Goal performance is strongest when commitment to goals is strongest. Commitment can be enhanced by reinforcing the importance of the outcome and by enhancing self efficacy. Commitment can also be increased by making a public commitment to the goal,[23] and by receiving support from leaders.[24] Self-efficacy can be enhanced by providing adequate training to increase mastery, observing positive role models, and hearing persuasive communication from experts or peers who express confidence in your ability to achieve the goal.[25]

Feedback

Regular feedback also enhances performance. When people realize they are falling short of their goals, they normally increase their effort or shift to a more effective strategy.[26]

In summary, goal setting will be most effective when five processes are followed:

1. Allow aspirational goals to evolve over time.
2. Allow some latitude in setting learning goals to acquire the skills and knowledge necessary to tackle a goal.
3. Set challenging and specific performance goals with input from experts if possible. Include short term and intermediate measurable milestone targets. Limit performance goals to activities that are under your control.
4. Seek feedback and monitor progress. Increase effort or modify strategies if goals are not being met.
5. Enhance commitment through public statements of commitment and inspiring comments from leaders.

   • A health promotion program can support the Set Goals step by offering goal setting sessions in group, print and web format. Aspirational goals typically begin to emerge during the initial Get Ready step. Learning and performance goals take form during the *Build Skills* step.

Step 4. Build Skills

If you were going to learn a new language, what would you do? The best strategy would be to immerse yourself in a culture that speaks that language, so you could hear people speak, watch how their lips and face move as they express each of the words and phrases, learn about their customs so you could better understand the underlying meaning of phrases. You would also need to learn grammar rules and vocabulary. Using books, tapes or a language coach might help you. You would also need to practice, practice, practice. If you were going to learn how to play soccer, you could start by watching others play. You would need to learn the rules by reading manuals and talking to people. At some point you would need to meet people who play soccer so you could play with them. To get good, you need to learn the individual moves, how to dribble with your feet, how to trap (or catch) a ball with your feet or any other part of your body (except your hands), how to pass or take a shot on goal. If you want to get really good, you need to learn how to dribble past a defender with speed or finesse, how to kick a ball that is six feet off the ground by doing a modified back flip, or put spin on the ball when you kick it, so it changes direction in mid air to go over or around a defender. Having the right books, a coach, and patient teammates really helps during this process. Eventually, you need to internalize the rules, know the rules without thinking, so you don't go off-sides, commit a foul, or get yourself thrown out of the game. To play at the highest level, you need to master the individual moves so you perform them instinctually when an opportunity presents itself. You also need to learn mental toughness so you can keep playing full speed when you are exhausted, hurt, or way behind.

Changing a health behavior is a lot like learning a new language or playing a new sport, except it is usually a lot harder, because you need to break habits you have formed over decades of time. If you could immerse yourself in a culture that supports your new lifestyle, it would be a lot easier, but that is not an option for most people. So you have to find or build subcultures that can support you, and teach you how to resist the influences of the cultures that have supported the unhealthy habits you have learned and practiced for decades. Think about it. You have indeed honed those old habits through decades of practice, practice,

practice. They are part of you. You perform them without thinking. They are comfortable. They are part of your identity. You need to learn new habits, and learning new habits usually takes months and often takes years. In the case of quitting smoking or chewing tobacco, you also have to overcome a chemical addiction to nicotine. Weight loss is even more complicated because you cannot just quit eating. You must learn how to eat differently. If you are going to be successful in changing your health habits, you need to build new skills.

The skill building process has three basic stages: learning, practicing and building support. Celebrating progress in moving through these stages reinforces each of them. The stages are described in more detail below.

Learning

One of the first steps in learning is figuring out how you like to learn and how much help you need. The key is to match the complexity of the change you want to make with the amount and form of help you draw upon. If you want to change something simple, like starting to floss your teeth every night, you can probably get a brochure from your dentist or simple instructions on the web. If you want to lose 100 pounds, you need more help. Individually directed options include reading, listening to tapes, or following web-based programs. Expert-directed options include working with a counselor or coach through individual or group sessions on the telephone or face-to-face. People are more likely to stick with learning formats suited to their learning style and schedule. Most people benefit from some direct interaction with a real person, even if most of their learning is self-directed. Utilizing the most scientifically validated strategies can have tremendous benefit. For example, people who try to quit smoking cold turkey are successful about 5% of the time, while those who use a combination of behavioral therapy and medication are successful about 30% of the time.[27]

Practicing

The simple act of practicing a new behavior is an important step in building confidence that you can perform the behavior. This is called enhancing self-efficacy.[28] The higher the level of self-efficacy, the longer the newly acquired behavior will be practiced before relapse.

Building Support and Reinforcement

Most people are successful in continuing a behavior if they have access to a physical environment that makes that behavior easy to perform, and a network of people to encourage them. Making sure these pieces are in place during the skill building stage can increase the chances of maintaining these new behaviors long term. For example, if you want to exercise on a regular basis, you need a place to do it. Some people can be successful walking or running in their neighborhoods and doing calisthenics without equipment. Other people need the equipment provided by a fitness center. Similarly, some people can maintain their programs on their own but most people benefit from having a network of friends to join them in workouts. The same concepts apply to all health behaviors. For example, to eat a nutritious diet, you need to have access to grocery stores and cafeterias that sell the right food. If you live with other people, they need to at least tolerate the foods you choose to eat.

Celebrating Progress

Recognizing and celebrating milestones is very reinforcing for many people. Milestones might include (1) making a commitment to change; (2) developing a change plan; (3) learning the skills you need to change; (4) trying out each new skill for the first time; (5) practicing each new skill on a regular basis; (6) achieving performance goals – for example, exercising for 30 minutes, three times a week for a full week; and (7) making incremental progress in achieving an aspirational goal (i.e., losing a certain number of pounds, reaching different strength levels, etc.). For many people, just pausing to reflect on the effort you have exerted to reach this goal, and realizing you have achieved it, is a sufficient celebration. Many people like to include some more significant celebrations. The key is to choose celebrations that you value, support your wellness goal and are healthy for you in general. Many cultures around the world equate celebration with splurging on food…usually high fat, sweet food, or drinking lots of alcohol. Why not? Its fun and it feels great…at first. It also leads to all the health problems discussed in this chapter. Splurging on food might not be a great way to celebrate your wellness milestones, especially if you are trying to lose weight. Working through each of these issues during the Build Skills stage increases the chances of maintaining long-term behavior change.

- A health promotion program can support the *Build Skills* step by offering skill building programs for each of the health change areas (fitness, nutrition, stress management, weight control, quit smoking, etc.) in multiple learning formats (i.e., print, web, telephonic, video, face to face, etc.)

Step 5. Form Habits

Dieting doesn't work. Virtually everyone who goes on a diet to lose weight fails. They fail not because they don't lose weight. In fact, most well-conceived diets do produce weight loss… for a few weeks or months. Diets usually fail because most people revert to their old eating habits when they reach their weight goal… and they regain their weight. People succeed in losing weight and keeping it off when they change how they eat…forever. The same is true for getting fit. Working out for a month or a year gets you in shape for that month or year, but when you stop exercising, you eventually get out of shape. The key to successful long-term health behavior change is to build your

newly formed health skills into habits you practice every single week, and in most cases, every single day.

When you add a new positive behavior to your life, it often takes months of diligent discipline to keep practicing the new behavior. An addictive behavior, like smoking cigarettes, can take as much as 5 to 12 years of diligent discipline to change permanently. Most of the time you feel the immediate rewards of your new behavior, and that keeps you going, but remaining disciplined is draining work for most people. If you can build the new behavior into your routine, you take away the need to discipline yourself.

Your routines change over the span of a lifetime, and you need to adapt with these changes in routines to form new habits around exercise. A high school student involved in sports works out during varsity sports practices. Going to practice becomes the habit. A college student enrolled in gym classes is physically active during those classes. The changing schedule of classes does not matter because the habit formed becomes taking a gym class. An adult involved in a team sport forms the habit of going to team practice. Over time, getting a regular workout becomes one of the important ingredients in a successful day and is squeezed in regardless of the challenges.

- Health promotion programs can support the *Form Habits* step through programming, community networks, policy changes and enhancing the physical environment. Programming options include offering ongoing classes on nutritious cooking, aerobics, yoga, ballroom dancing, and other types of physical activity and support groups for people who have quit smoking or lost weight. Community networks can include sports teams and leagues, discounts negotiated with local fitness centers, and improved access to fresh produce markets.

Physical environment supports can include cafeterias that serve nutritious foods, work sites built to make stairs more accessible than elevators and floor plans that encourage other forms of walking. Policy supports can include smoke free policies, health insurance coverage of health promotion services, and many other options.

Step 6. Help Others

The final step in the Renewing Health Behavior Change Process is helping others. Helping others can take the form of serving as a peer mentor, organizing or leading a support group or an activity group, learning how to teach a skill building course, serving on a planning committee, helping to promote a program, or many other forms. Helping others has at least four benefits.

First, it reinforces a newly adopted behavior. Everything you learn to help yourself become a leader can help you learn how to maintain the new behavior in your own life. Additionally, knowing that other people are depending on you makes you want to serve as a good role model for the new behavior and reinforces your commitment to that behavior.

Second, helping others provides an inspiration for others to change. When people see that someone else has been successful in changing their behavior and has progressed beyond that to helping other people, it increases their belief they can be successful in making the same kind of change.

Third, helping other people seems to have a direct protective effect on health, especially for older adults.[29] Helping others also allows people to show compassion, which seems to have a direct positive impact on health.

Finally, as more and more people extend themselves to help others, more people can be helped.

- Health promotion programs can support the *Help Others* stage by making it very clear that peer leaders are critical to the success of the program, carving out defined leadership opportunities, training people how to serve in these roles, and thanking them for the contributions they make.

Ongoing Renewal

Helping Others is listed as the sixth and final step in the Renewing Health Behavior Change Process but there is really no final step. The Process is illustrated in a circle, because it is really an ongoing process. When you are successful in achieving one health behavior change, this is a good time to reflect on progress, celebrate success, renew commitment to that change, take a deep breath, and ask yourself if you are ready to tackle another health behavior change. The satisfaction and self-confidence that comes from feeling successful in making the first change will often propel you through the difficult early stages of the next change. Other great times to reflect on health and get ready to make another change are anniversary dates and the beginning of the new year.

- A health promotion program can support the overall Renewing Health Behavior Change Process by making the steps in the process clear, encouraging people to move through each of the six steps, and providing tools to help people document and celebrate their progress through the steps.

AWARENESS, MOTIVATION, SKILLS AND OPPORTUNITIES

In 1984[30], I suggested that we think of health promotion programs in terms of three components: Awareness, Behavior Change and Supportive Environments. In 2005, I started advocating that we shift the paradigm to think in terms of four areas: Awareness, Motivation, Skills and Opportunity (AMSO), i.e. the AMSO Framework.[31] The purpose of this change in terminology is to shift the focus of health promotion from the work of health promotion providers to the experiences of the people and organizations served. The AMSO Framework is illustrated in the form of a triangle to evoke the image commonly used to describe how money should be allocated in different investment vehicles in an investment portfolio. Within the facial image of the Face of Wellness Model, the AMSO Framework represents the nose (Figure 3-5).

Awareness

The origins of health promotion are in health education, and as the term implies, health education focuses on making people aware of the risks of unhealthy behaviors such as eating an unhealthy diet, drinking excessively and smoking, as well as the benefits of positive behaviors such as regular health screenings, physical activity and stress management. Our belief was that people would make the right choices if they just had the right information, i.e. the right education. Most health promotion programs in the 1970s and 1980s were based on an educational model, and many still are. Over time, we have learned that education is not enough to change behavior for most people. Most people know that they SHOULD exercise. Most smokers know that smoking causes many forms of cancer, respiratory problems, and heart disease, and that it is likely to contribute to their early demise. If knowledge were enough, no one would smoke and everyone would exercise.

This is not to say that education is not important. Education plays at least two important roles. First, effective education campaigns do make people aware of health risks and health improvement opportunities. For people who are considering making a behavior change, education can help them weigh the pros and cons of making the change, and lead them to the resources they need to support their change efforts. Second, education campaigns can be critical in mobilizing organization- or nation-wide change efforts in building broad support for an idea or plan. For example,

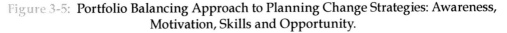

Figure 3-5: Portfolio Balancing Approach to Planning Change Strategies: Awareness, Motivation, Skills and Opportunity.

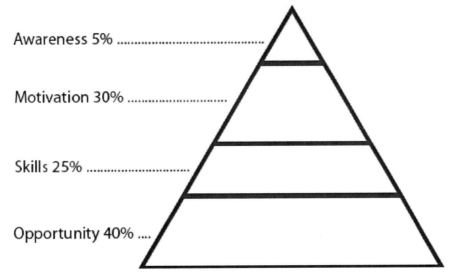

Awareness 5% ....

Motivation 30% ....

Skills 25% ....

Opportunity 40% ....

when people realized that secondhand smoke is not just irritating, but a Class A carcinogen, efforts to create smoke-free workplaces were perceived as strategies to protect workers instead of strategies to punish smokers. Despite the limited impact of education on behavior change, it is still important to improve the effectiveness of education efforts, and excellent progress has been made in this area. Improvements have included learning how to tailor messages to address people's individual needs, providing multiple formats in which to convey content (lecture, print, audiotape, Internet, e-mail, etc.), and harnessing data management and communication capabilities to store, manage, retrieve, and deliver data. Despite these developments, education simply is not enough to change behavior for most people, and managers need to realize this in designing and evaluating programs.

Motivation

When a person is motivated to make a behavior change, s/he will strive to gain the knowledge and skills necessary to make that change, and will create the opportunity to make it possible. If a person is not motivated to change, all the knowledge and skills in the world will still not cause change. For example, testing of the Theory of Planned Behavior[32] developed by Fishbien and Aizen has shown that attitudes and norms have little effect on behavior unless a person has intentions to change. Knowledge of the importance of motivation and measuring motivation has improved substantially in the past few decades. One of the most important developments in this area has been articulation of the concept of motivational readiness to change, as articulated in the *Transtheoretical Model* by Prochaska and DiClemente.[33] This model shows us that different strategies are important to motivate people to change at different levels of readiness to change. For example, it shows us that people who are not thinking about change in the near future

(precontemplation) have no interest in hearing about how to change their behavior, but those thinking about changes (contemplation) might be interested in this information. It also shows us that enhancing self-efficacy is important to those getting ready to make changes (preparation), those in the process of making changes (action), and those who are working to maintain changes (maintenance).

Progress has also been made in explaining how *intrinsic* and *extrinsic incentives* motivate people to join programs and change behaviors. For example, a review by Matson-Koffman et al.[34] showed that financial incentives have the impact of significantly increasing participation rates. This probably occurs because incentives capture the attention of people who are thinking about making changes (contemplators) and accelerates their decision to make a change, and possibly even those not thinking about making a change (precontemplators) because they are attracted by the money. Matson's review also showed that financial incentive programs do not increase behavior change success rates in most cases. This is not surprising for two reasons. First, if incentives attract people who are less committed to making a change into programs, we would expect fewer of those people to succeed. Second, financial incentive programs are based on the assumption that money is important to everyone. To a certain extent, this is true. To those with modest incomes, a few hundred dollars can make a big difference in helping to meet basic needs in any given week or month, but over the course of a year, this translates to only a few dollars a week, and will not make much difference in any budget. Millions of people with limited incomes find a way to spend $20 to $100 dollars a week, or $1000 to $5000 a year, on cigarettes. If money were a sufficient motivator, no one would smoke. For a wealthy person, a financial incentive of a few hundred dollars is little more than a pleasant gift; it makes no impact on other spending decisions. To be effective in producing significant change, a financial reward would need to be large enough to impact someone's financial well-being, and this is just not feasible for most health promotion programs.

The prevalence of financial incentives in workplace health promotion programs is likely to increase significantly over the next decade because of Section 2705 of the Affordable Care Act passed in 2010. Section 2705 confirmed in statute what had previously been articulated only in federal regulations, i.e. that employers are permitted to offer a differential in health plan premiums of up to 20% for employees who meet health standards compared to employees who do not. These standards can be set by employers, but typically include choosing to participate in a program, not smoking, having a recommended weight, and having normal biometrics. The maximum premium differential is scheduled to increase to 30% in 2014 and the Secretaries of Treasury and Health and Human Services were given authority to increase the amount to 50% in 2014. Given the findings of a growing body of research,[35] implementation of these policies is likely to significantly increase participation in health promotion programs. For example, Seaverson et al [36] found that participation rates in health risk assessments were in the 20% - 40% range for workplace programs that had strong leadership support and well designed marketing programs and 70% to 90% and higher for programs that also offered financial incentives. The 90% and higher participation rates were achieved by employers who provided a financial incentive by reducing the amount of the health plan premium or deductible. Employer adoption of these programs took a big jump as soon as the Affordable Care Act passed. According to a survey of large employers in 2009, 36% offered financial incentives for participating in programs and 8% for achieving health goals in 2009. By 2012, those values jumped to 80% for participation and 38% for health outcomes.[37]

Despite the effectiveness of financial incentives in motivating people to participate in programs, we should not over rely on financial or other extrinsic incentives. The biggest shortcomings in our efforts to motivate people have been our focus on extrinsic rewards such as money and gifts, which capture short-term attention, rather than intrinsic rewards that are part of a person's basic values. If we want to be effective in motivating people, we need to first understand their passions in life, long-term goals, and current priorities. For example, I spent a year in Seoul, Korea, as a visiting professor in the department of preventive medicine of a university. Although most of the faculty in my department did not smoke, the smoking rate among physician professors in departments of preventive medicine in Korea as a whole was close to the smoking rate of men in general, which was over 60%. Lack of knowledge of the health risks of smoking was clearly not the issue with these physicians; I quickly learned that discussions of the health risks of smoking were fruitless. After a few months of observing the culture, I realized the importance within the Korean culture of being a good role model, especially among physician educators. When I asked my smoking colleagues about the message their smoking behavior was sending to their medical students, their patients, and their own children, they were far more receptive to thinking about quitting. Discussing smoking in this context shifted them from precontemplation to contemplation.

This strategy could probably work with anyone. For example, I once met an older woman who was sedentary and overweight. She had no interest in exercise and had become content with the belief that she always had been and always would be overweight. The priority in her life was spending time with her grandchildren. When she realized that playing with her grandchildren for a few hours exhausted her, and that she might not live long enough to attend her granddaughter's wedding, she decided to start a regular exercise program . . . in the form of playing with her grandchildren. Another example: A friend in college started smoking when he was in high school and continued smoking when he went to college. He was strong and energetic and felt impervious to any health risks smoking might cause in twenty or thirty years. He did not stop smoking until he got a serious crush on a beautiful young woman. She made him leave the room whenever he smoked, her feelings were hurt when he said the food she cooked for him was bland, and she hated kissing him because his mouth smelled so bad. He decided to quit smoking because he thought he would lose her. He was sure he had made the right decision when he realized how much money he was saving and now had available to take her out on dates. These examples illustrate that improving health is often not the motivation for many behavior changes, even though most health professionals think improving health is a primary motivator. If we are to be successful in helping people change their health behaviors, we must understand their passions, long-term goals, and current priorities. The process of Motivational Interviewing developed by Miller and Rolnick[38] provides an excellent framework for this process. Some health promotion professionals are beginning to apply this important process in their programming efforts. Describing optimal health in terms of the five dimensions of optimal health, and encouraging each individual to put their passions in the heart of their programs is also likely to engage many people. The challenge, of course, is the high cost of taking the time to do this on a one-to-one basis. It may be possible to develop computer-based strategies for this work. Some health promotion providers have developed online tailoring programs that do much of this.

Enhancing self-efficacy is another way to enhance motivation.[25] *Self-efficacy* is the belief that one can do something, like exercise regularly, quit smoking, give a speech, etc. *Behavioral efficacy* is the belief that a specific behavior will produce a specific outcome – for example, that quitting smoking will reduce the likelihood of developing lung cancer. The higher level of self-efficacy and behavioral efficacy, the greater the motivation.

Our overall understanding of how to motivate people in the context of a health promotion program is probably the biggest gap in our health promotion knowledge. If we can fill this gap, we are likely to see the participation and success rates soar.

Skills

The biggest shortcoming of awareness programs is that they tell people WHAT to do, but not HOW to do it. Skill-building programs show people HOW—how to perform the actual behaviors they should perform, how to integrate these behaviors into their lives, and how to change their environment and surroundings to create opportunities to practice the behaviors they need to practice. Skill building strategies are discussed above as the third step of the individual Renewing Health Behavior Change Process.

Opportunity

Earlier editions of this textbook[30,39,40] articulated the concept of a supportive environment as one that includes supportive culture, policies, facilities, and programming. Given the goal discussed earlier of shifting the focus of the work of health promotion professionals from an internal focus on the work they do to the perspective of the people they serve, this edition uses the broader concept of opportunity.

Having access to opportunities to practice a healthy lifestyle is one of the most important factors in helping a person advance from building new skills (step 4 above) to forming habits (step 5 above).

A person who is highly motivated to practice a healthy lifestyle and has well-developed skills to integrate these practices into his or her life can do a lot to create the opportunities necessary to make this a reality.

However, sometimes a person's life situation is so demanding, or his or her physical surroundings so limited, that creating the necessary opportunities is very difficult, even for a highly motivated and skilled person. Most people are only moderately motivated and moderately skilled and need even more support to make a behavior change. They need convenient access to affordable, delicious, nutritious foods; safe and fun places to be physically active; smoke-free air to breathe at home, work, and play; exposure to supportive friends and family, and to a culture that values and rewards good health; freedom from media, advertising, and other marketing influences that are peddling risky behaviors; time to devote to healthy endeavors that are difficult to integrate into daily routines; and sufficient protection from the stresses of finances, overly demanding work, abusive social situations, and safety threats to be able to focus on good health practices.

At the other extreme, an abundantly supportive environment can cause an unmotivated, unskilled person to practice very healthy habits. At a health spa, it's easy to eat delicious, low-calorie, nutritious food at every meal, because that is all that is served. It is easy to go for a swim when you wake up, go for a long hike before lunch, do yoga before a late afternoon nap, and take time to reflect on the priorities of life in the evening. There are talented and charming experts to guide you, interesting, motivated people to join you, and all the time you need to do whatever you want. The biggest shortcoming of a spa experience is that the wonderful supports that make it easy to practice a healthy lifestyle stay at the spa when you leave. For some people, the experience of eating well, exercising regularly, and relaxing in a spa setting shows them that it is possible to do these things, and gives them a sense of the physical and emotional rewards these things provide. This enhances their self-efficacy and behavioral efficacy. This sense of enhanced self-efficacy and behavioral efficacy

increases motivation to continue performing these behaviors. If the spa can also teach people the skills to integrate the new behaviors into their lives and continue them as part of a normal life, successful maintenance is much more likely. The other great shortcoming of a spa situation is that most people do not have the financial resources to spend the $1000-per-day or higher fees charged by the best spas. It is possible to create supportive environments in any workplace or community setting if there is sufficient will. The cost is on the order of $200 to $400 per person per year for a comprehensive program, including the awareness, skill-building, motivational, and supportive environment components. In a workplace setting, supportive environments will include physical environments, organizational policies, organizational culture, and ongoing programs and structures that encourage healthy lifestyle, and strategies to ensure that employees feel a sense of ownership for the program (Table 3-4). Workplace health promotion programs have so much potential to improve the health of employees because employees spend a large portion of their waking hours at work, usually over a long span of time. They develop close long-term relationships with work colleagues and can be influenced in positive ways by the organizational culture. However, employees are exposed to many influences beyond the workplace that create an abundance of opportunities to develop positive or negative health habits. Health promotion programs will have the greatest successes if they account for all these many influences and opportunities.

POSSE²: THE DIMENSIONS OF OPPORTUNITY

POSSE² is a pneumonic device created to organize a vast range of factors that influence the opportunities a person is able to access. POSSE² is defined as "a large group with a common interest" by the Merriam Webster

Table 3-4: Elements of a Supportive Environment.

Physical Environments

Healthy food in cafeteria
Smoke-free environment
Ergonomically sound furniture
Protection from injury hazards
Opportunities to be physically active

Organization Policies

Medical coverage of preventive services
Consumer-driven health plan
Absenteeism policy that rewards being healthy
Smoke-free environment
Flexible benefits and flextime
Management policies that moderate stress

Organization Culture

Healthy role models
Incentive systems
Communication systems
Peer support

Ongoing Programs and Structures

Health promotion department
Coaching and mentoring
Employee assistance programs
Child care programs
Recreation programs

Employee Ownership and Involvement

Program design
Program promotion
Program delivery
Program leadership
Program evaluation

Dictionary,[41] and as "your crew, your homies, people who sometimes have your back" by the Urban Dictionary.[42] The six components of POSSE[2] are listed and discussed below.

P: Peers
O: Organizations
S: State
S: Society
E: Environment
E: Equality

P: Peers

The health behaviors and attitudes of close friends and co-workers, especially people we consider our peers, have a significant impact on our health habits. This is clearly illustrated in a series of studies conducted by Nicholas Christakis, James Fowler and colleagues on the impact of the health habits of friends, family members, and neighbors on each other, drawing from data in the Framingham Heart Study.[43] The Framingham study involved 12,067 people spanning three generations, with longitudinal data on health habits and health outcomes collected eight times between 1973 and 2003. As shown in Figure 3-6, an individual is nearly 175% more likely to become obese if a close friend (referred to as "mutual" friend in the Figure) becomes obese. As the strength of the emotional connection to the person becoming obese decreases, the association also decreases. For example, the individual is 50%-75% more likely to become obese when a same sex friend, a same sex sibling or ego-perceived friend (someone you consider a friend but they do not consider you a friend) becomes obese. The likelihood of becoming obese does not increase substantially or at all when an opposite-sex friend, an immediate neighbor, or an alter-perceived friend (someone who considers you a friend but you do not consider a friend) becomes obese.[44] This team found similar but less pronounced patterns for tobacco use,[45] depression,[46] and alcohol use.[47]

O: Organizations

Employers have a tremendous influence on the health habits of their workforces. Channels of influence include the formal health promotion programs they offer, access to fitness centers and other places to be physically active, nutritious food served in cafeterias, protection from exposure to toxic substances including second hand tobacco smoke, policies related to absenteeism, medical insurance, and environmental sustainability as well as the management style of leaders and the core values and mission of the organization.

Despite the magnitude of its influence, employers represent just one of the organizations that influence people's health habits. For families with children, schools, child care centers, entertainment outlets, grocery stores and restaurants all have a powerful influence. For families of faith, churches, synagogues, mosques and other religious centers shape priorities in life, increase access to services and influence health choices in other ways. Social clubs, professional networks, food and entertainment outlets all influence people's attitudes and perceptions as well as their access to programs and services. Employers need to learn how to leverage these influences, or overcome them, to be successful in enhancing the health of their employees.

S: State

Employee health is influenced by "the state" through laws and regulations at the local, state and national level.

At the national level, health practices are influenced by policies related to agriculture, transportation, education, environmental protection, tobacco, pharmaceuticals, social safety net, integration of health promotion into Medicare, Medicaid and private health insurance plans, support for medical research as well as specific campaigns on fitness, nutrition, tobacco use and other health behaviors. For example, the Affordable

Figure 3-6: Probability of Becoming Obese if Others Become Obese.

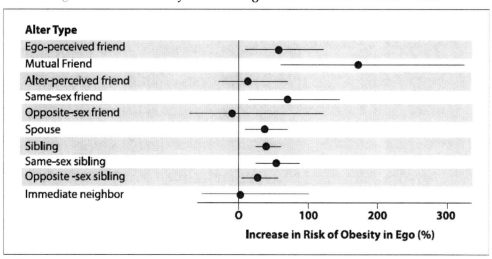

Chrisakis NA, Fowler JH.N Engl J Med.2007; 357; 370-379.

Care Act passed in March of 2011 included 38 specific provisions that integrate health promotion into national health policy. These provisions include development of an annual National Prevention Strategy, providing grants to help small employers develop health promotion programs, allowing employers to provide reduced health plan premiums to employees who meet health goals, providing reimbursement for Medicare beneficiaries to have an annual wellness exam and access to lifestyle change programs, testing the impact of health promotion programs on health and costs for Medicaid recipients and many other provisions.[48]

At the state level, important policies include gun safety, road speed limits, motorcycle helmet rules, Medicaid eligibility and scope of services covered, pollution protection and tobacco policy support. For example, there is significant variation by state in requiring smoke free workplaces and public places, amounts of state taxes charged on tobacco sales, support for tobacco prevention and cessation efforts, allowing employers to set their own policies about hiring smokers, and the portion of the tobacco Master Settlement Agreement (MSA)

devoted to tobacco prevention and cessation efforts. For example, the Centers for Disease Control and Prevention (CDC) developed recommendations for how much each state should spend on state tobacco prevention programs based on the size of its population, the amount it receives annually from the MSA, and the cost and effectiveness of various tobacco prevention and treatment strategies. In 2012, Alaska ranked 1st (best) spending $10.8 million, 101% of the 10.7 million recommended by CDC. Ohio tied for 50th (worst) with Missouri, Connecticut, District of Columbia, Nevada, and New Hampshire, spending $0 on these programs. Under Governor John Kasich, Ohio became the only state in the nation that did not provide support to allow its residents to access the national 1-800-QUITNOW telephone quit line.[49] Earlier, in 2008, under the leadership of then Governor Ted Strickland, the Ohio legislature dismantled the Ohio Tobacco Prevention Foundation, one of the most effective state level tobacco prevention organizations ever created, and used the funding to support the Governor's budget priorities.[50] Declines in the smoking rate leveled off shortly after these policy changes were implemented.

Local policies include zoning laws allowing mixed use real estate developments, active transportation options and construction of sidewalks, bike paths and pedestrian malls, prohibition of use of toxic ingredients in restaurants, smoke-free work and public place policies, excise taxes on tobacco, protection from pollution and outreach campaigns in each of the healthy lifestyle areas. Policies in New York City are probably the most effective in the nation in terms of promoting healthy lifestyle.[51]

Employers have the choice of being passive or active citizens in establishing local and state health policies, and to some extent in national health policies. For example, under the leadership of CEO Dr. Toby Cosgrove, the Cleveland Clinic decided to become very active in state and local tobacco policy. They established smoke-free campuses at their nearly 100 hospital and clinic locations in 2005, developed an intensive tobacco treatment program for patients, helped pass a state law establishing smoke-free policies in all work and public places and helped pass a county law increasing excise tax on cigarettes in 2006, provided free nicotine replacement therapy (NRT) for all residents in Cuyahoga County (county in which most Cleveland Clinic hospitals and clinics are located) who called the state quitline (1-800-QUITNOW) in 2007, and stopped hiring smokers in 2008. Collectively, these policies drove smoking rates in Cuyahoga County from 26% in 2003 to 15% in 2009. By way of comparison, rates dropped from 25% to 21% for the rest of the State of Ohio and 22% to 18% for the United States during the same time period. By getting involved in these state and local policy efforts, the Cleveland Clinic was able to help its employees quit smoking and also to reinforce its image as a strong proponent of smoke-free living. These efforts to fight tobacco are consistent with the Cleveland Clinic's ongoing ranking as the #1 heart center in the nation.

S: Society

In addition to being strongly influenced by peers, people are also influenced by broad cultural norms of the society in which they live, ethnic norms of the people with whom they interact and celebrities prominent in the media.

Physical Activity

At the beginning of the running craze in the United States, running a marathon (26.2 miles) was considered the rare feat of highly developed athletes and an estimated 25,000 completed a marathon in 1976. Over the years, peoples' view of the marathon evolved to the point that people believed running a marathon was within the grasp of the average healthy person. In 2011, an estimated 518,000 finished a marathon.[52] Despite the fact that a large portion of the population remains sedentary, the portion of the population that is very active has increased substantially.

Tobacco Use

In the mid 1970s when the workplace health promotion field started to take hold in the United States, second-hand smoke was considered annoying by many non-smokers, but there were minimal restrictions on smoking in homes, restaurants, workplaces, even hospitals. Asking someone to not smoke, even in your own home, was considered to be rude. These norms have completely flipped; smoking is known to be deadly,[53] smoking is unusual in most work and entertainment settings, and smoking without asking is considered rude in most settings. In fact, restrictions for entire states are very common. Comprehensive (workplace, restaurant, bars) smoke-free laws in effect increased from zero on December 31, 2000,[54] to 23 states by July 1, 2012. Furthermore, 29 states prohibit smoking in workplaces, 34 in restaurants, 29 in bars and 15 in casinos. An estimated 81% of the population of the United States is covered by smoke-free laws at the state or local level.[55] Not surprisingly, tobacco use is highest in the states that have the weakest smoking policies.[56]

Ethnic Norms

People's health habits are strongly influenced by ethnic and cultural norms in their families and communities related to expression of emotions, asking for help, and helping others, the significance of food, and the extent to which one's views should be imposed on others. For example, cultural value of familismo, respeto, simpatia and personalismo make Hispanic/ Latino families want to protect their families from second hand smoke BUT also make them reluctant to ask neighbors to refrain from smoking.[57]

Celebrity Role Models

Celebrities have a significant impact on many people. For example, as Oprah Winfrey lost and gained weight over the past few decades, many people, especially women, have tracked and emulated her methods.[58] Similarly, the constant exposure of women to the perfect bodies of starlets can lead some women, especially young women, to dissatisfaction with their own bodies and sometimes to eating disorders or excessive exercising.[59] Increased visibility of fit women can also have positive effects. For example, when Sushmita Sen became the first Indian women named Miss Universe in 1994, it stimulated a shift toward a positive view of fitness in the Indian culture, a culture that has historically favored spiritual and intellectual development over fitness.

For employers, the key is to be aware of the impact of these broad societal influences, harness them when possible, and be prepared to overcome them when necessary.

E: Environment

There is a growing body of evidence that the natural, built and policy environment has a significant impact on physical activity and eating habits, and an emerging literature showing that these habits can be improved by changing these environments. This field of inquiry was largely created by the Robert Wood Johnson Foundation through their programs in Active Living by Design,[60] Active Living Research[61] and more recently in Healthy Eating Research.[62] Growth is fastest in the active living research, with the number of research studies published growing from 30 in 2000 to 678 in 2010.

The basic idea of active living is that routine physical activity has been engineered out of many people's lives. In the 1950s and 1960s, most children walked to school every day. By the 1980s, most children took the bus or were driven. People used to live in complete neighborhoods that allowed them to walk to the store, to a movie or restaurant and sometimes to work. Today, many communities are so spread out that a car is necessary to go any place. Many communities are built for cars rather than pedestrians or bicycles. Rather than walk to the corner for the bus or subway, people back out of their garages, drive to work and often park in the basement of the buildings where they work. Safety from crime is also a concern that keeps many people from walking, especially in poor neighborhoods. People use remote clickers to turn on the TV, send emails at work rather than walking down the hall and surf the net to do research rather than browse through the library. Many of these advances have significantly improved productivity, but they have also increased sedentary behaviors. One of the landmark studies in this area examined the relationship between sprawl, health behaviors, and health conditions, and involved 206,992 adults in 448 counties. It showed that people who lived in counties with greater sprawl walked less, and had higher rates of obesity and hypertension. In fact, people who lived in low sprawl areas like Manhattan and Washington, DC weighed an average of 6 pounds less than people living in high sprawl counties based on sprawl related factors.[63]

Many buildings are designed to maximize efficiency in moving from one section to another, with elevators in clear view and staircases often hidden and sometimes not very pleasant.

Large grocery stores are the predominant source of food for most people. They provide the advantage of a wide variety of food in one place, but access is sometimes limited for people who do not have cars, or who live in poor neighborhoods.

Community design and food access is governed largely by federal, state and local government laws related to transportation, zoning, agriculture, and building codes-areas that are beyond the expertise of the typical health promotion program manager, and even the leadership of many organizations. However, most employers do have control over the design of their own offices and the food served in their own cafeterias. Employers also have the choice to become more involved in shaping their environments through advocacy at the local, state and federal level.

Employers need to be aware of the impact of the built and natural environment on the health habits of their employees and either harness them or be prepared to overcome them.

E: Equality

There is a growing body of evidence that poverty has a strong impact on a wide range of health problems and that income inequality has an additional independent effect. This evidence comes to light at the same time income inequality is worse in the United States than almost any other developed nation. Additional details on the health impact of income inequality and recent increase in income disparities in the United States are shown in the Appendix 3-B titled "Causes of Income Inequality in the United States and Resulting Health Effects."

Income inequality is relevant to workplace health promotion programs in several ways. Employees who have very low incomes or who live in states or local areas, or perhaps who work in organizations in which income inequality is high, may have elevated levels of health problems and lower levels of social trust. Additional financial resources and staff time may be required to establish trust with these employees, engage them in programs, and reverse the negative effects of their situations. Employers need to be aware of the impact of poverty and inequality on their employees and be prepared to reduce it or overcome its effects.

RELATIVE IMPORTANCE OF DIFFERENT STRATEGIES

No empirical studies have been conducted to directly test the relative importance of awareness, motivation, skills and opportunity in stimulating sustained behavior change. However, drawing from the findings of the systematic process used to develop the framework described here, I feel confident concluding that awareness is by far the least important factor, opportunities are the most important, and motivation is slightly more important than skills. One way to think about the relative importance of these factors is in the context of multivariate analysis. If these four factors could explain all the variation in successful lifestyle change, my hypothesis is that awareness would be responsible for 5% of the change, motivation for 30%, skills for 25% and opportunity for 40%. Another way to think of this is in the context of an investment portfolio; 5% of efforts and resources should be invested in enhancing awareness, 30% in enhancing motivation, 25% in building skills and 40% in providing opportunities to practice healthy lifestyles.

CONCLUSION AND IMPLICATIONS

The underlying purpose of this integrated model is to create positive movement and sustained momentum for people and organizations. The five dimensions of optimal health will capture people's attention. At worst, they will laugh and say "That's flaky." More likely, they will see the dimensions as reflecting priorities in their own life, and will look closer into programs built around these concepts. The six steps in the Renewing Health Behavior Change Process are specifically designed to keep people moving forward to building one positive behavior after another into their lives. The AMSO Portfolio Balancing Framework is designed to stimulate organizations to continually reflect on their programs to make sure they are investing the appropriate resources in areas that are most likely to make a difference, especially to stimulate people who are not health nuts...a description that probably fits most of the people reading this chapter.

Historical Roots of an Aspirational Vision of Health

The historical roots of an aspirational vision of health came from the early work of Bill Hettler, John Travis and Don Ardell, who came together to create the National Wellness Institute at the University of Wisconsin, Stevens Point in 1977. Hettler was a physician who directed the student health service. In 1976, he described six dimensions of wellness (Figure 3A-1) in a brochure intended for his student patients. These included physical, spiritual, emotional, social, intellectual and occupational health. He discussed this six-dimensional model widely in presentations, but apparently did not publish any written work on the dimensions until years after others had begun to write about it.[1] A few years earlier, apparently in 1972, John Travis, a physician and the founder of what has been described as the first wellness center in the United States, articulated a continuum of health in which premature death was shown on the left and high-level wellness on the right (Figure 3A-2). Traditional medicine typically focused on moving people to the mid point, helping them overcome disabilities, symptoms and signs of disease, to a point of no discernable illness, but also no discernable wellness. The emerging field of wellness would help them move through that neutral point toward high-level wellness through awareness, education and growth.[2] Early work in the health promotion field was inspired by Hetler's six dimensions of wellness and Travis's illness-wellness continuum.

In 1995, O'Donnell, inspired by a personal comment from Noreen Clark, the then chairman of the Department of Health Behavior and Health Education at the University of Michigan, suggested that illness and wellness were actually not part of the same continuum and that a person did not need to pass though a point of no discernable disease to begin to move toward high-level wellness, or as he called it, optimal health.[3] For example, a person could have a terminal disease, but also be highly evolved in their emotional, spiritual, intellectual and social health. He suggested that a health matrix, with illness on one axis and wellness on the other axis,

Figure 3A-1: The Six Dimensions of Wellness.

might be a more accurate conceptualization than one continuum (Figure 3A-3). Optimal health is shown in the top right corner of this matrix. People would strive to achieve the highest level of freedom from illness and highest level of wellness to move as close as possible to optimal health. Using this matrix better allows clinicians to better apply health promotion principles in working with sick patients. For example, despite living with the physical deterioration caused by cancer, diabetes or heart disease, there is no reason a person cannot excel in the other dimensions of optimal health. In fact, enhancing their social, intellectual, emotional and spiritual health may help them manage their physical disability. Physical activity, nutritious diet, not using tobacco or other toxic substances will facilitate recovery as well. These principles also apply to helping someone recover from an injury, heart attack or other acute but resolvable disease.

Figure 3A-2: Illnes-Wellness Continuum.

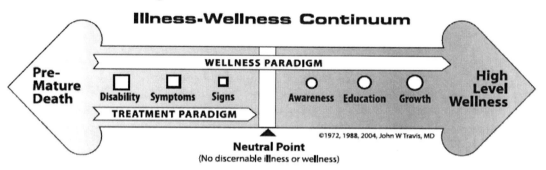

Figure 3A-3: Optimal Health Matrix.

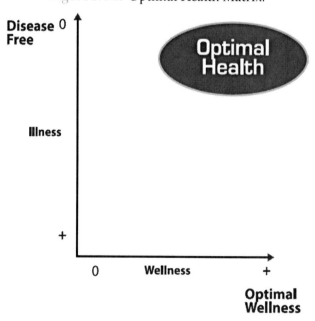

REFERENCES

1. National Wellness Institute. The six dimensions of wellness model. Available at: http://www.nationalwellness.org/index.php?id_tier=2&id_c=25. Accessed August 30, 2012.

2. Ardell D. Meet John Travis, doctor of wellbeing. *Prevention.* 1975;4:62–69.

3. O'Donnell MP. *How to Design Workplace Health Promotion Programs.* Keego Harbor, MI: American Journal of Health Promotion, Inc; 1995.

APPENDIX 3-B

Causes of Income Inequality in the United States and Resulting Health Effects

Excerpt from O'Donnell MP. Erosion of Our Moral Compass, Social Trust, and the Fiscal Strength of the United States: Income Inequality, Tax Policy, and Well-Being. *Am Jour Health Promot.* 2012, 26, 4, iv-xi.

INCREASES IN INCOME DISPARITIES IN THE UNITED STATES

The Occupy Wall Street movement[1] has focused attention on the dramatic and growing income disparities between the rich and the poor, and to a large extent between the rich and everyone else, and that the outcome of our federal spending and tax policies is to make the rich richer and the poor poorer. In fact, of the 34 nations that make up the Organization for Economic Co-operation and Development (OECD) only China, Mexico and Turkey have higher income disparities than the United States. The top 10% of Americans earn an average of $114,000/year, 15 times the $7,800 earned by the lowest 10%. The difference has gotten worse over the past 30 years; it was 12 times more in the 1990s and 10 times more in the 1980s. This disparity exists despite a 30% increase in hours worked by the lowest 10% in the past decade, and a 1% drop in hours worked by the top 1%. The income gap is more extreme for the top 1%, who earn an average of $1.3 million and collectively earn 18% of all income for the entire nation, more than two times the 8% of all income they collectively earned in 1980. During the same period, the highest marginal income tax rates in the U.S.

dropped from 70% to 35% and capital gains rates dropped from 25% to 14%; the result being that high income earners are able to keep a higher portion of the income they are earning.[2] The story on accumulated wealth is even more extreme. A recent analysis of the most current data (2007) from the Survey of Consumer Finances[3] found that the top 20% of wealth holders own 87.2% of all the wealth in the United States, the top 1% owns 69%, and the richest 400 individuals have as much wealth as the entire bottom 50%. One family, the six heirs to the Walmart fortune, have as much wealth as the entire bottom 30% of the population of our nation.[4] We expect to see that disparities are even more extreme when data from 2011 is released. For example, the fortune of the Walmart heirs increased from $70 billion to $93 billion between 2007 and 2011.

To exacerbate the problem, the U.S. does relatively little to help people with low income. For example, the direct financial support provided to people with low-incomes represented just 6% of their household incomes, compared to an average of 16% in the OECD nations. Spending on public services like health care and education was 13.4% of GDP, about average for the OECD nations.[5] It is shocking but not surprising that an estimated 14.7% of children in the U.S. live in poverty,[6] despite the widely accepted finding that successful early childhood development is the best predictor of future success in life. We have also allowed the evisceration of our once great K-12 education system, seen cuts in state funding of a state college and university system that was once the envy of the world, allowed the core of many of our great cities to decay, and done little to stop the erosion of our infrastructure of roads, bridges and energy supports. Neglect in these areas hurts all of society, but has the greatest impact on those with lowest incomes.

GROWING EVIDENCE OF THE IMPACT OF INEQUALITY ON HEALTH AND OTHER ASPECTS OF QUALITY OF LIFE

The final factor that has made me realize I have had my head in the sand is my growing understanding of the impact of income inequality on health and other aspects of quality of life. I have learned the most in this area by reading the work of Richard Wilkinson. Richard Wilkinson is a long-time collaborator with Michael Marmot on the study of social determinants of health, and the leader of a series of studies that show the devastating impact of income inequality. The findings of these studies are described brilliantly in his book titled *The Spirit Level: Why Greater Equality Makes Societies Stronger*[7], which he co-authored with Kate Pickett. Together, they have created the Equality Trust to make these findings more visible and to rally people to look for strategies to reduce inequality. The findings from their research, slide decks and access to their original data sets are available on their website: http://www.equalitytrust.org.uk. The overall conclusion of their work is that differences in income between rich and poor, rather than per capita income per se, is one of the most powerful predictors of life expectancy, infant mortality, obesity, mental illness, teenage birth rate, homicides, imprisonment, education scores, social mobility and trust. Collectively, these factors make up an "Index of health and social problems." Their analysis begins with examining the relationship between the per capita income of a nation and life expectancy.

They found that there is a strong relationship between income and life expectancy for low-income nations, with the poorest nations having life expectancies in the 40s and richer nations having life expectancies over 70. However, once per capita incomes reach about $10,000 per year, higher per capita incomes do not seem to have much impact on life expectancy. Once a per capita income has reached this baseline level, income inequality is more important than per capita income in explaining life expectancy. Most of their global analysis is based on 23 nations. They started with the 50 wealthiest nations of the world, dropped those with populations of less than 3 million people and those that did not have good data on income inequity and the other outcome variables in their analysis, which is described below.

They have analyzed and reported these relationships for their sample of 23 nations and for the 50 states in the United States. The strength of the relationships is remarkably strong, reaching statistical significance for all of these outcomes, and explaining 18% to 86% of the variances in the individual factors and 76% of the variance in the Index of health and social problems. Using data from the developed nations, but not from the individual U.S. states, they found statistically significant relationships between income inequality and drug use, calorie intake, child well-being, juvenile homicides, child mental illness, public expenditures on health care, paid maternity leave, child conflict, recycling, peace index, spending on police, social expenditures, women's status, high school dropout, pugnacity and spending on foreign aid.

The consistency of these relationships is remarkable. Variances of this magnitude mean that income inequality is an important predictor for all these outcomes, and probably the most important factor for some of them. I was stunned, and quite frankly ashamed, that the United States ranked so poorly on so many of these values. This certainly does not jive with the view so many Americans hold, including me, that the United States is the greatest nation in the world. It leaves me trying to think of the ways in which we are the greatest, and after reading this work, I am challenged in that task. The biggest shock for me was how poorly we rank in foreign aid as a percent of GDP...dead last among the 23 nations in their study! We are also the worst in income inequality, social mobility, and the rates of imprisonment, teenage births, mental illness, obesity, homicides, infant mortality, and overweight children. In addition, the U.S. is almost the worst in illegal drug use, child well-being, educational testing scores, child conflict, recycling, ecological footprint and life expectancy. We are about average on women's status and the level of trust. The only areas the U.S. ranks at the top are income per capita, military spending per capita and medical care spending per capita.

DAMAGING EFFECTS OF INEQUALITY

Why does inequality have such a strong impact? Inequality seems to have a devastating and cascading effect on health and other factors for at least five reasons.

First, poverty, independent of inequality, causes many health problems. These problems leave poor people with lower resilience to recover from the additional risks caused by inequality. For example, medical conditions that are higher for people with low income include obesity,[8] asthma,[9] diabetes,[10] hypertension,[11] human immunodeficiency virus infection,[12] and coronary heart disease and stroke,[13] as well as preterm birth[14] and adolescent pregnancy.[15] Smoking rates are higher among people with lower incomes and less education,[16] as are death by homicide[17] and premature death by any cause. Rates of disease and death are higher for these groups partly because of poor health habits, but also

because of lack of access to clean and safe housing[18] and clean air,[19] and poor access to regular medical care,[20] nutritious foods, and formal education.[21]

Second, inequality causes people to judge themselves negatively relative to other people, a phenomenon called "social evaluative threat" which in turn has been shown to trigger release of cortisol and proinflammatory cytokine.[22] Cortisol impedes immune functions, increases the risk of heart disease and threatens other physiological systems. Chronic inflammation has been linked to increased rates of autoimmune disorders including rheumatoid arthritis, lupus and polymyalgia rheumatica, asthma and the inflammatory bowel diseases, ulcerative colitis, Crohn's disease, cardiovascular disease, bacterial endocarditis, cancer, urinary infections or cystitis and may increase risk of a squamous cell bladder cancer.[23] An indirect impact of social evaluative threat is that defending one's honor becomes more important, and can lead to physical injuries caused by fighting and the additional stress caused by hostile interactions.

Third, the importance of maintaining status increases the social pressure to divert limited financial resources from food, rent, utilities, medical care and other necessities of basic living that will preserve good health, to buying nice clothes, cars, toys for kids or entertainment to raise status, or to drugs, alcohol or cigarettes to help cope with the stress. This temptation to divert resources from basic needs to entertainment and luxuries is much lower in poor nations in which incomes are low for all people because these discretionary luxuries are rare, not promoted through ubiquitous advertising and rarely purchased by peers. As such, the standard of living of a typical family in a poor nation that has low levels of income inequality might be similar to the standard of living of a poor person in the United States (which has high income inequality) in an absolute sense, but the person living in the poor nation does not suffer the negative consequences of income inequality because their standard of living is the same as everyone else they encounter.

Fourth, a pregnant woman experiencing the elevated stress caused by inequality generates cortisol and other stress related hormones and toxins. This combination can cause lasting damage to her fetus, increasing the likelihood of low birth weight, premature birth, or other congenital defects. This is in addition to the damage to the fetus caused by malnutrition. This makes it very difficult for this woman's child to ever catch up.

Fifth, early childhood development is impacted directly by poverty. For example, Goodman and Gregg found that the most important factors affecting child development are birth weight, mother suffering from post-natal depression, being read to every day at age 3 and having a regular bed time at age three[24] and that all of those factors are related to socio-economic status. Recovering from these setbacks compounds the challenges of a child born into poverty. For example, one of the findings of the 1970 British Cohort Study was that children in high socioeconomic (SES) status families maintained or improved their cognitive abilities relative to their peers as time passed, while those from low SES families dropped. More specifically, a cohort of children from high SES family who tested at the 10th percentile at 22 months, averaged scores at the 55th percentile at 118 months, while those from low SES families who started out at the 10th percentile, averaged scores at the 28th percentile at 118 months. Similarly, high SES children who tested at 90th percentile at 22 months, averaged scores at the 68th percentile at 118 months while low SES children who started at the 90th percentile, averaged scores at the 39th percentile at 118 months.[25] It is important to acknowledge the racial bias in cognitive testing in interpreting these findings, [26] but it is hard to not conclude that poverty has a depressing impact on cognitive development. This childhood development

effect is exacerbated by the fact that social standing and peer acceptance is especially important to adolescent children. Those with depressed cognitive development tend to have lower social status, which produces more stress and the physical problems caused by stress, as well as increased temptation to perform risky behaviors to get attention or join gangs to enhance social relationships.

Racial discrimination is no doubt closely aligned with income inequality. Wilkinson does not specifically address racial discrimination in his book and a thorough review of this is beyond the scope of this paper, but a few key points need to be acknowledged. The most obvious link between income inequality and racial discrimination is that oppressed racial groups have lower incomes,[27] and thus suffer from all the negative income inequality effects described above. In addition, some people are victims of discrimination because of their race, independent of their income. In addition to increased threats of violence and exclusion from many opportunities, this discrimination creates the same type of stress caused by social evaluative threat, and the resulting physical consequences. For people with high and middle incomes who suffer racial discrimination, this subjects them to stresses they would otherwise be able to avoid. For people with low income, it increases the stress they already endure from poverty and income inequality.

REFERENCES

1.   Occupy Wall Street. The revolution continues world wide. Available at: http://occupy-wallst.org/. Accessed December 22, 2011.

2.   Congressional Budget Office. Trends in federal tax revenues and rate, December 2, 2010. Available at: http://www.cbo.gov/doc.cfm?index=11976. Accessed October 1, 2012.

3.   Board of Governors of the Federal Reserve. Survey of consumer

finances. Available at: http://www.federalreserve.gov/econresdata/scf/scf_2009p.htm. Accessed December 12, 2011.

4. Allegretto S. The few, the proud, the very rich. Center on Wage and Employment Dynamics. December 5, 2011. Available at: http://blogs.berkeley.edu/2011/12/05/the-few-the-proud-the-very-rich/. Accessed December 12, 2011.

5. Organization for Economic Co-operation and Development. Divided we stand: why inequality keeps rising. December 2011. Available at: http://www.oecd.org/document/51/0,3746,en_2649_33933_49147827_1_1_1_1,00.html. Accessed October 1, 2012.

6. Annie E. Casey Foundation. Promoting opportunity for the next generation, 2011 KIDS COUNT data book. State profiles of child well-being. Available at: http://www.aecf.org//media/Pubs/Initiatives/KIDS%20COUNT/123/2011KIDSCOUNTData Book/KCDataBook2011.pdf. Accessed August 23, 2011.

7. Wilkinson R, Pickett K. *The Spirit Level: Why Greater Equality Makes Societies Stronger.* New York, NY: Bloomberg Press; 2009.

8. Freedman DS. Obesity — United States, *1988-2008. MMWR Morb Mortal Wkly Rep.* 2011;60(suppl):73-77. Available at: http://www.cdc.gov/mmwr/pdf/other/su6001.pdf. Accessed August 23, 2011.

9. Moorman JE, Zahran H, Truman BI, Molla MT. Current asthma prevalence — United States, 2006-2008. *MMWR Morb Mortal Wkly Rep.* 2011;60(suppl):84-86. Available at: http://www.cdc.gov/mmwr/pdf/other/su6001.pdf. Accessed August 23, 2011.

10. Beckles GL, Zhu J, Moonesinghe R. Diabetes — United States, 2004 and 2008. *MMWR Morb Mortal Wkly Rep.* 2011;60(suppl):90-93. Available at: http://www.cdc.gov/mmwr/pdf/other/su6001.pdf. Accessed August 23, 2011.

11. Keenan NL, Rosendorf KA. Prevalence of hypertension and controlled hypertension — United States, 2005-2008. *MMWR Morb Mortal Wkly Rep.* 2011;60(suppl):94-98. Available at: http://www.cdc.gov/mmwr/pdf/other/su6001.pdf. Accessed August 23, 2011.

12. Hughes D, Dean HD, Mermin J. H. Fenton KA. HIV infection — United States, 2005 and 2008. *MMWR Morb Mortal Wkly Rep.* 2011;60(suppl):87-89. Available at: http://www.cdc.gov/mmwr/pdf/other/su6001.pdf. Accessed August 23, 2011.

13. Keenan NL, Shaw KM. Coronary heart disease and stroke deaths — United States, 2006. *MMWR Morb Mortal Wkly Rep.* 2011;60(suppl):62-66. Available at: http://www.cdc.gov/mmwr/pdf/other/su6001.pdf. Accessed August 23, 2011.

14. Martin JA. Preterm births — United States, 2007. *MMWR Morb Mortal Wkly Rep.* 2011;60(suppl):78-79. Available at: http://www.cdc.gov/mmwr/pdf/other/su6001.pdf. Accessed August 23, 2011.

15. Ventura SJ. Adolescent pregnancy and childbirth — United States, 1991-2008. *MMWR Morb Mortal Wkly Rep.* 2011;60(suppl):105-109. Available at: http://www.cdc.gov/mmwr/pdf/other/su6001.pdf. Accessed August 23, 2011.

16. Garrett BE. Cigarette smoking — United States, 1965-2008. *MMWR Morb Mortal Wkly Rep.* 2011;60(suppl):109-113. Available at: http://www.cdc.gov/mmwr/pdf/other/su6001.pdf. Accessed August 23, 2011.

17. Logan JE, Smith SG, Stevens MR. Homicides—United States, 1999–2007. *MMWR Morb Mortal Wkly Rep.* 2011;60(suppl):67–72. Available at: http://www.cdc.gov/mmwr/pdf/other/su6001.pdf. Accessed August 23, 2011.

18. Raymond J, Wheeler W, Brown MJ. Inadequate and unhealthy housing, 2007 and 2009. *MMWR Morb Mortal Wkly Rep.* 2011;60(suppl):21–27. Available at: http://www.cdc.gov/mmwr/pdf/other/su6001.pdf. Accessed August 23, 2011.

19. Yip FY, Pearcy JN, Garbe PL, Truman BI. Unhealthy air quality—United States, 2006–2009. *MMWR Morb Mortal Wkly Rep.* 2011;60(suppl):28–31. Available at: http://www.cdc.gov/mmwr/pdf/other/su6001.pdf. Accessed August 23, 2011.

20. Moonesinghe R, Zhu J, Truman BI. Health insurance coverage—United States, 2004 and 2008. *MMWR Morb Mortal Wkly Rep.* 2011;60(suppl):35–37. Available at: http://www.cdc.gov/mmwr/pdf/other/su6001.pdf. Accessed August 23, 2011.

21. Beckles GL, Truman BI. Education and income—United States, 2005 and 2009. *MMWR Morb Mortal Wkly Rep.* 2011;60(suppl):13–17. Available at: http://www.cdc.gov/mmwr/pdf/other/su6001.pdf. Accessed August 23, 2011.

22. Dickerson SS. Emotional and physiological responses to social-evaluative threat. *Soc Pers Psychol Compass* [serial online]. Blackwell. March 2008. Available at: http://www.blackwell-compass.com/subject/socialpsychology/article_view?article_id=spco_articles_bpl095. Accessed January 6, 2012.

23. Leserman J, Petitto JM, Golden RN, Gaynes BN, et al. Impact of stressful life events, depression, social support, coping, and cortisol on progression to AIDS. *Am J Psychiatry.* 2000;157:1221–1228. doi:10.1176/appi.ajp.157.8.1221. Available at: http://ajp.psychiatryonline.org/article.aspx?articleID=174261. Accessed January 6, 2012.

24. Goodman A, Gregg P, Washburn E. Children's educational attainment and the aspirations, attitudes and behaviours of parents and children through childhood in the UK. *Longit Life Course Stud.* 2011;2:1–18.

25. Feinstein L. Inequality in the early cognitive development of British children in the 1970 cohort. *Economica.* 2003;70:3–97.

26. Morgan ATA, Marsiske M, Dzierzewski J, et al. Race-related cognitive test bias in the ACTIVE study: a MIMIC model approach. *Exp Aging Res.* 2010;36:426–452. Available at: http://www.ncbi.nlm.nih.gov/pmc/articles/PMC2941916/. Accessed January 6, 2010.

27. U.S. Census Bureau. Income, expenditures, poverty, & wealth, the 2012 statistical abstract. Available at: http://www.census.gov/compendia/statab/cats/income_expenditures_poverty_wealth.html. Accessed January 6, 2012.

Glossary

Face of Wellness Model: Graphic image resembling a face with two eyes and a nose, consisting of the circular illustrations of five dimensions of optimal health and the renewing behavior change process and the triangular illustration of the AMSO Framework.

AMSO & POSSE[2] Framework: Awareness, Motivation, Skills and Opportunity and Peers, Organizations, States, Society, Environment and Equality.

Dimensions of Optimal Health: Physical, Social, Emotional, Spiritual and Intellectual

Renewing Behavior Change process: Get ready; Measure your health; Set goals, Build skills, Form habits, Help others.

Optimal health matrix: Graphic illustration showing illness on the vertical axis and wellness on the horizontal axis, with optimal health in the upper right quadrant, illustrating that wellness and illness are different constructs that wellness can enhance even in the presence of a terminal disease.

Supportive environment: Natural, built, cultural and policy environments that support positive health practices because they make healthy choices easy.

Built environment: Human made surroundings including sidewalks, roads, paths, streets, buildings, and green spaces, that influence the degree to which people are physically active, have access to nutritious foods, interact with each other, feel safe and practice other health habits.

Aspirational goals: Lofty dreams about what could be, like running a marathon, always having a positive outlook on the world, becoming a vegetarian, or fitting into a wedding gown on 30th anniversary.

Learning goals: Desire to acquire specific knowledge, like how to cook nutritious foods, train for a triathlon, mindfulness protocols.

Performance goals: Specific behavior goals like walking for at least 30 minutes 6 days a week, eating five fruits and vegetables every day, being smoke free within 45 days.

Benchmarking: Comparing programming strategies and results among different organizations to determine common and most successful approaches (also called "best practices").

Learning Objectives

After reading this chapter, readers will be able to do the following:

1. Describe the six steps on the renewing health behavior change process.
2. Describe the elements of the AMSO POSSE[2] Framework.
3. Describe the five dimensions of optimal health.

Discussion Questions

1. What strategies can be used to enhance each of the five dimensions of optimal health in a work setting?
2. What strategies can be used to implement each of the six stages of the behavior change process?
3. What are the advantages and disadvantages of the workplace as a setting to enhance each of the five dimensions of optimal health? What other settings can be drawn upon to enhance each of the dimensions?
4. From a behavior change perspective, what is the relative importance of each of the elements in the AMSO POSSE[2] Framework?
5. From an overall health perspective, what is the relative importance of each of the five dimensions of optimal health?
6. How might the definition of optimal health be refined in its next stage of evolution?

REFERENCES

1. O'Donnell MP, Bishop CA, Kaplan KL. Benchmarking best practices in workplace health promotion. *Am J Health Promot.* 1996:11(4):TAHP-1–TAHP-8.
2. O'Donnell MP. Health impact of workplace health promotion programs and methodological quality of the research literature. *Art Health Promot.* 1997;1:1–7.
3. Wilson MG, Holman PB, Hammock A. A comprehensive review of the

effects of worksite health promotion on health-related outcomes. *Am J Health Promot.* 1996;10:429–435.

4.   Wilson MG. A comprehensive review of the effects of worksite health promotion on health-related outcomes: an update. *Am J Health Promot.* 1996;11:107–108.

5.   Aldana SG. Financial impact of health promotion programs: a comprehensive review of the literature. *Am J Health Promot.* 2001;15:296-320.

6.   The Health Project Web site. C. Everett Koop Award Winners. Available at: http://www.thehealthproject.com/index.html. Accessed August 15, 2012.

7.   O'Donnell MP. Definition of health promotion. *Am J Health Promot.* 1986;1:3.

8.   Naditch MP. The StayWell Program. In: *Behavioral Health.* New York: John Wiley & Sons; 1984:1071–1078.

9.   The Twelve Traditions. *AA Grapevine.* 1949:6(6).

10.   Prochaska JO, Velicer WF. The transtheoretical model of health behavior change. *Am J Health Promot.* 1997;12:38-48.

11.   National Heart Lung and Blood Institute. Diseases and conditions index Web site. Available at: http://www.nhlbi.nih.gov/health/dci/Diseases/ms/ms_whatis.html. Accessed October1, 2012.

12.   Heaney C, Goetzel R. A review of health-related outcomes of multi-component worksite health promotion programs. *Am J Health Promot.* 1997;11:290-307.

13.   Rothkopf E, Billington M. Goal-guided learning from text: inferring a descriptive processing model from inspection times and eye movements. *J Educ Psychol.* 1979;71:310–327.

14.   Bryan J, Locke E. Goal setting as a means of increasing motivation. *J Appl Psychol.* 1967;51:274–277.

15.   LaPorte R, Nath R. Role of performance goals in prose learning. *J Educ Psychol.* 1976;68:260–264.

16.   Wood R, Locke E. Goal setting and strategy effects on complex tasks. In: Staw B, Cummings L, eds. *Research in Organizational Behavior.* Vol 12. Greenwich, Conn: JAI Press; 1990:73–109.

17.   Seijts GH, Latham GP, Tasa K, Latham BW. Goal setting and goal orientation: an integration of two different yet related literatures. *Acad Manage J.* 2004; 47:227–239.

18.   Kanfer R, Aclerman PL. Motivation and cognitive abilities: an integrative/aptitude-treatment interaction approach to skill acquisition. *J Appl Psychol.* 1989;74:657-690.

19.   Seijts GH, Latham GP. The effect of distal learning, outcome, and proximal goals on a moderately complex task. *J Organ Behav.* 2001;22:291–302.

20.   Locke EA, Latham GP. A theory of goal setting and task performance. Englewood Cliffs, NJ: Prentice Hall; 1990.

21.   Wagner J, Gooding R. Effects of societal trends on participation research. *Adm Sci Q.* 1987;32:241–262.

22.   Locke EA, Alavi M, Wagner J. Participation in decision-making: an information exchange perspective. In: Ferris G, ed. *Research in Personnel and Human Resources Management.* Vol 15. Greenwich, CT: JAI Press; 1997:293-331.

23.   Hollenbeck J, Williams C, Klein H. An empirical examination of the antecedents of commitment to difficult goals. *J Appl Psychol.* 1989;74:18–23.

24.   Roman WW, Latham GP, Kinne SB. The effects of goal setting and supervision on worker behavior in an industrial situation. *J Appl Psychol.* 1973;58:302–207.

25.   Bandura A. *Self-Efficacy: The Exercise of Control.* New York, NY: Freeman; 1997.

26.   Matsui T, Okada A, Inoshita O. Mechanism of feedback affecting task performance. *Organ Behav Hum Perform.* 1983;31:114–122.

27. U.S. Dept of Health and Human Services, Office of the Surgeon General. Clinical practice guideline: treating tobacco use and dependence: 2008 update. Available at: http://www.surgeongeneral.gov/tobacco/treating_tobacco_use08.pdf. Accessed August 30, 2012.

28. Bandura A. Self-efficacy: toward a unifying theory of behavior change. *Psychol Rev.* 1977;84:191–215.

29. Brown LB, Neese RM, Vinokur AD, Smith DM. Providing social support may be more beneficial than receiving it: results from a prospective study of mortality. *Psychol Sci.* 2003;14:320–327.

30. O'Donnell MP, Ainsworth T. *Health Promotion in the Workplace.* Albany, New York: John Wiley and Sons; 1984.

31. O'Donnell MP. A simple framework to describe what works best: improving awareness, enhancing motivation, building skills, and providing opportunity. *Am J Health Promot.* 2005;20: suppl 1-7 following 84, iii.

32. Aizen I. From intentions to actions: a theory of planned behavior in action. In: Kiehl J, Bechman J, eds. *Action Control: From Cognition to Behavior.* New York, NY: Springer-Verlag; 1985:11–39.

33. Prochaska J, Velicer W. The transtheoretical model of health behavior change. *Am J Health Promot.* 1997;12:38–48.

34. Koffman D, Lee J, Hopp J, Emont S. The impact of including incentives and competition in a workplace smoking cessation program on quit rates. *Am J Health Promot.* 1998;13:105–111.

35. Taitel MS, Haufle V, Heck D, et al. Incentives and other factors associated with employee participation in health risk assessment. *J Occup Environ Med.* 2008;50:863–872.

36. Seaverson EL, Grossmeier J, Miller TM, Anderson DR. The role of incentive design, incentive, value, communications strategy, and worksite culture on health risk assessment participation. *Am J Health Promot.* 2009;23:343-352.

37. Towers Watson. 2011/2012 Staying@Work survey report: a pathway to employee health and workplace productivity. Available at: http://www.towerswatson.com/united-states/research/6031. Accessed August 16, 2012.

38. Miller W, Rolnick S. *Motivational Interviewing: Preparing People to Change Addictive Behavior.* New York, NY: Guilford; 1991.

39. O'Donnell MP, Harris JS. *Health Promotion in the Workplace.* 2nd ed. Albany, NY: Delmar Publishers; 1994.

40. O'Donnell MP. *Health Promotion in the Workplace.* 3rd ed. Albany, NY: Cenage; 2002.

41. POSSE². Merriam-Webster dictionary Web site. Available at: http://www.merriam-webster.com/dictionary/posse. Accessed August 31, 2012.

42. POSSE². Urban Dictionary Web site. Available at: http://www.urbandictionary.com/define.php?term=posse. Accessed August 31, 2012.

43. Framingham Heart Study Web site. Available at: http://www.framinghamheartstudy.org/. Accessed August 31, 2012.

44. Christakis NA, Fowler JH. The spread of obesity in a large social network over 32 years. [published online ahead of print July 25, 2007]. *N Engl J Med.* 2007;357:370–379.

45. Christakis NA, Fowler JH. The collective dynamics of smoking in a large social network. *N Engl J Med.* 2008;358: 2249–2258.

46. Rosenquist JN, Fowler JH, Christakis NA. Social network determinants of depression [published online ahead of print March 16, 2010]. *Mol Psychiatry.* 2011;16:273–281.

47. Rosenquist JN, Murabito J, Fowler JH, Christakis NA. The spread of alcohol

consumption behavior in a large social network. *Ann Intern Med.* 2010;152:426–433, W141.

48. O'Donnell MP. Integrating health promotion in the national agenda: the perspective of a grass roots advocate. *Health Educ Behav.* 2012;39:518-22.

49. U.S. state and local issues. Campaign for Tobacco Free Kids Web site. Available at: http://www.tobaccofreekids.org/what_we_do/state_local/. Accessed August 17, 2012.

50. O'Donnell MP. Fool me once, shame on you. Fool me twice, shame on me [Editor's Notes]. *Am J Health Promot.* 2008;23:iv.

51. New York City Dept of Health and Mental Hygiene Web site. Available at: http://www.nyc.gov/html/doh/html/home/home.shtml. Accessed August 17, 2012.

52. Running USA's A-nnual Marathon Report. Available at: http://www.runningusa.org/index.cfm?fuseaction=news.details&ArticleId=332&returnTo=annual-reports. Accessed August 20, 2012.

53. The health consequences of involuntary exposure to tobacco smoke: a report of the Surgeon General. Atlanta, GA: U.S. Dept of Health and Human Services, Centers for Disease Control and Prevention, Coordinating Center for Health Promotion, National Center for Chronic Disease Prevention and Health Promotion, Office on Smoking and Health; 2006.

54. State smoke-free laws for worksites, restaurants, and bars—United States, 2000-2010. *MMWR Morb Mortal Wkly Rep.* 2011;60;472–475. Available at: http://www.cdc.gov/mmwr/preview/mmwrhtml/mm6015a2.htm#tab1. Accessed October 1, 2012.

55. American Nonsmokers Rights Foundation. Summary of 100% smokefree state laws and population protected by 100% U.S. smokefree laws, July 1, 2012. Available at: http://www.no-smoke.org/pdf/SummaryUSPopList.pdf. Accessed October 1, 2012.

56. Giovino GA, Chaloupka FJ, Hartman AM, et al. Cigarette smoking prevalence and policies in the 50 states: an era of change—the Robert Wood Johnson Foundation ImpacTeen Tobacco Chart Book. Buffalo, NY: University at Buffalo, State University of New York; 2009. Available at: http://impacteen.org/statetobaccodata/chartbook_final060409.pdf. Accessed August 20, 2012.

57. Baezconde-Garbanati LA, Weich-Reushé K, Espinoza L, et al. Secondhand smoke exposure among Hispanics/Latinos living in multiunit housing: exploring barriers to new policies. *Am J Health Promot.* 2011;25(5 suppl):S82–S90.

58. Oprah's weight loss confession. Available at: http://www.oprah.com/health/Oprahs-Weight-Loss-Confession/. Accessed August 20, 2012.

59. National Eating Disorders Web site. Available at: http://www.nationaleating-disorders.org/. Accessed August 20, 2012.

60. Active Living by Design Web site. Available at: http://www.activelivingbydesign.org/. Accessed August 20, 2012.

61. Active Living Research. Available at: http://www.activelivingresearch.org/. Accessed August 20, 2012.

62. Healthy Eating Research Web site. Available at: http://www.healthyeatingresearch.org/. Accessed August 20, 2012.

63. Ewing R, Schmid T, Killingsworth R, et al. Relationship between urban sprawl and physical activity, obesity, and morbidity. *Am J Health Promot.* 2003;18:47–57.

CHAPTER

4

How to Design and Finance Workplace Health Promotion Programs

Michael P. O'Donnell

INTRODUCTION

The purpose of this chapter is to describe a process that can be used by any employer or consultant to design a workplace health promotion program. It incorporates the AMSO Framework and draws on the definition of health promotion articulated by the American Journal of Health Promotion[1] (See Table 4-1). The process also reflects the findings of a benchmarking study conducted by the author on the best workplace health promotion programs.[2]

The goal of that study was to identify the best *workplace health promotion programs* in the United States and determine what made them different from the hundreds of

Table 4-1: Definition of Health Promotion.

"Health Promotion is the art and science of helping people discover the synergies between their core passions and optimal health, enhancing their motivation to strive for optimal health, and supporting them in changing their lifestyle to move toward a state of optimal health. Optimal health is a dynamic balance of physical, emotional, social, spiritual, and intellectual health. Lifestyle change can be facilitated through a combination of learning experiences that enhance awareness, increase motivation, and build skills and, most important, through the creation of opportunities that open access to environments that make positive health practices the easiest choice."

Source: M. O'Donnell, *American Journal of Health Promotion*, 2009.

other programs in place. The eight elements unique to these programs are shown in Table 4-2. These elements are organized in a matrix in terms of the impact of the element on program outcome and the level of control a typical program manager would have over building that element into their program. For example, linking the goals of the program to the business goals of the organization has a major impact on the effectiveness of the program and is also something the typical program manager can control. The manager can articulate the goals of the organization and align the program goals to support these organization goals. Not surprisingly, another factor that was very important in determining the success of the program was strong top management support. Unfortunately, in the short term, the typical program manager has little control over how much support they receive from top management. Interestingly, having a large program budget was only moderately important in determining the success of a program. Most of the programs studied did have generous budgets, but many of the programs not deemed among the "best" also had strong program budgets. A strong program budget is important, but it is not sufficient to make a program successful.

The striking finding of this study was that management-related factors were more important than programming factors in determining the success of the program. The typical health promotion program manager who is trained as a health expert tends to focus on the health dimensions of a program and often neglects how the program ties into the organization. A team putting together a new health promotion program should build each of these eight qualities into their new program.

The design process described here has three basic stages: preparing for the design process, collecting data and determining the program content and management structure for the program.

PHASE I: STRUCTURING THE DESIGN PROCESS

The design process described here is fairly elaborate and participatory. It assumes that the organization is starting at the beginning, not yet having decided even whether it is ready to develop a health promotion program. Each organization will have to adapt this process to meet its specific situation and the protocols it normally follows to develop a program.

Before an organization starts the design process, it should prepare for the design process by answering four basic questions:

1. How ready is the organization to develop a health promotion program?
2. Are the program outcome expectations realistic?

Table 4-2: Characteristics of Best Workplace Health Promotion Programs.

	Low Impact	Medium Impact	High Impact
High Control		• effective communicaton • communicate evaluation results	• link programs to business goals
Medium Control		• evaluation component	• incentive program
Low Control		• strong budget	• supportive culture • top management support

3. How participative a process does the organization want to follow in designing the program?
4. How extensive a design process does it wish to follow?

Each of these questions is discussed in the paragraphs that follow.

Stages of Readiness

Table 4-3 shows the various *stages of readiness* in which an organization might find itself and the action it should take for that level of readiness. This is not an exhaustive list of stages, but it covers the full range of situations.

At one extreme, an analyst or program proponent might find that the organization or key decision makers are not at all interested in health promotion. Starting a design process would be a waste of time. Although a *feasibility study* might uncover some good financial arguments for the program and some pockets of support, it would probably not be taken seriously if no interest exists and would be difficult to complete without a fair degree of cooperation. The analyst or proponent could probably best use his or her time selling the concept.

In another case, the decision makers might be totally sold on the concept and committed to developing a program, but, because of lack of knowledge of program options and benefits, employees might have little interest in the programs. The proponent might de-emphasize the cost/benefit part of the research and follow a design process committed to heavy employee participation.

In some companies, extensive research on feasibility and employee interests may have been completed, and the desired program has been outlined. Collecting extensive additional data and taking months to analyze it might exhaust the patience of the leadership and allow excitement to develop a program to dissipate. The effort might be most successful if it bypasses much of the research and design phases described here and proceeds directly to implementation.

Finally, if the organization is committed to developing a program but resources are inadequate to develop a comprehensive one, the program designer might do additional research to establish the need and secure the resources for a more comprehensive program.

Each organization should determine its stage of readiness within the continuum shown in Table 4-3 and enter the design process at the appropriate stage.

Setting Realistic Goals

As a discipline, workplace health promotion is in the mid-adolescent stage. Some significant programs have been in place for almost 50 years, and the vast majority of large workplaces have some form of program.[3] Health promotion programs are found in all types of large and small, white- and blue-collar, public and private sector organizations. As a science, health promotion is pushing from its late childhood to early adolescence. Major teaching institutions offer health promotion majors; major research institutions are involved in health promotion; thousands of studies have been published on the health impact of programs; behavior

Table 4-3: Stages of Organizational Readiness.

Stage	Action
Not interested	Sell the concept or wait
Interested in concept but not sure if it will work	Conduct feasibility study
Sold on concept	Conduct needs assessment
Impatient for program	Implement quickly

change theory is finally being translated into practical applications and health promotion concepts have been integrated into national policy. In clinical settings, intensive health promotion techniques have even been able to reduce heart disease.[4] Despite this progress, the science of workplace health promotion still has many limits. In fact, as our science has improved, the limits of our current programs become more clear.

It *is* realistic to

- Engage a large portion of employees in programs
- Help a significant portion of participants to improve in some areas, including
  - Quit smoking
  - Reduce dietary fat consumption
  - Reduce blood pressure
  - Reduce cholesterol
  - Reduce absenteeism
  - Increase seat belt use
  - Increase levels of physical activity
  - Reduce heavy alcohol use
  - Reduce medical costs
  - Learn how to better manage stress

It *may not* be realistic to see a substantial number of employees

- Lose weight
- Improve fitness
- Increase fruit and vegetable consumption

It is *not* realistic to:

- Expect no relapses to past poor health behaviors
- Reverse significantly deteriorated health conditions in less than five years
- Expect major improvements in health conditions without major effort
- Expect health improvements to continue after a program is discontinued

It is also *not* realistic to:

- Expect 100% participation in programs
- See major reduction in health care expenditures within a few years without major investments in the programs
- See increased job output from all participants in the program

As we perfect our methods, improve our diffusion of knowledge among health promotion professionals, and perfect our execution, we should expect lower relapse rates, greater success in reversing significantly deteriorated health conditions, and higher participation rates in programs. We should never expect major payoffs to the sponsoring organization without a significant investment of resources.

The program developer must also be assertive, yet realistic about getting clarification on what top management will agree to in the design and implementation of the program. The developer should be assertive by insisting that health promotion be treated as an investment that will benefit the organization, not as an extravagant benefit for employees that can be cut when money is short. The organization may discover through the health promotion program that it should enhance some of its communication practices, refine its organization structure, or do a better job of involving employees in its decision making. Although the need for these changes might be recognized as a result of the health promotion program, they are changes that will ultimately facilitate the organization's basic goals.

Major shifts that benefit the health promotion program but detract from the organization's basic mission or clash with its culture should not be expected. For example, allowing employees flextime or time off work to participate in programs might have a significant impact on success of the program but may be impractical in many organizations. Flexible (or cafeteria) benefits may generate funds for the health promotion program by allowing employees to apply some of their benefit dollars to programs. However, if the cost of developing and managing a flexible benefit program is greater than the projected benefits of the health promotion program, it has little chance of being implemented.

The ultimate corporate goal of the health promotion program is to make the organization better able to achieve its strategic goals.

Therefore, the health promotion program must be molded to fit the organization. The organization will not be molded to fit the health promotion program.

Table 4-4 shows the likelihood of achieving various organization goals with each of the different levels of programs. For example, the table suggests it is unlikely that an awareness program will reduce medical care costs but it is probable that a program that utilizes all four

Table 4-4: Impact of Program Levels on Achieving Organization Goals.

Organization Goals	Level I Awareness Only	Level II 2-3 AMSO Elements	Level III 4 AMSO Elements
Enhance Image			
General visibility	unlikely	maybe	very probable
Recruiting	maybe	maybe	very probable
Institutional relationships	unlikely	maybe	maybe
Related product image	unlikely	maybe	probable
Enhance Productivity			
Morale	probable	probable	very probable
Turnover	unlikely	maybe	very probable
Absenteeism	maybe	probable	very probable
Physical stamina	unlikely	probable	probable
Emotional hardiness	unlikely	maybe	probable
Desire to work	maybe	maybe	very probable
Reduce Medically Related Costs			
Medical crises	unlikely	maybe	probable
Medical premiums	maybe	probable	very probable
Disability costs	maybe	probable	very probable
Workers compensation costs	maybe	maybe	probable
Life insurance	unlikely	maybe	maybe

elements of the *AMSO Framework* will reduce medical care costs. This table will help the design team and management set realistic goals for the program. The typical struggle occurs when top management wants to achieve a wide range of ambitious organization goals but wants to invest a small amount of money. This chart helps them realize significant programs will be required to achieve significant organization goals. If there is a mismatch between goals and budget, one of the two must change. This table should be used during the initial planning stages and later in the process when actual program content is being developed.

Employee Involvement in the Design Process

Participation by employees in the design process is essential to the success of the program. Employees must know that the program is designed to meet *their* needs and that *their* involvement is critical to the success of the program.

The degree of employee involvement in the design process for the health promotion process should be significant in all organizations but should fall within the range of employee involvement in other comparable decision processes in that organization. The range of participation levels is listed in Table 4-5.

The employees' level of authority within this design process might be further defined or limited to developing components of the program. For example, top management might have authority to set financial budgets; a consultant or subject-matter expert might have authority to determine specific curriculum and protocols; and the employees on the design committee might have authority to determine specific topics, program components, types of promotional efforts, and operational protocols.

Employee Committee

An *Employee Health Promotion Committee* can provide a very effective mechanism to ensure employee involvement in the design process. The committee will probably be most effective and efficient if it has at least six and no more than sixteen members, representing the types of employees listed here.

- Top management spokesperson
- Health benefits manager
- Education and training manager
- Recreation programs coordinator
- Recruiting employment manager
- Medical department coordinator
- Employee association(s) representative
- Union representative(s) (if a large portion of employees is represented by unions)
- Employee(s)-at-large representing various departments
- Middle management representative(s)
- Facilitator
- Communication manager
- Technical expert

A smaller committee is easier to manage; a larger committee may provide better representation of important interest groups.

Table 4-5: Degree of Employee Participation in the Design Process.

1. Top management directs process and makes all decisions
2. Top management directs process and makes all decisions but seeks input
3. Top management retains decision making but shares direction of process
4. Top management shares decision making and direction of process
5. Employees direct process and decision making

Committees provide an excellent mechanism for involving employees in decision making, for generating ideas, and for stimulating input from many interest groups. Committees can also be very time-consuming and get bogged down in the decision making process. Committees will be most effective if their purpose and degree of authority in each area covered is clearly stated and if they are coordinated by an experienced facilitator. Table 4-6 shows the topics of meetings of an actual committee in which the participation level (from Table 4-5) was "Top management shares decision making and direction of the process with employees."

Knowledge and Expertise Required to Design a Health Promotion Program

Employees on the committee should be given authority to set goals and policies to the extent approved by the organization. They should be involved in selecting program topics and developing program protocols, but they should be careful not to exceed their level of knowledge and skill in clinical and organizational areas of health promotion. The individuals responsible for designing the program should have expertise in all of the following areas:

- Organizational theory
- Group process
- Operations management
- Communication and marketing methods
- Motivation techniques
- Design process
- Clinical aspects of health promotion, including
  - health assessment
  - fitness
  - nutrition
  - stress management
  - smoking cessation
  - medical self-care
  - social health

Table 4-6: Topics of Meetings in Typical Design Process.

Meeting Number	Topics Covered at Meeting
1	Stimulus for program Role and process clarification Education on health promotion
2	Education on health promotion Presentation of data collected to date
3	Education on health promotion Data collection plan
4	Report on data collection findings
5	Synthesis: Organization and health improvement goals
6	Synthesis: Program content and administrative structure
7	Discussion of proposal 1st draft
8	Discussion of proposal 2nd draft
9	Ratification of 3rd draft to be sent to top management

Few organizations will have all of these knowledge areas represented within their existing staff. They can develop or acquire knowledge in these areas by educating existing staff, hiring new staff members with the necessary knowledge, or working with a consultant.

Magnitude of the Design Process

An extensive design process will not be necessary for all organizations. Organizations that have already completed some phases of the process described above can skip those stages. Organizations that know ahead of time that they want a very simple program do not need an extensive process. Organizations working with external vendors can sometimes rely on the vendor's expertise and shorten some of the steps. Each organization must determine the extent of the process appropriate for its needs but err on the side of a more extensive process. The process described here is probably most appropriate for an organization with 4,000-10,000 employees. Smaller or larger employers or those developing less-comprehensive programs can follow the same framework but adjust the magnitude of the design process accordingly.

Extra time and resources spent on collecting data will provide additional baseline data for later measures of program success. Extra time and resources spent in the design process will increase the opportunity for employee involvement and the likelihood of an appropriate design. Extra time and resources spent on implementation will increase the chances of having a program that is introduced effectively. A surprisingly large number of employers simplify this process and rely on vendors for guidance on many of the issues described here. While this saves significant time in the short run, it reduces the employer's understanding of the intricacies of the program and increases the employer's dependence on the vendor.

Developing and implementing a health promotion program in moderate- to large-sized organizations normally takes 6 to 18 months but can sometimes take years. The typical development timetable is shown in Table 4-7. The time can be on the short side if management is committed to moving quickly and resources are available to design and implement a program. The timetable can be compressed significantly if pressure to reduce medical care costs is severe, or if an outside group, like the health insurance vendor, implements a turnkey program. In many cases, however, there is a longer period of "gestation" in which management is becoming familiar with the health promotion concept and is not yet ready to develop a program. In general, the process takes longer in larger organizations, especially if data is required from multiple locations, multiple levels of approval are required, and programs are implemented over time at different locations.

Table 4-7: Development Timetable.

Stage of Development	Timetable
Gestation	0-24 months
Assessment	2-12 months
Design	2-12 months
Approval	1-12 months
Implementation	3-36 months

PHASE II: COLLECTING DATA— CONDUCTING A FEASIBILITY STUDY OR NEEDS ASSESSMENT

The second major step in the design process is collecting data to gather the information necessary to design the program. This can take the form of a **feasibility study** or a **needs assessment**. In some instances, the data collection may be designed to determine if the organization should or should not develop a program. In these cases the data collection might be called a "feasibility study." In other circumstances the decision to develop the program may have already been made, and the data collection may be designed to determine how the program should be developed. This data collection might be called a "needs assessment."

The specific focus and the use of the information derived from these two types of studies will be slightly different, but the tools and process used for both will be very much the same. Moreover, a comprehensive feasibility study can answer both whether or not a program should be developed and how it should be developed. Organizations that have already decided to develop a program can make slight adaptions to this approach in data collection.

If an organization expects to evaluate the effectiveness of its program in achieving stated goals, it should expect to collect some data in addition to the basic data collected for the feasibility study.

The feasibility study answers the basic question: Is it feasible for this organization to develop and operate a health promotion program? Five specific questions are addressed in dealing with this basic issue:

1. What are the organization's goals and motives for considering the development of a program?
2. Is a health promotion program a cost-effective investment for this organization?

3. What are the levels of support, need, and interest among employees, middle managers, and top managers?
4. Does the organization have access to the necessary resources within the organization and the community?

If the answers to the first four questions indicate that the program is feasible, the last question is:

5. What are the key factors that should be considered during the actual program design process?

In addition to answering the basic feasibility questions, this study provides much of the background information required for the design process and provides an opportunity to promote the health promotion program among many of the people who will be crucial to its success. It also provides much of the baseline data against which future progress can be measured.

The time and other resources spent on the feasibility study should be determined by the quality of information required and by the impact of that information on the eventual design process. A basic study will take an experienced analyst 40-120 hours over 4-16 weeks if needed data is readily available. If the study is for a large organization, if data are not available, if a major investment needs to be made in the program, or if there is significant controversy surrounding the prospect of a program, the study can take far more time.

Clarification of Motives and Goals

"We want to have a health promotion program. Let's design one like XYZ Company. The program can reduce our medical care costs, enhance our image, and improve our productivity." This is the typical summary of an employer explaining the concept of and goals for a health promotion program. Unfortunately, if the concept and goals are not further clarified before a program is developed, achieving any of the stated benefits will be almost entirely coincidental.

To be successful, the employer's position should be rephrased. "We want to reduce medical care costs, improve our productivity, and enhance our image. We will develop a health promotion program designed to achieve these goals." With this approach, the employer decides which benefits are most important and then designs a program specifically to achieve them.

It is all right for the organization to:

- Think the health promotion concept makes sense and, therefore, to want to develop a program.
- Be altruistic and want to improve the well-being of its employees by sponsoring a health promotion program.
- Expand the goals of the program after it has had more experience with the program and better understands the potential benefits.

However, in designing the programs, the goals must be clarified and the design process must be directed by the goals. If not, there is much less chance the program will benefit the organization. Major problems in the mismatch of design and goals occur for the following reasons:

- Most managers and executives don't know enough about health promotion programs to realize the time required for the design process.
- Most health promotion program designers don't understand organizations well enough to know the range of benefits that may result from the programs—nor do they understand program design or health promotion well enough to design the program to achieve specific goals.

- Most health promotion program designers don't understand group process well enough to help the organization articulate the goals for the program.
- Many organizations don't adequately clarify the goals of any of their activities.

If the goals of the program are going to be adequately clarified, significant effort will be required to direct the goal clarification process. This will include convincing top management that goal clarification sessions are necessary. The extent of the goal clarification process and the overall program design process will, of course, depend on the extent of the program to be designed.

Most of the goals of the program can be categorized under two headings: *management goals* and *health goals*. Management goals will include reduction in medical care costs, enhanced image, and improved productivity. Health goals will address the level of health change desired and the specific *area* of change, such as nutrition or fitness. Management and health goals will not always be achieved through the same program design, and the relative priorities of the two will certainly impact the focus of the program.

For example, if the management goal of reducing medical care costs were the primary goal, the following process might be followed:

1. Analyze past, current, and projected health care expenditures for patterns and high-cost areas.
2. Determine current and projected future health conditions of employees as they relate to health care expenditures. This is done through health screenings and by reviewing medical insurance and worker's compensation records.
3. Determine which health conditions have the greatest impact on cost and

which can be successfully addressed by health promotion programs.

4. Perform a cost/benefit analysis to determine which programs produce benefits that are greater than their cost.
5. Investigate methods to correct or prevent the high-cost health conditions that cannot be affected by health promotion.
6. Develop methods to track the impact of the program on health care costs.
7. Develop health promotion programs that will have the greatest impact on medical care costs. These will probably include special programs for employees with the highest medical care costs, smoking cessation, hypertension control, prevention of lower back problems, auto safety, and general injury prevention programs.

If the goal is a health goal, such as reducing the incidence of heart attacks, the following very different process might be followed:

1. Determine causes of heart attacks.
2. Determine which of these causes can be affected by health promotion programs.
3. Conduct screening of employees to identify cardiac risk factors.
4. Determine which programs are most effective in reducing the cardiac risk factors in the employee population.
5. Investigate methods to correct the cardiac risk factors that cannot be reduced by the health promotion program.
6. Develop methods to track the impact of the programs on cardiac risk factors.
7. Develop the programs that will have the greatest impact on cardiac risk factors. These will probably include nutrition, smoking cessation, fitness, stress management, hypertension control, and social support enhancement.

If the goal is a management goal to enhance the image of the organization, the following process might be followed:

1. Determine the groups and individuals whose perception of the organization is most important.
2. Determine the components of a health promotion program most likely to shape this group's perception and develop these programs.
3. Develop mechanisms to capitalize on the image value of the program.
4. Investigate methods to enhance image other than the health promotion program.
5. Develop methods to track the impact of the program on image.
6. Develop other non-health promotion programs that will have the greatest impact on image.

In most cases there will be multiple goals. The challenge to the program designer is to accurately determine the relative priorities of the goals and to design the program to achieve the appropriate balance of benefits in each of the goal areas.

In virtually every case, a third major consideration–in addition to the health and organization goals–will be limits on the human, financial, spatial, and time resources available for the program. These will limit the range of program options considered and will force the programs to be designed in such a way that they achieve the greatest possible return on investment.

The importance of clarifying motives and goals is illustrated by the results of the benchmarking study. The most successful programs tied their program goals to the organization's goals. If the goals are not clarified, the goals cannot be aligned.

It is often difficult for an organization to clarify the goals of a proposed health promotion program. This is true because most executives do not have a precise understanding of the potential benefits of a health promotion program. Also, all large organizations are composed of many decision makers or top managers. It would not be unusual for one manager to expect the health promotion program to reduce medical care costs by 15 percent and another manager within the same organization to expect the program to have no impact on medical care costs. One solution to this problem is to have a clear protocol for clarifying goals. The five-step process outlined here has been used effectively by a number of organizations to clarify goals.

Cost/Benefit Analysis Projections

Like any other program in the organization, the health promotion program should not be a frill. It should pay for itself in terms of the benefits it brings to the organization. Some of these benefits will be tangible and measurable, such as reduced medical care costs or reduced absenteeism. Others will be more difficult to measure but equally valuable, such as improved image. Projecting the financial returns a program may generate is not simple, but it can and should be done as part of the feasibility study to determine if the program is a good investment for the organization.

Levels of Support and Areas of Interest

Broad-based and strong support among all levels of employees is critical to the success of the health promotion program. Measuring the level of support during the research phase will show how support figures into the overall design strategy. If support is very strong, that alone may be enough to convince those in power that a program should be developed. If support is very weak but all other measures in the feasibility study indicate that a health promotion program makes sense, program designers should be prepared to allocate a significant portion of resources to promotion of the program. Support should be measured at three levels:

1. Top management
2. Middle management
3. General employee population

Support at all levels is important, but support from top management is probably the most important if the program is going to get off the ground. This support means much more than just agreeing with the concept of the program. Positive answers to all of the following questions show strong support. For example, will top management agree to the following:

- Will they act as a role model by participating in the program?
- Will they promote the program regularly through formal and informal statements of support?
- Will they provide financial backing for the program?
- Will they provide administrative support through facilities maintenance, financial access to communication channels, and effective supervision?
- Will they be open to reviewing and possibly changing policies that do not encourage a healthy lifestyle?

Table 4-8 shows a more detailed set of questions that can be used in structured interviews with top managers. These interviews will also provide an opportunity to articulate the mission, long-term goals, and current priorities of the organization.

Middle managers are the final gatekeepers to the employees' participation in the program. The key question that must be answered about their support is: Will these managers allow, facilitate, and encourage their employees to participate in the programs?

Table 4-8: Questions to Ask Top Managers.

1. Program Content
    - What is your concept of a health promotion program?
    - What kinds of programs would work best for this organization?
    - What level of programs (awareness, behavior change, supportive environments) makes the most sense for this organization?

2. Support
    - Would you personally participate in the program?
    - Would you encourage the managers who report to you to participate in the program and to encourage their employees to participate?
    - Would you be available to help in promoting the program to employees in general?
    - Would you be available to troubleshoot if the program needs help?
    - How strong do you expect support for the program to be at each level of the organization?

3. Benefits
    - What do you see as the qualitative and quantitative benefits of a health promotion program for this organization? What percentage improvements would you see in medical care costs and productivity?

4. Budget
    - How much would you budget for the program?

5. Strategy
    - What do you recommend to make the program successful?
    - What do you see as possible obstacles to be aware of and overcome?

6. Organization Priorities
    - What is the organization's mission?
    - What are the organization's long-term goals?
    - What are the organization's current priorities?

Among the general employee population, the questions of support are simple ones: Do employees want the programs? Will they participate?

As simple as these questions are, measuring support is difficult because most people don't know what a health promotion program is and, worse yet, harbor false impressions. This was evidenced by one senior manager whose young wife was involved in competitive aerobics classes. He said he didn't want to do aerobics because he thought he would look silly wearing tights and dancing to music. He didn't realize aerobics includes a wide range of cardiovascular exercises (like running, swimming, and bicycling) and that none of these programs required wearing skimpy attire. Another middle manager did not want to take a stress management class because she equated this with meditation, which she felt was a form of faddish Eastern religion. She envisioned the group discussions as threatening encounter groups with sexual overtones. Another senior manager was afraid of health promotion programs because he thought he would have to build a fitness facility and talk people into becoming body builders. Another employee was nervous about participating in a health screening because she thought the results would be shared with her supervisor. Many employees have been concerned about participating in health screenings because they were concerned about losing medical insurance coverage.

Support must sometimes be measured indirectly because of these misconceptions. If a top manager wants to focus effort on reducing medical care costs and has a strong concern for her own well-being and the well-being of her employees, she can probably be counted as an advocate of the program because she supports what it stands for. An employee who wants to exercise more, stop smoking, eat better, or learn to relax and who also feels comfortable accepting guidance from her employer would probably be a supporter of the program even though she does not know what it is.

Personal interviews are probably the most accurate method to measure support in this context. The interview allows the analyst to assess the employees' understanding of the programs and factor that knowledge into the interpretation of their comments. The analyst also has the opportunity to explain the elements of a program and clear up any misconceptions. Unfortunately, interviews take a lot of time. They should be used with members of top management and key non-managers, but time usually will not permit extensive interviews with the general employee population.

Questionnaires are the most practical tool to use with large groups of employees, but they do have some limitations. One of the biggest limitations is that the analyst does not know how the employee's understanding of the questionnaire or misconceptions about health

promotion programs might bias the answers. Validity and reliability testing can reduce this problem, but most health promotion managers do not know how to perform these tests. Also, response rates to such questionnaires are often less than 30% of the employee population. This is problematic because those who do not respond often have different opinions and practices than those that do respond. Group interviews, called focus groups, can supplement the information provided by questionnaires.

Questionnaires for managers might address the following issues:

- Perceptions of levels of specific problems in the organization in areas that may be impacted by the health promotion program
- Beliefs on the potential impact of a health promotion program in the organization's specific problem areas
- Managers' general level of support for the program
- Program content interests

Points to address in questionnaires sent to employees should cover the following:

- Current health practices in each health area (e.g., exercise, nutrition, etc.)
- Interest in improving health practices in each health area
- Interest in participating in programs sponsored by the employer in each health area
- Perception of how well the employer is encouraging positive health practices in each health area

Questionnaires to measure employee's health practices, interests, and levels of perceived organizational support can be developed internally or purchased from external vendors. External vendors can also take on the time-consuming task of tallying and summarizing responses. Developing a high-quality questionnaire is difficult and time consuming and should not be attempted unless the developer is skilled in this area. Newly developed questionnaires should be refined for clarity through pilot testing and analyzed for psychometric properties (validity and reliability) through further testing. Without this type of testing, it is not likely that the information collected by the questionnaire will be very useful. Also, it is critical that responses are received from a sufficiently large sample.

Vendors selling standardized questionnaires should be asked to demonstrate that their questionnaires have strong psychometric properties. Also, standardized questionnaires should be used only if they include the specific information relevant to the program design effort.

A growing number of vendors can develop custom questionnaires to address individual needs of different organizations, process the responses, and provide summary reports for a reasonable cost.

Some organizations use a *health risk assessment* (HRA) to collect information to design a program. This is a tempting strategy because the HRA does measure employee health risks and provide computer tallies of the results. This is now financially feasible because the cost of an online HRA is so low, however, because the HRA requires so much information from employees, the response rate is often low and biased toward people who are interested in making health improvements. As discussed later, response rates can be increased significantly with the appropriate promotion and incentives, but this is sometimes difficult to do during the planning process, i.e. before a program is fully launched.

Discussing specific questionnaire content is beyond the scope of this chapter. However, any questionnaire attempting to measure employee health behaviors and interest in participating in programs will be of limited value if it does not measure the employees readiness to change each health behavior.[5] Understanding stage of readiness to change is critical to preparing the types of programs most appropriate for the population and for projecting participation rates.

Access to Resources

The resources required to develop and operate the program include money, space, technical knowledge, and staff to run the programs. The organization's ability to finance the program is independent of the cost/benefit value of the program. In addition to recognizing the cost/benefit value, the organization must have access to liquid assets to develop and operate the program. An organization might project it will earn $2 for every $1 it invests in the program; but if it does not have sufficient cash reserves, it may not be able to start the program.

Space is often a problem for organizations located in or close to urban areas, especially when they want to provide fitness facilities. Fortunately, many programs do not require fitness facilities or extensive space.

Technical knowledge on program design, curriculum development, and health assessment—among other areas—is necessary to develop the program. Skilled staff are required to operate it. The organization must have these resources within its employee group or be able to contract for them in the community. Contracting for these services will not be a problem for most organizations in urban settings in the United States but may be difficult for organizations in small towns or in countries that do not have extensive health promotion capabilities.

Program Development Issues

After the organizational goals are clarified, the cost/benefit analysis is completed, levels of interest are measured, and support and access to resources are determined, the organization should be able to determine if it is feasible to develop a health promotion program. If it determines that the program is feasible, it should then address program development issues. The basic program development question it must answer is: If the health promotion program seems to be a good investment of the organization's resources and the organization can draw all the necessary resources from itself and the community, how should it proceed in developing the program? More specifically:

- What departments and individuals should be involved in developing the program?
- What are the various combinations of community and organizational resources that can be used to develop the program?
- Which of the program focus options seem to be most appropriate for achieving the stated organization and health goals?
- What will be the major obstacles to overcome in developing the program?

The answers to these questions give management a clear view of what is required to move to the next step — developing program content.

PHASE III: PROGRAM DESIGN— DEVELOPING PROGRAM CONTENT AND MANAGEMENT STRUCTURE

Program design is the third major phase in developing the program. Although this phase is described as having finite limits — starting after the feasibility study and ending before implementation — the actual design of the program will continue to evolve as it becomes integrated into the organization. This evolution will be visible if the program has a scheduled evaluation and readjustment phase or is implemented on a pilot or phased-in basis. The program will continue to evolve in all cases, even when the evolution is not visible.

Results of the Program Design Phase

Just as the feasibility study produces a guide to lead into the program design phase, the program design phase produces a plan for implementation. The plan should be directed by a clear statement of the health change or lifestyle goals and the organizational goals of the program. Specific descriptions of program contents, program and corporate-level management systems, financing arrangements, use of outside vendors, participant policies, and an implementation schedule should be included. In many cases, specific program curricula will be developed during the design phase. This will often be less true if the program is going or phased in slowly or if course curricula are to be supplied by an outside vendor.

Factors Influencing Program Design

The importance of clearly stating the program's organizational and health improvement goals in such a way that they can guide the design process has been discussed. Unfortunately, it is often very difficult to position the program's goals as the primary factor impacting the design of the program. Myriad political forces can often skew the focus of the design. A good program designer may be able to recognize these forces and channel them to support, rather than derail, the stated goals of the program in many cases. In other cases, the program designer may be able to recognize but not influence these factors.

Quality of the Design Process

The first challenge will be to ratify stated program goals that reflect the needs of the organization. Top management may have priorities different from managers and employees. The design team's lack of understanding of health promotion programs may further confuse the goal ratification process. The impact of these difficulties can be reduced by educating the design team on the history, operation, and expected benefits of health promotion programs.

Securing Employee Support

The problem of securing employee and middle-management support for programs proposed by top management is common for many programs in most large organizations. Extensive management processes have been developed to address this problem. The impact of the problem can be reduced if it receives appropriate attention. This is especially important in the design and implementation of a health promotion program because it affects each participant in a very personal way. The most effective strategy is probably to involve employees and managers in all aspects of the design and management of the program, to design the program to meet their specific needs, to keep them well-informed of program developments and make transparency a centerpiece of the program.

Impact of the Program on Design Committee Members' Jobs

The development of a program can have a major impact on the jobs of managers operationally linked to the program, e.g., benefits managers, facilities managers, training directors, and managers of employee health. The new program may increase their power base, threaten their turf, increase their workload, or expose the quality of their work. In fact, in most cases, a new health promotion program will focus new attention on the management of medical care costs, rates of absenteeism and turnover, and productivity levels. This is one of the spin-off

benefits of the health promotion program. The program often provides a non-threatening environment in which to address these problems. Nevertheless, the initial exposure of these problems is often very threatening to the manager(s) in charge of these areas.

Knowledge and Experience of Design Committee Members

The background of the design team members will have a major impact on their input into the design process. A facilities manager may have an orientation toward fitness facilities, a training director toward classes, a nurse or physician toward screening programs, and a recreation leader toward sports and other fun events. Any exposure team members have had to other programs will further influence their input. If the same group were on a team designing a computer system, their biases would have less impact on their input because they would not feel knowledgeable about computers and would defer to those with technical expertise. However, most people feel they know a lot about health and health habits and can personalize the program to their own situation. Consequently, they are more vocal and allow their own personal preferences to affect their input.

Profitability and Organization Transitions

Unrelated cycles of the organization will make a difference in the design of the program. These cycles can postpone the development of the program, speed up the process, or shift its focus. For example, a pending corporate relocation might postpone the program's development until the move is made. However, the construction of *new* corporate facilities and the initiation of new management programs that usually accompany such a move might facilitate implementation of the program. A high-profit year can free funds to develop the program. A low-profit year can make funds difficult to come by. Ironically, an organization in a poor profit situation especially needs to enhance productivity, reduce medical care costs, and correct image problems that health promotion programs address. Further, the cost of a health promotion program is usually not so great that it would be a significant drain on funds. Nevertheless, in tight financial times, new programs and programs not contributing directly to the core business of the organization are often discontinued or delayed.

DESIGN OPTIONS: PROGRAM CONTENTS

Design decisions made during the design phase focus on the contents of the program, the organizational system to manage the program, and the policies governing participation in the program. The three major decisions made about program contents center on (a) the desired level of impact of the program, (b) the desired intensity of the program, and (c) the topics covered by the program.

Level of Impact

The most important decision on program content is the level of impact desired. As discussed earlier, programs that focus on enhancing *awareness* have the impact of increasing knowledge but have very little impact on behavior. *Skill building* programs help people change specific health behaviors, such as quitting smoking, starting to exercise, learning to manage stress, etc. Unfortunately, after people complete these programs, they often revert to their previous unhealthy lifestyles.[6] People will be much more likely to continue to practice healthy lifestyles on a long-term basis when they have *opportunities* that make the healthy choice the easiest choice.

Supportive cultural environments were one of the eight characteristics of the most successful programs discovered in the benchmarking study. The most successful programs take a comprehensive approach.[7] Also, as shown in Table 4-4, it is important to stress that programs with all four elements of the AMSO framework are ones most likely to achieve the organizational goals that most employers want to achieve.

Level of Intensity

The level of intensity of the program is determined by the degree of success desired in the health change goal and the level of intensity needed to achieve success. For example, in smoking cessation, systematic reviews of the literature have shown that quit rates increase as the number of minutes of counseling increase to 300, as the number of sessions increase to eight, the number of professionals leading the program reaches three, and a combination of behavior therapy and medication are used.[8] A supportive environment that includes extensive exercise facilities, frequent incentives to practice healthy behavior, and top management support will have a greater chance of success than a less intensive program. Factors determining the level of intensity include the quantity of resources invested, staff levels provided, and time spent by the participants in the programs. The increased intensity of the program will translate to increased success to the extent that the program is well designed. The most appropriate level of intensity will also be determined by the health conditions and health practices of specific employees. Given that a small portion of the employees are responsible for a majority of the medical care costs, it will be advisable to provide high-intensity programs to these employees if the goal of the program is to reduce medical care costs or to reach those with the greatest health risks.

Program Topics

Selection of topics will be relatively easy once the program goals are clearly stated and the desired level and intensity of the program are determined. Table 4-9 shows the type of programs that might be most appropriate for different health goals. Table 4-10 shows the type of programs that might be most appropriate for different organization goals. Both of these tables of programs were developed by a health promotion design committee designing an actual program. They are not intended to be the only programs appropriate for the health and organization problem areas shown. In many cases the program's health goals are not very specific and are instead directed toward improving employees' overall well-being. In those cases, a broad range of topics is normally advisable, and program topics might be selected based on what is expected to be most popular.

Also, it is valuable to be able to offer programs that are appropriate to each of the major stages of readiness to change for each of the health behavior areas. For example, the needs assessment might show that 25% of the employees are smokers, and that 40% of smokers are in the precontemplation stage, 40% are in the contemplation, and 20% are in preparation. Only the employees in preparation will likely be ready to quit and would want to participate in a formal quit-smoking program. In an organization with 1,000 employees, these values would translate to 250 smokers, 50 of whom are ready to quit. If half of them were able to sign up for a quit-smoking course right away, that would translate to 25 smokers. A classic face-to-face quit program focusing on

Table 4-9: Programs Most Appropriate for Health Goals.

Hypertension Medical evaluation and prescription Nutrition & fitness Weight control Smoking cessation Stress management	Obesity Fitness Nutrition Self-esteem training Stress management Weight control
Stress Fitness Childcare Employee assistance program (EAP) Policy review Stress management	Smoking Smoking policy Smoking cessation Fitness Weight control Stress management

Table 4-10: Programs Most Appropriate for Organization Goals.

High Medical Care Costs	Low Morale	Low Productivity
Medical self-care Risk rating Hypertension control Injury control Smoking policy Smoking cessation Medical coverage	Dependent care facilities & programs Visible fitness facilities Employee Assistance Programs (EAPs) Policy review Incentive programs Recreation programs Other visible programs	Policy review Fitness programs Dependent care facilities & programs Stress management Comprehensive programs

quitting smoking would thus be helpful to only 10% of all the smokers. A core advantage of most web-based and telephone coaching approaches is that they are designed to serve the needs of employees at all of the stages of readiness to change. An additional advantage is that there are no minimum numbers of employees that can participate at one time, and maximums can usually be handled if some warning is given... although there are some limits to the number of telephone coaches that can be available at any one time on short notice. Table 4-11 shows strategies that might be appropriate for each of the stages of readiness to change. These strategies can be adapted to each of the health behavior areas.

Table 4-11: Strategies Based on Motivational Readiness to Change.

Precontemplation
  - Unconditional acceptance
  - Indirect comments

Contemplation
  - Enhance behavioral efficacy
  - Enhance self efficacy
  - Expose social networks
  - Aspirational goal setting

Preparation
  - Learning goal setting
  - Enhance self efficacy
  - Enhance behavioral efficacy
  - Introduce to social networks

Action
  - Performance goal setting
  - Skill building
  - Engage in social networks

Maintenance
  - Maintain social networks
  - Offer leadership opportunities
  - Reinforce self efficacy
  - Reinforce behavioral efficacy

Communication, Incentives and Supportive Cultures

The final three components of the best programs in benchmarking are effective communication efforts, incentive efforts, and supportive cultures.

Effective communication programs serve the basic purpose of enhancing employee awareness about the links between health behaviors and health outcomes, but equally important, they make employees aware of many program offerings available to help them improve health practices. The most effective communication efforts are tailored to the individual characteristics of employees, including their personal priorities in life, and their motivational readiness to change. The best communication programs need to be ubiquitous to reach a large portion of the employee population, and meet high quality standards to convey a high quality health promotion program.

The primary impact of incentive programs is to enhance participation. This is critically important because only the employees in preparation will be ready to join actual programs, and this typically represents a small portion of the population, perhaps as low as 20% of employees. Incentives may be an effective way to attract the attention of the other 80% of the employees. Incentives can be intrinsic, focusing on internal values, or extrinsic, focusing on cash awards and prizes. They can take the form of simple, small-prize giveaways to people who attend an event, cash to people who complete a health screening, chances in lotteries for larger prizes, discounts on health plan premiums, or other forms. Well designed incentive programs have been shown to push participation rates to the 70% to 90% range,[9,10] however, there is little evidence that incentive programs have much impact in actually changing health behaviors.[11]

People's health behaviors are strongly influenced by the behavioral norms of their friends, family, co-workers and society at large. It is more difficult to eat junk food, take the elevator and smoke when everyone around you is eating nutritious food, taking the stairs and never smoking. Organizations with the best health promotion programs have been able to create organization cultures that facilitate positive health practices and have programs consistent with behavior change theories.

DEVELOPING A MANAGEMENT STRUCTURE

Important management decisions to be made during the design process include where to place the program in the organizational structure, how much staffing is required, how to build strong top management support, how to finance the program, how often to use

vendors and consultants, who will be eligible to participate, what will be the necessary operating procedures, and how to evaluate the program. Each of these issues is discussed briefly below.

Location in the Organizational Structure

The placement of the health promotion program in the organization will depend on the focus of the program and the related organizational goals; rank within the organizational hierarchy; and personalities, images, and workloads of various departments.

Program Focus and Goals

It makes sense to pair the program with the department most closely responsible for achieving the health or organizational goals the program is designed to achieve. If the program goal is educational, the training and development department might be most appropriate. A program centered on health screening and risk reduction might fit best in the medical or employee health department. A fitness facility with very little programming could be supervised by the facility's management department. The benefits department might be appropriate if the program is designed to reduce health care expenditures. A recreation-centered program might fit well within the employee association. If the program focus is broader and is designed to improve the overall well-being of the employees, direct management by the human resources department probably makes the most sense.

Organizational Hierarchy

The health promotion program should be at a level high enough in the organization that the manager has direct access to top management when necessary and is on the same level as line managers supervising the employees who will be enrolled in the programs.

Personalities, Images, Work Loads of Managers and Departments

A new health promotion program is in a precarious position. Because it is a new concept that is sometimes not very well-understood, much of its long-term success will depend on how well it is positioned at its inception. Ideally, the department responsible for the health promotion program should have a positive image. The manager supervising the program director should be well-respected, very supportive of the concept, a good role model, and have sufficient time to give strong support for the program during its inception.

Linkages with Other Departments

The health promotion program will normally be designed to achieve numerous organizational goals, including reducing health care expenditures, improving the corporate image, reducing absenteeism, and increasing work output. In most cases, specific departments in the organization are responsible for each of these areas. Therefore, each of these departments should be linked to the health promotion program. Additionally, other departments–such as communications, public relations, and plant management–will be important to the successful day-to-day operation of the program and should also be linked to the program. Finally, the participation of the employees from all departments in the organization is critical to the growth and survival of the program. Linkages to all of these staff support departments and to line managers in other departments should therefore be established.

The optimal mechanism for the linkage to each of these groups will be different in each case. Committees are appropriate in some cases; however, in order to be effective, they should have clear tasks and be well-managed. Recruiting key managers and employees to serve as volunteers in responsible operational roles in the program can also work.

If the program is managed by a support department such as human resources, additional links should be made directly to top management. One method is to appoint a top line manager as a figurehead leader of the program. The program manager would be responsible for all administrative functions, but the figurehead top manager would be available for troubleshooting and public relations efforts. This is analogous to the city manager/mayor form of government used in some cities or the executive director/honorary national chairperson of a national campaign.

Staffing Levels

The benchmarking study determined that the best programs have approximately one full-time professional staff person for every 1800 employees. This figure is also consistent with the staffing ratio recommended by a number of major program management companies.

Modeling Best Programs to Build Top Management Support

Having strong top management support is one of the characteristics of the best health promotion programs. Which came first? In most cases, the former *preceded* the latter. Many programs become excellent because they have strong top management support. Regardless of the current level of top management support, program developers should focus on this point as they develop their program. First, they should tell top management that strong support is one of the eight ingredients for a successful program. This may motivate some top managers to become more involved. Second, developers should ask top managers what they need to do to insure strong support from top management, make sure those things are done, and make sure top management knows these things are being done. As discussed earlier, one of the most important factors in developing top management support is linking the program to the organization's goals and making top management aware of how the program is supporting those goals.

Program Budgets and Funding

Budgets

There are no standardized recommendations on how much to budget for a comprehensive health promotion program. However, examining the budgets of successful programs can provide some guidance.

A meta analysis of 22 programs that had *returns on investment (ROI)* of 3.27 in medical cost savings and 22 programs that had returns on investment of 2.73 in absenteeism reduction reported annual budgets that averaged $144 per person and $132 per person (2009 dollars) respectively. Despite their success in producing impressive savings, their level of comprehensiveness is not known.[12]

The benchmarking study found that the average annual budget among the best programs was approximately $200 per eligible employee (not per participant) in 1996 dollars. This is consistent with the author's experience that an internally managed comprehensive program that includes awareness, motivation, skill building and opportunities costs approximately $205 (in 2012 dollars) per employee (not per participant) in an organization with at least 4,000 employees. These figures include staff salaries but do not include office space, employee benefits, overhead benefits, staff recruitment, initial training costs, or the cost of top management's supervision of the program. If fitness facilities are included, this will add an additional $100 to $200 per employee (not per participant), including amortization of construction costs over 15 years but not including land acquisition or space costs. Fitness facility costs can often be reduced by charging employees a modest membership fee.

Despite the significant expansion of the scope of the typical program in the past decade, the cost of the typical comprehensive program has not increased substantially in that period. Cost increases have been moderated in part by the cost effectiveness of web based HRAs and skill-building programs, which can often be provided for 10% to 20% of the cost of paper and pencil HRAs and in-person skill building programs. The rate of increase has also been much lower than the annual increase in medical care costs. As a result, the ability of programs to break even and to produce substantial returns on investment in medical cost savings has improved over the last decade.

Program Funding

Employers fund health promotion programs through four basic approaches, and often supplement this funding with a variety of these sources. These are listed and described below.

1. Perfunctory budgeting strategies.
2. Projected medical cost savings and productivity enhancements.
3. Integration into health plan premium.
4. Not hiring smokers.
5. Health plan supplements, vendor guarantees, employee fees.

Perfunctory Budgeting Strategies

Most employers, especially small- and medium-sized employers, fund their health promotion efforts the same way they fund every other relatively small operational purchase they make. Cost of health promotion programs are similar to the costs of office supplies, office furniture, landscaping, office parties, sports leagues, interior decorating. Given a cost of $250 per employee per year for a comprehensive program, employers realize that health promotion programs are a cost effective way to help employees improve their health, and to attract and retain the most talented workforce. The cost is half the cost of a 1% raise for a person who makes $50,000 a year and 4% of the $6000/ covered life they spend for employee health insurance each year. Employers who purchase health promotion programs with this mindset, focus on getting the best price for the program that meets their needs, and typically monitor employee participation and satisfaction, but do not attempt to measure medical cost savings or productivity enhancements. This approach is most common among small to medium sized employers who self fund their health plans.

Projected Medical Cost Savings and Productivity Enhancements

Most large employers think of their health promotion programs as investments that are likely to reduce medical costs and absenteeism, help attract and retain the best employees, and possibly enhance productivity. They are under extreme pressure to control the rate of increase in their medical care costs, and are often familiar with the literature which shows that more than 60 well-designed programs have reduced medical costs and absenteeism[13] and nearly two dozen programs have seen medical care cost savings of approximately $3 for every dollar invested plus absenteeism cost savings nearly as high, producing a total ROI of 6:1.[14] They also know that savings are not likely in the first year, breakeven is possible in the second year, and net savings are likely to be realized by the third year of the program. They might not expect to see savings of this order of magnitude from their own programs, and they usually realize that few if any product lines in their own organization produce ROIs of 6:1, but they do believe it is very likely their investment in health promotion will save more than it costs in hard dollars. They are also aware that a well-designed program can enhance employee well-being and morale. These employers work hard to get the best possible price from the vendors they hire and usually focus programs in areas that will produce financial returns. Most of them are not prepared to spend the several hundred thousand dollars necessary to conduct a well designed study on the financial return of their programs, but they do want to closely monitor effective implementation of program components, expect high levels of employee participation and satisfaction, and focus on changes in employee health risks and health conditions. They are interested in their vendors' estimates of cost savings, but may not take them too seriously.

Integrate into Health Plan

The author predicts an emerging trend, especially among large self-insured employers, in which the full cost of the health promotion program will be included in the organization's medical plan costs. The $250/person/year typical annual cost of a comprehensive health promotion program represents only 4% of the typical $6000/employee/year cost of a typical health plan. This puts the low cost of the health promotion program, relative to health plan costs, into sharp focus. The employer, then, has the option of passing some, or all, of the program cost to employees in the form of slightly higher premium payments. For example, if the employer covered 70% of the health plan cost and employees covered the 30% balance, and the same formula was applied to the health promotion program, the employee would cover $83.33 (30% x $250) of the cost, or $7/month. If the program is successful in reducing medical costs as expected, the cost increase should pay for itself in the second year and produce savings in excess of costs by the third year, resulting in no net cost to the employee or employer.

An important enabler of this emerging trend is the integration of health promotion financial incentives into medical plan premiums among large self-insured employers. Through these incentives, the amount of an employee's health plan premium is in part tied to their success in achieving health goals or participating in programs to achieve those goals. The net result is that employees who achieve all of their health goals or choose to participate in programs to achieve those goals, pay the lowest premiums, and employees who choose not to participate pay the highest premiums. A survey of large employers showed that 36% offered financial incentives for participating in programs and 8% for achieving health goals in 2009 and this grew to 80% for participation and 38% for health outcomes in 2012.[15] The major stimulus of this growth is Section 2705 of the Affordable Care Act (ACA), which confirmed in statute what was previously only in federal regulation, that employers can provide a discount on the total health plan cost for employees who participate in programs or meet health standards. The ACA confirmed the discount to be 20% through the end of 2013, specified that it would increase to at least 30% in 2014 and allowed the Secretaries of Health and Human Services and Treasury to increase the differential to as high as 50% in 2014. Regulations guiding the implementation of section 2705 were released on behalf of the Departments of Treasury, Health and Human Services, and Labor May 29, 2013, and published in the Federal Register on June 3, 2013, just a few weeks before this text went into production.[16] As such, employers and consultants are still sorting through the exact meaning of the 36 dense pages of legalese and are trying to translate what is allowed and prohibited into incentive program design. A further complication is that the agencies expect to release additional "subregulations" based on questions posed by the public or misinterpretations caused by incomplete detail in these regulations. In addition, the Equal Employment Opportunity Commission (EEOC) has not yet released its regulations. Some employers are delaying implementation of new incentive programs until the dust settles on these issues, while others are moving forward. Appendix 4-A provides a description of an approach to integrate financial incentives for health promotion programs into health plan premiums that is consistent with the regulations, cost neutral to employers, and likely to motivate the vast majority of employees to get involved in the health promotion program. This approach is likely to be refined in the coming months and years. This approach is grounded in empirical literature related to program participation and equity.

Program Participation

Two separate studies showed that health promotion programs with well-designed marketing efforts and strong support from top management had participation rates in the 20% to 40% range, while those that also offered financial incentives to participate had rates in the 70% to 90% range;[17] those in the 90% range integrated their incentives into the health plan design. [18] Using this approach to providing incentives could lead to near universal participation in health promotion programs among employees who work in organizations that offer this approach, and thus significant improvements in the health of these employees.

Health Plan Cost Equity

A study of 46,026 employees in six different organizations found that employees with no health risk factors had medical costs 70% lower than those with multiple risk factors.[19] This means that employees who are working hard to successfully manage their health but are required to pay the same premium as other employees, are being forced to subsidize employees who are not even willing to participate in programs to improve their help. Offering a 20%, 30%, or 50% premium discount to employees who achieve health goals or participate in programs to try to improve, reduces the inequity, but also continues to provide a more than fair arrangement for those who choose not to participate.

Not Hire Smokers

The American Civil Liberties Union estimated that at least 6,000 employers had policies of not hiring smokers.[20] Some, including hospitals and voluntary health organizations, adopted these policies to be consistent with their health missions. Some employers take this approach to reduce exposure of employees and customers to second hand smoke and to encourage their employees to quit. Second hand smoke alone kills an estimated 53,000 people per year, more than are killed by car crashes.[21] Smoking remains the top preventable cause of death in the United States, killing more than 400,000 people each year. This is more each year than all the deaths of all Americans in all of the foreign wars in our history.[22] Most smokers (79.3%) expect to quit at some point, a majority (58.4%) plan to do so within the next 6 months, and many of them (46.8%) actually try to quit each year,[23] so many smokers who already have jobs in these companies welcome such a policy because it gives them an extra nudge to quit. Other employers, including manufacturers who deal with toxic explosive chemicals adopt these policies for safety reasons. Finally, some employers don't hire smokers to save money. The Centers for Disease Control and Prevention estimated the annual direct medical costs of smoking at $1,623 in 1998 dollars, and the indirect costs, including time off work for smoking breaks, at $1,760 [24] for a total of $3,383 per year per smoker. Not hiring smokers provides an immediate payoff to any employer who hires new employees on a regular basis. For example, an employer with 1,000 employees, annual turnover rate of 15%, a smoking rate of 20% among new hires, and an average annual cost of $3,000 per smoker (reduced from the $3,383 estimate of CDC) who implemented a policy of not hiring smokers would save $90,000 in the first year, an additional $166,500 in the second year, and an additional $231,525 in the third year. The policy would save a total of $3,269,373 by the 10th year, $769,373 more than had been spent on the comprehensive employee health promotion during that decade. This is in addition to medical cost savings produced by the health promotion program, which would be expected to be in the $7 million range for the decade.[25]

Employers who adopt these policies report that they have few negative repercussions, among existing employees or in their communities, especially when they assure existing employees who smoke that they will not be forced to quit smoking and that their smoking status will not impact job security. However, some employers choose not to implement these policies because they are concerned about employee or community backlash.

Furthermore, not hiring smokers might not be advisable for organizations with labor shortages, especially if they need to hire large numbers of blue-collar workers, or other workers with high smoking rates. Also, employers should be aware of laws governing hiring in their states. Twenty-one states (Alabama, Alaska, Arizona, Arkansas, Delaware, Florida, Georgia, Hawaii, Idaho, Iowa, Kansas, Maryland, Massachusetts, Michigan, Nebraska, Ohio, Pennsylvania, Texas, Utah, Vermont, Washington), have no restrictions on not hiring smokers. The remaining 29 states and the District of Columbia have passed laws elevating smokers to protected status. Not hiring smokers in those states is prohibited unless the reason is job related.[26]

Health Plan Funding, Employee Fees and Vendor Guarantees

Health Plan Funding

Some employers are able to supplement program funding with contributions from health plans and employee fees and secure guarantees of savings or reimbursement of costs from vendors. For example, a survey of a national representative sample of 730 employers reported that 47.7% of employers that had health promotion programs listed their health plan as the primary funder of their health promotion program.[27] Similarly, in a more recent survey of 1,515 firms, 87% of all firms reported that most of their wellness benefits are provided by their health plan.[28] The portion was 88% for firms with 3-199 employees, 68% for firms with 200 or more employees and 56% for firms with 5,000 or more employees. The programs offered by health plans at no cost are typically online portals that can include health risk assessment screenings; skill building programs on fitness, nutrition, stress management, weight control, smoking cessation and medical self-care; and online chat groups. These programs can provide a valuable supplement to the program elements provided by the employers, but do not, by themselves, provide all the components necessary for a comprehensive program.

Employee Fees

Employers tend to avoid charging employee fees for most components of their health promotion program because they want to remove all barriers to entry. In fact, they often give employees financial incentives to join the programs. However, it is not unusual to charge fees for membership to onsite health clubs or for programs that provide nutritious meals.

Vendor Guarantees

An emerging trend that may or may not last, is for vendors to guarantee medical care cost savings that exceed program costs in exchange for sharing a portion of those savings with the vendor. Employers are normally required to follow specific implementation protocols to qualify for the guarantee. This is an interesting approach that could motivate late adopting employers to implement programs, however, there is minimal documentation on the success of this approach. One of the unintended consequences of this approach might be that employers would have an incentive to show that programs have not saved money while vendors would have an incentive to show they do save money. This could lead to conflicts between employers and providers,

and different interpretations of the same data. Vendor guarantees are described in more details in Appendix 4-C.

Given the range of funding options available to employers, and the high likelihood of a positive financial return, the financial barriers to implementing a health program might be described as minimal, at least for moderate to large employers.

Use of Vendors and Consultants

In the United States, vendors and consultants are available to serve virtually all the employer's needs related to the health promotion program. They can design the program, hire staff, build facilities, manage programs, conduct health screenings, provide face-to-face and online skill-building programs, supply materials and equipment, and evaluate programs. They can do this on a turnkey basis or piece-by-piece.

The criteria and methods used to determine whether to use vendors, how much to use them, and how to select them should be the same as those used in evaluating the use of vendors for other projects. The employer's experience in going through the same questions in developing the organization's health insurance plan, its computer capabilities, or its facilities can be helpful. The individual responsible for these decisions should have some knowledge of health promotion and be skilled in dealing with vendors. However, health promotion programs are different from computer systems in that they impact employees in a very personal way. If outside vendors are used to provide programs, effective integration of the human factor needs to be a top criteria in vendor selection. Employees need to feel that they, and not the vendor, own the program.

When all the hidden costs of an internally managed program are considered, the costs of managing a program internally and externally are comparable. Working with an outside vendor also has the additional advantages of being able to get a program started quickly without hiring new staff, and being able to terminate it when the contract period has passed, without needing to layoff any staff. It is not surprising that a large portion of workplace health promotion programs are now managed by external vendors.

Eligibility for the Program

The magnitude of the program and the method of deciding who is eligible to participate in the program should be determined during the design phase. The program can be made available to all employees or only to selected employees. The program can also be offered to spouses, children, unmarried partners, and retirees. The eligibility policy should be determined by the goals for the program and the resources available to develop it. The program might start as a small pilot project and grow on a phased-in basis until it becomes available to all employees and family. In other cases, it might start small and stay small. It might be offered to employees in one division or location; to top management; to employees with specific health conditions; to a random cross section of all employees; or on a first-come, first-served basis.

Family participation is important if a core program goal is improving health habits because it is very difficult for an employee to change a health habit without the support of close family members. This is especially true for tobacco use and nutrition. Similarly, involving the family is important if the goal is to reduce medical care costs because spouses and dependents might account for up to three-quarters of all medical claims. Given the growing pressure for most employers to reduce their medical costs, the general trend over the past decade has been for employers to engage as many employees in programs as

fast as possible, and to be less concerned about the marginal program costs for each additional employee. Employers have begun to work to engage spouses and children, but most have had only limited success.

Operating Procedures

Procedures for operating the program should be outlined during the design phase. These procedures will include staffing plans, scheduling, promotional methods, facilities maintenance, budgeting, materials and equipment management, and evaluation methods. Some of the details of these procedures will be refined during implementation and initial operation.

Evaluation Plan

An evaluation effort is an important part of every health promotion program. The benchmarking study showed that the best programs have evaluation efforts in place, and equally important, that they communicate their evaluation results. In addition to measuring the impact of the program on health outcomes, the evaluation effort should measure the extent to which it addresses the organization's long-term goals and current priorities. Of course, these findings should be communicated to top management.

The evaluation plan—including what will be evaluated, when it will be evaluated, how, by whom and for what purpose—should be specified as the program plan is developed. If the evaluation plan is not developed and approved as part of the basic program plan, it will be very difficult to start the evaluation once the program is up and running. Also, some baseline measures will need to be recorded before programs are launched so that progress against these values can be assessed. If the evaluation plan is not developed, it will be difficult to know which baseline measures need to be taken.

Approximately 5 to 10% of the program budget should be allocated to program evaluation to effectively monitor the implementation of the program and its effectiveness.

Modeling other Successful Programs

A useful exercise for advanced program developers is to review what has been written about the most highly recognized programs. The Health Project has assembled descriptions of programs that have been awarded the prestigious C. Everett Koop Award based on the success of these programs in improving health, reducing medical costs and enhancing productivity. These are featured on their website.[29]

Scorecards developed by the Health Enhancement Research Organization (HERO) and the Centers for Disease Control and Prevention (CDC) provide an excellent reference for planning a program. These scorecards were developed primarily to audit and guide the refinement of existing programs, but they can also be used proactively to serve as a road map for the development of new programs. They are briefly described in Appendix 4-D.

CONCLUSION

One of the biggest challenges facing all health promotion professionals is adapting their content training in exercise, education, psychology, nutrition, nursing, or any other clinical area to work settings. Very few of these professionals receive training in management procedures. This becomes very evident when they attempt to design a workplace health promotion program. Fortunately, protocols like those described here have been developed that work. Our challenge in health promotion program design is not so much to develop better design techniques but to make health promotion professionals aware that they exist and to improve their ability to follow them.

The next challenge for employers will be to reach beyond the workplace, into the schools, faith communities, and the other organizations in which people spend their time when they are not at work, and in which spouses and children spend their time. These efforts might even include collaborating with the employers of spouses. The goal of these outreach efforts would be to weave a web of support that reaches people several times each day with the most effective strategies where they work, shop, study, worship and relax.

APPENDIX 4-A

Integrating Financial Incentives into Health Plan Design based on Section 2705 of the Affordable Care Act and subsequent regulations

Prepared with input from James Pshock

INTEGRATE INTO HEALTH PLAN

The author predicts an emerging trend, especially among large self-insured employers, in which the full cost of the health promotion program will be included in the organization's medical plan costs. The $250/person/year typical annual cost of a comprehensive health promotion program represents only 4% of the $6000/employee/year cost of a typical health plan. This puts the low cost of the health promotion program, relative to health plan costs, into sharp focus. The employer, then, has the option of passing some, or all, of the program cost to employees in the form of slightly higher premium payments. For example, if the employer covered 70% of the health plan cost and employees covered the 30% balance, and the same formula was applied to the health promotion program, the employee would cover $83.33 (30% x $250) of the cost, or $7/month. If the program is successful in reducing medical costs as expected, the cost increase should pay for itself in the second year and produce savings in excess of costs by the third year, resulting in no net cost to the employee or employer.

An important enabler of this emerging trend is the integration of health promotion financial incentives into medical plan premiums among large self-insured employers. Through these incentives, the amount of an employee's health plan premium are in part tied to their success in achieving health goals or participating in programs to achieve those goals. The net result is that employees who achieve all of their health goals or choose to participate in programs to achieve those goals, pay the lowest premiums, and employees who choose not to participate pay the highest premiums. As mentioned in Chapter 3, a survey of large employers showed that 36% offered financial incentives for participating in programs and 8% for achieving health goals in 2009 and this grew to 80% for participation and 38% for health outcomes in 2012.[1] A more recent survey showed that providing financial rewards for not using tobacco grew from 32% of large employers in 2011 to 42% in 2012 and are projected to grow to 54% by 2014 and 71% by 2016.[2] The major stimulus of this growth is Section 2705 of the Affordable Care Act (ACA), which confirmed in statute what was previously only in federal regulation, that employers can provide a discount on the total health plan cost for employees who participate in programs or meet health standards. The ACA confirmed the discount to be 20% through the end of 2013, specified that it would increase to at least 30% in 2014 and allowed the Secretaries of Health and Human Services and Treasury to increase the differential to as high as 50% in 2014. Regulations guiding the implementation of section 2705 were released on behalf of the Departments of Treasury, Health and Human Services, and Labor on May 29, 2013, and published in the Federal Register on June 3, 2013.[3] Employers and consultants are still sorting through the exact meaning of the 36 dense pages of legalese and are trying to translate what is allowed and prohibited into incentive program design. A further complication is that the agencies expect to release additional "sub-regulations" based on questions posed by the public or misinterpretations caused by incomplete detail in these regulations. In addition, the Equal Employment Opportunity Commission (EEOC) had not yet released its regulations when this book went to press in May of 2014. Some employers are delaying implementation of new incentive programs until the dust settles on these issues, while others are moving forward. Appendix 4-A provides a description of an approach to integrate financial incentives for health promotion programs into health plan premiums that is consistent with the regulations, cost neutral to employers, and likely to motivate the vast majority of employees to get involved in the health promotion program. This approach is likely to be refined in the coming months and years.

This approach is grounded in empirical literature related to program participation and equity. Three important studies are summarized below.

Program Participation

Two separate studies showed that health promotion programs with well-designed marketing efforts and strong support from top management had participation rates in the 20% to 40% range, while those that also offered financial incentives to participate had rates in the 70% to 90% range;[4] those in the 90% range integrated their incentives into the health plan

design.[5] Using this approach to providing incentives could lead to near universal participation in health promotion programs among employees who work in organizations that offer this approach, and thus significant improvements in the health of these employees.

Health Plan Cost Equity

A study of 46,026 employees in six different organizations found that employees with no health risk factors had medical costs 70% lower than those with multiple risk factors.[6] This means that employees who are working hard to successfully manage their health are required to pay the same premium as other employees and are being forced to subsidize employees who are not even willing to participate in programs to improve their help. Offering a 20%, 30%, or 50% premium discount to employees who achieve health goals or participate in programs to try to improve, reduces the inequity, but also continues to provide a more than fair arrangement for those who choose not to participate.

Section 2705 of the Affordable Care Act confirmed that group health plans, including self-insured employers, may adjust health plan premiums based on employees participating in health promotion programs and achieving health goals. Final regulations describing how this law could be applied were published in the Federal Register on June 3, 2013. The recommendations on how to integrate these new regulations into health plan premium design are described below, with three cautions. 1) These recommendations were written a few months after the regulations were released, and will no doubt be refined as the intention of specific sections of the regulations become more clear. 2) The agencies expect to release sub-regulations based on questions from the public and misinterpretations of the regulations. 3) The Equal Employment Opportunity Commission has not yet released it regulations.

KEY PROVISIONS OF THE FEDERAL REGULATIONS

The federal regulations are presented in a format and tone that no doubt makes sense to lawyers and regulators, but are baffling to the typical health promotion professional. The key elements of the federal regulations are summarized below in greatly abbreviated form, and in terms that are more likely to be understandable to health promotion professionals.

INTENTION OF THE FEDERAL REGULATIONS

Language in the federal regulations make it clear that the authors of the regulations want to make it possible for employees who chose to participate in health promotion programs to receive the full discount, even if they do not achieve specified health goals. On page 33160, they state the following: "The intention of the Departments in these final regulations is that, regardless of the type of wellness program, every individual participating in the program should be able to receive the full amount of any reward or incentive, regardless of any health factor." They operationalize this intention through the concept of a "reasonable alternative standard," which essentially allows anyone who does not meet any health goal an alternative method (or alternative standard to meet) to earn the discount if they are willing to work toward that goal by participating in programs or making progress toward the goal. However, later language makes is clear that the authors of the regulations are not attempting to eviscerate discounts based on achieving health outcomes. On page 33165 they state the following: "The requirement to provide a reasonable alternative standard to all individuals who do not meet or achieve a particular health outcome is not intended to transform all outcome-based wellness

programs to participatory wellness programs." These two intentions in the regulations, which initially seem contradictory, should guide the design of any incentive program integrated into a health plan premium structure.

TYPES OF INCENTIVE STRUCTURES

The federal regulations recognize three basic types of incentive structures (although they refer to these types of incentive programs as types of "wellness programs" instead of incentive structures). 1) Participatory. The most basic incentive program is based on a reward or discount being provided based on an employee merely participating in a program, such as a health screening, a lecture series, etc, without any requirement to meet a health goal. 2) Health Contingent -Activity-Only. The next level of incentive program is based on a reward or discount being provided based on an employee completing an activity such as a running program, following a specific diet, etc. This type of incentive might be offered as the initial incentive or as reasonable alternative standard for employees who fail to achieve a specific health outcome 3) Outcome Based. The final level of incentive program is based on achieving a specific health goal, such as not using tobacco, having normal biometric values, normal weight, passing a fitness test, etc.

The only restrictions on Participatory incentives are to make them available to all "similarly situated individuals" (ie employees covered by the health plan, and their covered dependents if the health promotion program and incentive program is extended to them), and accommodating people who have medical issues that make it difficult to participate. Health Contingent-Activity-Only and Outcome-Based incentive programs must meet five criteria: 1) allow people the opportunity to qualify at least once a year, 2) limit rewards to 30% of the total health plan premium, or 50% if tobacco use is part of the incentive, 3) be offered in the context of a health promotion program with a "reasonable design" that is likely to help the employee improve their health, 4) provide an "alternative standard" that an employee can meet if they are not able to perform the original activity or achieve the health standard. For Health-Contingent Activity Only, the alternative standard can be limited to situations with medical issues. For outcomes-based, the alternative cannot be limited to situations with medical issues. For Outcomes-Based Incentives, the employer can require physician verification of a medical reason the employee cannot perform the activity, but cannot require this for not meeting the health goal. 5) the means to achieve the alternative standard must be included in all promotional documents that describe the details of how to earn the incentive. The reward limits and the alternative standard are described in more detail below.

AMOUNT OF DISCOUNTS

Through the end of 2013, the maximum reward or discount was 20% of the total value of the health plan premium, including the employer and employee contribution. Beginning in 2014, the maximum discount increased to 30%, with the provision that an extra 20% can be added to programs that target tobacco use, for a total of 50%. The employer has the option of presenting these amounts from a positive perspective as incentives or discounts, or a negative perspective, as surcharges or penalties. The incentives can also take the form of contributions to health savings accounts, or expanded forms of health coverage.

According to language on page 33163 of the regulations, the full amount of the discount must be "paid" in the year in which it is earned, even if the employee meets the standard at the end of the year and after cycling through a series of alternative standards over the span of the year. If necessary, it can be "paid" retroactively or prorated over the balance of a plan year. However, language written

in a Frequently Asked Questions document released on January 9, 2014, seems to indicate that the amount of the discount can be reduced or even eliminated if an employee does not attempt to meet the alternative standard by the deadline set by the employer.[7] In the original regulations, the regulators acknowledged that there may be confusion on this point, and future sub-regulations may be necessary. The discount can be limited to the premium for the employee or can include the premium for spouses and dependents if they have convenient access to all aspects of the program. Employers have discretion on how to allocate the reward based on the "performance" of the individual family members in meeting or not meeting the various standards. Besides the requirement to include tobacco use in rewards of 50% versus 30%, there are no limitations on how the 30% reward can be allocated to various elements of the incentive program.

REASONABLE ALTERNATIVE STANDARD

A reasonable alternative standard to earn the reward must be offered to all employees who are not able to meet the initial standard for Outcome-Based standards. The alternative standard can be in the form of another incentive program with the same or a different structure. For example, for an employee who cannot meet the Outcome-Based standard of BMI of 25, the alternative standard could be meeting a fitness standard (another Outcome-Based standard), making progress in reducing weight to achieve a BMI of 27 (another Outcome-Based), participating in a program to increase physical activity or eating more nutritious foods (Activity-Only standard), or listening to a series of lectures on weight management (Activity-Only standard in this context because it is for people who failed the BMI standard). A reasonable alternative standard must also be offered for Activity-Only and Participatory incentives for employees who have a medical issue that makes meeting those standards difficult or inadvisable. The alternative standard must always be "reasonable" and the opinion of the employee's personal physician must always prevail in the selection of the alternative standard if there is a disagreement.

RECOMMENDED INCENTIVE STRUCTURE

Guiding Principles

The recommended incentive structure described below is designed with the goal of complying with the provisions in the regulation, motivating employees to be engaged in efforts to improve health, making the full cost of the incentive cost neutral to the employer, and having a premium structure that covers a portion of the cost of the health promotion program. The approach described here assumes that reductions in employer medical care costs would need to come from reduced medical care utilization caused by improved health or wiser use of medical care by employees, rather than shifting those costs to employees. Some employers may choose to include some additional cost shifting in their incentive structure, but that approach is not reflected here.

This approach is based on a series of parallel incentive programs with the alternative standard for each of them being a related effort that benefits the employee's health.

Behavior and Health Conditions Targeted

Keeping the incentive program structure simple makes it easy for employees to understand and makes data management less cumbersome. A structure that focuses on one behavior (a Participatory incentive), which is participating in a health screening, and three health contingent standards (Outcome-Based incentives) that can be measured objectively, might be the optimal balance of comprehensiveness and simplicity.

Those health standards might be (1) no tobacco or nicotine use, (2) body mass index (BMI) ≤ 27.5 or passing a fitness test, and (3) biometrics in the normal range, including blood pressure, cholesterol, triglycerides, and glucose. Values for all of these standards would need to be measured through screenings, not self reported, to avoid creating an incentive for employees to lie in a self-report. These are briefly described below.

Health Screening

The health screening needs to be conducted at least once a year, and measure all the health values covered by the other elements of the incentive program, including cotinine or another objective measure of tobacco use. Receiving an incentive for participating in a health screening is a Participatory level incentive, so no alternative standard is required unless an employee has a medical condition that makes it inadvisable to participate in the health screening.

Tobacco/Nicotine Use

The standard to receive the tobacco use incentive should be no measureable cotinine detected in the health screening. This would apply to employees using nicotine replacement therapy to quit smoking. Measurement of cotinine could be excluded from the health screening for employees who acknowledge they use tobacco or nicotine replacement therapy. This is an Outcome-Based level incentive, which requires an alternative standard option. The alternative standard should be the opportunity to participate in a tobacco cessation program. Receiving an incentive to participate in the tobacco cessation program is a health contingent activity-only level incentive and requires another activity level alternative standard for employees who have a medical issue that makes an element of a tobacco cessation program inadvisable, an alternative must be offered. For example if it would be inadvisable for an employee to use nicotine replacement therapy, a program that did not use nicotine replacement therapy must be offered.

Recommended Weight

The standard to receive the recommended weight standard should be BMI of 27.5, or when possible, a comparable level from the direct measurement of body fat through an objective standard, with the employer choosing the measurement approach. The 27.5 BMI is recommended rather than the usual 25 BMI to provide slack for those who are moderately overweight and to recognize the inconsistent findings on the links between overweight (but not obesity) and health. Use of body fat percentage is probably the most accurate method to prevent misclassifications for employees who are heavy because of extensive muscle rather than excess fat. Unfortunately, this approach may not be feasible because of the time and skill required for this approach. Waist, or waist/hip ratio measurements may be an alternative approach. The alternative standard for this Outcome-Based level incentive would be another Outcome-Based level incentive of passing a fitness test. Passing a fitness test as an alternative standard is recommended because compelling research has shown that lack of fitness is a more important predictor of mortality than being overweight.[8] The alternative standard for this Outcome-Based level incentive might include a range of options including making progress in losing weight or improving fitness (another Outcome-Based level), participating in a program to improve fitness and lose weight (an Activity-Only level or Participatory program, depending on the focus of the program). The choice of Outcome-Based, Activity-Only, or Participatory level incentives should be guided by the resources and overall philosophy of the health promotion program staff. The number of levels of alternative standards to be met

should be guided by what the field learns over time about how long program participants will embrace vs. reject these multiple levels, and the culture of the employer organization.

Biometric Values

The standard for biometric values incentive might be the recommended normal values for blood pressure, cholesterol, glucose or Hemoglobin A1c, and possibly triglycerides. If the philosophy of health promotion programs is to motivate employees who have measureable abnormal medical conditions to seek medical care from a physician, and to not interfere with the patient-physician relationship, the alternative standard for this Outcome-Based level incentive should be complying with appropriate medical care from a physician (an Activity-Only level incentive). Following the advice of ones personal physician is also the final default alternative standard specified in the federal regulations for any Outcome-Based incentive. Another option is to combine the requirement to comply with physician advice with participation in programs to improve nutrition, fitness, manage stress, or lose weight.

Amounts of Incentives

The regulations allow considerable leeway on the amount of the incentive applied to individual components. A maximum incentive of 50% of the health plan premium provides more than enough to capture employee's attention and motivate them to become engaged in programs. Assuming average total medical care premium costs of $6000/person, 50% would be $3000... an amount that is probably more than enough to engage most employees. In earlier recommendations, when the maximum incentive levels were expected to be 20% or 30%, the author recommended incentives of 5%-7.5% for participating in the screening, and 5%-7.5% for achieving each of the three health goals.[9] This was based in part on personal experience that $300 is probably enough to motivate most employees to participate in each distinct program, like participating in a health screening, or a tobacco cessation program. Given the new limit of 50%, it may be reasonable to increase the ranges, but not because of any cohesive rationale that justifies why they should be raised. Below are the ranges that might be considered.

Participating in a health screening:	5%–15%
No tobacco use:	5%–20%
Meeting weight standard:	5%–10%
Meeting biometric standard:	5%–10%

These ranges should be revised based on employers' practical experience and findings of the empirical literature in the coming years.

REFERENCES

1   Towers Watson. 2011/2012 Staying@ Work Survey Report: A Pathway to Employee Health and Workplace Productivity. Available at http://www.towerswatson.com/united-states/research/6031. Last accessed August 16, 2012.

2   Towers Watson/National Business Group on Health. 2013/2014 Staying@Work U.S. executive summary report. Available at: http://www.towerswatson.com/en-US/Insights/IC-Types/Survey-Research-Results/2013/09/2013-2014-stayingatwork-us-executive-summary-report. Accessed March 11, 2014.

3   Incentives for Nondiscriminatory Wellness Programs in Group Health Plans, Federal Register, Vol 78, No. 106, June 3, 2013. Available at https://www.federalregister.gov/articles/2013/06/03/2013-12916/incentives-for-nondiscriminatory-wellness-programs-in-group-health-plans. Accessed June 12, 2013.

4   Taitel, MS, Haufle V, Heck D et al. Incentives and other factors associated with employee participation in health risk assessment. *J Occup Environ Med* 2008. 50:863–872.

5   Seaverson, ELD, Grossmeier J, Miller TM, and Anderson DR. The role of incentive design, incentive, value, communications strategy, and worksite culture on health risk assessment participation. *Am J Health Promot* 2009. 23:343.

6   Goetzel RZ , D. R. Anderson DR, Whitmer RW, et al. The relationship between modifiable health risks and health care expenditures: an analysis of the multi-employer HERO health risk and cost database,. *J Occup Environ Med* 1998. 40:843–854.

7   United States Department of Labor, FAQs about Affordable Care Act Implementation (Part XVIII) and Mental Health Parity Implementation: Wellness. January 9, 2014. Available at: http://www.dol.gov/ebsa/faqs/faq-aca18.html. Accessed March 11, 2014.

8   Sui, X. , et al. Cardiorespiratory fitness and adiposity as mortality predictors in older adults. *JAMA* 2007. 298:2507–2516.

9   O'Donnell MP. Making the Impossible Possible: Engaging the Entire Population in Comprehensive Workplace Health Promotion Programs at No Net Cost to Employers or Employees. *Am J Health Promot*: July/August 2010, Vol. 24, No. 6, pp. iv-v.

APPENDIX 4-B

Proposed Regulations to Guide Implementation of Wellness Incentives in the Affordable Care Act

On November 20, 2012, proposed regulations to guide the implementation of the Wellness Incentives (Section 2705 from the Affordable Care Act) were released by the Departments of Treasury, Labor and Health and Human Services for public comment.[1] Comments were due by January 25, 2013. The proposed regulations include 16 significant revisions to the statute, two of which impact the approach proposed in Appendix 4-A. The expectation is that at least one more revision and probably two will be released based on comments submitted. The final regulations are expected to be released by January 1, 2014, because all provisions in the statue will be in effect on that date. Employers should develop programs based on the provisions in the statute until the final regulations are released.

PARTICIPATION IN PROGRAMS BEING SUFFICIENT FOR THE FULL DISCOUNT

The proposed regulations recommend that employees who do not meet health standards, eg. they use tobacco, are overweight, etc., be able to qualify for the health standard and receive the full premium discount by participating in a wellness program to help them meet the standard. This revision to the statute eviscerates the concept of different levels of rewards for participating in programs versus meeting the health standard. This change was opposed by most employer groups and supported by some patient advocate groups. If this rule is retained in the final regulations, the approach described in Appendix 4-A would need to be modified to eliminate the different levels of discount for meeting the health standard versus participating in a program.

MAXIMUM DISCOUNT INCREASED FROM 30% TO 50%

The proposed regulations recommend that the maximum discount in effect on January 1, 2014, be increased from 30% to 50% on the condition that one of the health standards is being tobacco free. As such, the maximum discount for meeting all other health standards would be 30%, thus allowing 20% for being tobacco free. The statute in the Affordable Care Act allows a maximum discount of 20% until January 1, 2014, specifies that the maximum will increase to at least 30% on that date, and gives the Secretaries of Treasury and Health and Human Services the authority to increase the maximum to 50% on that date. Reactions to this proposed rule were mixed, with no clear pattern of supporters and opponents, and many not commenting. In the author's opinion, the 50% level discount is not necessary from a motivation perspective, so the recommended approach would not need to be modified from what is described in Appendix 4-A. Also, given the fact that few employers offer discounts at the 20% range now permitted, it is unlikely that most employers will increase the discount to the full 50%. However, if the 50% maximum is retained, some employers are likely to increase to the maximum and that the overall average discount among all employers is likely to increase.

REFERENCE

1. Incentives for Nondiscriminatory Wellness Programs in Group Health Plans. Federal Register/Vol. 77, No. 227/ Monday, November 26, 2012/Proposed Rules. 70620-70642.

Vendor Savings Guarantees

Steven P. Noeldner

INTRODUCTION

In the early 2000s, disease management/medical condition management providers started offering employers guarantees that their programs would save money in excess of their costs. In recent years, health promotion providers have started to offer similar savings guarantees. There are no known surveys on the prevalence of savings guarantee agreements, however, they seem to be common among 1) large national providers who offer comprehensive health promotion programs that are expected to improve or eliminate health risk factors and reduce medical care costs[1] and 2) very large self-insured employers (i.e. 3,000 or more employees). They are most common when the health promotion provider is a health insurance carrier or a national vendor and when a consultant releases a national request for proposal (RFP) on behalf of the employer and includes the savings guarantee as a preferred element of the RFP. Savings guarantees are sometimes offered to medium sized employers (1,000 to 2,999 employees), and sometimes by regional health promotion providers, but not very often. Savings guarantees are rarely, if ever, offered by providers who specialize in individual program components, such as health risk assessments, screening programs, individual behavior change programs, fitness center management, and other limited services; or when the employer is small, fully- insured and/or is part of a pooled health insurance group.

STRUCTURE OF AGREEMENTS

Risk and Flow of Payments

It is common for health promotion providers that offer savings guarantees to put at risk some financial stake, typically a percentage of the fees they charge, to support the savings guarantee to their clients. The amount of the financial stake varies considerably depending upon such factors as the amount of program fees collected by the vendor, whether or not the vendor is competing with other vendors for the business, and the negotiating skills of the employer or consultant representing the employer. When providers offer savings guarantees with some of their fees at risk, they typically build additional revenue into their fee structure to cover their financial risk. Some vendors may increase their service fees to the employer by an amount equivalent to their fees at risk, while others may only increase fees by a fraction of their fees at risk. The magnitude of the increase in service fees may also be influenced by the provider's perception of how its fees will compare to those of competitors vying for the client's business.

In one common model for a medical cost savings guarantee, the health promotion provider and employer agree on a fixed percentage of the annual program fees that will be refunded to the employer if the cost savings for the program do not meet or exceed agreed upon targets. For example, savings targets may be expressed in terms of Return on Investment (ROI) and set at 0.8:1 for the first program year, 1.5:1 for the second program year, and 2:1 for the third program year. The percent of service fees that is eligible for refund may, for example, start at 5% in year one and increase in the second and third years. This is consistent with the idea that as health promotion programs mature, greater cost savings are expected and more weight (greater fees at risk) is placed on savings as a program outcome. If the provider builds extra revenue into its service fees to cover the savings guarantee, then when savings targets are met, the excess fees are retained by the provider as additional profit.

Another relatively new, but emerging approach is gain-sharing. In this model, the provider and employer agree in advance on a savings calculation methodology and on the proportions of savings attributed to the health promotion program the employer and provider will share. One example of a gain-sharing split might be 30% to the provider with 70% retained by the employer. In this arrangement, the employer would pay the provider its share of the cost savings (gain) after the program period (typically annually). Gain-sharing would be in lieu of a provider raising its service fees to cover fees it puts at risk for achieving a savings target.

Employer Requirements

Providers that offer savings guarantees often require the employer to agree to a number of conditions. A multi-year contract, typically a minimum of three years, is common. A variety of implementation elements may be required of the employer as well, such as having a structured communication plan, incentives for employees to participate, a high percentage of accurate contact information, and in some cases, a minimum participation rate (although employers may expect the provider to be responsible for participation rates if the employer is providing incentives and promotional support).

Evaluation Methodology

There are a number of factors that should be considered when a savings guarantee is established. The methodology used to calculate cost savings will determine how precise – and believable – the outcome will be. The methodology selected should also dictate the savings target. Robust methodologies that control for confounding influences typically yield more precise (and often more conservative) results compared to methodologies that predict or estimate cost savings.

Selecting an appropriate evaluation methodology on which both provider and employer agree is an important first step. A variety of factors should be considered, including what type of data is available (e.g., health care claims data, time-over-time health risk assessment results for the same individuals, etc.), the number of program participants, and the evaluation resources available to the provider or employer (e.g., capable evaluation staff, statistical analysis technology, funding, etc.).

Health Risk Assessment (HRA) Data

Wellness or lifestyle management program providers historically have utilized individual-level HRA data from participants who completed the HRA both at the beginning and the end of an evaluation period (e.g., program year) to estimate health care cost savings for risk factors that have been reduced or eliminated. Most "predictive" methodologies have been developed using health care costs associated with individual health risk factors as reported in the landmark Health Enhancement Research Organization (HERO) studies near the end of the 1990s.[2,3]

While these predictive methodologies are useful and may provide good directional estimates of program cost savings, they are subject to a number of challenges to their precision. For example, how the estimated cost savings for any individual health risk factor is allocated over time – e.g., assigning some portion of the total cost savings in the first year a health risk was eliminated, compared to assigning portions of the total cost savings over a number of years – could influence the magnitude of the ascribed savings in any one program year.

Health Care Claims Data

The use of actual medical and pharmacy claims data is far superior to costs tied to proxy measures such as self-reported health habits. As such, a growing number of health promotion providers are now using claims data to evaluate cost savings.

Trend Analysis vs. Matched Controls

Even when individual-level health care claims data are available, there are different approaches to determining cost savings. Until recently, some form of health care cost trend analysis was often utilized to calculate cost savings, or more precisely, cost avoidance for those who participated in a health promotion program.

Trend analysis typically compares the employer's health care cost experience prior to the implementation of a health promotion program to its cost experience after the program has been in place for a year or more. The difference between the "expected" trend that might have occurred if no program had been implemented, and the "actual" health care costs measured during the evaluation period, is assumed to be associated with the impact of the health promotion program.

While trend analysis may appear to be an attractive methodology, it is subject to a number of potentially confounding influences. Factors that can influence the accuracy of the results of the trend methodology include differences from base line to intervention period in health plan design (e.g., cost sharing, mix of plan types offered, provider networks, etc.), health plan carrier (if it changed), and composition of the employee population (e.g., healthier employees are added to the workforce, less healthy employees depart).

A more robust alternative to the health care cost trend analysis is the matched-control, multivariate regression analysis methodology, which typically yields a more precise (and conservative) analysis of health care cost savings associated with health promotion program participation. This is a claims-based, multi-step methodology which first uses statistical techniques to find close matches between program participants and non-participants (controls). Some factors typically used for matching include age, gender, health status (or risk score), and health care costs. After a closely-matched control group is identified, the difference in costs for participants from the baseline period (prior to the program) to the end of the evaluation period (at least one program year) is compared to the difference in cost for controls from baseline to the end of evaluation period. This "difference-in-difference" value is considered the cost savings associated with program participation.

Savings Targets

The amount of the savings target will be influenced both by the quality of the program and evaluation methodology. In the author's experience, less precise predictive or estimation methodologies sometimes result in higher savings values than those calculated using more rigorous matched-control regression analysis. Because of the potential for numerous confounding influences when using the trend-based methodology, calculated savings using this methodology are typically higher than when using the matched-control regression analysis methodology. Similarly, predictive methodologies that assign a savings value to reduced or eliminated health risks, often provide inflated estimates of true cost savings and should have savings targets adjusted accordingly. This trend is not consistent with the published literature. For example, in a meta-analysis involving 22 studies on the impact of health promotion programs on medical care costs, the studies with randomized experimental designs had ROIs averaging 3.36, while those with non-randomized designs had ROIs of 2.38.[4]

Evaluator

Most cost savings evaluations are done by the vendors that provide the health promotion programs. Rarely does the employer conduct the analysis, primarily because it lacks the necessary expertise or resources. On occasion, larger employers that have made substantial investments for their health promotion programs, engage a third-party evaluator, usually a data analysis or consulting firm. When a third-party is the evaluator, the methodology used is typically a more robust, matched-control regression analysis.

CHALLENGES, RISKS AND OPPORTUNITIES

Accurate measurement of health care cost savings associated with health promotion programs is a challenging endeavor. The resources required to gather and analyze data are considerable. Most employers and vendors don't have adequate expertise to conduct a robust savings analysis, and the considerable cost of an analysis can erode savings generated by the program. Typically, only employers that have invested substantially in their programs, or expect very large gross savings amounts, will pay for a robust savings analysis to verify their program's financial outcomes.

One notable threat to the successful utilization of savings guarantee agreements is the potentially adversarial relationship it may establish and foster. If the employer has an opportunity to be refunded some of its program fees if the vendor misses the savings target, it may not be fully motivated to provide the support needed for the program to succeed. Conversely, if the vendor has fee revenue or a portion of a gain-share at stake, it may be motivated to utilize an imprecise evaluation methodology, or even falsify or skew the interpretation of results to avoid refunding fees, or to achieve a greater "gain".

If an employer can justify the expense of a precise cost savings evaluation using a robust methodology (ideally conducted by a qualified third party), a gain-sharing arrangement with the vendor may establish the most positive and productive employer-vendor relationship. Gain-sharing can motivate both employer and vendor to do all they can, separately and collectively, to assure the success of health promotion programs. If the employer is unable or unwilling to commit the resources needed to conduct a robust savings analysis, it may be reasonable to forgo a savings guarantee to avoid higher vendor service fees to cover the vendor's fees at risk for the savings guarantee.

RECOMMENDED APPROACH

The following approach may be used to support decision-making about the appropriateness and approach to savings guarantees.

1. Decide if a savings guarantee is desired by the employer and acceptable to the vendor.
2. If yes, review the skill level available to design and execute the study and the quality of data available.
3. Develop a study methodology that matches the skill level, available data and the financial terms of the guarantee, as well as protocols to resolve disagreements.
4. Confirm the party responsible for each element of the study methodology.

REFERENCES

1. Serxner S, Gold D, Meraz A, Gray A. Do employee health management programs work? *Amer J Health Promot.* 2009;23:TAHP-1-8,iii.
2. Anderson DR, Whitmer RW, Goetzel RZ, Ozminkowski JR, et al. The

relationship between modifiable health risks and group-level health care expenditures. *Amer J Health Promot.* 2000;15:45-52.

3.   Goetzel, R.Z., Anderson, D.R., Whitmer, R.W., Ozminkowski, J.R., Dunn, R.L., Wasserman, J., HERO Research Committee (1998). The relationship between modifiable health risks and health care expenditures. *Journal of Occupational and Environmental Medicine,* 40(10), 1-12.

4.   HERO Best Practice Scorecard in Collaboration with Mercer. The Health Enhancement Research Organization site. Available at: http://www.the-hero. org/scorecard_folder/scorecard.htm. Accessed September 11, 2012.

HERO Scorecard and CDC Scorecard

HERO SCORECARD

The HERO Best Practice Scorecard© was developed as a tool to help employers improve the quality of their health promotion programs by documenting program components, primarily from a management perspective. The Scorecard can be used as an inventory to catalogue a program's components, an indicator of success in implementing program components and as a comparative benchmarking tool to compare a program with peer employers. HERO has published several reports summarizing findings drawn from the database of responses.

In version 3.1, the core questionnaire has 62 questions organized into six major sections: strategic planning (10 questions), leadership engagement (6 questions), program level management (8 questions), programs (22 questions), engagement methods (13 questions), and measurement and evaluation (3 questions). It also has an optional section on outcomes, with more detailed questions on participation rates in the various program areas, program costs, and impact of programs on health risks and medical costs.

The Scorecard was developed through a collaborative process involving several dozen leading authorities in health promotion who volunteered their time and expertise to HERO (Health Enhancement Research Organization), and Mercer who provided expertise in health promotion and technical support to produce the tools. The first edition was developed in 2006. Version 3.1 was released in March of 2012 and version 4 was in development at the time this book was published. More details can be found at the HERO Scorecard website:[1] http://www.the-hero.org

After completing the Scorecard online a report is sent to the user showing the score for their organization and average scores for all other organizations. The Scorecard and a follow-up report with scores for the individual user organization and average aggregate scores for all other organization users are provided at no charge to all users. More detailed reports with aggregated responses for each question, breakdowns of scores by industry, geographic region, and employer size can be purchased.

THE CDC WORKSITE HEALTH SCORECARD: AN ASSESSMENT TOOL FOR EMPLOYERS TO PREVENT HEART DISEASE, STROKE, & RELATED HEALTH CONDITIONS

The CDC Worksite Health ScoreCard[2] was developed to help employers determine if they have implemented evidence based interventions and strategies. It focuses primarily on the components of individual program interventions but includes a short section on organization level design.

The questionnaire contains 100 questions that assess the extent to which evidence-based strategies have been used in programs. The strategies include counseling services, environmental supports, policies, health plan benefits, and other worksite programs shown to be effective in preventing heart disease, stroke, and related health conditions. The 100 questions are organized into 12 major sections: organizational supports (18 questions), tobacco control (10 questions), nutrition (13 questions), physical activity (9 questions), weight management (5 questions), stress management (6 questions), depression (7 questions), high blood pressure (7 questions), high cholesterol (6 questions), diabetes (6 questions), signs and symptoms of heart attack and stroke (4 questions) and emergency response to heart attack and stroke (9 questions). Users tally their own scores manually and there is no mechanism to add scores to a central database.

All of the items in the questionnaire are tied to strategies that have been documented in the scientific literature to be effective. From a scoring perspective, the relative value of each item is weighted to reflect both the magnitude of impact of the approach and the quality of published evidence supporting its impact. References to the scientific literature are provided for each topic area. The questionnaire was field tested with a sample of 93 very small, small, medium, and large worksites for validity and reliability, and feasibility of adopting the strategies highlighted in the tool.

The Appendix of the Scorecard includes an example of the strategies, processes, communications and evaluation elements that might be in a plan to achieve several specific health goals. It also includes sample program budgets, and blank templates that can be used to prepare plans and budgets.

The CDC Scorecard was developed by a team of professionals at CDC and Emory University. It was released in September of 2012. More information can be found at The Worksite Health Scorecard website: http://www.cdc.gov/dhdsp/pubs/worksite_scorecard.htm

APPENDIX-E

HERO Scorecard

The HERO Best Practice Scorecard © was developed as a tool to help employers improve the quality of their health promotion programs by documenting program components, primarily from a management perspective. The Scorecard can be used as an inventory to catalogue a program's components, an indicator of success in implementing program components and as a comparative benchmarking tool to compare a program with peer employers. HERO has published several reports summarizing findings drawn from the database of responses.

In version 4.0,, the core questionnaire has 64 questions organized into six major sections: 1) strategic planning (7 questions), 2) organization and cultural support (8 questions), 3) programs (14 questions), 4) program integration (6 questions) 5) participation strategies (21 questions), and measurement and evaluation (8 questions). It also has optional section on program costs, outcomes, outcome measures, and financial impact.Users complete the Scorecard online. A report is sent to the user showing the score for their organization and average scores for all other organizations.

The Scorecard was developed through a collaborative process involving several dozen leading authorities in health promotion who volunteered their time and expertise to HERO (Health Enhancement Research Organization), and Mercer who provided expertise in health promotion and technical support to produce the tools.

The Scorecard and a follow-up report with scores for the individual user organization and average aggregate scores for all other organization users are provided at no charge to all users. More detailed reports with aggregated responses for each question, breakdowns of scores by industry, geographic region, and employer size can be purchased.

More details can be found at HERO Scorecard website:*http://www.the-hero.org/scorecard_folder/scorecard.htm.

REFERENCES

1. Centers for Disease Control and Prevention. *The CDC Worksite Health ScoreCard: An Assessment Tool for Employers to Prevent Heart Disease, Stroke, and Related Health Conditions.* Available at: http://www.cdc.gov/dhdsp/pubs/worksite_scorecard.htm. Accessed September 11, 2012.
2. Baicker K, Cutler D, Song Z. Workplace wellness programs can generate savings. Health Aff (Millwood). 2010 Feb;29(2):304-11. Epub 2010 Jan 14.

Glossary

AMSO Framework: See Chapter 3.

Feasibility Study: Process to determine if it is possible to develop a wellness program that is likely to achieve health and organization goals.

Needs assessment: Process to determine the health needs of employees and/or the organizational needs of the employer.

---

*NEXT GENERATION HERO Employee Health Management (EHM) Best Practices Scorecard in Collaboration with Mercer. Available at: http://www.the-hero.org/scorecard_folder/scorecard.htm. Accessed November 13, 2014.

Motivational readiness to change: See Chapter 9.

Cost effectiveness, cost benefit analysis: See Chapter 6.

Participation rates: Percentage of employees who participate in a program.

Relapse rates: Percentage of people who make a successful behavior change (like quitting smoking), then revert to the previous behavior (like smoking again).

Organization priorities: See Chapter 2.

HRA: Health risk assessment questionnaire that documents health practices and estimates the impact of these practices on future health.

Benchmarking: See Chapter 3.

Incentives: See Chapter 10.

Meta-analysis: Statistical method of combining data from multiple studies of the same variables and reanalyzing the data with the larger combined data set.

Learning Objectives

After reading this chapter, readers will be able to do the following:

1. Describe the three phases in designing a workplace health promotion program.
2. Describe four methods employers can use to finance a health promotion program.
3. Describe two scorecards that can be used to critique the structure and program elements of a health promotion program.
4. Describe the three major elements that need to be determined in developing program content?

Discussion Questions

1. How much time and effort should be invested in designing a workplace health promotion program?
2. How does an employer decide the optimal level of intensity in program offerings?
3. What is the relative importance of top management support versus employee engagement in the success of a program?
4. What are some strategies to engage employees in a program?
5. What are some strategies to build leadership support for a program?
6. How long does it take to design and implement a program?

REFERENCES

1. O'Donnell MP. Definition of Health Promotion 2.0: Embracing Passion, Enhancing Motivation, Recognizing Dynamic Balance, and Creating Opportunities. *Amer J Health Promot.* 2009;24:iv–iv.
2. O'Donnell M, Bishop C, Kaplan K. Benchmarking best practices in workplace health promotion programs. *Am J Health Promot.* 1997;1:TAHP-1-8.
3. Linnan L, Bowling M, Childress J, Lindsay G, et al. Results of the 2004 National Worksite Health Promotion Survey. *Am J Public Health.* 2008; 98:1503–9.
4. Gould L, Ornish D, Scher W, Brown S, et al. Changes in myocardial perfusion abnormalities by positron emission tomography after long-term, intense risk factor modification. *JAMA.* 1995; 274:894–901.
5. Prochaska J, Velicer W. The transtheoretical model of health behavior change. *Am J Health Promot.* 1997;12:38–48.

6. O'Donnell M. Health impact of workplace health promotion programs and methodological quality of the research literature. *Am J Health Promot.* 1997;1:TAHP-1-8.

7. Heaney C, Goetzel R. A review of health related outcomes of multi-component workplace health promotion programs. *Am J Health Promot.* 1997;11:290-307.

8. U.S. Department of Health and Human Services. Clinical Practice Guideline: Treating Tobacco Use and Dependence: 2008 Update. Available at: http://www.surgeongeneral.gov/tobacco/treating_tobacco_use08.pdf. Accessed August 23, 2012.

9. Seaverson ELD, Grossmeier J, Miller TM, Anderson DA. The role of incentive design, incentive value, communications strategy, and worksite culture on health risk assessment participation. *Am J Health Promot.* 2009;23:343-52.

10. Taitel MS, Haufle V, Heck D, Loeppke R, Fetterolf D. Incentives and other factors associated with employee participation in health risk assessment. *J Occup Environ Med.* 2008;50:863–872.

11. Matson D, Lee J, Hopp J. The impact of incentives and competitions on participation and quit rates in worksite smoking cessation programs. *Am J Health Promot.* 1993;7:270-280.

12. Baicker K, Cutler D, Song Z. Workplace Wellness Programs Can Generate Savings. *Health Aff.* 2010;29:304-311.

13. Chapman LS. Meta-Evaluation of Worksite Health Promotion Economic Return Studies: 2012 Update. *Am J Health Promot.* 2012;26:TAHP-1-TAHP-12.

14. Baicker K, Cutler D, Song Z, Workplace Wellness Programs Can Generate Savings, Health Affairs, 29, no. 2 (2010): 304-311.

15. Towers Watson. 2011/2012 Staying@Work Survey Report: A Pathway to Employee Health and Workplace Productivity. Available at: http://www.towerswatson.com/united-states/research/6031. Accessed August 16, 2012.

16. Incentives for Nondiscriminatory Wellness Programs in Group Health Plans, Federal Register, Vol 78, No. 106, June 3, 2013. Available at: https://www.federalregister.gov/articles/2013/06/03/2013-12916/incentives-for-non discriminatory-wellness-programs-in-group-health-plans. Accessed June 12, 2013.

17. Taitel, M. S., V. Haufle, D. Heck, et al. Incentives and other factors associated with employee participation in health risk assessment. *J Occup Environ Med* 2008. 50:863–872.

18. Seaverson, E. L. D., J. Grossmeier, T. M. Miller, and D. A. Anderson. The role of incentive design, incentive, value, communications strategy, and worksite culture on health risk assessment participation. *Am J Health Promot* 2009. 23:343.

19. Goetzel RZ, Anderson DR, Whitmer RW, Ozminkowski RJ, et al. The relationship between modifiable health risks and health care expenditures: an analysis of the multi-employer HERO health risk and cost database. *J Occup Environ Med.* 1998;40:843-854.

20. ACLU briefing paper 12.The 'Lectric Law Library site. Available at: http://www.lectlaw.com/files/emp08.htm. Accessed August 24, 2012.

21. Secondhand Smoke (SHS) Facts. Centers for Disease Control and Prevention site. Available at: http://www.cdc.gov/tobacco/data_statistics/fact_sheets/secondhand_smoke/general_facts/. Accessed August 18, 2010.

22. Centers for Disease Control and Prevention (CDC).Cigarette smoking-attributable morbidity—United States,

2000.*MMWR Morb Mortal Wkly Rep.* 2003;52:842–844.

23. McClave AK, Whitney N, Thorne SL, Mariolis P, et al. Adult tobacco survey — 19 States, 2003–2007. *MMWR SurveillSumm.* 2010;59:1–75.

24. Centers for Disease Control and Prevention (CDC). Annual smoking-attributable mortality, years of potential life lost, and economic costs--United States, 1995-1999. *MMWR Morb Mortal Wkly Rep.* 2002;51:300-3.

25. O'Donnell MP, Roizen MF. The SmokingPaST Framework: Illustrating the Impact of Quit Attempts, Quit Methods, and New Smokers on Smoking Prevalence, Years of Life Saved, Medical Costs Saved, Programming Costs, Cost Effectiveness, and Return on Investment. *Am J Health Promot.* 2011;26:e11-e23.

26. State Smoker Protection Laws. American Lung Association site. Available at: http://www.lungusa2.org/slati/appendixf.php. Accessed August 24, 2012.

27. Linnan L, Bowling M, Childress J, Lindsay G. Results of the 2004 National Worksite Health Promotion Survey. *Am J Public Health.* 2008;98:1503-9.

28. Henry J. Kaiser Family Foundation, Health Research and Educational Trust. Employer Health Benefits 2011 Annual Survey. Kaiser Family Foundation site. Available at: http://ehbs.kff.org/pdf/2011/8225.pdf. Accessed August 24, 2012.

29. C. Everett Koop National Health Award. The Health Project site. Available at: http://www.thehealthproject.com/index.html. Accessed August 23, 2012.

CHAPTER

5

Management Processes

William Baun

INTRODUCTION

The last decade brought difficult economic times for many companies,[1] workforces are being threatened by aging and noncommunicable diseases (cancer, cardiovascular, chronic pulmonary, diabetes, and mental illness)[2] and a growing epidemic of workplace stress.[3] These challenges are causing a shift in the health and productivity orientation of workplace health promotion programs from a limited risk management perspective to a holistic focus on the total value of worker health. This shift also underscores the importance and significant need for health promotion programs in middle-sized and small businesses, feeding the last decade of health promotion program growth in companies of all sizes.[1,4] A recent Rand Health Review sponsored by the U.S. Departments of Labor and Health and Human Services[5] suggests that programs have become very common and achieved a high penetration in the United States, and that program uptake is expected to continue as the Affordable Care Act increases employment-based coverage and promotes workplace health promotion/prevention efforts.[6] This review also suggests that the "innovations of the health promotion industry have outpaced its underlying evidence base," suggesting a

need for health promotion program managers with better integration skills, and a different mix of management/leader competencies than outlined in the management chapter in the third edition of this book, which was published in 2002.[7] The purpose of this chapter is to give program managers a sense of the skills necessary to manage a program. It is organized around five core elements that have been distilled from competency standard guidelines developed by groups in the United States,[8] Australia,[9] and Europe.[10] These five elements are listed below.

1. Management of Your Job and Growth
2. Management of People, Collaborators, and Stakeholders
3. Management of the Health Promotion Unit/Department
4. Management of the Program Design, Development, and Delivery
5. Management of the Reporting Process

ELEMENT 1: MANAGEMENT OF YOUR JOB AND GROWTH

Peter Drucker, one of the most influential writers on the subject of management, suggested that "managing oneself" is one of the most important responsibilities of being a successful manager.[11] Successful managers understand that their success is not about the work, but the results of the work. They have learned to build on their strengths, and the strengths of their staff, partners, and stakeholders. Good programs aren't built off weaknesses, but strengths that produce real results and continually gain the support of program champions. Tom Rath's book *Strengths Finder 2.0* was the result of the Gallup team looking at "what's right with people."[12] It was based on Gallup's 40 years of studying human strengths and developing and validating strength assessments. The book outlines 34 themes that represent what's right with people, or the dominant talent that successful people start with and build from. Rath calls the raw or dominant talents that we continue to strengthen throughout life *multipliers*. Successful program managers use their multipliers to ensure success, but also understand their weaknesses, and have implemented several strategies to ensure their weaknesses don't become major roadblocks. Many have found career paths or positions that allow them to avoid their weaknesses. A manager's job requires many different skills, and many managers have learned to partner with individuals that have skills their teams need, but are their weaknesses. For some a good hire is a team member that brings needed skills and is excited about using these skills to strengthen the team.

Project Management

Project management is an important element of a health promotion manager's role. Managers must clearly know their project management temperament. Are they starters, improvers, or finishers? Like strengths, understanding project management temperament can help managers coordinate projects by maximizing the temperament they bring to a project and supplementing it by collaboration with others who bring other temperaments, increasing potential success. Managers need to continually update their project management skills through training. Many will find that their companies have a specific project management model that is used throughout the company. A manager's

personal library should include a few project management books. There are many good project management books; managers might ask their supervisor for a suggestion, or look to see what's in their supervisor's library. The 4th edition of *Project Management for Dummies* was just released in 2013.[13] Figure 5-1 is a schematic of the life cycle of project management and the different processes that must be managed.[14] The schematic underlines the importance of understanding and negotiating the project's objectives at initiation phase; of establishing a project's scope and organizing a work team to help meet the project specifications throughout the execution phase; and finally, of ensuring the project finishes on time, and on budget.

Work Life Effectiveness

Health promotion managers need to strive for work life effectiveness, an outcome of resilience and disciplined daily wellness practices. Wellness can be defined in many different ways, and it is important that health promotion managers take responsibility and accountability for their health and well-being. O'Donnell[15] suggests that optimal health is a dynamic balance of the physical, emotional, social, spiritual, and intellectual health. Table 5-1 expands O'Donnell's model and raises work life effectiveness issues that managers must make into a high priority in their daily management effectiveness practices. The good news, bad news is that others expect health promotion managers to "walk their talk" and be true health and well-being role models, and for some managers their life is like living in a fish bowl. Program managers need to participate in their programming and not just manage it, for through participation they have opportunities to fulfill their role as a health and well-being role model.

Mentors

Oprah Winfrey said, "I think mentors are important and I don't think anybody makes it

Figure 5-1: **Project Management Processes.**

Initiating

- Negotiate objective
- Understand what is negotiable and what is not
- End up with the how and why

Planning

- Project charter
- Project scope
- Work structure
- Sequence of work (critical path, etc.)
- Gantt chart

Executing

- Build project team
- Manage task and deliverables
- Keep on schedule, budget, etc.

Controlling

- Performance baselines, schedule, costs, etc.
- Manager risk
- Maintain quality

Re-planning

Closing

- Administrative close
- Lesson learned

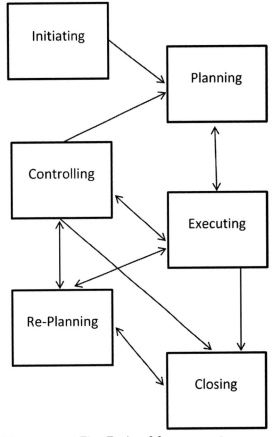

Source: Adapted from Michael S. Dobson Project Management Five Project Management Processes, 2003.

in the world without some form of mentorship. Nobody makes it alone. Nobody has made it alone. And we are all mentors to people even when we don't know it."[16] Traditionally, mentoring was a partnership between two people supporting personal and/or professional developmental/growth strategies. Mentors shared their experiences, technical knowledge, organizational relationships, and gave feedback and tips for mentee success. Mentors served as trusted advisors, providing a sounding board for day-to-day issues encountered on the job, and provided an alternative perspective on issues. They helped with both problem identification and problem solving, and facilitated a mentee's journey through political minefields. Today managers will find mentors still willing to serve in the

Table 5-1: Work Life Effectiveness Priorities.

Dimension	Priorities to Be Managed
Physical	Fitness Physical activity Nutrition Weight management Medical self-care Appropriate screenings Know your numbers Substance abuse Second- and third-hand smoke Sleep
Emotional	Stress management Relaxation Emotional crisis management Accepting and expressing feelings Adjust to change Joy and happiness
Social	Communities Families Friends Diversity Positive relationships Giving back/passing on Life of harmony with others
Intellectual	Mental growth and stimulation Formal educational achievement Lifelong learning Cultural activities Exploration of new ideas Exploration of new skills Being creative
Spiritual	Love Hope Charity Life of meaning Live our values each day Values guide decisions Mindfulness Meditation or prayer Accept views of others

Source: Adapted from O'Donnell MP. Definition of health promotion 2.0: embracing passion, enhancing motivation, recognizing dynamic balance, and creating opportunities. *Am J Health Promot.* 2009;24:IV.

traditional mentor role, but the types of mentors have grown. Peer mentors are health promotion managers at the same experience level, but with an expertise in an area that the mentee does not hold. An example would be the University of Texas System health promotion manager who has experience in managing hypertension programs, something our program manager at MD Anderson Cancer Center would like to be mentored around. Another mentor type is group mentoring or mentoring circles. This is when individuals are linked to more experienced colleagues. Many companies set up Excel (Microsoft, Redmond, WA) mentoring circles to help individuals throughout the company grow their Excel skills. Another mentoring type is virtual mentoring, which has moved everything online. Virtual mentoring transcends groups and organizational boundaries because it can involve multiple mentors and networks. Some companies have set up virtual communities online as mentoring communities. Flash mentoring is a onetime meeting or discussion on broad strategic issues, career goals, or specific advice for managing an issue. An example would be when a manager is having a vendor delivery issue and sits with another manager at lunch for a quick review of options they've used in a similar experience. Many companies are setting up reverse mentoring, which pairs a seasoned employee with a younger professional. The younger professional is considered the mentor and provides the seasoned professional ideas and concepts relative to new technologies and trends. The last mentor type is speed mentoring and can be set up by a company or association to help individuals explore potential mentoring relationships. Speed mentoring is like speed dating; individuals have the opportunity to move around a room getting to know many different potential mentors. There are lots of options for managers to have a mentoring relationship or multiple mentoring relationships, the key is for them to proactively set up a mentor and grow!

Training

There are many ways to grow into being a better manager. Many companies have a management and leadership development training curriculum divided into different levels that managers are required to complete. In some companies, noncompletion of these training curricula can negatively affect annual performance evaluation scores. Many associations such as the Society for Human Resource Management (https://www.shrm.org/Pages/default.aspx) and the American Management Association (http://www.amanet.org/) offer leadership and management courses at their conferences, as well as online. Course participants gain certificates or certifications in a variety of leader and manager skill areas that facilitate personal growth. Health promotion managers also need very specific management skills around population health management, which include needs assessment, program planning, communications and marketing, program delivery, and program evaluation and reporting. Again, there are many different educational and training opportunities. Many university systems cater to the full-time worker and offer class after work and/or on the weekends. There are many master's level health promotion degrees that are totally online. The specialized certificate and certifications in worksite health promotion or wellness continue to grow. A full mix of member associations and health promotion companies offer a variety of face-to-face workshops, Webinars, and online courses. Many of these organizations have training health promotion professionals as part of their mission. A few of the organizations that have been involved in training worksite health promotion professionals for many years are listed below.

- *American Journal of Health Promotion* (https://www.healthpromotionjournal.com/)

- National Wellness Institute (http://www.nationalwellness.org/)
- International Association of Worksite Health Promotion (http://www.acsm-iawhp.org/i4a/pages/index.cfm?pageID=1)
- Wellness Councils of America (https://www.welcoa.org/)
- Health Enhancement Research Organization (http://www.the-hero.org/)

Recognizing Faults

Marshall Goldsmith[17] in his book *What Got You Here Won't Get You There* starts with a set of habits that hold leaders back until they recognize that what got them into a management position is not going to grow them into being better managers. Goldsmith suggests that most managers tend to have a set of faults that are simple to correct and that the fix is a skill set within each human being, but recognition of the fault is a must. In order for managers to grow into better managers they must recognize and be willing to work on their faults. Below is a list of top faults that Goldsmith has seen in leaders over the years in his role as an executive coach. Consider how these issues can stymie leader and team growth.

- Being a winner at all costs, even when it doesn't matter, sets leaders up to ensure others fail at the expense of their success.
- The need for leaders to always add their two cents in every discussion, leads to disempowered staff.
- Needless sarcasms and cutting remarks, which leaders might think make them sound sharp and witty can decrease staff confidence in themselves and/or the team, and can create a sarcastic environment.
- The need for leaders to constantly be telling others how smart they are gets

team members wondering why the need for a team.
- Negativity or telling staff why something won't work leads to a staff that becomes timid and shy at being creative.
- Withholding information to maintain an advantage over others leads to a team that stops sharing.
- Leaders that claim credit for things they don't deserve build teams that back off from supporting their leaders.
- Playing favorites leads to staff members that don't collaborate well.
- Not listening says to staff members, "I don't respect you, your ideas, or your work," and staff/manager communications decrease.

ELEMENT 2: MANAGEMENT OF PEOPLE, COLLABORATORS, AND STAKEHOLDERS

Successful managers get people moving by energizing and mobilizing them with a leadership style that inspires a shared vision, enables others to act, and encourages an emotional engagement that fosters teamwork.[18] But it's not enough to get people moving; good leaders are effective in growing and strengthening their programs, and also growing the people associated with these programs. In the book *How the Best Leaders Make Everyone Smarter* Wiseman and Mckeown[19] suggest a leadership continuum with multipliers on one end and diminishers on the other end. Multipliers are people who attract the best talent, and use them to the fullest extent, doing a good job of preparing them and helping them grow. In contrast, diminishers resolve to be the smartest person on the team and tend to drain the intelligence and capabilities of others. Diminishers sometimes have a terrific track record of promotion, but the capability gap between themselves and the people just below them is huge. Health promotion managers have the full responsibility to pursue, attract, build, and grow the talent in their integrated teams.

Talent—Workforce Planning

Program managers should work closely with their human resources department to ensure they understand how individuals are hired, brought onboard, and supported through training or development opportunities. The size of an employee population influences the level of staffing in the health promotion program. Job audits and workforce-planning processes help evaluate current and future staffing needs and focus on getting the right number of people with the right competencies in the right job, at the right time.[20] The process begins with identifying the critical positions and deciding if they will be full-time, part-time, or a mix. Full-time positions generally have two categories: those that have a clear career path, and those that do not have a career path. Career path positions are composed of sequential jobs that are interrelated and lead to higher-level positions requiring more knowledge and skills, which are developed in the job. A good example would be the five potential steps from the entry-level health promotion specialist's position that leads to coordinator, administrator, manager, and finally, health promotion director. An emerging senior-level position that has been added to this sequence in some organizations is called *wellness officer, chief wellness officer,* or *chief health officer*. It has grown out of the strategic emphasis being placed on employee health and well-being.[21] Institutions including the Cleveland Clinic, MD Anderson Cancer Center, Ohio State University, and Oklahoma State University have created these positions to help better guide their health promotion efforts within their employee populations and the communities they serve. Part-time staff might include intervention leaders, specialty class teachers, student interns, or clerical help who only work several days a week. In many health promotion programs there may be more part-time staff than full-time staff because this provides a cost-effective way to gain the professionalism necessary to offer a comprehensive program and reduce the financial burden. It also provides the program manager a way to tinker with new intervention concepts or program pilots without having to dedicate significant resources to salaries. Staff salaries typically represent 18% to 52% of the operating budget and the use of part-time and temporary positions can help keep salary expenses in the low range.[22] Once the job audit or workforce plan has been completed, it is time to develop job descriptions and/or position descriptions.

Talent—Job Descriptions and Position Descriptions

A job description outlines the purpose, duties, responsibilities, relationship with other staff, physical condition requirements, and salary ranges. A well-written job description will help attract the right candidate and can serve as an outline for performance expectations, job training and development, and career advancement. It also can provide a reference point for compensation decisions.[23] In some organizations, the job description serves as the description of the general position (health promotion specialists, health promotion administrator), and the position description describes specific tasks and responsibilities of a particular job (specialist's position: exercise physiologist, wellness educator). Both are important to the next stage of talent, which is recruitment.

Talent—Recruitment, Screening/ Interviews, and Onboarding

The major goal in recruitment is to inform well-qualified candidates that a job exists. Recruitment is now online in many organizations. It is not uncommon to recruit from within an organization or use employment agencies, search firms, computerized databases, and professional association job bank career centers for senior positions. The recruitment process sometimes starts a barrage of phone calls and e-mails concerning the position, in addition to applications and resumes. Managers need to have an effective system for screening and documenting these different contact points. The immediate supervisor for the position being offered, or a selection committee, normally completes the screening. The first step is rating each applicant on a check list of necessary qualifications, reducing the initial field of applicants to those who are most qualified. The next step is usually a telephone interview that ensures the person is still interested in the position and validates the candidate's qualifications. Some organizations check the applicant's credentials and references before face-to-face interviews. Others do this after finalists are identified. Many organizations have adopted behavioral-based interview processes that focus on experiences, behaviors, knowledge, skills, and abilities that are job related. The behavioral interview process is based on the belief that past behavior and performance predict future behavior and performance. Behavioral interviewing revolves around questions designed to solicit examples of how a candidate has used an important skill, instead of traditional questions such as "Tell me about your strengths and weaknesses," which are easily rehearsed by candidates.[24] It is not uncommon in the interview process for candidates to teach a class, provide coaching, or an exercise prescription. Depending on the position, many companies will have applicants participate in in-depth interviews with participants and committee members. If the position will be part of a health promotion team, allowing a team to interview candidates and have a voice in the hiring decision can help to reveal strengths and weaknesses seen by one's peers, and increases support

for the person selected. Job offers are usually made after the in-depth or team interviews and sometimes involve a negotiation process managed by the human resources department. After an employee has been hired it is important that an onboarding process be used to familiarize newly hired persons with company policies, procedures, business goals, and work expectations.

Onboarding is completed in many different ways, including through a class, Internet, or a handbook that describes the company and explains the benefits. Effective onboarding provides the first step in helping the new hire become a productive employee. Many companies set up mentoring relationships or formal on-the-job training opportunities to ensure that new employee gain the culture competencies necessary to be a successful employee. It is not unusual for a new employee to be given a probationary period of 60 to180 days. During the probationary period, a new employee can often be terminated at will.

Talent—Employee Development, Coaching, and Performance Appraisals

Studies have shown that the best employee development results are achieved when the manager is actively involved in the process.[25] Employee development requires a balance between an individual's career needs and goals and the organization's needs and goals. It is generally composed of training that is focused on helping employees acquire new skills and knowledge, and education that is more formal and designed to develop an individual in a broader sense. An effective approach is to have employees design an annual development strategy with their manager. It might include online, onsite, or offsite training courses, and possible workshops or conferences. It might also include industry certification or potential licensure. It may also make sense to plan for team-building efforts to help the group come together as a team. Team learning requires trust, good communications, and the willingness to work and grow together on team skills.

Coaching for performance is a process that focuses on "future possibilities and not past mistakes."[26] It is a process in which knowledge and skills are transferred to help employees grow. It can be a guided self-discovery process or job shadowing; both create opportunities for learning. Coaching is not a process of telling employees what to do, but a combination of enabling and building awareness that fosters self-responsibility and accountability.

Performance appraisals are an important component of employee development because they provide the employee with feedback on performance and progress. Appraisals are normally completed by the immediate supervisor and sometimes they include feedback from other team members, using 360-degree or related processes. A performance appraisal system should include formal and regularly scheduled assessments mixed with informal spontaneous feedback. Records of performance appraisal are sometimes recorded online and often include values or expected employee behaviors, combined with specific goals agreed upon between the supervisor and employee. Completing performance reviews is often perceived as a challenging and difficult process for supervisors but essential in helping employees understand their strengths and weaknesses and setting goals for future development. If done well, they can enhance employee morale and engagement. Key to a successful appraisal feedback process is for the manager to focus on dialogue and planning for the future rather than completing the appraisal form based on the past. Appraisals are most effective when they are a cooperative effort between the manager and employee, and focus planning solutions that will ensure employee growth, productivity, and success.[27] Team evaluation scheduled periodically can help teams reflect on their performance as a team and review their progress on purpose and goals.

Stakeholder the Lifeblood

Typically, stakeholders are clients, employees, and partners or vendors. These are groups and individuals that are affected by, concerned about, or have a vested interest in a health promotion program. Developing a stakeholder strategy that maximizes value can lead to the program by creating a cooperative ecosystem in which each group benefits and overall program values are maximized. The six steps described below can guide development of a stakeholder strategy.[28]

1. Identify stakeholder groups.
2. Create a value proposition for each stakeholder group.
3. Determine what the program needs from each group, and what stakeholder groups might expect to gain from the program.
4. Identify stakeholder capabilities, strengths, and weaknesses.
5. Consider the differences between the groups, and potential gaps that might affect program performance.
6. Determine a set of key performance indicators for each group, and for the team as a whole.

Partnerships are stakeholders that have become closer allies and usually set up through a formal agreement. Vendors are special partners that help fill the gap between what can be provided internally and ultimately must be accomplished to meet the program goals. Six factors can be considered in vendor selection[29]:

1. First impressions: professional image, philosophy, fit to your need, expertise, reputation
2. Product quality: documentation, success rate, qualified staff, customization
3. Customer service: reliability of contact person, willingness to find solutions, process and past data

4. Technology effectiveness: sound technologic foundation, compatibility
5. Performance: track their progress with minimal effort, report on effectiveness, outcomes, financial impact
6. Product cost and value: competitively priced, volume and per-unit cost, do results justify costs

Management of a High Performance Team

Highly integrated health promotion teams require high-impact leaders who can pull together the internal staff and the variety of internal and external stakeholders into a high performance team. These leaders must have a clear vision of the future and its alignment with the overall organizations goals. They must be able to create blueprints for action and use language that increases trust between groups, encourages forward thinking, and creates a team energy that nudges program champions forward. High-impact leaders ask good questions, are good listeners, and let others speak first. They follow through on their commitments and work hard to be confident and dependable. Most important, they are genuine, even when they have to talk about the hard things or face up to nonperforming teams or team members.[30]

Maximizing the Creativity and Innovation of Integrated Teams

Teams need sufficient time to explore their different perspectives, play with ideas, and overcome the losses that potentially occur from groups that work independently, but are mutually dependent upon each other. Teams that are successful at rapid creativity and innovation have aligned the team structure, standardized the creative team process, and ensured ample practice of team creativity and innovation. Health promotion managers focused on increasing team creativity and innovation must consider where their teams are most creative and innovative and what triggers or creates these moments. *The Critical Thinking Toolkit* of the American Management Association[31] provides activities to help increase a team's creativity. Managers provoke new thinking by going beyond brainstorming and bringing creative approaches and tools to their teams. Teams are more creative when they are able to eliminate worn-out preconceived ideas, by listing what's in the box, so they can start to think "outside the box." New ideas must be explored, even when it is uncomfortable to do so, and teams need to try to avoid all group think. Group think can extinguish the creative capital of a team by creating a team of homogeneous thinkers. The trick is for managers to support their team in idea generation, but keep them focused on ideas that will yield practical, actionable results. Field trips or excursions into work environments are good ways to force staff to experience different sensory inputs combining sight, smell, taste, touch, and hearing, adding an experienced-based richness to the creative process.[32]

ELEMENT 3: MANAGEMENT OF A HEALTH PROMOTION UNIT OR DEPARTMENT

As workplace health promotion has expanded in many different types and sizes of companies, the science supporting the field has demonstrated that program success is driven by a complex interplay of intrapersonal, interpersonal, organizational, and cultural factors.[33] A strong program infrastructure is critical in providing a foundation from which the day-to-day operation can be effective. But behind the consistent daily operation must be a strategic plan that provides a vision aligned with the business priorities and that drives program participation and engagement.[34]

The Basics of Strategic Planning

Strategic planning is the process a health promotion team uses to envision its future and articulate its goals. It is probably least effective when the process only involves a small number of senior leaders. Diverse teams generate ideas that can lead to more robust strategies and maximize the opportunity for the buy-in from the full integrated team. Strategic plans are based on trends, barriers, opportunities, connections, and events that help the team make decisions today that create a purpose-driven future and culture.[35]

In 2004, the senior leadership of Dow Chemical led a strategy planning process that resulted in approval of a corporate health promotion strategy that specified a set of health and resiliency behaviors they hoped their employees would adopt. Their larger goal was to achieve a global culture of health. The strategy was driven across the globe by a Healthy Workplace Index that scores worksites on nine components (tobacco policy enforcement, physical activity, access to healthy foods, case management of medical conditions, health assessment participation, medical surveillance participation, workplace exposure index, supportive work environment, and stress management). Dow's senior leaders, including the board of directors, understood that their support for the program was critical, but also understood that all employees must embrace these concepts for the program to became a part of the Dow culture and value system.[36]

An effective strategic planning answers six questions:

1. Where are we now or what is our current situation?
2. How did we get here?
3. Where do we want to go or what are our strategic objectives?
4. How do we get from where we are to where we want to go?
5. What obstacles will we have to overcome, or what problems will we have to solve?
6. What additional knowledge, skills, or resources will we need to achieve our strategic objectives?[37]

Answering these questions requires creativity, analysis, and a willingness to be honest and collaborative. Many companies have established strategic planning processes, which can be adopted and used to facilitate the health promotion strategic planning process. Using the same process throughout the organization will help it be understood and accepted throughout the organization. Table 5-2 provides a planning model that was adapted from Robert Leonard Goodstein and colleague's Applied Strategic Planning Model.[38] Several of the components are described below.

Visioning

Michael Hyatt,[39] in his blog concerned with helping leaders leverage influence, suggests that vision and strategy are both important, but with a clear vision you attract the right strategy. Vision always comes first. Visioning is a word picture of the future and sets the overall direction of the program. A good vision helps staff and stakeholders set program destination or program goals. Good visions are not so much about what they are, but what the vision does. Peter Senge[40] describes vision as a reflection of our deeper intentions, a tool for orienting our energies and efforts. Good vision statements must effect present actions, while representing the desired future. For example, the wellness vision statement of the San Francisco General Hospital and Trauma Center is: "A sustainable, vibrant, healthy, engaged, and compassionate community."[41]

Core Values

Core values guide the thoughts and actions of individuals and groups within the program.

Table 5-2: Strategic Planning Model.

Step	Title	Description
1	Preplanning	Answers questions critical to the planning process: Who should be involved? How will absent stakeholders be involved? How long will it take? What information is needed? Who needs to collect and develop the data? How much commitment to the planning process is present?
2	Environmental monitoring	What is happening in their environments that might affect them? Factors to consider are the social demographic and technologic factors, industry and market segmentation factors, the competition, and the organization's history, strengths, and weaknesses.
3	Vision scan	What are the personal and organizational values found in the team? How does the department approach its work? What is the culture of the organization and how does it affect program operation? Who are the stakeholders and what are their fundamental beliefs relative to health and wellness?
4	Mission formulation	What function does the department perform? For whom are these functions performed? How are these functions performed? Why does the department exist?
5	Strategic process modeling	This is the department's first attempt to consider in some detail the paths and channels by which the mission is to be accomplished. Included should be critical success indicators, strategic goals, and the program lines.
6	Performance audit	Once the future has been envisioned, a clear understanding of the current performance is critical. This will include analysis of internal strengths, weaknesses, and external opportunities and threats. It is also important to include an analysis of competitors.
7	Gap analysis	What gaps are present between the current performance and the envisioned future?
8	Integrated action plan	A grand strategy that is a comprehensive approach guiding the department's future by integrating the various parts of the plan.
9	Contingency planning	Contingency planning provides scenarios for each major possibility based on the trends, threats, and opportunities being analyzed.

Source: Adapted from Goodstein L, Nolan T, Pfeiffer J. Applied strategic planning model. In: *Applied Strategic Planning: A Comprehensive Guide*; San Diego, Cal. Pfeiffer & Company. 1992: 1-35.

Values define the standard of behavior, or code of conduct, that help the program team enjoy working together. They provide guidelines for preventing and resolving interpersonal issues and are the foundation for high trust, and high performance. Values are the foundation for strengthening relationships within the program team, and with internal and external stakeholders. An example of core values would be the University of Texas MD Anderson Cancer Center core values of caring, integrity, and discovery. After agreement on core values the team should work on a program mission statement.

Mission Statement

The vision statement creates a tangible view of what the program wants to be, and the mission statement describes the conditions that will be true when it is achieved. It describes how the present will lead to the future and lists the broad goals and key measures of success. A good mission statement not only provides the purpose and quality standards, but also serves as a guiding star on the horizon that captures the soul of the program, inspiring change and progress. Good mission statements are customer/client driven, and sensitive to environmental and cultural forces. A powerful method to explore the program mission statement is to use the "five whys" technique. Start with a statement that describes the program and then asks "Why is it important?" five times. An example would be, "Our program provides health risk assessments to all employees," and the answers to each of the five whys will bring the mission closer to the true purpose of the program. Use real-life examples to communicate your team's mission. If it is made up of a lot of buzzwords, jargon, or unclear language, it will be hard to communicate and just cause confusion. In a recent article in Forbes, Patrick Hull[42] suggests there are four essential questions that your mission statement must answer: (1) What do

we do? (2) How do we do it? (3) Whom do we do it for? and (4) What value are we bringing?

Linking the program mission statement to the program strategy seems obvious, yet many program managers realize too late that their inability to garner management and employee support is directly related to their program's mission and goals. Short-term acceptance and long-term program survival depend on the program's ability to meet the basic mission and goals of the organization that it serves. The Centers for Disease Control and Prevention[43] suggests that there are six reasons organizations invest in workplace health promotion: (1) help employees take responsibility for lifestyle choices, (2) educate the workforce about hazards and wellness opportunities, (3) enhance employee productivity, (4) reduce absence and idleness, (5) reduce health care costs, and (6) shift health care paradigm from treatment to prevention. These six motives can better focus efforts in formulating a mission statement that is aligned with the company's mission and underscores the importance of the health promotion department. Once a mission statement has been written, program goals and objective must be addressed.

Goals and Objectives

Goals are specific and measureable accomplishments that can be achieved within a specified time and under specific cost constraints. Goals should complement the fulfillment of the mission statement and require team effort and individual commitment. It is important that individuals who are involved in goal achievement be active participants in the goals-setting process. Active participation in the goal-setting process produces an ownership that instills the motivation and commitment necessary to successfully reach the goals. The raw materials of goal setting are developed in answering the questions of "Who? What? When? How? and How much?" Well-defined goal statements are crucial to goal achievement and formulize the Who? When? and How? questions into clear motivating statements. Many teams use the SMART method to ensure that all the necessary elements are included in goal statements[44]:

S: Specific
M: Measurable
A: Action oriented
R: Realistic
T: Time and resource constrained

Goal statements can be divided into three different categories: essential, problem solving, and innovative. Essential goals are those that are necessary for continued and ongoing processes. An example of an essential goal in a worksite program would be to complete an health risk assessment (HRA) intervention on 75% of the workforce by the end of the third quarter, using existing staff and staying within budget. A problem-solving goal statement outlines the necessary activities needed to improve performance. An example would be to reduce the number of individuals that drop out of the diabetes support group from 50% to 20% by the end of the year without adding existing staff and staying within budget. The last goal statement category is innovative, and it focuses on improving current conditions. Unlike problem-solving statements it does not focus on a problem, but on ways to speed up processes, make a process cheaper, easier, or safer. An example of a worksite program innovative goal statement would be to change the current class registration system to an online system by the end of the year. Once goal statements have been written, objectives can be developed that become the tactical plans or methods used to reach and achieve the goals.

Tactical and Operational Plans

Tactical plans describe the tactics that will be used to activate a strategy and make it work. These plans break down the broader mission and goal statements into actionable chunks with a scope of less than 1 year. The strategic plan responds to the "What?" and the tactical plans responds to the "How?" Tactical plans should be very flexible documents, but use the SMART goal writing format to ensure specific goals with fixed deadlines. Tactical plans will list budgetary requirements, potential resources, and how these plans align with the current marketing, program delivery, and evaluation plans. Tactical plans lead to operational plans, which describe the day-to-day program operation. The operational plans become a roadmap that is focused on accomplishment of the goals outlined in the tactical plans within a realistic time frame. These could be single-use plans created for a single occurring event or they could be ongoing plans for activities, interventions, procedures, or policies that are ongoing and require continuous staff involvement and attention. Strong operation plans become the backbone of a health promotion team and successful operations management.

Operations Management

Operations management is the administration of business practices as efficiently as possible to maximize success.[45] In a health promotion program the manager must efficiently "operationalize" the daily tasks required to accomplish the operational, tactical, and strategic goals. Financial controls and budgeting are major elements of operations management. The financial and budgeting responsibilities are crucial to the success of programs. Through the budgeting process, planning becomes realistic and managers become involved and gain ownership in a crucial quality control system made up of different cost and profit centers. As the managers begin to understand the monthly financial statement they can better manage the relationships of cost, participation, and individual and group programming success.

Budget Planning

A budget is the formalized financial plan of the goals and objectives of the program. It is generally expressed in schedules of expenses, surplus or deficits, and product or service volume for a predetermined period. Many program budgets are drawn from a larger departmental budget, such as Human Resources, Occupational Health, or Facilities Management, and thus are generally initiated by a combination of a top-down and bottom-up approaches. The process can start with the health promotion staff members by having them review the programming, marketing, and promotional plans for the coming year. Each would build a budget for his or her program responsibilities, describing each component in terms of costs, revenue, and potential participation/engagement or services to be delivered. The manager then would add appropriate administrative costs (such as salaries, facility rent, and upkeep costs). This completed plan is then submitted to the next budgetary level for review.

Budget Types

There are several different budget types, but most health promotion programs will only deal with personnel, operating, and capital budgets. The personnel budget reflects all the costs related to staffing and, for most program budgets, is the largest. An operations budget focuses on the operations areas (equipment, programming, preventive maintenance, materials, supplies, etc.) and can be managed in various formats. The most common budget format is the line-item budget that groups different categories of expenditures. Another budget format found in health promotion programs is the functional-area budget. In a functional-area format, categories would be organized by functional areas such as marketing, program delivery, administration, personnel, and facilities and equipment. Another useful budget format in health promotion is the intervention-area budget format where allocations are broken down into intervention areas (stress, nutrition, physical activity, parenting, screening, case management, and other programming areas). Both the functional and intervention budget formats help the manager better understand how program resources are aligned to participation and engagement and allow for real-time adjustments. A capital budget reflects expenditures that are associated with equipment, facility, or new technology development projects. Capital budgets are often divided into categories of capital improvement and equipment. An example of a capital improvement might be additional space required for a lactation room or bike barn. In fitness centers, where equipment is replaced every 5 to 7 years owing to the high replacement costs and constant technology developments, staggering replacement strategies ensure centers have new pieces of equipment on the floor almost every year.

Implementing a Budget

A budget serves as a quality control tool and helps the team identify priorities and provides justification for decreasing or increasing programming expenditures. All programming decisions are based in part on budgetary performance standards. Efficient record management techniques and the use of computer spreadsheets and accounting programs help coordinate the implementation of a budget. Record management is concerned with specific procedures and processes for controlling and documenting expenditures and revenue: formal procedures for paying contract services, salaries, rent, and ordering and paying for supplies and materials. These procedures ensure proper records are maintained to provide a paper trail history of each budgetary action. Proper record management of supporting documents is vital to a successful budgetary process. There is a wide assortment of computer software programs providing budget management and analysis capabilities. Most of these programs have built-in graphic capabilities that create graphs and charts that can be used to enhance budget presentations. Managers should regularly report on the budget and budget variances to their staff to keep the program moving forward. A budget variance report shows the budgeted amounts compared to actual amounts spent. Typically, the report provides a dual set of dollar values representing data from the current period (month) and year-to-date data. Erroneous variations between the budgeted allowances and actual results should be explained and then corrected. Company policy often dictates when variance explanations are required, but it is good management to review each summary report and ensure expenditures have been accurately recorded.

Maintaining and Growing a Budget

The health promotion manager has the responsibility not only for planning a budget, but also for insuring that the assigned amounts are monitored and used for the specific resources. Budget efficiency is computed by calculating the ratio of the difference between the actual expenditure and budgeted amount, divided by the budgeted amount: Efficiency Ratio = Difference Between Actual and Budgeted Amounts.

Budget Amount

The budget efficiency ratio provides information about the performance of each line item and comparisons for budgetary periods. It can be influenced by many factors, but in health promotion programs, participation and engagement are the major determinants of expenditures and revenues. Program managers have three types of costs that make up their budgets and are defined as fixed, variable, and semivariable.[46] Fixed costs are those that remain constant over the reporting period and an example would be rent. Variable costs rise and fall in relation to changes in participation and engagement or other activities that change during the reporting period. An example

of variable costs would be the rise in use of health education materials during a month where several mini-health fairs are offered. Semivariable costs are those that are partially fixed, and partially variable. In bike barns or fitness centers, there is an expected level of soap usage that is predicted from participation. When participation levels increase, a variable amount of soap must be purchased to meet the demand. Managers should plot the performance of fixed, variable, and semivariable costs and revenues to gain a clear view of the budgetary process. These plots, combined with the monthly variance reports and computed efficiency ratios, provide the manager with data helpful in building a case for budget growth. Budget growth is tied to program success and the potential to increase multiple touches and dose response, both evidence-based strategies shown to decrease health risk and their related costs. Crucial to budgetary growth is the ability to meet senior management's program delivery expectations and continuing to educate them on their champion role in supporting new and more effective program options or expanding programs that work. Managers that effectively and efficiently administrate their budgets display the skills and understanding necessary to manage and build budgets and gain the backing of their champions. Champions that regularly receive program and budgetary reports will recognize the need for budget expansion and can mandate and support the necessary actions. Through shared employee stories, champions are continually reminded that the total value of the health promotion activities and services go way beyond return on investment (ROI), and program and budget growth are significant elements in the company's employee engagement strategy. When a manager relinquishes the budget responsibility to another staff member, it weakens the potential efficiency and growth of the program, for the manager loses the potential leverage within a budget. Only by observing and understanding the departmental expenditures and revenues that parallel participant engagement will the manager ensure budget efficiency and growth.

Facilities and Equipment

Facilities are not a component of all health promotion programs, but when a facility is included, the effectiveness of its management is directly related to program success. Each program component included in the program mix must be reviewed for facility and equipment requirements. Facilities should be reviewed for functional space requirements, participant accessibility, signage, and safety and emergency procedures. There are several sources (*Facility Planning Design for Health Physical Activity, Recreation, and Sport*, and *ACSM's Health Fitness Facility Standards and Guidelines*, 4th edition) that provide an extensive range of information on facility planning, from initiation of space planning with an architect to selection and supervision of contractors.[47,48] Most health promotion programs use training or facility department spaces for programming. Managers will review and outline their space and equipment (chair, tables, LCD, flip charts, computers) requirements and make requests through the appropriate department. Programs that offer fitness classes in training rooms will need to ensure chairs can be easily stacked and tables collapsed and moved off to the side to make room for the class. Portable exercise mats and equipment used in these classes should be stored in an area close to the class to make setup easier. Some programs have dedicated space for demonstration cooking areas, lactation rooms, stress-busting stations, power nap areas, game rooms, bike barns, fitness centers, community gardens, and outside fitness areas and walk/jog trails. Programs that have dedicated space must have comprehensive facility and equipment plans that not only maximize efficient use of the space, but also ensure the safety of participants and staff and reduce risk. Risk is associated with an event that could happen

in the future and is definitely undesirable. One of the best resources for the health and fitness professional on risk management is the book titled *Risk Management for Health/ Fitness Professionals: Legal Issues and Strategies*.[49] The authors use a four-step risk management process outlined in Figure 5-2 and composed of (1) assessment of liability exposure, (2) development of risk management strategies and plan, (3) implementation of the plan, and (4) regular evaluation of the plan to ensure risk is being managed daily. Managers must ensure staff recognize the importance of risk management and take ownership for reduction of risk in their programming. Unannounced risk management inspections and trainings around demonstration emergency situations build staff confidence and ownership for risk management.

Managers must also understand the needs and regulations for special and disability populations, relative to facility and equipment planning. Program accessibility is a major issue in program participation and engagement and the needs of special populations must be taken into account early in the facilities- and equipment-planning stages. The Administration on Aging reports that persons older than 65 years represent one in every eight Americans (12.9%) and in 2030 that number is expected to grow to 19%.[50] The Wall Street Journal[51] reports more than 18% of the labor force consists of individuals older than 65 years and this number is expected to grow. The Disability Compendium, published in 2013, indicates that 10.2% of the U.S. population is living with disabilities, and 35% of these individuals are working.[52] Successful programs ensure they meet the special needs of these populations. An example would be cancer survivorship programming that offers focused programming on the nutritional, work life effectiveness, and importance of physical activity to survivorship. Many programs, in collaboration with their human resource departments, offer training to special need

Figure 5-2: Major Components of the Four Risk Management Steps.

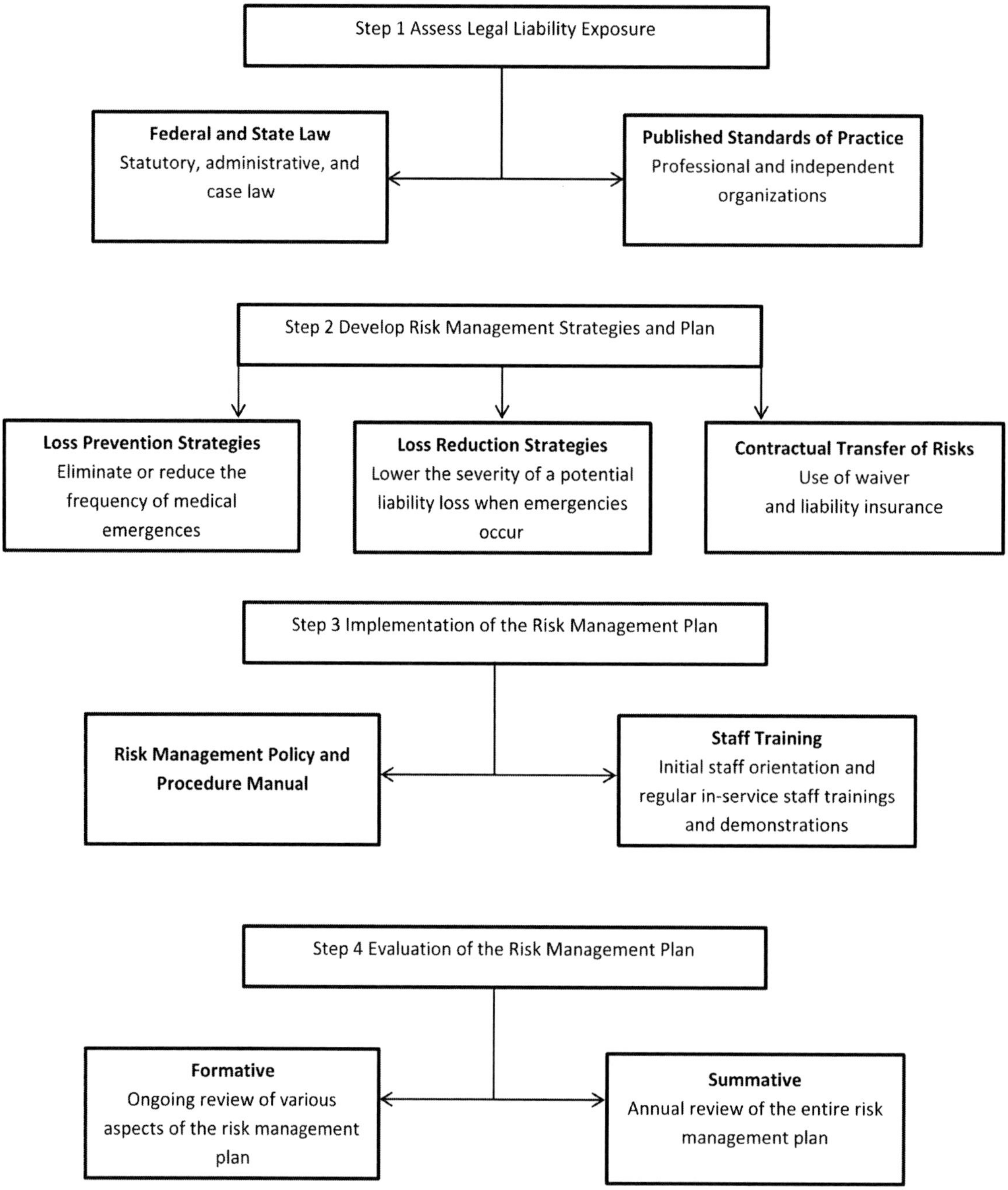

```
┌─────────────────────────────────────────────────────┐
│          Step 1 Assess Legal Liability Exposure       │
└─────────────────────────────────────────────────────┘

┌──────────────────────────┐        ┌──────────────────────────┐
│  Federal and State Law    │        │ Published Standards of Practice │
│ Statutory, administrative, and │ ←→ │ Professional and independent │
│        case law           │        │       organizations       │
└──────────────────────────┘        └──────────────────────────┘


┌─────────────────────────────────────────────────────┐
│   Step 2 Develop Risk Management Strategies and Plan  │
└─────────────────────────────────────────────────────┘

┌──────────────────────┐  ┌──────────────────────┐  ┌──────────────────────┐
│ Loss Prevention Strategies │ Loss Reduction Strategies │ Contractual Transfer of Risks │
│ Eliminate or reduce the │  │ Lower the severity of a potential │ Use of waiver │
│ frequency of medical │    │ liability loss when emergencies │ and liability insurance │
│     emergences       │    │        occur         │  │                      │
└──────────────────────┘  └──────────────────────┘  └──────────────────────┘


┌─────────────────────────────────────────────────────┐
│   Step 3 Implementation of the Risk Management Plan   │
└─────────────────────────────────────────────────────┘

┌──────────────────────────┐        ┌──────────────────────────┐
│ Risk Management Policy and │       │      Staff Training       │
│     Procedure Manual      │  ←→   │ Initial staff orientation and │
│                          │        │ regular in-service staff trainings │
│                          │        │    and demonstrations     │
└──────────────────────────┘        └──────────────────────────┘


┌─────────────────────────────────────────────────────┐
│     Step 4 Evaluation of the Risk Management Plan     │
└─────────────────────────────────────────────────────┘

┌──────────────────────────┐        ┌──────────────────────────┐
│        Formative          │        │        Summative          │
│ Ongoing review of various │  ←→   │ Annual review of the entire risk │
│ aspects of the risk management │   │    management plan        │
│          plan             │        │                          │
└──────────────────────────┘        └──────────────────────────┘
```

Source: Adapted from Risk Management for Health/Fitness Professionals: Legal Issues and Strategies (2009).

and disability employees on their employee rights under the law, company benefits support, and American with Disabilities Act accommodations. It is important that managers keep up with the Americans with Disability Act through the Federal Register.[53] There are several large employee benefit consulting groups (Towers Watson and Buckconsultant) that provide white papers and reports summarizing the different regulatory changes and can be very helpful for health promotion managers.[54,55]

The last function in successful management of facilities and equipment is preventive maintenance. This ranges from simply keeping employees comfortable in clean spaces to ensuring that equipment works. Effective preventive maintenance requires that the owners' manuals and warranty materials are catalogued for future use, and a listing of manufacturer representatives is maintained. These documents are usually kept in the policy and procedure manual. The policy and procedure manual documents the administrative actions expected in a variety of situations, from program planning, new member orientation, and emergency procedures. They should include the policies and procedures necessary to ensure safe and successful program operations. Policy and procedural titles should be friendly, using key words describing their primary contents. Policy and procedural statements should provide specific information regarding the issues and/or procedures that give step-by-step instructions. There are many different ways to organize a policy and procedure manual, but generally they are categorized by key areas with appropriate subsections. Table 5-3 provides a sample of potential categories that might be found in a policy and procedure manual in a health promotion program. Many different variables can be used to measure the success of a health promotion manager as the unit or department leader, but the bottom-line measure is the participants' experience

or satisfaction with the program and its staff. Participants can be thrilled about losing weight or getting off tobacco, but quickly forget their behavioral success with one bad lost-and-found experience, or a health coach that is late for too many coaching sessions. Good programming is the result of a team effort that is focused on delivering high-quality programs, but also excellence in the administrative aspects of the program that can engage participants daily through various programming, communication, and environmental activities. Health promotion managers must ensure their teams are trained, have the knowledge, and are inspired to administrate the programs they coordinate with excellence as their standard.

ELEMENT 4: MANAGEMENT OF PROGRAM DESIGN, PLANNING, AND DELIVERY

The major purpose of a health promotion program is to deliver integrated programs focused on total value of worker health. The World Economic Forum report titled *The Workplace Wellness Alliance: Investing in a Sustainable Workforce*[2] suggests that workplace wellness is a part of the solution to the human capital challenges employers are facing. Successful programs support the company's business goals and strategies, and are relevant to the needs and interest of employees and their families. Programming has been called an "art" and a "science" because of the mix of skills and experience required in planning and implementation. Program delivery is divided into three distinct stages: program design and planning, implementation, and evaluation.

Program Design and Planning

The initial stage of program design and planning is focused on understanding the needs of the organizational stakeholders, employee groups, and individual employees and their families.

Table 5-3: Example of Table of Contents for a Health Promotion Policy and Procedure Manual.

Key Area	Subsections
Staff management	Hiring New employee orientation Work schedules Annual employee evaluation Temporary workers Part-time workers Travel request Training request Vacation request Media inquiries Internships Termination
Facility management	Opening and closing procedures Key control Purchasing procedures Inventory control procedures Lost and found Cleaning schedule Preventive maintenance Emergency procedures
Participant/ client management	Program enrollment/registration Fee collection Participant data reporting Program follow-up procedures Coaching signup and follow-up Coaching schedule Group class schedule Group class signup
Program management	Screening and assessment setup procedures Screening and assessment reporting Program development worksheet Program proposal worksheet Annual staff planning retreat Committee charters Online communication procedures (all employee e-mails, newsletters, etc.)
Program evaluation	Coaching reports Group class reports Dose response reports Neighborhood report s Health risk assessment reports Annual medical care costs report Annual workers' compensation and disability report Annual absenteeism report Annual productivity report Annual program satisfaction report Annual employee recruitment and retention report

Chapter 4 "Designing Programs" and Chapter 13 "Health Assessment" provide concepts and strategies for linking and leveraging the different data sets that provide a snapshot of a company's health and well-being. The snapshot is used to identify different targets and initiate programs and activities that will engage the maximum number of employees and their families.[56] The Centers for Disease Control and Prevention[57] suggests that the program plan should be strategic and include broad techniques to achieve program goals, but also have a tactical focus to include steps necessary to implement and evaluate specific programs. They list six concepts that should be used in the development of a program plan.

1. Systematic linking of health and productivity metrics
2. Ensuring confidentiality of employee information
3. Leveraging and building on existing activities
4. Recognizing the diverse needs of individuals and groups
5. Providing multiple education and participant opportunities
6. Maintaining program accessibility and flexibility

Program planning can be initiated in many different ways, but if a committee has not been formed the first step would be to form a health promotion committee. Many programs start with a vision from the company president, or a senior champion. A committee is important for it creates a sense of ownership in the program for the employee population. The committee needs to be a good cross-section of the employee population, for a good mix provides the diversity necessary to have a strong voice across the needs and interest of the entire workforce. Committee members could be appointed, be volunteers, or formal and informal leaders that serve as the eyes and ears for the program. It is very important that the committee have enough members with formal power to work within the company culture to get things done and gain the resources it needs. Many health promotion programs in larger companies have dedicated staff, but the mid to small companies could have part-time staff, or an employee who only spends 25% of his or her time on health promotion. Whatever the staff situation, the committee structure is important in program design. In programs with a full staff, the manager would bring program plans to the committee to gain a sense of ownership, and enlist the support of the committee in promoting the plan throughout the company. In smaller programs where there is not a full-time staff, the committee would do the planning or it might get help from a consultant. There are many ways to organize the data collection and assessment phase, but a good way to integrate the data and present it to the committee or for a committee to organize it is a SWOT analysis.[58] SWOT stands for strengths, weaknesses, opportunities, and threats. The Centers for Disease Control and Prevention[59] has identified four key questions that help better prioritize the findings.

1. What are the key health and well-being issues affecting employees, employee teams, and employee families?
2. What factors at the worksite and within the community influence health?
3. What are the employees' health and safety concerns?
4. What strategies are most appropriate to address these health issues?

A well-orchestrated SWOT analysis will help identify health issue with high interest, high need, high leadership support, and high environmental support. Rarely do programs have all four, but programs that hit one or several of these have a greater opportunity for success. Program prioritization is an art of balancing needs, interests, leadership, and environmental supports. The health interest of a target group is important, but the needs identified in the data analysis process normally have more weight in program prioritizing. The level of leadership support is significant and their expectations can make or break a program, but it's also very important to consider the environment and if it's easy for individuals and teams to make and sustain healthy choices. The program mission statement could get driven by the program prioritization process and written when it is complete, or it could get written before the process begins and is driven by the vision of senior management or a champion. Think of the mission statement as the overall purpose for the program, providing the context or framework within which intervention strategies are formulated. The SMART goals reviewed earlier will be followed by objectives that describe precisely what is necessary to reach the goals. An example of goals and objectives:

Physical activity goal: Our workplace Be Well Program will promote an active lifestyle during the 2014 calendar year.

Objective 1: By March, 2014, a policy will be in place allowing flextime for physical activity.

Objective 2: By August 2014, a map with indoor walking routes and outdoor walking trails will be provided to all employees and placed on the Be Well Internet and Intranet sites.

Once the program goals and objectives have been written an overall program mix should be developed to reach the goals and objectives. Program mix refers to the program opportunities that will be offered to ensure program goals are reached. Figure 5-3 illustrates the concept of program mix.

It is wise in new programs to have a narrow program breadth and shallow program depth to allow programmers to concentrate their effort on doing a few programs well to ensure they gain the support of employees. As the program grows in popularity and success more program lines and options can be added, deepening the program depth and broadening the program lines. A comprehensive health promotion program will have a variety of program lines supported by different intervention options. Comprehensiveness is a best practice dimension and is listed in Table 5-4 "Best Practice Dimensions of a Workplace Health Promotion Program."[60] After a program mix has been developed it's good to put the program mix on an annual calendar and see how it would flow through the year.

A calendar places a program mix along a time line for program development, preprogram promotion, program registration, implementation/delivery, and program evaluation. Comprehensive programs can be complex and offer many different program opportunities during a month, and seeing them laid out in a calendar format serves as a

Figure 5-3: Program Mix.

Program Breadth Program Lines Available		
Program Depth Program Options Available	Narrow	Broad
Shallow	Few program lines and few options in each line	Several program lines, but few options in each line
Deep	Few program lines, but many options in each line	Several program lines, and many options in each line

Table 5-4: Best Practice Dimensions of a Workplace Health Promotion Program.

Leadership engagement throughout the organization: senior, middle, supervisors, ambassadors/champs, self-leadership
Program relevance that address critical factors driving participation and engagement
Partnerships with multiple internal and external stakeholders
Comprehensiveness including programs addressing awareness, motivation, skills, and opportunity
Implementation that is planned, coordinated, managed, and evaluated
Engagement promoting respect, trust, and facilitating program ownership
Communication strategy that brands the program, ensures visibility, ongoing communications, and multiple delivery channels
Data driven providing guidance through ongoing measurements, evaluation, and reporting
Compliance ensuring that the program meets regulatory requirements

Source: Adapted from Pronk N. Best practice design principles of worksite health and wellness programs. *ACSMs Health Fitness J.* 2013;18:1–5.

reality check. Many programs will use a 15- to 18-month program calendar to allow for better long-range planning and visioning. Program activities should be staggered throughout the year, weaving in national and state health themes. The U.S. Department of Health and Human Services[61] provides a National Health Observances calendar that is dedicated to raising awareness about important health topics.

Up to this point the program design and planning steps have all been focused on what is termed the "Big P" or total program. When the program calendar has been approved by staff and/or given an approving nod from the committee, it is time to hand out programming assignments, which is the little "p" of program design and planning. Little "p" programming can be managed more effectively, if a standard program planning check list is used by programmers. A check list can be developed that ensures programs

are designed on appropriate behavior change theory and evidence-based practices. There are many different program models that could be used at this stage,[62] but when a staff team or committee develop their own check list the pride and ownership for programming is significant. An example of a program planning check list developed by a health promotion team is provided in Table 5-5.

Program Implementation

The second stage of program delivery is implementation and is concerned with reach, program effectiveness, and sustaining participation and behavior change. Quintiliani[63] and others[64] have raised the importance of reach or involving a significant portion of the employee population and their families in successful workplace programs. Successful reach strategies work because they are customized to "fit" the work environment.

Table 5-5: Programming Planning Checklist.

Write out each of the following:
1. What is the major purpose of the program?
2. What is the need for the program?
3. What are the potential benefits of this program?
4. What are the two to four program goals? Include in each goal's statement appropriate metrics.
5. What are the program tactics? Brief program description, population or targets, marketing/promotion ideas, delivery ideas, and evaluation focus.
Program components to consider and describe if they will be used:
1. Program rules or requirements
2. Registration or orientation process
3. Participant goal setting
4. Participant barrier discovery process
5. Skill-building component
6. Educational component
7. Social support component
8. Motivational component
9. Environmental support component
10. Tracking systems
11. Necessary forms
12. Incentive systems
13. Celebration activities

A large hospital system with more than 80 different buildings needs a different reach strategy than a small printing business with one shop. Successful reach strategies use multiple touchpoint strategies that mix traditional and virtual health promotion programming. When designing a reach strategy it is important to consider community building. A closer look at the large hospital system with 80 different buildings finds it is actually made up of 15 different neighborhoods, and targeting these different neighborhoods as communities improves reach or maximizes participation and engagement numbers. Program effectiveness can be defined in many different ways and it is helpful for teams to consider how they will measure program effectiveness. The reality is that in most programs the effectiveness metrics will be different because of barriers in data collection and analysis. An example would be two large hospital systems where different buildings or neighborhoods have been targeted, but one system has only a paper pencil participation system, which makes participation very hard to track with large number of participants. Basically, they will be able to give only participation numbers to their senior management. But the other hospital uses a badge system, which allows specific tracking not just of participation but also of what type of neighborhood and departments are involved. The Rand Report on Workplace Wellness just released to the U.S. Congress[5] describes the possible importance of dose response on behavior change and cost savings. The more employees and their families participate and are engaged in wellness activities, the more opportunity for sustained behavior change. The hospital system that can track participation and engagement through its badge system can fine-tune tactics that increase dose response possibility in specific neighborhoods for specific high-risk behaviors.

Program Registration

Program implementation has several techniques that program managers must understand and manage well if programs are going to maximize program reach and effectiveness. Program registration is the first step in program implementation and should be kept simple and only require information critical to participation success. Many work environments now use employee badges, and registration for many programs will just be a badge swipe. Use of Internet portals to have individuals sign up for programs provides the opportunity to tie into exiting databases that already describe the participants' demographics, risk behaviors, and possibly, dose response history.

Program Kickoff, Orientation, New Program Participant Packet

Many programs fail because of bad or slow participant starts. Participants don't understand the purpose of the program, don't understand the rules of a challenge, or didn't realize the program had a substantial cost. Depending on the program and the population being targeted, there are lots of different ways to kick off programs. Health promotion committees and staff members should brainstorm in many different ways, and then test the ideas with different participants for feedback. Piloting several different kickoff scenarios is always a good idea and will significantly increase the opportunity for success. Face-to-face kickoff meetings or group program orientations always provide time for questions, but online program participant packets can also be just as effective.

Goal Setting

Goals will be covered in Chapter 8, but managers need to understand that individuals and groups involved in goals provide specific targets and serve as a frame of reference for decision making and performance feedback. A recent review article on health and wellness coaching found that patients or participants determined goal setting an important process in behavioral intervention in health care.[65] Goals are shared conceptions of intention and place value on the processes and outcomes involved in daily tasks. Team goals reviewed and tracked at team meetings provide a continual focus on results, and provide bonding and support opportunities. Goal reviews provide opportunities for feedback, revitalization, and the potential for updating or rewriting goal statements to fit the current situation or challenges. Behavior change is all about the small steps necessary to move forward, but goal statements need to have both long-range goals or vision, and short-range steps that make the long-range goals reachable. Every "little p" and "Big P" program needs goal statements on the organizational, group, and individual participant levels.

Incentives and Motivation

Chapter 10 will cover intrinsic and extrinsic incentives, so it won't be covered in great detail here, but the Affordable Care Act has expanded the penetration of health promotion programming into worksites of all sizes and increased the number of programs that reward workers who achieve health improvement goals.[66] It is important that managers understand the Genetic Information Nondiscrimination Act of 2008, and the Health Insurance Portability and Accountability Act of 1996 (HIPAA) and final rule Incentives for Nondiscriminatory Wellness Programs in Group Health Plans (2013).[67] The behavioral economics literature continues to grow, but it is clear from the research to date that it does not produce long-term behavior change.[68] Incentives have become a significant aspect of most health promotion programs and managers must be ready to manage them successfully. Keep the rules simple and focused on one goal at a time. Behavior change, such as weight loss requiring change in multiple behaviors (increase movement, decrease calories, increase plant-based food, etc.), makes it tough to manage effectively an incentive program based on multiple changes. Consider rewarding points instead of dollars or specific gifts that participants can redeem for something they value. It is important to design a program where everyone has an opportunity to be a winner. Programs can reward individuals for maintaining health habits, individuals that take first steps, or individuals for supporting others. Incentive programs can be designed so many different types of individuals win. Most important is to focus on the positive, recognizing and celebrating individual and team successes. Incentive programs can be designed to reward progress or penalize individuals for unhealthy behaviors or not making progress. Program managers need to be ready to manage incentive programs effectively, and be able to explain to all level of participants why an incentive program is just not another cost-shifting approach.[69]

Social Support/Networking Systems

Chapter 21 will discuss social norms and social support systems, and managers need to incorporate these strategies in their program designs to increase the opportunity for program success. Social contagion theory examines the power and engagement possibilities within the dynamic social networks of human behavior.[70] The sophistication and advancement of the social networking literature[71] have significantly increased the use of team or buddy systems and have provided a better understanding of delivering wellness programs in the home. In large employee-based programs, where population targets become employee neighborhoods developed within specific buildings, the sense of community developed through social support is significant and important in programming. Individuals must be trained how to support each other through the use of emotional, informational, and instructional cues, and being evaluative or providing feedback. Program managers should look for natural occurring social networks that could be used as a framework for programming. Social support can be both formal and informal, and sometimes the more powerful support may come from informal lunchtime-sharing groups focused on specific issues. A good example would be a "terrible two's" parent group that meets on every third Tuesday of the month to talk about issues relative to life with 2 year olds. Social support could be a team challenge that energizes and engages teams around a single wellness issue such as "move more." Team challenges can be powerful catalysts for health behavior change and can boost participation and engagement rates. Team challenges can be driven by formal or informal leadership buy-in that is translated into team ownership and pride for doing a health behavior change together. Managers need to offer a program mix with individual, group, and organizational level programming that helps grow social support networks by helping participants develop more positive relationships based on healthy choices within the worksite and/or at home.

Program Momentum

Program momentum is an important concept for managers to understand and build. Just like linear momentum in classical mechanics, program momentum is the product of mass and velocity. In large worksites it can take heavy promotion, and significant senior and middle management support to kick off an institutional program to get high participation quickly. In smaller worksites, the mass issue might be easier, but other issues become barriers to program momentum. Experienced programmers will develop a program mix that builds program momentum in a variety of different offerings, growing participation and engagement. A significant strategy to build and maintain program momentum is using program advocates, ambassadors, or champs. These individuals might serve on the program committee, but that is not a requirement. These individuals are the torch barriers for the program, and in their respective departments, divisions, hallways, neighborhoods, or communities they recruit program participants and work to decrease participation and engagement barriers.[72] The use of program champs has been raised throughout the best practice literature and should be a program strategy that managers master.[73]

ELEMENT 5: MANAGEMENT OF THE REPORTING PROCESS

The importance of collecting, analyzing, and reporting evaluation metrics throughout the "Big P" and "little p" program lifecycles has significant bottom-line importance for program managers. Chapter 6 will cover program evaluation, so it will not be covered in depth here. What program managers do with

the evaluation results is important and will be covered in this section. Let's start with "little p" programming. A weight loss challenge could collect a variety of different outcome and impact metrics. Reporting these results back to participants is important so they understand where they have succeeded and where they need more work. Weight loss is the result of behavior change involving a variety of different diet, movement, and emotional support skills. Providing participants with feedback specifically about growth in these skill areas or work that needs to be done to keep moving forward is important and needs to be part of the "little p" measurement reporting process. Staff programmers, or committees that design, develop, and implement programs will not get better without specific information about the administration of the program. This is called *process evaluation* and can look at a variety of different program parts. Did the registration process work? If not, why not? Did the buddy support program work? Why not? Did the celebration activity work? Was it at the right time? This information needs to be given to the specific programmer or committee members that implemented the program, so they can use the information to improve program success.

Program managers should be providing their supervisors a variety of different reports. They could be reporting on specific programs, or monthly reports that summarize team member reports. Some programs use a quarterly or semiannual reporting structure to keep senior management abreast of the program's growth and success, and ensure their ownership. Many companies use financial and product volume dashboards to keep employees informed on the important data that drives business success within their company. Dashboards are now being used by health promotion managers for the same purpose. Health promotion dashboards could follow risk stratification, participation and engagement rates, neighborhood or community penetration, participant satisfaction, and modifiable health care expenditures.[74] Program dashboards can be placed on health promotion Internet or Intranet sites to provide a transparent view of the program's growth and success. Dashboards can support the total value of worker health by providing a variety of different measurements that help expand an individual's view of the relationship between behavior change, health, and productivity. Managers need to consider several other terms that are being used in the health and productivity literature. Leading indicators provide a basis for the health promotion strategy and include the health risk, biometric screening results, and prevalence of chronic conditions. Lagging indicators are the financial, presenteeism, and productivity costs resulting from an inability to better manage the leading indicators. Parry and Sherman[75] suggest one more indicator they call "care indicators" or preventative care, program participation, employee engagement, and health care utilization. The care indicators represent the health promotion program elements that drive lagging indicators down. The use of leading, care, and lagging indicators by managers increases the tools they have to communicate to their supervisors, program champions, and senior management about program success. Unfortunately, most programs do not have access to the financial data necessary to build lagging indicators. These programs must rely on ROI calculators to provide estimates on the financial viability of the programs. The Centers for Disease Control and Prevention[76] in its Healthier Worksite Initiative provides cost calculators for depression, tobacco, alcohol, physical inactivity, and obesity.

CONCLUSION

The chapter reviewed current program management practices and promising practices that are being used to deliver integrated programs focused on total value of worker health.[77] The management literature is clear: good managers lead through a team and must manage themselves, as well as connections and collaborations outside of their control.[78] The chapter focused on the essential management competencies that are necessary to build and maintain a high performance team capable of startup, cross-promotion, maintenance, and growth of integrated programs. Managers are individuals who have both authority and responsibility for the actions of their departments, but also critical to their success is their ability to manage the department's interaction and integration with external and internal partners and stakeholders. This role challenges managers to be true leaders who, through their "big picture" work influence, but also provide direction and delegate actions to their subordinates. A manager's opportunity for success is significantly tied to his or her understanding and ability to manage the constraints and opportunities of cost, time, and people. The best managers have learned to mix their leadership and management skills, relying on their big picture abilities, and understanding the importance of managing the details.[79] Successful managers have increased their potential and the potential of their program by integrating these two roles. The synergistic relationship between leadership and management provides a balance in the program that increases the opportunity for continued program success and growth. The leaders/managers must engage others, commit their full energy, and create value and success through development of four roles:

- Visionary: Guiding organizational and individual growth through creation and communications of a compelling vision and strategy;
- Tactician: Ensuring that results are achieved by effectively planning work, delegating responsibility, reviewing performance, and improving systems and processes;
- Facilitator: Creating an environment of collaboration and partnership to ensure effective working relationships;

- Contributor: Creating organizational success by contributing their personal talents, experiences, and abilities.[80]

Successful managers become visionaries of a culture of health that inspires and guides the energy of their staff and partners to transform the workplace into an environment where healthy choice is the easy choice. In these environments, individual employees accept the responsibility and accountability for their health and also the supportive ownership for the health of their work teams and families.

Glossary

Competencies: Are the measurable or observable knowledge, skills, abilities, and behaviors critical to successful job performance.

Leadership: Process of social influence in which one person can enlist the aid and support of others in the accomplishment of a common task.

Mentee: A person who is being mentored.

Mentors: An experienced person who advises a less experienced colleague.

Multipliers: Are leaders who use their intelligence to amplify the smarts and capabilities of the people around them.

Onboarding: Mechanisms through which new employees acquire the necessary knowledge, skills, and behaviors to become effective organizational members and insiders.

Operational plans: Is the process of linking the strategic goals and objectives to the tactical goals and objectives and describe the day-to-day operation.

Program mix: Total opportunities offered in a health promotion program, as defined by program depth and breadth.

Stakeholder: A person, group, or organization that has interest or concern in an organization and can affect or be affected by the organization's actions, objectives, and policies.

Strategic plans: Is an organization's process of defining its strategy, direction, or making decisions about allocation of resources in pursuit of its strategy.

SWOT: An analysis structured planning method used to evaluate the strengths, weaknesses, opportunities, and threats.

Tactical plans: Is the process of taking the strategic plan and breaking it down into particular, short-term actions and plans.

Work life effectiveness: Learning to be more productive with your work life, and more effective with the time you do have.

Learning Objectives

1. Readers will be able to list the five elements of managing a health promotion program and briefly describe the relevance of each to program success.
2. Readers will be able to describe the importance of health promotion managers being able to effectively integrate staff, committee members, champs, and other stakeholders.
3. Readers will be able to briefly describe the integrations of strategic, tactical, and operations planning.
4. Readers will be able to define the measures of reach and effectiveness and tell how they are used in program management.

Discussion Questions

1. Peter Drucker suggests managing oneself is the most important responsibility of being a successful

manager. What are several of the key elements of managing oneself relative to the field of health promotion?

2. Managing the talent of a health promotion team combines many different skills. What are some of the key skills necessary in talent management?

3. What would be a strategic goal for a health promotion unit, and what would the tactical and operations goals supporting this strategic goal be?

4. The annual report showed that the tobacco cessation program reach and effectiveness was low. The manager has asked that a new program mix for tobacco cessation be developed. Develop a program mix for tobacco cessation in a mid-sized factory with 1200 employees located in four different buildings.

REFERENCES

1. Towers Watson & National Business Group on Health. Pathway to health and productivity: 2011/2012 Staying@Work Survey Report. December 2011. Available at: http://www.towerswatson.com/en-CA/Insights/IC-Types/Survey-Research-Results/2011/12/20112012-StayingWork-Survey-Report--A-Pathway-to-Employee-Health-and-Workplace-Productivity. Accessed September 28, 2013.

2. World Economic Forum. The Workplace Wellness Alliance investing in a sustainable workforce. 2012. Available at: http://www.weforum.org/reports/workplace-wellness-alliance-investing-sustainable-workforce. Accessed September 28, 2013.

3. American Psychological Association. Stress in America. November 2013. Available at: http://www.apa.org/news/press/releases/stress/. Accessed September 28, 2013.

4. Partnership for Prevention. Lead by example: the value of worksite health promotion to small- and medium-sized employers. 2011. Available at: http://www.prevent.org/data/files/initiatives/lbe_smse_2011_final.pdf. Accessed September 28, 2013.

5. U.S. Department of Labor and the U.S. Department of Health and Human Services. Occasional paper: a review of the U.S. workplace wellness market. 2012. Available at: http://www.dol.gov/ebsa/pdf/workplacewellnessmarketreview2012.pdf. Accessed September 28, 2013.

6. Centers for Disease Control and Prevention. Preventing chronic disease: promoting prevention through the Affordable Care Act: workplace wellness. 2012. Available at: http://stacks.cdc.gov/view/cdc/19776. Accessed September 28, 2013.

7. Baun WB. Program management of workplace health promotion programs. In: O'Donnell MP, ed. *Health Promotion in the Workplace*. Albany, NY: Delmar; 2002.

8. Becker C, Loy M. Important competencies for future health and wellness professionals: an investigation of employer desired skills. *Am J Health Educ*. 2004;35(4):228–233.

9. Australian Health Promotion Association. Core competencies for health promotion practitioners. 2009. Available at: http://www.healthpromotion.org.au/images/stories/pdf/core%20competencies%20for%20hp%20practitioners.pdf. Accessed September 28, 2013.

10. Executive Agency for Health and Consumers. *CompHP Professional Standards for Health Promotion Handbook: Developing Competencies and Professional*

Standards for Health Promotion Capacity Building in Europe. 2012. Available at: http://www.nuigalway.ie/health-promotion/documents/M_Barry/booklet_comphpa57_3_final_version.pdf. Accessed September 28, 2013.

11. Christensen CM. HBR's 10 must reads on managing yourself. Harvard Business Press books, 2011. Available at: http://hbr.org/product/hbr-s-10-must-reads-ebook-boxed-set/an/10917E-KND-ENG. Accessed March 9, 2014.

12. Rath T. *Strengths Finder 2.0.* New York, NY: Gallup Press; 2007.

13. Portny S. *Project Management For Dummies (Business & Personal Finance).* 4th ed. Hoboken, NJ: Wiley Publishing; 2013.

14. Dobson MS. *Project Management: How to Manage People, Processes, and Time to Achieve the Results You Need.* Avon, Mass: Adams Media Corporation; 2003.

15. O'Donnell MP. Definition of health promotion 2.0: embracing passion, enhancing motivation, recognizing dynamic balance, and creating opportunities. *Am J Health Promot.* 2009;24:IV.

16. Nova/Dulles SHRM. Establishing a mentoring program in your local SHRM chapter. 2012. Available at: http://www.shrm.org/Communities/VolunteerResources/Documents/324VA_NOVA_Dulles_Mentoring_Program_Toolkit_April2012.pdf. Accessed March 10, 2014.

17. Goldsmith M. *What Got You Here Won't Get You There.* New York, NY: Hyperion; 2007.

18. Kouzes J, Posner B. *The Leadership Challenge: How to Make Extraordinary Things Happen in Organizations.* 5th ed. San Francisco, Calif: Jossey-Bass 2012.

19. Wiseman L, Mckeown G. *Multiplers: How the Best Leaders Make Everyone Smarter.* New York, NY: HarperCollins; 2010.

20. Sinclair A, *Workforce Planning: A Literature Review.* 2004. Available at: http://www.employment-studies.co.uk/pdflibrary/mp37.pdf. Accessed December 12, 2013.

21. New calling: SHRM editorial: Wellness Officer. 2011. Available at: http://www.shrm.org/Publications/hrmagazine/EditorialContent/2011/0211/Pages/0211wells.asx. Accessed December 12, 2013.

22. Society for Human Resource Management. *2012 Employee Benefits.* 2012. Available at: http://www.shrm.org/research/surveyfindings/articles/documents/2012_empbenefits_report.pdf. Accessed December 12, 2013.

23. U.S. Small Business Administration. Writing effective job descriptions. 2013. Available at: http://www.sba.gov/content/writing-effective-job-descriptions. Accessed December 12, 2013.

24. National Institutes of Health Leadership & Management Behavioral Interview Guide. 2013. Available at: https://www.google.com/search?q=national+institutes+of+health+leadership+%26+management+behav&sourceid=ie7&rls=com.microsoft:en-us:IE-SearchBox&ie=&oe=&rlz=1I7RNLA_enUS529. Accessed December 12, 2013.

25. Gebelein SH, Nelson-Neuhaus KJ, Skube CJ, et al. *Successful Manager's Handbook: Develop Yourself Coach Others.* 8th ed. Minneapolis, Minn: PreVisor; 2010.

26. Whitmore J. *Coaching for Performance.* 4th ed. Boston, Mass: Nicholas Brealey Publisher; 2009.

27. Bacal R. *Manager's Guide to Performance Management.* 2nd ed. New York, NY: McGraw-Hill; 2012.

28. Springman J. Implementing a stakeholder strategy. 2011. Available at: http://blogs.hbr.org/2011/07/implementing-a-stakeholder-str/. Accessed December 12, 2013.

29.   Absolute advantage—anybody out there. 2004. Available at: http://www.absoluteadvantage.org/uploads/files/finding_the_vendor_thats_right_for_you.pdf. Accessed December 12, 2013.

30.   The Linkage Leader. 10 leadership techniques for building high-performing teams. 2008. Available at: http://www.linkageinc.com/thinking/linkageleader/Documents/PhilHarkins_10_Leadership_Techniques_for_Building_High_Performing_Teams_0506.pdf. Accessed December 12, 2013.

31.   Caroselli M. *The Critical Thinking Toolkit*. Chatsworth, Calif: American Management Association; 2009.

32.   Hines A, Bishop P. *Thinking About the Future: Guidelines for Strategic Foresight*. Washington, DC: Social Technologies; 2006.

33.   Sorensen G, Barbeau EM. Integrating occupational health, safety and worksite health promotion: opportunities for research and practice. *Med Lav.* 2006;97:240–257.

34.   Berry LL, Mirabito AM, Baun WB. What's the hard return on employee wellness programs? *Harv Bus Rev.* 2010;88(12):104–12, 142.

35.   Conversation Management. A purpose driven culture. 2013. Available at: http://www.theconversationmanager.com/2013/10/01/a-purpose-driven-culture/. Accessed December 14, 2013.

36.   Buck Consultants. Winning strategies in global workplace health promotion: a study of leading organizations. 2012. Available at: http://newsroom.cigna.com/images/9022/Winning-Strategies-in-Global-Workplace-Health-Promotion.pdf. Accessed December 14, 2013.

37.   Brian Thomas International. Six key questions in strategic planning. 2011. Available at: http://www.briantracy.com/blog/business-success/six-key-questions-in-strategic-planning/. Accessed December 14, 2013.

38.   Goldstein N, Nolan T, Pfeiffer J. Applied Strategic Planning: How to Develop a Plan That Really Works. New York, NY: McGraw-Hill; 1993.

39.   Hyatt M. Why vision is more important than strategy. 2012. Available at: http://michaelhyatt.com/why-vision-is-more-important-than-strategy.html. Accessed March 8, 2014.

40.   Senge P. What the vision does. 2009. Available at: http://www.awakin.org/read/view.php?tid=669. Accessed March 8, 2014.

41.   SFGH Community Wellness Program. Available at: http://sfghwellness.org/about/our-mission-vision. Accessed March 8, 2014.

42.   Hull P. Answer 4 questions to get a great mission statement. 2013. Available at: http://www.forbes.com/sites/patrickhull/2013/01/10/answer-4-questions-to-get-a-great-mission-statement/. Accessed March 8, 2014.

43.   Centers for Disease Control and Prevention. Sustainability. Available at: http://www.cdc.gov/sustainability/worksitewellness/. Accessed March 8, 2014.

44.   Whitaker R. Harvard study…smart goals and you, HBR 2012. Available at: http://www.aboutleaders.com/harvard-study-smart-goals-and-you/. Accessed March 8, 2014.

45.   Operations management: Investopedia defines operations management. 2014. Available at: http://www.investopedia.com/terms/o/operations-management.asp. Accessed March 8, 2014.

46.   Chenoweth DH. *Worksite Health Promotion*. 3rd ed. Champaign, Ill: Human Kinetics; 2011.

47.   Sawyer TH. *Facility Planning Design for Health Physical Activity, Recreation, and Sport*. Urbana, Ill: Sagamore Publishing; 2009.

48. American College of Sport Medicine. *ACSM's Health Fitness Facility Standards and Guidelines.* 4th ed. Champaign, Ill: Human Kinetics; 2012.

49. Eickhoff-Shemek JM, Herbert DL, Connaughton DP. *Risk Management for Health/Fitness Professionals: Legal Issues and Strategies.* Philadelphia, Pa: Wolters Kluwer/Lippincott Williams & Wilkins; 2009.

50. Department of Health & Human Services. Administration of aging: aging statistics. 2014. Available at: http://www.aoa.gov/AoAroot/Aging_Statistics/. Accessed March 9, 2014.

51. Wall Street Journal. More people over 65 are still working. 2012. Available at: http://blogs.wsj.com/economics/2012/10/08/more-people-over-65-are-still-working/. Accessed March 9, 2014.

52. Rehabilitation Research & Training Center. *2013 Annual Disability Statistics Compendium.* 2013. Available at: http://disabilitycompendium.org/docs/default-source/2013-compendium/download-the-2013-compendium.pdf?sfvrsn=0. Accessed March 9, 2014.

53. Federal Register. 2014. Available at: https://www.federalregister.gov/. Accessed March 9, 2014.

54. Towers Watson. 2014. Available at: http://www.towerswatson.com/en-US. Accessed March 9, 2014.

55. Buckconsultants. 2014. Available at: https://www.buckconsultants.com/. Accessed March 9, 2014.

56. Edington DW. Who are the intended beneficiaries (targets) of employee health promotion and wellness programs? *NC Med J.* 2006;67:425–427.

57. Centers for Disease Control and Prevention. Workplace health promotion: planning/workplace governance. Available at: http://www.cdc.gov/workplacehealthpromotion/planning/. Accessed March 13, 2014.

58. Bensoussan BE, Fleisher CS. *Analysis Without Paralysis: 12 Tools to Make Better Strategic Decision.* Upper Saddle River, NJ: Pearson Ed, Inc; 2012.

59. Centers for Disease Control and Prevention. Workplace health promotion assessment. Available at: http://www.cdc.gov/workplacehealthpromotion/assessment/. Accessed: March 13, 2014.

60. Pronk N. Best practice design principles of worksite health and wellness programs. *ACSMs Health Fitness J.* 2013;18:1–5.

61. U.S. Department of Health and Human Services. National health observances. Available at: http://healthfinder.gov/NHO/. Accessed March 13, 2014.

62. Bartholomew KL, Parcel GS, Kok G, et al. *Planning Health Promotion Programs: An Intervention Mapping Approach.* San Francisco, Calif: Wiley; 2011.

63. Quintiliani L, Sattelmain J, Sorensen G. The workplace as a setting for interventions to improve diet and provmote physical activity (Background paper prepared for the WHO/WEF joint event on preventing noncommunicable diseases in the workplace. 2007. Available at: http://www.who.int/dietphysicalactivity/Quintiliani-workplace-as-setting.pdf. Accessed March 14, 2014.

64. Hersey J, Williams-Piehotsa P, Sparling PB, et al. Promising practices in promotion of healthy weight at small and medium sized U.S. worksites. Prev Chronic Dis 2008;5:1–11.

65. Wolever RQ, et al. A systematic review of the literature on health and wellness coaching: defining a key behavioral intervention in healthcare. *Glob Adv Health Med.* 2013;3:38–57.

66. Health policy brief: workplace wellness programs the Affordable Care Act will expand the ability of employers to reward workers who achieve health improvement goals. *Health Affairs.* 2012; May 10:1–5.

67. Department of Labor. Incentives for nondiscriminatory wellness programs in group health plans. 2013. Available at: http://www.dol.gov/ebsa/pdf/workplacewellnessstudyfinalrule.pdf. Accessed March 14, 2014.

68. O'Donnell MP. Editor's notes: financial incentives for workplace health promotion: what is equitable, what is sustainable, and what drives healthy behaviors. *Am J Health Promot.* 2012;26:iv–vii.

69. Horwitz JR, Kelly BD, DiNardo JE. Wellness incentives in the workplace: cost savings through cost shifting to unhealthy. *Health Affairs.* 2013; 32:468–476.

70. Christakis NA, Fowler JH. Social contagion theory: examining dynamic social networks and human behavior. *Stat Med.* 2012;32:556–577.

71. Pachucki MA, Jacques PF, Christakis NA. Social network concordance in food choice among spouses, friends, and siblings. *Am J Public Health.* 2011;101:2170–2177.

72. Kuehl H, Mabry L, Dlliot DL, et al. Factors in adoption of a fire department wellness program champ-and-chief model. *J Occup Environ Med.* 2013;4:424–429.

73. Consensus statement. Guidance for a reasonable designed, employer-sponsored wellness program using outcome-based incentives. *J Occup Environ Med.* 2012;7:889–891.

74. Hunnicutt D. Developing a data dashboard the art and science of making sense. *Absolute Advantage.* 2007:34–40.

75. Parry T, Sherman B. A pragmatic approach for employers to improve measurement in workforce health and productivity. *Popul Health Manag.* 2011;15:61–64.

76. Centers for Disease Control and Prevention. Healthier worksite initiative: cost calculators. Available at: http://www.cdc.gov/nccdphp/dnpao/hwi/programdesign/costcalculators.htm. Accessed March 15, 2014.

77. Steps to a Healthier U.S. Workforce. Policy and Practice Working Group: examining the value of integrating occupational health and safety and health promotion programs in the workplace. 2005. Available at: http://www.saif.com/_files/CompNews/CNexamining.pdf. Accessed September 28, 2013.

78. HBR Blog Network. Harvard Business Review: good managers lead through a team. 2012. Available at: http://blogs.hbr.org/2012/04/good-managers-lead-through-a-t/. Accessed September 28, 2013.

79. HBR Blog Network. Harvard Business Review: true leaders are also managers. 2010. Available at: http://blogs.hbr.org/2010/08/true-leaders-are-also-managers/. Accessed September 28, 2013.

80. Wilson Learning. Integrated leadership: balance of essence and form. 2006. Available at: http://www.wilsonlearning.com/images/uploads/pdf/leadership_en.pdf. Accessed September 28, 2013.

CHAPTER

6

Health Promotion in the Workplace Program Evaluation

Ron Z. Goetzel, Enid Chung Roemer, Karen Kent, Andriana Hohlbauch, Maryam J. Tabrizi and Kristyn Smith

INTRODUCTION

An increasing number of employers are introducing workplace health promotion programs with the expectation that these programs will improve employee health, lower healthcare spending, and increase worker productivity as a by-product of workers remaining healthy or becoming healthy. As more resources are directed toward health promotion programs, the need for effective program evaluation, supported by necessary data collection, is paramount. Program evaluation helps ensure that scarce resources are applied in the most cost-effective way to improve health and achieve other organization goals. Furthermore, program administrators and decision-makers seek reassurance that both the *structure* of their program and the implementation *process* are adequate for achieving these desired outcomes. Thus, there

is a need for regular monitoring and reporting of program achievements to guide any necessary fine-tuning.

The job of determining if something "works" is often difficult, especially in a "real world" setting in which the evaluator lacks control of extraneous forces that may influence outcomes. This chapter explains scientifically rigorous, but practical, evaluation methods that can be used to simultaneously satisfy the business and research communities – to determine whether investment in employee health is a wise business decision in addition to being "the right thing to do."

Purpose, Scope and Format

This chapter provides a practical measurement and evaluation guide for health promotion program managers and external evaluators. The purpose of the chapter is multifold. For program managers not trained in advanced statistical methods and evaluation research, the chapter illustrates the complexity of conducting studies and provides tools and guidance to assist in their evaluation efforts. As an example, a program manager with little background in measurement theory can adapt the sample employee survey, found in the appendix of this chapter, to evaluate several key program success factors. The sample assessment relies upon participants' self-reported engagement in the program, satisfaction with its component parts, improved health habits, and other outcomes of interest to the program manager and sponsor.

For readers with advanced training in program evaluation, the chapter illustrates how techniques and principles used in other applied research studies can be adapted to workplace health promotion. A multidisciplinary team of experts with a variety of skills and backgrounds often needs to be assembled when conducting these studies. It is not unusual, for example, to include, as part of the team, experts in statistics, health services research, economics, epidemiology, psychology, medicine, public health, employee benefits, and health education. Whereas the typical program manager might not ever consider assembling such a team of diverse and talented people, the evaluator might call upon any one of them as an advisor or consultant to the evaluation project. The manager may also be able to identify individuals within the organization who possess the skills necessary to conduct good studies and draw upon their expertise when needed.

This chapter, an update of the prior Program Evaluation chapter published in the third edition of O'Donnell's <u>Health Promotion in the Workplace</u>,[1] places a greater emphasis on describing the three components of program evaluation: structure, process, and outcomes, with a particular focus on economic evaluations of worksite programs — specifically methods employed for conducting cost/benefit evaluations, otherwise known as return-on-investment (ROI) studies.

The chapter begins with a discussion of six issues that help guide the development of an evaluation plan. The rest of the chapter discusses basic and applied research principles including those relevant to study design, validity issues, structure evaluation, process evaluation, data collection procedures, descriptive and multivariate analysis, financial impact analysis, and presentation of findings.

Developing an Evaluation Plan

In developing an evaluation plan, the program manager should be prepared to address the following issues:

- Why should health promotion programs be evaluated?
- What are the arguments against conducting a program evaluation?
- Why do health promotion programs fail?
- How is agreement on program objectives achieved?
- How are health promotion goals aligned with an organization's mission?
- Can results from one program be generalized to another?

Each of these issues is discussed below.

Why Should Health Promotion Programs be Evaluated?

Evaluation studies serve four basic functions. First, they <u>support a "business case" for program introduction</u>. In a sense, program evaluation begins even before a program is put into place. In deciding whether to initiate a new program, the program champion needs to compile evidence of "problems" or needs within the organization that a health promotion program can solve.

Thus, program evaluation begins by gathering data to determine whether an investment in an intervention addresses a real problem for the organization. The program is then presented to senior management by using a variety of data sources to cost-justify the investment. Often a cost/benefit model is developed whereby investments needed to solve the problem are compared to the potential benefits realized by ameliorating the problem. This is referred to as prospective ROI analysis.

Second, program evaluations provide ongoing monitoring and measurement of program performance needed to fine-tune or renew program elements. Here, the focus is on "process" measures that assess how well the program is implemented and whether participants accept and like program elements. Data gathered are used by program planners and administrators and displayed as "dashboards" or "report cards" necessary to monitor progress. In addition, problems in the design and implementation of the program can be flagged early and corrected. This stream of data provides reassurance to program sponsors that their investment is being well managed and results are forthcoming.

Third, program evaluations are necessary to determine whether the right decision was made in starting the program and whether the program has been successful in achieving its objectives. At this point, the focus shifts from structure and process to outcome measures – the extent to which specific program objectives, developed early on, are met according to plan. This highlights the need for accountability of program implementers. At certain milestones, the evaluator presents evidence to the decision-making group that the program has, or has not, been successful in meeting its goals. At the conclusion of such a meeting, the decision-makers determine whether the program adds value to the organization.

Fourth, program evaluations contribute to the science of organizational and individual change. As individuals and groups develop exemplary programs, knowledge gained from evaluation of these programs is disseminated to others through scientific articles and public presentations at conferences. These communications of program achievements are most convincing when credible results accompany the description of the program's

design and implementation. Thus, the credibility of program achievements often hinges upon the strength of the evaluation design.

What are the Arguments Against Conducting a Program Evaluation?

Despite the many good reasons to perform program evaluations, there are also many reasons why an organization may choose not to do so. Some examples include:

1. Evaluation may be viewed as a low-priority activity that is expensive and distracting from the actual intervention. When decision-makers purchase health promotion programs, they may conjure up a vague idea of what they hope to accomplish, e.g., improve health, reduce costs, improve productivity, or heighten morale. However, once a conscious decision is made to invest in the program, their attention is almost entirely directed at the "nuts and bolts" of putting the program in place. The details of implementation, therefore, often overshadow concerns about evaluation. In addition, since the investment in the intervention is often substantial, persuading the decision-maker to pay for an additional expense directed at evaluation (which is classified as "administrative" rather than "programmatic") is challenging.

Finally, many organizations believe that program evaluation is unnecessary due to an inherent faith in the probable benefits of health promotion programs. They may have reviewed studies that discussed evaluations of similar programs and are satisfied that the same outcomes will apply to their situation. Consequently, they choose to invest in high level programming rather than evaluation. As noted earlier, this involves a leap of faith that may not be justified.

2. Potential negative results may undermine the program. The decision-maker,

as well as the program administrator, is naturally worried about what might happen if positive results fail to materialize. Program administrators may feel that if an investment is made in measurement, the evaluator and decision-maker are obligated to release the findings of that evaluation, even if those results are negative. For those who are uncomfortable with entering into situations where the outcome is uncertain, deciding to conduct an evaluation that may produce negative results may be off-putting. On the other hand, continuing a program that is not achieving positive outcomes is not defensible. The alternative to discarding a poorly performing program is to modify it so that it does achieve positive results. In either case, one should evaluate programs to identify their plusses and minuses, learn from the mistakes, and improve operation as needed.

3.   An evaluation may require <u>archival data that are often either difficult to access or unavailable</u>. There are legal or practical barriers to accessing person-level data. The evaluator may discover that historical data are only available from specific sources and in unusual formats. Thus, evaluators may face formidable administrative and legal obstacles.

Historical as well as contemporaneous data may be unavailable simply because they are not routinely collected by the organization. Furthermore, data may be available only in an inconvenient form, e.g., hard copy, at the organizational not individual level, or not linkable to any other data source. The evaluator therefore needs to gain the "buy-in" of key stakeholders including organizations' legal staff, chief financial officers, insurance administrators, vendors, and labor unions when designing the evaluation. This can be accomplished by assembling a cross-functional work team, within and outside the organization, to address these problems to avoid future frustrations and delays in the evaluation process.

4.   Evaluations that are perceived to be <u>academic, complex, intellectual and</u> <u>"ivory tower" exercises</u> can be disconcerting to executives who have neither the time nor interest to carefully review a description of complex methodology and accompanying lists of limitations and caveats. If they do not understand how results are obtained, decision-makers may be reluctant to support the study and its conclusions. Therefore, program sponsors need to be presented with an analytic approach that is understood by laypersons, often as a one-page executive summary, with accompanying recommendations, decision options, and next steps.

In the presentation to senior leaders, it is crucial to explain the objectives, methods, results, and implications for action in a way that motivates creative and productive organizational decision-making. The evaluation should address key questions posed by management and decisions that align with the data. The main point of the evaluation should be to answer the question, "did the program work?" and "how can I use the information moving forward?"

5.   It takes <u>time and resources</u> to conduct studies. Many U.S. corporations focus on quarterly results. An organization's economic climate, workforce composition, and strategic focus may change frequently. When told that they may have to wait several years for evaluation results on some financial measures, decision-makers may be reluctant to commit resources. In response, the evaluator may point out that large-scale initiatives require years to take hold and become engrained into the organizational fabric – short-term initiatives seldom produce long-term benefits. Therefore, a health promotion program, and its ongoing evaluation, also needs to be thought about as a multi-year endeavor. Additionally, the evaluation should be crafted so that research answers are delivered frequently as different programmatic milestones are reached leading to actionable recommendations.

6. The evaluation may be viewed as <u>intrusive or disruptive</u>. Assessment of program results should be accomplished by gathering the necessary data with the minimum amount of disruption and intrusion. Nonetheless, the decision-maker may be reluctant to allow proactive data gathering from individuals engaged in the program, and may be more opposed to gathering data from individuals who are not directly affected by the intervention, i.e., a control or comparison group. Disruption can be minimized or avoided by using available archival data for comparison purposes.

7. Often, to save <u>costs</u>, the organization may turn to its own staff to conduct the evaluation, even though they may lack the expertise to design and implement an appropriate study design. Consequently, little effort is directed at the evaluation project and the results are inconclusive. At worst, an inadequate evaluation may lead to misleading findings. Economic realities are important, but conversations about the potential costs and benefits of a good program evaluation that occur early on may help avoid "penny-wise" but "pound-foolish" strategies. Also, it is difficult for the person responsible for managing the program to be sufficiently neutral to conduct an unbiased evaluation.

In sum, while the initial intent of decision-makers may be to support a high-quality evaluation effort, plan execution may suffer when decision-makers fully grasp the cost and complexity of conducting an unbiased evaluation. Therefore, well-vetted, early decisions should be made about the scope of the evaluation effort. In particular, decision-makers should consider the potential consequences of gathering limited or misleading information from the program evaluation.

Why do Health Promotion Programs Fail?

There are many successful health promotion initiatives and probably just as many unsuccessful ones. The reasons for perceived or real failure often fall into one of three categories[2]:

1. The <u>theory</u> underlying the program design is inappropriate or inadequate. The approach to behavior change is flawed. Interventions are constructed based on program managers' intuition or "feel" instead of scientific evidence of program effectiveness or a widely accepted theory of behavior change. The intervention may not address underlying motivations for behavior change. The intervention may be too narrow or ill defined. The program may be insufficiently comprehensive, integrated, synergistic, or rational. In short, the structural underpinnings and theoretical foundation for the program may be so weak that no matter how hard the staff tries, a successful outcome is not achievable.

2. In other cases, the theoretical framework for the program may be adequate, and perhaps even elegant, but <u>program implementation</u> is flawed. For example, resources may not be adequate to do the job properly; the staff may not be well trained and supervised; the essential equipment may not be provided; the program may be too weak; opportunities for health improvement are lacking; or senior management may not be supportive of the effort. In short, the theory is fine but the execution is poor.

3. Finally, for some programs, design and execution are sound, but inadequate effort is made toward <u>documenting program success</u>. Improper measurement may take the form of poor instruments or tools to record program accomplishments. The overall design of the evaluation may be flawed. Consequently, the program is terminated not because it is ineffective, but rather because administrators lack the proper methods by which to evaluate it.

How is Agreement on Program Objectives Achieved?

Historically, organizations institute health promotion programs for a variety of reasons.

However, within any one organization, individual decision-makers may have different criteria for program success based upon their area of expertise and responsibility.

For example, a benefits director may wish to reduce healthcare or other costs; the personnel director may wish to curtail absenteeism; the human resources vice president may wish to reduce turnover and attract the best talent; the medical director may wish to prevent disease; and the president may wish to improve the company's image in the community.

Consequently, program evaluators may find that there is no one company spokesperson who effectively verbalizes a consensus opinion regarding the organization's health promotion goals and objectives. One of the most important initial tasks, therefore, for those who are designing the evaluation effort, is to help key decision-makers form a consensus opinion on conceptual and operational definitions of program success. Among those who need to be polled, and who often play a critical role in defining the requirements for a successful program, are the following:

- Economic buyer (the chief executive officer, chief financial officer, or vice president of human resources) – often, this individual is, or is close to, the "visionary" of the organization whose job it is to create a link between programmatic and organizational strategic objectives;
- Program administrator – the individual responsible for running the program who may be most knowledgeable about what a health promotion program can achieve;
- Medical or health science professional – the physician (medical director) or occupational health nurse who provides clinical supervision of the program;

- Human resources executive (benefits director, quality manager, or training professional) who provides corporate-level management and funding for the program; and
- Other interested parties who may include the fitness center director, general manager, company consultant or someone who has taken an active interest in the program and is willing to become its champion.

In building consensus among this diverse group of individuals, the evaluator must first understand the reasons for each person's advocacy of the program, and how that person expects the program will benefit the organization. The evaluator can then assemble these parties to articulate and build consensus on specific quantifiable and measurable outcomes. Once individuals are exposed to their colleagues' reasons for introducing the program, they may decide to collectively focus on a limited number of outcomes that can be reasonably accomplished and measured.

For example, if the benefits director, whose chief aim is to reduce medical care costs, accepts the idea that an effective way to achieve this aim is to reduce the number of people at high risk for specific diseases, then documenting health risk reduction for the population may be adequate to establish program success. To further support this approval, the program champion may show existing research that illustrates how reducing modifiable risk factors reduces medical costs. If, on the other hand, the link between risk and cost suggested by the research literature is not accepted by the group, then a more expensive and complicated medical claims analysis may be warranted.

In another example, an organization may introduce a program to increase worker morale where the main aim is to achieve high employee engagement. In that situation, the evaluation focus would be on structure- and process-related measures rather than outcomes.

How are Health Promotion Goals Aligned with Organizations Mission?

Experience in the field, supplemented by reports on "best practice" organizations, highlights the need to clearly connect health promotion programming with corporate mission and vision statements.[3-6] Best-practice health promotion teams start by reviewing their organizational mission, and then translating that mission into easily understood health promotion objectives clearly linked to the organization's purpose. These teams are explicit about how accomplishment of their program's objectives would directly benefit the organization as a whole.

For example, in manufacturing organizations, a case can be made that improving the health risk profile of workers can positively influence productivity and reduce safety incidents.[7-14] Similarly, in a high technology firm, a similar case can be made for improving physical and mental health as a means of enhancing worker creativity, alertness, focus, energy, and mood.

One way to "connect the dots" for human resources executives is to document the productivity costs of modifiable risk factors such as obesity, high stress, and smoking measured as:

- number of individuals absent or missing from work each day;
- organizational expenses associated with disability and workers' compensation claims; or
- reduction in the productive output of workers as measured in terms of specific products, services, new sales, and customer retention outcomes.[7-11]

Using several established methods, program advocates can "monetize" key health promotion measures and present them in financial terms. Further, they can calculate the savings opportunity resulting from influencing a change in health promotion outcomes and project an ROI from that investment. Demonstrating that health promotion can positively influence employee safety will also get the attention of risk managers and safety officers in the organization. Usually, it takes little convincing for a chief executive officer or chief financial officer to make the connection between healthy workers and safety, a business imperative.

To maintain senior management support for workplace health promotion, program metrics need to be presented regularly (preferably quarterly) to high-ranking executives. This ensures the program remains fresh and a high priority activity relevant to the business. It also underscores the importance of accountability for program success or failure. If health promotion program measures are linked to incentive compensation or employee bonus plans, they assume greater relevance. The astute program administrator is therefore urged to develop easy to understand performance metrics that are linked to achievable goals, and are central to the health promotion program's success as well as to overall business success.

Can Results from One Program be Generalized to Another?

Often, program managers are asked: "Why should we spend the money to prove that health promotion works if others have already shown that to be true?" An appropriate response would be, "If you assume that our program is similar in design and implementation to others that have preceded us, and you are willing to also assume our results are "close enough" to theirs, then, indeed, spending time and money on a new evaluation would be wasteful." However, few decision-makers are willing to concede that the results of another program apply to their "unique" situation. The reality is that there is great diversity in programs that fall under the broad umbrella term of workplace health promotion.

Thus, in thinking about the generalizability of results from one program to another, evaluators should take into account the enormous variability in program design, implementation, and intensity. It would be erroneous to assume that any one health promotion program is like any other. Consequently, evaluations of alternative program designs need to consider the effect that these various designs may have on specific outcomes of interest and overall program impact.

For example, some organizations offer on-site interventions while others deliver programs via the web, telephone, or by mail. Staff and facilities may be centrally delivered, community-based, or provided by vendors. Programs may be run by professionals or by volunteers. Program components may be coordinated under a central strategy or run as independent efforts. Singular topic areas may be offered in a variety of formats, e.g., classroom instruction, self-paced study guides, interactive sessions, by telephone, or through the Internet. Conversely, a similar program delivery mode (e.g., telephone counseling) may be employed, although various topics are discussed and interview techniques across topics differ.

Further, a variety of incentives for participation and behavior change may be offered. These may include individual prizes, team awards, and insurance premium rebates. In one organization, senior and middle management may be supportive of the initiative while in others they may be cynical and obstructive. Some companies may allow their employees time off for participation while others may only offer programs on employees' own time. Companies may require employee contribution (cost sharing) or make programs available free of charge. Finally, organizational factors such as the characteristics of the employee population and the work environment may determine the effectiveness of the program. For example, two organizations—one with a majority of shift workers who conduct all their business at

various external locations and the other with a majority of employees working conventional business hours at a central location—may achieve very different results with an identical program.

In short, there are many organizational and programmatic factors that either facilitate or hinder implementation and effectiveness. These need to be considered in attempting comparisons between program outcomes and in planning an evaluation effort. Importantly, when writing up results, program design and implementation particulars need to be described in detail.

PRINCIPLES OF APPLIED RESEARCH

This section reviews some general program evaluation principles used in applied research, that is, research done in the "real world" as opposed to a laboratory setting. As part of this review, alternative research designs and their relative merits are discussed, especially as they relate to study validity.

The Basic Questions of Research

In developing an evaluation plan, the researcher may get lost in the details of study design, sampling procedures, operational definitions, and statistical techniques. It is useful, therefore, to step back from the minutiae and ask some basic fundamental questions relevant to the measurement task at hand.

Developing a clear and cogent research question is a critical first step in formulating the research design. Broadly speaking, the research question may be as basic as, "Was the program successful in meeting its intended goals?" followed by more specific questions that can be tested empirically (i.e., verifiable from observation or experiment). These more specific questions often define the outcome and population of interest – for example, "Was the program successful at lowering absenteeism rates of employees at intervention worksites?"

Related to the research question is the hypothesis, or what one expects the intervention program to achieve, in measurable terms.[15] An example of a hypothesis might be "employee participation in the workplace health promotion program will reduce health risks by one percentage point (net) per year in each of ten risk factors."

To help evaluators approach the task of measurement in simple to understand language, we offer the following nine questions that experts and novices alike can ask when formulating a clear evaluation strategy:

1. What do I want to **KNOW**? What is the research question I hope to answer? What problem am I trying to solve? (*Focusing Question*)

2. What will the answer or solution to the problem **LOOK** like? What do I expect to happen as a consequence of the intervention? How much of a program effect will I see? For example, if healthcare cost reduction is the goal, what level of reduction is anticipated? (*Hypotheses*)

3. How will I **SEE** it? What is the basic design of my study? What are the operational definitions of the constructs of interest? How will I control for potential confounders or alternative explanations of results? (*Design*)

4. How will I collect and **RECORD** the data? How will the data be aggregated? What instruments will I use? What will the research database contain? (*Measures*)

5. How will I **CATEGORIZE** and analyze the data? How will the data be coded? What do I envision my results report to look like? How will the tables and graphs be constructed? What categories of data will be developed? What statistical techniques will be applied? How will I group the data? (*Data Analysis and Results*)

6. How will I **AFFECT** the data? How will I guard against introducing my personal bias into the study? Do I have a stake in study outcome? What can I do to minimize bias? What explicit limitations should be stated beforehand? (*Limitations*)

7. What will I **INFER** from the data? How will I interpret the results? What are the implications for action given alternative study outcomes? (*Discussion*)

8. What will I **FIND** out that I did not already know before I started? What is the "so what?" question being addressed? Is the evaluation, as structured, worth the effort? (*Conclusions*)

9. What can I **DO** with the information I learn – what are the implications for action? (*Implications*)

The final two questions, similar to the first one, force the evaluator to re-examine the importance of the study and to question the amount of effort necessary to conduct a credible evaluation. It is remarkable how often the above nine questions are not asked, hence not answered, before an extensive and resource consuming evaluation project is begun. In particular, the first question, asked quite innocently, may trip-up evaluators who have spent much time and effort conjuring elaborate designs and statistics that are directed at issues not easily operationalized and often unanswerable. Note, that following each question, a certain word or key phrase is shown in italics corresponding to sections of a manuscript that would describe the study in a scientific journal.

Applying Scientific Methods in Program Evaluation

In performing program studies, the evaluator is attempting to apply scientific methods to assess program effect. Scientific methods rely upon systematic formulation, testing, and modification of hypotheses. In trying to determine a cause and effect relationship between events, scientific methods attempt to "control" for competing explanations of observed phenomena, i.e., they take into account other possible "causes" for what is perceived as an outcome or effect.

Why should decision-makers be concerned with scientific methods when all they wish to determine is whether the program "worked?" When discussions take place among decision-makers on how these studies should be performed, the methods used, and the cost of performing analyses, program funders may advocate for a less rigorous approach. They may say, "We don't need a study that is of publishable quality," or "we just need some results – not a Nobel Prize masterpiece." This is a common dilemma faced by program evaluators and, in practice leads to a less rigorous evaluation methodology. This may produce "results" – but the results may be at best misleading and at worst wrong. If the aim of an evaluation is to estimate the "true" effects of the program, then more rigorous scientific methods should be considered and, if feasible, applied.[16]

Having stated the obvious, many studies are conducted without much attention paid to the rules of scientific inquiry. From a pragmatic standpoint, it is clear that these types of studies will continue to be performed to justify a program's continued existence. In many cases, the cost of scientifically rigorous studies would far exceed the cost of the intervention. Nonetheless, evaluators need to be aware of differences in study designs that affect study validity and how compromises in the application of scientific principles may hinder the ability to make useful decisions about the programs being evaluated. At the very least, evaluators need to explicitly state the limitations of their studies when presenting the findings.

EVALUATION TYPES

Organizing Framework

An organizing framework or theoretical model is helpful in illustrating the flow of program components –how they are expected to influence one another – and therefore the measurement points for the evaluation. This framework is sometimes referred to as a causal diagram or logic model.

The causal diagram can guide the identification of critical pathways and measures for testing study hypotheses. It is often displayed as a graphical representation of the relationships between variables, with arrows indicating the direction of "explanatory" and "outcome" variables. In these diagrams, time runs from left to right so that "causally" prior variables have arrows running from the left to the affected "outcome" variables on the right. Figure 6-1 below shows an example of a simple causal diagram related to the hypothesis, *"Employees participating in worksite health promotion reduce their health risks."*

The first box represents social, economic, behavioral, and other background characteristics of the population of interest that influence the likelihood of participation in the health promotion program or intervention. The middle box represents the intervention or the

Figure 6-1: Simple causal diagram.

program hypothesized to cause change. The last box – reduced health risks – is the outcome of interest.

There are, of course, other variables that can influence the outcome other than those included as part of the intervention, such as intervening life events, changes in norms, and other external influences. There are also variables that may mediate the influence of the intervention on the outcome, for example, whether the intervention is even noticed by workers and if the workplace offers sufficient opportunities to practice health-promoting behaviors. These variables can be added to the causal diagram to create a more complete representation of the relationships between various causes and effects.

Figure 6-2 shows an example of a logic model for workplace health promotion developed by the Centers for Disease Control and Prevention (CDC).

The model highlights the health promotion program in the top oval and recognizes that both individual and environmental interventions

are offered as part of the program's structure. However, just making the program available to employees is not sufficient for achieving the listed outcomes. Individuals must be aware of the program, participate in it, and be satisfied with component parts and its implementers. Moreover, the program must be attractive, accessible, and tailored to the needs and interests of the employees for it to be effective. These elements are illustrated under the heading "program implementation process."

The last set of model elements focuses on program outcomes. Workers who are exposed to the program must become engaged in it, be motivated to change their health behaviors, and gain knowledge about when to appropriately use healthcare services. If these preceding factors are in place, adoption of healthy lifestyles (e.g., exercising, eating healthy foods) and reduction of health risk behaviors (e.g., smoking, high alcohol consumption) would be expected to lead to improved physiological measures (e.g., blood pressure, cholesterol, blood glucose, weight); improved

Figure 6-2: Logic model: worksite wellness program.

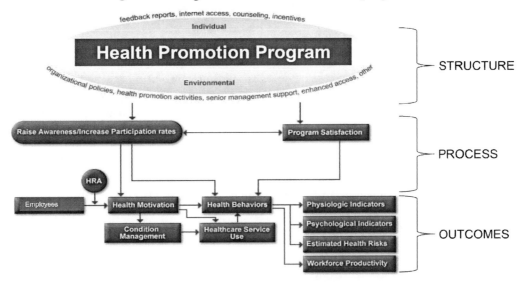

Modified Worksite Health Promotion (Assessment of Health Risk with Follow-Up) Logic Model adpoted by the CDC Community Guide Task Force.

psychological health (e.g., reduced stress, depression); reduced health risks for common illnesses such as heart disease and cancer; and improved productivity (e.g., fewer absences, more energy, and increased job quality when at work).

The model above illustrates a type of "checklist" that an evaluator can apply when identifying broad areas that need to be measured. It also highlights the sequence of events expected, with the *structure* representing the first step in identifying and establishing the program design; *process* indicating the second step of program implementation; and the final third step – highlighting desired program *outcomes*.

Evaluation Approaches

In determining whether a workplace health promotion program worked, the evaluator generally begins with the basic question, "What was the effect of the intervention?" As noted earlier, the answer is tied to program objectives. Those objectives may be stated as general principles such as "improve employee health," "reduce the rate of increase in healthcare costs," and "improve worker productivity." They may also be stated in more specific terms such as "reduce by 10% the number of employees with high blood pressure (140/90 and above) within one year" or "reduce the rate of increase in total healthcare costs by three percentage points over a three year period."

A focus on outcomes is central to good program evaluation. However, in addition to outcomes, the evaluator needs to consider the program framework or structure, as well as the process by which the program is delivered. Without the structure and process evaluation components, a program evaluation falls short of vital information to explain how any given component may have contributed to good or bad outcomes, and in turn, be able to identify the strategies for remedying the problems or replicating the successes.

In short, a comprehensive health promotion program evaluation needs to address structure, process, and outcome variables. The purpose and measures of each of these three components of program evaluation are described below.

Structure Evaluation

Definition and Purpose

Program structure is defined as the basic architecture or blueprint of the program – its "inputs." A structural evaluation is simply an assessment of the extent to which the program's critical components are in place according to plan, as laid out by program planners and implementers. This evaluation is often referred to as an "audit" of design plan compliance. Specifically, it collects organizational level data about worksite characteristics; health promotion policies, practices and program offerings; social and environmental supports for a healthy lifestyle; and program implementation and evaluation efforts.

Questions asked in a structure assessment typically include: What exactly is the intervention? How many content areas are covered? How is the program delivered to participants? How are topics addressed? Are core evidence-based program elements or promising practices included in the design? Who is eligible? What kind of social and environmental supports are in place to facilitate and incentivize engagement? These and similar questions need to be addressed when describing program features, design elements, and content.

Structure evaluation is sometimes referred to as the formative research phase of a comprehensive program evaluation. There are three broad purposes of formative research. First, it provides a preliminary evaluation of the intervention design *before* the intervention is implemented in order to increase the chance of achieving the program objectives. Specifically, this preliminary evaluation can provide information to: 1) refine the interventions to

make sure they meet the needs of the target population, 2) determine whether appropriate strategies are in place to maximize participation, 3) refine the implementation methods so they are appropriate to the setting, and 4) determine whether increased management support is needed.

The second purpose of formative research is to direct the design and logistics (i.e., data collection) of assessing the effectiveness of the program (the outcomes evaluation). Specifically, once the program structure and program implementation plans are mapped out, the data collection protocols can be developed to ensure all data sources, necessary tools, and resources are properly identified and aligned to capture the outcomes of interest.

The third purpose is to serve as a mechanism for collecting baseline structure variables (as described above) that may influence the execution of the intervention (i.e., facilitators and barriers), and in turn, affect the impact of the program. These baseline variables are important moderators and mediators that need to be considered when estimating the effectiveness of the intervention. Furthermore, results from this phase can inform the steps and strategies needed to maintain or refine the program design, structure, and processes.

Structure Evaluation Tools

There are several tools available in the public domain that assesses various aspects of program structure for workplace health promotion programs. Some cover multiple elements of structure. Some focus on one specific structural element while others include structure measures as part of a larger comprehensive program evaluation tool. Brief descriptions of some of those tools are provided below.

The Health Enhancement Research Organization (HERO) Employee Health Management Best Practice Scorecard© (The HERO Scorecard),[17] developed in collaboration with Mercer, is a questionnaire designed to help organizations learn about employee health management best practices, identify opportunities to improve their programs, and measure progress over time. The HERO Scorecard is comprised of 62 questions and covers six foundational areas of effective programs: (1) strategic planning, (2) leadership engagement, (3) program-level management, (4) program content, (5) engagement methods, and (6) measurement and evaluation.

The CDC Worksite Health ScoreCard (HSC) is a tool designed to help employers assess the extent to which they have implemented evidence-based health promotion interventions aimed at preventing heart disease, stroke, and related chronic conditions.[18,19] The HSC assists employers in identifying gaps in their health promotion programs and to prioritize high-impact strategies across the following 12 topics: (1) organizational supports, (2) tobacco control, (3) nutrition, (4) physical activity, (5) weight management, (6) stress management, (7) depression, (8) high blood pressure, (9) high cholesterol, (10) diabetes, (11) signs and symptoms of heart attack and stroke, and (12) emergency response to heart attack and stroke.

The Leading by Example (LBE) tool measures the extent to which leadership of the organization supports a health-promoting environment.[20,21] The LBE is a 13-item self-report questionnaire that uses a five point Likert scale (1=strongly disagree to 5=strongly agree) to measure perceived organizational support and management engagement in employee health promotion. The LBE includes four subscales: (1) business alignment with health promotion objectives; (2) awareness of the economics of health and productivity; (3) worksite support for health promotion; and (4) leadership support for health promotion.

The Environmental Assessment Tool (EAT) is a comprehensive assessment designed to evaluate the physical and social environment of a worksite in terms of support for health promotion by the organization[20] within three categories: physical activity, nutrition,

and organizational characteristics. The EAT contains questions related to work rules and requirements, current programs, and formal policies that support or facilitate healthy eating, physical activity, or both. The EAT also collects observational data of the physical environment to identify evidence of physical activity support (e.g., shower and changing facilities, on-site fitness centers, bike racks) and nutrition/weight management support (e.g., nutrition labels, point of purchase prompts for healthier items, access to healthy options at on-site food outlets).

The *Wellness Impact Scorecard* (WISCORE[SM]) was developed in 2009 by the National Business Group on Health (NBGH) to help large employers understand the impact of their wellness programs on employee health, quantify performance over time, and benchmark with peer companies.[22] The metrics assessed in the WISCORE are organized into three categories: (1) improving health (i.e., the program strategies, tactics, and communication methods), (2) participation (i.e., the participation and satisfaction rates), and (3) impact on the workforce (i.e., the outcomes related to changes in health behavior, biometrics, productivity, and medical trends).

Developing and conducting a tailored comprehensive structure evaluation using the appropriate tools is relevant for both establishing a baseline assessment and on-going annual reviews. Furthermore, these findings provide the building blocks for developing process evaluation protocols for monitoring, adjusting, and assessing program implementation.

Process Evaluation

Definition and Purpose

Process evaluation involves determining whether the execution of the program is progressing according to plan and whether the operation is smooth. Specifically, a process evaluation is used to determine measures of program fidelity, dose delivered, dose received, and reach.

Process Measures

Fidelity is a measure of program quality in terms of how well interventions are being implemented as planned. The purpose of measuring fidelity is to have the opportunity to adjust program implementation, when appropriate, and to determine the role of program fidelity on any observed changes in outcomes of interest. An instrument measuring fidelity includes a checklist of all intervention activities and protocols to which the program implementation team responds through an interview and/or self-report survey format. This fidelity instrument may include (but is not limited to) the following types of questions:

- Have the following interventions been implemented as planned (yes or no) and on schedule (yes or no)?
- Describe barriers and facilitators you experienced in implementing the programs. Were barriers addressed? If so, how? If not, are action plans in place?
- Were modifications made to any of the programs prior to or during implementation?
- List any additional programs implemented that were not part of the original plan/package.
- What worked or didn't work in communicating the intervention activities to employees?

The fidelity instrument is usually administered annually. Fidelity measures are typically qualitative in nature. However, where applicable, data are quantified (e.g., calculating the percentage of programs implemented out of total planned).

Dose delivered is a measurement of program completeness (i.e., the degree to which all aspects of an intervention are implemented). An instrument is tailored to list each program and all of its components to determine the dose level delivered in relation to program

completeness in terms of <u>frequency</u> (e.g., how often stress management classes were offered compared to how many were planned), intensity (e.g., did the stress management class include educational materials, follow-up, or combined with other resources as intended), and duration (e.g., what was the length of each session and how many sessions were offered compared to the planned schedule). Dose delivered data are typically collected at the same time, using the same methods, and on the same schedule as fidelity measures. The findings from dose delivered measurement are used to adjust program implementation as needed to ensure all components of the program are delivered as intended.

Dose received is a measurement of employee exposure to and satisfaction with the program provided. Specifically, the purpose of dose received is to measure the degree to which employees are aware of the available programs, level of participation (extent of interaction with and use of resources), reasons for engaging or not engaging, and overall evaluation of program quality and effectiveness of each component of the interventions received. As with fidelity and dose delivered measures, a dose received survey is tailored to the specifications of the program under evaluation. Dose delivered surveys, generally known as employee feedback surveys, may include questions such as:

- Do you remember receiving/seeing any of the following promotional information regarding the wellness program in the past 12 months? (*check all that apply*)
- In the past 12 months, did you participate in any of the following program offerings?
- If you participated in any program offerings, why did you choose to participate? (*check all that apply*)
- If you DID NOT participate in any program offerings, which of the

following would explain why you DID NOT participate? (*check all that apply*)
- In the last 12 months, how would you rate the program at your worksite?

Determining the answers to dose received measures is vital to understanding the findings related to perception of program quality, participation rates, and ultimately, program outcomes. For example, if participation rates were low, was it because employees were simply unaware of the programs? Or was it because they were dissatisfied with the program offerings, its quality, or other factors? Participant satisfaction will not only influence the individual's decision to participate in the program, it is also likely to affect the individual's decision to follow through on program recommendations and behavior change attempts. Thus, this element of process evaluation obtains the feedback necessary to identify the specific areas of program implementation requiring modification. This might include the need to improve communication strategies, change the types of programs offered and how they are delivered (e.g., on-site vs. off-site fitness center), or some combination of actions.

Reach is a measurement of participation rate across the employee population. The purpose of monitoring participation and attendance is to ensure that a sufficient number of the target population is reached, and quantifying how much of the eligible population participated in various program components.

In assessing participation, several key issues need to be addressed. The first is, "how is participation defined?" At one extreme, a participant can be viewed as someone who engages in "any" health promotion activity in a given year -- for example, completing an HRA. At the other extreme, an employee may be defined as an "active" participant -- for example, one who is routinely involved in health promotion programs by exercising regularly, attending health education classes, completing an on-line course, speaking to a health coach, and submitting weekly "activity logs" that record activities outside of work.

The rationale for adopting a more "liberal" definition of participation (i.e., engagement in "any" health promoting activities) is simple; program evaluators do not yet know whether any one intervention or combination of interventions will achieve the desired effect. For example, an individual who participates in only one activity in a given year, such as counseling following completion of an HRA, is told that he or she has high blood pressure and should immediately see a physician. The individual then follows the advice of the counselor, begins taking blood pressure medication, and, in turn, lowers his or her risk for stroke and heart attack. That individual's health outcome is positive even though participation in the health promotion programs was limited. In contrast, another individual may participate in several health promotion programs but do so because a financial incentive is linked to participation or because the person is "curious" about the program but not motivated to change behavior. That individual, while classified as an "active" participant, might gain little from exposure to the interventions.

Second, in addition to assessing "any" and "active" participation in a program, it is also helpful to flag participants in specialized high-risk intervention programs since these programs have been shown to have a significant impact on program results.[23-26] Further, it is useful to assess the intensity of program participation (e.g., number of visits to fitness centers, number of assessment materials returned, number of educational sessions attended, etc.) because the degree of program exposure has been shown to be correlated with program success, i.e., the more intensive the participation levels, the better the outcomes.[27] This "dose-response" relationship was shown in the evaluation performed for Chevron Corporation focused on its Health Quest fitness program.[28,29] In that

evaluation, individuals who participated in the program more frequently achieved the greatest cost savings.

Third, ideally, program participation data are captured efficiently by a management information system and integrated with other relevant databases (i.e., personnel or human resource files that help determine program eligibility, HRA data). A system can be designed that provides invaluable process and impact data across a number of dimensions. For example, the tracking system might include the demographic characteristics of participants, usage patterns for various programs (e.g., time of day, frequency of usage), whether first time users are being engaged in the program, and differential participation rates across time periods. Finally, by combining HRA and participation data, the evaluator can determine the extent to which the population at greatest risk is being reached by the program. This is achieved when the eligible population completes an HRA where high-risk status can be ascertained. The analytic function of identifying high-risk individuals and determining the extent to which they are participating in the program is critical in developing and evaluating a high-risk program.

Humanistic Measures

One rationale for introducing health promotion programs is that they help project an image of caring about employees' health and well-being. Offering health promotion programs is expected to instill a greater sense of loyalty toward the employer who has demonstrated a willingness to invest in the physical and mental health of the workforce. Positive sentiments toward the employer are expected to eventually achieve lower turnover, a reduction in absenteeism, and overall improved productivity.

Management is therefore interested in demonstrating that the program, which represents a human resource expense, is viewed positively and improves morale. Humanistic measures often include assessments of workers' perceived quality of life, resilience, attitude toward work, attitudes toward management, and self-assessed productivity. These measures may be included in the process evaluation, typically as part of the employee feedback survey or as part of the HRA. They may be measured using a pretest-posttest design in which the same attitudinal statements are examined before and after program introduction. Alternatively, employees may be asked post-hoc about the effects of the program on their productivity, morale, and attitudes toward management after the program has been in place for a given time period (e.g., one year). The sample employee feedback survey, found in the appendix, includes example humanistic measurement questions.

Outcome Evaluation

Variables of Interest

Behavior Change and Health Improvement

Ultimately, the most important and relevant aim of a workplace health promotion program is to improve the health and well-being of the target population (employees and more recently dependents). To achieve this aim, a significant portion of employees with poor health habits who are at high health risk need to be engaged by the program. Additionally, they need to attend to the behavior change messages sent and to respond positively to these messages.

Thus, one important test of program effectiveness is its ability to modify unhealthy habits and improve the risk profile of all employees, especially the highest risk members. Another marker of program effectiveness is its ability to keep low risk people at low risk and prevent them from moving into a high-risk category. In short, both improvements and

decrements in risks should be evaluated when measuring behavior change and risk reduction efforts, and the results should show a net positive effect. If high-risk individuals improve while low-risk individuals worsen in their risk profiles, the net effect could be zero or negative, and the program would be judged as either lacking impact, or worse, having a negative impact.

As noted above, one marker of program effectiveness is assessing the degree to which "at high risk" profiles improve over time. A way to test for, and express this change, is to compare the proportion of the population "at high risk" between at least two time periods, such as from baseline to one year later. This approach provides uniform reporting across measures, which is readily understood by non-research oriented audiences.

To determine program effectiveness in achieving health improvement and risk reduction, the first step is to collect valid and reliable baseline data on the target population's *health habits* such as diet, exercise, alcohol consumption, smoking status, seat belt use, and sleep patterns; *biometric characteristics*, which might include total cholesterol, blood pressure, and blood sugar; and *well-being* measures of stress, depression, and overall health status. Follow-up assessments should be performed after an appropriate time interval (preferably annually) and during the same season as the baseline assessment to avoid the problem of a seasonal effect on reported health habits and biometric measures.

For example, in a real world case, a baseline HRA was administered in the spring season of a year and a follow-up HRA right after the Christmas holiday. Not surprisingly, the Time 2 biometric and self-report health measures showed that subjects were more overweight, consumed more alcohol, practiced poorer eating and driving habits, and in general were in worse physical health, as compared to baseline.

Financial Outcomes

Program sponsors may, over time, reach the conclusion that improvement in the health and well-being of their workers leads to improvements in productivity and reductions in insurance benefit costs. These relationships are supported by research that links health risk values to medical expenditures and productivity decrements. Several ROI models have been created that are built on the empirical foundation that health risks are associated with higher medical costs and impaired productivity – and that improving the risk profile of a population leads to cost savings and potentially a positive return on investment (ROI).[30-34]

In spite of several studies focused on the economic impacts and ROI of workplace health promotion programs, skepticism remains high. The conventional wisdom expressed by many corporate benefits directors is that these programs are worthwhile because they improve morale and "probably" reduce health risks. However, they, and their benefit consultants, continue to express doubt about the economic returns attributable to programs. Part of the skepticism is derived from a lack of knowledge concerning the state of research findings in this area, especially in regards to newer methods employed in evaluating financial impact and ROI.

The problem is not the lack of research efforts at documenting cost savings from such initiatives; there are many studies, some large scale, which have taken on the challenge of documenting savings.[35] The problem is that these studies often contain methodological flaws in their design that call into question some of the conclusions presented. As noted below in the threats to validity section, these inherent limitations common to "real-life" research are related to difficulties of achieving internal and external validity (most notably, selection bias).

That said, program evaluators are still challenged to prove that health promotion saves money, or at least, pays for itself.

Economic markers that are commonly tracked in corporate environments include costs associated with healthcare utilization, absenteeism, turnover, workers' compensation, short and long-term disability, and employee productivity. These indicators may be tracked differently by different organizations, or different departments within the same organization, and the quality of data associated with each program is often lacking.

A wide range of financial outcome measures and data sources for these measures are discussed below and listed in Table 6-1 (adapted from the work by Fielding, 1986).[36]

Healthcare Utilization and Costs

Measures of healthcare utilization and costs include both inpatient and outpatient services (e.g., hospital admissions, annual doctor's visit, preventive screenings), emergency room visits, and pharmaceutical expenses. However, when measuring the impact of health promotion programs on healthcare utilization and costs, the evaluator encounters many issues unrelated to the health of populations. For example, to save money, companies often change their benefit plan provisions from year to year. They may switch claims administrators. They may impose a greater cost burden on consumers in the form of higher deductibles, co-payments, or coinsurance. The administrator may change the way in which claims are paid, data are collected, or managed care provisions are enforced. Employees may migrate from fee-for-service indemnity plans into consumer driven health plans that are less costly. The company may institute cost control measures such as utilization review systems or channeling workers into preferred provider networks. Providers in the community may increase their charges dramatically for the same services because they control a given market where there is little competition.

Another challenge with healthcare data is the wide variation in utilization among different segments of the population. Some employees

Table 6-1: Financial measures assessed in a health promotion evaluation.

Measures	
Absenteeism	Turnover
Disability	Workers' Compensation
Productivity	Healthcare Utilization and Cost
Possible Data Sources	
Personnel records	Human resource files
Payroll files	Supervisory ratings
Disability	Medical records
Insurance claims data	Benefits consultant reports
Self-report data	

may utilize a great number of medical services because of chronic health problems while others may use none. Traditionally, a small minority of the total covered population uses a disproportionately large amount of healthcare resources. This is sometimes referred to as the 80-20 rule, meaning about 80% of healthcare dollars are spent on 20% of the patient population.

Additionally, usage of resources often varies year to year as the health status of individuals fluctuates. Illnesses attributable to lifestyle practices, such as heart disease and cancers, may have evolved over a long period. Further, improvement in the company's healthcare experience may take several years to register once health habits are changed and utilization of services is subdued. In most cases, healthcare costs may actually increase in the first year of program introduction as employees become aware of problematic conditions such as hypertension or high cholesterol and seek medical attention. On the other hand, the company may realize short term savings when certain lifestyle practices are improved, such as not drinking and driving, wearing seatbelts,

seeking help for depression, taking actions to correct home safety problems, and seeking treatment for drug and alcohol abuse.

Most studies of the relationship between health promotion programs and medical care costs have used overall healthcare spending as the outcome variables. It is useful, however, to segregate costs associated with inpatient and emergency room care (expected to be reduced) as opposed to outpatient preventive service visits and pharmaceutical use (expected to increase). Segregating inpatient, emergency room, pharmacy, and preventive services costs makes it possible to detect increases or decreases in each individual utilization category. These different trends would be obscured if the costs were tracked as one lump sum.

Also, it is useful to focus on specific lifestyle-related diagnoses (LDGs) within the context of overall medical care expenditures in order to separate out when certain costs should or should not be factored into the calculations. An obvious example of costs that should not be included relates to "normal" obstetric care in which a healthy newborn is delivered without complications. In such circumstances, demographics of the workforce, fertility of the female population, and individual choice, as opposed to adverse lifestyle practices, will determine costs. In general, when conducting healthcare claims analyses, women who are pregnant at any point during the evaluation studies should be removed from the analysis, otherwise the results will be skewed on the high side, and not reflective of the actual healthcare costs due to unhealthy lifestyle practices.

Alternatively, data on pregnant women can be separated from the analytic sample and reviewed separately. The rate of complicated deliveries (e.g., those resulting in premature or low birth weight infants) will be affected by lifestyle practices of the mother (e.g., poor nutrition, smoking, or drinking alcohol) and should, therefore, be considered in evaluations of lifestyle-related medical care utilization and cost affecting pregnant women. In such studies, improving the lifestyle practices of the population is expected to reduce the rate of adverse pregnancy related outcomes and associated costs.

While some medical conditions have no known relationship to lifestyle habits and characteristics, the course of treatment and severity of illness for these conditions may be affected by modifiable health risks. For example, an individual who is physically, emotionally, and spiritually healthier than someone who is not will likely experience a faster recovery from illness and shorter hospital length of stay.[37] Therefore, we recommend that all health conditions be included in an overall analysis of program impact on healthcare utilization and costs.

It is not unusual for a smaller number of employees to have medical costs of several hundred thousand dollars because of complicated procedures such as an organ transplant or a severe illness requiring an extended stay in the intensive care unit. Individuals generating high claims, called outliers, can distort the overall analysis. As such, they are analyzed separately and results presented with and without outliers. In general, analyses that exclude outliers are more germane to workplace health promotion program evaluations because these programs aim to improve overall population health rather than be focused on particular subsets of populations that suffer from very costly and debilitating diseases.

Disability

When absenteeism due to illness or disability is prolonged, short- and long-term disability programs are triggered. Organizational compensation for short- and long-term disability is determined in different ways for different organizations, making cross-company comparisons of rates and costs difficult. Most companies differentiate between short- and long-term disability, but company policies as to when short-term disability ends and long-term disability begins vary from three months to more than one year. Employers also offer different benefit packages for disability. For those employers who have a flexible benefit structure, employees can choose the desired benefit level each year when enrolling in the program. There is also no standard system of reporting causes or types of disability. Some systems report specific ICD-9-CM diagnostic codes while others report broad categories of disability such as "back problem" or "cardiovascular disease."

In spite of these limitations, it is beneficial to track utilization of disability benefits and costs across time to determine whether the health promotion program is having any demonstrable effect on this program. Once again, comparison group studies are preferred over time series analyses when tracking disability costs because of the numerous factors cited above that may influence a company's disability experience.

Worker Safety

Safety is a paramount concern for employers, especially in high-risk industries such as manufacturing and construction. Employer's attention to worker safety is mandated by state and federal laws and recording of safety-related incidents is required by the Occupational Safety and Health Administration (OSHA). This concern over worker safety can be used as a leverage point for health promotion program managers and evaluators.

Where possible, program evaluators should report workers' compensation claim costs and incidence rates as indicators of the company's focus on prevention activities. However, it is often difficult to report these measures since laws differ from state to state and even within states for different occupational groups such as police and fire department employees. There is also variability in the coverage provisions for different categories of claims. For example, stress-related claims may be considered valid in one jurisdiction but not another.

For workers' compensation studies, when longitudinal studies are employed, we recommend comparing groups that have stable turnover rates and stable work assignments for the types of work performed in order to better isolate potential effects of the program on disability claims. Further, for the same reasons, stability in state statutes, company policies, and insurance carriers are important in these types of assessments. Finally, rather than studying program impacts on the broad category of disability, studies should focus on specific illnesses or disability areas that are targeted by the intervention programs. For example, the incidence of back problems, carpal tunnel disorders, strains, and sprains would be impacted by programs emphasizing proper lifting techniques, strength training programs, weight management, and ergonomic modification of the physical space. Health promotion programs that ally with other initiatives that aim to improve the organizational climate and work environment may also significantly impact workers' compensation claims and costs.[38]

Turnover

Turnover, particularly of well-trained employees, can be expensive[6,39] – estimated to cost as high as 20-30% of an employee's annual salary.[6,40] However, in some industries, for example retail or fast food, turnover costs are far lower and may, in fact be "negative" since newly hired employees for relatively low skill positions often accept lesser starting wages than more senior workers.

Tracking turnover may be difficult since organizations do not always record reasons for termination. As with absenteeism, the evaluator needs to be aware of other conditions that may have changed during the course of the study that may influence turnover rates, e.g., improved job security measures introduced into labor contracts; introduction of profit sharing or stock option benefits; future prospects for the company or industry; and overall employee morale related to views of senior management. In some sectors of the economy where turnover is traditionally very low, it is difficult to detect reductions in turnover regardless of the effectiveness of health promotion programs.

An example of a baseline turnover study graphic, where the company's experience is compared to norms, is shown in Figure 6-3. This graphic is taken from a "best practice" benchmarking study conducted in 1997 in cooperation with the American Productivity and Quality Center (APQC) based in Houston, TX. The project involved collecting a variety of health and productivity measures from several organizations and developing norms and best practice benchmarks for the organizations recruited for the project. The turnover graphic displayed as Figure 6-3 shows the cost of turnover for one of the employers in the database ($1,535 -- depicted as a diamond shape) compared to all other employers in the study. Also shown are separate costs for hourly and salaried employees as well as their turnover rates. This information was used to set a target for improving the turnover experience for the organization, operationally defined as the 25th percentile value for the group as a whole.

Figure 6-3: Sample baseline turnover analysis of employee norms vs. best practices.

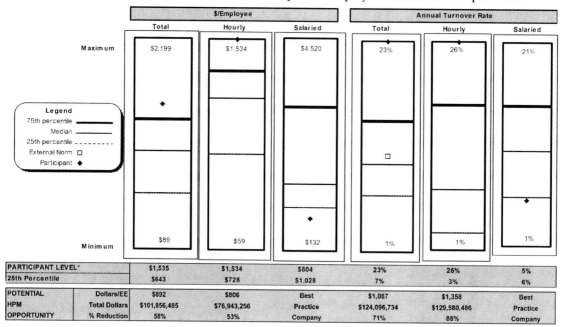

		$/Employee			Annual Turnover Rate		
		Total	Hourly	Salaried	Total	Hourly	Salaried
Maximum		$2,199	$1,534	$4,520	23%	26%	21%
Minimum		$89	$59	$132	1%	1%	1%
PARTICIPANT LEVEL*		$1,535	$1,534	$804	23%	26%	5%
25th Percentile		$643	$728	$1,028	7%	3%	6%
POTENTIAL	Dollars/EE	$892	$806	Best	$1,087	$1,358	Best
HPM	Total Dollars	$101,856,485	$76,943,256	Practice	$124,096,734	$129,580,486	Practice
OPPORTUNITY	% Reduction	58%	53%	Company	71%	88%	Company

Legend
75th percentile ─────
Median ─────
25th percentile ─ ─ ─ ─
External Norm ☐
Participant ◆

* Participant level metrics are calculated independently for Hourly. Salaried and Total.

Absenteeism

Prior to assessing program effects, agreement should be reached as to what constitutes absenteeism attributable to health and lifestyle factors, i.e., absenteeism for illness but not for jury duty, military leave, family medical leave act (FMLA), holidays, or vacation. This is becoming more difficult as many organizations have instituted paid time off (PTO) systems in which sickness absences, holidays, and vacation are all included in the same pool of days from which the employee may draw time off. Monetizing absenteeism is sometimes challenging because a prorated value benefit needs to be included for each hour lost to absenteeism.

Additionally, absenteeism rates may be influenced by a variety of factors other than employee illness or injury. Job satisfaction, general employee morale, changes in company policies toward absenteeism, and outbreaks of adult and children's illnesses in the community are all factors that may affect absenteeism rates.

Use of comparison groups exposed to similar social and environmental conditions is the best way to control for these potential confounders.

The evaluator should be aware that groups with higher than average absenteeism rates at baseline are most likely to exhibit rate reductions and subsequent cost savings from health promotion intervention. Groups with low rates may already have eliminated unnecessary days absent and may show little additional improvement.

An example of a baseline absenteeism analysis, where the company's experience is compared to norms, is shown in Figure 6-4. This graphic is also taken from the aforementioned APQC study. The data in the figure are displayed as described above; the organization's absence costs and rates relative to the other benchmark organizations.

Productivity

There are many definitions and measures related to worker productivity. The evaluator

Figure 6-4: Sample baseline analysis of absence rates and costs showing norms vs. best practices.

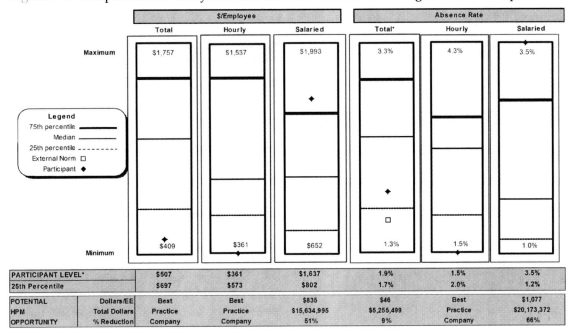

	$/Employee			Absence Rate		
	Total	Hourly	Salaried	Total*	Hourly	Salaried
Maximum	$1,757	$1,537	$1,993	3.3%	4.3%	3.5%
Minimum	$409	$361	$652	1.3%	1.5%	1.0%
PARTICIPANT LEVEL*	$507	$361	$1,637	1.9%	1.5%	3.5%
25th Percentile	$697	$573	$802	1.7%	2.0%	1.2%
POTENTIAL Dollars/EE	Best	Best	$835	$46	Best	$1,077
HPM Total Dollars	Practice	Practice	$15,634,995	$5,255,499	Practice	$20,173,372
OPPORTUNITY % Reduction	Company	Company	51%	9%	Company	66%

Legend
75th percentile ———
Median ———
25th percentile - - - - -
External Norm ☐
Participant ◆

* Participant level metrics are calculated independently for Hourly, Salaried and Total.

should consider "tapping into" existing quality and efficiency measures already used in the organization. Some of these may include internal measures of productivity (e.g., widgets produced per unit of time) or external measures of productivity (e.g., acceptance of widgets by customers expressed as revenues or profits per employee). Often, customer and even employee satisfaction can be used as a proxy for productivity, especially when these have been shown to be correlated with shareholder value.

Quality and productivity indicators are easier to track for some occupational groups than for others. For example, productivity can be measured for call center operators, computer data entry workers, insurance claims processors, and for individuals paid for individual output (e.g., garment or agricultural workers). For white collar workers, often referred to as "knowledge workers," measurement may involve the administration of validated self-report instruments, use of "beeper" studies where workers record what

they are doing (on or off task) whenever they are "beeped," and simulation studies where workers are asked to perform "real-life" tasks in a lab environment that simulates their real jobs. Some examples of instruments measuring productivity or presenteeism (being at work but experiencing reduced work quality/output due to health problems) can be found in Lerner et al.[41] and Koopman et al.[42], and research focused on health promotion program impacts on presenteeism is documented in studies by Pelletier[43] and Cancelliere.[44]

In measuring productivity, more than with any other outcome variable, multiple internal and external confounders may affect the data. These include market conditions; availability of capital and raw materials; quality of leadership and management practices; presence of economic incentives for increased productivity; overall morale; and labor-management relations. While productivity indicators can theoretically be compared across groups and over time, in real-life situations, such convenient comparison groups are rarely available. In short, the evidence is still inconclusive on how much health promotion programs impact productivity.[44]

Framework for Selecting Outcome Measures

Which of the above outcomes should be used in an evaluation effort? That decision will hinge upon the importance of each outcome to the decision maker; the availability of data in a "clean" and usable format; access to experts who can analyze and interpret the data; and funding for both program and evaluation efforts. Further, sensitivities regarding employee confidentiality and patient protection often emerge when requesting individual level personnel or medical claims data.

In general, it is recommended that as many measures as are reasonable be considered in a comprehensive evaluation project. Since the intervention is likely to affect many outcomes simultaneously, it is advantageous for the evaluator to gather data in multiple domains rather than relying on only one or two measures. In that way, a "rich" and multi-dimensional story can be told regarding program effects on a variety of issues of interest to various audience members. Additionally, a multi-measure "triangulation" approach reassures sponsors that several indicators are moving in the same direction, as they ought to. If a more limited list of success factors is selected for evaluation purposes, the evaluator should take special care to ensure that the outcomes identified directly coincide with program and organizational goals.

The disadvantage of a comprehensive evaluation approach is that scarce evaluation resources are then distributed across several measures rather than concentrated in any one area. However, a focused evaluation approach creates an opposite problem in which positive results are not known simply because they were not included in the evaluation. The main advantage of a multiple measure approach

is that different individuals' agendas are addressed simultaneously and the reasons behind program success or failure can more easily be determined. This, in turn, helps shape future program designs and implementation strategies.

STUDY METHODOLOGY

A study design is an analytic approach to conducting an investigation. In other words, it is a plan for data gathering and examination with the purpose of determining whether something that was supposed to happen actually did happen. In the case of evaluation research, a study design describes the protocol for collecting data and measuring constructs, and how researchers determine whether the program has been successful at meeting its stated goals. A well-developed study design is important for ensuring that findings are valid and consistent with the rules of inference. A robust study design established prior to study initiation assures that enough data are collected and the study has sufficient power to detect changes.

The purpose of a research design is to guide the evaluator on such issues as what data to collect, how often, from whom, and how the right comparisons are made. In addition, the design forces the evaluator to confront the issue of extraneous factors, or confounders, that may influence outcomes, and how these are controlled through an appropriate design.

Three broad research designs are typically used in evaluation studies: non-experimental (also referred to as pre-experimental or observational studies), quasi-experimental, and experimental. The advantages and disadvantages of alternative designs are discussed below with an emphasis placed on how these are applied to workplace health promotion evaluations. For the interested reader, a thorough review of statistical and design issues discussed here can be found in Kerlinger[45] and Campbell and Stanley.[46] Additionally, a more rigorous and technical review of methods that can be used to adjust for non-measurable factors like employee attitudes can be found in Heckman and Robb.[47]

Structure of the Study

Non-Experimental (Observational Studies)

Non-experimental, observational studies are the simplest and least expensive to perform. They are also the most widely used in health promotion evaluations. The most common among these is a design referred to as <u>one group, posttest only</u> illustrated below

$$X \quad O_2$$

where X is the "intervention" and O_2 is simply the "observation" or a recording of the experience following the intervention.

An example of a one group, posttest only evaluation is one where individuals are administered surveys at key program milestones after being exposed to the program. Surveys may ask such questions as, "How did the intervention change your health habits?" Responses to the survey are used to determine whether the interventions achieved their desired effects. The benefit of this design is that it is the least resource intensive to implement. The drawback is that it is the least capable of deducing cause and effect.

In a post-intervention survey, responses from employees about program effects are, by definition, subjective and prone to positive response bias – meaning, respondents are likely to say the program had a positive impact since they spent mental and physical energy participating in it. More objective measures may be taken in a post-intervention survey such as height, weight, blood pressure, and cholesterol; but there would be no way of knowing how these measures have changed due to the intervention without baseline assessments.

Feedback from surveys provides valuable information to program managers that can be used to improve the delivery of interventions. However, this design is of limited usefulness in evaluating whether a "change" has occurred since the approach does not address the question of what might have happened in the absence of the intervention. When a pre-experimental design is used, especially in survey research, special effort should be made to obtain opinions from a representative group of program-eligible individuals and especially from those who typically do not complete questionnaires.

A second and stronger non-experimental design is the one group, before and after or pretest-posttest only design.

$$O_1 \quad X \quad O_2$$

A pre-test (O_1) is administered to the target population followed by the intervention (X), and then a posttest (O_2). This evaluation design is the second most common form of evaluation in worksite settings. One prime example of this approach is the administration of a baseline Health Risk Assessment (HRA) as a first intervention in a comprehensive program. The HRA is subsequently re-administered after an appropriate time interval has elapsed, usually 12 to 24 months after the program is implemented. Other common applications of this design are evaluations of smoking cessation, exercise, nutrition or other behavioral change programs.

However, in a pre- and post- comparison of the intervention group, there may have been other external factors causing changes in outcomes besides the intervention that are not taken into account. For example, if during the intervention period there was an influenza outbreak that caused many employees to stay home (increase absenteeism rates) or visit their doctor for treatment (increase healthcare utilization), these behavior changes could be misinterpreted as attributable to the intervention. However, if there was a concurrent comparison group that also reacted to the influenza outbreak, the independent effects of the intervention could be determined.

Another non-experimental design is the longitudinal, repeated measures or time series analysis.

$$O_1 \ O_2 \ O_3 \ O_4 \quad X \quad O_5 \ O_6 \ O_7 \ O_8$$

With this design, a series of observations or measures (O_1, O_2, ...) are taken prior to the intervention (X) in order to establish a baseline. These are followed by another series of observations (O_5, O_6, ...). Ideally, the baseline measures are relatively stable so that any deviation from baseline may be attributed to the effects of the intervention.

For example, following a series of baseline measures, a stable absenteeism rate is established. The program is then introduced and absenteeism is reduced. The program is then withdrawn and absenteeism returns to its original baseline level. Because of these alterations in the program, effects are noted for specific outcomes of interest.

However, alternative explanations for these reductions are plentiful. These may be classified as changes attributable to other events or combinations of events occurring simultaneous with the study. For example, reductions in absenteeism rates may be associated with changes in company paid time off (PTO) policies; deterioration of overall economic conditions that make jobs harder to find and employees more likely to work harder to keep their jobs; and company layoffs that result in the least productive employees (those with the most absenteeism) being dismissed.

A variation of this evaluation design is the multiple time series design.

$$O_1 \ O_2 \ O_3 \ O_4 \quad X_1 \quad O_5 \quad X_2 \quad O_6 \quad X_3 \quad O_7 \ O_8 \ O_9$$

Here, as above, baseline measures are collected, an intervention takes place, and

follow-up observations are conducted. Additional interventions (X_2, X_3, ...) may be introduced at varying intensities to determine whether these induce changes in the outcomes.

For example, following a series of baseline measures, a stable aerobic exercise frequency measure is established at a worksite. A fitness program is then introduced and aerobic exercise frequency increases. The program is intensified (or modified) and aerobic exercise frequency increases further. The program is then withdrawn and exercise frequency returns to its original baseline level. Because of these alterations in program "dose," effects are noted for the specific outcome of interest. Ideally, a "dose-response" relationship is observed in which the more intensive the program, the more positive the outcomes. As above, alternative explanations for improvements or decrements need to be considered when interpreting study results.

Although pre/post and post-only approaches constitute pre-experimental designs, the pre/post design is considered the stronger option of the two. The pre/post design, typically employed in workplace evaluations, allows a comparison of outcomes at two time points rather than just one, which improves the validity of the evaluation.

Quasi-Experimental Design

The most common quasi-experimental design used in health promotion evaluation is the pretest and posttest with comparison group (also known as the non-equivalent control group design).

$$\begin{array}{ccc} O_1 & X & O_2 \\ \hline O_1 & & O_2 \end{array}$$

With this design, baseline measures are taken for two groups, one exposed to the intervention and the other not. Follow-up measures are also recorded for both groups. When feasible, a quasi-experimental design is one that most health promotion program evaluators adopt for measuring the effects of workplace health promotion programs in "real world" settings. A quasi-experimental design addresses the question, "What would have happened if we did nothing?" Changes in the participant group are compared to changes in a non-participant group. The key task, therefore, is to secure an appropriate group of non-participants, sufficiently similar to the participant group, to allow for valid estimates of what would have occurred absent an intervention.

The factor that distinguishes this approach from a true experimental design is the lack of random assignment of people to study and control conditions. In a worksite environment, one group of individuals might voluntarily enroll in the health promotion program while another group might elect not to join. Since participants are volunteering to take part in the health promotion program, they have, on their own accord, initiated a change process by indicating "readiness." This acknowledgement separates this group from those who have not yet decided they wish to change. One way to address the problem of self-selection is to classify all employees at a site offered a health promotion program as treatment subjects. As such, all employees at that site eligible for the program are compared to another group of employees at another site not eligible.

While this approach can help avoid problems related to different motivational levels between participants and non-participants, it still has inherent shortcomings. There may be several reasons why any given site is selected as the health promotion intervention or pilot site. The site may be led by a visionary general manager; employees may demand the program as part of their labor contract; the employees may be more highly compensated and willing to contribute to the cost of the program; the site may have a history of high benefit costs, which senior management is attempting to moderate; and so forth. Thus, selection bias at the site level is also problematic. However, if site selection is random, then many of the biases described above can be avoided.

The approach in which sites receiving a program are compared to those without the program, also known as "ecological studies" or "natural experiments," has been employed in several large-scale evaluations of health promotion programs, including those by Johnson & Johnson[48-51] and the Dow Chemical Company.[33,52-54]

Another approach for dealing with self-selection bias is to identify a comparison group with as many similar attributes to the intervention group as possible (i.e., "twins" of individuals exposed to the program) and then apply various statistical techniques to further control inherent differences between these groups. These steps increase the likelihood of achieving valid study outcomes. A method used by many evaluators to create statistical "twins" of participants from a pool of non-participants is known as propensity score matching. More details about how to conduct these types of analyses are presented later in this chapter (see Dealing with Threats to Validity).

As emphasized below, experimental (randomized) designs generally address most validity threats, but randomized designs require a great deal of effort and constant monitoring. While an excellent randomized trial is superior to quasi-experimental designs, poorly conducted randomized trials can be just as invalid as poorly controlled quasi-experimental studies. Quasi-experimental retrospective studies have the advantage of reporting what actually takes place in a real-life naturalistic setting as compared to a more sterile and at times contrived experimental laboratory environment. Further, quasi-experimental studies can take advantage of archival (administrative) data and therefore can leverage large databases to detect smaller changes over time and differences between groups. Additionally, quasi-experimental studies are far less costly to conduct than randomized trials and can be completed in a shorter timeframe.

Experimental Design

The most rigorous design is called experimental. Here, individuals are randomly assigned into the treatment or control group and observations are made before and after the intervention. Individuals in the intervention group are exposed to the workplace program while individuals in the control groups are not. Data are collected at baseline and at follow-up intervals after the intervention has been implemented. Intervention and control group outcomes are compared at baseline and then at each key study milestone. Differences between the groups at follow-up are attributed to the effect of the intervention rather than the unique characteristics of people exposed to the intervention.

This design addresses a common problem in "real-world" evaluations, namely biased results due to non-equivalence of the treatment and control groups at the start of an intervention. Conrad et al.[55] provide an excellent discussion of the threats to internal validity in workplace health promotion research when designs other than true experimental designs are used.

Diagrammatically, experimental design is configured as follows:

$$[R] \quad \begin{array}{lll} O_1 \;\; X \;\; O_2 & \text{Treatment} \\ \hline O_1 \quad O_2 & \text{Control} \end{array}$$

The [R] indicates that subjects have been randomly assigned to experimental and control groups above and below the line, respectively.

The strength of this approach is that, if subjects are truly randomly assigned, there should be no differences in the composition of the intervention and control groups at the beginning of the study that may independently influence outcomes. The effectiveness of randomization can be tested by comparing intervention and control group characteristics at baseline. If there are observable differences at baseline despite randomization, then the randomization process may be faulty. However, differences between groups can still be controlled for later on using statistical models.

Random assignment of individuals or groups of individuals to intervention and control conditions is considered the "holy grail" of research methods and appropriate for clinical studies in which drugs or alternative medical treatments are tested. The idea behind clinical trials is that the chemistry of the medicines or the science behind a medical intervention is what drives an effective treatment – not the behavior of the clinician. In fact, great pains are taken to ensure that clinicians that administer the intervention are as "neutral" as possible, meaning they do not influence the treatment in any way. In fact, when conducting "double blind" studies, clinicians do not know whether they are administering a drug or a placebo to their patients.

However, it is widely recognized that randomization is usually impractical in health promotion evaluations and may be illegal (unfair or unethical). It may be illegal when employers offer differential health benefit programs to some employees but not others. In health promotion programs, the interventions offered, e.g., getting people to quit smoking, lose weight, increase physical activity, and eat a healthy diet, are unquestionably helpful and very likely to lead to improved health and a better quality of life. Hence, senior managers at companies are generally unwilling to support randomization because by allowing a randomized trial they would be deciding, de facto, to allow some employees to benefit from a health improvement program while others would be denied that benefit.

On the other hand, randomized trials may be ethically justifiable when considerable uncertainty exists about the effects (either positive or negative) of an intervention, or when budgets for programs are limited. In the latter case, the organization may not have sufficient funding to introduce the program to all employees, so instead a lottery-based enrollment is applied, which can be construed as a fair way to randomize people into treatment and control conditions.

Operationally, this approach calls for the assignment of volunteers for a program at a given site into treatment and "waiting list" groups on a random basis. Hence, outcome measures are assessed for equally motivated individuals at baseline and after a given time interval – some of whom then participate in the program while others remain on a wait list until openings become available.

Unfortunately, this evaluation approach does not work for single-site interventions that are "environmental" or "culturally" based, since they involve changing policies and norms for the entire worksite in addition to providing health improvement programs to individuals. All of these changes are likely to also influence the behaviors of those on the waiting list. Consequently, the worksite itself is the "subject" of the evaluation rather than individuals at that site, since the aim of the program is to alter the culture and norms at that site, thus making it more health promoting.

An additional problem of using the "waiting list" approach is the collection of data from the control group. If the data collection effort is directed at archival data (e.g., absenteeism or healthcare records compiled routinely and stored historically), then comparisons of intervention and control groups are possible and uncomplicated. However, if the analysis calls for a comparison of data that need to be collected directly from employees (e.g., health risk assessments, biometric measures, satisfaction scores, worker attitudes, etc.) then potential contamination may occur. For example, when health measures are compared across sites, the collection of these data may be viewed by the participant as an intervention, especially if individual feedback is provided to both study and comparison group populations.

Longitudinal, repeated-measure time series can also be applied to quasi-experimental and experimental design in which several years of baseline data are collected.

Other Study Designs

The models discussed above assume a prospective evaluation design, meaning there is a start to the program and an end-point at which measurements are collected. Data collection occurs over many years and evaluation results reported regularly. But, what if the program is ongoing and there are no clear start and stop points? The study designs below can be used in those circumstances.

Retrospective Studies

A retrospective study is one that "looks back" in time and measures what happened historically to determine whether the program influenced the outcome. In a retrospective study, all of the data have already been accumulated and are now available for analysis. The evaluator's task is to summarize data from different milestones and record trends in health or costs during the observation period.

Cross-sectional Studies

Cross-sectional studies are conducted when researchers wish to take a "snapshot" picture of what is happening at any given point in time, and to report those data over a given time horizon. Cross-sectional studies are less useful than longitudinal studies for identifying causal relationships because the direction of causality (what is the cause and what is the effect) is unknown. However, cross-sectional studies can describe relationships between the variable of interest, for example smoking and drinking excessive amounts of alcohol (i.e., how many people smoke and drink vs. only smoke or only drink).

Qualitative Studies

Qualitative studies, sometimes referred to as formative research, aim to capture subjective data using such techniques as open-ended questionnaires, interviews, focus groups, or site visits. Investigators may review transcripts and notes to identify richly detailed themes that can inform new areas of inquiry or hypotheses. Qualitative studies typically complement quantitative data to provide a context for quantitative results. Qualitative studies are typically conducted as part of structure and process evaluations.

Multi-site Studies

For multi-site studies, evaluators measure the effect of the intervention at each site (e.g., several unique locations or business units across a large organization) by comparing outcomes to the control groups matched to each study site. Evaluators then pool the data from the multiple sites to measure an overall effect of the intervention.

Ideally, each site collects sufficient data to test the hypotheses of interest, and the site can therefore stand on its own in terms of study results. Pooling data across sites allows researchers to test for smaller effects and to see whether differences in outcome may be attributable to the unique characteristics of a site's population or the way in which the intervention was put in place. A multi-site study also allows researchers to make inferences about the relative effectiveness of interventions at each participating site – measure of the relationship between the amount of program "dose" and subsequent outcomes. It also allows the evaluator to make generalizations about the effectiveness of the intervention as a whole.

Using Multiple Designs in Evaluation Studies

When assessing multiple outcomes in health promotion evaluations, it is inevitable that several research designs will be used. For example, qualitative data related to satisfaction, interest, and awareness of the program are frequently collected using surveys administered to the population offered the program. The intent is to gauge the thoughts and opinions of those exposed to the program through surveys; the one-group post-test only design is most common in these cases. These surveys are typically administered at key milestones in the project, often at 12, 24, 36, 48, and 60 months, assuming a long-term evaluation is conducted.

In assessing the impact of the program on health behaviors and biometric measures, a quasi- or true-experimental design is preferred; in particular, when testing the effectiveness of a new program or intervention whereby volunteers are assigned to either the intervention (treatment) or comparison (control) group. For routine studies of program effects on health outcomes, a one-group pretest/posttest only design is used. The validity of such a design is enhanced when the following is achieved: high initial participation, high follow-up rates, and several iterations of the evaluation that allow evaluators to monitor changes periodically over a long time.

The pretest/posttest designs with comparison groups or time series analyses are also preferred for financial impact studies. The larger the number of comparison groups, and the greater the extent to which sites are arbitrarily assigned to treatment and comparison conditions to control for possible confounders, the stronger the design and the more valid the results.

Threats to Validity

The credibility of an evaluation study is based on the extent to which factors that threaten internal and external validity have been carefully considered and controlled. Those threats manifest themselves as potential confounders or alternative explanations of results. Consequently, the responsible evaluator will develop a plan that addresses these threats in the study design and acknowledge any shortcomings or limitations inherent in that design.

Validity is defined as the extent to which one measures what one thinks is being measured.[45] Internal validity refers to the extent to which the measured effect of the program reflects the true program effect. External validity refers to the extent to which the results observed in a given study can be generalized to other situations with different populations and under different conditions.

Campbell[56], Campbell and Stanley[46], Cook and Campbell[57], and others have published guides for establishing internal and external validity.[58] Conrad et al.[55] provide a review of these threats as they apply to health promotion research. The most important threats are summarized below.

Types of Threats

Selection Bias

When volunteers (or participants) to a health promotion program are compared to non-volunteers (non-participants), a questionable assumption is made that the outcomes being measured would be the same for these groups of people in the absence of a program. Since program participants self-select into health promotion interventions, they may be more motivated to change behaviors, interested in improving their health habits, and more cognizant of healthcare service use when compared to non-participants. Alternatively, employees may decide not to participate in a formal health promotion program because they think they already practice good health habits and would not benefit from a program directed at less knowledgeable individuals. Given these potential differences from the onset, any observed effects from the program may be attributed to these factors and therefore threaten the validity of the findings as being due to the program itself.

Attrition

Attrition is the effect of loss of subjects during the course of interventions due to dropout from the program. Those who drop out are often people who are least motivated or unsuccessful in achieving a desired behavior change. This threat can lead to a small sample size that may make it difficult to generalize findings beyond the small group of individuals who are retained in the sample. Similarly, depending on who drops out of the program, this may lead to a bias of the study results, specifically from actions or characteristics of those individuals who remain in the study.

Maturation

Maturation is the effect of subject aging on any of the values or measures recorded. For example, as people age they are likely to gain weight and be at greater risk for high blood pressure. Thus, these maturation tendencies can obscure the real impact of the program.

History

The threat of history involves factors in the environment, such as changing laws, cultural trends, or adaptation of worksite policies that may affect behaviors or attitudes of subjects. This threat is especially relevant when worksites in different locations or organizations are compared to one another.

Instrumentation

This threat involves changes in the way data are recorded, e.g., self-report vs. biometric readings, wording changes in a questionnaire, or changes in recording equipment or measurement tools.

Regression toward the mean

This is defined as the tendency of extreme values to move toward the average. People with very high values for blood pressure, cholesterol, or stress often achieve lower values when retested because extreme values tend to gravitate toward "normal," even in the absence of a program. For example, an individual reporting high stress at baseline may be in the midst of a stress-inducing life crisis. Getting through that crisis will likely result in a lower stress score at a later point in time when that individual is re-tested.

Regression toward the mean may not apply in some areas such as weight or smoking where high values (pounds or cigarettes smoked) tend to remain stable or even increase over time.

Treatment Fidelity

Threat to treatment fidelity occurs when there is variation in the ways in which the program is delivered across sites/locations that may influence outcomes.

Diffusion of Treatments

A spillover of effects from site to site or within sites may occur when control site individuals have access or exposure to intervention materials or programs offered to treatment subjects. This is sometimes referred to as a "contamination" effect.

Testing

The effect of taking readings or measures from subjects that might, by themselves, cause a change. The influence of testing on measures is sometimes referred to as the "Hawthorne Effect" in which any change in the work environment, or simply increased attention to a group of employees, will lead to a temporary increase in the measures of interest, such as productivity. (See for example Steele-Johnson.)[59]

Dealing with Threats to Validity

Some ways to deal with some of the most common threats to validity are described below.

To address *selection bias*, a standard approach commonly used in evaluations of workplace health promotion programs is to find "twins" for individuals exposed to the program from a pool of individuals without exposure or access to the program. This is done using propensity score matching or weighting methods. Introduced by Rosenbaum and

Rubin, propensity score methods, sometimes referred to as "twin-pair" or case controlled studies, use the conditional probability of being in the intervention group, based on observed variables, to match each participant to a non-participant or control subject.

To implement this method, the evaluator estimates a logistic regression model that predicts the likelihood that an individual would be a participant in the program based on available baseline variables that may include readiness to improve one's health behaviors and lower risk (individual readiness scale), health status, geographic location, self-reported quality of life, demographics, medical utilization, and spending patterns. The logistic regression model assigns each participant and control person a predicted probability of participation, also called a propensity score, which ranges from 0 to 1 (not at all likely to very likely to be a participant). Participants and non-participants are then matched, generally allowing each control group member to be matched to only one participant.

To determine whether participants and controls are well matched, various visual and numeric diagnostic tests are used to compare the "twins" before and after matching. A good match means there are few or no significant differences among the observed variables across the two groups after matching. Items examined may include categorical variables (e.g., gender, smoking status, physical inactivity, poor eating habits, stress, or social isolation). These matching variables are then tested for statistical significance using McNemar or Mantel Haenszel chi-square tests by comparing the proportion of people at high risk in the intervention group to those in the control group. For continuous variables (e.g., age, BMI, doctor visits or hospital admissions), t-tests are used to measure differences before and after matching. If significant differences remain after matching, adjustments can be made to the matching procedures and results are reevaluated. Once evaluators are satisfied with the matches, they create a baseline dataset that consists of participants and their matched controls and the two groups of individuals are followed over time.

Controlling for study *attrition* (i.e., where participants or non-participants drop out and thus do not contribute ongoing or follow-up data) can be accomplished by using a technique called "baseline observation carried forward" or BOCF. This method assumes that individuals who drop out of a study would have maintained their baseline values throughout the study period and those values are inserted into "missing data" fields. This assumption is problematic because many health risks (e.g., weight, blood pressure, cholesterol) may increase simply because of the aging process; therefore, it is likely that the BOCF substitution data are not reflective of the true values for those missing individuals.

Another method for handling missing follow-up data is called mean-based imputation, which assigns the mean values of the control group to participants who drop out. This approach also has limitations because attrition affects both treatment and control subjects and the results may be biased for both groups.

The impact of *maturation* can be reduced by carefully matching treatment and control subjects using age, or age ranges, as a matching criterion. The effects of *history* can be reduced by studying comparison group individuals from similar organizations, and for whom data are available for a similar time horizon as treatment subjects. Where possible, comparison groups should be drawn from the same region, industry, size, and other relevant dimensions, as those from the intervention groups.

To control for *instrumentation*, the same or very similar instruments and data collection procedures should be used at each measurement milestone. *Regression toward the mean* is controlled when treatment and

control subjects are matched at baseline and an extended and stable pre-intervention baseline period is established. This method provides a more accurate estimate of each subject's true baseline value before the intervention.

Treatment fidelity and *diffusion of treatments* are addressed by performing careful qualitative baseline assessments of treatment and control sites and collecting follow-up data once the intervention is underway. Finally, the effects of *testing* are reduced when both treatment and control subjects are administered the same instruments, at approximately the same time, so that the experience of being tested affects both groups equally.

Sample

Most evaluations focus on a distinct sample of the total population of interest. The population may be as broad as all workers in U.S. companies, blue-collar workers, teachers, or municipal employees. Since it is typically impossible to assess an entire population, or the universe of individuals belonging to a given broad class, a sample of that universe is selected and studied. For example, a study sample may consist of teachers in a given city who participate in a health promotion program and who voluntarily complete an HRA instrument. Several rules and guidelines apply for selecting a target population, developing an appropriate comparison group, recruiting subjects, establishing adequate sample sizes for the study and sampling from the universe of potential study participants in order to be able to generalize results to the larger group. These are described below.

Target Population

In establishing an evaluation plan, there must be a well-defined target population. This group may include all potential recipients of the program in addition to those who actively participate. For example, in a study that examines environmental influences on health (e.g., signs encouraging staircase use, healthy food options in cafeterias), all employees at a given site would constitute a target population since everyone is exposed to the intervention.

Even when the evaluation only focuses on program participants, it is necessary to be precise in defining the total eligible population so that accurate success rates are determined. For instance, when considering the "quit rate" for a given smoking cessation program, all attendees at the initial session would be included as the target population rather than only those who completed the program and participated through to the final session. Counting everyone who attends a first session of a program as a subject is referred to as an "intent to treat" design. In each follow-up assessment as many initial program participants as possible are then identified and tracked.

Informed Consent

When academic institutions conduct the evaluation, or when the study involves clinical trials, there may be a need to submit a study design document to the sponsoring organization's Institutional Review Board (IRB). Most IRBs will regard workplace health promotion research as a quality improvement or evaluation project that is "exempt" from IRB review. Nonetheless, the evaluator may need to complete forms or submit an application that reassures the IRB the study is ethical and legal, and complies with standard informed consent procedures. In extreme cases, the IRB may review the scientific merit of the study to ensure that the conduct of the study and potential benefits warrant the participant burden. However, most of the studies focused on workplace programs rely on de-identified secondary data sources (data collected for another purpose) and therefore most often receive an exemption from full IRB review or an expedited IRB review.

Comparison Group

As discussed earlier, a suitable comparison group is required for quasi-experimental studies. An ideal comparison group is composed of similar employees not offered the program. Other options for comparison groups include employees at other companies or published normative data (e.g., data on changes in smoking rates for the U.S. population, healthcare utilization trends for different industries, or employee absence rates derived from the Bureau of National Affairs).

A common method for evaluating health promotion programs is to compare participants to non-participants who may share the same site or location. However, this approach, while convenient, has its limitations. The characteristics of non-participants and participants can differ at the onset of the program (e.g., existing health habits, health risks factors, gender). This in turn affects how the results can be interpreted; that is, it would be more difficult to demonstrate that the program was the reason for the positive improvements on health for the participants because, for example, the participants were already healthier and more motivated to begin with compared to the non-participants. Diffusion of treatment is another limitation to this approach. While not engaged in the program, the comparison group is still exposed to and has access to it, which can dilute the result when evaluating the impact of the program.

Recruitment

Recruiting program participants is an art in itself. Picking the population to be studied can be done in either of two ways. The evaluator can either select the entire population offered the program (and an appropriate comparison group) or a sample of that population. When choosing to sample the population, what is an adequate sample size becomes the next question. That is, how many people does the evaluator need to recruit for the sample group in order to achieve results that reflect the entire population?

Sample Size and Power Calculations

Well-executed evaluations often require several types of data to be collected from or about intervention participants and non-participants. Depending upon the magnitude of the differences in outcomes expected from participants and non-participants, researchers may wish to collect data from hundreds or even thousands of subjects. There are two reasons why large samples may be desirable. First, the larger the sample size the greater the statistical power there is to detect any program impact. Second, the larger the sample, the more likely the evaluation results accurately reflect the target population and can be generalized to other settings or populations.

Random Sampling

Random sampling is a technique for picking research subjects in a way that each person has an equal chance of being selected. Computer programs are commonly used to select a random group of individuals from the total eligible population. Alternatively, most statistical textbooks include a table of random numbers that may be used for random selection of names.

How Sample Size can Effect Study Conclusions

If a large enough sample is not drawn initially when undertaking an evaluation study, then the conclusions drawn from that study may be tenuous. This is especially true when conventional (and more familiar) statistical tests are used in the analysis. For example, an evaluator may want to determine the effectiveness of a smoking cessation program using a Time 1/Time 2 cohort group design without using a comparison group (referred to earlier as "the one group, before and after pretest-posttest only design"). The initial population of 500 employees includes 150 smokers (30% of the total population). If the employer loses 10% of its employees a year through attrition or turnover, this would leave 122 individuals from the original smoker group after two years (150 x .90 x .90 = 122).

The evaluator now re-measures the remaining cohort group of 122 employees and determines a certain quit rate. Using established statistical formulas,* the evaluator determines (with a 95% level of confidence) that the true quit rate after two years is plus or minus 9%. Thus, if 30% of the remaining 122 individuals quit, then the evaluator can say that between 27.5% and 45.7% of the population quit.

The only way to decrease the error factor and more precisely estimate the true quit rate would be to increase the population sampled. If the number of people sampled is increased, then the error factor will decrease. For example, if the initial population is doubled from 500 to 1,000 and the number of smokers is increased to 300 from 150, then the number of smokers remaining in the study after two years is 243 (300*.9*.9). With a doubling of the initial study population, the error factor is reduced to 6.4% from 9.1%.

Sampling to Estimate the Prevalence of Risk Factors

One common circumstance requiring sample size determination is estimating the prevalence of a risk factor in a population. As above, formulas and calculators for establishing appropriate sample sizes can be found at various websites including the one listed as a footnote in the previous section and below.[¶] For quick reference, Table 6-2 is provided

---

*See for example the following website for guidance on how to calculate sample sizes: http://bphc.hrsa.gov/policiesregulations/performancemeasures/patientsurvey/calculating.html, accessed 10/6/13.

[¶] See for example the following website for guidance on how to calculate sample sizes: http://www.unc.edu/~rls/s151-2010/class23.pdf, accessed 10/6/13.

Table 6-2: Sample size requirements for health profiles and employee surveys.

Total Eligible Population	Sample Size
50	44
100	79
200	132
300	168
400	196
500	217
700	248
1000	278
2000	322
5000	357
10000	370

Note: The sample size estimates assume an error of 5% (e=.05), and an alpha level of .05, i.e., the results achieved will be within 5% of the true value at least 95% of the time. For example, when assessing smoking rates for a population of 1,000 individuals, the evaluator finds that 30% of the 278 randomly surveyed individuals smoke. The sample prevalence (in this case 30% smokers) will be within five percentage points (25% to 35%) of the population value, 95% of the time.

showing the sample size requirements for various populations.

Power Analysis for Evaluating Program Impacts

Another circumstance in which sample sizes would need to be determined is in comparing the changes between two groups. For example, in a smoking cessation program, the evaluator wishes to know if the quit rates are different for treatment and control groups. Determining the sample size in this case utilizes a statistical concept called power analysis.

Statistical power is the extent to which one is confident that a non-statistically significant difference between two groups does indeed reflect a lack of difference between those groups, as opposed to the non-difference being attributable to a too small sample size. Here again, the reader is referred to various

statistical textbooks or the Wikipedia site that offers a quick reference guide.[§]

Since formulas for calculating sample size are complicated, evaluators normally draw figures from tables such as those in Fleiss.[60] For example, the evaluator assumes that 25% of smokers in the treatment group and 10% in the comparison group will quit. The evaluator also sets the significance levels at .05 (i.e., 95% of the time results will not be due to chance alone), and the power to detect differences between groups at .80. Under these conditions, the evaluator would need 113 subjects in the treatment group and 113 subjects in the control group to detect differences in quit rates between groups, assuming the program was successful.

Estimating power and sample size requirements prior to initiating research is important because the small intervention

[§] See: http://en.wikipedia.org/wiki/Statistical_power, accessed 10/6/13.

group sizes common to health promotion programs, combined with relatively low rates of change frequently observed, often make it difficult to detect statistically significant differences between treatment and comparison groups. For additional discussion on this topic, the reader is referred to Konrad and DeFriese[61] and Cohen.[62]

Sample Sizes Needed for Analysis of Archival Data

The greater the variance or variability of an outcome of interest, the larger the sample size required to establish statistically significant differences in outcomes. Archival or administrative data such as medical expenditures, days of work lost due to illness, short-term disability rates, or work time lost due to safety incidents involving workers' compensation claims tend to have very large variances. In addition, underlying health risks and behavioral habits may vary considerably among individuals resulting in a large difference in healthcare costs between those who take good care of themselves and those who do not. The wide range of values for these outcomes means that the average values do not always reflect what is "typical" in terms of a person's experience.

Consequently, while studies of "more stable" outcomes (e.g., program satisfaction, employee attitudes, change in health risks) may require only *hundreds* of subjects, studies of medical claims or other administrative data often require *thousands* of subjects. Thus, the reader is cautioned that the final sample size for an evaluation should be governed by the sample size requirements for the variable of greatest interest. If that variable is healthcare costs, for example, it may require upward of 2,000 individuals to be included in the intervention group and an equal number in the comparison group. This assumes minimal attrition of subjects over time. If attrition is high, sample sizes exceeding 3,000 or even 4,000 people in both treatment and comparison groups may be needed.

Achieving High Survey Response Rates

Evaluations often rely upon survey instruments to collect information about participants and non-participants in a program. Examples include HRA questionnaires designed to measure health habits and other risk factors, as well as satisfaction and attitude surveys.

High response rates are more likely achieved when questionnaires are short (one to two pages), primarily composed of closed-ended questions (checklists, yes/no, rating scales), management is supportive of the survey process by allowing time off to complete the instrument, and completion is rewarded with incentives. Further, participants are more likely to offer opinions when surveys are anonymous or when confidentiality is assured. (For a discussion of ways to achieve high response rates in health promotion programs, see Thompson et al.[63] and Dillman.[64])

When low response rates are anticipated, because of general antipathy against survey instruments or low literacy rates for the population, the evaluator might consider structured interview protocols that are administered by telephone or in person. These techniques are also effective as follow-up measures to elicit additional feedback from erstwhile non-respondents. Often response rates can be greatly enhanced through person-to-person solicitation as opposed to written communications.

When response rates are low despite the best efforts to maximize them, survey analysts can use regression-based weighting techniques to assure that responses to the survey data adequately represent the population as a whole. With these techniques, more weight is given to people who responded to the survey even though their underlying propensity to respond was low. The rationale for this approach is that these individuals are more likely to represent non-respondents than are others who typically respond to surveys with little hesitation.

Kalton and Kasprzyk[65] describe the methods used to estimate the likelihood of responding to surveys and associated weighting techniques. Generally, the evaluator collects information on factors expected to influence response rates. For example, sometimes survey response varies by job type, salary, educational level, gender, or worker morale. The evaluator's job is to collect information on as many of these factors as possible so that they can be controlled for in the analysis of data.

Armed with these data, the evaluator then conducts a logistic regression analysis designed to estimate relationships between factors influencing response rates and whether or not the survey was completed. The logistic regression results are used to estimate each person's probability of completing the survey. These probabilities are then inverted (i.e., the ratio 1/probability is calculated) and the inverted probabilities become the survey weights. The weights assign more importance to those who were expected not to respond to the survey based on their demographic profile (i.e., the weights are higher for those least likely to respond).

Measures

Data Sources

It goes without saying that in order to measure program success, the evaluator first needs to gather the data. There are, fortunately, no shortages of data resident in many databases across organizations. There are, however, limited resources to extract, compile, and aggregate the needed data, and to link any one data source to all others.

Program administrators are burdened with the task of cajoling database keepers into releasing information necessary for analytic studies. Frequently, corporate attorneys who are brought into discussions, express reservations regarding the release of data because of the aforementioned concerns related

to privacy. Such scenarios reinforce the need for a clear data analysis plan that is communicated to corporate officials. The plans should include specific safeguards against potential disclosure of private information (i.e., adherence to federal laws such as the Health Insurance Portability and Accountability Act [HIPAA]).[66]

When collecting data for health promotion program evaluations, three principal sources are found:

1. *"Paper and Pencil" measures* may include program attendance records; data from HRA instruments; program structure questionnaires; and employee feedback surveys.
2. *Observation techniques* may include, for example, data collected from screenings of blood pressure, weight, cholesterol, and glucose; evidence of environmental support for healthy lifestyle at the workplace (signs encouraging stairway use, healthy options in cafeterias); or unobtrusive observations by parking lot security personnel who record the number of seat belt wearers entering a garage.
3. *Archival or administrative files* may include health insurance claims; personnel records; absence data; disability and workers' compensation filings; computerized attendance logs; electronic medical records; class enrollment forms; and normative databases.

Each of these data sources can be analyzed independently or, better yet, integrated with one another. Before expending time and effort in building integrated or relational databases on their own, organizations should ask and answer the "so what" question, i.e., how much time and effort is required to re-invent this wheel, and how will my internal data systems be used for decision making about program design and implementation? To avoid the cost of designing customized data acquisition and analysis systems, organizations can consider contracting with experienced data warehouse and data integration organizations. These companies often use proprietary data build and reporting systems but also rely upon "off the shelf" statistical computer packages such as SAS, SPSS, or STATA to link databases and conduct sophisticated data analyses.

Measurement Validity and Reliability

Social science research texts (Kerlinger[45]) devote considerable attention to ways of improving validity and reliability in measurement systems. Validity refers to the extent to which the measurement instrument is measuring what it intends to measure. Reliability is the extent to which an instrument is stable, dependable, and predictable in its "scoring" of a given trait or behavior, for any given individual over a period of time under consistent conditions.[45] The validity and reliability of measurement tools and procedures are of utmost importance in program evaluations because they are critical to reporting credible study findings. Surveys that do not adhere to the rigors of scientific assessment are likely to yield data of questionable value. The results reported may be misleading and in many cases worse than having no information at all.

For example, if an invalid instrument is used to measure emotional stress, and the measure underestimates the true stress experienced by the employee, program designers might conclude that a stress management program is not needed or may not work when, in fact, the opposite is true. If the measurement instrument is unreliable or invalid, then actual improvement may remain unrecognized when, in fact, it occurred. This could result in discontinuing a very effective program. Similarly, an ineffective program may be expanded even though actual improvement is suspect, given the measurement tools used.

Using existing validated measurement instruments saves the time otherwise required to test the psychometric properties of the measurement tools used. Several compendia of valid and reliable instruments have been compiled and should be referenced when deciding which tools or measures to use as part of the evaluation process. (See for example materials prepared by The Institute for Health and Productivity Management, Integrated Benefits Institute, and Care Continuum Alliance.)[67-69]

In addition, several industry trade organizations including the Health Enhancement Research Organization (HERO), Care Continuum Alliance (CCA), and National Committee for Quality Assurance (NCQA) have developed "core metrics" for gathering health risk, cost, productivity, and organizational data.[70,71]

Some of the ways validity and reliability can be established are described below.

Face Validity

Face validity is the extent to which the instrument appears to be measuring what it purports to measure. It more generally refers to the perception of validity by expert and non-expert observers (e.g., potential survey respondents) informing the evaluator that the tool appears to measure the concept of interest. Face validity is not a statistical measure, but a subjective impression.

Content Validity

Content validity refers to the extent an instrument addresses the full scope of relevant content areas of a given social construct. If a concept or trait that is to be measured encompasses many different areas, a content validity analysis determines whether all of these areas are addressed by the instrument. This analysis is typically performed by experts in the field who know the theoretical underpinning of a concept or trait and can determine whether each relevant component is considered in the instrument's design.

For example if an instrument is designed to measure a construct such as "general well-being," then a panel of experts will be employed to determine whether key component elements of this general concept (e.g., ability to cope with anxiety, overall depression, coping skills, social support network, etc.) are included in the construction of the measure.

Construct Validity

Construct validity refers to the degree to which theoretical elements of the construct under assessment are actually captured by the measurement tool. A statistical method used to assess construct validity is called factor analysis. Here, data from a large sample of respondents are analyzed to determine whether responses to different items on a survey instrument correlate with one another, indicating that they are likely measuring a common concept.

For example, the Connor Davidson Resilience Scale (CD-RISC) was tested using factor analysis and determined to include the following five factors as the theoretical components underpinning the broader trait called resilience: personal competence; trust in one's instincts; positive acceptance of change; control; and spiritual influence.[72]

Predictive Validity

Predictive validity is the extent to which the score on an instrument can be used to predict certain future outcomes or behaviors. In a strict study of predictive validity, the test scores are collected first; then the criterion measure is collected at a future point. For example, the ability of an employee satisfaction survey to predict health program completion rates is tested by examining the correlation between the ratings and actual program participation attendance records. If the correlation between program satisfaction at an early stage of the program and program completion rate is statistically significant, then the satisfaction instrument has predictive validity.

Test-Retest Reliability

Test-retest reliability is the extent to which an instrument captures similar responses from one administration to the next for the same person. It may be determined by retesting a group of individuals using the instrument shortly after the first measure is taken (ideally, within one or two days).

Inter-rater Reliability

Inter-rater reliability refers to the degree to which two or more independent raters reach agreement on an assessment. Inter-rater reliability is useful when refining a tool given to human judges by determining, for example, if a particular scale is appropriate for measuring a given variable of interest. If there is a high level of disagreement between raters, it may mean that the tool is not reliable or that the raters need to be re-trained (e.g., they are not using the same protocol when conducting their assessments), or the tool itself needs to be revised.

Internal Reliability

Internal reliability is defined as the consistency of results across items within a measure that are intended to measure one concept. To determine the internal consistency of the instrument, for any given respondent, responses to similar items on the instrument are compared to one another to test whether they are correlated. A high internal correlation ("alpha coefficient") determines that the instrument is internally consistent in assessing the trait or behavior of interest. Conducting internal consistency studies are far more efficient and less costly than studies of test-retest reliability and inter-rater reliability. Also, they are remarkably accurate. For example, Cochrane[73] showed that high levels of internal consistency often relate to high levels of other reliability measures, such as inter-rater reliability.

However, internal reliability measures, such as calculation of an alpha coefficient, are only relevant to survey instruments with multi-item scales that measure the same theoretical constructs. If a questionnaire measures multiple concepts, the alpha coefficient is determined for each concept. For example, a questionnaire on stress might measure exposure to stress, access to support resources, and coping skills. The alpha coefficient is then measured for each of these concepts. Similarly, alpha coefficients are less relevant to biometric screenings or other observational measures that rely upon multiple observations by the same person or independent observations of a given phenomenon by two or more persons.

Data Analysis

Data analysis is the process of systematically applying statistical techniques to inspect, describe, model, and evaluate data. Descriptive statistics are first applied to data to describe the basic characteristics of a study sample and provide simple summaries or observations. Descriptive statistics help inform inferential statistics that make predictions about a population from a study sample.

Univariate analysis involves the analysis of one variable such as the number of individuals who comprise the study sample in terms of their age or gender, while multivariate analysis involves the observation and analysis of more than one variable. Both descriptive and multivariate analyses are described below.

Descriptive Studies

Descriptive analyses are integral to an evaluation because they provide rich information regarding the study sample at each data collection point. Information from descriptive analyses can inform inclusion and exclusion criteria for the sample and specifications for multivariate models that follow. The process of identifying the study sample drawn from an administrative or archival database, conducting descriptive analyses, and displaying the results is described below.

Eligible Sample and Eligibility Trees

After the database is built, inclusion/exclusion criteria are applied to identify the relevant study population. Stringent eligibility criteria can lead to a significant loss of subjects. Thus, it is helpful to retain the original population in the database with flags that identify the criteria used for inclusion or exclusion of people into the final study sample.

Flags on the data also facilitate the creation of an eligibility tree, which is a diagram that shows how a final study sample was created from the original population based on inclusion/exclusion criteria. For a typical health promotion evaluation, the overall study population represents the employees at the organization on a given date. Each branch then describes the number of employees left in the pool after each exclusion criterion is applied. For example, one branch may be the number of employees who met the age criteria for the study. The number of "branches" on the tree will depend on the number of eligibility criteria applied to the sample. The last branch displays the final sample size used in the analysis.

Showing the eligibility tree is particularly relevant when the final sample size is significantly smaller than the original population. When included in study-related publications, the eligibility tree provides readers with a visual understanding of the generalizability of the study results. For example, if the study excluded all adults over age 65, readers know that the results are not applicable to this older age group.

Figure 6-5 is an illustration of an eligibility tree that starts with the original population at the top and contains branches for each eligibility criterion.

Sample Characteristics

Once the eligible sample has been determined, this pool of individuals is compared to the rest of the population not included in this analysis. The comparison identifies whether individuals in the sample are similar to the

Figure 6-5: **Sample eligibility tree.**

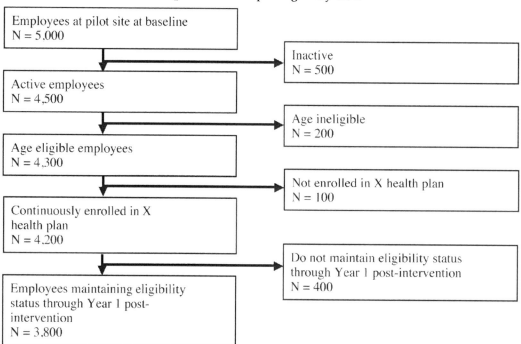

broader population. For example, if one of the eligibility criteria applied is completion of an HRA or other survey, this comparison provides information about whether the survey completers are similar in terms of demographic and work characteristics to the non-completers. Any differences should be made transparent in the presentations of results.

Comparisons between populations should include statistical analyses applied to continuous and categorical demographic or other relevant variables. Typically, continuous variables can include age, income, and measures of disease severity such as the Charlson Comorbidity Index (CCI),[74] number of Psychiatric Diagnosis Groups (PDG),[75] or Chronic Disease Score (CDS).[76] If the variables are normally distributed, they can be analyzed using an independent sample t-test; if they are not normally distributed, a non-parametric test is more appropriate.

Other descriptive variables that are categorical in nature include gender, race,

ethnicity, part-time/full-time status, job location, job type, age group, education, union status, and benefit plan choice. A chi-square analysis is used to evaluate the differences in the proportion of individuals in each category for those included in the sample and the original population.

A table of the eligible group's socio-demographics, work characteristics, and clinical characteristics can provide information about how similar the sample is to other populations. For categorical variables (e.g., gender, race/ethnicity, and work status), the table includes the percentage of the sample in each category. For continuous variables (e.g., age, clinical severity), the table includes the mean values, standard deviations, and the range (e.g., minimum and maximum values). Including age in the table as both a continuous variable (mean years of age) and a categorical variable (percent in each age group) may be useful for informing additional multivariate analysis or statistical models.

Characteristics of Participant Groups

After baseline characteristics of the eligible sample have been examined, each employee in the sample is identified as a participant or non-participant. Participation status is different from "exposure" status. Exposure status distinguishes employees at intervention sites from the control sites. Participation status distinguishes employees at the intervention sites who participated in any of the programs from those who did not participate. Participation status will vary by the specific program of interest, so program-specific participation flags are created. For example, an employee may be identified as a participant in the HRA program if the employee completed the HRA survey, but may be identified as a non-participant in a fitness intervention if the employee did not participate in any of the fitness programs offered.

Participation criteria are based on theory related to the level of engagement necessary for the program to have an influence on employee health. For example, the evaluation team may decide to identify an employee as a participant only if the employee enrolled *and* completed the specified program because program completion is assumed to affect one's future health status. Individuals who enrolled, but did not complete the program, would then be identified as non-participants.

A categorical or continuous measure of overall program exposure intensity can be created based on the number of programs in which the individual participated or the number of program interactions (e.g., coaching sessions). A mutually exclusive, hierarchical measure of program participation may also be appropriate. Such a categorical measure may be structured as follows: (1) only completed an HRA; (2) completed an HRA plus at least one coaching program; (3) completed an HRA and attended a fitness program; (4) completed an HRA and was engaged in an interactive web-based education program; and (5) completed an HRA and participated in an on-site screening and nurse feedback program. There are many ways program exposure intensity or dose can be captured based upon the above or a similar scheme.

The descriptive analysis informs which categories of participation are germane to the evaluation. For example, some programs that are poorly attended may be combined with others so that only the main participation categories are evaluated along with an "other" category containing low volume participation groups. Within the eligible sample, the percent participation for each program and each program intensity category can be ascertained, using the total number of individuals in each participation group as the numerator and the total eligible sample for the program as the denominator.

Descriptive Studies Focused on Structure and Process Evaluation

As described earlier, structure and process evaluation often includes an assessment of programs offered, policy changes, and other environmental supports for employee health promotion. These are measured in terms of program implementation fidelity; dose delivered; and dose received. When conducting organizational-level assessments of program structure and process, site-level data are collected for intervention and control locations, and these may be displayed at the department, building or floor level, depending on the uniqueness of the site and amount of variation expected. As in other studies, measures are collected at baseline and at each key milestone to facilitate the examination of changes over time in worksite culture and employee engagement.

Most of the data collected here are qualitative in nature and themes, patterns, and issues are then identified and summarized to determine facilitators and barriers contributing or impeding program impact. For example, an employee survey may reveal reasons why people did not participate in the program (e.g., lack of awareness, supervisor opposition, scheduling conflicts, and unappealing program). Some of these data can also be quantified, which can further illuminate the depth of the issues to be addressed (e.g., percent of survey respondents who cited "lack of supervisor support" as the primary reason for non-participation). These descriptive studies of structure and process data provide insights needed to improve structural elements or implementation strategies for the program.

Descriptive Studies Focused on Health Risks

Analysis of health risk information collected from employees who completed HRAs and their results from biometric screenings is a hallmark of health promotion programs. HRA and biometric data are used by program managers to identify employees who could benefit from interventions and tailor health improvement programs more generally. These data are also important for evaluation purposes because they are used to determine how health risks change over time and thus the impact of the program on health outcomes.

For each health risk, the proportion of workers at high risk is calculated. When biometric measures such as cholesterol, blood glucose, height/weight, and blood pressure are collected, the average values for each outcome is determined to provide additional information. Changes over time in percent at high risk are shown to be statistically significant using a chi-square analysis. Continuous measures such as weight, blood pressure, glucose, and total cholesterol can be evaluated using a repeated measures t-test. The changes in the proportion at high risk and in biometric values should be calculated overall, by site, and by treatment condition.

As above, descriptive statistics can determine the range and distribution of data. It is useful to have clinical input in determining what the clinical cut-offs should be for biometric measures collected during screenings. Trimming or censoring extreme values is advised since these are likely entered into the database incorrectly.

Descriptive Studies Focused on Financial Outcomes

Financial measures of healthcare utilization are typically evaluated on an annual basis and include counts of outpatient office visits, inpatient admissions, prescription drug scripts purchased, and emergency room encounters. The distribution of all values combined for each metric is the first step in the analysis. The range of values and potential outliers are also evaluated when looking at the data to ensure that the information appears to be reasonable and valid.

Additionally, the percentage of participants with zero office visits or hospital admissions should be examined to determine what type of multivariate model to use. For example, if a large group of individuals has no hospital admissions (i.e., greater than 20% of the sample), a simple Ordinary Least Squares (OLS) regression model may not be appropriate and a two-part model is needed; one that first estimates the likelihood of having an admission and then, for those with admissions, the number of admissions.

Once all of the outcome variable distributions have been examined, the percent of people without healthcare utilization has been determined, and potential outliers have been identified, a table of results is created. This table includes the average number of office visits, inpatient admissions, and emergency room visits overall, and by intervention site for each year of data collected. If employees at intervention sites are divided into participation groups, (high, low, or none) then comparison of outcomes by this distinction is included in a separate table. Similar to the other measures, changes over time are calculated by subtracting the Year 2 average values from the Year 1 average values. Simple repeated-measures t-tests can be used to determine significant changes over time overall, by intervention site, and by participation group.

After examining healthcare utilization, medical costs can be evaluated in a similar manner. In addition to total healthcare costs aggregated from individual level medical claims data, separate analyses are performed to summarize inpatient, emergency room, prescription drug, and office visits costs. Typically, total allowed amounts (also called covered charges) are examined as the key outcome measure for healthcare costs. These amounts include both the employer and employee portions of payments and are a true reflection of costs since they include copayment, coinsurance, and deductible amounts, but not the amount of premium paid by the employee for health insurance coverage.

Productivity-related costs can be calculated by examining expenditures related to workers' compensation claims, short-term disability, absenteeism, and presenteeism. These metrics report different aspects of time spent away from work except presenteeism, which measures on-the-job productivity losses. Absenteeism is either self-reported from a survey instrument (e.g., HRA) or available by analyzing human resources information systems where days away from work are coded as lost time due to illness or other reasons. Similar to the utilization metrics, the distributions of each cost outcome is examined to determine the validity and reasonability of the data. As with medical claims data, the range of values and outliers are analyzed by conducting descriptive studies that report minimum and maximum values for each variable to determine if the data are reasonable and whether outliers need to be removed.

Summary of Descriptive Studies

Descriptive studies measure the levels and degree of variance for each outcome of interest and each independent variable that may affect outcomes (e.g., participation, age, sex, clinical severity). Descriptive analyses can also provide information about the sample at baseline and how various measures change over time for the intervention and control groups. As noted, descriptive analysis may uncover data problems, such as potential outliers and extreme values, which need to be addressed prior to developing multivariate models.

While the descriptive analysis offers insight into outcome differences between groups, this type of analysis does not control for other factors that may also affect results. A multivariate analysis, described below, more accurately measures the influence of the intervention after controlling for potential confounders.

Multivariate Analysis

If the intervention and control groups are different at baseline in terms of age, sex, and clinical severity, those factors can influence the changes in outcome and make the intervention appear more or less effective than it really is. Therefore, it is necessary to hold those variables constant when determining the influence of the intervention. Multivariate analysis allows evaluators to predict changes in outcomes (e.g., healthcare costs) resulting from changes in independent variables (e.g., program participation), while holding the other independent variables constant.[77] Multivariate models also allow evaluators to assess the statistical significance of the estimated relationships between the intervention and expected outcomes; that is, the degree of confidence that the estimated relationships are reflective of true relationships, as opposed to chance.

Financial Impact Analysis

This section describes the manner in which financial analyses are conducted. A financial impact study requires sound methods to address each of the following issues:

Net Present Value and Cost-Benefit Ratio

In a cost-benefit analysis, cost and benefit data are combined in several ways to estimate the impact of the health promotion program. The two most popular methods to do this are by calculating the net present value (NPV) and the cost-benefit ratio (CBR), often referred to as the return-on-investment (ROI) analysis.

The NPV of the program is defined as the difference between the total discounted, inflation-adjusted benefits and costs of the program over its useful life whereas the CBR is the ratio of discounted, inflation-adjusted benefits to costs. Benefits and/or costs can be discounted or inflation adjusted depending on the preference of the organization. This ratio specifies the estimated number of benefit dollars received per dollar spent on the program. For example, if each dollar spent on a health promotion program yields $1.25 in reduced medical expenditures, 1.25 to 1.00 represents its CBR or ROI.

When reporting the financial impact of a health promotion program, some economists and policy makers prefer the NPV to the CBR for two reasons. First, the NPV provides information in simple dollar terms. Second, unlike the CBR, the NPV is not affected by the placement of negative benefits in the equation. Suppose, for example, two programs of equal size yield $100,000 in positive economic benefits, such as a reduction in the value of time lost to short-term disability. Both programs also yield $20,000 in negative economic benefits (e.g., an increase in medical costs needed to better manage disabling problems) and both programs cost $50,000 to implement. Using the NPV formula would yield identical results ($30,000), regardless of whether the $20,000 negative benefit figure is included on the cost side or the benefit side of the equation (i.e., ($100,000 - $20,000) - 50,000 = $100,000 + (-$20,000 - $50,000)). In contrast, the value of the CBR depends on which side the $20,000 in negative benefits are examined (i.e., ($100,000 - $20,000) / $50,000 is not equal to $100,000/($50,000 - $20,000)).

However, the term CBR tends to be more familiar to senior level managers, and thus is often the preferred statistic. Presenting both the NPV and CBR provides a more complete understanding of the impact of the health promotion program.

Inflation Adjustment and Discounting

Many interventions last for several years, with program-related costs incurred each year. Money spent on the program over multiple years, adjusted for inflation, illustrates the erosion of purchasing power over time. Adjusting for inflation can be accomplished by applying a price index value, which measures changes in prices over time, to program cost estimates to produce "constant" dollars (i.e., in the dollars of a base year). The index value equals 1.0 for the base year, which is usually defined as the first year of program operation. Cost estimates for each subsequent year are divided by the index value for the year in which the costs were incurred, to transform estimates to constant dollars. The inflation index developed by the Bureau of Labor Statistics' Gross Domestic Product Implicit Price Deflator can be found at www.bea.doc.gov/bea/dn/dpga.pdf.

When interventions span many years, costs incurred after the first year can be discounted as well as adjusted for inflation. Discounting later-year dollars is predicated on the assumption that consumers place a higher value on dollar costs incurred now versus the same dollar costs incurred later. The reason for this difference in value is that $1 spent now could otherwise have been invested to yield (for example), $1.05 next year (even after adjusting for inflation). Thus, today's dollars are worth more than next year's dollars. As a rule of thumb, a 3% discount rate is typically applied in economic analyses of health promotion programs.[78] Many organizations establish their own discount rate based on prevailing costs of borrowing money or investment opportunities.

Cost-Effectiveness

In cost-effectiveness analysis, sometimes referred to as a value-on-investment (VOI) analysis, cost and effectiveness estimates are combined to show the cost of each unit of improvement - for example, the cost of having a person quit smoking, the cost per unit drop in BMI, or the cost of preventing a newly diagnosed case of type-2 diabetes. The incremental cost-effectiveness ratio is defined as the difference in the average costs of two alternatives, divided by the difference in the average levels of effectiveness of those two alternatives. Generally, the program with the lowest incremental cost per health outcome achieved is preferred. Analyses can be discounted or not, depending on the preference of the employer. Examples of the incremental cost-effectiveness of various types of programs can be found in Hargreaves, et al.[79] (for mental health programs) and in Gold, et al.[80]

Cost-Utility

In a cost-utility analysis, the cost of the program is compared to the quality of health outcomes that are averted or produced as a result of the program.[81] This health improvement outcome is often measured as quality-adjusted life-years (QALYs), expressed as a cost per QALY gained. Quality of life measures may focus on social functioning, physical ability, psychological well-being, or other benefits gained from participation in a program. Cost-utility analysis allows for broad comparisons of a unified outcome across diverse programs. Traditionally, cost-benefit and cost-effectiveness analyses are more commonplace than cost-utility studies when assessing the economic impact of workplace health promotion programs.

Calculating Program Savings

The monetary benefits of a program are determined by estimating the dollar value of changes resulting from participation in the health promotion program. These monetary benefits may include savings from improvements in health status resulting in reduced medical expenditures; fewer wage replacement dollars spent because workers are absent from work less often; reduced productivity losses monetized in terms of time lost when workers perform at sub-optimal levels; lower payments for short-term or long-term disability programs; and fewer dollars spent for workplace injury treatment. The objectives of any particular health promotion program may suggest other potential monetary benefits.

Estimating program benefits can be complex since this requires differentiating between changes in outcomes that are due to the program from changes stemming from other factors. The inference that benefits obtained are due to program participation requires a quasi-experimental design that consists of comparing outcomes of an intervention group to that of a comparison group.

Calculating Program Expenses

Information on the financial investment or cost of the program is essential to determining financial impact of that intervention. Actual costs of all program components available to all employees – both fixed costs (e.g., fitness center) and variable costs (e.g., HRAs or individual counseling) – should be included in the program cost calculation. Below is a brief listing of distinct cost categories and accompanying examples as described by Wilson:[82]

1) Direct payments to the wellness organization and its vendor(s):

   - General program administration (including direct administrative costs and full-time-equivalents (FTEs) affiliated with the program;
   - Licensing of intellectual property;
   - Biometrics testing, laboratory costs and administration;
   - Health risk assessment tool administration;

- Health risk assessment tool analysis and feedback, overall and customized to individuals;
- Health risk assessments based in claims data and feedback, overall and customized to individuals; and
- Health coaching.

2) Internal costs incurred by the purchaser of a health promotion program:

- Full-time equivalent (FTE) for wellness coordinator;
- Other staff costs in addition to vendor costs;
- Physical plant and other space-related costs; and
- Claims costs related to preventive services (if considered part of cost).

3) Costs incurred by the participant (employee, spouse, etc.):

- Fees for entry into fitness center;
- Costs incurred for healthy food; and
- Costs for individualized coaching.

The above list is not exhaustive. Program costs may vary depending on the breadth of the program. In general, incentives for participation in a program, or for achieving certain health outcomes, should not be included in the calculation of program costs unless these are true out-of-pocket costs for the employer. Most often, incentives can be structured to make them cost-neutral. For example, a $500 incentive can be offered employees for participating in the program but that amount may not be a direct expense to the employer. Instead, the employer can structure the incentive as a credit on an insurance premium, which already accounts for the value of the incentive. Regulations related to the structuring of financial incentive programs for workplace health promotion programs were issued in 2013 and these regulations should be carefully followed when establishing these programs.[83]

Program costs are often expressed on a per participant basis (based on the number of individuals that actually participated in the program) or per eligible basis (based on the number of employees or individuals eligible to participate in the program). Ideally, a methodology for categorizing and tracking program costs should be developed prior to the commencement of the program to facilitate financial impact analyses.

Summary Approach to Conducting Financial Impact Studies

The above narrative may feel overwhelming to the reader. In an attempt to summarize and synthesize the many ideas presented thus far, this section provides a "Cliff's Notes" version for conducting a financial impact evaluation of workplace health promotion programs. The summary below borrows heavily from the work of Serxner, Gold and Parker,[84] three noted workplace health promotion program evaluators.

An economic evaluation relies upon identifying participants in the health promotion program and matching them to their counterparts ("twins") in a group not exposed to the program. The non-exposed sample can be selected from other organizations, businesses, units, or sites not offering intervention programs. After carefully matching individuals at baseline, treatment and comparison group pairs are followed over time and their financial, utilization, and productivity outcomes compared at key milestones – i.e., baseline, year 1, year 2, and so forth. To control for less than perfect matching at baseline, additional multivariate studies are conducted to "subtract out" remaining confounders, and the difference-in-differences between treatment and comparison subjects is calculated to derive program savings. The dependent variable is generally per person per year medical costs, absenteeism hours, or workers' compensation claims, as examples. The "delta" or difference between participants and non-participants' annual expenditures, for the entire study period, is then determined to be program savings (assuming participants' costs are lower than for non-participants) or expenses (assuming the opposite is true). Finally, aggregate savings (or expenses) are compared to program investment amounts to establish net savings (NPV) and a cost-benefit ratio (CBR).

Presentation of Results

When showing results of evaluation efforts, the presenter must be cognizant of the audience's interests and level of sophistication. High-level presentations to senior management generally focus on overall conclusions, presented in "bullet" format or as simple graphs. Typically, 15 - 30 minute presentations are adequate.

In contrast, presentations to middle managers and program administrators are more comprehensive. A two to three hour review of the data, and the methodology used to gather the data, is not unusual. This format allows sufficient time for discussion. The presenter should anticipate the questions foremost in the audience's mind, for example whether the focus should be placed on economic or health outcomes. Are there specific questions of interest that need to be answered? Which charts or graphs will have the greatest impact?

Use of audiovisual aids is recommended to enhance the understanding and engagement of managers and program administrators and a variety of media can be employed in the presentation of results. For example, audio or video testimonials by employees (or managers) on how the program has affected these individuals' quality of life is a very powerful presentation tool because it provides managers a sense of the program's impact from a humanistic or more personal level. Similarly, engaging managers in the health promotion process, through individualized health risk appraisals or "personal training" with feedback, can be a useful way of educating the decision makers on the relevance of the program by doing so on an individual basis.

It is imperative that all of the data, both positive and negative, be presented to decision makers. The credibility of the evaluation team hinges on its openness and honesty in presenting program results. If it is determined at a later date that misinformation was presented, or that critical information was omitted, then not only is the credibility of the evaluation team at stake but also that of the staff managing the program.

In presenting results, the evaluator needs to help the audience interpret findings to reach valid conclusions. To the evaluator, the conclusions may be obvious, only because the evaluator has been working with the data for some time. To the audience members who are first exposed to the potentially voluminous and complex findings, results may be confusing and even contradictory. Thus, the evaluator should summarize and draw conclusions from the data to help the audience verbalize possible implications for action. Finally, the evaluator should prepare the audience for future results by speaking about ongoing evaluation activities, other studies that are planned, or follow up to the analysis just presented.

Dashboards

Results obtained from the descriptive analysis are typically displayed in tables and charts. Key findings or indicators can also be summarized in a dashboard. A dashboard is a snapshot of the results, displayed graphically, and designed to be easily absorbed and interpreted by a manager who is not a statistician. Dashboards present data at the level of the entire sample or by intervention site. Highlighting one or two key measures or indicators for the overall sample can provide insight into how all employees fare in terms of health or healthcare utilization and costs regardless of job location. Similarly, highlighting the top three health risks across the entire sample may also be informative.

An intervention site dashboard may contain information specific to the intervention implemented at a specific location. For example, for an intervention site that has introduced weight reduction programs, the dashboard may include a comparison of participants and non-participants on measures related to nutrition, physical activity, and weight. Other examples of dashboard reports include "top 10" claims by prevalence or cost. Depending on the frequency of data collection and the needs of managers, dashboards can be reported monthly, quarterly, semi-annually, or annually.

EVALUATION COST AND TIMETABLE

Cost of Evaluation Studies

How much should be spent on health promotion program evaluation? Five to ten percent of the total intervention program budget is probably sufficient to cover evaluation costs, with higher amounts spent early on, when a baseline needs to be established and early results are presented to management.

The key drivers in establishing an evaluation budget are the overall size and intensity of the intervention program (i.e., is it a $50,000 or $5,000,000 program), and the requirements of program funders (i.e., general descriptive information or an evaluation worthy of publication in a peer reviewed journal). A $100,000 a year intervention program would require $5,000 to $10,000 to be spent annually for evaluation. This amount would cover the cost of surveys that ask about program participation, self-reported health improvements, effects on morale, and satisfaction with program components.

Studies that examine health improvements among program participants require that a follow-up health risk assessment be conducted, typically at 12-month intervals. The costs of doing this type of study include those associated with the retesting or rescreening as well as the analysis and interpretation of data. If the rescreening costs are classified as programmatic costs, since such rescreening is itself an intervention, then the costs of study preparation and data analysis can often be accomplished with the above $5,000 - $10,000 budget, assuming the availability of internal staff expertise to design the measurement instruments, distribute the survey, code the responses, analyze the data, and prepare a final report.

Financial impact studies are generally more elaborate and therefore more expensive to conduct. Typical retrospective absenteeism and medical claims studies can cost between $150,000 and $250,000 (in 2013 dollars including database build costs). More elaborate evaluation efforts that examine and relate multiple databases may cost many hundreds of thousands of dollars. Thus, when discussing evaluation activities directed at financial impact measures, program sponsors and evaluators need to be educated regarding the complexity of such studies and concomitant cost implications.

Analysis Timetable

Once all of the groundwork has been completed in planning the program, a plan for reporting results needs to be developed. Decision-makers need to be supplied with periodic briefings to track program performance and identify possible problems. Some program effects are likely to be seen almost immediately while others will take years to materialize. Immediate results are likely to be realized in self-reported health improvements, morale, and attitudes toward management. Risk reduction will take longer to document and will often occur in the following sequence described below.

The participant will enter a psychological state of "readiness" to change; educational materials and behavior change information will be reviewed and incorporated; new behaviors will be attempted; and finally the new behaviors will become integrated as part of the individual's behavioral repertoire – that is, become a habit. While some of these steps may be observed in the short term, the assessment of whether new behaviors are internalized and maintained may take several years. Effects on rates of cardiovascular and cancer disease prevalence may take many more years or even decades to discern. Concomitant medical care cost savings associated with the reduction of disease prevalence in the population are likely to be detected in two to three years.

If immediate results are required (i.e., within 12 months), changes in program awareness, satisfaction, participation, health improvements, and morale or attitude shifts should be visible. Within 24 months, improvements in absenteeism and disability rates (both occupational and non-occupational) are likely to be noticed. Within 36 months, healthcare cost savings should become evident. Since organizations generally plan and budget programs over a 12 month cycle, providing program achievement data sufficiently in advance of the budgeting cycle is recommended. (See Table 6-3 for a sample evaluation timetable.)

The timetable presented underscores the need to collect and report follow up measures as quickly as possible with an emphasis on an early effort at collecting baseline data, since these data often "evaporate" over time as files are purged or archived. Establishing a realistic evaluation timetable for management tempers leaders' expectations for program performance and lessens the pressures on program administrators.

SUMMARY COMMENTS

This chapter has stressed the importance of performing evaluation research using the most rigorous methods available. We underscored the need to profile representative samples, conduct studies with suitable comparison groups, control for confounders using advanced statistical methods, achieve very high follow-up rates, and collect data at multiple intervals in order to assess health changes over time and evaluate financial impact. These are the requirements for excellent scientific research. In short, much of the chapter describes what *ought* to be done, in an almost perfect world, when performing evaluation studies focused on workplace health promotion programs. When these rules and guidelines are followed, the final product will be more accurate and consequently more valuable.

However, what should be done in "real-life" research is not always what is done. Budgets for studies are often limited, or in some cases non-existent. The necessary expertise to perform rigorous evaluation studies is not always resident in-house, and there are no funds for expert consultants.

So, what should the "typical" program evaluator do? The answer is, be pragmatic. If the requirements for documentation are low, and the budget is limited, perform the minimum amount of studies to fulfill requirements, keeping in mind the rule of thumb that evaluation costs should equal approximately five to ten percent of the intervention costs in any given year. Such budget constraints should help form the boundary and scope conditions for the evaluation and establish realistic expectations.

When performing quick and low budget studies, the evaluator should strive to employ the most credible methods and resources available. Most importantly, evaluation results should be presented in an honest and forthright manner with acknowledgement of the inherent limitations of such research.

As final advice to the reader, the program evaluator is encouraged to design an evaluation protocol that achieves study goals in the most cost-effective manner and within the resource constraints established by the program funder. A discussion of methods and budgets forces all parties to clarify program goals at the project's initiation before expectations regarding

Table 6-3: Sample evaluation timetable.

Project Milestone	Outcome of Interest	Instrument/Technique
Before the Program Begins	Health Care Utilization/ Cost	Baseline Claims Analysis including a focus on Lifestyle Related Diagnoses (LDGs)
Baseline Measures	Human Resource Expenditures	Baseline Analysis of Human Resources Expenditures in the Following Areas: Absenteeism, Overall Health Care, Turnover, Workers' Compensation, Disability and Productivity, Human Resources Cost Analysis (HRCA)
	Interest/Attitude	Baseline Employee Interest and Attitude Survey
At Program Initiation	Employee Health Status	Health Risk Appraisal/Health Profile - Group Report
Year 1	Employee Health Status Biometric Measures	Follow-Up Health Profile - Group Report
	Participation Rate	Quarterly/Annual Participation Reports
		Human Resources Cost Trends
		Human Resources Cost Analysis (HRCA)
	Employee Satisfaction/ Attitudes	Employee Satisfaction Survey
Year 2	Employee Satisfaction	Employee Satisfaction Survey
	Human Resources Costs	HRCA
	Participation Rate	Quarterly/Annual Participation Reports
Year 3	Employee Satisfaction	Employee Satisfaction Survey
	Human Resources Costs	HRCA
	Participation Rate	Quarterly/Annual Participation Reports
	Return on Investment (ROI)	Medical care, absenteeism, disability, workers' compensation and productivity study

outcomes are crystallized. If the goal is to publish results in a top tier scientific journal, the highest level of rigor is required. If, on the other hand, the goal is to provide sufficient data to senior management regarding program accomplishments so that management can make an informed decision about future funding, then a far lower level of rigor is required.

For health promotion programs to succeed, they need clearly formulated action plans that are based on sound scientific theory and subject to thoughtful measurement and evaluation. Support for the program needs to come from the key stakeholders of an organization. In order to maintain their support, the evaluator needs to clearly understand their motivations for introducing and maintaining the program and the types of results they expect of the program. Since there are often multiple stakeholders within an organization, each of whom has different requirements of the program, it is recommended that multiple measures be applied to assess program achievements across different indicators. To the extent possible, program objectives and measures focused on those objectives should be clearly aligned with overall company mission and vision statements.

Keeping the program current, listening to the stakeholders and their shifting requirements and emphases, continuously collecting and reporting data on program results as they become available in each area of interest, using a variety of measures and reporting strategies, and varying presentation techniques and styles, are some of the techniques used to ensure that the program will continue to receive the attention and support of senior management.

Finally, evaluators need to recognize that they may not be able to do it all alone. Effective program evaluation requires the combined skills and talents of a variety of individuals. Experienced evaluators know that they need to seek the opinions of experts in the field and gain peer review of their designs and evaluation results. It is recommended that "second opinions" be secured at every stage of the evaluation process.

In closing, while health promotion program administrators, and the decision makers who fund these programs, have a need for data that support their investment decisions, they may not be very knowledgeable about ways to secure those data. They may feel that the data should be easy to obtain and feel frustrated when their expectations are not easily fulfilled. It is the responsibility of evaluators to inform and educate their funders on issues discussed in this chapter and to support their efforts at obtaining good information on program results. Working in partnership, evaluators, program managers, and decision-makers will gather quality data that support continued investment in employee health.

APPENDIX 6-A

Sample Employee Satisfaction Survey

PROGRAM AWARENESS

	Yes	No
1. Prior to seeing this survey, were you aware that your organization offered a health promotion program to its employees?	□	□

→ *If you replied "yes," proceed to question 2.*
→→ *If you replied "no, skip to question 8.*

2. In the past 12 months, do you remember receiving/seeing or hearing any of the following promotional information regarding the Health Promotion Program? *(check all that apply)*

	Yes	No
a. Announcements from program staff during meetings	□	□
b. Emails	□	□
c. Flyers sent to your home	□	□
d. Word of mouth from colleagues	□	□

e. Other (please specify): _____

PROGRAM PARTICIPATION

	Yes	No
3. In the past 12 months, have you participated in any of the Health Promotion Program offerings?	□	□

→ *If you replied "no," proceed to question 4.*
→→ *If you replied "yes," skip to question 5.*

4. Which of the following reasons explain why you chose *not* to participate in the Health Promotion Program? *(check all that apply)*

□ Did not know I could participate	□ Lack of interest
□ Lack of motivation	□ Was unaware of the program

☐ Program offerings were not available at my worksite or a worksite near me

☐ Programs were not scheduled at convenient times

→→ *Skip to question 8.*

5. Which of the following reasons explain why you chose to participate in the Health Promotion Program? (*check all that apply*)

☐ Interested in improving my health

☐ My friends/colleagues were participating

☐ My family encouraged my participation

☐ Felt pressure from management/senior leaders

☐ To earn the incentive

☐ Other (please specify):_____

PROGRAM SATISFACTION AND IMPACT

6. In the past 12 months, how satisfied were you with the overall Health Promotion Program?

Completely Satisfied	Somewhat satisfied	Neither satisfied nor dissatisfied	Somewhat dissatisfied	Completely dissatisfied
☐	☐	☐	☐	☐

7. In the past 12 months, what effect has the Health Promotion Program had on your...

	Very Negative Effect	Negative Effect	No Effect	Positive Effect	Very Positive Effect	Don't Know
a. Morale	☐	☐	☐	☐	☐	☐
b. Productivity	☐	☐	☐	☐	☐	☐
c. Satisfaction with your job	☐	☐	☐	☐	☐	☐
d. Satisfaction with your employer	☐	☐	☐	☐	☐	☐
e. Physical health	☐	☐	☐	☐	☐	☐
f. Mental health	☐	☐	☐	☐	☐	☐

8. In the past 12 months, in which of the following health improvement activities have you participated? *(check all that apply)*

	As part of the work-sponsored Health Promotion Program	Outside of work
a. Counseling or coaching with a health promotion professional	☐	☐
b. Regularly attended fitness classes or a gym	☐	☐
c. Joined a weight management program	☐	☐
d. Improved my eating habits	☐	☐
e. Began implementing stress management techniques (e.g., meditation, guided imagery)	☐	☐
f. Reduced alcohol consumption	☐	☐
g. Participated in a smoking cessation course	☐	☐
h. Participated in preventive screenings (e.g., cholesterol, diabetes)	☐	☐
i. Completed a Health Risk Assessment (HRA)	☐	☐

INCENTIVES

9. Please tell us how appealing each of the following incentives for improving health are to you, assuming equal monetary value.

	Not appealing at all	Somewhat appealing	Very appealing
a. Direct cash payments (as a check or extra compensation)	☐	☐	☐
b. Gift cards for retail businesses	☐	☐	☐
c. Entry tickets into a lottery for a grand prize (e.g., tablet)	☐	☐	☐
d. Gift items (e.g., pedometers, water bottles)	☐	☐	☐
e. Reduced premiums on health insurance	☐	☐	☐

YOUR OPINION COUNTS

10. Please tell us whether you agree or disagree with the following statements...

	Strongly agree	Agree	Neither agree nor disagree	Disagree	Strongly disagree
a. I would recommend my organization as a great place to work.	☐	☐	☐	☐	☐
b. My work environment allows me to maintain good health.	☐	☐	☐	☐	☐
c. I believe my organization cares about my physical and mental health.	☐	☐	☐	☐	☐

THANK YOU FOR COMPLETING THIS SURVEY!

Please email your completed survey to hpmanager@organization.com or mail a hardcopy to:

Your Organization
The Health Promotion Program Office
Room 123

Glossary

Applied research: Studies conducted in the "real world" as opposed to a controlled, laboratory setting.

Construct validity: Determination of whether theoretical elements of the concept being studied in the measurement instrument are captured by the measure. This type of validity can be established either qualitatively by an expert-panel or quantitatively using factor analysis.

Content validity: Whether a measurement instrument addresses all of the relevant content areas of the main concept being investigated.

Cost-benefit ratio: Comparison of the costs of providing a program to the benefits yielded from implementing the program. Often a return-on-investment (ROI) analysis is completed to represent the cost-benefit ratio in economic terms. *(See return-on-investment)*

Cost utility analysis: Assessment of the cost of the program compared to the quality of the health outcomes achieved or averted.

Dose delivered: A process measure of program completeness (i.e., the degree to which all aspects of an intervention are implemented).

Dose received: A process measure of employee exposure to and satisfaction with the program provided.

Evidence-based intervention or strategy: An intervention or strategy that has potential for impact, substantiated by evaluation and publication in a peer-reviewed journal.

Experimental research design: Research design in which individuals (or worksites) are randomly assigned to either an intervention or control group. Individuals in the intervention group are exposed to the program while individuals in the control group are not. Also known as a randomized-controlled trial.

Fidelity: A process measure of program quality that describes how well interventions are being implemented as planned.

Formative research: A preliminary evaluation of the intervention design before the intervention is implemented in order to increase the chance of achieving program objectives. Formative research helps tailor the program to meet the unique needs of the individuals and/or groups receiving the intervention.

Humanistic outcome measures: Self-assessed variables such as perceived quality of life, resilience, attitudes toward work, and attitudes toward management, morale, and productivity.

Instrument reliability: The consistency of a measurement instrument over multiple administrations over time. *(See internal consistency, inter-rater reliability, and test-retest reliability)*

Instrument validity: The extent to which a measurement tool is measuring what it is intended to measure. *(See content, construct, and predictive/criterion validity)*

Internal consistency: A type of instrument reliability used to determine whether responses to similar items on a measurement tool are correlated. Internal consistency is assessed using Cronbach's alpha (α) with values ranging 0.0 – 1.0, where higher values indicate higher internal consistency of the tool.

Inter-rater reliability: The degree of concurrence between scores on an instrument completed by two or more respondents. Inter-rater reliability is necessary when observational data such as responses to questions in an interview, counts of the number of healthy food items contained in a vending machine, or biometric measures are collected from multiple professional assessors.

Net present value: The difference amount between the total discounted, inflation-adjusted benefits (dollars saved) and costs (dollars invested) of the program over its useful life. NPV is used to compare the present value of money today to the present value of money in the future, taking inflation and returns into account.

Non-experimental (observational) research design: Study design in which intervention and control groups are observed and compared, however the researcher does not assign individuals to treatment or control groups.

Predictive/Criterion validity: The extent to which a measurement instrument can be used to predict certain outcomes or behaviors.

Process evaluation: Determination of whether the execution of the program is progressing according to plan and whether the operation is smooth. Specifically, a process evaluation measures program fidelity, dose delivered, dose received, and reach. *(See fidelity, dose delivered, dose received, and reach)*

Prospective research study: An analysis where new data are gathered at the start of a program and an end-point is determined.

Quasi-experimental design: With this design, the experience of a treatment group is compared to that of a comparison group but the causal impact of an intervention is estimated because participants are not randomly assigned to treatment and comparison groups.

Reach: A process measure of program participation rate.

Retrospective research study: Study design in which previously collected data are used to "look back" in time and measure what happened to determine whether the program influenced the outcome.

Return on investment (ROI): ROI is a ratio of how much you save, compared to how much you spend on a health promotion program.

Statistical power: The probability that your study results will lead to rejection of the false null hypothesis.

Structure evaluation: An assessment of the extent to which the program was implemented as planned. Oftentimes this type of evaluation is referred to as an 'audit' of program design compliance.

Test-retest reliability: The extent to which an instrument captures similar responses over time when no changes have been made to the instrument.

Learning Objectives

1. Readers will be able to describe the differences and importance of each of the three elements of program evaluation: structure, process, and outcome.
2. Readers will be able to describe methods employed in applied evaluation studies focused on health promotion programs and be able to distinguish between pre-experimental, quasi-experimental, and true-experimental research designs.
3. Readers will be able to articulate specific research questions, hypotheses, methods, and potential results that can emerge from health promotion program studies.
4. Readers will be able to list internal and external threats to validity commonly faced by program evaluators and list methods for addressing these threats.
5. Readers will be able to describe the various outcome measures important in evaluating health promotion programs.

Discussion Questions

1. Describe the factors that need to be considered when selecting a study

sample and comparison groups for an evaluation study.

2. Why would an evaluator need to measure both dose delivered and dose received, rather than just capture one or the other?

3. What are the issues/challenges around defining "participation"?

4. Net present value (NPV) and benefit-cost ratio (CBR) are two methods for estimating the impact of the health promotion program. What are the pros and cons to using each of these methods?

REFERENCES

1. O'Donnell MP. *Health promotion in the workplace*. 3rd ed. Albany: Delmar Thomson Learning; 2001.

2. Sloan RP, Gruman JC, Allegrante JP. *Investing in employee health : a guide to effective health promotion in the workplace*. 1st ed. San Francisco: Jossey-Bass; 1987.

3. Goetzel RZ, Shechter D, Ozminkowski RJ, Marmet PF, Tabrizi MJ, Roemer EC. Promising practices in employer health and productivity management efforts: findings from a benchmarking study. *J Occup Environ Med*. Feb 2007;49(2):111-130.

4. O'Donnell M. Benchmarking best practices in workplace health promotion. *Amer J Health Promot*. 1997(1):1-8.

5. O'Donnell M. How well do your programs contribute to the mission, long-term goals, and current priorities of the organization? *Amer J Health Promot*. 1999;14(1):IV.

6. Goetzel R, Guindon A, Humphries L, Newton P, Turshen J, Webb R. *Health and productivity management: Consortium benchmarking study best practice report*. Houston, TX: American Productivity and Quality Center International Benchmarking Clearinghouse;1998.

7. Boles M, Pelletier B, Lynch W. The relationship between health risks and work productivity. *J Occup Environ Med*. Jul 2004;46(7):737-745.

8. Burton WN, Chen CY, Conti DJ, Schultz AB, Pransky G, Edington DW. The association of health risks with on-the-job productivity. *J Occup Environ Med*. Aug 2005;47(8):769-777.

9. Goetzel RZ, Long SR, Ozminkowski RJ, Hawkins K, Wang S, Lynch W. Health, absence, disability, and presenteeism cost estimates of certain physical and mental health conditions affecting U.S. employers. *J Occup Environ Med*. Apr 2004;46(4):398-412.

10. Goetzel RZ, Gibson TB, Short ME, et al. A multi-worksite analysis of the relationships among body mass index, medical utilization, and worker productivity. *J Occup Environ Med*. Jan 2010;52 Suppl 1:S52-58.

11. Henke RM, Carls GS, Short ME, et al. The relationship between health risks and health and productivity costs among employees at Pepsi Bottling Group. *J Occup Environ Med*. May 2010;52(5):519-527.

12. Sorensen G, Landsbergis P, Hammer L, et al. Preventing chronic disease in the workplace: a workshop report and recommendations. *Am J Public Health*. Dec 2011;101 Suppl 1:S196-207.

13. Goetzel R. CDC and NIOSH Worklife Initiative. Landscape Assessment of Worker Health Protection and Promotion (WHPP) *Project Report prepared for the CDC* 2007.

14. Hymel PA, Loeppke RR, Baase CM, et al. Workplace health protection and promotion: a new pathway for a healthier--and safer--workforce. *J Occup Environ Med*. Jun 2011;53(6):695-702.

15. Strauss A, Corbin J. *Basics of qualitative research: Techniques and procedures for*

developing grounded theory. United States of America: Sage Publications, Inc.; 1998.

16. Ozminkowski RJ, Goetzel RZ. Getting closer to the truth: overcoming research challenges when estimating the financial impact of worksite health promotion programs. *Am J Health Promot.* May-Jun 2001;15(5):289-295.

17. *HERO Employee Health Management (EHM) Best Practices Scorecard in Collaboration with Mercer*: Health Enhancement Research Organization; 2006.

18. Roemer EC, Kent KB, Samoly DK, et al. Reliability and Validity Testing of the CDC Worksite Health ScoreCard: An Assessment Tool to Help Employers Prevent Heart Disease, Stroke, and Related Health Conditions. *J Occup Environ Med.* May 2013;55(5):520-526.

19. Worksite Health ScoreCard. In: Prevention CfDCa, ed. 2012.

20. Dejoy DM, Wilson MG, Goetzel RZ, et al. Development of the Environmental Assessment Tool (EAT) to measure organizational physical and social support for worksite obesity prevention programs. *J Occup Environ Med.* Feb 2008;50(2):126-137.

21. Della LJ, DeJoy DM, Goetzel RZ, Ozminkowski RJ, Wilson MG. Assessing management support for worksite health promotion: psychometric analysis of the leading by example (LBE) instrument. *Am J Health Promot.* May-Jun 2008;22(5):359-367.

22. *WISCORE, the Wellness Impact Scorecard*: National Business Group on Health (NBGH);2013.

23. Soler RE, Razi S, Hopkins DP, Griffith M, Aten A, Chattopadhyay SK, et al.; A systematic review of selected interventions for worksite health promotion. The assessment of health risks with feedback. *Am J Prev Med.* 2010;38(2S):S237-S262.

24. Pelletier KR. A review and analysis of the clinical and cost-effectiveness studies of comprehensive health promotion and disease management programs at the worksite: update VIII 2008 to 2010. *J Occup Environ Med.* Nov 2011;53(11):1310-1331.

25. Anderson LM, Quinn TA, Glanz K, et al. The effectiveness of worksite nutrition and physical activity interventions for controlling employee overweight and obesity: a systematic review. *Am J Prev Med.* Oct 2009;37(4):340-357.

26. Heaney CA, Goetzel RZ. A review of health-related outcomes of multi-component worksite health promotion programs. *Am J Health Promot.* Mar-Apr 1997;11(4):290-307.

27. Ozminkowski R, Goetzel R, Wang F, et al. The Savings Gained From Participation in Health Promotion Programs for Medicare Beneficiaries. *J Occup Environ Med.* 2006;48(11):1125-1132.

28. Wilson MG, Basta TB, Bynum BH, DeJoy DM, Vandenberg RJ, Dishman RK. Do intervention fidelity and dose influence outcomes? Results from the move to improve worksite physical activity program. *Health Educ Res.* Apr 2010;25(2):294-305.

29. Serxner SA, Gold DB, Grossmeier JJ, Anderson DR. The relationship between health promotion program participation and medical costs: a dose response. *J Occup Environ Med.* Nov 2003;45(11):1196-1200.

30. Carls GS, Goetzel RZ, Henke RM, Bruno J, Isaac F, McHugh J. The Impact of Weight Gain or Loss on Health Care Costs for Employees at the Johnson & Johnson Family of Companies. *J Occup Environ Med.* 2011;53(1):8-16 10.1097/JOM.1090b1013e31820451fd.

31. Baker KM, Goetzel RZ, Pei X, et al. Using a return-on-investment estimation model

to evaluate outcomes from an obesity management worksite health promotion program. *J Occup Environ Med.* Sep 2008;50(9):981-990.

32. Goetzel RZ, Ozminkowski RJ, Villagra VG, Duffy J. Return on investment in disease management: a review. *Health Care Financ Rev.* Summer 2005;26(4):1-19.

33. Goetzel RZ, Ozminkowski RJ, Baase CM, Billotti GM. Estimating the return-on-investment from changes in employee health risks on the Dow Chemical Company's health care costs. *J Occup Environ Med.* Aug 2005;47(8):759-768.

34. Ozminkowski RJ, Dunn RL, Goetzel RZ, Cantor RI, Murnane J, Harrison M. A return on investment evaluation of the Citibank, N.A., health management program. *Am J Health Promot.* Sep-Oct 1999;14(1):31-43.

35. Baicker K, Cutler D, Song Z. Workplace Wellness Programs Can Generate Savings *Health Affairs.* Feb 2010;29(2): 304-311.

36. DeJoy DM, Southern DJ. An integrative perspective on work-site health promotion. *J Occup Med.* Dec 1993;35(12):1221-1230.

37. Seligman MEP. *Flourish : a visionary new understanding of happiness and well-being.* 1st Free Press hardcover ed. New York: Free Press; 2011.

38. Bigos SJ, Battie MC, Spengler DM, et al. A prospective study of work perceptions and psychosocial factors affecting the report of back injury. *Spine (Phila Pa 1976).* Jan 1991;16(1):1-6.

39. *Avoiding the brain drain: What companies are doing to lock in their talent:* Kepner-Tregoe Business Issues Research Group; 1999.

40. Boushey H, Glynn S. *There Are Significant Business Costs to Replacing Employees.* Washington, DC: Center for American Progress; November 16, 2012.

41. Lerner D, Amick BC, 3rd, Rogers WH, Malspeis S, Bungay K, Cynn D. The Work Limitations Questionnaire. *Medical care.* Jan 2001;39(1):72-85.

42. Koopman C, Pelletier KR, Murray JF, et al. Stanford presenteeism scale: health status and employee productivity. *J Occup Environ Med.* Jan 2002;44(1):14-20.

43. Pelletier B, Boles M, Lynch W. Change in health risks and work productivity over time. *J Occup Environ Med.* Jul 2004;46(7):746-754.

44. Cancelliere C, Cassidy JD, Ammendolia C, Cote P. Are workplace health promotion programs effective at improving presenteeism in workers? A systematic review and best evidence synthesis of the literature. *BMC Public Health.* 2011;11:395.

45. Kerlinger F, Lee H. *Foundations of behavioral research.* 4th ed. New York, NY: Cengage Learning; 1999.

46. Campbell DT, Stanley JC, Gage NL. *Experimental and quasi-experimental designs for research.* Chicago: R. McNally; 1963.

47. Heckman JJ, Singer B, Social Science Research Council (U.S.). *Longitudinal analysis of labor market data.* New York: Cambridge University Press; 1985.

48. Bly JL, Jones RC, Richardson JE. Impact of worksite health promotion on health care costs and utilization. Evaluation of Johnson & Johnson's Live for Life program. *JAMA.* Dec 19 1986;256(23):3235-3240.

49. Isaac F. A role for private industry: comments on the Johnson & Johnson's wellness program. *Am J Prev Med.* Jan 2013;44(1 Suppl 1):S30-33.

50. Goetzel RZ, Ozminkowski RJ, Bruno JA, Rutter KR, Isaac F, Wang S. The long-term impact of Johnson & Johnson's Health & Wellness Program on employee health risks. *J Occup Environ Med.* May 2002;44(5):417-424.

51. Ozminkowski RJ, Ling D, Goetzel RZ, et al. Long-term impact of Johnson & Johnson's Health & Wellness Program on health care utilization and expenditures. *J Occup Environ Med.* Jan 2002;44(1):21-29.

52. DeJoy DM, Parker KM, Padilla HM, Wilson MG, Roemer EC, Goetzel RZ. Combining environmental and individual weight management interventions in a work setting: results from the Dow Chemical study. *J Occup Environ Med.* Mar 2011;53(3):245-252.

53. Goetzel RZ, Roemer EC, Pei X, et al. Second-year results of an obesity prevention program at the Dow Chemical Company. *J Occup Environ Med.* Mar 2010;52(3):291-302.

54. Goetzel RZ, Baker KM, Short ME, et al. First-year results of an obesity prevention program at The Dow Chemical Company. *J Occup Environ Med.* Feb 2009;51(2):125-138.

55. Conrad KM, Conrad KJ, Walcott-McQuigg J. Threats to internal validity in worksite health promotion program research: common problems and possible solutions. *Am J Health Promot.* Nov-Dec 1991;6(2):112-122.

56. Campbell DT. Factors relevant to the validity of experiments in social settings. *Psychol Bull.* Jul 1957;54(4):297-312.

57. Cook TD, Campbell DT. *Quasi-experimentation: Design and analysis issues for field settings.* Boston, MA: Houghton Mifflin Company; 1979.

58. Rossi PH, Freeman HL. *Evaluation: A systematic approach.* Newbury Park, CA: Sage Publications, Inc.; 1999.

59. Steele-Johnson D, Beauregard RS, Hoover PB, Schmidt AM. Goal orientation and task demand effects on motivation, affect, and performance. *J Appl Psychol.* Oct 2000;85(5):724-738.

60. Fleiss JL, Levin BA, Paik MC. *Statistical methods for rates and proportions.* 3rd ed. Hoboken, NJ: J. Wiley; 2003.

61. Konrad TR, Defriese GH. On the subject of sampling. *Am J Health Promot.* Nov-Dec 1990;5(2):147-153.

62. Cohen J. *Statistical power analysis for the behavioral sciences.* 2nd ed. Hillsdale, NJ: L. Erlbaum Associates; 1988.

63. Thompson B, Bowen DJ, Croyle RT, Hopp HP, Fries E. Maximizing worksite survey response rates through community organization strategies and multiple contacts. *Am J Health Promot.* Nov-Dec 1991;6(2):130-137.

64. Dillman DA. *Mail and internet surveys: the tailored design method.* 2nd ed. Hoboken, N.J.: Wiley; 2007.

65. Kalton G, Kasprzyk D. The treatment of missing survey data. *Survey Methodology.* 1986;12:1-16.

66. Health Insurance Portability and Accountability Act of 1996. In: Congress U.S., ed. *42 U.S.C. § 1320d-9* 1996.

67. *Practical Applications of the Health and Productivity Management Model. The Platinum Book* Institute for Health and Productivity Management (IHPM); 2011.

68. *Workforce Health and Productivity: How Employers Measure, Benchmark, and Use Productivity Outcomes.* Integrated Benefits Institute; 2011.

69. *Outcomes Guidelines Report v5.*: Care Continuum Alliance; 2010.

70. The Health Enhancement Research Organization. http://www.the-hero.org/index.html. Accessed 8/19/13.

71. Care Continuum Alliance. http://www.carecontinuumalliance.org/. Accessed 8/19/13.

72. Connor KM, Davidson JR. Development of a new resilience scale: the Connor-Davidson Resilience Scale (CD-RISC). *Depression and anxiety.* 2003;18(2):76-82.

73. Cochrane W. *Sampling Techniques.* 3rd ed. New York, NY: John Wiley & Sons, Inc.; 1978.

74. Charlson ME, Pompei P, Ales KL, MacKenzie CR. A new method of classifying prognostic comorbidity in longitudinal studies: development and validation. *Journal of chronic diseases.* 1987;40(5):373-383.

75. Ashcraft ML, Fries BE, Nerenz DR, et al. A psychiatric patient classification system. An alternative to diagnosis-related groups. *Medical care.* May 1989;27(5):543-557.

76. Von Korff M, Wagner EH, Saunders K. A chronic disease score from automated pharmacy data. *J Clin Epidemiol.* Feb 1992;45(2):197-203.

77. Rencher AC. *Methods of multivariate analysis.* 2nd ed. New York: J. Wiley; 2002.

78. Weinstein MC, Siegel JE, Gold MR, Kamlet MS, Russell LB. Recommendations of the Panel on Cost-effectiveness in Health and Medicine. *JAMA.* Oct 16 1996;276(15):1253-1258.

79. Hargreaves WA. *Cost-outcome methods for mental health.* San Diego: Academic Press; 1998.

80. Gold MR. *Cost-effectiveness in health and medicine.* New York: Oxford University Press; 1996.

81. Drummond M, O'Brien B, Stoddart G, Torrance G. *Methods for the Evaluation of Health Care Programmes.* 2nd ed. Oxford University Press; 1997.

82. Wilson T. Framework for Assessing the Financial Benefit of Wellness Programs. *Journal of Health and Productivity, Institute for Health and Productivity Management* 2009;4(2).

83. The Patient Protection and Affordable Care Act. Public Law 111-148. Washington, DC.

84. Serxner S, Gold D, Parker K. Financial Impact of Worksite Health Management Programs and Quality of the Evidence. In: JM R, ed. *Lifestyle Medicine.* 2nd ed. Boca Raton, FL: CRC Press; 2013:1325-1336.

CHAPTER

7

Communication and Marketing Strategies

Jessica Fitts Willoughby and Seth M. Noar

People encounter scores of messages each day telling them everything from what car they should buy to what toothpaste tastes the best. This barrage of messages targets not only our purchasing habits, but also our health habits. For instance, National Football League (NFL) players encourage children to play for 60 minutes a day; Sesame Street characters talk up the benefits of eating fruits and vegetables; and, drug store commercials promote the flu vaccine. But are such messages effective at changing attitudes, beliefs and/or behaviors, or do such messages fall on deaf ears?

Health communication campaigns have been defined as purposeful efforts to change attitudes, beliefs or behaviors in large populations through the use of communication strategies.[1] Though not all campaigns are successful, the research literature reveals that campaigns *can* be effective at changing attitudes, beliefs, and even behaviors.[2,3] Although there is not a recipe guaranteeing an effective health communication campaign, there are a number of elements that have been found to aid in the success of campaigns. These include the use

of audience segmentation, formative research, behavioral and message design theory, careful channel selection, strategic placement within channels, and process and outcome evaluation.

The purpose of this chapter is to provide an overview of the health communication campaign planning process, from both communication and marketing perspectives. It will provide the reader with the necessary tools to better assess, plan, and execute elements of campaigns including planning and program promotion. A campaign example is described at the end of the chapter.

CORE COMMUNICATION PRINCIPLES®

Core communication principles important in designing, implementing and evaluating campaigns, and a cohesive model incorporating all of them together, are described next.

DESIGN ELEMENTS
Messages and Use of Theory

Theories of health behavior should provide the foundation for a health communication campaign that aims to change behavior.[3,4]

The variables in these theories become the factors targeted for change in the campaign. For example, if a quit smoking campaign were based on the health belief model (HBM)[5] the campaign would include messages that effectively increase 1) one's perception of risk (*smoking will give you cancer*), 2) the severity of that risk (*cancer will cut your life short*), and 3) the benefits of quitting (*you'll add years to your life and have more money to spend on other things if you quit*). It would also provide messages that 4) reduce the barriers to quitting (*quitting is hard but this program can help make it easier*) and 5) provide cues to action (*enroll in this cessation program today and give it a try!*) to get the person to begin the process of trying to quit.

However, health behavior theories alone may be insufficient in health communication efforts because such theories do not provide insights into *how* to best change those factors – that is, how the specific messages should be articulated. For this, communication or persuasion theories can be especially useful. One example of a persuasion theory is the Elaboration Likelihood Model (ELM)[6], which describes how people processes information and how messages can be designed to best encourage persuasion. According to the ELM, persuasion can occur through either the central or peripheral route. If a person is highly involved (i.e., interested) in a topic as well as motivated and able to process the information, she is more likely to process a message centrally, which means that the arguments need to be strong because she is more likely to review the information critically and think about it. Consider the case where someone is shopping for a new car and is likely to have done a lot of research in this area. In this case, she is doing a lot of central processing of such information and thus the arguments in favor of buying a particular car need to be strong in order for her to be persuaded to make the purchase. When a person is successfully persuaded through the central route, the persuasion is more likely to have a lasting effect.[7]

If a person is less motivated or involved with the topic, she is more likely to process the message peripherally, which is a much more superficial form of message processing. What this means is that instead of a careful consideration of arguments, simple cues such as source credibility, source attractiveness, or length of argument may be most persuasive. Now think about the example of advertising about toothpaste. Most people are unlikely to do a lot of research on toothpaste, and thus peripheral cues such as an attractive spokesperson or claims about "tooth whitening" or "special plaque-reducing formula" may be enough to persuade her to buy a particular type of toothpaste. However, there is a catch here: when a person is persuaded through the peripheral route, that attitude change may not be long-lasting and is resistant to counter-persuasion, which means that the person may easily change his or her mind at a later date.[8]

Consider another example – the case of encouraging people to eat more fruits and vegetables. The ELM reminds us that while getting people to eat better may be a high priority for us, it is likely to be a low priority for many individuals. Thus, people are unlikely to centrally process our promotional materials that attempt to encourage such behaviors. Instead, we probably need to assume that people will process the promotional materials using peripheral processing. This would suggest that posters to try and encourage people to eat better use a source with high credibility, high attractiveness, and/or lots of arguments for why they should do so. However, messages should also contain information that provides a highly relevant reason why people should participate, so that if people are more inclined to process the messages more thoroughly, they could still be convinced.

There are also a number of other theoretical strategies that can be used to inform message design. The use of narratives and storytelling, for example, can increase persuasion.[9] Creating stories with particular elements such as a strong narrative and characters who model behaviors may increase the chances of behavior change, as has been evidenced through entertainment education, a communication strategy.[10,11] In entertainment education, practitioners aim to use entertainment formats, such as television shows or comics, to promote social change. Television programs that contain messages encouraging organ donation, for example, have been found to influence knowledge and even behavior change.[12]

Message framing, based on Prospect Theory,[13] is another communication strategy. Framing theory suggests that the way the *same* information is presented (emphasizing the positives of doing the behavior or the negatives of not doing the behavior) can differentially impact attitudes and behaviors.[14] Messages can be "gain" framed or "loss" framed. Gain framed messages typically emphasize the benefits of participating in a particular behavior – such as eating fruits and vegetables to improve daily energy.[15] Loss-framed messages instead emphasize the costs of not engaging in certain behaviors – such as having low energy as a result of not eating fruits and vegetables.[15] Loss-framed messages have been found to be most effective at promoting detection behaviors such as HIV testing[16] and mammography.[17] Gain-framed messages have been found to be most effective for prevention behaviors, such as participating in physical activity[18] and sunscreen use.[19]

These are just some example theories that can be helpful in designing messages for effective health communication. Ultimately, using health behavior theories as well as message design theories or strategies when developing a health communication campaign can help bolster health communication campaign effects.

Audience Segmentation

Carefully and clearly defining the campaign target audience is an important early step in the planning process.[2,3] Audience segmentation involves identifying the people most important to reach through the campaign, and understanding the characteristics they have in common. Audiences can be segmented based on a number of variables, including demographics (e.g., age, gender, race), psychosocial qualities (e.g., attitudes about the behavior), variables from theory (e.g., stage of readiness to change the behavior), and/or the behavior itself (e.g., people who engage in moderate, but not vigorous, exercise). Campaigns that segment audiences based only on demographic variables are less likely to be as effective as campaigns the draw on multiple variables, although audience segmentation based on demographics alone is quite common. Health issues often involve complexities that are not captured by gender, age and race. Considering additional variables is likely to result in audience segments that can be more effectively targeted with appropriate campaign messages.

Research has shown that campaigns that attempt to reach broad, general audiences often fail.[20] Segmenting the audience is thus very important because it allows health communicators to develop messages in ways that will resonate with that specific audience. This includes *what* information is presented, *how* it is presented, and *where* it is presented. Given that all other campaign decisions and elements will be affected by what audience is focused on, this is one of the most important decisions that a campaign designer makes.[21]

Formative Research

Formative research with the target audience is also crucial to the success of a health communication campaign.[3,22] There are two main types of formative research: preproduction research and production research.[22] In preproduction research, information is gathered on the attitudes and behavioral practices of the target audience and other factors important to the campaign.

In production research, also called *pretesting*, drafts of the actual materials being created for ultimate use in the campaign are tested. The focus is typically on attention, comprehension, interest, and perceived effectiveness of the messages. Pretesting materials with the target audience is then used to tailor the messages to the specific characteristics of the target audience.[22] In the absence of this feedback, it will be difficult to know what the audience thinks of the messages, and messages used may be ineffective, or worse, may lead to defensive responses among the target audience (e.g., reactance, denial).

Formative research can be conducted in a number of ways. For example, a campaign planner who wants to promote sunscreen use in young women may use in-depth interviews to talk to members of the target audience individually to learn why they do not use sunscreen consistently and what might encourage them to use sunscreen more often. Campaign planners can also use *focus groups* to garner feedback. Focus groups are carefully planned group discussions run by a facilitator that follows a guide constructed with particular goals in mind. Focus groups allow people to express their individual thoughts as well as build off of and react to the comments of others, and they may provide perspectives different from those in an individual interview.

Once draft messages are developed (from input from interviews or focus groups, as described above), pretesting is conducted with the target audience. Early pretesting may be conducted using qualitative methods, such as individual interviews or focus groups, in which audience members can react to messages and provide suggestions for refinement. *Intercept interviews* are another method to collect information. For example, young women outside a supermarket or at the beach can be asked what they think of the messages. These interviews can use structured questionnaires that ask members of the target audience to rate messages on various characteristics, such as ability to attract attention, credibility, and perceived effectiveness. These and other methods can be used to pretest messages, all of which can provide insights that help shape the direction of the campaign.

IMPLEMENTATION

Implementation of the campaign is the next step in the health communication process. Although a campaign may follow all the elements associated with effective design, if the target audience does not see the messages, preferably with multiple exposures, than the desired effects will likely not be achieved. In a meta-analysis (synthesis of research) conducted by Snyder and LaCroix (2013), the authors found that campaigns that had greater message exposure had greater success.[23] It is also important to note that exposure to campaign messages involves both reach and frequency. Reach refers to what proportion of the population is exposed to the message, while frequency refers to how often they are exposed. Ideally, a campaign will achieve both high reach and high frequency, i.e. much or most of the target audience will see, hear or experience the messages many times each. Indeed, low exposure to campaign messages is a factor that has likely doomed many campaigns of the past.[3,24]

Channel Selection

Exposure is directly related to the communication channels through which individuals are exposed to the messages. Clearly, channels need to be selected using a strategy that ensures members of the target audience will be repeatedly exposed. However, it is also important to strategically place messages within the selected channels.[3,21] For example, if a campaign is targeting an elderly population and encouraging walking instead of being sedentary, selecting television as a channel may be appropriate. However, within that channel, selecting MTV as a station on which to air the campaign messages would not be very wise because the primary audience of MTV is less than 30 years of age. Additionally, it would not make sense to air the messages at a time that they would not be viewed by the target audience (e.g., after midnight). While this point seems fairly obvious, it is a common mistake. For example, TV stations often air free public service advertising in the middle of the night, when very few people are watching TV.

Formative research can help prevent these kinds of mistakes. In such research, target audience members can be assessed as to 1) what communication channels they already use, such as Internet, email, social media, and TV, as well as the specifics of use, and 2) how they would prefer to receive information about a particular health promotion effort or program. This feedback is invaluable and will help the campaign designer in selecting appropriate communication channels, as well as strategically placing messages within those channels.

EVALUATION

Evaluation is another important part of the health communication campaign process.[3,4,25,26] In particular, two types of evaluation are important - process evaluation and outcome evaluation.[25] Process evaluation helps one to understand how a campaign was implemented and who was reached, and it has clear implications for effectiveness. That is, it can help with not only understanding outcomes of a campaign (why a campaign was effective or ineffective), but it can also be used to adjust campaign efforts as necessary to increase their effectiveness. For example, if one finds during process evaluation that messages are not being placed appropriately, or that the target audience is not being exposed to the messages, then the health communicator can take action to remedy the situation sooner rather than later.

Outcome evaluations are also incredibly important, as they help health communicators examine whether their health campaigns had the desired effects. In the scientific literature, quasi-experimental outcome evaluation studies are typically used, as true experiments are often not possible. While some studies have used fairly weak designs to evaluate campaigns,[26] those studies conducting rigorous evaluations of campaigns have helped us to understand under what circumstances campaigns can be most effective.[3,26,27] See the chapter on evaluation for more information on evaluation designs.

A COHESIVE MODEL

The Audience-Channel-Message-Evaluation (ACME) framework is a cohesive model that brings together all of the principles described above (see Table 7-1). The ACME model[21] suggests that the first choice often made in a campaign design – on audience segmentation – is likely the most important, as it has clear implications for the other domains, such as channel, message, and evaluation. For example, if a broad, diffuse audience is selected, it will be very difficult to choose channels that have a great chance of reaching that audience. Similarly, it will be challenging to compose messages that resonate with the entire audience. Thus, audience decisions should be made first and should be made very carefully.

In addition, ACME suggests that evaluation should not be an afterthought, but rather should be diffused throughout the entire campaign process. In fact, formative research is conceptualized in the model *as evaluation* (i.e., formative evaluation), as its purpose is to evaluate the audience on the behavior, messages, and channels. In this way, ACME suggests that at every stage of the campaign process, when possible, evaluation should accompany the associated activities, with formative (development stage), process (implementation stage), and outcome

Table 7-1: ACME Domains, Key Concepts, and Considerations in each Area.

Domain	Key Concepts	Considerations	Evaluation
Audience (who?)	Audience Segmentation	Who is the specific audience that the campaign will be directed toward?	Formative
		Is this audience homogenous or heterogeneous?	Formative
		How should the audience be segmented? Consider demographic, geographic, psychographic, attitudinal, cultural, and behavioral variables.	Formative
		Also consider attitudes/behavior, message and channel preferences, theory, etc.	Formative
		Once audience is segmented: What is known about the audience segment(s) attitudes/ behavior?	Formative
Channel (how?)	Channel/ component selection	What is known about the audience segment(s) channel preferences? What channel(s) should be used to reach the audience? What channel(s) contain(s) the desired communication properties? Should this be a media only or multi-component campaign?	Formative
	Strategic implementation	How can campaign messages be strategically placed within the selected channel(s) to reach the audience and achieve high message exposure? How can the campaign activities best be coordinated and rolled out? (e.g., short campaign bursts rather than long, diffuse campaign; coordinate timing of different channels/ components for synergy)	Formative
		Is the campaign being implemented correctly and effectively? Are any mid-course corrections in implementation needed?	Process
Message (what?)	Message Design	What is a clear message for the campaign (based on campaign goals)? What are audience members being asked to think/do?	Formative
		What behavioral determinants should the messages focus on (behavioral theory)?	Formative

Domain	Key Concepts	Considerations	*Evaluation*
		How can the messages be designed to be persuasive with the audience segment(s)(message design theory)?	Formative
		What kinds of message appeals and creative messaging appeal to the audience? What should the "look and feel" of messages be?	Formative
		What message sources have the most credibility with the audience segment?	Formative
		What should the campaign slogan be?	Formative
		What is known about the audience segment(s) general message preferences?	Formative
		How do audience members react to initial campaign materials (i.e., pretesting)?	Formative
Evaluation (did it work?)	Outcome Evaluation	Using a sensitive evaluation design, did the campaign impact the intended attitudes and/or behaviors?	Outcome

Note. Formative research activities should consider all types of data available – including original data, archival data, and the published literature, and should consider both qualitative and quantitative approaches for different activities.

evaluation (evaluation stage) accompanying all campaign activities at appropriate stages.

CORE SOCIAL MARKETING PRINCIPLES

Social marketing principles provide additional tools for developing health communication campaigns. Social marketing is the practice of using marketing principles to influence behavior for prosocial reasons, such as the betterment of society.[28,29] The term social marketing was coined in the 1970s to describe this practice, and has been defined as the "design, implementation, and control of programs calculated to influence the acceptability of social ideas involving considerations of product planning, pricing, communication, distribution and marketing research."[29] Social marketing

uses marketing principles and techniques to convince a target audience to voluntarily change behavior,[30] which is similar to the goal of health communication campaigns.

The social marketing approach can be summed up as consisting of the four Ps: product, price, place, and promotion (see Table 7-2). The first P, *product*, represents the needs and wants of the target audience and defining the product so it offers benefits to the audience.[31] The product should be something that is applicable to the target audience and something they would want. Often, the product is thought of as a tangible good, service, or behavior, but it can actually be seen as a "bundle of benefits" (p. 215) provided to the consumer. This means that perceptions of the product are based on what it has to offer, not just the physical product itself. *Price* includes weighing the direct and indirect costs of the product, service,

Table 7-2: The Four Ps of Social Marketing.

P	Definition	Physical Activity Example
Product	Set of benefits associated with behavior or service use	A program called *Walk After Work* encourages employees to be more active. Walking 30 minutes a day increases cardiovascular fitness and improves attitude/outlook.
Price	Cost exchanged for promised benefit as perceived by the consumer. Does not have to be monetary.	Thirty minutes spent walking takes away time from other activities; may be difficult for people who live in areas without walking paths, access to equipment, etc.
Place	Relates to the distribution of goods or services. Can include where or when the target action will be performed.	People can walk in a group or pairs for 30 minutes directly after work in and around the office.
Promotion	Types of communication used to describe benefits of products, pricing and place.	Posters, flyers and emails to people in the office promote the *Walk After Work* program, encouraging people to pair up and walk before heading home for the day.

or behavior, especially relative to the benefits. For example, tangible costs of exercising might include the cost of purchasing new clothing or a gym membership. Indirect costs might include loss of time to relax, less time with family and friends, and/or getting up earlier in the morning. Price is always considered from the consumers' perspective,[32] rather than from the marketer or anyone else's perspective.

Place refers to where services or goods are distributed, often referred to in social marketing as "action outlets."[32] These action outlets can include where or when members of the target audience will perform certain behaviors, receive related services, or gather necessary objects.[30] In the example in Table 7-2, a walking campaign promoted through the work setting might consider place issues such as where people will be able to walk as part of the program. It might include where and when participants can receive pedometers to track their steps. Place decisions can have implications for price as well, with places that are further away or more difficult to access

increasing the perceived or actual price for the consumer.[33]

Promotion is one of the most commonly thought of components associated with a social marketing campaign. In fact, some have misunderstood social marketing as *only* being a promotional strategy, but this is not the case (i.e., promotion is simply one of the four P's). Promotion itself includes all types of persuasive communication that are used to provide information on product benefits, pricing and place elements.[32] Promotional activities can involve public relations, advertising, promotional items, event planning, posters, commercials, face-to-face discussions and other methods of distributing information and persuasive communication.

APPLICATIONS TO HEALTH PROMOTION PROGRAMS

Looking at one specific case study of a health communication campaign that uses a social marketing framework can exemplify the approach and provide insights into the application of the principles discussed above. This particular case applies to a growing problem in the U.S. – the obesity epidemic. More than a quarter of adults in the U.S. are obese,[34] with obesity rates only expected to rise. Ironically, hospital employees are not immune to poor health. Doctors, for example, often avoid routine screenings and preventive care,[35,36] making them an important target audience. Responding to this problem, every year the education coordinator in a small regional hospital in the Northwest promotes walking as part of a campaign to increase physical activity levels of all hospital employees.

Each year, the walking campaign begins in October, a prime time to still be outside in this part of the country due to the crisp weather and lack of rain. The education coordinator uses a variety of communication methods to reach out to individuals. The *product* being marketed in this case is a behavior—uptake (or increase) in walking by hospital staff. The goal of the campaign is to increase awareness of the benefits of walking and to encourage staff members to sign up for the walking program. The program also allows them to log their physical activity and win prizes for participating. *Price* associated with the program is the time needed to add walking in during the day. Although the program did not cost participants anything directly (in terms of dollars), it does take away time from other activities such as working or being at home. Before beginning the walking campaign, the health educator received formative feedback through informal conversations with staff about goals and barriers to participation. This helped provide additional information on the items in the marketing mix. The target audience in this case was all hospital staff members. A concept of walking *together* came up in the formative research, so the health educator worked to create messages that showcased how walking could be a social experience and to create opportunities for staff members to walk together (i.e., planned

group outings). The campaign also used elements of theory, incorporating elements from the theory of planned behavior,[37] such as the fact that walking is a behavior that many others were participating in (targeting norms), that walking was good for staff members physically and socially as well (targeting attitudes) and that walking was an activity that anyone could do (targeting self-efficacy).

Place for campaign messages was determined based on the target audience—hospital staff members. Hospital staff spend a significant amount of time in common break rooms or checking emails. Thus, *promotion* in this case involved posters and email communications. In addition to placing posters throughout the hospital, the health educator specifically targeted break rooms, placing posters on bulletin boards, near refrigerators, and on tables, and sent emails recruiting people to participate in the walking program. People who signed up for the program also received weekly messages with walking tips (e.g., clothing options for colder weather) and encouraging messages (e.g., walking will give you increased energy to do other things you enjoy). Prizes were distributed periodically to participants who logged the most miles or to departments that had the greatest amount of participation. For example, one department received a "spa day" in which employees were treated to chair massages because of their high participation in the program. This type of reinforcement encourages the healthy behavior (according to social cognitive theory), and these kind of public events also reinforce social norms for walking at work.

Evaluation for this campaign was limited by budget constraints, as it is for many health communication campaigns. Process evaluation consisted of monitoring the number of people who opt-ed into the program and informal feedback about email message perceptions (e.g., were emails too frequent? Too long? Etc.). Outcome evaluation consisted of a short questionnaire sent via email to people who participated in the program to gather information on opinions toward and participation in the program. While it isn't clear if the program significantly increased these employees' health, people who responded to the questionnaire said they enjoyed the program and found the messages they received to be useful in encouraging them to keep walking, especially during the cold weather. Future campaigns have incorporated this feedback and encouraged people to set up walking "dates" and to walk together at various indoor settings (e.g., mall, local coliseum) during the colder weather.

The description of this campaign is just one example of a social marketing campaign and how the various elements of the marketing mix (i.e. the four Ps) can be applied to a real world campaign effort. As can be seen, the four Ps can be relatively easily translated from abstract concepts to concrete plans and activities, and they have broad applicability to all types of campaigns. As has been shown in this chapter, both core communication and marketing principles can be applied to campaigns, and using such principles can increase the chances of success. Applying communication and marketing approaches will greatly increase the chances of success in reaching one's audience with messages that resonate with them and potentially having a measurable impact.

CONCLUSION

There are a number of ways a health communicator can plan, implement, and evaluate a health communication campaign. There is not one road that guarantees a successful campaign. However, there is a clear set of principles that have been found to be associated with more effective health communication efforts, and these principles are embodied in both the communication campaign and social marketing approaches described in this chapter. To have the greatest chance of reaching their goals, health communicators would be wise to use one of these approaches

for the planning and implementation of their health promotion efforts.

Indeed, decades of research in communication and marketing have led to valuable insights regarding how to effectively communicate with people. Many of those insights are embodied in the ACME model and the social marketing four Ps. Those insights include an audience-centered approach – truly understanding an audience's motivations for or against the behavior and how the behavior fits into their real lives. A campaign that asks an audience to change their behavior without considering the broader context in which that behavior is embedded is likely to fail. Another important insight is the careful crafting, testing, and placement of messages. Especially in today's crowded media world, it is more important than ever to design the most effective messages possible and place them in channels that resonate with and provide multiple exposures to the target audience. A campaign that really connects with its audience and continually communicates through appropriate channels will have a good chance of reaching its goals. And finally, feedback is key – and this can be achieved through process evaluation. Continually examining campaign implementation indicators as well as asking audience members what is and is not working is a critical activity. Being responsive to such feedback can continually make a campaign effort stronger and more successful.

Glossary

Audience segmentation: Identifying who you want the campaign to target and what distinguishes them from other audiences; can be based on demographics, psychographics, Stages of Change, or other characteristics.

Channel: The medium through which you plan to reach out to your audience.

Formative research: Research conducted with the target audience to inform campaign design.

Health communication campaigns: Purposeful communication efforts to change attitudes and behaviors related to health.

Place: In social marketing, relates to the distribution of goods or services.

Pretesting: Testing preliminary messages with members of the target audience to garner feedback and influence later versions of messages.

Price: In social marketing, cost required in exchange for the benefit as perceived by the consumer.

Product: In social marketing, the set of benefits associated with adopting a behavior or using a service.

Promotion: Types of communication channels used to describe the benefits of a product, pricing and place information.

Social Marketing: Using marketing principles to influence behaviors for prosocial reasons.

Learning Objectives:

1. Define health communication campaigns, provide examples.
2. Understand the principles associated with effective health communication campaigns.
3. Understand the social marketing approach – i.e., the 4 p's.
4. Understand how to relate the principles in the chapter to various examples and your own projects.

Discussion Questions:

1. Of all the principles associated with effective campaign design, which do you think is the most important? Why?
2. Some health communication/social marketing campaigns have failed. If ignored, which principle(s) is most likely to doom a campaign? Why?
3. How are communication and social marketing principles similar? How are they different?
4. What about the hospital walking campaign made it a social marketing campaign? What elements were similar to other health communication principles discussed? How could that campaign have been improved?

REFERENCES

1. Rice RE, Atkin CK. *Public communication campaigns*. Vol 4. Thousand Oaks, CA: Sage Publications, Incorporated; 2013.
2. Randolph W, Viswanath K. Lessons learned from public health mass media campaigns: Marketing health in a crowded media world. *Annu Rev Publ Health*. 2004;25:419-437.
3. Noar SM. A 10-year retrospective of research in health mass media campaigns: Where do we go from here. *J Health Commun*. 2006;11:21-42.
4. Noar SM, Palmgreen P, Chabot M, Dobransky N, Zimmerman RS. A 10-year systematic review of HIV/AIDS mass communication campaigns: Have we made progress? *J Health Commun*. 2009;14(1):15-42.
5. Janz NK, Becker MH. The health belief model: A decade later. *Health Educ Behav*. 1984;11(1):1-47.
6. Petty RE, Cacioppo JT. The Elaboration Likelihood Model of Persuasion. *Adv Exp Soc Psychol*. 1986;19:123-205.
7. Perloff RM. *The dynamics of persuasion: Communication and attitudes in the 21st century*: Taylor & Francis; 2010.
8. Petty RE, Cacioppo JT, Strathman AJ, Priester JR. To think or not to think: Exploring two routes to persuasion. In: Shavitt S, Brock TC, eds. *Persuasion: Psychological insights and perspectives, 2nd edition*. Vol 2. New York: Allyn & Bacon; 2005:81-116.

9. Green MC, Brock TC. The role of transportation in the persuasiveness of public narratives. *J Pers Soc Psychol.* 2000;79(5):701.

10. Singhal A. *Entertainment-education and social change: History, research, and practice*: Routledge; 2004.

11. Singhal A, Rogers EM. *Entertainment-education: A communication strategy for social change*: Routledge; 1999.

12. Morgan SE, Movius L, Cody MJ. The power of narratives: The effect of entertainment television organ donation storylines on the attitudes, knowledge, and behaviors of donors and nondonors. *J Commun.* 2009;59(1):135-151.

13. Tversky A, Kahneman D. The framing of decisions and the psychology of choice. *Science.* 1981;211(4481):453-458.

14. Rothman AJ, Salovey P. Shaping perceptions to motivate healthy behavior: The role of message framing. *Psychol Bull.* 1997;121:3-19.

15. Salovey P, Williams-Piehota P. Field experiments in social psychology: Message framing and the promotion of health protective behaviors. *Am Behav Sci.* 2004;47:488-505.

16. Kalichman SC, Coley B. Context framing to enhance HIV antibody testing messages targeted to African American women. *Health Psychol.* 1995;14:247-254.

17. Schneider T, Salovey P, Apanovitch AM, et al. The effects of message framing and ethnic targeting on mammography use among low-income women. *Health Psychol.* 2001;20:256-266.

18. Robberson MR, Rogers RW. Beyond fear appeals: Negative and positive persuasive appeals to health and self-esteem. *J Appl Soc Psychol.* 1988;18:277-287.

19. Detweiler JB, Bedell BT, Salovey P, Pronin E. Message framing and sunscreen use: Gain-framed messages motivate beach-goers. *Health Psychol.* 1999;18:186-196.

20. Rogers EM, Storey JD. Communication campaigns. 1987.

21. Noar SM. An Audience–Channel–Message–Evaluation (ACME) Framework for Health Communication Campaigns. *Health Promot Pract.* 2012;13(4):481-488.

22. Atkin CK, Freimuth V. Guidelines for formative evaluation research in campaign design. In: Rice RC, Atkin CK, eds. *Public communication campaigns.* 4th Ed. ed. Thousand Oaks, CA: Sage Publications; 2013:21-68.

23. Snyder LB, LaCroix JM. How effective are mediated health campaigns? A synthesis of meta-analyses. In: Rice RE, Atkin CK, eds. *Public Communication Campaigns.* Vol 4. Thousand Oaks, CA: Sage; 2013:113-129.

24. Snyder LB, Hamilton MA, Mitchell EW, Kiwanuka-Tondo J, Fleming-Milici F, Proctor D. A meta-analysis of the effect of mediated health communication campaigns on behavior change in the United States. *J Health Commun.* 2004;9:71-96.

25. Valente TW, Kwan PP. Evaluating communication campaigns. *Public communication campaigns.* Vol 4. Thousand Oaks, CA: SAGE Publications, Inc.; 2013:83-97.

26. Noar SM, Palmgreen P, Zimmerman RS. Challenges in evaluating health communication campaigns: Defining the issues. *Commun Methods and Measures.* 2009;3(1-2):105-114.

27. Hornik RC. *Public health communication: Evidence for behavior change*: Lawrence Erlbaum; 2002.

28. Andreasen AR. Social marketing: Its definition and domain. *J Public Policy Mark.* 1994:108-114.

29. Kotler P, Zaltman G. Social marketing: an approach to planned social change. *J Mark.* 1971:3-12.

30. Kotler P, Roberto N, Lee NR. *Social marketing: Improving the quality of life.*

Thousand Oaks, CA: Sage Publications, Incorporated; 2002.

31. Siegel M, Lotenberg LD. *Marketing public health: Strategies to promote social change.* Sudbury, MA: Jones & Bartlett; 2007.

32. Grier S, Bryant CA. Social marketing in public health. *Annu Rev Publ Health.* 2005;26:319-339.

33. Lefebvre CR, Flora JA. Social marketing and public health intervention. *Health Educ Behav.* 1988;15(3):299-315.

34. Ogden CL, Carroll MD, Curtin LR, McDowell MA, Tabak CJ, Flegal KM. Prevalence of overweight and obesity in the United States, 1999-2004. *JAMA-J Am Med Assoc.* 2006;295(13):1549-1555.

35. Kay MP, Mitchell GK, Del Mar CB. Doctors do not adequately look after their own physical health. *Med J Aust.* 2004;181(7):368-370.

36. Richards J. The health and health practices of doctors and their families. *New Zeal Med J.* 1999;112(1084):96.

37. Ajzen I. The theory of planned behavior. *Organ Behav Hum Dec.* 1991;50(2):179-211.

CHAPTER

8

Pursuing Health-Related Goals

Michelle L. Segar and Winifred A. Gebhardt

INTRODUCTION

Most people attempt behavior change because they have some type of goal or desired outcome in mind.[1] For example, when people initiate a health-related behavior, such as exercising more or eating less palatable food, they hope to achieve some primary benefit or reward, such as feeling fitter or becoming more attractive (or both). Goals, thus, energize and direct human behavior.[2] Goals are considered to be the hub of the self-regulatory processes people use to control their thoughts, emotions, and impulses related to adopting new behaviors.[1,3]

However, most people who adopt a health-related goal eventually stop striving for it.[4-6] Typically people are very motivated when they first commit to a new goal and the behavior change attached to the goal. Eventually, however, competing demands start to override

health-related goals, undermining lasting behavior change.[7,8] Yet, achieving sustainable goal pursuit is crucial if health promotion initiatives are to result in healthy, happy, and energized employees; disease prevention and management; decreased health care costs; and a positive return on investments. Thus, successful health promotion professionals need to understand the fundamental role that goal pursuit plays in creating sustainable behavior change as well as how to achieve it.

This chapter translates key research that can help health promotion professionals design effective interventions, such as protocols, programs, campaigns, and even e-health algorithms, to enhance sustainable health-related behaviors. This chapter presents research that will help facilitate effective self-regulation, using the concept of *competing goals* as the primary conceptual framework. It includes a review of the relevant empirical literature and a discussion on how to apply this research into practice to optimize motivation and self-regulatory skills. The chapter ends by raising some unanswered questions that need to be addressed for an optimal understanding of goal pursuit, from the time even before an intention is formed until behavior is fully incorporated in the habitual pattern of the individual.

CONCEPTUAL FRAMEWORK: COMPETING GOALS

Self-regulation has been defined as "mental and behavioral processes by which people enact their self-conceptions, revise their behavior, or alter the environment so as to bring about outcomes in line with their self-perceptions and personal goals."[8] Behavior, therefore, is assumed to be goal oriented, and chosen to support the definition of the self.[9] Moreover, each person is unique with regard to the set of goals he or she chooses to pursue. Goals guide actions and give meaning (e.g., "I eat fruits and vegetables and do not drink, because I am a healthy and responsible person, and want to set a good example for my young children."). As such, goals are the organizing principles of behavior, and importantly, behavior can therefore only be understood by identifying the goals to which behavior is linked, i.e., contextualization of behavior within the personal goal structure of the individual.[10,11] Thus, self-regulation concerns the capacity of the individual to change his or her behaviors to bring them into alignment with individually or societally held standards, ideals, and goals.[12]

Everyday self-regulation involves the pursuit of many different goals.[7,11,13-16] For example, many health-related goals are simultaneously promoted to people: don't smoke, eat small portions, exercise regularly, avoid stress, get enough sleep, etc., and this quite long list of important health-related goals does not even include the many other daily goals and responsibilities that most people have (get your kids ready for school, get ready for work, work effectively, take care of parents, etc.).[17] *Competing goals* is an important framework that describes and addresses the process of goal pursuit within the context of all other valued goals.[13,17,18]

Thus, we hold numerous goals at any given moment. This fact may cause many people to not seriously consider adopting a new health goal. Similarly, when they do start a new health behavior, they eventually give up on it. From this perspective, health-related goals constantly compete for time, energy, and money with many other daily goals and responsibilities. To maintain health-related goals, it is crucial that people stay motivated to prioritize and protect their health-related goals from the other goals (goal shielding[19]) through all phases of behavioral change. In contrast, when people do not have to attend to a conflict between goals, their goal pursuit takes less effort and attention. Similarly, when goals coincide (i.e., goal facilitation[14,15]), for example, when the goal to exercise more through joining a gym is accompanied by the goal to meet people in the new city one has moved to, the goal to exercise is more protected from being overruled by other valued aims. Thus, the extent to which a health goal is mentally represented as a goal that serves other life aspirations and does not conflict with them is also likely to (positively) influence behavioral change. Therefore, to assist the process of goal pursuit, it is important to help people understand how their health-related behavior can help them better achieve their other daily roles and priorities. This will help make health-related goal pursuit more relevant and compelling for people to sustain.

REVIEW OF LITERATURE

The literature review that follows explains how the content, structure, context, and self-regulation of goals influence whether people prioritize their health-related goals among their other competing goals and responsibilities.

The Content of Goals

The *content* of goals, or the specific outcome that people hope to achieve from adopting a health-related behavior, strongly influences whether they stay motivated to pursue their goals or if they discontinue them. Goal contents theory[20] describes how people's goal contents influence their motivation and behavior and is one of the five subtheories of self-determination theory (SDT).[21]

SDT,[22] a comprehensive theoretical framework that evolved out of humanistic psychology, investigates motivation and behavior as connected with human growth and self-actualization. SDT is increasingly being used within health promotion and health care settings. It holds great promise for explaining, designing, and evaluating successful goal pursuit and behavior from lifestyle programs, coaching protocols and algorithms, and general marketing and communications.[23,24]

According to SDT, the primary mechanism through which behavior can be changed is through either supporting or thwarting three basic psychological needs: for competence, autonomy, and relatedness.[25] That is, people have a need to feel (1) *competent*, or capable of performing a behavior or achieving a desired outcome (i.e., self-efficacy); (2) *autonomous*, or self-governing and the originator of one's actions; and (3) *related* and connected to important others. When goal pursuit leads to fulfillment of these three fundamental needs, people are more likely to internalize the value of practicing that behavior and are motivated to maintain it.[26]

Goal contents theory distinguishes extrinsic from intrinsic goal content. In this line of research, *intrinsic* goals are inwardly focused on self-development; experienced as volitional; and reflect desired outcomes like enjoyment, feeling challenged, and being social. In contrast, *extrinsic* goals are outwardly focused and reflect trying to comply with external pressures, such as performing a behavior in order to get approval, meet attractiveness norms, and follow orders. In general, extrinsically motivating reasons for changing behavior feel controlling, whereas intrinsic goals are experienced as autonomous.[22]

Research shows that compared to extrinsic goals, intrinsic ones also predict greater needs satisfaction and psychological well-being and less depression and anxiety.[27-29] In the field of education, intrinsic goals have been shown to produce deeper engagement in learning activities and higher persistence in learning activities compared to extrinsic goals.[30] Similar positive findings have been seen for exercise. One Internet-based study investigated the effects from having intrinsic vs. extrinsic goals on well-being and exercise-related behaviors among male and female employees who were on average 41 years old (N = 410).[31] This cross-sectional study found that pursuing intrinsic exercise goals (i.e., skill development and social affiliation) relative to extrinsic exercise goals (i.e., image and social recognition) was positively associated with psychological need satisfaction in exercise, psychological well-being, and self-reported exercise behavior. When people strive toward extrinsic, relative to intrinsic goals, they may fail to get their basic needs met for competence, relatedness, and autonomy[31] because they tend to be more outwardly focused and compare themselves with others.[32] In general, extrinsic goals lead to worse psychological well-being compared to intrinsic goals.[33,34] Thus, in addition to making sustainable behavior less likely, extrinsic goals also have a psychological cost.

From a SDT perspective, goal content (i.e., intrinsic vs. extrinsic) is conceptually different from the behavioral regulation[21] (i.e., autonomous vs. controlled motivation) out of which goals are pursued. As depicted in Figure 8-1, SDT proposes a continuum of motives for initiating behavior, formally referred to as *behavioral regulations*. SDT broadly distinguishes between *controlled* (least self-determined) and *autonomous* (most self-determined) regulations. This continuum varies in the degree to which extrinsic regulations are more or less internalized into the self.[25] *Amotivation*, the first regulation on the left, refers to having no intention of or interest

Figure 8-1:   Self-Determination Theory Motive Continuum.

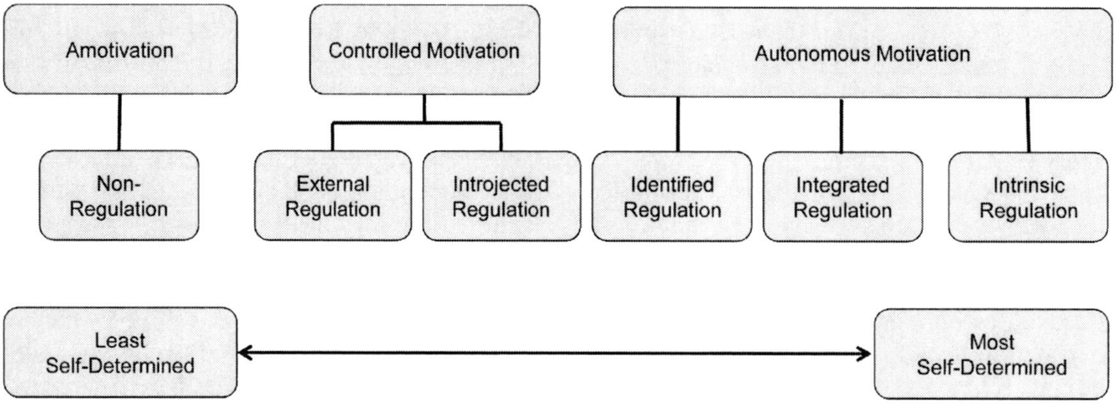

Adapted from Handbook of Self-Determination Research, Deci & Ryan 2002.

in changing behavior. *External regulation*, the first controlled regulation, refers to initiating a health behavior to fulfill an external demand or comply with an outside obligation (e.g., a drinker who is required to attend substance abuse counseling in order to keep his job). A less controlled, but very influential regulation is *introjected regulation*. It reflects people partially internalizing the value of performing the behavior but not in a deeper sense in which it is truly accepted as one's own. Introjected-based behaviors are performed to avoid guilt and shame and to attain feelings of worth. They often feel like "shoulds" and come out of socially constructed norms or pressures. An overweight woman who starts dieting because she feels pressure to lose weight as a way to get approval from her partner or employer would be considered as having introjected regulation.

In contrast, self-determined (e.g., autonomous) regulations reflect acting out of a sense of personal volition. When people feel self-determined toward performing a health behavior like exercising, it feels like a part of their identity (i.e., *integrated regulation*) and they place high value on doing it (i.e., *identified regulation*). A person who calls himself or herself an exerciser would have integrated regulation for exercising, and someone who exercises regularly because he or she values the

energy and focus it brings to daily life would have identified regulation toward exercising. *Intrinsic regulation* is distinct from the other autonomous motives because it reflects enjoying and/or receiving positive feelings and satisfaction from the act of actually doing the behavior.[25]

Yet people can strive for intrinsic and extrinsic goals for both autonomous and controlled reasons (i.e., regulations).[31] For example, people might go to the gym in order to lose weight (an extrinsic goal) because they value feeling and functioning better in their daily life (autonomous behavioral regulation) or because they feel pressured to lose weight by their employer or medical practitioner (controlled behavioral regulation). Thus, it is important to understand the greater aspiration people hope to achieve from pursing their health-related goals.

The Hierarchical Structure of Goals

Research shows that behavioral goals are organized in a *hierarchical* manner,[35] referring to a structure consisting of multiple levels. This means that when people strive to achieve an abstract goal ("be healthy") it is broken into subgoals ("stop smoking") until those subgoals are specific enough ("use a nicotine patch and work with a health coach") that they become actionable plans.

Thus, every goal is actually part of a larger goal hierarchy[13] that contains different levels. *Goal hierarchy* refers to any target goal linking to a goal at the level below and the level above the target. The level below reflects the specific plans for achieving that target goal, and the level above reflects the broader life values and aspirations that target goal aims to achieve.[36]

See Figure 8-2 for a depiction of a three-level goal hierarchy. Within this structure, the featured goal is the featured outcome of interest when initiating a new health-related behavior (e.g., having more energy every day)

that has both a lower and higher level in the goal hierarchy. This featured goal is called the *focal* goal. The lowest-level goal in the goal hierarchy is called the *subordinate* goal. The higher level in the hierarchy reflects the life value that the target goal aims to achieve and is called the *superordinate* goal.

According to Taylor et al.,[36] the featured focal goal asks: "What is it that I strive for?" The focal goal "to have more energy" gives a specific meaning and purpose to the subordinate goal of healthier eating. The superordinate goal asks: "Why do I want to achieve that for which I strive?" Although more abstract than the other lower-order goals,

Figure 8-2:   Three-Level Goal Hierarchy.

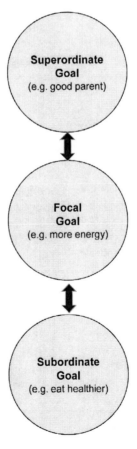

Reprinted with permission from Segar ML.

superordinate goals are highly motivational because they reflect people's life values and aspirations and are more closely tied to the self.[35] The superordinate-level goal for a health behavior reflects the deeper purpose of healthy eating, because it relates to their self-concept and core values, such as being a "good parent."[35] The subordinate goal seeks to answer, "How can I achieve that for which I strive?" This goal reflects the specific strategy or plan that is created as the means to achieve the target goal (i.e., "do physical activity for 15 minutes five times per week").

This hierarchical goal framework has predicted distinct types of behaviors, including health-related ones. One study sought to describe patient goal structures for managing hypertension.[36] A questionnaire was given to 240 patients in a hypertension clinic to identify the superordinate goals for their focal goal of regulating their hypertension and why they cared about these specific outcomes. This study identified 13 superordinate goals (promote health, prevent disease, longevity, quality of life, avoid premature death, active lifestyle, avoid medical interventions, self-reliance, meet family obligation, emotional health, prevent disability, overcome genetic predispositions, and personal goal) that clustered into three broad themes to (1) be autonomous, (2) fulfill family obligations, and (3) maintain overall quality of life and well-being. This study further investigated how these distinct goals were linked together to identify whether men and women reported valuing different goals. Men and women showed differences in the patterns for which goals were most important. "Family obligation" was the most important superordinate goal for women, followed by "quality of life." For men, "quality of life" was most important, followed by having an "active lifestyle." The study authors concluded that uncovering the hierarchical superordinate goal structures can offer insight into the deeply personal reasons why patients care about taking care of themselves, information that can

be used to develop messaging and strategies to foster effective self-management.

Another study focused on whether superordinate goals would predict longitudinal exercise behavior. This research assessed the superordinate goals for exercising among 226 working female employees (40–60 years old).[37] Participants were asked to identify their primary reason for exercising and then identify their superordinate goals for that reason. Exercise behavior was measured at three time points over 1 year. The three most important superordinate goals were related to improving health in the present moment, future aging in healthy ways, and daily quality of life. Results showed that participants who exercised to enhance their daily quality of life exercised about 20% more over 1 year compared to the participants who exercised in order to benefit their current and future health ($p < .01$). Although counterintuitive, these findings suggest that superordinate goals related to improving daily quality of life are more powerful motivators of sustained exercise than goals focused on improving current and future health among women who work full time.

Because goals are organized in a hierarchical structure, health coaches can explicitly link a client's potentially isolated focus goal for adopting a health behavior (e.g., quit smoking) with the client's higher life aspirations and values (e.g., live longer to enjoy grandchildren). This will help people create intrinsic goals and make them personally meaningful and compelling to pursue.[37] Goals, however, do not arise in a vacuum. People select and pursue specific goals based on what they have learned to value and achieve through socialization with the surrounding sociocultural context.[38,39] Therefore, it is important to understand the influential role of the context of people's goals.

The Context of Goals

In addition to thwarting or supporting people's psychological needs,[25] contexts such as culture, family, and workplaces socialize, or teach, people about what they should value and aspire to achieve.[38] Thus, the *context of goals* refers to the socializing agents and places that teach people about which goals they should pursue. This socialization determines the norms and pressures people face and thus what they most value.[40] Because socialization influences what people strive to achieve, it also influences what they prioritize on a daily basis.[38] In addition, socialization occurs primarily outside of conscious thought. Thus, people are often not aware of the ways in which their socialization influences what they value and prioritize and the goals they strive to achieve.[40] This makes socialization a powerful influence on people's daily goals, choices, and behavior.[39,41]

Because of this unconscious influence, health-related goals are inextricably influenced by external sources, such as cultural norms, the media, and health professionals.[42,43] For example, messaging by leading health organizations and the media has primarily promoted exercise as a behavior or vehicle for living a healthy life, preventing disease, controlling weight, and getting fit.[37] In contrast, when exercise is covered in the popular media, body sculpting and weight loss are the benefits emphasized most often. For example, the American Heart Association targets "overall health" as the primary reason women should adopt health behaviors like exercise and healthy eating in their women-specific "Go Red" campaign.[44]

In addition, the manner in which health promotion and health care professionals discuss and promote a health behavior influences how people perceive that health behavior, including the reasons why they would try to adopt it (i.e., their goals for that behavior).[43,45] One study investigated how socialization influenced which goals people strive to achieve from exercising.[41] Similar to other studies,[46,47] it found that 75% of study participants exercised specifically to achieve health- and weight-related goals, reflecting the dominant messaging about why people should exercise in society and in medical clinics.[48]

This research suggests that society and socialization powerfully influence which goals people strive to achieve through adopting health behaviors. Given this, it is crucial to consider the specific ways in which an organization's culture communicates about and socializes employees to adopt healthier lifestyles. SDT asserts that contexts tend to either thwart or support people's primary psychological needs, and thus greatly influence the type of motivation people develop.[26] Therefore, it is especially important for organizations to consider whether they are socializing people to feel autonomous about changing their behavior, adopting intrinsic vs. extrinsic goals, and helping individuals link their health goals with higher-level life goals they highly value.

Now that the content, structure, and context of goals have been reviewed, it is important to describe their key role in producing the self-regulation necessary for sustained goal pursuit.

The Self-Regulation of Goals

To successfully sustain a new behavior, it is not sufficient to have optimal goals and motivation. People must also continuously prioritize and negotiate (e.g., self-regulate) their new health-related behavior within their other many daily goals and tasks.[1,3] For any complex or time-intensive goal (e.g., regular exercise) to be successfully pursued, people must be capable of developing and implementing specific regulatory strategies such as planning and self-monitoring. It is important to understand what motivates people to enact these laborious processes that prioritize their health-related goals. It has been suggested that autonomy and health-related goals that are intrinsic (compared to extrinsic) better motivate more effective behavioral self-regulation.[34,49-51]

Two research groups at different universities independently investigated whether intrinsic, autonomous goals better predicted prioritizing and the self-regulation of exercise behavior than extrinsic ones.[49,52] Both studies assessed participants' specific goals for exercising, the extent to which they experienced their goals as self-determined and intrinsic, how much they planned exercise into their day, and how much they exercised. Specifically, both groups hypothesized that intrinsic goals, those reflecting outcomes that are deeply important to the people, such as "feeling energized" or "time with friends," better motivate exercise compared to goals that are more extrinsic and may feel controlling ("losing weight," etc.). One group conducted a cross-sectional study among male and female college students (n = 535) and the other studied full-time female employees who were on average 49 years old (n = 156). With different methods and study populations, both studies confirmed the same finding: intrinsic goals resulted in more exercise than extrinsic ones. But the primary finding of interest for both groups was that self-regulation strategies, such as planning, were responsible for (i.e., "fully mediated") the positive relationship between intrinsic goals and more exercise. In other words, people whose goals are more intrinsic (compared to extrinsic) do more exercise because they better prioritize it among their other competing goals through self-regulation techniques compared to less self-determined goals. These and other studies testify to the self-regulatory benefits from having self-determined goals.[53]

Another study investigated how regular exercisers differed from irregular exercisers in their self-regulation thoughts and practices. This research studied the importance participants attached to their exercise goal, the goal that most interfered with exercise, the amount of goal conflict they experienced (i.e., interference by another life goal with the exercise goal), and their level of self-regulation related to both their exercise and other life goals (n = 399).[54] The participants in the study were asked to identify the life goal that most interfered with exercising as well as their most important exercise goal.

Subsequently, they completed a self-regulation questionnaire (Goal Systems Assessment Battery)[54] for both the exercise goal and the competing life goal. Finally, they reported their level of weekly exercise participation. Not surprisingly, regular exercisers reported that they valued their exercise goal more than the irregular exercisers; they also appeared to be more effective at self-regulating their exercise behavior. Moreover, irregular exercisers were more motivated by their competing life goal, and consequently tended to self-monitor this goal more than their exercise goals, whereas regular exercisers were equally motivated for both types of goals and tended to self-monitor them both to a similar extent. This suggests that regular exercisers may have more enhanced self-regulatory skills, particularly when it comes to balancing exercise goals and other life goals. The authors concluded that irregular exercisers might become less sedentary if they could get help viewing their exercise goals within the context of their other competing life aspirations and goals.[17]

In addition to helping people create intrinsic goals and viewing them as part of their greater life aspirations, research shows it is also helpful to concurrently teach skills for specific self-regulation techniques, such as how to actively manage the conflicts that exist between the many daily goals people pursue. One such technique instructs people to proactively cope with the distractions that competing goals cause to a desired behavior. For example, Koestner et al. asked participants to prepare strategies for handling the distractions that would likely occur during the pursuit of their self-generated goals.[55] This method was found to positively affect the subsequent goal progress made by participants. This research further showed that goal progress was maximized when people both selected goals that were self-concordant (i.e., autonomous and reflecting personal core values) and created well-elaborated plans to implement their intentions. The authors concluded goal setters must simultaneously provide compelling answers to the questions "Why are you pursuing these goals?" and "How do you plan to initiate and maintain your goal-directed behaviors in the face of competing goals and other distractions?" That is, goal setters maximize their progress when they align their goals with personal interests and values and support their goals with specific plans that automatize their goal-directed behavior.

APPLICATIONS TO MOTIVATION

Motivation is energy and refers to the drive and desire people feel to strive toward their behavioral goals.[56] The following text reviews specific evidence-based techniques that can create motivating goals and the ongoing pursuit of health-related behavior.

Create an Autonomy—Supportive Environment

According to SDT, the key to success is not behavior change but helping people internalize the value of doing the behavior into their sense of selves and lives.[57] *Autonomy support* is a specific SDT-based technique that helps people take ownership of their decisions regarding their behavior and goals, and is a featured element in interventions based on SDT. Studies on smoking cessation show that when people feel autonomous about their behavior they stay tobacco free. Diabetes self-management and control (e.g., hemoglobin A1c), medication adherence, and weight management, among other health-related behaviors, are also associated with feeling autonomous and self-determined.[23,58,59] Similarly, in a nationally representative sample of women in New Zealand, feeling autonomous toward eating was associated with having a lower body mass index (BMI). Participants' BMI was lower by 2% for every 10-unit increase in autonomous regulation.[60] Thus, to achieve self-determined motivation and behavior, it is important for

organizations to create an autonomy-supportive environment that fundamentally treats people as the drivers of their own behavior rather than exerting pressure to comply with external norms or pressures.

In addition to supporting autonomy, however, it is also important to support the satisfaction of people's need for competence and relatedness.[25] Creating an environment that supports people's needs necessitates that counselors, coaches, and organizations create contexts that foster communication and methods that treat people as the source of their own behavioral choices. Specific strategies to supports people's needs include (1) emphasizing people having ownership, or taking personal responsibility, over their health-related behavior and other areas of life; (2) validating people's frame of reference without requiring them to achieve any specific health-related outcome; (3) helping people clarify their values and priorities; (4) helping people enhance their competence for a specific behavior by suggesting they set realistic goals, preview likely challenges, and develop strategies to prevent and/or overcome those challenges; (5) showing confidence that people have the potential to engage with and integrate new information; (6) showing authentic warmth toward people and fostering relatedness; (7) allowing people to determine their own solutions; and (8) minimizing the use of controlling language (i.e., "should, must, have to").[61,62]

The strategies to support people's needs from SDT listed above share some similarities with another method called *motivational interviewing* (MI).[63] MI is a counseling method that helps people move past ambivalence toward a health-related behavior change to create intrinsic motivation for that change. Readers interested in the similarities and differences between SDT and MI are advised to read a special journal on this topic.[64] One commonly used measure to determine whether the context (which might be an organization's culture, a clinician, a program, etc.) supports autonomy-based practices is the **Health Care Climate Questionnaire.** Different questionnaires are available to assess autonomy-supportive climates and many other SDT-based concepts.[65]

Challenge Introjected Thinking

Once people feel that their needs have been supported they will be more comfortable challenging their *introjected* thinking. *Introjects,* or introjected-based behaviors, undermine motivation because they are performed to avoid guilt and shame and to attain feelings of worth, often feeling like a "should."[25] In general, pursuing a health-related goal because of this type of pressure is not optimal for ongoing goal pursuit because it does not lead to self-determined motivation and makes behavioral sustainability less likely.[53] Introjected thinking undermines health behavior in many ways. Introjects often come from socially constructed norms and pressures, such as needing to be "a good provider" or "thin." Within SDT, helping people become mindful of their introjects is also thought to be important to fostering autonomy.[66]

Example Scenario

Dorothy is an employee who wants to exercise regularly, but she has an introject telling her that to be a "good wife and mother" her time outside of work should be dedicated to her family, and not be spent selfishly on herself. On the surface, being a good mother has nothing to do with exercising. Yet Dorothy's internalized belief system about her priorities generates guilt about exercising, which undermines her desire to take better care of herself. Because introjected thinking often directs behavior outside of conscious awareness, people need to become aware that they have these introjects directing their decisions. Dorothy's health coach helped her see that taking time to regularly exercise was in line with her value

of being a "good wife and mother," instead of undermining it. Dorothy was then able to realize that by exercising regularly, she would be better able to take care of her family as well as be an important role model for her children.

As this scenario showed, helping people identify their introjected behavior is important to adopting new beliefs about health behavior that will better support motivation and goal pursuit.

Emphasize Immediate Rewards Instead of Distant Ones

The many contexts in which people grow up, live, and work all teach them which goals to value and pursue.[39] Because certain types of goals and rewards are more motivating, organizations will be more successful if they are strategic about which ones they feature and promote in their wellness and health messaging and programs.[37,67] People are typically more motivated by rewards they will receive immediately rather than rewards in the future.[68,69] This notion relates to a behavioral economics called *delay discounting.* Delay discounting refers to people's tendency to select immediate gratification over rewards that are delayed sometime in the future.[68,70] Because people are biased to value the present more than the future and to seek instant over delayed gratification, helping people create goals from health behavior that aim to achieve immediate results, such as increased energy, instead of goals targeting outcomes that occur in the future (e.g., prevent cancer, lose weight) can benefit long-term behavioral adherence. The concept is called "*reward substitution,*" and is a strategy to replace a reward that is in the future from a target behavior with a reward that can be immediately experienced.

Example Scenario

A famous behavioral economist, Dan Ariely, discussed having hepatitis C and how he used reward substitution to better adhere to his treatment to get regular shots that had harsh side effects.[70] Ariely realized that he was not motivated to give himself these shots with debilitating side effects when the purpose of the shots was to avoid cirrhosis of the liver, an illness that wouldn't occur for another 20 years. Using reward substitution, Ariely changed the "reward," or goal for taking the shots, from a distant 20 years' time to immediately. His new plan was to watch movies all day on the days he gave himself the shots. This plan was reasonable because the side effects from the shots were so severe than he had difficulty working on the days of his shots. Once he substituted the "avoid severe health consequences in 20 years" goal to "watch my favorite movies all day today," Ariely stayed motivated to give himself these debilitating shots. At the end of his yearlong treatment his physician called him "the most compliant patient" he had ever seen.

Organizations can make their context more conducive for sustained goal pursuit by socializing people to practice healthy lifestyles as a way to achieve goals and benefits that they will notice immediately, such as feeling strong, being proud, or having energy. Repositioning healthy choices in this way is a form of *behavioral branding*, a process that influences the meaning of a specific health behavior and what people expect from doing it; rebranding health behaviors for their immediate rewards will make them more relevant and compelling to make a daily priority.[37,68]

Creating Intrinsic and Meaningful Goals

Given that people have a multitude of competing life goals and daily aspirations, it is important that organizations and professionals help their target audience understand the ways in which their health-related goals conflict with and contribute to the life values they most cherish. Personal projects is a relevant body of research that can help people create compelling goals. *Personal projects* refers to the specific goals, tasks, and projects that people are currently striving to achieve. A personal projects perspective explicitly treats people's health-related goals as a complex set of interconnected but often competing goals that reflect their life values (higher-level goals) and also generate plans (lower-level goals).[18]

Of central interest in the personal projects perspective is "the competitive nature of goal pursuit": any single health-related goal constantly competes for time, energy, and the (limited) cognitive resources available to people.[71] Once people understand the specific ways in which their health-related goals fit into and also compete with their larger personal goal structure, they are better able to create goals that feel intrinsic, meaningful, and compelling, so they stay motivated to pursue them.[17]

The three-level goal hierarchy discussed earlier can be leveraged to help people create meaningful, intrinsic goals that they will be motivated to sustain. *Goal facilitation*, or anticipating how a health-related goal contributes to the attainment of people's other goals, is a technique that can help convert health-related goals into top daily priorities.[17] For example, the goal to "park 20 minutes from work to walk every day" can facilitate other important goals, such as (1) spending time outside; (2) fitting in exercise; (3) saving money—no need to pay for parking; and (4) spending time with friends. This specific example is called *horizontal goal facilitation* because it reflects how a goal can help facilitate other goals on similar levels in the goal hierarchy. This is illustrated in Figure 8-3.

In contrast to horizontal facilitation, *vertical facilitation* relates to how a health-related goal contributes to the attainment of goals that are at a higher level of abstraction (e.g., superordinate goals). The lower-level goal of regular exercise aims to achieve the higher-order goals: to "be less stressed" and "have

Figure 8-3:   Horizontal Goal Facilitation.

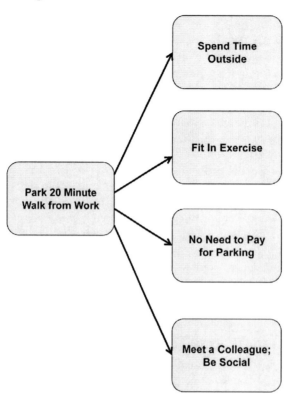

Reprinted with permission from Segar ML.

more energy." Furthermore, these goals can be made more meaningful and motivational by linking them to even higher-order goals tied to core values, such as: to "work well," "be a good parent," and "feel happy."[1] This example is illustrated in Figure 8-4.

Organizations and professionals can use goal facilitation to make health-related behaviors more personally relevant and compelling so they can better compete against people's other goals and priorities. In addition, taking a personal projects perspective on health-related goal pursuit increases people's awareness about how health-related behaviors fit within their greater life context, something that also helps build better skills to mindfully and successfully self-regulate and negotiate their health-related goals within their busy

lives.[15] More information about conducting personal projects analyses with people is available.[71-73]

APPLICATIONS TO SKILL BUILDING

The previous section reviewed strategies for fostering motivation or the energy needed to fuel the ongoing pursuit of health-related goals. Being energized or motivated to perform a health-related behavior, however, is not sufficient for creating sustained goal pursuit. People also need to have the skills to successfully prioritize and negotiate (i.e., better self-regulate) their health-related behavior. The following section discusses a few skills that are important to effective behavioral self-regulation.

Figure 8-4: Vertical Goal Facilitation.

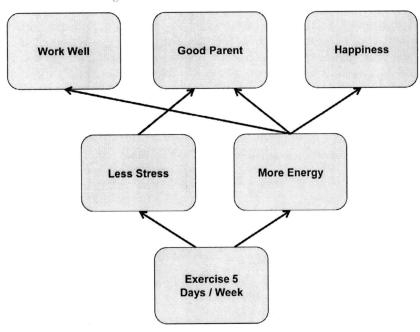

Reprinted with permission from Segar ML.

Mindfulness

The concept of *mindfulness* is often associated with promoting outcomes like stress reduction.[74] Mindfulness is also an essential skill for the ongoing pursuit of health-related behavior.[75] Mindfulness refers to having awareness about one's thoughts, beliefs, feelings, and behavior, which in turn helps people better self-regulate their behavior, monitor the things that lead to setbacks so they can "course correct" and progress toward their health-related goals.

Research shows that being more mindful increases the chances that intending to perform health-related behaviors will result in that behavior. For example, one study showed that having greater awareness of inner experiences and cues in the environment helped people carry out their intentions to exercise. In contrast, people who were less mindful were also less successful in exercising regularly because they did not have the awareness necessary to exert control and effectively self-regulate their

behavior when distracted from their goal to exercise.[76] Being mindful creates an important pause in time between a challenge in one's environment and the decision about how to respond to it. This pause permits people to choose how to respond instead of making a decision based on habit.

It is important to point out that contexts that support autonomy also foster mindfulness.[51] There are also many strategies and tools to help people become more mindful and skilled in overcoming their barriers. One intervention aimed to increase skills in mindfulness as a central component in a larger educational curriculum targeting increased physical activity that would be sustained. During the 6-week intervention, participants gained mindfulness skills through preplanning their future exercise behavior, as well as the specific challenges they would face to successfully achieving their plans every week. At the beginning of each session, participants were also asked to conduct weekly self-evaluations to further build their awareness of their barriers and effective strategies for overcoming them. Participants increased physical activity participation 44% from baseline to postprogram and 65% from baseline to the long-term study follow-up, on average 12 months after the program had ended ($p < .01$).[77] Helping individuals become aware of their barriers to physical activity and learn to develop strategies to overcome these things also promotes competence toward being physically active.[62]

Implementation Intentions

We now know that people process information and strive toward goals automatically, i.e., outside of their conscious awareness.[78-80] Furthermore, because self-regulation is often a struggle for self-control between emotional impulses and cognitive restraint, sustainable goal pursuit can be improved by reducing the need to use self-control.[79,81]

One evidence-based technique that reduces the need for self-control and helps people make challenging behavioral choices more automatic is called "implementation intentions." *Implementation intentions* (also called "if-then" planning) are the concrete strategies that people make to successfully initiate their behavior when certain situations arise. Implementation intentions are future oriented because they are developed before a situation occurs. Implementation intentions help people identify specific strategies and plans for what they will do and when they will do it. They are predeveloped responses to perform at very specific situational cues in order to overcome barriers (i.e., leaving at the planned time for a yoga class, declining a cigarette when offered).[82]

One intervention study evaluated whether implementation intentions could reduce dietary fat intake among female and male employees in a midsize company.[83] Participants (n = 264) filled out a questionnaire on dietary food intake and were then randomized into an experimental condition in which they had to create an implementation intention or a control group. Participants filled out the food intake measure again 1 month later. Fat intake, saturated fat intake, and the proportion of calories derived from fat decreased significantly in the experimental group but not in the control group after 1 month ($p < .05$). Given that there were no health professionals or other elaborate intervention elements in this study, the authors suggested that implementation intentions offer a low-cost intervention to change dietary behavior.

Example Scenario

Charlie and Gail work at the same organization. When their company started offering smoking cessation classes for free they both decided to enroll. As part of the program, Charlie and Gail were asked to develop "if-then" plans to help them be more prepared for the challenges to their desired cessation plans. In developing their plans, they first determined in which situations they would be most tempted to smoke and then they identified what alternative choices they would choose to avoid smoking in those specific situations. Charlie strategized for the end of every workday (the "when"), the time that he is most tempted to smoke as a form of relaxation with his friends. His plan (the "what") was to drive to the nearby park after work to take a relaxing brief walk instead of smoking with his friends. Gail's challenging situation was when her friends offered her a cigarette during the weekend. She decided that "if" one of her friends offered her a cigarette "then" she would say, "No thank you," and reach for a stick of the gum that she started carrying with her just for that situation. Because Charlie and Gail had their strategies in place when these challenging situations arose, they were prepared to choose their alternative plans without too much trouble.

If-then planning has been shown to create linkages in the mind between strategies and situational cues before the situations arise and make the desired response more automatic; this in turn reduces the need for self-control. If-then planning is thought to bridge the typical gap that occurs between people's intentions and their behavior.[82] The "if" part of if-then planning is to help people specify a specific time or place ahead of time as a way to help them notice this external cue when it occurs. The "then" part of if-then planning is thought to enhance competence (e.g., self-efficacy) by specifying and concretizing what action to take at the critical juncture.[84] Research using implementation intentions related to health-related behavior change shows that this type of very specific if-then planning is effective with different types of health behaviors.[85,86] Helping people become skilled in developing implementation intention is important to helping them successfully self-regulate their behavior. Implementation intentions are considered to be potent self-regulatory tools for overcoming the typical obstacles associated with goal-directed behavior. It is important to note, however, that implementation intentions are more effective when people strive to achieve intrinsic goals and feel autonomous in their behavioral pursuit.[55]

Social Connections with People

SDT considers relatedness to be one of people's three primary psychological needs.[25] In addition, receiving support and being connected to others when adopting new health-related goals provide camaraderie and enhance motivation.[26] Modern technology and social media have taken fostering relatedness to the next level. Helping people become skilled in using social networks, or online communities, to help them connect with other people to support their behavioral goal pursuit is a new and exciting technique to enhance motivation and self-regulation. There are numerous social media Web sites that combine tracking tools with community support. Tracking tools, in general, help people increase skills in self-regulating their behavior. The combination of social support from communities and tracking tools provides powerful support for challenges and camaraderie with peers who are also striving toward shared healthy-living goals.[87] Research on how participating in social networks impacts health-related behavior is still in its infancy but shows promise. One 16-week study on how social networks impact health-related behaviors collected data among adults with BMIs over 25 who also had type 2 diabetes or coronary artery disease.[88] All of the study participants (n = 324) wore enhanced pedometers and were asked to upload their step count (obtained from the pedometers) to a server. Participants could log in to the study Web site to view graphs of their walking progress, tailored motivational messages, and calculated steps. Half of the participants were randomized to have access to an online community where they could post and read messages. The other group did not have access to the online community. Both groups significantly increased their average daily step count from baseline to 16 weeks (mean 1888 ± 2400 steps), with no significant differences between the two groups. However, the group with access to the online community had 79% of their group complete and stay engaged in the intervention, compared to 66% of participants who did not have access to the online program, $p < .05$.

There are many social networks and online tracking tools, many of them free, to help people create relationships and use camaraderie to become more mindful of their goal pursuit so they can better achieve long-term success. There are resources available for professionals who want to build online communities in evidence-based ways.[87,89]

UNANSWERED QUESTIONS

Significant progress has been made in clarifying the underlying mechanisms of creating motivating goals, effective self-regulation, and ongoing goal pursuit. Yet the more we learn from research, the more questions that emerge regarding how to best translate the findings for optimal use in health promotion. The following section highlights two practical unanswered questions that relate to how to optimally facilitate the ongoing pursuit of health-related goals: (1) Should health promotion programs ask people to set learning or performance health-related goals? (2) Will health-related communications be more motivational and persuasive if they market different benefits and goals to men compared to women?

Should Health Promotion Programs Ask People to Set Learning or Performance Health-Related Goals?

An important question still to answer in health promotion is whether optimal behavioral outcomes will result from rewarding employees for learning how to integrate health behavior into their lives or for achieving specific biometric outcomes. Health promotion professionals can look to a 30-year body of research in work and education about the differing effects from setting performance compared to learning goals on motivation and sustained behavioral pursuit. Performance goals focus on achieving a specific outcome (e.g., a grade, weight goal, etc.), whereas, learning goals focus on mastering new tasks (e.g., eating five fruits and vegetables every day, being active for 15 minutes every day).[90]

Learning goals, in contrast to performance goals, emphasize the "how" of sustaining a new behavior. Learning goals guide people to discover the strategies, processes, and procedures necessary to perform a task effectively.[90] Learning goals focus people on mastering the task rather than worrying about achievement. More than three decades of research by Locke and Latham shows that when a task is complex and environments are dynamic, people who set learning goals have more intrinsic motivation, do better, and show

greater goal commitment than those who set performance goals.[90]

This general finding by Locke and Latham[90] in the area of work is also supported by a different but synergistic 30-year program of motivation research in the field of education studying the differential effects from having "mastery" (e.g., learning) or "achievement" (performance) goals led by Carol Dweck.[91]

Some health promotion programs ask and reward employees for specific outcomes like a reduction in weight or blood pressure. Yet the behaviors necessary to achieve those outcomes are very complex, such as changing dietary habits or integrating exercise into a busy life. Generalizing from these robust programs of research in work-related performance and education, teaching people to take a learning-goal approach might help them enjoy the process of striving toward their health-related goals and view their setbacks and challenges as opportunities to learn, instead of failures, something that builds resilience toward challenges and fosters ongoing behavior.[91] New research evaluating the pros and cons from giving employees learning vs. performance health-related goals will offer empirical evidence to more fully answer this question.

Will Health-Related Communications be more Motivational and Persuasive if they Market Different Benefits and Goals to Men Compared to Women?

In general, health-related communications tend to promote the same types of benefits from or goals for adopting healthy lifestyles to men and women. Yet research suggests that men and women differ on what types of health-related goals they value, which types of goals predict behavior, and what leads to relapse.[92-94] For example, research shows that men and women report distinct patterns of superordinate goals for managing hypertension.[36] As previously described, among women, "family obligation" was the most important superordinate goal, followed by "quality of life." For men, "quality of life" was most important, followed by having an "active lifestyle." Men and women do differ on what outcomes they find most motivating across many behaviors. Therefore, it is important to ask whether health promotion efforts would better engage and motivate more employees if they promoted different health-related goals to men and women.

A marketing experiment investigated this question by researching whether promoting physical activity as a way to achieve distinct goals differentially impacted motivation among a sample of midlife adult women and men who were overweight (BMI ≥ 25) or obese (BMI ≥ 30) (n = 1690).[95] Participants were randomized to read a single advertisement featuring one of the following three reasons to be physically active: (1) better health, (2) weight loss, or (3) daily well-being, and then were asked to report their level of intrinsic motivation (e.g., enjoyment or pleasure) toward being physically active. Overweight female participants who read the daily well-being advertisement reported higher intrinsic motivation compared to those reading the advertisement featuring weight loss as the reason to be physically active. In contrast, and contrary to hypotheses, overweight men who read the ads featuring "weight loss" and "health" reported higher intrinsic motivation more than the overweight men who read the "daily well-being" advertisement. There were almost no effects among obese participants. Although the effect sizes in this research were small, this proof-of-concept study suggests that promoting physical activity as a way to achieve daily well-being may improve overweight women's intrinsic motivation for being physically active.

In contrast to women, these findings suggest that overweight men might be more motivated to be physically active if health communications promoted physical activity as a primary way to achieve medical-related goals.

This explanation, however, is not supported by other research from behavioral economics showing that people, regardless of gender, tend to be more motivated by immediate experiences (e.g., increased energy, etc.) than abstract ones that take a long time to experience (e.g., disease prevention, etc.).[68,70] The research on masculine norms and behavior may help explain men's nonoptimal motivational response to the well-being advertisement. Research on masculinity shows that men want to avoid feeling "weak" and because of this they tend to not be comfortable acknowledging mental health issues.[96] Generalizing from this, the male participants might have interpreted the well-being advertisement promoting physical activity as a way to "reduce stress" and "lift mood" as reflecting mental health issues, and thus not felt motivated. To better understand whether gender differences should be considered as a fundamental health promotion strategy, it is important to have a much deeper understanding of which types of rewards and goals are most motivational to men compared to women. Research is currently underway to discover this information as key to optimally promoting health-related goal pursuit to both women and men.

SUMMARY AND CONCLUSION

Science related to goal pursuit has significantly advanced in the last three decades; much more is known about how to foster health-related behaviors that can be sustained over time. This chapter reviewed research to help professionals understand the core issues related to harnessing the power of health-related goal pursuit. It also discussed specific ways that this relevant research can be translated into concrete strategies to foster and support sustainable goal pursuit.

People will be more successful in sustaining health-enhancing behaviors if they remain focused on pursuing their goals. Therefore, understanding the core components of effective goal pursuit will help health promotion professionals be more successful in fostering health lifestyles that employees will be more likely to sustain. These components include:

1. The origin of goals, and how contexts such as organizations, the media, and even health apps influence which goals people consider valuable and strive to achieve.
2. The content of goals, the key difference between goals that are intrinsic vs. extrinsic, and the implications for developing controlled vs. autonomous regulations and motivation.
3. The structure of goals, and how the three-level goal hierarchy lends itself to helping individuals create and pursue meaningful goals that link to their core values.
4. The self-regulation of goals, and that certain goals positively and negatively impact self-regulation processes.

The chapter's organizing framework utilizes a competing goals perspective because it features the reality of promoting health to people: any desired health-related goal and behavior change constantly competes for time and energy, among other resources, with a multitude of other life goals and daily priorities.[17] Thus, to optimally foster the ongoing pursuit of health-related goals, these goals must be experienced as meaningful, relevant to, and supporting daily roles and life aspirations, as well as realistic to do.[1,37,97] Because any health goal is part of a larger hierarchy of goals,[7] professionals can explicitly link a potentially isolated focal goal for adopting a health behavior (e.g., exercise to regulate hypertension) with people's higher life aspirations and values (e.g., live longer to enjoy grandchildren).

How organizations and health professionals communicate about healthy living to employees is a primary socialization context that influences the content of the health-related goals people pursue, and whether these goals are experienced as self-determined or controlling. Research shows that intrinsic goals better support people's psychological needs and result in more autonomous motivation, better self-regulation, and more persistent goal pursuit than controlled goals.[33,34,36,52] Thus, it is crucial to consider how organizations and health promotion initiatives are socializing employees to adopt healthier lifestyles, especially the goals they should strive to achieve from health behaviors. Social marketing, coaching protocols, e-health games, and mobile apps, although all distinct intervention modalities, are also contexts that can resocialize people regarding their health-related goal pursuits by guiding them to explicitly link their health-related goals with their most cherished parts of living.

Glossary

Autonomy support: Techniques that support people taking ownership of their decisions regarding their behavior and goals; a featured element in interventions based on self-determination theory.

Behavioral branding: A process that influences what a specific health behavior means to people, what they expect from doing it, and whether they develop positive or negative feelings about that specific behavior.

Delay discounting: People's tendency to select immediate gratification over rewards that are delayed sometime in the future.

Goal: The end result or outcome that people hope to achieve from initiating a behavior or action.

Goal facilitation: Anticipating how one health-related goal contributes to the attainment of other goals.

Goal hierarchy: The idea that any target goal has a multilevel structure, consisting of one level above, reflecting life values, and one level below, reflecting the specific plan to achieve it.

Implementation intentions: Concrete future-oriented strategies that people create as a strategy to successfully initiate their desired behavior when challenging situations arise.

Mindfulness: Having awareness about one's thoughts, beliefs, feelings, and behavior, which in turn helps one better monitor the things that lead to setbacks and better progress toward their health-related goals.

Motivation: The drive and desire people feel to strive toward their behavioral goals.

Personal projects: The specific goals, tasks, and projects people are currently striving to achieve.

Reward substitution: A strategy to substitute a future reward from doing a behavior with a reward that will be immediately experienced.

Self-regulation: The mental and behavioral processes by which people enact their self-conceptions, revise their behavior, or alter the environment so as to bring about outcomes in line with their self-perceptions and personal goals.

Learning Objectives

After completing this chapter, you should be able to:

1. Describe the competing goals framework and why it helps inform developing sustainable goal pursuit.
2. Understand how the content of goals influences behavioral self-regulation and sustainable goal pursuit.
3. Discuss the primary tenets of self-determination theory, including humans' primary psychological needs, internalization, and how to foster autonomous regulations and motivation.

4. Identify the three levels in the goal hierarchy and how to leverage the highest level to make health-related goals more meaningful and motivational.
5. Appreciate the central role that contexts play in what people value and the goals they strive to achieve.

Discussion Questions

1. What are goals and how do they work through self-regulation to foster health-related behavior?
2. How can organizations support their employees' psychological needs?
3. Why is it important to consider competing goals when promoting health behavior?
4. How would you describe feeling autonomous?
5. How do introjects influence behavior?
6. Describe how you would use reward substitution to make a health-related behavior more relevant and compelling to your target audience.
7. Describe vertical facilitation, and give an example of it in your own life.
8. What is behavioral branding?
9. What is mindfulness and how is it related to self-regulating health-related behaviors?
10. What is one strategy to help self-regulation become more automatic and need less self-control?

REFERENCES

1. Carver C, Scheier M. On the structure of behavioral self-regulation. In: Boekaerts M, Pintrich P, Zeidner M, eds. *Handbook of Self-Regulation*. San Diego, Calif: Academic Press; 2000:41–84.
2. Scheier M, Carver C. Goals and confidence as self-regulatory elements underlying health and illness behavior. In: Cameron

L, Leventhal H, eds. *The Self-Regulation of Health and Illness Behaviour*. London, UK: Routledge; 2003:17–41.

3.   Cameron L, Leventhal H. Self-regulation, health, and illness: an overview. In: Cameron L, Leventhal H, eds. *The Self-Regulation of Health and Illness Behaviour*. London, UK: Routledge; 2003:1-13.

4.   Dishman R. The problem of exercise adherence. Fighting sloth in nations with market economies. *Quest*. 2001;53:279–294.

5.   Berlant N, Pruitt S. Adherence to medical recommendations. In: Cohen L, McChargue D, Collins F, eds. *The Health Psychology Handbook*. London, UK: Sage; 2003:208–222.

6.   Dunbar-Jacob J, Mortimer-Stephens MK. Treatment adherence in chronic disease. *J Clin Epidemiol*. 2001;54(suppl 1): S57–S60.

7.   Gebhardt WA. *Health Behaviour Goal Model: Towards a Theoretical Framework for Health Behaviour Change*. Leiden, The Netherlands; Leiden University; 1997.

8.   Gebhardt WA, Maes S. Competing personal goals and exercise behaviour. *Percept Mot Skills*. 1998;86:755–759.

9.   Forster J, Liberman N, Friedman RS. Seven principles of goal activation: a systematic approach to distinguishing goal priming from priming of non-goal constructs. *Pers Soc Psychol Rev*. 2007;11:211–233.

10.   Austin J, Vancouver J. Goal constructs in psychology: structure, process, and content. *Psychol Bull*. 1996;120:338–375.

11.   Gebhardt WA. Contextualizing health behaviors: the role of personal goals. In: de Ridder D, de Wit J, eds. *Self-Regulation in Health Behavior*. Chichester, UK: John Wiley & Sons; 2006:27-43

12.   Baumeister RF, Vohs KD. Self-regulation, ego depletion, and motivation. *Soc Personal Psychol Compass*. 2007;1:1–14.

13.   Maes S, Gebhardt WA. Self-regulation and health behavior: the health behavior goal model. In: Boekaerts M, Pintrich P, Zeidner M, eds. *Handbook of Self-Regulation*. San Diego, Calif: Academic Press; 2000:343–368.

14.   Riediger M, Freund AM. Interference and facilitation among personal goals: differential associations with subjective well-being and persistent goal pursuit. *Pers Soc Psychol Bull*. 2004;30:1511–1523.

15.   Presseau J, Sniehotta FF, Francis JJ, Gebhardt WA. With a little help from my goals: integrating intergoal facilitation with the theory of planned behaviour to predict physical activity. *Br J Health Psychol*. 2010;15:905–919.

16.   Shah JY, Kruglanski AW. Aspects of goal networks: implications for self-regulation. In: Boekaerts M, Pintrich PR, Zeidner M, eds. *Handbook of Self-Regulation*. San Diego, Calif: Academic Press; 2000:86-108

17.   Gebhardt WA. The role of goal facilitation and goal conflict in motivation. In: Brown LV, ed. *The Psychology of Motivation*. New York, NY.: Nova Science Pub Inc; 2007:1–11.

18.   Little, B.R. 1983. Personal projects: A rationale and method for investigation. *Environ. Behav*. 15(3), 273–309.

19.   Shah JY, Friedman R, Kruglanski AW. Forgetting all else: on the antecedents and consequences of goal shielding. *J Pers Soc Psychol*. 2002;83:1261–1280.

20.   Vansteenkiste M, Niemiec C, Soenens B. The development of the five mini-theories of self-determination theory: an historical overview, emerging trends, and future directions. In: Urdan T, Karabenick S, eds. *The Decade Ahead: Theoretical Perspectives on Motivation and Achievement*. Bingley, United Kingdom: Emerald Group Publishing Limited; 2010:105–165. *Advances in Motivation and Achievement*; vol 16.

21. Self-determination theory: formal theory: SDT's five mini-theories. Available at: http://www.selfdeter minationtheory.org/theory#formal Theory. Accessed July 15, 2013.

22. Ryan RM, Deci E. Self-determination theory and the facilitation of intrinsic motivation, social development, and well-being. *Am Psychol.* 2000;55:68–78.

23. Ng JYY, Ntoumanis N, Thogersen-Ntoumani C, et al. Self-determination theory applied to health contexts: a meta-analysis. *Perspect Psychol Sci.* 2012;7:325–340.

24. Patrick H, Canevello A, Williams GC. Testing the tenets of self-determination theory in the digital world to promote physical activity. *Ann Behav Med.* 2012;43:S143.

25. Deci EL, Ryan RM. The "what" and "why" of goal pursuits: human needs and the self-determination of behavior. *Psychol Inq.* 2000;11:227–268.

26. Deci EL, Ryan RM. Intrinsic motivation and self-determination in human behavior. New York, NY; Plenum; 1985.

27. Sheldon KM, Ryan RM, Deci EL, Kasser T. The independent effects of goal contents and motives on well-being: it's both what you pursue and why you pursue it. *Pers Soc Psychol Bull.* 2004;30:475–486.

28. Kasser T, Ahuvia A. Materialistic values and well-being in business students. *Eur J Soc Psychol.* 2002;32:137–146.

29. Vansteenkiste M, Soenens B, Duriez B. Presenting a positive alternative to materialistic strivings and the thin-ideal: understanding the effects of extrinsic relative to intrinsic goal pursuits. In: Lopez S, ed. *Positive Psychology: Exploring the Best in People.* Westport, CT: Greenwood Publishing Company; 2008:57–86.

30. Vansteenkiste M, Lens W, Deci EL. Intrinsic versus extrinsic goal contents in self-determination theory: another look at the quality of academic motivation. *Educ Psychol.* 2006;4:19–31.

31. Sebire SJ, Standage M, Vansteenkiste M. Examining intrinsic versus extrinsic exercise goals: cognitive, affective, and behavioral outcomes. *J Sport Exerc Psychol.* 2009;31:189–210.

32. Vansteenkiste M, Matos L, Lens W, Soenens B. Understanding the impact of intrinsic versus extrinsic goal framing on exercise performance: the conflicting role of task and ego involvement. *Psychol Sport Exerc.* 2007;8:771–794.

33. Sheldon KM, Elliot AJ. Not all personal goals are personal: comparing autonomous and controlled reasons as predictors of effort and attainment. *Pers Soc Psychol.* 1998;24:546–557.

34. Sheldon K, Kasser T. Goals, congruence, and positive well-being: New empirical support for humanistic theories. *J Humanist Psychol.* 2001;41: 30–50.

35. Carver C, Scheier M. *On the Self-Regulation of Behavior.* Cambridge, United Kingdom; Cambridge University Press; 1998.

36. Taylor SD, Bagozzi RP, Gaither CA, Jamerson KA. The bases of goal setting in the self-regulation of hypertension. *J Health Psychol.* 2006;11:141–162.

37. Segar M, Eccles J, Richardon C. Rebranding exercise: closing the gap between values and behavior. *Int J Behav Nutr Phys Act.* 2011;8:94:1–14.

38. Eccles J. Subjective task value and the Eccles et al. model of achievement-related choices. In: Elliot A, Dweck C, eds. *Handbook of Competence and Motivation.* New York, NY: Guilford; 2005:105–121.

39. Eccles JS, Wigfield A. Motivational beliefs, values, and goals. *Annu Rev Psychol.* 2002;53:109–132.

40. Coole D. The gendered self. In: Bakhurst D, Sypnowich C, eds. *The Social Self.* London, United Kingdom: Sage; 1995:123–139.

41. Segar ML, Eccles JS, Peck SC, Richardson C. Midlife women's physical activity goals: sociocultural influences and effects on behavioral regulation. *Sex Roles.* 2007;57:837–850.

42. McQuail D. *McQuail's Mass Communication Theory.* 5th ed. London, United Kingdom: Sage; 2005.

43. Baumann LC. Culture and illness representation. In: Cameron L, Leventhal H, eds. *The Self-Regulation of Health and Health Behaviour.* New York, NY: Routledge; 2003:242–253.

44. American Heart Association. Go red for women. Available at: http://www.goredforwomen.org/. Accessed June 15, 2013.

45. Rothman A, Kelly K, Hertel A, Salovey P. Message frames and illness representations: implications for interventions to promote and sustain healthy behavior. In: Cameron L, Leventhal H, eds. *The Self-Regulation of Health and Illness Behavior.* London, United Kingdom: Routledge; 2003: 278–296.

46. Koslow R. Age-related reasons for expressed interest in exercise and weight control. *J Appl Soc Psychol.* 1988; 18:349–354.

47. Segar ML, Spruijt-Metz D, Nolen-Hoeksema, S. Go figure? Body-shaping motives are associated with decreased physical activity participation among midlife women. *Sex Roles.* 2006; 54:175–187.

48. Russell NK, Roter DL. Health promotion counseling of chronic-disease patients during primary care visits. *Am J Public Health.* 1993;83:979–982.

49. Lutz RS, Karoly P, Okun MA. The why and the how of goal pursuit: self-determination, goal process cognition, and participation in physical exercise. *Psychol Sport Exerc.* 2008;9:559–575.

50. Sheldon KM, Houser-Marko L. Self-concordance, goal attainment, and the pursuit of happiness: can there be an upward spiral? *J Pers Soc Psychol.* 2001;80:152–165.

51. Ryan RM. A self-determination theory approach to psychotherapy: the motivational basis for effective change. *Can Psychol.* 2008;49:186–193.

52. Segar ML, Eccles JS, Richardson CR. Type of physical activity goal influences participation in healthy midlife women. *Women's Health Issues.* 2008;18:281–291.

53. Koestner R, Otis N, Powers TA, et al. Autonomous motivation, controlled motivation, and goal progress. *J Pers.* 2008;76:1201–1229.

54. Karoly P, Ruehlman L, Okun MA, et al. Perceived self-regulation and exercise goals and interfering goals among regular and irregular exercisers: a life space analysis. *Psychol Sport Exerc.* 2005;6:427–442.

55. Koestner R, Lekes N, Powers TA, Chicoine E. Attaining personal goals: self-concordance plus implementation intentions equals success. *J Pers Soc Psychol.* 2002;83:231–244.

56. Bagozzi R, Dholakia U, Basuroy S. How effortful decisions get enacted: the motivating role of decision processes, desires, and anticipated emotions. *J Behav Decis Mak.* 2003;16:273–295.

57. Teixeira PJ, Silva MN, Mata J, et al. Motivation, self-determination, and long-term weight control. *Int J Behav Nutr Phys Act.* 2012;9:22.

58. Williams GC, Freedman ZR, Deci EL. Supporting autonomy to motivate patients with diabetes for glucose control. *Diabetes Care.* 1998;21:1644–1651.

59. Williams GC. Improving patients' health through supporting the autonomy of patients and providers. In: Deci EL, Ryan RM, eds. *Handbook of Self-Determination Research.* Rochester, NY: University of Rochester Press; 2002:233–254.

60. Leong S, Madden C, Gray A, Horwath C. Self-determined, autonomous regulation of eating behavior is related to lower body mass index in a nationwide survey of middle-aged women. *J Acad Nutr Diet.* 2012; 2012 Sep;112(9):1337-46.

61. The art of health promotion: How do we both support autonomy and build accountability? A discussion with Dr. Edward Deci, co-founder of self-determination theory. Available at: http://www.healthpromotionjournal.com/index.php?com_route=view_video&vid=109. Accessed July 15, 2013.

62. Patrick H, Resnicow K, Teixeira PJ, Williams GC. Communication skills to elicit physical activity behavior change: how to talk to the client. In: *ACSM's Behavioral Aspects of Exercise.* New York, NY: Lippincott Williams & Wilkins; 2013.

63. Resnicow K, Davis R, Rollnick S. Motivational interviewing for pediatric obesity: conceptual issues and evidence review. *J Am Diet Assoc.* 2006;106: 2024–2033.

64. Patrick H, Williams GC. Self-determination theory: its application to health behavior and complementarity with motivational interviewing. *Int J Behav Nutr Phys Act.* 2012;9:

65. Self-determination theory. 2012. http://selfdeterminationtheory.org/ questionnaires. Accessed February 9, 2013.

66. Ryan RM, Deci E. A self-determination theory approach to psychotherapy: a motivational basis for effective change. *Can Psychol.* 2008;49:186–193.

67. Segar ML. Beyond smart goals: evidence-based insights into the "why" and "how" of helping individuals develop and pursue optimal health-related goals. Paper presented at: Art & Science of Health Promotion; April 11, 2012; San Diego, Calif.

68. Hariri AR, Brown SM, Williamson DE, et al. Preference for immediate over delayed rewards is associated with magnitude of ventral striatal activity. *J Neurosci.* 2006;26:13213–13217.

69. Rath T, Harter J. *Well-Being: The Five Essential Elements.* New York, NY; Gallup Press; 2010.

70. Ariely D. Why we do things that aren't in our best interests. 2010. Available at: http://bigthink.com/ideas/20760. Accessed June 14, 2011.

71. Presseau J, Sniehotta F, Francis J, Little B. Personal projects analysis: opportunities and implications for multiple goal assessment, theoretical integration, and behaviour change. *Eur Health Psychol.* 2008;10:32–36.

72. Little B, Salmela-Aro, K, Phillips, SD. *Personal Project Pursuit: Goals, Action, and Human Flourishing.* Mahwah, NJ; Lawrence Erlbaum Associates; 2007.

73. Little B. Personal projects assessment tools. 2013. Available at: http://www.brianrlittle.com/research/assessment-tools-2. Accessed January 20, 2013.

74. Baer RA, Carmody J, Hunsinger M. Weekly change in mindfulness and perceived stress in a mindfulness-based stress reduction program. *J Clin Psychol.* 2012;68:755–765.

75. Baer RA, Lykins ELB. Mindfulness and positive psychological functioning. In: Kashdan T, Steger M, Sheldon KM,

eds. *Designing Positive Psychology: Taking Stock and Moving Forward.* New York, NY: Oxford University Press; 2011:335–348.

76. Chatzisarantis NLD, Hagger MS. Mindfulness and the intention-behavior relationship within the theory of planned behavior. *Pers Soc Psychol Bull.* 2007;33:663–676.

77. Segar ML, Jayaratne T, Hanlon J, Richardson C. Fitting fitness into women's lives: effects of a gender-tailored physical activity intervention. *Women's Health Issues.* 2002;12:338–349.

78. Bargh JA, Gollwitzer PM, Lee-Chai A, et al. The automated will: nonconscious activation and pursuit of behavioral goals. *J Pers Soc Psychol.* 2001; 81:1014–1027.

79. Hofmann W, Friese M, Wiers RW. Impulsive versus reflective influences on health behavior: a theoretical framework and empirical review. *Health Psychol Rev.* 2009;2:111–137.

80. Hofmann W, Friese M, Wiers RW. Impulsive processes in the self-regulation of health behaviour: theoretical and methodological considerations in response to commentaries. *Health Psychol Rev.* 2011;5:162–171.

81. Hofmann W, Friese M, Strack F. Impulse and self-control from a dual-systems perspective. *Perspect Psychol Sci.* 2009;4:162–176.

82. Adriaanse MA, Gollwitzer PM, De Ridder DTD, et al. Breaking habits with implementation intentions: a test of underlying processes. *Pers Soc Psychol Bull.* 2011;37:502–513.

83. Armitage CJ. Evidence that implementation intentions reduce dietary fat intake: a randomized trial. *Health Psychol.* 2004;23:319–323.

84. Bayer UC, Gollwitzer PM. Boosting scholastic test scores by willpower: the role of implementation intentions. *Self Identity.* 2007;6:1.

85. Stadler G, Oettingen G, Gollwitzer PM. Intervention effects of information and self-regulation on eating fruits and vegetables over two years. *Health Psychol.* 2010;29:274–283.

86. Stadler G, Oettingen G, Gollwitzer PM. Physical activity in women: effects of a self-regulation intervention. *Am J Prev Med.* 2009;36:29–34.

87. Buis LR. The potential for Web-based social network sites and self-regulation for health promotion. *Am J Health Promot.* 2011;26:73–76.

88. Richardson CR, Buis LR, Janney AW, et al. An online community improves adherence in an internet-mediated walking program. Part 1: Results of a randomized controlled trial. *J Med Internet Res.* 2010;12:138–153.

89. Kraut R. Research on on-line communities. 2012. Available at: http://kraut.hciresearch.org/content/recent-articles-and-chapters. Accessed February 7, 2013.

90. Latham GP, Locke EA. New developments in and directions for goal-setting research. *Eur Psychol.* 2007;12:290–300.

91. Dweck CS. *Mindset: The New Psychology of Success.* New York, NY; Ballantine Books; 2007.

92. Nakajima M, al'Absi M. Predictors of risk for smoking relapse in men and women: a prospective examination. *Psychol Addict Behav.* 2012;26: 633–637.

93. Eccles JS, Harold RD. Gender differences in sport involvement: applying the Eccles' expectancy-value model. *J Appl Soc Psychol.* 1991;3:7–35.

94. Li KK, Concepcion RY, Lee H, et al. An examination of sex differences in relation to the eating habits

and nutrient intakes of university students. *J Nutr Educ Behav.* 2012;44: 246–250.

95. Segar ML, Updegraff J, Zikmund-Fisher B, Richardson C. Physical activity advertisements that feature daily well-being improve autonomy and body image in overweight women but not men. *J Obes.* 2012;2012:354721.

96. Mackenzie CS, Gekoski WL, Knox VJ. Age, gender, and the underutilization of mental health services: the influence of help-seeking attitudes. *Aging Ment Health.* 2006;10:574–582.

97. Sheldon KM, Elliot AJ. Goal striving, need satisfaction, and longitudinal well-being: the self-concordance model. *J Pers Soc Psychol.* 1999;76:482–497.

CHAPTER

9

Transtheoretical Model

James O. Prochaska and Janice M. Prochaska

INTRODUCTION

What motivates people to change? The answer to this question depends, in part, on where they start. What motivates people to begin thinking about adopting a healthy behavior can be different from what motivates them to begin preparing to take action. Once prepared, different forces can move people to take action. Once action is taken, what motivates people to maintain that action? Conversely, what causes people to regress or relapse to unhealthy behaviors? As individuals become motivated to think, to prepare or to act, what skills are needed to transform motivation into effective action?

To have a significant and sustainable impact on attaining healthy behaviors, a model of behavior change is needed to address the needs of entire workplace populations, not just the minority who are motivated to take immediate action for better health. The foundation of the Transtheoretical Model of Behavior Change (TTM) is the stages of change construct, which categorizes segments of populations based on where they are in the process of change. Principles and processes are applied to initiate

movement through the stages of change. Interventions based on TTM principles can produce programs that are interactive and broadly applicable for treatment of entire populations. The programs include computer tailored interventions (CTIs) delivered through various modalities, such as counselor guidance, telephonic coaching, the Internet, and mobile phones. The programs produce high impact on both single and multiple behaviors for disease prevention and management.

This chapter describes the TTM and all its constructs, reviews TTM's impacts on multiple behavior change programs, applies the TTM to motivation and skill building, and concludes with a discussion of future research issues.

CONCEPTUAL FRAMEWORK: CORE CONSTRUCTS OF THE TRANSTHEORETICAL MODEL

The TTM uses stages to integrate principles and processes of change across major theories of intervention; hence, the name Transtheoretical. This model emerged from a comparative analysis of leading theories grounded in psychotherapy and behavior change. Because more than 300 psychotherapy theories were found, the authors determined that there was a need for systematic integration.[1] Ten processes of change emerged, including consciousness raising from the Freudian tradition, reinforcement management from the Skinnerian tradition, and helping relationships from the Rogerian tradition.

In an empirical analysis of self-changers compared to smokers in professional treatments, researchers assessed how frequently each group used each of the ten processes.[2] Research participants indicated that they used different processes at different times in their struggles with smoking. These naive subjects were teaching us about a phenomenon that was not included in any of the multitude of therapy theories. They were revealing that behavior change unfolds through a series of stages.[3]

The TTM has concentrated on five stages of change, ten processes of change, decisional balance (the pros and cons of changing), self-efficacy, and temptation. Stage of change serves as the key integrating construct. While the time a person can stay in each stage is variable, the tasks required to move to the next stage are not. Certain principles and processes of change work best at each stage to reduce resistance, facilitate progress, and prevent relapse. Typically, only 20% or less of a population at risk is prepared to take action at any given time. Thus, if employers adopt action-oriented interventions they will disserve employees in the early stages. Strategies based on each of the TTM stages result in increased participation in the change process because they are tailored to each individual in the whole workplace population rather than the minority ready to take action. Since its initial development in the early 1980's hundreds of studies have been conducted on the strengths, weaknesses, and applications of the TTM. Some of these will be reviewed later in the chapter.

Stages of Change

The stage construct represents a temporal dimension. Change implies progress occurring over time. Traditionally, behavior change was often construed as an event, such as quitting smoking, drinking or over-eating, but the TTM recognizes change as a process that unfolds over time involving progress through a series of stages.

Precontemplation

People in the Precontemplation stage are not intending to take action in the foreseeable future, usually measured as the next six months. Being uninformed or under-informed about the consequences of one's behavior may cause a person to be in Precontemplation. Multiple unsuccessful attempts at change can lead to demoralization about the ability to change. Both the uniformed and under-informed tend to avoid reading, talking or thinking about their high risk behaviors. They are often characterized in other theories as resistant, unmotivated, or not ready for health promotion programs. The fact is, traditional employee population health promotion programs were not ready for such individuals and were not motivated to meet their needs.

Contemplation

Contemplation is the stage in which people are intending to take action in the next six months. They are more aware of the pros of changing, but are also acutely aware of the cons. In a meta-analysis across 48 health risk behaviors, the pros and cons of changing were equal in the Contemplation stage.[4] This weighting between the costs and benefits of changing can produce profound ambivalence that can cause people to remain in this stage for long periods of time. This phenomenon is often characterized as chronic contemplation or behavioral procrastination. Individuals in Contemplation are not ready for traditional action-oriented programs that expect participants to act immediately.

Preparation

Preparation is the stage in which people are intending to take action in the immediate future, usually measured as the next month. Typically, they have already taken some significant steps toward the behavior in the past year. These individuals have a plan of action, such as joining an exercise class, consulting a counselor, talking to their physician, buying a self-help book, or relying on a self-change approach. These are the employees who should be recruited for action-oriented programs such as traditional smoking cessation or weight-loss classes or clinics offered at worksites.

Action

Action is the stage in which people have made specific overt modifications in their lifestyles within the past six months. Since action is observable, the overall process of behavior change often has been equated with action. But in the TTM, Action is only one of five stages. Typically, not all modifications of behavior count as action in this model. In most applications, people have to attain a criterion that scientists and professionals agree is sufficient to reduce risk of disease. For example, reduction in the number of cigarettes or switching to low tar and nicotine cigarettes were formerly considered acceptable actions for reducing risks. Now the consensus is clear-only total abstinence counts, as those other changes do not necessarily lead to quitting and do not lower the risks associated with smoking as much as possible.

Maintenance

Maintenance is the stage in which people have made specific, overt modifications in their lifestyles, and are working to prevent relapse; however, they do not apply change processes as frequently as do people in Action. They are less tempted to relapse and grow increasingly more confident that they can continue their changes. Based on temptation and self-efficacy data, researchers have estimated that Maintenance lasts from six months to about five years. While this estimate may seem somewhat pessimistic, longitudinal data in the 1990 Surgeon General's report support this temporal estimate.[5]

A naturalistic design was used to follow-up every 12 months a population of smokers who quit on their own. After 12 months of continuous abstinence, 43% returned to regular smoking. It was not until 5 years of continuous abstinence that the risk for relapse dropped to 7 percent.[5]

Termination

Termination is the stage in which individuals are not tempted; they have 100 percent self-efficacy to do the healthy behavior. Whether depressed, anxious, bored, lonely, angry or stressed, individuals in this stage are sure they will not return to unhealthy habits as a way of coping. It is as if the habit was never acquired in the first place or their new behavior has become an automatic habit. Examples include people who have developed automatic seatbelt use or who automatically take their medications at the same time and place each day. In a study of 191 former smokers and alcoholics, researchers found that less than 20 percent of each group had reached the criteria of zero temptation and total self-efficacy.[6] The criterion of 100% self-efficacy may be too strict or it may be that this stage is an ideal goal for population health efforts. In other areas, like exercise, consistent condom use, and weight control, the realistic goal may be a lifetime of maintenance. Termination has not been given as much emphasis in TTM research since it may not be a practical reality for populations and it occurs long after interventions have ended.

Processes of Change

Processes of change are the experiential and behavioral activities that people use to progress through the stages. They provide important guides for intervention programs, serving as independent variables that are applied to move from stage to stage. Ten processes have received the most empirical support in our research to date. These processes come from various therapies[1] and include such theorists as Freud[7], Skinner[8], and Adler.[9]

Consciousness Raising

Consciousness raising involves increased awareness about the causes, consequences, and cures for a particular problem behavior. Interventions that can increase awareness include feedback from medical tests, education, and media campaigns. Sedentary people, for example, may not be aware that their inactivity can have the same risk as smoking a pack of cigarettes a day.

Dramatic Relief

Dramatic relief initially produces increased emotional experiences followed by reduced affect or anticipated relief, if appropriate action is taken, like ceasing the unhealthy behavior. Fear arousing photos on cigarette packs, personal testimonies, and feedback about making progress are examples of techniques that can move people emotionally.

Self-Reevaluation

Self-reevaluation combines both cognitive and affective assessments of one's self-image with and without a particular unhealthy habit, such as one's image as a "couch potato" versus an active person. Values clarification, identifying healthy role models, and imagery are techniques that can help people apply self-reevaluation. One might ask, "Imagine if you were free from smoking – How would you feel about yourself?"

Environmental Reevaluation

Environmental reevaluation combines both affective and cognitive assessments of how the presence or absence of a personal habit affects one's social environment, such as the effect of smoking on others. It can also include the awareness that one can serve as a positive or negative role model for others. Feedback sharing how one's risks compare to other's in the worksite can be helpful.

Social Liberation

Social liberation requires an increase in social opportunities or alternatives, especially for people who are relatively deprived and do not have adequate access to healthy alternatives. Providing healthy foods at discounted prices in the company cafeteria or family memberships to the YMCA are techniques that can increase healthy alternatives or social opportunities. Other policies and procedures can be used to help employee populations change; examples include smoke-free companies and walking paths or gyms in the workplace.

Self-Liberation

Self-liberation is both the belief that one can change and the commitment as well as re-commitment to act on that belief. New Year's resolutions, public testimonies or a contract are ways of enhancing what the public calls willpower. One might say, "Telling others about my commitment to take action can strengthen my willpower. Who am I going to tell?"

Counter Conditioning

Counter conditioning requires learning healthy behaviors as substitutes for problem behaviors. Examples of counter conditioning include nicotine replacement as a safe substitution for smoking or walking as a healthier alternative than "comfort foods" as a way to cope with stress.

Stimulus Control

Stimulus control removes cues for unhealthy habits and adds prompts for healthier alternatives. Examples are putting signs in company cafes that show the amount of calories or saturated fat in different choices.

Reinforcement Management

Reinforcement management provides positive consequences for taking steps in a positive direction. While reinforcement management can include the use of punishment, we found that self-changers rely on reward much more than punishment. Reinforcements are emphasized since a philosophy of the stage model is to work in harmony with how people change naturally. People expect to be reinforced by others more frequently than occurs, so they should be encouraged to reinforce themselves through self-statements like "Nice going – you handled that temptation." They also can treat themselves at milestones as a reinforcement to increase the probability that healthy responses will be repeated. Employers can use incentives to reward employees for participating in health promotion programs or for making actual changes.

Helping Relationships

Helping relationships combine caring, trust, openness, and acceptance, as well as support for healthy behavior change. Exercise teams, supportive calls from coaches, social media, and buddy systems can be sources of social support.

Decisional Balance

The process of reflection and weighing of the pros and cons of changing is decisional balance. Originally, TTM relied on Janis and Mann's model of decision making that included four categories of pros (instrumental gains for self, instrumental gains for others, approval from self, and approval from others).[10] The four categories of cons were instrumental costs to self and instrumental cost to others; and disapproval from self and disapproval from others. In a long series of studies attempting to produce this structure of eight factors, a much simpler structure was almost always found: the pros and cons of changing. Sound decision making requires the consideration of the potential gains (pros) and losses (cons) associated with changing a health risk behavior. For example, there are more than 50 objectively confirmed benefits of regular physical activity.[11] Each of these could become a pro in the decisional balance analysis. The more the list of pros outweighs the cons, the

better prepared one will be to take effective action.

Self-efficacy

Self-efficacy is the situation-specific confidence that people have while coping with high risk situations without relapsing to their unhealthy habit. This construct was integrated from Bandura's self-efficacy theory.[12]

Temptation

Temptation reflects the intensity of urges to engage in a specific habit while in the midst of difficult situations. Typically, three factors reflect the most common types of tempting situations: negative affect or emotional distress, positive social situations, and craving. Individuals can ask themselves how they will cope with emotional distress without relying on cigarettes or comfort foods to help them cope more effectively and thereby build their confidence or self-efficacy.

CRITICAL ASSUMPTIONS OF THE TTM

The Transtheoretical Model is also based on critical assumptions about the nature of behavior change and population health interventions that can best facilitate such change. The following are a set of assumptions that drive Transtheoretical theory, research, and practice:

1. Behavior change is a process that unfolds over time through a sequence of stages. Effective health promotion interventions need to match their help to individuals' stages as they progress over time.
2. Stages can be both stable and subject to change, just as chronic behavioral risk factors are both stable and subject to change. Workplace health initiatives can motivate change by enhancing

the understanding of the pros and diminishing the value of the cons.

3. The majority of at-risk populations are not prepared for action and will not be served by traditional action-oriented prevention programs. Helping individuals set realistic goals, like progressing to the next stage, will facilitate the change process.

4. Specific principles and processes of change need to be emphasized at specific stages for progress through the stages to occur.

These critical assumptions need to be taken into consideration when developing health promotion interventions for behavior change and to facilitate progress through the stages.

REVIEW OF THE EMPIRICAL LITERATURE

Each of the core constructs have been the subject of more than 200 studies across a broad range of behaviors and populations. Studies on the TTM include formative research and measurement, followed by intervention development and refinement, eventually leading to formalized efficacy and effectiveness trials.[13] A sample of those studies are reviewed below.

Stage Distribution

If interventions are to match the needs of entire populations, there is a need to know the stage distributions of specific high-risk behaviors. A series of studies on smoking in the 1980s and 1990s in the U.S. concluded that less than 20 percent of smokers were in the Preparation stage in most populations.[14,15] Approximately 40 percent of smokers were in the Contemplation stage and another 40 percent were in Precontemplation. In countries that have not had a long history of tobacco control campaigns, the stage distributions are even more challenging. In Germany, about 70 percent of smokers were in Precontemplation and about 10 percent of smokers were in Preparation, while in China, more than 70 percent were in Precontemplation and about 5 percent were in Preparation.[16,17] In a study of 15 health risk behaviors among 20,000 members of a Rhode Island HMO, only about 20% to 40% were ready for Action on each specific behavior.[18]

Integration of Pros and Cons and Stages of Change Across 12 Health Behaviors

Stage is not a theory; it is a construct. A theory requires systematic relationships between a set of constructs, ideally culminating in mathematical formulas that describe the relationships between them. Systematic relationships have been found between stages and the pros and cons of changing for 12 health behaviors. For all 12 behaviors, the cons of changing were higher than the pros for people in Precontemplation.[19] For all 12 behaviors, the pros were higher in Contemplation than Precontemplation. From Contemplation to Action for all 12 behaviors, the cons of changing were lower in Action than in Contemplation. For 11 of the 12 behaviors, the pros of changing were higher than the cons for people in Action. These relationships suggest that: to progress from Precontemplation, the pros of changing need to increase; to progress from Contemplation, the cons need to decrease; to progress to Action, the pros need to be higher than the cons. These same patterns of relationships have recently been replicated in a meta-analysis of the pros and cons of changing across the stages of change for 48 different health behaviors.[4]

Relationship Between Stages and Processes of Change

One of the earliest empirical integrations in the development of the TTM was the discovery of systematic relationships between the stages people were in and the processes they were applying.[3] This discovery allowed an integration of processes from theories that were typically seen as incompatible and in conflict. For example, Freudian theory relied almost entirely on consciousness raising for producing change. This theory was viewed as incompatible with Skinnerian theory that relied entirely on reinforcement management for modifying behavior. But self-changers did not know that those processes were theoretically incompatible and their behavior revealed that processes from very different theories needed to be emphasized at different stages of change. This integration suggests that in early stages of health promotion interventions, efforts should support the application of cognitive, affective, and evaluative processes to progress through the stages. In later stages, those programs should rely more on commitments, counter conditioning, rewards, environmental controls, and support to progress toward Maintenance or Termination.

Table 9-1 illustrates the processes that are most effective in helping people progress through each of the stages of change. To help people progress from Precontemplation to Contemplation, processes such as consciousness raising and dramatic relief need to be emphasized. Emphasizing reinforcement management, counter conditioning, and stimulus control processes in Precontemplation would represent a theoretical, empirical, and practical mistake. Conversely, such strategies would be optimally matched for people in Action. Integration of the processes and stages has not been as consistent as the integration of the stages with the pros and cons of changing. One of the problems is that there is great pressure in doing assessments to have as brief of measures as possible, especially when assessing 10 processes. Most often, each process is assessed with the minimum of two questions needed to measure a construct. But, with only two questions, reliability is clearly weakened, because reliability is so strongly related to the number of questions in brief scales. The weaker the reliability, the less consistently are replications likely to be produced. More research is needed to identify which variables, like number of questions used to measure each process, effect the pattern of integration between processes and stages of change.

Table 9-1: Processes of Change That Mediate Progression Between the Stages of Change.

Precontemplation	Contemplation	Preparation	Action	Maintenance
Consciousness Raising				
Dramatic Relief				
Environmental Reevaluation				
	Self-Reevaluation			
		Self-Liberation		
			Counter Conditioning	
			Helping Relationships	
			Reinforcement Management	
			Stimulus Control	

Note: Social Liberation can be helpful across all stages.

APPLIED STUDIES

A large, diverse body of evidence on the application of TTM has revealed several trends. The most common application have involved TTM computerized population level tailored interventions, that match intervention messages to individuals' particular needs across all TTM constructs.[20,21] They combine the best of population health with clinical health to provide individualized help. For example, individuals in Precontemplation could receive feedback designed to increase their pros of changing to help them progress to Contemplation. These interventions originally were printed either on site or mailed to participants at home, however a growing range of applications have been developed and evaluated using real time multimedia, computerized tailored interventions that can be delivered in clinic settings, worksites, schools or online at home.[22,23]

Increasingly, employers and health plans are making such TTM tailored programs available to entire employee populations. A recent meta-analysis of tailored print communications found that the TTM was the most commonly used theory across a broad range of behaviors.[24] TTM or Stage of Change Models were used in 35 of the 53 studies. In terms of effectiveness, significantly greater effect sizes were produced when tailored communications included each of the following TTM constructs: stages of change, pros and cons of changing, self-efficacy, and processes of change.[24] In contrast, interventions that included the non-TTM construct of perceived susceptibility had significantly worse outcomes. Tailoring non-TTM constructs like social norms and behavioral intentions did not produce significant differences.[24]

These findings illustrate the potential of the TTM to improve outcomes. Implementing this approach in workplace health promotion will require shifts in scientific and practice approaches including the following:

- from an action paradigm to a stage paradigm
- from reactive to proactive recruitment of participants
- from expecting participants to match the needs of programs to having programs match their needs
- from clinic-based to work-based behavioral health programs that apply the field's most powerful individualized and interactive intervention strategies; and
- from assuming some groups do not have the ability to change to making sure that all groups have easy accessibility to evidence based programs that provide stage-matched tailored interventions.

STUDIES CHALLENGING THE TRANSTHEORETICAL MODEL

Critics of the TTM have several core concerns. These include how well TTM constructs predict outcomes compared to non-TTM variables and whether TTM constructs (like processes of change) predict progress across stages of change in the way that TTM should predict. Their concerns are supported by some empirical studies, but some of the negative results in these studies can be explained by inappropriate methodology. Others have stronger methodology and provide useful detail that can be used to refine the TTM.

Farkas et al. and then Abrams et al. compared addiction variables to TTM variables as effective predictors of cessation over 12 to 24 months.[25,26] Addiction variables, including the number of cigarettes smoked and duration of prior quits (e.g., more than 100 days) were more effective than TTM variables in predicting cessation rates, suggesting that addiction models were preferable to TTM. Responses to these comparative studies have included concerns that Farkas et al. compared 14 addiction type variables to just the single stage variable from TTM.[27,28] The Abrams et al. study included self-efficacy and the Contemplation Ladder – an alternative measure of readiness or stage, as part of their addiction model, but failed to acknowledge that both of these constructs are part of TTM.[26] Also, from an intervention perspective, the amount of variance accounted for by predictor variables is less important than the amount of variance that can be controlled or changed through an intervention. For example, duration of previous quits (e.g., as 100 days) may be more predictive than stage, little can be done to change this historical variable, while a dynamic variable like stage is responsive to interventions.

In the first of a series of studies, Herzog and colleagues found that six processes of change were not adequate predictors of stage progress over a 12-month period.[29] In a second report, processes predicted stage progress but only when the Contemplation Ladder was used.[30] In the third report, TTM measures predicted 12-month outcomes, but self-efficacy and the Contemplation Ladder were not counted as TTM variables.[26] These findings conflict with other research that has found change processes and other TTM variables predict stage progress.[31-38] Johnson, J. L. et al. (2000) with their study explained some of the inconsistencies in previous research by demonstrating better predictions over 6 months vs. 12 months, and better predictions using all 10 processes of change instead of just a subset.[37]

One of the productive responses to studies critical of the TTM is to conduct further research. In response to the criticism that addiction severity levels are better predictors of long-term outcomes than stage of change, a series of studies was conducted to determine which types of effects predict long-term outcomes across multiple behaviors. To date, four such effects have been found.[39] The first is severity effect, in which individuals with less severe behavior risks at baseline are more likely to progress to Action or Maintenance at 24-month follow-up for smoking, diet, and sun exposure. This effect includes the severity of

addiction that Farkas et al. and Abrams et al. preferred.[25,26] The second is stage effect, in which participants in Preparation at baseline have better 24-month outcomes for smoking, diet, and sun exposure than those in Contemplation, who do better than those in Precontemplation. This effect is what Farkas et al. and Abrams et al. criticized.[25,26] The third is treatment effect, in which participants in treatment do better at 24 months than those randomly assigned to control groups for smoking, diet, and sun exposure. The fourth is effort effects in which participants in both treatment and control groups who progressed to Action and Maintenance at 24 months were making better efforts by using the TTM variables like pros and cons, self-efficacy, and processes at baseline. There were no consistent demographic effects across the three behaviors, indicating that no single demographic group did better across these multiple behaviors. What these results indicate is that either/or thinking (such as either severity or stage) is not as helpful as a more inclusive approach that seeks to identify the most important effects, whether they are based on TTM or on an addiction or severity model. These four effects are now being applied in TTM-tailored interventions for employees and other populations.

INCREASING IMPACTS WITH MULTIPLE BEHAVIOR CHANGE PROGRAMS

One of the greatest challenges for the application of any theory is to keep raising the bar, that is, to be able to increase the theory's impact on enhancing health. One potential is for TTM to treat multiple behaviors in a population, since populations with multiple behavior risks are at greatest risk for both chronic disease and premature death. Those multiple comorbid populations also account for a disproportionate percentage of health care costs. One estimate is that about 60 percent of health care costs are generated by about 15 percent of populations, who have multiple behavior risks and medical conditions.[41]

Historically, studies conducted on multiple behavior changes have been limited by reliance on the action paradigm, and the lack of applying the most promising interventions, such as interactive and individualized TTM-tailored communications.[42] From a TTM perspective, applying an action paradigm to multiple behaviors would indeed risk overwhelming populations, since action is the most demanding stage and taking action on two or more behaviors at once could be overwhelming. Furthermore, among individuals with four-health behavior risks, like smoking, diet, sun exposure, and sedentary lifestyles, less than 10 percent of the population was ready to take action on two or more behaviors.[43] The same thing was true with populations with diabetes who needed to change four behaviors.[44]

With a population of 1,277 overweight and obese patients proactively recruited in the U.S., we applied our first strategy for multiple behavior change. We call this the modular approach, where participants receive a separate TTM computerized tailored intervention (CTI) module for each of their risk behaviors related to healthy weight management. The treatment groups had significant changes at 24 months on healthy eating, exercise, and emotional eating. This study was the first to report results showing significant coaction in the TTM CTI group and significant changes in fruit and vegetable intake that were not treated. Also, this study reported a mean of about 0.8 behaviors changed per participant in the TTM group, which was 60% greater than the 0.5 behaviors in the control group.[45]

One of the most exciting developments in our knowledge of simultaneously changing multiple behaviors is the phenomena of coaction. Coaction is the increased probability that if individuals take effective action on one behavior (like exercise) they are more likely to take action on a secondary behavior (like

diet). We have found that significant coaction typically occurs only in our TTM treatment groups and not in control groups, suggesting it is likely to be treatment induced.[45-47]

With a population of 1,400 employees in a major medical setting, Prochaska's study made available online modular TTM CTIs for each of four behaviors (smoking, inactivity, BMI > 25, and stress) and three Motivational Interviewing (MI) telephonic or in-person sessions.[40] Employees chose which behaviors to target and how much time and effort spent on any behavior. At six months, both treatments outperformed the Health Risk Intervention (HRI) that included feedback on the person's stage for each risk and guidance on how they could progress to the next stage.

With a population of 1,800 students recruited from eight high schools in four states, Mauriello et al. applied a second generation strategy with exercise as the primary behavior receiving three online sessions of fully tailored CTIs.[46] The secondary behaviors of fruit and vegetables (F&V) intake and limited T.V. watching alternated between moderate and minimal (stage only) tailoring. Over the course of the six-month treatment, there were significant treatment effects in each of the three behaviors, but only changes in F & V were sustained at 12 months. Significant coaction was found for each pair of behaviors in the treatment group but none in the control group.

Prochaska et al. recruited 3,391 adults from 39 states who were at-risk for exercise and stress management.[47] This study applied a third generation strategy for multiple tailored behavior change. One treatment group received a fully tailored TTM CTI online for the primary behavior of stress management and only stage-matched for exercise. A second group received three sessions of optimally tailored telephonic coaching for exercise and stage matched for stress. This group also received smart goals for exercise based on the four effects. As noted earlier, the four effects predict long-term success across very different types of behaviors.[39]

Treatment, stage, severity, and effort are the four long-term predictors. Those in treatment are significantly more successful than controls; those in Preparation are more successful than those in Contemplation who are more successful than those in Precontemplation; those with less severe problems are more likely to progress to Action or Maintenance for their problems; and those making better efforts (e.g., on the pros and cons of changing) at baseline are more likely to change. These effects can produce smarter goals early on to help employees complete the intervention, progress from Precontemplation to Contemplation to Preparation, to reduce severity, to make better efforts on using the TTM change variables, and to make more progress across multiple behaviors.

In the Prochaska et al. study, the TTM exercise coaching outperformed the TTM online stress management which outperformed the controls.[48] Also, the exercise coaching produced significant effects on healthy eating and depression management, which were not treated. The mean number of behaviors changed per participant was 1.18 for exercise coaching, .8 for online stress management and .5 for controls. The last two results were remarkably similar to what was found in the Johnson, S.S. et al. study.[45] Finally, the same order of effective treatment was found for enhancing five domains of well-being: emotional health, physical health, life evaluation, thriving, and overall well-being. This study represents the greatest impact to date on decreasing multiple health risk behaviors and increasing multiple domains of well-being.

APPLICATIONS TO MOTIVATION

The stages of change can be applied to identify ways to motivate employees at each phase of planned intervention – recruitment, retention, and progress. More employees can be motivated to participate by changing paradigms and practices. The first paradigm that needs to be changed is the action-oriented paradigm that construes behavior change as an event that can occur quickly, immediately, discretely, and dramatically. The problem is that, with most unhealthy behaviors, fewer than 20% of the affected population is prepared to take action. When only action-oriented interventions are offered, they would usually meet the needs of fewer than 20% of at-risk population. To meet the needs of entire populations, programs must meet the needs of people at all stages of readiness to change, including the majority who are typically in the Precontemplation and Contemplation stages.

When offering programs for at-risk populations in each stage, communication campaigns need to let employees know that the programs can help them regardless of their level of readiness to change. Whether they are ready, getting ready or not ready to take action, the program can be of help. Without such stage-based recruitment messages, employees in Precontemplation or Contemplation are very likely to assume that the programs are action-oriented. Why sign up or show up if you are likely to fail in such a program.

Increasingly, employers have relied on financial incentives to increase motivation for participation in health promotion. From a TTM perspective, this makes sense since employees, by definition, are prepared to trade time for money. But employers are also correctly concerned that the use of such extrinsic motivation can increase participation dramatically, but may not increase successful outcome. So programs are needed that have the potential to transform extrinsic motivation into intrinsic motivation and external or social controls into internal or self controls.

The efforts of the U.S. Air Force to be smoke free provide an encouraging example. In one program, about 30,000 enlisted people were incentivized for being smoke free for the entire six weeks of basic training. Random urine samples were gathered to test for cotinine as biochemical verification of being abstinent. The incentive was powerful: failing the continine test would result in having to repeat basic training. All of the continine tests were negative, showing how powerful social controls and strong incentives can be. But the Air Force was faced with the fact that the recidivism rate at 12 months was very high – about 120%. This meant that some enlisted people started smoking after they enlisted.

To build on the six months of continuous abstinence, a brief but creative intervention was offered to an experimental group of about 7,000 enlisted people. One 45-minute session was spent discussing the pros of staying smoke-free. There were some significant pros or intrinsic incentives, such as smoke-free enlisted were promoted more and could be saving one month's salary. This intervention was mislabeled a relapse prevention program because all of the participants were abstinent in basic training and were assumed to be in the action stage. However, their "action" was under social control, such as external threats of having to repeat basic training. TTM is a model of intentional change where progressing to the action stage is primarily a function of the application of self-controls, like decision making. From a TTM perspective, an intervention designed to significantly increase the pros would be matched mostly to those in the Precontemplation stage who, compared to their peers in other stages, dramatically undervalue the pros. So this program was not effective with the whole population, but it produced about five times greater abstinence at 12-months in the treatment group compared to the control group for those in Precontemplation who were intending to go back to smoking as soon as basic training ended. The program was particularly effective with enlisted people of color. This brief intervention demonstrates how a simple principle of TTM, raising the pros in Precontemplation, can help transform social controls into self controls in the group that was not intending to stay quit.

What motivates employees to continue health behavior-change programs is receiving tailored interventions that match their stage of readiness to change. Our studies have found that stage-related variables were more reliable predictors than demographics, type of risk, severity, and other problem related variables. When interventions are matched to stage, people in the Precontemplation stage complete treatment at the same rates (about 75% to 85%) as those who start in Preparation.[42,49]

We have found that stage predicts the amount of successful action taken during and after intervention and is directly related to the stage of change at which the person started the program. A realistic goal is to help employees progress one stage. By setting goals that people are confident they can achieve, we can increase their motivation to progress. And, as they receive feedback on how they are progressing, we are helping to increase intrinsic motivation. The vast majority of smokers want to quit smoking, but the vast majority (80%) are not prepared to quit. Helping them progress frees them to go from wanting to preparing, and increasing their chances of success. If an employee moves relatively quickly, they may be able to progress two stages. We have found that, the likelihood of reaching action criteria (like abstinence) by six months is doubled for those who progress one stage in the first month. If they progress two stages, the likelihood that they will reach the action criteria increases about three times. Setting stage-matched goals enables more employees to enter a program, continue in a program, progress in a program, and continue to progress after the program ends.

One result for health professionals trained in the TTM can be a dramatic increase in their morale. They can see progress with most clients where they once saw failure when immediate action was the only criterion for success. They are much more confident that they have programs that can match the stages of all of their employees rather than the small number who are prepared to take immediate action.

A lesson here is that the models of behavior change selected should be good for the mental health of the health promotion professional as well as the employees. If health promotion professionals feel pressured to produce immediate action and transfer their pressure, most employees will not be reached, retained or changed. A majority can be helped to progress through relatively brief encounters, but only if realistic goals are set for both employees and the health promotion professionals. Otherwise, there is a risk of demoralizing and de-motivating both employees and health providers. Given the vast public health needs, another misuse is to limit programs only to those who are prepared to take immediate action.

APPLICATIONS TO SKILL BUILDING

The overarching skill in our TTM programs is teaching participants how to change. Our assumption is that the number one reason that the majority of people fail when they try to change is that they don't know how. When we ask public audiences how many have learned about the stages of change, only about 10% know about the stages. We find that the public continues to equate change with taking action. So, the first skill we teach is cognitive restructuring from an action model of behavior change to a stage model where change is understood as a process that unfolds over time and involves progress through a series of stages.

What others call skills, TTM usually labels as techniques for implementing principles and processes for progressing. Theoretically, there are an unlimited number of techniques, but only a limited number of dynamic constructs (like stages, pros and cons, self-efficacy, and processes of change) that drive change. TTM provides a systematic framework for applying techniques or building skills from across very different theories and approaches to health promotion. It is not particularly helpful to provider or participant to have a long laundry list of techniques that can be applied via what is called kitchen sink eclecticism, where a multitude of techniques are applied over time. With TTM, individuals are taught at least one technique or skill for applying each principle or process of change that can produce progress at a particular stage of change.

Imagine an employer wants you to help employees become proactive as health consumers. As discussed earlier, with employees who are in Precontemplation for making a particular behavior change, the first principle of progress that we emphasize are related to more intentional and effective decision making. One of the more innovative applications of TTM is a program designed to help employees become proactive health consumers.[50] This challenge includes helping employees to be proactive about their health by changing risk behaviors, which has been the primary emphasis of health promotion. It also includes being proactive about their health care so that they can get the best care at the best price for both preventing and managing chronic diseases. This requires skills in informed decision making and shared decision making.

As health care reform moves increasingly to Patient Centered Medical Homes and Accountable Care Organizations, providers and patients will need to change from a passive-reactive model of health and health care, where patients and providers react when the patient is feeling acutely ill, distressed or in pain. The passive patient is told what to do by the provider and reacts appropriately, if compliant (or in the Preparation stage), for a particular prescription.

Helping participants to be skilled in informed decision making starts with considerable consciousness raising in the form of education and information. The TTM program provides easy and immediate access to Internet sites that provide reliable and valid information for a broad range of health concerns. A concrete example is a 55-year old man who is getting pressure from his wife to get a PSA test to screen for prostate cancer. He goes on the Internet and learns that the U.S. Preventive Task Force recently changed with new recommendations that PSA testing not be given nationally to entire populations of men 50 and older, but only for those at high risk. The Task Force concluded that such routine prevention screening produced more harm than good and more costs than benefits. Our example may be asked a dramatic relief question about how he would feel about talking with his primary care physician to make a shared decision about whether he should have PSA screening. This individual may anticipate anxiety, because his self-image is that a good patient follows what his doctor orders. He can then be provided with strategies that activate self-re-evaluation, where he imagines starting to become more proactive and prepared for shared decision making.

Before he can make a commitment to share his decision with his doctor, this individual is provided counter conditioning exercises, where he practices how he might imagine being more assertive with this doctor. Such covert rehearsal can better prepare him to follow through on a commitment (self-liberation).He also spends some time considering who might provide a helping relationship to support him in the changes he is making. He may imagine his doctor's nurse with whom he could first start his discussion. Next, he imagines being reinforced by his wife and the nurse for the steps he is taking. More importantly, he begins to reinforce himself for all the progress he is making and imagines how much better he will feel as he becomes more skilled in informed and shared decision making. This includes the anticipation that he will be a more responsible health consumer who will increase the chances that he gets the best care at the best price.

Next we will shift from skill development at the individual employee level to the employer level. Many employers do not have human resources staff who have sufficient skills to

be informed decision makers to recommend high impact health promotion programs. Employers may be hearing from experts in the field that behavior change programs for health promotion do not work. Companies often turn to Benefits Brokers, who advise companies about wellness programs. Many brokers, however, apply a method that just checks off that a program includes: HRA with feedback (✓); 2. Telephonic coaching (✓); 3. Virtual coaching online (✓) or with mobile devices (✓), etc. Health promotion programs are often treated as commodities where there are no real differences in outcomes, only differences in costs.

Contrast that with a decision-making method that is rapidly emerging. This approach involves bench marking where employers making decisions about which health promotion program to adopt can compare the expected outcomes of a particular program against benchmarks. This approach has been advanced most by the National Task Force for Community Preventive Services (CHES) that is developing bodies of evidence for recommendations, expectations, and evaluations for population-based health promotion programs.[51]

One CHES team has developed a body of evidence that can serve as a benchmark for multiple behaviors (e.g., exercise, high fat diets, fruits and vegetables, and smoking) that were treated by the most common types of health promotion programs for populations of employees.[52] These interventions include health risk assessments with feedback (HRAF) repeated at least twice plus at least one additional health promotion intervention. This body of evidence can serve as a benchmark for average effects that employers could expect if they chose one of the most common types of health promotion programs.

Figure 9-1 presents the average outcomes at long-term follow-ups (about 2.75 years) for four risk behaviors (solid bar). Figure 9-1 also includes the results from the body of

Figure 9-1: **Comparative Outcomes of Health Promotion Interventions.**

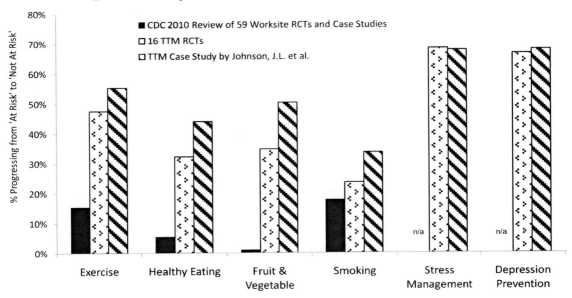

Johnson, J.L., Prochaska, J.O., Paiva, A.L., Fernandez, A.C., DeWees, S.L., and Prochaska, J.M. (2013) Advancing Bodies of Evidence for Population-based Health Promotion Programs: Randomized Controlled Trials and Case Studies. Population Health Management, 16, 373-380.

evidence we have developed in applying our TTM-based CTIs in population-based randomized controlled trials with 26 outcomes on six behaviors (smoking, high-fat diet, F/V, exercise, stress management, and depression prevention).[53] The patterned bars represent the average outcomes across trials for each behavior. Those outcomes can serve as benchmarks for our best practice of applying TTM CTIs to multiple health risk behaviors.

Figure 9-1 also includes the long-term outcomes from a real world dissemination study which applied our TTM CTIs to an employee population located in 23 sites across the U.S. In this case study, employees were motivated to participate starting in the first month with just an HRAF and biometrics then at least one session of a TTM CTI or coaching call the second year, and from year 3 on having to complete the HRAF, biometrics, plus three sessions of a TTM online session or

coaching call. (Over 80% of employees chose the online program). Figure 9-1 demonstrates clearly that our TTM-tailored population trials consistently produced much higher success rates (percent progressing from at-risk to health criteria at follow-up) than the average in the CHES/Soler et al. study.[52]

Figure 9-1 also shows that in the real world dissemination study the outcomes for four behaviors were higher than what we produced in our population trials and about equal to our results with stress and depression.[50-53] This type of graph can add benchmarks from bodies of evidence applying health promotion programs based on different theories and different treatment modalities. Decision makers can compare the results of their current programs to see if they are performing below average, above average or near or above benchmarks for best practices. They can also compare alternative approaches that they are considering to make much more informed decisions about the magnitude of outcomes they would be likely to attain from alternative interventions they are considering.

UNANSWERED QUESTIONS AND FUTURE RESEARCH

While research results to date are encouraging, much still needs to be done to advance behavior change through evidence-based efforts such as the Transtheoretical Model. Basic research needs to be done with other theoretical variables, such as processes of resistance, incentives, and problem severity, to determine if such variables relate systematically to the stages and if they predict progress across particular stages. More research is needed on the structure or integration of the processes and stages of change across a broad range of behaviors, including acquisition behaviors such as exercise, and extinction behaviors like what has been accomplished for smoking cessation.[54] Research needs to focus on modifications that may be needed in how TTM is applied to better address specific types of behaviors.

Since tailored communications represent the most promising interventions for applying TTM to entire populations, more research is needed comparing the effectiveness, efficiency, and impacts of alternative technologies. The Internet is excellent for individualized interactions at low cost but without incentives has not produced the high participation rates generated by person-to-person outreach via telephone or visits to primary care practitioners. Increasingly, employers are incentivizing employee populations to participate in more integrated Internet, telephone, and provider programs. Interventions that were once seen as applicable only on an individual basis are being applied as high impact programs for population health.

As TTM-tailored interventions are applied to more populations, research is needed on how diverse populations respond to stage-matched interventions and to high tech systems. Studies are needed on how programs might best be tailored to meet the needs of diverse populations. Comparing menus of alternative intervention modalities (e.g. telephone, Internet, mobile phones, person to person or workplace) may empower diverse populations to best match health-enhancing programs to their particular needs.

Changing multiple behaviors represents special challenges, such as the number of demands placed on participants and providers. Alternative strategies need to be tried beyond the sequential (one at a time) and simultaneous (all treated intensely at the same time). Integrative approaches are promising. For example, with the program Mastering Change in the Workplace, there are multiple behaviors (that is, being an ongoing learner, collaborative teamwork, and stress management skills) that need to be intervened on.[55] An integrated approach is needed to address change in the workplace. If behavior change is construct-driven (e.g., by stage or self-efficacy), what is a higher order construct that could integrate those more concrete behaviors? We are presently testing the concept of "living well" with college students as they work on the multiple behaviors of stress management, exercise, and healthy eating. As with any theory, effective applications may be limited more by our creativity than by the ability of the theory to drive significant research and effective interventions.

CONCLUSION

In this chapter, we described the fifteen core constructs of the TTM and how those constructs can be integrated across the stages of change. Empirical support for the basic constructs of TTM and for applied research was presented, along with conceptual and empirical challenges from critics of TTM. Applications of TTM-tailored interventions with entire workplace populations were explored with examples for single behaviors and for multiple health-risk behaviors. A major theme is that programmatically building and applying the core constructs of TTM at the individual level can ultimately lead to high-impact programs for enhancing health and well-being at the population level.

The Transtheoretical Model is a dynamic theory of change and it must remain open to modifications and enhancements as more students, scientists, and practitioners apply the stage paradigm to a growing number of diverse theoretical issues, public health problems, and at-risk populations.

Glossary

Accountable Care Organizations (ACOs): Groups of providers (e.g., physicians and hospitals) that agree to take collective responsibility for delivering and coordinating care for a designated population, and are held to benchmark levels of quality and cost.

Action Stage (overt changes): Individuals in this stage are overtly engaged in modifying their problem behaviors or acquiring new, healthy behaviors.

Coaction: The increased probability that if individuals take effective action on one behavior, they are more likely to take action on a second behavior.

Computerized Tailored Interventions (CTIs): CTIs use a computer to create individually tailored feedback from a feedback library using algorithms and pre-programmed, statistically derived decision rules.

Consciousness Raising Process: Finding and learning new facts, ideas, and tips that support the healthy behavior change.

Contemplation Stage (getting ready): Individuals in this stage are more likely to recognize the benefits of changing but still overestimate the costs of changing, and

therefore, are ambivalent and not yet ready to take action.

Counter Conditioning Process: Substituting healthier thoughts and behaviors for unhealthy thoughts and behaviors.

Decisional Balance: The process of reflection in weighing the pros and cons of the behavior change.

Dramatic Relief Process: Experiencing the negative emotions (e.g., fear, anxiety, worry) that go along with unhealthy behavioral risks or the positive emotions (e.g., inspiration) that go along with success in changing.

Environmental Reevaluation Process: Realizing the negative impact of the unhealthy behavior or the positive impact of the healthy behavior on one's social and phycical environment.

Maintenance Stage (keeping up the changes): Individuals in this stage have been able to sustain action for a while and are actively striving to prevent relapse.

Modular Multiple Behavior Change: Where participants receive a separate intervention for each of their risk behaviors.

Patient Centered Medical Homes: A health care setting that facilitates partnerships between individual patients and their personal physicians, and when appropriate, the patient's family to provide comprehensive patient centered care and coordinated care.

Precontemplation Stage (not ready): Individuals in this stage are not intending to take action in the foreseeable future.

Preparation Stage (ready): Individuals in this stage have decided to make a behavior change in the near future and have already begun to take small steps toward that goal.

Processes of Change: Ten cognitive, affective, and behavioral activities that people use to progress through the stages.

Reinforcement Management Process: Increasing the intrinsic and extrinsic rewards for the positive behavior change and decreasing the rewards for the unhealthy behavior.

Self-Efficacy: Confidence to make and sustain the new healthy behavior in difficult situations.

Self-Liberation Process: Believing in one's ability to change and making commitments based on those beliefs.

Self-Reevaluation Process: Realizing that the behavior change can enhance one's identity.

Stages of Change: Represents a temporal dimension – Readiness to take action.

Stimulus Control Process: Modifying one's environment to facilitate the healthy behavior and to reduce cues to engage in the unhealthy behavior.

Social Liberation Process: Realizing that social norms and environments are changing to support the healthy behavior change.

Termination Stage: Individuals are no longer tempted and have 100% self-efficacy to do the healthy behavior. This may not be achievable for some health risks and typically occurs long after interventions have ended.

Transtheoretical: Integration of processes and principles of change across major theories of intervention.

Transtheoretical Model of Behavior Change: A model that addresses the needs of the entire workplace population, not just the minority who are motivated to take immediate action for better health.

Learning Objectives:

1. To understand the core constructs of the Transtheoretical Model of Behavior Change

2. To learn about breakthroughs with the Transtheoretical Model from the 1980s to the present
3. To begin learning skills to master motivation and change

Discussion Questions:

1. What are the advantages of a stage paradigm vs. an action-oriented paradigm?
2. Historically, it was thought one could only change one behavior at a time. Evidence is now showing that multiple behavior change can happen. What are some new ideas that make this possible?
3. What stage of change are you in for a health risk behavior that you have? What TTM processes of change could you use to get to the next stage of change?

REFERENCES

1. Prochaska JO. *Systems of Psychotherapy: A Transtheoretical Analysis, 7th Edition.* Pacific Grove, CA: Brooks-Cole; 2009.
2. DiClemente CC, Prochaska JO. Self-change and therapy change of smoking behavior. A comparison of processes of change in cessation and maintenance. *Addict Behav.* 1982; 7: 133-142. doi:10.1016/0306-4603(82)90038-7.
3. Prochaska JO, DiClemente CC. Stages and processes of self-change of smoking: Toward an integrative model of change. *J Consult Clin Psychol.* 1983; 51: 390-395.
4. Hall KL, Rossi JS. Meta-analytic examination of the strong and weak principles across 48 health behaviors. *Prev Med.* 2008; 46(3): 266-274.
5. U.S. Department of Health and Human Services (DHHS). *The health benefits of smoking cessation: a report of the Surgeon General.* Washington, DC: U.S. Government Printing Office; 1990; 596.

6. Snow MG, Prochaska JO, Rossi JS. Stages of change for smoking cessation among former problem drinkers: A cross-sectional analysis. *J Subst Abuse*. 1992; 4: 107-116.

7. Freud A. *The ego and the mechanism of defense*. New York: International Universities Press; 1936.

8. Skinner BF. *Beyond freedom and dignity*. New York: Vintage; 1971.

9. Alder A. *Problems of neurosis*. London: Kegan Paul; 1929.

10. Janis IL, Mann L. *Decision Making: A Psychological Analysis of Conflict, Chance and Commitment*. London: Cassil & Collier Macmillen; 1977.

11. Pro-Change Behavior Systems, Inc. A Guide for Exercising Regularly. South Kingstown, RI; 2009.

12. Bandura A. Selfefficacy mechanism in human agency. *Am Psychol*. 1982; 37: l22l47. doi:10.1037/0003-066X.37.2.122.

13. Redding CA, Maddock JE, Rossi JS. The sequential approach to measurement of health behavior constructs: issues in selecting and developing measures. *Californian J Health Promot*.2006; 4(1): 83-101.

14. Velicer WF, Fava JL, Prochaska JO, et al. Distribution of smokers by stage in three representative samples. *Prev Med*. 1995; 24: 401-411.

15. Wewers ME, Stillman FA, Hartman AM, Shopland DR. Distribution of daily smokers by stage of change: Current population survey results. *Prev Med*. 2003; 36: 710-720. doi:10.1016/S0091-7435(03)00044-6.

16. Etter J-F, Perneger TV, Ronchi A. Distributions of smokers by stage: International comparison and association with smoking prevalence. *Prev Med*. 1997; 26: 580-585.

17. Yang G, Ma J, Chen A, et al. Smoking cessation in China: Findings from the 1996 national prevalence survey. *Tob Control*. 2001; 10(2): 170-174. doi:10.1136/tc.10.2.170.

18. Rossi JS. Stages of change for 15 health risk behaviors in an HMO population. Paper presentation at 13th meeting of the Society for Behavioral Medicine; 1992; New York, NY.

19. Prochaska JO, Velicer WF, Rossi JS, et al. Stages of change and decisional balance for twelve problem behaviors. *Health Psychol*. 1994; 13: 39-46.

20. Kreuter MW, Strecher VJ, Glassman B. One size does not fit all: The case for tailoring print materials. *Ann Behav Med*. 1999; 21(4): 276-283. doi:10.1007/BF02895958.

21. Skinner CS, Campbell MD, Rimer BK, Curry S, Prochaska JO. How effective is tailored print communication? *Ann Behav Med*. 1999; 21(4): 290-298. doi:10.1007/BF02895960.

22. Velicer WF, Prochaska JO, Bellis JM, et al. An expert system intervention for smoking cessation. *Addict Behav*. 1993; 18: 269-290.doi:10.1016/0306-4603(93)90029-9.

23. Mauriello LM, Sherman KJ, Driskell MM, Prochaska JM. Using interactive behavior change technology to intervene on physical activity and nutrition with adolescents. *Adolesc Med*. 2007; 8: 383-399. PMID: 18605653.

24. Noar SM, Benac C, Harris M. Does tailoring matter? Meta-analytic review of tailored print health behavior change interventions. *Psychol Bull*. 2007; 133(4): 673-693.

25. Farkas AJ, Pierce JP, Zhu SH, et al. Addiction versus stages of change models in predicting smoking cessation. *Addiction*. 1996; 91: 1271-1280. doi:10.1046/j.1360-0443.1996.91912713.x.

26. Abrams DB, Herzog TA, Emmons KM, Linnan L. Stages of change versus addiction: A replication and extension.

Nicotine Tob Res. 2000; 2:223-229. doi:10.1080/14622200050147484.

27. Prochaska JO, Velicer WF. On models, methods and premature conclusions. *Addictions.* 1996; 91: 1281-1283. PMID: 8854359.

28. Prochaska JJ, Velicer WF, Prochaska JO, Delucchi K, Hall SM. Comparing intervention outcomes in smokers treated for single versus multiple behavioral risks. *Health Psychol.* 2006; 25(3): 380-388. doi:10.1037/0278-6133.25.3.380.

29. Herzog TA, Abrams DB, Emmons KA, Linnan L, Shadel WG. Do processes of change predict stage movements? A prospective analysis of the transtheoretical model. *Health Psychol.* 1999; 18: 369-375. doi:10.1037/0278-6133.18.4.369.

30. Herzog TA, Abrams DB, Emmons KA, Linnan L. Predicting increases in readiness to quit smoking: A prospective analysis using the contemplation ladder. *Psychol Health*; 2000: 15(3): 369-381.

31. Prochaska JO, DiClemente CC, Velicer WF, Ginpil S, Norcross JC. Predicting change in smoking status for self changers. *Addict Behav.* 1985; 10: 407412. PMID: 4091072. doi:10.1016/0306-4603(85)90036-X.

32. Prochaska JO, Velicer WF, Guadagnoli E, Rossi JS, DiClemente CC. Patterns of change: Dynamic typology applied to smoking cessation. *Multivariate Behav Res.* 1991; 26: 83-107. doi:10.1207/s15327906mbr2601_5.

33. Prochaska JO, Velicer WF, Rossi JS, et al. Impact of simultaneous stage-matched expert system interventions for smoking, high fat diet, and sun exposure in a population of parents. *Health Psychol.* 2004; 23(5): 503-516. doi:10.1037/0278-6133.23.5.503.

34. Prochaska JO, Wright JA, Velicer WF. Evaluating theories of health behavior change: A hierarcl of criteria applied to the transtheoretical model. *Applied Psychology: An International Review.* 2008; 57(4): 561-588.doi:10.1111/j. 1454-0597.2008.00345x.

35. DiClemente CC, Prochaska JO, Fairhurst SK, Velicer WF, Valesquez MM, Rossi JS. The processes of smoking cessation: An analysis of precontemplation, contemplation, and preparation stages of change. *J Consult Clin Psychol.* 1991; 59: 295-304. doi:10.1037/0022-006X.59.2.295.

36. Dijkstra A, Conijm B, De Vries H. A match-mismatch test of a stage model of behavior change in tobacco smoking. *Addiction.* 2006; 101: 1035-1043. doi:10.1111/j.1360-0443.2006.01419.x.

37. Johnson JL, Regan R, Maddock JE, et al. What predicts stage of change for smoking cessation? *Ann Behav Med.* 2000; 22: S173. (Abstract).

38. Sun X, Prochaska JO, Velicer WF, Laforge RG. Transtheoretical principles and processes for quitting smoking: A 24-month comparison of a representative sample of Quitters, Relapsers and Non-Quitters. *Addict Behav.* 2007; 32:2707-2726. doi:10.1016/j.addbeh.2007.04.005.

39. Blissmer B, Prochaska JO, Velicer WF, et al. Common factors predicting long-term changes in multiple health behaviors. *J Health Psychol.* 2010; 15: 201-214. doi:10.1177/1359105309345555.

40. Prochaska JO, Butterworth S, Redding CA, et al. Initial efficacy of MI, TTM tailoring and HRI's with multiple behaviors for employee health promotion. *Prev Med.* 2008; 45: 226-231. doi:10.1016/j.ypmed.2007.11.007.

41. Edington DW. Emerging research: A view from one research center. *Am J Health Promot.*2001; 15(5): 341-349.

42. Prochaska JO, Velicer WF, Fava JL, et al. Counselor and stimulus control enhancements of a stage-matched expert system for smokers in a managed care setting. *PrevMed.* 2000; 32: 39-46.

43. Prochaska JO, Velicer WF. The transtheoretical model of health behavior change. *Am J Health Promot*. 1997; 12(1): 38-48. doi:10.4278/0890-1171-12.1.38.

44. Ruggiero L, Glasgow R, Dryfoos JM, et al. Diabetes self-management: Self-reported recommendations and patterns in a large population. *Diabetes Care*. 1997; 20(4): 568-576. doi:10.2337/diacare.20.4.568.

45. Johnson SS, Paiva AL, Cummins CO, et al. Transtheoretical model-based multiple behavior intervention for weight management: Effectiveness on a population basis. *Prev Med*. 2008; 46: 238-246. doi:10.1016/y.ypmed.2007.09.010.

46. Mauriello LM, Ciavatta MMH, Paiva AL, et al. Results of a multi-media multiple behavior obesity prevention program for adolescents. *Prev Med*. 2010; 51: 451-456. doi:10.1016/j.ypmed.2010.08.004.

47. Velicer, WF, Redding, CA, Paiva, AL, Mauriello, LM, Blissmer, B, Oatley, K, Meier, KS, Babbin, SF, McGee, H, Prochaska, JO, Burditt, C, & Fernandez, AC. Multiple Behavior Interventions to Prevent Substance Abuse and Increase Energy Balance Behaviors in Middle School Students. *Translational Behavioral Medicine: Practice, Policy and Research*. 2013; 01: 82-93.

48. Prochaska JO, Ever KE, Castle PH, et al. Enhancing multiple domains of well-being by decreasing multiple health risk behaviors. *Popul Health Manag*.2012; 15: 276-286.

49. Prochaska JO, Velicer WF, Fava JL et al. Evaluating a population-based recruitment approach and a stage-based expert system intervention for smoking cessation. *Addict Behav*. 2002; 26: 583-602.

50. Johnson SS, Cummins CO, Evers KE, Prochaska JM, Prochaska JO. Proactive Health Consumerism: An important new tool for worksite health promotion. *Am J Health Promot*. 2009; 23: 1-8.

51. Briss, P.A., ZaZa, S., Pappaioanou, M., et al. (2000). Developing an evidence-based Guide to Community Preventive Services – methods. *Am J Prev Med*.18(S1), S35-S43.

52. Soler RE, Leeks KD, Razi S, et al. A systematic review of selected interventions for worksite health promotion. The assessment of health risk feedback. *Am J Prev Med*. 2010; 38: S237-S262.

53. Johnson JL, Prochaska JO, Paiva AL, Fernandez AC, DeWees SJ, Prochaska JM. Advancing Bodies of Evidence for Population-based Health Promotion Programs: Randomized Controlled Trials and Case Studies. *Popul Health Manag*. 2013; 16: 373-380.

54. Rosen CS. Is the sequencing of change processes by stage consistent across health problems? A meta-analysis. *Health Psychol*. 2000; 19: 593-604. doi:10.1037/0278-6133.19.6.593.

55. Pro-Change Behavior Systems, Inc. Mastering Change: A Guide to Mastering Change in the Workplace. South Kingstown, RI; 2006.

CHAPTER
10

Intrinsic and Extrinsic Incentives in Workplace Health Promotion

Colleen M. Seifert and Joseph K. Hart

INTRODUCTION

Workplace health programs are designed around a goal that is common to both employers and employees: Improving individual health. To do so, the majority of worksite health promotion programs provided by large employers (over 1000 employees) use some sort of financial incentives for participation in health management programs, and fully 80% planned to do so in 2012.[1] Participation rates more than double for biometric screenings and health risk assessments when financial incentives are offered.[2] However, financial incentives might not be enough to drive fundamental changes in health behaviors, such as smoking cessation or disease and weight management programs. Even though participation would benefit employees and their employers, less than 20% of employees take advantage of these program opportunities.[3] Employees' lack of interest or reluctance to participate in health and wellness programs appears to be the main obstacle to changing health behaviors.[4] When they do participate, it is often because additional incentives are added to the program.

Why are incentives so important to workplace health promotion? It appears the fault lies not in the programs, but in human nature. In every arena of human behavior, people operate differently when they "should," compared to when they "want to." No one stays up late flossing, misses work to count their calories, or hides salads in their desk drawer at work. There are many "shoulds" in life that people may avoid, including taxes, church attendance, and spending time with family. The "stick" of the law, guilt, and social pressure are all tools used to help people perform tasks they should. Because it is more practical, programs turn to *incentives*, or rewards for behavior, to motivate individuals. In this sense, health promotion programs are no different from the many other activities in which people do not pursue the behaviors they "should."

The puzzling piece of this picture is that people also "want" to be healthy. They want to feel and look good, live as long as possible, and avoid negative health issues. So why do we need to pay people to pursue health goals? Participating in workplace programs results in better health, a highly positive reward; so, why are added incentives needed? This core question requires learning more about the nature of human motivation, and the roles of intrinsic and extrinsic incentives. This chapter starts with a review of major psychological theories of motivation as they relate to incentives. Next, the success of both intrinsic and extrinsic motivation in studies of health behavior change is reviewed. Finally, these concepts are applied to motivational theory, skill building, and initiating behavior change. The goal of the chapter is to review the complex issues of human motivation and the use of incentives, and provide a practical guide for making use of this knowledge within workplace health promotion programs.

CONCEPTUAL FRAMEWORK: INTRODUCTION AND HISTORICAL FOUNDATION OF THEORIES OF MOTIVATION

Imagine your life without alarm clocks, cell phones, or schedules. What would you do first when you awake? Biological needs for maintaining your body would likely come first, such as satisfying thirst and hunger, keeping warm or cool, and eating. Once beyond biological needs, you may soon want to talk to someone you care about (social belonging motivation[5]), or eventually feel the need to accomplish something during your day (achievement motivation[6]). How can we capture the variety of factors giving rise to our decisions to act?

Motivation is an inner state that arouses, directs, and maintains behavior.[7] Motivation is also related to a *goal*, or an intention or outcome that you desire, such as being financially independent, in a happy relationship, or getting the high score in a video game. Motivation affects behavior by directing it towards the goal, increasing effort, energy, and persistence, and improving performance. A critical aspect of motivation for health programs is that motivation determines *when* behaviors are likely to begin.

Just about any goal can be termed a motive for action as long as the person *chooses* to pursue it. Importantly, motivation is considered to arise with no external force compelling any action (that is, no one has a gun to your head). So it is *volitional,* occurring based on the individual's choice. By definition, motivation is an account of why we voluntarily choose to perform certain behaviors rather than others, and why we choose to act, or not to act. Even when the external environment is designed to maximize the likelihood of some behavior, the internal desire to pursue some goals and not others resides with the individual. As many health program managers know, "If you build it, it *doesn't* mean they will come." So what goes on within the individual such that motivation arises to spur action?

Cognitive Theories of Motivation

Many theories have been proposed to explain how and why people choose to perform specific behaviors when they do so. Many take a cognitive approach to motivation, rather than, for example, a biological approach. In a cognitive theory, thinking drives motivations. Taking the model of the human as active, curious, and responsive to perceptions, these theories explain motivation in terms of the goals, expectations, and explanations people generate. That is, people don't just "do;" instead, they "do for a reason." In fact, people so constantly generate explanations of their own behavior that they do so even when the behavior is actually motivated by chance. For example, in a supermarket study, people were asked to choose between two nylon stockings that were actually identical. They obliged, and when asked why they chose the one they did, they explained how the stocking they chose was superior to the other.[8] People want to know the *why* of their own behavior as well as others'. The need to understand and make sense of the world is central to cognitive theories of motivation.

These theories emphasize particular aspects of motivation, and suggest different strategies for health promotion.

Expectancy-Value Theory

Expectancy-Value Theory begins with the assumption that every person has a need for achievement, but in differing amounts.[9] Some people are motivated to appear at the top of the class, while others set their goal as a good performance. Expectancy-value Theory emphasizes two sources of motivation: Expectancy of success, and the value of that success. This is obviously a very individualized view in which the value of success can be very different for different individuals. Value is also affected by the perceived costs of pursuing the goal, which will again differ from person to person. What is given up by engaging in a behavior? If the costs are perceived as too high, the person may avoid the activity. Task value is further identified as attainment value, interest value, or utility value. So, the task may be seen as valuable because achieving it creates value (completing a marathon), allows you to go on to other goals (learning to swim in order to surf), or is inherently interesting.

These two factors combine to produce motivation towards a goal. They answer the question, "Why should I do this task?" If the task value and expectation for success are both high, high motivation will result, with more persistence and great effort expended. If both are low, then the resulting motivation is low, and the individual may decide not to participate. Expectancy-Value Theory would dictate several principles for health program design:

- Avoid "One Size Fits All" programs: Tailor programs to individuals' needs and values.
- Allow participants to assign their own personal value for the tasks.
- Help participants define tasks with high expectancy for success.

Attribution Theory

Attribution theory accounts for motivation through what people *believe* about why they succeed or fail at different tasks.[10] For example, if a person decides not to go to the gym today, she or he may attribute this action as resulting from getting out of work too late, or by condemning a weak will. An early theory called Locus of Control[11] noted that people differed in how they explained their successes and failures. People with high internal locus of control may blame a success or failure on an internal factor like will power, while people with high external locus of control may blame an external factor, like schedule. As a consequence, people may create different predictions about their future behavior depending on their perception of locus of control. If the problem is weak will (internal), then a person will likely feel they will not succeed in exercising tomorrow either; but, if the schedule is the problem (external), then they will feel more optimistic. A similar distinction is made between seeing the causes of events as localized in the present, or due to a more general, global cause. If a failure is explained as a local effect (the bus was late), execution of the plan successfully tomorrow may be anticipated. But, if the failure is seen as arising from a more global cause (such as fatigue from work), future failures may be anticipated. Finally, the stability of the attribution matters; missing a workout due to a rare late workday may preserve optimism for the future compared to attributing the cause to a demanding job.

In investigations of attributions, several patterns have been discovered. In general, people tend to attribute their successes to internal causes ("I worked hard") and failures to external causes ("The task was too hard").[12] People take credit for their successes, and blame the world for their failures. But attribution theory is most relevant when it comes to expectations for future success. In particular, when people feel the causes for failures are outside of their control and are unlikely to change, they have little motivation to try to change their behaviors. Rather than "mind over matter," attribution theory suggests, "Minds matter." People's beliefs about their future success play an important role in determining how hard they try to achieve it.[13] Some suggestions for health promotion programs from Attribution Theory include:

- Recognize participants' ability and effort as sources of their success.
- Help participants evaluate their failures when they occur.
- Determine realistic expectations for future behavior.

Protection-Motivation Theory (PMT)

When attributions and expectancies are focused on a threat, people are motivated to protect themselves from danger and fear. Just like other beliefs, how people think about negative threats to well-being can affect their motivation to resolve them. People "differ in their sensitivity and vulnerability to certain types of events, as well as in their interpretations and reactions."[14] In the case of Protection Motivation Theory (PMT), people's attributions or "appraisals" of threats make a difference in their ability to cope with or respond effectively to them.[15] PMT suggests that people try to control both the danger and the fear associated with the threat. As an extension of Expectancy-Value theory, PMT emphasizes people's own explanations and attributions, with the potential to lead to maladaptive behaviors such as avoiding the health *message* rather than the actual behavior.

Originally developed as a model of persuasion, Protection Motivation Theory has been developed extensively in the health promotion field as a means of influencing individuals through fear appeals. The notion was that people would be motivated to change their health behaviors by communication that 1) maximized the noxiousness of the event; 2) gave a high probability of the occurrence of the event; and 3) provided an effective response.[16]

For example, an informational program on smoking would be most effective by stressing the horrors of lung cancer, the likelihood of smoking leading to cancer, and the effectiveness of stopping smoking. But while fear may motivate behavior change, it can also produce *inaction* if there is no clear, achievable method to resolve the problem.[17] Further work has emphasized thinking about ways to cope with, and avert, the threat. Messages that focus on possible responses to threats, and on believing in one's own ability to succeed, can help to motivate behavior change.[18] Health promotion programs can help to address health threats by following these guidelines:

- Expose people to threatening information because it can motivate action.
- Emphasize positive steps to take to disable threats and the ability to succeed.
- Tailor threatening information to fit with individuals' needs and perceptions

Self-determination Theory

Self-determination Theory (SDT) describes three innate needs that must be met for optimizing human functioning: competence (ability to perform successfully), relatedness (social belonging), and autonomy.[19] Autonomy is the key principle that distinguishes this theory from others. The core of SDT is that people's behavior must be their own; that is, each person is the master of their own destiny, and the independence involved in making choices is the key to success as an individual. SDT emphasizes the right to freely choose a course of action; without this, motivation will be lacking.[20] The implications are that choice and self-regulation are critical for motivation.

SDT has a rich store of evidence to support its claims.[21] For example, classroom studies show that giving students self-determination in their activities promotes their interest in the material, and increases their preference for challenging tasks, conceptual learning, and creativity. It appears that the need to make one's own choices and decisions directly increases motivation. Drawing on these principles, health promotion programs can be enhanced when they:

- Present rules and instructions in an informational rather than controlling context.
- Provide opportunities for choices whenever possible.
- Evaluate performance in a non-controlling manner using positive feedback.
- Help participants feel competent as they master tasks and skills.
- Build on the desire to establish close emotional bonds and attachments with others.

Goal Orientation: Performance vs. Mastery

People differ in their "goal orientation," or how they decide to focus on and set realistic goals for themselves.[22] Setting goals improves performance by increasing focus on the task at hand and minimizing distractions, along with increasing effort towards the goal over time. Goal orientation acts at a "meta" level to direct attention to what needs to be done to be successful. For example, some individuals may be more oriented toward learning or mastery, and others towards performance or ability.[23] Performance goals suggest a motivation to "look good" and be favorably viewed by others, or at least a desire not to look bad. But a mastery goal orientation suggests a more genuine sense of personal achievement from becoming successful at a goal.[24] To foster a more beneficial goal orientation around mastery, some suggestions include:

- Relate programs to participants' needs, goals, and interests.

- Provide role models with interest in and enthusiasm for the program.
- Focus participants' attention on mastery goals rather than performance goals.

Individuals have been shown to hold a variety of goal orientations, including, work avoidance (doing as little as possible). The reasons behind individual differences in goal orientations may relate back to beliefs about one's own ability to change. Recent work on implicit theories of intelligence found that students with an "entity theory" think of their intelligence as an unchangeable internal characteristic, while others with an "incremental theory" believe their intelligence is malleable and can be increased through effort.[25] Which group is more likely to attempt challenging tasks, and achieve more intellectual growth? Similarly, participants in health programs who hear that people can successfully change their weight are likely to be more motivated than those reading the grim statistics about dieting failures.

Incentive Theories of Motivation

These cognitive theories attempt to account for motivation by examining what people think and believe, and how thinking affects action. An alternative view arises from a fundamental theory in psychology: Behaviorism.[26] The theory of behaviorism says any action can be explained by examining the rewards that follow it.[27] Wait until your dog sits, then give it a cookie, and you will see a lot more "sits" to come. Behaviorism has this as its core tenant: "Reward the behavior you want, and you will get more of it."[28] Consequently, a law of behavior is that higher incentives should lead to more effort, and result in better performance.[29]

Incentives are the rewards and punishments associated with different actions. Incentives for taking action can be hidden or explicit, and can work differently for different people (some people don't like ice cream!)[30] To impact behavior, a person must see a clear relationship between their action and the result. Two different types of incentives have been shown to motivate us: intrinsic and extrinsic.[31] *Intrinsic incentives* involve internal feelings, existing within the individual and driven by interest or enjoyment. These incentives motivate people to do things because happiness or good feelings follow. Donating money at the Salvation Army bucket leads to a warm feeling through knowing you are helping others, and a job that you love provides its own reward by helping you feel useful and needed. These behaviors reflect *intrinsic motivation*, or behaviors performed for the internal reward of what they feel like to the individual.

Extrinsic motivation refers to the desire to gain external rewards for performing a behavior, where "extrinsic" refers to an outcome or consequence arising outside of an individual. *Extrinsic incentives* are external rewards or punishments that motivate people to perform a specific action. So, an individual may work hard at a job because of the paycheck, or earn good grades in order to receive their parents' approval. In fact, a competition is inherently extrinsic because it depends on winning over another person. A foundational theorem from economics is that individuals respond to incentives:[32] There is a reason people do not need to be paid to play videogames, but must be paid to work at the Gap. Rewards motivate action, and money in particular is a very effective reward. Some have argued that money is such a strong incentive because it taps into our biological drives to trade and play.[33] People will reliably perform a broad range of behaviors for an extrinsic incentive.

From the behaviorist's vantage point, the world is organized around incentives.[34] Even our social relationships can be viewed as a form of exchanges based on incentives.[35] But despite people's natural tendency to attribute and explain their own behavior, the incentives that drive behavior may remain unrecognized. Typically, any behavior has both intrinsic and

extrinsic rewards, some hidden and some explicit. For example, brushing your teeth results in a clean-feeling mouth, and lower dental bills; and, running laps may earn points in the athletic club as well as provide a rush of endorphins. In general, the more different incentives for any behavior, the more frequently and regularly the behavior will occur.

Are intrinsic and extrinsic incentives equally valuable? That is, does paying someone to do something (extrinsic incentive) have the same psychological effect as their doing it because they enjoy it (intrinsic incentive)? And, do some kinds of incentives, both intrinsic and extrinsic, work better than others? The next section examines the effectiveness of both extrinsic and intrinsic incentives in promoting health behavior.

STUDIES OF EFFECTIVE INCENTIVES IN HEALTH BEHAVIORS

The health promotion literature includes many studies of the impact of both intrinsic and extrinsic incentives on behavior. Some guidelines for the use of incentives in health programs may be drawn from the evidence.

Effective Extrinsic Incentives in Health Behaviors

How effective are extrinsic incentives in promoting health behaviors? The question is not whether they work (they do!), but how well, and on what types of behaviors? A meta-review[36] examined the impact of economic incentives for motivating simple health behaviors and complex preventative medical procedures. The studies all involved preventive care and health promotion defined as healthy or physically at risk individuals who were not yet labeled with a diagnosis. Tertiary care, including self-care and management of diagnosed chronic illnesses such as diabetes and heart disease, was not included. The incentives included cash, gifts, lotteries, and other free or reduced-price goods and services. Most of the studies included incentives requiring a specific target behavior (e.g., getting a screening test), while 1/5th required the participant to attain a particular outcome (e.g., lab-verified abstinence). Preventive behaviors were divided into simple (directly accomplished, such as immunization) and complex (requiring sustained behavior change, such as a diet). Forty-seven studies were compared, and a positive result was found 73% of the time (74% for simple and 72% for complex). Successful incentives included rewards for participating and meeting goals, and discounts on the costs of preventive services. The authors concluded, "Economic incentives appear to be effective in the short run for simple preventive care" and for achieving distinct, well-defined behavioral goals."[20]

Incentives have a strong influence on participation rates, but how much financial incentive is "enough?" A large empirical study of 559,988 employees examined how differing levels of financial incentives influenced participation in health risk assessments offered by employers.[37] The results showed that smaller incentive values ($0-100) produced a steep positive trend in participation (see Figure 10-1). For incentives greater than $100, participation increased linearly, with diminishing returns at higher values. This suggests smaller incentives provide the most "bang for the buck" for one-time activities. A follow-up study demonstrated that factors such as the nature of communications about the incentive program can have significant impact on participation rates, and suggested variables such as company culture and

Figure 10-1: Health assessment participation rates as a function of level of incentive offered.

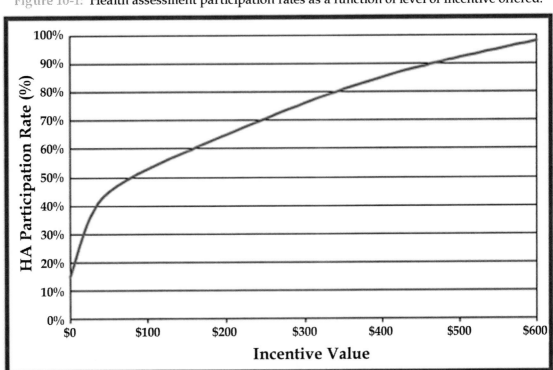

Source: Anderson DR, Grossmeier J, Seaverson ELD, Snyder D. The role of financial incentives in driving employee engagement in health management. *ACSM's Health Fit J. 2008;12(4):18-22.*

"integration into benefits programs" also play significant roles.[38]

Studies of behavior change show that incentives can work to increase attendance at programs such as smoking cessation[39] and weight loss programs.[40] A recent Randomized Clinical Trial (RCT) offered smokers a reward for participating in a five-session class (at $20 per class), with a $100 bonus for not smoking 30 days later.[41] Compared to a control group who were never paid, the incentive group had higher rates of program enrollment (43% versus 20%), completion (29% versus 12%), and quitting at 75 days (16% versus 5%). However, at six months, quit rates in the incentive group were not significantly higher (6.5% vs. 4.6%). The net effect of the incentives was to increase participation in the program, but without improving the rates of quitting smoking.

A review of research verified that incentives can increase healthy behaviors, but suggested that positive effects may diminish over time.[42] Monetary incentives appear to help motivate people to alter their lifestyle and lower cholesterol levels up to the measured six month period; however, evidence regarding incentives and weight loss is less conclusive. More encouraging results showed financial incentives work to motivate preventive care when there is clear proof of potential health gains, and guidelines are available.[43] These include preventative actions such as vaccinations, cancer screening and follow-up, tuberculosis diagnosis and treatment, pre- and postnatal care, and HIV and sexual health. The reviewed studies, mainly public programs aimed at low-income populations, suggest that financial incentives, even rather small ones, can influence health behaviors positively. But the lack of studies involving long-term follow-up means that relatively little is known about whether behavior changes last over time.

How well do incentives work for more habitual behaviors? A field study tested whether financial incentives could improve a notoriously challenging health behavior:

going to the gym.[44] All groups visited the lab for an informational session. After informing all participants about the benefits of exercise, members of one group had no further intervention; members of a second group were paid $25 to attend the gym at least once in the next week; and members of a third group were paid $25 to attend once and then another $100 to attend at least eight times in the next four weeks. Comparing gym attendance one week vs. five weeks after the informational lab visit, gym visits were more than *twice* as high for the high-incentive group. Importantly, as Figure 10-2 shows, the higher gym attendance rate was maintained eight weeks after all payments, suggesting that the effects of the financial incentive persisted past the incentive period.

In a second study, biometric measures were added to determine whether health outcomes improved along with attendance. This time, all participants were paid the same ($175), but some were required to attend the gym zero, one or eight times in the next month. Once again, the more frequent attenders showed a higher rate of gym use after the study ended, and the biometric scores improved more for them as well. These findings show that it may be possible to "nudge" people towards good habits through extrinsic incentives.[45]

Another study examined a variety of programs aimed at weight loss, smoking cessation, or seat belt use, comparing rewards to no-reward control groups.[46] Consistently, people receiving rewards showed better compliance at the beginning, but worse compliance in the long run compared to the no-reward groups, suggesting incentives help people to engage in behavior, but help less with persistence. However, there are logistical difficulties and higher costs for administering and measuring the impact of external incentives over longer periods of time. As a result, evidence from other health behavior studies is scarce. The available evidence includes studies of the workplace, and experimental economic

Figure 10-2: Average gym visits for the control group, one-time visit group, and eight-time visit group in Experiment 1.

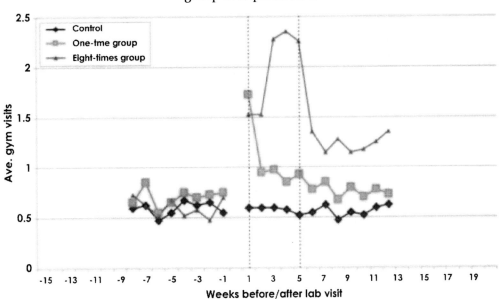

Source: Charness G, Gneezy U. Incentives to exercise. *Econometrica. 2009;77(3);909–931.*

or laboratory studies. These studies suggest extrinsic incentives may have the desired effects in the short run, but weaken longer-term intrinsic motivations.[47]

For example, a classic laboratory study paid participants to complete puzzles; later, when allowed to choose whether to complete them without payment, the individuals who had received incentives were less likely to perform the activity,[48] and other studies replicate this finding.[49,50] A review of 128 laboratory studies on the effects of extrinsic incentives provided for engaging in, completing, or meeting performance goals found that self-reported interest in the tasks was lower compared to control groups. The authors concluded, "Even when tangible rewards are offered as indicators of good performance, they typically decrease intrinsic motivation for interesting activities."[51] Evidence from economic studies suggests the effectiveness of incentives depends on how they are designed, the form in which they are given, and what happens after they are

withdrawn. [52] An economic analysis of fifty-one separate experimental studies of "pay for performance" plans for individual employees working in corporations found that incentives may reduce an employee's natural inclination to complete a task and derive pleasure from doing so, resulting in a negative impact on overall performance.[53] Dr. Bernd Irlenbusch from the London School of Economics stated that, "We find that financial incentives may indeed reduce intrinsic motivation and diminish ethical or other reasons for complying with workplace social norms such as fairness."[54]

The reason that extrinsic incentives may be problematic in maintaining behavior over the long term is that, as cognitive theories of motivation suggest, people *think about* why they choose to perform actions. A monetary bonus for having an inoculation means that the employee also thinks about the incentive as a *reason* for their decision to do it. Economic studies suggest that monetary incentives may have an indirect psychological effect that can "crowd out" the incentivized behavior.[55] Now, an employee may see the incentive as a major reason for having the inoculation, rather than the personal health benefit it offers. A laboratory study examined the effect of knowledge about the reward on individual's feelings about performing a task.[56] People were asked to perform a boring, difficult task, and were paid $20 to do so. Then, they were asked to convince someone else that the task was actually fun to do. This was awkward because these people knew they did it solely for the incentive. Other people were paid just $1 to perform the same boring task, and were also asked to convince others it was fun. These people could not rely on the incentive to explain to themselves why they had done the boring task; instead, they had to reconsider the task, and justify their decision to do it as something other than the $1 payment. These people were more likely to say that they really felt the task was not that bad, and they had actually enjoyed it. Without a large incentive, people were forced to provide their own motivational account for their behavior.

Another study, performed in both the U.S. and in India, asked people to perform a variety of tasks involving remembering strings of digits, performing motor skills, or playing creative games.[57] Different groups were given either small, medium, or large financial rewards based on their performance. For mechanical skills, where no thinking was involved, bigger rewards did lead to better performance. But if the task involved cognitive skills in even a rudimentary way, larger rewards led to poorer performance. For tasks involving thinking hard, being paid more backfired. One potential explanation for this finding is that people see the reward itself as information about the task, and they use that knowledge in reasoning about their performance. If it pays a lot, it must be difficult, so the pressure is on to perform well. In other cases, people may see a reward as information about whether they themselves or their behavior are valued by others,[58] such

as feeling underpaid for their work. The knowledge that one has performed a behavior in order to receive an incentive may alone be enough to change how an individual thinks or feels about engaging in that behavior again. For example, if a child is paid to brush their teeth daily, he or she may feel that dental care for health alone is less important. Because people reason about their own behaviors, adding external incentives into the mix may have unexpected influences on outcomes.

Effective Intrinsic Incentives in Health Behaviors

With extrinsic incentives, it is possible to be clear about the size and application of incentives on behavior; at the same time, field studies can be costly and logistically difficult to conduct. Studies of intrinsic incentives pose other challenges for empirical studies. It may be more difficult to quantify and measure intrinsic motivation reliably across many populations. For example, in a review examining nursing and allied health studies of motivations for health behaviors, over one-third of the studies found no significant role for motivation.[59] The absence of impact may be due to a lack of effectiveness, or to the difficulty in capturing the presence of the intrinsic incentives for individuals. As a result, evidence of the effectiveness of intrinsic motivation in health behavior change suffers from the difficulty of clearly capturing its meaning for individuals.

One approach is to simply ask people why they succeeded in changing their health behavior. In a review of 35 studies using self-report measures (including retrospective, prospective, and cross-sectional methods), the negative health consequences of smoking were found to be the primary concern of people attempting to quit.[60] Smokers cited reasons to explain their motivation to quit in terms of experiencing salient symptoms, wanting to feel better physically, seeing the illness or death of a family member or friend due to smoking, and concern about future health risks. The second most frequently mentioned reason was social concerns, such as family pressure, social pressure, effect on others, *responsibility* to others, and pregnancy. This review concludes that individual health concerns are the primary factor motivating quit attempts.

Another study examined women's persistence in physical activity through their experiences with a government-funded festival, and measured their participation in physical exercise six months later.[61] Through interview data, intentions to continue participating in physical exercise were connected to self-reports of feelings of "enhanced self-efficacy," support from activity leaders, and their own desire for improved health. A similar study examined older adult's motivations for sustaining physical activity levels.[62] Comparing those who were inactive, active, and sustained maintainers, the self-report results were that intrinsic motivation and self-determined extrinsic motivation (such as the desire to be able to travel) predicted older adults' ongoing activity levels. Older people in this study defined their own "extrinsic" or external incentives such as improved appearance and social or emotional benefits, but the factor contributing most to their later activity levels was their sense of enjoyment.

Another key factor in intrinsic motivation, as proposed in SDT (described above), is "autonomy," defined as having choices and self-initiation of actions.[63] In a Randomized Clinical Trial of dental hygiene training, one group received an intervention to improve their cleaning skills alone, and the other added an "autonomy-supportive" context during a single visit. This latter intervention was designed to facilitate feelings of autonomous motivation and self-perceived competence in the individual. The results showed those receiving the autonomy-supportive training decreased observed plaque and gingivitis over a 5.5-month period compared to the control group.[64] This one-time intervention, focusing on taking greater responsibility and self-initiative for dental home care, appeared to help people understand the importance of the behaviors; then, they were more likely to follow through with them, resulting in improved dental health.

Autonomy has also been found to be important in intrinsic motivation in other fields. In studies of business performance, intrinsic rewards have been found to be much stronger than financial rewards for increasing employee motivation.[65] Increasing intrinsic motivation in employees may lead to increased feelings of autonomy, making work more meaningful, demonstrating competence, and offering opportunities for professional development, gaining feedback, monitoring progress, and learning to reward themselves. Another domain showing robust effects of intrinsic motivation is learning and education, in which studies show that teachers can promote intrinsic motivation and foster mastery orientations.[66] Methods to enhance intrinsic motivation in learning involve asking students to plan ahead, take personal responsibility, set individual learning goals, and make choices.[67] Instructional practices that promote autonomy have been found to foster intrinsic motivation and lifelong learning.[68]

Another factor in intrinsic motivation based on SDT is "choice,"[69] the ability to make personal determinations regarding behavior. A meta-analysis of 41 studies including both children and adults showed that providing choice enhances intrinsic motivation, effort, task performance, and perceived competence, among other outcomes.[70] Eleven of these studies took place in the health behavior context, including exercise effort[71,72], aerobic classes,[73] and physical education programs.[74] For example, one study varied the music presented in a videocassette with aerobics dance instruction.[75] People led to believe the music was based on their own earlier choices reported higher intrinsic motivation than a control group. This incentive worked when people had merely the *perception* of choice, not actual choice. These studies suggest five guidelines for implementing choice in an intervention:[76] 1) a choice should not be highly effortful, 2) more choices are better than fewer (up to a point), 3) multiple choices yield greater benefits (up to a point), 4) avoid focus on controlling aspects of the environment, and 5) avoid pressure or dissimilar options.

APPLICATIONS TO MOTIVATION

Research in psychology has continued to develop theories about the nature of intrinsic motivation. In a series of studies, Reiss has identified a set of 16 separate intrinsic motivators, as shown in Table 10-1.[77] Reiss'

approach suggests that it is critical to look for these more specific themes within people's reports of intrinsic motivation. Affect, or the emotion we experience, is one of the important influences in motivation. "Fun" is a wonderful source of motivation for desirable behaviors that are also health promoting. Consider Volkswagen's experiment to see if making stairs more fun would spur subway riders to take them instead of the escalator (See Figure 10-3).[78] When ordinary stairs within a Stockholm subway station were changed into ones that functioned as piano keys, a 66% increase in use of stairs was observed. Other interventions based on Reiss' work may produce novel motivators for health behavior change.

Table 10-1: Reiss' 16 Intrinsic Motives.

Motive Name	Description	Intrinsic Feeling
Power	Desire to influence	Efficacy
Curiosity	Desire for knowledge	Wonder
Independence	Desire to be autonomous	Freedom
Status	Desire for social standing (including attention)	Self-importance
Social contact	Desire for peer companionship (desire to play)	Fun
Vengeance	Desire to get even (compete, win)	Vindication
Idealism	Desire to improve society (altruism, justice)	Loyalty
Physical exercise	Desire to exercise muscles	Vitality
Romance	Desire for sex (including courting)	Lust
Family	Desire to raise own children	Love
Order	Desire to organize (including rituals)	Stability
Eating	Desire to eat	Satiation
Acceptance	Desire for approval	Self-confidence
Tranquility	Desire to avoid anxiety, fear	Safe, relaxed
Saving	Desire to collect, value of frugality	Ownership

Source: Reiss S. Multifaceted nature of Intrinsic Motivation: The theory of 16 basic desires. Review of General Psychology. 2004; 8(3); 179-193.

Figure 10-3: **Stair use increased when a "fun" incentive (functional piano keys) was offered.**

Source: http://www.thefuntheory.com/piano-staircase by TheFunTheory.com-Rolighetsteorin.se.

Similarly, safety is another factor that can enhance intrinsic motivation.[79] For example, because biometric screenings are effective in detecting individuals in need of specific medical interventions, health professionals are puzzled about why some people don't take advantage of them. However, the possibility of finding a health problem may be so frightening that some people may avoid the opportunity to discover them. A review of 29 studies examining the role of anxiety, fear, and worry in breast cancer screening decisions concluded the components of cancer and the screening process that women fear may bear differing relationships to screening behavior.[80] Addressing emotions around the testing process and possible findings may encourage more people to participate.

Reiss points to "wonder," or the desire for knowledge, as a key intrinsic motivator. Logically, knowledge is the gateway to behavioral change because it precedes and informs the motivation to change behavior.[81] People faced with health issues seek out information on their own, increasingly through online sources.[82,83] Knowledge about potential health risks may be necessary to initiate the intrinsic motivation leading to an appropriate behavioral response.[84] For example, patients with no prior immunization history were more likely to have flu shots when given an informational brochure, and not when given an incentive.[85] In some cases, simply receiving needed information can be a powerful factor in motivating behavior change, or provide the *prerequisites* to successful behavior change.[86] Health behavior programs must move beyond educating about facts to knowledge management, or the provision of information in directly applicable, "how to" form. A specific proposal, Information Therapy, calls for the "timely prescription and availability of evidence-based health information to meet individuals' specific needs and support sound decision making.[87]

Malone[88] identified four basic sources of internal motivation -- challenge, curiosity, control, and fantasy -- each of which might be targeted by a wellness program. Just as with other behavior, health behavior may thrive when driven by the interest of the individual. Becoming a regular runner, or eating a vegan diet, may have positive health benefits, but may be originated through an interest of the individual. Just as it's difficult to select a movie for someone else, allowing a person's interests, hobbies, and "extracurricular" activities to direct changes may be necessary for the adoption of health changes. Part of this process is exposure to situations where interests are allowed to emerge. One model for the development of interests begins with triggering a situational interest, which over time allows the individual's interest to emerge, and eventually become sustained by the individual. Exposing people to novel situations in which they can explore and develop their own interests will allow new areas to emerge. This is a time consuming and expensive approach because there will be many mismatches, but the benefits of discovering a true interest, such as learning and loving tennis at age 40, is a lifestyle change that is tied to high motivation. One of the challenges in deciding the optimal combination of approaches is that no single study or set of studies has been able to determine which approaches work under what circumstances.

Health programs can be more intriguing when they create surprise and stimulate curiosity rather than provide the usual activities. A walking program based on "step counting" could be altered to match individual interests, such as combining it with a weekly tour of neighborhoods led by different participants, or shopping center "scavenger hunts" to find where products are sold, providing activity for the mind while incorporating the physical

activity goals. Humor, along with factors like surprise and attractive design, is a very effective motivator in facilitating behavior change.[89] Humor is highly valued by most people, and a wonderful anecdote to the usual seriousness of the work setting. It attracts people to events and helps bring them back, so it can be a positive and popular part of wellness programming.

APPLICATIONS TO SKILL BUILDING

Despite the risks of shifting attribution described earlier, incentives can sometimes work to foster good habits. For example, incentive programs may provide the initial motivation for a healthy lifestyle. Then, once people experience the positive aspects of a healthy lifestyle, their intrinsic motivation will help to make the changes more permanent. Ideally, incentives work by getting healthy habits started. According to behavioral theory, habits are formed by the gradual learning of associations between responses and rewards. As a result, a learner is tuned to attend to the features of contexts that predict when a response will be rewarded, as in operant conditioning[90] (e.g., physical settings, preceding actions). Once a habit is formed, perception of these contexts automatically triggers the associated response.

This explains why incentives are helpful in establishing new behavior: They provide an immediate reward that helps us learn that a behavior is valuable. It is much more difficult to train a habit when the reward is far removed from the behavior, such as working out for weeks before it feels any easier to run a lap. Some rewards may occur long after the initial behaviors are performed. That means it is difficult to associate the new behavior with the long-delayed reward. So to learn new habits, we have to repeat the behavior often enough that we experience the longer term reward. This explains why behaviors sometimes stop once incentives are removed: There is no longer any perceived reward for the behavior.

Luckily, however, people *think*. They can form a goal, and direct behaviors in service of those goals. Theories of habits suggest our goals can direct new habits by motivating repetition that leads to habit formation, and by promoting exposure to cues that trigger habits.[91] Doing so requires deliberate, thoughtful behavior that leads to the establishment of the habit. This may require more effort than people are willing to put in; but, there may be shortcuts to habit formation. One approach is to plan a new habit in advance, and to be very specific about intentions to implement the behavior. Research shows people are more likely to be successful in learning a habit when they plan some specific behaviors that lead to the desired outcomes.[92] In fact, behavior change has been shown to be much more likely when specific action plans are provided.[93] Providing specific direction places an "action trigger" in memory, so that the planned behavior can be spurred by cues in the world.[94]

A study of hip and knee replacement patients showed that simply asking them to plan when they would perform specific health behaviors cut their recovery time in half. Setting "action triggers" to remind them to follow their intended behaviors, such as when and where they would take a walk in the next week, led to faster recovery.[95] A meta-analysis of 8,155 participants in 85 studies found that those who set up "implementation intentions" for their behavior changes performed better than 74% of the people on the same task who did not develop specific action plans.[96] In a 2010 study, women measured their consumption of fruits and vegetables using food diaries for two years.[97] Half were informed about the importance of consuming more fruits and vegetables, and the other half were informed and then asked to plan *how* they would accomplish this increased level of consumption. Both groups improved their intake over the first four months (from less than half to one serving per day). But by setting their "action triggers" in advance, the planning group maintained a higher intake

up to *two years* later, while the information-only group returned to baseline levels. Adding instructions on planning very specific action steps greatly increased the effectiveness for long-term behavior change.

In fact, it may be possible to use people's tendency for cognitive explanations in creating new habits. First, get people to perform a habit, perhaps using incentives; for example, pay employees to avoid parking their cars in the company lot for a two-week period. Then, the creative ability of the human mind enters in: People may convince themselves that the new habit they have established during this period (walking, biking, or riding the bus to work) is something they actually prefer to do. Recall the psychological study discussed earlier in which people led to comply with requests (to say that they enjoyed a tedious task) later stated that they actually did enjoy the task.[98] That is, based on their behavior, they then increased their own internal sense of how much they enjoyed performing it. What determines our future actions is not only the value of the options, but also our (potentially biased) memories for our past actions.[99] In this sense, our actions do not merely reveal our preferences, but rather, *create* them. This suggests a path to the Holy Grail of wellness programs: a means to convince people they prefer options they currently do not. Of course, the circumstances must be just right to achieve this outcome. Specifically, if people can point to receiving an incentive as the reason for their action, then the effect of changing their attribution for their choice does not occur. At the least, getting people to perform behaviors increases accessibility of these actions in memory, and potentially, their influence on later habits.

UNANSWERED QUESTIONS

Motivation drives behavior. To see real changes in health outcomes, changes in behavior must be sustained, and that requires high levels of motivation. Many of the lessons discussed here about motivation have been developed in educational settings,[100] and may or may not be readily applicable to health and wellness programs in work settings. Given the difficulty of conducting longitudinal field studies of incentive use, the data are not yet available to determine when and how incentives can be successful in motivating long term behavior change.

There is sufficient evidence in the research literature to draw these conclusions:

1. Encourage people to take responsibility for their successes and failures, and help them view themselves as in charge of their own behavior and health.
2. Because an individual's beliefs about himself or herself matter, help individuals set personal goals for what they want to accomplish, and emphasize self-comparison and improvement.
3. Focus on effort rather than outcomes to allow people to attend to what they *can* control: their behavior (such as eating less, even though the scale may not show it).
4. Provide people with choices about their participation, and use variety *and* familiarity to capitalize on people's interests and enjoyment.
5. Avoid individual competitions; though they capture attention, they also emphasize social comparison and external standards, and deflect attention from more sustainable personal goals.
6. Emphasize feelings of competence by careful planning of specific steps and "action triggers."
7. Build small, incremental changes to reduce people's levels of intimidation and anxiety, and increase their level of confidence that they can achieve their goal.

In other words, one can view people as not simply either "healthy" or "unhealthy," but as capable of becoming "health*ier*!"[101]

A final component that has not been addressed is the role of other's expectations. When people are trying to achieve goals, the messages they receive about their likelihood of success or failure are important. In the educational domain, classic studies have shown that teachers who expect a lot from their students are rewarded by actual, not only perceived, student growth. Perhaps this tip from the best teachers -- expect a lot from every individual – will enhance the outcomes of health behavior programs. As Robert Rosenthal demonstrated, only those who we *believe* will "bloom" are those who become able to do so.[102]

CONCLUSION

Motivation is the key to long-term behavior change, and therefore, a critical component for successful health promotion programs. Psychological, educational, and economic studies have provided core constructs for theories of motivation. Specifically, cognition, or how people think about themselves and their behavior, plays a central role in determining the outcomes of attempts to influence behavior. There have been successful studies of behavior change using extrinsic incentives; however, some findings suggest the relationship between external incentives and longer term outcomes is complex. Studies of intrinsic incentives suggest that people who believe in their own capacity for change are more likely to accomplish it. For both types of incentives, more research is needed to understand the relationships between health promotion programs and successful behavior change.

Glossary

Action trigger: An external cue in the environment that spurs planned behavior.

Achievement motivation: The need to meet realistic goals and enjoy a sense of accomplishment.

Attribution Theory: The theory that motivation arises through what people believe about why they succeed or fail at different tasks.

Autonomy: Having the power of personal control and self-initiation of behaviors.

Behaviorism: The theory of behaviorism says actions occur based on their rewards.

Biometric measures: Biological indices of health functioning such as resting heart rate.

Choice: The ability to make personal determinations regarding courses of action.

Cognitive theory: An account of behavior that arises from human thought.

Entity theory: Intelligence is an unchangeable internal characteristic.

Expectancy-Value Theory: The theory that motivation comes from your expectancy of success, and the value of that success to you.

Extrinsic incentives: Rewards generated and provided outside of the individual.

Extrinsic motivation: An account of behavior based on its outcome arising outside of the person.

Goal orientation: Differing patterns of beliefs about one's goals, and the ability to set realistic goals.

Habits: Behaviors performed automatically.

Incentive Theories of Motivation: An account of motivation that explains behavior through its rewards.

Implementation intentions: Plans to execute specific actions in the future.

Incentives: The rewards and punishments associated with different behaviors.

Incremental theory: Intelligence is malleable and can be increased through effort.

Intrinsic incentives: Rewards generated and experienced internally.

Mastery: The goal orientation of genuine personal achievement from becoming successful at a goal.

Monetary incentives: The most common extrinsic incentive: Money.

Motivation: An inner state that arouses, directs, and maintains behavior.

Performance: The goal orientation of attending to performance or ability.

Protection-Motivation Theory: People's attributions or "appraisals" of threats make a difference in their ability to cope with or respond effectively to them.

RCT (Randomized Clinical Trial): An empirical study that includes assigning participants to treatment groups at random.

Reiss' Intrinsic Motives: A set of 16 inner motivations thought to drive behavior.

Self-determination Theory: The theory that three innate needs must be met for optimizing human functioning, including competence (ability to perform successfully), relatedness (social belonging), and autonomy.

Social motivation: The need to feel loved and to belong to social groups.

Theories of motivation: Accounts of the psychology behind our decisions to take action.

Learning Objectives

1. To understand the core constructs of cognitive theories of motivation
2. To learn about successful studies of incentives in health behavior change
3. To apply concepts from intrinsic motivation to wellness programs

Discussion Questions

1. Discuss how self-determination increases motivation on tasks. Think about some of your own experiences and talk about them with a partner.
2. What are some ways you can provide employees with choices that matter to them?
3. Identify three of Reiss' elements of motivation, and discuss how you might build them into health promotion programs.

REFERENCES

1. Towers Watson (2011/2012). Staying@WorkTM Survey Report, "Pathway to Health and Productivity." TW-NA-2011-19283.
2. Towers Watson. *Staying@Work™ Survey Report*, "Pathway to Health and Productivity," TW-NA-2011-19283, 2011/2012.
3. Towers Watson. *Staying@Work™ Survey Report*, "Pathway to Health and Productivity." TW-NA-2011-19283, 2011/2012.
4. The 15th Annual National Business Group on Health and the Towers Watson. *Survey Report*, "Purchasing Value in Health Care," TW-NA-2009-15565, 2010.
5. Baumeister RF, Leary MR. The need to belong: Desire for interpersonal attachments as a fundamental human motivation. *Psychol Bull.* 1995;117(3); 497–529.
6. McClelland DC. *The Achieving Society.* New York, NY: Free Press; 1961.
7. Woolfolk, A. *Educational Psychology*, 11th ed. Upper Saddle River, NJ: Pearson Education, Inc.; 2010.
8. Nisbett RE, Wilson TD. Telling more than we can know: Verbal reports on mental processes. *Psychol Rev.* 1977;84;231.
9. Murray, HA. *Explorations in Personality.* New York: Oxford University Press; 1938.
10. Heider, F. *The Psychology of Interpersonal Relations.* New York: John Wiley & Sons; 1958.
11. Rotter JB. Generalized expectancies for internal versus external control of reinforcement. *Psychol Monogr.* 1966; 8:1-28.
12. Weiner B. An Attributional Theory of Motivation and Emotion. New York: Springer-Verlag; 1986.
13. Wigfield A, Eccles JS, Schiefele U, Roeser RW, Davis-Kean P. Development of achievement motivation. In: Eisenberg N, ed. *Handbook of Child Psychology Vol. 3: Social, Emotional, and Personality Development* 6th ed. New York: John Wiley, Sons; 2006:933-1002.
14. Monat A, Lazarus R. *Stress and Coping: An Anthology.* New York: Columbia University Press; 1991.
15. Maddux JE, Rogers RW. Protection motivation theory and self-efficacy: A revised theory of fear appeals and attitude change. *J Exp Soc Psychol.* 1983:19:469-479.
16. Rogers RW. A protection motivation theory of fear appeals and attitude change. *J Psychol.* 1975;91:93-114.
17. Eagly, AH, Chaiken, S. *The Psychology of Attitudes.* Orlando, FL: Harcourt Brace Jovanovich; 1993.
18. Bartholomew LK, Parcel GS, Kik G, Gottlieb NH. *Planning Health Promotion Programs: An Integrative Mapping Approach.* New York: John Wiley, Sons; 2011.
19. Deci, EL, Ryan, RM. *Intrinsic Motivation and Self-Determination in Human Behavior.* New York: Plenum, 1985.
20. Ryan RM, Deci EL. Intrinsic and extrinsic motivations: Classic definitions and new directions. *Contemp Educ Psychol.* 2000;25:54-67.
21. Deci EL, Ryan R, eds. *Handbook of Self-Determination Theory Research.* Rochester, NY: University of Rochester Press; 2002.

22. Dweck, CS., & Elliott, ES. Achievement motivation. In: Mussen P, Hetherington EM, eds. *Handbook of Child Psychology.* New York: Wiley; 1983:643-692.

23. Pintrich PR. Multiple pathways, multiple goals: The role of goal orientation in learning and achievement. *J Educ Psychol.* 2000;92:544-555.

24. Pintrich, PR. An achievement goal theory perspective on issues in motivation terminology, theory, and research. *Contemp Educ Psychol.* 2000;25:92-104.

25. Dweck, CS. *Self-Theories: Their Role in Motivation, Personality, and Development.* Philadelphia: Psychology Press; 1999.

26. Skinner BF. Can psychology be a science of mind? *Am Psychol.* 1990;45;1209.

27. Skinner BF. Utopia through the control of human behavior. In: Rich JM, ed. *Readings in the Philosophy of Education.* Belmont, CA: Wadsworth; 1972.

28. Baum WM. *Understanding Behaviorism: Science, Behavior, and Culture.* New York, NY: HarperCollins College Publishers; 2003.

29. Gneezy U, Meier S, Rey-Biel P. When and why incentives (don't) work to modify behavior. *J Econ Perspect.* 2011; 25(4):191–210.

30. Atkinson JW. *An Introduction to Motivation.* Princeton, NJ: Van Nostrand; 1964.

31. Wigfield A, Guthrie JT, Tonks S, Perencevich KC. Children's motivation for reading: Domain specificity and instructional influences. *Journal of Educ Res.* 2004;97;299-309.

32. Bénabou R, Tirole J. Intrinsic and extrinsic motivation. *Rev of Econ Stud.* 2003;70(3);489-520.

33. Lea SEG, Webley P. Money as tool, money as drug: The biological psychology of a strong incentive. *Behav and Brain Sci.* 2006;29(02);161-209.

34. Skinner BF. *Walden Two.* New York: Macmillan, 1948.

35. Cook KS, Rice E. Social exchange theory. In: J. Delamater ed., *Handbook of Social Psychology.* Kluwer Academic/Plenum Publishers, New York, 2003:53-76.

36. Kane RL, Johnson PE, Town RJ, Butler M. A structured review of the effect of economic incentives on consumers' preventive behavior. *Am J Prev Med.* 2004;27(4):327–352.

37. Anderson DR, Grossmeier J, Seaverson ELD, Snyder D. The role of financial incentives in driving employee engagement in health management. *ACSM's Health Fit J.* 2008;12(4):18-22.

38. Seaverson ELD, Grossmeier J, Miller TM, Anderson DR. The role of incentive design, incentive value, communications strategy, and worksite culture on Health Risk Assessment participation. *Am J Health Promo.* 2009;23(5):343.

39. Curry SJ, Wagner, EH, Grothaus LC. Evaluation of intrinsic and extrinsic motivation interventions with a self-help smoking cessation program. *J Consult Clin Psychol.* 1991;59;318–24.

40. Follick MJ, Fowler JL, Brown RA. Attrition in worksite weight-loss interventions: The effects of an incentive procedure. *J Consult Clin Psychol.* 1984;52;139–40.

41. Volppl KG, Gurmankin Levy A, Aschl DA, et al. A Randomized Controlled Trial of financial incentives for smoking cessation. *Cancer Epidemiol Biomarkers Prev.* 2006;15(1):12–8.

42. Sutherland K, Christianson JB, Leatherman S. Impact of targeted financial incentives on personal health behavior: a review of the literature. *Med Care Res Rev.* 2008; 65(6 Suppl):36S-78S.

43. Sutherland K, Christianson JB, Leatherman S. Impact of targeted financial incentives on personal health behavior: a review of the literature. *Med Care Res Rev.* 2008;65(6 Suppl):36S-78S

44. Charness G, Gneezy U. Incentives to exercise. *Econometrica*, 2009:77(3);909–931.

45. Thaler RH, Sunstein CR. *Nudge: Improving Decisions about Health, Wealth, and Happiness.* Penguin Books; 2009.

46. Kohn A. *Punished by Rewards.* New York: Plenum Press; 1993.

47. Ariely D, Gneezy U, Loewenstein G, Mazar N. Large stakes and big mistakes. *Rev Econ Stud.* 2009:76;451-469.

48. Deci EL. Effects of externally mediated rewards on intrinsic motivation. *J Pers Soc Psychol*, 1971;18:105-115.

49. Wilson T, Hull J, Johnson J. Awareness and self-perception: Verbal reports on internal states. *J Pers Soc Psychol.* 1981:40;53-71.

50. Lepper M, Greene D, Nisbett R. Undermining children's interest with extrinsic rewards: A test of the 'Overjustification Hypothesis'. *J Pers Soc Psychol.* 1973;28;129-137.

51. Deci EL, Koestner R, Ryan RM. A meta-analytic review of experiments examining the effects of extrinsic rewards on intrinsic motivation. *Psychol Bull.* 1999;125(6):627-68.

52. Gneezy U, Meier S, Rey-Biel P. When and why incentives (don't) work to modify behavior. *J Econ Perspect.* 2011; 25(4):191–210.

53. Bowles S, Polania-Reyes S. Economic incentives and social preferences: Substitutes or complements? *J Econ Lit.* 2012;50(2):368-425.

54. Irlenbusch, B. London School of Economic's Department of Management, 2011. Available at http://www2.lse.ac.uk/newsAndMedia/news/archives/2009/06/performancepay.aspx. Accessed on 8/1/2013.

55. Gneezy U, Meier S, Rey-Biel P. When and why incentives (don't) work to modify behavior. *J Econ Perspect.* 2011; 25(4):191-210.

56. Festinger, L. *A Theory of Cognitive Dissonance.* Stanford, CA: Stanford University Press, 1957.

57. Ariely D, Gneezy U, Loewenstein G, Mazar N. Large stakes and big mistakes. *Rev Econ Stud.* 2009;76:451-469.

58. Benabou R, Tirole J. Incentives and prosocial behavior. *Am Econ Rev.* 2006;6(5);1652–78.

59. Carter KF, Kulbok PA. Motivation for health behaviours: a systematic review of the nursing literature. *J Adv Nurs.* 2002;40(3):316-330.

60. McCaul KD, Hockemeyer JR, Johnson RJ. Zetocha K, Quinlan K, Glasgow, RE. Motivation to quit using cigarettes: A review. *Addict Behav.* 2006;31(1):42-56.

61. Lloyd KM, Little DE. Keeping women active: An examination of the impacts of self-efficacy, intrinsic motivation, and leadership on women's persistence in physical activity. *Women Health.* 2010;50:652–669.

62. Dacey M, Baltzell A, Zaichkowsky L. Older adults' intrinsic and extrinsic motivation toward physical activity. *Am J Health Behav.* 2008;32:570–582.

63. Deci EL, Ryan RM. The "what" and "why" of goal pursuits: Human needs and the self-determination of behavior. *Psychol Inq.* 2000;11;227–268.

64. Munster Halvari AE, Halvari H, Bjørnebekk G, Deci EL. Self-Determined motivational predictors of increases in dental behaviors, decreases in dental plaque, and improvement in oral health: A Randomized Clinical Trial. *Health Psychol.* 2012;31(6);777–788.

65. Herzberg F, Mausner B, Bloch Snyderman, B. *Motivation to Work.* New Brunswick, NJ: Transaction Publishers; 2009.

66. Sansone C, Harackiewicz JM, eds. *Intrinsic and Extrinsic Motivation: The Search for Optimal Motivation and*

Performance. San Diego, CA: Academic Press; 2000.

67. Flowerday T, Schraw G. Effect of choice on cognitive and affective engagement. *J Educ Res.* 2003;96:207–215.

68. Dweck, CS. *Self-Theories: Their Role in Motivation, Personality, and Development.* Philadelphia: Psychology Press; 1999.

69. Deci EL, Ryan RM. *Intrinsic Motivation and Self-Determination in Human Behavior.* New York: Plenum Press; 1985.

70. Patall EA, Cooper H, Robinson JC. The effects of choice on intrinsic motivation and related outcomes: A meta-analysis of research findings. *Psychol Bull.* 2008;134(2);270-300.

71. Dwyer JJM. Effect of perceived choice of music on exercise intrinsic motivation. *Health Values.* 1995;19:18-26.

72. Thompson CE, Wankel LM. The effects of perceived activity choice upon frequency of exercise behavior. *J Appl Soc Psychol.* 1980;10:436-443.

73. Wheeler AS Effect of actual choice of music on females' aerobics intrinsic motivation. Unpublished master's thesis, Dalhousie University;1992.

74. Prusak KA, Treasure DC, Darst PW, Pangrazi RP. The effects of choice on the motivation of adolescent girls in physical education. *J Teach Phys Educ.* 2004;23:19-29.

75. Dwyer, JJM. Effect of perceived choice of music on exercise intrinsic motivation. *Health Values.* 1995;19(2):18-26.

76. Patall EA, Cooper H, Robinson JC. The effects of choice on intrinsic motivation and related outcomes: A meta-analysis of research findings. *Psychol Bull.* 2008;134(2);270-300.

77. Reiss S. Multifaceted nature of Intrinsic Motivation: The theory of 16 basic desires. *Rev Gen Psychol.* 2004; 8(3); 179-193.

78. Volkswagen, Inc. The Fun Theory. Available at: www.thefuntheory.com. Accessed on 8/1/2013.

79. Schuettler D, Kiviniemi M. Does how I feel about it matter? The role of affect in cognitive and behavioral reactions to an illness diagnosis. *J Appl Psychol.* 2006;36:2599-2618.

80. Nathan S. Consedine, Magai C, Yulia S. Krivoshekova, et al. Behavior: A critical review: Fear, anxiety, worry, and breast cancer screening, *Cancer Epi Biomarkers Prev.* 2004;13:501-510.

81. Seifert CM, Chapman LS, Hart JK, Perez P. Enhancing intrinsic motivation in health promotion and wellness. *Am J Health Promo.* 2012;26(3):TAHP1-TAHP10.

82. Cline RJW, Haynes KM. Consumer health information seeking on the Internet: The state of the art. *Health Educ Res.* 2001;16(6):671-692.

83. Hu Y, Sundar SS. Effects of online health sources on credibility and behavioral intentions. *Comm Res.* 2010;37(1):105-132.

84. Alexander J, Rothman AJ, Kiviniemi MT. Treating people with information: An analysis and review of approaches to communicating health risk information. *J Nat Cancer Inst Monogr.* 1999;25:44-51.

85. Moran WP, Nelson K, Wofford JL, et al. Increasing influenza immunization among high-risk patients: education or financial incentive? *Am J Med.* 1996;101:612–20.

86. Heath C, Heath D. *Switch: How to Change Things when Change is Hard.* NY: Broadway Books; 2010.

87. Kemper D, Mettler M. Information Therapy: Health Education One Person at a Time. *Health Promo Pract.* 2003 Jul;4(3):214-7.

88. Malone TW, Lepper MR. Making learning fun: A taxonomy of intrinsic motivations for learning. In: Snow RE, Farr MJ, eds. *Aptitude, Learning, and Instruction: Cognitive and Affective Process Analyses.* Hillsdale, NJ: Erlbaum; 1987:223-253.

89. Dalton A. Fun for a change. *Stanford Social Innovation Review.* 2010;8(2);63-65.

90.   Skinner, B. F. *The Behavior of Organisms:An Experimental Analysis.* New York: Appleton-Century-Crofts; 1938.

91.   Wood W, Neal DT. A new look at habits and the habit-goal interface. *Psych Rev.* 2007;114(4):843-863.

92.   Patalano AL, Seifert CM. Opportunistic planning: Being reminded of pending goals. *Cogn Psych.* 1997;34:1-36.

93.   Gollwitzer PM. Implementation intentions: Strong effects of simple plans. *Am Psychol.* 1999;54:493–503.

94.   Patalano AL, Seifert CM. Opportunism in memory: Preparing for chance encounters. *Curr Dir Psychol Sci.* 2001;10(6),198-201.

95.   Orbell S, Sheeran P. Motivational and volitional processes in action initiation: A field study of the role of implementation intentions. *J App Soc Psychol.* 2000;30:780-797.

96.   Gollwitzer P, Sheeran P, Webb TL. Implementation intentions and health behaviors. In: Connor M, Norman P, eds. *Predicting Health Behavior: Research and Practice with Social Cognition Models.* 2nd ed. Buckingham, UK: Open University Press; 2005.

97.   Stadler G, Oettingen G, Gollwitzer PM. Intervention effects of information and self-regulation on eating fruits and vegetables over two years. *Health Psychol.* 2010;29(3):274–283.

98.   Festinger L, Carlsmith JM. Cognitive consequences of forced compliance. *J Abnorm Soc Psychol.* 1959;58:203–211.

99.   Ariely D, Norton MI. How actions create – not just reveal – preferences. *Trends in Cogn Sci.* 2007;12(1):13-16.

100.   Wigfield A, Eccles JS. The development of achievement task values: A theoretical analysis. *Dev Rev.* 1992;12(3);265-310.

101.   Seifert CM, Hart, JK. A "health*ier*" program for health promotion and wellness. Unpublished manuscript.

102.   Rosenthal R. *On the Social Psychology of the Self-fulfilling Prophecy: Further Evidence for Pygmalion Effects and Their Mediating Mechanisms.* New York: MSS Modular Publications; 1974.

CHAPTER

11

Self-efficacy: Broad Implications for Research and Practice

Judith J. Prochaska, Kelly C. Young-Wolff and Wes Alles

INTRODUCTION: DEFINITION, HISTORY & BREADTH OF IMPACT

Self-efficacy is a major construct of psychological science and behavior change. In the late 1970s, Albert Bandura conceptualized self-efficacy as a person's perceived ability, or efficacy expectation, to perform on a task as a mediator of performance on future tasks.[1] That is, self-efficacy is a belief in one's own ability to succeed in specific situations. The nature of these beliefs, which are malleable, impacts one's likelihood to act.

Self-efficacy differs from other reflective constructs such as self-esteem and self-concept. Self-esteem refers to one's overall evaluation of self, an appraisal of one's own worth; whereas, self-concept reflects one's self-knowledge, more informational rather than attitudinal.

Self-efficacy is influenced by a reinforcing feedback loop with performance whereby increased self-efficacy results in improved performance and in turn, improved performance results in increased self-efficacy.

The flipside of the coin is that declines in self-efficacy predict declines in performance, and declines in performance lead to declines in self-efficacy. When the focus is on changing a behavior, this decline in performance may result in lapse or even relapse back to the problematic behavioral pattern. In turn, relapse may lead to feelings of self-defeat and low self-efficacy for efforts to re-engage in the behavior change process.

Over the nearly four decades since its initial conceptualization in the literature, the construct of self-efficacy has undergone broad scale dissemination, with impressive reach and relevance, and application to academic and work achievement, athletic performance, health behavior change, politics, environmental behavior, genetics, even aeronautics. Strecher and colleagues' review of 21 studies across a variety of health behaviors found that for each of the health behaviors, self-efficacy was a consistent predictor of both short and long-term success. They reported that manipulation of self-efficacy was consistently powerful in both the initiation and maintenance of behavior change.[2] Stajkovic and Luthans' meta-analysis[3] of 114 studies examined the predictive power of self-efficacy in the workplace. Significantly associated, they attributed self-efficacy to a

28% gain in work-related performance, greater than prior findings on work-performance enhancement via goal setting, feedback interventions, or organizational behavior modification.

A Medline search of the term "self-efficacy" yielded nearly 30,000 records and a search on Google yielded over 6.3 million hits (search date 2/21/13). To provide an introductory understanding of how self-efficacy is conceptualized in the public domain, we analyzed words in the first few paragraphs of the first 100 hits on Google, conducting semantic network analysis,[4] which treats a word as the unit of analysis. We started with 15,654 words and excluded function words such as 'the', 'a', 'to', etc. Figure 11-1 displays the semantic network of the terms that co-occurred most frequently (8 or more times). Line thickness indicates the frequency of word pair co-occurrence with the thinnest line indicating 8 connections and the thickest line indicating roughly 20 connections.

Figure 11-1:   Semantic Network of Key Introductory Words on "Self-Efficacy" Related Websites.

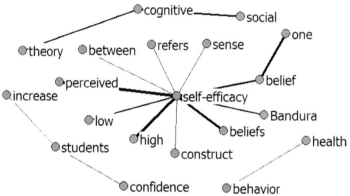

Acknowledgement: Ashley Saunders-Jackson, PhD, Stanford University.

In the resulting sociogram, we find self-efficacy at the center, networked directly and most strongly to keywords reflecting its definition (e.g., beliefs, perceived) and valence (e.g., high). Self-efficacy is also linked directly to Bandura, referenced as a point of origin. On the perimeter, three groupings of terms were found with high-frequency yet held few direct connections to the term "self-efficacy" suggesting these clusters were more conceptually discrete than other terms in the semantic network. These three groupings identify a theoretical home of self-efficacy (social cognitive theory) and key applied domains (health behavior and school achievement). From a snapshot of the more than 6 million web pages referencing self-efficacy on the Internet, it is notable how succinctly the concept can be distilled to a few central terms at the heart of the construct.

With an emphasis on theory and application, this chapter provides a conceptual framework that delineates the relationship of self-efficacy to motivation, cognition, and behaviors, followed by discussion of the factors that influence self-efficacy, including mastery and vicarious experiences, social persuasion, and physiological and emotional states. The chapter provides a brief review of the literature on the role of self-efficacy in behavior change, with relevance and application across different theoretical orientations. Lastly, it highlights specific applications of interventions targeting self-efficacy for motivation enhancement and skill building and with broadening to multiple risk behavior change, across diverse populations, and in diverse settings.

CONCEPTUAL FRAMEWORK

Relationship to Motivation, Cognitions & Health Behaviors

Self-efficacy is integrally and directionally related to motivation, thought patterns or cognitions, and engagement in health behaviors. Typically, high self-efficacy is associated with greater motivation to engage in a behavior as individuals anticipate they will be successful, while the reverse is true for low self-efficacy. The rare exceptions are the cases in which individuals with high self-efficacy are not as motivated to prepare for a task because of unrealistically high expectations that they will be successful, or when those with low self-efficacy are particularly motivated to learn more to gain greater familiarity with the task at hand.

Low self-efficacy tends to lead to increased stress,[5,6] poor planning,[7,8] avoidance,[9-12] and less persistence,[13-16] while high self-efficacy is associated with greater resolve in times of challenge.[13-16] In terms of failure cognitions, someone with high self-efficacy will attribute failure to external or situational factors, whereas a person with low self-efficacy will blame internal factors such as low ability.[17-18]

Self-efficacy is inextricably tied to goal setting and engagement in health behaviors such as exercise,[20-25] healthy nutrition,[26-28] quitting smoking,[29,30] using condoms,[31] and practicing stress management.[32,33] Specifically, self-efficacy influences decisions related to whether an individual will engage in a new health behavior and maintain the health behavior over time despite challenges.

Influences on Self-efficacy

Four primary influences are thought to contribute to the development and maintenance of self-efficacy.[34,35] These include mastery experiences, vicarious experiences, social persuasion, and physiological and emotional states. Each of these sources is reviewed below in greater detail.

The first, and most important is, mastery experiences, defined as performances that are successful. Information acquired from personal experiences provides the strongest contribution to perceptions of self-efficacy.[1,34] Individuals' beliefs in their ability to succeed on a task are largely based on prior experiences performing that task. This means that individuals who generally experience success enhance their confidence as each new experience is mastered. Repeated failures weaken self-efficacy, particularly when they occur before a strong sense of efficacy is established. Successful performances enhance self-efficacy by providing experiential evidence of one's capability of completing a task or managing a situation. Breaking a task down into small, graduated pieces early on is an effective way to highlight accomplishments and decrease frustration.[1] Mastery experiences are particularly reinforcing when a person encounters and overcomes obstacles or adversity. Compared with easily acquired successes, achievements that result from perseverance through difficulties and setbacks lead to a more resilient and enduring sense of personal efficacy.[34]

It is important to note that mastery experiences do not always boost self-efficacy, and personal failures do not always weaken self-efficacy. The influence of personal experiences on self-efficacy is also determined by a person's cognitive appraisal of the performance and their prior level of self-efficacy.[35,36] Individuals with high self-efficacy tend to view the outcomes of their behavior as controllable (e.g., via the amount of effort expended), which allows them to take credit for their achievements and mobilizes them to change their behavior following failures.[35,36] Conversely, people with low self-efficacy are more likely to view achievement outcomes as outside of their control (e.g., luck), and thus may be more prone to dismiss successes and experience helplessness following failures.[36]

Vicarious experiences or social modeling also shape self-efficacy.[1] Witnessing others successfully performing a challenging task or behavior can promote observers' beliefs in their ability to accomplish a similar activity, while watching others fail can lower one's sense of personal efficacy to perform an equivalent task.[34,37] Vicarious experiences are thought to provide more influential sources of efficacy information when models are comparable to observers with respect to characteristics such as age, sex, and ability.[1,34] Models who are dissimilar from the observers provide less relevant information about the observers' potential capabilities, and thus have a weaker impact on self-efficacy expectations.[34] Further, models who cope successfully with obstacles generate stronger self-efficacy beliefs in observers than models who complete tasks effortlessly without any mistakes.[34,36] While flawless models can teach useful strategies and skills,[38] those who succeed in spite of setbacks contribute to a more resilient sense of self-efficacy in the observer by modeling that success requires sustained effort.[34]

The third method of developing self-efficacy is called social persuasion. Persuasive information, including verbal encouragement, plays a role in shaping perceptions of self-efficacy. This comes about when someone offers encouragement to another person who is trying to achieve a task or goal. Statements such as, "You can do this," or, "You've succeeded in challenges like this in the past," provoke motivation, confidence, and commitment to succeed. Children's books or stories often focus on situations that involve a self-fulfilling prophecy. Children at a young age learn that believing in oneself is an important requisite to success. In particular, realistic positive feedback from professionals and significant others can increase confidence and help

one to more accurately interpret successful experiences as such.[35,39] On the other hand, unrealistic or excessively optimistic verbal encouragement from others that directly contradicts one's actual experience with a task or behavior can have the unintended result of undermining or weakening self-efficacy.[34] Verbal encouragement and social feedback may be most influential in boosting personal efficacy beliefs when coupled with concrete and effective skills and strategies for success on a specific task or goal.[34,36]

The fourth way to build self-efficacy relates to a conscious consideration of the individual's physical and emotional states.[1,35] This refers to the physical and emotional states prior to, during, and following behaviors directed toward goal achievement. A difficult challenge should not be considered when someone is fatigued, hungry, stressed or not feeling well. If it is determined that success is likely only under the best of conditions, then individuals should be encouraged to make the attempt when they are feeling up to the challenge.

RELEVANCE AND APPLICATION ACROSS THEORIES

Most prominent theories of health behavior include self-efficacy or related constructs. This section covers the relevance, integration, and application of self-efficacy in major theoretical models of behavior and behavior change. With broad investigation and application, the theories have been evaluated over multiple decades with demonstrated relevance to a wide variety of health related behaviors.

Social Cognitive or Social Learning Theory

A social psychologist, Bandura developed Social Cognitive Theory (SCT), built upon a triadic model of reciprocal causation. The model conceptualizes the ways in which humans acquire competencies, values, goal-oriented behaviors, motivation, and self-regulation. The triad includes: 1) personal factors, 2) environmental factors, and 3) behavioral factors. For example, factors related to the individual such as knowledge, attitudes, values, and beliefs elicit certain behaviors and in turn, the outcome of those behaviors influence one's knowledge, attitudes, values and beliefs. Similarly, the social environment has an influence on attitudes, values and behavior, and when behavior leads to success or 'failure', then perceptions about the environment are likely to be reinforced or altered. This dynamic interaction suggests that if we want to apply a new behavior to a task or goal, in order to increase the likelihood of success, we can shape the new behavior by altering its antecedents. Consequently, perceived self-efficacy can change throughout the lifespan; it can change from situation to situation; it can change from moment to moment; it can change depending on the task itself or the nature and significance of the goal.

Bandura[40] noted that previous models were uni-directional, indicating that either personal factors or environmental factors determined behavior. The unique aspect of his triad was that each of the three elements was proposed to be in a dynamic reciprocal circumstance with the other two. Thus, behavior itself, as well as the outcomes associated with behavior, also shape attitudes, beliefs, values, motivation, self-regulation, the social environment, and future behavior. This reciprocal interaction helps to explain why seemingly similar circumstances can create a different behavior within the same person. If the perceived intensity or importance of one variable is changed, the complex dynamic can shift the balance and a different behavior may be chosen.

The SCT recognizes that personal characteristics such as knowledge and attitudes play a role in behavior. The theory also recognizes that a person chooses a particular behavior, in part, because of environmental influences such as the social milieu and the observed behavior of others. This is especially true if the others who are being observed are similar to the person who is selecting a behavior. Given the dynamic connection between cognitive and personal factors, environmental influences, and previous behavior, the SCT also has been called the Social Learning theory.[41]

Bandura recognized that human beings are adaptive and resilient. It is expected that people will learn from varied behavioral experiences. If a chosen behavior does not turn out well, the individual may suffer some diminished self-efficacy. If a chosen behavior does turn out well, self-efficacy may be enhanced. In either situation, this experience will influence a person's perceived ability and goal directed behavior.

Transtheoretical Model

The Transtheoretical Model (TTM), developed by James Prochaska and Carlo DiClemente, both clinical psychologists, is an integrative model of intentional behavior.[42] TTM focuses on the decision making process and describes how people modify a problem behavior or acquire a positive behavior. In TTM, change is viewed as a process rather than an event and stage of change is the central organizing construct in the model. The five stages of change are:

- Precontemplation: individual has no intention to change in the near future, usually defined as in the next 6 months;
- Contemplation: individual intends to change in the next 6 months and hence recognizes the need for change (the pros of change), but also views the barriers (cons) as too large to change in the immediate future, defined as the next 30 days;
- Preparation: individual intends to change in the next 30 days and is taking active steps toward change (e.g., reducing the number of cigarettes smoked);

- Action: individual is actively engaged in the behavior change for less than 6 months time so remains at pretty high risk for relapse;
- Maintenance: individual has adopted the behavior change for at least 6 months time and so relapse is less of a risk.

A final stage of termination is part of the TTM though often not part of the studies conducted due to constraints with duration of follow-up in research. Termination is defined as no temptation and total self-efficacy. Approximately 20% of alcoholics or smokers reach that criteria - i.e. they have no temptation to go back to using and reach that criteria after 5 years. Explicitly, TTM integrates key constructs from other theories, including the processes of change, which are ten cognitive and behavior activities that facilitate change, the decisional balance (pros and cons), and self-efficacy.

In TTM, self-efficacy is represented either as one's confidence to change a behavior or, the converse, situational temptations to engage in the problem behavior, in different conditions or situations. Predictable changes

have been found in the self-efficacy concepts of confidence and temptation across the stages of change and in diverse populations with a wide range of risk behaviors. The TTM Situational Temptation Measure[43] assesses the intensity of urges to engage in a specific behavior (e.g., smoking) across a series of difficult conditions such as negative affect, social pressure, and boredom. Notably, both the self-efficacy and temptation measures were found to have the same structure,[44] whereby temptation declines from pre-action to the stages of action and maintenance, while self-efficacy climbs (Figure 11-2). Both constructs are especially sensitive to the change process in the post-action stages and are good predictors of behavioral relapse.

Health Belief Model

Created in the early 1950s by Godfrey Hochbaum, Stephen Kegels, and Irwin Rosenstock, social psychologists working in the U.S. Public Health Services, the Health Belief Model (HBM) was developed to explain why people do, or do not take action in response to public health campaigns.[45] These campaigns

Figure 11-2:   The Relationship between Stage of Change and the Self-Efficacy Concepts of Temptation and Confidence.

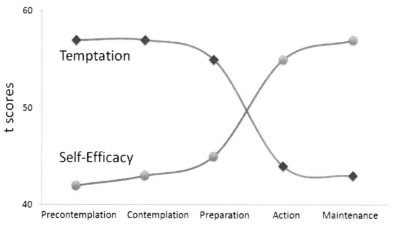

Acknowledgement: URI Cancer Prevention Research Center http://www.uri.edu/research/cprc/TTM/detailedoverview.htm.

most often focused on communicable disease through screening programs to prevent the spread of infection or immunizations to prevent the onset of disease. It was perplexing that more people did not participate in the programs despite being free of charge, offered in neighborhoods throughout many hours of the day, and with few barriers such as long lines, pain, or serious side effects.

One study of public health behavior examined the public's participation in a free screening program for tuberculosis.[46] The research team found that 82% of the people who believed they were susceptible to tuberculosis AND believed that early detection was beneficial participated by having a chest x-ray. In contrast, only 21% of the people who believed they were not susceptible and that early detection was not beneficial participated. The HBM was developed in response to these findings and posited that perceived susceptibility and perceived benefit were important drivers of action.

When the focus of prevention shifted from communicable disease to chronic disease, prevention design also had to change. Heart disease, cancer, stroke, accidents, and diabetes, the new prominent causes of death could not be prevented by a single screening or through a vaccination. Chronic disease is strongly related to lifestyle, and lifestyle change is difficult to initiate and retain. Lifestyle change requires strong motivation and commitment, both of which had to be accounted for in a new paradigm. Rosenstock added environmental cues and, in 1988, self-efficacy to the model after determining that these two factors increased HBM's predictive accuracy.[47]

`There is general agreement among those who work in public health that when individuals perceive they are susceptible, AND when it is perceived that the consequences of not taking action are significant, AND when it is perceived that the benefits of taking action outweigh the barriers (time, monetary cost, and risk associated with the intervention),

AND when there are cues to action, AND when they are confident that the recommendation can be achieved (self-efficacy), THEN it is highly probable that most individuals will take the steps that are necessary to protect themselves.[47-50]

Theory of Planned Behavior and Reasonable Action

HBM posited that beliefs had a direct effect on behavior. In contrast, the Theory of Reasoned Action (TRA) asserted that the effect of beliefs on behavior was mediated through intentions to perform that behavior. Martin Fishbein and Icek Azjen, both social psychologists, developed TRA in 1975. "Reasoned action" implies that with intent to change behavior, one has arrived at a place along a continuum of readiness where various pros and cons have been examined and weighed in advance and that a change in behavior has in some measure influenced the person's behavioral intention.[51]

The TRA primarily focused on attitudes and social norms. In 1985, Azjen modified the model to include perceived behavioral control (self-efficacy) and created the model known as the Theory of Planned Behavior (TPB). An important element of the TPB is that the environment can encourage individuals to move from a state of casual consideration (pre-readiness) to one where they are more actively considering adoption of a behavior. Of course, this also can work in the opposite direction, where knowledge and attitudes may be sufficiently strong to prompt a behavior change, but awareness that social norms do not support this behavior change inhibits one's readiness to act. In cases where knowledge, attitudes, and social norms are aligned in a positive direction, people develop strong behavioral intent and behavior change can be predicted.[52,53]

Armitage and Conner[54] conducted a meta-analysis of the TPB by reviewing 185 studies published through 1997. The TPB accounted for

27% of the variance in behavior and 39% of the variance in intention. Self-efficacy accounted for significant amounts of variance in intention and behavior independent of the theory of attitudes and subjective norms. A second meta-analysis determined that self-efficacy is a better predictor of exercise behavior than intention.[55]

HOW SELF-EFFICACY AFFECTS BEHAVIOR AND BEHAVIOR CHANGE: REVIEW OF THE EMPIRICAL LITERATURE

Application to Motivation

Self-efficacy is a critical proximal determinant of motivation to adopt health practices and change unhealthy behaviors.[56-57] According to Bandura,[34] self-efficacy contributes to motivation in three primary ways. First, self-efficacy influences the selection of goals and fosters motivation for behavior change. A person's *perceived* capability to make and maintain behavior change is thought to drive intentions for personal change to an even greater extent than *actual* ability.[34] People have low ambition to pursue health practices for which perceived self-efficacy is low, and tend to set and work toward health-related goals when they believe that they have what it takes to succeed. The act of setting specific, attainable goals incentivizes action and gives direction to behavior, leading to increases in self-efficacy and motivation to learn new skills.

Second, perceived self-efficacy affects the amount of effort that an individual devotes to a task.[34] Individuals with strong self-efficacy to carry out a specific behavior work harder and are more committed to their goals than those who lack self-efficacy. In turn, greater efforts and persistence contribute to higher achievement, which can generate subsequent increases in self-efficacy.[58,59]

Third, self-efficacy beliefs are crucial in maintaining a person's motivation to persevere following difficulties or in the absence of quick or easy results.[34] People who believe strongly in their ability to succeed on a task or make a health behavior change are more likely to interpret setbacks as a challenge to overcome, rather than as a failure. This is particularly relevant for relapse to addictive or unhealthy behaviors. The likelihood that stressful, risky situations will trigger relapse is highly contingent on abstinence self-efficacy, or a person's perceived capability to resist temptation and cope in more adaptive ways.[60,61] For example, substance abuse treatment studies provide considerable evidence that high self-efficacy predicts greater latency to relapse and greater post treatment abstinence (for review, see Kadden & Litt[62]). Self-efficacy is also paramount in determining whether an individual can bounce back in the event of a slip.[60] People with high self-efficacy tend to view relapse as a temporary misstep that can be managed, while those with low self-efficacy are more vulnerable to full-blown relapse to old problematic behaviors.[34]

Application to Skill Building

According to Bandura, self-efficacy is related to the building of skills in three key ways: (1) affecting an individual's motivation or choices to learn and engage in the new skill, (2) influencing how much effort is expended, and (3) determining how long an individual will persist in the face of obstacles or difficulties. Individuals' expectations that they have the capability to learn and maintain a new skill directly impact the likelihood that they will learn and adopt it (e.g., "I am capable of learning the necessary skills to start and follow through with an exercise plan"). This section describes key strategies for supporting the development of self-efficacy for skill building including the influences identified earlier of mastery experiences, vicarious experiences, social persuasion, and physical and emotional states; behavior modification strategies of goal setting, action plans, and self-monitoring; and, of increased attention recently, contingent monetary incentives.

Mastery of experience builds self-efficacy not merely for the specific situation, but more broadly for the next and every subsequent goal directed behavior. On a practical level, parents, educators, public health and health professionals can help others improve their health by establishing situations where the individual prepares a personal health improvement plan; has the opportunity to establish short term goals that are challenging but attainable; selects appropriate behaviors to overcome obstacles; and understands those adaptive behaviors that engendered success. Performance is greatest when goals are difficult enough that success brings satisfaction, but not so difficult that 'failure' is likely.[63]

As part of the development of self-efficacy, there should be many opportunities for vicarious learning by observing others' goal achievement. This provides external reinforcement that confidence, motivation, and commitment frequently result in attainment of a goal. If the successful person is similar to the individual who is observing this experience, the connection is even stronger. Vicarious experiences can be fostered in family, group, or classroom-based systems; via peer-to-peer counseling; using exemplary models; and even through virtual world avatars, described below in Applications to New Media.

Through this process, it is easy to imagine how people adopting healthier eating habits, for example, could encourage their friends, family, or coworkers to adopt healthier eating habits through their visibly changed behavior, especially if the new habits were accompanied by outwardly expressed attitudes extolling the virtues of healthy eating. These individuals, in turn, could encourage those around them in other social environments to adopt healthier behaviors, slowly creating healthier eating environments.

Verbal persuasion occurs when another person offers encouragement or positive reinforcement for wanting to attain a goal. Self-efficacy is not fixed – rather it responds to cognitive, social, and behavioral skills and is influenced by the environment. Further, it has been widely demonstrated that the higher the level of self-efficacy, the higher the performance accomplishments.[64] Verbal persuasion is an example of an environmental influence. When an individual gives encouragement or makes statements related to an expectation about someone else's ability to perform a task, assuming that the comment is plausible, that person's self-efficacy may be enhanced. Worksite based health promotion programs often involve behavior modification in groups where cognitive-behavioral techniques are employed. Often, these programs build verbal persuasion into the group process by encouraging participants to offer positive (but plausible) comments. In addition, some behavioral support groups build specific assignments into the curriculum, for instance, having a participant ask someone who was able to achieve a similar behavior change goal to serve as a guide or mentor.

Cognitive appraisals of physiological arousal are often utilized as a barometer to gauge performance ability. People often interpret high levels of arousal (e.g., increased heart rate, sweating) as a sign that they are unprepared or lacking the skills needed to succeed at a task or manage a situation,[34] and heightened physiological arousal can decrease self-efficacy by leading to the avoidance of the arousing task and increasing vulnerability to give up. For example, someone who has recently started an exercise routine may construe shortness of breath and racing heart as an indication of his or her inability to perform physically and eventually quit exercising.[39,65] Conversely, feelings of calmness or decreased arousal may be interpreted as a sign of confidence or ability to perform a task or behavior, contributing to increased self-efficacy. Having a negative physical and/ or emotional reaction to 'failure' diminishes confidence. Resilience and optimism on the other hand encourage the individual to pursue new tactics rather than to give up and accept 'failure'. Helping individuals modify their negative or inaccurate interpretations of physiological arousal and emotions may be a useful tool for reducing stress and increasing self-efficacy.[1,39]

Goal setting is an important requisite for the enhancement of self-efficacy. When goals are set too high or too low, they do not motivate and when goals are vaguely contemplated, commitment is diminished as obstacles arise. Successfully achieving a worthy goal both reinforces self-efficacy and enhances it for future challenges. One of the important skills related to goal setting is the ability to anticipate obstacles and apply pre-conceived alternative tactics to overcome them. An effective strategy in goal setting is to record progress and set backs in a journal, reflect on patterns to determine approaches that produce the best outcomes and then use this new knowledge to plan responses to future obstacles. Self-efficacy is affected by self-observation, self-judgment, and self-reaction to progress.

Action plans that clearly outline the steps needed to get to the desired outcome, and create situations that allow a person to gradually test out a new health-related behavior in an achievable way, can augment self-efficacy and lead to the development of new skills.[57] For example, a systematic review of intervention techniques for changing physical activity behavior determined that action planning (i.e., when, where, and how a person would perform an activity) and praising participants for their efforts toward achieving a specified goal were strongly predictive of both physical activity self-efficacy and physical activity behavior.[66]

Self-regulation is the application of an integrated learning process in which the learner observes, considers the situation and possible adaptations of behavior and then takes what is perceived to be prudent action. Self-monitoring is essential because it enables

the individual to process thoughts and feelings about how things are going and whether to continue on the pre-determined path or to make adjustments in the plan. Behavior change typically produces ambivalence at the very least. Active thought and conscious consideration enables the person to reflect on the change process, considering the perceived benefits against the perceived costs. The individual learns to apply reasoned judgment to behavior, this is likely to increase productive behaviors and decrease non-productive or counter-productive behaviors. Self-monitoring is a way of managing ambivalence, internal conflict, and the negative emotions that come with the possibility of "failure" to achieve a goal. Continual awareness through self-monitoring and persistent commitment through self-regulation improve the likelihood of goal attainment.[67] Self-regulatory skills have been found to be significantly associated with the volume of exercise and fruit and vegetable consumption in severely obese adults enrolled in a behavioral weight management program.[68] See Chapter 8 for more discussion on goal setting and self-regulation.

Monetary incentives are an increasingly common tool for engagement in health promotion activities, doubling or tripling participation rates, with potential implications for skill building.[69] Currently, most (63%) large firms (200+ employees) offer participatory wellness programs, in which employees receive incentives for engaging in wellness activities such as health screenings, exercise or quit smoking programs.[70] In the short-term, incentives for participation can advance clients' motivation or stage for making a behavior change; although in the long term, financial payment could potentially decrease intrinsic motivation. Though not directly addressed in relation to self-efficacy theory, monetary incentives may affect mastery experiences if they help people initiate a health behavior change and they see positive results. In multiple tobacco treatment trials, contingently-reinforced incentives, particularly those repeated over an extended period, are related to increased confidence with quitting smoking,[71-73] though changes in confidence seem to wane at the end of the anticipated contingency period. In a study comparing personalized feedback (intrinsic motivation), monetary incentives (extrinsic motivation), or both as an adjunct to self-help materials (control group), all motivation groups were more likely than the controls to report using the study cessation materials; those in the intrinsic motivation group were twice as likely as the other groups to report abstinence at both 3 and 12 months; and notably, the incentives did not increase cessation attempts and was associated with greater relapse among those who did quit.[74] The findings support concerns regarding the generalizability and sustainability of financial incentives for health behavior change. There also is evidence from weight loss trials that incentives can be counterproductive. In a 3-group study with 177 men and women, Jeffrey and Wing[75] compared standard behavioral therapy combined with food provision or incentives or both and found that although incentives led to increases in physical activity, they did not help people keep weight off in the long-term nor help people reduce barriers to change, which can affect self-efficacy. Though not centered on health behavior change, Mowen and colleagues[76] reported on the relationship between incentives, goal setting, and self-efficacy. They found that when people were paid under a piece-rate system (i.e., paid for completing small units along the way to a bigger goal), higher goals resulted in better performance than medium/easy goals. However, when people were paid only when completing the full goal, higher goals resulted in performance worse than that with medium/easy goals. It was interpreted that when monetary incentives are viewed as really far away (as it was with the hard goal), people may feel overwhelmed and less self-efficacious, and hence may not try as hard. Hence, the influence of monetary incentives on self-efficacy appears dependent on the *form* of monetary incentive given. A small study of a college telefund program examined monetary incentives added to goal setting to enhance performance of the student outbound callers. The study reported increases in both performance and self-efficacy; however, the individual contributory effects of goal setting versus financial incentives on productivity were not analyzed.[77] Given the broad adoption of incentives in worksite wellness programming, it is surprising how little research has examined the impact on self-efficacy, skill building, and behavior change. This issue is raised in the section on Unanswered Questions.

Application to Multiple Lifestyle Risk Behaviors

Lifestyle behaviors tend to cluster. For example, poor diet and inactivity levels commonly co-occur and most smokers (>90%) have at least one additional unhealthy behavior, or "risk factor." In the U.S., most adults have two or more behavioral risk factors.[78,79]

The co-occurrence of risk behaviors predicts a heightened risk of morbidity and mortality, as well as increased health care costs.[80] Given a window of intervention opportunity, a higher impact paradigm is to target multiple behaviors. Growing evidence suggests the potential for multiple-health behavior change (MHBC) interventions to have much greater impact on public health than single-behavior interventions.[81]

Constructs and concepts that generalize across risk behaviors and are instrumental for change, such as self-efficacy, have played a central role in interventions that target multiple risk behaviors for change.[81] The change process appears to be similar for different health behaviors, and it may be efficient to work on multiple behaviors at the same time in a single intervention. Lifestyle behaviors also may serve as a gateway to intervention on behaviors for which individuals have low motivation to change.[82] Confidence or self-efficacy gained from making changes in one behavior may serve to support changes in additional risks. In a three-year prospective study, individuals who quit smoking significantly increased their physical activity, whereas continued smokers did not.[83] Similar changes were not observed for diet or alcohol use.

In a study of smokers who were sedentary, a significant cross-behavioral association was found with self-efficacy. Individuals with high levels of confidence for quitting smoking also reported high confidence for changing their physical activity.[84] While the data were cross-sectional in nature, the authors concluded that the associations provide preliminary evidence for how change in one behavior may be related to change in another. Individuals working on increasing their physical activity seem motivated and confident about decreasing their smoking and vice versa.

The Mediterranean Lifestyle Program is an example of a successful population-level MHBC intervention.[85] This randomized clinical trial for postmenopausal women with type 2 diabetes employed SCT to guide intervention strategies to address healthful eating, physical activity, stress management, smoking cessation, and social support. Intervention participants made and maintained modest but significant improvements in self-efficacy related to nutrition, exercise, and illness management and at 12 and 24 months, demonstrated improvements in all targeted lifestyle behaviors except smoking (there were too few smokers to analyze effects of the intervention on tobacco use).

The PREVENT trial, which utilized SCT, broadened intervention goals to include raising participants' self-efficacy for changing multiple risks by helping them recognize the natural intersections among their risky health habits. General cognitive and behavioral skills also were taught for application in changing any of their risk behaviors.[86] While significant

changes were reported in multiple risk behaviors, mediating effects of self-efficacy on the behavioral changes observed were not reported.

MHBC research is still fairly early in development and growing rapidly. Harnessing of key constructs that generalize across behaviors and theories, such as self-efficacy, has aided the research in this area and informed intervention design and evaluation.

Application to Multiple Demographic Populations

Self-efficacy has been found to predict health-behaviors across multiple demographic populations. Results from several studies with adolescents, older adults, and high-risk populations are reviewed below.

Self-efficacy is an important construct in positive youth development.[87] High self-efficacy predicts a range of health-related skills among adolescents including greater consumption of fruits and vegetables, higher intake of calcium-rich foods,[88] lower fat intake,[89-91] smoking cessation,[92-94] drug addiction,[95] alcohol use,[96] internet usage,[97] physical activity,[98] and decisions to delay the initiation of sex.[99] Further, interventions that boost self-efficacy among adolescents predict increases in health-related skills. For example, Bricker and colleagues[100] conducted a telephone smoking cessation intervention that utilized multiple elements of SCT with 2,151 senior year high school smokers. The intervention significantly increased smokers' self-efficacy to resist smoking in social and stressful situations, and self-efficacy boosts accounted for over 55% of the interventions impact on smoking cessation ($p < 0.001$).

A large body of evidence supports the predictive role of self-efficacy in health-related behaviors among seniors.[101] Studies that specifically utilize SCT principles to target physical activity self-efficacy among older adults have been effective in boosting self-efficacy and increasing physical activity initiation and maintenance.[39] The positive contribution of self-efficacy to health behavior change is further demonstrated by results from a review of older adults' adherence to randomized controlled trials of exercise, indicating that exercise self-efficacy is one of the strongest predictors of exercise adherence in this population.[102]

Self-efficacy is an important predictor of a variety of health behaviors and behavior change among high-risk populations. For example, among persons with serious mental illness, low abstinence self-efficacy, defined as one's perceived ability to cope with difficulties (e.g., stress, urges, temptations) without using substances, is associated with significantly higher substance use.[103] Self-efficacy is also a critical predictor of sexual risk-taking behavior in the gay community and among high-risk youth.[104] For example, in a study of the sexual health practices of 414 homeless young men and women aged 16-20, condom use self-efficacy was positively associated with safe sex practices and sexual self-care (e.g., getting tested or treated for a sexually transmitted disease).[105] Further, clinical trial studies of smoking cessation have demonstrated that increases in self-efficacy among people living with HIV/AIDS substantially mediate treatment effects on smoking cessation.[106,107]

Application within Different Settings & Groups

There is also convincing evidence that self-efficacy predicts behavior and behavior change across a range of groups, including families, schools, and communities. Families provide a social context that is critical for health promotion. In particular, parental self-efficacy has been identified as a strong predictor of health behaviors among family members. Parental self-efficacy predicts parental competence and child adjustment,[108] and parents' perceived ability to provide healthy environments for their children impact children's health and adoption of a range of health-related behaviors. For example, working parents with low self-efficacy to plan meals and choose healthy foods at the grocery store are more likely to take their families to fast-food restaurants and less likely to prepare meals in advance, compared with working parents with high self-efficacy in this domain.[109] Further, parental confidence and perceived ability to act on their child's oral health needs is associated with child oral health status, including regular dental checkups and more frequent brushing.[110,111] A study of low-income pregnant women found that low breastfeeding self-efficacy (e.g., "I am not confident in my ability to breastfeed my baby") was strongly associated with low intentions to breastfeed.[112] Strong self-efficacy has also been associated with better self-care and healthier behaviors in the context of high family stress. For example, among individuals caring for family members with Alzheimer's dementia, greater caregiver self-efficacy beliefs related to obtaining respite and controlling upsetting thoughts were associated with engagement in a greater number of positive health behaviors.[113]

Schools provide a useful setting for conducting health behavior change interventions with children. A review of meta-analyses on school-based interventions for health promotion and weight control indicated that school-based interventions can successfully produce weight loss.[114] Further, interventions that utilized strategies to increase skills related to self-efficacy, including education, self-monitoring, goal setting, skill-building, and improving self-talk, were listed among those of most value. A systematic review of 24 school-based interventions for health-related behaviors, including physical activity and dietary behaviors, found that the majority of studies were informed by SCT, and all interventions led to improvements in one or more health-related behaviors.[115] Consistent with results from a previous review on school-based interventions for physical activity,[116] there was some evidence indicating that increases in self-efficacy mediated treatment effects on physical activity.

Communities provide an important context for the development of self-efficacy and health risk behaviors. According to Bandura,[34] communities are healthier when residents have a greater sense of collective efficacy, or belief in the ability of community members to support each other and work together to impact positive social change. Similar to self-efficacy, collective efficacy influences people's goals, effort to reach those goals, and resilience to keep fighting for the greater good of the community when collective efforts are unsuccessful or slow to show results .[34]

Lower collective efficacy is associated with greater community violence[117] and a number of negative health outcomes, including mortality,[118,119] lower birth weight,[120] earlier onset of sexual intercourse and a greater number of sexual partners,[121,122] greater self-reported victimization and homicide rates,[123] partner violence,[124] greater body mass index,[125] and poorer overall health.[126] Neighborhoods with low collective efficacy are hypothesized to contribute to poorer health among residents through a variety of mechanisms, including lower social support and decreased motivation to initiate or fight for positive health changes (e.g., political initiatives to increase neighborhood safety, walkability, access to parks).[125]

Theory-informed community-based interventions are an important avenue for increasing collective and individual self-efficacy and promoting health.[127-129] The Stanford Five-City Project provides a model example of a successful theory-informed community-based program.[129] This study tested the longitudinal impact of a SCT-based communitywide health education program on cardiovascular disease risk factors using a large sample of individuals from two treatment and two control California cities (Treatment: N = 122,800, Control: N = 197,500).[129] The education

program utilized multiple methods, including radio and television, newspapers, school-based programs for students and teachers, and education materials for parents. Results indicated that this low-cost intervention successfully increased knowledge of cardiovascular disease risk factors and reduced total mortality risk scores and coronary heart disease risk scores. Community-based studies that utilize serial dramas have also been successful in promoting health education, increasing self-efficacy, and fostering health behaviors in communities across the globe (for review, see Bandura[130]). Informed by SCT, these television dramas depict real-life health problems (e.g., transmission of AIDS), model healthy behaviors, and provide education and resources.

Application to New Media

An area with exciting potential and growing interest is the use of new media for increasing self-efficacy and supporting behavior change. Virtual Reality (VR) technologies and interactive digital games provide an innovative channel for promoting health-related behavior change.[131-133] Still in the early stages of development, initial research suggests that interactive game-based interventions hold promise to enhance self-efficacy and health-related behavior change.[133-135] A few examples are featured here.

VR technologies produce multi-sensory, interactive 3D environments that simulate real-world experiences.[133] Internet-based Virtual Worlds, developed using VR technologies, provide a platform for participants to interact using digitalized personal representations or "avatars".[134] Researchers have harnessed virtual world technologies to promote health behaviors, for example by rewarding avatars for engaging in health behavior (e.g., riding a bike).[134] A successful illustration of a comprehensive virtual world program designed to promote self-efficacy, physical activity and healthy diet is *Club One Island* (Johnston et al., 2012), an interactive weight loss community informed by the Social Cognitive Theory. Briefly, *Club One Island* immerses users in a 3D complex environment that mirrors the physical world and includes spaces such as restaurants, mini-mart convenience stores, and indoor and outdoor workout facilities. Users are provided with a professional team and access to weight-loss related educational tools 24 hours a day, seven days a week. Using a personalized avatar, users have opportunities to interact with and get encouragement from other users (e.g., during social support classes), practice healthy behaviors (e.g., controlling food intake at a party), make healthy choices while eating out (e.g., restaurant menu items use a stoplight model with red, yellow, and green color coding to reflect nutritional value), engage in physical activity (e.g., cycling, swimming, roller skating, surfing), and participate in a 12-week group weight loss program that includes healthy habit and physical activity classes led by certified health professionals.

Results from a 12-week trial that compared Club One Island to a similar weight loss community in the physical world indicated that both groups lost weight (virtual world: 8.6 lbs; physical world: 6.2 lbs). Further, virtual-world participants experienced significant increases in self-efficacy (related to physical activity and weight-loss), engagement in physical activity, consumption of fruits and vegetables, and breakfast, while the face-to-face group demonstrated no changes in these outcomes. Given that vicarious experiences provide more influential sources of self-efficacy when models are similar to the observer,[1,34] it is noteworthy that virtual world participants identified with their avatars and altered the physical appearance of their avatars as they lost weight in real life.[131] The provision of greater opportunities to vicariously master positive health behaviors and manage health-related challenges in the virtual world might account for the observed increases in self-efficacy and

health practices.[131] The following example comment from a virtual world participant supports this hypothesis:

"Usually when I'm on the treadmill at the gym, I walk for 5 minutes and run 1 minute, which is really challenging. This last time, I pictured my avatar running and I felt like my avatar and it made me feel stronger. I ran for 2 minutes easily."[131]

A variety of video games have been developed using behavioral change theories to motivate a wide range of positive health changes, from physical activity and nutrition to disease self-management (for review, see Baranowski et al.[132]; Lieberman[137]). Preliminary results indicate that behavior change video games can promote health-related self-efficacy and increase a variety of health behaviors.[132,137,138] For example, the game *"Squire's Quest! (SQ!)"* applies multiple elements of behavioral change theories (e.g., education, goal setting, mastery) to help children increase fruit and vegetable intake.[139] In this game, players are knights in training (squires) who must gain strength to save the king and queen from invaders by consuming more fruits and vegetables. In a 5-week randomized clinical trial with 1578 4th grade students, the treatment (25 minutes of play, 2 times per week) led to a 0.9 serving per day increase in actual fruit and vegetable consumption.[139]

Exercise video games, or exergames (e.g., *Wii Fit, Frisbee Golf, and Dance Dance Revolution*), provide another creative avenue for health promotion. These games require physical exertion from players and can be utilized with multiple demographic populations in a wide range of settings, including hospitals, schools and community centers.[137,138] These active-play video games provide opportunities for players to increase physical activity self-efficacy through mastery experiences, skill building, and social interactions.[137] Preliminary studies indicate that exergames show promise to increase physical activity self-efficacy, cardiovascular endurance, and fitness, but additional research is needed.[132] Accordingly, the American Heart Association has partnered with Nintendo of America to support further development and evaluation of active-play video games for health promotion.[137]

At this stage of development, interactive game-based interventions that are informed by empirically-based, theoretical frameworks appear to hold great promise to promote health-related self-efficacy and encourage behavior change. The long-term impact of these technologies for health promotion remains to be seen.

UNANSWERED QUESTIONS

Volumes of studies and public discourse exist concerning self-efficacy, yet understanding of this construct is not always solidified and put into practice. While most health educators are familiar with leading theories of behavior and behavior change and key constructs such as stage of change and intention, self-efficacy is less well understood. Perhaps the name of the construct is a barrier to understanding or confusion arises in distinguishing self-efficacy from self-concept and self-esteem. How can behavior change programs expect success if practitioners are not comfortable with the importance and practice of self-efficacy? This chapter was written with the goal of facilitating broader understanding and use of this key concept.

Despite the extensive research on this concept, a number of theoretical questions remain for the field. For example, there is growing interest in the influence of incentives on behavior adoption and maintenance, particularly with regard to employer wellness programs. As mentioned, a majority of employers offer incentives for participating in wellness programs, such as health screenings, exercise or quit smoking programs.[70] Guidelines within the Affordable Care Act, may shift this incentive strategy toward health-contingent wellness programs because they allow employers to charge a differential in health plan premium of at least 30% and possibly as high as 50% based on achieving or not achieving health behavior related goals (e.g., quit smoking, weight loss). It is likely that this will make it harder for individuals with low self-efficacy to benefit from incentives. Few studies have investigated the effect of incentive programs on self-efficacy and more research is needed, particularly in relation to internalized motivations and long-term maintenance of behavior change. A diversity of questions remains regarding the types, amounts, and frequency of incentives and for whom and what behaviors they are most effective. When incentives are offered, is participation comparable for people at all levels of performance and health or do only the confident, healthy and fit participate? Certainly, from the employer perspective, the return on investment is more likely to come from improvements among those who are at highest risk. Should the highest risk employees, therefore, be able to receive a larger incentive since they may contribute greater savings than employees who are healthy? (See Chapter 4 for more details on the amount and form of the premium differentials allowed)

The relationship between the work environment and employee health-related self-efficacy is another area in need of greater investigation. In what ways do employer-sponsored wellness programs use environmental influences to increase self-efficacy for behavior change (e.g., by providing opportunities for co-workers to share success stories of changing risk behaviors or adopting health behaviors)? How can employee self-efficacy and motivation to participate and engage in existing workplace wellness programs be bolstered? Given that a family culture of wellness also is important for employee health, should employer wellness programs encourage spouse, same sex domestic partners, and children to participate?

The workplace provides an important social context for the development and maintenance of healthy behaviors with great potential to harness new media interventions. While interactive game-based interventions have been successfully employed in a number of settings (e.g., schools, hospitals, community centers) to increase health related self-efficacy and support a range of positive health changes, the impact of these technologies for health promotion in the workplace is unknown. To what extent would employees utilize active play videos if they were readily available (e.g., in the break room)? Would active-play video games enhance physical activity self-efficacy among employees and contribute to greater collective efficacy in the workplace (e.g., via increased opportunities for mastery experiences, modeling, and positive social interactions)? Conversely, would active play video games in the workplace have the potential to promote a competitive work environment that contributes to lower collective self-efficacy and poorer health among employees (e.g., via lower social support, greater stress)?

The percentage of individuals working from home is rapidly rising in the United States,[140] as new information and communication technologies (e.g., live video chat) have made it increasingly feasible for employees to work remotely. Telecommuting is thought to have value in terms of recruiting and retaining employees, improving employee motivation, saving infrastructure costs, and decreasing sick days and commuting costs.[141-143] However, there are also concerns about the potential negative impacts of telecommuting on productivity, innovation, motivation, and collaboration. The CEO of Yahoo recently decided to end the company's work from home policy, igniting national controversy.[144] The benefits and limitations of working from home are not yet fully understood, leaving many questions unanswered about the impact of telecommuting on self-efficacy, motivation, morale, and public health. For example, does telecommuting increase self-efficacy and productivity and lead to greater health via reduced hassle, greater autonomy, and increased flexibility to engage in health behaviors? Alternatively, does working from home restrict opportunities for positive environmental influences on self-efficacy, such as social modeling and social support, or reduce the likelihood that employees engage in health behaviors? Future research that addresses these questions will be critical to better understanding the behavioral and societal health impacts of telecommuting.

CONCLUSION

Confidence shapes so much of a person's attitudes, beliefs, and expectations, and research has consistently demonstrated the important bidirectional influence of self-efficacy on performance and behavioral choices. Within this chapter, a variety of behavioral theories have been presented, each one suggesting that goal attainment can be influenced through self-efficacy. Self-efficacy, the perception of one's ability to achieve a goal, can be enhanced yet also is vulnerable to diminishment, particularly when the learner experiences difficulty and begins to believe that the goal may not be achievable.

Enhancing self efficacy should be part of every plan to make a lifestyle change for health improvement. An individual who experiences success after struggling with obstacles that could potentially thwart achievement of the goal, comes away from the experience with even stronger self-efficacy and more able to accept the next set of challenges. Individuals who are not successful may come away from the experience believing that they are not as capable as they previously thought. One role of an educator, coach, clinician, and even boss is to understand the powerful effects that self-efficacy can have on achievement and the powerful effects that either success or 'failure' can have on self-efficacy. In the science of health promotion, the process of behavior change is facilitated in a rich learning environment that is filled with challenge, opportunity, and pride of accomplishment. In the art of health promotion, self-efficacy is crafted with each successful learning opportunity and it is the facilitator's wisdom that enriches the lives of others by building self-efficacy one success at a time.

The behavioral theories described in this chapter form a crucial foundation for health promotion professionals who want to make a difference in the lives of others. Knowledge is rarely a motivator that alone encourages health improvement. Attitudes and intent more directly predict adoption and maintenance of health behaviors. After decades of research on self-efficacy, it is clear that this is a powerful determinant of health behavior and a strong predictor of successful behavior change. We look forward to continued investigation and understanding of the diverse applications of self-efficacy via new channels and media.

Chapter Summary

Self-efficacy, which is malleable and bidirectionally related to performance and environment, reflects an individual's confidence in being able to achieve a goal. Volumes of studies have demonstrated that self-efficacy is an essential construct that can predict successful accomplishment of a goal; as such, the leading behavioral theories in psychology include self-efficacy as part of the learning paradigm. Of the theories presented in this chapter, the Health Belief Model and the Theory of Reasoned Action were changed to include self-efficacy. The Health Belief Model added self-efficacy and environmental cues to the original conceptualization.[47] The Theory of Reasoned Action was re-created by Azjen and the name was changed to the Theory of Planned Behavior.[52] The Transtheoretical Model has always included self-efficacy.[42]

Not only are the models themselves inclusive of the self-efficacy construct, but

study after study focused on each of these theories has demonstrated a powerful relationship between self-efficacy and behavior change. Testing within each of these behavioral theories has shown self-efficacy to be predictive of successful behavior change for a variety of specific behaviors including quitting smoking,[29,30] healthy eating,[26-28] physical activity,[20-25] contraceptive behavior,[31] and many others. This is not to dismiss the importance of additional elements that are part of the behavioral theories, namely, perceived threat and outcome expectancy from the Health Belief Model; behavioral intention from the Theory of Planned Behavior; and the stages of change, decisional balance, and processes of change from the Transtheoretical Model.

Those with low self-efficacy: a) are less eager to set goals, b) enter the process with self-doubt and therefore are less motivated and committed, c) experience fear of failure throughout the process and when a setback does occur, view it as a 'self-fulfilling prophecy', d) view the change process as a psychological threat that can expose their inadequacies, and e) retain a negative outcome expectancy believing that even if the goal is achieved, the effort will not have been worth it. Those with low self-efficacy are likely to blame themselves for 'failure'. If the outcome is positive, they may attribute success to luck or some other external factor. Those with low self-efficacy are likely to have had only intermittent success with mastery of a challenge. As such, when an obstacle arises, those with low self-efficacy have a relatively small repertoire of behavioral choices that can be applied to the situation.

In contrast, those with high self-efficacy tend to have a history of positive experiences with mastering challenges. Because of their previous positive experiences with mastery, those with high self-efficacy tend to have a large repertoire of problem-solving tactics available to them. As such, when an obstacle arises, those who are confident employ one tactic after another, all the while remaining optimistic that one or more of the tactics will effectively remove the barrier, and they will accomplish the goal. Even if none of the responsive tactics effectively overcome the obstacle, those with high self-efficacy seem to have greater resilience, they remain hopeful, and they expect to achieve their goal. Confidence and commitment remain high.

Whether individually, with a coach, group, or online social network, key strategies to increase one's self-efficacy include: a) developing a change plan with challenging but reasonably attainable goals; b) learning from encounters with 'failure' along the way; c) persevering in the face of failure and viewing setbacks as temporary, d) conceptualizing behavior change as a process that will take time, e) remaining optimistic throughout the process believing in success despite an occasional setback, and f) retaining a positive outcome expectancy with the focus that when the goal is achieved, the effort will have been worth it. Going beyond the individual to community-level change, is collective efficacy, with great application and potential for engaging positive social change.

Glossary

Bandura, Albert: social psychologist who developed the model of self-efficacy also referred to as Social Cognitive Theory or the Social Learning Theory

Confidence & temptations: mirror image constructs used in measurement of self-efficacy in the Transtheoretical Model of behavior change, developed by Prochaska and DiClemente

Collective efficacy: Belief in the ability of community members to support each other and work together to impact positive social change

Goal setting: A process of assessment that indicates current status, desired future status, perceived barriers and perceived benefits; construction of a plan of behavior that includes long term goal and short term measurable objectives. Goal setting enhances self-efficacy and increases the likelihood that a goal will be achieved.

Mastery experiences: Performances that are successful; individuals who generally experience success enhance their confidence as each new experience is mastered

Physiological and emotional states: Physical and emotional reactions that occur prior to, during, and following behaviors directed toward goal achievement and play a role in promoting or reducing self-efficacy

Self-efficacy: a belief in one's own ability to succeed in specific situations

Social persuasion: Verbal encouragement and social feedback that can shape perceptions of self-efficacy

Vicarious experiences: indirect learning such as through social modeling; witnessing others successfully performing a challenging task or behavior can promote observers' beliefs in their ability to accomplish a similar activity

Virtual world: Interactive 3D environments that simulate real-world experiences using digitalized personal representations or "avatars"

Learning Objectives

- To define self-efficacy and discuss its application to supporting health behavior change
- To understand the role self-efficacy plays in leading theories of behavior and behavior change
- To identify key influences on self-efficacy
- To appreciate the broad application of self-efficacy across diverse groups

Discussion Questions

1. Define self-efficacy
2. Identify three leading models of behavior and behavior change that incorporate self-efficacy as a central construct
3. How are self-efficacy, motivation, cognitions, and behaviors inter-related?
4. What four key factors influence self-efficacy?
5. Give an example whereby self-efficacy has affected your success (or lack of success) with adopting and maintaining a new behavior
6. Identify three strategies you might try for increasing self-efficacy in a client to start a new exercise program
7. Why is setting specific, small step goals helpful for engaging in a new behavior?
8. In considering the central tenets of Bandura's self-efficacy construct, how might a virtual avatar enhance or reduce the likelihood of building self-efficacy?

REFERENCES

1. Bandura A. Self-efficacy: Toward a unifying theory of behavior change. *Psychol Rev.* 1977; 84(2):191-215.
2. Strecher VJ, McEvoy B, Becker MH, Rosenstock IM. The role of self-efficacy in achieving health behavior change. *Health Educ Q.* 1986; 13(1):73-92.
3. Stajkovic AD, Luthans F. Self-efficacy and work-related performance: A meta-analysis. *Psychol Bull.* 1998; 124(2):240-261.
4. Cancho RFI, Sole RV. The small world of human language. *Proc R Soc B.* 2001;268:2261-2265.
5. Bandura A, Reese L, Adams NE. Microanalysis of action and fear arousal as a function of differential levels of perceived self-efficacy. *J Pers Soc Psychol.* 1982; 43(1):5.
6. Bandura A, Taylor CB, Williams SL, Mefford IN, Barchas JD. Catecholamine secretion as a function of perceived coping self-efficacy. *J Consult Clin Psych.* 1985; 53(3):406-414.
7. Steel P. The nature of procrastination: A meta-analytic and theoretical review of quintessential self-regulatory failure. *Psychol Bull.* 2007; 133(1):65.
8. Lippke S, Wiedemann AU, Ziegelmann JP, Reuter T, Schwarzer R. Self-efficacy moderates the mediation of intentions into behavior via plans. *Am J Health Behav.* 2009; 33(5):521-529.
9. Bandura A. Human agency in social cognitive theory. *Am Psychol.* 1989; 44(9):1175-1184.
10. Ozer EM, Bandura A. Mechanisms governing empowerment effects: A self-efficacy analysis. *J Pers Soc Psychol.* 1990; 58(3):472-486.
11. Betz NE, Hackett G. Applications of self-efficacy theory to understanding career choice behavior. *J Soc Clin Psychol.* 1986; 4(3):279-289.
12. Lent RW, Hackett G. Career self-efficacy: Empirical status and future directions. *J Vocat Behav.* 1987; 30(3):347-382.
13. Bandura A, Cervone D. Self-evaluative and self-efficacy mechanisms governing the motivational effects of goal systems. *J Pers Soc Psychol.* 1983; 45(5):1017-1028.
14. Cervone D, Peake PK. Anchoring, efficacy, and action: The influence of judgmental heuristics on self-efficacy judgments and behavior. *J Pers Soc Psychol.* 1986;50(3):492.
15. Jacobs B, Prentice-Dunn S, Rogers RW. Understanding persistence: An interface of control theory and self-efficacy theory. *Basic Appl Soc Psych.* 1984;5(4):333-347.
16. Weinberg RS, Gould D, Jackson A. Expectations and performance:

An empirical test of Bandura's self-efficacy theory. *J Sport Psychol.* 1979;1(4):320-331.

17. Alden L. Self-efficacy and causal attributions for social feedback. *J Res Pers.* 1986;20(4):460-473.

18. McAuley E, Duncan TE, McElroy M. Self-efficacy cognitions and causal attributions for children's motor performance: An exploratory investigation. *J Genetc Psychol.* 1989;150(1):65-73.

19. Silver WS, Mitchell TR, Gist ME. Responses to successful and unsuccessful performance: The moderating effect of self-efficacy on the relationship between performance and attributions. *Organ Behav Hum Dec.* 1995;62(3):286-299.

20. Eyler AE, Wilcox S, Matson-Koffman D, et al. Correlates of physical activity among women from diverse racial/ ethnic groups. *J Womans Health Gend Based Med.* 2002;11(3):239-253.

21. McAuley E, Mailey EL, Mullen SP, et al. Growth trajectories of exercise self-efficacy in older adults: Influence of measures and initial status. *Health Psychol.* 2011;30(1):75.

22. White JL, Randsdell LB, Vener J, Flohr JA. Factors related to physical activity adherence in women: Review and suggestions for future research. *Women Health.* 2005;41(4):123-148.

23. Sniehotta FF, Scholz U, Schwarzer R. Bridging the intention–behaviour gap: Planning, self-efficacy, and action control in the adoption and maintenance of physical exercise. *Psychol Health.* 2005;20(2):143-160.

24. McAuley, E. Self-efficacy and the maintenance of exercise participation in older adults. *J Behav Med.* 1993;16(1): 103-113.

25. Kaplan RM, Atkins CJ, Reinsch S. Specific efficacy expectations mediate exercise compliance in patients with COPD. *Health Psychol.* 1984;3(3):223.

26. AbuSabha R, Achterberg C. Review of self-efficacy and locus of control for nutrition-and health-related behavior. *J Am Diet Assoc.* 1997;97(10):1122.

27. Anderson ES, Winett RA, Wojcik JR. Self-regulation, self-efficacy, outcome expectations, and social support: Social cognitive theory and nutrition behavior. *Ann Behav Med.* 2007;34(3):304-312.

28. Kreausukon P, Gellert P, Lippke S, Schwarzer R. Planning and self-efficacy can increase fruit and vegetable consumption: a randomized controlled trial. *J Behav Med.* 2012;35(4):443-451.

29. Gwaltney CJ, Metrik J, Kahler CW, Shiffman S. Self-efficacy and smoking cessation: A meta-analysis. *Psychol Addict Behav.* 2009;23(1):56.

30. Condiotte MM, Lichtenstein E. Self-efficacy and relapse in smoking cessation programs. *J Consult Clin Psych.* 1981;49(5):648.

31. Sheeran P, Abraham C, Orbell S. Psychosocial correlates of heterosexual condom use: A meta-analysis. *Psychol Bull.* 1999;125(1):90.

32. Benight CC, Bandura A. Social cognitive theory of posttraumatic recovery: The role of perceived self-efficacy. *Behav Res Ther.* 2004;42(10):1129-1148.

33. Chwalisz K, Altmaier EM, Russell DW. Causal attributions, self-efficacy cognitions, and coping with stress. *J Soc Clin Psychol.* 1992;11(4):377-400.

34. Bandura A. Exercise of personal and collective efficacy in changing societies. In: Bandura A, ed. *Self-Efficacy in Changing Societies.* New York, NY: Cambridge University Press; 1995:1-45.

35. Bandura A. *Self-Efficacy: The Exercise of Control.* New York, NY: Freeman; 1997.

36. Zimmerman BJ, Cleary TJ. Adolescents' development of personal agency. In Pajares F, Urdan T, eds. *Self-Efficacy Beliefs of Adolescents.* Greenwich, CT: Information Age Publishing; 2006:45-69.

37.   Schunk DH. Peer models and children's behavioral change. *Rev Educ Res.* 1987; 57(2):149-174.

38.   Oettingen G. Cross-cultural perspectives on self-efficacy. In Bandura A, ed. *Self-Efficacy in Changing Societies.* New York, NY: Cambridge University Press; 1995: 1-45.

39.   Lee LL, Arthur A, Avis M. Using self-efficacy theory to develop interventions that help older people overcome psychological barriers to physical activity: A discussion paper. *Int J Nurs Stud.* 2008;45(11):1690-1699.

40.   Bandura A. *Social Foundations of Thought and Actions: A Social Cognitive Theory.* Englewood Cliffs, NJ: Prentice-Hall; 1986.

41.   Bandura A. Self Efficacy. In: Ramachaudran VS, ed. *Encyclopedia of Human Behavior.* San Diego, CA: Academic Press; 1998.

42.   Prochaska JO, DiClemente CC. Stages and processes of self-change of smoking: Toward an integrative model of change. *J Consult Clin Psych.* 1983;51(3):390-395.

43.   DiClemente CC. Self-efficacy and the addictive behaviors. *J Soc Clin Psychol.* 1986; 4:302-315.

44.   Velicer WF, DiClemente CC, Rossi JS, Prochaska JO. Relapse situations and self-efficacy: An integrative model. *Addict Behav.* 1990;15(3):271-283.

45.   Rosenstock IM. Historical origins of the health belief model. *Health Educ Quart.* 1974;2(4):328-335.

46.   Rosenstock IM. Why people use health services. *Milbank Meml Fund Q.* 1966;44(3):94-124.

47.   Rosenstock IM, Strecher VJ, Becker MH. Social learning theory and the health belief model. *Health Educ Quart.* 1988;15(2):175-183.

48.   Janz NK, Becker MH. The health belief model: A decade later. *Health Educ Behav.* 1984;11(1):1-47.

49.   Maiman LA, Becker MH, Kirscht JP. Scales for measuring health belief model dimensions: A test of predictive value, internal consistency, and relationships among beliefs. *Health Educ Quart.* 1977;5:215-230.

50.   Becker MH. The health belief model and personal health behavior. *Health Educ Quart.* 1974;2(4):324-508.

51.   Azjen I, Fishbein M. *Understanding Attitudes and Predicting Social Behavior.* Upper Saddle River, NJ: Prentice Hall; 1980.

52.   Ajzen I. Theory of Planned Behavior. *Organ Behav Hum Dec.* 1991;50:179-211.

53.   Godin G, Kok G. The theory of planned behavior: A review of its applications to health-related behaviors. *Am J Health Promot.* 1996;11(2):87-98.

54.   Armitage CJ, Conner M. Efficacy of the theory of planned behavior: A meta analytic review. *Brit J Soc Psychol.* 2001;40(4):471-499.

55.   Hausenblas HA, Carron AV, Mack DE. Application of the theories of reasoned action and planned behavior to exercise behavior. *J Sport Exerc Psychol.* 1997;191(1):36-51.

56.   Bandura A. Exercise of personal agency through self-efficacy mechanism. In Schwarzer R, ed. *Self-efficacy: Thought Control of Action.* Washington, DC: Hemisphere; 1992a:3-38.

57.   Schwarzer R, Fuchs R. Changing risk behaviors and adopting health behaviors: The role of self-efficacy beliefs. In: Bandura A, ed. *Self-efficacy in changing societies.* New York, NY: Cambridge University Press; 1995: 259-288.

58.   Bandura A. On the functional properties of perceived self-efficacy revisited. *J Manage.* 2012;38(1):9-44.

59.   Turner KM, Nicholson JM, Sanders MR. The role of practitioner self-efficacy, training, program and workplace

factors on the implementation of an evidence-based parenting intervention in primary care. *J Primary Prevent.* 2011;32(2):95-112.

60. Marlatt GA, Baer JS, Quigley LA. Self-efficacy and addictive behavior. In: Bandura A, ed. *Self-Efficacy in Changing Societies.* New York, NY: Cambridge University Press;1995:289-315.

61. Marlatt GA, Gordon J. *Relapse Prevention: Maintenance Strategies in the Treatment of Addictive Disorders.* New York, NY: The Guilford Press; 1985.

62. Kadden RM, Litt MD. The role of self-efficacy in the treatment of substance use disorders. *Addict Behav.* 2011;36(12): 1120-1126.

63. Locke EA, Shaw KN, Saari LM, Latham GP. Goal setting and task performance: 1969-1980. *Psychol Bull.* 1981;90(1):125-152.

64. Locke EA, Frederick E, Lee C, Bobko P. Effect of self-efficacy, goals, and task strategies on task performance. *J Appl Psychol.* 1984;69(2):241-251.

65. Ewart CK. Role of physical self-efficacy in recovery from heart attack. In R. Schwarzer, ed. *Self-efficacy: Thought Control of Action.* Washington, DC: Hemisphere; 1992:259-288.

66. Williams SL, French DP. What are the most effective intervention techniques for changing physical activity self-efficacy and physical activity behavior-and are they the same? *Health Educ Res.* 2011;26(2):308-322.

67. Schunk DH. Goal setting and self-efficacy during self-regulated learning. *Educ Psychol.* 1990;25:71-86.

68. Annesi JJ. Relationships between self-regulation skills and physical activity and fruit and vegetable consumption in obese adults: Mediation of mood and self efficacy. *Psychol Rep.* 2011;108(1): 95-103.

69. O'Donnell MP. Financial incentives for workplace health promotion: What is equitable, what is sustainable, and what drives healthy behaviors? *Am J Health Promot.* 2012;26(5):iv-vii.

70. Kaiser Family Foundation, Health Research & Educational Trust. Employer Health Benefits 2012 Annual Survey. Available at http://ehbs.kff.org/pdf/2012/8346.pdf. Accessed April 17, 2013.

71. Lamb RJ, Morral AR, Galbicka G, Kirby KC, Iguchi MY. Shaping reduced smoking in smokers without cessation plans. *Exp Clin Psychopharm.* 2005;13(2):83-92.

72. Heil SH, Alessi SM, Lussier JP, Badger GJ, Higgins ST. An experimental test of the influence of prior cigarette smoking abstinence on future abstinence. *Nicotine Tob Res.* 2004;6(3):471-479.

73. Alessi SM, Badger GJ, Higgins ST. An experimental examination of the initial weeks of abstinence in cigarette smokers. *Exp Clin Psychopharm.* 2004; 12(4):276-287.

74. Curry SJ, Wagner EH, Grothaus LC. Evaluation of intrinsic and extrinsic motivation interventions with a self-help smoking cessation program. *J Consult Clin Psychol.* 1991;59(2):318-24.

75. Jeffrey RW, Wing RR. Long-term effects of interventions for weight loss using food provision and monetary incentives. *J Consult Clin Psychol.* 1995;63(5):793.

76. Mowen JC, Middlemist RD, Luther D. Joint effects of assigned goal level and incentive structure on task performance: A laboratory study. *J Appl Psychol.* 1981;66(5):598.

77. Lee C. The effects of goal setting and monetary incentives on self-efficacy and performance. *J Bus Psychol.* 1988;2(4): 366-372.

78. Fine LJ, Philogene SG, Gramling R, Coups EJ, Sinha S. Prevalence of multiple chronic disease risk factors: 2001 national health interview survey. *Am J Prev Med.* 2004;27(2, Suppl):18-24.

79.   Pronk NP, Martinson B, Kesller RC, et al. The association between work performance and physical activity, cardiorespiratory fitness, and obesity. *J Occup Environ Med*. 2004;46(1):19-25.

80.   Edington DW, Yen LT, Witting P. The financial impact of changes in personal health practices. *J Occup Environ Med*. 1997;39(11):1037-1046.

81.   Prochaska JJ, Prochaska JO. A review of multiple health behavior change interventions for primary prevention. *Am J Lifestyle Med*. 2011;5(3):208-221.

82.   Patterson, F. Multiple health behavior change in sequence: The case for physical activity and smoking cessation. *J Health Behav Pub Health*. 2013;3(1):1-4.

83.   Perkins KA, Rohay J, Meilahn EN, Wing RR, Mathews KA, Kuller LH. Diet, alcohol, and physical activity as a function of smoking status in middle-aged women. *Health Psychol*. 1993;12(5):410-415.

84.   King TK, Marcus BH, Pinto BM, Emmons KM, Abrams DB. Cognitive-behavioral mediators of changing multiple behaviors: Smoking and a sedentary lifestyle. *Prev Med*. 1996;25(6):684-691.

85.   Toobert DJ, Glasgow RE, Strycker LA, Barrera M Jr, Ritzwoller DP, Weidner G. Long-term effects of the Mediterranean lifestyle program: A randomized clinical trial for postmenopausal women with type 2 diabetes. *Int J Behav Nutr Phy*. 2007;4:1.

86.   Emmons KM, McBride CM, Puleo E, et al. Project PREVENT: A randomized trial to reduce multiple behavioral risk factors for colon cancer. *Cancer Epidem Biomar*. 2005;14(6):1453-1459.

87.   Tsang SK, Hui EK, Law B. Self-efficacy as a positive youth development construct: A conceptual review. *Scientific World Journal*. 2012;2012. doi:10.1100/2012/452327.

88.   Ievers-Landis CE, Burant C, Drotar D, Morgan L, Trapl ES, Kwoh CK. Social support, knowledge, and self-efficacy as correlates of osteoporosis preventive behaviors among preadolescent females. *J Pediatr Psychol*. 2003;28(5):335-345.

89.   Bere E, Klepp K. Correlates of fruit and vegetable intake among norwegian schoolchildren: Parental and self-reports. *Public Health Nutr*. 2004;7(8):991-998.

90.   Fitzgerald A, Heary C, Kelly C, Nixon E, Shevlin M. Self-efficacy for healthy eating and peer support for unhealthy eating are associated with adolescents' food intake patterns. *Appetite*. 2012;63: 48-58.

91.   Frenn M, Malin S, Bansal NK Stage-based interventions for low-fat diet with middle school students. *J Pediatr Nurs*. 2003;18(1):36-45.

92.   Engels RC, Knibbe RA, de Vries H, Drop MJ. Antecedents of smoking cessation among adolescents: Who is motivated to change? *Prev Med*. 1998;27(3):348-357.

93.   Solomon LJ, Bunn JY, Pirie PL, Worden JK, Flynn BS. Self-efficacy and outcome expectations for quitting among adolescent smokers. *Addict Behav*. 2006;31(7):1122-1132.

94.   Woodruff SI, Conway TL, Edwards CC. Sociodemographic and smoking-related psychosocial predictors of smoking behavior change among high school smokers. *Addict Behav*. 2008;33(2): 354–358.

95.   Hyde J, Hankins M, Deale A, Marteau TM. Interventions to increase self-efficacy in the context of addiction behaviours: A systematic literature review. *Health Psychol*. 2008;13(5):607-623.

96.   Connor JP, George SM, Gullo MJ, Kelly AB, Young RM. A prospective study of alcohol expectancies and self-efficacy as predictors of young adolescent alcohol misuse. *Alcohol Alcoholism*. 2011;46(2):161-169.

97.   Tsai M, Tsai C. Junior high school students' internet usage and self-efficacy:

A re-examination of the gender gap. *Comput Educ.* 2010;54(4):1182-1192.

98. Bauman AE, Reis RS, Sallis JF, Wells JC, Loos RJ, Martin BW. Correlates of physical activity: Why are some people physically active and others not? *The Lancet.* 2012; 380(9838):258-271.

99. Gilliam ML, Berlin A, Kozloski M, Hernandez M, Grundy M. Interpersonal and personal factors influencing sexual debut among mexican-american young women in the united states. *J Adolescent Health.* 2007;41(5):495-503.

100. Bricker JB, Liu J, Comstock BA, Peterson AV, Kealey KA, Marek PM. Social cognitive mediators of adolescent smoking cessation: Results from a large randomized intervention trial. *Psychol Assix Behav.* 2010;24(3):436.Easom, 2003.

101. Easom LR. Concepts in health promotion. perceived self-efficacy and barriers in older adults. *J Gerontol Nurs.* 2003;29(5):11-19.

102. Martin KA, Sinden AR. Who will stay and who will go? a review of older adults' adherence to randomized controlled trials of exercise. *J Aging Phys Act.* 2001;9(2):91-114.

103. O'Hare T, Shen C. Abstinence self-efficacy in people with severe mental illness. *J Subst Abuse Treat.* 2013.

104. Bandura A. Perceived self-efficacy in the exercise of control over AIDS infection. *Eval Program Plann.* 1990;13(1):9-17.

105. Rew L, Fouladi RT, Yockey RD. Sexual health practices of homeless youth. *J Nurs Scholarship.* 2002;34(2):139-145.

106. Stanton CA, Lloyd-Richardson EE, Papandonatos GD, de Dios MA, Niaura R. Mediators of the relationship between nicotine replacement therapy and smoking abstinence among people living with HIV/AIDS. *AIDS education and prevention: official publication of the International Society for AIDS Education.* 2009;21(3 Suppl):65-80.

107. Vidrine DJ, Arduino RC, Gritz ER. Impact of a cell phone intervention on mediating mechanisms of smoking cessation in individuals living with HIV/AIDS. *Nicotine Tobacco Res.* 2006;8(Suppl 1):S103-S108.

108. Jones TL, Prinz RJ. Potential roles of parental self-efficacy in parent and child adjustment: A review. *Clin Psychol Rev.* 2005;25(3):341-363.

109. Morin P, Demers K, Turcotte S, Mongeau L. Association between perceived self-efficacy related to meal management and food coping strategies among working parents with preschool children. *Appetite.* 2013.

110. Kakudate N, Morita M, Sugai M, et al. Development of the self-efficacy scale for maternal oral care. *Pediatr Dent.* 2010;32(4):310-315.

111. Silva-Sanigorski A, Ashbolt R, Green J, et al. Parental self-efficacy and oral health-related knowledge are associated with parent and child oral health behaviors and self-reported oral health status. *Community Dentistry and Oral Epidemiology.* 2012;41. doi: 10.1111/cdoe.12019.

112. Mitra AK, Khoury AJ, Hinton AW, Carothers C. Predictors of breastfeeding intention among low-income women. *Matern Child Health J.* 2004;8(2):65-70.

113. Rabinowitz YG, Mausbach BT, Thompson LW, Gallagher-Thompson D. The relationship between self-efficacy and cumulative health risk associated with health behavior patterns in female caregivers of elderly relatives with alzheimer's dementia. *J Aging Health.* 2007;19(6):946-964.

114. Katz D. School-based interventions for health promotion and weight control: Not just waiting on the world to change. *Annu Rev Public Health.* 2009;30:253-272.

115. Van Stralen M, Yildirim M, te Velde S, Brug J, Van Mechelen W, Chinapaw

M. What works in school-based energy balance behaviour interventions and what does not; A systematic review of mediating mechanisms. *Int J Obes.* 2011;35(10):1251-1265.

116. Lubans DR, Foster C, Biddle SJ. A review of mediators of behavior in interventions to promote physical activity among children and adolescents. *Prev Med.* 2008;47(5):463-470.

117. Dupéré V, Leventhal T, Vitaro F. Neighborhood processes, self-efficacy, and adolescent mental health. *J Health Soc Behav.* 2012;53(2):183-198.

118. Cohen DA, Mason K, Bedimo A, Scribner R, Basolo V, Farley TA. Neighborhood physical conditions and health. *Am J Public Health.* 2003;93(3).

119. Lochner KA, Kawachi I, Brennan RT, Buka SL. Social capital and neighborhood mortality rates in chicago. *Soc Sci Med.* 2003;56(8):1797-1806.

120. Buka SL, Brennan RT, Rich-Edwards JW, Raudenbush SW, Earls F. Neighborhood support and the birth weight of urban infants. *Am J Epidemiol.* 2003;157(1):1-8.

121. Browning CR, Leventhal T, Brooks-Gunn J. Sexual initiation in early adolescence: The nexus of parental and community control. *Am Sociol Rev.* 2005;70(5): 758-778.

122. Browning CR, Burrington LA, Leventhal T, Brooks-Gunn J. *J Health Soc Behav.* 2008;49(3):269-285.

123. Sampson RJ, Raudenbush SW, Earls F. Neighborhoods and violent crime: A multilevel study of collective efficacy. *Science.* 1997;277(5328):918-924.

124. Browning CR. The span of collective efficacy: Extending social disorganization theory to partner violence. *J Marriage Fam.* 2002;64(4):833-850.

125. Cohen DA, Finch BK, Bower A, Sastry N. Collective efficacy and obesity: The potential influence of social factors on health. *Soc Sci Med.* 2006;62(3):769-778.

126. Browning CR, Cagney KA. Neighborhood structural disadvantage, collective efficacy, and self-rated physical health in an urban setting. *J Health Soc Behav.* 2002:383-399.

127. Mozaffarian D, Afshin A, Benowitz NL, et al. Population approaches to improve diet, physical activity, and smoking habits A scientific statement from the american heart association. *Circulation.* 2012;126(12):1514-1563.

128. Fortmann SP, Flora JA, Winkleby MA, Schooler C, Taylor CB, Farquhar JW. Community intervention trials: Reflections on the stanford five-city project experience. *Am J Epidemiol.* 1995;142(6):576-586.

129. Farquhar JW, Fortmann SP, Flora JA, et al. Effects of communitywide education on cardiovascular disease risk factors. the stanford five-city project. *J Am Med Assoc.* 1990;264(3):359-365.

130. Bandura A. Health promotion by social cognitive means. *Health education and behavior.* 2004;31(2):143-164.

131. Johnston JD, Massey AP, DeVaneaux CA. Innovation in weight loss programs: A 3-dimensional virtual-world approach. *J Med Internet Res.* 2012;14(5).

132. Baranowski T, Buday R, Thompson DI, Baranowski J. Playing for real: Video games and stories for health-related behavior change. *Am J Prev Med.* 2008;34(1):74.

133. Rizzo S, Lange B, Suma EA, Bolas M. Virtual reality and interactive digital game technology: New tools to address obesity and diabetes. *J Diabetes Sci Technol.* 2011;5(2):256.

134. Morie JF, Chance E. Extending the reach of health care for obesity and diabetes using virtual worlds. *J Diabetes Sci Technol.* 2011;5(2):272-276.

135. Bordnick PS, Carter BL, Traylor AC. What virtual reality research in addictions can tell us about the future

of obesity assessment and treatment. *J Diabetes Sci Technol.* 2011;5(2):265-271.

136. Lieberman DA. Video games for diabetes self-management: Examples and design strategies. *J Diabetes Sci Technol.* 2012;6(4):802-806.

137. Lieberman DA, Chamberlin B, Medina E, Franklin BA, Sanner BM, Vafiadis DK. The power of play: Innovations in getting active summit 2011 A science panel proceedings report from the American Heart Association. *Circulation.* 2011;123(21):2507-2516.

138. Primack BA, Carroll MV, McNamara M, et al. Role of video games in improving health-related outcomes: A systematic review. *Am J Prev Med.* 2012;42(6):630-638.

139. Baranowski T, Baranowski J, Cullen KW, et al. Squire's quest!: Dietary outcome evaluation of a multimedia game. *Am J Prev Med.* 2003;24(1):52-61.

140. Mateyka PJ, Rapino MA, Landivar LC. *Home-based workers in the United States: 2010. Current Population Reports.* Washington, DC: U.S. Census Bureau; 2012:70-132.

141. Bailey DE, Kurland NB. A review of telework research: Findings, new directions, and lessons for the study of modern work. *J Organ Behav.* 2002;23(4):383-400.

142. Employers stop one in five workers from working from home. Trades Union Congress Web site. Available at http://www.tuc.org.uk/workplace/tuc-18523-f0.cfm. Accessed April 17, 2013.

143. Gajendran RS, Harrison DA. The good, the bad, and the unknown about telecommuting: Meta-analysis of psychological mediators and individual consequences. *J App Psychol.* 2007;92(6):1524-1541.

144. Lee A. Working from home: The end of an era? Forbes Web site. Available at http://www.forbes.com/sites/insead/2013/04/17/working-from-home-the-end-of-an-era/. Accessed April 17, 2013.

CHAPTER

12

Tailoring and Health Promotion in the Workplace

Laura Linnan, Jayne K. Jeffries and
Meredith Eastman

INTRODUCTION

Workplace interventions that use a tailored approach hold promise for meeting the complex needs of today's diverse workforce and the changing conditions of work. Tailored approaches to health promotion take into account the unique characteristics of employees and features of the workplace, eschewing one-size-fits-all approaches that are less responsive and appropriate to the realities of work in the 21st century. More than 60% of adults in the United States are employed, and workforce demographic characteristics are increasingly diverse. In the typical U.S. workforce, the number of women has stabilized, the average age is increasing, and estimates suggest that non-Hispanic whites will be just 51.7% of the population in 2050 (compared with 72.2% in 2000), so that the largest source of new workers will be young Hispanics.[1] As managers and decision makers face the increasing complexity these demographic shifts in workforce characteristics present, they must also take into account the changing

nature of work, which has a dynamic interplay with the changing workforce. Two examples will illustrate this point. Since the 1980s in the United States, industries have moved from a focus on production and manufacturing to a focus on service industries. And increased use of smart phones and other mobile devices has allowed employees to work at home or off-site in growing numbers, yet has simultaneously created a 24/7 on-call demand for access to workers so there is little to no "off-the-clock" time. As the workforce and work conditions evolve, there is a growing demand for new and more appropriate interventions that can accommodate these changing realities. Ideally, these new interventions should be able to work seamlessly with mobile technologies, accommodate the needs and interests of diverse types of workers, be accessible to as many employees as possible, and motivate recommended employee health changes in a cost-effective manner. Moreover, the ideal new interventions will motivate managers and other decision makers to make permanent changes in the work environment (and related to work conditions) that positively influence and support employee health. Healthy workers operating within a safe and healthy workplace has been the main goal of the National Institute of Occupational Health and Safety and their Total Worker Health program.[2] The idea of developing new interventions for managers and decision makers who intend to create health-supportive programs, policies, and work conditions is consistent with the needs and demands of the fast-paced changes happening in the work environment. Tailored interventions are one strategy that may be able to address, motivate, and sustain positive health changes at both the workplace and individual employee levels.

The purposes of this chapter are to provide a conceptual framework to briefly define tailored and targeted interventions; review the key components of a tailored intervention; summarize results from a selected review of the literature on general and worksite-specific tailored interventions; briefly describe how tailoring is believed to influence motivation and skill building; and present a summary of unanswered questions about the future of tailored interventions that may be addressed by researchers and/or practitioners.

Targeted and Tailored Interventions—Brief Description

Targeted health communications focus on specific segments of the workforce and offer messages and educational materials that address subgroup level workforce characteristics. Targeted communication strategies grew out of social marketing approaches in which messages were directed to specific segments of the workforce "audience" based on selected group characteristics. Since the 1980s, public health interventions have benefited from these social marketing strategies—and they have become important features of many community and worksite-based interventions. For example, different targeted health communication messages might be directed to segments of the workforce such as older workers, women, men, or blue-collar workers. Most workplace health interventions are able to target one or more of

these subgroups. Targeted interventions may combine more than one group characteristic, e.g., African American men who work the day shift, or women who are managers. Targeted strategies have proven both useful and effective as a way of addressing segments of workers based on one or more group characteristics. However, in the late 1990s and into the 2000s, major advances in computing capacity and other technologies made it easier to gather data, summarize data efficiently, and produce reports quickly—which made *tailored* intervention approaches more feasible. Since then, tailored interventions have grown in number and sophistication; though tailored interventions have never really replaced targeted interventions, they often operate alongside some targeted interventions.

Kreuter et al[3(p277)] defined *tailoring* as "any combination of strategies and information intended to reach one specific person, based on characteristics that are unique to that person, related to the outcome of interest, and derived from an individual assessment." Several components of this definition are noteworthy when contrasting tailored vs. targeted approaches. First, tailoring is focused on an individual, not a group. With tailoring, the information is designed for one specific person (e.g., Jane Doe—an individual worker) vs. all women who work. Second, tailored approaches are based on characteristics unique to an individual (e.g., Jane Doe reports that she does not eat at least five servings of fruits/vegetables a day) vs. targeted approaches that will focus on women generally, and may use population estimates to determine how many women do or do not eat at least five servings of fruits/vegetables a day. Finally, tailored approaches can be accomplished only by using some type of individual assessment of Jane Doe vs. a targeted approach for all women who work, which may be gleaned from general population-based estimates. Thus, tailored approaches are personalized to the individual who completes an assessment; and, although a targeted communication may be directed to an individual by name (i.e., personalized), the information provided is more general, and not directly relevant to specific data from a specific individual.

Targeted communications are limited to group-level variables (e.g., age, gender, race/ethnicity, department, type of worker, etc.), whereas tailored communications are limited only by the number and type of questions one can ask of an individual. Tailoring occurs on narrow and broad questions, but the strength in tailoring is the personal relevance of the information fed back to the person who completed the assessment. There are many different types of tailoring to consider. First, one might tailor based on individual health status indicators. Someone who has diabetes or hypertension may get a message that someone without that condition will not receive. Second, tailoring is often done based on behavioral risk factors. As a result, an individual who is already meeting national guidelines for physical activity will get a different message than someone who is not active. A smoker will get a very different message than a nonsmoker. Tailoring may be done based on key theoretically driven constructs such as self-efficacy (social cognitive theory) or stage of readiness to change (transtheoretical model of behavior change [TTM]) or some combination of theoretical constructs. Tailoring may be done based on key demographic characteristics such as age, race/ethnicity, gender, income, or job status. There are very few limits to the tailoring combinations that might be available for a given individual, as long as someone is asked during an exchange of information that occurs as part of an assessment; algorithms can be programmed to tailor a response using all available information provided.

In addition to variation in the factors on which one might use to tailor, tailored interventions vary in the type, timing, and amount of feedback provided. For example,

tailored feedback may be provided once or multiple times off the initial assessment responses. As a result, tailored feedback can be static or dynamic. *Static tailoring* occurs when an initial assessment is performed, tailored feedback is offered based on the initial assessment, and then any additional feedback/information provided uses responses from that same initial assessment. *Dynamic tailoring* occurs when an initial assessment is performed, tailored feedback is offered based on that initial assessment, and then additional assessments occur so that subsequent feedback is based on updated assessment responses. Dynamic (vs. static) feedback is believed to be more personally relevant over time. If someone is a smoker at the initial assessment but quits smoking 2 weeks later, static tailoring (i.e., lack of a follow-up assessment) will not capture the change in smoking status and will not be able to incorporate that important information in subsequent feedback. Thus, the personal relevance of the later feedback reports will be diminished if they do not include nonsmoking status information. Conversely, if responses to multiple assessments are available, the personal relevance of tailored feedback can be enhanced by acknowledging the individual is a nonsmoker, congratulating him or her for this successful change, and identifying resources to help maintain a nonsmoking status. Clearly, this will strengthen the personal relevance of the tailored intervention, and evidence suggests that dynamic (vs. static) feedback has enhanced effects on key behavior change outcomes.

Tailored interventions can also be developed and implemented at the organizational level. Specifically, if a workplace is the organizational unit to be assessed, it is also the unit to which tailored feedback is provided. Therefore, tailoring at the organizational level is not used to reach individual employees and engage them about their personal health behavior; rather, it is used to reach organizational decision makers to engage them about how their workplace could better support employee health and wellness. For example, the TTM (i.e., stage of readiness to change) is often used to provide tailored feedback to individuals; organizational readiness to change can also be measured and used to develop tailored recommendations for the workplace. Several ways of defining readiness at the organization currently exist,[4] though, based on the authors' review of the literature, readiness has been infrequently used to develop workplace-specific organizational strategies to improve employee health. In addition to readiness, other variables that can be used to tailor information and strategies for worksites include the current status of efforts to promote behavior change (e.g., number and quality of facilities for physical activity, existence of smoking cessation programs), workplace size, industry, and manager beliefs about workplace health promotion. A variety of assessment tools are available to obtain responses that clarify facts about workplace facilities, programs, and policies that are used to generate organization-specific guidance for benchmarking and program/policy improvement and recommend strategies for change. Some of these are discussed later in the chapter.

CONCEPTUAL FRAMEWORK— INDIVIDUAL AND ORGANIZATIONAL LEVELS

Figure 12-1 depicts a conceptual framework of tailored interventions that operate at both the individual (employee) and organization (workplace) levels. The majority of tailored workplace interventions operate on the individual level—i.e., an employee completes an assessment (see INPUT, Figure); then, based on the employee's responses to specific questions, a set of algorithms or decision rules are enacted (see PROCESS, Figure) such that the applied logic provides feedback that is personalized to the employee (see OUTPUT, Figure). The idea behind tailoring is that the more one can make

Figure 12-1: Tailoring Process and Outcomes.

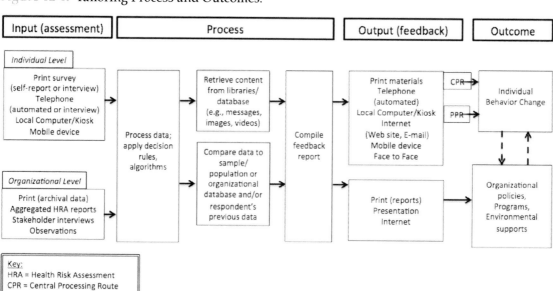

feedback personally relevant to the employee, the more likely it is to produce a host of positive results (see OUTCOME, Figure) such as improved awareness, motivation, and skills and (ultimately) desired behavior changes.

Figure 12-1 clarifies that many types of input sources are possible when tailoring interventions at the individual level. For example, assessments may be conducted with print formats, online, tablet, and free-standing kiosks or via surveys conducted in person or via phone. Data are processed by drawing upon *message libraries* written for all possible response options to the assessment questions. If someone answers a question that asks "On how many days per week do you get at least 30 minutes of moderate physical activity?" the response options may be 0, 1, 2, 3, 4, 5, 6, or 7 days per week. Because the national recommendations for being physically active are to get at least 150 minutes of moderate physical activity per week, then someone who says 0 is considered inactive, and will get a special message pointing out the risks of sedentary behavior. People who respond 1 to 4 days per week are not meeting the national recommendations, so they would get a tailored response that would inform them of the national recommendations and encourage them to increase moderate physical activity to at least 5 days per week. And, if someone responds that he or she is active 5, 6, or 7 days per week, then he or she is already meeting the national recommendations and would be encouraged to maintain this behavior over time. As a result, the output would be specifically shaped based on the responses provided to the assessment questionnaire. In some cases, additional programming logic is applied such that if different recommendations exist for men vs. women, messages would be pulled from the message libraries into the feedback (OUTPUT) that are unique to men or women. Moreover, in some cases, ex-smokers might get a different set of messages than will never smokers, or overweight individuals who do not eat vegetables might get different types of messages than healthy-weight individuals who eat recommended numbers of vegetables each day. As assessments are reapplied (i.e., dynamic tailoring), new messages are typically written for those who change behaviors in a positive direction, stay the same, or change in a negative (i.e., unhealthy) direction.

Tailored interventions may have variation in the types of assessments (INPUTS) or the data processing and data formats (e.g., written message libraries, video clips, photos or other graphics), as well as variation in the type, amount, and format of feedback provided (OUTPUTS). Typically, output at the individual level is available in a print version, such as a report or letter, offered in person or by phone as part of a coaching session. Sometimes, feedback is offered using a combination of methods including print, e-mail, or online reports or smart phone applications using responsive Web technology. The desired complexity, length, and type of feedback will often dictate what output format may be possible. For example, certain output formats are better at accommodating video clips, music, or images included as part of tailored feedback, whereas other formats are not. In addition, the characteristics and preferences of end users may drive certain decisions about the format of output. For example, older workers may be less interested in getting their feedback via smart phone than are younger workers. Usability testing prior to making final decisions on output is critically important. Behavior change outcomes at the individual level arise from the way in which tailored information is processed through central and peripheral routes, mechanisms described in greater detail in the Applications to Motivation and Skill Building section of this chapter.

The Figure 12-1 shows that both primary and secondary sources of data are available as inputs at the organizational level. Existing data from human resources files, absenteeism records, Occupational Safety and Health Administration reports, and other data sources may provide relevant and specific secondary data at the organizational level. The most commonly used source of data on the organization is information drawn from aggregate reports of individual health risk assessments (HRAs), questionnaires, and health screenings. The questionnaires often measure motivations, desires, and preferences of individuals, which can then be aggregated to reflect organizational-level characteristics. Data collected or reviewed as part of the input process are quite similar to those collected for individual-level tailoring. Specifically, primary or secondary data collected from the organization are compared against previous data collected for that organization or compared against organizations of a similar size or sector. Then, specific messages are prepared and a report is generated for management/decision makers. Recommendations for change in administration, management practices, policies, or the physical/social work environment are included and tailored to the unique characteristics of the organization. For example, if the input data revealed that the majority of employees in a manufacturing worksite were male, and less than 25% reported being physically active, recommendations might be to (1) enact a new benefit policy that would offer discounts on gym memberships, (2) dedicate a room at the plant and invest in basic strength training and aerobic fitness equipment for employee use, (3) consider endorsing a fitness break for 10 minutes every afternoon, (4) include an assessment as part of an annual health fair to benchmark key fitness measures, and (5) sponsor (pay for a joining fee) employees who participate in the Relay for Life fundraising event for the American Cancer Society and make sure key managers or leaders are part of the team to champion the effort. Taken together, these policies, programs, and/or environmental supports operate at the organizational level, are tailored to the types of workers and workplace, and are designed to support employee efforts to increase physical activity levels; thus, there is a reciprocal relationship between outcomes at the organizational and individual levels.

Tailored interventions at the individual and organizational levels offer excellent opportunities for creating awareness, increasing motivation, and promoting change. Some of the most relevant literature about the general impact of tailored interventions is summarized below and is followed by an updated review of tailoring specific to worksite-based interventions.

SUMMARY OF THE LITERATURE

Several of the earliest and leading researchers on the value and results of tailored interventions include Strecher et al,[5] who considered the effects of computer-tailored smoking cessation messages in family practice settings; Kreuter and Strecher,[6] who studied whether tailored behavior change messages enhanced the effectiveness of an HRA; Lipkus et al,[7] who investigated whether tailored interventions increase mammography use among women in a health maintenance organization; Brug et al,[8] who examined the impact of computer-tailored feedback on fat, fruit, and vegetable intake; Campbell et al,[9] who worked to improve dietary behavior in primary care settings via tailored messages; and Marcus et al,[10] who studied the efficacy of motivationally tailored physical activity intervention. An early, seminal paper on tailoring by Kreuter and Skinner[11] proposed a nomenclature for tailored interventions, and a book written by Kreuter and colleagues[3] became a one-stop how-to guide for developing tailored interventions. Together, these works helped launch a plethora of excellent practice and research on tailoring.

What have we learned in the past decade or more about tailored interventions? In general, reviews indicate that individuals who receive tailored interventions, regardless of the topic studied, tend to like and prefer them over nontailored materials. Specifically, tailored intervention materials are attractive to participants and are read at fairly high levels compared to nontailored interventions, understood, recalled, rated highly, and perceived as credible.[3,12-14] Second, tailored interventions produce better health outcomes, although with generally small effect sizes, over nontailored interventions.[13-18]

Although these early reviews were generally favorable, they revealed as many new questions about tailored interventions as they answered. For example, questions about the type and number of tailoring variables; the need to understand core features of tailored interventions; clarifying best types, timing, and amount of feedback provided; determining moderating effects of tailored interventions; and clarifying the extent to which the efficacy of tailored interventions change over time. In addition, these early literature reviews did not have the opportunity to apply meta-analytic techniques that would calculate precise effect estimates for the studies available for review.

Noar and colleagues[19] were among the first to apply meta-analytic techniques to summarize the tailoring literature when they reviewed 57 studies to assess the effects of tailored print health behavior change interventions. They found that tailored messaging accounted for approximately 7% of the variation in health behavior change in the overall sample, revealing that interventions with tailored messages were effective in stimulating health behavior change with a magnitude slightly less than a "small" effect.[20] When studies compared tailored message interventions to generic or targeted messages (k = 40 studies), the effect size was $r = .058$, which represents an odds ratio of 1.21. Combined with the consistency of evidence from the systematic reviews, a consensus of opinion is building that tailored print interventions have a positive effect, particularly when smoking cessation, dietary change, and screening behaviors (e.g., mammography and Pap tests) are concerned. Noar and colleagues[19] also examined characteristics of

the tailored intervention that were potential moderators of their effectiveness. For example, they found that output (i.e., feedback) in the form of pamphlets, newsletters, or magazines was more effective than booklets, manuals, or letters, as were print materials that were not lengthy. Pamphlets, newsletters, or magazines may have been more likely to feature appealing graphical formats to catch and retain readers' attention.[19] They found that studies with more intervention contacts, particularly those that include *ipsative* feedback (i.e., feedback messages that compare current responses with responses at previous time points), were more effective. And studies that tailored on attitudes ($Z = 2.38$, $p = .003$), self-efficacy ($Z = 4.40$, $p = .00001$), stage of change ($Z = 2.64$, $p = .004$), and social support ($Z = 9.88$, $p = .00001$) had significantly larger effect sizes than those that did not tailor on these concepts, whereas tailoring on perceived susceptibility produced smaller effect sizes ($Z = 6.87$, $p = .00001$).[19] Lustria et al[21] conducted a systematic review of computer-tailored behavioral interventions delivered over the Web with a special focus on implementation issues. Given the explosion of Web-based tailored interventions, and the many implementation factors to consider, such as level of sophistication, timing, user control (self-guided vs. expert-led), expert contact (type: mediated or face-to-face; nature: technical vs. expert), Web-related modalities (e.g., quizzes, e-mail, discussion boards) as well as traditional channels (e.g., phone, video, audio, print), tools for building self-regulatory skills, personal skill development tools (e.g., goal setting, testimonials, frequently asked questions), resource links and monitoring tools (e.g., diaries, data uploads, e-mail reminders), message tailoring strategies (e.g., risk factors, psychological states, health behaviors), and tailoring mechanisms (e.g., personalization, adaptation, feedback), ongoing research into the effectiveness of tailored approaches is needed. Web-based tailored interventions can facilitate implementation of tailored programs to a larger audience and may enhance effectiveness by allowing more options for interactivity with experts or computer nuances. Future studies are needed to examine the differential effects of Web-based tailoring on health outcomes versus non–Web-based and nontailored outcomes.

Krebs and colleagues[22] conducted a meta-analysis of 88 computer-tailored intervention studies that focused on smoking cessation, healthy eating, mammography screening, and physical activity. This rigorous review overcame many limitations of previous work. Results showed statistically significant effects for each behavioral outcome ($g = .16$ [95% confidence interval (CI) = .12–.19], $p < .001$ for smoking cessation; $g = .22$ [95% CI = .18–.26], $p < .001$ for healthy eating; $g = .13$ [95% CI = .08–.18, $p < .001$] for mammography; and $g = .16$ [95% CI = .10–.21, $p < .001$] for physical activity), though effects diminished over time. Dynamic tailored interventions increased efficacy over time (vs. static tailoring with tailored feedback based on one assessment). No differences were found by communication channel used to deliver feedback (i.e., print, phone, and computer were all equally effective). There was no negative impact on outcomes when combining up to three targeted behaviors. Future studies will need to consider how to help participants maintain health behavior changes, and what types of feedback features are most effective (e.g., graphics, visuals).

Selected Review of Tailored Interventions at the Workplace

This focused and selected literature describes how tailored approaches are being used in health behavior interventions in the workplace, including a brief description of their results (see Table 12-1). A PubMed, SCOPUS, and Google Scholar search was conducted using combinations of the terms "tailored," "intervention," "worksite," "employee," and "health risk appraisal," yielding 100 results. The reference lists of all selected articles were also reviewed to identify potentially relevant workplace intervention manuscripts that were not uncovered in the initial search strategy. To be included in this search, the articles (1) described a worksite-based intervention, (2) included a control or comparison group, and (3) focused on one or multiple health behaviors. Pilot studies (n = 10) were excluded. A total of 25 studies met these inclusion criteria. The Table shows the study population, health behavior(s), outcome variables, tailoring variables, feedback/information delivery methods, and results for each study. There is variation in the health behavior outcomes, the variables upon which tailored information was based, use of benchmarks for comparison, and mechanisms of feedback delivery. Nineteen described individual-level tailoring interventions,[24,26–28,31–33,35–38,40–47] four described organizational-level tailoring interventions,[23,25,34,39] and one described an intervention that included tailored interventions for both organization and individual levels.[30] A brief discussion of the tailoring variables, outcomes, benchmarks, feedback, health behaviors, and the results of these studies follows the Table.

Tailoring Variables

Tailoring variables used in the reviewed interventions included current health behaviors, barriers to lifestyle change, health preferences, theory-based psychosocial constructs, demographics, risk for a specific health outcome, and participant-selected goals. Ten studies used current employee health behaviors (e.g., physical activity) and their knowledge about health behaviors to tailor communications and/or strategies.[23,26,28,30,36–38,40,42,43] Lifestyle constraints (e.g., whether or not children live at home, whether meals are cooked at home) were used for tailoring in two interventions.[36,43] Health behavior preferences (e.g., whether

Table 12-1: Summary of Selected Review of Tailored Interventions at the Workplace.

Author	Population	Health Behavior(s)	Tailoring Variable(s)	Feedback/ Information Delivery Method	Benchmark	Outcome Variable(s)
Abood et al[23]	53 university staff members	Diet	Knowledge of nutrition, dietary behavior status, and perceived benefits and barriers (HBM)	Group classes, face-to-face counseling	None	Nutrition knowledge, dietary behaviors, specific health beliefs
Results: Intervention group showed significant change in perceived benefits, but not perceived barriers; scored significantly higher in nutrition knowledge posttest, and showed significant decrease in energy intake by approximately 840 kcal/day, total fat intake decreased by 45 g/day, and saturated fat and cholesterol decreased by 18 mg/day and 158 mg/day, respectively.						
Allen et al[24]	625 male employees age 45+ in 12 worksites	Prostate cancer screening	Personal risk for prostate cancer, pro/con ratings of screening, decisional consistency	Tablet computer, printout	Risk relative (less than average, average, more than average) to other men of same age	Prostate cancer screening decisional status; desire for involvement in decision making and decision conflict
Results: Intervention group showed significant increase in knowledge at follow up (10% improvement vs. 4% for controls; p=0.03). There were no significant differences between groups in changes in decisional status and marginally significant decreased decision conflict for the intervention group.						
Beresford et al[25]	18 transportation, manufacturing, utilities, personal,	Diet	Checklist of Health Promotion Environments at Worksites (CHEW)	Website	None	BMI

Author	Population	Health Behavior(s)	Tailoring Variable(s)	Feedback/ Information Delivery Method	Benchmark	Outcome Variable(s)
	household, and miscellaneous service companies					
Results: Response rates to the baseline survey among the 18 worksites are 81% on average.						
Campbell et al[26]	538 women at 9 small to midsized manufacturing workplaces	Diet, physical activity	Workplace, age, shift, health concerns, current health behaviors including fat, fruit and vegetable intake, frequency and duration of different types of leisure-time physical activity, smoking, cancer screening, and choice of behavioral priority for change. Psychosocial variables included behavior-specific barriers, outcome expectations, stage of change	Magazines	None	Fruit and vegetable consumption, fat intake, physical activity, smoking cessation, and cancer screening

Author	Population	Health Behavior(s)	Tailoring Variable(s)	Feedback/Information Delivery Method	Benchmark	Outcome Variable(s)
			(TTM), social support, informational needs, and community resources			

Results: At the 18 months, the intervention group increased fruit and vegetable consumption by 0.7 daily servings compared to no change in the control group (P < 0.05). Significant differences in fat intake were observed at 6 months (P < 0.05) but not at 18 months. The intervention group also demonstrated improvements in strengthening and flexibility exercise compared to the control. Rates of smoking cessation and cancer screening did not differ between study groups.

Author	Population	Health Behavior(s)	Tailoring Variable(s)	Feedback/Information Delivery Method	Benchmark	Outcome Variable(s)
Cho et al[27]	141 male Korean industrial workers	Diet, physical activity	Participant "health profile"	Face-to-face counseling	None	BMI, body fat, waist and hip circumference, blood pressure, total cholesterol, HDL cholesterol, LDL cholesterol, and triglycerides

Results: In the obese Apo E3 genotype group, body mass index, body fat (%), waist circumference, waist-hip ratio, and systolic blood pressure were decreased, as well as intakes of energy (P = .000) and carbohydrate (P = .005). High-density lipoprotein cholesterol (P = .004) level was improved in individuals with the Apo E2 genotype.

Author	Population	Health Behavior(s)	Tailoring Variable(s)	Feedback/Information Delivery Method	Benchmark	Outcome Variable(s)
De Bourdeaudhuij et al[28]	337 employees at 6 companies	Diet	Intentions, attitudes, perceived self-efficacy social	Computer (CD-ROM), printout	Recommended level of fat intake	Dietary fat intake

Author	Population	Health Behavior(s)	Tailoring Variable(s)	Feedback/Information Delivery Method	Benchmark	Outcome Variable(s)
			support benefits and barriers (TPB), knowledge related to low-fat diet, stage of change (TTM)			

Results: Analysis showed a steeper decrease in fat intake and percentage energy from fat between baseline and follow up in the computer-tailored group compared with the generic (non-tailored) intervention group (p < .001), and also compared with the no-intervention control group (p < .001).

Author	Population	Health Behavior(s)	Tailoring Variable(s)	Feedback/Information Delivery Method	Benchmark	Outcome Variable(s)
Glanz et al[29]	Employees at 111 work sites employing more than 28,000 workers in 16 states	Diet	Stage of change (TTM)	Not specified	None	% of energy from fat, fiber intake, fruit and vegetable intake

Results: Results at follow up showed a reduction in percentage energy from fat of 0.37 percentage points (p = .033), a non-significant increase in fiber of 0.13 grams/1000 kcal (p = .056), and an increase in fruit and vegetable intake of 0. 18 servings per day (p = .0001).

Author	Population	Health Behavior(s)	Tailoring Variable(s)	Feedback/Information Delivery Method	Benchmark	Outcome Variable(s)
Glasgow et al[30]	22 worksites (average 215 employees per site)	Diet, physical activity, smoking	Worksite: Turnover rate, % female, employees in different job categories, health promotion activities offered. Selection of	Face-to-face	Heart disease risk and healthy cholesterol levels per the U.S. DHHS National Cholesterol Education Program	Tobacco use, fat intake, cholesterol reduction, physical activity

Author	Population	Health Behavior(s)	Tailoring Variable(s)	Feedback/ Information Delivery Method	Benchmark	Outcome Variable(s)
			activities from the Take Heart Menu (motivational/ incentive, educational/skills training, policy/ environmental, and maintenance) Individual: total cholesterol, dietary fat intake, and tobacco use, perceived support from coworkers and supervisors for changing dietary and tobacco habits, intent to change, stage of change (TTM)			

Results: At the 2 year follow up period, there were significant differences between intervention and comparison worksites for decreases in fat intake (10% vs <2%, respectively; p=0.04), general improvement in eating patterns (p = .023) and in intentions to limit fat in one's diet (p = .046). There were no significant differences in cross-sectional analysis for cholesterol, physical activity, or smoking.

Author	Population	Health Behavior(s)	Tailoring Variable(s)	Feedback/ Information Delivery Method	Benchmark	Outcome Variable(s)
Irvine et al[31]	517 employees of a large	Diet	Stage of change (TTM), intention	Computer kiosk with	None	Fat intake, fruit and vegetable

Author	Population	Health Behavior(s)	Tailoring Variable(s)	Feedback/ Information Delivery Method	Benchmark	Outcome Variable(s)
	hospital system and of an international corporation		(TRA), self-efficacy (SCT), demographics	interactive programming (video, narrated text), tailored printout		consumption, stage of change to adopt low-fat diet, intention and self-efficacy to reduce dietary fat, and attitude towards importance of diet
	**Results:** Intervention demonstrated improved scores for all outcome measures as compared to the comparison group at 1 month follow up.
Kim et al[32]	2470 participants recruited through 43 companies and 13 community organizations	Diet, physical activity, weight loss, weight loss maintenance	Stage of change (TTM)	Telephone counseling	None	Fruit and vegetable intake, minutes of physical activity, weight and height
	**Results:** Results showed significant increase in fruit and vegetable consumption in the group receiving telephone counseling (1.13 servings per day) vs the group receiving (non-tailored) self-help materials only (0.88 servings per day, p=0.04). There were no differences in physical activity or weight loss between the two groups.
Kwak et al[33]	533 participants at 12 worksites	Diet, physical activity	Participant-selected energy balance-related behavioral change priority	Web and computer (CD-ROM)	"Healthy standards"	Body weight, skinfold thickness, and waist circumference

Author	Population	Health Behavior(s)	Tailoring Variable(s)	Feedback/Information Delivery Method	Benchmark	Outcome Variable(s)
Lemon et al[34]	806 employees at 6 hospitals	Weight gain prevention	Site-specific factors and priorities identified by leadership and employee advisory committees	Print newsletter, social marketing	None	BMI

Results: There was a significant greater reduction in skinfold thickness in the intervention group as compared to the control group at 12-and 24 months follow up (Unstandardized regression coefficients (B = -2.52, 95% C.I. -4.58, -0.45; p = 0.018; B = -4.83, 95% C.I. 6.98, -2.67; p < 0.001, respectively). And for changes in waist circumference both at 12 months (B = -1.50, 95% C.I. -2.35, -0.65; p < 0.001) and at 24 months (B = -1.30, 95% C.I. -2.18, -0.42; p = 0.005). No significant changes were observed for weight and BMI.

Author	Population	Health Behavior(s)	Tailoring Variable(s)	Feedback/Information Delivery Method	Benchmark	Outcome Variable(s)
Leslie et al[35]	655 staff members of medium-sized Australian University	Physical activity	Stage of change (TTM)	Email, interactive web quiz	None	Self-reported physical activity and sitting time

Results: No impact of intervention on change in BMI using intent-to –treat analysis. Intervention exposure was associated with a decrease of 0.012 BMI units for every 1-unit increase in intervention at 24-month follow up.

Author	Population	Health Behavior(s)	Tailoring Variable(s)	Feedback/Information Delivery Method	Benchmark	Outcome Variable(s)
Maruyama et al[36]	101 male office workers with metabolic	Diet, physical activity	Lifestyle, current diet habits, stage of change for	Face-to-face and web-based counseling	Participant-identified goals	Changes in food group intake and increased

Results: Overall, 327 were randomized to the website conditions and 250 completed the follow up survey. 46% visited the website over the trial period. A total of 4,114 hits to the website were recorded. Participants who entered the site spent on average 9 minutes per visit and visited 18 pages. Website use declined over time; 77% of all visits followed the first email.

Author	Population	Health Behavior(s)	Tailoring Variable(s)	Feedback/ Information Delivery Method	Benchmark	Outcome Variable(s)
	syndrome risk factors		physical activity and diet (TTM), self-efficacy for physical activity and diet change			number of ds; BMI and umbilical circumference, blood pressure, biochemical parameters

Results: Intervention group showed statistically significant positive changes in food group intake as compared to no-treatment comparison group (p=0.00). No significant changes were observed in number of steps. There were also significant differences in changes for body weight (p<0.05), BMI (p<0.05), Aspartate aminotransferase (AST) (p<0.05), insulin (p<0.05), and the homeostasis model assessment for insulin resistance (HOMA-IR) (p=0.00).

Author	Population	Health Behavior(s)	Tailoring Variable(s)	Feedback/ Information Delivery Method	Benchmark	Outcome Variable(s)
Mouttapa et al[37]	307 female university staff members	Diet	Demographics, current diet and physical activity habits, and participant-selected goals	Web, email-newsletter	None	Dietary intake (dairy, fruit, and vegetables) frequencies, weight loss

Results: Compared to the (no treatment) comparison group, the intervention group increased dairy intake frequency across the 3 assessments (F(2,304)=3.15; p < 0.05). Among participants who wanted to lose weight, weight loss in the intervention group was significantly higher compared to the control group from pretest to posttest (F(1,92) = 4.50; P < .05).

Author	Population	Health Behavior(s)	Tailoring Variable(s)	Feedback/ Information Delivery Method	Benchmark	Outcome Variable(s)
Neville et al[38]	365 Salt Lake County employees	Diet, physical activity, smoking	HRA measuring smoking, fruit and vegetable intake, and physical activity frequency	Print, face-to-face counseling	None	Self-reported dietary intake (fiber, fruit and vegetable, and cholesterol, physical activity, smoking

Author	Population	Health Behavior(s)	Tailoring Variable(s)	Feedback/ Information Delivery Method	Benchmark	Outcome Variable(s)
Park et al[39]	1463 employees from 21 retail chain stores	Stress, perceived health status	Site-specific needs identified through a participatory problem-solving intervention development process	Action plan worksheets	None	6 organizational climate dimensions (organizational support, coworker support, participation with supervisors, participation with others, communication, safety and health climate), and 2 wellbeing measures (job stress and perceived health status)

Results: Over the 8-year study period, a higher percentage of program participants reported eating 5 or more servings of fruits and vegetables (19% vs 26%, p=0.015) eating foods high in fiber (93% vs 98%, p<0.001), and being physically active 3 or more times per week (74% vs 85%, p<0.001) as compared to the general population. There was no significant difference in smoking or eating foods high in cholesterol.

Prochaska et al[40]	1400 employees of a medical	Inactivity, weight	HRA measuring inactivity,	Web, motivational	Peers who had made the most	% of participants who progressed

Results: There was a significant intervention effect on job stress (F=5.58, p=0.02)and perceived health status (F=8.20, p<0.004). Significant positive changes were also observed in organizational climate measures, with the exception of health and safety climate.

Author	Population	Health Behavior(s)	Tailoring Variable(s)	Feedback/Information Delivery Method	Benchmark	Outcome Variable(s)
	university	control, stress, smoking	BMI, stress and smoking; stage of change (TTM)	interviewing counseling (face-to-face or telephone)	progress for current TTM stage	from being "at risk" for a particular behavioral risk at baseline to being "at criteria" at 6 months

Results: At 6 month follow up, the HRA group (M = 1.445) had a significantly greater (p < .05) mean number of risks than the Motivational interviewing (M = 1.254) and the TTM (M = 1.319) groups.

Author	Population	Health Behavior(s)	Tailoring Variable(s)	Feedback/Information Delivery Method	Benchmark	Outcome Variable(s)
Purath et al[41]	286 female university employees	Physical activity	Stage of change (TTM)	Face-to-face counseling with booster phone call	None	Stages of change (TTM), blocks walked per day, vigorous and moderate weekend activity, minutes walked for exercise, and total minutes walked/week

Results: At 6-week follow-up, the control group demonstrated a 0.72 mean increase in stage of change, whereas the intervention group demonstrated a 1.34 mean increase in stage (p<0.001). There was a significantly different (p < .05) increase in blocks walked/day for the intervention group (7.31) as compared to the control (1.54). Hrs of weekend vigorous and moderate physical activity increased by .77 for the intervention group compared to .36 for the controls (p = .008). Change in minutes walked for exercise was also greater (p < .001) for the intervention group than for the controls, with an increase of 77.9 minutes/wk and 33.9 minutes/wk, respectively.

Author	Population	Health Behavior(s)	Tailoring Variable(s)	Feedback/Information Delivery Method	Benchmark	Outcome Variable(s)
Sorensen et al[42]	582 construction workers	Diet, smoking	Individual health behaviors,	Motivational interviewing	None	Fruit and vegetable

Author	Population	Health Behavior(s)	Tailoring Variable(s)	Feedback/ Information Delivery Method	Benchmark	Outcome Variable(s)
			intentions and self-efficacy to change, risk perceptions, social support, and nicotine addiction	telephone counseling, mail		consumption, smoking

Results: At 6-month follow-up, 8% of baseline cigarette smokers in the control group had quit, compared to 19% in the intervention group ($p = 0.03$) and the intervention group increased fruit and vegetable consumption by about 1.5 servings as compared to a slight decrease for the control group ($p < 0.001$).

Author	Population	Health Behavior(s)	Tailoring Variable(s)	Feedback/ Information Delivery Method	Benchmark	Outcome Variable(s)
Sternfeld et al[43]	787 employees in the administrative offices of a large healthcare organization	Diet, physical activity	Lifestyle constraints, current diet and physical activity, physical activity preference, stage of change (TTM)	Email, web	National recommend-ations	Self-reported changes in physical activity and fruit, vegetable, fats, and sugar intake

Results: Intervention group showed increase of 28 minutes/wk of moderate PA, 12.5 minutes/wk of vigorous PA, and 21 min/wk of walking as compared to control, intervention group showed increase of 28 minutes/wk of moderate PA, 12.5 minutes/wk of vigorous PA, and 21 min/wk of walking as compared to control group. Intake of saturated and trans fats declined.

Author	Population	Health Behavior(s)	Tailoring Variable(s)	Feedback/ Information Delivery Method	Benchmark	Outcome Variable(s)
Swartz et al[44]	351 participants recruited through large worksites	Smoking	Demographics	Web	None	Abstinence from smoking at follow up

Results: At 90-day follow up, the cessation rate was 24.1% (n=21) for the treatment group vs 8.2% (n=9) for the control group ($p=0.002$).

Author	Population	Health Behavior(s)	Tailoring Variable(s)	Feedback/ Information Delivery Method	Benchmark	Outcome Variable(s)
Thorndike et al[45]	330 employees of a large hospital	Diet, physical activity	Participant-selected goals	Web	None	% weight loss, time spent in

Author	Population	Health Behavior(s)	Tailoring Variable(s)	Feedback/Information Delivery Method	Benchmark	Outcome Variable(s)
			(for exercise and completion of weekly food logs); goals re-established every 3 months			physical activity, fruit and vegetable consumption, fatty and sugary food consumption

Results: There were no significant differences between intervention and control groups in outcomes measured at 1 year follow up.

Author	Population	Health Behavior(s)	Tailoring Variable(s)	Feedback/Information Delivery Method	Benchmark	Outcome Variable(s)
Tilley et al[46]	5042 employees at 28 worksites	Colorectal cancer screening	Stage of change (TTM)	Print (mailed booklet), phone	None	Completion of all recommended screenings (i.e., compliance), completion of at least one recommended screening (i.e., coverage)

Results: Intervention worksites demonstrated higher compliance and coverage as compared to control worksites. (OR=1.46, CI: 1.1-2.0 and OR=1.33, CI: 1.1-1.6, respectively).

Author	Population	Health Behavior(s)	Tailoring Variable(s)	Feedback/Information Delivery Method	Benchmark	Outcome Variable(s)
Yap et al[47]	73 employees from two distribution plants of a multi-national manufacturer	Physical activity	Need level (Maslow's Hierarchy of Needs)	Email	None	Stage of change (TTM), # of steps

Results: In the intervention group, 53.3% of the workers moved in stage of change, as compared to 19.2% in the comparison group (medium effect size = 0.353). There were no significant differences between the two groups in terms of increased step counts.

an individual prefers to get physical activity through structured exercise or through lifestyle activity) were used for tailoring in only one study.[43] Theory-based constructs were frequently used for tailoring, with 11 studies using stages of change from the TTM,[26,29–32,35,36,40,41,43,46] three studies utilizing self-efficacy from social cognitive theory,[28,36,42] one study using the health belief model,[23] one study using the theory of reasoned action,[31] one using the theory of planned behavior,[28] and five studies using constructs from other theories, sometimes unspecified (for example, social support or Maslow's hierarchy of need).[24,26,30,42,47] Demographics were used for tailoring in five interventions.[26,30,31,37,44] Risks for specific health outcomes or HRAs were used in four interventions.[24,27,38,40] Job characteristics,[26] specific organizational assessment tools (Checklist of Health Promotion Environments at Worksites [CHEW]),[25] and environmental/community resources[26] were each used in one instance. Lastly, participant-selected goals were used for tailoring in six intervention studies.[30,33,34,37,39,45]

Benchmarks for Comparison

Benchmarks can be useful in assessing change over time or in comparing outcomes against a standard or average. Various benchmarks were utilized in the selected studies to compare initial assessments against other data. The majority (19) did not have any specified benchmarks.[23–27,29,31,32,34,35,37–39,41,42,44–47] National recommendations were used in three studies, mostly with physical activity and diet.[28,30,43] Benchmark measures in three other studies were scores of peers,[40] progress towards self-identified goals,[36] and healthy standards.[33] Surprisingly, none of the interventions that used organization-level tailoring strategies mentioned the use of benchmarks, yet in practice one appeal of tailoring for worksites is based on the capacity to benchmark changes over time. Overall, benchmark measures were not consistently

used in the context of tailored workplace interventions. Greater use of benchmarks for comparison is one way in which tailored feedback to individuals and organizations might be enhanced.

Feedback/Information

Tailored feedback and information can be delivered in a variety of formats, with the most common forms of delivery being Web, counseling, and print. Counseling was among the most frequently used information delivery and feedback methods, with face-to-face interactions reported in seven studies,[23,27,30,36,38,40,41] telephone counseling in four studies,[32,40–42] and Web counseling occurring in one.[36] Print or mail was used for tailored health information in nine trials.[24,26,28,31,34,38,39,42,46] Eight studies used Web delivery for their employee communication.[25,33,35,37,40,43–45] Other studies reported the use of e-mail (4),[35,37,43,47] interactive kiosk (1),[31] CD-ROM (2),[28,33] and tablet computer (1).[24] One study did not specify how tailored information was delivered.[29]

Health Behaviors

A variety of health behaviors and conditions were targeted. Some of the most common health behaviors and conditions included diet (16 studies),[23,25–33,36–38,42,43,45] physical activity (12),[26,27,30,32,33,35,36,38,41,43,45,47] smoking (5),[30,38,40,42,44] weight management (3),[32,34,40] stress (2),[39,40] and cancer screening (2).[24,46] Some interventions focused on multiple health behaviors by combining efforts to improve physical activity and nutrition (6),[26,27,33,36,43,45] or other sets of multiple behaviors (6).[30,32,38–40] Thirteen studies focused on a single behavior to tailor worksite interventions.[23–25,28,29,31,34,35,37,41,44,46,47]

Results

Results reported in the studies reviewed show that tailored interventions were successful in increasing fruit and vegetable consumption,[26,29,31,32,36,38,42] reducing fat consumption,[23,26,28,30,31,43] increasing physical activity,[26,38,41,43] encouraging smoking cessation,[42,44] promoting disease screening,[46] reducing job stress,[39] improving perceived health,[39] and supporting weight loss.[27,36,37] Thus, tailored interventions were successful in changing behaviors that require continued commitment and maintenance, such as physical activity, as well as behaviors that are accomplished with a single action, such as disease screening. Results also revealed that tailoring was successful in addressing proposed mediators of behavior change such as knowledge,[23,24] perceived benefits,[23] and stage of change.[47] Not all studies, however, yielded positive results. Despite the aforementioned positive results, our review also included studies that found no advantage for tailoring in improving fruit and vegetable[45] or fat intake,[38,45] physical activity,[30,32,36,45,47] smoking cessation,[30,38,45] or weight loss.[32,33,34,45] Only two studies[34,45] reported no positive results for any of the outcomes they addressed.

It is important to note that results of the reviewed studies sometimes reflect a comparison between tailored and nontailored treatments and other times a comparison between a tailored intervention and no intervention. Therefore, we cannot conclude from this brief review that tailored interventions are significantly more likely to change behavior or its mediators than nontailored interventions. Additionally, publication bias against studies with null results raises the possibility that less successful tailored interventions are less likely to be found in the peer-reviewed literature. We can, however, conclude that the tailored interventions reviewed here yielded positive results for at least one outcome among the majority of studies reviewed. Given the generally positive results from this literature review, we expect the evidence base to grow for tailored interventions. Moreover, very little attention has been paid to the effects of organizational-level tailoring; this area is wide open for future research.

Summary

This brief review of worksite-based tailored interventions has described the variety of tailoring variables used, behavioral outcomes studied, and feedback mechanisms applied. It has also revealed that theoretical constructs are commonly used as tailoring variables, that benchmarks for comparison are underutilized, that tailored feedback can be delivered in a variety of ways, and that tailoring can be used to target change in several different behaviors simultaneously. Tailored interventions continue to show promise in effecting behavior change; however, results are relatively modest and somewhat mixed, which indicates the importance of conducting future research to improve the impact of tailored interventions. Specifically, both outcome and implementation studies would be beneficial: for example, studies that examine the effectiveness of benchmarks and of organizational-level tailoring, and those that explore whether certain tailoring variables or tailoring mechanisms are best suited for particular behaviors and populations. Future research into these areas will yield important information for health promotion practitioners in their efforts to implement effective tailored interventions in the worksite.

ASSESSMENT TOOLS FOR TAILORING

Individual Assessment Tools

Worksite-based tailored interventions employ many different types of assessment tools (INPUTS) as part of the tailoring process. Surprisingly, HRAs, which have been available for many years, were underutilized as individually focused assessment tools in this review of published studies of tailored worksite interventions. Only 2 of the 25 studies reviewed reported using HRAs.[38,40] It is important to point out that the published literature does not necessarily represent the reality of practice. Discussions with employers and health promotion vendors confirm that most employers use the aggregate reports from their HRAs to help guide development of their programs. HRAs provide a systematic approach to measuring and collecting information from individuals about key theory-driven constructs and health and risk behavior status, and typically offer feedback designed to motivate behavior change by sharing information, for example, that compares real, chronological age with an estimated age based on responses to the questionnaire via a series of algorithms. HRAs are routinely marketed to employers through insurers and other vendors, but the most recent national survey of worksites (conducted in 2004) revealed that only 19.4% of all employers utilized an HRA; these data varied widely by worksite size, such that 11.3% of those with 50 to 99 employees, 21.8% of those with 100 to 249, 30.1% of those with 250 to 749, and 45.8% of worksites with 750+ employees reported offering HRAs to employees ($p = .0002$).[48] Increased use of HRAs in assessing a workplace's employees would aid in developing tailored messages, serve as benchmarks for monitoring change at the individual and organizational levels, and help evaluate the change in employees (and aggregated change at the organizational level) over time.

Among the interventions reviewed, theory-based assessments were common, with 23 trials measuring theoretical constructs for the purposes of tailoring, and stages of change (from TTM) utilized by 11 studies. Surprisingly, job characteristics were included in the assessment for only one workplace tailored intervention reviewed, which yielded modest results.[30] Workplace-based interventions designed to take into account how the conditions of work might affect health behavior and leverage this information in tailored communications will be most effective if they capture relevant detail about job roles and responsibilities, shifts, and other characteristics.

Organizational Assessment Tools

Among the studies identified as doing tailored worksite interventions in this review, only one made use of a standardized organization assessment tool—the CHEW.[25] Although only one study used a standardized organization tool, these can be useful in developing organizational-level tailored interventions. Such assessment tools have grown in number and scope over the past decade. For example, the Centers for Disease Control and Prevention has developed a Worksite Health Scorecard (http://www.cdc.gov/dhdsp/pubs/worksite ecard.htm.) assessed April 22, 2014, and have recognized several other tools for this purpose: Designing Healthier Environments at Work Assessment Tool, Heart Check, and a Worksite Wellness questionnaire developed by Partnership for Prevention.[49] Others include the Environmental Assessment Tool,[50] methods to measure organizational stage of change/readiness,[4] and numerous tools developed by vendors and other nonprofits. Results from these assessment tools are typically summarized in report form for the workplace client or consultant or presented to management and/or an employee wellness committee at the organization. Results are used to identify gaps in support for employee wellness and to develop a set of strategies that are tailored to the unique characteristics of that workplace organization. As with individual-level assessments, results from organizational assessments can be compared against a variety of benchmarks, including national or industry averages or previous assessments. The idea of offering tailored interventions at the organizational level is not new, but there is little published literature on what the assessment tools include; which variables they use to tailor on; how, when, and in what format information is provided back to employers; and the impact of these tailored interventions on supporting changes in policies and programs and creating healthier work environments.

This is an area that demands additional research and has important implications for the practice of worksite wellness in the future. Use of standardized measurement tools facilitates the design of organizational-level tailored interventions and accurate comparisons across and within worksites.

APPLICATIONS TO MOTIVATION AND SKILL BUILDING

Motivation and skill building are both important steps on the pathway toward behavior change. For example, a full understanding of what motivates an individual to make a smoking quit attempt at a particular point in time and then follow through on the motivation includes a complex set of interactions that involves the larger social context (e.g., "Are policies about smoking in my state or town making it increasingly difficult to smoke?"), the community in which the individual resides (e.g., "Is the quitline in my state offering free nicotine replacement products and counseling services this month?"), the workplace at which the individual spends a majority of waking hours (e.g., "Has a new smoke-free policy at work been enacted that will limit my ability to smoke at work?"), interpersonal interactions (e.g., "How does my wife feel about my smoking during her pregnancy?"), and intrapersonal factors (e.g., "I am tired of smelling like smoke")—all of these factors may conspire to motivate a quit attempt.

The Elaboration Likelihood Model (ELM) is a useful theory to explain how tailoring works to enhance motivation to change behavior.[51] The ELM posits there are two routes to persuasion through which individuals process information. The *central* route is characterized by cognitive consideration of arguments presented and accesses the receiver's own memories and schemas to process information. The central route of processing results in more long-lasting changes in attitudes towards behavior change that are resistant to counterpersuasion.[52]

The receiver carefully evaluates the arguments, and this triggers issue-relevant thinking. The central route is activated through tailoring when the receiver is prompted to reflect on his or her own behavior and discrepancies with "ideal" behavior.[52] Thus, the personal relevance of health messaging is enhanced through tailored communication. The *peripheral* route is activated through mental "shortcuts" and bypasses careful thought and evaluation.[52] Processing through the peripheral route results in shorter-term changes in attitude. One way that tailoring uses the peripheral route of processing is by providing information in a way that conveys that the sender understands the receiver in terms of goals, desires, and barriers faced.[52] This enhances source credibility and reduces doubt in the mind of the receiver about new information or advice. Tailoring therefore incorporates central and peripheral processing routes to enhance personal relevance and inspire motivation to change health behaviors.

Tailored interventions have the ability to ask about the factors that are pushing someone toward wanting to change (benefits of change) as well as factors that might keep him or her from changing (barriers to change). Tailored interventions that (1) identify the most salient benefits, (2) validate those benefits and clarify how to overcome the barriers, and then (3) appropriately time the initial and follow-up messages in ways that move people along the pathway of change can be an important support for increasing motivation, activating the central and peripheral processing routes, and ultimately changing behavior. The studies reviewed in this chapter indicate that people prefer tailored interventions to generic, non-tailored interventions; they read and interact with the feedback more, and they exhibit small but statistically better changes in behaviors when compared with nontailored interventions around most, but not all, health outcomes. These changes could be attributed to the fact that messages are salient to the targeted individual because they integrate the environmental characteristics of the message (peripheral route) and the person's unique cognitive processes (central route). Together with an awareness that our workforce is becoming increasingly diverse, and because interventions must evolve with the changing work conditions, the authors remain enthusiastic supporters of tailored interventions as a core intervention strategy that is flexible enough to accommodate the changing realities of our workforce and type of work.

Likewise, tailored interventions may be quite useful when attempting to motivate organizations to adopt or implement healthy work environments, policies, and practices. Organizations are managed by people in leadership positions. Some organizations are hierarchical and autocratic, whereas others are decentralized and embrace a more democratic leadership style. These leadership differences matter when advocating for change in an organization. There is no one-size-fits-all approach to working with organizations, so the process of gathering information and insights about people, resources, policies, and practices is critically important. The assessment tools for gathering inputs to accomplish tailoring at the organizational level are relatively new in their development and not yet fully tested. A few exceptions exist; however, we have much to learn about motivating organizations to change via tailored interventions. In practice, health promotion practitioners have consistently attempted to identify organizational assets and strengths as a key component of our assessment efforts. They have engaged with managers and decision makers as well as mobilized employees from all subgroups of the workforce to get involved in the planning and delivery of worksite health promotion efforts;[53,54] yet, there has been little study of processes for engaging these groups in organizational decision making. Building on strengths of the organization is often an attractive idea to organizational leaders that can also be cost efficient. For example, if an organization decides to embark on developing a comprehensive wellness program, initial efforts to engage leaders involved with the safety committee around the idea of wellness promotion can save time, effort, and money if done well. The idea of tailoring at the macro level of the organization and how it works, along with tailoring individual programs offered (e.g., linking to the mission of the organization, logo, business plan) makes for a better fit and may help ensure long-term success. Tailoring at the organizational macro level using reliable, well-constructed messages through a quality and attractive presentation can combine central and peripheral processing routes at the organization level to ensure consistency of the wellness messages. At this point in time, these examples are more practice tested than empirically tested, so there is work to be done to build the evidence base on improving motivation and change at the organizational level with tailored workplace interventions. This type of work and gaps within research will fit nicely within the context of a growing interest in implementation and dissemination science. For example, health promotion practitioners might consider examining factors that enhance or inhibit organizational adoption and implementation of new technology within an organizational setting. Theories, lessons learned, and tailoring strategies may be gleaned from this body of literature and adapted for use by individuals who are planning worksite wellness programs.

In addition to building on strengths of individuals and organizations as a relatively untested tailoring approach, the authors advocate for continued personalization of the feedback provided, including culturally and contextually appropriate tailoring. For example, in a 24-hour manufacturing production facility with mostly blue-collar male workers, it is important to place feedback in the context of a busy production environment. Thus, both recommendations and feedback could be posted using pictures, stories, and testimonials from "real employees" working on a production line in a similar job. As expert computer systems continue to evolve, the precision of tailoring will be enhanced and opportunities to improve on feedback will be realized. With this extra precision comes the need for ongoing dialogue and message testing with the end user (e.g., individual worker or organizational decision maker). Conversations about preferences regarding the amount and type of feedback that is desired, acceptable, and effective are recommended. Pretesting tailored feedback could capture ways to improve messages that encompass peripheral and central route processing. Taking this technology to scale without adequate pretesting runs the risk of offending or disengaging the very people one intends to motivate. Establishing procedures for pretesting and then evaluating tailored intervention efforts is the key to continuous quality and impact improvement of tailored interventions.

UNANSWERED QUESTIONS

The field of tailored interventions emerged in the published literature in the late 1990s, and only a few workplace studies have focused specifically on tailored interventions at the individual level. Almost no research has been done to explain how tailored interventions might contribute to increasing adoption and improving the implementation and sustainability of effective workplace health promotion efforts. Acknowledging that this is a relatively new and still emerging field offers a wide array of research opportunities to begin to address a myriad of unanswered questions:

Assessment (Input)–Related Questions

- Is there a minimum "core set" of key variables that are essential to tailor on at the individual and organization levels for producing changes

behavioral outcomes? If yes, what are the theoretical guides serving as a foundation for those core set of variables?
- What are the best ways (e.g., formats and tools) for asking these core set of questions? Do we have adequate and affordable tools available or do we need to create new tools?
- How often should we ask the questions of individuals and organizational decision makers? What is the cost of these assessments, and is the burden on participants (individuals and organizations) reasonable?

Process-Related Questions

- Are there any standardized algorithms we can use to program the required output? What type of technology is needed to process these data most rapidly, with greatest accuracy and most cost efficiently?
- Are standardized message libraries available for use? What is the best way to do culturally and contextually appropriate pretesting of proposed messages prior to launch?

Feedback/Output–Related Questions

- What type, format, amount, and frequency of feedback are most preferred by individuals and organizations? Does preferred feedback outperform some other expert-driven feedback?
- Because dynamic feedback has proven to be more effective, is it practical or cost-effective to do repeated, ipsative feedback for individuals? Is ipsative feedback more effective for organizations? What is the return

on investment associated with more feedback? Are there any unintended consequences associated with too much or too frequent feedback?

Outcome-Related Questions:

- How can we maximize the effectiveness of tailored interventions? What are the mechanisms through which tailoring produces better outcomes? Would coaching or some other adjunct to the initial feedback be helpful? What is the cost-effectiveness of tailored vs. nontailored approaches?
- Is there a dose-response relationship between outcomes and amount of feedback provided? There is some evidence that up to three risk factors can be addressed at a time, and still other evidence to suggest that simultaneous (vs. sequential) behavior change goals are acceptable, but what is the best amount of feedback and the right combination of approaches for yielding success?
- Which subgroups are more/less likely to respond to tailored interventions at the individual and organization (worksite) levels? Are there other key moderating factors for understanding the effectiveness of these tailored interventions at work?
- What type of tailored intervention can produce lasting changes in targeted behavioral outcomes—that is, how can we improve maintenance via tailored interventions for individuals and organizations?

CONCLUSION

Tailored interventions are a relatively new and still emerging strategy for increasing awareness and motivation and influencing behavior change among employees and workplace decision makers. Early evidence suggests that tailored interventions are promising for acceptability, interest, and engagement among employees, as well as small but statistically significant changes in most health behavior outcomes. There has been very little work on tailored interventions for promoting healthy changes at the organizational (workplace) level, and this warrants further investigation. Tailoring at the individual and organizational levels follows the same general tailoring process—that is, assessment tools collect data; the data are processed and key messages are crafted; and feedback (output) is provided in a variety of formats that is uniquely customized to the individual employee or organization. Given the diversity of the workforce and the changing work environment, tailored interventions should be considered as part of a menu of intervention strategies included in comprehensive health promotion programs that are designed to improve worker and workplace health. When done well, all phases of the tailored intervention process should engage employees, managers, and decision makers in creating a vision and set of action steps for establishing a healthy and safe work environment. For example, completing the assessment sparks awareness among employees/managers, and the feedback can engage and encourage action. This chapter offers a conceptual framework for explaining how tailored interventions work, reviews the literature on tailored interventions generally as well as workplace-specific tailored interventions, and lists some of the unanswered questions that need to be addressed to move this approach forward. The authors hope the list of unanswered questions will stimulate scientists and practitioners to build evidence by evaluating any tailored interventions they are currently working with. We also intend for our list to be a starting point for scientists in designing studies that will push this important field forward.

Glossary

Assessment tool: An instrument that helps define and prioritize possible areas of improvement. For example, in the workplace an assessment tool may be used to identify workplace resources for healthy eating, physical activity facilities, or antismoking policies.[55]

Benchmark: A standard by which something can be measured or judged.

Health belief model (HBM): A psychological health behavior theory that focuses on individuals' perceived susceptibility to disease, perceived severity of disease, and perceived barriers and benefits of taking action.[56]

Health risk assessment (HRA): A systematic approach to collecting information from individuals that identifies risk factors, provides individualized feedback, and links the person with at least one intervention to promote health, sustain function and/or prevent disease. A typical HRA instrument obtains information on demographic characteristics, lifestyle, personal medical history, and family medical history.[57]

Message library: A collection of distinct health-related messages that map onto every possible response option that an individual could choose when completing an assessment tool (INPUT). Tailored reports assemble a unique set of messages drawn from the library of possible responses and are combined to create customized feedback based on responses to an initial assessment.[3]

Self-efficacy: The conviction that one can successfully execute a behavior required to produce an outcome.[58]

Tailoring: An intervention or behavior change strategy intended to reach one specific person (or organization), based on information unique to that person (or organization), related to the outcome of interest, and derived from individual assessment.[59]

Targeting: Information and behavior change strategies intended to reach a group of people based on a single characteristic of a group, such as age, gender, diagnosis, or ethnicity, or multiple group characteristics.[60]

Theory of reasoned action (TRA) and **theory of planned behavior (TPB):** Two closely related theories that focus on individual motivational factors as key determinants of the likelihood of performing a specific health behavior. Perceived behavioral control, attitudes, and subjective norms influence intention, which in turn predicts whether or not behavior change occurs.[61]

Transtheoretical model of behavior change (TTM): A theory that assesses an individual's readiness to take action to change a health behavior and offers strategies to guide the individual through six different stages of change: precontemplation, contemplation, preparation, action, maintenance, and termination.[62]

Learning Objectives

1. To learn the definition of tailoring and how it differs from targeting.
2. To clarify key components of tailoring at the individual and organizational levels.
3. To understand how tailoring for health behavior change has been used in worksite interventions.
4. To understand recommendations for future uses of tailoring in the workplace.

Discussion Questions

1. What are the challenges to implementing tailoring at the worksite?

2. What considerations should be made to determine the best communication strategy for providing tailored health information?

3. How could individual health behaviors and organizational supports for employee health be measured?

4. How could tailored approaches at both the individual and organizational level be combined to influence employee health behavior?

5. What types of information could be used to develop message libraries for tailored feedback?

6. What technological advances might improve tailored information and how it is delivered to employees?

REFERENCES

1. Toossi M. A new look at long-term labor force projections to 2050. *Mon Lab Rev.* 2006;129(19):19–39.

2. Centers for Disease Control and Prevention. Total Worker Health™. Available at: http://www.cdc.gov/niosh/TWH/default.html. Accessed May 29, 2013.

3. Kreuter MW, Farrell D, Olevitch L, Brennan L. What is tailored communication? In: *Tailoring Health Messages: Customizing Communication with Computer Technology.* Mahwah, NJ: Lawrence Erlbaum Associates Inc; 2000:1–23.

4. Weiner BJ, Amick H, Lee DSY. Review: conceptualization and measurement of organizational readiness for change: a review of the literature in health services research and other fields. *Med Care Res Rev.* 2008;65:379–436.

5. Strecher VJ, Kreuter M, Den Boer DJ, et al. The effects of computer-tailored smoking cessation messages in family practice settings. *J Fam Pract.* 1994;39:262–270.

6. Kreuter, MW, Strecher VJ. Do tailored behavior change messages enhance the effectiveness of health risk appraisal? Results from a randomized trial. *Health Educ Res.* 2005; 11: 97–105.

7. Lipkus IM, Rimer BK, Halabi S, Strigo TS. Can tailored interventions increase mammography use among HMO women? *Am J Prev Med.* 2000;18:1–10.

8. Brug J, Glanz K, Van Assema P, et al. The impact of computer-tailored feedback and iterative feedback on fat, fruit, and vegetable intake. *Health Educ Behav.* 1998;25:517–531.

9. Campbell MK, DeVellis BM, Strecher VJ, et al. Improving dietary behavior: the effectiveness of tailored messages in primary care settings. *Am J Public Health.* 1994;84:783–787.

10. Marcus BH, Bock BC, Pinto BM, et al. Efficacy of an individualized, motivationally-tailored physical activity intervention. *Ann Behav Med.* 1998;20:174–180.

11. Kreuter MW, Skinner CS. Tailoring: what's in a name? *Health Educ Res.* 2000;15:1–4.

12. Kreuter MW, Holt CL. How do people process health information? Applications in an age of individualized communication. *Curr Dir Psychol Sci.* 2001;10:206–209.

13. Rimer BK, Glassman B. Is there a use for tailored print communications in cancer risk communication? *J Natl Cancer Inst Monogr.* 1999;25:140–148.

14. Skinner CS, Campbell MK, Rimer BK, et al. How effective is tailored print communication? *Ann Behav Med.* 1999;21:290–298.

15. Ryan P, Lauver DR. The efficacy of tailored interventions. *J Nurs Scholarsh.* 2002;34:331–337.

16. Kroeze W, Werkman A, Brug J. A systematic review of randomized trials on the effectiveness of computer-tailored

education on physical activity and dietary behaviors. *Ann Behav Med.* 2006;31:205–223.

17. Revere D, Dunbar PJ. Review of computer-generated outpatient health behavior interventions: clinical encounters "in absentia." *J Am Med Inform Assoc.* 2001;8:62–79.

18. Brug J, Campbell M, van Assema P. The application and impact of computer-generated personalized nutrition education: a review of the literature. *Patient Educ Couns.* 1999;36:145–156.

19. Noar SM, Benac CN, Harris MS. Does tailoring matter? Meta-analytic review of tailored print health behavior change interventions. *Psychol Bull.* 2007; 133:673–693.

20. Cohen J. *Statistical Power Analysis for the Behavioral Sciences.* Hillsdale, NJ: Lawrence Erlbaum Associates Inc; 1988.

21. Lustria ML, Cortese J, Noar SM, Glueckauf RL. Computer-tailored health interventions delivered over the Web: review and analysis of key components. *Patient Educ Couns.* 2009;74:156–173.

22. Krebs P, Prochaska JO, Rossi JS. A meta-analysis of computer-tailored interventions for health behavior change. *Prev Med.* 2010;51:214–221.

23. Abood DA, Black DR, Feral D. Nutrition education worksite intervention for university staff: application of the health belief model. *J Nutr Educ Behav.* 2003;35:260–267.

24. Allen JD, Othus MK, Hart A Jr, et al. A randomized trial of a computer-tailored decision aid to improve prostate cancer screening decisions: results from the take the wheel trial [published online ahead of print August 17, 2010]. *Cancer Epidemiol Biomarkers Prev.* 2010;19:2172–2186. doi:10.1158/1055-9965.EPI-09-0410.

25. Beresford SA, Locke E, Bishop S, et al. Worksite study promoting activity and changes in eating (PACE): design

and baseline results. *Obesity,* 2007; 15(S1):4S–15S.

26. Campbell MK, Tessaro I, DeVellis B, et al. Effects of a tailored health promotion program for female blue-collar workers: Health Works for Women. *Prev Med.* 2002;34:313–323.

27. Cho SW, Kang JY, Park YK, et al. A 12-week worksite health promotion program reduces cardiovascular risk factors in male workers with the apolipoprotein E2 and apolipoprotein E3 genotypes, but not in apolipoprotein E4 genotype. *Nutr Res.* 2009;29, 542–550.

28. De Bourdeaudhuij I, Stevens V, Vandelanotte C, Brug J. Evaluation of an interactive computer-tailored nutrition intervention in a real-life setting. *Ann Behav Med.* 2007;33:39–48.

29. Glanz K, Patterson RE, Kristal AR, et al. Impact of work site health promotion on stages of dietary change: the Working Well trial. *Health Educ Behav.* 1998; 25:448–463.

30. Glasgow RE, Terborg JR, Strycker LA, et al. Take Heart II: replication of a worksite health promotion trial. *J Behav Med.* 1997;20:143–161.

31. Irvine AB, Ary DV, Grove DA, Gilfillan-Morton L. The effectiveness of an interactive multimedia program to influence eating habits. *Health Educ Res.* 2004;19:290–305.

32. Kim Y, Pike J, Adams H, et al. Telephone intervention promoting weight-related health behaviors. *Prev Med.* 2010; 50:112–117.

33. Kwak L, Kremers SP, Candel MJ, et al. Changes in skinfold thickness and waist circumference after 12 and 24 months resulting from the NHF-NRG In Balance-project. *Int J Behav Nutr Phys Act.* 2010;7:26.

34. Lemon SC, Zapka J, Li W, et al. Step ahead a worksite obesity prevention trial among hospital employees. *Am J*

Prev Med. 2010;38:27–38. doi:10.1016/j.amepre.2009.08.028.

35. Leslie E, Marshall AL, Owen N, Bauman A. Engagement and retention of participants in a physical activity website. *Prev Med.* 2005;40:54–59.

36. Maruyama C, Kimura M, Okumura H, et al. Effect of a worksite-based intervention program on metabolic parameters in middle-aged male white-collar workers: a randomized controlled trial. *Prev Med.* 2010;51:11–17.

37. Mouttapa M, Robertson TP, McEligot AJ, et al. The Personal Nutrition Planner: a 5-week, computer-tailored intervention for women. *J Nutr Educ Behav.* 2011;43:165–172.

38. Neville BH, Merrill RM, Kumpfer KL. Longitudinal outcomes of a comprehensive, incentivized worksite wellness program [published online ahead of print August 9, 2010]. *Eval Health Prof.* 2011;34:103–123. doi:10.1177/0163278710379222.

39. Park KO, Schaffer BS, Griffin-Blake CS, et al. Effectiveness of a healthy work organization intervention: ethnic group differences. *J Occup Environ Med.* 2004;46:623–634.

40. Prochaska JO, Butterworth S, Redding CA, et al. Initial efficacy of MI, TTM tailoring and HRI's with multiple behaviors for employee health promotion. *Prev Med.* 2008;46:226–231.

41. Purath J, Miller AM, McCabe G, Wilbur J. A brief intervention to increase physical activity in sedentary working women. *Can J Nurs Res.* 2004;36:76–91.

42. Sorensen G, Barbeau EM, Stoddard AM, et al. Tools for health: the efficacy of a tailored intervention targeted for construction laborers. *Cancer Causes Control.* 2007;18:51–59.

43. Sternfeld B, Block C, Quesenberry CP, et al. Improving diet and physical activity with ALIVE: a worksite randomized trial. *Am J Prev Med.* 2009;36:475–483.

44. Swartz LHG, Noell JW, Schroeder SW, Ary DV. A randomised control study of a fully automated internet based smoking cessation programme. *Tob Control.* 2006;15:7–12.

45. Thorndike AN, Sonnenberg L, Healey E, et al. Prevention of weight gain following a worksite nutrition and exercise program: a randomized controlled trial. *Am J Prev Med.* 2012;43:27–33. doi:10.1016/j.amepre.2012.02.029.

46. Tilley BC, Vernon SW, Myers R, et al. The Next Step Trial: impact of a worksite colorectal cancer screening promotion program. *Prev Med.* 1999;28:276–283.

47. Yap TL, Davis LS, Gates DM, et al. The effect of tailored E-mails in the workplace. Part I. Stage movement toward increased physical activity levels. *AAOHN J.* 2009;57:267–273.

48. Linnan L, Bowling M, Childress J, et al. Results of the 2004 National Worksite Health Promotion Survey. *Am J Public Health.* 2008;98:1503–1509.

49. Centers for Disease Control and Prevention. Healthy worksite initiative: environmental audits. Available at: http://www.cdc.gov/nccdphp/dnpao/hwi/programdesign/environmental_audits.htm. Accessed January 6, 2013.

50. Dejoy DM, Wilson MG, Goetzel RZ, et al. Development of the Environmental Assessment Tool (EAT) to measure organizational physical and social support for worksite obesity prevention programs. *J Occup Environ Med.* 2008;50:126–137. doi:10.1097/JOM.0b013e318161b42a.

51. Petty RE, Cacioppo JT. The elaboration likelihood model of persuasion. In: *Communication and Persuasion.* New York, NY: Springer; 1986:1–24.

52. Hawkins RP, Kreuter M, Resnicow K, et al. Understanding tailoring in

communicating about health [published online ahead of print March 17, 2008]. *Health Educ Res.* 2008;23:454–466. doi: 10.1093/her/cyn004.

53.   Linnan L, Weiner B, Graham A, Emmons K. Manager beliefs regarding worksite health promotion: findings from the Working Healthy Project 2. *Am J Health Promot.* 2007;21:521–528.

54.   Linnan L, Fava J, Thompson B, et al. (1999). Measuring participatory strategies: instrument development for worksite populations. *Health Educ Res.* 1999;14:371–386.

55.   Centers for Disease Control and Prevention. Workplace health promotion: assessment. Available at: http://www.cdc.gov/workplacehealthpromotion/assessment/index.html. Accessed January 6, 2013.

56.   Champion VL, Skinner CG. The health belief model. In: Glanz K, Rimer B, Viswanath K, eds. *Health Behavior and Health Education: Theory, Research, and Practice.* San Francisco, Calif: Jossey-Bass; 2008:45–62.

57.   Centers for Disease Control and Prevention. Healthier Worksite Initiative. Available at http://www.cdc.gov/nccdphp/dnpao/hwi/programdesign/health_risk_appraisals.htm. Accessed January 6, 2013.

58.   Bandura A. *Social Learning Theory.* Englewood Cliffs, NJ: Prentice Hall; 1977.

59.   Rimer BK, Kreuter MW. Advancing tailored health communication: a persuasion and message effects perspective. *J Commun.* 2006; 56(S1):S184–S201.

60.   Beck C, McSweeney JC, Richards KC, et al. Challenges in tailored intervention research. *Nurs Outlook.* 2010;58:104–110.

61.   Montaño DE, Kasprzyk D. Theory of reasoned action, theory of planned behavior, and the integrated behavioral model. In: Glanz K, Rimer B, Viswanath K, eds. *Health Behavior and Health Education: Theory, Research, and Practice.* San Francisco, Calif: Jossey-Bass; 2008:67–96.

62.   Prochaska JO, Redding CA, Evers KE. The transtheoretical model and stages of change. In: Glanz K, Rimer B, Viswanath K, eds. *Health Behavior and Health Education: Theory, Research, and Practice.* San Francisco, Calif: Jossey-Bass; 2008:97–117.

CHAPTER

13

Health Assessment

David R. Anderson, Erin L. D. Seaverson,
and Paul E. Terry

INTRODUCTION

Health assessment, broadly defined as an analysis of health-related data that evaluates health status, health risk, and health improvement priorities at the individual or organizational level, is a key element of worksite health promotion programs.[1] At the organizational level, health assessment is an important planning and evaluation process that provides information on many aspects of employee and organizational health and well-being. Health assessment data typically include health care utilization rates and costs, employee health-related risks, and employee health behavior, knowledge, attitudes, and intentions. At the individual level, health assessment can play an important role in a worksite health promotion program by creating "teachable moments" when the participating employee is especially receptive to health-related information and recommendations. In these teachable moments, such messages may act as catalysts for initiating behavioral changes that can result in health improvement or health risk reduction.

Historically, health risk assessment (HRA) and biomedical screening have been the most widely used sources of health assessment data in worksite health promotion. With advances in device, data, and networking technologies, however, there is a proliferation of other potential sources of health assessment data including mobile apps, health care and disability claims, laboratory tests from doctor visits, personal health record (PHR), electronic medical record (EMR), electronic health record (EHR), and electronic monitoring devices (e.g., activity trackers, blood pressure monitors, scales, and metabolic measures). Health assessment in worksite health promotion is moving toward integrating these diverse sources and extracting relevant data elements from each to provide a more complete and actionable understanding of every individual in the population, ranging from the very healthy to those with serious chronic health conditions.

The "Quantified Self" is a movement pursuing the use of technology to continually acquire data on a person's daily life, including inputs (e.g., food consumption), states (e.g., moods, blood pressure), and physical and mental performance. This movement is stimulating innovations in worksite health promotion that may lead to a deeper understanding of individual needs and more personalized interventions that better motivate participants and support changes in their health behaviors. For example, in an interview for the MIT Technology Review, Stephen Wofram, an early leader in the use of personal analytics, argued that most people are "leaving lots of digital trails" and "you're seeing people's lives played out in the level of the data."[2] In a widely read blog post among those interested in the quantified self, Wolfram shared a granular analysis of his habits in e-mailing, phoning, and meeting and included an analysis of his steps taken per day, all to share how personal analytics can "give us a whole new dimension to experiencing our lives."[3]

As in the broader health care market, business and economics are intertwined with science in decisions about worksite health promotion and, thus, health assessment. Employers have reported a desire to improve employee health and educate their employees to become better health care consumers as the major priorities for health and wellness initiatives.[4] These priorities support their longstanding goals of health care cost containment and, more recently, improved employee performance. This economic imperative introduces a fundamental difference between worksite health promotion and many other population health initiatives. While an axiom of population health is to provide "the greatest good for the greatest number," the economics of worksite health promotion factors

cost-effectiveness or cost-benefit into employer criteria for success.

The specific goals of a worksite health promotion program influence many aspects of an employer's health assessment approach. Health assessment dimensions will vary depending on whether the primary program goal is lowering health-related costs, improving population health, or increasing employee performance. Program goals influence the health issues and measures included in the health assessment, the populations targeted for measurement, ongoing surveillance, measurement intervals, and how the data get used.

The purpose of this chapter is to describe how health assessment can be used in worksite health promotion for strategic planning, program development, motivating individuals to change unhealthy behaviors, monitoring their progress, and evaluating outcomes. *HRA* has long been a core health assessment tool in worksite health promotion because it provides informative and action-oriented feedback both to the organization and to individual employees, based on an easily administered participant questionnaire. While Web and mobile technology will advance HRA design beyond the traditional approach of administering a single comprehensive HRA at the beginning of each program year, the underlying strategy of using self-reported employee health data to inform and motivate participants and to track population health is more compelling than ever. Because of its historical importance in worksite health promotion and essential role in the health behavior change process, HRA is an area of focus in this chapter. *Biomedical screening,* which can be implemented independently or in conjunction with HRA, is another important health assessment approach that is discussed in detail because of its wide use in worksite health promotion. A third area of focus is the growing use of *financial incentives* intended to increase health assessment participation and drive better population health outcomes.

PLANNING WORKSITE HEALTH ASSESSMENT

The role and implementation of health assessment varies considerably across different worksite health promotion programs. In some programs, gathering health assessment data occurs before planning, while in others the plans are developed first and health assessment serves as a baseline for measuring progress toward goals. Planning and evaluation overlap continuously in most cases, however, with health assessment serving both purposes. Ideally, both health assessment implementation and the overall program are driven by the employer's health improvement goals. In turn, health assessment procedures and instruments can be used to monitor progress toward goals and affirm and support the mission and direction of the program. Additionally, developing a program evaluation strategy begins with an analysis of how program interventions can be monitored with measurable outcome data such as those provided by health assessment.

Value of Health Assessment

Health assessment is a fundamental element of worksite health promotion programs because of its value in planning, program development, motivating individuals, and monitoring progress. Additionally, some aspects of health assessment, such as HRA and biomedical screening, provide tangible value to the employee and are usually perceived as a valuable employee benefit. Finally, to some extent health assessment can serve as an intervention by creating a "teachable moment" and call to action that provides direction for follow-up interventions.[5-7]

The value of the planning aspect of health assessment is found in the ability to link health assessment findings to planning and prioritizing interventions that can produce outcomes important to the organization. Health assessment data can identify which health risks and related conditions are currently driving health and productivity-related costs and, even more importantly, which are likely to drive future costs and performance levels. In turn, this information can be used to allocate program resources to achieve the greatest health impact and financial return on investment. Other chapters in this book provide more detail on targeted intervention strategies that can be used once an at-risk individual or population segment has been identified.

Health assessment data provide key metrics for measuring and monitoring individual progress and overall program impact. Initial health assessment data serve as benchmarks against which future measures can be compared. Individuals can monitor their progress and work with health professionals to improve their health behaviors and risk factors. Program management staff can monitor the overall impact of their program on key health and behavioral outcomes to determine if they are meeting organizational objectives.

Finally, health assessment in itself can be an important intervention. Individual health assessment results can create an opportunity to teach and motivate employees to make positive lifestyle changes. The health assessment data also provide program managers with information that can be used to target and tailor interventions to individual risks, readiness to change, and learning preferences. Various forms of health assessment are discussed in the following sections.

Health Assessment Framework

No single health assessment approach captures all of the information needed to effectively plan a worksite health promotion program. Furthermore, the nonexperimental, uncontrolled nature of most evaluations of worksite health promotion programs casts doubt on the validity of results based on any single measurement method. Accordingly, a worksite health assessment strategy that includes a variety of measurement tools is most likely to provide an adequate understanding of both short-term and long-term program needs and impact.[8-11] A truly comprehensive health assessment encompasses four domains of program evaluation, each with multiple measures: process measures, impact measures, outcome measures, and return-on-investment measures.[12]

Conducting a meaningful evaluation of a worksite health promotion program usually requires developing an analytic database that links individual employees' health-related claims data to their program data. Because true experimental designs are not usually feasible for worksite-based programs, this type of database is necessary to correlate program participation and changes in health risks to changes in health care utilization, health care costs, and productivity-related outcomes. Some employers place a high priority on having a detailed understanding of the impact of their health promotion program on health care costs and have the resources required to link program data with health care claims. For other employers, the cost and difficulty of such an analysis exceeds the benefit. The process of linking individual claims data with HRA and program participation data requires protocols that assure accuracy while protecting the confidentiality and privacy of highly sensitive health and medical data.

In addition to the practical difficulties of accessing data from employer-sponsored health promotion programs, confidentiality concerns make it very challenging for researchers not directly linked to the program to build an evidence base for the economic benefits of worksite health promotion programs. The need to instill confidence among employees that their HRA and other program data are private, however, is inherently greater than the need to study a relationship that explains only a fraction of the variation in medical resource use. If employees do not participate in

a worksite health promotion program because they fear misuse of program data, the issue of outcome evaluation will be irrelevant. Hence, both actual and *perceived* confidentiality are essential to success.

Worksite Health Assessment Approaches

Worksite health promotion program goals and related health assessment requirements vary considerably, depending on an organization's size and purpose. Small employers with modest program resources may rely almost entirely on the findings of population-based health assessments already conducted in industries like theirs or by their local or state health agencies. In addition to using normative data available in the public domain, small employers often use relatively informal assessment options ranging from observation to oral interviews, focus groups, and self-developed surveys. Larger employers, on the other hand, are more likely to plan and implement health promotion programs by using a subset of the assessment resources described below.

Health Risk Assessment

This popular health assessment approach uses computer technology to collect, analyze, and report on individual health risks and priorities. Since the advent of worksite health promotion, HRA data have almost exclusively been obtained from a comprehensive questionnaire, usually administered near the beginning of each program year, covering a broad range of self-reported health behaviors and risk factors (e.g., eating and exercise habits, weight, tobacco and alcohol use, stress, safety practices), personal health history, family health history (subject to federal Genetic Information Nondiscrimination Act regulations)[13], and intentions regarding changing specific health risks. As an adjunct to this self-reported health information, many organizations also collect biometric data at health screenings. Depending on the functionality of the HRA tool, biomedical screening data can either be self-reported or loaded directly into the HRA data record after collection at a health screening. Table 13-1 provides a sample of typical HRA questions. The benefits of an HRA to participants are that the educational feedback compiled from analysis of their data helps them understand the relationship between their personal health habits and their current and future health. Many HRAs offer recommendations for health action and provide tools participants can use to set personal health goals that will improve their health.[7,14] The organizational benefit of an HRA, in addition to its role in improving employee health, is that the tool provides a cost-effective method of collecting aggregate health information that can be used to plan a health promotion program and measure change over time.

While few question the value of HRA data in the health promotion process, advancing technology provides new possibilities for how it is collected and used. The ability to interact with individuals continually via a wellness program Web site or their mobile devices means individually relevant subsets of HRA data can be collected throughout the year in ways that have immediate value to the participant, such as brief risk-specific HRA modules integrated into intervention components such as coaching, worksite challenges, or Web-based "games" and trackers. These intervention components can be adjusted from health assessment and program data as frequently as useful and practical for the participant and practitioners. Examples include monitoring daily physical activities or eating habits, weekly weigh-ins, or random measures of stress and well-being. The ability to use technology to provide ongoing, dynamic, real-time feedback throughout the year, integrated into a continual stream of program interventions, offers the opportunity to transform HRA data collection from an annual event, perceived as a burden by many participants, to a series of engaging opportunities for them to get personally tailored and motivating feedback on their

health, which lead immediately to relevant intervention components.

Biomedical Screening

Many worksite health promotion programs offer biomedical health screening, sometimes on a stand-alone basis but most often in conjunction with an HRA. In the latter case, the biomedical measurements such as weight, blood pressure, cholesterol, and glucose values are combined with the HRA's self-reported behavioral and health history data in scoring the individual results. The recent proliferation of worksite biomedical health screening[15] is due in part to provisions of the 2010 Affordable Care Act (ACA) that permit the use of "health-contingent" financial incentives linked to these biomedical measures.[16] Some worksite health promotion programs, particularly those with onsite fitness centers, also include fitness testing in their health assessment protocol. Fitness testing is sometimes implemented along with other biomedical measures in the HRA-linked screening protocol, in which case it is typically made available to all who participate in the HRA. If fitness testing is implemented specifically to support fitness center operation, however, it is most commonly offered on a stand-alone basis to fitness center members at the time of initial enrollment to establish a baseline for exercise program prescription and periodically thereafter to monitor progress.

Employee Health and Interest Surveys

A census survey of health needs in an employee population or a random-sample survey, typically administered anonymously, is sometimes used to assess employee health needs and interests. These surveys may focus on a single issue, such as attitudes about a proposed corporate smoking policy, or encompass a broad range of issues such as health habits and psychological well-being, workplace safety, work-related stress, job satisfaction, health history, health awareness, attitudes about organizational health policies,

Table 13-1: Sample HRA Questions.

Physical Activity	Tobacco Use
In the past 7 days, how many days did you exercise? _____ days On days when you exercised, for how long did you exercise (in minutes)? _____ minutes per day ❑ Does not apply How intense was your typical exercise? ❑ Light (like stretching or slow walking) ❑ Moderate (like brisk walking) ❑ Heavy (like jogging or swimming) ❑ Very heavy (like fast running or stair climbing) ❑ I am currently not exercising	In the last 30 days, have you used tobacco? Smoked: ❑ Yes ❑ No Used a smokeless tobacco product: ❑ Yes ❑ No If Yes to either, Would you be interested in quitting tobacco use within the next month? ❑ Yes ❑ No
Sleep	**Depression**
Each night, how many hours of sleep do you usually get? ____ hours Do you snore or has anyone told you that you snore? ❑ Yes ❑ No In the past 7 days, how often have you felt sleepy during the daytime? ❑ Always ❑ Usually ❑ Sometimes ❑ Rarely ❑ Never	In the past 2 weeks, how often have you felt down, depressed, or hopeless? ❑ Almost all of the time ❑ Most of the time ❑ Some of the time ❑ Almost never In the past 2 weeks, how often have you felt little interest or pleasure in doing things? ❑ Almost all of the time ❑ Most of the time ❑ Some of the time ❑ Almost never Have your feelings caused you distress or interfered with your ability to get along socially with family or friends? ❑ Yes ❑ No

Source: Goetzel RZ, Staley P, Ogden L, et al. *A Framework for Patient-Centered Health Risk Assessments: Providing Health Promotion and Disease Prevention Services to Medicare Beneficiaries.* Atlanta, Ga: U.S. Department of Health and Human Services, Centers for Disease Control and Prevention; 2011.

and worksite health promotion programming preferences. Getting valid information on the population requires a high response rate to avoid overrepresenting health-oriented employees among survey respondents. Unlike an HRA, the direct benefit to the respondent is minimal, since the anonymous approach provides no opportunity for individual follow-up or ability to link the survey responses to other data such as health screening or claims. If the cost of health screening and HRA is a barrier, however, an employee health survey may be a low-cost substitute that provides some of the same planning and evaluation features. While HRA focuses primarily on health risks, interest surveys often gather information on employee preferences among alternative opportunities for learning at the worksite. A challenge for program planners is to match HRA findings about health problems with the types of programs that would be widely used by employees. It is helpful in meeting this challenge to survey employees' readiness to change[17,18] various health behaviors, as well as their learning preferences, if these measures are not in the HRA.

Emerging Health Assessment Approaches

With the recent growth of worksite health promotion, program designers are seeking other sources of individual health data that could provide a more comprehensive health assessment with the potential to increase population engagement and health impact. One data source growing in relevance is *claims administration* databases that capture medical, pharmacy, absence, disability, and workers compensation claims data. These databases provide information on medical diagnoses, health care services, and associated costs that may be combined with HRA and biomedical screening data to better stratify and target population segments across the entire health continuum from the healthiest employees, to those at varying degrees of risk for future

disease related to modifiable health behaviors, to those in early or predisease states (e.g., metabolic syndrome, prediabetes, morbid obesity), to those currently diagnosed with chronic health conditions. A second set of data sources is the various *electronic records* including the EMR, a patient record created by hospitals, physicians, and other health care providers; the EHR, a broader health record on patients or populations that includes demographics, medical history, medications and allergies, immunization status, laboratory test results, radiology images, vital signs, risk data such as tobacco use and weight, and billing information; and the PHR, which is an EHR maintained by individuals themselves. As these electronic data repositories become more standardized and accessible, they will increasingly become a health assessment data source or alternative single source of comprehensive health information needed for worksite health promotion. A third group of data sources is wearable *electronic devices* that automatically capture and transmit a growing range of individual health-related data such as physical activity, heart rate, blood pressure, body temperature, and other metabolic measures.

HRA and biomedical screening continue to be the most widely used health assessment approaches in worksite health promotion programs, with both offering the distinct advantage of informing and motivating the individual participant as well as providing aggregate data to the organization. As such, it is important to understand their limitations as well as their strengths. Because HRA and screening are usually voluntary, employees who participate are those most attracted by the features of these tools or the employer's communications about them. This general phenomenon, which statisticians call "selection bias," can yield aggregate health profiles that do not accurately reflect the total employee population. Despite this typical limitation, HRA and screening data can play a valuable role in documenting the value of worksite health promotion, as illustrated in seminal research that links health risks and health care costs.[19-21]

HEALTH RISK ASSESSMENT

HRA is a popular fixture in worksite health promotion programs. According to a recent national survey of employers, 81% of respondents reported that they have used HRA in their health promotion programs and another 7% plan to offer HRA in the near future.[15]

Early proponents of HRA innovation supported a change in its theoretical foundation from what had been a medically oriented, mortality-based assessment to a "habit-based" or behavioral approach that focuses on the health behaviors of the individual.[22] This shift was consistent with the experience of most worksite health promotion practitioners, who favor a more positive approach to providing individual feedback with an emphasis on individual assets rather than illness.

As the focus of HRA shifted from predicting causes of death to assessing modifiable health risks and behaviors, researchers documented the association between HRA results and health-related outcomes important to employers. Studies have linked a range of HRA-based risk measures to concurrent or prospective health care costs[19-21,23-25] and to absenteeism and presenteeism.[26-28] Such studies support the predictive validity of HRA and the potential for using HRA data to estimate the cost impact of health promotion programs, which is further supported by research showing changes in health care costs following changes in HRA results.[29,30] Another promising direction is the use of HRA data in "predictive modeling" of health care utilization and costs. While traditional HRA risk algorithms are based on the probabilities of long-term mortality or morbidity consequences of unhealthy lifestyle behaviors or risk factors, some HRA tools also

collect data predictive of short-term health care utilization (e.g., chronic conditions, health status, past utilization). This type of HRA data has been shown to be nearly as good as current health care claims data at predicting the next year's health care costs,[31] which has important implications for the evolution of worksite health promotion toward a more comprehensive population health management model.

HRA as a Behavior Change Intervention

Research has documented little effectiveness of HRA as a stand-alone behavior change intervention.[7] This lack of behavioral impact found in HRA research, however, may be because the tools used in relevant published research were developed by biomedical experts rather than experts in behavior change theory and practice.[5] Researchers have acknowledged the lack of behavior-change expertise in most past HRA development but express optimism about the potential to develop HRAs that are effective behavior change tools.[32] Analyzing the role of HRA feedback by using the Health Belief Model,[33] which conceptualizes health behavior change as a function of perceived threat of a negative health outcome and perceived benefits (minus perceived barriers) of preventive activity, Strecher and Kreuter[32] make three recommendations for designing behaviorally focused HRAs.

Their first recommendation is to "provide feedback designed to correct users' inaccurate perceptions of their own risk." A substantial amount of research indicates that most people underestimate their health risk.[34-36] Others—called the "worried well" in the health promotion profession—overestimate their risk and, consequently, often seek health care unnecessarily. If HRA feedback were designed to take advantage of what researchers have discovered about the causes of these inaccurate perceptions, Strecher and Kreuter[32] believe it could move users toward more accurate perceptions of their risk. Although acknowledging that changes in perceived risk alone are not sufficient to elicit behavioral changes, they believe it is an essential first step in the change process because people who underestimate their risk are generally less motivated to change.

Their second recommendation is to "provide feedback that establishes behavior change priorities when multiple risk factors exist,"[32] which is in alignment with current research.[7,14] The importance of this prioritization becomes clear when one reviews nonprioritized HRA feedback to high-risk participants—faced with a seemingly impossible list of firmly entrenched behaviors and risk factors the HRA recommends be changed, it is not surprising that many individuals are overwhelmed and consequently less likely to act on recommendations. As well as focusing high-risk participants on changing a small number of habits at a time, it is also important that the right criteria be used in establishing this prioritization. Strecher and Kreuter[32] identify five specific criteria they believe are important in prioritizing change recommendations: epidemiologic risk, readiness to make behavioral changes, self-efficacy for behavioral changes, quality-adjusted life years, and gateways to behavioral change. Further informing this risk prioritization and feedback, recent research by Prochaska and colleagues indicates that many people may be able to change up to three health behaviors simultaneously without diminishing the rate of change in any of the individual behaviors.[37]

With the exception of epidemiologic risk, for which HRA feedback has traditionally relied on mortality risk or morbidity risk, all of these criteria are psychosocial factors. Readiness to change (see Chapter 9 for more detail) refers to the importance of focusing behavioral recommendations on risks the employee is currently prepared to change while encouraging increased readiness to change for other risks,[17,18] a seemingly obvious notion that

has often been ignored in the health promotion profession. Self-efficacy (see Chapter 11 for more detail) refers to the individual's confidence he or she can succeed in modifying an unhealthy behavior or risk factor.[38] Quality-adjusted life years move beyond a narrow measure of mortality risk to take into account the individual's health-related quality of life during those additional years of life.[39] Gateways to behavioral change refer to the idea that certain key health-related changes, such as engaging in physical activity or reducing stress, may "open the gate" to making other changes such as quitting smoking, reducing depression, or losing weight.[40,41] While not yet established in health promotion, the gateway concept is central to game theory and is widely used in online games where people spend untold hours trying to attain ever higher levels in games that all begin with relatively simple gateways to future challenges.[42]

The third recommendation Strecher and Kreuter[32] make is to "provide feedback that enhances the user's ability to make recommended health behavior changes." The feedback many HRAs provide on recommended changes is weak in behavior change content, often just telling users what behaviors need to be changed to reduce their risk, with no individually tailored information on how best to go about making the changes. To become more effective as a behavior-change tool, an HRA needs to assess not only an individual's health risks, but also behavioral and psychosocial factors that affect their motivation and ability to change health behaviors, and HRA feedback needs to provide specific cues to action that capitalize on this additional information. For example, collecting information on barriers to change and addressing these barriers in educational feedback has been shown to increase positive behavior change.[43,44] Table 13-2 provides an example in which the participant's HRA feedback has been tailored to the contemplation stage of change.

Table 13-2: Sample HRA Feedback Tailored to Stage of Change.

The following is feedback to a currently sedentary HRA participant who is also overweight:

STEPS YOU CAN TAKE TODAY:

Imagine how your life would change if you lived an active lifestyle. The benefits of becoming more active include reducing your weight, developing stronger heart and lungs, improving your self-esteem, and feeling more energetic. Record these and other "pros" of living an active lifestyle and compare them to your list of "cons." Review this list frequently.

Source: HealthPath Health Risk Assessment, StayWell Health Management, LLC. Used with permission. Copyright ©2013 StayWell Health Management, LLC. StayWell and HealthPath are registered trademarks of StayWell Health Management, LLC.

The Optimal Role of HRA in the Change Process

By incorporating features into HRA feedback such as those recommended by Strecher and Kreuter,[32] as well as motivational approaches drawn from game theory and behavioral economics concepts, HRAs are likely to become more effective in stimulating a modest level of health-related behavior change. No matter how well behavioral science and individually tailored messaging are incorporated into HRA feedback design, however, most individuals will still require ongoing support and follow-up over an extended time period to successfully navigate the change process. For this reason, experienced health promotion practitioners consider HRA to be a potentially valuable educational and motivational tool for *initiating* the behavior-change process. They clearly recognize that many high-risk individuals and others attempting to change long-term unhealthy habits also need follow-up interventions focused on developing behavior change and maintenance skills.

Viewed from the conceptual framework of the stages of change model, HRA is most useful in helping participants move through the early stages of change—from precontemplation to contemplation and from contemplation to preparation. HRA can create positive movement through these stages by heightening participants' awareness about their susceptibility to poor health outcomes, consequences of their unhealthy behaviors, what they can do to reduce their risks, and the many benefits of change.[33] HRAs may also use principles of successful game design in supporting movement through stages of readiness by cueing action and providing intermittent reinforcement for progress toward goals.

When HRA includes behavioral and psychosocial data, these data can be used to fine-tune the intervention targeting process. For example, smokers who indicate a high state of readiness to quit smoking in the near future, and also request support, can be referred to a smoking cessation intervention. This approach to HRA feedback design that associates readiness to change with a recommendation into a stage-appropriate follow-up intervention has been shown to increase intervention effectiveness.[45,46] Additionally, depending on their preferences, HRA participants ready to quit smoking can be offered a group support program, one-on-one counseling, or Internet-based self-management smoking cessation tools. On the other hand, smokers not currently interested in quitting can be offered information about the health effects of smoking or, alternatively, appropriate programs targeting other risks they are ready to change.

Selecting the Right HRA

Worksite health promotion practitioners need to be vigilant in choosing an HRA that meets their organizational needs and supports the vision and mission of their health promotion program. Practitioners should examine each aspect of a proposed HRA tool by requesting empirical evidence from the designers on the effectiveness of the tool. The discussion of behavioral issues in HRA design earlier in this chapter provides ideas for important questions to ask in evaluating various HRA tools. Health promotion practitioners may also find helpful information to support their review of HRA tools in the Centers for Disease Control and Prevention (CDC) Community Guide on assessment of health risks,[47] a CDC report on HRA for Medicare use,[14] and an Agency for Healthcare Research & Quality HRA technology assessment.[48] Information on quality standards for HRA tools is also available from health care accreditation organizations such as the National Committee for Quality Assurance[49] and URAC.[50]

BIOMEDICAL SCREENING

Unlike self-reported HRA data, biomedical risk factors, such as elevated body weight, blood pressure, and cholesterol values, are "objective" measures of risk for future chronic conditions, such as diabetes, stroke, and heart disease, which drive a large portion of employer health care costs. These biomedical risk factors are also more immediate predictors of impending disease and related costs, since the normal progression is from unhealthy behaviors over an extended time frame to elevated biomedical risk factors to the emergence of chronic conditions. For these reasons, employers are increasingly focusing on the incidence of these biomedical risks in their workforce. The growth in the use of "health-contingent" wellness incentives, codified by the ACA of 2010,[16] has also driven higher rates of screening in worksite

health promotion. This incentive approach ties the attainment of a defined health factor target, such as a recommended cholesterol level, to financial incentives.

While biomedical screening in worksite health promotion has become more prevalent, it is not a new practice. HRA tools that evolved from the mortality-based tradition of prospective medicine were designed to provide mortality projections that depended substantially on biomedical screening data. In addition to being used in the HRA scoring algorithms, the results of screening tests are typically integrated with self-reported behavioral risk data in participants' feedback reports to provide a comprehensive assessment of their modifiable health risks.

Decisions about which biomedical measures to include in worksite health promotion have been strongly influenced by the recommendations of the U.S. Preventive Services Task Force.[51,52] In addition to these science-based recommendations, there are also practical considerations for the program planner in deciding whether to implement biomedical screening and in selecting which tests to offer. Screening opportunities, such as blood pressure or cholesterol tests, are popular because employees generally find getting feedback incorporating their vital measures to be much more interesting than feedback based entirely on their self-reported HRA data. For that reason, many program planners try to increase HRA participation by administering it in combination with a screening event or health fair.

Because some biomedical screening tests are costly or recommended less often than annually for most people (e.g., lipid measurement is recommended every 5 years for low-risk individuals), program planners may stagger the screening components from year to year. For example, low-cost screening measures, such as height, weight, and blood pressure, may be done annually with every HRA, while blood chemistries and fitness testing may be done in alternate years unless these are required annually to meet legal requirements when financial incentives are tied to achieving biometric health standards.

In some instances, the scientific evidence for performing clinical tests is equivocal and the recommended intervals for conducting the examinations are controversial. In these cases, employee preferences should be considered in determining the health screening protocol. For example, the American Cancer Society recommends mammograms annually for all women beginning at age 40 years, while the U.S. Preventive Services Task Force recommends screening every 1 to 2 years for women aged 40 years and older. Similar contradictions based on reviewing the same scientific evidence exist for stool occult blood tests, prostate-specific antigen tests, and digital rectal examinations. Given the absence of clear evidence for or against a particular clinical recommendation, the health promotion planner should try to accommodate the values of employees in determining the best approach. It is also important that program planners responsible for health screening distinguish between science-based recommendations and values-based personal choices.

Blood Pressure Screening

Given the prevalence and serious complications of hypertension, its ease of detection, and the effectiveness of treatment, periodic blood pressure screening is recommended for all persons aged 18 years or older.[53] Furthermore, the workplace has been identified as a useful setting for hypertension detection and follow-up programs both in the United States[54] and internationally.[55]

While blood pressure measurement can be highly accurate, potential sources of error must be considered. Sphygmomanometry (i.e., blood pressure measurement) errors can occur from machine or cuff malfunction.

All blood pressure–measuring equipment requires periodic calibration for proper functioning. Individual variation also needs to be taken into account. Coming to screening during a stressful work day or not allowing sufficient sitting time before taking a reading can elevate the measurement. "White coat syndrome," an elevated reading that some people experience from the anxiety produced from visiting a clinician, has also been shown to affect blood pressure.[56,57] Accordingly, rechecking elevated blood pressures at different times and under different conditions is standard protocol before a definitive diagnosis of hypertension would be made. Table 13-3 includes guidelines for blood pressure measurement from the U.S. Preventive Services Task Force.[58]

Normal blood pressure, which is a recommended level for good health, is considered by medical experts to be less than 120/80 mm Hg (i.e., systolic blood pressure value less than 120 mm Hg and diastolic value less than 80 mm Hg). Those with blood pressure between 120/80 and 139/89 mm Hg receive a classification of "prehypertension" to identify them as individuals who, while at high risk of developing hypertension, could adopt healthy lifestyle behaviors that would be likely to reduce their blood pressure or decrease the rate of progression to hypertensive levels. Anyone with blood pressure consistently at or above 140/90 mm Hg is considered to have hypertension and be "at risk" for related medical complications such as cardiovascular disease and kidney disease. Those consistently at or above 160/100 mm Hg are considered to be at *high* risk for such complications. Table 13-4 provides standards for use in worksite blood pressure screenings.[59] Recommended standards for blood pressure and other biomedical measures may change as scientific evidence grows, so verifying current guidelines for all included measures is an essential task in planning a screening.

Table 13-3: Guidelines for Sphygmomanometry[58].

> - Clients should be seated with bare arm at heart level or level with the midsternum.
> - Clients should have had no recent smoking, caffeine, or exertion and should rest quietly for 5 minutes before measuring.
> - An appropriate cuff size with the bladder encircling at least two-thirds of the arm should be used.
> - Measurement should be taken preferably with a mercury sphygmomanometer (a recently calibrated aneroid manometer or a validated devise can also be used).
> - Both systolic and diastolic pressures, using the disappearance of sound as the diastolic, should be recorded.
> - Two or more readings, separated by 2 minutes, should be averaged. If the first two readings differ by more than 5 mm Hg, additional readings should be obtained and averaged.

Weight and Body Composition Screening

Despite the widely publicized health consequences of obesity and billions of dollars spent annually on weight loss efforts, the prevalence of overweight has increased steadily in the United States in recent decades.[60] Most health complications of obesity are actually attributable to excess body fat, rather than excess weight per se, with considerable evidence that excess abdominal fat (i.e., "male-pattern" fat distribution) may further increase coronary heart disease (CHD) risk.[61] However, because body fatness is more difficult to measure than is weight in large populations and in work settings, many practitioners and researchers use body mass index (BMI) as a proxy for body composition. BMI is defined as weight in kilograms divided by height in meters squared and is highly correlated with total body fat. Even though BMI is the most widely used method for assessing risks due to overweight and obesity in large populations, this approach has been shown to misclassify some individuals. One report, using total fat percentage as the reference standard, found that 40% to 60% of patients were misclassified as nonobese when using BMI.[62] Conversely, a study using waist circumference categories as

a reference standard found that more than 60% of BMI-based risk classifications were false positives.[63] Yet another study suggests that the validity of BMI varies according to age and gender.[64]

In response to the increasing problem of obesity and these deficiencies of using BMI alone to classify weight-related risk, the National Institutes of Health issued guidelines on the identification, evaluation, and treatment of overweight and obesity in adults.[65] According to these guidelines, assessment of overweight involves the evaluation of three key measures: BMI, waist circumference, and risk factors for diseases and conditions associated with obesity. Periodic assessment is recommended every 2 years. The guidelines identify *overweight* for both adult men and women as a BMI of 25 to 29.9 and *obesity* as a BMI of 30 and above. A BMI of 30, which is approximately 30 pounds overweight through the middle of the height range, equals 221 pounds for a 6-foot person and 186 pounds for a 5-foot 6-inch person. The panel recognized that very muscular people could have a high BMI without health risk, which is partially addressed by adding waist circumference to the risk assessment process. A waist circumference of more than 40 inches in men and more than 35 inches in women

Table 13-4: Worksite Blood Pressure Screening Standards and Follow-up Criteria.

Classification	Blood Pressure	
	Systolic, mm Hg	Diastolic, mm Hg
Normal	<120	and <80
Prehyertension	120–139	or 80–90
Hypertension (stage 1)	140–159	or 90–99
Hypertension (stage 2)	≥160	or ≥100

Classification	Initial Blood Pressure, mm Hg*		Recommended Follow-up Criteria
	Systolic	Diastolic	Recommended Follow-up†
Normal	<120	and <80	Recheck in 2 y
Prehyertension	120–139	or 80–90	Recheck in 1 y‡
Hypertension (stage 1)	140–159	or 90–99	Confirm within 2 mo‡
Hypertension (stage 2)	≥160	or ≥100	Evaluate or refer to source of care within 1 mo
	>180	and >110	Evaluate and treat immediately or within 1 wk depending on complications and clinical situation

Source: Adapted from *The Seventh Report of the Joint National Committee on Prevention, Detection, Evaluation, and Treatment of High Blood Pressure*. NHLBI, U.S. Department of Health and Human Services; 2004. NIH Publication No. 04-5230. Available at: http://www.nhlbi.nih.gov/guidelines/hypertension/jnc7full.pdf
*If the systolic and diastolic categories are different, follow the recommendations for the shorter time follow-up (e.g., 160/86 mm Hg should be evaluated or referred to source of care within 1 month). Blood pressure measurement and follow-up criteria are based on the average of two or more readings.
†The scheduling of follow-up should be modified by reliable information about past blood pressure measurements, other cardiovascular risk factors, or target-organ disease.
‡Provide advice about lifestyle modifications.

is associated with increased risk in those who have a BMI of 25 to 34.9. The presence of associated risk factors—listed in Table 13-5—further increases the risk level of overweight or obese individuals.

Obesity can also be defined by an excessive percentage of body fat relative to total body mass, with suggested cut-points of 35% in women and 30% in men.[66] While hydrostatic (i.e., underwater) weighing has traditionally been considered the gold standard in accurate body fat measurement, it is not feasible for worksite testing. For worksite use, body fat can be estimated by using air-displacement

Table 13-5: Risk Factors Affecting Risk Level of Overweight and Obese Persons.[65]

Disease Conditions: Established CHD, other atherosclerotic diseases, type 2 diabetes, and sleep apnea; patients with these conditions are classified as being at very high risk for disease complications and mortality.

Other Obesity-Associated Diseases: Gynecologic abnormalities, osteoarthritis, gallstones and their complications, and stress incontinence.

Cardiovascular Risk Factors: Cigarette smoking, hypertension (systolic blood pressure ≥ 140 mm Hg or diastolic blood pressure ≥ 90 mm Hg, or the patient is taking antihypertensive agents), high-risk LDL cholesterol (≥160 mg/dL), low HDL cholesterol (<35 mg/dL), impaired fasting glucose (fasting plasma glucose of 110 to 125 mg/dL), family history of premature CHD (definite myocardial infarction or sudden death at or before 55 years of age in father or other male first-degree relative, or at or before 65 years of age in mother or other female first-degree relative), and age (men ≥ 45 years and women ≥ 55 years or postmenopausal). Person can be classified as being at high absolute risk if they have three of these risk factors.

Other Risk Factors: Physical inactivity and high serum triglyceride levels (>200 mg/dL). When these factors are present, patients can be considered to have incremental absolute risk above that estimated from the preceding risk factors. Quantitative risk contribution is not available for these risk factors, but their presence heightens the need for weight reduction in obese persons.

CHD indicates coronary heart disease; LDL, low-density lipoprotein; and HDL, high-density lipoprotein.

---

plethysmography (e.g., Bod Pod), electrical impedance testing, skin-fold caliper readings, body circumference measures, and infrared reflected-light technology.[67] While the accuracy of these measures is generally acceptable for worksite use, program planners should review reliability and validity information on their selected approach to identify factors (e.g., dehydration, recent food consumption) that affect its reliability and validity.[68]

Bod Pod is considered a new gold standard for body fat measurement that uses air displacement rather than hydrostatic weight.[69] The approach is more practical than hydrostatic weighing when precise measurement is desired, such as in research, health care, and health club settings. However, this approach may not be the optimal choice for many worksite applications. Costs associated with Bod Pod machines and/or testing (i.e., testing conducted at a facility with existing Bod Pod machines) can be a significant barrier. Logistical challenges of doing the testing in the worksite setting include portability, fasting requirements (minimum 3-hour fast required), and specific clothing recommendations not easily accommodated at the worksite.

Skin-fold measures are commonly used for estimating body fat because this method is easy to administer and inexpensive. Sites generally measured by a skin-fold caliper include the chest, axilla, triceps, subscapula, abdominal, suprailium, and thigh.[70] Tester technique, site selection, skin-fold size, leanness, age, and gender are all determinants of adipose density and predicted body-fat percentage. Based on their observations, Martin et al.[71] concluded that skin-fold thickness alone, without being converted into percentage fat, is a reasonably accurate indicator of body fat. These authors recommended using skilled technicians and making repeated measures on a number of body sites to ensure accuracy.

Bioelectrical impedance is another method for estimating body composition, which has the advantage of largely eliminating tester error. Unlike the skin-fold measure, which is quite consistent over brief measurement intervals, bioelectrical impedance values are affected by numerous variables including body position, hydration status, recent consumption of food and beverages, ambient air and skin temperature, recent physical activity, and electrical conductance of the examining table. Although bioelectrical impedance is popular with participants because of its technologic nature, it is not the best option in an uncontrolled setting, such as the worksite, if precise measurement is required (e.g., when incentives are linked to meeting a body-fat target).

Blood Chemistry Screening

A large and growing number of parameters of health and organ function can be measured with a small specimen of blood at very low cost. This makes it tempting to include all of these measures in periodic health screenings. The risk of measuring a large number of values, however, is that the "normal" range for each test is based on the statistical distribution of a measure with less than perfect reliability. There is a very real probability of one or two types of erroneous results on each test administered—a *false positive* where the test result is abnormal but the underlying condition is not present, or a *false negative* where the test result is normal but the underlying condition is present. The more tests administered to an individual, the greater the probability of one or more erroneous results. Further, administering a test to an asymptomatic person for a condition with a low prevalence rate means that the abnormal result will more commonly be a false positive. A false abnormal result on even one test can result in needless anxiety for the employee, as well as significant costs resulting from referring the employee to a physician for follow-up evaluation and even more testing.

For this reason, experienced worksite health promotion planners adhere to U.S. Preventive Services Task Force guidelines by

only conducting tests for conditions that are prevalent, potentially serious, and for which the test is reasonably specific and sensitive. (A "specific" test is one with a low rate of false positives; a "sensitive" test is one with a low rate of false negatives.) Follow-up testing is targeted to the subset of individuals determined to be at elevated risk for a specific condition. On the basis of these criteria, the blood chemistry tests recommended for population-wide use at the worksite include blood cholesterol (total, high-density lipoprotein [HDL] and low-density lipoprotein [LDL]) to screen for the very prevalent heart disease risk[72,73] and blood glucose to screen for the very serious and increasingly prevalent problem of diabetes.[51]

Blood Cholesterol Screening

Although the CHD mortality rate has decreased in recent decades, CHD remains by far the leading cause of death in the United States.[74] Along with smoking and hypertension, high blood cholesterol is a major risk factor for CHD,[75] and lowering blood cholesterol has been shown to significantly reduce CHD risk.[76]

The most recent recommendations of the expert panel for cholesterol management convened by the National Cholesterol Education Program established three categories for total blood cholesterol. Less than 200 mg/dL is "desirable" to lower one's risk for heart disease; 200 to 239 mg/dL is "borderline-high" and increases risk; 240 mg/dL or above is "high" risk.[72,73] Based on growing evidence that low HDL cholesterol levels also increase risk for CHD, the expert panel classified low HDL levels (<40 mg/dL) as a major risk factor for CHD and recommended including HDL with total blood cholesterol in initial screening. The expert panel further indicated that testing should only be done if accuracy of measurement, appropriate counseling, and follow-up could be assured.[72,73] While recommendations now include LDL cholesterol, owing to its central role in increasing CHD risk, accurate LDL measurement requires a fasting test that is often difficult to accommodate in workplace settings.[72]

Follow-up lipoprotein analysis and therapeutic prescription by a physician were recommended by the expert panel for all those initially screened who fell into the "high-risk" group owing to total blood cholesterol of 240 mg/dL and above, or owing to HDL levels less than 40 mg/dL. Those in the 200 to 239 mg/dL borderline-high range who had two or more CHD risk factors were also classified as high risk, with follow-up testing recommended. The expert panel guidelines and follow-up lipid analysis criteria are presented in more detail in Table 13-6.

The ratio of total cholesterol to HDL can also be used to assess risk. The goal is to keep the total cholesterol to HDL ratio below 5:1 with an optimal ratio at or below 3.5:1. However, the American Heart Association and the National Cholesterol Education Program both recommend evaluating risk based on absolute values of total cholesterol, HDL, and LDL because they are more meaningful to health professionals when defining appropriate treatment strategies.[72,73,77]

Blood Glucose Screening

Diabetes is one of the most serious and costly health problems in the United States. It is the seventh leading cause of death and is estimated to cost $116 billion annually in direct medical costs and $58 billion in indirect costs (disability, lost productivity, mortality).[78] Unfortunately, many people first become aware they have diabetes when they develop one of its complications, which include heart disease and stroke, blindness, kidney disease, nerve disease and amputations, and impotence. Of the estimated 25.8 million people in the United States who have diabetes, fully 7.0 million (27%) are not aware they have the disease.[78]

With the high economic and human costs of diabetes, it is critical to identify the large undiagnosed population and triage individuals to appropriate interventions. Fortunately,

diabetes screening can be accomplished with a simple blood glucose test. Testing can either be nonfasting or fasting (8 hours), with the latter recommended if practical. A fasting glucose level of less than 100 mg/dL is considered normal, and a result of greater than 125 mg/dL yields a provisional diagnosis of diabetes that must be medically confirmed. Those whose values fall in the 100 to 125 mg/dL range are classified as having impaired glucose tolerance, which is a risk factor for both diabetes and heart disease.[79] As in the case of blood pressure, individuals in this above-normal range are given a classification of prediabetes, indicating a relatively high risk for future development of diabetes. These high-risk individuals are encouraged to participate in structured programs of lifestyle change, including moderate weight loss, regular physical activity, and dietary strategies, to reduce total calorie, fat, and sugar intake while increasing consumption of dietary fiber and whole grains.

Although diabetes can be extremely destructive, many of its complications can be avoided or reduced for most diabetics solely through weight loss, improved nutrition, exercise and, possibly, other lifestyle modifications. A minority of those with diabetes may also require insulin and/or other medications to manage the disease.[79]

Fitness Testing

Some organizations conduct fitness testing before promoting exercise participation to screen for those at higher risk for a cardiac event during exercise, prescribe safe and effective exercise, and determine baseline functional capacity for ongoing monitoring and program evaluation. Fitness testing is particularly important for employers with on-site fitness facilities to manage the liability risk associated with exercise supervision. The components of a fitness test can include the following:

Table 13-6: Blood Cholesterol Screening and Follow-up Criteria.[72,73]*

Total Cholesterol, mg/dL		LDL Cholesterol, mg/dL		HDL Cholesterol, mg/dL	
		<100	Optimal	≥60	Protective
<200	Desirable	100–129	Near optimal/above optimal	40–59	Normal
200–239	Borderline High	130–159	Borderline high	<40	High risk
≥240	High	160–189	High		
		≥190	Very high		

Follow-up Recommendations for Adults With No Personal History of CHD[†]

Recommended Screening Interval	Description
More frequent than every 5 years	Individuals who have lipid levels close to those warranting therapy
Every 5 years	Individuals with no personal history of CHD[†]
Less frequent than every 5 years	Individuals who are not at increased risk and who have had repeatedly normal lipid levels

*LDL indicates low-density lipoprotein; HDL, high-density lipoprotein; and CHD, coronary heart disease.
[†]All individuals with CHD should be referred to their physician for follow-up.

- Functional test of cardiovascular endurance to measure or estimate aerobic capacity;
- Body composition and circumference measurements to determine body fatness and lean body mass (see earlier section); and
- Measurements of flexibility, strength, and muscular endurance to assess the function of joints and muscles.

Functional Capacity Test of Cardiovascular Endurance

Functional capacity tests are used to measure or estimate maximal oxygen uptake or aerobic capacity (VO_2max), the largest amount of oxygen one can use under the most strenuous conditions.[70] Normative information on aerobic capacity, which is useful in providing feedback on test results, has been developed by the American College of Sports Medicine.[80] There are four principles for testing functional capacity[81]:

1. The work must involve large muscle groups;
2. The work must be measurable and reproducible;
3. Test conditions must be such that the results are comparable and repeatable; and
4. Testing must be well tolerated and must not require unusual skill.

Fitness-testing laboratories affiliated with medical facilities typically conduct a maximal graded exercise test on a motor-driven treadmill or bicycle ergometer, combined with electrocardiographic (EKG) monitoring, blood pressure monitoring, and physician attendance to detect signs of subclinical heart disease. The U.S. Preventive Services Task Force recommends against using an exercise EKG for screening purposes in clinically healthy persons owing to its expense and the low probability that disease would be detected.[82]

Submaximal tests using a treadmill, bicycle ergometer, steps, or timed run or walk are much less useful for the diagnosis of asymptomatic coronary artery disease, but they can be used to reliably estimate functional capacity. Submaximal tests rely on attaining a steady state heart rate for a given work load, and then using the heart rate and work load data to project maximum heart rate and VO_2max from nomograms.[70] Distinct advantages of submaximal tests are that they are relatively inexpensive, do not require the presence of a physician, and may not require EKG monitoring. They are used most often and appropriately in young healthy populations or in mass testing outside of the laboratory environment. Bicycle ergometer testing uses a mechanically braked bicycle pedaled at a constant rate over increasing resistance. This method is more portable than treadmill testing and tends to produce less upper body movement, which makes heart rate and blood pressure measurements easier to obtain. However, this testing method may not be practical for workplace screenings owing to equipment transport and the time required for testing.

The easiest and least expensive submaximal tests are the field tests described by Balke[83] and Cooper[84] and later reviewed and modified by Kline et al.[85] Kline and his colleagues used a repeated, fast 1-mile track walk and treadmill-measured VO_2 to develop a predictive equation for estimating VO_2max in 30- to 69-year-old adults.

Field tests such as the timed 1-mile walk can be administered safely to most employees at a worksite and repeated whenever necessary to document changes in fitness but may not be practical for workplace screening events. Employees who are committed to a program of vigorous physical activity, but who are at high risk for heart disease because of their age and the presence of other coronary risk factors, should be referred to their physician for evaluation before beginning their program.

Flexibility and Muscle Strength Testing

Exercises that improve strength and flexibility can enhance performance, decrease the risks of vigorous aerobic exercise, and provide additional health benefits of their own. For example, back injury prevention programs, arthritis treatment programs, and the prevention of falls in the elderly typically include exercises that promote strength and flexibility. For this reason, tests of strength and flexibility can be useful as part of an overall fitness assessment. Testing standards and normative information are less well established for strength and flexibility testing than for aerobic fitness testing, but helpful information is available from the President's Council on Fitness, Sports & Nutrition.[86] Similarly, there is considerably less scientific documentation of the benefits of exercises to improve strength or flexibility than there is for aerobic exercise.

KEY APPLICATIONS OF HEALTH ASSESSMENT IN WORKSITE HEALTH PROMOTION

Periodic population-wide HRA (with or without biomedical screening), as well as more frequent, ongoing monitoring of high-risk employees identified in the population-wide assessment process, can be very helpful in planning worksite health promotion programs and targeting intervention components to employees who will benefit the most from them. Research has clearly established that targeting educational interventions is much more effective in attracting participation than less focused approaches, as well as being more effective in improving health outcomes.[87-89]

Key issues in maximizing the effectiveness of worksite health promotion programs include targeting the right employees for the right interventions, as well as maximizing levels of participation and risk reduction. HRA and biomedical screening can play a key role in segmenting the population, but only if participation in these assessment activities is consistently high. To achieve acceptable levels of participation, an increasing number of employers are offering financial incentives. Many are also attempting to encourage risk reduction through the use of incentives. This section explores the role of HRA and biomedical screening in targeting interventions, administering incentives, and monitoring program impact.

Focusing Efforts Based on Needs and Interests

Now that most worksite health promotion programs implement their HRA by using Internet technology, segmenting large employee populations for targeted follow-up is both easy and inexpensive. This makes comparing the value of short-term versus long-term health improvement strategies more important than ever. Given the relatively limited resources available for health promotion programming, it is likely that targeting the highest-risk employees for intensive intervention will come at the expense of programming for the general population. This strategy is usually justified by the argument that a small proportion of employees use a disproportionately large portion of total health care resources. While it may be true that a small number of employees with chronic conditions use most medical services, it is also likely that an even larger

number with poor health habits will suffer from these same conditions in the future. Accordingly, cost avoidance by keeping healthy employees healthy may be a better strategy for many organizations than the usual focus on risk reduction. Recent research makes it reasonable to conclude that even minimally improving the health practices of a large population, moving many individuals to just a slightly lower risk level or delaying the onset of new risks, can be more cost-effective than targeting only a small number of currently high-cost employees.[30] Research that carefully explores the balance point between these two alternatives, and how this point varies depending on population characteristics (e.g., compensation patterns, turnover rate), is very important to the health promotion and disease management fields.

Another compelling reason to question the logic of limiting resources to the highest-risk employees is the possibly false assumption that this will save the most money. For example, if clinical guidelines representing "best practices" for chronic conditions were fully implemented, many believe the total costs of care in the United States would increase dramatically.[90,91] The unfortunate reality of "usual care" for most chronic conditions is that patients do not receive the amount of care they need. Effective disease management often means more doctor visits, more expensive medication, more employee education, and more programming aimed at employee compliance with treatment regimens.

Today's most successful worksite health promotion programs use an approach to targeting interventions that preserves employees' choice and privacy while offering the support they are seeking. The HRA tool or screening process should offer participants easy options on whether and when they want to be contacted about programs related to their specific interests and risks. Fortunately, in addition to addressing the privacy issue, well-designed HRA instruments allow targeting based not only on participants' risks, but also on their readiness to change and other health-related, psychosocial, and behavioral factors. This enables the program planner to target follow-up interventions according to willingness to be contacted, but also to tailor the specific intervention to the participant's stage in the change process and other individual factors.

Use of Incentives to Increase HRA and Screening Participation and Health Improvement

Use of Incentives in Health Assessment

Two primary reasons underlie the growing number of employers using financial incentives to increase program participation and reward positive health outcomes. First, research has demonstrated that offering incentives increases participation rates, and that these rates increase as the amount of the incentive increases.[92] It is important to recognize that this research also showed that a supportive culture and strong communications substantially increased incentive effectiveness.[93-95] Second, the ACA[16] codified and expanded on the 2006 Health Insurance Portability and Accountability Act (HIPAA) rules on nondiscrimination in wellness program incentives. In addition to elevating the 2006 final HIPAA rules to statutory authority, section 2705 of the ACA allows employers to provide incentives (e.g., lower health plan premiums) if individuals meet a health factor standard, such as healthy weight, blood pressure levels, and cholesterol levels. See Chapter 3 for more details.

The administration of health-contingent incentives is still a relatively new concept, so guidelines continue to evolve concerning the best use of participatory versus health-contingent approaches. Advocates for tying incentives to the achievement of health factor standards argue that the higher costs paid by those who do not satisfy a health standard will provide the funding needed to keep wellness programs affordable.[96] However, it is precisely the concern that such cost differentials effectively shift costs from healthy to less healthy employees that has generated the greatest opposition to this approach. Specifically, public health advocacy groups have argued that health-contingent incentives will limit access to health insurance, undermining the intent of the ACA to increase access.[97] The ACA language acknowledges this concern, stating that "a reward contingent on meeting a standard related to a health factor creates a transfer from those who do not meet the standard to those who do meet the standard."

Progress-Based Incentives

Because health-contingent incentives tied to meeting a health factor standard have raised concerns about fairness and fear that those at greatest risk will "opt out" because they see the targets as impossible to achieve,[97,98,99] a third approach has been proposed. The progress-based incentive model seeks the common ground between participatory incentives and accountability for meeting health standard targets demanded by health-contingent incentives.[100] This model intends to engage all employees by making the incentive contingent on either achieving health standard targets or achieving an individually tailored health goal short of health standard targets. Providing annual biomedical screening data is a vital part of monitoring either health-contingent or progress-based incentives, since metrics are required to determine current status vis-à-vis incentive-related targets. The progress-based approach is best facilitated by health coaches trained in motivational interviewing skills, with physician oversight and review of progress goals set for those with medical conditions.

With physician involvement as needed, the coach and participant discuss baseline biomedical status and develop reasonably attainable goals. For example, if achieving a BMI of 30 within the next 12 months is an unreasonable target for an obese employee, the coach would work with the employee to set a reasonable individual health goal, such as losing 5% to10% of body weight during this period as the alternative standard. The focus in a progress-based design shifts from rewarding outcomes to rewarding progress toward outcome targets, which is also consistent with behavioral principles related to rewarding successive approximations toward a long-term goal.

A progress-based incentive design responds to detractors concerned that health-contingent wellness incentives represent a cost shift from the sick to the healthy. There may still be a cost shift, but a significant portion will be to shift costs from those who agree to engage to those who decline to do so. If an incentive is tied to achieving a recommended health factor standard, employees may simply seek a waiver based on health issues rather than attempting to achieve a goal they believe is out of their reach. Basing incentives on reasonable progress, on the other hand, not only addresses current health issues but also is responsive to the wide variation in individual capacity to change. Health status is influenced by physiological and genetic factors as well as lifestyle, so lifestyle changes made by one person can produce significantly different health outcomes than the same change by another person.[101] A progress-based approach starts where each employee is and rewards meaningful effort as well as ultimate outcome achievements.

The role of a well-designed health assessment process in support of progress-based incentives is to offer employees regular opportunities to demonstrate progress toward their individual goals and to provide useful aggregate data for employers detailing population-based progress toward organizational goals. To satisfy ACA provisions, incentives that require meeting

a health standard can only be used if they are accompanied by a "reasonably designed wellness program," which means the overall program must have a reasonable chance of improving population health.[102]

Monitoring and Follow-up

The most valuable HRAs are those with the built-in capability to provide comparisons over time. An HRA can serve as a catalyst for behavior change when employees benefit from seeing how their risks have improved or worsened since a previous assessment. Similarly, HRA technology should maintain time-over-time data in a database that allows employers to monitor aggregate-level progress of employees participating in specific programs, as well as change in the health of their total population and key population segments over various time periods.

CONCLUSIONS

For worksite health promotion programs to be successful, it is critical that HRA, biomedical screening, and other health assessment approaches be combined with behavioral interventions and used for follow-up and ongoing monitoring. It is also critical that health assessment be positioned positively within the organization to gain the greatest levels of participation and engagement. The contribution of health assessment in worksite health promotion can be summarized as follows:

1. Health assessment is a fundamental element of worksite health promotion programs because it provides a basis for program planning and development, serves as an intervention platform, and allows monitoring of both individual and organizational progress.
2. A well-designed health assessment process provides a cost-effective way

to collect the information required to tailor educational feedback and target follow-up interventions to support employee lifestyle change, medical self-care, health care decision support, and chronic disease management. It also provides the information required to determine whether these efforts are improving health.

3. Ongoing health assessment to measure time-over-time trends is a key component in evaluating worksite health promotion programs, providing information to support program design, quality improvement, and outcomes measurement.

4. The use of benefits-integrated financial incentives has been shown to substantially increase HRA participation rates. The ACA provisions allowing financial incentives to be linked to meeting a health factor standard have significantly increased employer use of biomedical screenings and HRA.

5. HRA and biomedical screening are the most widely used health assessment approaches for determining employees' health risks, health priorities, and readiness to change.

Glossary of terms

Health assessment: An analysis of health-related data that evaluates health status, health risk, and health improvement priorities at the individual or organizational level, is a key element of worksite health promotion programs.

Health risk assessment (HRA): Popular health assessment approach that uses computer technology to collect, analyze and report on individual health risk and priorities. Typically administered as a self-report questionnaire near the beginning of each program year, covering a broad range of health behaviors and risk factors (e.g., eating and exercise habits, weight, tobacco and alcohol use, stress, safety practices), personal health history, family health history (subject to Genetic Information Nondiscrimination Act regulations), and intentions regarding changing specific health risks.

Biomedical screening: Popular health assessment approach offered on a stand-alone basis or in conjunction with a HRA. Biomedical measurements such as weight, blood pressure, cholesterol and glucose values are collected to determine "objective" measures of risk of future chronic conditions like diabetes, stroke and heart disease.

Employee Health and Interest Surveys: Census or random-sample survey of health needs in an employee population, typically administered anonymously. Surveys may focus on a single issue, such as attitudes about a proposed corporate smoking policy, or encompass a broad range of issues such as health habits and psychological well-being, workplace safety, work-related stress and job satisfaction, health history, health awareness, attitudes about organizational health policies, and worksite health promotion programming preferences.

Affordable Care Act (ACA): The Patient Protection and Affordable Care Act (ACA), is a Federal law enacted March 23, 2010 that is aimed at increasing the number of Americans with health insurance coverage and reducing the overall costs of health care.

Genetic Information Nondiscrimination Act (GINA): A Federal law enacted May 21, 2008 that is designed to prohibit the use of genetic information in health insurance and employment.

Health Insurance Portability and Accountability Act (HIPAA): Federal law enacted August 21, 1996 that (1) protects health insurance coverage for workers and their families when they change or lose their jobs (Title I); and (2) requires establishing national standards for electronic health care transactions and national identifiers for providers, health insurance plans, and employers including maintaining the privacy and security of individually identifiable health information (Title II).

Claims administration databases: Databases that capture medical, pharmacy, absence, disability, and workers compensation claims data to provide information on medical diagnoses, health care services and associated costs. Claims data can be combined with HRA and biomedical screening data to better segment and target population segments across the entire health continuum.

Electronic Medical Records (EMR): Electronic patient record created by hospitals, physicians, and other health care providers.

Electronic Health Record (EHR): Broad electronic record on patients or populations including demographics, medical history, medications and allergies, immunization status, lab test results, radiology images, vital signs, risk data like tobacco use and weight, and billing information.

Personal Health Record (PHR): Broad health record maintained by individuals themselves that includes information similar to that in an EHR, e.g., demographics, medical history, medications and allergies, immunization status, lab test results, radiology images, vital signs, risk data like tobacco use and weight.

Progress-based incentives: Incentive model that combines participatory incentives and the health-contingent incentives with the intention to engage all employees by making the incentive contingent on achieving an individually tailored health goal that may be short of the typical target in the health standard.

Health Belief Model: Conceptualizes health behavior change as a function of perceived threat of a negative health outcome and perceived benefits (minus perceived barriers) of preventive activity.

Stages of Change Model: Conceptual framework of behavior change that postulates that individuals move through a series of five discrete stages in changing a problem behavior beginning from not being ready (precontemplation stage), to considering change (contemplation stage), to preparing for change (preparation stage), to taking action (action stage), to sustaining healthy behavior (maintenance stage).

Learning Objectives

1. Define the primary methods of assessment in worksite health promotion.
2. List the pros and cons of health risk assessment and biomedical screening in worksite health promotion.
3. Identify and summarize additional methods of health assessment such as employee surveys and claims administrative databases.
4. Describe the use of financial incentives to promote participation in health assessment.

Discussion Questions

1. Why is health assessment a fundamental element of worksite health promotion programs?
2. What benefits does ongoing health assessment provide to worksite health promotion programs?
3. What factors should be considered when designing incentive strategies for health assessment?
4. What are the most widely used health assessment approaches in worksite health promotion?

REFERENCES

1. U.S. Department of Health and Human Services, Public Health Service. 1992 national survey of worksite health promotion activities: summary. *Am J Health Promot.* 1993;7:452–464.

2. Stephen Wolfram on Personal Analytics. *MIT Technology Review.* Available at: http://www.technologyreview.com/news/514356/stephen-wolfram-on-personal-analytics. Accessed May 21, 2013.

3. Wolfram S. The personal analytics of my life. Stephen Wolfram blog. Available at: http://blog.stephenwolfram.com/2012/03/the-personal-analytics-of-my-life. Accessed May 21, 2013.

4. Towers Watson, National Business Group on Health. *Pathway to Health and Productivity 2011/2012 Staying@ Work Survey Report.* 2011. Available at: http://www.towerswatson.com/DownloadMedia.aspx?media={7BE638F3-9EA0-4BAE-A048-75 87BF501C1F. Accessed May 21, 2013.

5. Anderson DR, Staufacker MJ. The impact of worksite-based health risk appraisal on health-related outcomes: a review of the literature. *Am J Health Promot.* 1996;10(6):499–508.

6. Soler RE, Griffith M, Hopkins DP, Leeks KD. The assessment of health risks with feedback: results of a systematic review. In: Pronk NP, ed. *ACSM's Worksite Health Handbook: A Guide to Building Healthy and Productive Companies.* Champagne, Ill: Human Kinetics; 2009: 82-91.

7. Soler RE, Leeks KD, Razi S, et al. A systematic review of selected interventions for worksite health promotion: the assessment of health risks with feedback. *Am J Prev Med.* 2010;38(2 suppl):S237–S262.

8. Anderson DR, Jose WS. Comprehensive evaluation of a worksite health promotion program: the StayWell program at Control Data. In: Klarreich SH, ed. *Health and Fitness in the Workplace.* New York, NY: Praeger; 1987:284-298.

9. Hoover S, Jensen M, Murphy R, Anderson D. Evaluation: guidelines for the accountable health promotion professional. In: Opatz JP, ed. *Economic Impact of Worksite Health Promotion.* Champaign, Ill: Human Kinetics Publishers; 1994:99-120.

10. Goetzel RZ, Guindon AM, Turshen IJ, Ozminkowski RJ. Health and productivity management: establishing key performance measures, benchmarks, and best practices. *J Occup Environ Med.* 2001;43(1):10–17.

11. Goetzel RZ, Ozminkowski RJ, Pelletier KR, et al. Emerging trends in health and productivity management. *Am J Health Promot.* 2007;22(1):suppl 1–7, iii.

12. Grossmeier J, Terry PE, Cipriotti A, Burtaine JE. Best practices in evaluating worksite health promotion programs. *Am J Health Promot.* 2010;24(3):TAHP1–TAHP9, iii.

13. Regulations Under the Genetic Information Nondiscrimination Act of 2008. Vol 29. In: Commission EEO, ed. 2010.

14. Goetzel RZ, Staley P, Ogden L, et al. *A Framework for Patient-Centered Health Risk Assessments: Providing Health Promotion and Disease Prevention Services to Medicare Beneficiaries.* Atlanta, Ga: U.S. Department of Health and Human Services, Centers for Disease Control and Prevention; 2011.

15. National Business Group on Health, Fidelity Investments Benefits Consulting. *Employer Investments in Improving Employee Health Survey.* 2012.

16. Patient Protection and Affordable Care Act, 42 USC 300gg–11. 2nd ed. 2010:974.

17. Prochaska JO, DiClemente CC. Stages of change in the modification of problem

behaviors. *Prog Behav Modif.* 1992;28: 183–218.

18. Prochaska JO, Norcross JC, DiClemente CC. *Changing for Good: The Revolutionary Program That Explains the Six Stages of Change and Teaches You How to Free Yourself From Bad Habits.* 1st ed. New York, NY: W Morrow; 1994.

19. Anderson DR, Whitmer RW, Goetzel RZ, et al. The relationship between modifiable health risks and group-level health care expenditures; Health Enhancement Research Organization (HERO) Research Committee. *Am J Health Promot.* 2000;15(1):45–52.

20. Goetzel RZ, Anderson DR, Whitmer RW, et al. The relationship between modifiable health risks and health care expenditures: an analysis of the multi-employer HERO health risk and cost database. *J Occup Environ Med.* 1998;40(10):843–854.

21. Goetzel RZ, Pei X, Tabrizi MJ, et al. Ten modifiable health risk factors are linked to more than one-fifth of employer-employee health care spending. *Health Aff (Millwood).* 2012;31(11):2474–2484.

22. Terry PE. The role of health risk appraisal in the workplace: assessment versus behavior change. *Am J Health Promot.* 1987;2(2)18–36.

23. Brink S. *Health Risks and Behavior: The Impact on Medical Costs.* Brookfield, WI: Milliman & Robertson, Inc; 1987.

24. Golaszewski T, Lynch W, Clearie A, Vickery DM. The relationship between retrospective health insurance claims and a health risk appraisal-generated measure of health status. *J Occup Med.* 1989;31(3):262–264.

25. Vickery DM, Golaszewski T, Wright E, McPhee LE. Life-style and organizational health insurance costs. *J Occup Med.* 1986;28(11):1165–1168.

26. Bertera RL. The effects of behavioral risks on absenteeism and health-care costs in the workplace. *J Occup Med.* 1991;33(11):1119–1124.

27. Yen LT, Edington DW, Witting P. Prediction of prospective medical claims and absenteeism costs for 1284 hourly workers from a manufacturing company. *J Occup Med.* 1992;34(4):428–435.

28. Riedel JE, Grossmeier J, Haglund-Howieson L, et al. Use of a normal impairment factor in quantifying avoidable productivity loss because of poor health. *J Occup Environ Med.* 2009;51(3):283–295.

29. Edington DW, Yen LT, Witting P. The financial impact of changes in personal health practices. *J Occup Environ Med.* 1997;39(11):1037–1046.

30. Nyce S, Grossmeier J, Anderson DR, et al. Association between changes in health risk status and changes in future health care costs: a multiemployer study. *J Occup Environ Med.* 2012;54(11): 1364–1373.

31. Anderson DR, Mangen DJ, Grossmeier JJ, et al. Comparing alternative methods of targeting potential high-cost individuals for chronic condition management. *J Occup Environ Med.* 2010;52(6):635–646.

32. Strecher VJ, Kreuter MW. Health risk appraisal from a behavioral perspective: present and future. In: Hyner GC, Peterson KW, Travis JW, et al, eds. *SPM Handbook of Health Assessment Tools.* Pittsburgh, Pa: The Society of Preventive Medicine, The Institute for Health and Productivity Management; 1999:75–82.

33. Becker MH. The Health Belief Model and personal health behavior. *Health Educ Q.* 1974;2:324–472.

34. Avis NE, Smith KW, McKinlay JB. Accuracy of perceptions of heart attack risk: what influences perceptions and can they be changed? *Am J Public Health.* 1989;79(12):1608–1612.

35. Skinner CS, Kreuter MW, Kobrin S, Strecher VJ. Perceived and

actual breast cancer risk: optimistic and pessimistic biases. *J Health Psychol.* 1998;3(2):181–193.

36. Weinstein ND. Why it won't happen to me: perceptions of risk factors and susceptibility. *Health Psychol.* 1984;3(5):431–457.

37. Terry PE. The art of innovation. *Am J Health Promot.* 2012;26(5):TAHP-2–TAHP-6.

38. Bandura A. Self-efficacy: toward a unifying theory of behavioral change. *Psychol Rev.* 1977;84(2):191–215.

39. Kaplan R. Quantification of health outcomes for policy studies in behavioral epidemiology. In: Kaplan R, Criqui M, eds. *Behavioral Epidemiology and Disease Prevention.* New York, NY: Plenum; 1985:31-56.

40. Landsbergis PA, Schnall PL, Deitz DK, et al. Job strain and health behaviors: results of a prospective study. *Am J Health Promot.* 1998;12(4):237–245.

41. U.S. Department of Health and Human Services. *A Report of the Surgeon General: Physical Activity and Health.* Atlanta, Ga: Centers for Disease Control and Prevention; 1996.

42. McGonigal J. *Reality Is Broken: Why Games Make Us Better and How They Can Change the World.* New York, NY: Penguin Press; 2011.

43. Strecher VJ, Kreuter M, Den Boer DJ, et al. The effects of computer-tailored smoking cessation messages in family practice settings. *J Fam Pract.* 1994;39(3):262–270.

44. Skinner CS, Strecher VJ, Hospers H. Physicians' recommendations for mammography: do tailored messages make a difference? *Am J Public Health.* 1994;84(1):43–49.

45. Terry PE, Seaverson EL, Staufacker MJ, Gingerich SB. A comparison of the effectiveness of a telephone coaching program and a mail-based program. *Health Educ Behav.* 2010;37(6):895–912.

46. Terry PE, Seaverson EL, Staufacker MJ, Tanaka A. The effectiveness of a telephone-based tobacco cessation program offered as part of a worksite health promotion program. *Popul Health Manag.* 2011;14(3):117–125.

47. Task Force on Community Preventive Services. Guide to Community Preventive Services. Assessment of health risks with feedback to change employees' health. Available at: www.thecommunityguide.org/worksite/ahrf.html. Accessed February 28, 2013.

48. Oremus M. *Health Risk Appraisal Technology Assessment Report.* Rockville, Md: McMaster University Evidence-Based Practice Center Under Contract to the Agency for Healthcare Research and Quality, U.S. Department of Health and Human Services; 2011.

49. National Committee for Quality Assurance. Available at: http://www.ncqa.org/. Accessed February 28, 2013.

50. URAC. Available at: https://www.urac.org/. Accessed February 28, 2013.

51. U.S. Preventive Services Task Force. *Guide to Clinical Preventive Services: Second Edition.* Baltimore, Md: Williams & Wilkins; 1996.

52. U.S. Preventive Services Task Force. *Guide to Clinical Preventive Services, 2012.* Available at: http://www.ahrq.gov/professionals/clinicians-providers/guidelines-recommendations/guide/guide-clinical-preventive-services.pdf.

53. U.S. Preventive Services Task Force. Screening for high blood pressure in adults. Available at: http://www.uspreventiveservicestaskforce.org/uspstf/uspshype.htm. Accessed March 5, 2013.

54. Alderman MH, Lamport B. Treatment of hypertension at the workplace: an opportunity to link service and research. *Health Psychol.* 1988;7(suppl):283–295.

55. World Health Organization. *Global Brief on Hypertension.* Geneva, Switzerland: World Health Organization; 2013.

56. Grassi G, Bombelli M, Seravalle G, et al. Role of ambulatory blood pressure monitoring in resistant hypertension. *Curr Hypertens Rep.* 2013;15(3):232–237.

57. Muxfeldt ES, de Souza F, Salles GF. Resistant hypertension: a practical clinical approach. *J Hum Hypertens.* 2013;27(11):657-662.

58. The sixth report of the Joint National Committee on prevention, detection, evaluation, and treatment of high blood pressure. *Arch Intern Med.* 1997;157(21):2413–2446.

59. National High Blood Pressure Education Program. *The Seventh Report of the Joint National Committee on Prevention, Detection, Evaluation, and Treatment of High Blood Pressure.* NHLBI, U.S. Department of Health and Human Services; 2004. Available at: http://www.nhlbi.nih.gov/guidelines/hypertension/jnc7full.pdf.

60. Flegal KM, Carroll MD, Kit BK, Ogden CL. Prevalence of obesity and trends in the distribution of body mass index among U.S. adults, 1999-2010. *JAMA.* 2012;307(5):491–497.

61. Canoy D, Boekholdt SM, Wareham N, et al. Body fat distribution and risk of coronary heart disease in men and women in the European Prospective Investigation Into Cancer and Nutrition in Norfolk cohort: a population-based prospective study. *Circulation.* 2007;116(25):2933–2943.

62. Blijdorp K, van den Heuvel-Eibrink MM, Pieters R, et al. Obesity is underestimated using body mass index and waist-hip ratio in long-term adult survivors of childhood cancer. *PLoS One.* 2012;7(8):e43269.

63. Jitnarin N, Poston WS, Haddock CK, et al. Accuracy of body mass index-defined overweight in fire fighters. *Occup Med (Lond).* 2013;63(3):227–230.

64. Gallagher D, Visser M, Sepulveda D, et al. How useful is body mass index for comparison of body fatness across age, sex, and ethnic groups? *Am J Epidemiol.* 1996;143(3):228–239.

65. National Heart Lung and Blood Institute. *Clinical Guidelines on the Identification, Evaluation, and Treatment of Overweight and Obesity in Adults.* Bethesda, Md: National Heart, Lung and Blood Institute-NHLBI Information Center; 1999.

66. Wadden TA, Bell ST. Obesity. In: Bellack AS, Hersen M, Kazdin AE, eds. *International Handbook of Behavior Modification and Therapy.* New York, NY: Plenum; 1990:449-473.

67. Wagner DR, Heyward VH. Techniques of body composition assessment: a review of laboratory and field methods. *Res Q Exerc Sport.* 1999;70(2):135–149.

68. Heymsfield SB, Lohman TG, Wang ZM, Going SB. *Human Body Composition.* Champaign, Ill: Human Kinetics; 2005.

69. Fields DA, Goran MI, McCrory MA. Body-composition assessment via air-displacement plethysmography in adults and children: a review. *Am J Clin Nutr.* 2002;75(3):453–467.

70. Pollock ML, Wilmore JH. *Exercise in Health and Disease: Evaluation and Prescription for Prevention and Rehabilitation.* 2nd ed. Philadelphia, Pa: Saunders; 1990.

71. Martin AD, Ross WD, Drinkwater DT, Clarys JP. Prediction of body fat by skinfold caliper: assumptions and cadaver evidence. *Int J Obes.* 1985;9(suppl 1):31–39.

72. Grundy SM, Cleeman JI, Merz CN, et al. Implications of recent clinical trials for the National Cholesterol Education Program Adult Treatment Panel III guidelines. *Circulation.* 2004;110(2):227–239.

73. National Cholesterol Education Program. *Third Report of the National Cholesterol Education Program (NCEP) Expert Panel on Detection, Evaluation, and Treatment of High Blood Cholesterol*

in Adults (Adult Treatment Panel III) Final Report. NHLBI, U.S. Department of Health and Human Services; 2002. Available at: http://www.nhlbi.nih.gov/guidelines/cholesterol/atp3full.pdf.

74. Go AS, Mozaffarian D, Roger VL, et al. Heart disease and stroke statistics — 2013 update: a report from the American Heart Association. *Circulation*. 2013;127(1): e6–e245.

75. Kannel WB, Castelli WP, Gordon T. Cholesterol in the prediction of atherosclerotic disease: new perspectives based on the Framingham study. *Ann Intern Med*. 1979;90(1):85–91.

76. Frick MH, Elo O, Haapa K, et al. Helsinki Heart Study: primary-prevention trial with gemfibrozil in middle-aged men with dyslipidemia: safety of treatment, changes in risk factors, and incidence of coronary heart disease. *N Engl J Med*. 1987;317(20):1237–1245.

77. American Heart Association. What your cholesterol levels mean. Available at: http://www.heart.org/HEARTORG/Conditions/Cholesterol/AboutCholesterol/What-Your-Cholesterol-Levels-Mean_UCM_305562_Article.jsp. Accessed June 6, 2013.

78. Centers for Disease Control and Prevention. *National Diabetes Fact Sheet: National Estimates and General Information on Diabetes and Prediabetes in the United States, 2011*. Atlanta, Ga: U.S. Department of Health and Human Services, Centers for Disease Control and Prevention; 2011.

79. American Diabetes Association. Standards of medical care in diabetes-2011. *Diabetes Care*. 2013;36(suppl 1):S11–S66.

80. Thompson WR, American College of Sports M, Gordon NF, Pescatello LS. *ACSM's Guidelines for Exercise Testing and Prescription*. 8th ed. Baltimore, MD: Lippincott Williams & Wilkins; 2009.

81. McKiman MD, Froelicher VF. General principles of exercise testing. In: Skinner JS, ed. *Exercise Testing and Exercise Prescription for Special Casts: Theoretical Basis and Clinical Application*. Philadelphia, Pa: Lee and Febiger; 1987:3-19.

82. Chou R, Arora B, Dana T, et al. *Screening Asymptomatic Adults for Coronary Heart Disease With Resting or Exercise Electrocardiography: Systematic Review to Update the 2004 U.S. Preventive Services Task Force Recommendation*. Rockville, Md: Agency for Healthcare Research and Quality; 2011.

83. Balke B. *A Simple Field Test for the Assessment of Physical Fitness*. Oklahoma City, Okla: Civil Aeromedical Research Institute, Federal Aviation Agency; 1963.

84. Cooper KH. A means of assessing maximal oxygen intake: correlation between field and treadmill testing. *JAMA*. 1968;203(3):201–204.

85. Kline GM, Porcari JP, Hintermeister R, et al. Estimation of VO2max from a one-mile track walk, gender, age, and body weight. *Med Sci Sports Exerc*. 1987;19(3):253–259.

86. President's Council on Fitness, Sports & Nutrition. Available at: http://www.fitness.gov/index.html. Accessed April 15, 2013.

87. Erfurt JC, Foote A, Heirich MA, Gregg W. Improving participation in worksite wellness programs: comparing health education classes, a menu approach, and follow-up counseling. *Am J Health Promot*. 1990;4(4):270–278.

88. Erfurt JC, Foote A, Heirich MA. Worksite wellness programs: incremental comparison of screening and referral alone, health education, follow-up counseling, and plant organization. *Am J Health Promot*. 1991;5(6):438–448.

89. Heaney CA, Goetzel RZ. A review of health-related outcomes of

multi-component worksite health promotion programs. *Am J Health Promot.* 1997;11(4):290–307.

90. Terry P, Thorson D, Wegleitner T, Linck E. Decision support for preventive services—developing a U.S. Preventive Services Task Force-based computer assessment system for a group practice setting. *Group Pract J.* 1994;43(4):32–37.

91. Terry PE. A case for no-fault health insurance: from the "worried well" to the "guilty ill." *Am J Health Promot.* 1994;8(3):165.

92. Anderson D, Grossmeier J, Seaverson ELD, Snyder D. The role of financial incentives in driving employee engagement in health management. *ACSMS Health Fitness J.* 2008; 12(4):18–22.

93. Seaverson EL, Grossmeier J, Miller TM, Anderson DR. The role of incentive design, incentive value, communications strategy, and worksite culture on health risk assessment participation. *Am J Health Promot.* 2009;23(5):343–352.

94. Taitel MS, Haufle V, Heck D, et al. Incentives and other factors associated with employee participation in health risk assessments. *J Occup Environ Med.* 2008;50(8):863–872.

95. Wilhide C, Hayes JR, Farah JR. The use and influence of employee incentives on participation and throughput in a telephonic disease management program. *Popul Health Manag.* 2008;11(4):197–202.

96. O'Donnell MP. Making the impossible possible: engaging the entire population in comprehensive workplace health promotion programs at no net cost to employers or employees. *Am J Health Promot.* 2010;24(6):iv–v.

97. Carnethon M, Whitsel LP, Franklin BA, et al. Worksite wellness programs for cardiovascular disease prevention: a policy statement from the American Heart Association. *Circulation.* 2009;120(17):1725–1741.

98. American Heart Association. Position Statement on Financial Incentives Within Worksite Wellness Programs. Available at: http://www.heart.org/idc/groups/heart-public/@wcm/@adv/documents/downloadable/ucm_428966.pdf. Accessed March 4, 2013.

99. Hudson T, Hymel P, Loeppke R. ACOEM urges implementation of Affordable Care Act wellness provisions. Available at: http://www.acoem.org/Comments_AffordableCareActWellnessProvisions.aspx. Accessed March 4, 2013.

100. Terry PE, Anderson DR. Finding common ground in the use of financial incentives for employee health management: a call for a progress-based approach. *Am J Health Promot.* 2011;26(1):ev–evii.

101. Karavirta L, Hakkinen K, Kauhanen A, et al. Individual responses to combined endurance and strength training in older adults. *Med Sci Sports Exerc.* 2011;43(3):484–490.

102. Guidance for a reasonably designed, employer-sponsored wellness program using outcomes-based incentives. Consensus Statement of the Health Enhancement Research Organization; American College of Occupational and Environmental Medicine; American Cancer Society and American Cancer Society Cancer Action Network; American Diabetes Association; American Heart Association. *J Occup Environ Med.* 2012;54(7):889–896.

CHAPTER

14

Enhancing Fitness and Physical Activity

Mark G. Wilson, Jennifer L. Gay, David M. DeJoy and Heather M. Padilla

INTRODUCTION

The benefits of physical activity have been well documented in clinical and community studies spanning a century or more.[1] Physical activity has been shown to decrease the risk and/or incidence of cardiovascular disease, stroke, type 2 diabetes and metabolic syndrome, osteoporosis, obesity, depression, breast cancer and colon cancer.[1-3] As a result, physical activity has become a cornerstone of disease prevention and health promotion efforts.[4] Physical activity programs have been a foundation of workplace health promotion programs for three decades or more. National surveys have documented the prevalence of physical activity programs with 66% of large worksites offering programs in the latest survey.[5] Physical activity programs should be an integral part of comprehensive worksite health promotion efforts.

This chapter reviews elements of fitness, fitness prescriptions, and the prevalence of work-related physical activity, summarizes the health and financial impact of physical activity programs at work, and proposes strategies that include both skill (individual) and opportunity (environmental) enhancement strategies. It closes with a discussion of emerging trends in physical activity programs at work.

ELEMENTS OF FITNESS

Health-related fitness consists of the following elements[6-9]: 1) flexibility, the ability to have range of motion, 2) body composition, the relationship between fat and fat-free tissue and the comparison between the two, 3) muscular strength and endurance, capability to generate force and to make repeated contractions, and 4) cardiorespiratory endurance (aerobic power), the ability of the body to transport oxygen and perform work on a sustained basis (Table 14-1). These components, in addition to the dimensions of frequency, intensity, time (duration) and type (F.I.T.T. principles) provide a foundation for all physical activity programs.

FITNESS PRESCRIPTION DIMENSIONS

The foundations of any fitness program are frequency, intensity, time and type. These factors should be considered and incorporated into all physical activity prescriptions.

Frequency

Frequency refers to the number of sessions per week. The amount of improvement in oxygen

Table 14-1: Health benefits of fitness components.

Fitness Components	Definition	Program Examples	Known Health Benefits
Cardiorespiratory Endurance	Delivers oxygen and nutrients to the body for a sustained amount of time	Jogging or running groups Intramural sports such as basketball, softball or baseball, brisk walking, riding a bicycle, treadmill, stationary bicycle, elliptical Group fitness (e.g., Zumba)	Disease outcomes inversely related to regular physical activity include cardiovascular disease, thromboembolic stroke, hypertension, type 2 diabetes mellitus, osteoporosis, obesity, colon cancer, breast cancer, anxiety and depression.
Muscular Strength	Exert force for a brief period of time	Weight lifting Stair climbing	Bone health (lower risk of osteoporosis and fracture) Independence (particularly among older adults)
Muscular Endurance	Repeated contractions or continuous force	Bicycle riding, circuit weight training, free weights, push-ups, sit-ups, planks	Independence (particularly among older adults) Improved core body strength/reduced risk of lower back pain
Flexibility	Full range of motion	Stretching, group classes or individual practice of yoga or Pilates, golf	Injury prevention Independence (particularly among older adults)
Body Composition	Lean and fat mass	Combination physical activity and healthy eating programs	All-cause mortality Cardiovascular disease Type 2 diabetes mellitus Hypertension Some forms of cancer Stroke

uptake increases with the frequency of aerobic training. This can also occur in reverse with decreases in oxygen uptake occurring during periods of no exercise. If an individual misses a training session, it is best to try to get back into the workout regimen very soon.

Intensity

Exercise intensity refers to the level of stress achieved during the exercise period, and can be described in absolute or relative terms. Absolute intensity is typically measured using metabolic equivalents and assesses the amount of energy required to complete a task regardless of physiological capacity.[10] Relative intensity is ascertained through heart rate, perceived exertion and aerobic capacity.

Metabolic equivalent of task, or MET, quantifies intensity in terms of oxygen and caloric expenditure required to perform a certain level of work. The higher the MET, the more energy is being used to perform the action. For example, 1 MET designates a person at rest, usually sitting or lying down, 3 METS for walking at 2.5 mph (average pace), 5.5 METS mowing the lawn with a push-mower, and 9.8 METS for running at a 10-minute mile pace. The national guidelines state that to achieve health benefits of cardiorespiratory exercise, individuals should exercise at moderate- (4-6 METs) or vigorous-intensity (>6 METs).

A common way of measuring intensity is by heart rate. The heart rate method assumes there is a relationship between heart rate and oxygen consumption. The American College of Sports Medicine recommends exercise between 60% and 90% of age-related maximal heart rate.[11] A person's maximal heart rate is an estimated count of beats per minute that a person can attain without experiencing adverse reactions. Resting heart rate for adults is between 60 and 100 beats per minute. Both maximal and resting heart rates are dependent upon a number of factors including age, conditioning, and chronic health conditions.

For the majority of aerobic enthusiasts, this form of monitoring exercise intensity provides a safe, effective, and quick way of ensuring that they are reaping the health benefits of their exercise program through adequate effort levels. To determine what heart rate range is best for any individual, the four-step Karvonen process[12] can be used.

1. The *maximum heart rate* (HR_{max}) is the maximum number of heart beats a minute that an individual can achieve without severe problems through exercise stress and depends on age. The most accurate way of measuring maximum heart rate is via a cardiac stress test, but crude estimates can be predicted for maximal heart rate by subtracting the age of the individual from 220 (for women), or subtracting half the age from 205 (for men). [For example for a 40 year old woman: 220 – 40 = 180]

2. The basal or resting heart rate (HR_{rest}) is the number of heart beats per minute while the subject is relaxed but awake. It can be measured easily with a watch that has a second hand. Subtract the resting heart rate in beats per minute from the predicted maximal heart rate to calculate the maximal heart rate reserve. The best time to estimate the resting heart rate is in the morning. [Continuing for example: 180 - 60 = 120]

3. For most healthy adults, 60% to 90% of predicted maximal heart rate is the optimal range. To determine the range for the individual in the example, multiply the predicted maximal heart reserve (120) rate by 60% to determine the lower end of the range and by 90% to determine the upper end of the range. [120 x .60 = 72 and 120 x .90 = 108]

4. Finally, add the resting heart rate back into the heart rate range at the lower and upper ends of the range to estimate the aerobic training zone. [72 + 60 = 132 and 108 + 60 = 168]

The rate of perceived exertion (RPE) method is another simple method that can be used to determine intensity. It is performed by asking the individual to rate the feelings of exertion caused by an aerobic activity using a scale ranging from 6-20 that describes intensity of the exercise.[13] On this scale a rating of 6 to 7 would be considered "very, very light", 12 to 13 "somewhat hard", 15 to 16 "hard", and 19 to 20 "very, very hard". To exercise at 60% to 80% of maximal heart rate, the individual should be in the range of 12 to 15.

Time

Duration refers to the length in time of the physical activity session. For most adults, the intensity and duration of exercise are normally inversely related: the higher the exercise intensity, the shorter the duration of the exercise.[10] Thus, the duration of an activity can be increased when the activity is performed at lower intensities. One hour following a workout, an individual should feel rested. Performing too much too soon may lead to greater fatigue and injury, and reduced adherence rates.

Type

Mode refers to the type of activity performed during a physical activity session. The mode is dependent upon the individual's physical activity goals. For example, to improve muscular strength and endurance, weight training might be the focus of activity, while goals centered on weight reduction and improving cardiorespiratory endurance will include activities such as running, biking, and swimming. A variety of activities, such as running, cycling, swimming, hiking, cross country skiing, and dancing are recommended to allow a person to maximize health effects of physical activity (i.e., aerobic endurance, muscular strength and endurance, flexibility, body composition).[10,14]

PREVALENCE OF PHYSICAL ACTIVITY AND INACTIVITY

Recommendations on the optimal levels of physical activity continue to evolve over time.

The 2008 Physical Activity Guidelines for Americans[15] released by the Department of Health and Human Services provides guidelines in four areas pertaining to physical activity:

1) Avoid sedentary behavior and inactivity
2) Engage in at least 150 minutes of physical activity that is of moderate-intensity or 75 minutes of vigorous-intensity, or a combination each week
3) Participate in physical activity in bouts of at least 10 minutes
4) Engage in activities that strengthen muscles

Using these guidelines as standards, approximately one-third of adults engage in recommended levels of either moderate- or vigorous-intensity physical activity. A fourth of adults engage in no leisure-time physical activity.[16] These rates are markedly worse than the goals established by the *Healthy People 2020* objectives for the nation (Table 14-2).[17]

An important limitation of these guidelines and most population wide measurements of physical activity is the focus on vigorous to moderate "exercise" per se and not physical activity throughout the day, including during work. For example, Caban-Martinez and colleagues[18] examined leisure-time physical activity by occupation in a study of more than 150,000 workers in the U.S. but neglected to measure physical activity related to work. Across all labor sectors the amount of leisure-time physical activity was less than needed to meet guidelines. Only 31% of male and 36% of female workers met the Healthy People 2010 leisure-time physical activity guidelines and these levels vary significantly with the occupation (Table 14-3).[18] However, not much is known about the extent of work-related physical activity.

The increasing use of technology and concerns of workplace safety has led to a decrease in work-related physical activity at work. Similarly, more workers in the United

Table 14-2: Healthy People 2020 Objectives for the Nation relevant to workplaces.

Objective Number	Objective	Target Level
PA 1	Reduce the proportion of adults who engage in no leisure-time physical activity	32.6%
PA 2	Increase the proportion of adults who meet current Federal physical activity guidelines for aerobic physical activity and for muscle-strengthening activity	
PA 2.1	Increase the proportion of adults who engage in aerobic physical activity of at least moderate intensity for at least 150 minutes/week, or 75 minutes/week of vigorous intensity, or an equivalent combination	47.9%
PA 2.2	Increase the proportion of adults who engage in aerobic physical activity of at least moderate intensity for more than 300 minutes/week, or more than 150 minutes/week of vigorous intensity, or an equivalent combination	31.3%
PA 2.3	Increase the proportion of adults who perform muscle-strengthening activities on 2 or more days of the week	24.1%
PA 2.4	Increase the proportion of adults who meet the objectives for aerobic physical activity and for muscle-strengthening activity	20.1%
PA 12	Increase the proportion of employed adults who have access to and participate in employer-based exercise facilities and exercise programs	Developmental*
PA 15	Increase legislative policies for the built environment that enhance access to and availability of physical activity opportunities	Developmental
PA 15.1	Increase community-scale policies for the built environment that enhance access to and availability of physical activity opportunities	Developmental
PA 15.2	Increase street-scale policies for the built environment that enhance access to and availability of physical activity opportunities	Developmental
PA 15.3	Increase transportation and travel policies for the built environment that enhance access to and availability of physical activity opportunities	Developmental

*Objective is new with no targeted level.

Table 14-3: Percent of U.S. workers by gender meeting the Healthy People 2010 recommended leisure-time physical activity levels of U.S. worker groups from the 1997-2004 National Health Interview Survey.[a]

Occupation	Male		Females	
	Estimated U.S. worker population	**% Exercise[b]**	**Estimated U.S. worker population**	**% Exercise[b]**
Total	67,295,584	36	58,028,885	31
Officials and administrators public admin	403,134	43	369,713	31
Managers administrators, except public administration	7,272,533	41	5,048,892	36
Management related occupations	2,145,080	42	2,940,700	35
Engineers	1,770,314	44	202,275	45
Architects and surveyors	185,286	47	39,178	43
Natural mathematical/ computer scientists	1,828,875	46	787,830	42
Health diagnosing occupations	757,642	51	293,948	46
Health assessment/treating occupations	431,252	45	2,869,192	38
Teachers, librarians, counselors	2,143,317	52	4,665,859	41
Writers, artists, entertainers, athletes	1,169,655	47	1,110,940	44
Other professional specialty occupations	1,481,366	48	1,438,179	38
Health technologists/ technicians	368,284	42	1,468,113	32
Technologists, technicians except health	1,786,063	39	833,058	36
Supervisors and proprietors	2,273,853	36	1,521,792	27
Sales representatives, commodities and finance	2,618,251	43	1,562,285	39
Other sales	2,326,746	37	3,769,708	26

Occupation	Male		Females	
	Estimated U.S. worker population	% Exercise[b]	Estimated U.S. worker population	% Exercise[b]
Computer equipment operators	168,339	35	203,739	28
Secretaries, stenographers and typists	58,321	34	2,572,932	29
Financial records processing occupations	212,772	36	1,866,976	28
Mail and message distributing	503,481	34	368,265	27
Other administrative support	2,952,905	37	8,254,599	28
Private household occupations	33,520	41	643,231	27
Police and firefighters	1,199,680	55	216,625	42
Other protective service occupations	692,925	37	263,074	28
Food service	2,169,299	34	3,131,848	26
Health service	283,035	40	2,330,125	25
Cleaning and building service	1,633,057	27	1,400,367	20
Personal service	479,408	41	2,241,124	32
Farm operators and managers	700,736	25	139,259	33
Farm workers and other agricultural workers	1,575,327	25	360,481	26
Forestry and fishing occupations	134,988	27	4708	c
Mechanics and repairers	4,398,967	32	200,529	31
Construction and extractive trades	5,563,509	31	147,746	35
Precision production occupations	2,548,881	31	802,467	21

Occupation	Male		Females	
	Estimated U.S. worker population	% Exercise[b]	Estimated U.S. worker population	% Exercise[b]
Machine operators/ tenderers, except precisions	2,842,681	27	1,471,483	16
Fabricators, assemblers, inspectors, samplers	1,622,158	29	987,253	18
Motor vehicle operators	3,426,034	28	495,220	27
Other transportation, except motor vehicles	181,507	39	3421	[a]
Material moving equipment operators	1,078,483	28	74,679	18
Construction laborers	1,006,417	26	24,992	29
Freight, stock, material handlers	2,867,505	30	902,081	20

[a] Confidence intervals, standard errors for each prevalence estimate are provided at the Miami NIOSH Research Website: http://www.rsmas.miami.edu/groups/nichs/niosh/.

[b] Sample size based on participants who self-reported leisure-time physical activity.

[c] Prevalence not reported when subgroup sample size is less than 25.

Table adapted from Caban-Martinez et al. 2007. Leisure-time physical activity levels of the U.S. workforce. Preventive Medicine 44: 432-436.

States are employed in service sector occupations that do not require as much manual labor as jobs that produce goods such as manufacturing and construction.[19] Increasing opportunities for physical activity at the workplace may allow more people to reach the recommended levels of physical activity. Worksite interventions to increase physical activity are not new. However, these interventions have almost exclusively focused on increasing physical activity through formal exercise rather than integrating activity into work or daily living.

Physical Activity and Work

Few studies have directly examined the amount of work-related physical activity in working populations. Work-related physical activity has often been estimated indirectly by reviewing job titles or position descriptions. One review of the occupational physical activity literature reported consistently low levels of physical activity at work, even in occupations classified as highly active.[20] Another study documented the prevalence of work-related physical activity, showing a decrease over the last five decades (Figure 14-1).[19]

One limitation of studies on occupational physical activity is the reliance on self-report instruments that can result in over-estimating moderate-to-vigorous intensity activity and under-estimating light-intensity activity, the type usually performed in work settings. In a step toward standardized classifications

Figure 14-1: Occupational METs and energy expenditure since 1960.

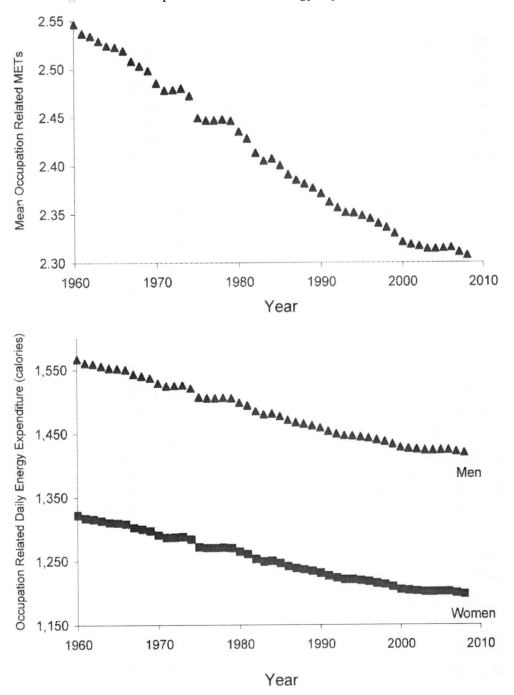

Figure from Church et al. 2011. Trends over 5 decades in U.S. occupation-related physical activity and their associations with obesity. PLoS 6: e19657.

of occupational activity, Tudor-Locke and colleagues[21] assigned MET values to each occupation in the census occupational classification system (Table 14-4). They found that one-third of workers had completely sedentary occupations, and another 47% engaged in primarily light-intensity activities while at work. There is an opportunity to engage workers in more physical activity while on the job, through active transportation and general conduct of life.

A more recent development in occupational physical activity studies is the notion of compensation. More specifically, researchers are asking whether there is an inverse relationship between occupational physical activity and leisure-time physical activity, such that the more activity a person does on the job, the less s/he will do during free time. While this may be a concern, the evidence so far has not supported a compensation effect. On the contrary, analysis by Wolin and Bennett[22] found that the two types of physical activity were positively associated; the more occupational activity performed, the greater amount of leisure-time physical activity. This finding has been supported by self-report and objectively measured physical activity data.[23,24]

A current trend in occupational activity studies is the examination of sedentary time, usually assessed as sitting time, as a separate behavior and health risk factor from physical activity. Sedentary behavior is prevalent among office workers, making up more than 80% of work time.[25] Furthermore, employees are more likely to be sedentary during work time than when not at work.[26] Sitting time is associated with increased waist circumference and metabolic risk profiles including blood pressure, cholesterol and blood glucose.[27] However, risk can be reduced when sitting time is interrupted by frequent but brief breaks of walking at a normal pace.[28] While research on the health impact of sedentary time is relatively new, early findings support the notion that physical activity, even at a low intensity, is

better than being sedentary in terms of risk for chronic disease.

HEALTH AND FINANCIAL IMPACT OF FITNESS PROGRAMS

The National Worksite Health Promotion Survey indicated that 20% of organizations were offering physical activity programs or activities in 2004.[5] As with previous national studies, this varied considerably based on the size of the organization with 66% of large organizations (750+ employees), 29% and 24% of medium sized organizations (250-749 and 100-249), and 9% of small organizations (50-99) reporting programs.

Impact of Fitness Programs on Health

The impact of workplace physical activity programs has been examined over the last three decades. Hundreds of studies summarized in multiple critiques of the literature conducted by varied investigators have supported the effectiveness of worksite programs. Shephard[29] reviewed 52 studies from 1974 to 1994 and found that well designed worksite fitness programs can be effective for improving health outcomes in program participants. Proper and colleagues[30] reviewed 15 randomized controlled trials and 11 nonrandomized controlled trials from 1980 to 2000 and reported strong evidence for the positive effect of worksite programs on physical activity and musculoskeletal disorders.

Conn and colleagues[31] conducted a meta-analysis of 138 studies encompassing 38,231 participants from 1969–2007 and reported significantly positive effects on physical activity behaviors and fitness, health outcomes (lipids, anthropomorphic measures) and organizational outcomes (job stress and work attendance). This was updated with a meta-analysis of 358 intervention studies from 1960 to 2007 that concluded that interventions designed to

Table 14-4: Activity codes and MET values assigned to 2002 Census Occupational Classification System.

Occupation group title from 2002 Census Occupational Classification System	2002 census codes	Range of assigned MET values	Summary MET values*
1 Management	0010--0430	1.5-3.0	1.73
2 Business and financial operations	0500--0950	1.5-2.5	1.67
3 Computer and mathematical	1000--1240	1.5-2.5	1.58
4 Architecture and engineering	1300--1560	1.5-2.5	1.64
5 Life, physical, and social science	1600--1960	1.5-2.5	2.03
6 Community and social services	2000--2060	1.5-2.5	2.08
7 Legal	2100--2150	1.5	1.50
8 Education, training, and library	2200--2550	2.5	2.50
9 Arts, design, entertainment, sports, media	2600--2960	1.5-3.5	2.13
10 Healthcare practitioner and technical	3000--3540	1.5-3.0	2.22
11 Healthcare support	3600--3650	2.0-4.0	2.83
12 Protective service	3700--3950	2.0-5.0	2.56
13 Food preparation and serving related	4000--4160	2.0-3.5	2.58
14 Building and grounds cleaning and maintenance	4200--4250	2.5-4.5	3.58
15 Personal care and service	4300--4650	1.5-3.0	2.53
16 Sales and related occupations	4700--4960	1.5-2.5	2.00
17 Office and administrative support	5000--5930	1.5-4.5	1.83
18 Farming, fishing, and forestry	6000--6130	2.5-8.0	3.67
19 Construction and extraction	6200--6940	2.5-8.0	4.29
20 Installation, maintenance, and repair	7000--7620	1.5-8.0	3.19
21 Production	7700--8960	1.5-4.0	2.69
22 Transportation and material moving	9000--9750	1.5-7.5	2.68

*Published previously[7].
Table adapted from Tudor-Locke et al. 2011. Assigning metabolic equivalent values to the 2002 census occupational classification system. J Phys Act Health 8: 581-586.

increase physical activity in worksites were moderately effective.[32] Hutchinson and Wilson conducted a meta-analysis of 29 studies from 1999 to 2009 and found that the workplace is a suitable environment for making changes in the physical activity, nutrition and health of employed individuals.[33] Finally, the Community Preventive Services Task Force recommended the creation of or enhanced access to places for physical activity at the worksite based on strong evidence of their effectiveness in increasing physical activity and improving physical fitness.[34] All of these studies examined the impact of increasing exercise rather than building activity into work or daily living.

Physical Activity and Work-Related Outcomes

Researchers typically examine physical activity and work-related outcomes from one of two perspectives. First, physical activity can be viewed as an aspect or characteristic of a particular job or occupation. From this perspective, almost any health or safety outcome could be linked to the level and type of physical activity associated with a given job or occupation. In essence, physical activity is treated as a working condition or occupational exposure. Job features, such as heavy lifting, repetitive motions, awkward postures, or prolonged standing or sitting, can be viewed as job demands or exposures that may affect employee health and well-being. A second perspective entails viewing physical activity as a lifestyle component, with the idea that leisure time physical activity or inactivity may enhance or detract from worker health and productivity. Interestingly, much of the early research on physical activity and health concentrated on work-related physical activity virtually to the exclusion of non-work physical activity.

This pattern changed abruptly around 1970, when most researchers turned their attention to leisure-time physical activity and formal exercise.[35] Part of this shift may have been related to decreases in work related physical activity caused by the ubiquitous spread of information technology in the workplace and the transition to a service-based economy. In many workplaces, there has been a concerted effort to "engineer" physical activity out of jobs in the hopes of reducing injuries and boosting productivity. The shift to leisure-time physical activity also roughly parallels the emergence of disease prevention and health promotion as major public health priorities.

Occupational Physical Activity

In one of the earliest studies, Morris and colleagues[36] in England examined mortality data for a variety of different occupations which they categorized into three levels of physical activity: heavy, intermediate, or light. Their results showed that death from coronary artery disease at ages 45 to 64 were more than twice as common among workers in "light" occupations compared to those in "heavy" occupations. When these analyses were expanded to include other causes of death, "light" workers once again displayed higher rates for a variety of other diseases, including lung cancer, diabetes, duodenal ulcer, and cirrhosis of the liver.[37] Fatal accidents were the major exception to this pattern, with much higher levels occurring to workers in the "heavy" activity category.

However, some researchers did not find the same positive health effects associated with physically active jobs.[38,39] To help alleviate possible confounding due to socioeconomic factors and other differences between occupations, some researchers sought to compare active and inactive workers with the same or similar jobs. For example, Kahn[40] compared letter carriers and postal clerks, and Morris and colleagues[36] compared bus drivers and bus conductors. In both of these studies, coronary disease mortality rates were higher among those with more sedentary work activities. More recent modern and sophisticated studies continue to show conflicting results.[41,42]

Overall, jobs and occupations considered to be physically demanding have higher rates of accidents and injuries than less active jobs and occupations.[43] This pattern is perhaps most apparent for non-fatal injuries with the highest rates occurring in natural resources and mining, transportation/warehousing and construction (Figure 14-2). The health care and social assistance sectors also have relatively high rates of injury, with many of the injuries involving patient handling and lifting. It is not possible to confirm that higher rates of injuries are caused by the level of physical activity because people in these jobs are exposed to a variety of hazards, including working at heights or in confined spaces, mechanical and electrical hazards, and adverse environmental conditions. The picture for fatalities is complicated somewhat due to

the large number of fatal work-related injuries involving motor vehicles. Motor vehicle crashes account for about one-third of all work-related fatal accidents.[44]

Injury prevention strategies in the workplace typically fall into three categories: 1) direct hazard or engineering controls that seek to eliminate or control the hazard itself, often through the engineering or design of equipment and processes; 2) administrative controls such as worker training or scheduling; and 3) the provision of personal protective equipment or devices. According to the traditional hazard control hierarchy,[45] hazard controls are usually preferred over administrative controls, and administrative controls are usually preferable to personal protection approaches. Injury prevention strategies have often focused on making ergonomic modifications to tools, equipment,

Figure 14-2: Incidence rates for nonfatal occupational injuries and illnesses involving days away from work, selected industries, 2010.

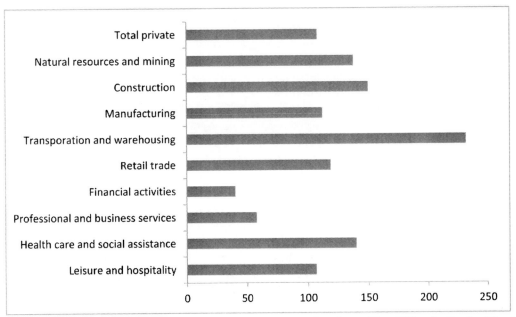

Source: Bureau of Labor Statistics, U.S. Department of Labor. The Editor's Desk, Nonfatal occupational injuries and illnesses requiring days away from work in 2010 on the Internet at http://www.bls.gov/opub/ted/2011/ted_20111117.htm. Accessed March 13, 2013.

and jobs, and/or by limiting the magnitude or duration of exposure; for example, by introducing work or exercise breaks into the workday. Much of the research on injury prevention has focused on computer-related work tasks and musculoskeletal complaints and injuries. Ergonomic interventions can be quite effective, especially when they provide for active employee involvement in problem identification and control activities.[46,47] Research also supports the usefulness of exercise and rest breaks in reducing injury and absences, but does not show one to be more beneficial than the other.[48,49] Some other injury prevention approaches, such as safe lifting education and back supports, have shown quite limited benefits.[50]

Exercise programs alone or in combination with other intervention modalities are frequently used as rehabilitation or return-to-work strategies for injured workers, particularly those with musculoskeletal injuries. These efforts are sometimes referred to as work hardening programs. There have been several systematic reviews of this literature, and these reviews have yielded generally mixed results concerning effectiveness.[51-53] Conclusions on the benefits of different types or doses of exercise are particularly difficult to draw. Programs closely tied to the specific jobs and work settings tend to be more effective than general or home-based exercise programs. Multi-modal interventions that combine exercise with other intervention strategies are often more effective than single modality interventions. The difficulty in drawing firm conclusions on the specific benefits of exercise on returning to work after an injury may be due to the fact that return-to-work is ultimately a complex process involving a host of medical, psychosocial, organizational, and economic factors.[54] These complexities aside, evidence is quite consistent showing that returning to work by itself has beneficial effects on employee health.[55]

Economic Evidence

There is very limited research on the economic impact of physical activity programs as separate programs that are independent from comprehensive health promotion programs.[56] Shephard[57] reviewed 14 company-sponsored fitness programs and reported cost-benefit ratios ranging from $1.07 to $5.58. Proper et al.[58] found some evidence for reduced absenteeism associated with worksite physical activity programs but no impact on productivity. More recently, a study of Swedish dental office employees engaging in 2.5 hours of physical activity during work hours experienced a decrease in the number of sickness absence days and spells of sickness absence. Overall, there was a 22% reduction in costs per employee.[59] In a cohort study, Tuomi et al.[60] reported increases in productivity associated with leisure time physical activity.

More often, worksite health promotion programs involve multiple components consistent with a socio-ecological model. Multicomponent programs that include physical activity have shown positive effects and do generate economic impact.[61-64] Many of these programs are discussed in other chapters in this text.

CONCEPTUAL FOUNDATION FOR PHYSICAL ACTIVITY INTERVENTIONS

The conceptual foundation for effective physical activity programs is the same foundation that has been discussed for other health promotion programs and is highlighted by studies conducted by Goetzel and Terry. Goetzel and colleagues[65] conducted an inventory of promising practices from 39 large organizations identified as being leaders in offering health and productivity management programs to their employees. They found seven promising practices which include: 1) integrating programs into the organization's operations, 2) simultaneously addressing individual, environmental, policy, and cultural factors, 3) targeting several health issues, 4) tailoring programs to address specific needs, 5) attaining high participation, 6) rigorously evaluating programs, and 7) communicating outcomes to key stakeholders.

Terry and colleagues[66] examined 22 organizations from a pool of 111 that offered comprehensive health promotion programs with complete program data to identify best practice program components. They identified nine comprehensive program quality components that distinguished 'best-practice' programs from 'common-practice' programs. These components included: 1) comprehensive program design, 2) management support, 3) integrated incentives, 4) comprehensive communications, 5) dedicated onsite staff, 6) multiple program modalities, 7) health awareness programs, 8) biometric health screenings, and 9) vendor integration.

Programs to increase physical activity in workplaces will have greater impact if they are multi-level, tailored to the individual's or group's needs, target several health issues along with physical activity (e.g. healthy eating, weight management, stress reduction) and incorporate evidence-based strategies. Multi-level strategies can maximize program effectiveness by including skill enhancement and opportunity enhancement strategies.

SKILL ENHANCEMENT STRATEGIES
Physical Activity Program Guidelines

Physical activity programs should be targeted to impact the fitness element that is relevant to the target audience and outcome. For example, workers who are at increased risk for back injury should be offered strength training or flexibility programs. Workers who wish to lose weight, should be steered toward aerobic training programs. The remainder of this section discusses additional suggestions for programs in these three areas.

Cardiorespiratory Endurance (Aerobic training)

Aerobic exercise is defined as any activity that rhythmically utilizes large muscle groups for a continuous period. The selection of the mode of exercise should be dependent on the individual's goals, past exercise experiences, budget, current fitness level, and preferences.[6] The most common forms of aerobic exercise include walking, running, swimming, and biking. Cardiorespiratory endurance may be the most important health-related component of physical activity due to its impact on coronary heart disease risk factors and other chronic diseases.[67]

Muscular Strength and Endurance (Strength training)

Muscular performance involves the effectiveness of how our muscles use energy and entails both muscular strength (the maximal level a muscle can exert a force) and endurance (the muscle's ability to make repeated contractions against resistance). For strength, a key concept behind muscular performance is the resistance or overload principle. Resistance may come in the form of an external force, such as a barbell, or one's own body weight. The goal is to increase the load a muscle can bear in order for that area of the body to become larger, stronger, and work more efficiently against such force. Through progressive resistance training, increasing the force or "overloading" the muscle will in turn improve strength. For endurance, interval training, which involves short times of exertion that are followed by recovery periods, can be used. Endurance is built through an individual increasing the number of times they can perform the repetitions. Training for the healthy adult includes performing contractions at moderate-to-slow speed, through the full range of motion, and using a normal breathing pattern during lifting movements.

Flexibility

Flexibility is defined as the body's ability to move freely over a wide range of motion void of stiffness and resistance. Flexible muscles are less prone to soreness and injury and can help to improve overall muscular performance due to ability to lengthen and stretch. Stretching may be performed as often as an individual desires and should focus on the area(s) of the body which needs improvement in range of motion. Five to ten minutes of pre-exercise stretching can help reduce the risk of injury during vigorous exercise bouts, and stretching at the end of a workout can prevent muscle soreness. The optimal way of working on the flexibility of a muscle is through slow, gentle stretching, without bouncing. Keeping a stretch slow and controlled throughout the range of motion is important in avoiding hyperextension or pushing a joint beyond its limits. The "sitting toe-touch" is an example of a flexibility stretch that examines the limberness of the lower back and hamstrings. This test can be used to assess an individual's lower body flexibility and as a means of developing an exercise program that can help improve the stiffness of these muscles and prevent future injury or lower back pain.

Physical Activity Programs

Table 14-5 lists a variety of physical activity program strategies commonly implemented in workplaces and their fitness benefits (discussed above). Tailoring strategies to address the goals of each individual increases participation in and adherence to programs. For example, someone who wants to increase strength and muscle mass is more likely to achieve these goals in a strength training program than a stretching program.

At the same time, comprehensive programs designed to achieve multiple fitness benefits (e.g. cardiorespiratory endurance and flexibility)

can impact multiple health risks, achieving benefits beyond individual expectations. Provided that the cost of the programs doesn't exceed the benefits, multi-strategy programs can motivate individuals to be more physically active long term.

Overcoming Barriers

In study after study, both in the United States and internationally, adults identify similar barriers to physical activity participation: motivation, lack of energy or willpower, fatigue, lack of childcare, and not having safe places to be active.[68-74] As a result, skill-building strategies are essential for changing behavior, particularly for overcoming barriers.[75]

Skills that are important for increasing activity include time management, goal setting, relapse planning and prevention, accountability and experiential learning. These skills are derived from several theories in health promotion including Social Cognitive Theory[76] and Self-Determination Theory.[77] These theories both posit that the built and social environments influence health behaviors. From a self-determination perspective, the social context of work environments can facilitate choices for being active during work breaks, as well as camaraderie among workers. Providing autonomy and feelings of social support among workers can increase motivation and therefore physical activity participation.

Goal-setting is another frequently used component of physical activity interventions and have been used successfully in hospital, fitness center, and home-based settings with a variety of populations.[78-81] Goal-setting content can be delivered in-person, to groups or using a computer-based system.[78,79,81] Goal-setting asks an individual to set goal(s) for an activity that is specific as to time (when it will happen), place (where it will happen), and specific strategy (how it will happen). An individual who sets a goal of 'walking their dog around the neighborhood every night after dinner for ½ hour' is much more likely to achieve that goal than someone who sets

Table 14-5: Physical activity program strategies and primary fitness benefits.

Strategies	Cardio-respiratory Endurance	Muscular Strength	Muscular Endurance	Flexibility	Body Composition
Basketball	X				X
Brisk walking	X				
Circuit weight training		X	X		
Crossfit	X		X		X
Dancing	X				
Functional fitness training		X	X		X
Golf				X	
Group fitness classes (e.g. Zumba)	X			X	X
Jogging or running groups	X				X
Pilates				X	
Push-ups, sit-ups, planks			X		
Riding a bicycle	X		X	X	X
Soccer	X				X
Softball / baseball	X				X
Stair climbing		X	X		
Stretching exercises				X	
Swimming	X	X	X		X
Tennis	X				
Volleyball	X				X
Walking to work	X				
Weightlifting		X			
Yoga				X	

the goal of 'walking more after work'. Agreeing to walk with a partner increases accountability and the likelihood the goal will be achieved.

Role modeling and experiential learning, as well as accountability, are also commonly used strategies to increase physical activity behavior. Role modeling is a technique in which individuals who are successfully maintaining physically active lifestyles are featured as examples of what is possible. This can be used alone or in conjunction with experiential learning, in which program participants are able to try out different activities and experience how it feels to be active. Role modeling can be presented in-person or via telephone, internet, or print media while experiential learning is conducted in-person. Other skills such as accountability, relapse planning, self-monitoring and time management are usually incorporated into an intervention as part of a multiple-skill program. A combination of individually-tailored motivational programs rooted in behavior change theory and environmental prompts have shown slightly better outcomes than either strategy alone.[82]

OPPORTUNITY ENHANCEMENT STRATEGIES

Worksites are a unique setting because the organization has considerable control over the environment in which its employees work. This includes the social and organizational environment as well as the physical environment. This affords an employer a great opportunity to enhance the environment to encourage employees to be more physically active. Even for those workers who work in non-traditional work environments, such as police officers who will patrol an area or crews who repair power lines, opportunities arise to foster physical activity.

A broad range of strategies can be used to increase people's opportunities to be more physically active. These opportunity enhancement strategies range from traditional approaches like providing onsite fitness centers and increasing the attractiveness of stairways to creating company policies and norms related to sitting and standing. All of these strategies can be categorized into two

broad categories: a) designing or modifying the worksite to impact employees who work at that location or b) instituting policies across the organization that impact all employees at all of the organization's worksites. The first category focuses on engineering the worksite and the second on engineering the organization.

Engineering the Worksite

An employee's individual workspace influences their physical activity. For example, an increasingly common occurrence in many workspaces is the standing desk. Raising the level of the employee's desk requires them to stand for longer periods of the day, expending greater levels of energy and avoiding the debilitating effects of sitting. The overall benefit to the employee depends on the time spent in that workspace and the amount of time chairs are used. A number of worksites allow employees to incorporate exercise equipment into their workspace. This may take the form of stationary bicycles, treadmills, stepping devices, etc. that enable the individual to move without leaving their workspace. Although some of these can be expensive and utilize substantial space, there is some evidence of their effectiveness in increasing overall energy expenditure.[83] Computer software is being developed that would serve as a cue to activity. This software prompts the individual every 30 minutes to stand, reducing the long periods of uninterrupted sedentary behavior.[68]

Opportunities also exist in break rooms, hallways, conference or meeting rooms, stairways, etc. Modifications to these spaces have the potential to impact a larger part of the workforce. Research has shown that worksites with a greater number of physical activity environmental and policy supports (onsite fitness centers, shower facilities, lockers, safe bicycle storage, stairs, etc.) have higher levels of physical activity among their employees.[69]

Perhaps the most common environmental support for physical activity is an onsite fitness facility. Staffed facilities with trained fitness professionals and offering fitness programs (i.e. spin classes, Zumba, etc.) increase their effectiveness in reaching inactive workers.[70,80] Working with fitness facilities located in the community (i.e. YMCA) to arrange employee discounts or modified hours of operation can provide opportunities for employees to be physically active closer to their home.

Stairs that are attractive, centrally located and well lit are more likely to be used. Point of decision prompts (i.e. signs, posters) posted at the stairs are effective for increasing the percentage of people taking the stairs.[71,72] Some worksites are beginning to place copiers and printers in central locations (work rooms) so that employees will have to walk to pick up their printed document. Other organizations are scheduling walking meetings in which the meeting takes place on a walk rather than at a table and the length of the meeting is a distance covered rather than time. Worksites have organized exercise breaks in which employees leave their workstation to participate in an organized activity session or participate as part of a regularly scheduled meeting.[73] These types of brief breaks in which all employees participate together have been found effective for reducing weight, BMI, and blood pressure.[74]

A number of worksites have modified their outdoor space to include walking areas or trails, moved parking farther away from the buildings, discontinued shuttle services from building to building and/or set up outdoor meeting areas. The City of New York has developed Active Design Guidelines to encourage architects and building designers to create healthier buildings and streets (http://www.nyc.gov/html/ddc/html/design/active_design.shtml) and some worksites have adopted these strategies for their buildings. This can be coordinated with community efforts to create active living communities that encourage physical activity for everyone throughout the day (http://www.activelivingresearch.org). However, to be maximally effective these strategies should be part of a larger organizational effort to foster a healthy active work culture.

Engineering the Organization

Creating an organizational culture that values physical activity complements the physical environment and makes physical activity the easy choice. The organizational environment encompasses all employees, wherever they may be located. Pronk and Kottke[75] recommend developing a "human centered culture" which promotes respect, embraces diversity, engages workers, develops trust and optimizes a culture that improves health and productivity through the inclusion of physical activity strategies.

Policies have a strong influence on an organization's culture. Sallis and colleagues[76] have recommended policies to support physical activity that revolve around 1) safety (i.e. safe places to walk, bike lane design), 2) availability/access to facilities and programs (for all employees), 3) support for personal transportation (i.e. biking, walking), 4) support for incidental activity indoors (i.e. stairways), and 5) incentives for physical activity. Although difficult to implement sometimes, policies can show the organization's commitment to the health and safety of its employees. Policies that encourage employees to walk, bicycle, and take public transportation to work can positively impact activity levels as well as employee morale.

Finally, incentives have the power to create opportunity. Incentives often include providing the employee an object (i.e. t-shirt, lunch bag, water bottle) for signing up, participating, and/or completing a specific program, although the effectiveness of such type of incentives on behavior change is not proven. Other incentives could include giving employees time to devote to being physically active through strategies such as flextime or allowing employees to exercise on work time.

EMERGING TRENDS AND UNANSWERED QUESTIONS

It is time to reevaluate how we view and measure activity at work. How can we reengineer activity back into our workday without compromising workplace safety? How can we change the workplace culture so that taking the stairs is preferred over taking the elevator? How do we incent employees to park further away from their building? Can we use computers to increase, rather than decrease? These questions and others are being addressed by worksite practitioners from a variety of disciplines. For example, occupational safety researchers have examined how to positively impact safety climate[77,84] and economists are researching how to incent individuals to perform positive behaviors in the growing field of behavioral economics.[85,86]

The ecological model can provide a framework which can guide future research. The ecological model provides a comprehensive framework for understanding the multiple, interacting factors that determine health behavior. These multiple levels of influence include intrapersonal, interpersonal, organizational, community, and public policy.[87] Opportunities to study and impact emerging trends in physical activity at work exist at every level.

At the *intrapersonal* level, technology is providing individuals with access to incredible amounts of information. An employee's smart phone doubles as an accelerometer documenting their activity from the time they wake until the time they sleep. Their watch tracks their heart rate and blood pressure. Their shoes can track the number of steps they take each day. These personal tracking devices can be downloaded daily (or hourly) into a computer application that provides instant feedback on their activity. Applications on employee's smart phones allow them to take a picture of their lunch and receive feedback on

the calories and nutrients of that meal. What is the impact of these increasing levels of feedback on individual behavior and how could they be used to increase physical activity? How do they impact our ability to measure activity at work?

At the *interpersonal* level, social media are becoming the norm with work-related social media sites proliferating. These sites provide a mechanism to communicate with a variety of individuals who may work for another organization or in another state (or country!). Social media is allowing individuals to share information about their activities and monitor the activities of other colleagues. Research has documented the impact of social norms on behavior, but little is known about the impact of these technological delivery mechanisms (phones, tablets, computers, etc.) on physical activity levels. Can we use social media as we have team competitions to increase activity levels of employees?

At the *organizational* level, many organizations have undertaken modifications to the physical environment to foster activity (as discussed above). However, very little work is being conducted on ways to redesign specific jobs to make them more active. Considerable research has been conducted on how to redesign jobs to make them safer, what would be the impact if organizations redesigned jobs to make them more active? How would increases in physical activity levels at work impact physical activity levels outside of work or at home?

At the *community* level, the idea of an active living community is drawing considerable attention, even though there is little evidence to support impact of such a community on physical activity. Considerable challenges revolve around bringing disparate groups (transportation, urban planning, recreation, economic development, environment health, etc.) to the table to discuss strategies for building an active community, let alone determining how to pay for it. The goal would be to create active living communities where individuals could work, live and play in a setting that supported rather than discouraged activity throughout the day. How would these active communities effect crime, housing, transportation, tax revenues or the quality of life of their residents?

Finally, at the *public policy* level, provisions in the Patient Protection and Affordable Care Act are serving as an incentive to organizations to closely examine plan design and how it might impact employee health, accelerating this trend. As a result, many organizations are modifying their benefit plan to offer discounts on medical insurance premiums to those participating in health promotion programs including physical activity programs. What will be the impact of these new plans on participation in worksite physical activity programs? Can we have a meaningful impact on physical activity rates nationwide through worksite programs?

CONCLUSIONS

The workplace provides a unique setting which can be exploited to foster physical activity at a number of levels over an extended period of time. As such, work organizations should carefully consider how to integrate physical activity promotion into their overall business planning process. Successful efforts can significantly improve the health and productivity and decrease injuries in their employees[81], positively impacting the bottom-line. Adapting strategies tested in other settings, with other populations and other health risks, can stimulate a paradigm shift that could open new avenues for promoting physical activity in employees.

Glossary

Active transportation: The use of human-powered forms of travel such as walking, cycling, skating, skiing, and manual wheelchairs.

Aerobic capacity: The maximal capacity for oxygen consumption by the body during maximal exertion. Also known as VO2max.

Aerobic metabolism: A process occurring in the mitochondria that uses oxygen to produce energy (ATP). Also known as cellular respiration.

Cardiorespiratory endurance: The ability of the body to sustain prolonged exercise.

Hazard Control Hierarchy: A method to protect workers from injury that includes elimination, engineering (extra ventilation or isolation), warnings (displays, alarms, and lights), administrative (policies/procedures), and personal protective equipment (respirators, ear plugs, and gloves). Elimination of hazards should be accomplished, and if this cannot happen, the remaining steps should be followed in order with personal protective equipment as a last resort.

Light-intensity activity: Any physical activity more strenuous than sleeping and less strenuous than a brisk walk.

Metabolic syndrome: A group of risk factors that raises your risk for heart disease and other health problems, such as diabetes and stroke. You must have at least three metabolic risk factors to be diagnosed with metabolic syndrome. These risk factors include: abdominal obesity, high triglyceride level, low HDL cholesterol level, high blood pressure, and high fasting glucose level.

METs (Metabolic Equivalent of Tasks): A unit used to estimate the metabolic cost (oxygen consumption) of physical activity. One MET equals the resting metabolic rate of approximately 3.5 ml of O2 x kg-1 x min -1.

Muscular strength: The ability of a muscle to exert force.

Muscular endurance: The ability of a muscle to resist fatigue.

Musculoskeletal disorders: An injury of the muscles, tendons, ligaments, nerves, joints, cartilage, bones, or blood vessels in the arms, legs, head, neck, or back that is caused or aggravated by work tasks such as lifting, pushing, and pulling.

Moderate-intensity physical activity: On an absolute scale, physical activity that is done at 3.0 to 5.9 times the intensity of rest. On a scale relative to an individual's personal capacity, moderate-intensity physical activity is usually a 5 or 6 on a scale of 0 to 10.

Occupational injuries: An injury or illness is considered by the Occupational Safety and Health Administration to be work-related if an event or exposure in the work environment either caused or contributed to the resulting condition or significantly aggravated a pre-existing condition.

Perceived exertion: A subjective measure of how hard a person feels their body is working. It is based on the physical sensations a person experiences during physical activity, including increased heart rate, increased breathing rate, increased sweating, and muscle fatigue.

Social Cognitive Theory (SCT): Addresses both the psychosocial dynamics influencing health behavior and methods for promoting behavioral change. Within SCT, human behavior is explained in terms of behavior, personal factors (including cognitions), and environmental influences all interacting. The crucial personal factors are the individual's capabilities to symbolize behavior, to anticipate the outcomes of behavior, to self-regulate behavior, and to reflect on and analyze experience.

Sedentary: Doing or requiring much sitting; not physically active.

Self-Determination Theory (SDT): A broad framework for the study of human motivation and personality. SDT focuses on how social and cultural factors facilitate or undermine people's sense of volition and initiative, in addition to their well-being and the quality of their performance. Conditions supporting the individual's experience of autonomy, competence, and relatedness are argued to foster the most volitional and high quality forms of motivation and engagement for activities, including enhanced performance, persistence, and creativity.

Socio-ecological model: An approach to health promotion that offers a broad perspective to address public health challenges. The Socio-Ecological Model recognizes that public health challenges are too complex to be adequately understood and addressed from single level analyses, and this approach integrates multiple levels of influence. The levels of influence include intrapersonal (knowledge, beliefs, attitudes), interpersonal (family, friends, peer interactions), organizational (rules, regulations, and informal structures), community (social norms of a formal or informal group).

Vigorous-intensity physical activity: On an absolute scale, physical activity that is done at 6.0 or more times the intensity of rest. On a scale relative to an individual's personal capacity, vigorous-intensity physical activity is usually a 7 or 8 on a scale of 0 to 10.

Work hardening programs: An inter-disciplinary, individualized, job specific program of activity with the goal of returning to work. Work hardening programs use real or simulated work tasks and progressively graded conditioning exercises that are based on the individual's measured tolerances. Work hardening provides a transition between acute care and successful return to work and is designed to improve the biomechanical, neuromuscular, cardiovascular and psycho-social functioning of the worker.

Learning Objectives

After reading this chapter, the reader will be able to:

1. Describe the prevalence of physical activity in employed populations
2. Discern the difference between leisure- and work-related physical activity
3. Relate the health and financial benefits of physical activity to the worker and organization
4. Describe skill enhancement strategies that may be effective in their organization
5. Describe opportunity enhancement strategies that may be effective in their organization

Discussion Questions

1. Why has little attention been paid to work-related activity by worksite health promotion professionals?
2. What strategies could be most effective in your workplace to increase physical activity?
3. What strategies could be used to change the culture and make your workplace an active living workplace?

REFERENCES

1. *Physical activity and health: a report of the surgeon general.* Atlanta, GA: U.S. Department of Health and Human Services, Public Health Service, CDC, National Center for Chronic Disease Prevention and Health Promotion; 1996.

2. Centers for Disease Control and Prevention. Physical activity and health. Available at http://www.cdc.gov/physicalactivity/everyone/health/index.html. Accessed January 4, 2013.

3. Marcus BH, Simkin LR, Rossi JS, Pinto BM. Longitudinal shifts in employees' stages and processes of exercise behavior change. *Am J Health Promot.* 1996; 10(3):195–200.

4. McGinnis JM, Foege JM. Actual causes of death in the United States. *JAMA.* 1993; 270(18):2207–2212.

5. Linnan L, Bowling M, Childress J, et al. Results of the 2004 National Worksite Health Promotion Survey. *Am J Public Health.* 2008; 98(8):1503–1509.

6. Robergs RA, Roberts SO. *Exercise physiology: exercise, performance, and clinical applications.* St. Louis, MO: Mosby; 1997.

7. Bouchard C, Shephard RJ, Stephens T, eds. *Physical activity, fitness, and health. International proceedings and consensus statement.* Champaign, IL: Human Kinetics; 1994.

8. Collingwood TR. Fitness programs. In: O'Donnell MP, Harris JS, eds. *Health promotion in the workplace.* 2nd ed. Albany, NY: Delmar; 1994:240–270.

9. Wilmore JH, Costill DL. *Physiology of sport and exercise.* Champaign, IL: Human Kinetics; 1994.

10. Powell KE, Paluch AE, Blair SN. Physical activity for health: What kind? How much? How intense? On top of what? *Annu Rev Publ Health.* 2011; 32:349–365.

11. American College of Sports Medicine. *ACSM's Guidelines for Exercise Testing and Prescription.* 8th ed. Philadelphia: Lippincott, Williams, and Wilkins; 2009.

12. Karvonen M, Kentala E, Mustala O. The effects of training on heart rate; a longitudinal study. *Ann Med Exp Biol Fenn.* 1957;35(3):307–315.

13. Borg GAV. Psychophysical bases of physical exertion. *Med Sci Sport Exer.* 1982; 14:377–387.

14. Haskell WL, Lee I-M, Pate RR, et al. Physical activity and public health: updated recommendation for adults from the American College of Sports

Medicine and the American Heart Association. *Med Sci Sport Exer*. 2007; 39(8):1423–1434.

15.   Physical Activity Guidelines Committee. *Physical activity guidelines advisory committee report, 2008*. Washington, DC: U.S. Department of Health and Human Services; 2008.

16.   *2011 Behavioral Risk Factor Surveillance System Survey Data*. Atlanta, GA: Centers for Disease Control and Prevention; 2012.

17.   U.S. Department of Health and Human Services. Office of Disease Prevention and Health Promotion. Healthy People 2020. Washington, DC. Available at http://www.healthypeople.gov/2020/topicsobjectives2020/objectiveslist.aspx?topicId=33. Accessed January 3, 2013.

18.   Caban-Martinez AJ, Lee DJ, Fleming LE, et al. Leisure-time physical activity levels of the U.S. workforce. *Prev Med*. 2007;44(5):432–436.

19.   Church TS, Thomas DM, Tudor-Locke C, et al. Trends over 5 decades in U.S. occupation-related physical activity and their associations with obesity. *PLoS One*. 2011; 6(5): e19657. Available at doi:10.1371/journal.pone.0019657. Accessed January 4, 2013.

20.   Castillo-Retamal M, Hinckson EA. Measuring physical activity and sedentary behaviour at work: a review. *Work*. 2011; 40(4):345–357.

21.   Tudor-Locke C, Ainsworth BE, Washington TL, Troiano R. Assigning metabolic equivalent values to the 2002 census occupational classification system. *J Phys Act Health*. 2011; 8(4):581–586.

22.   Wolin KY, Bennett GG. Interrelations of socioeconomic position and occupational and leisure-time physical activity in the National Health and Nutrition Examination Survey. *J Phys Act Health*. 2008; 5(2):229–241.

23.   Kirk MA, Rhodes RE. Occupation correlates of adults' participation in leisure-time physical activity: a systematic review. *Am J Prev Med*. 2011; 40(4):476–485.

24.   Van Domelen DR, Koster A, Caserotti P, et al. Employment and physical activity in the U.S. *Am J Prev Med*. 2011; 41(2):136–145.

25.   Parry S, Straker L. The contribution of office work to sedentary behaviour associated risk. *BMC Public Health*. 2013; 13(1):296.

26.   McCrady SK, Levine JA. Sedentariness at work: how much do we really sit? *Obesity*. 2009; 17(11):2103–2105.

27.   Healy GN, Wijndaele K, Dunstan DW, et al. Objectively measured sedentary time, physical activity, and metabolic risk. *Diabetes Care*. 2008; 31(2):369–371.

28.   Healy GN, Dunstan DW, Salmon J, et al. Breaks in sedentary time. Beneficial associations with metabolic risk. *Diabetes Care*. 2008; 31(4):661–666.

29.   Shephard RJ. Worksite fitness and exercise programs: a review of methodology and health impact. *Am J Health Promot*. 1996; 10(6):436–452.

30.   Proper KI, Koning M, van der Beek AJ, Hildebrandt VH, Bosscher RJ, van Mechelen W. The effectiveness of worksite physical activity programs on physical activity, physical fitness, and health. *Clin J Sport Med*. 2003; 13(2):106–117.

31.   Conn VS, Hafdahl AR, Cooper PS, Brown LM, Lusk SL. Meta-analysis of workplace physical activity interventions. *Am J Prev Med*. 2009; 37(4):330–339.

32.   Conn VS, Hafdahl AR, Mehr DR. Interventions to increase physical activity among healthy adults: meta-analysis of outcomes. *Am J Public Health*. 2011; 101(4):751–758.

33.   Hutchinson AD, Wilson C. Improving nutrition and physical activity in

the workplace: a meta-analysis of intervention studies. *Health Promot Int.* 2012; 27(2):238–249.

34. Guide to Community Preventive Services. Environmental and policy approaches to increase physical actvity: creation of or enhanced access to places for physical activity combined with informational outreach activities. Available at: http://www.thecommunityguide.org/pa/environmental-policy/improvingaccess.html. Accessed August 2, 2012.

35. Powell KE, Thompson PD, Caspersen CJ, Kendrick JS. Physical activity and the incidence of coronary heart disease. *Annu Rev Publ Health.* 1987; 8:253–287.

36. Morris JN, Heady JA, Raffle PA, Roberts CG, Parks JW. Coronary heart-disease and physical activity of work. *Lancet.* 1953; 265(6796):1111–1120.

37. Morris JN, Heady JA. Mortality in relation to the physical activity of work: a preliminary note on experience in middle age. *Br J Ind Med.* 1953; 10(4):245–254.

38. Chapman JM, Goerke LS, Dixon W, Loveland DB, Phillips E. The clinical status of a population group in Los Angeles under observation for two to three years. *Am J Public Health.* 1957; 47:33–42.

39. Stamler J, Lindberg H, Berkson D, Shaffer A, Miller W, Poindexter A. Prevalence and incidence of coronary heart disease in strata of the labor force of a Chicago industrial corporation. *J Chronic Dis.* 1960; 11:405–420.

40. Kahn HA. The relationship of reported coronary heart disease mortality to physical activity of work. *Am J Public Health* 1963;53:1058–1067.

41. Fletcher JM, Sindelar JL, Yamaguchi S. Cumulative effects of job characteristics on health. *Health Econ.* 2011; 20(5):553–570.

42. Holtermann A, Hansen JV, Burr H, Sogaard K, Sjogaard G. The health paradox of occupational and leisure-time physical activity. *Br J Sports Med.* 2012; 46(4):291–295.

43. Castillo D, Pizatella T, Stout N. Injuries. In: Levy B, Wegman D, Baron S, Sokas R, eds. *Occupational and environmental health: recognizing and preventing disease and injury.* 5th ed. Philadelphia: Lippincott, Williams, and Wilkins; 2006:471–87.

44. Centers for Disease Control and Prevention. Motor Vehicle Safety. Available at: http://www.cdc.gov/niosh/topics/motorvehicle/. Accessed January 3, 2013.

45. Goetsch DL. *Occupational safety and health for technologists, engineers, and managers.* 5th ed. Columbus, OH: Pearson, Prentice Hall; 2005.

46. Rivilis I, Van Eerd D, Cullen K, et al. Effectiveness of participatory ergonomic interventions on health outcomes: a systematic review. *Appl Ergon.* 2008; 39(3):342–358.

47. Westgaard RH, Winkel J. Ergonomic intervention research for improved musculoskeletal health: A critical review. *Int J Ind Ergonom.* 1997; 20(6):463–500.

48. Barredo RDV, Mahon K. The effects of exercise and rest breaks on musculoskeletal discomfort during computer tasks: an evidence-based perspective. *J Phys Ther Sci.* 2007; 19(2):151–163.

49. Swanson N, Sauter S. The effects of exercise on the health and performance of data entry operators. In: Luczak C, ed. *Work with display units '92.* Amsterdam: Elsevier; 1993:288–291.

50. Van Poppel MN, Hooftman WE, Koes BW. An update of a systematic review of controlled clinical trials on the primary prevention of back pain at the workplace. *Occup Med.* 2004; 54(5):345–352.

51. Schonstein E, Kenny D, Keating J, Koes B, Herbert RD. Physical conditioning

programs for workers with back and neck pain: a cochrane systematic review. *Spine*. 2003; 28(19):E391–5.

52. Oesch P, Kool J, Hagen KB, Bachmann S. Effectiveness of exercise on work disability in patients with non-acute non-specific low back pain: Systematic review and meta-analysis of randomised controlled trials. *J Rehabil Med*. 2010; 42(3):193–205.

53. Schaafsma F, Schonstein E, Whelan KM, Ulvestad E, Kenny DT, Verbeek JH. Physical conditioning programs for improving work outcomes in workers with back pain. *Cochrane Database Syst Rev*. 2010; (1):CD001822.

54. Pransky GS, Benjamin KL, Savageau JA. Early retirement due to occupational injury: who is at risk? *Am J Ind Med*. 2005; 47(4):285–295.

55. Rueda S, Chambers L, Wilson M, et al. Association of returning to work with better health in working-aged adults: a systematic review. *Am J Public Health*. 2012; 102(3):541–556.

56. Pronk NP. Physical activity promotion in business and industry: evidence, context, and recommendations for a national plan. *J Phys Act Health*. 2009; 6:S220–S235.

57. Shepard R. Twelve years experience of a fitness program for the salaried employees of a toronto life assurance company. *Am J Health Promot*. 1992; 6(4):292–301.

58. Proper KI, Staal BJ, Hildebrandt VH, van der Beek AJ, van Mechelen W. Effectiveness of physical activity programs at worksites with respect to work-related outcomes. *Scand J Work Env Hea*. 2002; 28(2):75–84.

59. Von Thiele Schwarz U, Hasson H. Effects of worksite health interventions involving reduced work hours and physical exercise on sickness absence costs. *J Occup Environ Med*. 2012; 54(5):538–544.

60. Tuomi K, Vanhala S, Nykyri E, Janhonen M. Organizational practices, work demands and the well-being of employees: a follow-up study in the metal industry and retail trade. *Occup Med*. 2004; 54(2):115–121.

61. Pelletier KR. A review and analysis of the health and cost-effective outcome studies of comprehensive health promotion and disease prevention programs at the worksite: 1991-1993 update. *Am J Health Promot*. 1993; 8(1):50–62.

62. Pelletier KR. A review and analysis of the health and cost-effective outcome studies of comprehensive health promotion and disease prevention programs at the worksite: 1993-1995 update. *Am J Health Promot*. 1996; 10(5):380–388.

63. Pelletier KR. A review and analysis of the clinical and cost-effectiveness studies of comprehensive health promotion and disease management programs at the worksite: 1995-1998 update (IV). *Am J Health Promot*. 1999; 13(6):333–45.

64. Pelletier KR. A review and analysis of the clinical and cost-effectiveness studies of comprehensive health promotion and disease management programs at the worksite: 1998-2000 update. *Am J Health Promot*. 2001; 16(2):107–116.

65. Goetzel RZ, Shechter D, Ozminkowski RJ, Marmet PF, Tabrizi MJ, Roemer EC. Promising practices in employer health and productivity management efforts: findings from a benchmarking study. *J Occup Environ Med*. 2007; 49(2):111–130.

66. Terry PE, Seaverson ELD, Grossmeier J, Anderson DR. Association between nine quality components and superior worksite health management program results. *J Occup Environ Med*. 2008; 50(6):633–641.

67. Bishop JG, Aldana SG. *Step Up to Wellness: a stage-based approach.* Boston, MA: Allyn and Bacon; 1999.

68. Evans RE, Fawole HO, Sheriff SA, Dall PM, Grant PM, Ryan CG. Point-of-choice prompts to reduce sitting time at work: a randomized trial. *Am J Prev Med.* 2012; 43(3):293–297.

69. Crespo NC, Sallis JF, Conway TL, Saelens BE, Frank LD. Worksite physical activity policies and environments in relation to employee physical activity. *Am J Health Promot.* 2011; 25(4):264–271.

70. Marshall AL. Challenges and opportunities for promoting physical activity in the workplace. *J Sci Med Sport.* 2004; 7(1 Suppl):60–66.

71. Anderson LM, Quinn TA, Glanz K, et al. The effectiveness of worksite nutrition and physical activity interventions for controlling employee overweight and obesity: a systematic review. *Am J Prev Med.* 2009; 37(4):340–357.

72. Kwak L, Kremers SPJ, Van Baak MA, Brug J. A poster-based intervention to promote stair use in blue- and white-collar worksites. *Prev Med.* 2007; 45(2-3):177–181.

73. Yancey AK, Lewis LB, Sloane DC, et al. Leading by example: a local health department-community collaboration to incorporate physical activity into organizational practice. *J Public Health Manag Pract.* 2004; 10(2):116–123.

74. Lara A, Yancey AK, Tapia-Conye R, et al. Pausa para tu Salud: reduction of weight and waistlines by integrating exercise breaks into workplace organizational routine. *Prev Chronic Dis.* 2008; 5(1):A12.

75. Pronk NP, Kottke TE. Physical activity promotion as a strategic corporate priority to improve worker health and business performance. *Prev Med.* 2009; 49(4):316–321.

76. Sallis JF, Bauman A, Pratt M. Environmental and policy interventions to promote physical activity. *Am J Prev Med.* 1998; 15(4):379–397.

77. DeJoy DM, Della LJ, Vandenberg RJ, Wilson MG. Making work safer: testing a model of social exchange and safety management. *J Safety Res.* 2010; 41(2):163–71.

78. Duncan K, Pozehl B. Effects of an exercise adherence intervention on outcomes in patients with heart failure. *Rehabil Nurs.* 2003; 28(4):117–122.

79. Annesi JJ. Effects of computer feedback on adherence to exercise. *Percept Mot Skills.* 1998; 87(2):723–730.

80. Petosa RL, Suminski R, Hortz B. Predicting vigorous physical activity using social cognitive theory. *Am J Health Behav.* 2003; 27(4):301–310.

81. Jette AM, Lachman M, Giorgetti MM, et al. Exercise-it's never too late: the strong-for-life program. *Am J Public Health.* 1999; 89(1):66–72.

82. Marcus BH, Williams DM, Dubbert PM, et al. Physical activity intervention studies: what we know and what we need to know: a scientific statement from the American Heart Association Council on Nutrition, Physical Activity, and Metabolism (Subcommittee on Physical Activity); Council on Cardiovascular Disease in the Young; and the Inderdisciplinary Working Group on Quality of Care and Outcomes Research. *Circulation.* 2006; 114(24):2739–2752.

83. McAlpine DA, Manohar CU, McCrady SK, Hensrud D, Levine JA. An office-place stepping device to promote workplace physical activity. *Brit J Sport Med.* 2007; 41(12):903–907.

84. DeJoy DM, Schaffer BS, Wilson MG, Vandenberg RJ, Butts MM. Creating safer workplaces: assessing the determinants and role of safety climate. *J Safety Res.* 2004; 35(1):81–90.

85. Trial AR, Volpp KG, John LK, Troxel AB, Norton L, Fassbender J. Financial incentive–based approaches for weight loss. *JAMA*. 2008; 300(22): 2631–2637.

86. Volpp KG, Asch DA, Galvin R, Loewenstein G. Redesigning employee health incentives – lessons from behavioral economics. *New Engl J Med*. 2011; 365(5):388–390.

87. Sallis JF, Owen N, Fisher EB. Ecological models of health behavior. In: Glanz K, Rimer BK, Viswanath K, eds. *Health Behavior and Health Education. Theory, research, and practice*. 4th ed. San Francisco: Jossey-Bass; 2008:465–482.

CHAPTER

15

Worksite Nutrition Programs

Anastasia M. Snelling and Kristin Kirkpatrick

INTRODUCTION

The nutrient qualities of the foods we eat have a profound impact on our lifetime risk of developing health conditions such as hypertension, hypercholesterolemia, cancer, heart disease, diabetes, obesity, and overall mortality. Worksite nutrition programs can educate employees regarding healthy food and lifestyle choices, and can support behavior changes at both the individual and the family level. Worksite nutrition programs have been shown to help increase fruit and vegetable consumption,[1] increase awareness or knowledge of healthy eating habits,[2] provide short-term improvements in body weight[3] and decrease health care costs.[4]

This chapter discusses the components of effective worksite nutrition education strategies, the variability of worksite nutrition education programs, and research findings of worksite nutrition education program evaluations. (Weight control programs are discussed in depth in Chapter 17.) Chapter sections summarize current nutrition guidelines and their relationship to chronic disease, identify current practice and research on

nutrition programs at the worksite, provide the theoretical foundations for worksite nutrition programs, and describe various types of worksite nutrition programs. This chapter aims to stimulate creative applications and advances in worksite nutrition education practice and research. Improved food consumption in working populations requires building on and extending past efforts in this area.

NUTRITION AND HEALTH: IMPACT OF NUTRITION ON HEALTH

An estimated 80% of chronic diseases are caused by people's personal behaviors. These include tobacco and alcohol use, unhealthy diet choices, lack of physical activity and poor management of chronic psychological stress. Further, 75% of health care costs are due to chronic diseases.[5,6] Although much remains to be learned about the role of specific nutrients in decreasing the risk of chronic disease and achieving optimal health, a large body of evidence supports the health enhancing value of diets composed of whole-grains, legumes, vegetables and fruits, and a limited consumption of refined starches, red meat, full-fat dairy products, and foods and beverages high in added sugars and salt. Such diets have been associated with decreased risk of a variety of chronic diseases.[7]

Despite the documented health benefits of a nutritious diet, many Americans have poor dietary habits and consume excess calories, which leads to obesity and an increased risk of several chronic diseases. Obesity rates have more than doubled in the past 30 years,[8] increasing the rates of obesity-associated chronic conditions that lead to rising health care costs. More than one-third of Americans are obese.[9] In 2008, medical costs associated with obesity were estimated at $147 billion; medical costs for people who are obese were $1,429 higher than those of normal weight.[10] Several trends may explain this dramatic increase in obesity levels, including decreases in physical activity levels, increases in the availability of quick, processed food options, and increases in portion size. If these trends continue, almost half of all Americans are projected to be obese by the year 2030.[11] Nutrient-related obesity and the associated chronic diseases have high personal and social costs, reducing quality of life and work productivity while increasing health care costs, premature disability, and death.

In the United States and many other industrially developed countries, programs to promote healthful dietary patterns have become public health priorities. This is because five of ten leading causes of death (coronary heart disease, kidney diseases, cancer, stroke, and adult-onset diabetes) are nutrition related see Table 15-1.[12] If we include alcohol consumption as a dietary behavior, then accidents, suicide, and cirrhosis of the liver would also be counted among the leading causes of death that could be prevented by dietary change.

Major conclusions from rapidly evolving laboratory, clinical, and epidemiological research linking diet to major chronic diseases are reviewed below. Advances in molecular biology and an expansion in the number of very large epidemiological studies of diet and disease are producing a steady stream of new, and often unexpected, findings. With increased news coverage on health studies, many new findings receive immediate, exaggerated attention, without the benefit of additional years or decades of follow-up research to confirm or refute their accuracy. Thus, the first half of this chapter focuses on associations between diet and disease for which there is *substantial agreement* among nutritional scientists, clinicians, and public health officials.

Table 15-1: Number of Deaths For Leading Causes of Death, 2010 Final Data.

Heart Disease	597,689
Cancer	574,743
Chronic lower respiratory diseases	138,080
Stroke (cerebrovascular diseases)	129,476
Accidents (unintentional injuries)	120,859
Alzheimer's disease	83,494
Diabetes	69,071
Nephritis, nephrotic syndrome, and nephrosis	50,476
Influenza and Pneumonia	50,097
Intentional self-harm (suicide)	38,364

Source: National Center for Health Statistics.

Cardiovascular Disease

The direct relationship between diet and cardiovascular disease is well documented. Evidence demonstrates higher levels of risk for cardiovascular disease and stroke with several diet-related chronic conditions such as hyperlipidemia, diabetes, hypertension and metabolic syndrome. Dietary factors directly affecting risk include the type of fat consumed in the diet - specifically saturated fat, as well as the amount of sodium, refined carbohydrates and overall calories. One study found that replacing saturated fats with polyunsaturated fats was protective against the risk of heart disease.[12] Consumption of omega 3 fatty acids through fatty fish as opposed to supplementation,[13] and adherence to a Mediterranean diet, rich in fruits, vegetables, whole grains and moderate consumption of alcohol[14] both appear to be protective. Plant-based omega 3 fatty acid consumption has also been associated with a decreased risk of sudden cardiac death.[15] Plant based sources of omega 3 alpha Linolenic Acid include walnuts, soybeans and flaxseed.

A high sodium diet, primarily from processed food, is associated with an increased risk for heart disease and stroke.[16] Further, over-consumption of sugar[17] and artificial sweeteners[18] appears to increase the risk for vascular events.

Cancers

Cancer is a leading cause of death worldwide, accounting for 7.6 million deaths (around 13% of all deaths) in 2008. Lung, stomach, liver, colon and breast cancers cause the most cancer deaths each year.[19] Although genetic and environmental factors account for many cancers, diet plays a large role in the development of cancer. The most consistent finding, for many cancers, is the protective effect of vegetables, especially non-starchy leafy greens and cruciferous vegetables such as broccoli, cauliflower, brussel sprouts and kale. High intake of leafy vegetables,[20] as well

as carotenoid rich foods such as carrots, sweet potatoes and tomatoes,[21] can reduce the risk of cancer. Additionally, though still controversial, an overwhelming body of evidence shows that whole sources of soy in the diet can lead to a reduction in breast cancer risk as well.[22] Foods high in fiber such as whole grains, fruits and vegetables are associated with a decreased risk of prostate,[23] colon[24] and esophageal cancers.[25] Additionally, recent evidence suggests that diets high in saturated fats such as red meat and processed meats[26] increase the risk of pancreatic cancer and mortality from cancer.[27] Evidence also links fried foods to increased risk of prostate cancer.[28] Finally, current research on alcohol consumption suggests that risk of specific cancers such as breast[29] and endometrial cancers[30] may be more closely tied to consumption amounts than previously thought. The U.S. Dietary Guidelines for Americans 2010,[31] list as well as the American Cancer Society[32] recommends no more than one drink per day for women or two drinks per day for men.[31]

Obesity

Obesity is defined as weight that is greater than what is generally considered healthy for a given height.[33] Adult obesity rates have grown from 15 percent in 1980 to 34 percent in 2008[33] and remain one of the most critical current public health problems. Obesity is a complex condition but is ultimately the result of chronic excess energy intake. Maintaining a balance between energy intake and expenditure can be difficult for person's leading sedentary lifestyles, especially given the ready availability of low price, processed, high-calorie foods. However, recent studies have shown that many factors beyond energy intake and expenditure are to blame for the current obesity epidemic. Diets high in fruits, vegetables, whole grains, and lean sources of protein are associated with better adherence of maintaining a healthy weight.[34] Further, low carbohydrate diets have also been shown to be just as effective as low fat diets,[35] which has historically been a popular weight loss choice. However, current research indicates that general over-consumption of calories may be more to blame than the source of these calories from specific macronutrients.[36] Americans are eating more of their calories away from home, a factor that researchers believe may be significantly increasing the risk of obesity.[37] This is especially true with the increased availability of fast food.[38] Additionally, over consumption of sweetened beverages is associated with an increase in pediatric obesity[39] and increased consumption of artificial sweeteners is associated with an increased risk of weight gain.[40]

As for most other associations between diet and disease, there is considerable variability across individuals in their susceptibility to obesity. However, it is clear that once a person becomes obese, it is very difficult to lose weight and maintain significant weight loss. Weight loss has been associated with both the prevention of certain chronic conditions such as hypertension and may even play a role in the reversal of conditions such as diabetes and hyperlipidemia.[41] Thus, prevention of obesity is a diet-related goal appropriate for everyone.

Diabetes

The prevalence of diabetes in the United States has dramatically increased in the past 20 years and researchers believe that if trends continue, 1 in 3 adult Americans will have diabetes by 2050.[42] The most recent Centers for Disease Control survey indicates that 25.8 million people in the United States have diabetes, accounting for 8.3% of the population. Of these, an estimated 7 million individuals are undiagnosed.[43] Diet composition, weight management and physical activity levels play critical roles in both the prevention and management of diabetes.[44] The Diabetes Prevention Program (DPP), a large prevention study of people at high risk for diabetes, showed that lifestyle interventions that focus on weight loss and increasing physical activity reduced the likelihood of developing type 2 diabetes by 58% during a 3-year period. The reduction was even greater (71%,) among adults aged 60 years or older.[45,46] From a dietary perspective, tight blood glucose control is critical to the management of both type 1 and type 2 diabetes. The Mediterranean diet appeared to be consistently effective for preventing diabetes, as well as useful in the management of the disease,[47] due to its high intake of legumes,[48] fruits, vegetables and whole grains.[49] Typical foods in the Mediterranean diet may also play a role in decreasing risk for cardiovascular disease and certain types of cancer.

Osteoporosis

Osteoporosis is a weakening of the bones that may cause bones to be brittle and break easily. This disease mainly affects post-menopausal women but can impact men as well. Individuals' risk of osteoporosis may be caused by a variety of factors, including excess weight, insufficient exercise, cigarette smoking and estrogen use.[50] Many measures to reduce osteoporosis risk are diet related, however, nutrient intake must be accompanied by physical activity.[51] Inadequate calcium and vitamin D intake may be risk factors for osteoporosis. The best sources of calcium in the diet include low or non-fat dairy products such as milk, yogurt and cottage cheese. Calcium can also be consumed through plant-based food including broccoli, collard greens, soy milk[52] and legumes. Vitamin D is needed for proper absorption of calcium and is best obtained through sun exposure; in addition, foods high in vitamin D include fatty fish,[53] low fat milk, fortified cereals and eggs. Further evidence is needed to determine if Vitamin D or calcium from dietary supplements helps reduce the overall risk of osteoporosis.[54]

Other Diet-Related Concerns for Working Adults

For working adults and their families, food consumption patterns should be a more general concern for a variety of reasons. For example, for women of childbearing age, optimal nutrition plays a role in both fertility and pregnancy outcomes. Dental health, child growth and development, and even surgical outcomes can be affected by diet and nutritional status. Food safety, whereby some infectious diseases may be avoided, can also contribute to overall health. Finally, dietary patterns are an integral part of one's culture, shared meals are a method of social cohesion, and food can provide great pleasure.

Economic Consequences of Nutrition-Related Disease

The United States spends more for health care than any other country[55,56] with cardiovascular disease, cancer and diabetes accounting for 75% of these costs.[57] Further, experts believe that while 16% of the U.S. GDP in 2005 was spent on health care, more than 20% will be spent in 2015 if trends continue.[58]

There are substantial economic consequences, both to individuals and to society at large, from poor dietary practices. For individuals, socio-economic level, education, and access to medical care can influence food choices and development of chronic conditions. For employers, consequences of employees' poor dietary practices include absenteeism, reduced productivity, disability, and high health care utilization. While it is difficult to calculate the exact proportion of disease that is attributable to poor dietary practices, the total economic costs of diet-related diseases are enormous. See Tables 15-2 and 15-3.[59,60] America spends $150 million annually on healthcare linked to obesity.[59] Additionally, productivity losses related to personal and family health problems cost U.S. employers $1,685 per employee per year, or $225.8 billion annually.[60]

GUIDELINES FOR HEALTHY EATING PATTERNS

Developing dietary guidelines can be controversial. This is especially true when scientific data are inconclusive or when significant economic interests are at stake. Governmental agencies, professional and scientific organizations, and voluntary health organizations have all developed and communicated recommendations and guidelines for healthful diets.

Since the early 1900s, the government has produced a food guide to translate scientific guidelines into an educational tool for the general public. The food guide, developed by the United States Department of Agriculture (USDA), has changed over the decades to reflect the changing food supply in the United States. In 2010, USDA introduced the Myplate icon.[61] MyPlate is divided into sections of approximately 30 percent grains, 30 percent vegetables, 20 percent fruits and 20 percent protein, accompanied by a smaller circle representing dairy. These guidelines are recommended for the general adult population. See Figure 15-1.

To develop dietary guidelines that are linked to the prevention and management of chronic conditions, expert panels convened by the U.S. Departments of Agriculture and Health and Human Services achieved consensus around seven overarching recommendations in "Nutrition and Your Health: Dietary Guidelines for Americans'.[62] First developed in 1980 and revised every five years, these guidelines provide consistent, current and comprehensible messages to educate the public about nutrition and health.[62] These guidelines provides the public with the connection of specific nutrients with chronic conditions. The ten guidelines, and details about each recommendation, are listed in Table 15-4.[62]

A third nutrition education tool, the Nutrition Facts on food labels, incorporates the Dietary Guidelines and the myplate icon

Table 15-2: Estimated Direct and Indirect Costs of Major Cardiovascular Diseases, United States, 2010.

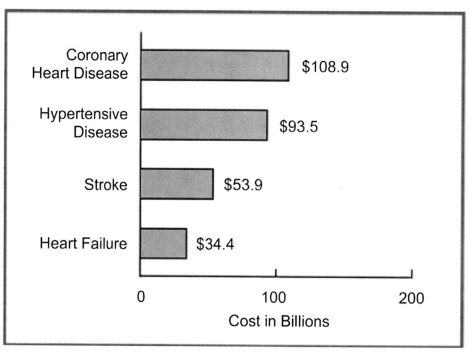

Source: Heldenrelch PA, Trogdon JG, Khavjou OA, Butler J, Dracup K, Ezekowitz MD, et al. Forecasting the future of cardiovascular disease in the United States: a policy statement from the American Heart Association. *Circulation* 2011;123(8):933–944.

Table 15-3: Snapshot of Obesity-Related Costs.

Country	Obesity-Related Costs (% of total spending on health care)	Publication Year
Brazil	3.0–5.8	2007
China	3.4	2008
Canada	2.9	2001
France	0.7–1.5	2000
Japan	3.2	2007
Sweden	2.3	2005
U.S.	20.6	2012

Source: Cawley J, Meyerhoefer C. The medical care costs of obesity: an instrumental variables approach. *J Health Econ.* 2012; 31:219-30;
Withrow D, Alter DA. The economic burden of obesity worldwide: a systematic review of the direct costs of obesity. *Obes Rev.* 2010. DOI: 10.1111/j.1467-789X.2009.00712.x.

Figure 15-1: Dietary Guidelines for Americans.

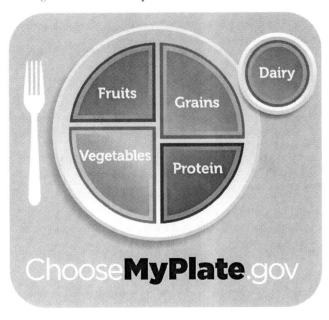

See Figure 15-1[61] messages in relationship to a specific food and its ingredients.[63]

The concepts below can guide the development of worksite nutrition programs.

- Address important and well-established dietary risk factors from major diseases
- Be generally applicable to healthy adults and be prepared to engage licensed dietitians and nutritionists who prescribe specific diets for diabetes or cardiovascular disease
- Be consistent with cultural norms of employee population(s)
- Avoid popular fads and extreme scientific viewpoints
- Be feasible for worksite implementation
- Provide knowledge and education that is consistent with the foods available at the worksite

To effectively address the leading causes of chronic conditions, the following areas are the most important for worksite health promotion:

- Weight management (covered in Chapter 17)
- Reduction in total fat, saturated fat, and cholesterol
- Reduction of salt and sodium
- Reduction in refined grains
- Reduction of foods with added sugars or minimal nutrient density
- Increase in consumption of fresh fruits, vegetables, legumes, healthy fats, whole grains and lean sources of protein
- Increase in calcium consumption

Current Diet Trends

Some progress has been made in the past few decades toward improving the *quality* of the U.S. diet. These include increases in the availability of fresh fruit and vegetables and food choices with whole grains, lower-fat or sugar content, and the elimination of trans-fats in foods.[64]

Table 15-4: Dietary Guidelines for Americans: Foods and nutrients to increase.

Individuals should meet the following recommendations as part of a healthy eating pattern while staying within their calorie needs.
1. Increase vegetable and fruit intake.
2. Eat a variety of vegetables, especially dark-green and red and orange vegetables and beans and peas.
3. Consume at least half of all grains as whole grains. Increase whole-grain intake by replacing refined grains with whole grains.
4. Increase intake of fat-free or low-fat milk and milk products, such as milk, yogurt, cheese, or fortified soy beverages.[6]
5. Choose a variety of protein foods, which include seafood, lean meat and poultry, eggs, beans and peas, soy products, and unsalted nuts and seeds.
6. Increase the amount and variety of seafood consumed by choosing seafood in place of some meat and poultry.
7. Replace protein foods that are higher in solid fats with choices that are lower in solid fats and calories and/or are sources of oils.
8. Use oils to replace solid fats where possible.
9. Choose foods that provide more potassium, dietary fiber, calcium, and vitamin D, which are nutrients of concern in American diets. These foods include vegetables, fruits, whole grains, and milk and milk products.

Other positive changes are the labeling of trans-fats,[65] and menu labeling[66] at some chain restaurants. However, negative changes to the food environment include increases in foods that are categorized as minimal-nutrient dense foods, and increases in foods that are higher in sugar, fat, and sodium content in relationship to the overall caloric content.[67]

The average energy intake was 2,504 kilocalories (kcals) for men and 1,771 kcals for women in 2007-2008. These levels have remained relatively stable for the past decade. The average carbohydrate intake was 47.9% of total kilocalories (% kcals) for men and 50.5% for women while fat intake was 33.6% and 33.5% of total kcals for men and women, respectively.[68]

In 2009, an estimated 32.5% of U.S. adults consumed the recommended amount of fruits (3-5 servings per day) and 26.3% of adults consumed the recommended amount of vegetables (2-4 servings per day). This has remained relatively unchanged over the past decade.[69]

The most alarming nutrition-related change in health of the U.S. population has been the profound increase in obesity, which is considered a risk factor for cardiovascular disease, certain cancers, and diabetes. Weight status is based on body mass index (BMI). Overweight is defined as a BMI of 25-29.9 and obesity is defined as a BMI of 30 or higher. Obesity rates increased from 22.9 in 1988-1994 to 30.5% in 1999-2000. The prevalence of overweight also increased during the same period from 55.9% to 64.5%.[70] The reasons for this marked rise are complex and multidimensional, but certainly involve both increased total energy intake and decreased physical activity. (Chapter 17 explores obesity and these factors in more detail.)

Since the early 1990s, more attention has been given to developing the programs and infrastructure required to promote healthful dietary change. Early examples of social marketing campaigns include the "5 A Day for Better Health" program, a large, national effort to promote increased consumption of fruits and vegetables,[71] the development and dissemination of such nutrition education materials as the my plate icon, Dietary Guidelines for Americans, and the Nutrition Facts food label.[61-63] As part of a broad program to improve public health overall, the Healthy People 2020 Objectives identify specific goals for nutrition education at the worksite. These objectives state that worksite nutrition and physical activity programs should be designed to improve health-related behaviors and health outcomes. An associated developmental goal is to increase the proportion of worksites that offer "nutrition or weight management" classes or counseling. Worksite nutrition education programs are becoming more commonplace; in 2004 22.7% of worksites surveyed in a national survey program reported offering nutrition education programs and 21.4% offered a weight management program.[72]

Worksite nutrition intervention programs should follow established health and nutrition guidelines and reflect an accurate and timely understanding of the social and economic trends that affect employees' food choices and other diet-related behavior. Food choices and eating are very complex behaviors with multiple drivers, including, but not limited to, convenience, cost, taste, availability, and nutrition. A trend that influences food choices and calorie consumption is the number of meals consumed outside the home. On average, 41% of the typical U.S. household food budget is now allocated to food obtained away from home (an increase from 25% in 1970).[73] The percentage of daily energy obtained from

home-prepared foods decreased from 77% in the late 1970s to about 65% in the mid-1990s. Forty percent of individuals consume at least three meals away from home each week and 40% consume four or fewer meals at home each week.[73]

Worksites, schools, restaurants (including fast food), and supermarkets all provide a variety of meals to consumers. Unfortunately, food served in restaurants tends to be higher in sugar, fat, and sodium and lower in fruits, vegetables, and whole grains. Fortunately, the food industry has developed a small market of products that do conform to healthful dietary guidelines, especially in terms of containing less total fat and saturated fat. In addition, the new Nutrition Facts food labels make it easier for consumers to compare across brands and types of convenience foods. This helps them be able to choose foods with superior nutritional characteristics. This is one area in which worksite nutrition programs can directly affect the quality of their employees' diets: by making available tasty and convenient meals and snacks that are consistent with healthful dietary guidelines in employee cafeterias, vending machines and work-sponsored meals.

THEORETICAL FOUNDATIONS FOR WORKSITE NUTRITION PROGRAMS

While many early reports of worksite nutrition interventions did not cite a particular theory or model as the basis for the strategies they employed, the application of sound behavioral science theory in worksite nutrition programs is becoming increasingly common practice.[74-76] In fact, intervention research conducted in occupational settings has been a major force in advancing understanding of the theoretical foundations for dietary behavior and of methods to measure relevant theoretical constructs.[77-86] Successful nutrition intervention programs have evolved to reflect these approaches over the past several decades.

Worksite nutrition programs that employ an ecological perspective for health promotion are more likely to be effective.[87-88] Nutrition interventions should not only target individual factors, but should also affect organizational and environmental factors that influence dietary behavior.[89] In the 1980s and 1990s, worksite nutrition education programs focused heavily on the individual person using a traditional face-to-face model emphasizing nutrition knowledge; more recently there is a focus on organizational and environmental approaches to reach a broader audience.

Several behavior change theories are particularly useful for explaining the processes of changing eating patterns in worksite settings: Social Cognitive Theory, the Transtheoretical Model, the Health Belief Model and the Social Ecological Model. The central elements of each theory and how they can be used to formulate worksite nutrition programs are described below.

Social Cognitive Theory

The principles of Social Cognitive Theory, Bandura's contemporary version of the social learning theory, postulate that there are dynamic relationships among personal factors, the social and physical environments, and behavior.[90] The key social cognitive theory construct of reciprocal determinism means that a person can be both an agent for change and a respondent to change. Thus, changes in the environment, examples of role models, and reinforcements can be manipulated to promote healthier behavior. Also, self-efficacy, or a person's self-confidence about the ability to successfully carry out a behavior even when faced with challenges,[91] can be improved through program activities that incorporate goal setting, feedback, external rewards, and self-reward.[92] Skill-building activities such as cooking demonstrations, problem-solving discussions, reading food labels, and self-monitoring are rooted in Social Cognitive

Theory. (See Chapter 11 for more details on self-efficacy.)

One skill that warrants more attention in worksite nutrition education programs is the skill of food selection, which is becoming more challenging as front-of-the-package marketing and labeling is increasing. The Food and Drug Administration regulates the Nutrition Facts panel required on all food products. This information is standardized across all foods to provide shoppers with a quick and easy way to compare similar products. More recently, marketing changes are resulting in front-of-the-package labeling that includes messages from the food manufacturer, the food stores' own icon that labels healthy items, or other associations that endorse products that follow different guidelines. Food manufacturing labels might include messages such as Cheerios' claim about lowering cholesterol, or Safeway's "Simple Nutrition Labeling" system based on select government guidelines, or the American Heart Association "check" that endorses products that are lower in saturated fat, fat, and sodium. Other skills, such as selecting foods at restaurants or food preparation, can be readily incorporated in worksite nutrition programs. This type of education provides employees practical nutrition information tailored to their lifestyles. Several recent large worksite nutrition programs have applied constructs from social cognitive theory to their programs, including self-regulation, self-efficacy, outcome expectations, and social support.[93-95]

Transtheoretical Model of Behavior Change

The Transtheoretical Model of Behavior Change (TTM) can be helpful in designing, delivering, and evaluating interventions to help employees adopt more healthful diets. An important element within the TTM is the stages of change construct, a heuristic model that describes a sequence of steps in successful behavior change: precontemplation (no intention to change); contemplation (thinking about changing); preparation (planning for change); action (adopting new habits); and maintenance (ongoing practice of new, healthier behavior).[96] The stages of change construct suggest that interventions should be designed to match employees' state of readiness to change. Beyond the stage of change construct, other constructs within the TTM are the processes of change, decisional balance, temptation, and self-efficacy. (See Chapter 9 for a detailed discussion on the Transtheoretical Model of Behavior Change.)

Over the past fifteen years, there has been a substantial increase in research applying the stages of change model to dietary behavior.[97] The stages of change algorithms have been validated for fruit and vegetable consumption, dietary fat, fiber, and calcium consumption. Population studies rely most on the stages of change construct, however decisional balance, self-efficacy, and process of change have all been studied. Research using a stage-based dietary intervention appears to support a stage-based approach to improving dietary behaviors. This research has been done primarily using fruit and vegetable consumption and to a lesser extent on other nutrition behaviors.

Health Belief Model

Developed approximately sixty years ago, the Health Belief Model (HBM) was an attempt by social psychologists at the United States Public Health Service to better understand a widespread reluctance of people to access disease prevention services.[98] The HBM is described as a value-expectancy theory because it suggests that behavior results from an individual's *value* of the outcome of the behavior and the *expectation* that a particular action or actions will lead to the outcome. The constructs within the HBM are perceived susceptibility, severity, benefits and barriers, self-efficacy, and cues to action. Many worksite programs begin with identifying health risks through a health risk appraisal instrument

then refer individuals to educational programs based on these risks. This approach aligns with this model by first identifying risks and the perceived severity, benefits, and barriers to behavior change. Studies have demonstrated that by implementing programs based on the HBM, positive nutrition changes were made to target cardiovascular disease and cancer risks.[99-100]

Social Ecological Model

The Social Ecological Theory of Planning is based on the interrelationships of human beings and their environments,[101] recognizing that within the environment there are physical, social, economic, and cultural forces that have the potential to alter health outcomes. The environment is important, but not to the exclusion of the individual. This theory includes the individual attributes such as genetics, behaviors, and knowledge; other social and environmental factors are also acknowledged in the theory, such as environmental settings, sectors of influence, and norms and cultures within society. The Social Ecological Theory has made an important contribution to the field of health promotion, particularly in regards to the design of interventions to improve health behaviors. No longer are programs designed only with the individual in mind; program planners must assess other factors in the work environment that may either hinder or facilitate the behavior change process.

Measurement of Nutrition Behaviors

Nutrition behaviors are a complex set of behaviors. It can be challenging to measure the degree to which an intervention is having its intended outcome(s). There are several different approaches to measuring nutrition behavior, including observations, purchase or sales records, food diaries, food surveys, apps, or 24-hour recalls. Selecting the appropriate method for the nutrition education intervention will depend on personnel as well as other resources. First, program planners should identify what nutrient or food item the program is targeting to change, for example if the program seeks to increase fruit and vegetable consumption, selecting an app or food survey that only collects data on fruit and vegetables is a good approach. However, if the program seeks to change overall nutrient consumption, a food diary or 24-hour recall would be recommended. Regardless of the method selected, each has its limitations. One major limitation to most of these methods is the issue of self-report. Other limitations include personnel time, training for some methods such as conducting a 24-hour recall, use of validated instruments, and analyzing nutrient consumption for example when using a food analysis program. Measuring the food or nutrient change as a result of an intervention can provide evidence of the impact of the nutrition education program.

WORKSITE NUTRITION PROGRAMS

Skill Enhancement Strategies

Theory and research suggest that the most effective worksite health promotion programs are those that use multiple strategies and aim to achieve multiple levels of awareness, information transmission, skill development, and supportive environments and policies.[102] Programs differ based on the goals and objectives of the organization and the available personnel and financial resources dedicated to the program. Typically, nutrition programs are implemented as part of a broader, multicomponent and multiple-focus worksite health promotion program, often paired with physical activity interventions.

Over the past few decades, much has changed in the way worksite nutrition programs are delivered, yet little has changed in the *content* of the nutrition education messages. Programs have evolved to incorporate new social media outlets when delivering program

content and there is a growing emphasis on environmental changes and the use of multiple program elements (i.e. counseling, exercise, social support, health screenings). Amidst these changes, nutrition education content has stayed relatively stable, with an emphasis on increasing the consumption of fruits and vegetables while decreasing fat, saturated fat, simple sugar, and sodium.

The majority of published evaluations of worksite nutrition programs examine four types of interventions: group education, group education with individual counseling, environmental-based programs, and group education combined with environmental supports.[88] Across these types of programs, certain emerging issues and trends warrant consideration. These issues relate to choices regarding the approach to worksite nutrition interventions and contrast "traditional" methodologies with more innovative models. These approaches, described below, focus on building skills and knowledge to improve food choices, and creating opportunities within the environment to make it easier for employees to make healthy choices.

Individual approaches to worksite nutrition programs were among some of the first nutritional interventions introduced in the worksite and were by far the most common during the 1990s. These programs focused primarily on individuals at high risk for nutrition-related health problems, or on self-selected groups of motivated and interested people. These approaches tended to employ intensive interventions, including screening, individual counseling, and classes, often involving medical personnel.

More recently, there is recognition that worksite nutrition programs should be more broad, targeting all employees. With this shift, many worksite health promotion programs include health screenings and the use of health risk appraisals to identify each individual's health portfolio. Screenings often include blood pressure, body mass index (measuring height and weight), cholesterol screening and education/counseling efforts. Financial incentives linked to these screenings are often used to increase levels of employee participation.[103]

The primary health focus of many worksite nutrition education programs (after weight management) is cardiovascular risk reduction.[104-105] Program components include increasing nutrition knowledge, behavioral skills, goal setting, self-monitoring, cooking demonstrations, and social support. Although the program components are similar to prior decades, different strategies are implemented to focus on reducing cardiovascular risk factors. Levin et al (2010)[106] placed participants on a low-fat vegan diet and provided weekly dietary instruction and group support whereas Thorndike et al (2011)[105] used a competition-based approach that included both nutrition guidance and a pedometer program. More studies report using a behavioral focus on diet and exercise that is consistent with the message that healthy eating and regular exercise work synergistically to reduce cardiovascular risk.[104-106]

Another approach to delivering skill-enhancing interventions is through a web-based platform. Web-based interventions have expanded the available venues for providing nutrition education interventions. Franklin et al (2006),[107] used an email-only intervention to increase physical activity and fruit and vegetable consumption. Results indicate that sustained participation document the feasibility, broad reach, employee acceptance, and potential value of using electronic communications for health promotion in the workplace. Another study demonstrated the impact of an email worksite nutrition intervention that showed modest, yet significant improvement in stages of change and fruit and vegetable consumption.[107] The program delivers messages weekly to participants' emails and included nutrition information, dietary tips tailored to the individual, and goal setting

strategies. Although still in the infancy phase of design, implementation and evaluation, using emails to reach employee populations has great potential especially due to the increase in the number of workers who telecommute. Further, email interventions may offer an opportunity to reach dependents.

Opportunity-Enhancement Interventions

To complement the individual-based interventions, opportunity-enhancement or environmental approaches are becoming recognized as key components to effectively changing health behavior. Since the dietary behavior of employees is determined by conscious choices and unconscious processes, changing the employees' physical environment has the potential to influence both conscious and unconscious behaviors and habits that lead to improved nutrition choices.[108] Less intensive but broader-reaching programs can achieve small and large changes in a wide audience and thus result in broader population impact. The environmental and organizational context is also important in shaping, maintaining, and reinforcing individual change. Modification of cafeterias, dining facilities, catered lunches, and vending services, along with other supportive policies and incentives, are increasingly a focus of programs to encourage healthy eating patterns.[109-112] Collectively, these strategies are aimed at reducing barriers or increasing opportunities for healthy choices, making healthy choices more accessible and restricting the number of unhealthy choices.

Three general types of nutrition policy and environmental interventions can be implemented in the workplace: food access strategies (improving the healthfulness of available foods, decreasing the number of unhealthy products, establishing healthy catering policies), nutrition information policy and strategies (food labeling, point-of-choice nutrition information), and economic strategies (incentives, pricing to encourage healthy choices).[109-112] A key feature of each of these interventions is the potential to reach all employees at the point of purchase or at the time of selection. This approach is consistent with Edington (2010)[113] who recommends that programs focus not just on the high-risk pool but on promoting the health of all employees.

Food access strategies increase the availability of nutritious foods in cafeterias and vending machines, use recipe modifications to improve the composition of foods that are already available, or establish policy guidelines for foods served at company functions (i.e., catering policies). Point-of-choice programs provide nutrition information to individuals at the point of food selection or purchase, thereby increasing awareness and prompting people to select more healthful foods.[114-116]

The Affordable Care Act now requires that certain chain restaurants and similar retail food establishments with 20 or more locations disclose certain nutrient information for standard menu items.[117] They are required to list calories, fat content, and sodium levels of menu items at the point of purchase. One study evaluated the real-life impact of menu labeling after new regulations were implemented and found some improvement, although most entrées continue to exceed recommended nutritional guidelines.[118] Although the impact of menu labeling has not been evaluated at the worksite as an intervention to improve the consumption of healthy foods, this federal action may lead the way for nutrient information to become more available at other places where food is purchased, such as a company cafeteria.

Many large organizations outsource their food service to management companies and have little or no involvement in the selection. Health promotion professionals need to be involved in selecting a food service provider that is aware of and committed to providing healthful nutrition options. Some food service providers have begun to make healthier options more available to employees, however, employers should drive this movement and continue to develop the scope and variety of healthier food offerings to the employees.

Economic strategies that reduce the prices of healthier choices compared to unhealthy products have been evaluated as an environmental approach. Price changes can be applied in company cafeterias or vending machines. Kottke et al (2013)[119] reduced the price of salad bar by 50% for one month and used sales data to measure the effect. Using sales data to detect changes in salad bar sales as a result of the price change indicated that salad bar sales increased by 366%. The data suggests that efforts to increase salad bar consumption by reducing price may be an effective strategy. French (2010)[120] applied a price change to food choices available in vending machines by decreasing the cost of low-fat items by 10%, 25%, and 50%. This study reported a significant increase in lower-fat snack sales as a result of the price reduction. Further, as the prices were reduced, the percentage of lower-fat snack sales increased. Both studies suggest that decreasing the cost of healthy food options appears to promote consumption of these foods.

THE IMPACT OF WORKSITE NUTRITION PROGRAMS

Information about the impact of worksite nutrition programs is increasingly available from large field trials that address nutrition and other risk factors. During the mid 1990s, there were several new trials of worksite nutrition programs to reduce the risks of cardiovascular disease and cancer and to lower employees' elevated cholesterol levels. (As noted earlier, weight control interventions are described in Chapter 17). These large trials used a variety of measures and designs and units of analysis. These trials generally showed positive results, including increased consumption of fruits, vegetables, and fiber and lower-fat eating.[121-124]

A rigorous, comprehensive literature review of worksite nutrition programs published in 2007 found 47 worksite nutrition studies that reported nutrition and health outcomes.[125] The sheer number of studies is evidence of the increasing availability of nutrition education programs offered and evaluated in worksites. To be included in the review, studies had to (1) include diet, physical activity or both, (2) be offered at the worksite, and (3) provide data on at least one weight outcome (i.e. BMI) measured at least 6 months from the beginning of the program.

Studies were divided by time frames with a third being shorter than six months, a third 6-9 months, and the final third longer than 12 months. Study participants were primarily white-collar employees, with slightly more women than men. Of these studies, about a third were targeted to reduce cardiovascular risk factors through informational and behavioral skill interventions.

These studies examined worksite nutrition programs using different types of interventions: self-instruction, group education, environment-based studies with pricing strategies, and the combination of different program elements. The purpose of the intervention in 34% of the studies was CVD risk reduction, 26% weight control, and 19% physical fitness. Program intensity, defined as the number of contacts with the program participants, ranged from two to five in 43% and more than five contacts in 55% of the studies. The behavioral focus was on diet and physical activity in 57% of the studies, on diet only in 21%, and physical activity only in 21%. The three types of interventions were coded as informational, behavioral skills, and policy or environmental. Sixty-nine percent offered both the informational and behavioral skills, while only four studies included a policy or environmental component. The evaluations used a variety of measures and designs and varied as to whether individuals or worksites were the unit analysis.

Analysis of the results using all study designs were reported by three outcomes: weight in pounds, BMI, and change in percent body fat. Fifteen studies used weight status as an outcome measure and the pooled summary effect on change in weight favored the intervention group. Among the studies using BMI as an outcome measure, the results favored the intervention group. In both groups, there was modest but consistent positive change to weight reduction. Twelve studies reported on change in percent body fat, and consistent with the other studies, a modest reduction of 1% decrease was reported across studies at 12 months.

In the second stage of this analysis, 31 randomized control trials compared a treatment group with an untreated control group. Of the 31 studies, only 17 studies were used in the meta-analysis due to adequate variance data or the small number of outcome measures. Changes in weight status was reported either through changes in pounds or BMI. The meta-analytic result, using a random effects model, indicates a change of -2.8 pounds (95% CI=-4.63, -0.96) in favor of the intervention group at 6-12 months. The pooled effect from three of the randomized control trials that focused on physical activity alone was -2.24 pounds (95% CI=-6.39, +2.00), compared with -3.18 pounds (95% CI=-5,88, -0.50) in five randomized control trials where the intervention focused on both diet and physical activity.

Offering multiple program components appeared to result in greater weight loss, however the results were not consistent. Structured programs for behavioral skills development or physical activity showed greater benefits than unstructured or self-directed approaches.

Environmental Changes

Two systematic reviews on worksite environmental interventions have been conducted.[109,114] Engbers et al (2005)[109] reviewed 10 trials that were conducted to trigger healthy dietary change. These trials reached larger numbers of employees, ranging from 250 to 2800 employees. The environmental modifications included strategies such as the promotion and expansion of healthy food in the company cafeteria, labeling of foods, changes in the vending machines, and educational posters and bulletins. These programs lasted between 12-24 months. Results indicate significant effect on nutrition knowledge, and on fruit and vegetable consumption and fat intake.[109] However, due to the multicomponent nature of these interventions, it is not possible to attribute the effects solely to environmental changes.

Matson-Koffman et al (2005)[114] focused on environmental interventions for cardiovascular health in multiple locations. Twelve of the studies occurred at the worksite. The studies involved offering healthier food choices and point-of-purchase nutritional information on menus, posters, or table flyers. Four of the studies showed that labeling and price reduction of heart-healthy foods led to increased purchases by employees. Two of the studies showed a significant decrease in self-report dietary fat intake, four showed a significant increase in employee fruit and vegetable consumption, and one study showed a significant increase in fiber intake.

Emerging Findings and Unanswered Questions

Research provides evidence that worksite nutrition programs can increase fruit/vegetable consumption, decrease fat consumption, and increase healthy food purchases that result in decreased BMI. However, many questions remain. Continued research is needed to understand how to successfully engage all employees to practice consistent nutrition behaviors to improve the quality of their health and manage health care costs. Further, all employees, from the low-risk population to those who have multiple chronic conditions, need to be engaged in worksite nutrition programs. Beyond health status, other employee variables such as age, type of job, race/ethnicity, location, must be integrated into research studies to understand how best to reach the employee population. Dependents are another target population that few research studies have included yet these individuals contribute to the overall health care costs of an organization.

Five of the ten leading causes of death and disability are linked to food patterns, either over or under consumption of select nutrients. Research continues to confirm the critically important role nutrition plays in achieving and maintaining good physical health. Current research is investigating the correlation between diet and cognition as well as understanding the relationship between physical activity and diet and dementia and Alzheimer's Disease[126] and if certain foods are addictive.[127] However, consistent through the years are the nutrient recommendations to reduce total fat, saturated fat, sodium, and sugar in the diet while increasing the consumption of fruit, vegetables, and fiber. More research will continue to provide evidence on the impact of nutrition on a specific disease. Using this research as the basis for nutrition education programs will be important for connecting nutrition and health.

Nutrition education programs will continue to be evaluated and questions still remain on how best to measure their impact; weight status, reducing blood cholesterol, or blood pressure are desirable outcome measures. However, questions remain on how best to measure food or nutrient consumption to understand the impact of nutrition education programs. As noted earlier, many of these measures are self-report questionnaires which is a limitation to assessing the effect of the intervention.

Nutrition interventions, both skill and opportunity enhancement strategies, have changed over the past few decades. Primarily, more skill and behavior interventions tend to be delivered with less emphasis on knowledge alone. Questions that are emerging surround how best to deliver this content given the rapid change of technology and social media. Health promotion professionals need to understand how to incorporate these tools into program design to continue to reach people where they work, whether it is in a traditional office environment, their home, or on the road. The opportunity-enhancement strategies are an area that has seen the most growth in the past decade and has many unanswered questions with great potential to reach a broad audience. Emerging questions include can the cost of healthy foods be modestly reduced while increasing the cost of minimal-nutrient dense foods? Can we limit the amount of sugar-sweetened beverages available for purchase in an organization? What role does a farmer's market have on promoting access and consumption of local fruits and vegetables when available at a corporate worksite? How can the food culture within an organization support its goal to create a culture of health to support the corporate mission while managing health benefits?

Worksite health promotion practitioners need to deliver comprehensive programs that incorporate nutrition education. Strategies are needed to identify how best to incorporate nutrition topics within other interventions rather than teaching health as separate topics.

Many questions remain regarding how best to deliver worksite nutrition education programs to improve or maintain the health of employees. Amidst all of these questions, it is evident that nutrition programs are an important component of an overall worksite health promotion program, and these programs are a proven strategy for organizations to manage their health care benefit package.

SUMMARY

As discussed in this chapter, nutrition-related health issues are among the most significant and challenging public health issues today. This chapter identifies some of the dilemmas that challenge health promotion professionals as they work in this field. To address these challenges, a wide range of worksite nutrition education programs have been developed, implemented, and tested with varying degrees of success. The worksite health promotion efforts in the 1990s and early into the 21st century significantly contribute to our knowledge of effective design, implementation, and evaluation of the worksite nutrition programs. Although there is no universally acceptable, feasible, and effective worksite nutrition enhancement program that is suitable for every worksite, there are guidelines for effective programs that should be followed.

First, nutrition interventions must be targeted to the audience the program serves, and must take into account contextual factors. Food selection decisions are made for many reasons other than just nutrition: taste, cost, convenience, and cultural factors all play significant roles. The design and implementation of worksite nutrition programs must take these issues into consideration. Including the target audience in discussions of changes to the food environment or the design of educational programs will lead to a greater acceptance of these interventions. The health promotion motto "know your audience" has a true and valuable meaning.

Second, change occurs in incremental stages and even small changes make a difference in health status. Many people have practiced a lifetime of less-than-optimal nutrition behaviors. It is unreasonable to expect that significant changes will occur during the course of a program that lasts only a few months. Programs need to pull the workforce along the continuum of change, being sure to be just in front of those most ready to change with attractive, innovative offerings. Creating a culture of health within the organization will broaden the reach of the program to all employees.

Third, the underlying program philosophy should not blame the victim. For many employees, easy access to fresh, wholesome, nutritious foods is quite limited. In some cases, for example, low-fat dairy products cannot be found in the cafeteria. In such cases, it is of limited value to adopt a program solely oriented toward modifying individual choice e.g., teaching and persuading employees to choose low-fat dairy products. A more productive strategy would also include environmental change efforts, such as expanding the availability of more nutritious food choices. When this is done in conjunction with individual skill training, long-lasting and meaningful changes can be expected.

Fourth, worksite nutrition programs must engage and hold the attention of the audience to sustain program success. Engagement can be achieved through using humor, competition, skill building (e.g, cooking classes) or fun activities that employees can enjoy and remember. Employees will participate and refer co-workers to the next event, if they can have fun while learning new nutrition behaviors and skills that are achievable. Emerging communication technologies are opening up new channels for engaging the interest of workers in better nutrition. Worksite e-mail support and motivation systems, "Internet buddies," and interactive Web-based approaches can be used creatively to promote healthful eating. The communication of nutrition information, no matter how important it is to good health, is secondary to attracting and retaining the interest and enthusiasm of the audience.

Glossary

Body Mass Index: (BMI) is a number calculated from a person's height and weight that indicates weight status.

Cardiovascular disease: A group of diseases that involve the heart or blood vessels.

Dietary Guidelines for Americans: A set of diet guidelines that balances calories and physical activity and is the cornerstone of federal nutrition policy.

Food Labeling: Used to inform consumers of the nutrient content of foods.

Hypertension: A condition whereby the force of the blood against an artery wall is high enough where it can cause health problems.

Menu Labeling: Nutrient information on select foods that is listed on the menu.

Myplate icon: The USDA food graphic that provides guidance on daily eating.

Nutrient recommendation: The amount of each nutrient recommended to sustain and promote health.

Nutrition skills: The application of nutrition knowledge and food selection or preparation.

Osteoporosis: A disease of the bones, in which bones become weak and may lead to increased fracture.

Point-of-purchase information: Found at the time a consumer buys an item and informs the consumer of the nutrient composition of the food.

Saturated Fat: A triglyceride that has no double bonds between the carbon chains. Saturated fats are found primarily in animal-based foods.

Total Fat: The amount of fat an individual consumes over a period of time.

Worksite nutrition Programs: Individual and environmental activities that promote healthy eating practices.

Learning Objectives

1. To describe the nature and magnitude of health, economic, and quality-of-life problems due to poor nutrition.
2. To describe current guidelines for healthy eating patterns and key barriers to and supports for good nutrition.

3. To outline theoretical bases and range of options for effective worksite nutrition interventions.
4. To review recent and current strategies for worksite nutrition programs, the evidence regarding their impact, and contemporary "best strategies".
5. To introduce the design and conduct of worksite nutrition program evaluation.

Discussion Questions

1. Identify the relationship of nutrients and the following conditions:
   a. Cardiovascular disease
   b. Hypertension
   c. Osteoporosis
   d. Cancer
2. Describe how eating patterns have changed over time and how these changes have influenced disease patterns.
3. Describe the MyPlate Icon and the Dietary Guidelines for Americans. What is the relationship between these two nutrition guidelines?
4. Identify the following theories and models
   a. Social Cognitive Theory
   b. Health Belief Model
   c. Transtheoretical Model of Behavior Change
   d. Social Ecological Model
5. Describe the difference between skill enhancement and opportunity enhancement strategies.
6. Identify how worksites are implementing skill enhancement strategies and opportunity enhancement strategies to promote sound nutrition practices.
7. What results do we know of the impact of these strategies on improving nutrition behavior and health outcomes?

8. Identify emerging issue and unanswered questions.
9. What are the guidelines for nutrition education programs at the worksite?

REFERENCES

1. Sorensen G, Stoddard A, Peterson K, et al. Increasing fruit and vegetable consumption through worksites and families in the treatwell 5-a-day study. *Am J Public Health.* 1999;89(1):54-60.
2. Nakade M, Muto T, Hashimoto M, Haruyama Y. Internet-based education program of nutrition as a workplace health promotion tool- a review of the literature. *Int. Congr. Ser.* 2006;1294:135-138.
3. Benefict MA, Arterburn D. Worksite-based weight loss programs: a systematic review of recent literature. *Am J Health Promot.* 2008;22(6):408-416.
4. Henke RM, Goetzel RZ, McHugh J, Isaac F. Recent experience in health promotion at Johnson & Johnson: lower health spending, strong return on investment. *Health Aff.* 2011;30(3):490-499.
5. Berry LL, Mirabito AM. Partnering for prevention with workplace health promotion programs. *Mayo Clin Proc.* 2011;86(4):335-337.
6. 2009 Almanac of Chronic Disease. Partnership to Fight Chronic Disease Web site. Available at: http://www.fightchronicdisease.org/sites/fightchronicdisease.org/files/docs/PFCDAlmanac_ExecSum_updated81009.pdf. Accessibility verified April 23, 2013.
7. Ford ES, Bergmann MM, Kroger J, Schienkiewitz A, Weikert C, Boeing H. Healthy living is the best revenge. *Internal Med.* 2009;169(15):1355-1362.
8. Eyre H, Kahn R, Robertson RM. Preventing cancer, cardiovascular disease, and diabetes: a common agenda

for the American Cancer Society, the American Diabetes Association, and the American Heart Association. *Diabetes Care.* 2004;27(7):1812-1824.

9. Adult Obesity Facts. Center for Disease Control and Prevention Web site. Available at: http://www.cdc.gov/obesity/data/adult.html. Accessibility verified April 23, 2013.

10. Finkelstein EA, Trogdon JG, Cohen JW, Dietz W. Annual medical spending attributable to obesity: payer-and service-specific estimates. *Health Aff.* 2009;28(5):w822-w831.

11. Finkelstein EA, Khavjou OA, Thompson H, et al. Obesity and severe obesity forecasts through 2030. *Am J Prev Med.* 2012;42(6):563-570.

12. Jakobsen MU, O'Reilly EJ, Heitmann BL, et al. Major types of dietary fat and risk of coronary heart disease: a pooled analysis of 11 cohort studies. *Am J Clin Nutr.* 2009;89:1-8.

13. Kris-Etherton P, Harris WS, Appel LJ. Fish consumption, fish oil, omega-3 fatty acids, and cardiovascular disease. *Circulation.* 2002;106:2747-2757.

14. Kris-Etherton P, Eckel RH, Haward BV, St. Jeor S, Bazzarre TL. Lyon diet heart study: benefits of a Mediterranean-style, national cholesterol education program/American Heart Association Step I dietary pattern on cardiovascular disease. *Circulation.* 2001;103:1823-1825.

15. Albert CM, Oh K, Whang W, et al. Dietary α-linolenic acid intake and risk of sudden cardiac death and coronary heart disease. *Circulation.* 2005;112:3232-3238.

16. He J, Ogden LG, Vupputuri S, Bazzano LA, Loria C, Whelton PK. Dietary sodium intake and subsequent risk of cardiovascular disease in overweight adults. *JAMA.* 1999;282(21):2027-2034.

17. de Koning L, Malik VS, Kellogg MD, Rimm EB, Willett WC, Hu FB. Sweetened beverage consumption, incident coronary heart disease, and biomarkers of risk in men. *Circulation.* 2012;125:1735-1741.

18. Gardener H, Rundek T, Markert M, Wright CB, Elkind MSV, Sacco RL. Diet soft drink consumption is associated with an increased risk of vascular events in the Northern Manhattan study. *J Gen Intern Med.* 2012;27(9):1120-1126.

19. Cancer. World Health Organization Web site. Available at: http://www.who.int/mediacentre/factsheets/fs297/en/. Accessibility verified April 23, 2013.

20. Masala G, Assedi M, Bendinelli B, et al. Fruit and vegetables consumption and breast cancer risk: the EPIC Italy study. *Breast Cancer Res Treat.* 2012;132:1127-1136.

21. Nishino H, Murakoshi M, Tokuda H, Satomi Y. Cancer prevention by carotenoids. *Arch Biochem Biophys.* 2009;483(2):165-168.

22. Lee SA, Shu XO, Li H, et al. Adolescent and adult soy food intake and breast cancer risk: results from the Shanghai Women's Health study. *Am J Clin Nutr.* 2009;89(6):1920-1926.

23. Raina K, Ravichandran K, Rajamanickam S, Huber KM, Serkova NJ, Agarwal R. Inositol hexaphosphate inhibits tumor growth, vascularity, and metabolism in TRAMP mice: a multiparametric magnetic resonance study. *Cancer Prev Res.* 2013;6:40.

24. Hansen L, Skeie G, Landberg R, et al. Intake of dietary fiber, especially from cereal foods, is associated with lower incidence of colon cancer in the HELGA cohort. *Int J Cancer.* 2012;131(2):469-478.

25. Bravi F, Edefonti V, Randi G, et al. Dietary patterns and the risk of esophageal cancer. *Ann Oncol.* 2012;23:766-770.

26. Ollberding NJ, Wilkens LR, Henderson BE, Kolonel LN, Marchand LL. Meat consumption, heterocyclic amines and

colorectal cancer risk: the multiethnic cohort study. *Int J Cancer.* 2012; 131(7):e1125-e1133.

27. Pan A, Sun Q, Bernstein AM, et al. Red meat consumption and mortality: results from 2 prospective cohort studies. *Arch Intern Med.* 2012;172(7):555-563.

28. Stott-Miller M, Neuhouser ML, Stanford JL. Consumption of deep-fried foods and risk of prostate cancer. *Prostate.* 2013;1-10.

29. Chen WY, Rosner B, Hankinson SE, Colditz GA, Willett WC. Moderate alcohol consumption during adult life, drinking patterns, and breast cancer risk. *JAMA.* 2011;306(17):1884-1890.

30. Friberg E, Wolk A. Long-term alcohol consumption and risk of endometrial cancer incidence: A prospective cohort study. *Cancer Epidemiol Biomarkers Prev.* 2009;18:355.

31. The Dietary Guidelines for Americans. The United States Department of Agriculture Web site. Available at: http://www.cnpp.usda.gov/Publications/DietaryGuidelines/2010/PolicyDoc/Chapter3.pdf. Accessibility verified April 23, 2013.

32. American Cancer Society. *Alcohol and Cancer.* Available at: http://www.cancer.org/acs/groups/content/@healthpromotions/documents/document/acsq-017622.pdf. Accessibility verified July 18, 2013.

33. Obesity and Overweight. Center of Disease Control and Prevention Web site. Available at: http://www.cdc.gov/nchs/fastats/overwt.htm. Accessibility verified April 23, 2013.

34. Epstein LH, Gordy CC, Raynor HA, Beddome M, Kilanowski CK, Paluch R. Increasing fruit and vegetable intake and decreasing fat and sugar intake in families at risk for childhood obesity. *Obes Res.* 2012;9(3):171-178.

35. Nordmann AJ, Nordmann A, Briel M, et al. Effects of low-carbohydrate vs low-fat diets on weight loss and cardiovascular risk factors: a meta-analysis of randomized controlled trials. *Arch Intern Med.* 2006;166(3):285-293.

36. Thompson WG, Rostad Holdman N, Janzow DJ, Slezak JM, Morris KL, Zemel MB. Effect of energy-reduced diets high in dairy products and fiber on weight loss in obese adults. Obes Res. 2005;13(8):1344-53.

37. Kong A, Beresford SA, Alfano CM, et al. Self-monitoring and eating-related behaviors are associated with 12-month weight loss in postmenopausal overweight-to-obese women. *J Acad Nutri Diet.* 2012;112(9):1428-1435.

38. Odegaard AO, Koh WP, Yuan J, Gross MD, Pereira MA. Western-Style Fast Food Intake and Cardiometabolic Risk in an Eastern Country. *Circulation.* 2012; 126 (2):182-188.

39. Ludwig DS, Peterson KE, Gortmaker SL. Relation between consumption of sugar-sweetened drinks and childhood obesity: a prospective, observational analysis. *Lancet.* 2001;357(9255):505-508.

40. Swithers SE, Davidson TL. A role for sweet taste: calorie predictive relations in energy regulation by rats. *Behav Neurosci* 2008;122(1):161-73.

41. Anderson JW, Konz EC. Obesity and disease management: effects of weight loss on comorbid conditions. *Obes Res.* 2001; 9 Suppl 4:326S-334S.

42. CDC. Diabetes: Successes and Opportunities for Population-Based Prevention and Control: At A Glance 2011. Available at: http://www.cdc.gov/chronicdisease/resources/publications/AAG/ddt.htm. Accessibility verified April 23, 2013.

43. CDC 2011 National Diabetes Fact Sheet. Available at: http://www.cdc.gov/diabetes/pubs/factsheet11.htm?loc=diabetes-statistics. Accessibility verified April 23, 2013.

44. Skyler JS, Bergenstal R, Bonow RO, et al. Intensive glycemic control and the prevention of cardiovascular events: implications of the ACCORD, ADVANCE, and VA Diabetes Trials: A position statement of the American Diabetes Association and a Scientific Statement of the American College of Cardiology Foundation and the American Heart Association. *J Am Coll Cardiol.* 2009; 53(3):298-304. Available at http://circ.ahajournals.org/content/119/2/351.short. Accessibility verified April 23, 2013.

45. CDC 2011 National Diabetes Fact Sheet: General Information. Available at: http://www.cdc.gov/diabetes/pubs/general11.htm#gen_c. Accessibility verified April 23, 2013.

46. Perreault L, Pan Q, Mather KJ, et al. Effect of regression from prediabetes to normal glucose regulation on long-term reduction in diabetes risk: results from the Diabetes Prevention Program Outcomes Study. *Lancet.* 2012; 379 (9833):2243-2251.

47. Salas-Salvadó J, Bulló M, Babio N, et al. Reduction in the incidence of type 2 diabetes with the Mediterranean diet: results of the PREDIMED-Reus nutrition intervention randomized trial. *Diabetes Care.* 2011; 34 (1) 14-19.

48. Jenkins DJ, Kendall CW, Augustin LS, et al. Effect of Legumes as Part of a Low Glycemic Index Diet on Glycemic Control and Cardiovascular Risk Factors in Type 2 Diabetes Mellitus, A Randomized Controlled Trial. *Arch Intern Med.* 2012;172(21):1653-1660.

49. Martinez-Gonzalez MA, Fuente-Arrillaga C, Nunez-Cordoba JM, et al. Adherence to Mediterranean diet and risk of developing diabetes: prospective cohort study. *BMJ.* 2008; 336(7657):1348-1351.

50. Hannan MT, Felson DT, Dawson-Hughes B, et al. Risk Factors for Longitudinal Bone Loss in Elderly Men and Women: The Framingham Osteoporosis Study. *J Bone Miner Res.* 2010; 15 (4): 710-720.

51. Taku K, Melby MK, Nishi N, Omori T, Kurzer MS. Soy isoflavones for osteoporosis: An evidence-based approach. *Maturitas.* 2011; 70 (4): 333-338.

52. Chan KM, Anderson M, Lau EMC. Exercise interventions: Defusing the world's osteoporosis time bomb. *Bull World Health Organ.* 2003; 81:827-830. Available at **http://www.scielosp.org/pdf/bwho/v81n11/v81n11a09.pdf**. Accessibility verified July 18, 2013.

53. Farina EK, Kiel DP, Roubenoff R, Schaefer EJ, Cupple LA, Tucker KL. Protective effects of fish intake and interactive effects of long-chain polyunsaturated fatty acid intakes on hip bone mineral density in older adults: the Framingham Osteoporosis Study. *Am J Clin Nutr.* 2011; 93 (5):1142-1151.

54. Ross CA, Manson JE, Abrams SA, et al. The 2011 Report on Dietary Reference Intakes for Calcium and Vitamin D from the Institute of Medicine: What Clinicians Need to Know. J *Clin Endocrinol Metab. 2011; 96 (1):53-58.*

55. Marvasti FF, Stafford RS. From Sick Care to Health Care — Reengineering Prevention into the U.S. System. *N Engl J Med.* 2012; 367:889-891.

56. Promoting Cardiovascular Health in the Developing World: A Critical Challenge to Achieve Global Health. Washington, DC: The National Academies Press; 2010. Available at: http://www.ncbi.nlm.nih.gov/books/NBK45693/. Accessibility verified April 23, 2013.

57. Healthy People 2020 Website. Available at: http://www.healthypeople.gov/2020/default.aspx. Accessibility verified April 13, 2013.

58. Almanac of Chronic Disease, Partnership to Fight Chronic Disease. Executive Summary. 2009. Available at: http://

www.fightchronicdisease.org/sites/fightchronicdisease.org/files/docs/PFCDAlmanac_ExecExe_updated81009.pdf. Accessibility verified April 23, 2013.

59. Trust for America's Health, The Robert Wood Johnson Foundation. F as in Fat: How Obesity Threatens America's Future. 2011. Available at: http://healthyamericans.org/reports/obesity2011/Obesity2011Report.pdf. Accessibility verified April 23, 2013.

60. Stewart WF, Ricci JA, Chee E, Morganstein D. Lost productive work time costs from health conditions in the United States: results from the American Productivity Audit. *J Occup Environ Med.* 2003;45(12):1234-46.

61. Dietary Guidelines for Americans. United States Department of Agriculture Web site. Available at: http://www.cnpp.usda.gov/dietaryguidelines.htm. Accessibility verified April 23, 2013.

62. United States Department of Agriculture MyPlate Web site. Available at: http://www.choosemyplate.gov/. Accessibility verified April 23, 2013.

63. Nutrition Facts Label Programs & Materials. Food and Drug Administration Web site. Available at: http://www.fda.gov/Food/ResourcesForYou/Consumers/NFLPM/default.htm. Accessibility verified April 23, 2013.

64. Nutrient Content of the U.S. Food Supply, 2005. Center for Nutrition Policy and Promotion, USDA. Available at: http://www.cnpp.usda.gov/Publications/FoodSupply/FoodSupply2005Report.pdf. Accessibility verified April 23, 2013.

65. Trans Fat Now Listed With Saturated Fat and Cholesterol. Food and Drug Administration Web site. Available at: http://www.fda.gov/Food/ResourcesForYou/Consumers/NFLPM/ucm274590.htm. Accessibility verified April 23, 2012.

66. Menu & Vending Machines Labeling Requirements. Food and Drug Administration Web site. Available at: http://www.fda.gov/Food/IngredientsPackagingLabeling/LabelingNutrition/ucm217762.htm. Accessibility verified April 23, 2013.

67. Krebs-Smith SM, Reedy J, Bosire C. Healthfulness of the U.S. food supply little improvement despite decades of dietary guidance. *Am J Prev Med.*2010; 38(5):472-477.

68. CDC NCHS Data Brief. Trends in Intake of Energy and Macronutrients in Adults From 1999-2000 Through 2007-2008. Available at: http://www.cdc.gov/nchs/data/databriefs/db49.htm. Accessibility verified April 23, 2013.

69. CDC Morbidity and Mortality Weekly Report. State-Specific Trends in Fruit and Vegetable Consumption Among Adults, United States, 2000-2009. Available at: http://www.cdc.gov/mmwr/preview/mmwrhtml/mm5935a1.htm. Accessibility verified April 23, 2013.

70. Flegal KM, Carroll MD, Ogden CL, Johnson CL. Prevalence and Trends in Obesity Among U.S. Adults, 1999-2000. *JAMA.* 2002; 288(14):1723-1727.

71. Linnan L, Bowling M, Childress J, et al. Results of the 2004 National Worksite Health Promotion Survey. *Am J Public Health* 2008; 98(8):1503–1509.

72. Social Marketing Campaigns such as "5 a Day for better health" Havas S, Heimendinger J, Reynolds K, et al. 5 a day for better health: a new research initiative. *J Am Diet Assoc.* 1994; 94.

73. Appelhans BM, Waring MO, Schneider KL, et al. Delay discounting and intake of ready-to-eat and away-from-home foods in overweight and obese women. *Appetite* 2012; 59 (2):576-584.

74. Anderson ES, Winett RA, Wojcik JR. Self-regulation, self-efficacy, outcome expectations, and social support: Social cognitive theory and nutrition behavior. *Ann Behav Med.* 2007; 34 (3):304-312.

75. Glanz K, Seewald-Klein T. Nutrition at the worksite: An overview. J Nutr Edu. 1986;18(2):S1-S12.

76. Glanz K, Eriksen M. Individual and community models for dietary behavior change. *J Nutr Edu.* 1993;25: 80-80.

77. Glanz K, Kristal AR, Tilley BC, Hirst K. Psychosocial correlates of healthful diets among male auto workers. *Cancer Epidemiol Biomarkers Prev.* 1998;7(2): 119-26.

78. Glanz K, Patterson RE, Kristal AR, et al. Stages of Change in Adopting Healthy Diets: Fat, Fiber, and Correlates of Nutrient Intake. *Health Edu Behav.* 1994;21(4):499-519.

79. Kristal AR, Glanz K, Curry SJ, Patterson RE. How Can Stages of Change be Best Used in Dietary Interventions? *J Am Dietetic Assoc.* 1999;99(6):679-684.

80. Kristal AR, Patterson RE, Glanz K, Heimendinger J, Hebert JR, Feng ZD, Probart C. Psychosocial correlates of healthful diets: baseline results from the Working Well Study. *Prev Med.* 1995; 24(3):221-228.

81. Sorensen G, Stoddard A, Macario E. Social Support and Readiness to Make Dietary Changes. *Health Edu Behav.* 1998;25(5):586-598.

82. Terborg JR, Hibbard J, Glasgow RE. Behavior Change at the Worksite: Does Social Support Make a Difference? Am J Health Promot. 1995;10(2):125-131.

83. Abood DA, Black DR, Feral D. Nutrition Education Worksite Intervention for University Staff: Application of the Health Belief Model. *J Nutr Edu Behav.* 2003;35(5):260-267.

84. Sorensen G, Stoddard A, Lederman R, et al. Increasing Fruit and Vegetable Consumption Through Worksites and Families in the Treatwell 5-a-day Study. *Am J Public Health.* January 1999; 89(1):54-60

85. Block G, Block T, Wakimoto P, Block CH. Demonstration of an E-mailed worksite nutrition intervention program. *Prev Chronic Dis.* 2004;1(4):A06.

86. Glanz K, Kristal AR, Sorensen G, Palombo R, Heimendinger J, Probart C. Development and validation of measures of psychosocial factors influencing fat- and fiber-related dietary behavior. *Prev Med.* 1993;22(3):373-87.

87. Stokols D. Translating Social Ecological Theory into Guidelines for Community Health Promotion. *Am J Health Promot.* 1996;10(4):282-298.

88. McLeroy KR, Bibeau D, Steckler A, Glanz K. An Ecological Perspective on Health Promotion Programs. *Health Edu Behav.* 1988;15(4):351-377.

89. Sallis J, Owen N. Ecological Models. In: Health behavior and health education: Theory, research, and practice. 2nd ed. San Francisco: Jossey-Bass, Inc; 1997: 403-424.

90. Bandura A. Social foundations of thought and action: A social cognitive theory. Englewood Cliffs: Prentice Hall; 1986.

91. Bandura A. Self-efficacy: The exercise of control. New York: W.H Freeman; 1997.

92. Anderson E, Winett R, Wojcik J. Self-Regulation, Self-Efficacy, Outcome Expectations, and Social Support: Social Cognitive Theory and Nutrition Behavior. *Ann Behav Med.* 2007;34(3): 304-312.

93. Brug J, Steenhuis L, van Assema P, Glanz K, De Vines H. Computer-tailored nutrition education: differences between two interventions. *Health Edu Res.* 1999;14(2):249-256.

94. Sorensen G, Emmons K, Hunt M, Johnston D. Implications of the Results

of Community Intervention Trials. *Ann Rev Public Health.* 1998;19(1):379.

95. Tilly B, Vernon S, Glanz K, et al. Worksite cancer screening and nutrition intervention for high-risk auto workers: Design and baseline findings of the Next Step Trial. *Prev Med.* 1997;26:227-335.

96. Prochaska J, DiClemente C, Norcross J. In search of how people change: Applications to addictive behaviors. *Am Psychol.* 1992;47:1102-1114.

97. Spencer L, Wharton C, Moyle S, Adams T. The transtheoretical model as applied to dietary behaviour and outcomes. *Nutr Res Rev.* 2007;20(1):46-73.

98. Janz NK, Becker MH. The health belief model: A decade later. *Health Ed Q.* 1984;11(1)1-47.

99. Rosenstock IM. The health belief model and nutrition education. *J Can Diet Assoc.* 1982 Jul;43(3):184-92.

100. Sharifirad G, Entezari MH, Kamran A, Azadbakht L. The effectiveness of nutritional education on the knowledge of diabetic patients using the health belief model. *J Res Med Sci.* 2009 Jan;14(1):1-6.

101. Stokols D. Establishing and maintaining healthy environments: Toward a social ecology of health promotion. *Am Psychol.* 1992;47:6-22.

102. Centers for Disease Control and Prevention. Workplace Health Promotion. Available at: http://www.cdc.gov/workplacehealthpromotion/. Accessibility verified July 1, 2013.

103. Harvard Health Publications. Money talks: Financial incentives for health. Available at: http://www.health.harvard.edu/newsletters/Harvard_Mens_Health_Watch/2011/May/money-talks-financial-incentives-for-health. Accessibility verified July 1, 2013.

104. Engbers L. Foot Steps The effects of a worksite environmental intervention on cardiovascular risk indicators. Wagenimgen: Ponsen & Looijen B.V.: 2006.

105. Thorndike AN, Healey E, Sonnenberg L, Regan S. Participation and cardiovascular risk reduction in a voluntary worksite nutrition and physical activity program. *Prev Med.* 2011;52(2):164-6.

106. Levin SM, Ferdowsian HR, Hoover VJ, Green AA, Barnard ND. A worksite programme significantly alters nutrient intakes. *Public Health Nutr.* 2010;13(10):1629-1635.

107. Franklin PD, Rosenbaum PF, Carey MP, Roizen MF. Using sequential email messages to promote health behaviors: evidence of feasibility and reach in a worksite sample. *J Med Internet Res.* 2006; 8(1).

108. Kremers SP, de Bruijn GJ, Visscher TLS, van Mechelen W, de Vries NK, Brug, J. Environmental influences on energy balance-related behaviors: A dual-process view. *Int J Behav Nutr Phys Act.* 2006;3:9.

109. Engbers LH, Van poppel MN, Chin a paw MJ, Van mechelen W. Worksite health promotion programs with environmental changes: a systematic review. *Am J Prev Med.* 2005;29(1):61-70.

110. Glanz K., Lankenau B, Foerster S, Temple S, Mullis R, Schmid T. Environmental and policy approaches to cardiovascular disease prevention through nutrition: opportunities for state and local action. *Health Edu & Behav.* 1995;22(4):512-527.

111. Glanz K, Mullis RM. Environmental interventions to promote healthy eating: A review of models, programs, and evidence. *Health Edu Q.* 1988;15(4):395-415.

112. Snelling A, Bachtel J, Karch R. Promoting Better Nutrition in the Workplace: Employer Strategies. *Natl Bus Group.* 2004;2(2):1-15.

113. Edington DW. Zero Trends, Health as a Serious Economic Strategy. Health

Management Research Center University of Michigan; 2009.

114. Matson-Koffman DM, Brownstein JN, Neiner JA, Greaney ML. A Site-specific Literature Review of Policy and Environmental Interventions that Promote Physical Activity and Nutrition for Cardiovascular Health: What Works? *Am J Health Promot.* 2005;19(3):167-193.

115. Glanz K, Hewitt AM, Rudd J. Consumer behavior and nutrition education: An integrative review. *J Nutr Edu.* 1992;24:267-277.

116. Mayer J, Dubbert P, Elder J. Promoting nutrition at the point-of-choice: A review. *Health Edu Q.* 1989;16:31-43.

117. Federal Register. Food labeling: Nutrition labeling of standard menu items in restaurants and similar retail food establishments. Available at: https://www.federalregister.gov/regulations/0910-AG57/food-labeling-nutrition-labeling-of-standard-menu-items-in-restaurants-and-similar-retail-food-estab. Accessibility verified July 1, 2013.

118. Bruemmer B, Krieger J, Saelens BE, Chan N. Energy, saturated fat, and sodium were lower in entrées at chain restaurants at 18 months compared with 6 months following the implementation of mandatory menu labeling regulation in King County, Washington. *J Acad Nutr Diet.* 2012;112(8):1169-76.

119. Kottke TE, Pronk NP, Katz AS, Tillema JO, Flottemesch TJ. The effect of price reduction on salad bar purchases at a corporate cafeteria. *Prev Chronic Dis.* 2013;10:E25.

120. French SA, Harnack LJ, Hannan PJ, Mitchell NR, Gerlach AF, Toomey TL. Worksite environment intervention to prevent obesity among metropolitan transit workers. *Prev Med.* 2010;50(4):180-5.

121. Sorensen G, Thompson B, Lichtenstein E, et al. Work Site-Based Cancer Prevention: Primary Results from the Working Well Trial. *Am J Public Health.* July 1996;86(7):939-946.

122. Jeffrey RW, French SA, Raether C, Baxter JE. An environmental intervention to increase fruit and salad purchases in a cafeteria. *Prev Med.* 1994;23:788-792.

123. Biener L, Glanz K, McLerran D, et al. Impact of the Working Well Trial on the Worksite Smoking and Nutrition Environment. *Health Edu Behav.* 1999;26(4):478-494.

124. Tilley B, Glanz K, Kristal A, et al. Nutrition intervention for high-risk auto workers: Results of the Next Step Trial. *Prev Med.* 1999;28:284-292.

125. Anderson LM, Quinn TA, Glanz K, et al. The effectiveness of worksite nutrition and physical activity interventions for controlling employee overweight and obesity: a systematic review. *Am J Prev Med.* 2009;37(4):340-57.

126. Morris MC. Diet and Alzheimer's disease. *Med Gen Med.* 2004; 6(1): 48-54.

127. Ifland JR, Preuss HG, Marcus MT, et al. Refined food addiction: A classic substance use disorder. *Medical Hypotheses.* 2009;72(50): 518-526.

CHAPTER
16

Stress Management in the Workplace

**Sokratis Dinos, Richard Citrin, and
Kamaldeep Bhui**

INTRODUCTION

Although work provides a range of benefits such as increased income, social contact, and sense of purpose, it can also have negative effects on mental health, particularly in the form of stress. Estimates from The National Institute of Occupational Safety and Health in the United States[1] indicate that 40% of American workers report their job is very or extremely stressful, 25% view their jobs as the number one stressor in their lives, and three-fourths of American employees believe that workers have more on-the-job stress than a generation ago. A similar trend was found in the United Kingdom (UK) where work stress–related illnesses resulted in nearly 10.4 million lost working days between 2011 and 2012.[2] The estimated economic costs as a result of stress at work are considerable.[3] In the United Kingdom, the cost in 2007 was estimated to be approximately .9% of UK Gross Domestic Product.[4] Work stress can lead to physical illness, as well as psychological distress and mental illness.[2] There are various forms of work stressors related to different work contexts, and these may be unique to an organization or an industry.

This chapter discusses approaches to understanding and tackling work-related stress and its impact on health, with an emphasis on mental health and well-being. It starts with a short discussion of the factors associated with stress, then describes theoretical models of stress that account for the individual physiological and psychological responses to stressors, and the interaction between the individual and environment.[5] Then the chapter focuses on describing stress management intervention programs that (1) target the individual (e.g., stress awareness training, relaxation techniques, and cognitive behavioral therapy [CBT]) or the organization (e.g., workplace adjustments or conflict management approaches in a specific organization), and (2) are delivered at primary, secondary, or tertiary levels.[6-12] More recent approaches to work stress emphasize the need for employees to improve their health and well-being outside of the workplace as a way of managing stressful work environments. The concept of resilience, sustained health, and well-being despite adversity is becoming popular because it places proportionate responsibility on employees themselves. This approach encourages employees to take up public health approaches to health and well-being, and to factor in their work situations, which can sometimes be inherently stressful. For example, growing workloads and demands are inevitable if there are fewer people in the workforce. It is clear that the way people manage their lives and work, and the balance between the two, is as important as employers' efforts to guard against work stress. The chapter then discusses specific groups who may be at higher risk of developing stress at work and also discusses how organizations currently view stress management programs and how they have adopted these programs on behalf of their employees. Finally, a discussion on the evidence for stress management programs points out evidence gaps to encourage future research.

FACTORS ASSOCIATED WITH STRESS

A large body of research documents the factors associated with work stress. Most research suggests that factors such as job strain, highly demanding jobs, long working hours, roles involving lack of involvement in decision making and low social support from managers and/or colleagues, effort-reward imbalance, and high job insecurity, (which becomes even more prominent at times of local or global financial crisis) have a significant impact on work stress–related anxiety and depressive illnesses.[13] A systematic review found a significant relationship between stress-related disorders and high job demands, low supervisor and coworker support, lack of job control, and a high effort-reward imbalance. Repetitive work was not found to be a risk factor.[14]

Some additional but more specific factors that are implicated in work-related common mental disorders involve concepts such as organizational injustice,[15] bullying,[16] and discrimination.[17,18] This type of research relates work practices that are perceived unfair and discriminatory.[19] Furthermore, the link between stress at work and coronary heart disease has been well documented in previous research.[16,20] For example, Kivimaki et al.[16] found that people who experience stress at

work have a 50% higher risk of heart disease than people who do not.

A large body of research has also documented that some social groups are more vulnerable than others in experiencing stress at work, leading to the development of mental health and behavioral problems at work for these groups. This research has mainly focused on exposure to experiences of discrimination and stigmatization.[21] Most of the research on vulnerable groups at work has focused on gender, ethnicity or ethnic minority status, sexuality, age, mental illness, and learning disability. These factors, such as age and gender, can also interact, with older women being at higher risk of discrimination and stereotyping.[22-25] Research has found, for example, that black African–Caribbean women may be particularly at risk of work stress and its consequences because of the potential for gender and/or racial bias, which has been apparent for some time.[18] Research has shown that work experiences of discrimination, harassment, and stigmatization can have deleterious effects and lead to great vulnerability, depressive and anxiety disorders, distress, low self-esteem, and alcohol and substance abuse.[21,26] Negative workplace interactions that are experienced routinely, and that seem minor when taken in isolation, together have even been linked to a greater risk of stress-induced mental health problems than major life events.[27] There are a lot of similarities between different vulnerable groups on how harassment and/or discrimination at work impacts on mental health, which are manifested, for example, through one's sex in the case of sexual harassment, race or ethnicity in the case of racial discrimination, and so on.[28]

THEORETICAL FOUNDATIONS FOR THE IMPACT OF PSYCHOSOCIAL RISK FACTORS AT WORK

The literature on work-related stress proposes a number of models to explain the presence and consequences of psychosocial risk factors for stress at work. Many stress management interventions or programs are based on these models. Work stress models present stress as a stimulus in the environment such as dealing with a demanding job (e.g., situational stress) or as a response to a stimulus from the environment (e.g., subjective appraisal of the situation). Some models present work-related stress as a transaction between stimulus and response (i.e., transactional models) and frame stress as a transaction between the individual and his or her environment.[29]

A great deal of research on work-related stress is concerned with demand-control balance or job strain[30] and the effort-reward imbalance (ERI).[31] These models of stress consider factors such as job characteristics, for example, a demanding role, low control and social support; and negative life experiences and demands outside of work, such as caring responsibilities.[8,9,12,32]

The job strain model presents stress as an interaction between objective pressures in the work environment, such as excessive workload and highly demanding work environments, and the individual's latitude or power in decision making (e.g., the ability to control or be involved in the decision making).[33] Therefore, according to this model, highly stress-inducing jobs are those that place heavy demands on the individual without allowing the opportunity for involvement or shaping of the work structure. The job strain model was later developed further to include the concept of social support from managers and colleagues.[34] Social support acts as a moderator in the interaction between demand and control and minimizes the impact of a highly demanding job that has low decision latitude. This model suggests that control over decision making and greater occupational social support can enhance well-being in the work environment.[13] On the other hand, the ERI model posits that an imbalance between the amount of effort that is expended at work and the perceived rewards received

can result in work-related stress.[31,35] Therefore, stress can be described as a manifestation of the poor fit between a person's expectations and his or her environment.[6] Stress is then seen to arise owing to a discrepancy between the inputs and outputs and the mediating appraisal of stress, personal skills to manage it, and environmental demands and rewards. A recent systematic review investigated the job strain and the ERI model in relation to stress at work and cardiovascular illness.[36] Meta-analytic findings based on the job strain and the ERI model showed a relationship between work stress and cardiovascular illness. In particular, psychosocial factors at work, including both individual factors (e.g., coping, overcommitment) and working conditions (e.g., workload, time pressure, organization of work), showed a significant association with cardiovascular morbidity and mortality.

Transactional theories have further refined the interactional models in order to make them more dynamic and account for the ongoing relationship between individuals and their work environment.[13,32,37] Transactional models, as those proposed by Lazarus[38] and Cox and Ferguson,[39] conceptualize stress as something that unfolds over time within a series of transactions between a person and his or her environment. Stress is therefore elicited and maintained by the individual's actions and perceptions as well as the characteristics of the work environment. The transactional theories incorporate structural elements with a process-based account of stress.[40]

STRESS MANAGEMENT INTERVENTIONS AND THEIR IMPACT ON HEALTH

Interventions to tackle stress depend on the specific conceptualizations of stress adopted. Cahill,[7] Cooper et al.,[10] and Marine et al.[11] describe categories of stress management interventions that target the individual or the organization and whether these are acting at primary, secondary, or tertiary preventive levels (see Table 16-1).

Individual interventions include elements such as stress awareness training or CBT for psychological and emotional stress. Organizational interventions are those that affect whole populations or groups of people and include workplace adjustments or conflict management approaches in a specific organization. Some interventions target both the individual and organization and may include, for example, policies to secure a better work-life balance and peer-support groups. Therefore, interventions may introduce the implementation of new human resources policies, redesign management practices to involve employees in decision making, as well as focus on classic health promotion programs.[42]

Stress management interventions further specify actions at primary, secondary, or tertiary preventive levels.[41] Primary interventions aim to prevent the causal factors of stress, secondary interventions aim to reduce the severity or duration of symptoms, and tertiary or reactive interventions aim

Table 16-1: Model for Categorizing Stress Management Interventions*.

Level	Primary Prevention	Secondary Prevention	Tertiary Prevention	Outcome Measures
Organizational	Improving work content, fitness programs, career development	Improving communication and decision making, conflict management	Vocational rehabilitation, outplacement	Productivity, turnover, absenteeism, financial claims
Individual and organizational interface	Time management, improving interpersonal skills, work/home balance	Peer support groups, coaching, career planning	Posttraumatic stress assistance programs, group psychotherapy	Job stressors such as demands, control, support, role ambiguity, relationships, change, burnout
Individual	Pre-employment medical examination, didactic stress management	Cognitive behavioral techniques, relaxation	Rehabilitation after sick leave, disability management, case management, individual psychotherapy	Mood states, psychosomatic complaints, subjective experienced stress, physiological parameters, sleep disturbances, health behaviors

Adapted from De Jonge J and Dollard MF. *Stress in the Workplace: Australian Master OHS and Environment Guide.* Sydney, Australia; CCH; 2002.[41]

*Individual and organizational interface interventions and outcomes were summed under individual employee interventions and perceptions with the exception of the provision of support or skill training provided by the organization.

to provide rehabilitation and maximize functioning among those with chronic health conditions.[43] Individual and organizational stress management interventions, which have been evaluated empirically, are described below. It is important to note that stress management interventions do not necessarily aim to remove stress at the workplace because stress at work can be a result of a number of factors, some of which may be unavoidable (e.g., highly demanding job). Therefore, the aims are to present interventions and suggest programs that will aid the management of stress and enhance well-being.

INDIVIDUAL STRESS MANAGEMENT INTERVENTIONS: SKILL ENHANCEMENT STRATEGIES

Individual interventions are aimed at the individual employee. Such interventions usually take the form of self-management techniques. It is important to note that these interventions are sometimes implemented by the organization and sometimes adopted by the individual independently of the organization. As already discussed, these can be implemented at the primary level (e.g., organizational and/or stress management skills training intended to avoid stress), secondary level (e.g. exercise, healthy diet, or meditation all designed to minimize stress), and tertiary level (e.g., one-to-one psychological therapy, such as CBT, intended to remediate stress levels).

Physical Activity

The relationship between physical activity and stress has been studied extensively. However, the impact of physical activity on work stress is less studied. Promoting physical activity and encouraging individuals to take ownership of health risk behaviors and decisions about health, well-being, and family outside of work may be a promising stress management intervention for work-related stress. A synthesis of several

reviews[44] showed that organizational measures to increase physical activity show promising results. For example, Cancelliere et al.[45] found that exercise (e.g., back pain exercise programs, supervised worksite exercise such as aerobics, and self-directed worksite exercise) has a positive impact on improving presenteeism. Furthermore, Bhui et al.[44] found that the only organizational intervention to show convincing effects on absenteeism was physical activity programs,[46] whereas additional individual stress management techniques (i.e., mental imaging, CBT, and in vivo exposure) have a more useful role in secondary prevention.[44]

Relaxation Interventions

Relaxation interventions can take several forms and can involve a number of techniques including mindfulness-based stress reduction, meditation, yoga, imagery techniques, music, dance, and others. These interventions aim to reduce stressful thoughts as well as somatic responses including increased heart rate, blood pressure, tense muscles, and aches and pains that could be stress related or exacerbated by stress. Yung and Keltner[47] and Yung et al.[48] tested the impact of a relaxation program on the mental health of nurses. This consisted of techniques on relaxing the muscles as well as cognitive relaxation techniques using mental imagery of peaceful scenes. Results showed that the treatment groups receiving training in muscle and cognitive relaxation reported significantly lower levels of anxiety and mental health symptoms at 1-month follow-up period than the control group that received no intervention. Meditation is also appearing more frequently in the literature as a form of individual stress management intervention. In particular, mindfulness-based stress reduction (MBSR) is a structured program based on meditation. Grossman et al.[49] conducted a systematic review to investigate the relationship between MBSR and health-related problems and found MBSR to be significantly related to coping with clinical and nonclinical problems including stress. Similarly, Gelderloos et al.[50] conducted a review on the benefits of transcendental meditation in treating and preventing substance abuse. The review found 24 studies that included surveys as well as longitudinal and randomized controlled studies. All 24 studies showed a significant positive effect on well-being, self-esteem, and perceived sense of control.[50]

Workplace Counseling, CBT, and Employee Assistance Programs (EAPs)

Counseling, CBT, and EAPs tend to be targeted at the tertiary level. The aim of these interventions is to treat and/or reduce symptoms related to possible mental health symptoms that may be experienced by the employee. These interventions are very often provided by outside professionals contracted with the organization and can be directed at alleviating the symptoms at the individual level or removing the stressors at the workplace.[51] There is relatively little information on how to intervene at the organizational level in order to prevent or reduce the occurrence of work stress–related consequences.

CBT is an intervention very often used to provide the individual with necessary tools and/or training to cope with or manage stress and is primarily used as a tertiary form of support. CBT techniques include challenging negative thoughts, physical and relaxation techniques, and solution-focused and goal-oriented training. In a recent review, Bhui et al.[44] concluded that cognitive behavioral programs consistently produced larger effects at the individual level than other types of interventions, for example, relaxation. In particular, Murphy[52] found that multimodal interventions or combination strategies that involved CBT (along with one or more other techniques such as relaxation, meditation, and biofeedback) produced the most consistent,

significant results, a result that was not supported by one meta-analytic review.[53] It needs to be noted that CBT and physical activity interventions are better defined in the literature than stress management interventions to reduce stress, and therefore are more scientifically measurable. This may account for the relatively higher success rate of CBT. Similarly, the optimal duration of the interventions and timing of measurement of outcomes are not well defined in the literature.[44]

ORGANIZATIONAL STRESS MANAGEMENT INTERVENTIONS: OPPORTUNITY ENHANCEMENT STRATEGIES

Organizational stress management interventions are implemented for groups of people within an organization or for the whole organization with the aim to reduce psychosocial risk factors that can impact on the mental health of employees.[54] Such interventions can be implemented at the human resources policy level as well as the job structure/nature/task level.[42] Organizational interventions can also be categorized in terms of their implementation, at primary, secondary, or tertiary levels.[55] Organizational level interventions are discussed below.

Risk Assessment and Organizational Strategies

Risk assessment strategies are considered primary interventions, normally involve an entire organization, and have the goal of creating a culture of well-being. They strive to offer a wide range of approaches to protect against the development of mental health problems. Such assessment strategies may include elements such as job redesign, change of organizational culture, improvement of communication between management levels and departments, control latitude, collective decision making, work-life balance policies, and flexible working hours. In a systematic review of such assessment strategies, and in particular job redesign, participative management through team working, and collective decision making, Bambra et al.[56] found that many studies reported no net impact. For example, job redesign interventions had positive and negative impacts. The positive impact was related to the variety that it added to the job. However, adding this variety increased job demands without increasing job control. Therefore, any effect on mental health was either small or statistically nonsignificant. Similarly, participative management improved social support at the workplace but health-related indicators did not change significantly.

Other organizational design strategies can take the form of psychosocial intervention programs[57] aiming to reduce or manage stress through strategies related to communication and social support, role clarity, and control latitude over task. Psychosocial interventions can more specifically involve participatory action research (PAR) and "socio-technical" interventions.[57,58] PAR methods involve the identification of workplace stressors and subsequent plans of removing or reducing them. As the name suggests, both the identification of stressors, as well as plans to remove them through interventions, can only succeed with the participation of all employees within an organization, regardless of status and seniority. A successful example of PAR to reduce stress and enhance well-being was the involvement of bus drivers in Scandinavia in the change of the job design such as bus routes, bus lanes, bus stops, etc.[59] Other review studies have also suggested that PAR appears to be one of the most successful organizational interventions.[60-62] Sociotechnical interventions focus primarily on changes to working conditions or work environments such as work schedules, workload, and work processes. Research evidence suggests that such interventions are beneficial.[58]

Furthermore, such interventions may include technologic improvements,[58] as well as ergonomics such as posture,[63] but research findings on their impact on stress and mental health are scarce and mixed. Both PAR and sociotechnical interventions are broadly based on the demand-control[30] and/or demand-control-support or iso-strain model.[34] Although the aforementioned research findings[59-62] are supportive of the individual components of the model (i.e., control, demand, and support), additional findings on their interaction are lacking.

Organizational Health Promotion Programs

As documented in the other chapters of this book, offering comprehensive organization-level health promotion programs to reduce stress and increase job satisfaction has become increasingly popular in the past 3 decades. Health promotion programs can involve a single health-related component (e.g., on-site gym or off-site gym membership, nutrition, stress reduction classes) or a combination of components (e.g., gym, seminars on health nutrition), with the aim to promote health-related activities[64] and reduce stress indirectly by improving mental health in general. Empirical studies have used a number of methodologies to evaluate the impact of health promotion programs on stress, and in most cases yielded mixed results or were inconclusive.[64,65] Two meta-analytic reviews[46,66] found that participation in organizational health promotion programs was associated with decreased absenteeism and increased job satisfaction.

In a recently completed North American survey on workplace wellness by Towers Watson and the National Business Group on Health,[67] the authors reported that there is a greater recognition of the role of organizational health promotion programs within corporations. However, they also identified that there remains a significant gap between the recognition by employers of the burden of stress carried by their employees and the effectiveness of the actions they are taking to address stress issues in the workplace. While employers recognize that excessive workloads, poor work-life balance, and 24/7 technology access fuel high stress levels, they are finding that actions they may take to address these concerns have yielded little or no benefit related to stress. In fact, the authors report that fewer than 10% of companies working to address stress in the workplace report any significant benefit from their efforts. The role of technology in creating a new architecture of work-home connections needs more investigation, especially around decision making. The role of deliberation and consultation is diminishing if decisions are expected more immediately, and their number in a working day increases.

Organizational Resilience

As mentioned above, resilience strategies have the potential to address workplace stress issues by examining both individual and organizational approaches to stressful and adverse events. Resilience approaches shift the conversation around stress from the concept of "managing" stress to recognizing and acknowledging that challenging events will occur in the workplace. Therefore, employees and employers must prepare, navigate through, and recover quickly from those events.

In the mid 1970s, Salvatore Maddi,[68] who was a psychology consultant for Illinois Bell, approached a senior leader at the company, Carl Horn, about initiating a study of how employee health and performance would be affected during times of corporate stress. Both Maddi and Horn anticipated that federally mandated deregulation of the communications industry would lead to the divestiture of all local Bell Telephone companies from the American Telephone and Telegraph Corporation (AT&T). Both Maddi and Horn recognized that

this event would provide a testing ground to identify salient issues around how employees handle stressful work situations.

Maddi developed a research protocol to study the impact of this event on employee well-being. His plan was to design a naturalistic study that provided longitudinal data on the impact of stress caused by the divestiture and its associated stress on the health and performance of employees at Illinois Bell. Beginning in 1975, employees were invited to participate in a study on employee well-being. They were not given specific details about the focus of the study. Approximately 450 employees volunteered and were tested by using a variety of psychological assessments that measured personality, stress, motivational levels, and social interaction patterns. Additionally, the researchers collected job performance reports, along with medical evaluation data, which were obtained from annual medical physical examinations that were provided by the company during that period.

The researchers had collected 6 years of data by 1981 when the long-expected divestiture of AT&T occurred. More than half of the workforce of 26,000 employees was laid off. In the first several years the company experienced organizational difficulties in establishing clear strategies and objectives on how to manage employees. It was reported, for example, that several employees had 10 or more different managers during the first year of divestiture. The researchers continued to collect data for an additional 6 years following the breakup of the company, providing 12 years of longitudinal data.

The researchers found that approximately two-thirds of the employees experienced psychological, medical, and performance decrements as a result of the workplace challenges. Serious medical conditions, such as heart attacks, stroke, and suicide, along with psychological maladies such as depression, divorce, and drug-related difficulties, were also reported by this group. Workplace performance declined, with many employees in this group reporting feeling disengaged, uninterested, and lacking commitment to their work. The remaining one-third of the participants in the study demonstrated successful approaches to the changes. If they had decided to stay with the company, they tended to take on additional leadership and management responsibilities. Their performance also improved and they reported excitement and enjoyment of the challenges they confronted on a daily basis. These employees appeared to thrive in the high stress environment with their health, performance, and reported their psychological well-being as excellent. The researchers determined that the high performers were resilient in the face of the workplace stress and that they could be described as possessing "hardiness," which they viewed as a key basis for resilience.

Finally, Maddi and his team identified three key constructs as being important to the employees who successfully managed the organizational changes. These included an ability to (1) *commit* to the project at hand and to fully engage in the challenges they were facing, (2) identify ways to find *control* of situations as much as possible and avoid falling into situations where they were powerless, and (3) see the work situation as a *challenge*, which would represent an opportunity for new learning.

DISCUSSION: EMERGING FINDINGS AND UNANSWERED QUESTIONS

In a review of systematic reviews, Bhui et al.[44] found that, overall, individual interventions show larger effects than organizational interventions or mixed interventions; benefits were seen mainly at the individual level through one-to-one interventions, such as CBT, although some studies did show organizational benefits.[44] In particular, organizational interventions such as management skills training and support for staff, along with methods to cope with work stress, all seem significant components for stress management programs. Where positive impacts were seen at individual levels, findings were not entirely convincing about their positive benefit because the effect could not entirely be attributed to improved management standards or working relationships.[11,51] On the other hand, some organizational interventions, such as health promotion programs, show more consistent evidence for positive mental health and in reducing absenteeism rate.[69,70]

One of the main reasons for the insufficient evidence of the effects of workplace interventions and/or programs on stress is related to the design and implementation of such studies. Most frequently, the time frames used in evaluation research of this type are too narrow to detect effectiveness. For example, evaluations of individual interventions may appear more beneficial because they are often limited by lack of follow-up data[51] and reliance upon subjective rating skills. Benefits may be short lived and overstated by the participants. On the other hand, organizational interventions may appear less beneficial because they may take longer to bring about positive effects than most research has allowed for.[51,53] Therefore, the benefits may occur, but are not detected because they are not measured. Moreover, most of these interventions and/or programs are not implemented for research purposes and do not allow for experimental designs such as controlled trials. Therefore, randomization of employees or blinding of treatments is very difficult to implement, if at all possible.[71]

Some additional limitations can be found at the outcome measurement level and in particular in the diversity of the tools used to measure stress and common mental disorders. For example, in a recent review of reviews[44] for both organizational and individual interventions at the workplace, only 23 reviews were selected of 7845 identified potential publications for inclusion. These included 499 primary studies. Most reviews concluded that drawing meta-narrative or meta-analytic conclusions was difficult because of this diversity in outcomes, intervention, and methods. Furthermore, a small improvement in sickness absence statistics and/or measures might yield substantial benefits for business viability and provision of services.[45] Although many reviews at face value have been evaluating the same evidence, they do not all identify the same primary studies, and therefore do not always reach the same conclusions.[44] Selection bias may be an important explanation for this. For example, organizations with the most stressful work environments are less likely to participate in research than organizations with little stress among employees. Consequently, organizations with low baseline stress levels would make any effects from targeted interventions more difficult to capture. However, preliminary support was found in one meta-analytic review that interventions conducted with employees at high levels of baseline stress appeared to be at least as effective as interventions conducted with employees at low levels of baseline stress.[53] Establishing what works for whom and the maintenance of these effects need further research.[62]

Finally, there is a relative lack of studies with employees who have been treated for stress-related or mental health problems, as well as health care workers and law enforcement officers who perhaps need specific attention given the unique circumstances and stressors to which they are exposed at work. The few methodologically rigorous studies that have been conducted with patients have not included nontreatment control groups but have instead compared two treatment types.[44]

Improving Public Health

Many stress management policies focus on the individual worker taking personal responsibility for general health, exercise,

nutrition; reducing alcohol consumption and use of nicotine; being part of the community; and remaining engaged in learning opportunities. The anticipated impact of such interventions is to increase resilience, which in turn may enable people to continue to work longer without the adverse effect of employment resulting in work stress or related physical health problems.

Public Health England[72] has begun to take a different approach regarding policies and plans related to work stress. It was established in April 2013 and consists mainly of scientists, researchers, and public health professionals. The emphasis of Public Health England is on positive psychology and heightened performance rather than only on illness, work stress, and pathology. Actively tackling obesity, smoking, alcohol use, inactivity, and a lack of learning opportunities is all part of this approach, but methodologic evaluation will be needed to determine whether having a mandated approach to educating employees about stress will yield improved health and workplace performance.

CONCLUSIONS

Overall, comprehensive health promotion programs and cognitive behavioral therapy appear to be the most effective organizational and individual-level targeted interventions, respectively, for both organizational and individual outcomes related to stress.[44] Encouragement of physical activity at an organizational level seems to reduce absenteeism. Interventions need to be developed that can provide consistent and stronger effects on organizational outcomes such as absenteeism. There are a number of gaps in the literature, particularly studies investigating the influence of specific occupations, different-sized organizations, and different sectors of organizations (public, private, and not for profit). Studies of management practices seemed not to show strong effects, but there are still insufficient studies in this area.

Research needs to take into account factors such as gender, sexuality, ethnicity, age, and socioeconomic status in relation to stress management interventions. Discrimination in the workplace can take different forms and can happen on the basis of one's sex, sexuality, race/ethnicity, or age, to name a few. While there may be an interplay between gender, race/ethnicity, and age, other sources of discrimination (e.g., sexual orientation) merit future attention. Therefore, multiple social statuses, such as sex, sexuality, age, and race/ethnicity (and education and income, which have not been addressed in this section), may influence cumulatively specific psychiatric vulnerabilities among individuals at the workplace in ways that are not yet understood.

Glossary

Cognitive behavioral therapy (CBT): A psychotherapeutic approach that deals with troublesome emotions, behaviors, and cognitions through techniques to cope with or manage these emotions, behaviors, and cognitions

Demand-control-support model: Social support acts as a moderator in the interaction between demand and control and minimizes the impact of a highly demanding job that has low decision latitude

Effort-reward imbalance (ERI) model: Presents work-related stress as an imbalance between the amount of effort that is expended at work and the perceived rewards received

Employee assistance programs (EAPs): Programs such as counseling services offered by employers to help employees deal with problems that may impact on their work performance and well-being

Job redesign: Initiatives by employers to redesign how work is carried out and what it involves in order to reduce work-related stress

Job strain model: Presents work-related stress as an interaction between objective pressures in the work environment, such as excessive workload and highly demanding work environments, and the individual's latitude or power in decision making

Primary prevention: Interventions aiming to prevent the causal factors of stress-related symptoms at work

Psychosocial intervention programs: Programs aiming to reduce or manage stress through strategies related to communication and social support, role clarity, and control latitude over task

Relaxation interventions: Interventions involving a number of techniques (e.g., meditation, yoga, dance) to reduce stress-related symptoms

Resilience: The ability to recover quickly from stress-related illness

Return to work: Returning to work after illness absence

Secondary prevention: Interventions aiming to reduce the severity or duration of stress related symptoms at work

Tertiary prevention: Interventions aiming to provide rehabilitation and maximize functioning among those with chronic stress-related or health conditions impacting on work

Transactional models: The conceptualization of stress as something that unfolds over time within a series of transactions between the person (e.g., individual actions and perceptions) and his or her environment (e.g., work characteristics)

Learning Objectives

1. To outline traditional concepts and theories about the origins of work stress and interventions

2. To identify the prevalence of work-related stress and its impact on health

3. To describe models of work stress and the available evidence about their application on work environments

4. To identify evidence-based individual and organizational programs used to reduce or manage work-related stress

5. To identify evidence-based primary, secondary, and tertiary prevention programs for the management of work-related stress

6. To contrast these traditional concepts and theories with new approaches that attend to well-being, resilience, and public health approaches

7. To propose new directions for intervention research and evaluation

Discussion Questions

1. What is the prevalence of work-related stress and how does it impact on health and well-being?

2. How effective are individual and organisational stress management interventions in reducing work-related stress?

3. What is the impact of primary, secondary and tertiary prevention programmes on work-related stress?

4. How do sociodemographic characteristics and job type influence stress at work?

5. What is the impact of stress management interventions in different sized organisations and different sectors (e.g. public private and not for profit)?

6. Is it possible to design robust controlled trials to measure the impact of stress management interventions at the workplace?

REFERENCES

1. Centers for Disease Control and Prevention 2010. Stress at work. Available at: http://www.cdc.gov/niosh/docs/99-101/. Accessed 05/28/2014.

2. Health and Safety Statistics 2011/2012. National statistics 2013. Available at: http://www.hse.gov.uk/statistics/dayslost.htm. Accessed 05/28/2014.

3. Health and Safety Executive. Stress-related and psychological disorders, Health and Safety Executive 2009. http://www.hse .gov.uk/statistics/causdis/stress/. Accessed 05/28/2014.

4. Jordan J, Gurr E, Tinline G, et al. *Beacons of Excellence in Stress Prevention: Research Report 133.* London, England: Health & Safety Executive Books; 2003.

5. Cooper C, Dewe P. Well-being—absenteeism, presenteeism, costs and challenges. *Occup Med (Oxford).* 2008;58(8):522–524.

6. Cox T. Organizational culture, stress, and stress management. *Work Stress.* 1991;5(1):1–4.

7. Cahill J. Psychosocial aspects of interventions in occupational safety and health. *Am J Ind Med.* 1996;29(4):308–313.

8. Stansfeld SA, Fuhrer R, Head J, et al. Work and psychiatric disorder in the Whitehall II study. *J Psychosom Res.* 1997;43(1):73–81.

9. Stansfeld SA, Bosma H, Hemingway H, Marmot MG. Psychosocial work characteristics and social support as predictors of SF-36 health functioning: the Whitehall II study. *Psychosom Med.* 1998;60(3):247–255.

10. Cooper CL, Dewe PJ, O'Driscoll MP. *Organizational Intreventions. Organizational Stress: A Review and Critique of Theory, Research, and Applications.* Thousand Oaks, Calif: Sage; 2001.

11. Marine A, Ruotsalainen J, Serra C, Verbeek JH. Preventing occupational

stress in healthcare workers. *Cochrane Database Syst Rev.* 2006;(4):CD002892.

12. Karasek R. Low social control and physiological deregulation—the stress-disequilibrium theory, towards a new demand-control model. *Scand J Work Environ Health.* 2008;34(6):117–135.

13. Stansfeld S, Candy B. Psychosocial work environment and mental health—a meta-analytic review. *Scan J Work Environ Health.* 2006;32(6):443–462.

14. Nieuwenhuijsen K, Bruinvels D, Frings-Dresen M. Psychosocial work environment and stress-related disorders, a systematic review. *Occup Med (Oxford).* 2010;60(4):277–286.

15. Ylipaavalniemi J, Kivimäki M, Elovainio M, et al. Psychosocial work characteristics and incidence of newly diagnosed depression: a prospective cohort study of three different models. *Soc Sci Med.* 2005;61(1):111–122.

16. Kivimäki M, Virtanen M, Vartia M, et al. Workplace bullying and the risk of cardiovascular disease and depression. *Occup Environ Med.* 2003;60(10):779–783.

17. Bhui K, Stansfeld S, McKenzie K, et al. Racial/ethnic discrimination and common mental disorders among workers: findings from the EMPIRIC Study of Ethnic Minority Groups in the United Kingdom. *Am J Public Health.* 2005;95:496–501.

18. Wadsworth E, Dhillon K, Shaw C, et al. Racial discrimination, ethnicity and work stress. *Occup Med (Oxford).* 2007;57(1):18–24.

19. Ybema JF, van den Bos K. Effects of organizational justice on depressive symptoms and sickness absence: a longitudinal perspective. *Soc Sci Med.* 2010;70(10):1609–1617.

20. Chandola T, Britton A, Brunner E, et al. Work stress and coronary heart disease: what are the mechanisms? *Eur Heart J.* 2008;29(5):640–648.

21. Mays VM, Cochran SD. Mental health correlates of perceived discrimination among lesbian, gay, and bisexual adults in the United States. *Am J Public Health.* 2001;91(11):1869–1876.

22. Schuman E, Kleiner B. Is age a handicap in finding employment? *Equal Opportun Int.* 2001;20(5–7):48–52.

23. Duncan C, Loretto W. Never the right age: gender and age-based discrimination in employment. *Gend Work Organ.* 2004;11(1):95–115.

24. Walker A. Towards and international political economy of ageing. *Ageing Soc.* 2005;25:815–839.

25. Wood G, Wilkinson A, Harcourt M. Age discrimination and working life: perspectives and contestations—a review of the contemporary literature. *Int J Manag Rev.* 2008;10(4):425–442.

26. Rospenda KM, Richman JA, Shannon CA. Prevalence and mental health correlates of harassment and discrimination in the workplace: results from a national study. *J Interpers Violence.* 2009;24(5):819–843.

27. Nawyn SJ, Richman JA, Rospenda KM, Tonda LH. Sexual identity and alcohol-related outcomes: contributions of workplace harassment. *J Subst Abuse.* 2000;11(3):289–304.

28. Rospenda KM, Richman JA. Harassment and discrimination. In Barling J, Kelloway EK, Frone MR, eds. *Handbook of Work Stress.* Thousand Oaks, Calif: Sage; 2005:149–188.

29. Cooper CL. *Theories of Organisational Stress.* Oxford, England: Oxford University Press; 1998.

30. Karasek RA. Job decision latitude, and mental strain: implications for job redesign. *Admin Sci Quart.* 1979;24(2):285–308.

31. Siegrist J. Adverse health effects of high effort-low reward conditions at work. *J Occup Health Psychol.* 1996;1:27–43.

32. Siegrist J. Chronic psychosocial stress at work and risk of depression: evidence from prospective studies. *Eur Arch Psychiatry Clin Neurosci.* 2008;258(5):115–119.

33. Karasek R, Theorell T. *Healthy Work-Stress, Productivity and the Reconstruction of Working Life.* New York, NY: Basic Books; 1990.

34. Johnson JV, Hall EM, Theorell T. Combined effects of job strain and social isolation on cardiovascular disease morbidity and mortality in a random sample of the Swedish male working population. *Scand J Work Environ Health.* 1989;15(4):271–279.

35. Siegrist J. A theory of occupational stress. In: Dunham J, ed. *Stress in the Workplace: Past, Present and Future.* London, England: Whurr Publishers; 2001.

36. Backe EM, Seidler A, Latza U, et al. The role of psychosocial stress at work for the development of cardiovascular diseases: a systematic review. *Int Arch Occup Environ Health.* 2012;85:67–79.

37. Cox T, Griffiths A, Barlow C, et al. *Organisational Interventions for Work Stress.* Sudbury, United Kingdom: HSE Books; 2000.

38. Lazarus RS. Psychological stress in the workplace. *J Soc Behav Pers.* 1989;6(7):1991–2013.

39. Cox T, Ferguson E. Individual difference, stress and coping. In: Cooper C, Payne L, eds. *Personality and Stress: Individual Differences in the Stress Process.* Chichester, United Kingdom: John Wiley & Sons; 1991:7–29.

40. Cox T. Stress research and stress management: putting theory to work. *HSE Contract Research Report.* 1993;61:29.

41. De Jonge J, Dollard MF. *Stress in the Workplace: Australian Master OHS and Environment Guide.* Sydney, Australia: CCH; 2002.

42. Landsbergis PA. Unhealthy work: causes, consequences, cures. In: Shnall PL, Dobson M, Rosskam E, eds. *Interventions to Reduce Job Stress and Improve Work Organization and Worker Health.* New York, NY: Baywood Publishing; 2009:193–209.

43. Whitehead M. A typology of actions to tackle social inequalities in health. *J Epidemiol Commun Health.* 2007;61(6):473–478.

44. Bhui K, Dinos S, Stansfeld SA, White P. A synthesis of the evidence for managing stress at work: a review of the reviews reporting on mental health and absenteeism. *J Environ Public Health.* 2012; 2012, p.515874.

45. Cancelliere C, Cassidy JD, Ammendolia C, Cote P. Are workplace health promotion programs effective at improving presenteeism in workers: a systematic review and best evidence synthesis of the literature. *BMC Public Health.* 2011;11(1):395–434.

46. Conn VS, Hafdahl AR, Cooper PS, et al. Meta-analysis of workplace physical activity interventions. *Am J Prev Med.* 2009;37(4):330–339.

47. Yung PMB, Keltner AA. A controlled comparison on the effect of muscle and cognitive relaxation procedures on blood pressure: implications for the behavioural treatment of borderline hypertensives. *Behav Res Ther.* 1996;34:821–826.

48. Yung PMB, Yi Fung M, Chan MFT, Lau BWK. Relaxation training methods for nurse managers in Hong Kong: a controlled study. *Int J Ment Health Nurs.* 2004;13:255–261.

49. Grossman P, Niemann L, Schmidt S, Walach H. Mindfulness-based stress reduction and health benefits: a meta-analysis. *J Psychosom Res.* 2004;57:35–43.

50. Gelderloos P, Walton KG, Orme-Johnson DW, Alexander CN. Effectiveness of the transcendental meditation program in preventing and treating substance

misuse: a review. *Subst Use Misuse.* 1991;26(3):293–325.

51. Martin A, Sanderson K, Cocker F. Meta-analysis of the effects of health promotion intervention in the workplace on depression and anxiety symptoms. *Scan J Work Environ Health.* 2009;35(1): 7–18.

52. Murphy LR. Stress management in work settings: a critical review of the health effects. *Am J Health Promot.* 1996;11(2):112–135.

53. van der Klink JJ, Blonk RW, Schene AH, van Dijk FJ. The benefits of interventions for work-related stress. *Am J Public Health.* 2001;91:270–276.

54. Marine A, Ruotsalainen J, Serra C, Verbeek J. Preventing occupational stress in healthcare workers [review]. *Cochrane Database Syst Rev.* 2006;(3):1–42.

55. Stranks J. *Stress at Work: Management and Prevention.* Oxford, England: Elsevier Butterworth-Heinemann; 2005.

56. Bambra C, Egan M, Thomas S, et al. The psychosocial and health effects of workplace reorganisation: a systematic review of task restructuring interventions. *J Epidemiol Community Health.* 2007;61(12):1028–1037.

57. Parkes KR, Sparkes TJ. *Organisational Interventions to Reduce Work Stress: Are They Effective? A Review of the Literature.* Sudbury, United Kingdom: HSE Books; 1998.

58. Kawakami N, Araki A, Kawahima M. Effects of work-related stress reduction on depressive symptoms among Japanese blue-collar workers. *Scand J Work Environ Health.* 1997;23:54–59.

59. Poulsen K, Jensen S, Bach E, Schostak J. Using action research to improve health and the work environment for 3500 municipal bus drivers. *Educ Action Res.* 2007;15(1):75–106.

60. LaMotagne A, Keegel T, Louie A, et al. Systematic review of the job stress intervention literature 1990-2005. *Int J Occup Envion Health.* 2007;13:268–280.

61. Semmer N. Job stress interventions and the organisation of work. *Scan J Work Environ Health.* 2006;32(6):515–527.

62. Egan M, Bambra C, Thomas S, et al. The psychosocial and health effects of workplace reorganisation: a systematic review of organisational-level interventions that aim to increase employee control. *J Epidemiol Community Health.* 2007;61(11):945–954.

63. Evanoff BA, Bohr PC, Wolf LD. Effects of a participatory ergonomics team among hospital orderlies. *Am J Ind Med.* 1999;35:358–365.

64. Wolfe R, Parker D, Napier N. Employee health management and organizational performance. *J Appl Behav Sci.* 1994;30: 22–42.

65. Altchiler L, Motta R. Effects of aerobic and nonaerobic exercise on anxiety absenteeism, and job satisfaction. *J Clin Psych.* 1994;50:829–840.

66. Parks KM, Steelman LA. Organizational wellness programs: a meta-analysis. *J Occup Health Psychol.* 2008;13(1): 58–68.

67. Towers Watson and The National Business Group on Health. *The Health and Productivity Advantage: Staying at Work Report.* New York, NY; 2010.

68. Maddi SR. *Hardiness: Turning Stressful Circumstances into Resilient Growth.* New York: Springer Briefs in Psychology; 2013.

69. Bell BC, Blanke D. The effects of a worksite fitness program on employee absenteeism. *Health Val.* 1989;13:3–11.

70. Lynch WD, Golaszewski TJ, Clearie AF, et al. Impact of a facility based corporate fitness program on the number of absences from work due to illness. *Occup Med (Oxford).* 1990;32:9–12.

71. Kompier M. Job design and wellbeing. In: Schabracq MJ, Winnubst JAM, Cooper

CL, eds. *The Handbook of Work and Health Psychology*. 2nd ed. Chichester, United Kingdom: Wiley & Sons Ltd; 2003: 429–454.

72.   Public Health England, 2013. Available at: https://www.gov.uk/government/organisations/public-health-england. Accessed 05/28/2014.

CHAPTER
17

Addressing Obesity at the Workplace

Ed Framer, Gordon Kaplan and Nico Pronk

INTRODUCTION

In the United States today, more than one-third of adults are obese, and adult obesity rates have more than doubled since the late 1970s. In addition, 17% of children and adolescents are obese, and childhood obesity rates have tripled during the course of a single generation.[1] Some researchers project continued growth in the prevalence of obesity in the United States between 2010 and 2030, with obesity prevalence perhaps rising by as much as an additional 33% to a record 51% by 2030.[2] Such an increase, compared to maintaining the prevalence at 2010 rates, would increase annual medical care expenditures by as much as $550 billion. However, other emerging data indicate that the prevalence of obesity in the United States appears to be leveling out.[3,4] The reasons behind this observed plateau, however, remain unknown and appear to be independent of current treatment or prevention strategies. Treatment options, despite showing statistically significant results in trials, have not been able to curb the population trend toward increased weight. Worksite obesity treatment programs are no exception. Despite some evidence of successful programs, obesity remains largely resistant to programmatic solutions designed to treat or prevent it.

To quote Albert Einstein, "The significant problems we face cannot be solved at the same level of thinking that was used when we created them."[5] The appropriate fix is not necessarily driven by what or who caused the problem, or even by narrow theoretical definitions of the problem itself. For example, until very recently obesity has been largely treated as an individual-level problem in need of individual-centered treatment. This remains true whether the treatments are delivered in one-to-one or one-to-many (i.e., group) formats. The expected adjustments to lifestyle behaviors, psychological processes, or even the surrounding environment too often remain largely the responsibility of each adult individual. But can an individual focus, no matter whether delivered as a 1-to-1 or 1-to-20 or even 1-to-30 intervention, be expected to get the job done? In fact, it is not likely to succeed in the face of a combined overweight and obesity rate of over 65% in the United States. It is highly doubtful that more than 65% of us are "broken" at an individual level, either biologically or psychologically, and thus able to be fixed with individually based treatments alone. Solutions are more likely to come from a wide variety of changes made at the level of families, groups, workforces, communities, the nation, and even the world that will collectively impact on the way individuals behave and make decisions.

Obesity exerts a heavy toll on individuals, populations, and society as a whole. Cawley[6] summarizes the insights gleaned from various lines of obesity research from a wide variety of perspectives, including anthropology, economics, government, psychology, and sociology. Cawley's conclusions echo those made by the Institute of Medicine, which recognize that obesity carries stigma and is associated with:

- lower quality of life and work performance,
- increased chronic disease burden and medical care costs,
- reduced physical, social, and emotional functioning,
- lost productivity costs,
- reduced longevity, and
- premature mortality.[6,7]

Obesity imposes a significant burden on employers. Almost two-thirds of the increase in the national expenditures in health care over the past two decades can be attributed to the increase in obesity rates.[8] Despite the fact that most, if not all, of the increased costs are eventually borne by the workers themselves as costs are passed on to them through forgone earnings,[9] employers still have to manage increases in total cost of medical care; deal with financial challenges associated with employees not being at work or being less than optimally productive; and address the administrative challenges associated with worker replacements and retention. Excess obesity-related costs, when combined with absenteeism, are estimated to be in the range of $400 to more than $2000 per employee per year.[10] For example, in one manufacturing site, obesity-related absenteeism and presenteeism, indicators of indirect costs, were associated with a 4.2% productivity loss, which converted into a loss of

$506 (in 2008 dollars) per employee per year.[11] Other indicators of reduced work performance have been associated with obesity or obesity-related health factors (physical inactivity, poor cardiorespiratory fitness) as well, including overall job performance, quality or quantity of work performed, quality of interpersonal interaction with coworkers, extra effort exerted, and work loss days.[12] Furthermore, obesity is associated with increased chances of injury on the job, asthma, musculoskeletal disorders, immune system responses, neurotoxicity, stress, cardiovascular disease, and cancer.[13] Taken together, these data suggest that obesity exerts a heavy toll on both employees and their companies. This toll results from reduced physical, mental, and emotional health, and is collected as excess medical care expenditures, reduced productivity, and impaired overall performance at work.

The rationale for addressing obesity at the workplace is compelling. As a complex social system, the workplace can reach large numbers of people, directly or indirectly, frequently, and over long periods of time.[14,15] The organizational context may be leveraged for the purpose of health improvement through the use of organizational policies, leadership roles, benefits designs, human resource functions, incentive strategies, and communications. When considering these opportunities carefully and strategically, norms or cultures conducive to health may be created[16-19] and leveraged to address obesity from both prevention and treatment/management perspectives.

Purpose, Scope, and Format

The purpose of this chapter is to present a comprehensive discussion of obesity and its relationship to the workplace setting and the broader community, with a special emphasis on employer concerns. As such, the review of the evidence base for successful individual or small group interventions is limited. The interested reader may find additional examples of these reviews elsewhere.[20-27] The chapter is not meant to be a how-to manual for implementing obesity initiatives. For that, we have provided selected resources to assist those interested in applying our recommendations (see Table 17-1). The scope of this chapter is intentionally broad. It includes a review and discussion of:

- a conceptual framework for reducing obesity;
- trends in prevalence;
- changes in energy balance–related behaviors at work;
- the impact of obesity on health and cost outcomes;
- the business case for obesity

Table 17-1: Open Access and Web-Based Resources Available to Support Workplace Obesity Programs.

Topic	Open Access Source
CDC LEAN Works program	http://www.cdc.gov/leanworks/
CDC Nutritious Eating Toolkits	http://www.cdc.gov/nccdphp/dnpao/hwi/toolkits/nutrition.htm
CDC Steps to Wellness: A Guide to Implementing the 2008 Physical Activity Guidelines for Americans in the Workplace	http://www.cdc.gov/nccdphp/dnpao/hwi/toolkits/pa-toolkit.htm
CDC increasing fruit and vegetable consumption	http://www.cdc.gov/nccdphp/dnpao/hwi/toolkits/gardenmarket/index.htm
CDC stairwell walking	http://www.cdc.gov/nccdphp/dnpao/hwi/toolkits/stairwell/index.htm
CDC walkability audit	http://www.cdc.gov/nccdphp/dnpao/hwi/toolkits/walkability/index.htm
CDC lactation support program	http://www.cdc.gov/nccdphp/dnpao/hwi/toolkits/lactation/index.htm
State of Iowa being active and eating smart tools	http://www.idph.state.ia.us/iowansfitforlife/common/pdf/healthy_worksites_toolkit.pdf
State of North Carolina Eat Smart, Move More	http://www.eatsmartmovemorenc.com/Worksites.html
New Hampshire Healthy Worksite toolkit	http://www.dhhs.nh.gov/dphs/nhp/worksite/index.htm
State of Minnesota Healthy Minnesota Toolkit	http://www.health.state.mn.us/divs/hpcd/NGAtoolkit/toolkit.pdf
NIH weight management resources	http://www.nhlbi.nih.gov/health/public/heart/obesity/wecan/tools-resources/weight-management.htm

Topic	Open Access Source
Harvard School of Public Health–The Obesity Prevention Source	http://www.hsph.harvard.edu/obesity-prevention-source/obesity-prevention/worksites/worksites-obesity-prevention-recommendations-complete-list/
NIOSH Total Worker Health program	http://www.cdc.gov/niosh/twh/

*CDC indicates Centers for Disease Control and Prevention; NIH, National Institutes of Health; and NIOSH, National Institute for Occupational Safety and Health.

prevention and treatment from an employer's perspective;

- considerations of successful program design elements or principles; and
- obesity in the context of the complex social system of the workplace and the larger community of which it is part.

To guide the discussion, we present a conceptual framework that illustrates the salient components and elements.

A Conceptual Framework

Addressing obesity at the worksite holds promise, but should be considered carefully and strategically in order to ensure optimal health outcomes, equity across employees and dependents, and avoidance of unintended consequences. Therefore, a delineation of an overall approach is well advised. Figure 17-1 presents a conceptual framework designed to guide the overall strategy and implementation for obesity at the workplace as discussed in this chapter. The framework is constructed based on evidence derived from the scientific literature and informed by insights that stem from best practices and case examples. This framework will also serve as a guide for the remainder of this chapter. Briefly, the model presents, from left to right, activities, outputs, impacts, and outcomes. Activities fall under three main headings: (1) multilevel activities that can influence individuals, groups, the organization as a whole, and the community; (2) activities

that address vision and engagement, involving leadership, cultural norms and values, and worker involvement; and (3) activities that improve the work environment through changes in the physical, psychosocial, and socioeconomic environments, as well as efforts at the policy and advocacy levels. Collectively, these activities are intended to improve weight-related behaviors that in turn positively affect energy balance of individuals as well as the population. Once these collective forces are generating improvements, a variety of outcomes may be observed, including improved health, enhanced well-being, increased function, improved job performance and productivity, reduced health care utilization and costs, and enhanced corporate culture and image.

What will it Take to Generate Successes in the Short and Long(er) Term?

It is important to recognize that obesity is the result of a complex set of interrelated factors that extend far beyond the employee and the workplace. It is affected by food marketing, television viewing, use of video games, policy, food prices, behavioral economics, food availability, bias, stigma, and discrimination, just to name a few. Success in the short term may be achieved, for example, by engaging overweight or obese employees in weight loss challenges or team competitions. At the same

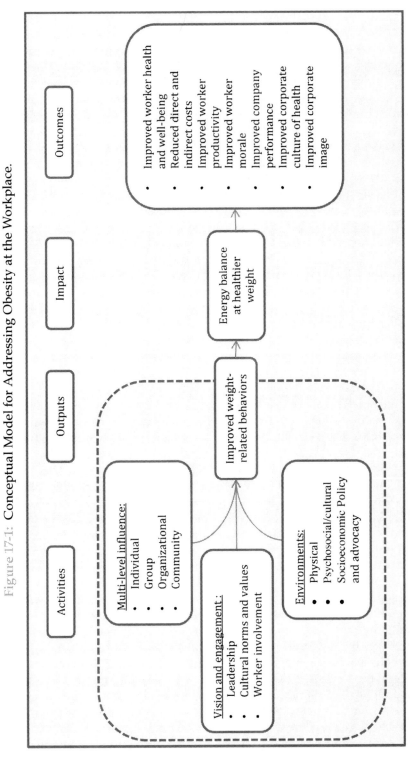

Figure 17-1: Conceptual Model for Addressing Obesity at the Workplace.

time, achieving more meaningful, longer-term weight loss and weight loss maintenance will require the use of strategies and incentives suited for those goals.

Given the generally intractable nature of obesity,[28] to address it effectively, programs and services will require sustained, multilevel, comprehensive efforts. Worksite interventions have demonstrated the ability to influence obesity for the short term. For example, a meta-analysis of 80 studies with follow-up periods of at least a year or more showed weight losses of 11 to 18 pounds and weight maintenance of 6.5 to 13 pounds.[29] Although not trivial, these amounts represent limited success for someone who is 30 to 50 or even more pounds overweight. As such, they are not likely to represent a meaningful solution to the issue of obesity. In a systematic review of the summarized findings from 11 clinical trials and 11 observational studies involving 480,142 participants, Hutfless and colleagues[27] found that short-term weight loss has been achieved from low-fat diets, eating fewer meals away from home, eating more fruits and vegetables, monitoring heart rate during exercise, and participating in group lifestyle sessions with reminder text messages, but also that the strength of the evidence is low. Realistically, both short- and longer-term success may be expected only when activities follow the basic approach outlined in the conceptual framework (Figure 17-1). At the activity level, this calls for individual-level programs to be supported by peers and others who are part of a team while the organization provides both supportive policies and an environment in which the employees can participate in health-promoting activities. Their individual and group-based efforts also need to be reinforced through engaging community-based resources, such as walking trails, local fitness centers, and access to healthy food options. Company leaders can support weight management activities, which can also be placed within a broader context of health promotion program options

addressing other risk factors. This approach frames weight management options to be one health improvement among many, and it allows employees more freedom in making participation choices rather than being singled out for having a specific risk (i.e., obesity). This strategy fosters the creation of a corporate culture that supports health and well-being. In addition, successes in managing other health risks are also likely to have a beneficial impact on weight management. Finally, changes in organizational policy and the physical and psychosocial environments that support a healthy weight may be the most important factors to be considered when it comes to longer-term success. When organizational policies that support health and well-being are written, implemented, and enforced, specifically promoting physical activity, reducing prolonged sitting, and making healthful food choices, it is highly likely that a supportive physical and psychosocial work environment will emerge. That is, organizational health policy will shape the work environment.

By themselves, individual-level programs are unlikely to be an adequate intervention. The cost of individual treatment is too high and the long-term results too poor. These observations are supported by Heinen and Darling[30] and Yancey et al.[31] Both of these large reviews of workplace approaches to obesity make the point that although the workplace is a particularly important arena in which to tackle obesity and health, what is needed is an emphasis on workplace policies and cultures—that is, organizational-level approaches. Heinen and Darling specifically state that "policy development is needed to accelerate change, especially for smaller employers (those with fewer than 500 employees), which represent the majority of U.S. employers..."[30]

Before presenting recommendations that address the issue of overweight and obesity in the workforce, it will be beneficial to put these recommendations in context by outlining the extent of the problem and its impact on health and costs. The reader may also see the previous version of this chapter for additional details.[32]

THE PROBLEM

Defining Overweight and Obesity

Obesity is a condition defined as an excess of body fat over desirable levels. It has taken center stage as a national health problem because of its relationship to a broad spectrum of health problems. This relationship has been acknowledged for decades and it continues to be refined. In addition, debate continues over the best metric or metrics to use when discussing obesity and its relationship to health and to health care and productivity costs. Metrics that have been considered include weight; weight adjusted for height; percentage body fat; and various indices of body fat type such as waist-to-hip ratio, sagittal abdominal diameter (the distance from the small of the back to the upper abdomen), and waist circumference. Despite academic debate, however, overweight and obesity have traditionally been defined by body mass index (BMI), a metric defined as weight in kilograms divided by height in meters squared. BMI has been extensively researched and has long been established as a valid approach to stratifying individuals with regard to the risk posed by their weight on their physical and emotional health.[33] Figure 17-2 displays the current definitions for BMI ranges. BMI is not a perfect metric, particularly not in the range of 25 to 29.9, where those classified as overweight may not always be overfat by percentage body fat criteria. BMIs of 30 or greater are much less likely to result in such errors. All of this notwithstanding, BMI does have the advantage of being easy and inexpensive to obtain across a variety of settings. Thus, it remains the metric of choice for stratifying weight with regard to health risk and population goals, both in the United States[34] and throughout the world.[35] For these reasons, BMI provides a reasonable metric for use by employers faced with decisions about offering interventions and incentives to their employees. It also works when setting goals and demonstrating the impact of their wellness programs on employee health and productivity.

The Increasing Prevalence of Overweight and Obesity

Since the 1900s, the United States[36] and global[37] prevalences of overweight and obesity have increased dramatically. Recent surveys estimate that two-thirds of American adults have BMIs exceeding 24.9 kg/m² (overweight) and approximately one-third exceed 29.9 kg/m² (obese).[36] Wang and coworkers extrapolate that if past trends were to continue, the prevalence of obesity among adults would increase from its present level of about 32% to approximately 50% by 2030.[38] Although there are recent data to suggest that in the United States increases

Figure 17-2: BMI Classifications (NIH, 1998).

< 18.5 kg/m²	Underweight
18.5-24.9 kg/m²	Desirable weight
25.0-29.9 kg/m²	Overweight
30.0-34.9 kg/m²	Obesity (Class 1)
35-39.9 kg/m²	Obesity (Class 2)
>= 40.0	Extreme Obesity (Class 3)

may be leveling off,[3,4,39,40] this provides little reassurance given current high levels of overweight and obesity.

Similar trends apply to the worksite situation. Both the 2006 Medical Expenditure Panel Survey (MEPS) and the 2008 U.S. National Health and Wellness Survey (NHWS) reflect working-age populations and hence are representative of employees and worksite situations across the nation. Finkelstein et al. analyzed data from these surveys and found the prevalence of overweight to be 38.0% and 35.6% and for obesity to be 28.5% and 34.8% for the MEPS and NHWS, respectively.[41] Consequently, weight management represents an important health improvement opportunity among employees and a critical risk factor to consider when addressing health-related cost concerns among employers.

The Health Hazards of Overweight and Obesity

The health risks of obesity have been studied extensively and are well recognized.[33,42] According to the National Institutes of Health, being overweight or obese substantially increases the risk of morbidity from hypertension, dyslipidemia, type 2 diabetes, coronary heart disease, stroke, gallbladder disease, osteoarthritis, sleep apnea, respiratory problems, and certain cancers including endometrial, breast, prostate, and colon cancers.[33] A few examples will serve to illustrate this situation. Landsberg et al. cite the American Heart Association as estimating that at least 75% of the incidence of hypertension is related directly to obesity.[43] Geiss et al.[44] found obesity to be a major factor in new incidences of type 2 diabetes. Jensen et al.[45] found that being overweight or obese was associated with significantly increased risk for acute coronary events across all levels of behavioral lifestyle risks (physical inactivity, smoking, unhealthy diet). Anandacoomarasamy et al.[46] document the associations between obesity and a variety of musculoskeletal disorders. They also note the importance of weight loss in addressing these problems. In addition to these physical health effects, the quality of life for obese individuals is lower than for their nonobese counterparts,[47] and they continue to experience social stigmatization and discrimination.[48] Recent analyses support the overall conclusion that obesity increases health risks. The International Association for the Study of Obesity recently provided a review of the strength of the associations between excess weight and a number of disease outcomes. These include ischemic heart disease, stroke, diabetes mellitus, chronic obstructive pulmonary disease, and several cancers (lung, breast, colon and rectum, mouth and oropharynx, esophagus, endometrium [uterus, womb], kidney, and gallbladder).[49]

Obesity is also associated with increases in all-cause mortality.[33,49] In 1998, the National Institutes of Health recognized overweight and obesity as a major contributor to preventable deaths in the United States, calling it a major public health challenge. It also remains a target in the list of recommendations issued by the Surgeon General for improving the health of Americans.[34] The association of obesity with mortality is found across increasing age groups,[50] suggesting that it may never be too late to address this health problem. Greenberg estimates that young and middle-aged adults who are obese will reduce their life expectancy by 9.44 years.[51] Although there is some disagreement about the mortality risk posed by being overweight — with some finding such a relationship[52] but others not[53] — there is less controversy about the increased morbidity risk posed by overweight.[54,55] Unfortunately, many studies reporting on the impact of overweight and obesity on mortality do not adequately adjust for cardiorespiratory fitness. As a result, it is unclear if the protective effects of being physically fit can offset the negative impact of too much weight. A recent study by Sui and colleagues provides some insight on this issue.[56]

Their conclusions indicate that fitness has a strong inverse association with mortality. This pattern is changed little by adjustments for adiposity or fat distribution. Hence, both fitness and BMI represent strong and independent risk factors of all-cause mortality. In addition, they found that higher levels of fitness provided a protective effect on mortality in both normal-weight and overweight subgroups. This was not the case for the obese categories; however, they noted that their sample sizes and observed death rates were not sufficient to draw firm conclusions for the obese (BMI ≥ 30) groups.

Fortunately, losing weight provides strong health benefits for people who are obese. Juonala et al.[57] found that individuals who were obese in childhood and remained obese as adults were at increased risk for type 2 diabetes, hypertension, dyslipidemia, and carotid-artery atherosclerosis. On the other hand, those who achieved desirable weight status as adults had no greater risk for these conditions than those who had never been obese.[57] Other research also shows that interventions that successfully reduce BMI and maintain these reductions are associated with improved health parameters (i.e., reduced morbidity).[58] In addition, benefits are known to occur even with modest weight losses on the order of 5% to 10% of initial body weight.[59,60] It has been noted that intentional weight loss is difficult for most people to maintain,[61,62] and concern has been expressed that weight cycling may increase health risk.[63] However, recent research indicates that the latter is not the case.[64,65] Finally, a recent 8-year longitudinal cohort analysis indicated that among employees who successfully reduced their body weight from a BMI above 30 kg/m² to below 30 kg/m² in the first 4 years of the study, the likelihood of developing diabetes declined by 78%. On the other hand, among those who gained weight and became obese in the first 4 years of the study, the likelihood of developing diabetes in the second 4 years of the study increased by 885%.[66] Therefore, efforts to reduce body weight should not be abandoned

because of the difficulty associated with weight loss and weight loss maintenance.

The Etiology of Obesity

It is not the intention of this chapter to rehash theories of the etiology of obesity. Authorities agree that causes for the dramatic increase in the prevalence of both overweight and obesity over the past several decades are multifactorial and interactive. They include genetic, hormonal, environmental, behavioral, social, and even political factors. From this general understanding of the nature of the problem, it becomes clear that solutions will also need to be broad, multifactorial, and interactive, as our conceptual framework illustrates.[67] This chapter may also shed some light on the impact of the employer and worksite within the constellation of interventions that will need to be applied in pursuit of a reversal of the current obesity epidemic.

THE COSTS OF OBESITY

Societal Costs

Obesity is a significant driver of health care costs in the United States. Compared with nonobese individuals, obese individuals have higher utilization of health care services even when controlling for health status and sociodemographic variables.[68] In an analysis of data from the Health and Retirement Study, Andreyeva et al. found that obesity-related health care costs increased with increasing degree of obesity, with class 1 (BMI = 30–35), class 2 (BMI = 35–40) and class 3 (BMI > 40) showing increases in health care expenditures above normal weight of 25%, 50%, and 100%, respectively.[69] Arterburn et al. also found that aggregate obesity-related U.S. health care expenditures among morbidly obese adults exceeded $11 billion in 2000.[70] Finkelstein et al. reported an increase in the estimated medical costs of obesity from $78.5 billion in 1998 to $147 billion by 2008.[71] Finally, data from the MEPS showed increases in the average annual health care expenditure for the obese population (rising from $3458 to $5148) and the overweight population (rising from $2792 to $3636) when comparing the years 2001 and 2006. Overall health care expenditures increased by 82% and 36% for obese and overweight adults respectively versus only 25% for normal-weight adults, also reflecting the increase in the prevalence of overweight and obesity in the population.[72] Based on their estimates of projected increases in the incidence of diabetes, cardiovascular disease, and cancers due to projected increases in obesity over the next two decades, Wang et al. predict increased health care costs of $48 billion to $66 billion per year in the United States.[38] This underscores the importance of preventing obesity. Weight loss may also help reverse the trend. For example, Dall et al. report that among 4.6 million military beneficiaries, 1.1 billion dollars in medical costs in 2006 was attributed to obesity; based on their predictive modeling, they further estimate that among overweight and obese beneficiaries, lifetime medical expenditures would decline $440 for each permanent 1% reduction in body weight.[73] Validation of this projection awaits further confirmation from other studies.

The Cost to Employers

Published studies are uniform in demonstrating that obese workers cost employers significantly more than their nonobese counterparts in terms of both direct medical costs and increased productivity losses.[74] Kaplan et al. summarized earlier research,[32] and more recent studies continue to demonstrate the costs that obesity poses for employers. For example, in a study of self-insured employers that included 88,984 employees, Durden et al. estimated that the incremental combined direct medical and indirect costs for overweight, obese, and severely obese employees were $1550.92, $2223.58, and $3391.52 per year, respectively.[75] Again, in a cross-sectional analysis of the 2006

MEPS and the 2008 NHWS, Finkelstein et al.[41] found an annual cost attributable to obesity among full-time employees of $73.1 billion. They also found an incremental increase in costs with increasing BMI and that those with a BMI > 35 represented 37% of the obese population but were responsible for 61% of excess costs.

Effectively addressing obesity among employees is likely to result in cost savings. For example, Carls et al.[76] showed that over a 6-year period, employees who moved into high risk status (BMI ≥ 30) had 9.9% higher annual cost increases compared with those who remained at lower risk status. In addition, those who moved from high to lower risk status had annual cost increases that were 2.3% lower than those who remained at high risk status.[76] Even with pending changes in how employers provide health care coverage for their employees, obesity will continue to be an economic issue because of its association with productivity costs.[77-80]

ACTIVITIES

There can be no disagreement that the population prevalences of overweight and obesity have continued to rise over the past 30 to 40 years.[2,36,37,81] Further, there seems to be no individual-based treatment for obesity that can quickly, reliably, and cost-effectively reach the majority of people who need it. Instead, it appears that we have a population-based, cultural, and environmental issue that we must deal with by developing and using a substantially different approach. The following categories will be used to organize the types of strategies needed for this approach: Awareness, Motivation, Skills, and Opportunity.[82]

Awareness

Awareness programs are those that help employees understand the impact of various behaviors and decision making on success in maintaining a healthy body weight. Behaviors such as food choices, physical activity, sleep, and alcohol use have direct impacts on metabolism and weight regulation. Specific to physical activity and food choices, promotional activities designed to raise awareness include the use of pamphlets, fliers, posters, and signage to saturate the workplace with messages.[83] E-mails, instant messages, texts, and tweets can also extend the reach of such communications. Prompts and reminders have also shown to be highly effective in raising awareness, thereby adding to the likelihood that individuals will change behavior (see Community Preventive Services Task Force findings at http://www.thecommunityguide.org/worksite/index.html). Specifically for physical activity behavior, prompts have proven to be an effective and low-cost tactic to increase positive behavior.[84] Examples of these approaches to increase awareness for physical activity behavior include marking walking paths inside and outside company buildings, creating prompts for people to use the stairwells instead of escalators or elevators, and providing equipment to monitor body weight (e.g., scales located in bathrooms). Other examples more specifically tailored to dietary behavior include healthful food choice labeling in corporate cafeterias, equipment (scales) to use to measure foods and control portion sizes, and text messages set to be received just prior to lunchtime that remind people to select healthful food options (yumPower program at www.yumpower.com). In a recent study, stair prompts were associated with a 3.21% increased likelihood of stair use.[85]

Motivation

What is motivation? The *Oxford Dictionary* defines motivation as "the reason or reasons one has for acting or behaving in a particular way."[86] The reason(s) one has for behaving in specific ways can have a direct impact on the success or lack thereof in behavior changes, including weight loss and weight maintenance. Reasons for acting may be internally or externally focused. Intrinsic motivation refers to internally based motivation that is driven by an interest or enjoyment in the task itself or that follows from its naturally occurring results. Extrinsic motivation comes from outside of the individual. Common extrinsic motivators are external rewards (for example, money or grades) for showing the desired behavior, or the threat of punishment following misbehavior. Intrinsic and extrinsic motivators or rewards are not to be confused with operant reinforcers (which increase the rate of the behavior that occurred just before the reinforcer was delivered) or punishers (which decrease the rate of the behavior that occurred just before the punisher was delivered). Things that we refer to as motivators or rewards, at least as far as health promotion programming goes, usually increase program participation. Although participation is critical to program success, participation in a program is not tantamount to successful behavior change. For example, although participating in a weight loss program may be a prerequisite to successful weight loss and weight maintenance for many people, developing the necessary weight-focused behaviors and sustaining them over time is an additional requirement that goes beyond simple program participation.

Intrinsic motivation may be stimulated by having people reflect on issues that are important to them, for example, by asking the question, "As you think about your health, consider what matters to you. Now how can you achieve those things you are wanting?" An individual may be able to uncover those things that allow him or her to pursue improved health because of his or her interest in doing so, not because of anyone else's agenda or some other external reason. Specific examples of how to stimulate acting on obesity using intrinsic motivation may include personal health coaching, virtual health coaching, seminars, employee assistance programs, or referral to community resources. However, being motivated for any reason is not the same as defining healthy behaviors or skills (behaviors or more often groups of behaviors) and then developing them or increasing their frequency if they already exist. What is being motivated, whether the motivation is intrinsic or extrinsic? The usual result of motivation in weight loss situations is participation in a program, project, or treatment. Participation and eventually personal engagement are prerequisites to learning, behavior change, weight loss, weight maintenance, and health improvement.

Extrinsic motivation may include financial incentives for individuals to achieve by participating in a worksite health promotion program. Such incentives may be integrated into a health care benefits design (e.g., preferential deductible or copay option), reduced health care premium, cash incentives, or other rewards including material goods or chances to win as part of a lottery. Other extrinsic motivators include competitions, which are extrinsic motivators because they encourage the performer to win by defeating others, not simply to enjoy the intrinsic rewards of the activity. However, extrinsic motivation is too easily relied on to do all the work in getting people to change their behavior. It only works as long as the rewards are employed, are arranged to take advantage of the ways that people respond to such reward/ punishment systems, and remain valued when balanced against the behavioral costs required to maintain behaviors that may take much effort over sustained periods to generate success. Thus, many extrinsic motivational interventions are likely to succeed only in the short term. That doesn't mean they shouldn't be used, just that they need to be a component of a broader, more comprehensive health promotion strategy.

Skills

A range of strategies exist to support people in acquiring and implementing the skills needed to live a more physically active lifestyle, increase access to more healthy and nutritious food options, and optimize the chances to sustain those skills over time. The final criteria in judging the success of skill-building efforts are whether calorie deficits can be generated in order to lose weight and whether the participant can learn to maintain energy balance long term.[32] The two preceding chapters in this book have addressed the areas of healthy eating and physical activity, and much of what they present is relevant for skill development in weight management programming. Skill building may occur at the individual or personal level, but may also apply to groups or teams at the workplace or the family unit at home. Examples of such efforts include the adoption of journaling and tracking when trying out a new behavior; researching specific questions related to problems or barriers encountered in attempting to adopt a new behavior; and the creation of a group or support team at work, at home, or in the community in order to ensure sufficient social support to successfully adopt a new behavior. Such efforts can be supported by various tools and resources. For example, the use of electronic pedometers and accelerometers is pervasive. Many of these tools can be considerably enhanced by using Web-based or virtual programs — for example, the use of Web- and phone-based applications for tracking from wearable devices that measure and record food choices and physical activities. The tracking of weight using digital scales connected to the Internet may also be enhanced by connecting these to health coaching call centers.[87] Managing obesity requires a net calorie intake and calorie expenditure that allow for a dynamic energy balance at the participant's target weight.

Opportunity

Opportunity refers to the ways in which employers can support employees to be more active, have better access to healthful food options, and in general stimulate more healthy work environments. The surrounding physical and social cues, supports, and rewards take on a very important emphasis. Related to physical activity, examples of opportunity include the creation of inviting stairwells as a physical activity–friendly environment, the provision of an on-site fitness center or discounts at local fitness facilities, the provision of bike racks and bike-to-work incentives, and access to locker rooms and shower facilities at the workplace. Other, more recent developments include the use of sit-stand devices to reduce prolonged sitting time at work. Recent trials have shown evidence of effectiveness of this strategy to reduce sedentary behavior and, in the process, improve workplace performance.[88,89]

For nutrition, examples of opportunity include the labeling of healthy food choices in vending machines, providing preferential pricing for healthful food options,[90] coordination of local farmers' markets at the workplace, organizational policies to mostly or only allow healthy foods to be served at company events, and employer coalitions to support healthy weight and physical activity in the community.

Another major area of opportunity is explicit action on the part of company leadership to set a forward-looking vision for the health promotion program, then commit the company to an approach that ensures high levels of engagement. Such approaches should be pursued at multiple levels of the organization so as to make sure that middle managers and front-line staff are involved in the overall program. Table 17-2 gives examples of how the different activity areas can be operationalized within the model shown in Figure 17-1.

OUTPUTS, IMPACT, AND OUTCOMES

The conceptual framework presented in Figure 17-1 illustrates how the overall strategies implemented at the workplace result in activities and tactics that generate specific outputs. These outputs subsequently impact energy balance and drive health-related outcomes, including but not limited to a healthier body weight. The output section in this framework describes the collective input of all activities—individual-level, management activities, leadership, and changes in the physical and psychosocial or cultural environment. Improved weight-related behaviors include higher levels of physical activity and reductions in prolonged sitting time. They also include increases in healthier food choices that result in a level of calorie intake that is more easily balanced against total energy expenditure. Additionally, other behavior closely related to energy input and expenditure is also improved, including sleep, stress management skills, problem-solving skills, and decision-making skills.[6] These behaviors play an important role in optimizing the chances that individuals can succeed at short-term weight loss and longer-term weight maintenance.

Successful outcomes are an important consideration in creating a business case for investment in obesity programs by the employer. Through the efficient and ongoing use of assessment and evaluation, the following examples of outcomes may be tracked and reported on[91,92]:

- Worker health and well-being
- Reduced health care costs
- Improved productivity
- Improved employee morale
- Improved company performance
- Improved corporate culture
- Improved corporate image in the community

None of these outcomes, however, will occur if there is little employee participation or program engagement. The following program elements are examples of how participant experiences manifest themselves into long-term program engagement[93–101]:

Table 17-2: Activities (to Support Individuals in Maintaining Healthy Weights)*.

Activity Type	Worksite Focus	Intervention Level	Examples
Increasing awareness	Participants	Individual	Providing feedback reports showing employees' health risks, strengths, and suggested next steps based on their answers on an HRA.
		Group	Lunch and learn sessions for weight management.
		Organization/ company	Displaying company-wide HRA completion rates and explaining the relationship to the company's vision for a healthy workforce.
		Community	Inviting spouses to participate in weight management activities provided for employees.
	Vision, culture, and engagement	Individual	Sending periodic prompts to at-risk employees' e-mails of the availability of health coaching for weight management.
		Group	Sharing weight-related wellness challenge participation and outcome metrics comparing departments within a company.
		Organization/ company	Providing a clear endorsement from senior leadership of various company policies that support maintaining a healthy body weight.
		Community	Posting signs showing opportunities and reasons for involvement in community activities (for example, community fun runs, farmers' markets, etc.) that support healthy weight management.
	Environments	Individual	Encouraging individuals to use a company-endorsed mobile app for tracking food intake as part of weight management.
		Group	Healthy weight informational campaigns.
		Organization/ company	Posting signs promoting healthy food and activity choices in common areas (cafeterias, break rooms, etc.)
		Community	Providing employees with maps of the local community showing places for safe walking/biking.

Activity Type	Worksite Focus	Intervention Level	Examples
Enhancing motivation	Participants	Individual	Training health advocates/coaches to use motivational interviewing techniques to help individuals who are overweight/obese explore their values and behavioral intentions with respect to making lifestyle changes to better manage their weight.
		Group	Team competitions for weight loss and weight maintenance.
		Organization/company	Celebrating individuals' successes at a company-sponsored awards event.
		Community	Working through local business group (e.g., Chamber of Commerce) or city/county government agencies to sponsor a competition for employers focused on healthy weight management.
	Vision, culture, and engagement	Individual	Encouraging employees to set specific goals for healthy living that will have a beneficial impact on their weight.
		Group	Using wellness champions within company sites to promote participation in healthy weight activities.
		Organization/company	Arranging benefits designs to reinforce the maintenance of healthy body weights and/or modest weight loss.
		Community	Being visible, as a company leader, participating in community-based events that promote being active.
	Environments	Individual	Have people post the reasons why they want to be more active at their work station.
		Group	Sharing success stories.
		Organization/company	Arranging for a special incentive (e.g., a trip to climb Pike's Peak) for all employees who earn a designated amount of wellness credits from wellness program participation.
		Community	Allowing employees to earn wellness credits for participating in local fun runs.

Activity Type	Worksite Focus	Intervention Level	Examples
Building skills	Participants	Individual	Providing individual coaching to increase fruit/vegetable intake.
		Group	Providing on-site group-based weight management programs during the workday.
		Organization/company	Providing a Fitbit device for employees to track their daily activity.
		Community	Providing a health coach-guided grocery store tour.
	Vision, culture, and engagement	Individual	Using gamification to engage employees in healthy weight programs.
		Group	Using gamification to initiate team competitions to avoid weight gain during the month of December.
		Organization/company	Providing healthy weight group-based activities on company time.
		Community	The company's sponsoring a community-based healthy nutrition initiative that brings schools and families together using farmers' markets.
	Environments	Individual	Sharing and highlighting success stories.
		Group	Group-based walking clubs.
		Organization/company	Organizational campaigns to increase stair use.
		Community	Engaging local health care providers and hospitals to provide hypertension management education courses that address obesity and lifestyle behaviors for prevention and management.

Activity Type	Worksite Focus	Intervention Level	Examples
Creating supportive environments	Participants	Individual	Advising/allowing employees to keep walking shoes at their workstations so they can take advantage of opportunities to be more active.
		Group	Setting up a bulletin board where people can anonymously share the tactics they have found to be successful in managing their own weight.
		Organization/company	Setting a company policy that allows employees to conduct business meetings during walks.
		Community	Providing a voucher for participating in a local Weight Watchers (or other reputable weight management) group.
	Vision, culture, and engagement	Individual	Giving feedback to individuals participating in a company-sponsored exercise challenge that compares their progress with that of other participants.
		Group	Sponsoring company teams to participate in community events related to healthy living (walk to cure cancer, marathon clubs, etc.)
		Organization/company	Ensuring supportive company policies for healthy nutrition options at the workplace.
		Community	The organization's joining a local employer coalition with the goal to improve community resources for active living.
	Environments	Individual	Decorating stairwells, provide signage, and prompt stair use.
		Group	Making fruit available for all meetings lasting 4 or more hours.
		Organization/company	Adopting a company-wide practice of not having unhealthy foods served during company meetings.
		Community	Providing memberships to local fitness clubs as part of the employee benefits package.

*Note that some activities may fit more than one type/focus/level combination. HRA indicates health risk assessment.

- Incentives design
- Program options and activities
- The way in which the program is implemented
- The way in which leadership participates and supports the program
- The manner in which employees are represented in decision making regarding the program
- The way communications are designed to ensure employees stay up to date; and
- The manner in which all programmatic activities are experienced by the users

What Resources Are There Available Through Open Access?

A large array of resources in the public domain provides information on weight management–related programs and services. Most come from nonprofit sources, frequently government sources, and are available at no cost via the Internet (see Table 17-1). In particular, the Centers for Disease Control and Prevention provide several worksite health promotion programs with an emphasis on obesity. Additionally, the National Institute for Occupational Safety and Health has introduced the Total Worker Health (TWH) program, which is designed to integrate worker health protection and health promotion. Many excellent resources are available through that program as well. Obesity has an impact on both worker health and worker safety, and it qualifies as a special area of interest of TWH.

CONCLUSIONS

The weight control chapters in the first three editions of this book focused primarily on what interventions could be offered at the worksite to overweight/obese employees and their spouses. In the past decade, it has become increasingly apparent that this approach is inadequate and severely limited in

the potential for impacting the problem.[32] The conclusions of this chapter are straightforward but broad in scope. They can be summarized as follows:

- Overweight and obesity continue to be significant problems for employers! All developed countries have witnessed epidemic rises in the prevalence of overweight and obesity, and it is also becoming a problem in developing countries.[102,103] This is important because the workforce in both national and multinational companies is increasingly an overweight workforce.
- Research continues to demonstrate the deleterious health impacts of obesity. In addition, obesity shares common causality with and is an etiological path for those major chronic medical conditions that account for the majority of premature death in developed countries, including heart disease, diabetes, stroke, and many forms of cancer.[7]
- These medical consequences translate into significant financial consequences that ultimately matter to individuals, families, employers, the United States, and other countries throughout the world. Obese individuals have reduced quality of life, decreased productivity, and significantly increased costs of medical care. These effects persist—often for years.
- In a world that is increasingly competitive, reduced productivity and increased medical costs for employers are unacceptable.
- Whenever a majority of a population is overweight or obese, treatment-based solutions will never be adequate. The results of this approach are modest weight losses that are not well maintained. Thus, any impacts on long-term health, productivity,

and health care costs are likely to be minimal.

So what will be necessary to significantly impact the broad scope of overweight and obesity? What role do employers need to play?

- Significant change will take sustained efforts. Just as successful companies have annual goals as well as longer-range goals and strategies to grow their business, achieving success in weight management requires both a short-term and long-term focus.
- To be maximally effective, the strategy should be multilevel, addressing the influences on obesity at the individual, small group (interpersonal), organizational (worksite) and community levels. This is necessary because successful and sustainable individual behavior change not only requires motivation and planning, but most often also requires improvements to the physical, psychosocial, and organizational environments. (See Figure 17-1.)
- Employers need to expand their understanding that creating an environment supportive of healthy weight management requires more than putting a few low-fat foods in the vending machines or even providing a nice walking track. Although such interventions are part of a more comprehensive approach to environmental support, to date, much of what passes for environment support remains piecemeal. Maximizing the supportiveness of the work environment requires an integrated, systems approach. Building healthy weight management into the company's corporate vision and mission statements, including the development of a culture of health in which engagement in healthy weight

management behaviors becomes normative, is critical for long-term success in this area.[104]

- It will also be useful, perhaps even necessary, for employers to reach out into the community, to political entities and to other employers within the community, to share weight management initiatives and to pool resources. Attaching value and integrating with wider organizational, community, and even regional and national initiatives is still largely missing from corporate thinking in the area of weight management. This concept is growing, and will likely come to full flower over the next 10 to 15 years.[105]
- Lastly, employers should embrace policy as the front line for achieving healthy workforces, whether this be at the corporate level or at local and national governmental levels.[106]

Although helping employees achieve and maintain healthy body weights is far from a simple task, it must be integrated into a company's short- and long-range business strategy such that this goal can eventually be achieved.

Glossary

Abdominal Obesity: Waist circumference of ≥35 inches in women and ≥40 inches in men. Abdominal obesity is considered a cardiovascular risk factor in the most recent American Heart Association/American College of Cardiology obesity guidelines. A body mass index (BMI) of 25 to 34.9 and the presence of abdominal obesity places the person at greater cardiovascular risk than expected from BMI alone.

Absenteeism: Days or part days where an employee is not present during his or her expected working time.

Body Mass Index: The BMI is a measure of weight adjusted for height. It is calculated by dividing weight (in kilograms) by the square of height (in meters). It is the most common metric used to define overweight and obesity and to demonstrate their relationship with health outcomes and health care and productivity costs.

Obesity: A condition defined as an excess of body fat over desirable levels. However, it is defined operationally in terms of BMI. BMIs ≥ 30 are considered obese.

Overweight: Defined operationally as a BMI between 25.0 and 29.9.

Presenteeism: Time when an employee is present at work but is less than fully productive.

Risk factor: A measurable medical or behavioral indicator that is predictive of health status. When elevated, risk factors predict poorer health outcomes and increased health care costs. Risk factors are of two general types: modifiable and nonmodifiable. Nonmodifiable risk factors include, but are not limited to, age, gender, race/ethnicity, and family and personal health history. Modifiable risk factors include, but are not limited to, lifestyle behaviors such as tobacco use, physical activity, or diet composition as well as medical indicators such as weight, blood pressure, blood lipids, or blood glucose.

Learning Objectives

After reading this chapter, the reader:

1. Will be able to discuss the costs of obesity to the individual, employer, and society.
2. Will be able to articulate the logic and importance of a population-based versus a purely clinical approach to treating obesity at the worksite.
3. Will be able to discuss the value of treating and managing obesity across

multilevel activities that can influence individuals, groups, the organization as a whole, and the community.

Discussion Questions

1. How do population-based strategies and tactics differ from a clinical approach to obesity management and reduction?
2. How does the Awareness, Motivation, Skills and Opportunity model pertain to this chapter's population-based approach to obesity management and reduction?
3. What role do employers need to play if worksite obesity management is to succeed in the future?

REFERENCES

1. Overweight and obesity. Centers for Disease Control and Prevention Web site. Available at: http://www.cdc.gov/obesity/. Accessed December 21, 2012.
2. Finkelstein EA, Khavjou OA, Thompson H, et al. Obesity and severe obesity forecasts through 2030. *Am J Prev Med.* 2012;42:563–570.
3. Kern E, Chan NL, Fleming DW, Krieger JW. Declines in student obesity prevalence associated with a prevention initiative—King County, Washington, 2012. *Morb Mortal Wkly Rep.* 2014; 63:155–157.
4. Thomas DM, Weedermann M, Fuemmeler BF, et al. Dynamic model predicting overweight, obesity, and extreme obesity prevalence trends. *Obesity.* 2014;22:590–597.
5. Calaprice A, ed. *The Ultimate Quotable Einstein.* Kindle ed. Princeton, NJ: Princeton University Press; 2011.
6. Cawley J. *The Oxford Handbook of the Social Science of Obesity.* New York, NY: Oxford University Press Inc; 2011.

7. Institute of Medicine. *Accelerating Progress in Obesity Prevention: Solving the Weight of the Nation*. Washington, DC: National Academies Press; 2012.

8. Thorpe KE, Howard DH. The rise in spending among Medicare beneficiaries: the role of chronic disease prevalence and changes in treatment intensity. *Health Aff.* 2006;25:w378–w388.

9. Baicker K, Chandra A. Myths and misconceptions about U.S. health insurance. *Health Aff.* 2008;27:w533–w543.

10. Finkelstein EA, Fiebelkorn IC, Wang G. The costs of obesity among full-time employees. *Am J Health Promot.* 2005;20:45–51.

11. Gates DM, Succop P, Brehm BJ, et al. Obesity and presenteeism: the impact of body mass index on workplace productivity. *J Occup Environ Med.* 2008;50:39–45.

12. Pronk NP, Martinson B, Kessler RC, et al. The association between work performance and physical activity, cardiorespiratory fitness, and obesity. *J Occup Environ Med.* 2004;46:19–25.

13. Schulte PA, Wagner GR, Ostry A, et al. Work, obesity, and occupational safety and health. *Am J Public Health.* 2007;97:428–436.

14. Pronk NP. Physical activity promotion in business and industry: evidence, context, and recommendations for a national plan. *J Phys Act Health.* 2009;6(suppl 2):S220–S235.

15. Pronk NP, Kottke TE. Physical activity promotion as a strategic corporate priority to improve worker health and business performance. *Prev Med.* 2009;49:316–321.

16. Crimmins TJ, Halberg J. Measuring success in creating a "culture of health." *J Occup Environ Med.* 2009;51:351–355.

17. Hoebbel C, Golaszewski T, Swanson M, Dorn J. Associations between the worksite environment and perceived health culture. *Am J Health Promot.* 2012;26:301–304.

18. Pronk NP, Allen CU. A culture of health: creating and sustaining supportive organizational environments for health. In: Pronk NP, ed. *ACSM's Worksite Health Handbook. A Guide to Building Healthy and Productive Companies*. 2nd ed. Champaign, Ill: Human Kinetics; 2009:224–230.

19. Pronk NP. Population health management and a healthy workplace culture: a primer. In: *Engaging Wellness. Corporate Health and Wellness Association*; 2012. Available at: www.wellnessassociation.com. Accessed Month 05, 2013.

20. Lemmens VE, Oenema A, Klepp KI, et al. A systematic review of the evidence regarding efficacy of obesity prevention interventions among adults. *Obes Rev.* 2008;9:446–455.

21. Brown T, Avenell A, Edmunds LD, et al. Systematic review of long-term lifestyle interventions to prevent weight gain and morbidity in adults. *Obes Rev.* 2009;10:627–638.

22. Arem H, Irwin M. A review of Web-based weight loss interventions in adults. *Obes Rev.* 2011;12:e236–e243.

23. Hebden L, Chey T, Allman-Farinelli M. Lifestyle intervention for preventing weight gain in young adults: a systematic review and meta-analysis of RCTs. *Obes Rev.* 2012;13:692–710.

24. Perez LG, Arredondo EM, Elder JP, et al. Evidence-based obesity treatment interventions for Latino adults in the U.S. A systematic review. *Am J Prev Med.* 2013;44:550–560.

25. Wadden TA, Butryn ML, Byrne KJ. Efficacy of lifestyle modification for long-term weight control. *Obes Res.* 2004;12(suppl):151S–162S.

26. Young MD, Morgan PJ, Plotnikoff RC, et al. Effectiveness of male-only weight

loss and weight loss maintenance interventions: a systematic review with meta-analysis. *Obes Rev.* 2012; 13:393–408.

27. Hutfless S, Gudzune KA, Maruthur N, et al. Strategies to prevent weight gain in adults—a systematic review. *Am J Prev Med.* 2013;45:e41–e51.

28. Bassett MT, Dumanovsky T, Huang C, et al. Purchasing behavior and calorie information at fast-food chains in New York City, 2007. *Am J Public Health.* 2008;98:1457–1459.

29. Franz MJ, VanWormer JJ, Crain AL, et al. Weight-loss outcomes: a systematic review and meta-analysis of weight-loss clinical trials with a minimum 1-year follow-up. *J Am Diet Assoc.* 2007;107:1755–1767.

30. Heinen L, Darling H. Addressing obesity in the workplace: the role of employers. *Milbank Q.* 2009;87:101–122.

31. Yancey AK, Pronk NP, Cole BL. Workplace approaches to obesity prevention. In: Kumanyika S, Brownson RC, eds. *Handbook of Obesity Prevention: A Resource for Health Professionals.* New York, NY: Springer; 2007:317–347.

32. Kaplan GD, Brinkman-Kaplan V, Framer EM. Workplace weight management. In: O'Donnell MP, ed. *Health Promotion in the Workplace.* 3rd ed. Albany, NY: Delmar Thomson Learning; 2002:293–337.

33. National Institutes of Health. Clinical guidelines on the identification, evaluation, and treatment of overweight and obesity in adults—the evidence report. *Obes Res.* 1998;6:51S–209S.

34. Healthy People 2020. Surgeon General Web site. Available at: http://www. healthypeople.gov/2020/topicsobjectives 2020/objectiveslist.aspx?topicId=29. Accessed April 13, 2013.

35. World Health Organization. Physical status: the use and interpretation of anthropometry. Geneva, Switzerland: WHO; 1995. Available at: http://www. who.int/childgrowth/publications/ physical_status/en/. Accessed April 13, 2013.

36. Flegal KM, Carroll MD, Ogden CL, Curtin LR. Prevalence and trends in obesity among U.S. adults, 1999–2008. *JAMA.* 2010;303:235–241.

37. Finucane MM, Stevens GA, Cowan MJ, et al. National, regional, and global trends in body-mass index since 1980: systematic analysis of health examination surveys and epidemiological studies with 960 country-years and 9.1 million participants. *Lancet.* 2011;377:557–567.

38. Wang YC, McPherson K, Marsh T, et al. Health and economic burden of the projected obesity trends in the USA and the UK. *Lancet.* 2011;378:815–825.

39. Yanovski SZ, Yanovski JA. Obesity prevalence in the United States—Up, down, or sideways? *N Engl J Med.* 2011;364:987–989.

40. Flegal KM, Carroll MD, Kit BK, Ogden CL. Prevalence of obesity and trends in the distribution of body mass index among U.S. adults, 1999–2010. *JAMA.* 2012;307:491–497.

41. Finkelstein EA, DiBonaventura M, Burgess SM, Hale BC. The costs of obesity in the workplace. *J Occup Environ Med.* 2010;52:971–976.

42. NHLBI Obesity Education Initiative. The practical guide. Identification evaluation and treatment of overweight and obesity in adults. 2000. NIH publication 00-4084.

43. Landsberg L, Aronne LJ, Beilin LJ, et al. Obesity-related hypertension: pathogenesis, cardiovascular risk, and treatment—a position paper of the Obesity Society and the American Society of Hypertension. *Obesity.* 2013;21:8–24.

44. Geiss LS, Pan L, Cadwell B, et al. Changes in incidence of diabetes in U.S. adults, 1997–2003. *Am J Prev Med.* 2006; 30:371–377.

45. Jensen MK, Chiuve SE, Rimm EB, et al. Obesity, behavioral lifestyle factors, and risk of acute coronary events. *Circulation.* 2008;117:3062–3069.

46. Anandacoomarasamy A, Caterson I, Sambrook P, et al. The impact of obesity on the musculoskeletal system. *Int J Obes.* 2008;32:211–222.

47. Bentley TGK, Palta M, Paulsen AJ, et al. Race and gender associations between obesity and nine health-related quality-of-life measures. *Qual Life Res.* 2011;20:665–674.

48. Carr D, Friedman MA. Is obesity stigmatizing? Body weight, perceived discrimination, and psychological well-being in the United States. *J Health Soc Behav.* 2005;46:244–259.

49. The global epidemic. International Obesity Taskforce Web site. Available at: http://www.iaso.org/iotf/obesity/obesitytheglobalepidemic/. Published 2009. Accessed April 9, 2013.

50. Masters RK, Powers DA, Link BG. Obesity and U.S. mortality risk over the adult life course. *Am J Epidemiol.* 2013;177:431–442.

51. Greenberg JA. Obesity and early mortality in the U.S. *Obesity.* 2013;21:405–412.

52. de Gonzalez AB, Hartge P, Cerhan JR, et al. Body-mass index and mortality among 1.46 million white adults. *N Engl J Med.* 2010;363:2211–2219.

53. Flegal KM, Kit BK, Orpana H, Graubard BI. Association of all-cause mortality with overweight and obesity using standard body mass index categories. A systematic review and meta-analysis. *JAMA.* 2013;309:71–82.

54. Heir T, Erikssen J, Sandvik L. Overweight as predictor of long-term mortality among healthy, middle-aged men: a prospective cohort study. *Prev Med.* 2011;52:223–226.

55. Zajacova A, Dowd JB, Burgard SA. Overweight adults may have the lowest mortality—do they have the best health? *Am J Epidemiol.* 2011;173:430–437.

56. Sui X, LaMonte MJ, Laditka JN, et al. Cardiorespiratory fitness and adiposity as mortality predictors in older adults. *JAMA.* 2007;298(21):2507–2516.

57. Juonala M, Magnussen CG, Berenson GS, et al. Childhood adiposity, adult adiposity, and cardiovascular risk factors. *N Engl J Med.* 2011;365:1876–1885.

58. Eilat-Adar S, Eldar M, Goldbourt U. Association of intentional changes in body weight with coronary heart disease event rates in overweight subjects who have an additional coronary risk factor. *Am J Epidemiol.* 2005;161:352–358.

59. Loria BE, Millen CA, Nonas F, et al. 2013 AHA/ACC/TOS guideline for the management of overweight and obesity in adults: a report of the American College of Cardiology/American Heart Association Task Force on Practice Guidelines and the Obesity Society. *Circulation.* 2013;1–69. Available at: http://circ.ahajournals.org/content/early/2013/11/11/01.cir.0000437739.71477.ee.citation. Accessed November 12, 2013.

60. Tzotzas T, Evangelou P, Kiortsis DN. 2011. Obesity, weight loss and conditional cardiovascular risk factors. *Obes Rev.* 1992;12:e282–e289.

61. Weiss EC, Galuska DA, Khan LK, et al. Weight regain in U.S. adults who experienced substantial weight loss, 1999-2002. *Am J Prev Med.* 2007;33:34–40.

62. Katan MB. Weight-loss diets for the prevention and treatment of obesity. *N Engl J Med.* 2009;360:923–925.

63. Brownell, K.B. 2010. The humbling experience of treating obesity: should we persist or desist? *Behav Res Ther.* 48, 717–719.

64. Field AE, Manson JE, Laird N, et al. Weight cycling and the risk of developing type 2 diabetes among adult

women in the United States. *Obes Res.* 2004;12:267–274.

65. Stevens VL, Jacobs EJ, Sun J, et al. Weight cycling and mortality in a large prospective U.S. study. *Am J Epidemiol.* 2012;175:785–792.

66. Rolando L, Byrne DW, McGown PW, et al. Health risk factor modification predicts incidence of diabetes in an employee population: results of an 8-year longitudinal cohort study. *J Occup Environ Med.* 2013;55:410–415.

67. Rutter H. Where next for obesity? *Lancet* 2011;378:746–747.

68. Bertakis KD, Azari R. Obesity and the use of health care services. *Obes Res.* 2005:13;372–379.

69. Andreyeva T, Sturm R, Ringel JS. 2004. Moderate and severe obesity have large differences in health care costs. *Obes Res.* 2005;12:1936–1943.

70. Arterburn DE, Maciejewski ML, Tsevat J. Impact of morbid obesity on medical expenditures in adults. *Int J Obes.* 2005;29:334–339.

71. Finkelstein EA, Trogdon JG, Cohen JW, Dietz W. Annual medical spending attributable to obesity: payer- and service-specific estimates. *Health Aff.* 2009;28:w822–w831.

72. Stagnitti MN. *Trends in Health Care Expenditures by Body Mass Index (BMI) Category for Adults in the U.S. Civilian Noninstitutionalized Population, 2001 and 2006.* Rockville, Md: Agency for Healthcare Research and Quality; 2009. Statistical brief 247. Available at: http://www.meps.ahrq.gov/mepsweb/data_files/publications/st247/stat247.shtml. Accessed May 04, 2013.

73. Dall TM, Zhang Y, Zhang S, et al. Weight loss and lifetime medical expenditures: a case study with TRICARE prime beneficiaries. *Am J Prev Med.* 2011; 40:338–344.

74. Gabel JR, Whitmore H, Pickreign J, et al. Obesity and the workplace: current programs and attitudes among employers and employees. *Health Aff.* 2009;28:46–56.

75. Durden ED, Huse D, Ben-Joseph R, Chu B. Economic costs of obesity to self-insured employers. *J Occup Environ Med.* 2008;50:991–997.

76. Carls GS, Goetzel RZ, Henke RM, et al. The impact of weight gain or loss on health care costs for employees at the Johnson & Johnson Family of Companies. *J Occup Environ Med.* 2011;53:8–16.

77. Milliman and Robertson Inc. Health risks and behavior: the impact on medical costs. Milwaukee, Wis: Milliman and Robertson Inc; 1987.

78. Tucker LA, Friedman GM. Obesity and absenteeism: an epidemiologic study of 10,825 employed adults. *Am J Health Promot.* 1998;12:202–207.

79. Pelletier B, Boles M, Lynch W. Change in health risks and work productivity over time. *J Occup Environ Med.* 2004; 46:746–754.

80. Jans MP, van den Heuvel SG, Hildebrandt VH, Bongers PM. Overweight and obesity as predictors of absenteeism in the working population of the Netherlands. *J Occup Environ Med.* 2007;49:975–980.

81. Fryar CD, Carroll MD, Ogden CL. *Prevalence of Overweight, Obesity, and Extreme Obesity Among Adults: United States, Trends 1960–1962 Through 2009–2010.* National Health Statistics Health E-Stats September 2012.

82. O'Donnell MP. A simple framework to describe what works best: improving awareness, enhancing motivation, building skills, and providing opportunity. *Am J Health Promot.* 2005;20(1):1–12.

83. Pratt CA, Lemon SC, Fernandez ID, et al. Design characteristics of worksite environmental interventions for obesity prevention. *Obesity.* 2007;15:2171–2180.

84. Soler RE, Leeks KD, Buchanan LR, et al. Point-of-decision prompts to increase

stair use: a systematic review update. *Am J Prev Med.* 2010;38(2S):292–300.

85. Zimring C, Joseph A, Nicoll GL, Tsepas S. Influences of building design and site design on physical activity: research and intervention opportunities. *Am J Prev Med.* 2005;28(2, S2):186–193.

86. Motivation. Oxford Dictionary Web site. Available at: http://www.oxforddictionaries.com/us/definition/american_english/motivation. Accessed January 6, 2014.

87. VanWormer JJ, Martinez AM, Benson GA, et al. Telephone counseling and home telemonitoring: the weigh by day trial. *Am J Health Behav.* 2009; 33:445–454.

88. Neuhaus M, Healy GN, Dunstan DW, et al. Workplace sitting and height-adjustable work stations: a randomized trial. *Am J Prev Med.* 2013;46:30–40.

89. Pronk NP. Integrated worker health protection and promotion programs: overview and perspective on health and economic outcomes. *J Occup Environ Med.* 2013;55(12 suppl):S30–S37.

90. Kottke TE, Pronk NP, Katz AS, et al. The effect of price reduction on salad bar purchases at a corporate cafeteria. *Prev Chronic Dis.* 2013;10:120214. doi: http://dx.doi.org/10.5888/pcd10.120214.

91. Program measurement and evaluation guide: core metrics for employee health management. Health Enhancement Research Organization Web Site. Available at: http://www.the-hero.org/learning_series/HERO-CCA-Guide-StakeholderPublicComment.pdf. Published February 2014. Accessed February 27, 2014.

92. Pronk NP, ed. *ACSM's Worksite Health Handbook: A Guide to Building Healthy and Productive Companies.* 2nd ed. Champaign, Ill: Human Kinetics; 2009.

93. Carnethon M, Whitsel LP, Franklin BA, et al. Worksite wellness programs for cardiovascular disease prevention: a policy statement from the American Heart Association. *Circulation.* 2009;120:1725–1741.

94. Task Force on Community Preventive Services. A recommendation to improve employee weight status through worksite health promotion programs targeting nutrition, physical activity, or both. *Am J Prev Med.* 2009;37:358–359.

95. Levi J, Vinter S, St. Laurent R, Segal LM. *F as in Fat: How Obesity Policies Are Failing in America 2008:* Washington, D.C.: Trust for America's Health; 2008.

96. U.S. Dept of Health and Human Services. *The Surgeon General's Vision for a Healthy and Fit Nation.* Rockville, Md: U.S. Dept of Health and Human Services, Office of the Surgeon General; 2010.

97. Wellness Council of America. WELCOA's 7 benchmarks of success: developing results-oriented wellness programs one company at a time. *Absolute Advantage.* 2006;01:3–29.

98. World Health Organization. *The Challenge of Obesity in the WHO European Region and the Strategies for Response.* Copenhagen, Denmark: World Health Organization; 2007.

99. World Health Organization WEF. *Preventing Noncommunicable Diseases in the Workplace Through Diet and Physical Activity: WHO/World Economic Forum Report of a Joint Event.* Geneva, Switzerland: WHO Press; 2008.

100. Anderson LM, Quinn TA, Glanz K, et al. The effectiveness of worksite nutrition and physical activity interventions for controlling employee overweight and obesity: a systematic review. *Am J Prev Med.* 2009;37:340–357.

101. Creating healthy states: actions for governors. National Governors Association Web site. Available at: http://www.nga.org/files/live/sites/

NGA/files/pdf/0602CREATING
HEALTHYSTATESACTIONS.PDF;
jsessionid=586712D3AEDE991D0BAA8
ED1815224BC. Published 2005. Accessed
February 2, 2012.

102. Obesity. World Health Organization
Web site. Available at: http://www.
who.int/gho/ncd/risk_factors/
obesity_text/en/#. Published 2014.
Accessed February 24, 2014.

103. Global health risks: mortality and
burden of disease attributable to
selected major risks. World Health
Organization Web site. Available at:
http://www.who.int/healthinfo/
global_burden_disease/GlobalHeal
thRisks_report_full.pdf. Published 2009.
Accessed February 24, 2014.

104. Goetzel RZ, Tabrizi MJ, Roemer EC, et
al. A review of recent organizational
health assessments. *Am J Health Promot.*
2013;27(5):TAHP-2–TAHP-10.

105. Environmental scan: role of corporate
America in community health and
wellness. Institute of Medicine Web
Site. Available at: http://www.iom.
edu/~/media/Files/Activity%20Files/
PublicHealth/PopulationHealthImprov
ementRT/Background-Papers/
PopHealthEnvScan.pdf. Published
January 2014. Accessed February 27, 2014.

106. Terry PE, ed. Editor's desk: exploring
cultural boundaries: leadership and
organizational health policies. *Am J
Health Promot.* 2014;28(3):TAHP-1–
TAHP-12.

18

Tobacco Prevention and Control in the Workplace

Brian King

INTRODUCTION

Tobacco use is the leading cause of preventable disease, disability, and death in the United States.[1] However, despite the known health risks associated with tobacco use, approximately one in four American adults currently uses some form of tobacco, and one in five uses cigarettes.[2,3] The severity of this public health problem is compounded by the fact that the harmful effects of tobacco use do not end with the user.[4,5] Approximately two-fifths of Americans are exposed to secondhand smoke from burning tobacco products, which has been shown to cause adverse health effects in adults and children who do not smoke.[6]

Given that many adults spend the majority of their day in the workplace and the prevalence of tobacco use among workers is comparable to that of the general population,[7] the workplace represents an important setting for the implementation of evidence-based strategies to prevent and control tobacco use.[8] The primary objectives of workplace tobacco control interventions are traditionally focused on encouraging tobacco users to quit and reducing exposure to secondhand smoke among employees and the general public. Secondary objectives may include reducing tobacco use initiation and behavior among other subpopulations, such as visitors of the workplace and employee's family members.[7]

This chapter provides an overview of the prevalence of tobacco use and secondhand smoke exposure in the United States, the impact of these behaviors on workers and the general population, and best practices and effective strategies for addressing this important public health problem in the workplace. The chapter also discusses emerging areas in the field of tobacco control, as well as opportunities for the future advancement and sustainment of workplace tobacco control interventions.

IMPACT OF TOBACCO USE ON HEALTH

Tobacco use imposes substantial health and financial costs on society, all of which are completely avoidable. These costs are particularly pertinent to workplaces, a setting in which tobacco use and secondhand smoke exposure still persist in many states and localities across the United States.

Health Burden

Tobacco use causes significant morbidity and mortality.[1] The adverse health effects associated with tobacco use include heart disease, multiple types of cancer, pulmonary disease, developmental and reproductive problems, and the exacerbation of multiple chronic health conditions.[1] It has been estimated that more deaths are caused each year by tobacco use than by human immunodeficiency virus, illegal drug use, alcohol use, firearm-related incidents, infectious and toxic agents, and motor vehicle injuries combined.[9] Cigarette smoking alone has been estimated to cause 443,000 deaths, or nearly one of every five deaths, per year in the United States.[10] This estimate includes deaths from lung cancer (128,900), ischemic heart disease (126,000), chronic obstructive pulmonary disease (92,900), other cancers (35,300), stroke (15,900), and other diagnoses (44,000).[10]

The adverse health effects associated with tobacco are not limited to the user. Exposure to secondhand smoke from burning tobacco products causes heart disease and lung cancer in nonsmoking adults and sudden infant death syndrome, acute respiratory infections, ear problems, and more severe asthma in children.[4] Each year, secondhand smoke exposure causes an estimated 3400 lung cancer deaths and more than 46,000 heart disease deaths among American adults who do not smoke.[10] Even brief exposure to secondhand smoke can have immediate adverse effects on the blood and blood vessels, increasing the risk of having a heart attack.[4,11] In 2006, the U.S. Surgeon General concluded that there is no risk-free level of secondhand smoke.[4]

Financial Burden

Tobacco use and secondhand smoke exposure also impose substantial financial costs on society. During 2001–2004, the total economic burden of adult cigarette smoking in the United States was approximately $193 billion per year, including $96 billion in direct health care expenditures and $97 billion in productivity losses attributed to diseases caused by smoking.[10] Nonsmokers' exposure to secondhand smoke alone has been estimated to cost the U.S. economy approximately $10 billion per year, including $5 billion in medical expenditures and an additional $5 billion in disability losses.[12] In contrast, investments in comprehensive statewide tobacco control programs, which can lead to substantial reductions in tobacco-related morbidity and mortality when fully funded at levels recommended by the U.S. Centers for Disease Control and Prevention,[8] totaled only $641.1 million in 2010.[13] It is also important to consider that the aforementioned estimates of smoking-attributable costs are likely understated because they do not account for expenditures related to the use of noncigarette tobacco products, such as cigars and pipes, or the costs associated with tobacco use and secondhand smoke exposure among children and adolescents.

PREVALENCE OF TOBACCO USE AND SECONDHAND SMOKE EXPOSURE

Tobacco Use

Population-based surveys have been used extensively to document the prevalence and trends in tobacco use at both the national and state levels in the United States.[8] These surveys traditionally obtain data from household or telephone interviews, which rely on self-reported tobacco use.[14] Although underreporting may occur among subpopulations for which there is a high societal demand for abstinence, such as individuals with heart disease or pregnant women, the impact of these situations on survey estimates is small and self-reported data have been shown to provide valid estimates of tobacco use in the general population.[15,16]

Cigarettes are the most commonly used tobacco product in the United States.[2] Although cigarette smoking has declined considerably over the past several decades (Figure 18-1),[17] the magnitude of the decline has slowed in recent years and disparities in prevalence still exist across states.[18,19] An estimated 19.0% (43.8 million) of U.S. adults were current cigarette smokers in 2011.[3] Of these, 77.8% (34.1 million) smoked every day, and 22.2% (9.7 million) smoked some days.[3] Smoking prevalence in 2011 was 21.6% among males and 16.5% among females. By race/ethnicity, prevalence

was highest among non-Hispanic American Indians/Alaska Natives (31.5%), followed by non-Hispanic whites (20.6%), non-Hispanic blacks (19.4%), Hispanics (12.9%), and non-Hispanic Asians (9.9%). Prevalence was lower among adults aged 65 or more (7.9%) and 18 to 24 years (18.9%) compared to those aged 25 to 44 (22.1%) and 45 to 64 years (21.4%). Prevalence was higher among adults living below the federal poverty level (29.0%) compared with those living at or above this level (17.9%), and higher among those with a disability (25.4%) compared with those with no disability (17.3%). By state, prevalence ranged from 11.8% in Utah to 29.0% in Kentucky in 2011.[3]

Disparities in cigarette smoking also exist among U.S. working adults.[20] During

Figure 18-1: Current Cigarette Smoking Among U.S. Adults ≥18 years old, overall and by sex, 1965-2011.

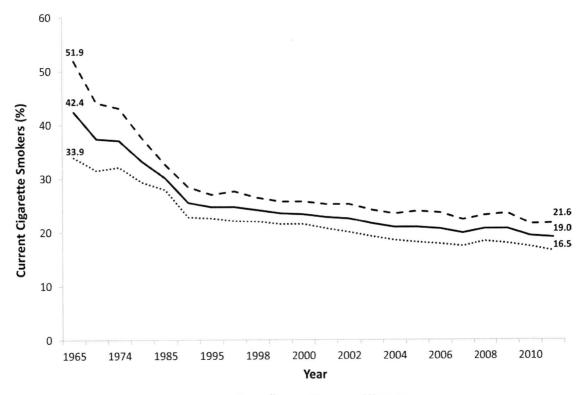

Source: Centers for Disease Control and Prevention (CDC). National Health Interview Survey.

2004–2010, age-adjusted cigarette smoking prevalence among working adults was 19.6%; prevalence was highest among those with less than a high school education (28.4%), with no health insurance (28.6%), living below the federal poverty level (27.7%), and aged 18 to 24 years (23.8%).[20] Differences in smoking prevalence also exist across industry and occupation groups.[20] For example, during 2004–2010, smoking prevalence ranged from 9.7% in education services to 30.0% in mining; by occupation group, prevalence ranged from 8.7% in education, training, and library to 31.4% in construction and extraction (Figure 18-2).[20]

Although less common than cigarette smoking, the prevalence of other forms of tobacco use has increased in the United States in recent years.[2] During 2009–2010, an estimated 25.2% of U.S. adults reported currently using any form of tobacco, including cigarettes, cigars, chewing tobacco, water pipes, snus, or pipes. By product type, current use among U.S. adults was 6.6% for cigars, 3.4% for chewing tobacco, 1.5% for water pipes, 1.4% for snus, and 1.1% for pipes.[21]

Secondhand Smoke Exposure

Exposure to secondhand smoke can be assessed using multiple methods, including

Figure 18-2: Current Cigarette Smoking Among Working U.S. Adults ≥18 years old, by occupation group, 2004-2010.

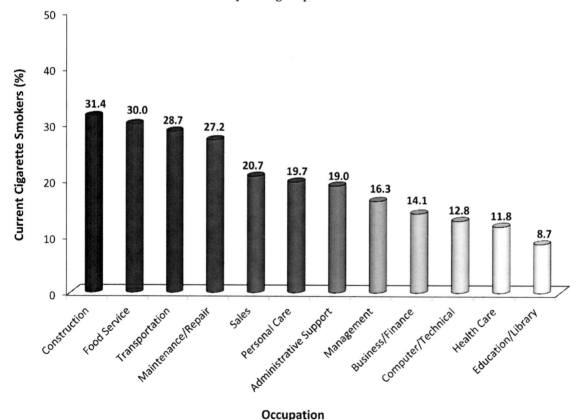

Occupation

Source: Centers for Disease Control and Prevention (CDC). National Health Interview Survey.

biomarkers, self-reported surveys, and environmental monitoring.[22-24] The most scientifically valid measure of secondhand smoke exposure is a biomarker known as cotinine, which is a metabolite of nicotine that can be assessed in the blood (serum), urine, or saliva.[22] The proportion of U.S. nonsmokers with detectable levels of serum cotinine has declined over time, from 87.9% during 1988–1991 to 40.1% during 2006–2007.[4,6] This decline is attributable to many factors, including decreased smoking prevalence, increased local and state laws prohibiting smoking in indoor workplaces and public places, increased voluntary smoking restrictions in workplaces and homes, and changes in public attitudes regarding the social acceptability of smoking.[4] However, despite this decline, approximately 88 million U.S. nonsmokers remained exposed to secondhand smoke during 2006–2007.[6]

Disparities in secondhand smoke exposure exist across subpopulations.[4,6] For example, levels of exposure are generally higher among males than females, among non-Hispanic blacks than non-Hispanics whites and Mexican-Americans, among children aged 3 to 11 years and youths aged 12 to 19 years than adults aged 20 or more years, and among those living below the federal poverty level than those at or above the poverty level.[6] In addition to sociodemographic disparities, variations in exposure also exist by occupation.[25,26] During 2001–2002, average cotinine levels were highest among blue-collar workers, followed by service workers and white-collar workers; levels were lowest among farm workers.[25]

Population-based surveys are also frequently used to assess exposure to secondhand smoke that has occurred in the past.[23] In contrast to biomarkers, surveys allow for inquiries into the frequency and duration of secondhand smoke exposure in specific environments, such as workplaces.[23]

For example, an estimated 14.8% of adults aged 20 years and older reported being exposed to secondhand smoke in the home or workplace during 2003–2004, with 5.4% reporting exposure only in the home and 8.5% reporting exposure only in the workplace.[27] Similarly, during 2009–2010, 20.4% of U.S. nonsmoking workers reported being exposed to secondhand smoke in the workplace within the past 7 days; those most likely to be exposed to secondhand smoke in the workplace included males, non-Hispanic blacks, Hispanics, younger adults, and those with less education.[28]

Environmental monitoring can also provide useful information on the extent of secondhand smoke in workplaces.[24] The measurement of airborne nicotine, a tobacco-specific constituent, is frequently used to confirm the presence and cumulative level of secondhand smoke in a variety of workplaces.[29] A review of studies of airborne nicotine in workplaces found that levels in smoke-free venues were approximately 2 to 6 times lower than in smoke-permitted offices, 3 to 8 times lower than in smoke-permitted restaurants, and 10 to 40 times lower than in smoke-permitted bars.[30] Particulate matter is also a widely used measure of secondhand smoke exposure in workplaces, particularly hospitality venues such as restaurants, bars, and casinos.[24] Particulate matter differs from airborne nicotine in that it can be measured in real time and can be used to determine both the presence and severity of exposure.[24] The specific class of particulate matter that is assessed is $PM_{2.5}$ or particles less than 2.5 µm in diameter.[24] The U.S. Environmental Protection Agency has established an average 24-hour $PM_{2.5}$ exposure standard of 35 µg/m³; levels above this standard are considered unhealthy.[31] For comparison, research has shown that levels of indoor air quality in smoking-permitted bars can average around 329 µg/m³.[32]

THEORETICAL FOUNDATION FOR WORKPLACE TOBACCO CONTROL INTERVENTIONS

Workplace tobacco control interventions can help to encourage tobacco users to quit and reduce exposure to secondhand smoke among employees and the general public. However, not all workplace tobacco control interventions are equally successful, and those that are most effective are founded upon a clear understanding of tobacco use, secondhand smoke exposure, and the environmental context of both behaviors.[8] Such interventions are best developed and implemented using strategic theoretical frameworks and are recurrently improved through evaluation. A clear understanding of key theories of health behavior can help facilitate this process.

Multiple models and theoretical frameworks exist for the purposes of health promotion and may be applied when designing workplace tobacco control interventions.[33,34] Identifying a model and/ or theoretical framework depends upon the factors that are to be addressed and the setting in which the intervention or program will take place. Some of the most commonly used theoretical frameworks used in the context of tobacco control include, but are not limited to, the transtheoretical model,[35,36] theory of planned behavior,[37] and social-ecological model.[38] Development of workplace tobacco control interventions may be informed by a single model or theoretical framework, or may encompass more than one model and/or theoretical framework.[33,34]

The transtheoretical model of health behavior change is frequently used in the context of workplace tobacco control.[35,36] An important construct within the model is the idea of people being at different stages of motivational readiness to change, or "stages of change." Transition between stages is circular, not linear, and individuals or workplaces can enter or exit at any point in the continuum of change. There are six distinct stages (precontemplation, contemplation, preparation, action, maintenance, and termination),[35,36] and the most effective interventions are those that are tailored to the specific point in the continuum of change in which an individual currently resides. In this manner, the model can be used both to understand the situation at hand and to set realistic goals to facilitate movement to the next stage.[35,36] The following scenario provides an example of the application of the transtheoretical model of behavior change in the context of a workplace tobacco cessation intervention.

Example Scenario

A company is interested in implementing a workplace-based tobacco control intervention with the ultimate goal of establishing a corporate culture that supports cessation for all employees. The company establishes a working group to achieve this goal, which is composed of employees, management, and administrative personnel. After preliminary discussions, the working group decides to utilize the stages of change approach to help better understand why employees who use tobacco have not taken part in past cessation efforts initiated by the company and to develop a cessation program that reaches more tobacco users. To achieve the first goal, they utilize an employee survey to identify current and former smokers, classify them according to a specific stage of change, and then tailor specific messages, strategies, and programs to each stage. An overview of each stage, including the work group's intended interventional approach, includes the following:

Precontemplation: Workers in the precontemplation stage include current tobacco users who report having no interest in quitting. This stage is composed of those who are unaware of the dangers of tobacco use or have not been prompted to think about behavior change; this stage also includes those who are persistent or recalcitrant tobacco users who are not receptive to direct messages about the health risks of tobacco use. Meaningful interventional approaches for individuals in the first group include direct efforts to educate workers about the dangers of tobacco use and secondhand smoke exposure and to increase awareness and the need for behavioral change. In contrast, meaningful interventional approaches among persistent or recalcitrant tobacco users may include indirect measures, such as education about the health effects of secondhand smoke exposure on other people, the financial costs of tobacco use, or the successes that other individuals have had in quitting.

Contemplation: Workers in the contemplation stage include tobacco users who are thinking about quitting in the near future. These individuals require motivation and encouragement to help assist them in making specific cessation plans. Possible interventional approaches for workers in the contemplation stage include the development of materials and activities focused primarily on motivation and stressing the benefits of cessation, including health risk appraisals, health fairs, or one-time "free sample" cessation seminars for workers considering quitting.

Preparation: Workers in the preparation stage include tobacco users who are ready to plan a quit attempt and require assistance in developing concrete action plans and goals. Interventional approaches for workers in the preparation stage include improved access to cessation group resources, medication coverage, or flexible benefit credits to finance cessation interventions.

Action: Workers in the action stage include tobacco users who have already implemented a specific action plan for cessation. These individuals are best assisted with resources that offer relevant feedback, problem solving, social support, and reinforcement related to their quit attempt. Meaningful interventions for workers in the action stage include access to on-site or community, intranet, or telephone-based counseling services.

Maintenance: Workers in the maintenance stage include former tobacco users who have successfully quit using tobacco. These individuals have achieved the desired change and are best assisted with resources that assist with coping, reminders, and avoiding relapse. Possible interventional approaches for workers in the maintenance stage include access to on-site or community, intranet, or telephone-based counseling services, and coverage of proven drug therapies to sustain long-term cessation.

Termination: Workers in the termination stage include former tobacco users who have been tobacco free for at least 5 years, have 0% temptation to use tobacco, and have 100% self-efficacy to remain tobacco free.[39] Although relapse rates among former smokers who have been abstinent over 5 years are approximately 5% or less and relapse rates decline as the duration of abstinence increases, fluctuations between abstinence and tobacco use are not uncommon. The utility of intervening with former smokers who have relapsed after 5 years is uncertain and such interventions should be targeted at those at most risk for late relapse, such as those with comorbidities (e.g., history of mental illness or alcohol abuse).[39]

As this scenario demonstrates, the stages of change approach can be used to address tobacco use among a diverse set of employees at varying levels of readiness to quit. However, the theory of planned behavior can also be applied in the context of a workplace tobacco control intervention.[37] The theory of planned behavior is an extension of the theory of reasoned action,[40] which asserts that the best predictor of behavior is intention. More specifically, intention is the cognitive representation of a person's readiness to perform a given behavior, such as tobacco use, and is the immediate antecedent of the behavior. This intention is determined by three factors: the individual's attitude toward the behavior, his or her subjective norms, and his or her perceived behavior control.[40] In the context of workplace tobacco control, interventions can be implemented to influence each factor, including activities to inform and encourage cessation among tobacco users, to denormalize tobacco use in the workplace, and to improve access to cessation resources to improve tobacco users' perceptions of their ability to quit.

The social-ecological model can also be applied in the context of workplace tobacco control interventions.[38] Socio-ecological models assist with the identification of determinants at different system levels and suggest relationships between and among those levels. In doing so, these types of models take into account the complexities of health determinants and environmental influences on health, and help create environmental conditions that support and promote effective and sustainable behavior change.[41] For example, interventions at the intra level, which include factors such as age, education, and income, can focus on skills training and enhanced access to cessation resources among tobacco users. At the inter level, interventions can be instituted to enhance awareness and knowledge of the dangers of tobacco use and secondhand smoke exposure among all workers. Finally, at the workplace level, initiatives such as smoke-free policies can be implemented to help achieve an organizational culture that supports tobacco prevention and control.

IMPACT OF WORKPLACE TOBACCO CONTROL INTERVENTIONS

Research suggests that workplace tobacco control interventions can be effective in promoting tobacco cessation and improving the productivity of employees. However, the benefits of these interventions do not end with the tobacco user. Workplace tobacco control interventions can also lead to improvements in the health of the general population and substantial cost savings to both employers and society.[4,42,43]

Employees

Tobacco use impacts employee productivity and absenteeism, increases the use of disability leave, and increases overall health care costs among workers.[1] Cigarette smoking alone costs an estimated $97 billion in productivity losses each year in the United States,[10] and studies have found that current smokers miss more days of work and experience more unproductive time at work compared with both former and never smokers.[44] For example, men who smoke use 4 more sick days per year than nonsmoking men, and women who smoke use 2 more sick days per year than nonsmoking women.[44]

Studies have shown that implementing smoke-free policies can have immediate benefits on workers' health.[7] For example, within 3 months of the adoption of a statewide comprehensive smoke-free law in New York State, saliva cotinine among a convenience sample of nonsmoking restaurant, bar, and bowling facility workers decreased from 3.6 ng/ml to 0.8 ng/ml, and the prevalence of self-reported sensory irritation symptoms among these individuals declined from 88% to 38%.[45] Similarly, 78% of bartenders with prior sensory symptoms reported no symptoms 1 month after the adoption of California's smoke-free bar law.[46] In addition, smoke-free workplace policies can reduce tobacco consumption and increase cessation.[47-49] A study of U.S. workers found that those who worked in smoke-free workplaces were twice as likely to quit smoking as those in smoke-permitted workplaces,[47] and a multi-country study found that a workplace smoke-free policy led to a 3.8% reduction in smoking prevalence and 3.1 fewer cigarettes smoked per day among continuing smokers.[49]

In addition to smoke-free policies, other workplace interventions to support employees who use tobacco have also been shown to be effective. For example, a telephone-based health coaching tobacco cessation program that was provided as part of a workplace health promotion program by 10 large U.S. employers achieved a 32% quit rate among program participants compared to 18% among nonparticipants, with the quit rate being highest (44%) among program completers who were ready to change at baseline.[50] The use of workplace-based incentives and competition, when implemented alone, has not been shown to reduce tobacco use among workers.[51] However, there is still sufficient evidence to suggest that workplace-based incentives and competitions in combination with additional interventions are effective in increasing the number of workers who quit using tobacco.[51] These findings, in addition to those pertaining to smoke-free policies, provide evidence that workplace tobacco control interventions can be effective, especially for employees who are ready to change their existing tobacco use behaviors.

Employers

Tobacco use increases the costs of doing business for most employers. Employees who smoke have significantly higher absentee, injury, accident, and disciplinary rates compared to nonsmoking employees.[44,52-54] One study of U.S. employees found that the average annual cost for lost productivity was nearly twofold higher for smokers compared to nonsmokers, with more than half of these costs being the result of unproductive time at work.[44] However, the costs associated with tobacco use among employees extends beyond productivity; tobacco use increases both employer and employee medical care costs, including greater hospital admissions, longer hospital stays, higher average outpatient payments, and higher average insurance payments.[55] In addition to these effects of tobacco use, allowing smoking in the workplace can also lead to decreased productivity and health among workers as a result of secondhand smoke exposure, higher fire insurance premiums, and increased maintenance costs.[4]

Multiple studies have documented the potential cost savings associated with reducing tobacco use among employees and implementing smoke-free policies. For example, a study that assessed the potential costs to employers averted by implementing a smoke-free workplace policy in Scotland found that employee smoking resulted in annual costs of $858 million in lost productivity, $77 million in absenteeism, and $8 million in fire damage.[56] Similarly, the U.S. Environmental Protection Agency concluded the collective net benefit from smoke-free policies ranged from $48 billion to $89 billion per year in the United States in 1994, and a separate U.S. study found that employers could potentially save $10,246 per year for every smoker who quits because of a smoke-free workplace policy.[57,58] The cost savings of smoke-free policies relative to other workplace tobacco control interventions has not been extensively studied; however, one study found that Minnesota's smoke-free workplace policy was approximately nine times more cost effective per smoker than a free nicotine replacement therapy program, with the workplace policy generating 10,400 quitters at a cost of $799 per quitter and the latter program generating 18,500 quitters at a cost of $7020 per quitter.[59]

Some opponents of smoke-free workplace policies contend that such restrictions will have an adverse economic impact on businesses, particularly those in the hospitality industry.[4] However, evidence from peer-reviewed studies examining objective measures such as taxable sales revenues and employment levels shows that smoke-free policies and regulations do not have a negative economic impact on the hospitality industry, with some studies even documenting a positive impact on these indicators following policy implementation.[4,60]

General Population

The benefits of workplace tobacco control interventions extend beyond just workers and employers. The general public is susceptible to secondhand smoke exposure in workplaces in which smoking is permitted. Research indicates that smoke-free laws reduce self-reported and objectively measured secondhand smoke exposure in the general population of nonsmoking adults and children.[61-63] The implementation of such policies has also been shown to lead to reductions in hospitalizations and emergency room visits for heart attacks and asthma in the general population.[11,64-66] In addition to improved health through less exposure to secondhand smoke exposure as a result of smoke-free policies, the general public also benefits from cost savings associated with reduced health care expenditures, increased productivity, and lower health insurance premiums.[4,10]

SKILL ENHANCEMENT STRATEGIES

Providing support for employees who wish to reduce their tobacco consumption or quit using tobacco completely is a crucial component of any workplace tobacco control intervention. Quitting smoking is beneficial to health at any age, and cigarette smokers who quit before age 35 years have mortality rates similar to those who never smoked.[1,67] Since 2002, the number of former U.S. smokers has exceeded the number of current smokers,[68] and in 2010, 68.8% of current cigarette smokers said they would like to completely stop smoking and 52.4% had tried to quit smoking in the past year.[69] Employers can draw on a number of evidence-based interventions to help employees quit tobacco use, including enhanced access to tobacco cessation counseling, medications, and workplace cessation programs and resources.

Tobacco Cessation Counseling

Individualized screening for tobacco use and tobacco cessation counseling with a health provider are effective methods with which to help tobacco users successfully quit. Even brief 3-minute counseling sessions during clinic visits have been shown to be effective in reducing smoking rates, with effectiveness increasing with session length and frequency.[70] For example, success rates for those quitting smoking with no assistance ("cold turkey," 5%) are markedly lower than for brief (1–3 minutes, 14.4%) and intense (300 minutes, 25.5%) counseling.[43,70] The U.S. Public Health Service's Clinical Practice Guideline, *Treating Tobacco Use and Dependence*, outlines a five-step approach known as the "5 A's" for health professionals to help their patients quit tobacco use.[70] The approach encourages health professionals to *ask* patients if they use tobacco, *advise* them to quit, and *assess* their willingness to quit. If the patient is willing to make a quit attempt, the clinician should *assist* the patient by offering medication and providing or referring for counseling or additional treatment, and *arrange* for follow-up contact to prevent relapse. Considerable effort has been expended over the past decade to integrate the 5 A's model into clinical practice through medical education, enhanced health systems quality, and health plan benefit design.[70,71]

However, only three out of five adults are screened for tobacco use by a health care provider, and among current tobacco users, only one in five report receiving tobacco counseling during their clinician visit.[72] Accordingly, the workplace provides a unique opportunity for identifying and assisting tobacco users who might not otherwise have access to a health professional. For example, tobacco users can be identified using employee health risk appraisals, and provided with follow-up counseling and treatment. Follow-up approaches could include referral to outside organizations or telephone quitlines or bringing a health educator or tobacco cessation counselor to the workplace. Quitlines, which can initiate and reinforce tobacco users' efforts to quit, are housed in all 50 U.S. states.[73] However, several states have considered stopping funding and some have restricted the availability of services.[74] For example, the Ohio quitline was once free to all smokers, but now provides services to only certain individuals free of charge, including Medicaid recipients and pregnant women.[75] Telephone sessions typically follow a standardized counseling approach, and can be combined with other interventions, such as distributing cessation materials, formal individual or group counseling sessions, or tobacco cessation medications.

Tobacco Cessation Medications

The average success rate when using medication to quit smoking is 25%, and the combination of medication and counseling for tobacco cessation is 1.4 times more effective than for medication alone.[70] Effective tobacco cessation medications include nicotine replacement therapy and prescription nonnicotine medications. Nicotine replacement therapy works by providing a substitute source of nicotine, without the harmful components of tobacco products, and can reduce or eliminate the withdrawal symptoms many tobacco users have when quitting. Nicotine replacement therapy products such as patches, gum, and lozenges can be purchased over the counter, whereas nicotine inhalers and nasal spray require a prescription. In contrast, nonnicotine medications, such as sustained-release bupropion (Zyban) and varenicline (Chantix), are available by prescription only.[76] The U.S. Food and Drug Administration has approved all of the seven aforementioned products for smoking cessation.[76]

Employers can enhance employee access to approved tobacco cessation medications by providing services or coverage for, or reimbursing the costs associated with, nicotine replacement therapy and non–nicotine-containing medications. Enhanced access to these medications is best achieved through full coverage under employee medical insurance plans.[70] Such actions align with recent national initiatives to increase the number of persons in the United States with access to proven cessation medications. For example, effective September 2010, the 2010 Patient Protection and Affordable Care Act required non-grandfathered private health plans to offer cessation coverage without cost sharing.[77] Effective January 2014, the act also bars state Medicaid programs from excluding U.S. Food and Drug Administration (FDA)–approved cessation medications, including over-the-counter medications, from Medicaid drug coverage.[77]

Tobacco Cessation Program and Resources

In addition to improved access to tobacco cessation counseling and medication, other educational and social support initiatives can also be instituted in the workplace to help employees who use tobacco to quit. For example, employers can implement cessation programs and resources in collaboration with public health partners, such as local chapters of the American Lung Association or American Heart Association, public health departments, community health centers, and local hospitals and universities. Such programs can be developed to address tobacco use among all employees, or tailored to fit a particular workplace site or group, by establishing employee steering committees to provide advice and feedback. Workplace events can also be planned to coincide with public health awareness events throughout the year, such as the American Cancer Society's Great American Smokeout (November),[78] or the World Health Organization's World No Tobacco Day (May).[79] Competitions and incentives for smoking cessation can also be implemented in the workplace; however, early success with these programs tends to dissipate when rewards are no longer offered, and such efforts have not been shown to enhance long-term tobacco cessation rates when implemented alone.[51,80]

OPPORTUNITY ENHANCEMENT STRATEGIES

The two primary purposes of workplace tobacco control interventions are to encourage tobacco users to quit and to reduce exposure to secondhand smoke. Two opportunity enhancement strategies that can lead to the successful realization of these objectives include the provision of health benefits to support tobacco cessation and the implementation of tobacco-free policies.

Health Benefits to Support Tobacco Use Cessation

Efforts to make evidence-based interventions more affordable can increase interest in the utilization of these treatments and promote tobacco cessation among employees.[70] One way to improve the affordability of these interventions in the workplace is to reduce tobacco users' out-of-pocket costs, which has been shown to be effective in increasing the use of tobacco cessation therapies, the number of people who attempt to quit using tobacco, and the number of people who successfully stop using tobacco.[70] The reduction of out-of-pocket costs is best achieved through the provision or enhancement of employee benefits, with the two most crucial components being full coverage of both clinical counseling and FDA-approved medications for tobacco cessation.[81,82] In addition to reducing out-of-pocket costs, full coverage of medications mitigates existing barriers governing the packaging and sale of over-the-counter nicotine replacement products. These barriers, including restrictions

on the types of outlets that can sell these products, high cost due to large package size requirements, and concerns about safety resulting in part from extensive labeling requirements, all contribute to low utilization rates.[83]

Most tobacco users are dependent on nicotine, and research suggests that nicotine is as addictive as heroin or cocaine.[84] Accordingly, quitting tobacco use is difficult and all tobacco users may require multiple attempts before they are ultimately successful. Tobacco users often relapse because of stress, weight gain, and withdrawal symptoms such as irritability, anxiety, difficulty concentrating, and increased appetite.[70] However, tobacco users can learn from previous quit attempts and be better prepared to overcome the challenges that caused them to relapse. Moreover, different medications and counseling methods work for different people.[70] Therefore, making multiple cessation options available on a recurrent basis can enable employees who use tobacco to find a specific treatment or combination of treatments that best suits their needs and that increases the likelihood they will quit for good.

Tobacco-Free Policies

The implementation of a tobacco-free policy, which completely prohibits the use of tobacco of any kind on workplace property, is an evidence-based and sustainable approach for eliminating nonsmokers' exposure to secondhand smoke in the workplace and reducing tobacco use among employees.[4,8] Tobacco-free policies can be established by private, nongovernment, and government groups and entities, and are more effective than tobacco restrictions, which only limit tobacco use to designated areas instead of prohibiting it from the entire property.[8]

The most frequently implemented types of tobacco-free policies are smoke-free policies, which prohibit combustible tobacco use, or smoking, in indoor areas of a workplace.[4] Smoke-free policies are implemented with the intent of protecting people from secondhand smoke exposure in public areas. These policies can vary in scope, and in some cases include exemptions for specific venue types or separate ventilated areas.[4] Comprehensive smoke-free policies, which prohibit smoking in all indoor areas of workplaces and public places, including restaurants and bars, are the most effective.[4] In 2002, Delaware became the first state to implement a comprehensive smoke-free policy,[85] and as of January 1, 2013, 26 states and the District of Columbia had instituted such laws (Figure 18-3).[86] Comprehensive smoke-free policies have also been instituted in over 500 localities, and approximately 49% of the U.S. population (149.7 million individuals) was covered by a state or local comprehensive smoke-free policy as of January 1, 2013.[87] However, gaps in coverage, especially in the southern United States and in states with laws that preempt local smoking restrictions, are contributing to disparities in secondhand smoke protections.[88] Data from the Current Population Survey suggest that although three-fourths of U.S. white-collar workers were covered by smoke-free policies during 1993–1999, only 43% of the country's 6.6 million food preparation and service occupation workers benefited from this level of protection.[89]

Comprehensive smoke-free policies are associated with reductions in self-reported respiratory symptoms and improved lung

Figure 18-3: Laws Prohibiting Smoking in Indoor Workplaces, by state, 2012.

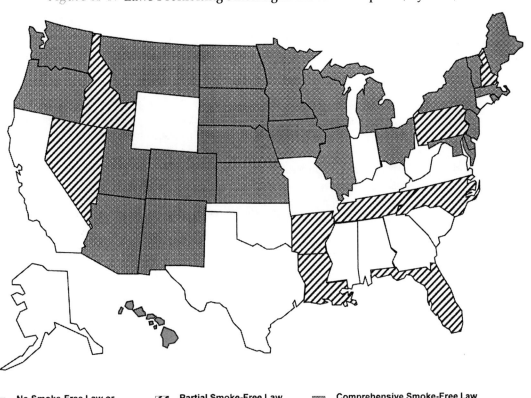

☐ No Smoke-Free Law or Major Exemptions   ▨ Partial Smoke-Free Law (Some Workplaces)   ▦ Comprehensive Smoke-Free Law (All Workplaces, including Bars and Restaurants)

Source: Centers for Disease Control and Prevention (CDC). State Tobacco Activities Tracking and Evaluation (STATE) System.

function among nonsmoking hospitality workers and with declines in hospitalizations and emergency room visits for heart attacks and asthma in the general population, and do not have an adverse economic impact on the hospitality industry.[4,90,91] Such policies are also popular among the public; during 2009–2010, 81.6% of American adults thought workplaces should be smoke free, with state-specific prevalence ranging from 68.6% (Kentucky) to 89.1% (California).[92] Studies also show that smoke-free policies can facilitate smoking cessation and the adoption of voluntary smoke-free home rules.[4,90,91] Irrespective of these benefits, tobacco-free policy adoption should be combined with tobacco cessation campaigns and referral programs in order to maximize cessation efficacy.[7]

DEVELOPING AND IMPLEMENTING A WORKPLACE TOBACCO CONTROL INTERVENTION

The process for developing and implementing a workplace tobacco control intervention involves a series of sequential steps, which can be divided into four primary phases: preparation, implementation, maintenance, and evaluation.[93] Although distinct from one another, the steps are interdependent and crucial for the successful realization of an effective and sustainable workplace tobacco control intervention. A more detailed discussion can be found in the sections of this text on program design (Chapter 4) and evaluation (Chapter 6).

Preparation

The first step in developing a workplace tobacco control intervention is to secure commitment from management, union leaders, and any other key stakeholders or groups. Methods for enhancing interest and support among these individuals could include the provision of information on the dangers of tobacco use and secondhand smoke exposure, including the potential health and economic benefits that could be realized by a workplace tobacco control intervention. Once commitment has been secured, a working group should be established with representatives from all sectors of the workplace, including management officials, union representatives, and employees. Given the known disparities in tobacco use and secondhand smoke exposure in the population, efforts should also be made to ensure that the working group is inclusive of all population groups, including men and women, ethnic minorities, and current, former, and never tobacco users. The working group will ultimately be tasked with developing the interventional approach, while making sure to utilize existing workplace resources where appropriate. In some instances, senior management may also determine the interventional approach beforehand and then form a work group to determine how best to implement it. Irrespective of the approach, the inclusion of a formal needs assessment, or systematic process for determining goals and establishing priorities for action, is ideal.

During the development of an interventional approach, several key factors should be considered, including the objective of the intervention, the type of intervention, how smoking cessation will be addressed, and the timeline and procedures for implementation of the intervention, enforcement, and evaluation. To help inform this process, the working group should consider reviewing lessons learned and best practices from other workplaces that have implemented similar interventions, as well as conducting a survey among employees to obtain workplace-specific information on the prevalence of tobacco use and attitudes, beliefs, and preferences toward a tobacco control intervention. For example, if a large proportion of smokers identify stress as their main reason for using tobacco use, the working group can make an effort to identify causes of stress in the workplace, work to remove or modify these sources, and offer workplace stress management seminars in concert with the provision of tobacco cessation support. Once a plan for the intervention is developed, it should be presented in writing, and approved by management, union leaders, and any other key stakeholders or groups prior to implementation.

Implementation

Following the development and approval of the tobacco control intervention, an official implementation date should be announced. At least 4 to 6 months should be allowed between the time of the announcement and implementation, depending upon the size of the organization and the magnitude of change associated with the intervention. During this lead time, the details of the intervention can be reinforced through messages in company media, including paycheck inserts, company newsletters, posters, and e-mails. It is crucial that these materials frame the intervention in a manner that focuses on the act of smoking, rather than the smoker, as well as on health and safety instead of individual rights. Details of the impending intervention can also be accompanied by materials on the dangers of tobacco use and secondhand smoke, and information on resources to support employee tobacco cessation, such as quitlines.

Prior to the official implementation date, training should be provided for middle managers and supervisors on policy communication and enforcement, when applicable. For example, the training could include role-play scenarios on how to advise visitors of a smoke-free policy and how to address noncompliance. To help mark the start of the intervention, a workplace-wide kickoff event can be held on the official implementation date. To help capitalize on existing resources and cessation support services, the kickoff could coincide with a national public health awareness event, such as the Great American Smokeout or World No Tobacco Day.[78,79]

Maintenance

Equitable enforcement of a workplace tobacco control intervention is crucial for ensuring its long-term sustainability and effectiveness. In the case of smoke-free policies, efforts should be made to ensure that enforcement is equitable across job categories and that no differentiation is made between smoking breaks and other forms of breaks. The successful maintenance of a smoke-free policy also requires the continued provision of smoking cessation educational opportunities and resources once the policy has been implemented to fully support employees in their attempts to quit tobacco and to prevent relapse. In the case of other forms of tobacco control interventions, such as employee health benefits, efforts should be made to ensure that employees have full and continued access to these resources following the official implementation date.

Evaluation

Evaluating a workplace tobacco control intervention can provide useful information on interventional effectiveness and cost efficiency, help maintain accountability to both the employer and employees, and also assist in identifying ways to improve the intervention.[94,95] Three types of potential evaluations for developing and implementing a workplace tobacco control intervention include formative, process, and summative. Formative evaluations are used in the introductory stage of interventional development to identify the most suitable strategies for a particular workplace. An example of a formative evaluation would be an employee survey on tobacco use and attitudes, beliefs, and preferences toward a specific workplace tobacco control intervention. In contrast, process evaluations focus on interventions that are currently underway to determine if any adjustments need to be made to the approach. Examples of process evaluations could include assessments of the number and types of employees who participated in a tobacco cessation class, or participant satisfaction or complaints associated with the class. Finally, summative evaluations focus on whether an intervention was effective and achieved the objectives that it initially set out to accomplish. Examples of summative evaluations could include a cost-benefit analysis or an assessment of changes in the number of employees who use tobacco, the quantity of tobacco that they use, and intentions to quit among continuing tobacco users.

The information obtained from evaluating the intervention should ultimately be used to revise and improve the existing intervention or to better inform strategies to implement such interventions in the future. The evaluation results are best compiled in the form of a written report that outlines key lessons learned and best practices for the development and implementation of the specific workplace tobacco control intervention.

EMERGING AREAS IN WORKPLACE TOBACCO CONTROL

The science and practice of tobacco control is dynamic and continues to rapidly evolve over time. Accordingly, tobacco prevention and control efforts must change over time to reflect both the current state of scientific knowledge and changing social norms related to tobacco use. Several decades ago, the primary focus of tobacco control interventions was to educate people about the adverse health effects of tobacco use and to promote cessation at the individual level, whereas the current emphasis is on policy approaches to address tobacco use and secondhand smoke at the population

level.[96] In recent years, new issues have emerged in the field of tobacco control that can influence workplace health promotion, including disparities in the adoption and coverage of tobacco control interventions, the proliferation of tobacco-free hiring policies, and the introduction of novel tobacco products into the U.S. marketplace.

Disparities

Socioeconomic status is significantly associated with tobacco-related knowledge, consumption, and cessation,[97,98] and disparities in adult mortality have also been linked to the effects of tobacco use.[99] Possible reasons for these inequalities include variations in educational attainment, propensity and self-efficacy toward tobacco cessation, and deprivation.[100]

Few studies have evaluated the relationship between socioeconomic status and interventional strategies to reduce tobacco use and secondhand smoke exposure in the workplace. The limited number of studies that have been conducted suggest that secondhand smoke exposure and smoke-free policy noncompliance are disproportionately higher among individuals with lower socioeconomic status, particularly those with lower income or less education or those who live in rural areas.[101-103] Current smokers with higher socioeconomic status have been found to be more likely to be covered by a smoke-free policy in the workplace; however, the same study found no variations in the prevalence of smoke-free bar and restaurant policies, or the rate of adoption of such policies, across socioeconomic groups.[104]

Disparities in access to workplace-sponsored smoking cessation programs have also been noted in the literature. Data from the 2006 Current Population Survey indicate that the percentage of U.S. workers who reported that their employer offered any help to employees who want to quit smoking was higher for white-collar occupations

(19.8%) compared to both blue-collar (13.5%) and service occupations (10.6%).[105] These disparities in access to smoking cessation programs, in addition to variations in smoke-free policy protection, suggest that continued efforts are needed to ensure that workplace tobacco control interventions reach all subsets of the population, particularly among lower wage earners and lower socioeconomic populations.

Tobacco-Free Hiring Policies

In addition to policies and restrictions on the use of tobacco in the workplace, a growing number of organizations have chosen to extend the breadth of workplace tobacco control efforts by instituting policies that specifically bar tobacco users from employment.[106] In some instances, employers have enforced such policies using cotinine testing, which can test positive as the result of tobacco use, secondhand smoke exposure, or the use of nicotine replacement therapy such as the nicotine patch.[106]

Proponents of tobacco-free hiring policies, many of which are health care and tobacco control organizations, contend that such policies help denormalize tobacco use and ensure that employees are able to act as advocates or role models of the organization. Potential savings from reduced health care benefit costs have also been cited as potential advantages of such policies.[106] In contrast, opponents claim that tobacco-free hiring policies disproportionately limit the employment opportunities of tobacco users and may exacerbate unemployment and job insecurity among subpopulations with a higher prevalence of tobacco use,[106] including lower socioeconomic groups and racial minorities such as American Indians and Alaska Natives.[3]

In some states, the adoption of tobacco-free hiring policies is prohibited through legislation that prevents employers from discriminating against employees for using tobacco products. As of January 1, 2013, 29 states and the District of Columbia had enacted laws that protect tobacco users from tobacco-free hiring policies (Figure 18-4).[107] The scope of these "smoker protection laws" varies by state; however, most explicitly prohibit employers from firing an employee or refusing to hire a job candidate for using tobacco during nonwork hours and when the individual is off the employer's property. In New York and Colorado, there is no law that specifically addresses the use of tobacco by employees, but tobacco users are protected under broader legislation that prohibits discrimination against an employee who is engaging in a lawful activity.[107]

Novel Tobacco Products

Despite continued declines in the prevalence of cigarette smoking among adults in the United States, the consumption of noncigarette products has stalled (e.g., smokeless tobacco),[2] or in some cases increased (e.g., cigars), in recent years.[108] During the same time period, various novel tobacco products, such as snus and electronic cigarettes, have also been introduced into the marketplace and have gained popularity.[109] Snus is a smokeless tobacco product that does not require the user to spit,[110] and an electronic cigarette, or e-cigarette, is a battery-powered device that provides inhaled doses of nicotine and other additives to the user.[111]

Public health professionals are concerned that the use of emerging products like snus and e-cigarettes will encourage smoking initiation, perpetuate the use of nicotine among tobacco users who might otherwise quit, and counter the effectiveness of smoke-free policies.[111,112] In addition, snus use has been shown to cause certain cancers,[113,114] and potentially harmful constituents have been identified in some e-cigarette cartridges.[115] In contrast, proponents of these products contend that they are less harmful to health than combustible tobacco products, such as cigarettes, and may help some smokers to quit.[116,117]

Figure 18-4: Laws Prohibiting Employers from Discriminating Against Employees Who Use Tobacco, by state, 2012.

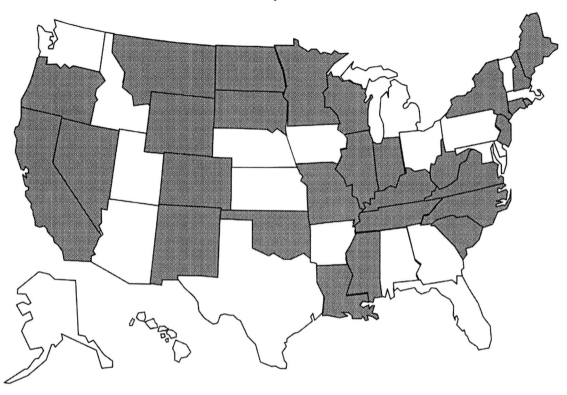

Law Prohibiting Employers from Discriminating
Against Employees who Use Tobacco

Source: American Lung Association.

In recent years, a growing number of states, localities, and private institutions have made efforts to address the use of emerging tobacco products in the workplace. For example, as of January 2013, over 740 U.S. colleges and universities have instituted tobacco-free policies that prohibit the use of all types of tobacco, including smokeless products such as snus, on their campuses.[118] Several national public health organizations, including the American Cancer Society, American Heart Association, and American Lung Association, have also advocated for the inclusion of e-cigarettes into existing and future smoke-free legislation.[119] In January 2010, New Jersey became the first U.S. state to enact legislation that specifically prohibits the use of e-cigarettes in public places and workplaces,[120] and the U.S. Department of Transportation banned the use of e-cigarettes on commercial flights as of February 2011.[121]

CONCLUSION

The workplace represents an ideal setting in which to develop and implement interventions to address tobacco use and secondhand smoke exposure. Although progress has been made over the past several decades in reducing tobacco use and implementing comprehensive smoke-free policies in indoor environments, enhanced efforts are still needed to reduce the health and economic toll of tobacco in the United States. Research suggests that approximately 20% of working adults in the United States smoke cigarettes, and the same percentage report being involuntary exposed to secondhand smoke in the workplace.

Workplace tobacco control interventions, including tobacco-free policies, employee health benefits to support tobacco use cessation, and tobacco cessation programs and resources, are cost-effective mechanisms with which to improve the health and productivity of both workers and the general public. Such strategies can also yield significant cost savings to employers and society through reductions in tobacco-related illnesses, increased productivity among employees, and declines in maintenance and insurance expenditures. Support for employees who use tobacco, including full health benefits for cessation counseling and FDA-approved medications, is a particularly important component. Aside from improving the health of the tobacco user and the employer's bottom line, providing this support demonstrates the employer's commitment to enhancing the health of all employees, as well as an understanding of the highly addictive nature of nicotine and the difficulty of quitting tobacco use.

Workplace tobacco control interventions are best developed and implemented with involvement from all sectors of the workplace, including management officials, union representatives, and employees. The inclusion of all key stakeholders will ultimately help achieve a comprehensive approach to workplace health that ensures tobacco-free employees, a tobacco-free work environment, and an organizational culture that values health, safety, and wellness.

Glossary

5 A's: A five-step approach for health professionals to help their patients quit tobacco use. The approach encourages health professionals to *ask* patients if they use tobacco, *advise* them to quit, and *assess* their willingness to quit. If the patient is willing to make a quit attempt, the clinician should *assist* the patient by offering medication and providing or referring for counseling or additional treatment, and *arrange* for follow-up contact to prevent relapse.

Biomarker: A specific physical trait used to measure or indicate the effects or progress of a disease or condition. Cotinine is an example of a type of biomarker used to assess recent secondhand smoke exposure.

Comprehensive smoke-free policy: A policy or law that completely prohibits tobacco smoking in all indoor areas of workplaces and public places, including restaurants and bars.

Cotinine: A type of biomarker that is the most scientifically valid measure of recent secondhand smoke exposure. Cotinine is a metabolite of nicotine that can be assessed in the blood (serum), urine, or saliva of adults and children.

Electronic cigarette (e-cigarette): A battery-powered device that provides inhaled doses of nicotine and other additives to the user.

Environmental monitoring: The assessment of the actual or potential exposure of an individual to materials that may be present in his or her environment. Examples of environmental monitoring include the measurement of airborne nicotine, a tobacco-specific constituent, or airborne particulate matter, both of which can be used to determine the presence and magnitude of secondhand smoke in a specified environment.

Nicotine: A highly addictive substance that is present in tobacco products.

Nicotine replacement therapy: Therapeutic products that provide a substitute source of nicotine to the user, without the other harmful components of tobacco products, and can reduce or eliminate the withdrawal symptoms many tobacco users have when quitting. Types of nicotine replacement therapy include patches, gum, and lozenges, which can be purchased over the counter, as well as inhalers and nasal spray, which require a prescription from a health professional.

Nonnicotine medication: Therapeutic medications that do not contain nicotine and can reduce or eliminate the withdrawal symptoms many tobacco users have when quitting. Types of nonnicotine medications include sustained-release bupropion (Zyban) and varenicline (Chantix), both of which require a prescription from a health professional.

$PM_{2.5}$: Airborne particulate matter less than 2.5 µm in diameter. $PM_{2.5}$ is frequently used in environmental monitoring to determine the presence and severity of secondhand smoke in a specified environment. The U.S. Environmental Protection Agency has established an average 24-hour $PM_{2.5}$ exposure standard of 35 µg/m³.

Quitline: A telephone helpline offering treatment for tobacco addiction. Some quitlines also offer free access to nicotine replacement therapy such as nicotine patches.

Secondhand smoke: The combination of smoke emitted from the burning end of a cigarette or other smoked tobacco product and the smoke exhaled from the lungs of smokers. Secondhand smoke is involuntarily inhaled by nonsmokers, can linger in the air for hours after smoked tobacco products have been extinguished, and contains at least 250 chemicals that are known to be toxic to humans.

Snus: A type of smokeless tobacco product that does not require the user to spit.

Tobacco-free hiring policy: A policy that specifically bars tobacco users from employment. In some states, the adoption of tobacco-free hiring policies is prohibited through legislation that prevents employers from discriminating against employees for using tobacco products.

Tobacco-free policy: A policy that completely prohibits the use of tobacco of any kind on a specified property such as a workplace. Tobacco-free policies can be established by private, nongovernment, and government groups and entities, and are more effective than tobacco restrictions, which only limit tobacco use to designated areas instead of prohibiting it from the entire property.

Learning Objectives

After completing this chapter, you should be able to:

1. Describe the adverse health effects associated with tobacco use and secondhand smoke exposure, as well as the prevalence of these risk factors among workers and the general population.
2. Identify a theoretical framework and provide an example of its application in the context of a workplace tobacco control intervention.
3. Discuss multiple evidence-based interventions that can help people to quit tobacco use.
4. Name a workplace tobacco control intervention and describe the steps for its development and implementation.
5. List three emerging areas in the field of tobacco control and explain how each can influence workplace health promotion.

Discussion Questions

1. What are the adverse health effects associated with tobacco use and

secondhand smoke exposure and the prevalence of these risk factors among workers and the general population?

2. What is an example of a theoretical framework, and how can it be applied in the context of a workplace tobacco control intervention?

3. What are two evidence-based interventions that can help people to quit tobacco use?

4. What is an example of a workplace tobacco control intervention, and what are the steps for its development and implementation?

5. What are three emerging areas in the field of tobacco control, and how can each influence workplace health promotion?

REFERENCES

1. US Dept of Health and Human Services. *The Health Consequences of Smoking: A Report of the Surgeon General*. Atlanta, Ga: US Dept of Health and Human Services, CDC; 2004.

2. US Dept of Health and Human Services. *Results from the 2011 National Survey on Drug Use and Health: Summary of National Findings*. Rockville, MD: Substance Abuse and Mental Health Services Administration; 2012.

3. Centers for Disease Control and Prevention. Current cigarette smoking among adults—United States, 2011. *MMWR Morb Mortal Wkly Rep.* 2012;61:889–894.

4. US Dept of Health & Human Services. *The Health Consequences of Involuntary Exposure to Tobacco Smoke: A Report of the Surgeon General*. Atlanta, Ga: US Dept of Health and Human Services, Centers for Disease Control and Prevention, Coordinating Center for Health Promotion, National Center for Chronic Disease Prevention & Health Promotion, Office on Smoking and Health; 2006.

5. US Dept of Health and Human Services. *How Tobacco Smoke Causes Disease: The Biology and Behavioral Basis for Smoking-Attributable Disease: A Report of the Surgeon General*. Atlanta, Ga: US Dept of Health and Human Services, CDC; 2010.

6. Centers for Disease Control and Prevention. Vital signs: nonsmokers' exposure to secondhand smoke—United States, 1999–2008. *MMWR Morb Mortal Wkly Rep.* 2010;59:1141–1146.

7. Hopkins DP, Razi S, Leeks KD, et al. Smokefree policies to reduce tobacco use. A systematic review. *Am J Prev Med.* 2010;38:S275–S289.

8. Centers for Disease Control and Prevention. Best practices for comprehensive tobacco control programs—2007. Atlanta, Ga: US Dept of Health and Human Services, CDC; 2007.

9. Mokdad AH, Marks JS, Stroup DF, Gerberding JL. Actual causes of death in the United States. *JAMA.* 2004;291:1238–1245.

10. Centers for Disease Control and Prevention. Smoking-attributable mortality, years of potential life lost, and productivity losses—United States, 2000–2004. *MMWR Morb Mortal Wkly Rep.* 2008;57:1226–1228.

11. Institute of Medicine. *Secondhand Smoke Exposure and Cardiovascular Effects: Making Sense of the Evidence*. Washington, DC: National Academies Press; 2009.

12. Behan DF, Eriksen MP, Lin Y. Economic effects of environmental tobacco smoke. American Academy of Actuaries. Available at: http://www.soa.org/research/research-projects/life-insurance/research-economic-effect.aspx. Accessed January 10, 2013.

13. Centers for Disease Control and Prevention. State tobacco revenues

compared with tobacco control appropriations—United States, 1998–2010. *MMWR Morb Mortal Wkly Rep.* 2012;61:370–374.

14. Yee SL, Schooley M. *Surveillance and Evaluation Data Resources for Comprehensive Tobacco Control Program.* Atlanta, Ga: Centers for Disease Control and Prevention; 2001.

15. Giovino G. Epidemiology of tobacco use in the United States. *Oncogene.* 2002;21:7326–7340.

16. Caraballo RS, Giovino GA, Pechacek TF, Mowery PD. Factors associated with discrepancies between self-reports on cigarette smoking and measured serum cotinine levels among persons aged 17 years or older: Third National Health and Nutrition Examination Survey, 1988–1994. *Am J Epidemiol.* 2001;153: 807–814.

17. Garrett BE, Dube SR, Trosclair A, et al. Cigarette smoking—United States, 1965–2008. *MMWR Morb Mortal Wkly Rep.* 2011;60:109–113.

18. Centers for Disease Control and Prevention. Vital signs: current cigarette smoking among adults aged ≥18 years—United States, 2005–2010. *MMWR Morb Mortal Wkly Rep.* 2011;60:1207–1212.

19. Centers for Disease Control and Prevention. State-specific prevalence of cigarette smoking and smokeless tobacco use among adults—United States, 2009. *MMWR Morb Mortal Wkly Rep.* 2010;59:1400–1406.

20. Centers for Disease Control and Prevention. Current cigarette smoking prevalence among working adults—United States, 2004–2010. *MMWR Morb Mortal Wkly Rep.* 2011;60:1305–1309.

21. King BA, Dube SR, Tynan MA. Current tobacco use among adults in the United States: findings from the National Adult Tobacco Survey. *Am J Public Health.* 2012;102:e93–e100.

22. Avila-Tang E, Al-Delaimy WK, Ashley DL, et al. Assessing secondhand smoke using biological markers. *Tob Control.* 2013;22:164–171.

23. Avila-Tang E, Elf JL, Cummings KM, et al. Assessing secondhand smoke exposure with reported measures. *Tob Control.* 2013;22:156–163.

24. Apelberg BJ, Hepp LM, Avila-Tang E, et al. Environmental monitoring of secondhand smoke exposure. *Tob Control.* 2013;22:147–155.

25. Wortley PM, Caraballo RS, Pederson LL, Pechacek TF. Exposure to secondhand smoke in the workplace: serum cotinine by occupation. *J Occup Environ Med.* 2002;44:503–509.

26. Arheart KL, Lee DJ, Dietz NA, et al. Declining trends in serum cotinine levels in US worker groups: the power of policy. *J Occup Environ Med.* 2008;50: 57–63.

27. Max W, Sung HY, Shi Y. Who is exposed to secondhand smoke? Self-reported and serum cotinine measured exposure in the U.S., 1999–2006. *Int J Environ Res Public Health.* 2009;6:1633–1648.

28. Homa DM, King BA, Dube SR. *Secondhand Smoke Exposure and Attitudes Toward Smoke-Free Policies in Workplaces.* Paper presented at: 2012 National Conference on Tobacco or Health; August 15–17, 2013; Kansas City, Mo.

29. Hammond SK. Exposure of U.S. workers to environmental tobacco smoke. *Environ Health Perspect.* 1999;107:329–340.

30. Hammond SK, Sorensen G, Youngstrom R, Ockene JK. Occupational exposure to environmental tobacco smoke. *JAMA.* 1995;274:956–960.

31. US Environmental Protection Agency. *Area Designations for 2006 24-Hour Fine Particulate (PM2.5) Standards.* Washington, DC: US Environmental Protection Agency; 2006.

32. Connolly GN, Carpenter CM, Travers MJ, et al. How smoke-free laws improve air quality: a global study of Irish pubs. *Nicotine Tob Res.* 2009;11:600–605.

33. McKenzie JF, Neiger BL, Thackeray R. *Planning, Implementing, and Evaluating Health Promotion Programs: A Primer.* 6th ed. Boston, Mass: Pearson Education Inc; 2013.

34. Glanz K, Rimer BK, Lewis FM. *Health Behavior and Health Education: Theory, Research, and Practice.* 3rd ed. San Francisco, Calif: John Wiley & Sons; 2002.

35. Prochaska JO, Velicer WF. The transtheoretical model of health behavior change. *Am J Health Promot.* 1997;12:38–48.

36. Zimmerman GL, Olsen CG, Bosworth MF. A "stages of change" approach to helping patients change behavior. *Am Fam Physician.* 2000;61:1409–1416.

37. Topa G, Moriano JA. Theory of planned behavior and smoking: meta-analysis and SEM model. *Subst Abuse Rehabil.* 2010;1:23–33.

38. Kothari A, Edwards N, Yanicki S, et al. Socioecological models: strengthening intervention research in tobacco control. *Drog San Soc.* 2007;6:iii1–iii24.

39. Wetter DW, Cofta-Gunn L, Fouladi RT, et al. Late relapse/sustained abstinence among former smokers: a longitudinal study. *Prev Med.* 2004;39:1156–1163.

40. Ajzen I. The theory of planned behavior. *Organ Behav Hum Decis Process.* 1991;50:179–211.

41. Stokols D. Translating social ecological theory into guidelines for community health promotion. *Am J Health Promot.* 1996;10:282–298.

42. Warner KE, Smith RJ, Smith DG, Fries BE. Health and economic implications of a work-site smoking-cessation program: a simulation analysis. *J Occup Environ Med.* 1996;38:981–992.

43. O'Donnell MP, Roizen MF. The SmokingPaST Framework: illustrating the impact of quit attempts, quit methods, and new smokers on smoking prevalence, years of life saved, medical costs saved, programming costs, cost effectiveness, and return on investment. *Am J Health Promot.* 2011;26:e11–e23.

44. Bunn WB, Stave GM, Downs KE, et al. Effect of smoking status on productivity loss. *J Occup Environ Med.* 2006;48:1099–1108.

45. Farrelly MC, Nonnemaker, Chou R, et al. Changes in hospitality workers' exposure to secondhand smoke following the implementation of New York's smoke-free law. *Tob Control.* 2005;14:236–241.

46. Eisner MD, Smith AK, Blanc PD. Bartenders' respiratory health after establishment of smoke-free bars and taverns. *JAMA.* 1998;280:1909–1914.

47. Bauer JE, Hyland A, Li Q, et al. A longitudinal assessment of the impact of smoke-free worksite policies on tobacco use. *Am J Public Health.* 2005;95:1024–1029.

48. Frieden TR, Mostashari F, Kerker BD, et al. Adult tobacco use levels after intensive tobacco control measures: New York City, 2002–2003. *Am J Public Health.* 2005;95:1016–1023.

49. Fichtenberg CM, Glantz SA. Effect of smoke-free workplaces on smoking behaviour: systematic review. *BMJ.* 2002;325:188–194.

50. Terry PE, Seaverson EL, Staufacker MJ, Tanaka A. The effectiveness of a telephone-based tobacco cessation program offered as part of a worksite health promotion program. *Popul Health Manag.* 2011;14:117–125.

51. Leeks KD, Hopkins DP, Soler RE, et al. Worksite-based incentives and competitions to reduce tobacco use.

A systematic review. *Am J Prev Med.* 2010;38:S263–S274.

52. Halpern MT, Shikiar R, Rentz AM, Khan ZM. Impact of smoking status on workplace absenteeism and productivity. *Tob Control.* 2011;10:233–238.

53. Ryan J, Zwerling C, Orav EJ. Occupational risks associated with cigarette smoking: a prospective study. *Am J Public Health.* 1992;82:29–32.

54. Ryan J, Zwerling C, Jones M. Cigarette smoking at hire as a predictor of employment outcome. *J Occup Environ Med.* 1996;38:928–933.

55. Penner M, Penner S. Excess insured health care costs from tobacco-using employees in a large group plan. *J Occup Med.* 1990;32:521–523.

56. Parrot S, Godfrey, C, Raw M. Costs of employee smoking in the workplace in Scotland. *Tob Control.* 2000;9:187–192.

57. United States Environmental Protection Agency (EPA). *The Costs and Benefits of Smoking Restrictions: An Assessment of the Smoke-Free Environmental Act of 1993 (H.R. 3434).* Washington, DC: Office of Air and Radiation; 1994.

58. Weis WL. Can you afford to hire smokers? *Pers Adm.* 1981;26:71–73,75–78.

59. Ong MK, Glantz SA. Free nicotine replacement therapy programs vs implementing smoke-free workplaces: a cost-effectiveness comparison. *Am J Public Health.* 2005;95:969–975.

60. Scollo M, Lal A, Hyland A, Glantz S. Review of the quality of studies on the economic effects of smoke-free policies on the hospitality industry. *Tob Control.* 2003;12:13–20.

61. Centers for Disease Control and Prevention. Reduced secondhand smoke exposure after implementation of a comprehensive statewide smoking ban—New York, June 26, 2003–June 30,

2004. *MMWR Morb Mortal Wkly Rep.* 2007;56:705–708.

62. Haw SJ, Gruer L. Changes in exposure of adult non-smokers to secondhand smoke after implementation of smoke-free legislation in Scotland: national cross sectional survey. *BMJ.* 2007;335:549.

63. Akhtar PC, Currie DB, Currie CE, Haw SJ. Changes in child exposure to environmental tobacco smoke (CHETS) study after implementation of smoke-free legislation in Scotland: national cross sectional study. *BMJ.* 2007;335:545.

64. Tan CE, Glantz SA. Association between smoke-free legislation and hospitalizations for cardiac, cerebrovascular, and respiratory diseases: A meta-analysis. *Circulation.* 2012;126:2177–2183.

65. Lightwood JM, Glantz SA. Declines in acute myocardial infarction after smoke-free laws and individual risk attributable to secondhand smoke. *Circulation.* 2009;120:1373–1379.

66. Mackay DF, Irfan MO, Haw S, Pell JP. Meta-analysis of the effect of comprehensive smoke-free legislation on acute coronary events. *Heart.* 2010;96:1525–1530.

67. Doll R, Peto R, Boreham J, Sutherland I. Mortality in relation to smoking: 50 years' observations on male British doctors. *BMJ.* 2004;328:1519–1528.

68. Centers for Disease Control and Prevention. Cigarette smoking among adults—United States, 2002. *MMWR Morb Mortal Wkly Rep.* 2004;53:427–431.

69. Centers for Disease Control and Prevention. Quitting smoking among adults—United States, 2001–2010. *MMWR Morb Mortal Wkly Rep.* 2011;60:1513–1519.

70. Fiore MC, Jaen CR, Baker TB, et al. *Treating Tobacco Use and Dependence: 2008 Update. Clinical Practice Guideline.*

Rockville, Md: US Dept of Health and Human Services, Public Health Service; 2008.

71. Curry SJ, Keller PA, Tracy Orleans CT, Fiore MC. The role of health care systems in increased tobacco cessation. *Annu Rev Public Health. 2008;29:411–428.*

72. Jamal A, Dube SR, Malarcher AM, et al. Tobacco use screening and counseling during physician office visits among adults — National Ambulatory Care Survey and National Health Interview Survey, United States, 2005–2009. *MMWR Morb Mortal Wkly Rep.* 2012;61:38–45.

73. North American Quitline Consortium. Increase reach of tobacco cessation quitlines: a review of the literature and promising practices. Available at: http://c.ymcdn.com/sites/www.naquitline.org/resource/resmgr/issue_papers/naqc_issuepaper_increasingre.pdf. Accessed March 25, 2013.

74. Campaign for Tobacco Free Kids. Quitlines help smokers quit. Available at: http://www.tobaccofreekids.org/research/factsheets/pdf/0326.pdf. Accessed March 25, 2013.

75. Ohio Dept of Health. Ohio tobacco quit line. Available at: http://www.healthyohioprogram.org/healthylife/tobc2/cessation/quit.aspx. Accessed March 25, 2013.

76. US Food and Drug Administration. FDA 101: smoking cessation products. Available at: http://www.fda.gov/forconsumers/consumerupdates/ucm198176.htm. Accessed March 25, 2013.

77. US House of Representatives. Patient Protection and Affordable Care Act. Available at: http://housedocs.house.gov/energycommerce/ppacacon.pdf. Accessed March 25, 2013.

78. American Cancer Society. Great American Smokeout. Available at: http://www.cancer.org/healthy/stayawayfromtobacco/greatamericansmokeout/index. Accessed March 25, 2013.

79. World Health Organization (WHO). World No Tobacco Day. Available at: http://www.who.int/tobacco/wntd/en/. Accessed March 25, 2013.

80. Cahill K, Perera R. Competitions and incentives for smoking cessation. *Cochrane Database Syst Rev.* 2011;(4): CD004307.

81. Task Force on Community Preventive Services. Effectiveness of reducing patient out-of-pocket costs for effective therapies to stop using tobacco. The Guide to Community Preventive Services. Available at: www.thecommunityguide.org/tobacco/cessation/outofpocketcosts.html. Accessed March 25, 2013.

82. US Dept of Health and Human Services, Agency for Healthcare Research and Policy, The United States Preventive Services Task Force. Counseling to prevent tobacco use. Available at: http://www.uspreventiveservicestaskforce.org/uspstf/uspstbac2.htm. Accessed March 25, 2013.

83. Kozlowski LT, Giovino GA, Edwards B, et al. Advice on using over-the-counter nicotine replacement therapy-patch, gum, or lozenge to quit smoking. *Addict Behav.* 2007;32:2140–2150.

84. US Dept of Health and Human Services. *The Health Consequences of Smoking: Nicotine Addiction: A Report of the Surgeon General.* Rockville, Md: US Dept of Health and Human Services, Centers for Disease Control and Prevention, Coordinating Center for Health Promotion, National Center for Chronic Disease Prevention & Health Promotion, Office on Smoking and Health; 1988.

85. Centers for Disease Control and Prevention. State smoke-free laws for

worksites, restaurants, and bars — United States, 2000–2010. *MMWR Morb Mortal Wkly Rep.* 2011;60:472–475.

86. Centers for Disease Control and Prevention. State Tobacco Activities Tracking & Evaluation (STATE) system. Available at: http://www.cdc.gov/tobacco/state_system/index.htm. Accessed March 25, 2013.

87. American Nonsmokers' Rights Foundation. Summary of 100% smokefree state laws and population protected by 100% U.S. smokefree laws. Available at: http://www.no-smoke.org/pdf/SummaryUSPopList.pdf. Accessed March 25, 2013.

88. Centers for Disease Control and Prevention. Comprehensive smoke-free laws — 50 largest U.S. cities, 2000 and 2012. *MMWR Morb Mortal Wkly Rep.* 2012; 61:914–917.

89. Shopland DR, Anderson CM, Burns DM, Gerlach KK. Disparities in smoke-free workplace policies among food service workers. *J Occup Environ Med.* 2004;46:347–356.

90. International Agency for Research on Cancer. *Evaluating the Effectiveness of Smoke-Free Policies.* Lyon, France: International Agency for Research on Cancer; 2009.

91. Goodman PG, Haw S, Kabir A, Clancy L. Are there health benefits associated with comprehensive smoke-free laws. *Int J Public Health.* 2009;54:367–378.

92. King BA, Dube SR, Tynan MA. Attitudes toward smoke-free workplaces, restaurants, and bars, casinos, and clubs among U.S. adults: findings from the 2009–2010 National Adult Tobacco Survey. *Nicotine Tob Res.* 2013;15: 1464–1470.

93. Health Canada. *Towards a Healthier Workplace: A Guidebook on Tobacco Control Policies.* Ontario, Canada: Health Canada Publications; 2007.

94. National Cancer Institute. *Theory at a Glance: A Guide for Health Promotion Practice.* Washington DC: US Dept of Health and Human Services, National Institutes of Health; 2005.

95. Task Force on Community Preventive Services. *The Guide to Community Preventive Services: What Works to Promote Health.* New York, NY: Oxford University Press; 2005.

96. Farquhar J. The evolution of tobacco use and control in the United States: an interview with Dr. John Farquhar. Interview by Jamie Hwang. *Am J Health Promot.* 2005;19:255–259.

97. Siahpush M, McNeill A, Hammond D, Fong GT. Socioeconomic and country variations in knowledge of health risks of tobacco smoking and toxic constituents of smoke: results from the 2002 International Tobacco Control (ITC) Four Country Survey. *Tob Control.* 2006;15:iii65–iii70.

98. Siahbpush M, McNeill A, Borland R, Fong GT. Socioeconomic variations in nicotine dependence, self-efficacy, and intention to quit across countries: findings from the International Tobacco Control (ITC) Four Country Survey. *Tob Control.* 2006;15:iii71–iii75.

99. Jha P, Peto R, Zatonski W, et al. Social inequalities in male mortality, and in male mortality from smoking: indirect estimation from national death rates in England and Wales, Poland, and North America. *Lancet.* 2006;368:367–370.

100. Layte R, Whelan CT. Explaining social class inequalities in smoking: the role of education, self-efficacy, and deprivation. *Eur Sociol Rev.* 2009;25:399–410.

101. Moussa K, Lindstrom M, Ostergren PO. Socioeconomic and demographic differences in exposure to environmental tobacco smoke at work: the Scania Pulic Health Survey 2000. *Scand J Public Health.* 2004;32:194–202.

102. Shavers VL, Fagan P, Alexander LA, et al. Workplace and home smoking restrictions and racial/ethnic variation in the prevalence and intensity of current cigarette smoking among women by poverty status, TUS-CPS 1998–1999 and 2001–2002. *J Epidemiol Community Health.* 2006;60:34–43.

103. Harris JK, Geremakis C, Moreland-Russell S, et al. Demographic and geographic differences in exposure to secondhand smoke in Missouri workplaces, 2007–2008. *Prev Chronic Dis.* 2011;8:A135.

104. King BA, Hyland AJ, Borland R, et al. Socioeconomic variation in the prevalence, introduction, retention, and removal of smoke-free policies among smokers: findings from the International Tobacco Control (ITC) Four Country Survey. *Int J Environ Res Public Health.* 2011;8:411–434.

105. Alexander LA, Crawford T, Mendiondo MS. Occupational status, work-site cessation programs and policies and menthol smoking on quitting behaviors of U.S. smokers. *Addiction.* 2010;105: 95–104.

106. Voigt K. Nonsmokers and "nonnicotine" hiring policies: the implications of employment restrictions for tobacco control. *Am J Public Health.* 2012;102: 2013–2018.

107. American Lung Association. State "smoker protection" laws. Available at: http://www.lungusa2.org/slati/appendixf.php. Accessed March 25, 2013.

108. Centers for Disease Control and Prevention. Consumption of cigarettes and combustible tobacco—United States, 2000–2011. *MMWR Morb Mortal Wkly Rep.* 2012;61:565–569.

109. McMillen R, Maduka J, Winickoff J. Use of emerging tobacco products in the United States. *J Environ Public Health.* 2012;2012:989474.

110. Foulds J, Kozlowski L. Snus—what should the public-health response be? *Lancet.* 2007;369:1976–1978.

111. Etter JF, Bullen C, Flouris AD, et al. Electronic nicotine delivery systems: a research agenda. *Tob Control.* 2011;20: 243–248.

112. Timberlake DS, Zell JA. Review of epidemiologic data on the debate over smokeless tobacco's role in harm reduction. *BMC Med.* 2009;7:61.

113. Boffetta P, Hecht S, Gray N, et al. Smokeless tobacco and cancer. *Lancet Oncol.* 2008;9:667–675.

114. Luo J, Ye W, Zendehdel K, et al. Oral use of Swedish moist snuff (snus) and risk for cancer of the mouth, lung, and pancreas in male construction workers: a retrospective cohort study. *Lancet.* 2007;369:2015–2020.

115. Cobb NK, Byron MJ, Abrams DB, Shields PG. Novel nicotine delivery systems and public health: the rise of the "e-cigarette." *Am J Public Health.* 2010;100:2340–2342.

116. Cahn Z, Siegel M. Electronic cigarettes as a harm reduction strategy for tobacco control: a step forward or a repeat of past mistakes? *J Public Health* Policy. 2011;32:16–31.

117. Gartner C, Hall W. The potential role of snus in tobacco harm reduction. *Addiction.* 2009;104:1586–1587.

118. American Nonsmokers' Rights Foundation. U.S. colleges and universities with smokefree and tobacco-free policies. Available at: http://www.no-smoke.org/pdf/smokefreecolleges universities.pdf. Accessed March 25, 2013.

119. American Cancer Society, American Heart Association, Campaign for Tobacco-Free Kids, and American Lung

Association. Policy Guidance document regarding e-cigarettes. Available at: http://www.ttac.org/tcn/tfp/2010/may-2010/pdfs/Policy_Guidance_E-Cigarettes.pdf. Accessed March 25, 2013.

120. State of New Jersey 213th Legislature. Assembly Committee Substitute for Assembly, Nos. 4227 and 4228. Adopted November 23, 2009. Available at: http://www.njgasp.org/E-Cigs_A4227.pdf. Accessed March 25, 2013.

121. 76 *Federal Register* 179 (2001). Thursday, September 15, 2011. Available at: http://airconsumer.ost.dot.gov/rules/E-cigarette%20NPRM.pdf. Accessed March 23, 2013.

Health Decision Support: Health and Medical Decision Support and Chronic Condition Self-Management

Paul E. Terry, Stefan Gingerich and
Judith Hibbard

INTRODUCTION

Over the past several centuries, those with medical or health concerns have seldom lacked ready access to advice. Whether from the shaman or witch doctor, from housewives talking across the backyard fence, from late-night infomercials, or from a family member who happens to be a nurse, recommendations for how to care for a flu or a fever and home remedies for back pain or gout have always been easy to come by. Assessing whether such readily available answers are safe or effective is a different story. Indeed, the era of digital content proliferation and portable, immediate access to information democratizes decision support and self-management on one hand while promulgating buyer-beware dilemmas on the other. Ironically, such abundance and ready access to health and medical advice may make decision making only marginally less risky than in the past but ever more complicated.

What has not changed is that the consumer remains the ultimate arbiter of health decisions, and the consumer's ability to protect self-interests hinges on that individual's cues to action along with their motivation and ability. These are the domains that health educators reading this chapter need to be professionally equipped to support. Developing, evaluating, and implementing medical decision support systems and chronic condition self-management programs follow most of the tenets found throughout this book on workplace health promotion. For brevity, these overlapping constructs of chronic condition self-management and health care or medical decision support are referred to as "decision support." For clarity, this chapter is divided into four main parts:

I. Introduction
II. Evidence to Support the Use of Decision Support
III. Advice for Worksite Health Practitioners
IV. Condition-Specific Decision Support Programs

Interest in improving and supporting health care consumer decision making has spawned an extraordinary profusion of research, programs, products, and services over the past two decades. The need for and value of activating consumers to be smarter consumers of health care derive from decades of related research, advocacy, and health education program development. Review of studies from the 1990s and early 2000s in this chapter demonstrates how research has increased conceptual clarity concerning what is meant by activated consumerism and decision support. From there, the best examples of well-designed decision support programs from the past decade are provided to illustrate how decision support technologies and tools are becoming a mainstream part of how worksite health promotion is transforming and contributing to innovation in health care delivery. No longer is the health promotion professional the educator gathering and disseminating needed information. Rather, our charge is that of a curator and coach, supporting clients in making an overwhelming plethora of health content useful, actionable, and relevant to the consumer's personal needs, values, and goals.

Definition of Decision Support

The concept of decision support resides at the crossroads between medical care and personal health management. Accordingly, decision support is defined using precepts from these related fields. The medical side of the definition is the easy side to describe because it simply references the science of diagnosing, treating, and curing disease. The self-management part of the definition is somewhat more difficult because it is a field spawned from consumer and market need, fueled by entrepreneurs, substantiated by medical providers, and abetted by fast growing social media, digital apps, and self-monitoring devices.

Given there are no professional societies or expert consensus panels dedicated to determining a definition for health care decision support, pieces must be borrowed from related disciplines to formulate a definition for decision support. For example, in a consensus panel dedicated to defining health education, Green and Kreuter[1] defined health education as "any combination of learning experiences designed to facilitate voluntary action conducive to health." Until such time that health decision support has an authoritative panel dedicated to its identity, for this chapter, *decision support* will be defined as any combination of learning experiences designed to facilitate the personal diagnosis, treatment, self-management, and cure of illness.

A critic less schooled in the principles of personal empowerment and individual responsibility could view this definition of health care decision support as practicing medicine without a license. To address this concern, it is important to distinguish between health care decision support for chronic conditions versus acute emergencies versus self-limiting conditions. Teaching others the ability to distinguish between these conditions and discern what can be treated alone and what needs professional attention is at the heart of health care decision support.

Acute, emergency conditions that require medical attention benefit from decision support that teaches people how to identify life-threatening problems and act quickly. When conditions are self-limiting, they will go away without medical intervention and decision support has a role in providing comfort. For chronic health conditions, i.e., those lasting 6 months or longer, decision support offers therapeutic as well as comforting benefits. Involving patients in self-care of chronic health problems is, after all, the most critical component of treating problems that have no cure.

Naturally, whether a condition is chronic, acute, or self-limiting, there is a very important role for medical professionals. Decision support is not meant to fill this role but exists because health care is necessarily complex and important, and because sometimes patients need help understanding how to best address whatever health concern they have.

Why is Decision Support Needed?

The advent of health care decision support, with its attendant self-care books, training sessions, and subsequent online and apps-based decision support media, corresponds to the changes in United States health policy priorities. Whereas lifestyle and individual responsibility were the watchwords of the 1980s and early 1990s, in the first decade of the 21st century there has been a movement toward wellness, population health, and "accountable care" models of health insurance reimbursement.

Policy makers have come to realize that the promise of citizens and patients taking control of their lifestyles is not only difficult but takes considerable time to accomplish. To address a small but costly portion of this issue, disease management vendors began providing programs of varying quality and demonstrable outcomes. Employers were eager for expansions, so an array of programs and interventions was offered to encompass a broader spectrum of care services. These services have been identified as a "continuum of care" spanning from wellness through health risk and disease burden levels. Today, employers and other health care purchasers view population health management as a promising practice to improve health outcomes and to keep down overall health care costs.[2]

In this milieu of policy and program innovations striving to balance individual versus social responsibility for health, and lifestyle versus condition management, medical decision support will play an increasingly vital role in population health management. Table 19-1 illustrates the differences between the various health management programs that are commonly available for employees today.

Today millions of people (35% of U.S. adults) use the Internet every day to self-diagnose and decide on a course of action. According to the Pew Internet Project, half of those who do this form of online triage follow up with a visit to the clinic and 40% of those who see a health professional have their self-diagnosis confirmed.[3] From the vantage point of a worksite health practitioner, this poses both opportunities and threats relating to the health and productivity of a workforce. Though common sense cannot be taught and hypochondria cannot be solved, employees can be equipped with guidelines, including cautions, for making health care decisions. Clearly, use of the Internet and other decision support tools increases convenience and reduces costs related to face-to-face visits with health professionals, but unfettered information seeking can produce unneeded anxiety and a missed opportunity for a correct diagnosis or treatment. To wit, if 40% of self-diagnosis can be confirmed by doctors, what about the other 60% of self-diagnosis via the Web?

Most worksite health promotion programs have made it a priority to improve online self-diagnosis. However, significant priorities for American worksite health promotion include the primary goal of improving employee health and a secondary goal of reducing health care costs. This trend, along with the proliferation of health-related apps and tools and the inherent difficulty of diagnosis (60% self-misdiagnosis), speaks to the need for decision support. Just as many clinics are responding to online demand for medical information, employers too are reinvesting in onsite clinics, telephonic health coaching, and other electronic or virtual methods that can reliably substitute for a clinic waiting room.

At the same time, the quality of medical care has become a major issue in evaluating employee benefits. Decision support tools have generally been shown to have favorable effects on consumer satisfaction and certain health outcomes. In addition, for conditions that will resolve on their own, decision support and

Table 19-1: Differentiating Decision Support and Employee Health Management Programs.

Programs	Primary Related Theories	Cost and Prevalence of Conditions Addressed	Time Needed for Program Impact	Resource Use Implications
Health care decision support	• Sick-role theory • Theory of Reasoned Action • Health Belief Model	Low cost, high prevalence conditions; primarily self-limiting conditions (e.g., colds, flu, fevers, headaches, earaches)	Short-term impact (hours to a few days before changes)	Good evidence of cost-effectiveness
Demand Management Programs	• Health Belief Model • Expectancy Theory	Moderate to high cost, moderate prevalence conditions; both self-limiting and chronic conditions (e.g., backaches, chronic pain syndrome, adult asthma)	Short to intermediate term impact (weeks to months before changes)	Weak or no evidence of cost-effectiveness; suggestive evidence supporting individual case management
Chronic condition self management	• Trans-theoretical Model • Organizational Change Theories • Value Expectancy Frameworks	High cost, high prevalence conditions; primarily chronic conditions (e.g., diabetes, congestive heart failure, pediatric asthma, hyperlipidemia)	Intermediate to long-term impact (months to years before changes)	Suggestive evidence of cost-effectiveness for select conditions (e.g. CHF, pediatric asthmas); cost increases likely for many conditions
Health Promotion or Disease prevention programs	• Social Learning Theory • PRECEDE/ PROCEED • Trans-theoretical Model • Social Marketing	Lifestyle conditions, (e.g., smoking, diet, exercise, clinical preventive services such as immunizations, blood pressure measurement)	Long-term impact (many years before changes)	Good evidence of long-term cost-effectiveness for select conditions like exercise and early detection of hypertension; equivocal evidence for obesity, diet

employee education are likely to be the most cost-effective and consumer-friendly way to reduce unnecessary use of health services, all of which improves the overall quality of medical care. The remainder of this chapter discusses the scientific evidence related to decision support in these contexts, beginning with tactics that have been shown to help employees build their skills at understanding their health issues.

EVIDENCE TO SUPPORT THE USE OF DECISION SUPPORT

The Patient Activation Measure (PAM)

Some people are very proactive about managing their health and others are quite passive. Given this variability, researchers have developed ways to measure people's ability and willingness to self-manage. One very useful measure for this is the Patient Activation Measure (PAM).[4]

What is Activation or Engagement?

Consumer engagement and activation are widely used terms, yet they are often poorly defined and used to denote different ideas. In this section they are used interchangeably to indicate the same concept: individuals who fully participate and are able to effectively manage their health and health care. The full definition of *activation* is "the degree to which an individual understands his or her own role in maintaining and promoting personal health and the extent to which he/she possesses the necessary knowledge and a sense of self-efficacy for taking on this role."[4] This global concept involves beliefs about one's role, as well as knowledge and self-efficacy for taking stewardship of one's own health.

This definition was used to create a measurement tool, the PAM, which is now widely used as a metric for assessing patient activation or engagement. The PAM is a 13-item questionnaire that scores patients on a 0 to 100 scale. The score incorporates responses to 13 statements about beliefs, confidence in managing health-related tasks, and self-assessed knowledge. Examples include "When all is said and done, I am the person who is responsible for taking care of my health"; "I am confident that I can tell whether I need to go to the doctor or whether I can take care of a health problem myself"; and "I am confident that I can tell a doctor the concerns I have even when he or she does not ask." Responses are degrees of agreement or disagreement.[5] The measure has proven to be reliable and valid across different languages, cultures, demographic groups, and health statuses.[6-12] The PAM opens up opportunities for innovative and effective ways to intervene with and support individuals, and ultimately to improve health decisions, health behaviors, and health outcomes.

The Importance of Activation

The nutritional value of diets, physical activity level, and adherence to treatment regimens will largely determine people's health outcomes. For example, it is estimated that people with diabetes who are able to manage their diet, be physically active, and comply with medication regimens to maintain near normal blood sugar levels will gain, on average, an additional 5 years of life, 8 years of sight, and 6 years free from kidney disease.[13] At the same time, many of the behaviors required of patients to maintain their health necessitate the acquisition of new knowledge and skills. For example, with new pharmaceutical approaches to treat conditions such as diabetes and asthma, patients must manage complex drug regimens by themselves. Similarly, with shorter hospital stays, patients often return home sicker and must manage posthospital drug, feeding, and wound care regimens on their own.

Multiple cross-sectional studies from a variety of settings and different population groups indicate that engagement or activation, as measured by the PAM, is correlated with a full range of health behaviors and many health outcomes. For example, the PAM score is significantly correlated with many preventive behaviors (screenings, immunizations, etc.), healthy behaviors such as diet and exercise, health information–seeking behaviors, and disease-specific self-management behaviors.[14-19] Higher activation scores have also been linked with having fewer unmet medical needs, having a regular source of care, and higher participation in physical therapy after spine surgery.[20,21] The findings linking activation and health behaviors remain statistically significant even after controlling for sociodemographic factors and insurance status. Findings have also been replicated in studies conducted in several countries.[6-12] Further, activation scores are predictive of outcomes within condition-specific patient groups, such as those with multiple chronic conditions and those with a serious mental health diagnosis, heart disease, HIV, multiple sclerosis, chronic obstructive pulmonary disorder (COPD), cancer, inflammatory bowel syndrome, hypertension, asthma, and diabetes.[22-28]

Conversely, lower activation scores are correlated with the use of costly health care services, such as emergency department use, hospitalizations, and being rehospitalized within 30 days of discharge.[6,14,26,28] A study by Kaiser Permanente that examined whether activation scores could predict future behavioral and health outcomes for diabetes patients found that baseline PAM scores were significant predictors of multiple diabetes outcomes.[26]

Increasing Consumer Activation

Interventions designed to increase individuals' activation have been shown to be effective.[28-33] Terry and colleagues showed that a worksite intervention with a focus on skill development, changing social norms, and the physical environment, including health coaching for high risk individuals, increased activation levels and improved behaviors.[32] Other studies show that tailoring support and education to the individual's level of activation is effective in increasing activation and improving outcomes.[28,33]

A key insight from the patient activation research is that starting where the individual is on the activation continuum and encouraging behavioral change that is realistic and achievable is an effective approach for helping individuals increase in activation and improve decision making and health outcomes. Strategies that segment a population based on activation level and that use different interventions for the different segments have also been shown to be successful.

Because the concept of activation or engagement is such an important element in supporting health decisions and behavior change, finding ways to effectively and efficiently increase activation in employee and patient populations has become a priority. Employers looking to increase activation among their employees are, no doubt, hoping to improve employee health, make the health care experience more efficient, and encourage the appropriate utilization of health care. The next section discusses other decision support interventions that have been studied for their ability to improve health care utilization patterns.

Decision Support and Appropriate Utilization of Health Care

Numerous studies over many years show that educating employees about self-care, particularly about home remedies for symptom management of self-limiting conditions, can be effective in reducing unnecessary clinic visits.[34-36] Even though decision support programs in the past 10 years have addressed a broad range of acute and chronic conditions, the primary reason for their use has been to keep people out of the doctor's office. Accordingly, decision support that teaches people to care for acute self-limiting conditions—those that will go away without a doctor's visit—has been among the most studied and popularized types of programs. A focus on this aspect of decision support derives from studies showing that educating consumers about managing self-limiting conditions will, on average, save money. However, decision support may also play a role in increasing appropriate utilization for certain types of health conditions.

In a randomized study of over 14,000 managed care members, Terry and Pheley found the use of decision support material reduced unnecessary utilization of services for certain conditions (such as colds and flu) but increased visits for such conditions as fever and sore throat.[34] This selective increase in utilization would have been a positive finding had it been the intended purpose of the intervention. Although fevers and sore throats can occasionally indicate more serious problems, the authors suggested that special care needs to be taken in how self-care messages are presented to achieve the desired outcome.

The potential for decision support to lead to more appropriate utilization, rather than to reduce overall utilization, was also demonstrated in a community-based study. After a community-wide intervention in which residents were provided a self-care book and advised about access to a nurse-phone service, Hibbard reported that use of a self-care manual was as likely to increase utilization as it was to reduce utilization.[37] The intervention community was more likely to access a self-care book, but there were no significant differences in the use of a phone service. The conscientious consumer, considering risk and benefits, may be making a perfectly reasonable choice to visit and rule out the possibility of having a more serious illness. Education, then, depending on the goals of the program developers, can be a means of increasing utilization.

Impact of Decision Support Programs on Health and Satisfaction

Numerous studies have demonstrated the effectiveness of decision support interventions on asthma, common respiratory symptoms (e.g., cough, congestion), diabetes, heart failure, and some musculoskeletal diseases.[38-42] It is less clear whether decision support education interventions are effective for other conditions, such as arthritis and COPD.[43,44]

This discrepancy, where decision support has been effective for some health conditions but not for others, may be partially explained by studies showing that outcomes from decision support programs can be modified by patient-level factors. Some factors that have been shown to influence decision support intervention effectiveness are literacy, numeracy, depressive symptoms, rural or urban living situations, and age.[40,45-47] And, as discussed in the PAM section earlier, a patient's level of personal activation is a variable that can both be tested and improved via decision support programs.[48]

The challenge of assessing reasons for more or less effectiveness in decision support offerings is also complicated by the interaction between the patient, all of his or her characteristics, and the characteristics of the intervention itself. A self-management intervention written in Spanish will obviously be less effective in Portland, Maine, than in El Paso, Texas. Less obviously, an online self-management intervention may be less effective for osteoporosis than for asthma, not because of the targeted disease but because of the average age of the people with the disease. However, at least one study demonstrated that older adults (age 60–75) benefited from self-management interventions for diabetes just as much as their younger counterparts.[49] So it is important for the worksite health practitioner to consider the target population, as well has the research evidence for that population, before making determinations about which decision support intervention to use.

Another key indicator of intervention success is patient satisfaction. Studies have shown that satisfaction with care is strongly associated with the quantity and quality of patient education that physicians provide, and that patients are most satisfied when they consider the physician a partner in exchanging information rather than an authority who controls the relationship.[50-55] Unfortunately, even though patient education is highly valued by patients, they seldom ask physicians to provide additional instructions.[56] The inability to ask for more education seems to persist regardless of a patient's health status.[57] Accordingly, the worksite health practitioner can play a vital role in enabling employees to better utilize their health care providers and their health system's resources. Many health systems have patient education departments and Web-based patient instruction available that is intended to augment and strengthen patient/physician interactions. Employers aiming to improve employee health care decision making should connect with their major health systems to ensure that patient education resources are well communicated and utilized.

Decision Support for Acute and Self-Limiting Conditions

Some of the most common reasons for visiting a health care provider include conditions that will resolve without medical intervention. These are called "self-limiting conditions" and can include coughs, knee pain, and stomach symptoms that could be targeted by decision support materials.[58] Decision support interventions can improve the appropriate utilization of health care by 7% to 17% depending on the health conditions being evaluated.[34-36] So it makes sense that many decision support interventions focus on common symptoms and potentially self-limiting conditions.

A study of uncomplicated acute bronchitis in adults showed that a comprehensive education program targeted at unnecessary antibiotic use resulted in significant improvements.[59] Certain self-care behaviors, such as use of cough suppressants and analgesics, were not affected by the comprehensive program, but there was a significant decline in antibiotic prescription use at the comprehensive intervention site. Because of the increasing resistance of many microorganisms to treatment, largely attributable to the overuse and misuse of antibiotics, employers need to be as concerned as health professionals about unnecessary antibiotic use.

An exploratory trial by Yardley and colleagues assessed the potential of an "Internet doctor" (i.e., Web-based decision support tool) to improve patients' ability to self-manage minor symptoms.[42] The Internet doctor tool was associated with higher satisfaction levels and better patient understanding of his or her illness. Although the trial was exploratory, in the sense that follow-up studies are necessary, the results suggest that tailored, Internet-based medical advice may be able to help patients understand and manage acute symptoms more effectively.

Still, it is difficult for many employees and other patients to determine when and when not to seek medical care, and physicians fear they may be neglecting a potentially serious health threat in cases where consumers are trained in self-management but illness symptoms persist, especially with conditions that the consumer/patient believes to be self-limiting. To examine this concern, Vickery and colleagues studied the utilization practices of participants who had been provided self-care education and who had fewer subsequent clinic visits.[60] By tracking postintervention claims data, this study demonstrated that the short-term utilization reduction effects of education did not result in delayed care seeking for truly problematic conditions.

Decision Support for Chronic Conditions

Some of these problematic conditions are truly chronic, and require the use of medical services. The evidence for and against decision support for the more-prevalent chronic conditions of asthma, arthritis, and diabetes is reviewed later in this chapter. Other, less common chronic conditions are sometimes considered within the purview of worksite health decision support programs, and some are briefly discussed below.

Perhaps the most frequently studied example of successful decision support for intensive medical self-management are programs that were developed to support those living with HIV/AIDS. A now-iconic example came from Gifford and colleagues, who were among the first to demonstrate the tremendous value of making the patient a partner in health care decision making.[61] In a randomized controlled study, 71 men with symptomatic HIV/AIDS were taught wide-ranging disease self-management and physician-patient communication skills. The main outcome measure comparing the intervention and control groups was symptom status. The treatment group was significantly more successful in controlling symptoms and showed increased self-efficacy for managing symptoms that occurred.

Similar positive effects of self-management education on self-efficacy and psychosocial function have been shown for patients with heart disease.[62] One study showed that in addition to increasing consumer competence, decision support through a pharmacy of a U.S. Army health system significantly increased commitment to seeking preventive services and improved opinions about the health care system.[63] This study offered an early example that employees who are actively informed consumers tend to have better outcomes and view the health system more positively.

And although heart disease is, unfortunately, a very common condition, an exemplary study of patients with Parkinson's disease shows how a minimal intervention on a less-common condition can positively affect life-changing decisions.[64] This randomized controlled trial used a through-the-mail approach to provide patient information, customized letters from physicians, and computer-generated disease assessments. The intervention group had significantly increased exercise, reduced side effects, and decreased Parkinson's symptoms. As important, from an employer's perspective, the education groups decreased their time off work and increased their quality-of-life scores.

When considering the business case for offering decision support to employees, the financial return on investment will continue to be challenging in workplaces because they are not conducive to randomization and research trials.[65] Still, this Parkinson's study, like those from the more-prevalent chronic conditions offered above, suggests that there is substantial validity for making the investment because the overall value, not only the financial returns, can readily be found in healthier, happier, and more productive employees.[66,67] Worksite health promotion professionals will continue to look to new technologies as a method for producing positive behavior changes at increasingly lower costs.

Pros and Cons of Emerging Decision Support Technology

Decision support programs have traditionally been delivered directly to the consumer as a way to offer standardized consumer information about self-management of common health problems.[68-70] However, many new media channels for decision support interventions have emerged in recent years. Several of these newer media channels have shown promise in improving individual health,[31,47,71-73] but each of them must be considered in the larger employee context if they are to be used to maximum effectiveness.

Table 19-2 outlines the types of educational modalities available as they relate to the goals and learning needs of the employee health management program. The column headings in the table, including group educational

Table 19-2: Decision support Program Framework. Preferred Strategy Index: 1= Primary Strategy, 2= Supportive Strategy, 3=Ineffectual.

	Individual Counseling and Clinical Visits	Group Programs	Newsletter	Self-Care Books, Videos, Pamphlets	Internet/ Apps/ Expert Systems	Support Groups/ Social media	Phone Counseling and Education Services
Acute-Self-Limiting Conditions	3	2	2	1	1	2	1
Acute-emergent conditions	1	3	2	2	1	2	1
Chronic Diseases	1	1	3	2	2	1	2
Lifestyle change/ unhealthy habits	2	1	3	2	3	1	2
Location variables: Worksite-based self-care	3	1	2	1	2	2	1
Community-based self-care	2	2	3	1	3	3	2
Health care-based self-care	1	3	2	1	2	2	1

campaigns, social media–abetted "flash mobs for health," worksite contests, and other media campaigns, are ingredients in an employee health program's ongoing plan of health care consumerism and decision support.

Each of these ingredients has pros and cons associated with its use and will vary in effectiveness for different health concerns. Much evidence to date is positive in that participants in intervention groups have shown improvements in their self-care behaviors, at least in the short term. However, the overall population effectiveness of any intervention is also largely a function of the number of people the intervention can touch. With each new technology there is usually a significant lag between the time that the technology and the intervention are introduced and the time that the general population, i.e., all employees, is ready to adopt them.

The newest technologies, therefore, will outpace the ability for researchers to study their effects on health. It may be several years before these technologies have been studied enough to draw conclusions as to how well they promote self-care behaviors among employees, patients, or community members. This is apparent from a review of the potential of text messaging for improving interventions for chronic illness management. In one study, de Jongh et al.[71] found positive but very limited evidence that this intervention modality can help people effectively manage their conditions. The authors concluded that more research was needed, as only four studies fit the study inclusion criteria.[71]

The Internet has been commonplace a bit longer than text messaging, and information is available concerning the effectiveness of education provided via this format. In a review of studies on the effectiveness of Web-based learning for health-related matters, Chumley-Jones et al. concluded that little evidence exists to suggest that Web-based learning is superior to more traditional methods (e.g., person-to-person or paper-based instruction)

but that it should be utilized as another tool in the educator's toolbox, and that all of those tools should be used in the proper context.[74] This study was published in 2002 and the effectiveness of Web-based instruction has likely improved. Still, other studies have produced similar findings and suggest that Internet instruction is not inherently better than traditional learning methods. Worksite-based research, for example, has shown that differences in outcomes between phone-based coaching and materials-based decision support relate to consumer readiness for change and other characteristics.[75,76] Lorig et al. conducted a randomized trial on 958 participants to assess an intervention that targeted multiple chronic conditions and used many of these education tools (i.e., Web-based, in person, and print).[73] Participants in the intervention group had less pain and less shortness of breath than their nonintervention counterparts. So it appears that a balanced approach, using multiple modes of education such as online, in person, and/or print, may yield the greatest population-level health improvement.

In order to improve health from any intervention, consumers must also have a ready access to the intervention technology, and because there will inevitably be a growing list of prerequisites for each new technology, many considerations must be made. For example, text message interventions require a mobile telephone that receives text messages (preferably for free). Interventions that use mobile apps require a smart phone and the ability to download the app, along with any data plan requirements and fees associated. Every one of these interventions requires that the person using the intervention has the skill to use the intervention appropriately, e.g., knows how to use the mobile app in question.

Despite these challenges, many new technologies are less expensive than traditional print-based interventions on a per-participant basis, and the reach of these new technologies is almost unimaginable. For example, many mobile apps are free[72] to download and have already been developed, and Internet-based interventions have practically unlimited scalability. Some text-message interventions are provided free from the vendor but the participant/employee may need to pay a fee for receiving texts.[77] The bottom line is that worksite health practitioners should embrace new media and carefully consider how to capitalize on these opportunities to enhance the total impact of their decision support offerings.

ADVICE FOR WORKSITE HEALTH PRACTITIONERS

Integration of Decision Support with Care Delivery Systems

The potential impact of decision support depends greatly on risk stratification. Advances in electronic health records, laboratory data sets, and health care claims processing systems have enhanced health assessment and risk stratification capabilities that can inform decision support interventions. This will likely increase employee engagement and participation, and result in improved health outcomes and reduced health care costs.

Still, the worksite is only one aspect of the potential use of these new technologies as they relate to decision support. Data collected at worksite clinics or physician offices or at broader, regional levels, such as accountable care organizations or patient-centered medical homes, can also be used to identify individuals for decision support interventions. Increasingly, end-user medical devices such as smart phones, iPads, personal computers, and digital televisions—all utilizing mobile apps—can be used to augment decision support and offer employees the ability to communicate with physicians, caregivers, and other program participants.[78]

The growing interest in supporting the health consumer's emerging role in shared decision making in health care is captured by a new body of research most often described as patient-centered outcomes research (PCOR). The Patient-Centered Outcomes Research Institute, the primary federal agency for funding this type of research, used a consensus development approach, including active involvement of consumers, to develop the following definition: "Patient-Centered Outcomes Research (PCOR) helps people and their caregivers communicate and make informed health care decisions, allowing their voices to be heard in assessing the value of health care options."[79]

PCOR researchers and patient advocates have framed a series of questions that capture the decision support needs of patients and health care consumers. In turn, researchers use these questions as a backdrop for assessing whether research interests are closely aligned with the needs and interests of patients. The PCOR questions also offer a useful framework for health promotion professionals attempting to organize what decision support resources should be available for employees:[79]

1. "Given my personal characteristics, conditions, and preferences, what should I expect will happen to me?"
2. "What are my options, and what are the potential benefits and harms of those options?"
3. "What can I do to improve the outcomes that are most important to me?"
4. "How can clinicians and the care delivery systems they work in help me make the best decisions about my health and health care?"

Several tools have emerged that help patients answer these questions and meet the goals of PCOR. An instructive example is the popular Web site Patients Like Me[80] (http://www.patientslikeme.com/). Designed as a place for "making healthcare better for everyone through sharing, support and research," this free Web site allows patients to connect with others with similar conditions to track the history and progress of their condition and to learn more, primarily from other patients, about living with and treating their condition.

Patient-centered care advocates believe sites such as this "democratize" decision making and make information more accessible and transparent. Critics of such sites are concerned about unfettered sharing of inaccurate, even dangerous, health and medical advice.

Finding Effective Decision Support for a Population

Considering the potential benefits and detriments to both new and old decision support, how is a worksite health practitioner to identify the right resources? First and foremost, it is necessary to make sure that decision support and other educational interventions are integrated into health care delivery. The ideas related to the need for data integration are not new, and the merits of integrating decision support into health care delivery have been long established.[81] Employers seeking to differentiate between health care providers and to increase the quality of care offered to employees need to be proactive in seeking health systems with an orientation toward understanding the decision support needs and preferences of employees. Providing consumers with current and relevant decision support, such as discussed earlier in this chapter, is an often overlooked variable in distinguishing quality, but can be one of the most valuable parts of employee interactions with the health system.

Whether in reference to medical decision support or chronic condition self-management programs, there are several actions that worksite health practitioners can take in deciding about decision support approaches:

- Assess employee learning styles, educational needs, health risks, health interests, health status, and individual attributes such as socioeconomic status, generational differences, and differences such as race, ethnicity, or sexual orientation.
- Develop and test educational content through an iterative process that measures and draws from the user experience. Determine how health decision support and self-management systems complement, or could be redundant with, other health care delivery strategies aimed at educating and supporting the consumer.
- Evaluate decision support information across multiple modalities such as phone-based, Internet-based, materials-based, group programs, or individual instruction in health improvement and disease management.
- Use continuous quality improvement methods to measure and improve consumer activation, reduce unnecessary utilization of health services, and increase appropriate use of health services.
- Deploy program evaluation at regular intervals, at least annually, for quality assurance and education system redesign.

Finally, there's the ever-present workplace issue of cost-benefit balance. When deciding about the kinds of programs that best support employees, there is always a tradeoff between an intervention program's time requirements, the intensity of the offering, and the reality of a busy workforce. A less intensive program that attracts and retains many participants will likely yield greater health benefits than a comprehensive program in which only a few people are willing to participate. For employers referring their employees for service or providing such services at the workplace, the intensity of the educational approach and the cost benefit of increasing levels of intensity should be carefully considered.

Likewise, many studies show the effectiveness of a comprehensive educational approach while neglecting to show the attrition rates. Simply put, the less time it takes to get through a program, the more likely employees will complete the program and, thus, improve their health or health behaviors. The next section provides a review of programs for chronic conditions most commonly of concern to a contemporary workforce, with a focus on those interventions that can realistically be sponsored by employers, given the fact that employers and employees have a limited amount of time to devote to such interventions.

CONDITION-SPECIFIC DECISION SUPPORT PROGRAMS

Asthma

Asthma is garnering considerable attention from employers and health systems because of its high prevalence and the very high costs associated when it is poorly managed. Increases in asthma morbidity and mortality have been blamed, in part, on the history of poor patient compliance with recommended treatment regimens. Educating patients and making them active partners in the health care team are critical to the successful management of asthma. The National Asthma Education Program identified four asthma management components that are necessary for an effective program: pharmacologic therapy, lung function measurement, patient education, and environmental modifications.[82] These components form the foundation of the *step care* approach, which is a widely used term in asthma education to describe how the level of treatment needs to correspond to the level of severity of the illness.[83] Patient education is considered critical in each of the steps because adherence to therapy is considered the best way to prevent unnecessary utilization of medical

services for employees with asthma. From the perspective of a workplace health promotion program, improved asthma management also relates to improvements in worker productivity and presenteeism.

Given the wide acceptance among health care providers and consumer advocates that asthma education is vital for improving outcomes, it is not surprising that asthma self-management has been a popular focus for start-up companies offering asthma apps. A challenge in patient education generally, and with the use of apps in particular, is the need to tailor educational content to the widely varying needs of individuals. For example, in a review of mobile apps specifically geared towards helping patients manage their asthma, Huckvale et al. concluded that "[no] apps…combined reliable, comprehensive information…with supportive tools for self-management."[72] The authors noted that there was no single app that stood out; each had its benefits and detriments. This is not surprising given that the steps approach in asthma needs to address the symptoms unique to every individual and should adjust educational content to the different learning needs of the individuals.

A number of studies clearly demonstrate a more traditional high-touch approach to asthma decision support works. One widely recognized controlled trial comparing individual and group education was designed to improve poor self-management practices among patients.[84] Patients with moderate to severe asthma were randomly assigned to one of three groups with six to eight members per group. Group one received classroom instruction, group support, behavior contracting, and at-home activities. The second group received individual instruction delivered in three to five customized counseling sessions drawing from the same content as the small group education. The third group was a control group, and received either an asthma chapter or no education. Significant improvements in use of a metered dose inhaler were achieved by groups one and two at a 5-month follow-up, and improvements in symptom measures for these two groups occurred by the 1-year follow-up. Physician evaluation of study participants indicated that asthma status was measurably improved for 52% of those in group education compared to 44% and 42% improvements in the individual counseling group and control group, respectively. The study showed the small-group education session to be somewhat more effective than the individual counseling and that both forms of education were significantly more effective than the control groups. Both treatment groups had fewer symptom days (19% treatment vs. 27% control), a reduction in acute visits per year, and lower overall hospitalization rates.

Although many studies indicate the benefits of self-care instruction in asthma management, the effect of education on changes in morbidity and mortality remains controversial. To address this concern, one study focused on the role of asthma self-management in the behavior of patients during acute asthma attacks.[85] This cross-sectional study used a comprehensive questionnaire to associate asthma knowledge with self-reported behavior during asthma attacks. Knowledge scores were positively correlated with medical care factor and the likelihood of the patient's having a written action plan for asthma management. The key variables that are associated with decision support (an action plan, use of peak flow meter, and supply of medication) were positively associated with behaviors appropriate to an asthma attack. The authors noted that, although their findings lent support to asthma education initiatives, they still found a troublesome gap between knowledge of asthma management and the rate at which patients were doing the right things during asthma attacks. This result reinforces the need to design chronic disease–based decision support programs that emphasize behavior changes as well improved knowledge.

Arthritis

Millions of American workers have arthritis that has been undiagnosed and/or undertreated. If employers are to invest additional resources into improving arthritis management, the programs must prove to be effective at reducing arthritis symptoms and demonstrate that they are cost-effective, as well. As with other chronic conditions, the test of cost-effectiveness relates to reduced medical costs and improved employee productivity associated with improved condition management.

James Fries, one of the more prolific authorities in health care decision support, designed a study to determine if mail-delivered arthritis self-management programs could positively affect patient outcomes and decrease medical costs.[86] In this randomized controlled trial, at 3-month intervals, retirees in the intervention group received health assessment questionnaires and individualized, computer-processed letters recommending self-care practices. After 6 months, intervention group participants had 16% fewer doctor visits than the control group. Numerous health measures improved, including pain, functional status, vitality, exercise, and self-efficacy scores. The authors noted that their findings were similar to those attained through traditional group education programs. Considering the many barriers to involving employees in traditional education programs, the success of a consumer direct approach holds great promise.

In a longer-term study, Lorig and colleagues studied the effects of self-management programs 4 years after the intervention.[87] Using self-administered instruments designed to measure health service utilization, health status, and psychological states, sustained improvement was shown in the intervention groups whereas no similar gains were found in the control group. Specifically, those who had been taught arthritis self-management skills had 40% fewer doctor visits and 20% reduction in self-reported pain. Patient savings were estimated to be $648 for rheumatoid arthritis patients and $189 for osteoarthritis patients.

Accruing such savings through effective education interventions has long been a goal in health reform proposals. Specifically, if medical service providers can demonstrate improved population level health outcomes at a lower cost, some payment reform systems reward these providers with increased reimbursement. Employers were among the first to experiment with such pay-for-performance approaches in negotiations with service providers, and progressive employers will likely continue to apply these behavioral economics principles to both providers and employees to advance condition-specific programs such as arthritis management.

Developing and implementing self-management programs for chronic arthritis has led to the examination of several other alternative delivery approaches. For example, most often patient education is provided one-on-one by the costliest of medical providers—the doctor. A less-costly option, providing education with an arthritis user specialist, has been tested for inner-city patients with arthritis of the knee.[88] The education participants received individualized 30- to 60-minute education sessions and brief phone contacts after 1 and 4 weeks. The intervention group had significantly lower scores for resting knee pain and disability, and, as in the Fries study described above,[86] the magnitude of effects compared favorably to more time-consuming and labor-intensive programs.

Studies such as these showing the effectiveness of arthritis self-management programs are critical to the continued funding and development of employee decision support strategies, but interventions are sometimes met with concerns about how many people such programs can benefit. To address this question, a study of the Arthritis Self-Help Course (ASHC), a 6-week program sponsored by the Arthritis Foundation, was conducted to assess the long-term cost benefits

from a societal perspective.[89] A decision model was developed to assess per-person program costs along with estimated physician costs and time and transportation costs. The ASHC was analyzed over a 4-year time span and computed to save $320 per patient related to increased productivity because of better-managed arthritis. Increased productivity was defined in this study as cost savings that would benefit society. Researchers further computed a health care cost savings of $267 per patient.

Perhaps it seems intuitively obvious that when employees are taught self-care they will use fewer health care resources. The results of these well-designed and -executed arthritis studies should convince even the shrewdest health services purchaser that decision support is an investment, not merely an added cost.

Diabetes

Diabetes is among the costliest of the chronic conditions. In terms of employee education time and treatment intensity, diabetes is among the most difficult to medically manage and the most complex to self-manage.[90] Perhaps that is why leaders in the field of diabetes management have essentially developed a "formula of who is to teach what, when, and how, and how to assess suitable outcomes."[91] Accordingly, clinicians caring for those living with diabetes are more likely to be certified diabetes educators, whereas health professionals conducting disease self-management programs for other conditions are often not certified experts.

This level of sophistication for diabetes education has resulted in more studies for diabetes self-management programs than for other conditions. Program planners and researchers developing diabetes interventions can take advantage of the American Diabetes Association's (ADA's) "National Standards for Diabetes Self-Management Education."[92] These standards consist of 10 directives designed to help ensure that organizations providing diabetes self-management education are doing so in an effective and consistent manner. Taken as a whole, the standards represent very clear directions that organizations should follow to help ensure their diabetes self-management education programs have the best chance of being effective. However, the task force assigned to review and approve the standards pointed out in their first guiding principle for the standards that "diabetes education is effective...at least in the short term." Although the task force was not explicit in their definition of "short term," in this context it likely means 1 to 6 months after the intervention occurs. Future research should focus on how to extend these short-term impacts so diabetes self-management becomes ingrained in the daily behavior of patients. This, of course, is not a concern unique to diabetes.[38,43]

Because of the ADA's national standards, diabetes education has formal requirements (and sanctions) intended to reduce practice variation and to increase effectiveness in patient education. Several of the national standards are designed to elicit patient self-care behavior. Standard 8, for example, requires that the "participant and instructor(s) will together develop a personalized follow-up plan for ongoing self-management support." In one experiment, trained health coaches using motivational interviewing methods coached patients living with diabetes and demonstrated that such a collaborative approach has positive effects on goal setting, goal acquisition, and health outcomes.[93] This type of collaborative approach is explicitly encouraged throughout the ADA guidelines because diabetes is a lifelong management challenge that requires ongoing goal setting and monitoring.

Given the intricacy of diabetes in self-care and the high health stakes involved in effective management, patient education needs to account for the patient's self-efficacy as much as the patient's knowledge and skills. To this end, a 6-week patient empowerment program was studied in a randomized controlled trial to assess if participation in the program would improve attitudes toward diabetes as well as lower blood glucose levels.[94] The study found that the intervention group had a statistically significant improvement based on self-efficacy and attitude subscales, along with significant reductions in glycated hemoglobin levels, compared to the control group. Such a finding lends support to the need for including psychosocial supports and education in the self-care portfolio for people with diabetes.

One of the most commonly accepted devices (both socially and behaviorally) for facilitating positive self-care is the diabetes self-management record. Records are checklists for diabetes self-management that include dates, times, and sometimes a point system for behaviors such as exercise, reading food labels, checking meat portion size, abstaining from beverages with added sugar, and many other diabetes control goals. One study used a record with 39 adults to self-monitor behaviors such as exercise, glucose control, fat consumption, sugar/carbohydrate consumption, and other eating practices.[95] Diabetes management scores were higher among the record-keeping group than the control group, and the behaviors were maintained as least 6 weeks postintervention.

The American Diabetics Association's national standards in diabetes education positively influenced the content of diabetes education programs offered throughout the country. Employers can play an instrumental role in advancing the quality of diabetes management by advocating reimbursement of quality service. For example, the inclusion of an annual eye examination for people with diabetes to detect diabetic retinopathy has been included in the Health Plan Employer Data and Information Set. This is a tool that was developed to make health plans more accountable to employer purchasers. Many managed-care companies will reimburse diabetes education only if it occurs at ADA-recognized medical practices or hospitals.

CONCLUSIONS

This chapter has focused on the role of health consumer decision support, given cost containment is a primary objective for many workplace health promotion programs. Well-designed decision support interventions include the identification and surveillance of high risk employees, focused education, and routine follow-up. Each of these elements is needed to reduce unnecessary medical visits and improve health outcomes. When programs are designed to affect long-term savings, decision support programs designed to increase utilization of preventative services should also be considered.

Most decision support tools, whether apps, monitoring devices, or books, teach about the need for both preventive exams and instructions about self-care of common problems. For most populations, preventive services such as mammograms, colon exams, flu shots, cholesterol tests, and other such exams are underutilized. It is as likely that encouraging use of these services will lead to more clinical visits as it is that discouraging doctor visits for a cold or flu will decrease clinical visits.

The workplace health promotion program planner developing an overall employee health management strategy should consider decision support in the context of goals for increasing utilization in some areas and decreasing utilization in other areas. Moreover, the best decision support programs will be fully integrated with the other workplace health promotion services the employer offers. When offered in the context of a supportive environment and when well integrated with employer sponsored health insurance, the decision support programs described in this chapter will be experienced as one of the most valuable benefits available to employees.

Glossary

Activation: The degree to which an individual understands his or her own role in maintaining and promoting personal health and the extent to which he/she possesses the necessary knowledge and a sense of self-efficacy for taking on this role.

Decision support (or medical decision support, or condition self-management): Any combination of learning experiences designed to facilitate the personal diagnosis, treatment, self-management, and cure of illness.

National Standards for Diabetes Self-Management Education: Ten directives developed by the American Diabetic Association to help ensure that organizations providing diabetes self-management education are doing so in an effective and consistent manner.

Patient Activation Measure (PAM): A 13-item validated questionnaire that measures a patient's level of activation using a 100-point scale.

Patient-centered outcomes research: Field of research that helps people and their caregivers communicate and make informed health care decisions, allowing their voices to be heard in assessing the value of health care options.

Step care: Asthma management strategy that simplifies self-management by educating employees about therapeutic alternatives and gradually increasing medication doses until management is achieved.

Learning Objectives

1. Define decision support, or medical condition self-management.
2. Name three conditions for which scientific evidence clearly supports the effectiveness for decision support interventions.
3. Explain the importance of the Patient Activation Measure as it relates to decision support.
4. Name three modes of decision support and the types of conditions for which

each one might be a primary strategy of a worksite health practitioner.

Discussion Questions

1. Decision support is defined as any combination of learning activities designed to facilitate the personal diagnosis, treatment, self-management, and cure of illness. Describe the scientific rationale for this definition.
2. Whereas the health promotion professional used to be an educator who gathered and disseminated needed information, the role has changed to that of a curator and coach. Why has the health promotion professional's role changed in the past decade?
3. How do you distinguish between health care decision support for chronic conditions versus acute emergencies versus self-limiting conditions? Why is it important for health care consumers to understand these differences?
4. Use of the Internet and other decision support tools increases convenience and reduces costs related to face to face visits with health professionals. Yet if 40% of self-diagnosis can be confirmed by doctors, what about the other 60% of self-diagnosis via the Web?
5. One approach to costs associated with health care utilization would be to use decision support to design a "zero-sum game" with a goal of having a decrease in unneeded visits canceling out the costs related to increases in appropriate visits. How would that work? What kind of clinical visits would you try to decrease and what kind would you want to see increase?
6. Having a high PAM score is significantly correlated with most preventive behaviors: healthy behaviors such as diet and exercise, health information–seeking behaviors, and disease-specific self-management behaviors. So it is good to have a high activation score, but is there any downside to having lower activation scores?
7. Would "high touch" or "high tech" be preferable for working with someone with a low activation score? Why?
8. Name three pros and three cons related to Internet-based decision support.

REFERENCES

1. Green LW, Kreuter MW. *Health Promotion Planning: An Educational and Ecological Approach.* 3rd ed. Mountain View, Calif: Mayfield; 1999.
2. Felt-Lisk S, Higgins T. *Exploring the Promise of Population Health Management Programs to Improve Health.* Princeton, NJ: Mathematica Policy Research; 2011.
3. Fox S, Duggan M. *Health Online 2013.* Washington, DC: Pew Research Center's Internet & American Life Project; 2013.
4. Hibbard JH, Stockard J, Mahoney ER, Tusler M. Development of the Patient Activation Measure (PAM): conceptualizing and measuring activation in patients and consumers. *Health Serv Res.* 2004;39(4, pt 1): 1005–1026.
5. Hibbard JH, Mahoney ER, Stockard J, Tusler M. Development and testing of a short form of the patient activation measure. *Health Serv Res.* 2005;40(6, pt 1):1918–1930.
6. Begum N, Donald M, Ozolins IZ, Dower J. Hospital admissions, emergency department utilisation and patient activation for self-management

among people with diabetes. *Diabetes Res Clin Pract*. 2011;93:260–267.

7. Rademakers J, Nijman J, van der Hoek L, et al. Measuring patient activation in the Netherlands: translation and validation of the American short form Patient Activation Measure (PAM13). *BMC Public Health*. 2012;12:577.

8. Fujita E, Kuno E, Kato D, et al. Development and validation of the Japanese version of the Patient Activation Measure 13 for Mental Health. *Seishin Igaku*. 2010;52:765–772.

9. Maindal H, Sokolowski I, Vedsted P. Translation, adaptation and validation of the American short form Patient Activation Measure (PAM13) in a Danish version. *BMC Public Health*. 2009;9:209.

10. Steinsbekk A. Patient Activation Measure [in Norwegian]. *Tidsskr Nor Laegeforen*. 2008;128:2316–2318.

11. Rogvi S, Tapager I, Almdal TP, et al. Patient factors and glycaemic control — associations and explanatory power. *Diabet Med*. 2012;29:e382–e389.

12. Ellins J, Coulter A. *How Engaged Are People in Their Health Care? Findings of a National Telephone Survey*. Oxford, UK: Picker Institute Europe; 2005.

13. *AADE Guidelines for the Practice of Diabetes Self-Management Education and Training (DSME/T)*. Chicago, Ill: American Association of Diabetes Educators; 2010.

14. Greene J, Hibbard JH. Why does patient activation matter? An examination of the relationships between patient activation and health-related outcomes. *J Gen Intern Med*. 2011;27:520–526.

15. Hibbard JH, Mahoney ER, Stock R, Tusler M. Do increases in patient activation result in improved self-management behaviors? *Health Serv Res*. 2007;42:1443–1463.

16. Fowles JB, Terry PE, Xi M, et al. Measuring self-management of patients' and employees' health: further

validation of the Patient Activation Measure (PAM) based on its relation to employee characteristics. *Patient Educ Couns*. 2009;77:116–122.

17. Mosen DM, Schmittdiel J, Hibbard JH, et al. Is patient activation associated with outcomes of care for adults with chronic conditions? *J Ambul Care Manage*. 2007;30:21–29.

18. Becker ER, Roblin DW. Translating primary care practice climate into patient activation: the role of patient trust in physician. *Med Care*. 2008;46:795–805.

19. Hibbard JH, Cunningham P. *How Engaged Are Consumers in Their Health and Health Care, and Why Does It Matter?* Washington, DC: Center for Studying Health System Change; 2008.

20. Skolasky RL, Mackenzie EJ, Wegener ST, Riley LH. Patient activation and adherence to physical therapy in persons undergoing spine surgery. *Spine*. 2008;33:E784–E791.

21. Hibbard JH. Using systematic measurement to target consumer activation strategies. *Med Care Res Rev*. 2009;66(1 suppl):9S–27S.

22. *Chronic Care: A Call to Action for Health Reform*. Washington, DC: American Association of Retired People Public Policy Institute; 2009.

23. Stepleman L, Rutter M-C, Hibbard JH, et al. Validation of the patient activation measure in a multiple sclerosis clinic sample and implications for care. *Disabil Rehabil*. 2010;32:1558–1567.

24. Green CA, Perrin NA, Polen MR, et al. Development of the Patient Activation Measure for mental health. *Adm Policy Ment Health*. 2009;37:327–333.

25. Munson GW, Dittus RS, Roumie CL. Activation and perceived expectancies: correlations with health outcomes among veterans with inflammatory bowel disease. *J Gen Intern Med*. 2009;24:809–815.

26. Remmers C, Hibbard JH, Mosen DM, et al. Is patient activation associated with future health outcomes and healthcare utilization among patients with diabetes? *J Ambul Care Manage.* 2009;32:320–327.

27. Marshall R, Beach M, Saha S, et al. Patient activation and improved outcomes in HIV-infected patients. *J Gen Intern Med.* 2013;28:668–674.

28. Shively MJ, Gardetto NJ, Kodiath MF, et al. Effect of patient activation on self-management in patients with heart failure. *J Cardiovasc Nurs.* 2013;28:20–34.

29. Druss BG, Zhao L, von Esenwein SA, et al. The Health and Recovery Peer (HARP) program: a peer-led intervention to improve medical self-management for persons with serious mental illness. *Schizophr Res.* 2010;118(1–3):264–270.

30. Frosch DL, Rincon D, Ochoa S, Mangione CM. Activating seniors to improve chronic disease care: results from a pilot intervention study. *J Am Geriatr Soc.* 2010;58:1496–1503.

31. Lorig K, Ritter PL, Laurent DD, et al. Online diabetes self-management program: a randomized study. *Diabetes Care.* 2010;33:1275–1281.

32. Terry PE, Fowles JB, Harvey L, Xi M. The ACTIVATE study: results from a group randomized controlled trial comparing a traditional worksite health promotion program with an activated consumer program. *Am J Health Promot.* 2011;26:e64–e73.

33. Hibbard JH, Greene J, Tusler M. Improving the outcomes of disease management by tailoring care to the patient's level of activation. *Am J Manag Care.* 2009;15:353–360.

34. Terry PE, Pheley A. The effect of self-care brochures on use of medical services. *J Occup Med.* 1993;35:422–426.

35. Vickery DM, Golaszewski TJ, Wright EC, Kalmer H. The effect of self-care interventions on the use of medical service within a Medicare population. *Med Care.* 1988;26:580–588.

36. Fries JF, Koop CE, Beadle CE, et al. Reducing health care costs by reducing the need and demand for medical services. The Health Project Consortium. *N Engl J Med.* 1993;329:321–325.

37. Hibbard JH. Breaking through boundaries. Paper presented at: 6th Annual Park Nicollet Health Conference; October 21, 1999; Minneapolis, Minn.

38. Gibson PG, Powell H, Coughlan J, et al. Self-management education and regular practitioner review for adults with asthma. *Cochrane Database Syst Rev.* 2003(1):CD001117.

39. Sieber W, Newsome A, Lillie D. Promoting self-management in diabetes: efficacy of a collaborative care approach. *Fam Syst Health.* 2012;30:322–329.

40. Tung HH, Lin CY, Chen KY, et al. Self-Management Intervention to Improve Self-Care and Quality of Life in Heart Failure Patients. *Congest Heart Fail.* 2013;19(4):E9–E16.

41. Wallace AS, Seligman HK, Davis TC, et al. Literacy-appropriate educational materials and brief counseling improve diabetes self-management. *Patient Educ Couns.* 2009;75:328–333.

42. Yardley L, Joseph J, Michie S, et al. Evaluation of a Web-based intervention providing tailored advice for self-management of minor respiratory symptoms: exploratory randomized controlled trial. *J Med Internet Res.* 2010;12:e66.

43. Bischoff EW, Akkermans R, Bourbeau J, et al. Comprehensive self management and routine monitoring in chronic obstructive pulmonary disease patients in general practice: randomised controlled trial. *BMJ.* 2012;345:e7642.

44. Nolte S, Elsworth GR, Newman S, Osborne RH. Measurement issues in

the evaluation of chronic disease self-management programs. *Qual Life Res.* 2013;22(7):1655–1664.

45. Cavanaugh K, Wallston KA, Gebretsadik T, et al. Addressing literacy and numeracy to improve diabetes care: two randomized controlled trials. *Diabetes Care.* 2009;32:2149–2155.

46. Egede LE, Osborn CY. Role of motivation in the relationship between depression, self-care, and glycemic control in adults with type 2 diabetes. *Diabetes Educ.* 2010;36:276–283.

47. Schillinger D, Hammer H, Wang F, et al. Seeing in 3-D: examining the reach of diabetes self-management support strategies in a public health care system. *Health Educ Behav.* 2008;35:664–682.

48. Harvey L, Fowles JB, Xi M, Terry PE. When activation changes, what else changes? The relationship between change in Patient Activation Measure (PAM) and employees' health status and health behaviors. *Patient Educ Couns.* 2012;88:338–343.

49. Beverly EA, Fitzgerald S, Sitnikov L, et al. Do older adults aged 60 to 75 years benefit from diabetes behavioral interventions? Diabetes Care. 2013;36(6):1501-1506.

50. Abramowitz S, Cote AA, Berry E. Analyzing patient satisfaction: a multianalytic approach. *Qual Rev Bull.* 1987;13:122–130.

51. Anderson LA, Zimmerman MA. Patient and physician perceptions of their relationship and patient satisfaction: a study of chronic disease management. *Patient Educ Couns.* 1993;20:27–36.

52. Robbins JA, Bertakis KD, Helms LJ, et al. The influence of physician practice behaviors on patient satisfaction. *Fam Med.* 1993;25:17–20.

53. Savage R, Armstrong D. Effect of a general practitioner's consulting style on patients' satisfaction: a controlled study. *Brit Med J.* 1990;301:968.

54. Schauffler HH, Rodriguez T, Milstein A. Health education and patient satisfaction. *J Fam Pract.* 1996;42:62–68.

55. Weingarten SR, Stone E, Green A, et al. A study of patient satisfaction and adherence to preventive care practice guidelines. *Am J Med.* 1995;99:590–596.

56. Kalet A, Roberts JC, Fletcher R. How do physicians talk with their patients about risks? *J Gen Intern Med.* 1994;9:402–404.

57. Zapka JG, Palmer RH, Hargraves JL, et al. Relationships of patient satisfaction with experience of system performance and health status. *J Ambul Care Manage.* 1995;18:73–83.

58. Centers for Disease Control and Prevention. *National Ambulatory Medical Care Survey: 2010 Summary Tables.* Hyattsville, MD: Ambulatory and Hospital Care Statistics Branch, National Center for Health Statistics; 2011.

59. Gonzales R, Steiner JF, Lum A, Barrett Jr PH. Decreasing antibiotic use in ambulatory practice: impact of a multidimensional intervention on the treatment of uncomplicated acute bronchitis in adults. *JAMA.* 1999;281:1512–1519.

60. Vickery DM, Golaszewski TJ, Wright EC, Kalmer H. A preliminary study on the timeliness of ambulatory care utilization following medical self-care interventions. *Am J Health Promot.* 1989;3:26–31.

61. Gifford AL, Laurent DD, Gonzales VM, et al. Pilot randomized trial of education to improve self-management skills of men with symptomatic HIV/AIDS. *J Acquir Immune Defic Syndr Hum Retrovirol.* 1998;18:136–144.

62. Clark NM, Janz NK, Becker MH, et al. Impact of self-management education on the functional health status of older adults with heart disease. *Gerontologist.* 1992;32:438–443.

63. Steinweg KK, Killingsworth RE, Nannini RJ, Spayde J. The impact on

a health care system of a program to facilitate self-care. *Mil Med.* 1998; 163:139–144.

64. Montgomery Jr EB, Lieberman A, Singh G, Fries JF. Patient education and health promotion can be effective in Parkinson's disease: a randomized controlled trial. *Am J Med.* 1994;97:429–435.

65. Grossmeier J, Terry PE, Anderson DR, Wright S. Financial impact of population health management programs: reevaluating the literature. *Popul Health Manag.* 2012;15:129–134.

66. Terry PE, Xi M. An examination of presenteeism measures: the association of three scoring methods with health, work life, and consumer activation. *Popul Health Manag.* 2010;13:297–307.

67. Terry PE, Parry T, Nyman JA, Kelley B. Return on investment case study: the visionary CEO and the dubious CFO. *Am J Health Promot.* 2012;27(1):TAHP7–TAHP11.

68. Lorig K, Kraines RG, Brown BW Jr, Richardson N. A workplace health education program that reduces outpatient visits. *Med Care.* 1985;23:1044–1054.

69. Lynch WD, Vickery DM. The potential impact of health promotion on health care utilization: an introduction to demand management. *Am J Health Promot.* 1993;8:87–92.

70. Terry PE. The effect of a materials-based intervention on knowledge of risk-based clinical prevention screening guidelines. *J Occup Med.* 1994;36:365–371.

71. de Jongh T, Gurol-Urganci I, Vodopivec-Jamsek V, et al. Mobile phone messaging for facilitating self-management of long-term illnesses. *Cochrane Database Syst Rev.* 2012;12:CD007459.

72. Huckvale K, Car M, Morrison C, Car J. Apps for asthma self-management: a systematic assessment of content and tools. *BMC Med.* 2012;10:144.

73. Lorig KR, Ritter PL, Laurent DD, Plant K. Internet-based chronic disease self-management: a randomized trial. *Med Care.* 2006;44:964–971.

74. Chumley-Jones HS, Dobbie A, Alford CL. Web-based learning: sound educational method or hype? A review of the evaluation literature. *Acad Med.* 2002;77(10 suppl):S86–S93.

75. Jeffery RW, McGuire MT, Brelje KL, et al. Recruitment to mail and telephone interventions for obesity in a managed care environment: the Weigh-To-Be project. *Am J Manag Care.* 2004; 10:378–382.

76. Terry PE, Seaverson EL, Staufacker MJ, Gingerich SB. A comparison of the effectiveness of a telephone coaching program and a mail-based program. *Health Educ Behav.* 2010;37:895–912.

77. National Healthy Mothers Healthy Babies Coalition. text4baby. Available at: www.text4baby.org. Accessed January 16, 2013.

78. *Implementation and Evaluation: A Population Health Guide for Primary Care Models.* Washington, DC: Care Continuum Alliance; 2012.

79. Patient-Centered Outcomes Research Institute. http://www.pcori.org/research-we-support/pcor/. Accessed May 16, 2013.

80. PatientsLikeMe. Available at: http://www.patientslikeme.com/. Accessed June 14, 2013.

81. Terry PE, Healey M. Comparing a physician-delivered and consumer-direct approach to self-care education. Paper presented at: Minnesota Health Services Research Conference; February 23, 1999; Minneapolis, Minn.

82. Bone RC. The bottom line in asthma management is patient education. *Am J Med.* 1993;94:561–563.

83. National Heart Lung and Blood Institute. *Asthma Care Quick Reference.* Available at:

http://www.nhlbi.nih.gov/guidelines/asthma/asthma_qrg.pdf. Accessed July 16, 2013.

84. Wilson SR, Scamagas P, German DF, et al. A controlled trial of two forms of self-management education for adults with asthma. *Am J Med.* 1993;94:564–576.

85. Kolbe J, Vamos M, Fergusson W, et al. Differential influences on asthma self-management knowledge and self-management behavior in acute severe asthma. *Chest.* 1996;110:1463–1468.

86. Fries JF, Carey C, McShane DJ. Patient education in arthritis: randomized controlled trial of a mail-delivered program. *J Rheumatol.* 1997;24:1378–1383.

87. Lorig KR, Mazonson PD, Holman HR. Evidence suggesting that health education for self-management in patients with chronic arthritis has sustained health benefits while reducing health care costs. *Arthritis Rheum.* 1993;36:439–446.

88. Mazzuca SA, Brandt KD, Katz BP, et al. Effects of self-care education on the health status of inner-city patients with osteoarthritis of the knee. *Arthritis Rheum.* 1997;40:1466–1474.

89. Kruger J, Helmick CG, Callahan LF, Haddix AC. Cost-effectiveness of the arthritis self-help course. *Arch Intern Med.* 1998;158:1245–1249.

90. Assal JP, Jacquemet S, Morel Y. The added value of therapy in diabetes: the education of patients for self-management of their disease. *Metabolism.* 1997;46(12, suppl 1):61–64.

91. Flack JR. Effect of diabetes education on self-care metabolic control and emotional well-being. *Diabetes Care.* 1990;13:1094.

92. Funnell MM, Brown TL, Childs BP, et al. National standards for diabetes self-management education. *Diabetes Care.* 2009;32(suppl 1):S87–S94.

93. Melko CN, Terry PE, Camp K, et al. Diabetes health coaching improves medication adherence: a pilot study. *Am J Lifestyle Med.* 2010;4:187–194.

94. Anderson RM, Funnell MM, Butler PM, et al. Patient empowerment. Results of a randomized controlled trial. *Diabetes Care.* 1995;18:943–949.

95. Bielamowicz MK, Miller WC, Elkins E, Ladewig HW. Monitoring behavioral changes in diabetes care with the diabetes self-management record. *Diabetes Educ.* 1995;21:426–431.

CHAPTER

20

Employee Assistance Programs: Serving at the Nexus of Employers and Employee Well-Being

Beverly Younger

INTRODUCTION

In applying the question, "what works best in workplace health promotion?" to Employee Assistance Programs (EAPs), we need to begin with an understanding of its evolution and purpose. A look back at EAP's roots reveals they are tightly intertwined with business goals and practices, yet are constantly evolving, becoming better positioned to support a healthy, motivated and functioning workforce. Today's EAPs evolved from the work of welfare secretaries to care for and appease employees during the industrial strife of the early 1900's, to Occupational Alcoholism Programs with a singular focus on alcoholism in the mid 20th century, to broad-brush EAPs that address a wider array of employees' problem from the 1970's on.[1] Throughout this progression, there has always been a dual focus in EAPs on employee well-being and employer goals, understanding that these two are interdependent.

Today's Employee Assistance Programs are defined as "professional services provided to employees with the interdependent goals of improving employees' and family members' overall well-being, as well as enhancing the work organization's functioning and productivity."[2] EAPs are the norm in businesses now, with 78% of Human Resource professionals reporting that their businesses currently have an Employee Assistance Program.[3]

Employee Assistance Programs, and the professionals that support them, represent a conscious, disciplined approach to intervening at the intersection of the employee/employer relationship. That process continues to diversify, becoming multifaceted through the prism of time and experience. The EAP field and its practitioners appear to be following a natural trajectory, incorporating an even broader, systemic understanding of the interdependence of individual, family, organizational, community, and environmental well-being.

Purpose

This chapter provides the reader with the established and emerging work-related practices that fall under the auspices of "Employee Assistance Programs." Drawing upon a growing body of research, we discuss EAPs' impacts on both individual and organizational well-being. In addition, O'Donnell's Awareness, Motivation, Skills and Opportunities (AMSO) Behavioral Change Model is applied to the core EAP technology, critiquing the benefits of EAPs within this framework.

Scope

This chapter provides a roadmap of classic and emerging components, and a discussion of their potential to create well-being in workplaces. We explore the range of problem types generally addressed by EAP practitioners, as well as the service delivery models. The information sources are primarily U.S. publications. Although EAPS now serve employees around the globe, research and knowledge of global needs and services are just starting to emerge. Lastly, the four components of the AMSO Behavioral Change Model are each applied to EAPs, determining the extent to which they promote awareness, enhance motivation, build skills and create opportunities.

Format

This chapter's content starts with a discussion of the types and prevalence of concerns that employees and families member may bring to an EAP counselor, focusing on the individual and immediate family member concerns. These problem areas are explored for their prevalence among workplaces and EAP caseloads, and the effects of the problem areas on health functioning at work. A review of relevant theory and an application of open systems theory provide a foundation for the critical analysis of EAPs' potential impact. The diversification of EAP models is reviewed to understand evolving service delivery. The core technology and practices of EAPs are reviewed, followed by a discussion of EAP effectiveness.

TYPES AND PREVALENCE OF EMPLOYEE PERSONAL CONCERNS ADDRESSED BY EAPS

Early EAPs had a narrower substance abuse focus, utilizing a constructive confrontation approach, motivating employees with alcohol problems and performance problems to seek treatment. The current broad brush EAP model is more holistic in scope, using a problem identification or assessment process to identify employee needs.

Drawing from a cross-program EAP database representing 600 organizations and 500,000 employees, the prevalence of primary EAP presenting problems include:

- Alcohol and Drugs - 4.4%
- Psychological/Emotional - 26.8%
- Family/Marital/Relationship - 27.4%
- Work-Related - 25.5%
- Other Problems: Including legal, financial, medical and miscellaneous - 15.9%[4]

Employee utilization rates, or the percentage of employees using an EAP, also vary considerably. In one study comparing utilization rates among external EAP providers, the rates ranged from 1.3% to 13.0% of all eligible employees, with the average utilization rate in 2010 of 6.0%.[5]

Alcohol and Other Drugs (AOD) Concerns

The common use of the term "alcohol and other drugs" (AOD) signifies a broad range of addictive substances that lead to substance abuse or dependence among employee populations. The Substance Abuse and Mental Health Services Administration (SAMHSA) defines substance abuse as problematic substance use behaviors that are evident "at work, home and school," and dependence as "health and emotional problems associated with substance use," made more serious by the "psychological and physiological effects of tolerance and withdrawal."[6]

Prevalence of Alcohol and other Drug Problems

Consider for a moment how common it may or may not be in today's workplace to see a co-worker coming into work late, smelling strongly of alcohol and unable to function in a meeting. The visibility of the effects and the prevalence of substance abuse and dependence in workplaces may vary greatly, dependent upon the organization, location or the specific population's values and norms.

The reported use rate of alcohol, cocaine and other addictive substances actually remains fairly steady over time among young adults. A fairly significant slice of U.S. workers, or 8.4% (about 1 in 9) of employed individuals, are dealing with a substance abuse or dependence problem.[6] The prevalence among working individuals is similar to that found in the U.S. population of people age 12 or older, equaling 8.0%.[6] For comparison sake, diabetes affects 8.3% of the U.S. adult population across all age groups.[7]

EAP studies indicate that about 3% to 4% of EAP primary presenting problems include an alcohol or drug problem.[4,8,9] EAP utilization for substance abuse appears relatively small, given that one of every nine employees is likely to be affected by substance abuse or dependence, and given that the field was built upon the goal of addressing alcoholism.

On a positive note, a recent Brief Intervention Group (Big) initiative is promoting the use of SBIRT or Screening, Brief Intervention and Referral to Treatment model. Pilot studies using SBIRT found that about 18 to 20% of EAP clients screened positive for a moderate to high risk of alcohol use, significantly increasing the identification of alcohol problems.[10]

A targeted alcohol and substance use screening allow EAPs to more effectively tap into the underground nature of substance abuse concerns in the workplace. Currently, about 1 in 4 EAP external providers use SBIRT routinely within their intake process.[5]

Alcohol and other Drugs Impact on Health

High alcohol use, binge drinking or alcohol use disorders are associated with the following:

- Risky behaviors: Including driving while impaired, unintentional and intentional injuries, sexually transmitted diseases, impulse control problems and poor social functioning.[11,12]
- Medical problems: Including respiratory and cardiovascular problems and diseases, liver disease, thyroid functioning, metabolic syndrome, cancer, neoplasms and neurological problems.[11,13,14]

Often hidden behind other primary care presenting problems, alcohol and drug problems are costly to society. Affected individuals not only have higher rates of mental and physical illnesses, but also are more likely to use acute care, and are less likely to perform self-care effectively.[15] Spending by federal and state governments for all alcohol, drug and tobacco abuse-related health costs in 2005 amounted to $216 billion dollars, accounting for 58% of all costs related to AOD abuse, with only 2% of this amount spent directly on treatment itself.[15]

Alcohol and other Drugs Impact on the Workplace

Employees under the influence of alcohol and/or drugs are clearly less able to work effectively and safely. On-the-job substance abuse effects across studies include:

- Decreased morale and increased conflicts among co-workers

- Decreased on-the-job safety, affected by an increase in workplace accidents
- Increased absenteeism, lateness or early departures
- Decreased productivity or increased work strain.[16-18]

The most recent report by the Substance Abuse and Mental Health Services Administration on the hard costs of alcohol and drug use to the workplace equaled $134 billion, including healthcare, absenteeism, productivity, job turnover and disability costs.[19] Substance abuse and dependence are significant health concerns, directly impacting employees and employers, needing ongoing workplace prevention and interventions.

Mental Health Concerns

Mental illness or behavioral health disorders are defined as "a health condition that is characterized by alterations in thinking, mood, or behavior (or some combination thereof), that is mediated by the brain and associated with distress and/or impaired functioning."[20] Mental illnesses vary in severity and persistence, having correspondingly varied impacts on personal function and well-being.[20]

Over time, its causes have shifted from an internal psychodynamic fixation or crisis, to the impact of poor parenting, to an acknowledgement of the role of environmental stressors. More recently, mental illness may be attributed to genetic and neurological causes or conditions. For individuals with a chronic or severe mental illness, a better understanding of the etiology of mental illness and the rise of more sophisticated and better funded models of care have had a positive impact. While stigmatized labels, e.g., "he's just crazy," continue to be used, public health campaigns and national legislation spread the understanding that mental illness is a health condition rather than an internal weakness.

The policy of deinstitutionalization and the rise of community mental health centers in the 50's and 60's, and community support systems in the early 80's, led to expectations that people with chronic mental illnesses could be supported in communities and in workplaces.[21-23] Regardless, the majority of their attempts at employment ended in job termination, even with the aid of supportive employment services.[23] Good intentions of the Americans with Disabilities Act to support disabled individuals in employment failed to influence managers' tendency to discriminate more toward those with a mental disability than those with a physical disability.[24] Employees affected by mental health problems continue to struggle to stay employed.

Not every employee accessing an EAP counselor will be dealing with a chronic mental illness. For example, among EAP clients diagnosed with depression, one study found that only 20% were rated as severely depressed.[25] Yet, over one-third of them met the criteria for some degree of clinical depression. Mental health problems are one of the most significant concerns that modern Employee Assistance Programs and their counselors face.

Prevalence of Mental Health Concerns

A little over one-fourth (26.2%) of the U.S. residents have been identified as coping with a mental illness at some point in their lifetime, and 22.3% of that group are considered to have a severe mental illness.[26] This is three times the prevalence rate of substance abuse in the U.S. population.

Among U.S. workers, 9.4% of women were affected by any type of depression, with women being two times more likely to suffer from any type of depression than men, and three times more likely to suffer from major depression.[27] National studies on the prevalence of depression and mental illness among employed individuals are scarce, which is concerning given the high incidence of mental illness in the U.S. population. In one study, 26.8% of clients presented a psychological/emotional problem as a primary EAP concern,[4] corresponding closely to the national prevalence rate.

Impact of Mental Health Concerns on Health

The relationship between mental and physical illness may be causally cyclical, such that either may beget or complicate the other; mental illness leading to poor eating, exercise and health habits, and long-term physical illness negatively affecting emotional well-being. Depression is associated with a sedentary lifestyle[28] and therefore many of the health concerns that such a lifestyle may trigger. Obesity is common among people with serious mental illnesses, along with other illnesses such as tuberculosis, hepatitis, and osteoporosis.[29] The risk for people with mental illnesses of developing a serious medical condition varies from 50% to 90%, occurring often at a younger age and leading to an early death.[30]

A recent trend in the increase of suicides in the United States is a serious, emerging public health concern, and one which EAPs must address as well. Among middle-aged adults, the suicide rate increased by approximately 30% from 1999 to 2010, making suicide a more frequent cause of death than motor vehicle accidents.[31]

Impact of Mental Health Concerns on the Workplace

Major depression costs employers an estimated $36.6 billion and bipolar disorder cost an estimated $14.1 billion in lost productivity per year.[32] On the job, people dealing with depression may exhibit clinically based symptoms, such as poor concentration, a limited attention span, and reduced motivation.[33] Such symptoms may easily be misperceived as disinterest or poor performance. In a study comparing the workplace effects of bipolar disorder to major depression, absenteeism and its associated costs were higher for employees diagnosed with bipolar disorder.

Yet, the higher prevalence of major depression among employees led to higher costs for the employer.[32] The same study determined that presenteeism (or the tendency to be present but limited in functioning) was an even greater problem than absenteeism in lost days across both diagnostic groups.

It is also necessary to consider the impact of social stigma, as discrimination also has a significant effect on both the mentally disabled employee and the workplace. In a review of almost 2 million allegations of workplace discrimination filed with the Equal Employment Opportunity Commission (EEOC) from 1992 to 2008, about 12% of those filed were filed by those with a known mental illness.[34] The costs of discrimination apply to all involved parties, including the impacted individual, their family, the community and the employer.

Family and Interpersonal Concerns

In the latter half of the 20th century, the significant shift toward dual working parents and single parents led to an increase in work/family stressors. Today, the families of employees are relevant to EAP professionals in two ways; first as potential clients and second as the focus of broader Work-Life services often added to the core EAP services. Family access to the EAP has existed since the emergence of the broad-brush programs, with one source estimating that about 10% of EAP clients are family members.[35] Child care, elder care and other work-life services are often integrated into modern EAPs.[35]

Family and Interpersonal Concerns Prevalence

The definition of "a family problem" is relative to the perceptions of people going through them and is, therefore, hard to quantify. Divorce may be a blessing for some and a tragedy for others. The arrival of a child may increase both stress and joy. Family concerns are a significant focus of Employee Assistance

Programs, with 27.4% of primary problems presented as "family/marital/relationship."[4] Clearly, family concerns are one of the core reasons that employees and their family members reach out to EAPs.

Two sources of family stress are relevant to EAPs - transitions in the family (marriage, divorce, child birth, relocation, illness and death, and dependent elders) and the constant push/pull between work and family needs. Newer family research emphasizes that the number of familial transitions has the greatest negative impact on children's behaviors.[36] There is significant evidence of changes occurring in U.S. families, including the significant shift in family structure as a result of increased divorces toward the end of the last century.

The divorce rate increased 136%, from 2.2 in 1960 to 5.2 in 1980, but had dropped 31% by 2006.[36] Yet, marriage rates have also decreased from 8.2 to 6.8 marriages per 1000 individuals in the same time period, a decrease of about 17%.[37] National trends evidenced by the U.S. Census during 2000 – 2012 indicate:[38]

- An increase in unmarried partner households of both opposite and same sex
- An increase in one-person households
- A decrease in family size, and a decrease in the number of households with children under age 18
- An increase in multigenerational households
- An increase in households with people over 65 years or older.

Young adults are delaying marriage and childbirth. Households may consist of adult children and/or older parents, changes possibly triggered by the 2007 recession. Families continue to be in a state of flux. Whether an employee is a single householder, an unmarried partner, a single parent, or a householder with both children and responsibilities for elderly

parents, the potential for work-life stressors are evident. The prevalence of work-life conflict is well documented.[39] About 50% of parents in one study concurred that they experienced work-family conflicts.[40]

How work-family conflict is defined varies, including positive or negative spill-over, work to non-work interference, work-family imbalance,[41] and even a bidirectional approach from work-to-family or family-to-work.[39]

Impact of Family and Interpersonal Concerns on Health

Divorce is one of the most significant family problems associated with negative health outcomes. In comparison to married individuals, people who are divorced have more health problems overall, including depression, substance abuse and a higher mortality level.[36] The mechanism appears to be similar to most stressors, impacting the biological processes that in turn affect overall health and well-being.[42]

Single parenting directly affects work-to-family and family-to-work conflicts. When the health of a single parent becomes a concern, the interdependent nature of work/family/health concerns becomes highly evident, with the parent likely to delay his or her own medical care in order to make the required work hours, to afford childcare and to have time to parent the child or children. In one study, single mothers "were twice as likely as mothers in couple families to describe their health as 'not good.'"[43]

Impact of Family and Interpersonal Concerns on the Workplace

Summarizing across studies, Bianchi and Milkie noted that there is a direct work performance impact with employees experiencing family-to-work conflict, with women's performance being more affected.[39] And in a similar meta-analysis, job satisfaction, organizational commitment, burnout, absenteeism, and work-related strain were associated with work-to-family or family-to-work conflicts.[44]

The impact of work on health is clear. What may be a more relevant concern is whether EAPs, employers and employees can effectively collaborate to address the daily tug of war between work and families in U.S. homes and workplaces.

Violence and Trauma

While violence is commonly described as a form of human physical aggression, the definition of the trauma is more complex, with the word often used to describe both causes and effects. Someone may experience a life-threatening trauma that creates internal psychological and physiological trauma reactions. "Traumatic events" are used herein to refer to the wide range of negative events occurring in employees' lives that are perceived as harmful and/or life threatening, and "trauma" is used to describe the resulting psychological or physical harm.

Over the years, EAPs became actively involved in responding to violence in the workplace, as well as providing services for employees and families dealing with any type of traumatic event, including natural disasters, war, riots, hurricanes, earthquakes or tsunamis, suicides, or sudden deaths of co-workers on the job. While these occurrences are not every day realities for most employees, the overall prevalence of exposure to traumatic events is believed to be high. Breslau reported that 80% of the U.S. population has experienced one or more events that involved a serious threat to self or others.[45] The prevalence of trauma cases served by EAPs is unknown.

Studies on violence in the workplace did not appear in research literature until the 1980's, but the term is now a part of our modern lexicon. The Bureau of Justice Statistics defines workplace violence as "nonfatal violence (rape/sexual assault, robbery, and aggravated and simple assault) against employed persons age 16 or older that occurred while they were at work on duty."[46] This provides a clear delineation of violence relevant to the workplace, but leaves out other types of violence impacting employees and their families, including sexual harassment, and family and community violence.

Prevalence of Violence

Workplace violence has been on the decline since 1993, with nonfatal workplace violence 75% lower in 2009 than in 1993, following a trend in violence reduction in the U.S. as a whole.[46] Workplace homicides decreased by 39% in the same time period.[46] Jobs with the highest risk for violence include law enforcement officers, security guards and bartenders, and workplace violence is more likely to be perpetrated by strangers.[46]

Bank robberies are a form of workplace violence that may trigger significant trauma reactions among employees. The FBI reports that 5,086 bank robberies occurred during 2011, with injuries sustained by 45 employees and 15 customers nationally, but included no mention of the larger number of employees witnessing and potentially traumatized during bank robberies.[47]

Domestic violence and sexual assault are two forms of violence impacting women particularly, both causing trauma and affecting one's ability to work. In the general population, the downward trend of intimate partner violence mirrors that of most types of violence, with a fairly consistent decline of 64% since 1993. The rate of domestic violence in the U.S. from 1993-2010 was 3.6 per 1000 people (over 12 years of age), with women accounting for four-fifths of the victims.[48]

Sexual assault is a significant problem in the U.S., with one of every six women reporting being raped during their lifetime, and approximately 300,000 women and 91,000 men raped on average per year.[49] Domestic violence and sexual assault may also occur on the job. Statistics on these crimes occurring in the workplace are limited. The majority of violent perpetrators in the workplace are strangers (53% for males, 41% for females) or work colleagues (26% for males, 32% for females), with a small number of perpetrators being an intimate partner or relative of the victim (1.4% for males, 2.4% for females).[46]

However, the second leading cause of female workplace homicides is death caused by a "personal relation," accounting for 33% of all workplace murders of female employees, with 78% of those perpetrated by intimate partners specifically.[50] The uniqueness of these risks, and the complex dynamics associated with them, require special expertise and knowledge for effective responses and prevention efforts.

In addition to the effects of violence, employees also face death on the job due to accidents, health conditions, or suicides. In 2011, 4,609 workers died on the job, equaling a total of 13 deaths per day in the U.S.[51] Whether co-workers witness the death itself, or suffer the loss without witnessing it, trauma and grief reactions are likely. A recent report indicates that workplace suicides are the highest annual total ever reported, equaling 270 cases in 2010.[51]

Sexual harassment is included in this category of violence and trauma due to the often aggressive aspect of harassers' behaviors, and the tendency for victims to experience psychological trauma symptoms as a result. Sexual harassment includes sexually-related aggressive actions happening in work-related circumstances, perceived by the victim as a psychological threat, with workplace ramifications.[52] McDonald found huge variances in the incidence of sexual harassment, with 40 to 75% of women and 13 to 31% of men in the U.S. reporting sexual harassment.[52] Perception of the threat and responses to it are not only based on victim's perceptions, but on society's definitions as well.

Impact of Violence and Trauma on Health

The most commonly recognized reaction to traumatic events is posttraumatic stress disorder or PTSD, an acronym that has become well known through the media stories of soldiers returning from combat zones with disabling symptoms. The types of symptoms associated with PTSD include the following:[53]

1. Re-experiencing the traumatic events: Including flashbacks, nightmares and fearful thoughts.
2. Avoidance symptoms: Avoiding stimuli associated with the trauma, numbness, blocking or forgetting the event and others
3. Hyperarousal symptoms: Being easily startled, feeling nervous or tense, reactive anger and sleep disturbance.

The overall prevalence of PTSD in the U.S. population is estimated by the American Psychological Association to be 8%.[54]

In the workplace, some of the highest rates of violence occur in the health care sector. In a study on violence against nurses, while 17% met the criteria for PTSD, 95% of the nurses who were victims of a violent event on the job experienced at least one PTSD symptom.[55] Employees victimized by bank robberies report similar symptoms, including emotional, behavioral, and physiological symptoms both during and after the events.[56]

The physiological effects reported by people experiencing PTSD point to a direct impact on well-being. Research on victims of intimate partner violence (IPV) reveal a relationship between IPV and poor physical health, substance use and depressive symptoms; this relationship is influenced by demographics such as ethnicity and income.[57]

Impact of Violence and Trauma on the Workplace

According to Wald, employees dealing with PTSD symptoms caused by any trauma have been found across studies to have difficulties working effectively, particularly in being able to come to work after the trauma, ranging from missing a day of work to months of missed work, to being completely unable to return to work.[58] The effect of violence and traumas in employees lives is a significant health concern overall.

And, intimate partner violence is associated with absenteeism, tardiness, decreased productivity, and increased job turnover.[59] Employees with performance problems triggered by abuse may receive disciplinary actions or even face termination, as domestic violence victims are often held responsible or blamed for the crimes committed against them. This bodes poorly for employees coping with violence at home who need the financial resources that stable employment provides if they choose to break free from the abuse. Hopefully, increased knowledge and understanding of the effects of PTSD on the job will lead to the same empathic provision of medical and psychological care that is given to people dealing with physical illness or disabilities.

Work Related Stressors and Work Stress

The work environment obviously has the capacity for contributing to stress and disease in individuals, yet businesses and government regulators have been historically slow to respond. In the U.S., the development of labor laws focused first on the conditions affecting women and children, broadening their focus over time to all workers. In the late 1800's, states began passing laws relevant to the protection of the safety and health of workers. Early health hazards addressed by legislation and government regulation were exposure to harmful chemicals and gases.[60]

Currently, OSHA does require employers to document injuries and illnesses that are triggered by workplace violence or terrorist attacks, and also to record work-related stressors when the employee provides documentation of a mental illness that is work-related.[61] This is a significant step toward acknowledging that work environments and the very nature of the work itself (rather than only chemicals used in the work process) may trigger serious health concerns.

Prevalence of Work Stressors and Work Stress

As noted above, 25.5% of EAP clients presented a work-related concern as their primary problem. This means that one-fourth of the various EAPs' clients perceived their main concern to be a problem directly related to their work.

Although there is a discussion of work-related stressors in some developed countries across the globe, there are apparently no prevalence statistics on work stress from U.S. government agencies. In Great Britain, the Health and Safety Executive defines work-related stress "as a harmful reaction that people have to undue pressures and demands placed on them at work."[62] The prevalence of work-related stress among all work-related illnesses was rather high, equaling 40% of the 428,000 reports of work-related illnesses in the 2011/12 year. Jobs identified as having high prevalence rates included human service positions, such as teachers, nurses and welfare and housing professionals. Primary triggers of work stress included the pressure of the work itself, limited management support, violence and bullying on the job.[62]

Impact of Work Stressors on Health

The word "stress" has the same dual nature as the word "trauma," at times referring to both the cause (stressor) and the effect (stress reaction). Here, we define work stressors as those inherent in the job itself. These may include "high job demands, low job control, low co-worker support, low supervisor support, low procedural justice, low relational justice and a high effort-reward imbalance."[63]

The effects of stressful job realities include "mental health, psychological distress, (trait) anxiety, depression, (prolonged) fatigue, job satisfaction and emotional exhaustion (burnout)."[64] Our emerging understanding is that employees who have less control over the job process and higher work outcome expectations or demands are more likely to suffer a negative stress reaction.

The assumed relationship between stress and health is still being confirmed, although it is widely assumed. In workplace research, one study indicated that there is a relationship between psychosocial work factors and cardiovascular disease.[65] Another provided evidence that women in high demand jobs with low control had a higher risk of type 2 diabetes.[66]

A recent compilation focused on the Allostatic Load framework, which supports the finding that workplace stressors have a primary impact on felt symptoms of anxiety as well as stress hormones, and a secondary impact on physiological mechanisms such as blood pressure, cholesterol and body mass index, with tertiary disease effects including "cardiovascular disease, depression and mortality."[67] After many years of research in this area, interdisciplinary sciences are beginning to close the loop on the causal processes between work stress and disease.

Impact of Work Stressors and Stress on the Workplace

In studying work stressors and stress reactions, a cyclic relationship between the environment and workers emerges, e.g., work-related stressors trigger psychological distress, which in turn negatively impacts employees' ability to work. Current evidence indicates that increased job demands and decreased job resources are associated with an increase in burnout. In addition, burnout tends to predict the duration of employees' absenteeism, a tendency for involuntary absenteeism, and longer absences. On the positive side, a sense of work engagement is associated with less frequent absences, and an increase in job resources is related to an increase in work engagement.[68]

Will employers find this compelling? EAPs are beginning to emphasize this complex cycle by focusing more fully on the interaction between the work environment, employee health and well-being, and work performance.

A Comprehensive Focus on the Whole Person in the Environment

Left out of the above discussion are several other problem types that may either be presented to EAP counselors or assessed by them. These may include major health problems, disability, financial and legal concerns, immigration issues, expatriate needs, educational concerns and even community or housing problems.

The breadth of the focus of EAPs begs for a redefinition toward holism and wellness. EAP professionals struggle with a fear of losing the important emphasis on serious, even life-threatening issues such as alcoholism, chemical dependency, mental illness, and trauma, with the ever present need for information, advice, and support that today's workplaces and communities tend to lack. A more integrated, holistic approach in EAP assessment would allow EAPs to assess predictably related problems, such as domestic violence and work-related problems, or sexual harassment and health concerns, and to offer interventions that prevent the causal overflow across a presented problem and potential, ensuing problems.

THEORETICAL SUPPORT FOR EAPS

Historically, the theory driving the primary EAP intervention of constructive confrontation was social control theory, which asserts that "social processes emerge that are overtly aimed at maintaining a predictable social order by discouraging individual deviance and encouraging individual conformity."[69] The term "constructive confrontation" was coined to describe the process of using progressive positive discipline to motivate employees to use treatment to get sober and keep their jobs.[69]

EAPs and the use of constructive confrontation in combination with treatment became, then, a form of therapeutic control.[70]

Yet, this theory is not one that could be logically applied to describe today's EAPs, which have stretched their focus to include family issues, personal stress, and almost any personal issue that demanded an EAP counselor's attention, including assisting employees who have no performance problems. Tracing the theoretical influences on modern EAPs and their integration with other workplace services, Gornick and Blair state that "the larger society themes that guided this convergence are systems, connectedness, interconnectedness (or interdependence) and the reciprocal interaction of the individual and the whole.[71]

Drawing upon Open Systems theory, as defined by Katz and Kahn , homeostasis is a system's tendency toward growth that ensures survival. The balancing of input and output, and sufficiently open -- but not too open -- boundaries, helps with the development of negative entropy, or the successful importation of energy that keeps the organization alive and functioning, avoiding decay and death. Equifinality symbolizes the many ways that systems can solve problems and move towards growth. Singular, standardized solutions tend to fail as they do not adapt to changing environmental conditions. Differentiation and specialization are the essence of creative solutions. And, integration and coordination help large, complex systems work.[72]

EAPs support homeostasis through the balancing of the organization's input or employees, by helping them adapt individually to their work-life situations, by addressing work-life conflicts and supporting the work-life balance. Emerging EAP delivery models demonstrate differentiation and specialization as well as the principle of equifinality within the business world, selecting tailored services that match organizational needs. In partnership with businesses, today's EAPs have the potential to prevent entropy of the system's human components and to develop negative entropy or growth through promoting organizational well-being along with employee well-being.

EAP MODELS, CORE TECHNOLOGY, AND EMPIRICAL SUPPORT FOR CURRENT SERVICE PROVISION

The Ongoing Evolution of EAP Models of Service Delivery

Internal, External and Blended or Hybrid Models

Early Occupational Alcoholism Programs and the emerging broad-brush Employee Assistance Programs were often internal programs housed within a larger business' personnel or medical department. In a 1988 study of internal and external EAPs, 82% of all EAPs were categorized as internal programs.[73]

In the 1980's, internal EAPs were more alcohol problem-focused, served more male and minority clients, and provided more consultation and training to unions. External EAPs (or those located outside the company, provided by external consultants or firms) were more consistently broad-brush in focus, worked with more self-referred employees with mental health and legal concerns, and had a higher percentage of female, higher ranked, and white clients.[73]

The rise of external EAPs was driven by corporate downsizing and outsourcing of internal services, and also by the appearance of health maintenance organizations (HMOs) and managed behavioral healthcare (MBH) plans.[2] Employees who selected an HMO or managed care plan, had access to psychiatric and substance abuse treatments using gate-keeping or pre-approval mechanisms.[1] Stringent reimbursement limits, based upon diagnosis and severity, limited "length of stays" and reduced benefit costs dramatically.[1,74]

MBH gate-keeping functions overlapped somewhat with EAP continuum of care planning.

Managed care providers began to offer low-cost external EAP services, thereby creating major competition for internal EAPs and emerging external EAPs. Some external EAP companies managed to stay in business by creatively extending their EAP model to include MBH gatekeeping.

Within larger corporations that maintained internal EAPS, the blended or hybrid EAP model began to appear. The blended or hybrid model has management and staff working inside the corporation, which oversee external EAP contracted services.[75] In a 2008 survey of over 500 EAP professionals, only 28.8% described their work setting as an internal program.[76] With over 70% of EAPs in external or blended models, the shift away from internal models is clear.

Recently, the corporate-like structure of large external EAP vendors has served to dramatically extend the market range of EAPs. In a study of external vendors, each of the 11 largest external vendors had contractual responsibility for more than one million lives, with those offering both managed care and EAP services averaging more than three million covered lives.[5]

The externalization of EAPs, and fierce competition led to what some now call the "commoditization" of EAP services. The cost of service is often based on a highly competitive per employee per year rates, leading external EAP service providers to set limits on sessions offered in order to prevent a financial loss.[77] Successful EAP firms also bundle EAP services with other sought-after services such as work-life and wellness programs, creating a menu of services designed for each purchaser. Many EAP professionals are concerned that the commoditization of EAP services are altering

its core technology and, ultimately, the quality of services delivered.[78]

European EAP Models

The delivery of EAP services in Europe has followed a similar pattern to that in the United States, although the adoption of EAPs in these countries emerged in the early 1990's. EAPs in Europe have also shifted from a primary focus on alcohol and drug abuse to professional counseling services for the wide range of problems discussed in this chapter. In addition, their professionals report the same concern about the devaluation and commoditization of EAP services.[79]

Union, Member or Peer Assistance Programs

Member assistance programs (MAPs) or peer assistance programs (PAPs) have existed side by side with EAPs throughout the years, with an emphasis on member well-being that is similar to that of EAPs. The primary goal of MAPs is to provide employees resources and services in order to support job retention, as well as their job rights. MAPs tend to draw upon volunteer and peer counselors, rather than licensed professionals, and often refer members to professionals in the community.[80]

MAPs face challenges in declining union membership, with a severe drop in the manufacturing sector, but a significant gain in the healthcare sector.[81] With little published data to draw upon related to MAP services, information about their utilization and effectiveness is limited.

An Overview of Core Technology: EAP Interventions

EAP services have matured as the service model has evolved, with greater definition and some degree of emerging standardization. A published description of eight EAP core technologies serves as a standard for EAP service delivery in the U.S., and as a model for growing international services.[82] The accreditation of programs through the Council on Accreditation[83] also supports standards that promote the quality of care. Standards and accreditation together promote quality and preserve the essence of what makes EAPs unique in workplace services. These technologies are reviewed below.

Problem Identification/Assessment

Problem identification or assessment is the first step in EAP core service delivery. The essential components of problem identification/assessment include gathering standard clinical information, including the level of risks to self or others, past history impact on both self and job performance, relevant history and current observed mental/emotional status.[84]

The use of screening tools is altering the clinical EAP process, using tools that are now more sophisticated and widely available. Amaral and Attridge make a strong case for the use of brief, standardized screening tools to increase the identification of the chronic problems that more frequently impact employees' performance and functioning.[85] For example, the use of S-BIRT, or the Screening, Brief Intervention and Referral to Treatment process used when screening for alcohol problems, significantly increases the identification of positive alcohol findings.[86]

Short-term Problem Resolution

While early EAPs saw their role more as problem identification and referral, EAP counselors today usually meet with clients and resolve some less complex concerns directly, using short-term counseling techniques. The use of multiple EAP sessions with a client also allows for more extensive assessments and motivation building with clients. Counseling services are now part of the core technology, with 73% of EAPs rating their use of counseling services as "high."[87]

Referral to External Resources and Coordination of Care

The process of referrals and coordination of care with external resources continues to be an essential part of the EAP core technology, depending on the client's needs for external treatment, community services or other resources. Coordination of care with external treatment providers, through referral, linkage, and case management, are also a hallmark of EAP service.

Monitoring and Follow-Up Services

While the practice of monitoring mandatory clients was created by internal EAPs, it is also included in the service delivery of external EAP referrals. In a study of over 300 external EAP clients drawn from 20 employer groups, mandatory referrals made up about 15% of the sample.[88]

Follow up, on the other hand, is routinely used for all EAP clients, providing a longer-term feedback loop that serves to confirm service outcomes and re-engage clients when additional services are needed.

Drug-Free Workplace and Substance Abuse Professional (SAP) Services

EAPs often incorporate substance abuse professional (SAP) services under their auspices. The U.S. Department of Transportation created this new role, assigning SAPs the responsibility to clinically assess, refer and monitor treatment for employees who test positive for drugs or alcohol within companies subject to DOT regulations. SAPs also monitor employees' return-to-work after treatment and any ongoing testing.

Crisis Intervention

EAPs have been offering comprehensive trauma responses for over 30 years for employees who witnessed or were affected by robberies, tornadoes, plane crashes, violence, and death or trauma on the job. Critical Incidence Responses are the prevention activities, and incident and aftermath responses for individual, group and management levels.[89] Another term frequently used for specific techniques that reduce trauma and increase functioning after disaster is psychological first aid.[90]

Training of and Consultation with Organizational Leadership

As internal EAPs became more established within corporate structures, their role widened to include that of consultants and educators about workplace human behaviors and relationships. In this way, the internal EAP began to serve as a management tool.[91] The training and consultation role is still considered a core technology, and 87% of surveyed EAP professionals indicated that they offer management consultation and other organizational level support.[87]

Program Promotion and Education

Program promotion and education keep the EAP visible. Communications with employees are highlighted through web pages and newsletters. This core technology incorporates prevention and education mechanisms, serving to increase client utilization, intervene early, educate employees about policies and services, and support the continuation of the program as a whole.[92]

EAP Outcomes and Effectiveness

Employee Assistance Programs, emerging initially from their paraprofessional, workplace-based model to more sophisticated external clinically-based models, have gradually standardized both services and measurement of the quality and effectiveness of their services. EAP evaluations focus on the core services of short-term problem resolution, including referrals and coordination of care, yet some evaluate work unit or organizational level outcomes, such as critical incident response services. As discussed in Emerging

Issues and Concerns section at the end of the chapter, EAP research is suffering from limited empirical rigor in its evaluation design and methods.

Basic EAP Service Evaluation: Clinical Outcomes

Many internal and external Employee Assistance Programs are using pre/test (at intake) and post/test (during follow-up) measures to determine the changes in their clients' clinical outcomes and work-related outcomes over time. There has been fairly consistent evidence over the years of positive clinical outcomes in pre/post comparisons, generally with a census sample of all program participants, but with limited use of control/comparison groups.

There are several recent promising clinical outcomes results. Harlow's pre/post-test study of a random sample of 882 EAP clients from 100 different employers included a non-randomized comparison group of employees who had not received EAP services in the past.[93] The EAP clients scored statistically significantly higher ($p \leq .05$) on all 12 subscales of a Treatment Outcome Profile after using services than before services, on self-reported measures of quality of life, level of functioning, symptomology and satisfaction. The EAP client group scored significantly lower than the comparison groups upon intake. The post-test scores of both EAP and non-EAP employees were statistically the same on post-test scores, indicating EAP clients decreased symptoms and increased functioning to equal that of the average employee in the comparison group.

Greenwood, Deweese and Inscoe's pre/post-test study of 321 clients from 20 employer groups used a composite survey measuring self-reports of psychosis and depression/anxiety symptoms, daily living/role functioning, relationship functioning, and impulsive/addictive behaviors, on intake and one month after intake.[88] The pre/post-test differences indicated statistically significant positive outcomes across all subscales (p ≤ .01). No comparison or control group was utilized.

Selvik, Stephenson, Plaza and Sugden's study of almost 60,000 EAP clients from over 400 federal agencies used multiple measures, including general health status, work and social relationships and global assessed functioning.[94] The sample consisted of all clients using the Federal Occupational Health EAP services who completed both pre- and post-test assessment forms. No comparison or control group was utilized. The pre/post-test results increased significantly after services across all measures (p ≤ .01), with 74% improvement in social relationship functioning, 31% improvement in general health status, and 10% improvement in global assessed functioning.

Work-Related Individual Outcomes

EAPs are expanding their evaluation processes to capture evidence that services have a direct impact on the business outcomes. Work-related measures are now common, with many using self-reported estimates of missed days, ability to function at work, or in some cases actual employer data on absences and productivity. In Sharar, Pompe, and Lenox's (2012) study, the Workplace Outcome Suite (WOS), consisting of five item scales designed uniquely for EAPS, was used in a pre/post comparison of 197 participants (no comparison group was utilized). Work measures included self-reported absenteeism, presenteeism, work engagement, life satisfaction and workplace distress.[95] All measures except work engagement showed a statistically significant improvement (p ≤ .05).

Some studies have focused on employer-related costs, or the ability of EAPs to offset regular employer costs, such as healthcare plan utilization dollars or productivity costs. In a two-year study of 2,205 employees, comparing mental health and substance abuse healthcare benefits of all EAP users to a comparable sample of non-EAP users of, Dainas and Marks found that the total healthcare costs were approximately $2,200 per year lower for each employee using the EAP than for non-EAP-using employees.[96]

Productivity measures, and an absenteeism/tardiness measure in Selvik, Stephenson, & Sugden's study showed statistically significant improvement (p ≤ .01) of client-reported absenteeism/tardiness after using EAP services.[94] The pre/post study of 60,000 EAP clients demonstrated a 62% decrease in time away from work after using EAP services, equaling 87,140 whole or partial days gained.

Purchasers of external EAP services are increasingly expecting a promise of savings, and tend to ask for industry reports rather than formal research studies. Although often carried out by external evaluators, these are generated for and utilized by businesses in the selection of EAP services. For example, Davidson Trahaire Corpsych's Workplace Health and Wellness Report included a sample of 4,700 people using EAP services across customer organizations and demonstrated an average savings per person of $10,187 in work productivity costs (p ≤ .01) in their pre/post evaluation.[97] While not meeting the criteria for experimental design, these reports are driving the field in delivering data frequently required by brokers and corporate decision-makers.

Group or Organizational Level Intervention Outcomes

In addition to evaluations aimed at the individual EAP services, others have taken on the task of documenting effects of group or organizational level effects, such as the evaluation of psychological first aid or critical incident responses. In a random representative sample, longitudinal posttest-only study of 1,681 employees affected by the World Trade Center 9/11 disaster, employees receiving brief worksite crisis intervention services had reduced risks for substance abuse, psychological and emotional symptoms, PTSD symptoms and other functioning measures in comparison to those not receiving these services (p ≤ .05).[98]

In addition to lack of rigor in research, the impact of services, such as management training or organizational level change processes, are limited in the EAP evaluation literature. The question "Do EAP core technologies alter the organization's functioning and effectiveness overall?" remains largely unanswered.

EAPS AND THE AMSO FRAMEWORK

The historical focus of EAPs follows the same path that progressive businesses have followed, from exercising social control to promoting a healthier, engaged and potentially happier workforce. While employees may not have evolved to the point of whistling joyfully while they work, there is a new social contract developing in workplaces, and the EAP is one of the important tools in promoting well-being at work. The following is an analysis of the modern EAP as viewed through the lens of the AMSO Framework, around which this text is organized, discussing the degree to which EAPs in the new millennium serve as health promotion agents.

EAPs and Awareness

Awareness is defined as educating people of the "risks of unhealthy behaviors...as well as the benefits of positive behaviors" (Chapter 3). Employee Assistance Programs have always had an educational component of their own, and some coordinate their outreach and awareness efforts with their corporate wellness programs or initiatives partners. Many EAP professionals may consider education and training efforts as a form of outreach or marketing to increase EAP utilization.

In today's reality, lunchtime EAP seminars on substance abuse or depression have been replaced with webinars, easily documented by a Google search on the topic of "EAP webinars." A recent search resulted in 148,000 entries, with EAP webinars on topics such as stress management, relationship issues, financial concerns, and even a unique webinar for those recently affected by the Boston marathon bombings.

Awareness raising activities are also excellent opportunities to reach the more vulnerable employee populations, those suffering from serious mental health problems, substance abuse, eating disorders, domestic violence or even those coping with workplace harassment or discrimination. From an open systems theory perspective, it is part of the process of communication across internal or external systems boundaries to encourage the flow of energy and resources, both within the system and externally in employees' families and communities.

EAPs and Motivation

Constructive confrontation was a core EAP intervention, during a time when social control mechanisms were natural but rather conflictual fixtures in workplaces. When a union worker tested positive for alcohol or drugs, contentious negotiations between management and the union would flare up over the decision to refer the worker to the EAP or to fire them outright. Younger (personal correspondence, 2013) recalls working in the late 1980's with a human resource manager whose desk had a prominent sign that conveyed the message, "What part of "No" don't you understand?" His philosophy echoed the hard-line sentiment of management that the simplest way to deal with a problem employee was to terminate them. Working as EAP counselors in this setting, we used the employee's fear of being fired and constructive confrontation techniques to break through denial, to motivate employees to utilize treatment and 12 Step programs, ultimately saving their jobs and, in some cases, their lives.

One of the common counselor jokes asks the question, "How many counselors does it take to change a light bulb," which is answered by the refrain, "Only one, but it has to want to change." The discussion of the AMSO model in Chapter 3 acknowledges that intrinsic and extrinsic incentives are now used in health promotion to encourage employees' motivation to change, adding to the individual's desire to change through increasing the positive rewards associated with the change.

This mirrors the larger historical shift that Hansen (2004) described as "the transition of EAPs from a form of governance characterized by a pastoral mode of control and care to a neoliberal form of discipline, marked by an increasing reliance on the motivation of workers towards self-management, self-monitoring and self-correction."[99] As corporate culture and counseling processes changed, EAPs shifted from the negative reinforcement model of constructive confrontation to being a supportive resource for those ready to change, relying more on clients' intrinsic motivators.

While intrinsic motivation is an important EAP focus, financial incentives or employee perks may not fit as well with EAP services as they do with wellness programs. The principle of self-determination is now more integrated into the counseling approach of licensed EAP clinicians, which conflicts to some degree with the idea of using incentives to encourage EAP utilization.

As acknowledged in Chapter 3, the health promotion knowledge base is still lacking "an overall understanding of how to motivate people." This is also true of the EAP field as well, as we need new theories and evidence-based interventions that empower clients to achieve their goals for change.

EAPs and Skill Enhancement Strategies

Skill enhancement strategies are about integrating new behaviors successfully into daily life. Once people embrace the drive to change, they begin the process of learning a new dance of behaviors, gradually increasing a sense of self-efficacy in altering their behaviors day by day. It is important to consider that skill enhancement strategies are not always applicable to the broad range of problems that people now present to EAP counselors. A client dealing with a bitter divorcing spouse, coping with the daily stress of a dominant co-worker, or pressed to take care of an aging parent's needs may have limited control over the stressors in their lives. Health behavior models look to changes in oneself but rarely address how to cope with the realities that one has limited ability to change.

The Transtheoretical Model of health behavior change, for example, assumes that people can be supported in their movement through stages of change such as precontemplation, contemplation, preparation, action, maintenance and termination.[100] Yet, this model and others assume the solution to the client's problem is something alterable through their own behavior, which is not the case with situations that involve external conditions to which individuals need to adapt, confront, heal from, or accept. The complexity of human environments and behaviors requires additional, less linear strategies at times. EAP clinicians need alternate theories and short-term intervention models that support their clients in coping with the psychosocial complexities of life.

A subset of EAP clients' presenting problems, including alcoholism and drug addiction, does require significant behavioral changes on the part of the client. These clients will be referred to treatment providers that rely on behavioral and other types of interventions. The EAP role becomes a supportive one, creating a holding space for change through treatment referrals, direct linkage, and follow-up. EAPs counselors who incorporate knowledge of skill enhancement strategies will be more effective in supporting clients through the change process.

EAPS and Opportunity Enhancement Strategies

Opportunities to practice healthy lifestyles can be created by the individual and can exist naturally in supportive environments, some of which can even be abundant in presenting opportunities for change. Employer benefits and employee services are two enhancement strategies in work environments that can enrich the opportunities for health and wellness.

EAPs that work on integrating their programs with work-life, disability, wellness or other supportive employer functions may supercharge their ability to serve as opportunity enhancers. Theoretically, integration and coordination improve system performance. There is a movement toward integration by EAPs, with the goal of coordinating their delivery with a variety of employee services. Gornick & Blair note that a common purpose is often found across EAPs, work-life and health and productivity management programs.[71] Coordinating and integrating programs or services should lead to more flexible, creative services with additional programmatic energy and resources to offer employees, due to less energy being wasted on competition between them, and less resources diverted to multiple programmatic structures.

Combined EAP and wellness programs have been found to be effective, and are more likely to act as opportunity enhancers as a result. The Fairview Health Services company integrated a health management team, EAP team, occupational health team, employee benefits team, and vendor partners to deliver an array of services utilizing integrated Health Risk Assessment, promotion, communication, classes, and a common phone center.[101] Employees responded to this seamless service, increasing EAP utilization from 4.3% to 5.9%, with 82% of employee participating in some aspect of the Fairview Alive integrated array of services. Strong cost benefits included savings of $340 per employee on medical costs, $188 per employee on workers' compensation costs, and $230 per employees on absenteeism costs.[101]

Per Emery's version of open systems theory, organizations that are purposefully seeking ideal solutions and acknowledging interdependence will consciously design systems that are harmonious.[102] A principle-based approach is needed to overcome the competition and strong boundaries currently preventing integration of employee services, which ultimately improve the product that employees receive.

EMERGING ISSUES AND CONCERNS

The lack of empirically rigorous research is a core challenge for EAPs in documenting their ability to build organizational well-being and increase productivity in the workplace. If one examines the historical emergence of EAPs within U.S. industries, the reason for this deficit becomes clearer. The first wave of Occupational Alcoholism Programs and the second wave of internal Employee Assistance Programs were business-based, slowly maturing from paraprofessional to clinical staff, and internally managed. Early EAPs routinely submitted basic internal business reports, focused on process numbers (utilization) and service quality (generally client satisfaction), which were often acceptable to employers well into the mid-1990's.

As EAPs shifted over time toward more competitive, clinically-based external models, and as businesses grew in their demand for return-on-investment statistics, EAPs began to develop effectiveness and business value measures. Design limitations caused by external EAP service models and lack of access to organizational data continue to limit evaluation rigor today. As a result, the EAP field still lacks the elusive return-on-investment findings that business brokers shopping among services frequently now request.

Evaluation of services is complicated even further by ongoing changes in what EAPs deliver. What is needed most is an exploration and redefinition of EAP services as currently offered, within expanded and integrated service models and within new international markets, and a fresh look at where EAP fits within the scope of health and wellness workplace services.

Regardless of evaluation limitations and ongoing evolution, EAPs are well established in the business world. EAP implementation is also on the rise globally, partially due to a growing concern for employee well-being. Among employers in Australia, Canada, Europe, Latin America and Africa/Middle East countries, the top ten Global Wellbeing Priorities include stress, workplace safety, work/life issues and depression/anxiety, with stress being the number one concern.[103] EAPs are perceived as a solution in emerging markets, with 37% of global human resource professionals planning to expand EAP and Work-Life services internationally.[104]

As EAPs move into new locales, challenges abound regarding the need to design culturally relevant services. In developing countries, EAPs may require re-naming to fit the lingual and cultural realities. Or, they may be provided by non-licensed individuals in regions where licensed clinicians and behavioral health treatment systems are practically non-existent. Challenges to the core technology are predictable in developing countries.

In Bangalore, India, for example, an innovative consulting business now offers a variety of programs to employers, including a service called "Women Development Programs," responding to the emerging personal stressors caused by large numbers of women entering the workplace (Interweave, Ltd., personal correspondence, 2013). In patriarchic environments, the hiring of female workers by transnational companies comes with personal tensions and conflicts for women coping with a work/life balance uniquely different from that seen in the U.S. and Europe.

The reworking of the EAP model internationally may cause new challenges for U.S. EAP professionals, who are undergoing a type of identity crisis, struggling to maintain, assert and demonstrate the value of their core technology, while the winds of change blow strongly around them. Some in the EAP field are calling for holding to standards and the retention of core technology.[105]

Redefinitions and expansion of EAP services, if reframed, may ultimately be beneficial for employees and employers. Larger external EAP providers are now offering employers the ability to tailor an integrated set of EAP, Work/Life, wellness, disability management and others contractual employee services to fit the needs of the customer organization. Delivery of integrated services may include a centralized call center with greater ease of movement across needs and services. Digital delivery of services is expanding rapidly, addressing the needs of younger employee populations through video and web-based individual and group counseling (Mahieu & Taranowski, 2013).[5]

In addition, many EAP professionals are calling for an expanded EAP focus to more effectively address the multi-systemic and interdependent nature of personal stressors, work stress and individual and organizational well-being.[106,107] Efforts to integrate EAP and health promotion strategies are still evolving.

Utilizing the AMSO model, EAPs may expand employee awareness of resources through EAP outreach mechanisms, and draw more heavily upon new evidence-based clinical models like motivational interviewing and health behavior change theories that enhance client skills. And, to become an effective, integrated member of the health promotion team, EAPs offer employers a holistic array of integrated services to enhance opportunities for wellness.

Lastly, a challenge for the future will be the ability of businesses, EAPs and health promotion services to effectively expand the focus beyond the individual employee's problems or well-being to the larger organizational environment. Awareness of person-environment interdependency and causality, tools for motivating employers to create healthy work environments, enhancing organizational and management behaviors that promote individual well-being, and enhancing opportunities for organizational growth will lead to a new dimension of wellness.

SUMMARY

EAPS have been serving within businesses for over 50 years, focused on improving the behavioral health and well-being of employees and their families. With a historical emphasis on the work environment, there is an increasing tendency to expand and market the EAP model as an integrated service package with a variety of other contracted services, including work-life, wellness, disability management and others, partnering with employers to create versatile programs formed to fit the unique needs of their organization and employees.

The rigor of EAP evaluation research has been slow to develop, and will require EAP professionals and researchers to more effectively measure the value of EAPs, while simultaneously continuing to evolve the service delivery model. The high incidence of depression and mental health concerns, the need for ongoing transformation of services toward integration with other health promotion services and benefits, and the unique demands of emerging international markets are the challenges faced by this important work-enhancing service.

Glossary

Blended EAPs: Employee Assistance Programs that have some internal component, such as an EAP manager who is an employee of the organization offering the EAP to its employees, and some external components, such as externally contracted EAP affiliates working with the internal program. This is also called a "hybrid" EAP.'

Broadbrush Employee Assistance Programs: The current EAP model with a holistic approach that provides services to employees for a wide variety of personal concerns or problems.

Critical Incident Response: A planned response involving the selection of one to several interventions to address the needs of individuals, groups, organizations or communities affected by a life-threatening stressor or event, with the goal of preventing or reducing traumatic effects and restoring functioning.

Constructive Confrontation: An EAP process of using the evident consequences of employees' substance abuse, along with progressive positive discipline, to motivate employees to use treatment to get sober and keep their jobs.

EAP Core Technology: The set of Employee Assistance services processes historically defined by the members of the EAP professional field that differentiates EAP services from other types of behavioral healthcare or workplace services.

Employee Assistance Program: Professional services provided to employees with the interdependent goals of improving employees' and family members' overall well-being, as well as enhancing the work organization's functioning and productivity.

External EAPs: Employee Assistance Programs that are provided by an outside firm or consultants that are not owned by or directly affiliated with the employer organization receiving the services.

Gatekeeping: Pre-approval mechanisms that employees had to go through prior to receiving access to behavioral healthcare services.

Hybrid EAPs: Employee Assistance Programs that have some internal component, such as an EAP manager who is an employee of the organization offering the EAP to its employees, and some external components, such as externally contracted EAP affiliates working with the internal program. This is also called a "blended" EAP.'

Internal EAPs: Employee Assistance Programs that are housed inside a business organization, managed and/or staffed by internal counselors who are employees of the organization.

Mandatory Referrals: This is the process of supervisors or managers referring employees with observed performance problems to the EAP, as a part of the progressive discipline process, with the expectations that the employee's personal concerns may be contributing to the performance problem. These are also called supervisory or management referrals.

Occupational Alcoholism Programs (OAPs): Early workplace programs developed from peer outreach by recovering employees to employees affected by alcoholism, using constructive confrontation and supervisor referrals to motivate employees into treatment.

Presenteeism: A recently developed workplace measurement indicating employees tendency to be present physically yet diminished in their ability to function due to personal problems or lack of motivation.

Psychological First Aid: The actions implemented after a trauma of any kind to prevent or diminish the emotional, psychological and physiological effects of the trauma.

Work Engagement: The capacity for employees to perform job tasks and requirements effectively, and to interact positively in work environments, based on an internal state of motivation.

Work-Life Programs or Services: A program or services available to employees and family members that aim to reduce the work-life stressors by providing supportive resources and by creating more flexible work environments that support a more balanced family life.

Learning Objectives

1. To gain a comprehensive understanding of the unique role of Employee Assistance Programs in workplace health promotion, with an emphasis on their development over time, problems and needs addressed, the core technology provided, and the outcomes of EAP services.
2. To analyze the benefits and limitations of EAPs in addressing current needs and emerging trends.
3. To view EAP services within the lens of AMSO framework.
4. To consider the potential for EAPs to expand their focus to address a broader, more holistic health promotion going forward.

Discussion Questions

1. What are Employee Assistance Programs? What services do they provide? What type of problems do they address?
2. How prevalent are the problems addressed by EAPs in the U.S. in general and among employee populations?
3. What are the effects of these problems on employee health and on the work process or workplaces?
4. What are the services that make up EAP core technology? What are influences and trends affecting EAP service delivery?
5. What are the outcomes of EAP services? What benefits and limitations

exist in service effectiveness and in measuring effectiveness?

6. How well does the AMSO framework explain the relevance of EAP services?

7. What are the emerging trends in EAPs and needs for these services?

REFERENCES

1. Maiden RP. The evolution and practice of occupational social work in the United States. *Empl Assist Q.* 2001;17:119–161.

2. Younger BJ. Employee Assistance Programs. In: Cautin R, Lilienfeld S, eds, *Encyclopedia of Clinical Psychology*, NY, NY: Wiley-Blackwell; (Accepted).

3. Society for Human Resource Management. 2012 employee benefits: the employee benefits landscape in a recovering economy. 2012. Available at: http://www.shrm.org/research/surveyfindings/articles/documents/2012_empbenefits_report.pdf. Accessed January 02, 2013.

4. Amaral T. EAP Data Warehouse report. Personal archives. 2013.

5. Mahieu K, Taranowski CJ. External Employee Assistance Program vendors: a study of RFI data from 2009–2010. *EASNA Res Notes.*2013;3(3): 1–7. Available at: www.easna.org. Accessed March 15, 2013.

6. Substance Abuse and Mental Health Services Administration. Results from the 2011 National Survey on Drug Use and Health: volume I. Summary of national findings. Rockville, Md: U.S. Dept of Health and Human Services; 2012:17. Available at: http://www.samhsa.gov/data/nsduh/2k11results/nsduhresults2011.pdf. Accessed May 7, 2013.

7. Centers for Disease Control and Prevention. *National Diabetes Fact Sheet: National Estimates and General Information on Diabetes and Prediabetes in the United States.* Atlanta, GA: U.S. Department of Health and Human Services, CDC, 2011. Available at http://www.cdc.gov/diabetes/pubs/pdf/ndfs 2011.pdf 2011. Accessed November 3, 2013.

8. Merrick E, Hodgkin D, Hiatt D, et al. Integrated employee assistance program/managed behavioral health plan utilization by persons with substance use disorders. *J Subst Abuse Treat.* 2011;40:299–306. Available at: http://www.journalofsubstanceabusetreatment.com. Accessed January 15, 2013.

9. Prottas D, Diamante T, Sandys J. The U.S. domestic workforce use of employee assistance support services: an analysis of ten years of calls. *J Workplace Behav Health.* 2011;26:296–312. doi:10.1080/15555240.2011.618431.

10. Goplerud E, McPherson TL. Workplace alcohol screening, brief intervention, and EAPs: the BIG (Brief Intervention Group) Initiative. Washington, DC; George Washington University, Center for Integrated Behavioral Health Policy and Ensuring Solutions to Alcohol Problems: 2010. Available at: http://sphhs.gwu.edu/departments/healthpolicy/dhp_publications/pub_uploads/dhpPublication_8BE05199-5056-9D20-3D696151640F7376.pdf. Accessed January 20, 2013.

11. Blazer DG, Wu LT. The epidemiology of at-risk and binge drinking among middle-aged and elderly community adults national survey on drug use and health. *Am J Psychiatry.* 2009;166:1162.

12. Quintana DS, McGregor IS, Guastella AJ, et al. A meta-analysis on the impact of alcohol dependence on short-term resting-state heart rate variability: implications for cardiovascular risk. *Alcohol Clin Exp Res.* 2013;37(s1):E23–E29. doi:10.1111/j.1530-0277.2012.01913.x.

13. Caspers KM, Yucuis R, McKirgan LM, et al. Lifetime substance misuse and 5-year

incidence rates of emergent health problems among middle-aged adults. *J Addict Dis*. 2009;28:320–331.

14. Kodama S, Saito K, Tanaka S, et al. Alcohol consumption and risk of atrial fibrillation: a meta-analysis. *J Am Coll Cardiol*. 2011;57:427–436.

15. Clark RE, Connell EO, Samnaliev M. Substance abuse and healthcare costs knowledge asset. The Robert Wood Johnson Foundation's Substance Abuse Policy Research Program. 2010. Available at: http://saprp.org/knowledgeassets/knowledge_detail.cfm?KAID=21. Accessed February 7, 2013.

16. Frone MR, Brown AL. Workplace substance-use norms as predictors of employee substance use and impairment: a survey of U.S. workers. *J Stud Alcohol Drugs*. 2010;71:526–534. Available at: http://www.jsad.com. Accessed March 15, 2013.

17. Jacobson JM, Saco P. Employee assistance program services for alcohol and other dug problems: implications for increased identification and engagement in treatment. *Am J Addict*. 2012;21:468–475. doi:10.1111/j.1521-0391.2012.00256.x.

18. Osilla KC, Miles JN, Zellmer S, et al. Exploring productivity outcomes from a brief intervention for at-risk drinking in an employee assistance program. *Addict Behav*. 2010;35:194–200. doi:10.1016/j.addbeh.2009.10.001.

19. Substance Abuse and Mental Health Services Administration. Substance use, dependence or abuse among full-time workers. National Household Survey on Drug Abuse: the NHSDA Report. Rockville, Md: U.S. Department of Health and Human Services; 2002. Available at: http://www.DrugAbuseStatistics.samhsa.gov. Accessed February 5, 2013.

20. Finch, RA, Phillips, K. *An Employer's Guide to Behavioral Health Services: A Roadmap and Recommendations for Evaluating, Designing, and Implementing Behavioral Health Services*. Washington, DC: National Business Group on Health; 2005.

21. Bachrach LL. The biopsychosocial legacy of deinstitutionalization. *Hosp Community Psychiatry*. 1993;44:523.

22. Morrissey JP, Goldman HH. Cycles of reform in the care of the chronically mentally ill. *Hosp Community Psychiatry*. 1984;35:785.

23. Becker DR, Drake RE, Bond GR, et al. Job terminations among persons with severe mental illness participating in supported employment. *Community Ment Health J*. 1998;34:71–82.

24. Maiden RP, Younger B. The Americans with Disabilities Act: government intent—smaller business response. *Empl Assist Q*. 1996;12:1–18.

25. Lam RW, Wolinsky D, Kinsella C, et al. The prevalence and impact of depression in self-referred clients attending an Employee Assistance Program. *J Occup Environ Med*. 2012;54:1395–1399. doi:10.1097/JOM.0b013e3182611a69.

26. Kessler RC, Chiu WT, Demler O, et al. Prevalence, severity, and comorbidity of 12-month DSM-IV disorders in the National Comorbidity Survey Replication. *Arch Gen Psychiatry*. 2005;62;617. doi:10.1001/archpsyc.62.6.617.

27. Stewart WF, Ricci JA, Chee E, et al. Cost of lost productive work time among U.S. workers with depression. *JAMA*. 2003;289:3135–3144. doi:10.1001/jama.289.23.3135.

28. Roshanaei-Moghaddam B, Katon WJ, Russo J. The longitudinal effects of depression on physical activity. *Gen Hosp Psychiatry*. 2009;31:306–315. doi:10.1016/j.genhosppsych.2009.04.002.

29. Scott D, Happell B. The high prevalence of poor physical health and unhealthy lifestyle behaviours in individuals with

severe mental illness. *Issues Ment Health Nurs*. 2011;32:589. doi:10.3109/01612840. 2011.569846.

30. Viron MJ, Stern TA. The impact of serious mental illness on health and healthcare. *Psychosomatics*. 2010;51:458–465. doi:10.1016/S0033-3182(10)70737-4.

31. Centers for Disease Control and Prevention. Suicide among adults aged 35–64 years—United States, 1999–2010. *MMWR Morb Mortal Wkly Rep*. 2013;62: 321–325. Available at: http://www. cdc.gov/mmwr/preview/mmwrhtml/ mm6217a1.htm. Accessed February 18, 2013.

32. Kessler RC, Akiskal HS, Ames M, et al. The prevalence and effects of mood disorders on work performance in a nationally representative sample of U.S. workers. *Am J Psychiatry*. 2006;163:1561–1568. doi:10.1176/appi.ajp.163.9.1561.

33. Gilbody S, Bower P, Rick J. Better care for depression in the workplace: integrating occupational and mental health services. *Br J Psychiatry*. 2012;200:442. doi:10.1192/ bjp.bp.111.103598.

34. Hurley JE. *An analysis of ADA Title I allegations of workplace discrimination as filed with the EEOC by persons with mental illness*. Richmond, Virginia: Commonwealth University; 2011. Available from: ProQuest Digital Dissertations. Virginia Commonwealth University, Richmond, VA, Accessed February 21, 2013. Publication Number: 3490715.

35. Attridge M, Amaral T, Bjornson T, et al. History and growth of the EAP field. *EASNA Res Notes*. 2009;1(1):1–4.

36. Amato, PR. Research on divorce: Continuing trends and new developments. *J Marriage Fam*. 2010; 72:650–666. doi:10.1111/j.1741-3737. 2010.00723.x.

37. Centers for Disease Control and Prevention. National marriage and divorce rate trends. 2013. Available at: http://www.cdc.gov/nchs/nvss/ marriage_divorce_tables.htm. Accessed March 21, 2013.

38. Lofquist D, Lugaila T, O'Connell M, et al. Households and families: 2010. 2010 Census Briefs. U.S. Census Bureau, U.S. Dept of Commerce. 2012. Available at: http://www.census. gov/prod/cen2010/briefs/c2010br-14.pdf. Accessed March 21, 2013.

39. Bianchi SM, Milkie MA. Work and family research in the first decade of the 21st century. *J Marriage Fam*. 2010;72:705–725. doi:10.1111/j.1741-3737.2010.00726.x.

40. Bellavia GM, Frone MR. Work-family conflict. In: Barlin J, Kelloway EK, Frone MR, eds. *Handbook of Work Stress*. Thousand Oaks, Calif: Sage; 2005:113–148.

41. Moen P, Kelly E, Tranby E, Huang Q. Changing work, changing health: can real work-time flexibility promote health behaviors and well-being? *J Health Soc Behav*. 2011;52:404-429. doi:10.1177/0022146511418979.

42. Sbarra DA, Law RW, Portley RM. Divorce and death: A meta-analysis and research agenda for clinical, social, and health psychology. *Perspect Psychol Sci*. 2011;6:454–474. doi:10.1177/1745691611414724.

43. Hoxhallari L, Conolly A, Lyon N. Families with children in Britain: findings from the 2005 Families and Children Study (FACS). No. 424. Corporate Document Services. 2007. Available at: http:// www.familieslink.co.uk/download/ july07/New%20definition%20of%20 mother.pdf. Accessed January 7, 2013.

44. Amstad FT, Meier LL, Fasel U, et al. A meta-analysis of work-family conflict and various outcomes with a special emphasis on cross-domain versus matching-domain relations. *J Occup Health Psychol*. 2011;16:151–169. doi:10.1037/a0022170.

45. Breslau N. The epidemiology of trauma, PTSD, and other posttrauma disorders. *Trauma Violence Abuse.* 2009;10:198–210. doi:10.1177/1524838009334448.

46. United States Department of Justice, Bureau of Justice Statistics. Special report: workplace violence, 1993–2009. NCJ233231. 2011. Available at: http://bjs.gov/content/pub/pdf/wv09.pdf. Accessed April 14, 2013.

47. Federal Bureau of Investigation. Bank crime statistics (BCS): federally insured financial institutions, January 1, 2011–December 31, 2011. 2012. Available at: http://www.fbi.gov/stats-services/publications/bank-crime-statistics-2011/bank-crime-statistics-2011, Accessed April 14, 2013.

48. U.S. Dept of Justice, Bureau of Justice Statistics. Special report: intimate partner violence, 1993–2010. NCJ239203.2012. Available at: http://www.bjs.gov/content/pub/pdf/ipv9310.pdf. Accessed April 14, 2013.

49. Tjaden P, Thoennes N. Extent, nature, and consequences of rape victimization: findings from the national violence against women survey. united states; 2006. Available at: https://www.ncjrs.gov/pdffiles1/nij/210346.pdf. Accessed April 14, 2013.

50. Tiesman HM, Gurka KK, Konda S, et al. Workplace homicides among U.S. women: the role of intimate partner violence. *Ann Epidemiol.* 2012;22:277–284. doi:10.1016/j.annepidem.2012.02.009.

51. U.S. Dept of Labor, Bureau of Labor Statistics. Revisions to the 2010 census of fatal occupational injuries (CFOI) counts. 2010. Available at: http://www.bls.gov/iif/oshwc/cfoi/cfoi_revised10.pdf. Accessed May 7, 2013.

52. McDonald P. Workplace sexual harassment 30 years on: a review of the literature. *Int J Manag Rev.* 2012;14(1):1–17. doi:10.1111/j.1468-2370.2011.00300.x.

53. U.S. Dept of Health and Human Services, National Institute of Mental Health. Post-traumatic stress disorder (PTSD). Available at: http://www.nimh.nih.gov/health/publications/post-traumatic-stress-disorder-ptsd/nimh_ptsd_booklet.pdf. Accessed April 3, 2013.

54. American Psychiatric Association. *Diagnostic and Statistical Manual of Mental Disorders: DSM-IV-TR.* Washington, DC: American Psychiatric Association; 2000. doi: 10.1176/appi.books.9780890423349.

55. Gates DM, Gillespie GL, Succop P. Violence against nurses and its impact on stress and productivity. *Nurs Econ.* 2011;29:59. Available at: http://ldihealtheconomist.com/media/nv01.pdf. Accessed March 21, 2013.

56. Tabanelli, M. C., Bonfiglioli, R., & Violante, F. S. (2013). Bank robberies: A psychological protocol of intervention in financial institutions and principal effects. *Work: A Journal of Prevention, Assessment and Rehabilitation.* Work 00 (2013) 1–11. doi:10-3233/WOR 131625.

57. Lacey KK, McPherson MD, Samuel PS, et al. The impact of different types of intimate partner violence on the mental and physical health of women in different ethnic groups. *J Interpers Violence.* 2013;28:359–385. doi:10.1177/0886260512454743.

58. Wald J. Anxiety disorders and work performance. In: Schultz, Izabela Z., Rogers, E. Sally (Eds.). *Work Accommodation and Retention in Mental Health.* New York, NY: Springer; 2011:121–140.

59. Lindquist CH, McKay T, Clinton-Sherrod AM, et al. The role of Employee Assistance Programs in workplace-based intimate partner violence intervention and prevention activities. *J Workplace Behav Health.* 2010;25:46–64. doi:10.1080/15555240903538980.

60. U.S. Dept of Labor, Occupational Safety and Health Administration. Reflections on OSHAs history. 2009. Available at: http://www.osha.gov/history/OSHA_HISTORY_3360s.pdf. Accessed April 13, 2013.

61. U.S. Dept of Labor, Occupational Safety and Health Administration. Detailed frequently asked questions for OSHA's injury and illness recordkeeping rule. Available at: http://www.osha.gov/recordkeeping/detailedfaq.html. Accessed March 21, 2013.

62. Health and Safety Executive. Health and safety statistics. 2012. Available at: http://www.hse.gov.uk/statistics/index.htm. Accessed March 22, 2013.

63. Nieuwenhuijsen K, Bruinvels D, Frings-Dresen M. Psychosocial work environment and stress-related disorders, a systematic review. *Occup Med (Lond).* 2010; 60:277-286. doi:10.1093/occmed/kqq081.

64. Häusser JA, Mojzisch A, Niesel M, et al. Ten years on: a review of recent research on the Job Demand-Control (-Support) model and psychological well-being. *Work Stress.* 2010;24:1. doi:10l1090/02678371003683747.

65. Backé E, Seidler A, Latza U, et al. The role of psychosocial stress at work for the development of cardiovascular diseases: a systematic review. *Int Arch Occup Environ Health.* 2012;85(1): 67-79. doi:10.1007/s00420-011-0643-6.

66. Heraclides A, Chandola, T, Witte DR, et al. Psychosocial stress at work doubles the risk of Type 2 diabetes in middle-aged women evidence from the Whitehall II Study. *Diabetes Care.* 2009;32:2230-2235. doi:10.2337/dc09-0132.

67. Ganster DC, Rosen CC. Work stress and employee health: a multidisciplinary review. *J Manag.* 2013;39:1085-1112. doi:10.1177/0149206313475815.

68. Schaufeli WB, Bakker AB, Van Rhenen W. How changes in job demands and resources predict burnout, work engagement, and sickness absenteeism. *J Organ Behav.* 2009;30:893–917. doi:10.1002/job.595.

69. Beyer JM, Trice HM. A field study of the use and perceived effects of discipline in controlling work performance. *Acad Manag J.* 1984;27:743-764. Available at: http://www.jstor.org.libproxy.usc.edu/stable/255876. Accessed March 23, 2013.

70. Conrad P. Medicalization and social control. *Annu Rev Sociol.* 1992;18:209–232. Available at: http://www.jstor.org.libproxy.usc.edu/stable/2083452. Accessed February 7, 2013.

71. Gornick ME, Blair BR. Chapter 1: employee assistance, work-life effectiveness, and health and productivity: a conceptual framework for integration. *J Workplace Behav Health.* 2005;20:1-29. doi:10.1200/J490v20n01 01.

72. Katz D, Kahn RL. *The Social Psychology of Organizations. Contemporary Sociology.* New York, NY: Wiley; 1980.

73. Straussner SL. A comparative analysis of in-house and contractual Employee Assistance Programs. *Empl Assist Q.* 1988;3(3–4):43-56.

74. Goldman W, McCulloch J, Sturm R. Cost and use of mental health services before and after managed care. *Health Aff.* 1998;17:40-52. doi:10.1377/hlthaff.17.2.40.

75. Attridge M. Employee Assistance Programs: Evidence and current trends. In: Gatchel RJ, Schultz IZ, eds. *Handbook of Occupational Health and Wellness.* New York, NY: Springer Science+Business Media; 2012:441–467.`

76. Employee Assistance Professional Association. *A Comprehensive Study of Employee Assistance Professionals.* Arlington, Va. 2008. Available at: http://www.eapassn.org. Accessed April 12, 2013.

77. Attridge M, Amaral T, Bjornson T, et al. Pricing options for EAP services. *EASNA Res Notes.* 2010;1:1–4.

78. Masi DA. Redefining the EAP field. *J Workplace Behav Health.* 2011;26:1–9.

79. Buon T, Taylor J. A review of the Employee Assistance Programme (EAP) market in the UK and Europe. Robert Gordon University. 2007. Available at: http://www.buon.net/files/RGUEAEFttt pdf. Accessed May 7, 2013.

80. Golan M, Bacharach Y, Bamberger P. Peer assistance programs in the workplace. In: Houdamont J, Leka S, eds. *Contemporary Occupational Health Psychology: Global Perspectives on Research and Practice.* West Sussex, UK: John Wiley & Sons.; 2010:169–187

81. Rosenberg J. Organized labor's contribution to the human services: lessons from the past and strategies for the future. *J Workplace Behav Health.* 2009;24:113-124.doi:10.1080/15555240902849057.

82. Employee Assistance Professional Association. Definitions of an employee assistance program (EAP) and EAP core technology. 2011. Available at: http://www.eapassn.org/i4a/pages/index.cfm?pageid=521. Accessed January 25, 2013.

83. Employee Assistance Society of North America (EASNA). *Selecting and Strengthening Employee Assistance Programs: A Purchaser's Guide.* Arlington, Va: Employee Assistance Society of North America; 2009.

84. Employee Assistance Professionals Association, Inc. (EAPA). EAPA Standards and Professional Guidelines. 2010. Available at: http://www.eapassn.org/files/public/EAPASTANDARDS10.pdf. Accessed January 25, 2013.

85. Amaral T, Attridge, M. *A New Research-Driven Approach to Workplace Behavioral Health Services: Does This Present an Opportunity or Challenge for EAPs?* Yreka, CA: EAP Technology Systems, Inc. Unpublished report; 2010. Research brief.

86. Greenwood GL, Goplerud E, McPherson TL, et al. Alcohol screening and brief intervention (SBI) in telephonic employee assistance programs. *J Workplace Behav Health.* 2010;25:233–240. doi:10.1080/15555240.2010.518480.

87. Attridge M, Burke, J. Trends in EAP services and strategies: An industry survey. *EASNA Res Notes.* 2011;2:1–9.

88. Greenwood KL, DeWeese P, Inscoe PS. Demonstrating the value of EAP services: a focus on clinical outcomes. *J Workplace Behav Health.* 2006;21:1–10. doi:10.1300/J490v21n01_01.

89. Jacobson JM, Attridge M. Employee assistance programs (EAPs): an allied profession for work/life. In: Sweet S, Casey J, eds. *Work and Family Encyclopedia.* Chestnut Hill, Mass: Sloan Work and Family Research Network; 2010. Available at: http://wfnetwork.bc.edu/encyclopedia_entry.php?id=17296&area=All. Accessed April 17, 2013.

90. Attridge M, VandePol B. The business case for workplace critical incident response: A literature review and some employer examples. *J Workplace Behav Health.* 2010;25:132–145. doi:10.180/15555241003761001.

91. Attridge M, Amaral T, Bjornson T, et al. The business value of EAP: a conceptual model. *EASNA Res Notes.* 2010; 1(10): 1–4.

92. McCann B, Azzone V, Merrick EL, et al. Employer choices in Employee Assistance Program design and worksite services. *J Workplace Behav Health.* 2010;25:89–106. doi:10.1080/15555241003760979.

93. Harlow KC. The effectiveness of a problem resolution and brief counseling

EAP intervention. *J Workplace Behav Health.* 2007;22:1-12. doi:10.1300/J490v22n01_01.

94. Selvik R, Stephenson D, Plaza C, et al. EAP impact on work, relationship, and health outcomes. *J Empl Assist.* 2004;34:18–22. Available at: http://www.eapassn.org/public/pages/index.cfm?pageid=403. Accessed January 22, 2013.

95. Sharar D, Pompe J, Lennox R. Evaluating the workplace effects of EAP counseling. *J Health Productivity.* 2010;6(2):1–4. Available at: http://hdl.handle.net/10713/2602. Accessed February 7, 2013.

96. Dainas C, Marks D. Abbott Laboratories' EAP demonstrates cost effectiveness through two studies and builds the business case for program expansion. *Behav Health Manag.* 2000;20:34-41.

97. Davidson Trahaire Corpsych. EAP return on investment summary. 2013. Available at: http://www.davcorp.com.au/media/17992/dtc_eap_return_on_investment_summary_-_2013.pdf. Accessed April 7, 2013.

98. Boscarino JA, Adams RE, Figley CR. A prospective cohort study of the effectiveness of employer-sponsored crisis interventions after a major disaster. *Int J Emerg Ment Health.* 2005;7:9-22. NIHMSID: NIHMS116409.

99. Hansen S. From 'common observation' to behavioural risk management: workplace surveillance and employee assistance 1914–2003. *Intern Sociol.* 2004;19:151–171. doi:10.1177/0268580904042898.

100. Prochaska JO, Velicer WF. The transtheoretical model of health behavior change. *Am J Health Promot.* 1997;12:38–48. doi:http://dx.doi.org/10.4278/0890-1171-12.1.38.

101. Eischen BD, Grossmeier J, Gold DB. Fairview Alive—an integrated strategy for enhancing the health and well-being of employees. *J Workplace Behav Health.* 2005;20:263–279. doi:10.1200/J490v20n03_04.

102. Emery M. The current version of Emery's Open Systems Theory. *Syst Pract Action Res.* 2000;13:623–643. doi:1094-429X/00/1000-0623.

103. Global Corporate Challenge. Global workplace health and wellness report. 2013. Available at: www.gettheworldmoving.com. Accessed April 22, 2013.

104. ComPsych. Global trends report: global workforce needs are universal. 2012. Available at: www.compsych.com. Accessed January 23, 2013.

105. Kurzman PA. Employee Assistance Programs for the new millennium: Emergence of the comprehensive model. In *Soc Work Ment Health.* 2013:11. Soc Work Ment Health. 2013;11:381-403. doi:10.1080/15332985.2013.780836.

106. Jacobson JM, Jones AL. Standards for the EAP profession: isn't it time we all start speaking the same language? *J Workplace Behav Health.*2010;25:1–18. doi:10.1080/15555240903538741.

107. Nobrega S, Champagne N, Azaroff LS, et al. Barriers to workplace stress interventions in Employee Assistance practice: EAP perspectives. *J Workplace Behav Health.* 2010;25:282–295. doi:10.1080/15555240.2010.518491.

CHAPTER

21

Social Relationships: Harnessing their Potential to Promote Health

Catherine A. Heaney

We all live in a socially connected world. Sociological and epidemiological investigations have long shown the health benefits of social connections.[1] For example, a lack of social ties has been consistently associated with all-cause mortality.[2] Additionally, many studies provide evidence that social ties help to maintain psychological well-being.[3] More recently, the notion of "social contagion" has suggested that social ties also influence individuals' health beliefs and health behaviors.[4]

Throughout the last decades, we have come to understand the mechanisms through which these health benefits accrue. This chapter starts with definitions, key terminology and descriptions of the various ways that social relationships can benefit health and influence health behavior. Next, it focuses on how the health-enhancing power of social relationships is experienced in the workplace. Lastly, it describes potential strategies for harnessing the power of social relationships to enhance the efficacy of worksite health promotion efforts.

RELEVANT CONCEPTS AND PROCESSES

Several key terms have been used in studies of the health-enhancing components of social relationships.[1] The term *social integration* has been used to refer to the existence of social ties. The term *social network* refers to the web of social relationships within which individuals live. Often social networks are conceptualized as "egocentric" with a focal individual at the center and that person's social ties emanating from the center. Another way of drawing a social network is to sketch out the social ties within a specific group or community. This approach is termed "sociometric" and includes social ties that do not involve any one focal individual.[5]

Figure 21-1 shows an example of an egocentric and sociometric social network at work. In the first part of the figure, all network members have a tie to Person A, as well as some ties among each other. This is the egocentric network. When the second portion of the network is added, there are network members who are connected to other members but have no direct tie to Person A. The complete figure depicts the sociometric network. Using a sociometric approach allows for investigation of potential effects of Supervisor B or Coworker E on the beliefs and behaviors of Person A.

No matter how social networks are conceptualized, they can be described in terms of the characteristics of specific social ties (dyadic characteristics) and in terms of the characteristics of the network as a whole. Examples of dyadic characteristics include the extent to which resources and support are both given and received in a relationship (reciprocity); the extent to which a relationship is characterized by emotional closeness (intensity or strength); the extent to which a relationship is embedded in a formal organizational or institutional structure (formality); and the extent to which a relationship serves a variety of functions (complexity). Examples of characteristics that describe a whole network include the extent to which network members are similar in terms of demographic characteristics such as age,

race, and socioeconomic status (homophily); the extent to which network members live in close proximity to the focal person (geographic dispersion); and the extent to which network members know and interact with each other (density).[5,6]

Many social processes unfold through social networks, and it is these social processes that have the potential to affect health. These social processes can be grouped into two categories: (1) processes that do not include overt attempts to influence others or to provide support and (2) processes that rely on individuals' intentional interpersonal behaviors. The first category includes the processes of behavioral imitation, social comparison, and conformance to perceived social norms. The second category includes the provision of social support, social undermining, and intentional attempts to influence others' attitudes and behaviors. Each of these processes is described below.

Processes Involving no Intent on the Part of Social Network Members

Behavioral Imitation

Behavioral imitation of others has long been a part of psychological learning theories.

Figure 21-1: Example of egocentric and sociometric networks in the workplace.

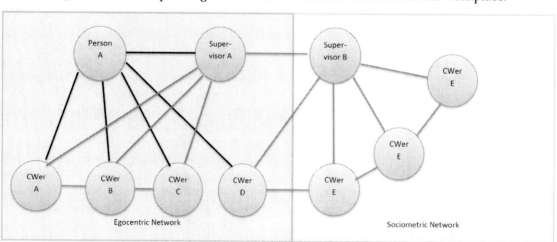

Albert Bandura, in his social cognitive theory, suggests that we engage in vicarious learning by watching others.[7] We see what works for them and then try it ourselves. Interestingly, such imitation may result from an intentional process of the learner or from a subconscious, physiologically-driven process. When we see someone engaging in a behavior, mirror neurons are activated. The brain practices doing something that, in reality, we are only watching.[8] Ultimately, this makes it easier to engage in the same behavior. This biological hardwiring of behavioral imitation makes it one of the simplest and often subliminal processes through which social ties affect behavior.

Social comparison

In the 1950s, the psychologist Leon Festinger first posited the importance of people comparing their own attributes, skills, opinions and behaviors to those of others.[9] Since then, social psychologists have actively investigated both the motivations for and consequences of social comparison. The social cognition explanation for why people engage in social comparisons is that it is simply easier than making comparisons to absolute standards or benchmarks.[10] For example, if a person is trying to assess if he or she is a physically active person, it is easier to compare one's own level of activity to the activity levels of others with whom you interact than it is to find and understand an absolute standard (e.g., the federal guidelines for health-promoting physical activity) and assess whether or not one meets that standard. Of course, the two types of comparisons may lead to quite different results.

Reviews of the social comparison literature suggest several different motivations for engaging in social comparisons: (1) to gain accurate self-evaluations; (2) to create or maintain a positive self-image; and (3) to facilitate self-improvement.[11] Each of these motivations suggests a different strategic choice of whom to compare oneself. If you are motivated by the need for an accurate self-evaluation, you are likely to compare yourself to similar others. For example, if you want an accurate assessment of your athleticism, you will want to compare yourself to others of the same age and gender. However, if you are motivated to create a positive self-image, you may strategically compare yourself to those who are worse off. In the case of assessing athleticism, you might compare yourself to friends or coworkers who do not regularly exercise. Lastly, if you are motivated by the need for self-improvement, you might be inspired by comparisons with professional athletes. Research shows that we all use these various types of comparisons to serve our own purposes.[11]

While we may make different social comparisons depending on our motivations, we also have a default comparison that we rely on the most often. This default comparison is composed of those in our peer group with whom we have the most contact. Thus, our families, close friends and coworkers are often chosen as those to whom we compare ourselves. In this way, without even trying, these social relationships influence our own self-assessments. As one social psychologist recently stated, "Social comparison is a remarkably ubiquitous process which influences how people think about themselves, how they feel, what they are motivated to do, and how they behave".[10]

Social Norms

Social norms are the standards against which the appropriateness of specific behaviors, states or beliefs are assessed. These standards are socially defined in a number of ways. A "descriptive norm" refers to the extent to which a behavior, state or belief is present among the members of the reference group for the norm. Reference groups can range from all of humanity to very specific groups of people with whom an individual interacts. An "injunctive norm" refers to the extent to which a behavior, state or belief is approved of by the members of the reference group for the norm.[12] The subjective norm construct in Fishbein and Ajzen's Theory of Planned Behavior is an injunctive norm. It is constructed of a person's beliefs about what others in their social networks expect of him or her.[13]

Descriptive norms depict what is happening, without any explicit judgment as to appropriateness. In spite of this lack of intentional social control, research suggests that people tend to not want to deviate from descriptive norms. For example, Ball and colleagues[14] found that individuals' perceived social norms about physical activity and healthy eating were associated with their own physical activity and eating behavior. That is, people who perceived other people to be engaging in healthier behaviors tended to engage in the same behaviors more often themselves. The same has been found for safety behaviors at work; the more employees perceived their coworkers to be performing safety behaviors, the more likely they were to perform them themselves.[15]

The presumed power of social norms to shape behavior is the major underpinning for social norms theory and social norm marketing.[16] Social norms theory applies to situations where people tend to misperceive a descriptive norm. Research suggests that when people are considering how often an unhealthy or risky behavior is being performed by their peers, they tend to over-estimate the prevalence. On the other hand, people tend to underestimate the extent to which healthy behaviors are being performed. People then modulate their own behavior to be in conformity with these misperceived norms. Social norm marketing provides information about an accurate descriptive norm in order to disabuse people of their misconceptions and to influence their behavior to be more in line with the accurate norm. Note that this type of message, providing normative information as the primary means to bringing about change,

differs from more traditional informational campaigns or fear-arousing efforts. It does not focus on expected consequences of the behavior but rather on the prevalence of the behavior itself. This type of social norm marketing has been used extensively on college campuses to help students re-align their descriptive norms about binge drinking and to bring their drinking behavior into line with their newly-perceived accurate social norms.[16,17]

Obviously, social norms marketing is only appropriate if the actual descriptive norm is originally misestimated. Additionally, if people find out that their behavior is already "better" than the norm, there is the risk of an undesirable boomerang effect; people may increase their undesirable behaviors or decrease their desirable ones in order to be more in conformance with the descriptive social norm. By invoking an injunctive norm, such boomerang effects can be minimized. A study of household energy consumption demonstrates this effect. All households received a feedback card that included information about how much energy they had used and the average household energy usage in their neighborhood. For those households with above average usage, this normative information resulted in decreased energy use. For those households with below average usage, there was a significant boomerang effect of increased usage. However, when households with below average usage received a hand drawn happy face on their feedback card (indicating the desirability of their behavior), this boomerang effect was eliminated.[18] While the target behavior in this study was not a health behavior, it shared many characteristics of healthy lifestyle behaviors. Energy usage behaviors are private, recurring behaviors that have both a clear personal benefit (i.e., lower energy bills) and unambiguous social approval. Thus, social norm marketing that includes information about both descriptive and injunctive norms has great potential for health promotion.

Processes Involving Intentional Interactions by Social Network Members

Social Support

The term "social support" is used in common parlance to indicate verbal and non-verbal expressions of care and concern. In the professional literature, social support has been defined in many ways. According to the classic typology first put forth by sociologist James House,[19] social support refers to four categories of supportive behaviors:

- *Emotional support* involves the provision of empathy, love, trust, and caring.
- *Instrumental support* involves the provision of tangible aid and services that directly assist a person in need.
- *Informational support* is the provision of advice, suggestions, and information that a person can use to address problems.
- *Appraisal support* involves the provision of information that is useful for self-evaluation purposes, i.e., constructive feedback, and affirmation.

Social support is always intended (by the provider of the support) to be helpful, thus distinguishing it from intentional negative interactions (e.g., social undermining behaviors such as angry criticism and hassling.)[6] Whether or not the intended support is perceived or experienced as helpful by the receiver is an empirical question, and indeed, negative perceptions and consequences of well-intended interpersonal exchanges have been identified.[20] Although the provision of social support, particularly informational support, can attempt to influence the thoughts and behaviors of the receiver, such informational support is provided in an interpersonal context of caring, trust, and respect for each person's right to make his or her own choices. This quality distinguishes social support from some other types of social influence that derive from the ability to provide or withhold desired resources or approval.

Many empirical studies consistently show the positive influence of social support on both mental and physical health.[21] The results of these studies are so compelling that Robert Putnam, a Harvard professor, stated in his classic book *Bowling Alone (2000)*:

> "...the positive contributions to health made by social integration and social support rival in strength the detrimental contributions of well-established biomedical risk factors like cigarette smoking, obesity, elevated blood pressure and physical activity."[22]

And:

> "The bottom line from this multitude of studies: As a rough rule of thumb, if you belong to no groups but decide to join one, you cut your risk of dying over the next year *in half*. If you smoke and belong to no groups, it's a toss up statistically whether you should stop smoking or start joining."[22]

By meeting basic human needs for companionship, intimacy, a sense of belonging, and reassurance of one's worth as a person, as well as providing important tangible and instrumental resources for living, supportive ties enhance well-being and health, regardless of a person's stress level. This is often termed the main effect or direct effect of social support on health. Another important health-promoting function of social support is its influence on how people respond to stress. The stress process, as posited in Richard Lazarus's Transactional Model of Stress[23], is depicted in Figure 21-2.

This model of the stress process begins when a person is exposed to environmental

Figure 21-2: Stress buffering roles of social support as adapted from the transactional model of stress.

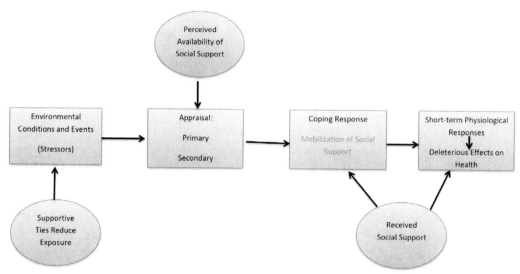

conditions or events that are potential stressors. These include major life events such as starting a new job, daily hassles like getting caught in traffic, and chronic role stressors such as not knowing what is expected of oneself on the job. Supportive social ties may reduce the frequency and duration of exposure to these potential stressors. For example, a supportive supervisor may ensure that an employee is not given too much work to do or confusing instructions about how to accomplish the work. According to Lazarus, potential stressors are appraised by the person experiencing them for the extent to which they are potentially harmful or threatening (primary appraisal) and the extent to which the demands of the potential stressor can be handled or addressed (secondary appraisal). This is the second point in the stress process where social support may play a role. If the focal person perceives that others in the social network will be ready and willing to provide social support, it may influence his or her assessment of the resources and opportunities available to mitigate the demands of the stressor. For example, if an employee perceives that coworkers will stay

late to help complete a project, the project will be appraised as less stressful.

If a stressor is appraised as stressful, then the person is likely to engage in coping responses. These coping responses are defined as "...cognitive and behavioral efforts to manage specific external or internal demands (and conflicts between them) that are appraised as taxing or exceeding the resources of a person.[24] And this provides the third point at which supportive ties affect the stress process. One type of coping response is to mobilize social support. The employee struggling with work overload may (1) seek advice on how to streamline the work process (informational support) from her supervisor, (2) request assistance in completing the work (instrumental support) from her coworkers, and/or (3) call her spouse for expressions of sympathy and caring (emotional support). Such support mobilization may help to solve the problem and reduce the likelihood of the person experiencing deleterious effects on health.

This may be particularly important for health in that people sometimes engage in risky or unhealthy behaviors (e.g., smoking or substance use) as unconstructive coping responses. The receipt of social support may reduce the performance of these behaviors. Lastly, by providing feedback that connotes caring, understanding or affirmation, supporters may decrease the distress that employees suffer when faced with difficult situations. In these various ways, social support buffers against the ill health effects of exposure to potential stressors.

Although the direct effects and the buffering effects of social support were initially investigated as either/or relationships, evidence suggests that social support has both types of effects, and that the predominance of one effect over the other depends on the target population, the situation being studied, and the ways in which the social relationship concept is measured.[25,26]

Social Undermining

In 1984, Karen Rook was among the first researchers to focus on negative social interactions as an important determinant of health.[27] Ten years later, Vinokur and colleagues[28] explicated the concept of social undermining to include behaviors aimed at another person that (1) displayed negative affect, (2) indicated a negative evaluation of the person, or (3) hindered the attainment of the person's goals. As with social support, social undermining is an intentional act.[29] At the workplace, displays of social undermining might include getting yelled at or criticized by a supervisor, being belittled or ostracized by one's coworkers, or not receiving needed work supplies when they are readily available to others.

Recipients of social undermining often experience psychological distress and feelings of helplessness.[29] Exposure to social undermining has also been associated with an increase in alcohol and drug use,[30] a decrease in healthy eating and exercise behaviors,[31] and increased susceptibility to infectious disease.[32]

As a matter of fact, several of these studies have shown that social undermining may be more strongly associated with these outcomes than is social support. More recently, negative social interactions have been related to heightened chronic inflammatory responses that may lead to increased risk of hypertension, coronary heart disease, and diabetes.[33]

Social Influence

Many social interactions involve efforts to influence the thoughts and behaviors of others, including the social processes described above. However, there are types of social influence that have not yet been described that unfold through the social ties of social networks. The most widely cited typology of social influence was developed by French and Raven.[34] In French and Raven's formulation, interpersonal power is considered the basis of social influence. They suggest several types of interpersonal power: referent, informational, legitimate, coercive/reward, and expert power.

Two of these sources of interpersonal power have been touched upon already. Referent power has its roots in the term "reference group", which is used to describe groups with which we identify and feel psychologically involved. They are groups to which we refer for our norms and values. There is considerable evidence that, because of private acceptance or internalization, we behave more consistently with a set of norms when they are communicated by referent others--- that is, people with whom we feel similar and trusting. This type of power is at work in the social norm marketing process described earlier. Another source of interpersonal power that we have already introduced is informational power. This type of power stems from access to information, the ability to clearly communicate the information, and the ability to use logical argument to effect change. It is the basis of informational social support.

Legitimate power is a source of interpersonal influence derived from a socially negotiated role, a set of social agreements regarding a position or role that invests those in that role with the power to direct the behavior of others. The terms *obliged, should* and *ought* may signal the existence of legitimate power.[35] This type of power is found in worksites where one's position within the hierarchy can provide supervisors legitimate power over their subordinates. There is little research on the effectiveness or consequences of the use of legitimate power, however its presence should be acknowledged and taken into account when developing worksite interventions to promote health.

Workplace hierarchies also provide opportunities for the use of coercive/reward power. Coercive power stems from the perception that another person has the ability to create a negative consequence for noncompliance with desired behavior. Negative consequences may include disapproval, ridicule, criticism, other unpleasant or embarrassing social interactions, or the withholding of material resources. Reward power is the flip side of coercive power and stems from the ability to provide desired resources in return for compliance. Such rewards may include access to information, services, favors and monetary incentives. Coercive and reward power may lead to short-term compliance with desired behaviors but are unlikely to lead to internalization of new behaviors and norms. Therefore, the need for continual surveillance is quite high and the likelihood of maintenance of the new behaviors is quite low.[34]

The last source of interpersonal power is expert power. This form of power exists when a person believes that another person knows "better" than she does. Statements from people with expert power are accepted whether or not a persuasive argument is presented. This contrasts with informational power where influence results from consideration of the content of the information being exchanged.[34] In worksites, health care professionals are considered experts in health; safety professionals are considered experts in safety. However, when employees comply with the wishes of these professionals solely because they are perceived to be experts, the employees are less likely to perceive themselves to have internal control over and personal responsibility for their actions. Thus, attitude change or behavior change resulting from expert suggestion may be short-lived and easily reversed in the face of other social challenges.[35]

SOCIAL RELATIONSHIPS AT THE WORKPLACE

Social networks at work typically include supervisors, coworkers, and people whom the employer is serving (e.g., clients, customers, patients, or students). They may also include formal helpers at the workplace such as occupational health professionals (including health educators) and human resource professionals. Each of these types of social relationships at work can play a role in promoting employee health. These social ties can promote health through both their general everyday interactions and through their social exchanges specific to health and health behavior. This section discusses how social network members at work can engage in ways that are generally health promoting. The last section addresses how they can help each other attain specific health behavior change goals.

Supervisors

Supervisors serve a very important role in social networks at the workplace. Figure 21-1 shows that many network members have ties to the supervisor. This figure portrays only a small work group. The influence of a supervisor would be even more widespread in a larger department where all employees report to one supervisor. Given this position of network centrality and the potential for supervisors to make decisions that affect the whole network, supervisors are often considered "high impact leverage points"[36] for implementing change within the networks. The ways that they behave and the decisions they make can have far-reaching consequences for the health and well-being of many employees.

Organizational researchers have long been interested in leadership styles and how they influence organizational and employee work-related outcomes.[37] More recently, attention has turned to how leadership styles and supervisory behaviors are associated with employee health and well-being. Reviews of this literature show a strong correlation between leader behavior and the well-being of their employees.[38] For example, Gilbreath and Benson[39] created an overall measure of supervisory behavior that included elements of leadership, communication, social support, empowerment, group maintenance and consideration (appreciation) for employees. They found that scores on this scale were associated with the health and well-being of the supervisors' employees, as measured by a health questionnaire.

But what exactly should supervisors who want to promote the health of their employees be doing? Transformational leadership, one of the most frequently studied styles of leadership behavior, has been consistently linked with employee well-being.[37] This style of leadership includes engaging in ethical decision-making, inspiring others through imparting a vision, providing intellectual stimulation, and treating others with consideration (e.g., empathy and compassion). Nyberg and colleagues[40] defined good leadership as "consideration for individual employees, provision of clarity in goals and role expectations, supplying information and feedback, ability to carry out changes at work successfully, and promotion of employee participation and control". In a prospective analysis of data from Sweden, they found that good leadership predicted a lower risk of subsequent heart disease among the supervisors' employees. Kelloway and his colleagues[41] used a simpler, less encompassing measure of positive leadership. In focus groups, health care workers were asked to identify supervisors' actions that resulted in the employee feeling better or more positive at work. This resulted in a 5-item scale measuring the extent to which supervisors thank their employees, praise them, cheer them up when needed, go out of their way to help them, and compliment them. Scores on this scale predicted subsequent positive employee affect.

These ways of conceptualizing good leadership clearly include aspects of social support behaviors. Interestingly, they do not explicitly address the need to minimize social undermining, although this is likely to be important in promoting employee health. Table 21-1 summarizes the behaviors that are likely to promote employee health if addressed in training programs for supervisors. Generally, behaviors that enhance the sense that the employee is appreciated and cared

Table 21-1: Health-promoting supervisor behaviors.

Behaviors that supervisors should perform	Behaviors that supervisors should avoid
• Providing positive feedback when appropriate • Offering assistance or guidance when needed • Communicating information important to the job • Showing care and concern for employee well-being	• Withholding social contact from or ostracizing an employee • Ridiculing or insulting • Criticizing in unhelpful ways • Acting unfairly (e.g., withholding resources from one employee that are readily available to others)

for will be helpful. Employees do not expect nor want their supervisors to behave like therapists.[42] Instead, they seem to desire and benefit from supervisors taking the time to acknowledge positive contributions rather than focusing solely on problems and mistakes. While social undermining can rarely be totally eliminated, increasing the ratio of supportive to undermining behaviors is likely to be health-promoting. Psychologist Barbara Fredrickson[43] suggests that a ratio of at least 3 to 1 will promote well-being.

Coworkers

Coworker support has been positively associated with employee well-being[19] and coworker undermining has been shown to reduce well-being.[44] Coworker behavior is generally less strongly associated with employee health and well-being than is supervisor behavior.[29] However, coworkers are in a unique position to understand the types of support that are needed. Sociologist Peggy Thoits[26] has offered a comprehensive approach to identifying an effective source of support. She contends that support is more likely to be effective if it stems from people who are socially similar to the support recipients and who have experienced similar stressors or situations. These characteristics enhance the "empathic understanding" of the support provider, making it more likely that the support proffered is in concert with the needs and values of the recipient. Empathic understanding is particularly relevant to the exchange of emotional support, but also applies to instrumental and informational support. Thus, combining the suggestions provided in Table 21-1 with the naturally occurring empathic understanding arising from experiencing the same jobs can be a potent source of health promoting social interactions.

Because of the relevant knowledge and experience of coworkers, they can also be salient role models for performing health behaviors within the constraints of the job. This knowledge

and experience provides them with credibility in terms of providing informational support or exerting informational influence.

Customers and Clients

In employment sectors where interactions with clients or customers are of short duration and limited intensity, employees would rarely nominate clients as members of their social networks. However, in jobs where the employee-client relationship is better established, clients can be both sources of stress and sources of support. In terms of stress, clients can place onerous demands on employees. These demands can be particularly stressful in a social context where employees are discouraged from giving voice to their authentic negative emotions (such as anger, irritation or frustration). In a setting where "the customer is always right", employees experience what is termed *emotional labor*[45] or the work of hiding authentic emotions or showing inauthentic emotions during job-relevant tasks. In terms of support, clients can be important providers of praise and other positive feedback. Many organizations are now creating formal mechanisms whereby employees receive positive feedback from satisfied clients.

Formal Helpers

Considerable debate has focused on whether professional helpers are effective sources of social support. Worksite health interventions may attempt to enhance the social support available to participants by linking them with professional helpers. Professional helpers often have access to information and resources that are not otherwise available in the social network. However, professional helpers are rarely available to provide social support or exert social influence over long periods of time. Additionally, professional-lay relationships are not typically reciprocal and may involve large power differentials or lack the "empathic understanding" described above. Having said this, it certainly behooves the efforts of formal helpers if they follow the dictates of (1) providing as little social undermining as possible, (2) exchanging social support that is appropriate to the job, and (3) using referent power and informational power in their efforts to influence others.[35]

SOCIAL EXCHANGES SPECIFIC TO HEALTH BEHAVIOR

Although the evidence for the effect of general everyday supportive behaviors on various indicators of health and well-being is strong and consistent, the research investigating the effect of general support on health behaviors is inconsistent and inconclusive.[46] Behavior-specific social interactions are more consistently associated with health behaviors. For example, smokers who perceive that their spouses or close friends support their efforts to quit are more likely to succeed in their cessation efforts.[47,48] People who are trying to lose weight are more successful if members of their social network support them in their weight management efforts.[49,50] Thus, it is logical to incorporate strategies to use social relationships to enhance the effectiveness of worksite health promotion programs. Table 21-2 presents the various available strategies.

Interventions to *enhance existing relationships* in order to support health behavior change sometimes focus on the individual trying to make the change. These focal individuals engage in activities to build skills for effective support mobilization. For example, cardiac patients can be counseled on how to strengthen their social networks in order to enhance their ability to manage their illness.[51] Smokers can be taught how to ask for support for their cessation efforts.[52] Another technique is to recruit social network members into the program and to assist them in developing skills in support provision. For example, significant others have been incorporated into smoking cessation programs[53] and friends and family members have been recruited into weight loss

programs[54] in order to provide support for behavior change. In a recent study, engaging in collaborative planning for increasing physical activity with a friend or family member resulted in more physical activity and greater weight loss.[55]

The worksite provides natural groups of people (e.g., work teams) that can be utilized in health promotion efforts. In a worksite weight loss program, participants who joined as part of a group lost more weight than did participants who joined as individuals.[56] Competitions among teams have been used as part of a multi-component program to bolster health behavior change.[57] These competitions may motivate team members to exchange more support with each and to avoid social undermining (e.g., choosing not to smoke in front of a coworker who is trying to quit).

Interventions that are designed to *develop new social network linkages* are most useful when the existing network is small, overburdened, or simply unable to provide effective support. Some interventions introduce "mentors" or "advisors" who are people who have already coped with the situation being experienced by the focal individual. This is the strategy used in Alcoholics Anonymous when participants choose other successful participants to be their sponsors to help guide their recovery.[58] Mentoring has become a highly valued and popular strategy for supporting others in the community (e.g., Big Brothers/Big Sisters[59]) and the workplace (e.g., established employees mentoring new employees[60]). However, it is a strategy that is not often used in workplace health promotion programs. Thus, it provides an untapped potential source of support for employees trying to engage in health behavior change.[61] Chapter 22 describes how mentoring strategies can be implemented in worksite health promotion programs.

Other interventions to develop new social linkages introduce "buddies" who are experiencing the same stressor or life transition or behavior change goal as the focal person and

Table 21-2: Strategies for Mobilizing the Power of Social Relationships in Worksite Health Promotion Programs.

Intervention Strategies
Enhancing Behavior-Specific Social Support
• Increasing support mobilization
• Enhancing existing social ties
• Developing new social ties
Building Healthy Social Norms
• Recalibrating misperceived norms
• Making healthy role models salient
Encouraging Healthy Social Comparisons
• Encouraging healthy role models
Facilitating Healthy Social Influence
• Recruiting natural helpers

are at the same stage of change. For example, in some smoking cessation programs and weight control programs, participants are encouraged to "buddy up" with another participant (with whom they had no previous relationship) to provide support and encouragement to each other.[62] Self-help or mutual aid groups provide a new *set* of network ties. Usually, people come together in self-help groups because they are facing a common stressor or because they want to bring about similar changes, either at the individual level (e.g., individual weight loss) or at an organizational level (e.g., increased safety at the workplace). In self-help or mutual aid groups, the roles of support provider and support recipient are mutually shared among the members. Thus, the ties often entail high levels of reciprocity. Such groups can be particularly effective for participants who cannot mobilize social support from their other social relationships. Support groups have been used sparingly in the worksite health promotion arena and with somewhat mixed results. For example, employees who chose to participate in a diabetes prevention program using a support group format were not as successful in reducing their risk for diabetes as those who chose to use a similar one-on-one counseling program.[63]

Recently, internet-based support groups have gained in popularity. People with common interests join a virtual community to share experiences and exchange support. Although there is little evidence of their effectiveness to date,[64] they are likely to be a continuing trend in how people seek information and support for specific life transitions and health problems. Research is needed to identify important components of internet support groups, and for whom and under what circumstances they can have health promoting effects. The growth of social media has been recognized as a potentially important opportunity for furthering health promotion goals, particularly as worksites become more geographically dispersed and employees have less occasion to have face-to-face interactions with their coworkers. However, at this time, few rigorous evaluations of these efforts have been conducted.[65]

As discussed above, efforts to *build healthy social norms* have been implemented in college settings. These efforts are limited in worksite health promotion efforts. Perhaps this is because existing descriptive norms for many health behaviors are poor and thus would not inspire conformity to the desired behavior. However, every worksite most likely has employees who are "success stories" for healthy lifestyles. Making these success stories more salient through worksite communication channels (e.g., newsletters, work team meetings, worksite bulletin boards) may encourage employees to begin to question their perceived norms. Some approaches are described in Chapter 22.

By being healthy role models, members of a social network can provide opportunities for *healthy social comparisons*. As mentioned previously, people tend to compare themselves to those with whom they interact. Thus, people tend to notice if a supervisor participates in the lunchtime fitness class or if coworkers choose salads for lunch in the cafeteria rather than a bag of potato chips. Such observed behaviors may be subconsciously imitated by others and/or may inspire self-improvement in others. If employees are made aware of the potential influence that their own behaviors can have on others, it may provide another altruistic motivation for engaging in healthy behaviors at the workplace.

Lastly, workplace health promotion efforts are likely to benefit from *facilitating healthy social influence*. Such influence is likely to stem from referent others (people that we trust and admire and with whom we feel similar) who are knowledgeable about health issues. These referent others are often natural helpers--- members of social networks to whom other network members naturally turn for advice, support and other types of aid.[66] One of the first tasks in natural helper interventions is to identify the people who currently fill these helping roles. Although various strategies have been used to do this,[67] they commonly

ask people in the community for the names of people who demonstrate the characteristics of natural helpers. The participation of community members in the identification process is critical. Those people whose names are repeatedly mentioned can be contacted and recruited. Once the natural helpers are recruited, the health professional can provide the needed information on specific health topics, health and human service resources available in the community, community problem-solving strategies, and can engage in a consultative relationship with the natural helpers. The natural helpers then serve as lay health advisors.[68] Such an approach has been used successfully in the workplace for increasing vaccination among health care workers[69] and for increasing participation in worksite health promotion activities among women in small blue-collar worksites.[70]

Awareness, Motivation, Skills and Opportunities (AMSO) Framework

At this point, it should be clear that social relationships influence each of the phases of the AMSO framework. For example, through exchanges of informational support, people learn new information about risk behaviors, healthy behaviors and how to engage in behavior change efforts. Through social comparison processes, people gain motivation to set challenging goals and work hard to attain them. Social norm marketing can change awareness about the social acceptability of a behavior and enhance motivation to choose a healthy alternative. Simple behavioral imitation can help employees begin to practice new skills. Supportive supervisors can create opportunities for employees to try out new healthy behaviors and can encourage them to persist in their efforts even when the employees experience setbacks. These are but a few examples of the pervasive influence that social relationships can have on health promotion efforts.

EMERGING FINDINGS AND UNANSWERED QUESTIONS

This chapter has explicated the various mechanisms through which social relationships can influence employee health and well-being. These mechanisms suggest strategies that can be incorporated into workplace health promotion efforts in order to optimize effectiveness. Some of these strategies necessitate a willingness on the part of worksite health promotion professionals to extend beyond their comfort zones and to take their mission beyond their traditional boundaries. For example, health promotion professionals might need to partner with those responsible for leadership training in order to work toward developing supervisors who promote the health of their employees. How can health promotion professionals obtain a "seat at the table" for these types of organizational activities? In addition, some of these strategies can only be accomplished with the support and commitment of upper management. For example, identified natural helpers might need time off from work to attend trainings and to conduct health promotion activities. What are the best ways of garnering upper management support for harnessing the power of social relations for promoting employee health?

While there are various strategies for strengthening social relationships available for health promotion professionals to consider, there is not a lot of research to aid in deciding which strategy to use in any given situation. How should you choose between a program to encourage healthy role models and one that tries to build new social ties? Indeed, there is unlikely to be a generic intervention that is effective with different people in various contexts. Instead, programs to enhance social networks need to be tailored to the needs and preferences of the employees being served. Thus, involving these employees in the planning and development of the programs is likely to increase program acceptability and effectiveness.

Lastly, with widespread access to the internet and the rise in popularity of social media, the role of virtual social interactions and internet-based exchange of social support is just beginning to be explored and evaluated. To what extent will computer-mediated relationships prove to be health promoting? Can all of the mechanisms described in this chapter for enhancing the health promoting aspects of social relationships take place in a virtual environment? These are some of the exciting questions that await research-based answers.

Glossary

Behavioral imitation: A process, either intentional or subconscious, through which we learn by watching and mirroring others' behaviors

Descriptive social norms: The extent to which a behavior, state or belief is present among members of one's social group

High impact leverage point: Members of social networks who have the potential to affect the health and well-being of many other members.

Injunctive social norms: The extent to which a behavior, state or belief is approved of by one's social group

Stress buffering: A process whereby social support reduces stress and/or its adverse health consequences.

Social comparison: Basic psychological process through which people compare their own attributes, skills, opinions and behaviors to those of others

Social influence: Efforts to influence the thoughts and behaviors of others.

Social integration: Existence of social ties

Social network: Web of social relationships within which individuals live.

Social norm marketing: A process through which accurate information about a descriptive norm is provided in order to correct people's misperceptions about the norm.

Social support: Intentional behaviors that provide emotional aid, tangible aid and services, and information

Social undermining: Intentional behaviors that display negative affect, indicate a negative evaluation of a person, or hinder a person's attainment of goals.

Learning Objectives

1. To describe the various processes through which social relationships influence health
2. To understand how supervisors, coworkers, customers and clients, and health professionals at work can enhance employee health and well-being
3. To discuss how the health-promoting power of social relationships can be optimally utilized in worksite health promotion programs.

Discussion Questions

1. Research consistently shows that people with social support available to them live longer, healthier lives. Why has it been so difficult to build effective strategies for increasing the social support available to those who do not naturally have it?
2. How can social norm marketing be applied in the workplace to promote healthy behaviors?
3. Who are the "high impact leverage points" in your social network? What behaviors should they perform in order to effectively promote the health of social network members?

4. Some of the strategies discussed in this chapter involve worksite health promotion professionals working beyond their traditional organizational boundaries. What challenges might be involved? How might those challenges be addressed?

REFERENCES

1. Berkman L, Glass T, Brissette I, Seeman TE. From social integration to health: Durkheim in the new millenium. Social Science and Medicine 2000;51:843-57.
2. berkman l, Glass T. Social integration, social networks, social support and health. In: Berkman L, Kawachi I, eds. Social Epidemiology. New York: Oxford University Press; 2000.
3. Kawachi I, Berkman LF. Social ties and mental health. Journal of Urban Health: Bulletin of the New York Academy of Medicine 2001;78:458-67.
4. Christakis NA, Fowler JH. The spread of obesity in a large social network over 32 years. The New England Journal of Medicine 2007;357:370-9.
5. Smith KP, Christakis NA. Social Networks and Health. Annual Review of Sociology 2008;34:405.
6. Heaney C, Israel B. Social Networks and Social Support. In: Glanz K, Rimer BK, Viswanath K, eds. Health Behavior and Health Education: Theory, Research and Practice. 4th ed. San Francisco, CA: Jossey-Bass; 2008.
7. Bandura A. Social Foundations of Thought & Actiopn: A Social Cognitive Theory: Pearson; 1985.
8. Iacoboni M. Mirroring People: The New Science of How We Connect with Others. New York: Farrar, Strauss & Giroux; 2008.
9. Festinger L. A theory of social comparison processes. Human Relations 1954;7:117-40.

10. Corcoran K, Crusius J, Mussweiler T. Social comparison: Motives, standards and mechanisms. In: Chadee D, ed. Theories in Social Psychology. Chichester UK: Blackwell Publishing Ltd.; 2011: 119-39.

11. Taylor S, Wayment HA, Carrillo M. Social comparison, self-regulation, and motivation. In: Sorrentino RM, Higgins ET, eds. Handbook of motivation and cognition. New York: Guilford Press; 1996:3-27.

12. Cialdini RB, Reno RR, Kallgren CA. A focus theory of normative conduct: Recycling the concept of norms to reduce littering in public places. Journal of Personality and Social Psychology 1990;58:1015-26.

13. Fishbein M, Ajzen I. Predicting and Changing Behavior: The Reasoned Action Approach. New York: Taylor & Francis; 2010.

14. Ball K, Jeffery RW, Abbott G, McNaughton SA, Crawford D. Is healthy behavior contagious: Associations of social norms with physical activity and healthy eating. The International Journal of Behavioral Nutrition and Physical Activity 2010;7.

15. Fugas CS, Silva SA, Meliá JL. Profiling Safety Behaviors: Exploration of the Sociocognitive Variables that Best Discriminate Between Different Behavioral Patterns. Risk Analysis 2013;33:838-50.

16. Berkowitz AD. Applications of social norms theory to other health and social justice issues: Jossey-Bass, San Francisco, CA; 2003.

17. Wechsler H, Nelson TF, Lee JE, Seibring M, et al. Perception and reality: A national evaluation of social norms marketing interventions to reduce college students' heavy alcohol use. Journal of Studies on Alcohol 2003;64:484-94.

18. Schultz PW, Nolan JM, Cialdini RB, Goldstein NJ, Griskevicius V. The constructive, destructive, and reconstructive power of social norms. Psychological science 2007;18:429-34.

19. House J. Work Stress and Social Support. Reading, MA: Addison-Wesley; 1981.

20. Hagihara A, Miller AS, Tarumi K, Nobutomo K. Social support has both positive and negative effects on the relationship of work stress and alcohol consumption. Stress and Health: Journal of the International Society for the Investigation of Stress 2003;19:205-15.

21. Tay L, Tan K, Diener E, Gonzalez E. Social relations, health behaviors, and health outcomes: A survey and synthesis. Applied Psychology: Health and Well-Being 2013;5:28-78.

22. Putnam R. Bowling Alone: The Collapse and Revival of American Community. New York: Simon & Schuster; 2000.

23. Lazarus R, Folkman S. Stress, Appraisal, and Coping. New York: Springer Publishing Co.; 1984.

24. Lazarus R. Emotion and Adaptation. Oxford UK: Oxford Univeristy Press; 1991.

25. Cohen S, Wills TA. Stress, Social Support, and the Buffering Hypothesis. Psychological Bulletin 1985;98:310-57.

26. Thoits PA. Mechanisms Linking Social Ties and Support to Physical and Mental Health. Journal of Health and Social Behavior 2011;52:145-61.

27. Rook KS. The Negative Side of Social Interaction: Impact on Psychological Well-Being. Journal of Personality and Social Psychology 1984;46:1097.

28. Vinokur AD, Price RH, Caplan RD. Hard times and hurtful partners: How financial strain affects depression and relationship satisfaction of unemployed persons and their spouses. Journal of Personality and Social Psychology 1996;71:166-79.

29. Duffy MK, Ganster D, Pagon M. Social undermining in the workplace. Academy of Management Journal 2002;45:331-51.

30. Oetzel J, Duran B, Jiang Y, Lucero J. Social support and social undermining as correlates for alcohol, drug, and mental disorders in American Indian women presenting for primary care at an Indian health service hospital. Journal of Health Communication 2007;12: 187-206.

31. Stanforth D, Mackert M. Social undermining of healthy eating and exercise behaviors. Heaney & Fitness Journal 2009;13.

32. Cohen S, Frank E, Doyle WJ, Skoner DP, Rabin BS, Gwaltney JM, Jr. Types of stressors that increase susceptibility to the common cold in healthy adults. Health Psychology 1998;17:214-23.

33. Chiang JJ, Eisenberger NI, Seeman TE, Taylor SE. Negative and competitive social interactions are related to heightened proinflammatory cytokine activity. Proceedings of the National Academy of Sciences 2012;109:1878-82.

34. French FRP, Raven B. The Bases of Social Power. In: Cartwright D, Zander A, eds. Group Dynamics. New York: Harper & Row; 1959.

35. van Ryn M, Heaney CA. Developing effective helping relationships in health education practice. Health Education and Behavior 1997;24:683.

36. Stokols D. Translating social ecological theory into guidelines for community health promotion. American Journal of Health Promotion 1996;10:282-98.

37. Kelloway EK, Barling J. Leadership development as an intervention in occupational health psychology. Work & Stress 2010;24:260-79.

38. Kuoppala J, Lamminpää A, Liira J, Vainio H. Leadership, job well-being, and health effects—A systematic review and a meta-analysis. Journal of Occupational and Environmental Medicine 2008;50:904-15.

39. Gilbreath B, Benson PG. The contribution of supervisor behaviour to employee psychological well-being. Work & Stress 2004;18:255-66.

40. Nyberg A, Alfredsson L, Theorell T, Westerlund H, Vahtera J, Kivimäki M. Managerial leadership and ischaemic heart disease among employees: the Swedish WOLF study. Occupational and environmental medicine 2009;66:51-5.

41. Kelloway EK, Weigand H, McKee MC, Das H. Positive leadership and employee well-being. Journal of Leadership & Organizational Studies 2013;20:107-17.

42. Vincent-Hoper S, Heaney C. Supportive leadership behavior and employee well-being: A mixed methods approach. 2013.

43. Fredrickson B. Positivity: Top-Notch research reveals the 3-to-1 ratio that will change your life. New York: Crown Publishers; 2009.

44. Sakurai K, Jex SM. Coworker incivility and incivility targets' work effort and counterproductive work behaviors: The moderating role of supervisor social support. Journal of Occupational Health Psychology 2012;17:150-61.

45. Hochschild A. The Managed Heart: Commercialization of Human Feeling. Berkeley CA: University of California Press; 1983.

46. Tamers SL, Beresford SAA, Cheadle AD, Zheng Y, Bishop SK, Thompson B. The association between worksite social support, diet, physical activity and body mass index. Preventive Medicine 2011;53:53-6.

47. Albertsen K, Borg V, Oldenburg B. A systematic review of the impact of work environment on smoking cessation, relapse and amount smoked. Preventive Medicine: An International Journal Devoted to Practice and Theory 2006;43:291-305.

48. Hennrikus D, Pirie P, Hellerstedt W, Lando HA, Steele J, Dunn C. Increasing support for smoking cessation during pregnancy and postpartum: Results of a randomized controlled pilot study. Preventive Medicine 2010;50:134-7.

49. Lemon SC, Zapka J, Li W, Estabrook B, Magner R, Rosal MC. Perceptions of worksite support and employee obesity, activity, and diet. American Journal of Health Behavior 2009;33:299-308.

50. Fuemmeler BF, Mâsse LC, Yaroch AL, et al. Psychosocial mediation of fruit and vegetable consumption in the body and soul effectiveness trial. Health Psychology 2006;25:474-83.

51. ENRICHD. Enhancing recovery in coronary heart disease (ENRICHD) study intervention: Rationale and design. Psychosomatic Medicine 2001;63:747-55.

52. Houston TK, Ford DE. A tailored Internet-delivered intervention for smoking cessation designed to encourage social support and treatment seeking: Usability testing and user tracing. Informatics for Health & Social Care 2008;33:5-19.

53. McBride CM, Baucom DH, Peterson BL, et al. Prenatal and Postpartum Smoking Abstinence: A Partner-Assisted Approach. American Journal of Preventive Medicine 2004;27:232-8.

54. Wing RR, Jeffery RW. Benefits of recruiting participants with friends and increasing social support for weight loss and maintenance. Journal of Consulting and Clinical Psychology 1999;67:132-8.

55. Prestwich A, Conner MT, Lawton RJ, Ward JK, Ayres K, McEachan RRC. Randomized controlled trial of collaborative implementation intentions targeting working adults' physical activity. Health Psychology 2012;31:486-95.

56. Rigsby A, Gropper DM, Gropper SS. Success of women in a worksite weight loss program: Does being part of a group help? Eating Behaviors 2009;10:128-30.

57. Leeks KD, Hopkins DP, Soler RE, Aten A, Chattopadhyay SK. Worksite-based incentives and competitions to reduce tobacco use: A systematic review. American Journal of Preventive Medicine 2010;38:S263-S74.

58. Tonigan JS, Rice SL. Is it beneficial to have an Alcoholics Anonymous sponsor? Psychology of Addictive Behaviors 2010;24:397-403.

59. Grossman JB, Tierney JP. Does mentoring work? An impact study of the Big Brothers Big Sisters program. Evaluation Review 1998;22:403-26.

60. Allen TD, Finfelstein LM, Poteet ML. Designing Workplace Mentoring Programs: An Evidence-Based Approach. Chichester UK: Blackwell Publishing; 2009.

61. Allen J. Wellness Mentor Resource Manual. Burlington, Vermont: Human Resources Institute, LCC; 2008.

62. May S, West R, Hajek P, McEwen A, McRobbie H. Randomized controlled trial of a social support ('buddy') intervention for smoking cessation. Patient Education and Counseling 2006;64:235-41.

63. Dallam GM, Foust CP. A comparative approach to using the Diabetes Prevention Program to reduce diabetes risk in a worksite setting. Health Promotion Practice 2013;14:199-204.

64. Salzer MS, Palmer SC, Kaplan K, et al. A randomized, controlled study of Internet peer-to-peer interactions among women newly diagnosed with breast cancer. Psycho - Oncology 2010;19:441.

65. Neiger BL, Thackeray R, Van Wagenen SA, et al. Use of social media in health promotion: Purposes, key performance indicators, and evaluation metrics. Health Promotion Practice 2012;13:159-64.

66. Israel B. Social networks and social support: Implications for natural helper and community level interventions.

Health Education Quarterly 1985;12: 65-80.

67. Eng E, Young R. Lay health advisors as community change agents. Family & Community Health 1992;15:24-40.

68. Eng E, Parker E, Harlan C. Lay health advisor intervention strategies: A continuum from natural helping to paraprofessional helping. Health Education and Behavior 1997;24:413.

69. Slaunwhite J, Smith S, Fleming M, Strang R, Lockhart C. Increasing vaccination rates among health care workers using unit "champions" as a motivator. 2009.

70. Tessaro IA, Taylor S, Belton L, et al. Adapting a natural (lay) helpers model of change for worksite health promotion for women. Health Education Research 2000;15:603-14.

22

Transforming Organizational Cultures to Support Good Health

Judd Allen

INTRODUCTION

Interest in the role of culture in workplace health promotion is growing. A recent survey of 1,248 organizations representing about 13 million employees found that 81 percent intended to focus on developing a wellness culture.[1] The purpose of this chapter is to describe what we know from a practice perspective about shaping cultures to improve health. This practical approach is complemented by the more scholarly approach taken in Chapter 21, Social Relationships: Harnessing their Potential to Promote Health.

The chapter begins with a definition of culture and reviews core cultural dimensions, then describes several techniques that show promise in culture change. Next, a brief review of the published literature on this topic is provided, followed by a discussion of how these concepts can be applied to enhancing motivation and building skills. The chapter concludes with a suggested research agenda.

"Key Strategy" comments throughout the chapter offer recommendations for how culture concepts could be put to work.

DEFINING CULTURE

The word *culture* has the same root as the farming word *cultivate*.[2] Extending the farming metaphor, the goal of health promotion is to create cultures – fertile ground – in which interests in and information about healthy lifestyles – the good seeds – are likely to take root and flourish. The goal is to shift cultures' influences from being neutral toward or working against healthy behavior. In a wellness culture, individual initiative to adopt healthier lifestyles is nurtured by the social environment. In a wellness culture, social influences lead people toward healthy behavior. We have seen this phenomenon in the use of car safety belts in the United States. It is now the norm to wear safety belts; 25 years ago, this was not the case.[3] Weak wellness cultures offer little or no guidance about health practices. In many cultures, for example, physical activity is left up to individual preferences. In such a culture, someone pursuing increased physical activity would have to fend for him- or herself. He or she would have to develop habits that are not rooted in household priorities, norms or support systems. Some cultures are directly unsupportive; unhealthy cultures push back against healthy intentions. Such a culture draws people toward unhealthy behavior. We have seen this negative influence in the ways Americans overeat. Efforts to eat healthier are often undermined by the culture. For example, American culture tends to support fast food, which is low in nutrition and high in calories.[4]

WE LIVE IN A WEB OF CULTURES

Whenever two or more people come together with a common purpose, a culture is likely to emerge.[5] Families, schools, friends, churches, workplaces, neighborhoods, states and nations all contribute to this cultural fabric.[6] Household cultures, family cultures, work cultures, community/neighborhood cultures, ethnic cultures and national cultures all influence health behavior. Any one person adapts to the many cultural influences in his or her environment. A child is likely to find that what works in the playground culture may not work at church, at home or even in the classroom culture. Similarly, an adult employee is likely to learn that the cultural rules at work differ from department to department.

Key Strategy: When trying to change a culture, it is helpful to determine which cultural zones of influence have the largest impact on health behaviors. For example, it is likely that household and family culture play a large role in determining whether someone gets a sufficient amount of sleep.

CULTURES ARE COMPLEX SYSTEMS

Culture is composed of a dynamic constellation of social influences (see Figure 22-1). Among these influences are: (1) shared values (i.e., priorities); (2) norms (i.e., "the way we do things around here"); (3) cultural touch points (i.e., formal and informal policies and procedures); (4) peer support (i.e., assistance in achieving a healthy lifestyle and other goals); and (5) climate (i.e., social cohesion).[7] These cultural influences form an integrated web. To successfully bring about culture change, multiple influences must be engaged. Health promotion programs designed to address only one aspect of the culture are

Figure 22-1: **Cultural Dimensions.**
Cultivating Healthy Behavior

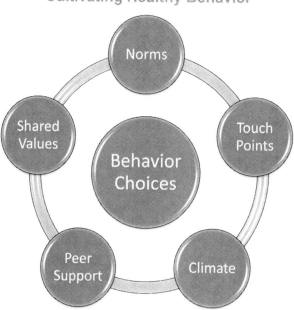

likely to be undermined by those aspects of the culture that have not been realigned with wellness. For example, a prohibition on smoking is likely to have unintended negative consequences, such as poor morale among smokers, if other influences are not aligned with smoking cessation goals. In the case of no-smoking rules, the addition of options such as affordable smoking cessation programs can help create a successful no-smoking culture.

Key Strategy: Each cultural influence represents a strategic opportunity to create a wellness culture. Multiple influences must be engaged. We can, for example, identify unhealthy norms and then shift touch points (formal and informal policies and procedures) so that healthier norms will take root in the culture.

SHARED VALUES

In a wellness culture, the health and well-being of people is among the top priorities. For example, employees in a technology company that has a wellness culture would likely report that the organization's priorities are serving the customer, innovating quickly, making a profit, and supporting the health of its people. In a wellness culture, employees see how attention to wellness drives business decisions.

Fortunately, there are many benefits for groups, organizations and communities that add health and well-being to their list of priorities. Wellness is a strategy for controlling health-care costs, delivering greater productivity, enhancing teamwork, saving lives, and improving the corporate image.

Key Strategy: Don't undersell wellness. Develop a full value proposition that will resonate with a cross-section of employees. It is important to help employees make a connection between the benefits of wellness and their own values and interests.

NORMS

Norms are the building blocks of culture. The behavioral expectations that norms create shape important health behaviors such as how much we eat, participation in physical activities, and how effectively we manage stress. In a wellness culture, the goal is to change norms for unhealthy behavior and to develop or maintain norms that support healthy practices.

Norms frequently operate outside our awareness. Normative behavior is seen as "the way we do things around here." We act without thinking. A wellness culture brings important health norms into the open.

Key Strategy: It is difficult to change norms. The best strategy is to focus on one or two norm change goals. Other norm change goals can be added in future rounds of culture change.

CULTURAL TOUCH POINTS

Cultural touch points are formal and informal policies and procedures that shape day-to-day behavior. Ten of the primary cultural touch points are listed on the following page. Integrating wellness concepts into these touch points will align the overall culture of the organization with wellness:

Rewards and Recognition

Are healthy choices being rewarded and recognized?

Are positive practices undermined through rewards for unhealthy choices?

Pushback

Does the culture include unintended penalties for healthy choices?

Is unhealthy behavior challenged?

Modeling

Do leaders demonstrate healthy choices in their own behavior?

Are unhealthy behaviors being modeled by mistake?

Recruitment and Selection

Do we have a reputation as being a good place for health-oriented people?

Are people made aware that support for healthy lifestyles is one of the primary benefits of joining the group/organization?

First Impressions and Orientation

Are new people made aware of all the programs and activities that support wellness?

Are people assisted in their efforts to integrate healthy activities into their new roles and responsibilities?

Learning and Training

Are people taught the skills they need to excel at practicing healthy behaviors?

Is training in unhealthy practices (such as going without sleep or taking safety shortcuts) being offered by mistake?

Information and Communication

Are people given the feedback they need to set individual and group wellness goals?

Are people kept abreast of wellness activities and opportunities to support the wellness initiative?

Traditions and Symbols

Are there wellness traditions?

Are there old traditions that might be adjusted so that they do not undermine wellness?

Relationship Development

Are friendships and teams being formed around healthy activities?

Are relationship-forming opportunities mistakenly being organized around unhealthy activities?

Resource Commitment

Do people have the time, space and equipment they need to adopt healthy lifestyles?

Does the allocation of resources send the mistaken message that healthy lifestyles are not important?

Key Strategy: A new health behavior will take root in a culture when enough touch points are aligned with that behavior. Change unsupportive touch points and reinforce existing positive influences to reach the tipping point.

PEER SUPPORT

Peer support is the practical and emotional assistance offered by close family, friends, housemates, and coworkers. Words of encouragement and the willingness to adopt similar goals are examples of emotional support. Helping with childcare responsibilities or clearing a space for exercise equipment are examples of instrumental support. Creating a wellness culture often involves increasing the quantity and improving the quality of peer support.[8] A buddy system, team activities and support groups are examples of wellness activities that enhance peer support.

Key Strategy: Family, friends and coworkers can make important contributions to the success of wellness programs. Programs that include mutual support help build a wellness culture. Keep in mind that helping also benefits the person offering assistance, by reinforcing his or her own healthy behavior.

CLIMATE

The social cohesiveness of a culture plays an important role in enhancing people's well-being and capacity to grow. People can achieve more when they get along and work well together. In contrast, when there are high levels of mistrust and divisiveness, it is difficult for individuals to follow through on their wellness goals.[9,10] A bad climate can undermine even the best wellness program by making it unlikely that people will cooperate. Three overlapping climate factors have been identified as being critical to individual and organizational growth:[11]

- **A sense of community** exists when people get to know one another, feel that they belong and trust one another.
- **A shared vision** exists when people are inspired by a common purpose, see how they are making a contribution to that purpose and feel that their personal values are well represented.
- **A positive outlook** exists when people celebrate accomplishments, approach challenges as opportunities for improvement, and look forward to the future.

Key Strategy: Health promotion should help build a positive climate by adopting approaches that focus on strengths rather than risks,

connect to the mission of the organization and give people opportunities to help one another.

TOOLS FOR CREATING WELLNESS CULTURES

A Systematic Approach to Normative Change

Establishing and strengthening wellness norms is an important culture change goal. The Human Resources Institute, LLC, has developed and tested an approach to do this through its Normative Systems model.[12] The components are briefly described below.

Just as good farming practice requires more than simply planting a seed, awareness of the culture's influence must be followed by an ongoing process of changing the many ways the culture shapes behavior. Phase I includes developing an understanding of the current norms, setting norm change goals and developing leadership support. In Phase II, the vision for the new culture can be planted

Figure 22-2: Normative Systems.

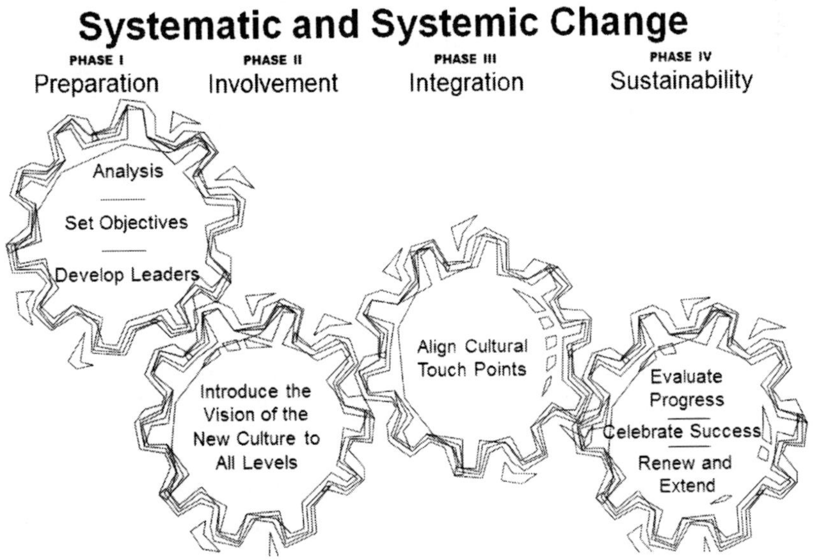

Systematic and Systemic Change

| PHASE I | PHASE II | PHASE III | PHASE IV |
| Preparation | Involvement | Integration | Sustainability |

Analysis
Set Objectives
Develop Leaders

Introduce the Vision of the New Culture to All Levels

Align Cultural Touch Points

Evaluate Progress
Celebrate Success
Renew and Extend

Reprinted with permission from the Human Resources Institute, LLC.

among the members of the culture. In Phase III, programs, policies and procedures are aligned so that the new norm can take root. In Phase IV, change is assessed, progress is celebrated and new goals are developed. This virtuous cycle of normative change builds a wellness culture.

Key Strategy: Norms are influenced by complex systems that can be highly resistant to change. A systematic approach makes it easier to manage this complexity. A wellness culture can be built one norm at a time.

Develop Wellness Leaders

A survey asked employers about the benefit of 200 variables that are believed to influence wellness program outcomes. Of theses factors, the ones correlated with positive financial outcomes and health outcomes were the level of senior leadership support and strength of the culture. Of the companies studied, just 25 percent reported that their senior leadership and culture were "very supportive" of their employee health management strategy. A majority (66 percent) of organizations with strong leadership and cultural support reported improvements in health behavior, compared with only 26 percent of organizations with little or no support. Half of organizations with strong leadership and cultural support reported a net positive impact on medical trends, versus only 14 percent of organizations with little or no cultural support.

Leaders have important roles to play in creating wellness cultures. In his book, *Zero Trends: Health as a Serious Economic Strategy,* Dee Edington identified important executive functions associated with a culture of health.[13] He concluded that senior management can:

- Set the vision and priorities for the wellness initiative.
- Pick wellness champions who will have responsibility for carrying the program forward.

- Allocate a budget and other resources needed for success.

Not all leadership responsibilities are specific to senior management. Managers, opinion leaders and members of wellness committees also can support wellness cultures. Judd Allen and David Hunnicutt identified four key functions of wellness leadership:[14]

- Sharing the vision of what the wellness program is, why it is important and how people can participate.
- Serving as a role model by participating in the wellness program and adopting healthier lifestyles.
- Aligning organizational programs, policies and procedures so they support wellness.
- Celebrating individual and group progress.

Key Strategy: Don't assume that senior management, middle management, wellness committee members or anyone else is clear about their role in creating a wellness culture. Help them develop their wellness leadership skills. This will increase joint ownership of wellness within the organization and give more people an active role.

Mobilize Peer Support

Friends, family, coworkers and housemates can play an important role by offering effective support for lifestyle improvement without being professional counselors or health experts.[15] Effective support goes beyond being a sympathetic listener. For example, people can be trained to use effective wellness coaching skills. A wellness buddy, peer coach or mentor can help with:

- Choosing wellness goals.
- Engaging a role model in a conversation about how he or she achieved similar goals.

- Addressing barriers to change.
- Locating and then increasing exposure to supportive environments.
- Avoiding and working through setbacks.
- Celebrating progress.

Key Strategy: Develop a buddy system or mentoring program as part of your health promotion program. Have people pair up for mutual support. Partners don't need to have the same goals. Instead, you can offer a common framework for support by teaching core peer support skills.

Support Family and Household Wellness

For many people, it is hard to imagine making a lifestyle change without support at home. In a similar way, families have an influence that transcends location. Those who live alone are likely to be influenced by family members even when they live miles away.[16] Families and household cultures operate in ways very similar to organizational cultures.[17] They develop norms, priorities, peer support, touch points and a climate.

Key Strategy: Invite household and family members to participate in worksite health promotion programs. Include households and family in peer support initiatives. A member of a household or family can offer effective peer support. In a similar way, an employee could serve a wellness leadership function at home by helping to create a wellness vision, serving as a role model, aligning informal touch points and celebrating progress. Leadership skills for bringing wellness home may reach employees' dependents.

Engage Community Wellness

Most communities offer a vast array of wellness resources.[18] Health-oriented restaurants, fitness facilities, exercise paths, volunteer opportunities, sports clubs, farmers' markets, education seminars and yoga classes are just some of the many resources available in most communities. Employers can support local business and wellness professionals by encouraging employees to take advantage of community resources.

There are times when it is necessary for employers to connect with outside community resources to support employee wellness. For example, Union Pacific Railroad determined that it would be beneficial to work with local restaurants to accommodate its shift workers.[19] This effort included a request to include healthier food options on the late-night menu. Employers seeking to establish wellness traditions sometimes support community fundraising activities such as walks and running races. Such public events make a statement about the organization's support for wellness.

Key Strategy: Health promotion programs need to help connect people to community wellness resources and address those aspects of community life that undermine the general welfare. A wellness culture does not exist in social isolation.

PUBLISHED LITERATURE ON CULTURE AND CULTURE CHANGE

Many of the ideas presented in this chapter have been developed and tested by the Human Resources Institute, LLC, and several hundred of its clients over four decades. Most of the evidence is provided in case studies.[20,21] Unfortunately, little empirical research has been conducted to measure the relative benefits of culture change approaches in comparison to or in addition to individual-focused approaches to worksite health promotion. A brief review of some of this literature is provided below. Key strategies that emerge from this literature are also provided.

The wellness culture approach integrates many strands of thinking in behavioral science disciplines, including anthropology, sociology, social geography, and psychology. These disciplines offer unique perspectives and supportive research that addresses the impact of the social environment on health. A recent literature review counted the number of articles published in a sample of health promotion journals that addressed some aspect of creating a wellness culture.[22] Articles met the inclusion criteria if the article addressed "things that would change a social group's values, beliefs, and practices related to health." By this very inclusive criterion, many of the articles addressed culture change even though almost none of these articles mentioned the word *culture*. Percentages by journal are listed below.

- 50 percent of articles in the *American Journal of Health Promotion*.
- 30 percent of articles in the *American Journal of Public Health*.
- 15 percent of articles in the *Journal of Occupational and Environmental Medicine*.

Measuring Wellness Cultures

A recent review of the literature[23] concluded that "Few instruments measure organizational health culture or its sub-components, and have published evidence for reliability and validity." One exception is the Lifegain Wellness Culture Survey (also known as the Lifegain Health Culture Audit), which measures five core dimensions of culture – values, norms, touch points, peer support and climate.[24] Its validity and reliability have been measured in several studies.[25,26]

Other questionnaires measure specific dimensions of culture. These fall into two categories:

- Health Climate: These instruments examine social cohesion as it relates to organizational effectiveness and personal well-being.[27,28,29]
- Health Environment: One instrument, Heart Check, is a checklist of programs, policies and procedures

that have been found to reduce cardiovascular risk behaviors such as smoking and physical inactivity.[30] Many of the items are formal policies and procedures that are related to cultural touch points.

A study comparing the Heart Check and the Lifegain Wellness Culture Survey found that both questionnaires are reliable and valid measures that independently contribute to an overall picture of the health environment.[31]

Key Strategy: Measuring culture involves both quantitative and qualitative assessment. Questionnaires and checklists can be used for the quantitative measures. Group and individual interviews can then be used for gaining insights into how best to address goals identified by the quantitative assessment(s).

Wellness Cultures Exist Today

Cross-cultural comparisons provide evidence for the value of wellness cultures. These comparisons have shown that there are places where people tend to live longer, happier and healthier lives.[32] These include the Italian island of Sardinia; the city of Loma Linda, California; the Nicoya peninsula of Costa Rica, Japan's island of Okinawa, and the Ikaria region of Greece. Although each of these cultural environments has unique norms and traditions, they all also have a lot in common. For example, they all have norms for healthy eating, physical activity and regular social engagement. Although there are lessons to be learned about how we should live as individuals, perhaps the greatest lesson is about the importance of culture in helping people achieve their full health potential.

Key Strategy: We can learn a lot from successful wellness cultures found around the world. They show that wellness cultures are achievable. They also open our eyes to possibilities in our own cultures.

The Role of Social Networks in Health

In their book *Connected*, Nicholas Christakis and James Fowler review groundbreaking research based on 30 years of data from the Framingham Heart Study, one of the longest-running epidemiological studies.[33] They found that close friends have a powerful impact on each other's behavior, even when they live hundreds of miles apart. People tend to be successful in making lifestyle changes at the same time as those in their network make similar changes. If a social network is moving toward obesity or unhappiness, the unhealthy behavior is likely to be "contagious." If, as would be the case in a wellness culture, people are moving together in the direction of positive practices such as increasing physical activity or stopping smoking, individual success is more likely.

Key Strategy: We need to engage our friends, family and coworkers in healthy lifestyles. Much more can be accomplished when we make healthy changes together.

Culture Keeps Healthy Behavior Going

Dee Edington and his associates at the Health Management Research Center at the University of Michigan found that one of the most effective strategies to improve the health of a population, and control the related medical costs, is to keep the healthy people healthy.[34] Using a lifeboat analogy, we have been pulling people into the lifeboat while allowing others to fall overboard. They found that we need to help the healthy people stay healthy in addition to helping the unhealthy people improve their health. A program that is exclusively directed at helping higher-risk people lower their health risks neglects opportunities to reduce health risks in the overall population.

Key Strategy: A wellness culture makes healthier lifestyles easier to achieve and maintain for people in all risk categories. Creating a wellness culture is a key way to stem the flow toward new unhealthy practices.

Engagement

Getting people to participate in health promotion activities can be challenging. A survey of 442 employers who offer health promotion programs found that approximately 61% completed a health risk assessment (HRA) questionnaire, 53% completed a biometric screening, but only 22% participated in lifestyle coaching sessions[35] This illustrates that engaging employees in health promotion efforts is a challenge. Many people are unable or unwilling to participate in health promotion activities such as assessments and educational offerings. There are a number of mechanisms through which a wellness culture has the potential to enhance engagement:

- In a wellness culture, healthy lifestyles are a top-level priority. A shared value for wellness makes it more likely that time, space and financial rewards are made available for those seeking to participate.
- In a wellness culture, support for healthy behavior is part of the norms and day-to-day operations. These influences permeate the environment. Positive influences reach those who might otherwise be hard to reach.
- In a wellness culture, people get along with and trust one another. The positive cultural climate makes participating in healthy worksite activities more enjoyable and desirable.
- In a wellness culture, the likelihood of lasting lifestyle change is increased. A higher success rate leads to greater enthusiasm for wellness goals. While

individuals' motivation and skills are helpful, long-term outcomes depend largely on whether the physical and social environments support healthy behavior.

Key Strategy: Define engagement so that a person is engaged if they pursue wellness at home, at work, with friends and in the community. Unlike an approach that focuses exclusively on activities at the workplace, participants are encouraged to address their needs and join in activities wherever it makes the most sense. From this perspective, anyone either pursuing a healthy lifestyle or helping someone else achieve such a goal is "engaged." A focus on environmental support makes a health promotion program less dependent on individuals' participation in formal program activities at work.

Lowering Health Risks and Improving Financial Outcomes

According to Terry, Seaverson, Grossmeier and Anderson, health promotion programs begin to pay for themselves when the prevalence of certain health risks is reduced 1 to 2 percent a year.[36] A review of the literature found that when worksite health promotion programs incorporate more cultural elements in their strategies, employee health risks are reduced by as much as 5 percent per year.[37] This reduction in health risks is 2.5 times as much as was found for standard practice programs.

Key Strategy: A greater amount of lasting behavior change achieved with a supportive culture would make a stronger business case for health promotion.

Positive Cultural Climate Offers Health Benefits

The climate dimension of culture (i.e., sense of community, shared vision and positive outlook) is likely to do more than just improve the likelihood of successful culture change. There is substantial evidence that social connections are essential to health and happiness. Social connectedness may be one of the most powerful determinants of life expectancy, ill health and recovery from illness. Dean Ornish's book *Love and Survival* provides a review of the research linking social connection to health.[38] Robert Putnam summarizes the general finding in his book *Bowling Alone*: "People who are socially disconnected are between two and five times more likely to die from all causes, compared with matched individuals who have close ties with family, friends, and the community."[39] This evidence supports the health promotion goal of strengthening the social connections provided by families, friends, coworkers and communities.

Key Strategy: Health promotion should be organized in such a way that healthy activities and mutual support for wellness goals create and strengthen relationships.

Combining Individual and Culture Initiatives

The culture approach is not a substitute for health promotion activities that are directed at individual change, such as personal health assessments and wellness coaching. The goal is to combine support for the individual with supportive environments at work, at home, among friends and in the community. The approaches are mutually supporting. Ajzen and Fishbein recognize this balanced approach in their Theory of Reasoned Action.[40] According to this theory, behavior is linked to individual intention to act, individual attitudes and perceptions about what is normal conduct. The Theory of Reasoned Action has been shown to be a good predictor of behavior. It seems likely that substantial and lasting health improvements depend on the individual and the culture.

Key Strategy: Offer programs that address both individual change and bring about culture change.

The Role of Culture in Enhancing Motivation and Building Skills

Culture appears to play an important role in motivation. In the United States, for example, cultural support for self-improvement helps explain why so many Americans make New Year's resolutions and buy self-help magazines in large quantities. One study estimated that 80 percent of adults in the United States attempt lifestyle improvement goals annually.[41] Motivation for healthy lifestyles appears to be strong. The study found that nutritious eating, weight loss, increased physical activity, stress management and improved social relationships are the most common goals in the United States. These goals also reveal the unhealthy behaviors with the highest prevalence in the population. The same correlation appears for unhealthy behaviors that are less common. For example, 68.8% of smokers say they want to quit smoking and 52.4% actually quit for one day in 2010.[42]

When the culture undermines lasting lifestyle change, it undermines motivation. For example, unsuccessful diets and failed attempts at quitting smoking are likely to undermine enthusiasm for weight management and smoking cessation. Those contemplating health goals may, on the basis of past experience, believe that success is unlikely. Executives and managers may be reluctant to back health promotion if they have previously had limited success in achieving wellness goals.[43] Health-care professionals may be reluctant to prescribe lifestyle change if they perceive that their patients will be unsuccessful in carrying out their recommendations.[44]

The culture may also be distracting people from important wellness goals. Time spent in front of televisions and computer screens may, for example, crowd out opportunities

for fitness. Similarly, the high cultural value placed on work may be undermining interest in social activities, vacations and other healthy interests. Health promotion programs often compete with other activities that are highly valued in the culture.

A poor cultural climate also undermines health promotion activities. Where a sense of community and a positive outlook are relatively absent, for example, members of a culture may be uncomfortable completing personal health assessments. In such a low-trust environment, employees may be concerned that personal health information will be used against them. And in such a poor cultural climate, employees may seek to limit their contact with the worksite. Anything optional or considered extra is unlikely to be treated with enthusiasm.

Culture may influence what is considered motivating. In some work cultures, such as that found in many marketing departments, economic incentives are highly effective. The amount of money required to incentivize an activity varies by cultural group. In other cultures, job stability is an important motivator. In yet other cultures, healthy lifestyle goals may be motivated by personal vanity. In some cultures, the impact of unhealthy behaviors on the health of children may be an important motivation for goals such as quitting smoking. In yet other cultural groups, such as older workers, compliance with a doctor's recommendations is an important motivation for pursuing healthier lifestyle choices.

The culture plays a role in informal learning. For example, recipes are sometimes handed down from generation to generation. Sometimes these traditional foods need to be adjusted so that they do not undermine health. Culture also plays an important role in conveying skills related to key health behaviors such as relaxation. Some cultures, for example, embrace regular meditation and prayer, while others do not.

The culture plays an important role in people's receptivity to and exposure to health promotion education. For example, in American culture men are often less interested in support group programs. Buddy systems and sports teams are often developed to reach men. In American culture leadership support tends to be seen as critical to success. As a result, programs directed at developing leadership support tend to be well received in the United States. Some workplaces have strong cultural prohibitions against interrupting work. Employees in such workplaces will find it hard to attend an education seminar during work hours.

A Research Agenda and the Future of the Wellness Culture Approach

Up to this point, the wellness culture approach has been based primarily on the experience of practitioners. For practitioners to progress to the next level of effectiveness and adoption, rigorous research needs to be conducted on all the topics discussed in this chapter. For example, one promising area of study would be to examine the extent to which each of the cultural touch points influences motivation, skills and health behavior. Another area of research would study culture in its entirety, including shared values, norms, touch points, peer support and climate. This research would test what has been learned by practitioners who have attempted to create wellness cultures. Other possible questions to test are below.

What is the impact of culture on health behavior and health conditions, in quantitative terms, relative to other elements of a health promotion program?

Can a wellness culture reduce the likelihood that people will adopt new health risks such as becoming overweight?

Can a wellness culture increase lifestyle change initial success rates and the longevity of new healthy lifestyle practices?

Does a wellness culture benefit those people who are not participating in health promotion activities?

What combination or amount of changes to cultural touch points are needed to change cultural norms?

What are the mechanisms through which culture impacts health behavior? Does culture improve motivation to change health habits? Does it help people acquire the skills to change habits, or does it cause people to change habits unconsciously, perhaps in compliance with behavioral norms?

If culture impacts health conditions in addition to health behaviors, through what mechanisms does this occur? Does it operate through health behaviors, by creating emotional contexts that are less stressful, or some other mechanism?

What is the relative importance of adopting a systematic approach versus addressing culture influences individually?

Robert Allen was one of the early pioneers in applying culture change approaches to wellness. His words seem prophetic more than 25 years after his death: "If we work together to support wellness, our human need for one another will no longer be an obstacle to overcome, but rather a virtue to be celebrated."[45] There is much work yet to be done in developing culture-based approaches that are rooted in solid research. Let's do this together.

Glossary

Culture: A web of social influences on attitudes and behavior. The five interrelated dimensions of culture are shared values, norms, cultural touch points, peer support and climate. Most people belong to multiple cultures.

Cultural Climate: The level of social cohesiveness of a culture, as seen in the sense of community, shared vision and positive outlook. Individual and organizational growth are more likely when these climate factors are present.

Cultural Touch Points: Formal and informal influences on behavior within a culture. The 10 primary touch points are: (1) rewards and recognition, (2) pushback, (3) modeling, (4) recruitment and selection, (5) first impressions and orientation, (6) learning and training, selection, (7) information and communication, (8) traditions and symbols, (9) relationship development, and (10) resource commitment. A tipping point in culture change is reached when enough touch points are aligned to establish a new norm.

Cultural Values: The priority placed upon specific goals within a culture. In worksite health promotion, an important objective is to make support for employee health one of the top cultural values.

Norms: Expected and accepted behavior within a culture. The goal is to strengthen norms for healthy lifestyle choices and to weaken norms for unhealthy behavior.

Normative Systems: An action-research process for bringing about sustained change. The process can be organized into four phases: (1) analysis, objective setting and leadership development; (2) introduction and engagement; (3) integration; and (4) evaluation, renewal and extension. Each cycle in the culture change process helps build the wellness culture.

Peer Support: Assistance provided to achieve healthy lifestyle goals. Both emotional and instrumental support can be offered by friends, family, housemates and coworkers. The goal is to increase both the quantity and the quality of peer support.

Learning Objectives

1. To be able to identify five dimensions of culture.
2. To be able to identify 10 cultural touch points.
3. To be able to identify six peer support skills.
4. To be able to identify three qualities of a healthy cultural climate.
5. To be able to identify four wellness leadership skills.

6. To be able to identify three unique benefits of a wellness culture.

Discussion Questions

1. There is a lot of interest in creating wellness cultures. Why do you think this approach is gaining popularity?
2. Personal health assessments, tailored health information and individual coaching can co-exist with collective efforts to create wellness cultures. What do you think is the right mix of efforts focused on individual change and efforts focused on creating wellness cultures? What is your reasoning? What additional evidence is needed to determine the best approach?
3. Health promotion programs organized for individuals could be reformulated to help individuals to find or create wellness cultures among their friends, at home and in the community. What are the pros and cons, if any, of incorporating wellness culture concepts into programs that focus on individual change?
4. Most people attempt wellness goals each year. A fraction of these goals are achieved. However, many people believe that most people are not interested in wellness. Do you think people are underestimating peoples' desire for wellness? How, if at all, does culture play a role in all this?

REFERENCES

1. Buck Consultants, LLC. Working Well: A Global Survey of Health Promotion and Workplace Wellness Strategies. Available at www.hreonline.com/pdfs/04012011Extra_BuckSurvey.pdf. Published November 2010. Accessed May 2, 2012.

2.   Culture. Merriam-Webster Dictionary. http://www.merriam-webster.com/dictionary/culture. Accessed December 17, 2012.

3.   Solomon MG, Leaf WA, Nissen WJ. National Occupant Protection Use Survey. Available at www.nhtsa.gov/people/injury/research/buckleup/ii_trends.htm. Published July 2001. Accessed December 17, 2012.

4.   Schlosser E. *Fast Food Nation: The Dark Side of the All-American Meal.* New York, NY: Houghton Mifflin Company; 2001.

5.   Allen RF, Kraft C. *Beat the System! A Way to Create More Human Environments.* New York, NY: McGraw Hill; 1980.

6.   Barker R, Shoggen P. *Qualities of Community Life.* San Francisco, CA: Jossey-Bass; 1973.

7.   Allen J. *Wellness Leadership.* Burlington, VT: Healthyculture.com; 2008.

8.   Allen J. *Healthy Habits, Helpful Friends: How to Effectively Support Wellness Lifestyle Goals.* Burlington, VT: Healthyculture.com; 2008.

9.   Moos R. Conceptualization of human environments. *AM PSYCHOL.* 1973; 28(8): 652-665.

10. Ornish D. *Love and Survival: The Scientific Basis for the Healing Power of Intimacy.* New York, NY: Harper Collins; 1998.

11. Allen RF, Allen J. A sense of community, a shared vision and a positive culture: core enabling factors in successful culture based health promotion. *Am J Health Promo.* 1987; 1(3): 40-47.

12. Allen RF, Linde S. *Lifegain: The Exciting New Program That Will Change Your Health and Your Life.* Burlington, VT: Human Resources Institute Press; 1981: 230-241.

13. Edington DW. *Zero Trends: Health as a Serious Economic Strategy.* Ann Arbor, MI: Health Management Research Center; 2009: 36-37.

14. Allen J, Hunnicutt D. *Fostering wellness leadership: a new model.* Special Report.

Omaha, NE: Wellness Councils of America; 2006.

15. Allen J. *Healthy Habits, Helpful Friends: How to Effectively Support Wellness Lifestyle Goals.* Burlington, VT: Healthyculture.com; 2008.

16. Christakis NA, Fowler JH. *Connected: The Surprising Power of Our Social Networks and How They Shape Our Lives.* New York, NY: Little, Brown and Company; 2009.

17. Allen J. *Bringing Wellness Home: How to Create a Household Subculture That Supports Wellness Lifestyle Goals.* Burlington, VT: Healthyculture.com; 2009.

18. WellnessNow databases of local wellness resources. Available at www.gotowellnessnow.com.

19. Allen J. Wellness Leadership Video: Defining Management's Role in Creating Healthier and More Productive Cultures. Produced by Vermont Educational Television. Available from Healthyculture.com. 1999.

20. Allen RJ, Allen RF. Achieving health promotion objectives through culture change systems. *Am J Health Promo.* 1986; 1(1): 42-49.

21. Holtyn K, Allen J, Fetzer B, Heirich M. *Reaping the Rewards of Worksite Wellness: A Special Report from Hope Health and Holtyn Associates.* 2011.

22. Terry PE. Do health promotion professionals have the wherewithal to change organizational cultures? *Am J Health Promot : The Art of Health Promotion.* 2012; 26(6): 11-12.

23. Aldana SG, Anderson DR, Adams TB, et al. A review of the knowledge base on healthy worksite culture. *J Occup Env Med.* 2012; 54(4): 414-419.

24. Allen J. Building supportive cultural environments. In: O'Donnell MP, ed. *Health Promotion in the Workplace,* 3rd ed. Albany, NY: Delmar Publishers, Inc.; 2001: 202-217.

25. Golaszewski T, Hoebbel C, Crossley J, Foley G, Dorn J. The reliability and validity of an organizational health culture audit. *American Journal of Health Studies.* 2008; 23(3): 116-123.

26. Hoebbel C, Golaszewski T, Swanson M, Dorn J. Associations between the worksite environment and perceived health culture. *Am J Health Promot.* 2012; 26(5): 301-304.

27. Moos R. Conceptualization of human environments. *Am Psychol.* 1973; 28(8): 652-665.

28. Ribisl KM, Reischl TM. Measuring the climate for health at organizations: Development of the worksite health climate scales. *J Occup Med.* 1993; 35(8): 812-824.

29. Allen RF, Allen J. A sense of community, a shared vision and a positive culture: Core enabling factors in successful culture based health promotion. *Am J Health Promot.* 1987; 1(3): 40-47.

30. Golaszewski T, Fisher B. Heart Check: the development and evolution of an organizational heart health assessment. *Am J Health Promot.* 2002; 17: 132-153.

31. Hoebbel C, Golaszewski T, Swanson M, Dorn J. Associations between the worksite environment and perceived health culture. *Am J Health Promot.* 2012; 26(5): 301-304.

32. Buettner D. *Blue Zones: Lessons for Living Longer from the People Who've Lived the Longest.* Washington, DC: National Geographic Society; 2008.

33. Christakis NA, Fowler JH. *Connected: The Surprising Power of Our Social Networks and How They Shape Our Lives.* New York, NY: Little, Brown and Company; 2009.

34. Edington DW. *Zero Trends: Health as a Serious Economic Strategy.* Ann Arbor, MI: Health Management Research Center; 2009: 36-37.

35. The HERO Best Practice Scorecard: An introduction and progress report. *The HERO Employee Health Management Best Practice Scorecard: 2010 Annual Report.* Edina, MN: The Health Enhancement Research Organization; 2010.

36. Terry PE, Seaverson EL, Grossmeier J, Anderson DR. Association between nine quality components and superior worksite health management program results. *J Occup Env Med.* 2008; 50: 633-641, as cited in Aldana SG, Anderson DR, Adams TB, Whitmer W, Merrill RM, George V, Noyce J. A review of the knowledge base on healthy worksite culture. *J Occup Env Med.* 2012; 54(4): 415.

37. Terry PE, Seaverson EL, Grossmeier J, Anderson DR. Association between nine quality components and superior worksite health management program results J Occup Enc Med. 2008; 50: 633-641, as cited in Aldana SG, Anderson DR, Adams TB, Whitmer W, Merrill RM, George V, Noyce J. A review of the knowledge base on healthy worksite culture. *J Occup Env Med.* 2012; 54(4): 415.

38. Ornish D. *Love and Survival: The Scientific Basis for the Healing Power of Intimacy.* New York, NY: Harper Collins; 1998.

39. Putnam R. *Bowling Alone: The Collapse and Revival of American Community.* New York, NY: Simon & Schuster; 2000.

40. Ajzen I, Fishbein M. *Understanding Attitudes and Predicting Social Behavior.* Englewood Cliffs, NJ: Prentice-Hall; 1980.

41. Allen J. The mentoring model. *Absolute Advantage.* 2004; 3(5): 52-55.

42. Centers for Disease Control and Prevention. Quitting Smoking Among Adults—United States, 2001–2010. Morbidity and Mortality Weekly Report [serial online] 2011;60(44):1513–19. Available at http://www.cdc.gov/tobacco/data_statistics/mmwrs/byyear/2011/mm6044a2/intro.htm Accessed March 1, 2013.

43. Inman L, Weiner B, Graham A, Emmons K. Manager beliefs regarding worksite health promotion: Findings from the Working Healthy Project 2, *Am J Health Promot.* 2007; 21(6): 521-528.

44. Allen J, Allen RF. From short term compliance to long term freedom: Culture–based health promotion by health professionals. *Am J Health Promot.* 1986; 1(2): 39-47.

45. Allen RF. Distinguished alumni commencement ceremony address. Plattsburgh State University of New York. Plattsburgh, NY; May 1981.

CHAPTER

23

Special Challenges and Opportunities for Small Business

Mari Ryan

INTRODUCTION

Despite the growth of health promotion programs in workplace settings, such programs continue to be rare among small employers. This is true for at least five basic reasons.

- First, and most importantly, the ability to control medical care costs by keeping employees healthy is muted for small employers because they are not self-insured. If a large self-insured employer reduces its employees' medical utilization, the savings go straight to its bottom line. If a small employer reduces employees' medical utilization, the savings go straight to the bottom line of its insurance provider. Seeing these savings may

increase the likelihood that the insurance provider will be willing to renew the contract when it expires, and may even reduce the amount of the premium increase when the contract is renewed; but most likely, the reduced utilization will have no direct impact on medical insurance costs. Small employers do benefit when the health of their employees improves, and these benefits are discussed in this chapter; but the savings in medical insurance cost are not among them.

- Second, small employers rarely have the infrastructure of a central human resources department to study and understand the financial return that is likely to result from a wellness program, let alone to design and implement a program.

- Third, small employers often have limited discretionary resources available to launch health promotion programs, even when they do anticipate tangible benefits.

- Fourth, the size of small employers makes it impossible to negotiate volume-based discounts enjoyed by larger employers, and in fact the small budget of the whole program makes the small employer unattractive to most health promotion vendors.
- Fifth, most of the research and best practice guidelines are based on the experience of large employers, so the optimal approach for small employers is not clear.

Despite these challenges, some strategies have been developed to address them and some small employers have implemented successful programs.

This chapter describes the challenges small business face in implementing health promotion, as well as the advantages and some initiatives to support development of programs.

PREVALENCE AND ECONOMIC CONTRIBUTION OF SMALL BUSINESS

Of the nearly 6 million businesses in the United States in 2010, most fall into the category of micro or small business with fewer than 20 employees, as shown in Table 23-1.[1]

Small businesses are a key element of the U.S. economy; they employ nearly half of the nation's private sector workforce; provide half of the nation's nonfarm, private real gross domestic product; create most of the new jobs; and produce a significant share of innovations.[2]

THE BUSINESS CASE FOR SMALL EMPLOYERS OFFERING HEALTH PROMOTION PROGRAMS

As with any business, the dominant concern of small business owners is staying focused on the production of goods and/or services that contribute to the company's bottom line. Their interests focus on maximizing those elements that contribute to productivity. Of small business owners who currently offer or used to offer a health promotion program, 93% of these small business owners believe that the health of their employees is important and positively impacts their bottom line.[3]

A series of surveys conducted in 2012 showed that small business owners feel that the most significant motivators for implementing health promotion programs include:

- improved overall employee health,
- lower health care costs in the long term,

Table 23-1: Number of Firms and Employment.

Employment Size	Firms by Size, %	Workers by Size, %
0–4	62.3	5.3
5–9	16.9	5.7
10–19	10.8	7.4
20–99	8.3	16.6
100–499	1.4	14.2
500+	0.3	50.9

- increased productivity,
- improved morale,
- enhanced employee recruitment and retention.

Additional benefits include reduced absenteeism and reduced cost associated with disability claims.[3,4] Another survey, conducted by the Small Business Majority—a nonprofit advocacy group focused on small business issues—found that 67% of small business owners indicated they would be interested in a workplace health promotion program if it helped lower health insurance costs.[5]

HEALTH INSURANCE LANDSCAPE FOR SMALL BUSINESSES

The rising cost of health insurance has been the top concern for small business owners from 1987 through 2012.[6] The cost of health insurance increased 103% between 2001–2011, outpacing wages and inflation. Also, the number of small businesses offering health insurance has been in constant decline as health insurance becomes increasingly unaffordable.

In the health insurance world, small business health insurance is "guaranteed issue," meaning that the insurer has a legal obligation to accept any small business that applies for insurance. Guaranteed issue does not however limit how much is charged to those who choose to enroll. Beginning in 2014, under provisions of the Affordable Care Act, all group health plans must offer policies to all applicants, regardless of health status.[7]

Most small businesses are fully insured, meaning that the insurance company, rather than the employer, assumes the risk of covering all medical expenses. In these cases, group insurance rates are established by a mechanism called *community rating*. Community rating spreads the risk by setting the same premiums for an entire community or group of subscribers. An insurer charges all people covered by the same type of health insurance policy the same premium without regard to age, gender, health status, occupation, or other factors. The insurer determines the premium from the health and demographic profile of the geographic region or the total population covered under a particular policy that it insures. Under community rating, higher-cost groups (e.g., groups made up of older or sicker people) are averaged out with lower-cost groups (e.g., groups made up of younger or healthier people). The anticipated expenses of all participants are pooled together and then spread out equally across all participants. Regardless of their success in improving health and reducing medical utilization, the community rating mechanism prevents their premium from being reduced.

Small businesses are less likely to offer health insurance than larger organizations. In 2012, an estimated 98% of large firms (>200 employees) offered health insurances, compared to 61% of small firms (3–199 employees). Furthermore, the rate has been declining, dropping from a high of 68% in 2000.[8] Within the category of small firms, the smaller the firm, the less likely they are to offer health insurance benefits, as shown in Table 23-2.[7] Beginning in 2014, the Affordable Care Act will require businesses with 50 or more full-time equivalents to offer health insurance. The Small Business Tax Credit in the Affordable Care Act is intended to encourage the smallest companies with the lowest paid workers to offer health benefits. The credit is available to businesses with 25 or fewer employees with average wages below $50,000. In 2013 the tax credit will be 35% (up to 25% for nonprofits) to offset the cost of health insurance. The credit increased to 50% (35% for nonprofits) in 2014.[9,10]

The federal government and some state governments have undertaken initiatives to improve the small group health insurance market in an effort to control costs. One approach has been to consolidate purchasing power by forming purchasing cooperatives. This provides the benefit to the insurer of a larger, potentially less volatile and more stable

Table 23-2: Percentage of Small Firms Offering Health Insurance Benefits.

Size of Firm	Percentage Offering Health Insurance
3–9	50
10–24	73
25–49	87
50–199	94

risk pool and reduces administrative costs. An additional feature of cooperatives is to provide the ability to offer multiple health plans, thereby providing employees with a choice of plans.[11]

The Affordable Care Act requires that states establish health insurance exchanges to serve both individuals and small businesses by 2014, or allow access to the federally operated exchange. The public and private exchanges already established in New York, Connecticut, Massachusetts, and Utah illustrate the feasibility of this approach, but currently serve a small portion of the existing market.[12]

Small employers have come to depend upon their insurance providers as a resource for prevention and health promotion programs in order to reduce the increasing burden of health-related cost growth. Small employers, often lacking human resource professionals on staff, depend on benefit brokers as a source of information on health promotion programs and for plan design guidance. Providing additional education on the value, benefits, and best practices on health promotion programs may be a worthwhile investment that will benefit both the insurers and the small businesses.[13]

OTHER CHALLENGES AND BARRIERS TO IMPLEMENTING HEALTH PROMOTION IN SMALL WORKSITES

Small businesses, generally less well capitalized than larger businesses, tend to have a shorter-term bottom-line orientation, fewer available internal resources, and less information about health promotion programs. As such, they often do not understand the requirements and benefits of implementing a results-oriented health promotion program.

The barriers cited by small business owners are clustered around several major issues, including the following[3]:

- Forty-six percent of business owners responding to a recent survey indicated lack of employee interest as a key barrier to implementing health promotion programs.
- The difficulty in administering programs was cited as a barrier by 21% of respondents to the same survey.
- Concerns over privacy and/or the singling out of individual employees also present strong barriers to health promotion initiatives.

Further insight to this matter resulted from a December 2011 event held by the Trust for America's Health and the Small Business Majority advocacy organizations. Stakeholders including government, small business owners, public health, unions, insurers, and brokers discussed the opportunities and challenges for increasing the number of small businesses offering health promotion programs. The group identified the following key factors as contributing to low adoption rates for small businesses:

- *Limited access to meaningful data:* Little research exists on small business health promotion programs, resulting in the absence of a strong case for support to small employers.
- *Lack of awareness:* Small business owners and their employees are unaware of the benefits a health promotion program can provide.
- *Lack of information on incentives:* While many credible research studies exist for large organizations demonstrating measurable ROI and financial incentives, there is no such research available demonstrating the same incentives for small employers.
- *Limited resources and administrative infrastructure:* Small businesses often do not have human resource departments and administrative resources necessary to support health promotion programs. They may not even offer health insurance.
- *Variability among size and workforce makeup:* There is a dearth of effective, adaptable, and scalable models for small business health promotion, suited to the various sizes and types of workforces found in small businesses.

A significant outcome of the December 2011 convening was the development of a logic model (Figure 23-1) illustrating how the many interconnected aspects of workplace health promotion fit together and the roles specific stakeholders can play in increasing adoption of programs by small businesses.[14]

This model demonstrates how the aspects of worksite health promotion fit together and the specific roles stakeholders can have in increasing the adoption of health promotion programs. At the core is individual choice, surrounded by the workplace and community environment. An integrator function is proposed to ensure that prevention and health promotion activities are coordinated, complementary, and not duplicative.

ADVANTAGES OF IMPLEMENTING HEALTH PROMOTION IN SMALL WORKSITES

Despite all the challenges and barriers small employers encounter, some understand the impact of health promotion programs on the health of their employees and on their bottom line, and remain interested in establishing programs. Small businesses have a number of unique social and organizational features that favor the implementation of health promotion programs. These include the unique social nature of a small workplace, with high levels of interaction and interdependency between employees, and the fact that it may be easier to shift the culture in a small organization.

The typically flat organizational structure of small businesses generally facilitates and expedites decision-making. Deciding upon and implementing a health promotion program within a small organization can be accomplished more rapidly than in larger organizations. The influence of the business owner can more directly encourage employees to participate and help demonstrate the connection between good health and business success. Because of the smaller number of employees, communication is often easier and more efficient. Gathering the necessary data and understanding interests of employees is a less cumbersome and less expensive process in smaller organizations.

Most significantly, small businesses that follow established best practices guidelines have been able to achieve similar health risk reduction outcomes as demonstrated in large and medium-sized employers.[15]

SMALL BUSINESS INTEREST AND ACTIVITIES IN WORKSITE HEALTH PROMOTION

A number of surveys conducted in 2012 help explain the scope of health promotion

Figure 23-1:   Improving the Health of Small Business Employees: Targeting Interventions to Where Individuals Live, Learn, Work, Play, and Pray.

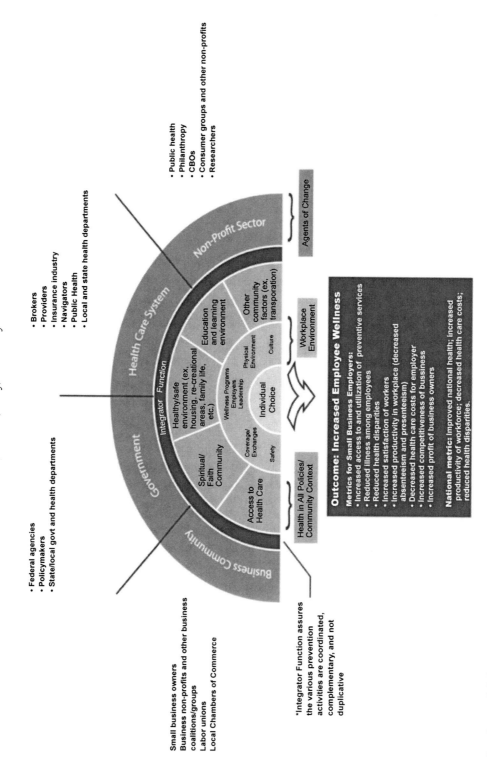

Logic model developed as a result of the December 14, 2011 small business workplace wellness convening (TFAH/SBM)

programs being offered in small businesses and the viewpoint of business owners.

A 2012 survey of 800 small business owners conducted by the Small Business Majority found that 51% were "very interested" or "somewhat interested" in establishing a workplace health promotion program at their business.[5]

In a 2012 survey of 1005 business owners, conducted by the National Small Business Association (NSBA), 93% of business owners acknowledged the importance of their employees' health to their businesses' bottom line, yet just 22% (Figure 23-2) were offering programs at the time of the survey. Employers also recognized the impact of the use of sick time on their business. While small employers in this survey report employees take few sick days, this often means they are coming to work sick. When they do take sick days, the impact to productivity is immediately evident.

Interestingly, this survey indicated that the smallest employers, those with two to nine employees, had the highest confidence (39%) in their ability help employees manage their health and well-being, compared with employers with 10 to 49 employees (29% confidence) and 50 to 100 employees (21% confidence).

The top health concerns cited in the NSBA survey are as follows:

- High stress levels (42%)
- Psychological well-being (13%)
- Weight management (11%)
- Alcohol and other drug habits (11%)
- Smoking habits (9%)
- Don't know/unsure (15%)

When asked which programs they would most likely invest in, business owners indicated stress management (26%) followed by health, education, prevention or screenings (24%), and weight management programs (12%).[1]

A 2012 national survey on workplace health promotion initiatives conducted by the Alliance for a Healthier Minnesota showed similar results to the previous surveys. In this survey, 27% of businesses with fewer than 100 employees and 52% of businesses with 199 to 499 employees have a worksite health promotion initiative in place. Interest in developing a worksite health promotion programs in the next 1 to 3 years was reported by 62% of employers with 1 to 99 employees and 74% of employers with 100 to 499 employees. In this survey, the top three health conditions of greatest concern to the employees

Figure 23-2: **Status of Health Promotion Programs.**

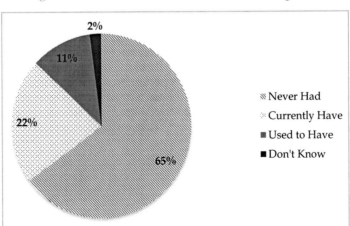

were overweight and obesity, stress and other mental health issues, and lack of exercise and fitness.[16]

STRATEGIES TO INCREASE ADOPTION

Because small businesses lack the internal resources and expertise to develop and implement worksite health promotion programs, linking these businesses to a variety of existing community resources may be a viable strategy. In the last 5 years, there have been a number of initiatives that focus on bringing health promotion programs to the small business sector.

These initiatives emanate from various sources, and include:

- Small business health insurance group purchasing collaboratives
- Government-sponsored grants or tax credits
- Government-sponsored and community-based demonstration projects
- Connecting small businesses with already existing community resources.

These initiatives are described below.

Small Business Purchasing Collaboratives

Purchasing collaboratives are based upon improving purchasing power by banding together. Group purchasing collaboratives are not new. Professional associations, chambers of commerce, and like organizations have served as a source of a variety of products and services for sole proprietors and small businesses for decades. These products and services may include office supplies, electricity and natural gas, and worker's compensation coverage.[17]

As previously discussed, small businesses have struggled with providing affordable health care to their employees. As a result, a variety of sources have been created for small businesses and these continue to evolve in the forms of group purchasing associations or collaboratives, and public and private exchanges.

The Connecticut Business and Industry Association (CBIA) is an example of an organization providing small employers with cost-effective options, including health insurance and health promotion programs. With 10,000 member companies, they provide health insurance to 5,500 employers with subscriber enrollment of more than 80,000. Their flagship product is Health Connection, which offers both a choice of health plans and insurers. In 2010, CBIA added free health promotion programs to the offering. The program is designed to create awareness of the link between healthy behaviors and employer/employee productivity, cost savings, and a positive work environment. The program uses a variety of best practice approaches including health promotion champion, employee health portal, health assessment, incentives, and awareness/education and behavior change campaigns.

Government-Sponsored Pilot Projects

National Healthy Worksite Program

The Affordable Care Act provides for funding of a demonstration project called The National Healthy Worksite Program (NHWP), carried out under the supervision of the Centers for Disease Control and Prevention. NHWP is designed to assist employers in implementing evidence-based prevention and health promotion strategies that will lead to specific, measureable health outcomes to reduce chronic disease rates. The program recruited 100 small, medium, and large employers from eight communities across the United States, and provides resources and technical assistance to implement comprehensive health promotion programs. An ongoing evaluation element of the program will study the impact of the program and track changes in employee knowledge, behavior, and productivity, as well as changes in employer health and safety culture. Evaluation efforts will also document best practices for implementing core workplace health programs and identify challenges experienced by employers and strategies to overcome them.[18]

Saint Lawrence Health Initiative, New York

The Saint Lawrence Health Initiative (SLHI), in Saint Lawrence County, New York, conducted a pilot with the goal of testing the feasibility of providing comprehensive health promotion services to micro businesses. Situated on the Canadian border in northern New York State, Saint Lawrence County has a population of just over 110,000. Its largest city, Potsdam, has a population of approximately 16,000.

The pilot, funded by the New York State Department of Health, was conducted between August 2010 and June 2012, with nine businesses employing a total of 280 employees participating. The number of employees in the participating companies ranged from 10 to 73. The industry segments included agriculture/mining, local governments, service, wholesale/retail/sales, and health care. The average wage of the employee participants was $28,557.

The project achieved or exceeded all of the project objectives, as shown in Table 23-3.

As a result of the project, SLHI developed service offerings to bring health promotion programs to other businesses in the region.[19,20]

Community-Based Worksite Health Promotion Projects

State and local governments often provide resources to support underserved populations. There is increasing recognition that small businesses represent an "underserved population." A number of new initiatives are being piloted across the United States to

Table 23-3: Saint Lawrence Health Initiative Project Objectives and Outcomes.

Objective	Outcome
At least 25% of employees who completed a health risk assessment will reduce at least one chronic risk factor.	Fifty percent of participants reported eliminating at least one risk factor as measured by time 1, time 2 health risk assessments.
The micro business will show a positive return on investment.	Measuring impact from reductions in obesity and fewer smokers on productivity, the return on investment was shown to be $1.22 for every dollar invested. Projections for future years are expected to provide a return of $2.50 for every dollar invested.
The project will validate the proposed price per employee ($150) to provide comprehensive worksite health promotion services to micro employers.	Preliminary results showed that the cost to deliver the services was $137.62 per employee per year.
The SLHI will have signed commitment worksites employing at least 500 people, a number sufficient to sustain a full-time coordinator.	Six of the nine businesses participating in the pilot committed to an ongoing program.

encourage small business adoption of health promotion programs. Several of these are described below.

Maine Micro Employer Worksite Health Promotion Program

In parts of rural Maine, locals like to say that wildlife outnumbers people. With small towns spread far apart, there are few resources available to small businesses. Somerset County, Maine, is just such a place. Half of the businesses in the county employ fewer than five employees, and 89% employ fewer than 10 employees. In 2011, the Greater Somerset Public Health Collaborative in partnership with The Maine Health Access Foundation and Medical Care Development developed a community-based employee health promotion program for micro businesses and demonstrated that small businesses within a community can join together to offer their workers health promotion activities that would not normally be economically feasible for groups their size. This model complements national health reform, which proposes models to allow small employers to group together to purchase health insurance coverage.

The program began by gathering environmental data from worksites, using a modified HERO scorecard. Employees engaged in the program by completing an interest survey. With these data collection steps, the project team worked with employers to create a 6-month plan for their business. The work plan identified environmental and policy interventions, such as fire escape routes, smoke detectors, tobacco use and substance abuse policies; and ways to communicate frequent and simple prevention messages, such as newsletters and bulletin boards. Employees engaged with community resources on specific targeted health issues, resulting in 52% of participants realizing improvements in their overall health promotion scores.[21]

By creating a project that gave small employers the opportunity to obtain worksite health promotion programs similar to those existing in larger companies, a complementary product prototype was developed. This product can be used to offer a full spectrum of health, health promotion, and medical care protection for small and very small employers.

Fall River Small Worksite Health Promotion Project

Fall River is a city of fewer than 100,000 persons on the south coast of Massachusetts. The industrial revolution brought economic prosperity to the city in the 1800s, but in the 20th century it became better known for its high crime rates and stagnant economy. The Greater Fall River Small Worksite Health Promotion Project is a public health project funded by the University of Massachusetts Lowell Center for Promotion of Health in the New England Workplace, a National Institute for Occupational Safety and Health-funded Center of Excellence. The project engaged 20 micro business employers (5–25 employees) during a 6-month period. By providing technical assistance, tools, and connection to community resources, the pilot measured 10 program elements including employer response to the invitation and response for and against participating, employee engagement and participation, and the helpfulness and effectiveness of using community-based resources to engage employees in smaller worksites in worksite health promotion.

Demonstration projects such as these are beginning to provide much-needed insight into the needs of small businesses and are spawning promising models that may be expanded to large numbers of small businesses.

Government Grants and Tax Credits

In the past few years, federal and state legislatures have been experimenting with ways to encourage small businesses to implement health promotion programs. Two approaches have been used: direct tax credits and grant programs. Early efforts from several states are described below. At the federal level, the Affordable Care Act authorized $200 million for small business health promotion grants for the years 2011–2015. However, the president's 2012 budget did not include appropriation for these grants owing to budget constraints.

While a number of states have proposed tax credits for health promotion programs, few have actually implemented them. In 2009 and 2010 nine states (Connecticut, Iowa, Illinois, Massachusetts, Maine, Pennsylvania, Washington, Wisconsin, and District of Columbia) proposed tax credits or exemptions for worksite health promotion programs.[22] Of those states, only Maine and Massachusetts have enacted the legislation. The Massachusetts tax credit is effective with the 2013 tax year,[23] while the Maine tax credit took effect in 2014.

In 2007, the Indiana General Assembly passed a bill enacting the Small Employer Qualified Health Promotion Program Tax Credit. This credit provided an incentive for employers with 2 to 100 full-time employees to implement a "certified health promotion program" to benefit employees. The credit applied to 50% of the program costs and was funded by a cigarette tax introduced the same year. Employers submitted applications for review by an advisory committee to receive certification based on program criteria. The criteria included data collection, awareness and education interventions, incentive programs, and evaluation. The program ran during the 2007–2011 tax years. Of the 626 applicants, 393 businesses received tax credits totaling $908,505. A moratorium was placed on the tax credit during the 2011 calendar year owing to budget constraints.

The Ohio Bureau of Workers Compensation offers a Workplace Health Promotion grant program to Ohio employers. This program assists employers with the creation and implementation of a workplace health promotion program. The program's goals are to:

- limit and control the escalating cost of workers' compensation claims by helping employers develop health promotion programs for their employees;
- reduce health care costs for employers, and improve the health and well-being of the workforce.

Participating employers may receive $300 per participating employee over a 4-year period, with a maximum of $15,000 per company. Employers are required to submit aggregate reports of health-risk appraisal, biometrics, and employee demographics and a year-end narrative case study report to qualify for funding into the next year. The data collected from this program will be used to establish health promotion program best practices and to determine the effectiveness of the programs. Participating employers are required to share aggregate health risk data and costs. The program has an economic stimulus effect in that employers may not self-administer any portion of the program, thereby encouraging the use of external service providers. Through November 2012 the program had approved 161 applications for funding of more than $600,000, with 90% of the approved businesses having fewer than 200 employees.[24]

CONCLUSION: CAUTIOUSLY OPTIMISTIC FUTURE FOR HEALTH PROMOTION IN SMALL BUSINESS SETTINGS

Small businesses will continue to be a key element of the U.S. economy and its development, as they represent most firms in the United States and employ most workers in this country. Small business owners recognize that the health of their employees has a direct impact on the profitability of their business. They are increasingly becoming more concerned about the costs of health care and are seeking ways to support and encourage health lifestyles for their employees. The health insurance landscape presents challenges to small business owners, not just from a cost perspective, but also because even if they can help improve the health of their employees, the cost benefit is not reflected in their premiums, so there is no financial incentive through premium reduction for their employees.

The inherent structure and nature of a small business, with high levels of interaction and interdependency between employees and flat organizational structure, provide a friendly environment in which to implement a health promotion program. Barriers such as lack of resources and expertise, lack of employee interest, and lack of awareness of the benefits are keeping small businesses from adopting health promotion programs.

While there are many promising practices and incentives for small business health promotion programs, much work needs to be done before this segment of the workforce can realize the full benefits of worksite health promotion. Current efforts, such as demonstration projects and experiments with grant funding and tax credits, hopefully will provide good data to help us better understand the impact and appropriate approaches to implementing health promotion programs in small businesses. Until such data are available, small businesses will continue to struggle with implementing results-oriented programs that lead to healthier employees. Strong leadership and advocacy for small businesses, along with recognition of the critical role they play in our economy, will require collaboration of all stakeholders. Only then will small businesses enjoy the same benefits of worksite health promotion experienced by large employers, and only then will we truly be able to reverse the chronic disease and health cost trends.

Glossary of Terms

Affordable Care Act: A federal statute signed into law in March 2010, the law included multiple provisions that would take effect over a matter of years, including the expansion of Medicaid eligibility, the establishment of health insurance exchanges, and prohibiting health insurers from denying coverage owing to preexisting conditions.

Community rating: A rule that prevents health insurers from varying premiums within a geographic area, based on age, gender, health status, or other factors.

Gross domestic product (GDP): The monetary value of all the finished goods and services produced within a country's borders in a specific time period, though GDP is usually calculated on an annual basis.

Guaranteed issue: A requirement that health plans must permit you to enroll regardless of health status, age, gender, or other factors that might predict the use of health services. Except in some states, guaranteed issue does not limit how much you can be charged if you enroll.

Micro business: A business that employs fewer than 10 employees.

Small business: A small business concern is one that is independently owned and operated, is organized for profit, and is not dominant in its field. While the parameters for a small business vary, the business typically employs fewer than 500 employees.

Self-insurance: Self-insurance is a risk management method in which a calculated amount of money is set aside to compensate for the potential future loss.

Learning Objectives

After reading this chapter, readers will be able to:

1. Discuss the challenges and opportunities for worksite health promotion in small businesses

2. Discuss the types of initiatives that are being used to increase adoption of worksite health promotion programs in small businesses

3. Discuss the health insurance environment for small businesses

Discussion Questions

1. What are the values and benefits to small businesses of implementing worksite health promotion programs?

2. What approaches can be used to support and encourage small businesses to adopt worksite health promotion programs?

3. How can connecting small business with community resources help small businesses overcome resource constraints?

4. What are some ways that the best practices used by large businesses be adopted or adapted for small businesses?

REFERENCES

1. U.S. Census Bureau. Statistics of U.S. businesses, 2010. Available at: http://www.census.gov/econ/susb/. Accessed December 15, 2012.

2. The small business economy, 2009. United States Small Business Administration, Office of Advocacy. Available at: http://archive.sba.gov/advo/research/. Accessed April 27, 2013.

3. National Small Business Association. Wellness program impacts bottomline. Available at: http://www.nsba.biz/?p=4224. Accessed September 28, 2012.

4. State of worksite wellness in America. Minnesota Department of Health. Available at: http://statesofwellness.healthiermn.com/. Accessed December 6, 2012.

5. Small Business Majority, Opinion Poll. Small business owners' views on implementing the Affordable Care Act. June 14, 2012. Available at: http://www.smallbusinessmajority.org/small-business-research/healthcare/small-business-owners-views-on-aca.php. Accessed June 20, 2012.

6. National Federation of Independent Businesses. Small biz problems and priorities. Available at: http://www.nfib.com/research-foundation/priorities. Accessed December 15, 2012.

7. Kaiser Family Foundation. Health insurance market reforms: guaranteed issue. June 2012. Available at: http://www.kff.org/healthreform/8327.cfm. Accessed April 27, 2013.

8. Kaiser Family Foundation/Health Research and Educational Trust. Employer health benefits: 2012 annual survey. Available at: http://ehbs.kff.org/. Accessed October 1, 2012.

9. Healthcare.gov. Small business and the Affordable Care Act. Available at: http://www.healthcare.gov/news/factsheets/2011/08/small-business.html. Accessed December 23, 2012.

10. Internal Revenue Service. Small business health care tax credit. Available at: http://www.irs.gov/uac/Small-Business-Health-Care-Tax-Credit-for-Small-Employers. Accessed December 23, 2012.

11. The Commonwealth Fund Economic and Social Research Institute. Health insurance purchasing cooperatives. Available at: www.commonwealthfund.org/usr_doc/wicks_coops.pdf. Accessed December 23, 2012.

12. Jost T. Employers and the exchanges under the small business health options program: examining the potential and the pitfalls. *Health Aff.* 2012;31(2): 267–274.

13. Hughes MC, Patrick DL, Hannon PA, et al. Understanding the decision-making process for health promotion

programming at small to mid-size businesses. *Health Promot Pract.* 2011;12(4):512–521.

14. Trust for America's Health and Small Business Majority. Striving for a healthier America through availability and uptake of workplace wellness programs in the small business community: convening highlights. December 14, 2011. Available at: www.smallbusiness majority.com/_docs/resources/031312_ SBM_TFAH_Workplace_Wellness.pdf. Accessed March 31, 2012.

15. Health Enhancement Research Organization. HERO Employee Health Management Best Practice Scorecard Annual Report 2012. Available at: www. the-hero.org/scorecard_folder/2012_ annual_report.pdf. Accessed August 4, 2012.

16. The States of Worksite Wellness in America. Alliance for a Healthier Minnesota. Available at: http:// statesofwellness.healthiermn.com/. Accessed December 7, 2012.

17. Butler B. Co-op may spell savings in health insurance. *Worcester Business Journal.* April 12, 2012. Available at: http:// www.wbjournal.com/article/2012 0123/PRINTEDITION/301239989. Accessed January 12, 2013.

18. Centers for Disease Control and Prevention. National Healthy Workplace. Available at: www.cdc.gov/ nationalhealthyworksite/index.html. Accessed: January 12, 2013.

19. Saint Lawrence Health Initiative. Healthy small business pilot. Available at: http://www.gethealthyslc.org/. Accessed April 2, 2013.

20. Work Well Investments Web site. Available at: www.workwellinvestments. com. Accessed April 2, 2013.

21. Health Enhancement Research Organization. HERO Webinar, January 23, 2013. Interview with program administrators, May 2012. Available at: http://www.the-hero.org/learning_ series/community_based_model.html. Accessed February 20, 2013.

22. National Conference of State Legislatures. 2006-2010 health promotion legislation. Available at: http://www. ncsl.org/issues-research/health/ wellness-legislation-2010-state-activity. aspx. Accessed October 12, 2012.

23. Commonwealth of Massachusetts, Department of Public Health. Small business Wellness Tax Credit. Available at: http://www.mass.gov/ wellnesstaxcredit. Accessed March 20, 2013.

24. Ohio Bureau of Workers Compensation. Workplace Wellness Grant Program. Available at: www.ohiobwc.com/ employer/programs/safety/wellness grants.asp. Accessed November 9, 2012.

INDEX